MARKETING MANAGEMENT: A COMPREHENSIVE READER

Jagdish N. Sheth
Brooker Professor of Research
Graduate School of Business
University of Southern California

Dennis E. Garrett
Assistant Professor of Business Administration
University of Oklahoma

Published by
SOUTH-WESTERN PUBLISHING CO.

CINCINNATI   WEST CHICAGO, IL   DALLAS   PELHAM MANOR, NY   LIVERMORE, CA

658.819
M341

Copyright © 1986
by SOUTH-WESTERN PUBLISHING CO.
Cincinnati, Ohio

All Rights Reserved

The text of this publication, or any part thereof, may not be reproduced or transmitted in any form or by any means, electronic or mechanical, including photocopying, recording, storage in an information retrieval system, or otherwise, without the prior written permission of the publisher.

ISBN: 0-538-19230-5

Library of Congress
Catalog Card Number: 85-62011

1 2 3 4 5 6 7 FG 2 1 0 9 8 7 6
Printed in the United States of America

PREFACE

Today's marketing managers are faced with unprecedented challenges and opportunities. No longer can marketers survive in the increasingly competitive marketplace by relying only on a few time-honored maxims, such as "Give the customer what he wants!" and "Rely on the product life cycle to guide your product decisions!" Marketing in today's turbulent environment requires a higher level of sophistication and sensitivity.

Fortunately, marketing managers have at their disposal the necessary resources to meet and overcome these challenges. In the academic realms of marketing, valid and applicable theories of marketing practice are being refined for eventual use by marketing practitioners. Indeed, the link between the applied and the theoretical worlds of marketing is growing stronger as members of both worlds realize the mutual benefits available from greater interaction. Also, new people are entering the profession with high-quality undergraduate and, quite often, graduate training in the marketing discipline. Finally, the communications revolution has unlocked the doors to vast storehouses of information which marketing managers may employ to solve complex problems.

In this new era there are four major revolutions in marketing that must be recognized and dealt with by marketing managers:

1. The Emergence of the Strategic Orientation. For at least the past twenty years, marketing has been dominated by the consumer orientation. Based on the venerable "marketing concept," the consumer orientation exhorted marketers to ascertain consumers' needs before attempting to produce and market goods for the public's consumption. As a result of the dominance of the consumer orientation, marketing theorists during this period concentrated on a micro-level analysis of the intricacies of consumer behavior, including such diverse topics as perceived risk, information processing, brand loyalty, and cognitive dissonance.

While the consumer orientation contributed a great deal to our understanding of the marketing process, in the 1980s there is a definite shift from the consumer orientation to the strategic orientation. The strategic orientation emphasizes that effective marketers must not only be aware of the needs of the consumers but also be cognizant of the challenges posed by competitors in the marketplace. Thus, marketers must somehow create a distinct competitive advantage in the market in order to ensure long-run survivability. To fashion such a competitive advantage, marketers must evaluate the opportunities present in the market and then critically analyze the resources available to exploit these opportunities. Thus, the strategic orientation explicitly acknowledges that there is now a heightened level of competition for consumers' attention and patronage.

2. *The Emphasis on Functional Integration.* The era of the functional specialist in marketing may be gone forever. No longer is it acceptable to recruit and train marketers to specialize in a very narrow aspect of the organization's broad marketing effort. For instance, until recently, a marketer could become an expert in sales management in a company and never be required to understand or interact with fellow marketing specialists in other functional cells within the organization, such as pricing or distribution. However, enlightened executives have now begun to stress the benefits that may accrue from increased integration of the basic marketing functions of product development, pricing, promotion, and distribution. By promoting greater interchange between these functional areas, marketing managers are able to achieve synergistic benefits and avoid inconsistencies created by inadequate communication and understanding. Therefore, modern marketers face the challenge of becoming experts in all functional areas of their organization's marketing program.

3. *The Emergence of the Stakeholder Perspective.* Increasingly, marketing practitioners must serve more and more constituents, both internal and external to the organization. For example, in addition to serving the needs and wants of the customers in the marketplace, marketing practitioners must worry about the unintended side effects of their marketing practices on the society. In other words, in addition to communicating about the products and services, marketing also influences the social and economic behavior of the society. Therefore, marketing must be concerned about the public opinion and social criticism inherent in implementing any strategy. Similarly, marketing practitioners must be conscious of the impact of their marketing practices on their employees' morale and dedication. After all, very few employees like to be associated with a company whose marketing practices are criticized or debated in the public forum.

4. *The Emphasis on Refined Theoretical Application.* The boundaries of marketing have expanded considerably within the past decade. There is general agreement among marketing scholars and practitioners alike that marketing may be beneficial to more areas than just for-profit business ventures. However, as marketing has been applied to a broader range of settings and issues, questions have been raised concerning the need to modify the basic principles of marketing to fit the specific requirements of the various problems. For instance, scholars are once again debating if the same marketing programs may be applied to both domestic and international markets. Likewise, arguments have been raised which suggest that marketing theories and principles must be modified if they are to be maximally beneficial to the supposedly unique

needs of consumer goods, industrial goods, and services marketing. Also, the possible distinctions among for-profit, not-for-profit, and social marketing are potential grounds for creating more specific theories of marketing for each arena.

Therefore, modern marketing managers must question how applicable the basic theories and principles of marketing are to their particular area of application. For example, if a marketer involved in international marketing accepts and applies his or her company's domestic marketing program in international markets, the outcome may be disastrous for both the marketer's career and the company's performance.

As these four major trends in marketing suggest, modern marketing managers must be well educated if they plan to prosper in this era of increased competition and sophistication. The purpose of this readings book is to expose students of marketing to the latest viewpoints regarding the paramount questions which marketing practitioners must address. Therefore, we have selected articles for inclusion in this readings book that are generally much more rigorous and provocative than those readings usually found in most marketing management readings books. Given the special challenges that marketing students of the 1980s will face when they enter the "real world of marketing," we firmly believe that the level of marketing education must be continually upgraded. Thus, this readings book is specifically designed to allow students to form their own opinions regarding the four major trends in marketing presented above. Although the readings in this book will demand a great deal of thought and analysis from marketing students, the eventual rewards from their efforts in terms of successful careers should be just compensation.

Jagdish N. Sheth
Dennis E. Garrett

CONTENTS

PART ONE/Marketing Strategy, Planning, and Control — 1

Section A/Major Issues in Managerial Marketing — 2

1. Top Management's Concerns About Marketing: Issues for the 1980s. *Frederick E. Webster, Jr.* — 3
2. The Misuse of Marketing: An American Tragedy. *Roger C. Bennett and Robert G. Cooper* — 17
3. The Effectiveness of Marketing's "R&D" for Marketing Management: An Assessment. *John G. Myers, Stephen A. Greyser, and William F. Massy* — 33

Section B/Strategic Marketing Concepts — 57

4. Marketing, Strategic Planning and the Theory of the Firm. *Paul F. Anderson* — 59
5. The Evolution of Strategic Marketing. *Subhash C. Jain* — 81
6. Diagnosing the Product Portfolio. *George S. Day* — 97
7. A Margin-Return Model for Strategic Market Planning. *Jagdish N. Sheth and Gary L. Frazier* — 114

Section C/Marketing Programs and Controls — 131

8. The Major Tasks of Marketing Management. *Philip Kotler* — 133
9. How to Plan and Set Up Your Marketing Program. *Edward S. McKay* — 146
10. Organizing the Marketing Function. *Barton Weitz and Erin Anderson* — 159
11. The Marketing Audit Comes of Age. *Philip Kotler, William Gregor, and William Rodgers* — 182

Section D/Managing Market Information — 203

12. Toward Strategic Intelligence Systems. *David B. Montgomery and Charles B. Weinberg* — 207

13. Decision Support Systems for Marketing Managers. *John D. C. Little* — 228

PART TWO/Marketing and the Environment — 261
Section E/Social Responsibility — 262

14. The Dangers of Social Responsibility. *Theodore Levitt* — 263
15. Marketing: A Social Responsibility. *Thaddeus H. Spratlen* — 278
16. Framework for Analyzing Marketing Ethics. *Gene R. Laczniak* — 300
17. A Managerial Approach to Macromarketing. *Jehiel Zif* — 319

Section F/Regulation of Marketing — 337

18. Reasonable Rules and Rules of Reason: Vertical Restrictions on Distributors. *John F. Cady* — 339
19. Marketing and Product Liability: A Review and Update. *Fred W. Morgan* — 359
20. Regulation in Advertising. *S. Watson Dunn* — 377
21. The Concerns of the Rich/Poor Consumer. *Lee E. Preston and Paul N. Bloom* — 403

PART THREE/Managing the Marketing Mix — 425
Section G/Managing the Product from Birth to Death — 427

22. Market Segmentation: A Tactical Approach. *Frederick W. Winter* — 429
23. New Product Models for Test Market Data. *Chakravarthi Narasimhan and Subrata K. Sen* — 440
24. Positioning Your Product. *David A. Aaker and J. Gary Shansby* — 466
25. Product Life Cycle Research: A Literature Review. *David R. Rink and John E. Swan* — 479
26. The Death and Burial of "Sick" Products. *R. S. Alexander* — 501

Section H/Pricing Perspectives: Managerial Versus Consumer — 513

27. Techniques for Pricing New Products and Services. *Joel Dean* — 515

28. Buyers' Subjective Perceptions of Price. *Kent B. Monroe* — 530

29. Economic Foundations for Pricing. *Thomas Nagle* — 551

30. Pricing Research in Marketing: The State of the Art. *Vithala R. Rao* — 576

Section I/Management of the Distribution Function — 599

31. Get Leverage from Logistics. *Roy D. Shapiro* — 600

32. Perspectives for Distribution Programming. *Bert C. McCammon, Jr.* — 612

33. An Integrative Model of the Channel Decision Process. *J. Taylor Sims, Herbert E. Brown, and Arch G. Woodside* — 632

34. Distributor Portfolio Analysis and the Channel Dependence Matrix: New Techniques for Understanding and Managing the Channel. *Peter R. Dickson* — 649

Section J/Special Topics in Promotion — 667

35. New Ways to Reach Your Customers. *Benson P. Shapiro and John Wyman* — 668

36. Effectiveness in Sales Interactions: A Contingency Framework. *Barton A. Weitz* — 683

37. Sales Force Management: Integrating Research Advances. *Adrian B. Ryans and Charles B. Weinberg* — 714

38. Today's Top Priority Advertising Research Questions. *Diane H. Schmalensee* — 738

39. Marketing and Public Relations. *Philip Kotler and William Mindak* — 759

40. The Association Model of the Advertising Communication Process. *Ivan L. Preston* — 774

PART FOUR/Broadening the Marketing Context — 797

Section K/Nonprofit and Social Marketing — 799

41. The Marketing of Social Causes: The First 10 Years. *Karen F. A. Fox and Philip Kotler* — 800

42. A Model of Strategy Mix Choice for Planned Social Change. *Jagdish N. Sheth and Gary L. Frazier* — 819

43. Strategies for Introducing Marketing into Nonprofit Organizations. *Philip Kotler* — 840

44. Strategic Management for Multiprogram Nonprofit Organizations. *Robert E. Gruber and Mary Mohr* — 855

Section L/International Marketing — 867

45. Are Domestic and International Marketing Dissimilar? *Robert Bartels* — 868

46. The De-Americanization of Marketing Thought: In Search of a Universal Basis. *Nikhilesh Dholakia, A. Fuat Firat, and Richard P. Bagozzi* — 878

47. The Globalization of Markets. *Theodore Levitt* — 889

Section M/Industrial Marketing — 907

48. Fundamental Differences Between Industrial and Consumer Marketing. *Industrial Marketing Committee Review Board* — 908

49. The Industrial/Consumer Marketing Dichotomy: A Case of Insufficient Justification. *Edward E. Fern and James R. Brown* — 917

50. The Development of Buyer-Seller Relationships in Industrial Markets. *David Ford* — 934

51. Situational Segmentation of Industrial Markets. *Richard N. Cardozo* — 952

Section N/Services Marketing — 967

52. Marketing Intangible Products and Product Intangibles. *Theodore Levitt* — 968

53. Classifying Services to Gain Strategic Marketing Insights. *Christopher H. Lovelock* — 980

54. The Marketing of Services. *Kenneth P. Uhl and Gregory D. Upah* — 999

PART ONE
Marketing Strategy, Planning, and Control

Strategic marketing, which involves planning the future destiny of marketing, has become extremely important in recent years. This future-oriented process requires four areas of understanding. The first is the assessment of the changing environment and its impact on corporate business, goals, and strategy. The second is the formulation of the business mission and objectives in light of the changing environment, including such fundamental issues as what business you are in and what business you should be in. The third area of understanding relates to the formulation of a strategy to achieve the business mission. This area emphasizes the identification of competitive strengths and weaknesses. Finally, the fourth area of understanding is strategy implementation. This area often refers to the structural reward system and action plans for carrying out the strategy.

In this part, we have identified major issues that are facing the marketing practice as well as the role of marketing planning, control, and information.

SECTION A
Major Issues in Managerial Marketing

There are three distinct issues facing the marketing professionals in practice.

First, what is the role of marketing within the organization? In an organization in which marketing is a corporate philosophy (everything in business revolves around customer satisfaction), it is relatively easy to assert that the marketing department plays a very critical role. Unfortunately, the same is not true in organizations that equate marketing with selling and treat it as a functional discipline. As a functional entity, marketing has to compete with engineering, manufacturing, finance, and legal departments for top management's attention.

Second, how productive is the marketing function? Compared with other functions in the organization, marketing is often unable or unwilling to provide a numerical measure for its productivity. For example, we still don't fully understand how advertising works and, therefore, we are unable to establish a direct causal link between advertising and sales. Similarly, there is an unwillingness on the part of the sales force to allocate its time separately for generating new business versus maintaining existing business or for selling one product line versus other product lines.

Third, can marketing provide an accurate assessment of the marketplace, including customer and competitive behavior? In other words, how good is marketing's market intelligence system? While most corporations have an abundance of information on their customers, it is still difficult to assess what customers really need or want. Furthermore, most organizations do not even have a formal competitive analysis department to understand the other half of market behavior.

This section is, therefore, devoted to understanding the challenges encountered by marketing professionals, especially within their own organizations.

1 — Top Management's Concerns About Marketing: Issues for the 1980s

Frederick E. Webster, Jr.

Reprinted from the *Journal of Marketing*, published by the American Marketing Association, Vol. 45 (Summer 1981), pp. 9–16. Reprinted by permission.

This article reports the findings of a study of top managers' views of the marketing function. The potential value of these findings lies in that they focus attention on a number of issues of concern to top management, helping to define research hypotheses and productive areas of inquiry. Many of these issues have not received the research attention they need and deserve.

It is valuable, from time to time, for marketing academicians to attempt a validity check on their own views of the field as compared with marketing managers who are an important set of beneficiaries, ultimately, of the results of research in marketing (and who frequently provide the financial support needed to conduct the research). How else can academicians be sure that their efforts are meaningful and useful? Are we concerned about and working in areas that management is interested in? It also is helpful to know which issues will be most likely to generate management interest and support in the future.

A recent study by the Marketing Science Institute identified marketing managers' principal areas of concern as: improving marketing productivity; government regulation and marketing practice; effective corporate communications with a variety of constituencies; and integrating marketing and strategic planning with a companywide marketing orientation (Greyser 1980). The current research suggests that top management has a somewhat different view of major issues facing marketing management in the 1980s.

PURPOSE OF THE RESEARCH

The research reported here was designed to determine how a sample of chief executive and operating officers in a variety of American corporations viewed the marketing function. It was intended that the interviews should reveal the major issues and concerns that these top managers see facing the marketing function. The purpose was not to gather data that would tell marketing managers how to do their job better or to determine the degree of acceptance of particular analytical and decision making techniques. Rather, the purpose was to report to marketing managers and scholars that set of issues that is currently foremost in the thinking of top managers as they direct and evaluate the marketing management function. These findings thus have some specific implications for marketing managers as they prepare for the challenges of the 1980s, and they suggest a number of areas and hypotheses for future research.

SAMPLE AND INTERVIEWS

Interviews were conducted by the author with chief executive officers, chief operating officers, or other members of top management (with titles such as Vice Chairman and Executive Vice President-Director) in a total of 21 corporations. Approximately one-third of these executives had marketing management backgrounds. While large, multinational firms dominated the sample, a number of smaller, primarily industrial products firms were also included. In addition, nine trustees of the Marketing Science Institute interviewed top management representatives of their own firms and reported the results to the author. These interviews were conducted using the same interview guide used by the author. The total sample, therefore, includes 30 top managers. The companies included in the sample are:

- AMCA International Corporation
- American Can Corporation
- Champion International Corporation
- Connecticut Mutual Life Insurance Company
- DeLorean Motor Company
- Donaldson Company
- Eastman Kodak Company
- Economics Laboratory
- Emery Air Freight Corporation
- General Electric Company
- General Foods Corporation
- General Mills, Inc.
- Gillette Company
- Gould, Inc.
- Graco, Inc.
- International Business Machines Corporation
- International Paper Company
- ITEK Corporation
- S. C. Johnson & Son, Inc.

- Markem Corporation
- Mobil Oil Corporation
- Norton Company
- Philip Morris Incorporated
- Provident National Bank
- Quaker Oats Company
- Joseph E. Seagram & Sons, Inc.
- Sentry Insurance
- Toro Company
- Union Carbide Corporation
- Xerox Corporation

This is clearly a convenience sample. Although there was some attempt to obtain a sample that contained a reasonably broad variety of industries and functional backgrounds among the respondents, the sample is by no means representative in a statistical sense. Likewise, the interpretation of the research results is highly subjective and impressionistic. It is obviously improper to generalize from these findings to all top managers, and it must also be recognized that comments about the rank order of importance of issues discussed are based on the author's interpretation of comments, not on hard quantitative measures of importance. All the same, it is likely that these findings have value as indicators of current concerns and as guides to research questions and hypotheses of some importance, because of the nature of the executives interviewed, not easily accessible to academic researchers, and the companies they represent. More research with executives at this level of the corporate hierarchy was called for by Jerry Wind in a *JM* editorial considering research priorities in marketing for the 1980s (Wind 1980).

Each interview took from one to three hours. While each was conducted according to a standard interview guide, each also tended to follow its own logic. Themes once established were persistent. The respondents were cordial and open and in all instances, seemed truly interested in the research and the research questions. An important motive for participating in this research was an interest in comparing one's thoughts and opinions with others who have similar responsibilities.

These managers do not spend a great deal of time thinking about the marketing function in the abstract; they focus on the problems of their own businesses and see marketing, when asked to think about it, in that light. Thus, they were not talking about marketing as it is studied and taught so much as marketing as it is practiced, intertwined with other business problems and functions. A good portion of these executives had trouble separating marketing from corporate strategy and planning, which would seem to underscore the concern of some authors that marketing scholars in the 1980s need to examine more closely the relationships between marketing and corporate strategy, and to support the observation that academic marketing researchers have been too concerned about tactical decisions rather than truly important strategic issues (Day and Wind 1980).

MARKETING COMPETENCE MORE IMPORTANT IN THE FUTURE

Despite the tendency of the research questions to focus on issues and concerns, a large majority of the respondents found the opportunity to express positive opinions and support for the marketing function in their businesses. In those firms where marketing is well-established and professional marketing competence is longstanding, such as in the large consumer package goods firms, it is clear that marketing is the prime line management function and that marketing competence is the key competitive weapon. In some other large firms, often with a mix of consumer and industrial products and markets, marketing was seen as a critical strategic area that would become more important in the more competitive, slower growth markets of the 1980s. But, there was also a sense in many of these firms that marketing management competence would have to improve. The executives in this second group of companies, having been somewhat critical of their marketing managers' performance in the past, would typically add that the responsibility for marketing failures and disappointments had to be shared with top management—i.e., themselves. A third group of top managers, typically those in smaller companies serving industrial markets (although not all of the smaller companies are in this set and not all firms in this set are small), saw a lack of marketing orientation as a historical weakness of their firms, but still stressed that increased marketing competence was a key priority for them for the 1980s.

In summary, there was virtually unanimous agreement, expressed spontaneously in most instances, that the marketing management function was a critical strategic function and that it would become even more so in the 1980s. (Perhaps some of this represents a bias introduced by the respondents' perceptions that the interviewer was identified with the marketing function, but care was taken to avoid leading questions and to minimize this potential problem.) Several respondents expressed the opinion that the financial management orientation that tended to dominate corporate strategy in the 1970s may have created a relatively short-term orientation that left firms in a somewhat weakened position to meet market conditions of the '80s. In the words of one respondent, "This led to an overstatement of the financial considerations versus what you can accomplish with good marketing." Other writers have recently noted that management's excessive concern for short-term, financial performance has created a competitive weakness for American firms as they enter the more competitive world markets of the 1980s (Hayes and Abernathy 1980, Mauser 1980).

MAJOR ISSUES AND CONCERNS

Although a given individual's major concerns were usually expressed in ways specific to his business, there was a surprising degree of consensus in the interviews as to the major issues facing marketing management. These issues will be highlighted and summarized first, next discussed briefly, and then some underlying questions will be defined. The principal issues that were uppermost in the minds of the executives interviewed can be summarized, in order of priority, as follows:

- Marketing managers are not sufficiently innovative and entrepreneurial in their thinking and decision making.
- The productivity of marketing expenditures appears to be decreasing as marketing costs, especially for advertising media and field selling, rise.
- Marketing managers are generally unsophisticated in their understanding of the financial dimensions of marketing decisions and lack a bottom-line orientation. They tend to focus more on sales volume and market share changes than on profit contribution and return on assets.
- The product management system, and the marketing competence it brought, are no longer the exclusive properties of the firms that developed the system. For those firms who have used it the longest, the system may have become an inhibitor of innovative thinking.
- Marketing people with MBA degrees tend to think alike, to be risk averse, to want to move into general management too quickly, and not to want to pursue careers in sales and sales management.
- The acceptance of the marketing concept as a management philosophy is still incomplete, especially in smaller, more technically oriented, and industrial (vs. consumer) firms.

Each of these concerns, summarized here and asserted as conclusions supported by admittedly subjective data, has significant implications for marketing managers as well as for marketing teachers/scholars, in their roles as educators and researchers.

Lack of Innovative and Entrepreneurial Thinking

The lack of innovative and entrepreneurial thinking by marketing people was expressed as a major concern by a majority of these respondents and came up in the discussion in several different contexts, including:

- failure to provide proper stimulation and guidance for R&D and product development;
- failure to exploit and develop markets for new products developed by R&D;
- inability to define new methods for promoting products to customers in the face of major increases in the costs of media advertising and personal selling;
- a general unwillingness to stick one's neck out and take a necessary risk;
- a failure to innovate in distribution and other areas in order to keep up with the changing requirements of industrial customers doing business on a multinational basis;
- a tendency for product managers and higher levels of management in the product management organization, all of whom have similar education, training, and experience, to approach problems in the same way;
- attempting to meet significant new competition with traditional ways of doing business;
- inability to refine and modify product positioning.

These observations about the lack of innovative and entrepreneurial thinking by marketing people echo a management concern expressed by other authors, that American managers in general have emphasized short-term financial results and developed an institutionalized aversion to risk (Hayes and Abernathy 1980). If it is indeed true that marketing managers do not often think in an innovative and entrepreneurial fashion, part of the problem must be found in the systems used to direct, evaluate, and control marketing performance. In addition, one must look to the organizational arrangements made to facilitate two-way communication between marketing and research and development. Several of the respondents noted these connections and commented that these were a top management responsibility. One chief executive observed that the budget planning and review process encouraged marketing managers to stick to the proven path; truly innovative and distinctive marketing approaches have a low probability of surviving the hierarchical budget planning process.

Marketing Productivity

The second major set of issues identified by these business leaders concerned the declining productivity of marketing expenditures in the face of increased costs of doing business and, as noted above, failure to find innovative, more efficient approaches for communicating with customers. For the large, consumer package goods marketers the issues centered around increased media costs, particularly the costs of broadcast media. For firms in such areas as insurance and business machines, the concern was for the increased costs of fielding a national sales organization, especially in those cases where unit product prices were decreasing significantly. While the use of sophisticated decision models and analytical techniques was not a major concern of these top executives, positive or negative, none of the respondents felt, when asked, that such models and techniques had made significant contributions to the efficiency of marketing expenditures. A few, however, did describe marketing experiments currently underway to assess the productivity of advertising expenditures.

These impressions held by this sample of top managers are not inconsistent with the conclusions of marketing scholars who have looked at the contributions of management science to marketing. Myers, Greyser, and Massy (1979, p. 27) in their report on the American Marketing Association's Commission on the Effectiveness of Research and Development for Marketing Management noted that "A significant amount of marketing research effort, new knowledge development, model-building, and theorizing has had relatively little impact on improving marketing management over the [1955–1980] period." It is possible that a major part of the problem is that significant developments of potentially high relevance have simply not been reported in the literature that top management reads, nor has it been adequately communicated to them by their marketing staffs. It may also be significant to note that the most frequently cited work on marketing productivity analysis is still a small textbook published over 15 years ago (Sevin 1965). (See also Bucklin 1978 and Heskett 1965.) There appears to be little or no connection at the moment between marketing productivity analysis and concepts and techniques of management science developed in the last two decades.

Financial Performance

A third set of issues focussed on marketing managers' lack of understanding of the financial dimensions of corporate strategy and management decision making. The major criticism was that marketing managers do not understand basic concepts of financial management and are unable to consider the financial consequences of their decisions. As a result, they are said to concentrate on sales volume and market share objectives rather than such measures of profitability as profit contribution margin, R.O.I., and return on assets employed by business segment (i.e., product, customer, region, etc.).

There is much more to this concern than these most obvious issues. A central dimension is performance evaluation and the relationship between what marketing managers emphasize in their decision making and how they are evaluated and rewarded. A second dimension concerns how much emphasis should be placed on financial considerations by marketing managers. Some of these executives expressed a concern that marketing people could place too much emphasis on financial dimensions, worrying about things other than how to get orders, build market share, and improve competitive effectiveness, which should be their major concerns. Yet another consideration is the way in which top management has changed the signals as they relate to marketing management. In the words of one respondent, "We used to say to them, 'You get the sales and profit margins and we'll worry about how to finance them.' Not any more."

Related to this is the fact that some top managements have had difficulty assessing the tradeoffs between current, short-term financial performance—sales volume, contribution margin, and cash flow—and future, long-term financial performance—market share and long-range return on investment. As a result,, their marketing organizations have been receiving confused, changing, and conflicting signals. Astute top managers do tend to recognize this problem and take a major share of the blame for the less than satisfactory marketing performance that often resulted.

The Product Manager System and the MBA

Concern about the functioning of the product management system of marketing organization is relatively straightforward and is also intertwined with a concern about the nature of MBA-trained managers. The product manager system per se no longer conveys the inherent competitive advantage that it held for those large consumer package goods firms that innovated the concept. Their smaller and newer competitors have copied the system and hired away some of the talent developed by the leaders. As these systems mature, higher levels of management are staffed by persons who have been promoted from lower levels of the product management organization. Thus, several levels of management can have very similar training and experience. These former product managers can tend to continue to dabble in the details of product management to a degree that hinders the effectiveness of management at the lower levels.

According to some of the executives interviewed in the larger, consumer package goods firms, product managers used to come from many areas within the firm—sales, manufacturing, engineering, and others—as well as from outside. Today in contrast the standard source is the top 20 or 30 MBA programs in leading universities throughout the country. Among the opinions expressed by these top management representatives about the MBA talent being recruited by their organizations are that MBAs all tend to think alike, to approach problems the same way, to obscure a problem with excessive numbercrunching and analysis, to want to move into general management too quickly, to be unwilling to stay in a position long enough to develop competence and learn the details of the business, and to have no interest in sales and sales management careers. These are familiar concerns about MBAs, but that does not make them invalid.

Not only do these concerns about MBA aspirations and performance relate to the performance of the product manager system. They also relate directly to the observation that marketing managers do not like to take risks and are unable to approach problems in an innovative and entrepreneurial fashion.

Incomplete Acceptance of the Marketing Concept

As noted earlier, there was virtual unanimity among these executives that marketing is the critical management function in their firms from a strategic viewpoint and that it is likely to become even more important in the current decade. In the most sophisticated marketing organizations (i.e., the consumer package goods firms primarily), marketing is the line management function and the marketing concept is the dominant and pervasive management philosophy. In the rest of the companies in the sample, however, there appeared to be an incomplete acceptance of the marketing concept.

In the most obvious situation, the respondent executive could point to an absence of any senior executive with clear responsibility for marketing within the organization. In these instances, there had been a history of strong production-, technical- (engineering or R&D), or sales-oriented thinking dominating the firm. Another symptom of the problem was an absence of any market segmentation strategy. There also were a few cases where the respondent executive felt that marketing weakness was due to a failure by top management to devote the necessary financial and managerial resources to the marketing task.

In the industrial products and services firms especially, and also in some of the consumer products firms, marketing and sales were organizationally distinct, with sales being seen as a line function and marketing as a staff responsibility, often associated with the corporate planning function. The marketing function in these circumstances was said to be responsible for long-range marketing planning and market development, whereas the sales function was responsible for current year sales volume and profit performance through the implementation of marketing plans through specific sales and promotion programs. Not all of these top managers would agree that the separation of marketing and sales within the organization is evidence of incomplete acceptance of the marketing concept.

One senior executive made the important observation that getting the marketing concept understood and accepted is still the biggest challenge faced by any organization, despite the fact that the concept is now more than a quarter-century old. In his extensive experience in the top ranks of both industrial and consumer products firms, he noted that marketing "tends to degenerate into a sales orientation and an exclusive concern for marketing communications." He felt that there was an inevitable tendency in industrial firms for large customers, because of their importance, to bring pressures on the firm that create a very short-term orientation and a concern for specific orders and problems. He also pointed to sheer numbers of sales personnel compared with marketing as another reason why sales tends to dominate marketing. While these particular observations are attributable to a single CEO, they capture a set of issues of concern to a significant portion of this sample.

SOME IMPLICATIONS AND SUGGESTIONS FOR FUTURE RESEARCH

Although these concerns of top management are interesting for their own sake, and suggest some directions in which the marketing profession might look to find areas for improved management effectiveness, they also point to some underlying basic issues. These issues can be phrased as questions requiring further research and discussion.

How Does Management Performance Evaluation Impact on Marketing Performance?

There has been only minimal cooperation between organizational behavior and marketing scholars as revealed in the research literature, yet some of the most interesting and important issues of marketing decision making may be those that relate to the human side of enterprise. Criticism of marketing for failure to innovate and take risks is an obvious area where behavioral issues are at the core, not technical issues of marketing science and decision making. Part of the issue here is to explore relationships between various corporate financial goals and marketing performance as they are mediated through formal and informal performance appraisal systems. While recent months have seen some discussion of this issue in the management literature, it is an area that needs a great deal more management attention and academic research. Investigators need to look at relationships between measures of a firm's innovativeness, such as the rate of new product introductions, and how management in that firm is evaluated and rewarded. Marketing scholars need to become familiar with the work of scholars in organizational behavior on such topics as risk taking, organizational structure, and innovativeness, and integrate this into their own investigations of marketing performance and organizational effectiveness.

How Serious Is the Problem of Decreasing Productivity of Marketing Expenditures?

The assertion that marketing productivity has declined needs to be tested by careful analysis of changes in marketing costs and marketing effectiveness. Expenditure patterns need to be documented, adjusted for inflation, and related to changes in market share, sales volume, profit margin, and other measures of performance. A concern for such macro issues of marketing strategy and marketing performance has largely been left to the economists. Marketers have tended to focus their attention on the nuances of inter-brand competition and the battle for market share, and have not addressed some of the broader issues defined and outlined in this study.

At the minimum, marketers should be able to sort out the effects of cost inflation per se from the rest of the equation of marketing effectiveness that relates marketing dollar expenditures to marketing performance measures, if they are to deal with the charge of declining productivity. It is not likely that most marketing managers can defend themselves adequately against this charge, whether warranted or not, because they probably could not demonstrate any relationship between expenditures on marketing activities and traceable sales and profit results. The real issue here may not be productivity per se but an inability to measure cause-effect relationships between marketing expenditures and results.

What Has Happened to the Product Manager System?

There are several projects here for ambitious marketing scholars. A first step would be simply to track changes that have occurred in the nature and scope of product manager organizations in those firms that first developed such systems. A second step could be to trace their diffusion to other firms in the consumer packaged goods area and then beyond that to industrial product firms, providers of financial services, and other types of organizations, looking for adaptations that reflected the new environment of application. A third stage could define problems inherent in the system as perceived by product managers and their superiors in the organization. These descriptive stages could provide the base from which to investigate some more subtle and complex issues such as whether these systems stifle innovation and discourage risk taking. One hypothesis worth testing is that the training programs used by companies to develop product managers (not MBA programs) tend to develop rote approaches to problem analysis and solution. The issues here clearly trace back to issues of performance evaluation.

What Are the Barriers to Implementation and Maintenance of a Marketing Viewpoint in an Organization?

The obvious wisdom of customer orientation, market segmentation, and long-term strategic thinking based on sound market information, which are the hallmarks of the marketing concept, is hardly ever questioned, yet a substantial portion of this sample of some of the nation's top managers reports frustration in getting that viewpoint implemented. Students of organizations and human behavior are seldom surprised by the gap between theory and practice, concept and implementation, but the difficulties of implementing the market concept need to be understood in much greater detail. An important dimension to examine here is the central role played by the chief executive officer in promoting a marketing viewpoint, developing a truly integrated marketing organization, and supporting the marketing management team, especially as it competes with strong managers in engineering, R&D, production, sales, and other areas for scarce financial resources.

Some observers would argue that the emergence of strong strategic planning departments has weakened the position of the marketing department in the corporate hierarchy. That issue needs to be examined carefully. The conclusion will probably depend on the extent to which marketing is perceived to be part of, if not completely absorbed by, strategic planning. Another interesting issue here is whether a strong planning function serves as a stimulus or a barrier to innovative thinking. A reasonable hypothesis would be that it is intended to be the former but usually proves to be the latter.

SUMMARY AND CONCLUSIONS

These chief executives and operating officers believe that marketing is the most important management function in their businesses, and they see it becoming more important in the future. Whether they come from a marketing background or not, they believe that the development and maintenance of an effective marketing organization is a major requirement for success in the economic environment of increased competition and slow growth that will be characteristic of most markets in the 1980s. Having said that, however, these executives are critical of their marketing managers for a failure to think creatively and innovatively and to understand the financial implications of their decisions. They see marketing costs increasing faster than the effectiveness of those expenditures. They worry that the product management system may be becoming obsolete and express frustration with the difficulties of instilling and maintaining a true marketing orientation in their businesses. As CEOs and COOs, they feel a personal responsibility for the quality of their marketing managers and their performance and suspect that they have been guilty of giving conflicting signals to the marketers in their organizations because they, the top executives, have not resolved the complex tradeoffs between short-term and long-term measures of financial performance.

Against this background of management concerns, marketing managers and teachers/scholars in the field can assess their own activities, interests, and priorities. There are suggestions here that managers need to become more willing to take risks and more innovative and entrepreneurial in their thinking. Marketing managers need to devote more attention to financial analysis relevant to their decisions, especially relating to measures of return on investment and return on assets employed. This is a question of developing the necessary knowledge of financial management concepts as well as an issue of management attitude and viewpoint.

Those marketing managers who have the benefit of an MBA education may wish, in addition, to examine their own priorities and career plans. Does the career plan allow for adequate time to develop the necessary skills and understanding of the business to progress toward higher levels of marketing and general management? Does it recognize the importance of understanding the customer, the marketplace, competition, and distribution—knowledge that can often best be gained by significant exposure to field sales situations? MBAs must be sensitive to the way they are perceived by other members of the organization and must take steps to change the basis for those perceptions as well as the perceptions themselves.

For marketing academicians, some sobering self-analysis may also be in order. Are we asking the right questions? Marketing is different from finance and production, the other areas of management decision making where operations research and econometrics have been applied so forcefully and effectively. Marketing management is still more art than science and has yielded slowly to attempts to make it more scientific. Marketing data are by their very nature less precise, and cause-and-effect relationships are usually time-lagged and hard to pin down. Yet marketers aspire to the same degree of rigor that has characterized the analysis of their colleagues in these other functions. The result may have been a significant sacrifice of relevance (Mauser 1980).

The issues identified in this research as central in the thinking of top management are, by and large, qualitative, messy issues relating to organization, management direction and control, performance evaluation, goal-setting, etc. There is a real need for marketing researchers to refocus their attention on issues such as these, not just increasingly sophisticated issues of research methodology.

REFERENCES

Bucklin, Louis P. (1978), *Productivity in Marketing*, Chicago: American Marketing Association.

Day, George S. and Yoram Wind (1980), "Strategic Planning and Marketing: Time for a Constructive Partnership," *Journal of Marketing*, 44 (Spring), 7–8.

Greyser, Stephen A. (1980), "Marketing Issues," *Journal of Marketing*, 44 (January), 89–92.

Hayes, Robert H. and William J. Abernathy (1980), "Managing Our Way to Economic Decline," *Harvard Business Review*, 58 (July–August), 67–77.

Heskett, J. L., ed. (1965), *Productivity in Marketing*, Columbus: College of Commerce and Administration, The Ohio State University.

Mauser, Ferdinand (1980), "Marketing Issues: The Marketing Fraternity's Shortfall," *Journal of Marketing*, 44 (Fall), 97–98.

Myers, John G., Stephen A. Greyser, and William F. Massy (1979), "The Effectiveness of Marketing's 'R&D' for Marketing Management: An Assessment," *Journal of Marketing*, 43 (January), 17–29.

Sevin, Chester H. (1965), *Marketing Productivity Analysis*, New York: McGraw-Hill.

Wind, Yoram (1980), "Marketing in the Eighties," *Journal of Marketing*, 44 (January), 7–9.

2   The Misuse of Marketing: An American Tragedy

Roger C. Bennett and
Robert G. Cooper

Business Horizons, Vol. 24 (November–December 1981), pp. 51–61. Copyright 1981 by the Foundation for the School of Business at Indiana University. Reprinted by permission.

    The automobile industry, a microcosm of the American economy, entered 1981 in a state of shock. At one time, the industry, like America, was efficient, industrious, innovative, and very profitable. But by 1981 this was no longer true. Imports took 30 percent of the market; $80 billion was needed for design and retooling; Chrysler obtained a federal loan guarantee; and Ford and General Motors reported record losses. What is happening in the North American auto industry may offer a glimpse in miniature of what ails the entire U.S. economy.
    Has America lost its competitive edge? In the *Harvard Business Review*, two writers argued that America's economic malaise can be traced to a failure of the entrepreneurial spirit, a lack of technological innovation, and a shortsighted view of the future.[1] Pundits claim that the auto industry is in trouble because of cheaper imports that get better fuel economy.[2] This is too simple an answer. A more incisive diagnosis reveals the hard truths. The European and Japanese car makers have simply been better competitors: they anticipated market needs; they built a better product—one that is more reliable, has better workmanship, and is better engineered; and they did it efficiently. In short, these manufacturers delivered better value to the American consumer. While "domestic auto makers regarded small cars as low-technology, cheaply designed products aimed mainly at buyers unable or not willing to purchase a large vehicle,"[3] the foreign manufacturers produced high quality small cars that were recognized as better by the American consumer.
    The auto makers are not the only vulnerable companies in North America. In countless other manufacturing industries, North American firms are facing tough competition from foreign producers supplying products which offer better value. The television receiver industry, once dominated by domestic suppliers (RCA, GE, Sylvania, and others) has faced an onslaught of foreign brands for over a decade. Now Sony, Hitachi, and Toshiba appear to be the product leaders, with American consumers actually paying a *price premium* for certain of these "superior" imported goods. The same thing has happened in many other markets. Electronic goods and other moderate- to high-technology items such as

cameras, small kitchen appliances, stereo equipment, motorcycles, and bicycles are a few that come to mind. Industrial products face similar competition: Japanese and French tire makers have made major inroads into the U.S. industrial tire market based not on price, but on product and technological superiority. Even America's computer industry is nervously watching Japanese computer makers take aim at the U.S.

The failure to deliver product value to the customer is the prime reason for this lack of competitiveness. Twenty years of adherence to the marketing concept may have taken its toll on American enterprise.[4] The marketing concept has diverted our attention from the product and its manufacture; instead we have focused our strategy on responses to market wants and have become preoccupied with advertising, selling, and promotion. And in the process, product value has suffered.

In this article we examine how this has happened and we look at some of the major changes that are needed to correct the problem. In apportioning the blame, we are particularly scornful of the efforts of our own profession, namely marketing academics. We suggest that many professors, in relative isolation from the business community, have rigorously and expertly pushed back the frontiers of knowledge, but in the wrong direction. We personally have sometimes been involved in this ourselves. *Nostra culpa.* We have since seen the light, and in this article, one of our many messages is an appeal for others to do the same.

THE MARKETING CONCEPT: CULPRIT?

Three decades ago, the marketing concept was advanced as a guide to corporate strategy. What is this "marketing concept" that has had so much impact on American business direction? Simply stated, it is the business philosophy that places the customer at the top of the corporate organizational chart. It states that the firm should be "market oriented" and the "satisfaction of customer needs is the key to corporate profits." The philosophy begins with the argument that corporate fortunes are decided largely by the customers because customers through their purchase "votes," decide the fate of the firm. Further, the most effective way to create a customer is to market products aimed directly at his needs and wants. An integrated program of product, price, promotion, and distribution is considered to be essential to this approach.

The intuitive logic of the marketing concept is difficult to refute. It is impossible to name any commercially successful product or invention that failed to cater to some type of human need. Of course, many of the "needs" were after-the-fact explanations for the product's success, and often the need was not readily apparent at the time of the invention or product development.

This strict adherence to the marketing concept has damaged American business. It has led to a dearth of true innovation and it has shifted the strategic focus of the firm away from the product to other elements of the marketing mix, elements that can be manipulated very successfully in the short run but which leave the business vulnerable in the longer term.

PRODUCT INNOVATION: THE VICTIM

The impact of a market-responsive strategy has been most strongly felt in the field of product innovation. According to a recent U.S. Senate report, product strategies in the U.S. now emphasize short-term returns at the expense of significant innovations.[5] A market-driven new product strategy provides little encouragement for technological discoveries, inventions, or significant breakthroughs; the "technology push" model has given way to the "market pull" model. Two researchers, Donald A. Marquis and Sumner Myers,[6] report that of 567 new products they studied, about three-quarters were derived by using the market pull model; this study was made in 1969, and we suspect the figure is even higher today.

The market pull model is the antithesis of the technology push approach. With the latter, scientific discovery or the availability of new technology leads to the development of a product. Ideas come from scientists and engineers, not from consumers. This does not mean that these companies push ahead developing products for which there is no demand. But the initial impetus for a good new product does not always come from the consumer. Indeed, we argue that innovative ideas will rarely arise there. Technology push proves a far more fertile ground for new ideas. Well-known examples of technology push are the laser and transistor, two scientific breakthroughs which are used in a number of successful products.

The market pull model generally yields good results, especially for industries such as packaged goods. And it seems to work in the short run. But whether such a model is desirable for a company or an entire industry in the long run, and whether it suits high technology and more complex product classes, is certainly debatable. Yet, encouraged by the successes of these market-oriented new products, higher technology and industrial goods firms are now emulating the model. As one senior R&D manager in a huge multinational firm put it: "Our consumer division has a market pull new product model that really works. Now we in the industrial division want to do the same."

Much industrial R&D, as a result, has become a technological response to requests from the marketing department. One effect has been the diminished investment in R&D by American industry, dropping from 2.07 percent of GNP in 1960 to only 1.76 percent today. Another result, with serious implications, is that much of the R&D community, after two decades of being shackled, may have lost its creative and inventive capability. As one senior manager said: "Our advertising says we're the 'discovery company.' Hell, we haven't discovered anything for fifteen years!"

A market-oriented R&D strategy necessarily leads to low-risk product modifications, extensions, and style changes. Product proliferation, a disease of the seventies, has been one result. Market-derived new product ideas will usually result in the ordinary. Market researchers have become expert at encouraging consumers to verbalize their wants and needs, but people tend to talk in terms of the familiar, about what is around them at a particular moment. For example, ask a commuter what new product ideas he would like to see in the area of rapid transit and, chances are, he will list a number of improvements to his bus or subway system—tinted glass windows, air conditioning, better schedules, and the like. Rarely will he be able to think in terms of totally new and

The Market Pull Model

The market pull model has been perfected by the packaged goods industry. They search the market for clues and examine people's needs exhaustively. The result is usually a carefully focused product that is moderately successful. As an example, consider the market pull model for the development of a new breakfast food by a hypothetical company:

Step 1: Do extensive market research to identify an unsatisfied need, segment, or niche in the marketplace. Using sophisticated market research tools if necessary (multidimensional scaling, trade off analysis, and so on), determine the ideal product's attributes. Let the market "design" the product.

Example: for breakfast foods, a semi-sweet, easily prepared, baked breakfast product, with attributes somewhere between toast and a sweet roll.

Step 2: Ask the R&D group to develop a product that meets these market specifications exactly. No technological breakthroughs or inventions are necessary—just give the market what it says it wants.

Solution: a waffle-like product, frozen, suitable for a toaster, with a sweet filler, say strawberry jam.

Step 3: The next few steps involve the refinement of the product design (including consumer preference taste tests) and verifying the financial attractiveness of the project (test marketing, for example).

Final Step: Launch the product. Position it in people's minds as a great tasting, "fun" breakfast food, which is easy to prepare (hot from your toaster). Give it a name to reflect its position: "Pop-Toasties." Package it attractively, and saturation advertise on television.

imaginative urban transportation systems. The latter are the domain of the engineer, scientist, and designer.

Managers therefore learn only about the familiar needs of consumers, expressed in the consumer's own terms, for a particular point in time. As a source of innovative and significant new product ideas, the consumer is limited in three ways:

1. Consumers' perceptions of their needs are restricted to the familiar, to items consumers can relate to. By definition, a true innovation is very often out of the scope of the normal experience of the consumer.
2. Consumers' ability to express these needs, to verbalize what they want, particularly when they do not know what is technologically feasible, is limited.
3. Because of the dynamic nature of these expressed needs, they may well have changed by the time the new product is designed, tested, and manufactured, the Edsel being a classic example.

The eventual result of a market-based R&D strategy is the slow death of product innovation. Original and creative new products, once the lifeblood of American enterprise and one key to America's competitive success in the world, are sadly missing. Consider some more evidence:

In 1960, industry's expenditures for R&D were 87.5 percent of those spent on advertising. By 1977, the proportion had fallen to 75 percent. America is spending a relatively constant percentage of its GNP on advertising, while the proportion devoted to R&D is falling.

We have decided that it is easier to *talk about* our new products than actually to develop them. And so we spend billions more convincing the customer that the product is "new and improved" rather than spending the money in the lab to develop a significantly superior product. In the world of new products, we have become a society of tinkerers and cosmeticians rather than true product innovators.

SHIFTED FOCUS

The strategic focus has shifted away from the product, away from its design, development, and manufacture. Lacking significant product advantages, many firms have been forced to rely on the other selling tools: advertising, promotion, and distribution. And through the supporting elements of the marketing mix, the firm maintains its competitive edge. We call this approach a "non-product strategy," even though the approach is more tactical than strategic.

An example of a company that went from product leadership to relying on other elements of the marketing mix with unfortunate results is the Singer Sewing Machine Company. At one time, Singer *owned* the sewing machine market. It invented the sewing machine, and the name Singer almost became a generic term for sewing machine. The firm was the undisputed product and market leader.

During the fifties and sixties, Singer turned away from product as its core or central strategy. Distribution and a worldwide chain of Singer stores became a leading component of its strategy. And so did heavy advertising and promotion, mostly featuring Singer sales and dollar rebate specials; remarkably little advertising focused on product attributes and quality. As a result, product leadership—technology, design, and quality—began to falter.

The Europeans attacked the high end of the market with technologically superior and better quality machines. Names such as Bernina, Pfaff, and Necchi became synonymous with product reliability. The Japanese, meanwhile, took aim at the middle and lower ends of the market, offering machines comparable to Singer's, but often of higher quality, and usually at lower prices. Today, the major market contender for Singer's dominance is a private brand machine sold by a national retailer, but made in Japan.

The dilemma in which Singer finds itself occurred because the company created a product leadership void in the industry: it turned its attention to promotion, advertising, and merchandising, and left the door open to others to develop and manufacture superior products. Singer moved to a non-product strategy with serious consequences.

In fact, this non-product strategy may succeed, although normally in the short run and in domestic markets. After all, how can one go wrong simply doing what the customers say they want? For a decade or two, cosmetic changes and style updates, backed by intense advertising and promotion, will keep the product competitive. Success in the home market is guaranteed...for a while.

The American automotive industry went through this phase between 1955 and the late 1970s. The "new" models were unveiled each fall with great fanfare and little that was substantially and technologically new. In contrast, and with much less hoopla, foreign car manufacturers were busily perfecting new technologies: fuel injection, the diesel engine, front-wheel drive, pollution-free engines (rather than catalytic converters that attempt to deal with the pollution once it has been created), fuel-efficient engines, better quality control methods. The American auto industry's credo appeared to be: where our product is lacking, we will make up the difference by aggressive selling and heavy promotion. In recent years, the hard sell and dollar rebates signified trouble in the automobile industry.

Such a non-product strategy does not work well in international markets either. Here, a product must stand on its own much more than in the home market. Several studies have reported that the product offering (and this includes price) is the key to international success. One reason is different customer expectations. Europeans, for example, are often characterized as being more interested in the functional and technological aspects of products than are North American consumers.

More important, the other elements of the marketing mix are not likely to be as effective abroad. Advertising is bound to be less concentrated and hence less influential as many and diverse markets are attacked; the firm also loses some control over its promotional, selling, and distribution efforts as it moves to foreign lands and relies on intermediaries. In third-world and state-controlled economies, the normal supporting elements of the marketing mix are likely to be either ineffectual or controlled by others. Product must compete against product; and so product strategy becomes preeminent.

Unfortunately for many North American firms, our global economy and the multinational corporations are rapidly making the notion of a "home market" obsolete. As one British manager put it: "Our home market has become someone else's international market. Either we must build products for international markets or not build products at all." The same is happening on this side of the Atlantic. *World Products* are the logical outcome. The implications are clear: if America's home market is really an international market, then the rules of international competition apply. More than ever, a non-product strategy begins to fail.

The non-product strategy is weak also because it is a short-term solution. The strategy fails because no market remains stable forever; needs change and technology moves ahead. Somewhere, a company—at home or abroad—introduces a new product that represents a significant improvement over existing ones: a front-wheel-drive car; a radial tire; a word processing machine. The product may be better because it is a technological breakthrough. It might be simply a significant departure from existing designs. It almost certainly better anticipates users' needs. And the firms that have not heeded the central role of product strategy are suddenly vulnerable. The product cosmeticians and tinkerers are suddenly left in the wake of the firms seeking the technological advances.

A familiar example illustrates this point well. The American kitchen used to be dominated by American products, heavily promoted and, incidentally, sold at a relatively low price. But, in the last five years, of the three major technological innovations, two—the food processor and the convection oven—came from overseas, and the third—the microwave oven—illustrates the problem that U.S. manufacturers have in competing. The Japanese producers dominate the market.

THE ROOTS OF DISASTER

In the short space of twenty-five years, American business has shifted from a product strategy to one which emphasizes non-product variables.

Why the sudden reorientation? The marketing concept as a doctrine of business has been cited as one reason. But this is merely an explanation of a phenomenon, and not its cause.

We submit that two major forces have created this non-product movement. One is the fault of business educators. The other is the method used to evaluate academics.

Let us look first at management education. For the last twenty years, business schools have been the fastest growing educational units on university campuses. In the 1950s, schools of engineering led the way; but today management is king. The dramatic growth in graduates is further evidence: in 1950, only 4,000 MBAs graduated in America; by 1979, this number had grown to almost 50,000. Add to this the many undergraduate programs and executive training courses and we begin to appreciate the extraordinary growth of management education. The influx of graduates of these schools and courses into American business is bound to have had an impact.

Have you ever wondered what management teachers—those people charged with educating today's and tomorrow's managers—concern themselves with? Consider a recent convention of marketing educators, the 1980 American Marketing Association convention in Chicago. A quick perusal of the program reveals some startling facts. Over 50 percent of the sessions were devoted to techniques: understanding and reaching the consumer, measuring the consumer's behavior and desires, and developing new models and methodologies in this area; 18 percent to educational methods; 5 percent to techniques of planning and strategy; only 4 percent to general marketing strategy; and *nothing at all* to new products.

This breakdown is probably a fair representation of the interests of America's marketing academics, interests that become the thrust of the classroom teaching experience. It comes as no surprise to learn that today's marketing graduate, while quite expert in techniques of marketing research, quantitative decision making and consumer behavior, has very little feel for long-term competitive strategies. Moreover, the new MBA knows almost nothing about product strategy, design management, and the role of technological innovation. The graduate is a technician, not a strategist, and feels more at home playing with the elements of the marketing mix than developing bold new strategies with new products and new markets.

Similar problems beset other important areas of management education. For example, the finance educator appears to be going the route of the theoretical economist; production is no longer production, but operations research; and so on. We are educating a generation of number pushers and tacticians and calling them managers.

Behind this clear movement towards concentrating on theoretical trivia is the academic measurement system itself. The heart of academic research is the scientific method where everything can be assigned a number, measured, controlled, replicated, validated, and relied upon. So professors and others who aspire to academic advancement tend not to concern themselves with those areas where the scientific method is most difficult to apply. They search for problems that will yield the "correct" methodology rather than seeking new and better ways of looking at the major problem areas that beset managers. The academic evaluation system, then, is at the root of the problem.

The second force underlying the preoccupation with non-product tactics is the way managers themselves are evaluated. First, most performance measures are made over the short term. One year is about the maximum period over which performance is measured: this year's sales versus last year's; ROI for the year; and so on. And the best way to show "good results" in the short term is to gain or hold market share through tactical moves—advertising, promotion, selling—while cutting costs in the manufacture of the product, sometimes at the expense of product quality. The short time horizon tends to discourage strategic development and significant product innovation, whose costs may be incurred today, but whose payoffs are years away. As one senior manager, in charge of product and business development of a multinational firm, said: "Our firm is committed to yesterday's bottom line; and managers are measured on the past, not future performance."

A second aspect of management evaluation is the way managers themselves evaluate investments and expenditures. Today the manager is provided with myriad evaluative tools to help in making decisions about resource allocation. Of course, the criteria used in these decisions are closely related to the ways used to evaluate individuals. And quantifiable measures, such as short-term profitability, are usually included in the measurement system. Uncertainty and the future are handled poorly by most quantitative evaluation techniques. For example, it is usually difficult to predict the sales that an innovative product may generate. Lacking certain sales data as an input to the usual IRR or ROI calculations tends to make the evaluation come out negative. The result is that the short-term projects with highly certain outcomes are favored at the expense of riskier, long-term expenditures or investments.

The kind of training managers receive today coupled with the way managers are evaluated, and how they, in turn, evaluate resource allocations are largely responsible for the shift from product strategy and technological innovation. Instead of genuine advances, we witness a tactical and short-term orientation, one where the focus is on cosmetic product changes, advertising and promotion, and cutting production costs.

THE SOLUTION: PRODUCT VALUE

The essence of business is to deliver a product which satisfies a need and whose market value exceeds its cost. In the transaction between buyer and seller, it is the product's value that the customer pays for. Thus *product value* is an important concept to business. According to the Concise Oxford Dictionary, the term "value" means "worth, desirability, utility." Price and cost are essentially concerned with money, while value is concerned with worth and desirability, and is a subjective matter.[7] The marketplace provides a rough measure of the worth or value of a product: the price a product can command is a monetary measure the customer places on the product. Profits are thus the difference between a product's value (measured by its price) and the product's cost. The firm's task becomes the maximization of the spread between the value of a product and the cost to manufacture and deliver. The role of a business is the modulation of value, price, and cost of a product.

The ability to provide a product with superior value, but at competitive costs (or the same value at lower costs) is the key to long-run business success. A product has properties or attributes that can be translated into value. One such attribute is usefulness: a product may supplement or magnify a human effort, save time, or produce an otherwise unachievable result. Another value-inducing attribute is security: protection, safety, reliability. Availability is a third value-inducing attribute: people pay a premium for immediate delivery. Other value-inducing attributes include rarity (a Paris original or a limited edition); custom make (such as a made-to-measure suit); and original, creative work (a fine painting).

The manufacturer's task is to maximize the product's value for a given cost. He can do this by improving availability—fast delivery or more stock in inventory. Alternately, since value is in the eye of the beholder, often advertising and marketing communication will convince the buyer of the product's value. Advertising can actually increase the value of the product to the buyer by emphasizing certain desired attributes or by making existing attributes appear more important. But the product itself—its inherent attributes or properties—is by far the most important and enduring value-inducing element. Thus, the product should be the central or core element in the firm's competitive strategy. And the firm that strives to provide a higher value or "better" product has a more sound and longer lasting base for prosperity. Even the auto makers are learning the lesson. For example, GM's new chairman, Roger B. Smith, notes that attention to product quality along with fuel economy will be GM's product strategy in the future.

The critical role of having a superior and unique product has been reinforced by studies about what makes a new product a success.[8] Marketing skills and resources were assets; so were production and technological skills. And being in a growth market was a positive factor. But the most important characteristics that separated the successes from the failures were uniqueness and superiority—a product that did a unique task; performed better; lasted longer; saved the customer time or money; and so on. The point seems an obvious one. But is it? An inspection of the sample of products studied reveals that most firms were not developing unique and superior products. Product extensions and incremental developments are the rule rather than the exception in today's product development game. Other investigations have shown similar results.

MUST BE BETTER THAN COMPETITORS

The focus of a firm's competitive strategy should be on product and product value. The proponent of the marketing concept is right when he says the product must meet a market need. Otherwise it would have no value. But product value implies a comparison. And so it must do more than merely satisfy a need; the product must meet the needs *better* than the competitors' products. It is this focus on "being better" that is missing in the marketing concept.

A better or more highly valued product is a function of its attributes. And these in turn depend on the technology that goes into the product, the design and engineering that shape the product, and the product's manufacture (which determines quality of workmanship and product reliability). Note that the factors that create the superior value are the resources of the firm—R&D, engineering, design and production—and suggest an inward focus.

In contrast, a market-oriented philosophy urges us to look outward—to the marketplace—for new products and new opportunities. This may result in a product that meets a market need, but meeting a market need is a necessary but *not sufficient* condition for success. Being able to "do it better" is key—and here is where a focus on the firm's distinctive competencies and internal resources is required.

An example of the marketing concept taken to an extreme is the plight of certain universities and colleges in the U.S. Faced with declining enrollments, many colleges spotted new market needs, and in the tradition of a market orientation, developed new programs and courses. Continuing education was a favorite area. The trouble was that, in the case of many institutions, the expertise and material resources to deliver a good program in these new areas simply did not exist. And now many are in trouble, facing loss of accreditation. University administrators have learned what many businessmen now are experiencing: any astute organization can spot a market need; but only a minority can deliver a sound product for a particular need. Today the universities that focused on excellence rather than chasing market needs are in a sounder position.

It is time the firm stopped being so market driven, and began turning its attention back to its own internal areas of excellence. Let the firm do what it does best; let it build on its areas of strength; and let a preoccupation with technological, design, and manufacturing excellence dominate the desire to cater solely to market whims.

THE ROUTE TO RECOVERY

How can American business recapture its former prowess? One way is to reflect on the attitudes and approaches that once made American business the envy of the world. We must go beyond the market concept. The answer lies not just in satisfying customer needs but in providing a product of superior value to the marketplace. We must adopt a product value concept (which is, of course, very different from a production concept):

The product value concept is a business orientation that recognizes that product value is the key to profits. It stresses competing on the basis of customer need satisfaction with superior, higher value products. Value depends on the customer's perception of the product attributes, which are largely a function of the firm's technological, design, and manufacturing strengths and skills.

The implication, then, is that for long-term success, the firm must build on what it does best with the objective of delivering a superior quality, high value product. We borrow a familiar military strategic premise and argue that "the firm should operate from a position of power; it should build in areas where it can utilize its existing strengths." If concentrating on what the firm does best is essential for long-term success, then the corporation must be reasonably clear about what it is good at. Texas Instruments' success has been based on its strong production resources and its abilities to move down the learning curve rapidly. Of course, it also had to market the products it produced. Procter & Gamble recognized its success was due to its marketing abilities. But it also had to have good products. On the rare occasions that its products were not superior—Rely tampons and Pringle's New Fangled Potato Chips—disaster or relative failure resulted.

Let us take a look at a company that shifted its focus away from what it does best. Massey Ferguson was a leader in the 1930s, 40s, and 50s in combine harvester technology and in other aspects of farm machinery design. Indeed, Massey Harris merged with Ferguson in 1953 in order to enhance this leadership by obtaining access to Ferguson's hydraulic technology.

From the mid-sixties on, however, management diverted its attention to other markets. It became more heavily involved in diesel engines and concentrated aggressively on earth moving and construction equipment. An office equipment manufacturer was even acquired. Large investment was needed for the new businesses, and little top management time was left for the traditional business. Competitors, meanwhile, improved their products, fine-tuned their distribution systems, and began to leave Massey Ferguson behind. Larger, heavier, and more powerful farm equipment became available and Massey Ferguson began to find it difficult to compete.

In 1980, after several years of difficulties, it seemed the firm had reached a crisis. High interest rates and the recession proved damaging to a company that was highly leveraged and whose main lines were purchased by farmers on credit. The product line was not as strong competitively as it had been. And the dealer network was fraying. Management was trying to dispose of its peripheral businesses, begging money from government, and wondering what had happened to a proud old company.

What had happened was a failure to concentrate on providing a quality product in an area where it had leadership and expertise. Other aspects of the business took precedence. Massey Ferguson learned too late about building from a position of strength, about concentrating on what it did best.

The occasional company that has successfully moved into markets and products not based on traditional corporate resources has done so only after realizing the full implications of its move. IBM, for example, took three years after its decision to enter the computer field before it produced its first product. It hired a number of the available people with knowledge in the field during this period. And it built or acquired the necessary resources. To do this, of course, required top management commitment. As Tom Watson, Jr., IBM president said, "We realized we had to succeed at this or fail as a company."

This product orientation we propose leads to a view of the strategic planning process very different from the market driven approach accepted today. The strategic notions expressed in the famous 1960 article on marketing myopia represented an appealing but simplistic and one-sided solution. In today's complex world, the idea of building a business solely in terms of market needs does not necessarily work. According to this market-oriented strategic approach, the railroads should have seen themselves as providing transportation services to America (a market need); this would have taken them into trucking, airlines, and telecommunications, which are more viable businesses today. But the same logic would also have led them to car rentals, taxi fleets, and perhaps even the manufacture of transportation equipment or automobiles. These businesses are probably very wrong for railroads, simply because they do not build on the strengths and skills found in a railroad.

One very successful railroad in North America is Canadian Pacific. Now the world's largest privately-owned transportation firm, it was once just a transcontinental railroad. Following the "transportation concept," it expanded into trucking, airlines, ships, intermodal shipping, and telecommunications (including Telex). Note that this successful firm expanded only into areas that could build on its internal strengths. But the company was also successful in a number of non-transportation areas: mining operations, because lead and zinc were found on its land in the Rocky Mountains; hotels around the world, because it knew how to accommodate travelers; real estate development, partly because of its land holdings. These non-transportation areas are quite inconsistent with a market-oriented view of strategy, yet because they built on a resource the firm owned or some competence the firm possessed, these areas too were logical opportunities for exploitation.

A product orientation also focuses more attention on execution. Strategic choice—the right market and product concept—is only part of the battle. Being able to deliver the right product is the main issue. The emphasis here is on proper execution: sound technology, good industrial design, meticulous engineering, and workmanship and efficiency in production. Planning is important; but execution—"doing it right"—is equally critical, which brings us back to the necessity of basing strategy on what the firm does best.

Operationally, it is clear that changes are needed in a number of areas in order to achieve a product-value orientation. In the field of management education:

- Marketers must place less emphasis on the marketing concept as the *only* business philosophy. Let us downplay the marketing concept in texts, courses, and seminars. Instead, a product orientation—delivering product value based on what firms do well—should be taught. In addition, more emphasis on product strategy, technological innovation, management of technology, and industrial design is needed in business school curricula.
- The technology-push model must be reinvented as a viable route to new products in management courses. Typical management texts on new products sound as though market-pull were the *only* model.
- Academic research must be reoriented to deal with the problems and issues facing industry. Relevance, as well as academic rigor, should be the key. Instead of trying to be just as theoretical and elegant as their learned colleagues in the pure sciences, business academics should recognize that management is a profession. The audience for academic research should be far more frequently the practitioner, and not solely other academics.

In the business firm itself, many changes are possible. Most must begin with a change in attitude and our approach to doing business. Hence, these changes must be initiated from the top of the company. We suggest that, for most firms:

- The product value concept—delivering the most product value efficiently—should become the corporate credo.

- A competitive strategy based on product quality, design, and technology should be the long-term approach to domestic and international competition.
- R&D should not be strictly market oriented. Extensions, modifications and style changes in response to market wants will certainly be required. But a significant portion of R&D should be allocated to the long term: to the creation of innovative products, and even to scientific discovery, simply to keep the firm at the "state of the art."
- Performance measures for managers should be future oriented and not strictly short term. Yesterday's bottom line should not be the only criterion of evaluation. Provision should be made in evaluation systems to encourage wise, but forward-looking, thinking.
- Evaluation techniques for resource allocations should recognize the need for a balance between the lower risk, ordinary ventures and the more adventurous projects with longer term, but less certain, payoff. The usual ROI and discounted cash flow capital budgeting techniques need to be supplemented by evaluation approaches that permit subjective and non-quantitative inputs for these bolder projects.
- And above all, the firm must recognize what it does well. It must be aware of its distinctive competencies and unique resources. Having identified these areas of excellence, the firm should use these in its task of producing a product of superior value.

Perhaps, in the 1950s and 60s, many firms, especially those in industrial markets, had to become more market oriented. Management of that era was based on experiences of war and post-war shortages and a seller's market. A new outlook was needed.

By now, we have learned the lesson too well. In our efforts to cater to every whim of the consumer, we have become too concerned with the short term and the cosmetic. This attitude has been encouraged by academic institutions in their teaching and research activities. And it has been further reinforced by the essentially short-run nature of most corporate evaluation systems.

It is time for a new philosophy to emerge, based on the idea that product value is the key to success. Behind that concept lies the notion of providing superior products at competitive costs. Doing this requires the corporation to analyze its own skills and resources and to build from these positions of strength. While the firm cannot neglect market forces, the driving force must often come from elsewhere.

To achieve this change in philosophy will require a significant shift in attitudes and behavior. A good deal of what has been built up in recent years as a result of the marketing concept, our ideas of what constitutes good methodological research, and the control systems prevalent in most organizations today, will have to be reconsidered.

From the time of the introduction of the marketing concept in the late 1940s to its general acceptance in the early to mid-60s, fifteen years elapsed; many of its ramifications are still today working their way through corporate structures. For the sake of the economic health of America, we hope that the focus on product value occurs far more quickly.

ENDNOTES

1. Robert H. Hayes and William J. Abernathy, "Managing Our Way to Economic Decline," *Harvard Business Review*, July–August 1980: 67–77.
2. See "When It Comes to the Bottom Line on New Cars, Buyers' Yen for Imports Is Hardly Surprising," *The Wall Street Journal*, August 25, 1980: 32.
3. See "Detroit's New Sales Pitch," *Business Week*, September 22, 1980: 79.
4. Roger C. Bennett and Robert G. Cooper, "Beyond the Marketing Concept," *Business Horizons*, June 1979: 76–83.
5. Ellis R. Mottur, *National Strategy for Technological Innovation*, Report prepared for the U.S. Senate Committee on Commerce, Washington, D.C., October 1979.
6. Sumner Myers and Donald A. Marquis, "Successful Industrial Innovations: A Study of Factors Underlying Innovation in Selected Firms," *National Science Foundation*, NSF, 1969: 69–71.
7. Parts of this discussion based on: L. Bruce Archer, *Design Awareness and Planned Creativity in Industry* (Department of Industry, Trade and Commerce, Ottawa, and Design Council of Great Britain, London, 1974).
8. Robert G. Cooper, "The Dimensions of Industrial New Product Success and Failure," *Journal of Marketing*, Summer 1979: 93–103.

3 The Effectiveness of Marketing's "R&D" for Marketing Management: An Assessment

John G. Myers, Stephen A. Greyser, and William F. Massy

Reprinted from the *Journal of Marketing*, published by the American Marketing Association, Vol. 43 (January 1979), pp. 17-29. Reprinted by permission.

In 1976-1977, William F. Massy, then vice president of the American Marketing Association's Education Division, initiated a "blue ribbon" Commission to study the effectiveness of research and development for marketing management (Massy, Greyser, and Myers 1979). He enlisted Stephen A. Greyser to join the effort as co-chairman of the Commission. John G. Myers served as a Commission member along with many others[1] and became more deeply involved as the Education Vice President following Massy. This article draws heavily on the work of the Commission and presents some of our own reflections on the state of research utilization in marketing and its "effectiveness" over the 25[-year]-period from the early 1950s to the present.[2] It represents a summary of and observations on those elements of the Commission's work that we believe to be of broadest interest.

BACKGROUND AND MISSION

The Commission considered a retrospective look at marketing—where we are and how we got there—to be of potential value in enhancing the process of creating new marketing knowledge and disseminating/utilizing it. By understanding the process of knowledge-creation and diffusion and the barriers and blocks to the process, marketers should be able to learn something about how to make it work more effectively. The Commission was charged with both an *evaluation* function—to assess the effectiveness of research and development in marketing[3] for marketing management over the past quarter century—and a *prescriptive* function—to make recommendations of ways in which the generation and diffusion process could be improved.

The Commission accepted as a given the goal of the long-run relevance of knowledge created to practice in marketing. In this setting, knowledge implies all forms of academic and professional marketing research, and practice incorporates individuals and organizations such as line and staff marketing managers, senior corporation executives, and decision makers in government and nonprofit organizations. Its focus was thus on attempting to understand and evaluate the knowledge-creation and diffusion process in marketing. Where and how do changes originate? Where and with whom do ideas incubate and concepts become articulated? Where are the new methods tested and the techniques refined?

The concern for the study of these kinds of questions in marketing lies in the continuing serious debate as to the *relevance* of much of the knowledge-generating sector's activities to marketing management practice. It is obvious that a knowledge-creating sector does exist within marketing. Contrary to the views of many academics, the knowledge-creating sector is not solely, nor even largely, the province of academic researchers. Rather, it encompasses basic research mostly done in universities; applied and problem-oriented research in universities, research institutes, and government or nonprofit organizations; as well as problem-solving research in corporations, advertising agencies, marketing research firms, and consulting organizations. Attesting to a growth in quantity, albeit not necessarily in quality, of what is intended to be useful marketing knowledge over the past quarter-century was the creation of the AMA-sponsored *Journal of Marketing Research*, in addition to the *Journal of Marketing*; the advent of the multidisciplinary *Journal of Consumer Research* with its large proportion of marketing-based content; and an expansion of marketing-related articles in journals such as *Management Science* and *Operations Research*. But a fundamental question is whether all or most of these segments do create *useful* knowledge. Although terms like "useful," "effective," and "relevant" are hard to define tightly, there is little question that a hard-headed demand for demonstrations of relevance to practical marketing problems has, to a considerable degree, replaced a post World War II faith that knowledge is useful "in its own right." This is not to deny that much research—particularly basic research—is difficult to manage and inherently "wasteful" by post-hoc judgment. However, the Commission believed that it should be possible to trace *some* degree of impact of basic and other research on improvements in marketing management practice over a 25-year period.

Another way of expressing the driving force behind the Commission's work is to say that it was fundamentally interested in research accountability. Is the investment in knowledge-generation in the field of marketing worthwhile? Is the process self-generating (like a breeder reactor), or does it require explicit and continuing investments of time, talent and money? If the process is not now as effective as it should be, what are the barriers and blocks that prevent new knowledge and research from being utilized?

More specifically, the objectives of the Commission were:

- To identify changes in the marketing profession and practice over the past 25 years.
- To examine the nature and objectives of knowledge generation and R&D in marketing and provide examples of new knowledge developed during the period.
- To explain the process of knowledge-creation and the diffusion of knowledge in the field of marketing.
- To assess the contributions, or lack thereof, of marketing knowledge to marketing practice, and develop a list of recommendations directed to specific constituencies within the field.

The balance of this article is structured along these lines. Definitive conclusions in any of these areas are not easy, and not immediately amenable to the usual kinds of empirical research operations. The Commission employed a variety of methods and procedures to address each topic and illuminate the issues involved.

Methods

The work of the Commission involved five different operating methods and data generation procedures. First, commissioners and selected "friends" of the Commission[4] were polled for their opinions on four challenging questions: What were the major changes in the practice of marketing over the past 25 years? What major, new, useful approaches and techniques had been introduced over the period? What major problem areas remain? What major research approaches and techniques (in the commissioner's judgment) had failed to fulfill their promises?

Second, several face-to-face meetings of the commissioners were held during 1976 and 1977. Much attention, particularly in the later meetings, was given to the discussion and development of perspectives and viewpoints on the idea-generation and diffusion process in marketing.

Third, a study of changes in marketing journals and textbooks over the 25-year period was undertaken by the Commission's staff. The journal study involved content analysis at five-year intervals of the *Journal of Marketing*, *Journal of Marketing Research*, *Harvard Business Review*, and *Journal of Consumer Research*. Examined were "hot topics" at the beginning and end of the period, topics that appeared to be an ongoing source of interest as well as topics that seemed to fade and others that were introduced, and the business/academic affiliation of authors. Details of this study, as well as all other studies undertaken by the Commission, are given in its final report (Massy, Greyser, and Myers 1979). One self-evident watershed, however, was the 1964 founding of the *Journal of*

Marketing Research with its emphasis on reports of empirical research and multivariate data analysis.

The textbook study involved content analysis of 15 marketing textbooks (mostly those in multiple editions) ranging from Maynard and Beckman to Kotler, Enis, and Heskett. The period was characterized by a move from principles texts "about marketing" to managerial and decision-oriented texts "for marketing managers." Early texts covering institutional views and topics such as commodities and agricultural marketing were replaced by managerially-oriented texts emphasizing components of the marketing mix. Kotler's first edition (1967) extended this focus by incorporating much more behavioral science and quantitative material and was, in some sense, a precursor to a decade of quantitatively rigorous management science and marketing books. Consumerism, environmental issues, multinational marketing, and marketing for nonprofit organizations are characteristic new topics introduced in textbooks towards the end of the period.

A fourth type of effort involved a survey of AMA members on various aspects of idea generation and diffusion. The focus was on determining the amount of awareness and usage of 13 different types of analytical techniques, models, or research approaches. Here again, the details of this study are given in the main report (Massy, Greyser, and Myers, 1979).

Finally, attempts were made to elaborate on specific aspects of the overall project. Special interviews were conducted by the Commission staff to "track" the intellectual and applications evolution of new developments, in particular what many considered to be a highly successful example—that of conjoint analysis. Also, the Commission staff developed alternative skeletal views of the idea generation and diffusion process for use in Commission discussions of various conceptions of this process. Finally, the co-chairmen developed several "think pieces" on the types, nature, and functions of marketing research and the role of the marketing academic community.

How Marketing Practice Has Changed

Readers who are old enough to remember marketing in the 1950s will appreciate the diversity of changes that have taken place both in the marketing manager's environment and in the nature of the marketing operations themselves. They also might appreciate the difficulty of attempting to capture the nature and type of these changes in a few paragraphs! From the viewpoint of managerial practice, much that has changed is traceable to a change in managerial perspective contained in the familiar "marketing concept" with its emphasis on the identification and satisfaction of consumer wants and needs rather than on the "selling" of products. The implications of this externally focused attitude on how to run a business, and the basic idea that various components of marketing such as product, pricing, promotion, and distribution should be integrated into an overall comprehensive marketing plan, had far-reaching consequences for marketing practice and knowledge development over the period.

An external focus, for example, leads logically to a heightened awareness and stronger motivation for information-gathering and marketing research. This undoubtedly contributed to academic and professional concentration on understanding and predicting consumer behavior and was a major impetus in the creation of the consumer behavior field, the Association for Consumer Research, and numerous new consumer behavior textbooks and journals. The new focus gave increased stature and significance to marketing as a vital business function. Many of the aspects of a "profession" such as the scientific and explicit use of information in decision-making, the educational and university role in training managerial talent for marketing positions, and the numerous other trappings, are traceable to this change in overall managerial focus. The evolution of marketing research in some corporations from a purely data-gathering function to include complex decision models and multivariate analysis which characterize modern-day "marketing information systems" seems, in retrospect, a natural evolution of this fundamental idea. Another type of evolution is the application of marketing principles to nonprofit organization management, a trend particularly apparent in recent years.

An equally persuasive explanation for changes in marketing management practice and knowledge development can be found in technological innovations and in social, economic, and environmental changes that have occurred over the past 25 years. Perhaps the most significant innovations from the viewpoint of their effect on marketing management practice were the development of the computer and television. The 25-year period spans the time in which each of these inventions came into being on a commercial scale and had far-reaching impact on marketing (as well as on other aspects of the nation as a whole). Computers made possible the management of very large amounts of data both in terms of accessibility and analysis. This, in turn, stimulated the need for models, theories, and perspectives to guide the data collection and analysis process. Highly complex multivariate methods became feasible analysis alternatives, and a whole generation of model-builders, statisticians, and computer specialists began to look at marketing as an applications area in which to pursue their interests. Progress in adapting the computer to basic discipline studies on which marketing researchers continued to draw their inspiration and insight—economics, psychology, sociology, and others—further emphasized and expanded the important role of the computer.

Parallel reasoning could be applied to assessing the impact of television (as well as many other types of period-specific innovations or product-line extensions such as jet air freight and travel, the space program, etc.). Television created entire industries of market-related specialists in advertising, research, production, and so on. Methodologies developed in basic social science ranging from econometrics to pupilometrics and psychometrics were quickly adopted, refined, and in some cases rejected by marketing academics and commercial research firms doing television and advertising research. The marketing manager, for the first time, could direct messages to a mass market of millions of households via a total communications package (both audio and visual channels) at a comparatively low cost-per-thousand viewers reached. The absolute costs of television usage involving hundreds of thousands or millions of advertiser dollars increased marketing budgets accordingly. Many commissioners identified an overall increase in the scale of marketing operations as a characteristic change over the period. Obviously, when a marketing manager's budget has increased significantly, the requirements and opportunities for the use of marketing research data differ greatly.

Many other environmental factors affected marketing management over the period. Commissioners noted the increased role of government in marketing decision-making. Consumerism was a movement of the 1960s which impacted greatly on marketing. Energy and other shortages characterized manager concern towards the end of the period. Along with an overall increase in the scale of marketing operations, decisions became much more consequential or "risky" in terms of the stakes involved.

These are some of the major changes in marketing management practice and the forces that affected changes in practice over the period. The next question examined by the Commission concerned the nature and objectives of knowledge-generation and R&D in marketing and types of new knowledge that had been generated. The R&D on which the Commission focused does not refer to new technical inventions, chemical discoveries, and so on flowing from the nation's laboratories or what might be called the research and development associated with production. Rather, it refers to marketing research developments and new knowledge pertaining to advancement of marketing management practices.

MARKETING'S R&D

Throughout the balance of the article, the terms marketing R&D and marketing knowledge are used interchangeably. The R&D term is introduced to emphasize the fact that much of what a marketing manager considers "state-of-the-art" knowledge is *not* limited to the literature. Professionals in an applied field, such as marketing, do not rely solely (or even primarily) on journal materials as their source of knowledge—a fact often overlooked by academics for whom journals represent the major storehouse of new and accumulated knowledge. For marketing professionals, the proprietary research information resident in their companies (from both the company's own research and outside commercial sources) as well as the folklore and accumulated experience of managerial colleagues are important components of the "state-of-the-art." As will be seen, it is possible to document changes in marketing knowledge by examining journal materials, but extremely difficult or impossible to document important aspects of the total storehouse of knowledge generated over the period.

An equally difficult question concerns the effectiveness measure. What are, or should be, the objectives of knowledge-generation in marketing? We examine this controversial question next.

Objectives of Knowledge-Generation in Marketing

Although a viable argument can be made that knowledge development should be pursued for "its own sake" and much basic research in marketing is generated in this way, the Commission took the position that the objectives of knowledge-generation in our field should be to improve marketing management practice. Thus, even basic research if it is to be considered "effective" should, over the long run, contribute something to improved decision-making or other aspects of management practice. But how should "good" practice and management be defined? What is an effective marketing manager? More generally, what is an effective marketing organization? In either case, the usual criteria of sales and profits are often suspect because of the dynamics of markets and marketing operations. Good sales and good profits can result from "good luck"! The Commission's position was that management should be evaluated also on the basis of "good judgment" and the specific ways in which budgets and people are managed, plans developed, actions implemented, and operations controlled. As one CEO is reported to have said: "Don't tell me about sales and profits, tell me whether or not I have a good marketing operation."

Entire books have been written on the qualities of a good manager or, more generally, the "functions of the executive" (Barnard 1968). A marketing manager needs to possess a whole bundle of qualities captured in the notion of "leader"—the capacity to motivate people working under him or her, the capacity to efficiently manage large amounts of funds and expenditures, and the capacity to make difficult and risky decisions in an environment of great uncertainty. Increasingly, however, marketing managers must be capable of managing large amounts of complex data which can be used to reduce the uncertainty in decision-making. To do so, they need to be able to recognize and conceptualize important problems, and to distinguish the important from the trivial. In the Commission's view, they need a capacity to develop good "theories" or "models" of their operations, to be able to distinguish cause and effect, and understand the implications of their decisions.

The modern manager, in other terms, must be a good planner. The development of a good marketing plan where realistic and worthwhile objectives are carefully specified, the resources marshalled to carry them out, and control mechanisms introduced to evaluate them, is an important characteristic of good management. To this, we believe, should be added the capacity to guide research efforts, to marshall facts and data relevant to stated objectives, and the capacity to analyze and interpret complex information. The ideal manager must be able to bridge the gaps between an original theory/model specification, the research design actually used to generate data, and the interpretation of the final data results. The overriding point is that modern managers should display at least some of the characteristics of the scientist—a willingness to use theories, models, and concepts, a capacity to identify important problems, and a healthy respect for the value of objective information and research in seeking answers to problems. Managers need to know the "why" of their operations in the sense of a theory or model, the "what" in the sense of relevant facts and data that pertain to them, and the "how" in terms of the implications of implementation and control.

The difficulty of documenting that marketing managers were "better" at the end of the period than at the beginning should be obvious. The Commission did not attempt to test this proposition and we, frankly, don't know. We do know that more managers held the MBA degree, that there was much more marketing research information available, that the demands for in-company information systems and information to support decisions were higher, and that there was a marked rise in the size and scale of the marketing research industry generally. The criterion of "better practice" was thus left implicit rather than explicit in the Commission's deliberations, and the focus directed to better understanding the nature of marketing knowledge.

The Nature of Marketing Knowledge

Marketing "R&D" as referred to in this study encompasses a broad range of types of "knowledge" and ways in which it can be generated. Types of knowledge are in effect the "ends" to be achieved—the *objects* of research in marketing. The ways to generate knowledge represent the "means."

The Commission recognized two broad types of knowledge "objects" in this sense: (1) context-specific knowledge, and (2) context-free knowledge. Context-specific knowledge is specific to a particular firm or industry or specific to a particular managerial problem or situation: Does potato chip advertisement A generate more recall than advertisement B? Two subclasses of context-specific knowledge can be identified as (1a) product industry-specific, and (1b) situation-specific. Context-specific marketing knowledge is usually proprietary, particularly if it is current. It also is probably the most useful base of empirical evidence on which general facts and laws could eventually evolve. That is, by looking for regularities across product, industry, or situation-specific cases, we might come closer to more useful, relevant generalization in the field of marketing. There are examples of this type of work (Clarke 1976; Haley 1970), but it is comparatively rare.

Context-free knowledge encompasses three subclasses referred to as: (2a) general facts and laws, (2b) theories or conceptual structures, and (2c) techniques. Examples are the advertising-to-sales ratios of Fortune 500 companies, theories of buyer behavior, and factor analysis, respectively. What we know about the duration effects of advertising, and patterns of brand loyalty and switching from stochastic brand choice research fit the 2a category, and contrasting theories of advertising effects (hierarchy, low-involvement, conflict, and so on) fit 2b. Conjoint analysis, to be discussed later, is an example of what is considered 2c, a technique, although there is certainly a model or theory which motivates this approach to data collection. These latter types of knowledge-generation are largely, but not exclusively, the domain of academics and university research and make up the content of much of our journal materials.

The means of knowledge-generation can be broadly classified as different kinds of marketing research. We note that many recent marketing research textbooks make a distinction between "Basic" research and "Decisional" research (Churchill 1976; Green and Tull 1978; Tull and Hawkins 1976). Basic research usually involves *hypothesis-testing* of some kind, a prediction based on the hypothesis, devising a test of the prediction, conducting the test, and developing an analysis plan to determine whether the results are statistically significant at some researcher-specified confidence level. Decisional research, on the other hand, begins with a specification of alternative *solutions* to a marketing problem, the possible outcomes of each alternative, the design of a method to predict actual outcomes, and data analysis which relies more on Bayesian-type reasoning than on that of classical statistics. The decision-maker is often mostly interested in how the information changes his/her prior probabilities of likely outcomes than in statistical significance.

Although many "classic" data collection and analysis techniques are included in most marketing research textbooks, the decision-theory viewpoint, or "decisional" research, is becoming much more widely adopted, particularly where the emphasis is placed on the building of a model for which very specific demands are made on the data-collection process. Decisional research also differs in other fundamental ways. There is much more attention to considering trade-offs between the cost and value of the information which, in turn, implies less attention to replication and questions such as reliability and validity. The decision-maker is more interested in knowing the probability level of the results rather than whether they are statistically significant. Finally, the fact that the user of the research and researcher are in direct association with one another, distinguishes decisional from the basic or classical research. What seems evident is that marketing research textbooks are becoming more "decisional" than "basic" in these terms, and this appears to us to be a healthy trend.

A further delineation within the "decisional" category can provide a better understanding of a research taxonomy in marketing, namely distinguishing *problem-solving* research from *problem-oriented* research.

- Problem-*solving* research addresses a very specific applied issue or problem, and is usually proprietary in character; that is, it is usually done within a company or under contract by a commercial firm/consultant for a company. Advertising testing research is one example.
- Problem-*oriented* research addresses a *class* of issues or problems, and typically has at least limited generalizability across firms or situations. The topics examined are usually of a conceptual character, but oriented to applied problems—for example, an effort to classify the kinds of products and consumer purchase situations in which the hierarchy of advertising effects might operate in different ways.

The major criterion for assessing problem-solving research in marketing is whether it helps improve a specific business decision. For problem-oriented research, the criteria are whether it improves our understanding of particular kinds of phenomena in marketing (as an applied social science) and whether it contributes to advancements of theory and method in a basic discipline. The narrowness of the problem, the time frame for utility, and the context of the application all are factors differentiating problem-solving from problem-oriented research.

Two important conclusions flow from these views on the means and ends of marketing's R&D. First, there has been a progressively stronger *leveraged role* for research in marketing practice. With larger markets, more dollars are riding on marketing decisions. With more complex, highly segmented and fragmented markets, there is a higher premium on developing and reaching one's distinctive part in the market. And those companies which know how to harness the array of research tools, help develop and apply them ahead of others, and employ them swiftly and effectively in marketing decisions have an advantage over competition. Second, the huge growth of marketing research information and techniques has resulted in a multifaceted role for the marketing research manager. At least three separate missions can be discerned—facilitator, gatekeeper, and translator. *Facilitator* basically relates to planning and conducting studies and projects and bringing together managers and research specialists. *Gatekeeper* involves monitoring new research techniques and ideas, exploring, "filtering," and trying to apply some of them within the organization. The *translator* puts management issues and problems into researchable propositions and converts research findings into managerial terms.

Knowledge Development over the Period

As noted earlier, it is impossible to document the full scope of new knowledge developed over the 25-year period for much resides in the mind and mores of practicing managers. The overview in this section is largely confined to published materials. Suffice it to say, that marketing as a field is still characterized both by a management philosophy that emphasizes intuition, executive experience, and the "art" of marketing, and an emerging philosophy that emphasizes research, information-gathering, and what some call the "science" of marketing.

From this perspective, the Commission concluded that much had taken place during the 25 years in the direction of increased use and dependency on scientific marketing research information. The increased size and sophistication of commercial marketing research services as well as a general expansion in the industry was noted. A marked shift from trade to consumer research and from secondary to primary research took place. Much more use was made of test marketing before new product introductions. By the end of the period, most of the large consumer packaged goods corporations had some form of marketing information system, and were making increasing use of models and methods to simulate consumer and competitive reactions.

The development of the computer and television noted earlier as impacting on management practice also impacted heavily on knowledge-generation. *Marketing and the Computer* (Alderson and Shapiro 1963) contained papers by a new generation of eager, young students such as Al Kuehn, Ralph Day, Paul Green, Hans Thorelli, Purnell Benson, Bill Massy, and Arnie Amstutz and was, in retrospect, a major precursor of things to come. The largest commercial marketing research service, A.C. Nielsen, Inc., is currently also one of the largest worldwide users of computers. Television required the development of new theories of consumer behavior and communication, new methods to study its effects (e.g., dozens of new commercial services such as Burke's DAR, AD-TEL, ASI In-Theater Testing, etc.), and significant new models of advertising decision-making such as MEDIAC (Little and Lodish 1969).

ADBUG (Little 1970), POMSIS (Aaker 1968) and AD-ME-SIM (Gensch 1973) which utilized computer capacity to assist decision-making in television and mass media generally (for a recent review of related models, see Larreche and Montgomery 1977).

New knowledge in marketing, particularly that which has heavily impacted on changes in marketing practice, is very difficult to document. In medicine, the discovery of penicillin, X-rays, control of diseases like polio, tuberculosis, and syphilis are clearly definable events. In marketing, no "drug" has yet been invented that will "cure" the problem of new product failures. But it is, nevertheless, possible to trace some of the new ideas, theories, tools, and decision-aids introduced during the period.

Exhibit 1 shows a listing of 64 examples of knowledge development in marketing from 1952 to 1977 organized into four categories; (1) Discipline-Based Theories, (2) Managerial Frameworks and Approaches, (3) Models and Measurement, and (4) Research Methods and Statistical Techniques. This listing is illustrative only and is intended to provide a sampling of the variety of identifiable new theories, concepts, methods, and techniques. It is interesting to note the degree to which much that is "new" in marketing is closely related to new developments in the basic disciplines, particularly economics and psychology. Much new marketing knowledge is by definition an application and refinement of basic theories and methods in these social sciences and, in some instances, has had major impacts on the development of their theory and method. An interesting characteristic is the comparative speed by which marketing academics and professional researchers have adopted or "tried out" those ideas. In general, marketing knowledge generated over the period 1952 to 1977 changed principally in the degree to which it increased in quantitative and behavioral science sophistication. The introduction of a mangement science/engineering perspective to the field moved us closer to considerations of marketing as an applied science, and in general a "social engineering" view of the profession.

The next section deals with the third type of charge to the Commission: what is the nature of the knowledge-creation and diffusion process in marketing?

THE KNOWLEDGE-CREATION AND DIFFUSION PROCESS

The Commission recognized two major patterns by which new knowledge is created and diffused to line managers: knowledge that is essentially idea, concept, or methods-driven and problem-driven knowledge. The first can arise in the academic *or* professional sphere when someone has a good idea and the energy and persistence to pursue the research, testing, and publication required to disseminate it.[5] Examples of this in marketing are the idea of a "hierarchy of effects" and the subsequent expectancy-value models to explain consumer decision-making and information processing. Consumer information processing, in particular, is now a very popular marketing academic subject which, some might say, is being driven mostly by the inherent interest of researchers in attempting to understand this phenomenon.

The second type of new knowledge might arise when a manager needs to predict his brand share for a new product. This leads logically into sales forecasting techniques (and new developments in this area, Bass and Wittink 1975), which in turn leads to the concept and use of panel data and, for example, stochastic models of brand choice (Morrison 1965), basic concepts such as market segmentation (Frank, Massy, and Wind 1972; Myers and Nicosia 1968; Wind 1978b) and to a variety of other new models and methods developments (e.g., Silk and Urban 1978; Srinivasan and Shocker 1973). Much segmentation research during the early part of the period appeared to be basically "idea-driven" (researchers were more interested in testing new types of multivariate methods factor analysis, cluster analysis, latent structure analysis, Sheth 1977), whereas during the latter part, particularly with the publication of *Market Segmentation* (Frank, Massy, and Wind 1972), research appeared more problem-driven and efforts were concentrated on situation-specific-type variables.

To better understand the process, the Commission chose conjoint analysis as a means of studying one pattern of adoption and diffusion. It is an example of an idea or methods-driven pattern, even though the problem (deriving a preference function and/or determining the utilities, "part-worths," of attribute levels) has been a part of marketing since the days when marketers were told to "sell the sizzle and not the steak!" The example illustrates several important ideas such as the role of nonmarketing academics, the importance of consulting arrangements in the diffusion process, and the contributions of academic and professional researchers in getting a complex idea widely disseminated and used.

It is generally held that a breakthrough article on conjoint analysis was published in 1964 in the *Journal of Mathematical Psychology* (Luce and Tukey 1964). It was a breakthrough in the sense of a long tradition of psychological and attitude measurement perspectives going back to Thurstone and others (nonmarketing academics) who make up the field of psychometrics and mathematical psychology. The first major publication in marketing literature on the subject was a 1971 *Journal of Marketing Research* article (Green and Rao 1971).[6] Green and his colleagues focused on developing a "full-profile" approach to the fundamental task of generating part-worth utilities on sets of decision criteria or salient brand/product attributes. A professional researcher, Richard Johnson of Market Facts, Inc., Chicago, working independently from the Wharton group, developed a parallel procedure based on a "two-factor-at-a-time" approach which he called "trade-off analysis" and published the new

EXHIBIT 1. Examples of Knowledge Development in Marketing, 1952–1977

Discipline-Based Theories	Managerial Frameworks and Approaches	Models and Measurement	Research Methods and Statistical Techniques
Demand and Utility Theory	Marketing Concept	Stochastic Models of Brand Choice	Motivation Research and Projective Techniques
Market Segmentation	Marketing Mix—4Ps	Market Share Models	Survey Research
General and Middle-Range Theories of Consumer Behavior	Development of Marketing Cases	Marginal Analysis and Linear Programming	Focus Groups and Depth Interviewing
Image and Attitude Theory	DAGMAR	Bayesian Analysis	Experimental and Panel Designs—ANOVA
Theories of Motivation, Personality, Social Class, Life Style, and Culture	Product Life Cycle	Advertising Models, e.g., Mediac, Pomsis, Admesim, Brandaid, Acbug	Advances in Probability Sampling
Expectancy-Value Theory	Marketing Plan	Causal Models	Hypothesis Formulation, Inference, Significance Test
Theories of Advertising Processes and Effects	State Approaches to Strategy Development	Sensitivity Analysis and Validity Tests	Multivariate Dependence Methods—Multiple Regression and Multiple Discriminant Analysis, Canonical Correlation
Information Processing Theory	Product Portfolio Analysis	Response Functions	Multivariate Interdependence Methods—Cluster and Factor Analysis, Latent Structure Analysis
Attitude Change Theories (consistency and complexity theories)	Physical Distribution Management	Weighted Belief Models, Determinant Attributes	
	Marketing Information Systems	Simulation and Marketing Games	
Attribution Theory	Product Positioning and Perceptual Mapping	Multidimensional Scaling and Attitude Measurement	Advances in Forecasting Econometrics, and Time Series Analysis
Perceptual Processes	Segmentation Strategies	Sales Management Models, e.g., Detailer, Callplan	
Advertising Repetition	New Marketing Organization Concepts, e.g., Brand Management	New Product Models, e.g., Demon, Sprinter, Steam, Hendry	Trade-Off Analysis and Conjoint Analysis
Distribution Theory	Territory Design and Salesman Compensation	Bid Pricing Models	Psychographics and AIO Studies
Refutation and Distraction Hypotheses	Marketing Audit	Computer-Assisted Marketing Cases	Physiological Techniques—Eye Camera, GSR, CONPAAD
Theories of Diffusion, New Product Adoption and Personal Influence	Demand State Strategies	Product Planning Models, Perceptor, Accessor	Unobtrusive Measures, Response Latency, Nonverbal Behavior.
	Creative Approaches and Styles		
	New Search and Screening Approaches		
Prospect Theory	Refinements in Test Marketing Approaches		

procedure in *JMR* (Johnson 1974). What is important for our purposes is to note the location of each individual, one in a university environment and one in a commercial or "external" marketing research firm. Also of significance is the pattern, particularly of the marketing academic in this case, of essentially using real-world marketing applications as the laboratory for further testing and refining the methods reflected in numerous studies involving actual situation-specific decisions and data.[7] A similar pattern from the professional researcher viewpoint was going on through the normal process of a marketing research firm (Market Facts) dealing with numerous clients, many of whom were being introduced to the technique over the period via this channel. Both individuals also were appearing at conferences and presenting papers on the subject further enhancing the diffusion process. Robinson and Associates (Philadelphia), another "external" marketing research firm, was also an early adopter of conjoint analysis and introduced the technique to many of its clients. Wharton students, particularly graduating Ph.D.s who accepted positions at other universities across the country, were significant forces in the general refinement and diffusion of conjoint analysis. One estimate is that there have been, to date, over 300 commercial applications (separate and distinct studies) of conjoint analysis, and interest is still high and spreading to applications in the nonprofit and government sectors.

In sum, this is an example of one of the most successful types of new knowledge introduced over the period in terms of making a complex idea developed in a basic discipline of direct use and benefit to line marketing managers and marketing decision-making. The basic ingredients of the process are a methodological breakthrough in basic research, the adaptation and refinement of the ideas by a small "innovator group" of marketing academics and professionals, and subsequent diffusion to line managers involving external marketing research companies, internal marketing research departments, students, journals, consultants, meetings, and conferences.

What can be said generally about the efficiency and effectiveness of this system over the 25 years? First, the Commission concluded that much innovation, particularly as perceived by academics, never reaches line managers, and in retrospect, has contributed little to improvements in marketing management practice. Second, and discussed in the next section, there is a great deal of "promising" development which is used little by managers. Third, important new developments have come from *both* academics *and* professionals. In marketing there is a relatively small "*innovator group*" made up of both professionals and academics from which a significant number of the major new, useful ideas flow. Finally, the Commission concluded that neither the idea nor the problem necessarily comes first at the initiation stage, and problems and ideas find themselves in different ways. There is no single, dominant pattern. In some cases, particularly among academics, a technique is developed and then applied to a real-world problem. In others, a problem is posed, and a search for new solution techniques is initiated. In either event, much effort is needed to test and hone the development before it becomes widely adopted or commercially useful. Unfortunately, problems often reside with management people who are not well trained to articulate them to research people unfamiliar with management life. The Commission was struck by the discrepancies between the volume of new knowledge generated over the period and the comparatively low rate of adoption at the line manager level. Is this type of "failure rate" endemic to the field? What causes it? What can be done about it?

Barriers to Innovation and Diffusion

The Commission recognized two types of barriers to the diffusion and adoption process broadly classified as Structural and Organizational (S/O) barriers and Substantive and Communication (S/C) barriers. On reflection, we have become impressed with the seeming rediscovery of C.P. Snow's "two cultures" within the field marketing, not characterized so much as that of academic/business as that of researcher/manager. We are reminded of the "those who think and never act" and "those who act and never think" distinction. Into this mix must be poured the numerous types of research specialists that have arisen in marketing over the 25 years, many of whom communicate in a language inherently foreign to one another.

More specifically, the Commission recognized as S/O barriers the inherent differences in occupational roles and incentives among managers, researchers, and academics. In particular, the impact of the reward system and the drive to do research and publish for academics is a significant cause of the volume and type of research and new-knowledge generation in marketing. In some universities, only contributions to basic research carry any weight, and it is often nonmarketing academics (economists, psychologists, sociologists) who are doing the evaluating. Built-in barriers between line and staff people within an organization, the proprietary and confidential nature of much marketing research information in corporations, the lack of exposure to and formal quantitative training of line managers,[8] and other characteristics of line managers and their positions (too busy, conservative, inherent inertia, etc.) were seen as S/O barriers to the process.

Numerous Substantive and Communication (S/C) barriers were identified. A common theme was the inappropriateness of many quantitative models and techniques to marketing problems as perceived by marketing managers. The length of time needed to test, adapt, and make a new idea useful was mentioned. Some commissioners recognized current marketing journals as a barrier—our journals represent mostly

3 — The Effectiveness of Marketing's "R&D" for Marketing Management: An Assessment

academics talking to one another, and reflect the *supply* of new knowledge rather than the *demand* for it. The credibility of much academic work comes into question when trivial problems are given treatment equal to that given important problems. The annual AMA conference structure was singled out as a barrier in the sense that two, separate conferences, one for educators and one for professionals, are held. The lack of line manager membership in the AMA, and/or the lack of time to participate actively in such organizations by line managers, was another type of S/C barrier. Particularly for managers, there are few incentives or rewards for contributing to new knowledge *per se*, and attention is often focused on short-run sales and profit generation.

Many of these barriers and blocks reduce to attitudinal factors residing in the make-up of each of the participants. Managers, often uncomfortable with complex quantitative and abstract materials, or with no time to learn about them, are prone to dismiss much that could be valuable as academic nonsense. Patterns such as the "not invented here" syndrome, anti-intellectualism, and other defenses develop to rationalize the basic position. Researchers, particularly those who are scholarly-inclined, often write-off practical marketing problems as irrelevant to what they do, or as an interference with their scholarly progress. Patterns of "let them learn what I am doing" develop with little or no commitment to translating ideas into the practical world of the marketing decision-maker.

ASSESSMENT AND SOME RECOMMENDATIONS

Three broad observations appear germane to the overall charge to the Commission of assessing the effectiveness of marketing research and development for marketing management:

- Knowledge-generation in marketing, like in any other professional or academic field, is to some degree "inefficient." There will always be waste in the system in terms of false starts, blind alleys, and so forth. Throughout its work, the Commission held to an initial view that the most meaningful criterion—perhaps the only criterion—for assessing and making new investments in developing marketing knowledge was its ultimate contribution to marketing practice. At the same time, there was broad recognition that *basic* research both warranted and demanded support, even though many who engage in it do so with the principal (and sometimes sole) motivation of enriching knowledge rather than improving practice. The often indirect impacts on practice— despite the aforementioned inherent inefficiencies in and unpredictability of basic research to be "useful"—remain important enough to sustain and encourage it.

- All forms and types of marketing research increased in both quality and quantity over the 25-year period. In quality terms, the direction has been toward greater quantitative and behavioral science sophistication. This has been manifested in the professional marketing and marketing research community and particularly in the ways marketing is taught in business schools. The latter, in turn, feeds the world of practice at the entry level.
- A significant amount of marketing research effort, new knowledge development, model-building, and theorizing has had relatively little impact on improving marketing management practice over the period. Although controversial, this observation represents our interpretation of a widely-held belief among Commission members after many months of deliberation on events of the past 25 years. As one Commissioner noted, "There isn't a single problem area with regard to the practice of marketing management that marketing research or the world of technology and concepts has mastered." Another said, "The tendency (is) for many marketing decisions to be made either without any research or on the basis of extremely sloppy research. The fact that the vast majority of new products put on the market turn out to be failures may be a manifestation of the phenomenon."

In reflecting on these assessments, we recognize that marketing is still in a rather primitive state of development. Unlike our impression of some other business fields such as accounting and finance, there is still no unifying marketing theory or model which holds together the diversity of perspectives and viewpoints. Materials which are widely taught in the classroom such as Bayesian analysis do not appear to be widely used by practicing managers. Although there are numerous examples of what might be considered "successful" knowledge development, measured in terms of managerial adoption, we are struck by the degree to which much that has been developed and *could be* useful is *not* being used.

What the Commission in effect rediscovered in the management science/model-building area was a reaffirmation of what many model-builders themselves have long believed—comparatively few firms or practicing management people seem to be using their models. This is particularly true for early, complex model formulations that often went through a cycle of trial and rejection. The most recent model-building trend—to begin with relatively simple concepts and functions, to involve the manager in the model-building effort, and to establish long-run relationships with the client firm—appears to us to be a very healthy one. Many behavioral researchers might well go through a similar type of introspective process with respect to how their work impacts on marketing practice, and the degree of its adoption or nonadoption by marketing decision-makers.

On a more optimistic note, we see marketing at somewhat of a turning-point with respect to the effectiveness of its R&D efforts. A major barrier to the diffusion process, particularly in terms of utilizing formal models, is largely one of scale of operations, the sizeable investments of funds required to develop and maintain on-going data bases, and the teams of specialists needed to achieve an effective utilization of research and knowledge-generation resources. The basic combination of scale and a willingness to invest now appears to us to exist in many corporations, and there are numerous examples of the fully-integrated information system model which this implies.

In retrospect, then, the quarter-century contained a significant amount of "ineffectiveness" regarding marketing's R&D. *The contributions of research and knowledge-development at best can be characterized as mixed.* The impacts have been significant, but far less than "what might have been." The reasons lie primarily in the numerous types of barriers and blocks to the diffusion process. We think concerned people in the field should examine their own organizations with respect to both the S/O and S/C barriers. Many of the Commission's recommendations pertain to various ways to reduce these barriers.

Recommendations

There are numerous recommendations given in the Commission's full report. Many relate to the fundamental needs for open lines of communication between researchers and managers, the needs to find ways to break down the barriers and blocks to the idea-generation and diffusion process, and the needs for conscious effort, investment, and continuing funding to make the process work. In our view, the process is not like a breeder reactor, it is *not* self-generating; rather it requires conscious effort to sustain it. More sources need to be found for supporting research, particularly of the "problem-oriented" kind, and better ways need to be developed to bridge the gaps between knowledge-generation and knowledge-utilization.

Among the many recommendations, we view the following as particularly important and provide some of our own reflections on the implications and impact of each:

1. *More support should be provided for basic and "problem-oriented" research in marketing*. Both the professional and the academic marketing communities need to give "problem-oriented" research much more attention. The company role here goes beyond providing financial support, to contributing data and information on company experiences. In this way, more progress can be made to develop experience-based "conditional generalizations," i.e., knowledge and concepts that apply under specified kinds of product, market, or consumer conditions. On the aca-

demic side, more appreciation is needed of the "respectability" of such research for academic knowledge-building. (See item 5, below.)

On the whole, relatively few institutions—notably the Marketing Science Institute, the now phased-down National Science Foundation's Research Applied to National Needs program, the American Association of Advertising Agencies' Educational Foundation—exist with "problem-oriented" research as their major focus. Such marketing research typically is not "basic" enough to gain support from institutions principally geared to "harder" sciences; this appears to have been the experience at NSF. Yet problem-oriented research is usually not immediately practical enough to warrant support from company operating budgets. In short, "problem-oriented" research is a stepchild. So far, the limited success in gaining support for such research has been rooted in institutional systems, such as MSI's, that catalytically bring together conceptually-oriented professionals with practically-oriented academics (Greyser 1978).

This focus on "problem-oriented" research does not reduce the importance, in our view, of basic research. It *is* important over the long-run. We think, however, that business and academe alike have given too little recognition and value to problem-oriented research.

2. *Nontechnical reviews of new concepts, findings, and techniques in marketing should be published far more frequently. At the same time, publications that permit researchers to write to other researchers need to be preserved and encouraged.* This recommendation basically addresses both ends of the knowledge development/knowledge utilization spectrum. For the former, we underscore the importance of having an "archival resource" that not only provides a medium where new research results can be published, but also permits such work to be accessed readily by other researchers over time. "Relevance" is not the appropriate criterion on which to assess such journals. The *Journal of Marketing Research* is obviously a specific example.

At the other end, nontechnical reviews represent one way of attempting to break the technical jargon block which many Commissioners thought was a major impediment to good communication. Complex ideas must often be expressed in formal, mathematical terms, but they should be capable of being communicated in terms that a broader audience can understand. The "annual reviews" in fields such as psychology were cited as illustrations, as were some of the "state-of-the-art" articles in current journals, and the concept of the *Review of Marketing*.

3. *Senior executives of major companies in the consumer, industrial, and services sector should be encouraged to develop a climate within their organizations which is amenable to exploration of and experimentation with new research ideas and techniques. Further, practicing managers must become more appreciative of the value of "good theory," and develop more capacity to conceptualize, supervise, and interpret information relevant to decision-making.* Unless the right climate of receptivity is developed within the organization, there is little chance of significant adoption of new knowledge. People simply won't want to take the necessary risks of introducing new ideas. Moreover, an attitude which assumes that new ideas and techniques are automatically of low or no relevance to one's operations needs to be guarded against. Anti-intellectualism, in whatever forms it may take and for whatever motivations it may arise, appears to us not to be in the best interests of either the firm or the manager. This recommendation may have a "motherhood" (maybe even a "Pollyanna") character, but we think it needs restatement here.

4. *A "clearinghouse mechanism" should be established in which company data files can be made available to academic and professional researchers.* This is not a new idea, but one which the Commission recommends receive attention and effort. It would do much to meet the needs of academic researchers for empirical data, and consequently increase the usefulness (real and perceived) of their work.

   The difficulties of implementing such an activity are widely recognized. Major difficulties include the concerns of companies regarding proprietary information, and the lack of congruence of categories and questions from study to study (even ones done by the same company). Although much time and careful effort is necessary, we think these problems can be mitigated.

   One commissioner suggested that what is needed to facilitate a clearinghouse mechanism is some motivation for contributing companies. Conscious as we are that many company studies are underanalyzed (even in terms of their own objectives), we think one possible avenue would be for companies contributing data to suggest particular perspectives/approaches for consideration by researchers working with the data through the clearinghouse.

5. *Marketing educators and university administrators must be made aware of the crucial need to maintain open lines of communication with professional researchers and practicing managers. They should be persuaded to support teaching, consulting, and research activities which foster this communication and involve real-world marketing problems.* This recommendation relates in large part to our earlier com-

ments on "two cultures." In our view, too many academics think that "being practical" is not desirable (and may even be explicitly undesirable). For marketing academics, this tendency can become exacerbated when people from nonbusiness fields are involved, as in universitywide promotion reviews. Understanding practice, and contributing to it, can lead to major contributions to knowledge-development itself.

Conclusion

What do we hope will emerge from the Commission's work? First and foremost, our hope is for greater sensitivity to and concern for the state of research in marketing today—whether that research be basic, problem-oriented, or problem-solving. From such sensitivity and concern we think will emerge an improved climate for all research, both in universities and in the business community. In turn, professionalism in marketing decision-making will be enhanced—a goal that we believe should be shared by all in the field.

ENDNOTES

1. The Commission consisted of 18 people, eight from universities, including the two co-chairmen, four from independent research, consulting, and advertising firms, and six from operating companies. The four from independent firms were professional researchers while the six from operating companies were evenly split between management and research functions. Other members were: Seymour Banks (Leo Burnett Co.), Frank Bass (Purdue University), Robert Burnett (Meredith Corporation), Robert D. Buzzell (Harvard University), Henry J. Claycamp (International Harvester), Robert Ferber (University of Illinois), Ronald E. Frank (University of Pennsylvania), John G. Keane (Managing Change, Inc., President, AMA, 1976–77), Philip Kotler (Northwestern University), Lawrence Light (BBD&O, Inc.), Elmer Lotshaw (Owens-Illinois), William T. Moran (Ad Mar Research), Bart R. Panettiere (General Foods), W. R. Reiss (American Telephone & Telegraph), and Dudley M. Ruch (The Quaker Oats Company). Christopher Lovelock (Harvard University) served as staff director, and John Bateson, an HBS doctoral candidate and Marketing Science Institute research assistant, served as project assistant.
2. The 25-year reference period was chosen as a useful time span for several reasons. It was considered long enough to provide evidence for a thoughtful review of changes in marketing practice and knowledge without being too long to be inaccessible to memory. It also encompassed several important events in the development of marketing. The computer was beginning to emerge onto the business scene at the beginning of the period. The Gordon and Howell (1959) and Pierson (1959) reports were completed during the early part of the period, significantly affecting curricula in business schools. An acceleration of change in the practice of marketing management and marketing research also took place during this period.

3. By "research in marketing," we mean research addressed to any and all zones of the marketing field, rather than "marketing research" or "market research" alone, which typically imply research on consumers and/or on characteristics of markets.
4. Particularly useful communications were obtained from Charles R. Adler of the Eastman Kodak Company, Paul N. Reis of the Procter and Gamble Company, C.R. Smith of Nabisco, Inc., and William D. Wells of Needham, Harper & Steers, Inc.
5. An academic administrator once correctly observed that even the most brilliant ideas contain no social value if they remain lodged in the heads of their proponents!
6. This was preceded by several working papers and a paper published as early as 1968 by Green and his colleagues at Wharton.
7. This process of refinement has continued to the present and involves different types of data collection procedures, different types of scale assumptions (nominal, ordinal, interval, ratio), and basic extensions such as categorical conjoint measurement and second generation models such as componential segmentation. (See Wind 1978a.)
8. We note that the "average" brand or product manager in a major corporation may now be much more comfortable with quantitative techniques given the likely exposure to them in classroom situations over at least the past 10 years. One estimate is that there are about 25,000 marketing majors produced annually in the United States. If only 1000 per year are MBAs exposed to quantitative methods in our better business schools, there should be 10,000 managers out there for whom models and techniques are a familiar part of marketing knowledge.

REFERENCES

Aaker, David A. (1968), "A Probabilistic Approach to Industrial Media Selection," *Journal of Advertising Research*, 8 (September), 46–54.

Alderson, Wroe and Stanley J. Shapiro, eds. (1963), *Marketing and the Computer*, Englewood Cliffs, NJ: Prentice-Hall, Inc.

Barnard, Chester I. (1968), *Functions of the Executive*, Cambridge, MA: Harvard University Press.

Bass, Frank M. and Dick R. Wittink (1975), "Pooling Issues and Methods in Regression Analysis with Examples in Marketing Research," *Journal of Marketing Research*, 12 (November), 414–425.

Churchill, Gilbert A. Jr. (1976), *Marketing Research: Methodological Foundations*, Hinsdale, IL: The Dryden Press.

Clarke, Darral G. (1976), "Econometric Measurement of the Duration of Advertising Effect on Sales," *Journal of Marketing Research*, 13 (November), 345–357.

Frank, Ronald E., William F. Massy, and Yoram Wind (1972), *Market Segmentation*, Englewood Cliffs, NJ: Prentice-Hall, Inc.

Gensch, Dennis H. (1973), *Advertising Planning: Mathematical Models in Advertising Media*, Amsterdam: Elsevier Publishing Co.

Gordon, Robert A. and James E. Howell (1959), *Higher Education for Business*, New York: Columbia University Press.

Green, Paul E. and Vithala R. Rao (1971), "Conjoint Measurement for Quantifying Judgmental Data," *Journal of Marketing Research*, 8 (August), 355–363.

────── and Donald S. Tull (1978), *Research for Marketing Decisions*, Englewood Cliffs, NJ: Prentice-Hall, Inc.

Greyser, Stephen A. (1978), "Academic Research Marketing Managers Can Use," *Journal of Advertising Research*, 18 (April), 9–14.

Haley, Russell I. (1970), "We Shot an Arrowhead (#9) Into the Air," *Proceedings*, 16th Annual Conference, Advertising Research Foundation, New York, 25–30.

Johnson, Richard M. (1974), "Trade-Off Analysis of Consumer Values," *Journal of Marketing Research*, 11 (May), 121–127.

Kotler, Philip (1967), *Marketing Management: Analysis, Planning & Control*, Englewood Cliffs, NJ: Prentice-Hall, Inc.

Larreche, Jean-Claude and David B. Montgomery (1977), "A Framework for the Comparison of Marketing Models: A Delphi Study," *Journal of Marketing Research*, 14 (November), 487–498.

Little, John D. C. (1970), "Models and Managers: the Concept of a Decision Calculus," *Management Science*, 16 (April), B466–485.

────── and Leonard M. Lodish (1969), "A Media Planning Calculus," *Operations Research*, 17 (January–February), 135.

Luce, Duncan R. and John W. Tukey (1964), "Simultaneous Conjoint Measurement: A New Type of Fundamental Measurement," *Journal of Mathematical Psychology*, 1 (February), 1–27.

Massy, William F., Stephen A. Greyser, and John G. Myers (1978), *Report of the Commission on the Effectiveness of Research and Development for Marketing Management*, Chicago, IL: American Marketing Association.

Morrison, Donald G. (1965), "Stochastic Models for Time Series with Applications in Marketing," *Program in Operations Research*, Stanford University, Technical Report No. 8.

Myers, John G. and Francesco M. Nicosia (1968), "On the Study of Consumer Typologies," *Journal of Marketing Research*, 5 (May), 182–193.

Pierson, Frank C. et al. (1959), *Education of American Businessmen: The Study of University-College Programs in Business Administration*, New York: McGraw-Hill (Carnegie Series in American Education).

Sheth, Jagdish N., ed. (1977), *Multivariate Methods for Market and Survey Research*, Chicago, IL: American Marketing Association.

Silk, Alvin J. and Glen L. Urban (1978), "Pre-Test Market Evaluation of New Packaged Goods: A Model and Measurement Methodology," *Journal of Marketing Research*, 15 (May), 171–191.

Srinivasan, V. and Allan D. Shocker (1973), "Linear Programming Techniques for Multidimensional Analysis of Preferences," *Psychometrika*, 38 (September), 337–369.

Tull, Donald S. and Del I. Hawkins (1976), *"Marketing Research: Meaning, Measurement, and Method*, New York: Macmillan Publishing Co.

Wind, Yoram (1978a), "Marketing Research and Management: A Retrospective View of the Contributions of Paul E. Green," in *Proceedings of the Tenth Paul D. Converse Awards Symposium*. Alan Andreasen, ed., Urbana, IL: University of Illinois Press.

────── (1978b), "Issues and Advances in Segmentation Research," *Journal of Marketing Research*, 15 (August), 317–337.

SECTION B
Strategic Marketing Concepts

Strategic marketing concepts are highly useful to an organization that wants to focus on the future rather than the present or past strategies and activities.

The focus on the future can be achieved by several processes. First, we can focus on the anticipated changes in the environment of marketing, such as customers, competition, technology, and regulation. This environmental analysis should pinpoint threats and opportunities facing the organization's products, services, and market segments. Finally, the threats and opportunities generated by environmental changes can be translated into future marketing plans and programs, including new products, price and promotion changes, or distribution realignments.

A second approach is a portfolio analysis, in which multiple products or brands are classified into categories based on some strategic criteria such as market growth or market share. Once a picture of the current product or brand positions is obtained, it is possible to allocate resources disproportionately toward the future rather than the present realities.

Finally, it is possible to examine the future-oriented marketing programs and plans can be examined by imposing the corporate financial objectives, such as targeted growth and targeted profits or return on investment. The basic strategic outcome is to protect and grow in those products and markets in which targeted objectives of growth and profits are easier to attain and exit or turn around those products and markets in which they are difficult to attain.

The environmental analysis approach to strategic marketing is probably the most fundamental because it forces the organization to focus on external changes and take an adaptive posture. However, it suffers from two weaknesses. First, it is often confused with corporate strategic planning because the same external environment also tends to drive other business functions. Second, it is very difficult to forecast the future or emerging changes in the environment, and the techniques are closer to a crystal ball, rather than a computer, in their precision.

The product portfolio approach has the main advantage of being simple and extremely easy to communicate. It is also good with respect to focusing on strategic considerations such as industry growth and marketing share realities. However, it also suffers from several weaknesses. First, it ignores the corporate structure issues and their impact on resource allocation toward the future. Due to internal corporate political realities, it is often very difficult, if not impossible, to milk a cash cow product or to exit a brand name. Second, there is considerable debate as to the correct measures of strategic importance. For example, no one really knows whether market growth or market size should be used to measure market attractiveness. Similarly, no one really knows how to measure market share.

The corporate objective approach to strategic marketing is more pragmatic and brings the planning process closer to the reward system of the organization. It also is less ambiguous and easier to measure. As you would expect, however, it focuses too much on the internal needs and wants of the organization and too little on external realities. It also encourages a tendency to be less entrepreneurial and more managerial.

In this section, we have selected papers that describe and discuss various ways to think strategically in marketing.

4 Marketing, Strategic Planning and the Theory of the Firm

Paul F. Anderson

Reprinted from the *Journal of Marketing*, published by the American Marketing Association, Vol. 46 (Spring 1982), pp. 15–26. Reprinted by permission.

> Would you tell me, please, which way I ought to go from here? asked Alice.
>   That depends a good deal on where you want to get to, said the Cat.
>   I don't much care where, said Alice.
>   Then it doesn't matter which way you go, said the Cat.
>   Lewis Carroll—*Alice's Adventures in Wonderland*

The obvious wisdom of the Cheshire's statement reveals an important fact concerning strategic planning: without a clear set of objectives, the planning process is meaningless. Two authorities on the subject refer to strategy as "the major link between the goals and objectives the organization wants to achieve and the various functional area policies and operating plans it uses to guide its day-to-day activities" (Hofer and Schendel 1978, p. 13). Other strategy experts generally agree that the process of goal formulation must operate prior to, but also be interactive with, the process of strategy formulation (Ackoff 1970, Ansoff 1965, Glueck 1976, Newman and Logan 1971). Given the growing interest of marketers in the concept of strategic planning, it would appear fruitful to assess the current state of knowledge concerning goals and the goal formulation process.

Over the years, this general area of inquiry has fallen under the rubric of the "theory of the firm." One objective of this paper is to review some of the major theories of the firm to be found in the literature. The extant theories have emerged in the disciplines of economics, finance and management. To date, marketing has not developed its own comprehensive theory of the firm. Generally, marketers have been content to borrow their concepts of goals and goal formulation from these other disciplines. Indeed, marketing has shown a strange ambivalence toward the concept of corporate goals. The recent marketing literature pays scant attention to the actual content of corporate goal hierarchies. Even less attention is focused on the normative issue of what firm goals and objectives ought to be. Moreover, contemporary marketing texts devote little space to the subject. Typically, an author's perspective on corporate goals is revealed in his/her definition of the marketing concept, but one is hard pressed to find further development of the topic. There is rarely any discussion of how these goals come about or how marketing may participate in the goal formulation process.

This is not to say that received doctrine in marketing has been developed without regard for corporate objectives. The normative decision rules and procedures that have emerged always seek to attain one or more objectives. Thus it could be said that these marketing models implicitly assume a theory of the firm. However, the particular theory that serves as the underpinning of the model is rarely made explicit. More importantly, marketing theorists have devoted little attention to an exploration of the nature and implications of these theories. For example, the product portfolio (Boston Consulting Group 1970, Cardozo and Wind 1980), and PIMS (Buzzell, Gale and Sultan 1975) approaches that are so much in vogue today implicitly assume that the primary objective of the firm is the maximization of return on investment (ROI). This objective seems to have been accepted uncritically by many marketers despite its well-documented deficiencies (e.g., its inability to deal with timing, duration and risk differences among returns and its tendency to create behavioral problems when used as a control device; Hopwood 1976, Van Horne 1980). However, the concern expressed in this paper is not so much that marketers have adopted the wrong objectives, but that the discipline has failed to appreciate fully the nature and implications of the objectives that it has adopted.

As a result, in the last sections of the paper the outline of a new theory of the firm will be presented. It will be argued that the theories of the firm developed within economics, finance and management are inadequate in varying degrees as conceptual underpinnings for marketing. It is asserted that the primary role of a theory of the firm is to act as a kind of conceptual backdrop that functions heuristically to guide further theory development within a particular discipline. As such, the proposed model is less of a theory and more of a Kuhnian-style paradigm (Kuhn 1970). Moreover, for a theory of the firm to be fruitful in this respect it must be congruent with the established research tradition of the field (Laudan 1977). It will be demonstrated, for example, that the theories emerging from economics and finance are inconsistent with the philosophical methodology and ontological framework of marketing. However, the proposed model is not only fully consonant with marketing's research tradition, but, unlike existing theories, it explicitly considers marketing's role in corporate goal formulation and strategic planning. Thus it is hoped that the theory will be able to provide a structure to guide future research efforts in these areas.

ECONOMIC THEORIES OF THE FIRM

In this section three theories of the firm are reviewed. The first, the neoclassical model, provides the basic foundation of contemporary microeconomic theory. The second, the market value model, performs a similar function within financial economics. Finally, the agency costs model represents a modification of the market value model to allow a divergence of interests between the owners and managers of the firm. In this sense, it operates as a transitional model between the economically oriented theories of this section and the behavioral theories of the section to follow. However, all three may be classified as economic models since they share the methodological orientation and conceptual framework of economic theory. Note that each postulates an economic objective for the firm and then derives the consequences for firm behavior under different assumption sets.

The Neoclassical Model

The neoclassical theory of the firm can be found in any standard textbook in economics. In its most basic form the theory posits a single product firm operating in a purely competitive environment. Decision making is vested in an owner-entrepreneur whose sole objective is to maximize the dollar amount of the firm's single period profits. Given the standard assumptions of diminishing returns in the short run and diseconomies of scale in the long run, the firm's average cost function will have its characteristic U-shape. The owner's unambiguous decision rule will be to set output at the point where marginal costs equal marginal revenues. The introduction of imperfections in the product market (such as those posited by the monopolistically competitive model) represent mere elaborations on the basic approach. The objective of the firm remains single period profit maximization.

The neoclassical model is well known to marketers. Indeed, it will be argued below that the profit maximization assumption of neoclassical economics underlies much of the normative literature in marketing management. It will be shown that this is true despite the fact that neoclassical theory is inconsistent with the basic research tradition of marketing. Moreover, the neoclassical model suffers from a number of limitations.

For example, the field of finance has challenged the profit maximization assumption because it fails to provide the business decision maker with an operationally feasible criterion for making investment decisions (Solomon 1963). In this regard, it suffers from an inability to consider risk differences among investment alternatives. When risk levels vary across projects, decision criteria that focus only on profitability will lead to suboptimal decisions (Copeland and Weston 1979, Fama and Miller 1972, Van Horne 1980). As a result of these and other problems, financial economists have generally abandoned the neoclassical model in favor of a more comprehensive theory of the firm known as the market value model.

The Market Value Model

Given the assumptions that human wants are insatiable and that capital markets are perfectly competitive, Fama and Miller (1972) show that the objective of the firm should be to maximize its present market value. For a corporation this is equivalent to maximizing the price of the firm's stock. In contrast to the profit maximization objective, the market value rule allows for the consideration of risk differences among alternative investment opportunities. Moreover, the model is applicable to owner-operated firms as well as corporations in which there is likely to be a separation of ownership and control.

The existence of a perfectly competitive capital market allows the firm's management to pursue a single unambiguous objective despite the fact that shareholders are likely to have heterogeneous preferences for current versus future income. If, for example, some stockholders wish more income than the firm is currently paying in dividends, they can sell some of their shares to make up the difference. However, if other shareholders prefer less current income in favor of more future income, they can lend their dividends in the capital markets at interest. In either case shareholder utility will be maximized by a policy that maximizes the value of the firm's stock.

The value maximization objective is implemented within the firm by assessing all multiperiod decision alternatives on the basis of their risk-adjusted net present values (Copeland and Weston 1979, Fama and Miller 1972, Van Horne 1980):

$$\text{NPV}_j = \sum_{i=1}^{n} \frac{A_i}{(1+k_j)^i} \qquad (1)$$

where NPV_j equals the net present value of alternative j, A_i equals the net after-tax cash flows in year i, n is the expected life of the project in years, and k_j is the risk-adjusted, after-tax required rate of return on j. In the absence of capital rationing, the firm should undertake all projects whose net present values are greater than or equal to zero. Assuming an accurate determination of k_j, this will ensure maximization of the firm's stock price. The discount rate k_j should represent the return required by the market to compensate for the risk of the project. This is usually estimated using a parameter preference model such as the capital asset pricing model or (potentially) the arbitrage model (Anderson 1981). However, it should be noted that there are serious theoretical and practical difficulties associated with the use of these approaches (Anderson 1981; Meyers and Turnbull 1977; Roll 1977; Ross 1976, 1978).

From a marketing perspective this approach requires that all major decisions be treated as investments. Thus the decision to introduce a new product, to expand into new territories, or to adopt a new channel of distribution should be evaluated on the basis of its risk-adjusted net present value. While similar approaches have been suggested in marketing (Cravens, Hills and Woodruff 1980; Dean 1966; Howard 1965; Kotler 1971; Pessemier 1966), it has generally not been recognized that this implies the adoption of shareholder wealth maximization as the goal of the firm. Moreover, these approaches are often offered in piecemeal fashion for the evaluation of selected decisions (e.g., new products), and are not integrated into a consistent and coherent theory of the firm.

Despite the deductive logic of the market value model, there are those who question whether corporate managers are motivated to pursue value maximization. An essential assumption of the market value theory is that stockholders can employ control, motivation and monitoring devices to ensure that managers maximize firm value. However, in the development of their agency theory of the firm, Jensen and Meckling (1976) note that such activities by shareholders are not without cost. As a result, it may not be possible to compel managers to maximize shareholder wealth.

The Agency Costs Model

The separation of ownership and control in modern corporations gives rise to an agency relationship between the stockholders and managers of the firm. An agency relationship may be defined as "a contract under which one or more persons (the principal[s]) engage another person (the agent) to perform some service on their behalf which involves delegating some decision making authority to the agent" (Jenson and Meckling 1976, p. 308). In any relationship of this sort, there is a potential for the agent to expend some of the principal's resources on private pursuits. As such, it will pay the principal to provide the agent with incentives and to incur monitoring costs to encourage a convergence of interests between the objectives of the principal and those of the agent. Despite expenditures of this type, it will generally be impossible to ensure that all of the agent's decisions will be designed to maximize the principal's welfare. The dollar value of the reduction in welfare experienced by the principal along with the expenditures on monitoring activities are costs of the agency relationship. For corporate stockholders these agency costs include the reduction in firm value resulting from management's consumption of nonpecuniary benefits (perquisites) and the costs of hiring outside auditing agents.

The tendency of managers of widely held corporations to behave in this fashion will require the stockholders to incur monitoring costs in an effort to enforce the value maximization objective. Unfortunately, perfect monitoring systems are very expensive. Thus the stockholders face a cost-benefit trade-off in deciding how much to spend on monitoring activities. Since it is unlikely that it will pay the shareholders to implement a "perfect" monitoring system, we will observe corporations suboptimizing on value maximization even in the presence of auditing activities. This leads to implications for managerial behavior that are quite different from those predicted by the market value model. For example, the Fama-Miller model predicts that managers will invest in all projects that will maximize the present value of the firm. However, the agency costs model suggests that management may actually invest in suboptimal projects and may even forego new profitable investments (Barnea, Haugen and Senbet 1981).

The recognition that a firm might not pursue maximization strategies is a relatively new concept to the literature of financial economics. However, in the middle 1950s and early 1960s, various economists and management specialists began to question the neoclassical assumption of single objective maximization on the basis of their observations of managerial behavior. This led directly to the development of the behavioral theory of the firm.

BEHAVIORAL THEORIES OF THE FIRM

In this section two behaviorally oriented theories of the firm will be reviewed. While other approaches could also be included (Bower 1968, Mintzberg 1979), these models will lay the foundation for the development of a constituency-based theory in the last sections of the paper. The first approach is the behavioral model of the firm that emerged at the Carnegie Institute of Technology. The behavioral model can best be understood as a reaction against the neoclassical model of economic theory. The second approach is the resource dependence model of Pfeffer and Salancik (1978). The resource dependence perspective builds on a number of ideas contained in the behavioral model. For example, both approaches stress the coalitional nature of organizations. Moreover, both models emphasize the role of behavioral rather than economic factors in explaining the activities of firms.

The Behavioral Model

The behavioral theory of the firm can be found in the writings of Simon (1955, 1959, 1964), March and Simon (1958), and especially in Cyert and March (1963). The behavioral theory views the business firm as a coalition of individuals who are, in turn, members of subcoalitions. The coalition members include "managers, workers, stockholders, suppliers, customers, lawyers, tax collectors, regulatory agencies, etc." (Cyert and March 1963, p. 27).

The goals of the organization are determined by this coalition through a process of quasi-resolution of conflict. Different coalition members wish the organization to pursue different goals. The resultant goal conflict is not resolved by reducing all goals to a common dimension or by making them internally consistent. Rather, goals are viewed as "a series of independent aspiration-level constraints imposed on the organization by the members of the organizational coalition" (Cyert and March 1963, p. 117).

As Simon (1964) points out, in real world decision making situations acceptable alternatives must satisfy a whole range of requirements or constraints. In his view, singling out one constraint and referring to it as the goal of the activity is essentially arbitrary. This is because in many cases, the set of requirements selected as constraints will have much more to do with the decision outcome than the requirement selected as the goal. Thus he believes that it is more meaningful to refer to the entire set of constraints as the (complex) goal of the organization.

Moreover, these constraints are set at aspiration levels rather than maximization levels. Maximization is not possible in complex organizations because of the existence of imperfect information and because of the computational limitations faced by organizations in coordinating the various decisions made by decentralized departments and divisions. As a result, firm behavior concerning goals may be described as satisficing rather than maximizing (Simon 1959, 1964).

Cyert and March (1963) see decentralization of decision making leading to a kind of local rationality within subunits of the organization. Since these subunits deal only with a small set of problems and a limited number of goals, local optimization may be possible, but it is unlikely that this will lead to overall optimization. In this regard, the firm not only faces information processing and coordination problems but is also hampered by the fact that it must deal with problems in a sequential fashion. Thus organizational subunits typically attend to different problems at different times, and there is no guarantee that consistent objectives will be pursued in solving these problems. Indeed, Cyert and March argue that the time buffer between decision situations provides the firm with a convenient mechanism for avoiding the explicit resolution of goal conflict.

Thus in the behavioral theory of the firm, goals emerge as "independent constraints imposed on the organization through a process of bargaining among potential coalition members" (Cyert and March 1963, p. 43). These objectives are unlikely to be internally consistent and are subject to change over time as changes take place in the coalition structure. This coalitional perspective has had a significant impact on the development of management thought. Both Mintzberg (1979) and Pfeffer and Salancik (1978) have developed theories of the firm that take its coalitional nature as given. In the following section the resource dependence approach of Pfeffer and Salancik is outlined.

The Resource Dependence Model

Pfeffer and Salancik (1978) view organizations as coalitions of interests which alter their purposes and direction as changes take place in the coalitional structure. Like Mintzberg (1979) they draw a distinction between internal and external coalitions, although they do not use these terms. Internal coalitions may be viewed as groups functioning within the organization (e.g., departments and functional areas). External coalitions include such stakeholder groups as labor, stockholders, creditors, suppliers, government and various interested publics. Pfeffer and Salancik place their primary emphasis on the role of environmental (i.e., external) coalitions in affecting the behavior of organizations. They believe that "to describe adequately the behavior of organizations requires attending to the coalitional nature of organizations and the manner in which organizations respond to pressures from the environment" (Pfeffer and Salancik 1978, p. 24).

The reason for the environmental focus of the model is that the survival of the organization ultimately depends on its ability to obtain resources and support from its external coalitions. Pfeffer and Salancik implicitly assume that survival is the ultimate goal of the organization and that to achieve this objective, the organization must maintain a coalition of parties willing to "legitimize" its existence (Dowling and Pfeffer 1975, Parsons 1960). To do this, the organization offers various inducements in exchange for contributions of resources and support (Barnard 1938, March and Simon 1958, Simon 1964).

However, the contributions of the various interests are not equally valued by the organization. As such, coalitions that provide "behaviors, resources and capabilities that are most needed or desired by other organizational participants come to have more influence and control over the organization" (Pfeffer and Salancik 1978, p. 27). Similarly, organizational subunits (departments, functional areas, etc.) which are best able to deal with critical contingencies related to coalitional contributions are able to enhance their influence in the organization.

A common problem in this regard is that the various coalitions make conflicting demands on the organization. Since the satisfaction of some demands limits the satisfaction of others, this leads to the possibility that the necessary coalition of support cannot be maintained. Thus organizational activities can be seen as a response to the constraints imposed by the competing demands of various coalitions.

In attempting to maintain the support of its external coalitions, the organization must negotiate exchanges that ensure the continued supply of critical resources. At the same time, however, it must remain flexible enough to respond to environmental contingencies. Often these objectives are in conflict, since the desire to ensure the stability and certainty of resource flows frequently leads to activities limiting flexibility and autonomy. For example, backward integration via merger or acquisition is one way of coping with the uncertainty of resource dependence. At the same time, however, this method of stabilizing resource exchanges limits the ability of the firm to adapt as readily to environmental contingencies. Pfeffer and Salancik suggest that many other activities of organizations can be explained by the desire for stable resource exchanges, on the one hand, and the need for flexibility and autonomy on the other. They present data to support their position that joint ventures, interlocking directorates, organizational growth, political involvement and executive succession can all be interpreted in this light. Other activities such as secrecy, multiple sourcing and diversification can also be interpreted from a resource dependence perspective.

Thus the resource dependence model views organizations as "structures of coordinated behaviors" whose ultimate aim is to garner the necessary environmental support for survival (Pfeffer and Salancik 1978, p. 32). As in the behavioral model, it is recognized that goals and objectives will emerge as constraints imposed by the various coalitions of interests. However, the resource dependence model interprets these constraints as demands by the coalitions that must be met in order to maintain the existence of the organization.

Research Traditions and the Theory of the Firm

In reflecting on the various theories of the firm presented herein, it is important to recognize that one of their primary roles is to function as a part of what Laudan calls a "research tradition" (Laudan 1977). A research tradition consists of a set of assumptions shared by researchers in a particular domain. Its main purpose is to provide a set of guidelines for theory development. In so doing it provides the researcher with both an ontological framework and a philosophical methodology.

The ontology of the research tradition defines the kinds of entities that exist within the domain of inquiry. For example, in the neoclassical model such concepts as middle management, coalitions, bureaucracy and reward systems do not exist. They fall outside the ontology of neoclassical economics. Similarly, the concepts of the entrepreneur, diminishing returns and average cost curves do not exist (or at least are not used) in the resource dependence model. The ontology of the research tradition defines the basic conceptual building blocks of its constituent theories.

The philosophical methodology, on the other hand, specifies the procedure by which concepts will be used to construct a theory. Moreover, it determines the way in which the concepts will be viewed by theorists working within the research tradition. For example, the neoclassical, market value and agency costs models have been developed in accordance with a methodology that could be characterized as deductive instrumentalism. The models are deductive in that each posits a set of assumptions or axioms (including assumptions about firm goals) from which implications for firm behavior are deduced as logical consequences (Hempel 1965, p. 336). The models are also instrumentalist in that their component concepts are not necessarily assumed to have real world referents. Instrumentalism views theories merely as calculating devices that generate useful predictions (Feyerabend 1964, Morgenbesser 1969, Popper 1963). The reality of a theory's assumptions or its concepts is irrelevant from an instrumentalist point of view.

It is essentially this aspect of economic instrumentalism that has drawn the most criticism from both economists and noneconomists. Over 30 years ago concerns for the validity of the theory among economists emerged as the famous "marginalism controversy" which raged in the pages of the *American Economic Review* (Lester 1946, 1947; Machlup 1946, 1947; Stigler 1946, 1947). More recently, much of the criticism has come from proponents of the behavioral theory of the firm (Cyert and March 1963, Cyert and Pottinger 1979). Perhaps the most commonly heard criticism of the neoclassical model is that the assumption of a rational, profit-maximizing decision maker who has access to perfect information is at considerable variance with the real world of business management (Cyert and March 1963, Simon 1955). Moreover, these critics fault the "marginalists" for concocting a firm with "no complex organization, no problems of control, no standard operating procedures, no budget, no controller, [and] no aspiring middle management" (Cyert and March 1963, p. 8). In short, the business firm assumed into existence by neoclassical theory bears little resemblance to the modern corporate structure.

Concerns with the realism of assumptions in neoclassical theory have been challenged by Friedman (1953) and Machlup (1967). In Friedman's classic statement of the "positivist" viewpoint, he takes the position that the ultimate test of a theory is the correspondence of its predictions with reality. From Friedman's perspective the lack of realism in a theory's assumptions is unrelated to the question of its validity.

Machlup, in a closely related argument, notes that much of the criticism of neoclassical theory arises because of a confusion concerning the purposes of the theory (1967). He points out that the "firm" in neoclassical analysis is nothing more than a theoretical construct that is useful in predicting the impact of changes in economic variables on the behavior of firms in the aggregate. For example, the neoclassical model performs well in predicting the *direction* of price changes in an industry that experiences an increase in wage rates or the imposition of a tax. It does less well, however, in explaining the complex process by which a particular firm decides to implement a price change. Of course, this is to be expected since the theory of the firm was never intended to predict the real world behavior of individual firms.

Thus the question of whether corporations really seek to maximize profits is of no concern to the economic instrumentalist. Following Friedman, the only consideration is whether such assumptions lead to "sufficiently accurate predictions" of real world phenomena (1953, p. 15). Similarly, the financial economist is unmoved by criticism related to the lack of reality in the market value and agency cost models. The ultimate justification of a theory from an instrumental viewpoint comes from the accuracy of its predictions.

In contrast to the instrumentalism of the first three theories of the firm, the behavioral and resource dependence models have been developed from the perspective of realism. The realist believes that theoretical constructs should have real world analogs and that theories should describe "what the world is really like" (Chalmers 1978, p. 114). Thus, it is not unexpected that these models are essentially inductive in nature. Indeed, in describing their methodological approach Cyert and March state that they "propose to make detailed observations of the procedures by which firms make decisions and to use these observations as a basis for a theory of decision making within business organizations" (1963, p. 1).

Thus it can be seen that the theories of the firm that have been developed in economics and financial economics emerged from a very different research tradition than the behaviorally oriented theories developed in management. This fact becomes particularly significant in considering their adequacy as a framework for marketing theory development. For example, the discipline of marketing appears to be committed to a research tradition dominated by the methodology of inductive realism, yet it frequently employs the profit maximization paradigm of neoclassical economic theory. Despite the recent trend toward the incorporation of social objectives in the firm's goal hierarchy, and the recognition by many authors that firms pursue multiple objectives, profit or profit maximization figures prominently as the major corporate objective in leading marketing texts (Boone and Kurtz 1980, p. 12; Markin 1979, p. 34; McCarthy 1978, p. 29; Stanton 1978, p. 13). More significantly perhaps, profit maximization is the implicit or explicit objective of much of the normative literature in marketing management. While the terms may vary from return on investment to contribution margin, cash flow or cumulative compounded profits, they are all essentially profit maximization criteria. Thus such widely known and accepted approaches as product portfolio analysis (Boston Consulting Group 1970), segmental analysis (Mossman, Fischer and Crissy 1974), competitive bidding models (Simon and Freimer 1970), Bayesian pricing procedures (Green 1963), and many others all adhere to the profit maximization paradigm. It may seem curious that a discipline that drifted away from the research tradition of economics largely because of a concern for greater "realism" (Hutchinson 1952, Vaile 1950) should continue to employ one of its most "unrealistic" assumptions. In effect, marketing has rejected much of the philosophical methodology of economics while retaining a significant portion of its ontology.

It would seem that what is required is the development of a theory of the firm that is consistent with the existing research tradition of marketing. Such a theory should deal explicitly with the role of marketing in the firm and should attempt to explicate its relationship with the other functional areas (Wind 1981) and specify its contribution to the formation of corporate "goal structures" (Richards 1978). In this way it would provide a framework within which marketing theory development can proceed. This is particularly important for the development of theory within the area of strategic planning. It is likely that greater progress could be made in this area if research is conducted within the context of a theory of the firm whose methodological and ontological framework is consistent with that of marketing.

Toward a Constituency-Based Theory of the Firm

The theory of the firm to be outlined in this section focuses explicitly on the roles performed by the various functional areas found in the modern corporation. There are basically two reasons for this. First, theory development in business administration typically proceeds within the various academic disciplines corresponding (roughly) to the functional areas of the firm. It is felt that a theory explicating the role of the functional areas will be of greater heuristic value in providing a framework for research within these disciplines (and within marketing in particular).

Second, a theory of the firm that does not give explicit recognition to the activities of these functional subunits fails to appreciate their obvious importance in explaining firm behavior. As highly formalized internal coalitions operating at both the corporate and divisional levels, they often share a common frame of reference and a relatively consistent set of goals and objectives. These facts make the functional areas an obvious unit of analysis in attempting to explain the emergence of goals in corporations.

The proposed theory adopts the coalitional perspectives of the various behaviorally oriented theories of the firm and relies especially on the resource dependence model. As a matter of analytical convenience, the theory divides an organization into both internal and external coalitions. From a resource dependence perspective, the task of the organization is to maintain itself by negotiating resource exchanges with external interests. Over time the internal coalitions within corporate organizations have adapted themselves to enhance the efficiency and effectiveness with which they perform these negotiating functions. One approach that has been taken to accomplish this is specialization. Thus certain coalitions within the firm may be viewed as specialists in negotiating exchanges with certain external coalitions. By and large these internal coalitions correspond to the major functional areas of the modern corporate structure.

For example, industrial relations and personnel specialize in negotiating resource exchanges with labor coalitions; finance, and to a lesser extent, accounting specialize in negotiating with stockholder and creditor groups; materials management and purchasing specialize in supplier group exchanges; and, of course, marketing specializes in negotiating customer exchanges. In addition, public relations, legal, tax and accounting specialize to a greater or lesser extent in negotiating the continued support and sanction of both government and public coalitions. In most large corporations the production area no longer interacts directly with the environment. With the waning of the production orientation earlier in this century, production gradually lost its negotiating functions to specialists such as purchasing and industrial relations on the input side and sales or marketing on the output side.

The major resources that the firm requires for survival include cash, labor and matériel. The major sources of cash are customers, stockholders and lenders. It is, therefore, the responsibility of marketing and finance to ensure the required level of cash flow in the firm. Similarly, it is the primary responsibility of industrial relations to supply the labor, and materials management and purchasing to supply the matériel necessary for the maintenance, growth and survival of the organization.

As Pfeffer and Salancik point out, external coalitions that control vital resources have greater control and influence over organizational activities (1978, p. 27). By extension, functional areas that negotiate vital resource exchanges will come to have greater power within the corporation as well. Thus the dominance of production and finance in the early decades of this century may be attributed to the fact that nearly all vital resource exchanges were negotiated by these areas. The ascendance, in turn, of such subunits as industrial relations and personnel (Meyer 1980), marketing (Keith 1960), purchasing and materials management (*Business Week* 1975) and public relations (Kotler and Mindak 1978) can be explained in part by environmental changes which increased the importance of effective and efficient resource exchanges with the relevant external coalitions. For example, the growth of unionism during the 1930s did much to enhance the role and influence of industrial relations departments in large corporations. Similarly, the improved status of sales and marketing departments during this same period may be linked to environmental changes including the depressed state of the economy, the rebirth of consumerism, and a shift in demand away from standardized "Model-T type products" (Ansoff 1979, p. 32). More recently, the OPEC oil embargo, the institutionalization of consumerism, and the expansion of government regulation into new areas (OSHA, Foreign Corrupt Practices Act, Affirmative Action, etc.) has had a similar impact on such areas as purchasing, public relations and legal.

Thus the constituency-based model views the major functional areas as specialists in providing particular resources for the firm. The primary objective of each area is to ensure an uninterrupted flow of resources from the appropriate external coalition. As functional areas tend to become specialized in dealing with particular coalitions, they tend to view these groups as constituencies both to be served and managed. From this perspective, the chief responsibility of the marketing area is to satisfy the long-term needs of its customer coalition. In short, it must strive to implement the marketing concept (Keith 1960, Levitt 1960, McKitterick 1957).

Of course, in seeking to achieve its own objectives, each functional area is constrained by the objectives of the other departments. In attempting to assure maximal consumer satisfaction as a means of maintaining the support of its customer coalition, marketing will be constrained by financial, technical and legal considerations imposed by the other functional areas. For example, expenditures on new product development, market research and advertising cut into the financial resources necessary to maintain the support of labor, supplier, creditor and investor coalitions. When these constraints are embodied in the formal performance measurement system, they exert a significant influence on the behavior of the functional areas.

In this model, firm objectives emerge as a series of Simonian constraints that are negotiated among the various functions. Those areas that specialize in the provision of crucial resources are likely to have greater power in the negotiation process. In this regard, the marketing area's desire to promote the marketing concept as a philosophy of the entire firm may be interpreted by the other functional areas as a means of gaining bargaining leverage by attempting to impress them with the survival value of customer support. The general failure of the other areas to embrace this philosophy may well reflect their belief in the importance of their own constituencies.

Recently, the marketing concept has also been called into question for contributing to the alleged malaise of American business. Hayes and Abernathy (1980) charge that excessive emphasis on marketing research and short-term financial control measures has led to the decline of U.S. firms in world markets. They argue that American businesses are losing more and more of their markets to European and Japanese firms because of a failure to remain technologically competitive. They believe that the reliance of American firms on consumer surveys and ROI control encourages a low-risk, short run investment philosophy, and point out that market research typically identifies consumers' current desires but is often incapable of determining their future wants and needs. Moreover, the short run focus of ROI measures and the analytical detachment inherent in product portfolio procedures tends to encourage investment in fast payback alternatives. Thus Hayes and Abernathy believe that American firms are reluctant to make the higher risk, longer-term investments in new technologies necessary for effective competition in world markets. They feel that the willingness of foreign firms to make such investments can be attributed to their need to look beyond their relatively small domestic markets for success. This has encouraged a reliance on technically superior products and a longer-term payoff perspective.

From a resource dependence viewpoint the Hayes and Abernathy argument seems to suggest that the external coalitions of U.S. firms are rather myopic. If the survival of the firm is truly dependent on the adoption of a longer-term perspective, one would expect this to be forced on the firm by its external coalitions. Indeed, there is ample evidence from stock market studies that investor coalitions react sharply to events affecting the longer run fortunes of firms (Lev 1974, Lorie and Hamilton 1973). Moreover, recent concessions by government, labor and supplier coalitions to Chrysler Corporation suggest a similar perspective among these groups.

However, the real problem is not a failure by internal and external coalitions in recognizing the importance of a long run investment perspective. The real difficulty lies in designing an internal performance measurement and reward system that balances the need for short run profitability against long-term survival. A number of factors combine to bias these reward and measurement systems in favor of the short run. These include:

- Requirements for quarterly and annual reports of financial performance.
- The need to appraise and reward managers on an annual basis.
- The practical difficulties of measuring and rewarding the long-term performance of highly mobile management personnel.
- Uncertainty as to the relative survival value of emphasis on short run versus long run payoffs.

As a result of these difficulties, we find that in many U.S. firms the reward system focuses on short run criteria (Ouchi 1981). This naturally leads to the use of short-term financial control measures and an emphasis on market surveys designed to measure consumer reaction to immediate (and often minor) product improvements. In some cases the marketing area has adopted this approach in the name of the marketing concept.

However, as Levitt (1960) noted more than two decades ago, the real lesson of the marketing concept is that successful firms are able to recognize the fundamental and enduring nature of the customer needs they are attempting to satisfy. As numerous case studies point out, it is the *technology* of want satisfaction that is transitory. The long run investment perspective demanded by Hayes and Abernathy is essential for a firm that focuses its attention on transportation rather than trains, entertainment rather than motion pictures, or energy rather than oil. The real marketing concept divorces strategic thinking from an emphasis on contemporary technology and encourages investments in research and development with long-term payoffs. Thus, the "market-driven" firms that are criticized by Hayes and Abernathy have not really embraced the marketing concept. These firms have simply deluded themselves into believing that consumer survey techniques and product portfolio procedures automatically confer a marketing orientation on their adopters. However, the fundamental insight of the marketing concept has little to do with the use of particular analytical techniques. The marketing concept is essentially a state of mind or world view that recognizes that firms survive to the extent that they meet the real needs of their customer coalitions. As argued below, one of the marketing area's chief functions in the strategic planning process is to communicate this perspective to top management and the other functional areas.

IMPLICATIONS FOR STRATEGIC PLANNING

From a strategic planning perspective, the ultimate objective of the firm may be seen as an attempt to position itself for long run survival (Wind 1979). This, in turn, is accomplished as each functional area attempts to determine the position that will ensure a continuing supply of vital resources. Thus the domestic auto industry's belated downsizing of its product may be viewed as an attempt to ensure the support of its customer coalition in the 1980s and 1990s (just as its grudging acceptance of the UAW in the late 1930s and early 1940s reflected a need to ensure a continuing supply of labor).

Of course, a firm's functional areas may not be able to occupy all of the favored long run positions simultaneously. Strategic conflicts will arise as functional areas (acting as units at the corporate level or as subunits at the divisional level) vie for the financial resources necessary to occupy their optimal long-term position. Corporate management as the final arbiter of these disputes may occasionally favor one area over another, with deleterious results. Thus, John De Lorean, former group executive at General Motors, believes that the firm's desire for the short run profits available from larger cars was a major factor in its reluctance to downsize in the 1970s (Wright 1979). He suggests that an overwhelming financial orientation among GM's top executives consistently led them to favor short run financial gain over longer-term marketing considerations. Similarly, Hayes and Abernathy (1980) believe that the growing dominance of financial and legal specialists within the top managements of large U.S. corporations has contributed to the slighting of technological considerations in product development.

Against this backdrop marketing must realize that its role in strategic planning is not preordained. Indeed, it is possible that marketing considerations may not have a significant impact on strategic plans unless marketers adopt a strong advocacy position within the firm (Mason and Mitroff 1981). On this view, strategic plans are seen as the outcome of a bargaining process among functional areas. Each area attempts to move the corporation toward what it views as the preferred position for long run survival, subject to the constraints imposed by the positioning strategies of the other functional units.

This is not to suggest, however, that formal-analytical procedures have no role to play in strategic planning. Indeed, as Quinn's (1981) research demonstrates, the actual process of strategy formulation in large firms is best described as a combination of the formal-analytical and power-behavioral approaches. He found that the formal planning system often provides a kind of infrastructure that assists in the strategy development and implementation process, although the formal system itself rarely generates new or innovative strategies. Moreover, the study shows that strategies tend to emerge incrementally over relatively long periods of time. One reason for this is the need for top management to obtain the support and commitment of the firm's various coalitions through constant negotiation and implied bargaining (Quinn 1981, p. 61).

Thus, from a constituency-based perspective, marketing's role in strategic planning reduces to three major activities. First, at both the corporate and divisional levels it must identify the optimal long-term position or positions that will assure customer satisfaction and support. An optimal position would reflect marketing's perception of what its customers' wants and needs are likely to be over the firm's strategic time horizon. Since this will necessarily involve long run considerations, positioning options must be couched in somewhat abstract terms. Thus the trend toward smaller cars by the domestic auto industry represents a very broad response to changing environmental, social and political forces and will likely affect the industry well into the 1990s. Other examples include the diversification into alternative energy sources by the petroleum industry, the movement toward "narrowcasting" by the major networks, and the downsizing of the single family home by the construction industry. The length of the time horizons involved suggests that optimal positions will be determined largely by fundamental changes in demographic, economic, social and political factors. Thus strategic positioning is more likely to be guided by long-term demographic and socioeconomic research (Lazer 1977) than by surveys of consumer attitudes.

Marketing's second major strategic planning activity involves the development of strategies designed to capture its preferred positions. This will necessarily involve attempts to gain a competitive advantage over firms pursuing similar positioning strategies. Moreover, the entire process is likely to operate incrementally. Specific strategies will focus on somewhat shorter time horizons and will be designed to move the firm toward a particular position without creating major dislocations within the firm or the marketplace (Quinn 1981). Research on consumers' current preferences must be combined with demographic and socioeconomic research to produce viable intermediate strategies. For example, Detroit's strategy of redesigning all of its subcompact lines has been combined with improved fuel efficiency in its larger cars (*Business Week* 1980).

Finally, marketing must negotiate with top management and the other functional areas to implement its strategies. The coalitional perspective suggests that marketing must take an active role in promoting its strategic options by demonstrating the survival value of a consumer orientation to the other internal coalitions.

Marketing's objective, therefore, remains long run customer support through consumer satisfaction. Paradoxically, perhaps, this approach requires marketers to have an even greater grasp of the technologies, perspectives and limitations of the other functional areas. Only in this way can marketing effectively negotiate the implementation of its strategies. As noted previously, the other functional areas are likely to view appeals to the marketing concept merely as a bargaining ploy. It is the responsibility of the marketing area to communicate the true long run focus and survival orientation of this concept to the other interests in the firm. However, this cannot be accomplished if the marketing function itself does not understand the unique orientations and decision methodologies employed by other departments.

For example, the long run investment perspective implicit in the marketing concept can be made more comprehensible to the financial coalition if it is couched in the familiar terms of capital budgeting analysis. Moreover, the marketing area becomes a more credible advocate for this position if it eschews the use of short-term ROI measures as its sole criterion for internal decision analysis. At the same time, an appreciation for the inherent limitations of contemporary capital investment procedures will give the marketing area substantial leverage in the negotiation process (Anderson 1981).

In the final analysis, the constituency model of the firm suggests that marketing's role in strategic planning must be that of a strong advocate for the marketing concept. Moreover, its advocacy will be enhanced to the extent that it effectively communicates the true meaning of the marketing concept in terms that are comprehensible to other coalitions in the firm. This requires an intimate knowledge of the interests, viewpoints and decision processes of these groups. At the same time, a better understanding of the true nature of the constraints imposed by these interests will allow the marketing organization to make the informed strategic compromises necessary for firm survival.

REFERENCES

Ackoff, Russell (1970), *A Concept of Corporate Planning*, New York: John Wiley & Sons.

Anderson, Paul F. (1981), "Marketing Investment Analysis," in *Research in Marketing*, 4, Jagdish N. Sheth, ed., Greenwich, CT: JAI Press, 1–37.

Ansoff, Igor H. (1965), *Corporate Strategy*, New York: McGraw-Hill.

—— (1979), "The Changing Shape of the Strategic Problem," in *Strategic Management: A View of Business Policy and Planning*, Dan E. Schendel and Charles W. Hofer, eds., Boston: Little Brown and Company, 30–44.

Barnard, Chester I. (1938), *The Functions of the Executive*, London: Oxford University Press.

Barnea, Amir, Robert A. Haugen and Lemma W. Senbet (1981), "Market Imperfections, Agency Problems and Capital Structure: A Review," *Financial Management*, 10 (Summer), 7–22.

Boone, Louis E. and David L. Kurtz (1980), *Foundations of Marketing*, 3rd ed., Hinsdale, IL: Dryden Press.

Boston Consulting Group (1970), *The Product Portfolio*, Boston: The Boston Consulting Group.

Bower, Joseph L. (1968), "Descriptive Decision Theory from the 'Administrative' Viewpoint," in *The Study of Policy Formation*, Raymond A. Bauer and Kenneth J. Gergen, eds., New York: Collier-Macmillan, 103–148.

Business Week (1975), "The Purchasing Agent Gains More Clout" (January 13), 62–63.

—— (1980), "Detroit's New Sales Pitch" (September 22), 78–83.

Buzzell, Robert D., Bradley T. Gale and Ralph G. M. Sultan (1975), "Market Share: A Key to Profitability," *Harvard Business Review*, 53 (January–February), 97–106.

Cardozo, Richard and Yoram Wind (1980), "Portfolio Analysis for Strategic Product—Market Planning," working paper, The Wharton School, University of Pennsylvania.

Chalmers, A. F. (1978), *What Is This Thing Called Science?* St. Lucia, Australia: University of Queensland Press.

Copeland, Thomas E. and J. Fred Weston (1979), *Financial Theory and Corporate Policy*, Reading, MA: Addison-Wesley Publishing Company.

Cravens, David W., Gerald E. Hills and Robert B. Woodruff (1980), *Marketing Decision Making*, rev. ed., Homewood, IL: Richard D. Irwin.

Cyert, Richard M. and James G. March (1963), *A Behavioral Theory of the Firm*, Englewood Cliffs, NJ: Prentice-Hall.

────── and Garrel Pottinger (1979), "Towards a Better Microeconomic Theory," *Philosophy of Science*, 46 (June), 204–222.

Dean, Joel (1966), "Does Advertising Belong in the Capital Budget?" *Journal of Marketing*, 30 (October), 15–21.

Dowling, John and Jeffrey Pfeffer (1975), "Organizational Legitimacy," *Pacific Sociological Review*, 18 (January), 122–36.

Fama, Eugene and Merton H. Miller (1972), *The Theory of Finance*, Hinsdale, IL: Dryden Press.

Feyerabend, Paul K. (1964), "Realism and Instrumentalism: Comments on the Logic of Factual Support," in *The Critical Approach to Science and Philosophy*, Mario Bunge, ed., London: The Free Press of Glencoe, 280–308.

Friedman, Milton (1953), "The Methodology of Positive Economics," in *Essays in Positive Economics*, Chicago: University of Chicago Press.

Glueck, William (1976), *Policy, Strategy Formation and Management Action*, New York: McGraw-Hill.

Green, Paul E. (1963), "Bayesian Decision Theory in Pricing Strategy," *Journal of Marketing*, 27 (January), 5–14.

Hayes, Robert H. and William J. Abernathy (1980), "Managing Our Way to Economic Decline," *Harvard Business Review*, 58 (July–August), 67–77.

Hempel, Carl G. (1965), *Aspects of Scientific Explanation*, New York: Macmillan Publishing Co.

Hofer, Charles W. and Dan Schendel (1978), *Strategy Formulation: Analytical Concepts*, St. Paul, MN: West Publishing Company.

Hopwood, Anthony (1976), *Accounting and Human Behavior*, Englewood Cliffs, NJ: Prentice-Hall.

Howard, John A. (1965), *Marketing Theory*, Boston: Allyn and Bacon.

Hutchinson, Kenneth D. (1952), "Marketing as a Science: An Appraisal," *Journal of Marketing*, 16 (January), 286–93.

Jensen, Michael C. and William H. Meckling (1976), "Theory of the Firm: Managerial Behavior, Agency Costs and Ownership Structure," *Journal of Financial Economics*, 3 (October), 305–60.

Keith, Robert J. (1960), "The Marketing Revolution," *Journal of Marketing*, 24 (January), 35–38.

Kotler, Philip (1971), *Marketing Decision Making*, New York: Holt, Rinehart and Winston.

────── and William Mindak (1978), "Marketing and Public Relations," *Journal of Marketing*, 42 (October), 13–20.

Kuhn, Thomas S. (1970), *The Structure of Scientific Revolutions*, 2nd ed., Chicago: University of Chicago Press.

Laudan, Larry (1977), *Progress and Its Problems*, Berkeley, CA: University of California Press.

Lazer, William (1977), "The 1980's and Beyond: A Perspective," *MSU Business Topics*, 25 (Spring), 21–35.

Lester, R. A. (1946), "Shortcomings of Marginal Analysis for Wage-Employment Problems," *American Economic Review*, 36 (March), 63–82.

────── (1947), "Marginalism, Minimum Wages, and Labor Markets," *American Economic Review*, 37 (March), 135–48.

Lev, Baruch (1974), *Financial Statement Analysis: A New Approach*, Englewood Cliffs, NJ: Prentice-Hall.

Levitt, Theodore (1960), "Marketing Myopia," *Harvard Business Review*, 38 (July–August), 24–47.

Lorie, James H. and Mary T. Hamilton (1973), *The Stock Market: Theories and Evidence*, Homewood, IL: Richard D. Irwin.

Machlup, Fritz (1946), "Marginal Analysis and Empirical Research," *American Economic Review*, 36 (September), 519–54.

——— (1947), "Rejoinder to an Antimarginalist," *American Economic Review*, 37 (March), 148–54.

——— (1967), "Theories of the Firm: Marginalist, Behavioral, Managerial," *American Economic Review*, 57 (March), 1–33.

March, James G. and Herbert A. Simon (1958), *Organizations*, New York: John Wiley & Sons.

Markin, Rom (1979), *Marketing*, New York: John Wiley & Sons.

Mason, Richard O. and Ian I. Mitroff (1981), "Policy Analysis as Argument," working paper, University of Southern California.

McCarthy, E. Jerome (1978), *Basic Marketing*, 6th ed., Homewood, IL: Richard D. Irwin.

McKitterick, J. B. (1957), "What Is the Marketing Management Concept?" in *Readings in Marketing 75/76*, Guilford, CT: Dushkin Publishing Group, 23–26.

Meyer, Herbert E. (1980), "Personnel Directors Are the New Corporate Heroes," in *Current Issues in Personnel Management*, Kendrith M. Rowland et al., eds., Boston: Allyn & Bacon, 2–8.

Meyers, Stewart C. and Stuart M. Turnbull (1977), "Capital Budgeting and the Capital Asset Pricing Model: Good News and Bad News," *Journal of Finance*, 32 (May), 321–336.

Mintzberg, Henry (1979), "Organizational Power and Goals: A Skeletal Theory," in *Strategic Management*, Dan E. Schendel and Charles W. Hofer, eds., Boston: Little Brown and Company.

Morgenbesser, Sidney (1969), "The Realist-Instrumentalist Controversy," in *Philosophy, Science and Method*, New York: St. Martin's Press, 200–18.

Mossman, Frank H., Paul M. Fischer and W. J. E. Crissy (1974), "New Approaches to Analyzing Marketing Profitability," *Journal of Marketing*, 38 (April), 43–48.

Newman, William H. and James P. Logan (1971), *Strategy, Policy and Central Management*, Cincinnati: South-Western Publishing Company.

Ouchi, William G. (1981), *Theory Z*, Reading, MA: Addison-Wesley.

Parsons, Talcott (1960), *Structure and Process in Modern Societies*, New York: Free Press.

Pessemier, Edgar A. (1966), *New-Product Decisions: An Analytical Approach*, New York: McGraw Hill.

Pfeffer, Jeffrey and Gerald R. Salancik (1978), *The External Control of Organizations*, New York: Harper and Row.

Popper, Karl R. (1963), *Conjectures and Refutations*, New York: Harper & Row.

Quinn, James Brian (1981), "Formulating Strategy One Step at a Time," *Journal of Business Strategy*, 1 (Winter), 42–63.

Richards, Max D. (1978), *Organizational Goal Structures*, St. Paul: West Publishing Company.

Roll, Richard (1977), "A Critique of the Asset Pricing Theory's Tests: Part I," *Journal of Financial Economics*, 4 (March), 129–76.

Ross, Stephen A. (1976), "The Arbitrage Theory of Capital Asset Pricing," *Journal of Economic Theory*, 13 (December), 341–360.

——— (1978), "The Current Status of the Capital Asset Pricing Model (CAPM)," *Journal of Finance*, 33 (June), 885–901.

Simon, Herbert A. (1955), "A Behavioral Model of Rational Choice," *Quarterly Journal of Economics*, 69 (February), 99–118.

——— (1959), "Theories of Decision Making in Economics and Behavioral Science," *American Economic Review*, 49 (June), 253–83.

——— (1964), "On the Concept of Organizational Goal," *Administrative Science Quarterly*, 9 (June), 1–22.

Simon, Leonard S. and Marshall Freimer (1970), *Analytical Marketing*, New York: Harcourt, Brace & World.

Solomon, Ezra (1963), *The Theory of Financial Management*, New York: Columbia University Press.

Stanton, William J. (1978), *Fundamentals of Marketing*, 5th ed., New York: McGraw-Hill.

Stigler, G. J. (1946), "The Economics of Minimum Wage Legislation," *American Economic Review*, 36 (June), 358–65.

——— (1947), "Professor Lester and the Marginalists," *American Economic Review*, 37 (March), 154–57.

Vaile, Roland S. (1950), "Economic Theory and Marketing," in *Theory in Marketing*, Reavis Cox and Wroe Alderson, eds., Chicago: Richard D. Irwin.

Van Horne, James C. (1980), *Financial Management and Policy*, 5th ed., Englewood Cliffs, NJ: Prentice-Hall.

Wind, Yoram (1979), "Product Positioning and Market Segmentation: Marketing and Corporate Perspectives," working paper, The Wharton School, University of Pennsylvania.

——— (1981), "Marketing and the Other Business Functions," in *Research in Marketing*, 5, Jagdish N. Sheth, ed., Greenwich, CT: JAI Press, 237–64.

Wright, Patrick J. (1979), *On A Clear Day You Can See General Motors*, Grosse Pointe, MI: Wright Enterprises.

5   The Evolution of Strategic Marketing

Subhash C. Jain

Reprinted by permission of the publisher from "The Evolution of Strategic Marketing," by Subhash C. Jain, *Journal of Business Research*, Vol. 11 (December 1983), pp. 409–425. Copyright 1983 by Elsevier Science Publishing Co., Inc.

In the past few years an important change has taken place of deep concern to the marketing discipline: namely, the emergence of strategic marketing as a new field of endeavor. Strategic marketing as a major component of strategic planning gained prominence among business corporations in the 1970s. While in the 1960s marketing orientation was the password, today the stress is on strategic marketing.

The growing importance of strategic marketing has blurred the concepts of strategy and marketing. In the midst of this confusion such questions as these become pertinent: What is strategic marketing? How is it different from marketing management? How does it blend with marketing orientation? Does strategic marketing change the traditional concept of marketing? If so, what shape must the marketing concept be given? How does strategic marketing relate to corporate strategy? What lessons can be drawn by marketing academicians to train students in the discipline of strategic marketing?

These are difficult questions, and their answers require a thorough investigation and a book-length report. As a beginning, however, this article provides a normative framework to explain the position and role of strategic marketing in business corporations. An attempt will be made to relate strategic marketing to the broader discipline of marketing on the one hand, and to strategic planning and business policy on the other.

EMERGENCE OF STRATEGIC PLANNING

Strategic planning concerns the relationship of an organization to its environment. Theoretically, an organization monitors its environment, incorporates the effects of environmental changes into its corporate decision-making, and formulates new strategies. The 1950s and 1960s were, by and large, very good years for U.S. business. Stable conditions and an expanding economy at home made growth and profitability goals easy to accomplish. Also, the U.S. clout abroad, both among developed and developing countries, to a great extent enabled corporations to realize their goals overseas without too many problems. In brief, susceptibility to environment in the 1950s and 1960s remained minimal. Favorable across-the-board conditions left little need for strategic thinking.

Toward the end of the 1960s, however, conditions began to change. The mounting deficit of the federable government and the unfavorable balance of payments ultimately led to the fall of the dollar, which was devalued twice. The fixed exchange rate that assumed a price of $35 an ounce of gold was abandoned. The oil crisis deepened the problem and inflation made conditions even worse. In the midst of all these difficulties, businesses found themselves at the mercy of a fast-changing environment. This situation called for new ways to manage. Corporations soon began to experiment with the idea of strategic planning.

Strategic planning requires that company assets (i.e., resources) are managed to maximize the financial return through selection of a viable business in accordance with changes in social, economic, political and technological fields. In the practice of strategic planning, a corporation's obligations to its different publics (i.e., stockholders, employees, customers, community, suppliers, financiers, government, and society) and its internal conditions (i.e., resources, culture, capabilities, and vulnerabilities) serve as constraints.

State-of-the-art knowledge in conducting business is manifested in two areas: either in academia or in corporate corridors. Strategic planning developed principally among concerned corporations as a new tool in the midst of a difficult and fast-changing environment. Among the business corporations, General Electric and Texas Instruments stand out as leaders in conceptualizing strategic planning for use in the real world. Along with the manufacturing corporations, several consulting firms did much to advance the state of the art; notably, the Boston Consulting Group and Arthur D. Little, Inc. The continued emphasis on strategic planning among business corporations led business schools to incorporate this emerging discipline into their curriculum, mainly in the late 1970s. Today, most schools offer some instruction in strategic planning, either through a new course on the subject or by incorporating selected material into an existing course.

STRATEGIC MARKETING

One very important component of strategic planning is the establishment of the product/market scope of a business. It is here that strategic planning becomes relevant for marketers. Formally, strategic marketing deals with these questions:

1. Where to compete; definition of market. For example, entire market versus one or more segments.

2. How to compete. For example, an entirely new way of solving customer need by introduction of a new product or by a product similar to that of the competition but with improvements.
3. When to compete. For example, be first in the market or wait until primary demand is established.

There is nothing new about these decisions. In strategic marketing, however, they are approached from a different angle. For example, in marketing management, segmentation amounts to grouping customers by mainly using marketing-mix types of variables. Strategically, market segments are formed to identify the group(s) that would provide the company with a sustainable economic advantage over competition. To clarify the difference, Henderson uses the term *strategic segment/sector*. Henderson notes:

> A strategic sector is one in which you can obtain a competitive advantage and exploit it... Strategic sectors are the key to strategy because each sector's frame of reference is competition. The largest competitor in an industry can be unprofitable if the individual strategic sectors are dominated by smaller competitors.[1]

Further, these decisions formerly could be made routinely and corporations could afford to be less than systematic because the environment was fairly stable. Even if a company allowed a weak product to continue, it had enough leverage to live with it. But shifts in the environment (i.e., social, economic, political, and technological environments) and difficulties in attaining corporate objectives have forced such decisions as market entry and exit to be made systematically. Figure 1 compares the perspectives of marketing management and strategic marketing.

Traditionally, the resources and objectives of the firm, however defined, constituted an uncontrollable variable in developing a marketing mix. In strategic marketing, objectives are systematically defined at different levels after a thorough examination of necessary inputs. Further, resources are allocated to maximize overall corporate performance. Finally, the resulting strategies are formulated with a more inclusive view. As Abell and Hammond have said:

> A strategic market plan is *not* the same, therefore, as a marketing plan; it is a plan of *all* aspects of an organization's strategy in the market place. A marketing plan, in contrast, deals primarily with the delineation of target segments and the product, communication, channel, and pricing policies for reaching and servicing those segments—the so-called marketing mix.[2]

Experience in strategic planning has not only underlined the importance of these decisions, but has also developed a variety of decision-making approaches. As many concerned marketers found the marketing aspects of strategic planning to be profoundly different from those of marketing management, a new field of marketing began: strategic marketing.

The changing environment does not necessarily pose threats for business; it could as easily provide new opportunities. Scanning and monitoring the environment to develop product/market perspectives

FIGURE 1. Strategic Marketing and Marketing Management

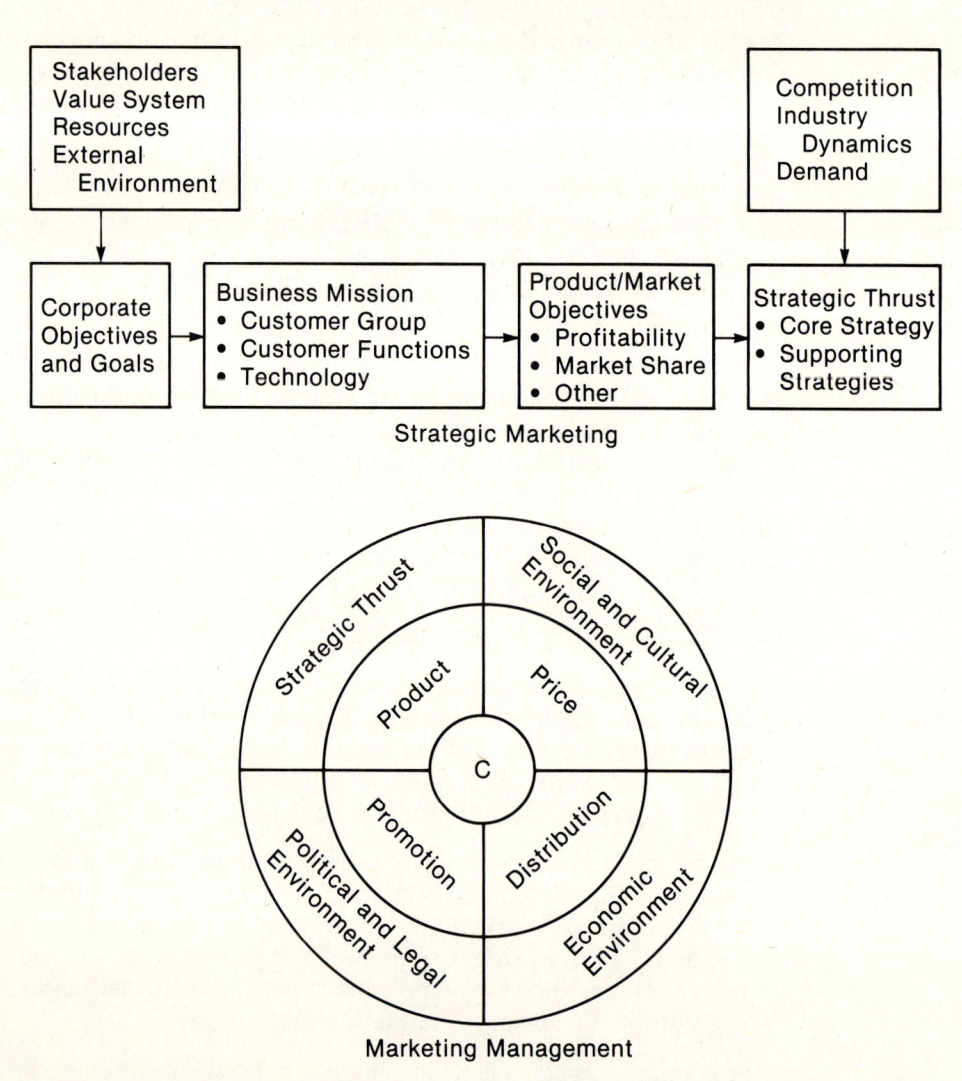

Strategic Marketing

- Stakeholders / Value System / Resources / External Environment → Corporate Objectives and Goals
- Business Mission: Customer Group, Customer Functions, Technology
- Product/Market Objectives: Profitability, Market Share, Other
- Competition / Industry Dynamics / Demand → Strategic Thrust: Core Strategy, Supporting Strategies

Marketing Management

Inner ring: Product, Price, Distribution, Promotion (center: C)
Outer ring: Strategic Thrust, Social and Cultural Environment, Economic Environment, Political and Legal Environment

does not necessarily mean, therefore, a defensive move. Rather it may be capitalization on a new opportunity.

Importance of Strategic Marketing

Strategic planning deals with the relationship of the organization to its environment and thus relates to all areas of a business. Among all these areas, however, marketing is most susceptible to outside influences. Thus, marketing concerns become pivotal in strategic planning. For example, a key question that must be raised in formulating strategic plans is, "What business are we in?" This question is directly related to a company's product/market perspective and, thus, the strategic perspective of the marketing side of business assumes significance in defining a company's purpose.

The experience of those companies well versed in strategic planning indicates that failure on the marketing front can block the way to the goals dictated by strategic plans. A prime example is provided by Texas Instruments. This company has been a pioneer in developing its system of strategic planning (popularly called OST system). Yet apparent marketing negligence forced it to adopt such a drastic measure as withdrawal from the digital watch business. A company can successfully ride on its technological leadership, manufacturing efficiency, and financial acumen with continued growth when the external environment is stable. As shifts in the environment take place, however, a lack of marketing perspective makes the best planned strategies treacherous. It has been put this way:

> Nowhere has that insensitivity been so clearly demonstrated as in the company's consumer products operations. The lack of marketing skills certainly was a major factor in the forthcoming demise of its watch business. T.I. did not try to understand the consumer, nor would it listen to the marketplace. They had the engineer's attitude.[3]

CHARACTERISTICS OF STRATEGIC MARKETING

Strategic marketing utilizes different perspectives from those of marketing management. Its salient features are:

Emphasis on Long-Term Implications

Strategic marketing decisions usually have a long-term focus. Thus commitments made today will have far-reaching implications. In the words of a marketing strategist, *strategic* marketing is a *commitment*, not an *act*. For example, it is not simply a matter of providing an immediate delivery to a favorite customer, but a decision to offer 24-hour delivery service to all customers alike.

In 1980, the Goodyear Tire Company made a strategic decision to continue its focus on the tire business. At a time when other members of the industry were deemphasizing tires, Goodyear opted for the opposite route.[4] This decision will have far-reaching implications for the company over the years. If its calculations were correct, its new entries should enable it to dominate the tire business not only in North America but to some extent in Western Europe as well (the home base of the Michelin tire, currently a strong challenger world-wide). On the other hand, if things turn sour, Goodyear may end up paying a high price for choosing greater involvement in tires than such competitors as Uniroyal and Firestone, who are now diversifying into other fields.

The long-term orientation of strategic planning requires greater concern for the environment. Environmental changes in the long run are more probable than in the short run. In the short run one may assume that environment will remain stable but that is not at all likely in the long run.

Proper scanning and monitoring of the environment requires strategic intelligence inputs. Strategic intelligence differs from traditional marketing research in that it requires much deeper probing. For example, simply knowing that a competitor has a cost advantage is not enough. Strategically, one should find out how much flexibility the competitor has in further reducing its price.

Corporate Inputs Required

Strategic marketing decisions require inputs on three corporate aspects: corporate culture, corporate publics, and corporate resources. Corporate culture refers to the style, whims, fancies, traits, taboos, customs, rituals, etc., of top management which over time come to be accepted as corporate-wide culture. At Pepsico, Inc., for example, the culture emphasizes the tough fight to win. Managers who can't stand involvement in the on-going fight against the competition for market shares may not have a bright future with the company. On the other hand, at the J.C. Penney Company, the corporate culture stresses stability. If a person cannot do well in the store, he may be transferred to a catalog unit in the hope things might work out there. The cultural attachment to stability is so strong at J.C. Penney that a manager may be fired for being aggressive and showing outstanding performance.[5]

Corporate publics are the various stakeholders with an interest in the organization. Typically customers, employees, vendors, governments, and society constitute the stakeholders. Corporate resources include the human, financial, physical, and technological resources of the company.

These three corporate aspects set the degree of freedom a marketing strategist has in making choices, e.g., which market to enter, which business to divest, which business to invest in, etc. The use of corporate-wide inputs in formulating marketing strategy also helps in maximizing overall benefits for the organization.

Varying Roles for Different Products/Markets

Traditionally, it was assumed that all products exert effort to maximize profitability. Strategic marketing starts from the premise that different businesses have varying roles for the company.[6] For example, some may be in the growth stage of the product life cycle; some, in the maturity stage; others, in the introduction stage. Each position in the life cycle requires a different strategy and produces different expectations. Products in the growth stage need extra investment, while those in the maturity stage should generate a cash surplus. Although this was understood conceptually for many years, it has been articulated for real-world application only in recent years—different products serve different purposes. The lead in this approach was provided by the Boston Consulting Group (BCG) in the form of a portfolio matrix, whereby products are split into a two-dimensional matrix of market share and growth rate, both measured on a continuous scale from high to low.[7]

The framework is based on the assumption that the firm with the highest market share relative to its competitors should be able to produce at the lowest cost. Conversely, firms with a low market share relative to competition will be high-cost producers. By comparing relative market share positions (high/low) with market growth rates (high/low), the firm can position its different businesses on a 2×2 matrix. An important characteristic of this framework is that it classifies businesses into four categories, reflecting their cash use and cash generation capabilities. The BCG matrix essentially has two properties: (a) it ranks diverse businesses according to uniform criteria; (b) it provides a tool to balance a company's cash flows by showing which businesses are likely to be cash providers and cash users.

The practice of strategic marketing seeks first to examine each product/market before determining its appropriate role. Further, different products/markets are synergistically related to maximize total marketing effort. Finally, each product/market is paired with a manager who has the proper background and experience to manage it.

Strategic Marketing Is Conducted Simultaneously at Different Levels in the Organizations

Strategic marketing is mainly conducted at the strategic business unit (SBU) level.

SBU Concept. Since formal strategic planning first began to make inroads in corporations in the 1970s, a variety of new concepts has been developed for ascertaining the opportunities of a corporation and speeding up the process of strategy development. These newer concepts create problems of internal organization. In a dynamic economy all the functions of a corporation (i.e., R&D, finance, and marketing) are interrelated. Optimizing some functions instead of the whole company prevents superior corporate performance. Such an organizational perspective permits only the chief executive officer to think of the corporation as a whole. Large corporations have tried many structural designs to broaden the scope of the chief executive in dealing with these complexities. One such design is the profit-center concept. Unfortunately, the profit-center concept emphasizes short-term consequences and optimizes the profit center rather than the corporation as a whole.

The strategic-business-unit concept has been developed to overcome the difficulties posed by the profit-center type of organization. Thus, the first step in integrating product/market strategies is to identify the SBUs or "strategy centers." This amounts to identifying natural businesses in which the corporation is involved. SBUs are not necessarily synonymous with existing divisions or profit centers. An SBU is composed of a product or product lines identifiably independent from other products or product lines in terms of competition, prices, substitutability of product, style/quality, and impact of product withdrawal. It is around this configuration of products that a business strategy should be designed. In today's organizations, this strategy could encompass products found in more than one division. By the same token, some managers may find themselves managing two or more natural businesses. This does not necessarily mean that divisional boundaries need to be redefined; often a strategic business unit can overlap division, and a division can include more than one unit.

Strategic business units may be created by applying a set of criteria consisting of price, competitors, customer groups, and shared experience. To the extent that price changes in a product entail a review of the pricing policy of other products, these products may have a natural alliance. If the various products/markets of a company share the same group of competitors, they may be amalgamated into an SBU for the purpose of strategic planning. Likewise, products/markets sharing a common set of customers belong together. Finally, products/markets in different parts of the company having common R&D, manufacturing, and marketing components may be included in the same SBU. For illustration, consider the case of a large diversified company, one division of which manufactures car radios. The following possibilities exist: the car radio division, as it stands, may represent a viable SBU; alternatively, luxury car radios with automatic tuning may constitute a different SBU from the SBU for standard models; or it may be that other areas of the company, such as the TV division, are combined with all or parts of the car radio division for the creation of an SBU.

Close Relationship Between Strategic Marketing and Finance Function

Strategic marketing decision-making is closely related to the finance function. The importance of maintaining a close relationship between marketing and finance, and for that matter with other functional areas of a business, is nothing new. But in recent years, frameworks have been developed which make it convenient to simultaneously relate marketing to finance in making strategic decisions.

The Boston Consulting Group's experience-curve concept and portfolio matrix provide a means for making finance-oriented marketing decisions related to the product/market perspective.

PROCESS OF STRATEGIC MARKETING

Strategic marketing concentrates on the market to serve, the competition to be tackled, and the timing of market extry/exit and related moves. Marketing management deals with developing a marketing mix to serve the designated market. Of course, the development of a marketing mix should be preceded by a definition of the market. Traditionally, however, market has been loosely defined. In an environment of expansion, even marginal operations could exist profitably. Therefore, there was no reason to be precise, especially since the task of defining the market is difficult. In addition, corporate culture emphasized short-term orientation, which by implication stressed a winning marketing mix rather than an accurate definition of the market. A viable definition of the market to be served, however, proves beneficial in the long run.

To illustrate how problematic it may be to define a market, consider *Wisk*. The market for Wisk can be defined in many different ways: for example, laundry detergent market, liquid laundry detergent market, and pre-wash treatment detergent market. In each market the product would have a different market share and would be challenged by a different set of competitors. Which definition of the market would be most viable for a long-term healthy performance is a question that strategic marketing would address. As Henderson has said:

> A market can be viewed in many different ways, and a product can be used in many different ways. Each time the product-market pairing is varied, the relative competitive strength is varied too. Many businessmen do not recognize that a key element in strategy is choosing the competitor whom you wish to challenge, as well as

TABLE 1. Salient Differences Between Strategic Marketing and Marketing Management

Point of Difference	Strategic Marketing	Marketing Management
1. Time frame	Long range, i.e., decisions have long-term implications	Day-to-day, i.e., decisions have relevance in a given financial year
2. Orientation	Deductive	Inductive
3. Decision Process	Primarily bottom-up	Mainly top-down
4. Relationship with Environment	Environment considered ever-changing and dynamic	Environment considered constant with occasional disturbances
5. Opportunity Sensitivity	On-going to seek new opportunities	Ad hoc search for a new opportunity
6. Organizational Behavior	Achieve synergy between different components of the organization, both horizontally and vertically	Pursue interests of the decentralized unit
7. Nature of Job	Requires high degree of creativity and originality	Requires maturity, experience, and control orientation
8. Leadership Style	Requires pro-active perspective	Requires reactive perspective
9. Mission	Deals with what business to emphasize	Concerns running a delineated business

choosing the marketing segment and product characteristics with which you will compete.[8]

Table 1 summarizes the differences between strategic marketing and marketing management. Strategic marketing differs from marketing management in many respects: orientation, philosophy, approach, relationship with the environment and other parts of the organization, and the management style required. For example, strategic marketing requires a manager to forgo short-term performance in the interest of long-term results.

According to Figure 1, strategic marketing starts with a definition of the business. Conceptually, this task may be performed at the corporate level. Given overall corporate objectives, the business mission may be defined based on three factors: customer group(s) to be served (e.g., household with school-age children); customer functions to be attended (e.g., heavy duty laundry); and alternative technologies (e.g., pre-wash treatment). Thereafter, the business mission will become the focus for delineating product/market objectives. Essentially, product/market objectives can be defined in terms of profitability, market share, growth, or in such other terms as technological leadership, social contribution, strengthening of national defense, or international economic development.

The product/market objectives along with competitive strengths, industry dynamics, and demand form the basis for determining strategic thrust. After trade-offs between alternative strategies have been determined, the chosen strategy usually will focus on one area of the marketing mix (i.e., product, price, promotion, or distribution). For example, the preferred strategy may be to reduce prices to maintain market share. Here the emphasis of the strategy is on pricing. Thus, pricing may be labelled as *core strategy*, i.e., area of primary concern. However, in order to make an integrated marketing decision, appropriate changes may have to be made in product, promotion, and distribution areas. The strategic perspective in these areas could be called *supporting strategies*.

Strategic marketing ends with the development of core strategy. Thereafter, the marketing management function takes over.

STRATEGIC MARKETING IN THE CORPORATE SETTING

This section describes where strategic marketing fits into the corporate environment vis-a-vis strategic planning. Supposedly, the planning system of each corporation is differently designed to work within its own internal and external environment. Given that, the role and position of strategic marketing would vary from corporation to corporation. Discussed here are only common "tenets" or "ground rules" basic to the strategic marketing function in a complex environment. No attempt is made to present a representative model; rather, general inferences are drawn based on my study of strategic marketing practices in nine corporations.

Origin of Strategic Marketing

Strategic marketing, as the textbook may suggest, did not originate in a systematic fashion. As already noted, the difficult environment of the early 1970s forced management to try to formally organize strategy development. Presumably, strategic planning should have begun with marketers in the driver's seat. It so happened, however, that the pioneering frameworks of strategic planning focused on finance. Certainly, the frameworks required marketing inputs which were gathered as needed or simply assumed. But financial bias of strategic planning systems demoted marketing to something as necessary but not important to the long-term perspective of the corporation. For example, most strategic planning approaches emphasized cash flow and return on investment. Of course, cash flow and return on investment must be examined vis-a-vis market share. The perspectives of such marketing matters as market share, however, were either obtained on an ad hoc basis or assumed as constant. Put another way, marketing inputs such as market share became the result instead of the cause. For example, the argument would go that market share *must* be increased to meet the cash-flow target. This perspective of strategic planning led many marketers to conclude that strategic planning occupied the driver's seat, forcing marketing to the back seat.

In a few years, as strategic planning was established, corporations began to realize that there was a missing link in the planning process. Without properly relating the strategic planning effort to marketing, the whole process tends to become static. Business exists in a dynamic setting and, by and large, it is only through marketing inputs that perspectives of changing social, economic, political, and technological environments can be brought into the strategic planning process.

Seven of the nine companies that I recently interviewed indicated that they were disillusioned by the lack of marketing orientation in their strategic planning system. Interestingly, three of these seven companies are firms that marketers traditionally refer to as truly marketing-oriented. A senior executive in one of these companies, a front runner in strategic planning, went so far as to say: "I am disheartened to admit that we have never been marketing-oriented. We are sales pushers."

In brief, the role of strategic marketing in the corporate setting vis-a-vis strategic planning is still emerging. My interviews with executives in the nine companies have led me to conceptualize the position of strategic marketing as shown in Figure 2.

With the advent of strategic planning, the role of marketing at the corporate level declined. Empirical evidence of this event is provided by Rich. In his study of twenty forest-products companies in 1979, he found that not one had a marketing executive with a title of Vice President at the corporate level. As Rich has noted:

> The highest level at which most marketing executives were found was just under the head of a strategic business unit be it at the group or at the division level. Those few marketing executives who were found up at the corporate level tended to be one of three types. The first type was a "V.P. Distribution Division" and was found in companies with strong captive distribution systems. His job was overseeing the distribution, usually at the wholesale level, of all or some of the products of the company's mills. Sometimes he drew on outside sources of supply as well. The second type carried a title such as "Manager of Marketing Planning" and reported to a "Director of Strategic Planning" who came under the CEO. The third type, sometimes carrying the title "Marketing Service Manager," reported to the president or executive vice-president, but his duties were confined mainly to handling important national accounts,

5 — The Evolution of Strategic Marketing

that is, large customers who bought from many different divisions of the company. Such national account sales managers, however, were more likely to be found down at the group level.[9]

According to Rich, this had not been true in the 1960s, when in every company except one a vice-president of marketing reported directly to the president. He further noted that the highest marketing executive was a vice-president or director of marketing who reported to the SBU head. Marketing and sales managers were involved mainly in day-to-day operations and occasionally in the strategic planning of the SBU. In brief, with the emergence of strategic planning, the marketing function was gradually relegated to the background.

My research indicates that marketing is once again assuming more prominence but with a different perspective. Corporations are finding that marketing is not just an operations function relevant for day-to-day decision making. It has strategic content as well. In fact, many companies have had to pay a high price for ignoring the strategic aspect of marketing.

The new attitude toward marketing is reflected in its position within the organization. Five of the nine companies studied established a new position of corporate marketing. Two of these companies further split this office into director of marketing strategy and director of marketing operations. In one of them, the position is titled Vice-president of Mar-

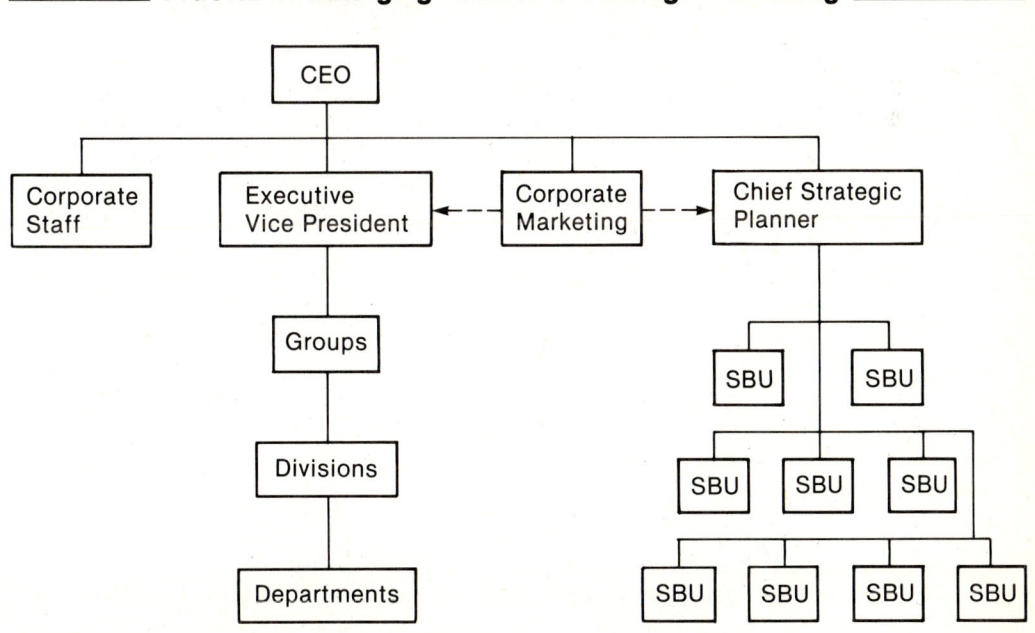

FIGURE 2. Emerging Position of Strategic Marketing

keting Strategy, while in another it is labeled Vice-president, Market Development. The fifth company lists this position simply as Vice-president, Corporate Marketing. In all five companies, this position has been established within the last three years. The major role that the new marketing executive plays is strategy-related in all five cases.

In the other four companies, the strategic role of marketing is duly acknowledged. Organizationally, however, marketing inputs for strategy formulation are brought in by appointing a person with strong marketing background as chief strategic planner. For example, in two of these four companies the chief strategic planner has been the vice-chairman, each one of whom had over twenty years' marketing experience at Procter and Gamble Company and at General Electric Company.

Even at the SBU level, many companies are appointing persons with marketing backgrounds as SBU head. Moreover, corporations are showing an acute need for relating strategic plans to the marketing perspective by scanning and monitoring marketing-related information.

In brief, while initially marketing got lost in the midst of emphasis on strategic planning, presently the role of marketing is better understood and is re-emerging with a new twist: strategic marketing.

Formal Instruction in Strategic Marketing

Marketing instruction traditionally has emphasized operational aspects. During the 1950s and 1960s, the business environment was favorable so that the marketing concept was given a short-term perspective. Business strategy then did not have to be explicitly defined. For this reason, a review of marketing decisions from a strategic angle rarely occurred.

The 1970s, however, brought home to business the importance of undertaking strategic planning. As strategic planning was accepted within corporations, its link to the marketing area became important. Now we are witnessing the broadening of the marketing discipline into two related parts: strategic marketing and operational marketing. At the cost of oversimplification, operational marketing is what is currently emphasized in marketing courses as marketing management. Strategic marketing, on the other hand, deals with the dynamic relationship between a company's offering and its environment, i.e., product/market perspective in a changing environment. Strategic marketing is intimately related to corporate-wide strategy. Further, all strategic marketing decisions must be reviewed and considered for their financial implications.

Clearly marketing academicians should pay heed to the new dimensions being added to their discipline. If marketing is to play its traditional dominant role among business corporations, the strategic aspects of marketing should be duly stressed both in instruction and research. New courses should be developed to instruct and train the future generation of marketers in strategic marketing. Strategic marketing is not a substitute for marketing management. It is an additional aspect of marketing that should be emphasized. More normative and empirical research needs to be undertaken on strategic marketing to advance the state of the art. Simultaneously, new study material should be developed both for college-level courses and executive training.

CONCLUSION

Organizational strategists must answer the crucial question: What business or businesses are we in? This concerns the product/market perspectives of the business—which is certainly a marketing-related matter. This question precedes concern with other functions such as finance, engineering, and manufacturing. Thus, regardless of the corporate mission, objectives, or goals, perspectives of marketing strategy are basic to overall organizational strategy. The strategic role of marketing should be distinguished from its traditional role. Toward this end, two types of marketing could be considered: marketing management and strategic marketing.

A recent criticism directed at corporation management in the United States is that top-level managers are often professional managers who know very little about the products and markets—that is, what their corporations produce and whom they serve.[10] As a matter of fact, lack of emphasis on marketing has created difficulties for many corporations in their strategic planning perspective.

One way to counteract this imbalance and inculcate strategic-marketing orientation in the strategy development process is to develop individuals with good product and market knowledge into strategic planners. One might use people with marketing background for executive development by transforming talented marketing people into managers of strategic business units. Alternatively, to ensure that marketing knowledge exists at corporate headquarters, a corporate-level marketing department could be established. Such a department would assess whether marketing-related concerns are duly addressed in formulating strategy.

REFERENCES

1. Henderson, Bruce D., *Henderson on Corporate Strategy.* Abt Books, Cambridge, Mass., 1981, p. 38.
2. Abell, Derek F., and Hammond, John S., *Strategic Market Planning.* Prentice-Hall, Englewood Cliffs, N.J., 1979, p. 9.

3. "When Marketing Failed at Texas Instruments," *Business Week* (June 22, 1981): 91. Also see: Uttal, Bro, Texas Instruments Regroups, *Fortune* (August 9, 1982): 40.
4. *Business Week* (September 25, 1978): 126.
5. "Corporate Culture," *Business Week* (October 27, 1980): 148.
6. Abell, Derek F., "Metamorphosis in Marketing Planning," in *Research Frontiers in Marketing: Dialogues and Directions,* Subhash C. Jain, ed., American Marketing Association, Chicago, 1978, pp. 257–259.
7. Wind, Yoram, and Mahajan, Vijay, "Designing Product and Business Portfolios," *Harvard Bus. Rev.* 58 (January–February, 1981): 155–165.
8. Henderson, Bruce D., "Metamorphosis in Marketing Planning," in *Research Frontiers in Marketing: Dialogues and Directions,* Subhash C. Jain, ed., American Marketing Association, Chicago, 1978, p. 4.
9. Rich, Stuart U., "Organization Structure and the Marketing Function in Forest Products Companies." A paper presented at the AMA Western Marketing Educators' Conference, San Jose, Ca., April 20, 1979.
10. "Following the Corporate Legend," *Business Week* (February 11, 1980): 62.

6   Diagnosing the Product Portfolio
How to Use Scarce Cash and Managerial Resources for Maximum Long-Run Gains

George S. Day

Reprinted from the *Journal of Marketing*, published by the American Marketing Association, Vol. 41 (April 1977), pp. 29–38. Reprinted by permission.

The product portfolio approach to marketing strategy formulation has gained wide acceptance among managers of diversified companies. They are first attracted by the intuitively appealing concept that long-run corporate performance is more than the sum of the contributions of individual profit centers or product strategies. Secondly a product portfolio analysis suggests specific marketing strategies to achieve a balanced mix of products that will produce the maximum long-run effects from scarce cash and managerial resources. Lastly the concept employs a simple matrix representation which is easy to communicate and comprehend. Thus it is a useful tool in a headquarters campaign to demonstrate that the strategic issues facing the firm justify more centralized control over the planning and resource allocation process.

With the growing acceptance of the basic approach has come an increasing sensitivity to the limitations of the present methods of portraying the product portfolio, and a recognition that the approach is not equally useful in all corporate circumstances. Indeed, the implications can sometimes be grossly misleading. Inappropriate and misleading applications will result when:

- The basic **assumptions** (especially those concerned with the value of market share dominance and the product life cycle) are violated.
- The **measurements** are wrong, or
- The **strategies** are not feasible.

This article identifies the critical assumptions and the measurement and application issues that may distort the strategic insights. A series of questions are posed that will aid planners and decision-makers to better understand this aid to strategic thinking, and thereby make better decisions.

——————— WHAT IS THE PRODUCT PORTFOLIO? ———————

Common to all portrayals of the product portfolio is the recognition that the competitive value of market share depends on the structure of competition and the stage of the product life cycle. Two examples of this approach have recently appeared in this journal.[1] However, the earliest, and most widely implemented is the cash quadrant or share/growth matrix developed by the Boston Consulting Group.[2] Each product is classified jointly by rate of present or forecast **market growth** (a proxy for stage in the product life cycle) and a measure of **market share dominance**.

The arguments for the use of market share are familiar and well documented.[3] Their basis is the cumulation of evidence that market share is strongly and positively correlated with product profitability. This theme is varied somewhat in the BCG approach by the emphasis on relative share—measured by the ratio of the company's share of the market to the share of the largest competitor. This is reasonable since the strategic implications of a 20% share are quite different if the largest competitor's is 40% or if it is 5%. Profitability will also vary, since according to the experience curve concept the largest competitor will be the most profitable at the prevailing price level.[4]

The product life cycle is employed because it highlights the desirability of a variety of products or services with different present and prospective growth rates. More important, the concept has some direct implications for the cost of gaining and/or holding market share:

- During the **rapid growth stage**, purchase patterns and distribution channels are fluid. Market shares can be increased at "relatively" low cost by capturing a disproportionate share of incremental sales (especially where these sales come from new users of applications rather than heavier usage by existing users).
- By contrast, the key-note during the **maturity stage** swings to stability and inertia in distribution and purchasing relationships. A substantial growth in share by one competitor will come at the expense of another competitor's capacity utilization, and will be resisted vigorously. As a result, gains in share are both time-consuming and costly (unless accompanied by a breakthrough in product value or performance that cannot be easily matched by competition).

PRODUCT PORTFOLIO STRATEGIES

When the share and growth rate of each of the products sold by a firm are jointly considered, a new basis for strategy evaluation emerges. While there are many possible combinations, an arbitrary classification of products into four share/growth categories (as shown in Exhibit 1) is sufficient to illustrate the strategy implications.

Low Growth/Dominant Share (Cash Cows)

These profitable products usually generate more cash than is required to maintain share. All strategies should be directed toward maintaining market dominance—including investments in technological leadership. Pricing decisions should be made cautiously with an eye to maintaining price leadership. Pressure to over-invest through product proliferation and market expansion should be resisted unless prospects for expanding primary demand are unusually attractive. Instead, excess cash should be used to support research activities and growth areas elsewhere in the company.

EXHIBIT 1. The Cash Quadrant Approach to Describing the Product Portfolio[a]

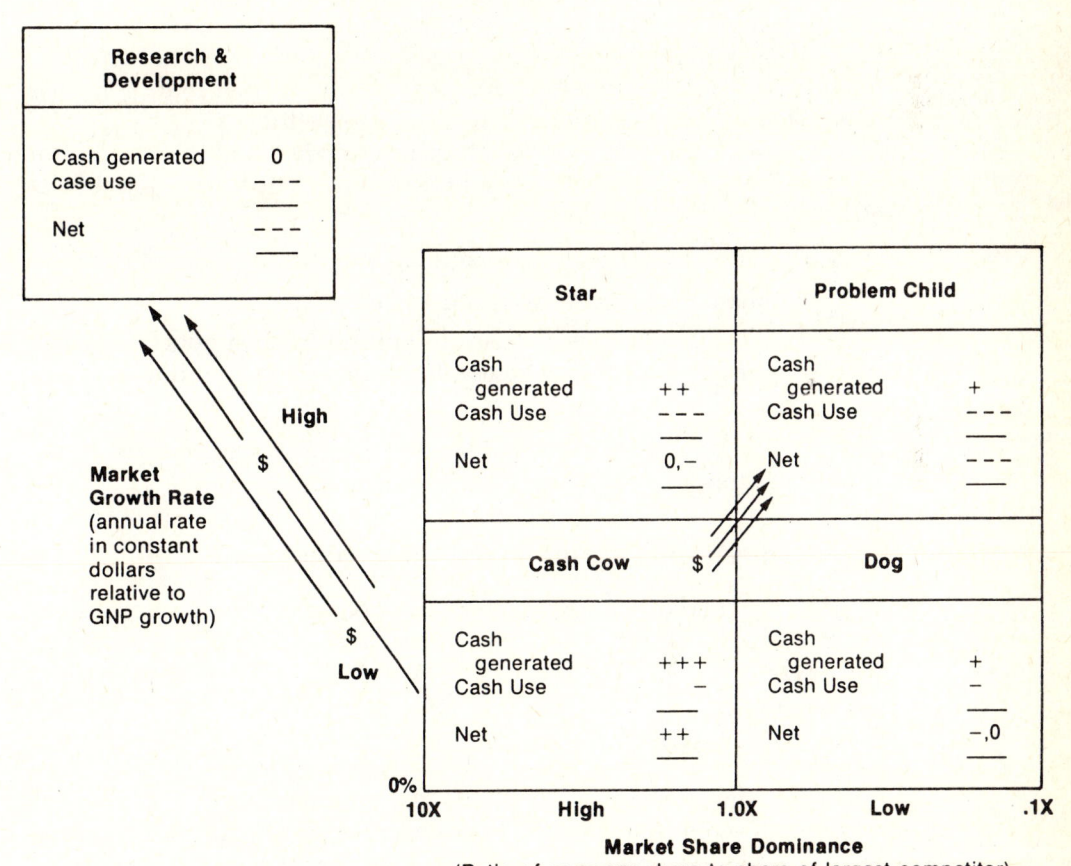

	Star	Problem Child
Cash generated	++	+
Cash Use	---	---
Net	0,−	---

	Cash Cow	Dog
Cash generated	+++	+
Cash Use	−	−
Net	++	−,0

Market Growth Rate (annual rate in constant dollars relative to GNP growth): High / Low, 0%

Market Share Dominance: 10X — High — 1.0X — Low — .1X
(Ratio of company share to share of largest competitor)

Research & Development
Cash generated case use   0
Net

[a] Arrows indicate principal cash flows.

High Growth/Dominant Share (Stars)

Products that are market leaders, but also growing fast, will have substantial reported profits but need a lot of cash to finance the rate of growth. The appropriate strategies are designed primarily to protect the existing share level by reinvesting earnings in the form of price reductions, product improvement, better market coverage, production efficiency increases, etc. Particular attention must be given to obtaining a large share of the new users or new applications that are the source of growth in the market.

Low Growth/Subordinate Share (Dogs)

Since there usually can be only one market leader and because most markets are mature, the greatest number of products fall in this category. Such products are usually at a cost disadvantage and have few opportunities for growth at a reasonable cost. Their markets are not growing, so there is little new business to compete for, and market share gains will be resisted strenuously by the dominant competition.

The slower the growth (present or prospective) and the smaller the relative share, the greater the need for positive action. The possibilities include:

1. Focusing on a specialized segment of the market that can be dominated, and protected from competitive inroads.
2. Harvesting, which is a conscious cutback of all support costs to some minimum level which will maximize the cash flow over a foreseeable lifetime—which is usually short.
3. Divestment, usually involving a sale as a going concern.
4. Abandonment or deletion from the product line.

High Growth/Subordinate Share (Problem Children)

The combination of rapid growth and poor profit margins creates an enormous demand for cash. If the cash is not forthcoming, the product will become a "Dog" as growth inevitably slows. The basic strategy options are fairly clear-cut; either invest heavily to get a disproportionate share of the new sales or buy existing shares by acquiring competitors and thus move the product toward the "Star" category or get out of the business using some of the methods just described.

Consideration also should be given to a market segmentation strategy, but only if a defensible niche can be identified and resources are available to gain dominance. This strategy is even more attractive if the segment can provide an entrée and experience based from which to push for dominance of the whole market.

Overall Strategy

The long-run health of the corporation depends on having some products that *generate* cash (and provide acceptable reported profits), and others that *use* cash to support growth. Among the indicators of overall health are the size and vulnerability of the "Cash Cows" (and the prospects for the "Stars," if any), and the number of "Problem Children" and "Dogs." Particular attention must be paid to those products with large cash appetites. Unless the company has abundant cash flow, it cannot afford to sponsor many such products at one time. If resources (including debt capacity) are spread too thin, the company simply will wind up with too many marginal products and suffer a reduced capacity to finance promising new product entries or acquisitions in the future.

The share/growth matrix displayed in Exhibit 2 shows how one company (actually a composite of a number of situations) might follow the strategic implications of the product portfolio to achieve a better balance of sources and uses of cash. The *present* position of each product is defined by the relative share and market growth rate during a representative time *period*. Since business results normally fluctuate, it is important to use a time period that is not distorted by rare events. The *future* position may be either (a) a momentum forecast of the results of continuing the present strategy, or (b) a forecast of the consequences of a change in strategy. It is desirable to do both, and compare the results. The specific display of Exhibit 2 is a summary of the following strategic decisions.

- Aggressively **support** the newly introduced product A, to ensure dominance (but anticipate share declines due to new competitive entries).
- Continue present strategies of products B and C to ensure **maintenance** of market share.
- Gain share of market for product D by investing in **acquisitions**.
- Narrow and modify the range of models of product E to **focus** on one segment.
- **Divest** products F and G.

Pitfalls in the Assumptions

The starting point in the decision to follow the implications of a product portfolio analysis is to ask whether the underlying assumptions make sense. The most fundamental assumptions relate to the role of market share in the businesses being portrayed in the portfolio. Even if the answers here are affirmative one may choose to not follow the implications if other objectives than balancing cash flows take priority, or there are barriers to implementing the indicated strategies.

What Is the Role of Market Share?

All the competitors are assumed to have the same overhead structures and experience curves, with their position on the experience curve corresponding to their market share position. Hence market share dominance is a proxy for the *relative* profit performance (e.g., GM vs. Chrysler). Other factors beyond market share may be influential in dictating *absolute, profit performance (e.g., calculators versus cosmetics)*.

The influence of market share is most apparent with high value-

EXHIBIT 2. Balancing the Product Portfolio

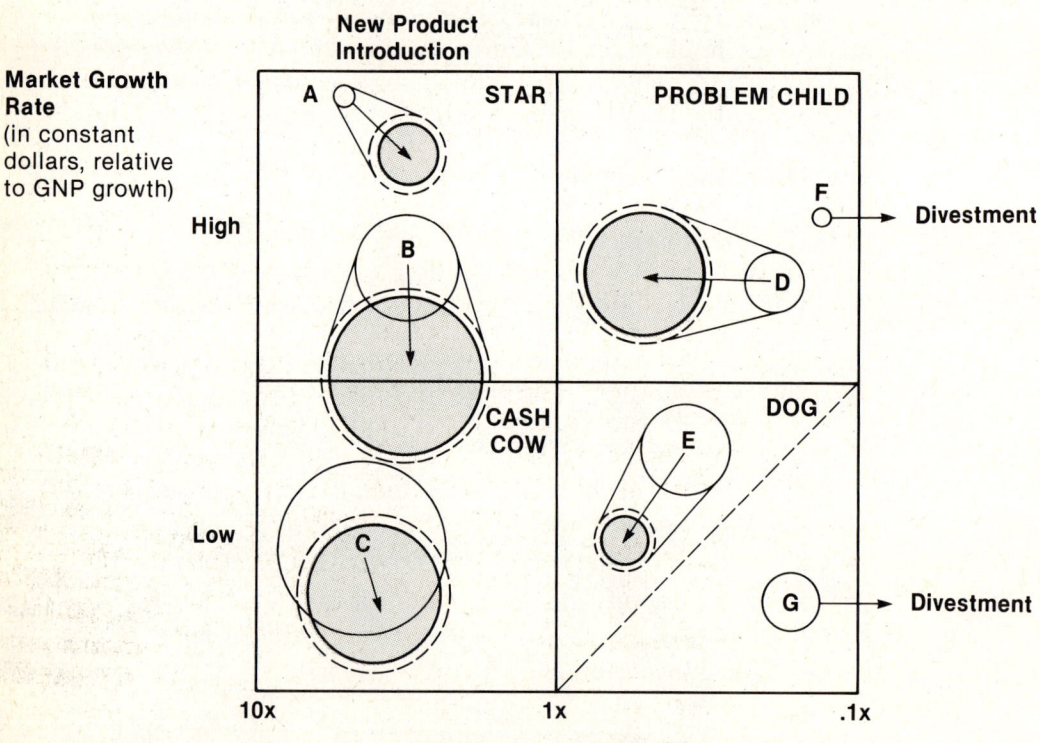

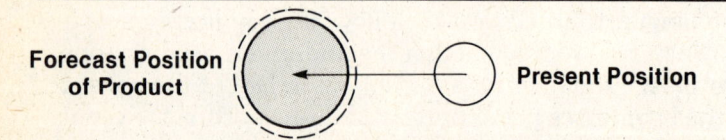

added products, where there are significant barriers to entry and the competition consists of a few, large, diversified corporations with the attendant large overheads (e.g., plastics, major appliances, automobiles, and semi-conductors). But even in these industrial environments there are distortions under conditions such as:

- One competitor has a significant technological advantage which can be protected and used to establish a steeper cost reduction/experience curve.
- The principal component of the product is produced by a supplier who has an inherent cost advantage because of an integrated process. Thus Dupont was at a cost disadvantage with Cyclohexane vis-à-vis the oil companies because the manufacture of the product was so highly integrated with the operations of an oil refinery.[5]
- Competitors can economically gain large amounts of experience through acquisitions or licensing, or shift to a lower (but parallel) cost curve by resorting to off-shore production or component sourcing.
- Profitability is highly sensitive to the rate of capacity utilization, regardless of size of plant.

There are many situations where the positive profitability and share relationship becomes very tenuous, and perhaps unattainable. A recent illustration is the building industry where large corporations—CNA with Larwin and ITT with Levitt—have suffered because of their inability to adequately offset their high overhead charges with a corresponding reduction in total costs.[6] Similar problems are also encountered in the service sector, and contribute to the many reasons why services which are highly labor-intensive and involve personal relationships must be approached with extreme caution in a product portfolio analysis.[7]

There is specific evidence from the Profit Impact of Market Strategies (PIMS) study[8] that the value of market share is not as significant for consumer goods as for industrial products. The reasons are not well understood, but probably reflect differences in buying behavior, the importance of product differentiation and the tendency for proliferation of marginally different brands in these categories. The strategy of protecting a market position by introducing line extensions, flankers, and spin-offs from a successful core brand means that product class boundaries are very unclear. Hence shares are harder to estimate. The individual brand in a category like deodorants or powdered drinks may not be the proper basis for evaluation. A related consequence is that joint costing problems multiply. For example, Unilever in the U.K. has 20 detergent brands all sharing production facilities and marketing resources to some degree.

When Do Market Shares Stabilize?

The operating assumption is that shares tend toward stability during the maturity stage, as the dominant competitors concentrate on defending their existing position. An important corollary is that gains in share are easier and cheaper to achieve during the growth stage.

There is scattered empirical evidence, including the results of the PIMS project, which supports these assumptions. Several qualifications must be made before the implications can be pursued in depth:

- While market share *gains* may be costly, it is possible to mismanage a dominant position. The examples of A&P in food retailing, and British Leyland in the U.K. automobile market provide new benchmarks on the extent to which strong positions can erode unless vigorously defended.
- When the two largest competitors are of roughly equal size, the share positions may continue to be fluid until one is finally dominant.
- There are certain product categories, frequently high technology oriented, where a dominant full line/full service competitor is vulnerable if there are customer segments which do not require all the services, technical assistance, etc., that are provided. As markets mature this "sophisticated" segment usually grows. Thus, Digital Equipment Corp. has prospered in competition with IBM by simply selling basic hardware and depending on others to do the applications programming.[9] By contrast, IBM provides, for a price, a great deal of service backup and software for customers who are not self-sufficient. The dilemma for the dominant producer lies in the difficulty of serving both segments simultaneously.[10]

WHAT IS THE OBJECTIVE OF A PRODUCT PORTFOLIO STRATEGY?

The strategies emerging from a product portfolio analysis emphasize the balance of cash flows, by ensuring that there are products that use cash to sustain growth and others that supply cash.

Yet corporate objectives have many more dimensions that require consideration. This point was recognized by Seymour Tilles in one of the earliest discussions of the portfolio approach.[11] It is worth repeating to avoid a possible myopic focus on cash flow considerations. Tilles' point was that an investor pursues a balanced combination of risk, income, and growth when acquiring a portfolio of securities. He further argued that "the same basic concepts apply equally well to product planning."

The problem with concentrating on cash flow to maximize income and growth is that strategies to balance risks are not explicitly considered.

What must be avoided is excessive exposure to a specific threat from one of the following areas of vulnerability:

- The economy (e.g., business downturns).
- Social, political, environmental pressures.
- Supply continuity.
- Technological change.
- Unions and related human factors.

It also follows that a firm should direct its new product search activities into several different opportunity areas, to avoid intensifying the degree of vulnerability. Thus, many companies in the power equipment market, such as Brown Boveri, are in a quandary over whether to meet the enormous resource demands of the nuclear power equipment market, because of the degree of vulnerability of this business compared to other possibilities such as household appliances.

The desire to reduce vulnerability is a possible reason for keeping, or even acquiring, a "Dog." Thus, firms may integrate backward to assure supply of highly leveraged materials.[12] If a "Dog" has a high percentage of captive business, it may not even belong as a separate entity in a portfolio analysis.

A similar argument could be used for products which have been acquired for intelligence reasons. For example, a large Italian knitwear manufacturer owns a high-fashion dress company selling only to boutiques to help follow and interpret fashion trends. Similarly, because of the complex nature of the distribution of lumber products, some suppliers have acquired lumber retailers to help learn about patterns of demand and changing end-user requirements. In both these cases the products/businesses were acquired for reasons outside the logic of the product portfolio, and should properly be excluded from the analysis.

Can the Strategies Be Implemented?

Not only does a product portfolio analysis provide insights into the long-run health of a company; it also implies the basic strategies that will strengthen the portfolio. Unfortunately, there are many situations where the risks of failure of these strategies are unacceptably high. Several of these risks were identified in a recent analysis of the dangers in the pursuit of market share.[13]

One danger is that the company's financial resources will not be adequate. The resulting problems are enormously compounded should the company find itself in a vulnerable financial position if the fight were stopped short for some reason. The fundamental question underlying such dangers is the likelihood that competitors will pursue the same strategy, because they follow the same logic in identifying and pursuing opportunities. As a result, there is a growing premium on the understanding of competitive responses, and especially the degree to which they will be discouraged by aggressive action.

An increasingly important question is whether government regulations will permit the corporation to follow the strategy it has chosen. Antitrust regulations—especially in the U.S.—now virtually preclude acquisitions undertaken by large companies in related areas. Thus the effort by ITT to acquire a "Cash Cow" in Hartford Fire and Indemnity Insurance was nearly aborted by a consent decree, and other moves by ITT into Avis, Canteen Corp., and Levitt have been divested by court order at enormous cost. Recent governmental actions—notably the *ReaLemon* case—may even make it desirable for companies with very large absolute market share to consider reducing that share.[14]

There is less recognition as yet that government involvement can cut both ways; making it difficult to get in *or out of* a business. Thus, because of national security considerations large defense contractors would have a difficult time exiting from the aerospace or defense businesses. The problems are most acute in countries like Britain and Italy where intervention policies include price controls, regional development directives and employment maintenance which may prevent the replacement of out-moded plants. Unions in these two countries are sometimes so dedicated to protecting the employment status quo that a manager may not even move employees from one product line to another without risking strike activity.

The last implementation question concerns the viability of a niche strategy, which appears at the outset to be an attractive way of coping with both "Dogs" and "Problem Children." The fundamental problem, of course, is whether a product or market niche can be isolated and protected against competitive inroads. But even if this can be achieved in the long-run, the strategy may not be attractive. The difficulties are most often encountered when a full or extensive product line is needed to support sales, service and distribution facilities. One specialized product may simply not generate sufficient volume and gross margin to cover the minimum costs of participation in the market. This is very clearly an issue in the construction equipment business because of the importance of assured service.

PITFALLS IN THE MEASURES

The "Achilles' Heel" of a product portfolio analysis is the units of measure; for if the share of market and growth estimates are dubious, so are the interpretations. Skeptics recognize this quickly, and can rapidly confuse the analysis by attacking the meaningfulness and accuracy of these measures and offering alternative definitions. With the present state of the measurements there is often no adequate defense.

What Share of What Market?

This is not one, but several questions. Each is controversial because they influence the bases for resource allocation and evaluation within the firm:

- Should the definition of the product-market be broad (reflecting the generic need) or narrow?
- How much market segmentation?
- Should the focus be on the total product-market or a portion served by the company?
- Which level of geography: local versus national versus regiocentric markets?

The answers to these questions are complicated by the lack of defensible procedures for identifying product-market boundaries. For example, four-digit SIC categories are convenient and geographically available but may have little relevance to consumer perceptions of substitutability which will influence the long-run performance of the product. Furthermore, there is the pace of product development activity which is dedicated to combining, extending, or otherwise obscuring the boundaries.

Breadth of Product-Market Definition? This is a pivotal question. Consider the following extremes in definitions:

- Intermediate builder chemicals for the detergent industry *or* Sodium Tri-polyphosphate.
- Time/information display devices *or* medium-priced digital-display alarm clocks.
- Main meal accompaniments *or* jellied cranberry.

Narrow definitions satisfy the short-run, tactical concerns of sales and product managers. Broader views, reflecting longer-run, strategic planning concerns, invariably reveal a larger market to account for (a) sales to untapped but potential markets, (b) changes in technology, price relationships, and supply which broaden the array of potential substitute products, and (c) the time required by present and prospective buyers to react to these changes.

Extent of Segmentation? In other words, when does it become meaningful to divide the total market into sub-groups for the purpose of estimating shares? In the tire industry it is evident that the OEM and replacement markets are so dissimilar in behavior as to dictate totally different marketing mixes. But how much further should segmentation be pushed? The fact that a company has a large share of the high-income buyers of replacement tires is probably not strategically relevant.

In general the degree of segmentation for a portfolio analysis should be limited to grouping those buyers that share situational or behavioral characteristics that are strategically relevant. This means that different marketing mixes must be used to serve the segments that have been identified, which will be reflected in different cost and price structures. Other manifestations of a strategically important segment boundary would be a discontinuity in growth rates, share patterns, distribution patterns and so forth when going from one segment to another.

These judgments are particularly hard to make for geographic boundaries. For example, what is meaningful for a manufacturer of industrial equipment facing dominant local competition in each of the national markets in the European Economic Community? Because the company is in each market, it has a 5% share of the total EEC market, while the largest regional competitor has 9%. In this case the choice of a regional rather than national market definition was dictated by the *trend* to similarity of product requirements throughout the EEC and the consequent feasibility of a single manufacturing facility to serve several countries.

The tendency for trade barriers to decline for countries within significant economic groupings will increasingly dictate regio-centric rather than nationally oriented boundaries. This, of course, will not happen where transportation costs or government efforts to protect sensitive industry categories (such as electric power generation equipment), by requiring local vendors, creates other kinds of barriers.

Market Served Versus Total Market?

Firms may elect to serve only just a part of the available market; such as retailers with central buying offices or utilities of a certain size. The share of the market served is an appropriate basis for tactical decisions. This share estimate may also be relevant for strategic decisions, especially if the market served corresponds to a distinct segment boundary. There is a risk that focusing only on the market served may mean overlooking a significant opportunity or competitive threat emerging from the unserved portion of the market. For example, a company serving the blank cassette tape market only through specialty audio outlets is vulnerable if buyers perceive that similar quality cassettes can be bought in general merchandise and discount outlets.

Another facet of the served market issue is the treatment of customers who have integrated backward and now satisfy their own needs from their own resources. Whether or not the captive volume is included in the estimate of total market size depends on how readily this captive volume can be displaced by outside suppliers. Recent analysis suggests that captive production—or infeeding—is "remarkably resilient to attack by outside suppliers."[15]

WHAT CAN BE DONE?

The value of a strategically relevant product-market definition lies in "stretching" the company's perceptions appropriately—far enough so that significant threats and opportunities are not missed, but not so far as to dissipate information gathering and analysis efforts on "long shots." This is a difficult balance to achieve, given the myriads of possibilities. The best procedure for coping is to employ several alternative definitions, varying specificity of product and market segments. There will inevitably be both points of contradiction and consistency in the insights gained from portfolios constructed at one level versus another. The process of resolution can be very revealing, both in terms of understanding the competitive position and suggesting strategy alternatives.[16]

Market Growth Rate

The product life cycle is justifiably regarded as one of the most difficult marketing concepts to measure—or forecast.

There is a strong tendency in a portfolio analysis to judge that a product is maturing when there is a forecast of a decline in growth rate below some specified cut-off. One difficulty is that the same cut-off level does not apply equally to all products or economic climates. As slow growth or level GNP becomes the reality, high absolute growth rates become harder to achieve for all products, mature or otherwise. Products with lengthy introductory periods, facing substantial barriers to adoption, may never exhibit high growth rates, but may have an extended maturity stage. Other products may exhibit precisely the opposite life cycle pattern.

The focus in the product portfolio analysis should be on the long-run growth rate forecast. This becomes especially important with products which are sensitive to the business cycle, such as machine tools, or have potential substitutes with fluctuating prices. Thus the future growth of engineered plastics is entwined with the price of zinc, aluminum, copper and steel; the sales of powdered breakfast beverages depends on the relative price of frozen orange juice concentrate.

These two examples also illustrate the problem of the self-fulfilling prophecy. A premature classification as a mature product may lead to the reduction of marketing resources to the level necessary to defend the share in order to maximize net cash flow. But if the product class sales are sensitive to market development activity (as in the case of engineered plastics) or advertising expenditures (as is the case with powdered breakfast drinks) and these budgets are reduced by the dominant firms then, indeed, the product growth rate will slow down.

The growth rate is strongly influenced by the choice of product-market boundaries. A broad product type (cigarettes) will usually have a longer maturity stage than a more specific product form (plain filter cigarettes). In theory, the growth of the individual brand is irrelevant. Yet, it cannot be ignored that the attractiveness of a growth market, however defined, will be diminished by the entry of new competitors with the typical depressing effect on the sales, prices and profits of the established firms. The extent of the reappraisal of the market will depend on the number, resources, and commitment of the new entrants. Are they likely to become what is known in the audio electronics industry as "rabbits," which come racing into the market, litter it up, and die off quickly?

PITFALLS FROM UNANTICIPATED CONSEQUENCES

Managers are very effective at tailoring their behavior to the evaluation system, *as they perceive it*. Whenever market share is used to evaluate performance, there is a tendency for managers to manipulate the product-market boundaries to show a static or increasing share. The greater the degree of ambiguity or compromise in the definition of the boundaries the more tempting these adjustments become. The risk is that the resulting narrow view of the market may mean overlooking threats from substitutes or the opportunities within emerging market segments.

These problems are compounded when share dominance is also perceived to be an important determinant of the allocation of resources and top management interest. The manager who doesn't like the implications of being associated with a "Dog," may try to redefine the market so he can point to a larger market share or a higher than average growth rate. Regardless of his success with the attempted redefinition, his awareness of how the business is regarded in the overall portfolio will ultimately affect his morale. Then his energies may turn to seeking a transfer or looking for another job, and perhaps another prophecy has been fulfilled.

The forecast of market growth rate is also likely to be manipulated, especially if the preferred route to advancement and needed additional resources is perceived to depend on association with a product that is classified as "Star." This may lead to wishful thinking about the future growth prospects of the product. Unfortunately the quality of the review procedures in most planning processes is not robust enough to challenge such distortions. Further dysfunctional consequences will result if ambitious managers of "Cash Cows" actually attempt to expand their products through unnecessary product proliferation and market segmentation without regard to the impact on profits.

The potential for dysfunctional consequences does not mean that profit center managers and their employees should not be aware of the basis for resource allocation decisions within the firm. A strong argument can be made to the effect that it is worse for managers to observe those decisions and suspect the worst. What will surely create problems is to have an inappropriate reward system. A formula-based system, relying on achievement of a target for return on investment or an index of profit measures, that does not recognize the differences in potential among business, will lead to short-run actions that conflict with the basic strategies that should be pursued.

ALTERNATIVE VIEWS OF THE PORTFOLIO

This analysis of the share/growth matrix portrayal of the product portfolio supports Bowman's contention that much of what now exists in the field of corporate or marketing strategy can be thought of as contingency theories. "The ideas, recommendations, or generalizations are rather dependent (contingent) for their truth and their relevance on the specific situational factors."[17] This means that in any specific analysis of the product portfolio there may be a number of factors beyond share and market growth with a much greater bearing on the attractiveness of a product-market or business; including:

- The contribution rate.
- Barriers to entry.
- Cyclicality of sales.
- The rate of capacity utilization.
- Sensitivity of sales to change in prices, promotional activities, service levels, etc.
- The extent of "captive" business.
- The nature of technology (maturity, volatility, and complexity).
- Availability of production and process opportunities.
- Social, legal, governmental, and union pressures and opportunities.

Since these factors are situational, each company (or division) must develop its own ranking of their importance in determining attractiveness.[18] In practice these factors tend to be qualitatively combined into overall judgments of the attractiveness of the industry or market, and the company's position in that market. The resulting matrix for displaying the positions of each product is called a "nine-block" diagram or decision matrix.[19]

Although the implications of this version of the product portfolio are not as clear-cut, it does overcome many of the shortcomings of the share/growth matrix approach. Indeed the two approaches will likely yield different insights. But as the main purpose of the product portfolio analysis is to help guide—but not substitute for—strategic thinking, the process of reconciliation is useful in itself. Thus it is desirable to employ both approaches and compare results.

SUMMARY

The product portfolio concept provides a useful synthesis of the analyses and judgments during the preliminary steps of the planning process, and is a provocative source of strategy alternatives. If nothing else, it demonstrates the fallacy of treating all businesses or profit centers as alike, and all capital investment decisions as independent and additive events.

There are a number of pitfalls to be avoided to ensure the implications are not misleading. This is especially true for the cash quadrant or share/growth matrix approach to portraying the portfolio. In many situations the basic assumptions are not satisfied. Further complications stem from uncertainties in the definitions of product-markets and the extent and timing of competitive actions. One final pitfall is the unanticipated consequences of adpting a portfolio approach. These may or may not be undesirable depending on whether they are recognized at the outset.

Despite the potential pitfalls it is important to not lose sight of the concept; that is, to base strategies on the perception of a company as an interdependent group of products and services, each playing a distinctive and suportive role.

ENDNOTES

1. Bernard Catry and Michel Chevalier, "Market Share Strategy and the Product Life Cycle," *Journal of Marketing*, Vol. 38 No. 4 (October 1974), pp. 29–34; and Yoram Wind and Henry J. Claycamp, "Planning Product Line Strategy: A Matrix Approach," *Journal of Marketing*, Vol. 40 No. 1 (January 1976), pp. 2–9.
2. Described in the following pamphlets in the *Perspectives* series, authored by Bruce D. Henderson, "The Product Portfolio" (1970), "Cash Traps" (1972) and "The Experience Curve Reviewed: The Growth-Share Matrix or the Product Portfolio." (Boston Consulting Group, 1973). By 1972 the approach had been employed in more than 100 companies. See "Mead's Technique to Sort Out the Losers," *Business Week* (March 11, 1972), pp. 124–30.
3. Sidney Schoeffler, Robert D. Buzzell and Donald F. Heany, "Impact of Strategic

Planning on Profit Performance," *Harvard Business Review* Vol. 52 (March–April 1974), pp. 137–45; and Robert D. Buzzell, Bradley T. Gale and Ralph G. M. Sultan, "Market Share—A Key to Profitability," *Harvard Business Review*, Vol. 53 (January–February 1975), pp. 97–106.
4. Boston Consulting Group, *Perspectives on Experience* (Boston: 1968 and 1970), and "Selling Business a Theory of Economics," *Business Week*, September 8, 1974, pp. 43–44.
5. Robert B. Stobaugh and Philip L. Towsend, "Price Forecasting and Strategic Planning: The Case of Petrochemicals," *Journal of Marketing Research*, Vol. XII (February 1975), pp. 19–29.
6. Carol J. Loomis, "The Further Misadventures of Harold Geneen," *Fortune*, June 1975.
7. There is incomplete but provocative evidence of significant share-profit relationships in the markets for auto rental, consumer finance, and retail securities brokerage.
8. Same as reference 3 above.
9. "A Minicomputer Tempest," *Business Week* January 27, 1975, pp. 79–80.
10. Some argue that the dilemma is very general, confronting all pioneering companies in mature markets. See Seymour Tilles, "Segmentation and Strategy," *Perspectives* (Boston: Boston Consulting Group, 1974).
11. Seymour Tilles, "Strategies for Allocating Funds," *Harvard Business Review*, Vol. 44 (January–February 1966), pp. 72–80.
12. This argument is compelling when $20,000 of Styrene Monomer can affect the production of $10,000,000 worth of formed polyester fiberglass parts.
13. William E. Fruhan, "Pyrrhic Victories in Fights for Market Share," *Harvard Business Review*, Vol. 50 (September–October 1972), pp. 100–107.
14. See Paul N. Bloom and Philip Kotler, "Strategies for High Market-Share Companies," *Harvard Business Review*, Vol. 53 (November–December 1975), pp. 63–72.
15. Aubrey Wilson and Bryan Atkin, "Exorcising the Ghosts in Marketing," *Harvard Business Review*, Vol. 54 (September–October 1976), pp. 117–27. See also, Ralph D. Kerkendall, "Customers as Competitors," *Perspectives* (Boston: Boston Consulting Group, 1975).
16. George S. Day and Allan D. Shocker, *Identifying Competitive Product-Market Boundaries: Strategic and Analytical Issues* (Boston: Marketing Science Institute, 1976).
17. Edward H. Bowman, "Epistemology, Corporate Strategy, and Academe," *Sloan Management Review* (Winter 1974), pp. 35–50.
18. The choice of factors and assessment of ranks is an important aspect of the design of a planning system. These issues are described in Peter Lorange, "Divisional Planning: Setting Effective Direction," *Sloan Management Review* (Fall 1975), pp. 77–91.
19. William E. Rothschild, *Putting It All Together: A Guide to Strategic Thinking* (New York: AMACOM, 1976).

7. A Margin-Return Model for Strategic Market Planning

Jagdish N. Sheth and
Gary L. Frazier

Reprinted from the *Journal of Marketing*, published by the American Marketing Assocation, Vol. 47 (Spring 1983), pp. 100–109. Reprinted by permission.

INTRODUCTION

A number of models or frameworks have recently emerged as tools for strategic market planning, such as the market share-growth matrix, the industry attractiveness-business strength screen, the PIMS analyses, and the strategic intelligence system approach (cf. Abell and Hammond 1979, Day 1977, Montgomery and Weinberg 1979, Wensley 1981). Although these models and frameworks are highly interesting and useful as diagnostic tools, they suffer from two major weaknesses. First, they are not adequately linked to the primary corporate goals of maintaining an adequate net profit margin and return on investment, due either to questionable assumptions and use of surrogate relationships or to methodological problems. Second, and perhaps more significantly, these models or frameworks provide strategic recommendations that are either too general (e.g., harvest, grow, divest) or often difficult to implement (e.g., disinvest "dogs").

This paper develops a model for strategic market planning using the corporate goals of margin and return on investment as its foundation. Based on whether or not an organization's net profit margin and return both reach targeted levels, the model shows how different strategic objectives should be sought and how different strategies should be utilized to achieve the organization's ultimate margin and return goals. It, therefore, attempts to alleviate two major weaknesses that exist in current models and frameworks dealing with strategic market planning.

THE MARGIN-RETURN MODEL

The two most common financial goals of all for-profit corporations are maintaining an adequate net profit margin and return on investment. The margin criterion reflects the company's financial performance on specific business activities. It is directly related to the efficiency of the company's purchasing, manufacturing, distribution and marketing operations. Perhaps the most important aspect of a firm's margin is that it reflects the company's cash flow position. The most common measure of net profit margin is the percent of sales revenue still remaining with the company after payment for all variable and controllable costs associated with its level of sales, such as cost of goods sold, operating expenses, short-term interest expenses and corporate tax. In short, the margin criterion reflects the financial impact of the firm's short-term tactical and operational decisions.

A firm's net profit margin will influence its return on investment. However, a firm's return also reflects other impotrant factors. First, it reflects the company's investment and capitalization policies and is generally indicated by the extent to which the company sinks capital into manufacturing, distribution, warehousing and human resources proportional to its level of sales. Second, it reflects the company's financial leverage decisions on issues such as its debt to equity ratio and the combination of various paper portfolios including common or preferred stocks, convertibles, bonds and debentures. Finally, it reflects the long-term financial viability of the corporation to sustain targeted growth and diversification objectives. In essence, the return criterion indicates the success of the company's attempt to declare and stake out its future mission and objectives, whereas the margin criterion indicates the company's present performance on strategic decisions made earlier.

The most common approach to measuring return on investment is the percentage recovery of capital assets (net profits divided by net worth) on an amortized basis (net present value).[1] It is directly anchored to the life cycles and depreciation schedules of embedded assets in manufacturing and distribution, manpower and the property holdings of the company.

The margin-return model is presented in Table 1. The basis for the model is whether or not a firm reaches targeted levels on both its net profit margin and return on investment.[2] Unlike the criteria utilized in the market share-growth matrix and the business screen analysis, the target levels established for satisfactory performance on margin and return are generally well-established and fairly consistent over time. Most companies tend to set a target level of net profits as a percentage of sales to reflect operations efficiency and similarly a target level of return as a percent of the capital asset base to reflect cost of capital and dividend policies. As Rappaport (1981) argues, targets should be set to preserve shareholder's value.

Current levels of margin and return can be inadequate indicators of the organization's actual value and probable future performance (cf. Rappaport 1981, Weston and Brigham 1972). For example, a firm's present return could be low because several of its major products have required heavy research and development expenditures and are in the introduction stage of their life cycle. A dangerously high leverage ratio will inflate a firm's return while increasing its future cost of capital and decreasing its future value as a result. Therefore, management should estimate what the firm's margin and return will look like over a several year span based on variations in the cost of capital, working capital and investment requirements per sales dollar, and environmental pressures on industry margins, as well as the riskiness of the investment before placing it in the model.

Distinctively different strategic objectives exist for each quadrant. The company can ask each functional area of the business such as marketing, personnel and manufacturing to identify specific strategies that would achieve the strategic objectives. In this paper the discussion is generally limited to marketing strategies and, therefore, strategic decisions related to the four Ps of the marketing mix (product, price, place and promotion).[3] Only in quadrant four where a functional orientation is inappropriate are nonmarketing strategies discussed.

In most cases a firm should seek the objectives and follow the strategies for the quadrant in which it is currently placed. However, where a firm is in danger of moving into a less desirable quadrant in the model (that is, it is near the boundary of two or more quadrants), a preemptive

TABLE 1. The Margin-Return Model

		Targeted Return	
		Satisfactory	*Unsatisfactory*
		Quadrant One	**Quadrant Two**

		1. *Market Enrichment*
		   a. Share protection strategy
		   b. Repositioning strategy
			1. *Volume Improvement*
			   a. Sales stimulation strategy
			   b. System selling strategy

	Satisfactory	2. *Marketing Expansion*
		   a. Multinational strategy
		   b. Full line strategy
			2. *Capital Restructuring*
			   a. Distribution productivity strategy
			   b. Reseller alignment strategy

Targeted Margin		**Quadrant Three**	**Quadrant Four**

		1. *Margin Improvement*
		   a. Repricing strategy
		   b. Cost control strategy
			1. *Corporate Retrenchment*
			   a. Overhead reduction strategy
			   b. Reorganization strategy

	Unsatisfactory	2. *Product Improvement*
		   a. Migration strategy
		   b. Vertical integration strategy
			2. *Corporate Restructuring*
			   a. Divestment strategy
			   b. Diversification strategy

strategy may be most appropriate to follow. Each quadrant of the model will now be examined in terms of the relevant managerial objectives and their corresponding strategies.

Satisfactory Margin and Return Situation

The situation described above is, of course, the ideal one for a company; it is above the targeted threshold level in its short-term operations efficiency as well as in its long-term strategic goals. Unfortunately, too many companies tend to become myopic over time if they remain in this ideal situation. While the company enjoys the benefits of good performance with respect to operations and strategy, it should also plan to ensure its continued viability. This can be achieved by setting and attempting to reach two objectives.

The Market Entrenchment Objective. The immediate strategic objective should be market entrenchment where the firm attempts to maintain and solidify its current position in the marketplace. When a company has achieved a satisfactory margin and return on its investment, there is a very strong likelihood that this success will invite relatively high competitive pressure. Competition may come from a variety of sources including new entrants, substitute products, forward integration by suppliers of raw materials and component parts as well as from large buyers who are tempted to engage in backward integration (Porter 1980). It is, therefore, vital for the company to set the market entrenchment objective with which to minimize competitive vulnerability from any of these sources.

There are two specific marketing strategies that can be used to achieve the market entrenchment objective. The first is a share protection strategy. Defending the company's market share can be achieved based on overall cost leadership and/or differentiation while focusing efforts on its major customers. For example, brands like Mennon (aftershave), Bic (ball-point pens) and Campbells (canned soups) have successfully defended their market share over time by engaging in overall cost leadership so that no company can offer the same product at a cheaper price without substantial financial loss. On the other hand, Monsanto has instituted a differentiation program for Lasso, its successful but mature herbicide, to protect its market share. This is reflected in its product positioning with large farmers through targeted advertising and rebates on purchases of 55 gallon drums of the herbicide. Similarly, Fieldcrest Mills, which manufactures bedspreads, sheets, blankets, rugs, and other fabric products, instituted an "account management" program with major department stores and mass merchandisers in which its salespeople were trained to build personal working relationships with several members in each of its key accounts. Finally,

IBM has always successfully minimized competitive inroads by creating industry specialization in its sales force and account management activities.

A second and slightly longer-term strategy to achieve market entrenchment is the repositioning strategy. In light of changing market needs and societal lifestyles, the firm attempts to enhance the position of its current product lines by changing and extending their image through mass advertising or personal selling. Some minor additions to the firm's product lines can also occur. While its current customer base may be emphasized, a slight extension to other target markets is also possible. For example, as a consequence of declining birth rates, an increase in working spouses and emergence of single adult households, Campbells is repositioning its soups from use as a meal supplement to use as a meal substitute product. A similar repositioning is currently practiced by Kelloggs to broaden and increase the consumption of cereals among adults.

The Market Expansion Objective. The market entrenchment objective to ward off potential competition is extremely useful in the short run if the share protection and repositioning strategies are effectively implemented. Unfortunately, competitive pressures tend to remain high due to the firm's satisfactory margin and return performance. Ultimately, the company must think strategically to convert a competitive (zero sum) game into a coexistive (positive sum) game. This can be achieved by setting the managerial objective of market expansion. A company in this quadrant will have the money, resources and borrowing capacity to fund a relatively costly expansion program.

There are again two fundamental strategies associated with this objective. The first is to redefine the market boundaries from the domestic to worldwide markets, a multinational strategy. This may include both marketing and manufacturing operations. For example, Coca-Cola has remained a profitable company by deciding several decades ago to bottle and distribute locally its soft drinks on a worldwide basis. In general, if a company belongs to an industry that is anchored to universal needs and wants, it is relatively easy to implement the multinational strategy. Examples include pharmaceuticals, heavy engineering and electronics.

The market expansion objective can also be achieved by expansion of the firm's product lines. This is referred to as a full line strategy. As the name implies, this strategy expands the range of products and services offered by the company. In high technology industries, it is usually associated with product line stretching. In the process the firm should seek out and serve each desirable target segment in the industry through a differentiated marketing approach (Kotler 1980). For example, after its successful entry into the medium sized, digital PBX market, Rolm Corporation has stretched its product line over a much larger continuum based on the number of telephone lines its digital switch can integrate and manage. It now offers a full line of PBX equipment appropriate for a wider range of businesses from small to large. A more recent illustration of line stretching strategy is IBM's manufacturing and marketing of personal computers.

A second mechanism of the full line strategy is to offer product assortments. Different products and services capable of satisfying different market needs are offered to the same target segment. The classic example, of course, was the emergence of Sears as the one-stop shopping place for practically everything that middle America needed and wanted.

The market expansion objective is clearly more risky than the market entrenchment objective because it requires significant changes in manufacturing, distribution and marketing operations in addition to greater capitalization of resources and manpower commitments. If a company is not careful in its expansion efforts, it can easily overextend itself and, as a result, move from the ideal quadrant to another less desirable quadrant in the model. For example, the failure of W. T. Grant Company is often attributed to a very rapid expansion policy. Numerous fast food chains have gone bankrupt in trying to expand their market coverage. We are also witnessing similar problems with many commercial airlines including the recent failures of Braniff and Laker. As inferred previously, market entrenchment should be effectively accomplished before an attempt at market expansion is undertaken; the short run objective must be achieved (or at least sought) before seeking the long run objective.

Satisfactory Margin but Unsatisfactory Return Situation

A company in quadrant two has a satisfactory net profit margin. However, due to heavy capitalization relative to sales volume, it is still below the targeted level of return on investment. In general, this situation is most common among companies in the early stages of their life cycles or companies that have undertaken major expansion programs.

The Volume Improvement Objective. The short run objective for a company in this quadrant is to increase asset turnover through volume improvement, since each incremental dollar of sales revenue will contribute toward reaching the targeted return objective. There are two basic marketing strategies available to the firm to achieve its volume improvement objective. The first is sales stimulation through aggressive selling and promotion to both intermediaries and end users. On one hand, it can utilize the push strategy with resellers of its products and services through sales contests and other sales incentive plans. On the other hand, it can also utilize the pull strategy by strong advertising and sales promotions addressed to the end users. A good example of the sales stimulation strategy is the Bell System's recent successful campaign for its profitable long distance service, using the slogan, "Reach out and touch someone." Similarly, McDonalds has attempted to increase sales volume in its fast food franchised outlets through use of a "sweepstakes" sales promotion.

Another marketing strategy to improve volume is system selling in which the company sells a group of related and complementary products to the same customer. In this context, system selling does not necessarily involve new product development or additions to the product line; the firm attempts to sell existing products as a group. Systems selling has become common in the office equipment business among suppliers such as Xerox, AT&T and others.

System selling, however, is not limited to industrial products. For example, Cole National Corporation's consumer products division consists of four major product lines: brass keys, colored keys, knives, and plastic letters, numbers and signs. In 1974 only four percent of its retail customers carried all four lines. To improve its asset turnover Cole instituted a systems selling approach that encouraged salespeople to engage in cross-selling. Each product line was related to the others in terms of special displays and relatively high margins for the retailer.

Two cautions are in order there. First, firms need assets to generate sales and if sales are increased, assets must also be expanded (e.g., raw material, work in process, finished goods inventories, delivery vehicles). Increases in sales beyond a safe range can actually hamper the firm in its drive to increase its return if increases in required assets are higher than the corresponding increase in sales. Second, the attempt to increase sales can result in a serious decrease in the firm's net profit margin if taken too far. Promotion expenses and any discounting in price must be carefully controlled so that the margin will not decrease below its targeted level.

The Capital Restructuring Objective. Unfortunately, there are situations where the volume improvement objective simply does not work due to temporary economic conditions. For example, the recent efforts by American automobile companies to stimulate sales through rebates and lower interest rates have been unsuccessful mostly because of high unemployment, high interest rates and a deep recession. It is also possible that the industry may be at a mature stage in its life cycle so stimulating sales may be more difficult. This is generally true of the appliance industry because it consists mostly of the replacement market.

In this situation a company can hope to improve its return on investment by instituting a capital restructuring program, definitely a longer run approach. Capital restructuring entails abolition of some of the firm's fixed, relatively noncontrollable costs of doing business. In the marketing area this objective can be carried out by focusing on the company's physical distribution, channel relationships and value-added services.

First, a company can attempt to restructure its capital through promoting distribution efficiency, a distribution productivity strategy. Here the emphasis is on decreasing the firm's level of current assets by effectively managing inventory and accounts receivable. Adopting improved inventory control procedures while coordinating the ordering process and order cycle with associated firms would decrease resources tied up in inventory. For example, Japanese automobile manufacturers are achieving significant savings in inventory costs by utilizing the "kanban" or "just in time" system of assembling the automobiles and shipping them to the marketplace (a policy since joined by domestic manufacturers). Some American companies in agribusiness such as Archer-Daniel Midland are reducing inventory as well as transportation costs through development of computerized software programs for shipment of grains through trucks, railroads and barges. Eli Lilly's physical distribution group recently instituted a material requirements planning inventory control system to lessen inventory levels within its distribution channel and, therefore, improve the firm's return.

A second way to achieve capital restructuring is the reseller alignment strategy, where the firm centers its efforts on decreasing levels of its fixed assets in the distribution channel. If the firm currently has a company owned physical distribution system, some trucks and warehouses could be sold while using independent distributors, trucking firms and some public warehousing. By streamlining its sales organization through the use of manufacturers' representatives and agents, or by instituting telemarketing programs (computerized telephone selling to dedicated accounts), a company can significantly reduce its fixed selling costs. Similarly, if a company has a corporate vertical selling system, it can convert it to a franchised selling system so that its capitalization in retail locations can be restructured. For example, IBM has given up its traditional vertical integration and district selling policy to end-users by adopting third party selling agreements with dealers such as Sears and Computerland for its personal computer line. To avoid a large amount of capital invested in distributing its products, Heinz uses food brokers to contact wholesaling establishments.

In some cases it is also possible to consolidate distribution and selling functions by joint agreements between two or more companies. For example, at one time Whirlpool Corporation and RCA had a joint selling and distribution program to minimize capitalization in the distribution and selling areas. Similarly, Pillsbury currently utilizes Kraft Foods' sales force and refrigerated trucks for its dough line instead of buying and maintaining its own fleet of trucks.

Finally, in the past companies have tended to provide a number of support services to the marketplace free of cost to the customer. This may include free delivery and installation, scheduled maintenance, liberal return or exchange policies, and credit float through its own credit cards. More and more firms are realizing that the hidden, uncontrollable costs of these support services are often staggering. For example, the Bell System discovered that the cost of installing the phone in the homes was prohibitive and it could not afford to continue to charge nominal fees as part of this support service. It has now instituted a program of designing modular jacks so that consumers can pick up and plug in their own telephones.

Capital restructuring is decidedly a much riskier corporate objective than volume improvement. First, it requires some reorganization and, therefore, there is generally strong resistance from all parties impacted by the decision. Second, the impact of strategies implemented to achieve capital restructuring is long-term; top management must have patience and confidence to sustain implementation. The temptation is often high to back away from continued support and sustenance of capital restructuring programs in the face of mounting opposition from all types of stakeholders and watchdogs. Third, capital restructuring strategies are inherently more risky since they require greater long-term capital commitments. For example, the jury is still out on whether Levi-Strauss Company will be able to survive and grow from its decision to align with convenience stores such as J.C. Penney and Sears. Much depends on the marketplace decision whether Levis is a specialty or convenience jean within the clothing business. Finally, fixed costs should not be reduced beyond a safe range as this will hamper the firm in having adequate capacity and customer coverage in a prosperous economy. In any case, an attempt at achieving the volume improvement objective should be made first.

Satisfactory Return but Unsatisfactory Margin Situation

In the third quadrant, a company is experiencing satisfactory return on investment but an unsatisfactory net profit margin. In general, this is true of mature industries and companies, partly due to depreciated book values of its capital assets, partly due to its lower interest rates on long-term debts secured under more favorable terms, and partly due to erosion of margins and a consequent profit squeeze created by intense price competition in the industry. A classic example of this is the present financial situation of the supermarket chains where net profits are generally less than two percent of sales, and yet most of them are still able to achieve a satisfactory return due to favorable mortgage rates and depreciated book values of buildings and fixtures. The company in this financial situation should set the following two objectives: margin improvement and product improvement.

The Margin Improvement Objective. This short run objective refers to increasing the gross margins as well as net profit margins of products and services. One way to improve product margins is through a repricing strategy. The price charged by the firm may be too low on certain products relative to the firm's cost of goods sold. Thus, tighter controls on pricing may be required along with a revision in pricing policy. Buyer selection and the evaluation of present customers become a relatively important consideration; current customers should be dropped if they are unwilling to buy the firm's products at acceptable prices. For example, in an attempt to ensure adequate gross margins, a number of wholesalers in the medical supply and equipment channel do not allow their salespeople to deviate from list price unless they receive prior approval from upper management.

Repricing can also be achieved in other ways. For example, one can change the packaging size or shape and the form of the product to improve the margin. Currently this is very commonly utilized by the carbonated beverage industry. It tends to charge different prices for soft drinks in cans as opposed to disposable plastic bottles. A more interesting repricing mechanism is the switch from selling to leasing durable products such as automobiles. The dealer tends to improve his/her margin by performing scheduled maintenance, as well as by providing property and casualty insurance as part of the lease price. With the significant increases in interest rates, many savings and loan institutions have developed "creative financing" programs such as variable term mortgages.

A second strategy to be used in reaching the margin improvement objective is the cost control strategy. This strategy increases the firm's net profit margin by reducing variable and controllable costs associated with the manufacturing and marketing of products and services. The focus of this strategy is on the productivity of different functional areas of the business. Because increasing sales volume in itself is not a primary goal here, promotion costs may be kept at relatively low levels. By increased efficiency in the firm's inventory control and logistics systems, ordering, warehouse, inventory carrying and delivery expenses can be decreased. Increases in fixed costs (e.g., purchase of computer control systems, newer delivery vehicles) can be incurred in the drive to decrease variable costs. For example, Stern and El-Ansary (1977) report that Marcor Corporation (formerly Montgomery Ward), in an attempt to improve its margins, achieved significant cost savings in its distribution center operations by utilizing computerization and automated handling equipment which reduced labor costs for order processing and filling. The W. H. Brady Company manufactures a broad line of products for industrial users that identify, inform, or instruct, such as nameplates, wire markers and safety signs. It is currently using a telemarketing program in low potential sales areas in an effort to lessen selling expenses.

The Product Improvement Objective. A second longer-term strategic objective for an improved net profit margin is product improvement. Implementation of this objective involves alterations in the company's product and market mix as well as its vertical relationships with suppliers, wholesalers and retailers.

First, a migration strategy should be considered. It entails assessment of margin contributions of each product or service, and adding or deleting products and services to improve the overall margin. For example, many supermarkets have added such product lines as L'eggs panty hose, delicatessens and even luncheon counters. In fact, major supermarket chains such as Jewel and Kroger are literally blurring the boundaries between grocery shopping and department store shopping by offering a wide assortment of nontraditional products such as housewares, cosmetics, clothing, cameras and electronic products.

In addition, the markets the firm is currently serving should be carefully evaluated. Customer selectivity should be the rule of the day so that unprofitable market segments are abandoned or given to competition by product pruning and selective selling approaches. Recently, many commercial banks have raised the minimum balances in interest bearing checking accounts to discourage very small depositors.

Similarly, some companies have learned to unbundle their offerings by eliminating many peripheral support services. For example, some supermarket chains have begun to offer highly selective products in "no frill" stores such as Aldi or Jewel. Similarly, some companies have eliminated low margin products or services. For example, several commercial airlines such as U.S. Air and Ozark Airlines have abolished first class sections in their planes. Libby, McNeill and Libby has recently sold some of its well-known canned fruit and vegetable lines because of low margins.

The migration strategy means many things, depending on the industry. It is often referred to as the planned obsolescence strategy in durable goods businesses. For example, in the automobile industry it is used to pass on the incremental costs associated with engineering improvements and regulatory requirements. It is also referred to as the cannibalization strategy in nondurable goods such as soaps and detergents, cosmetics and personal care products. In general, the marketer is interested in retaining loyal customers while motivating them to buy a better product that also has a higher margin. Finally, the migration strategy is sometimes referred to as a "moving up the ladder" strategy. In many retail stores, a customer for replacement of durable goods such as automobile tires, furniture, residential homes and cars is "steered" by salespeople to buy higher priced items that have higher margins and commissions.

Another way to achieve the product improvement objective is through a vertical integration strategy (forward or backward) that will provide economies of scale, increased control of sales and distribution activities, and overall cost efficiency in manufacturing and marketing operations. For example, many fast food franchising companies tend to engage in backward integration as a way to control costs of raw materials, supplies and cooking equipment. It is this vertical integration that gives McDonalds its greatest strength in french fries and hamburgers. Likewise, several packaged food companies have attempted forward integration by buying restaurants and fast food chains. Examples include Pillsbury's successful acquisition and marketing of Burger King and Quaker Oats' development of Magic Pan restaurants. Holiday Inn, in an attempt to ensure satisfactory margins, is evolving into a self-supply network that includes a carpet mill, a furniture manufacturing plant and numerous captive redistribution facilities.

Once again, it should be kept in mind that the product improvement objective is generally much more difficult and longer term as compared to the margin improvement objective. First, it requires significant changes in manufacturing and marketing operations. Second, it takes a considerably longer time period either to innovate new products or to integrate operations vertically. Finally, the strategies involved in product improvement often entail a considerable degree of capitalization. Therefore, any wrong decision may literally push the company into the fourth quadrant of an unsatisfactory margin and unsatisfactory return on investment. In that sense, the product improvement objective is similar to the market expansion and capital restructuring objectives of quadrants one and two respectively. The margin improvement objective must be sought before attempting to achieve the product improvement objective.

Unsatisfactory Margin and Return Situation

When a company finds itself in the fourth quadrant of the matrix, it has neither the margin nor capital leverage to fall back on. Under such financial conditions, more extreme measures are normally required. It is, therefore, not uncommon for a company in this situation to manifest crisis management. Furthermore, marketing as well as other business operations such as manufacturing or purchasing are relatively less useful in this situation. Instead, the company must focus on its management practices and procedures.

There are once again two strategic objectives a company can establish to survive and bounce back to a more desirable financial position. The first is corporate retrenchment and the second longer-term objective is corporate restructuring. Both are highly painful and unpleasant and require strong top management leadership. In fact, it is not unusual for many companies in this situation to hire a chief executive officer from outside the organization who can effectively act as a "hatchet man."

The Corporate Retrenchment Objective. This objective refers to organizational pruning and shaping so that the company becomes a more efficient, lean organization. One strategy for corporate retrenchment is overhead reduction. It requires systematic analysis of noncontrollable costs and finding ways to eliminate them. Reductions in staff personnel is the most obvious method of overhead reduction. Similarly, support systems such as consumer affairs and customer training may be eliminated or at least drastically reduced in funding. The overhead reduction process may entail closing a number of branches or outlets that are highly unprofitable, as A&P is still continuing to do. It may also require closing certain manufacturing plants and consolidating operations into fewer factories, as Firestone has done. Finally, it may be manifested in tougher negotiations with labor unions and seeking major wage and benefit concessions, as has been done recently by the three major automobile manufacturers.

A second strategy to achieve corporate retrenchment is reorganization. In general, it entails a greater degree of centralization, increased span of control, reduction in the number of hierarchical levels, and institution of incentive compensation plans. The general emphasis in the reorganization strategy tends to be one of focus and specialization. This strategy may also cause divesting of manufacturing or marketing operations to concentrate on the strengths of the organization. For example, many American companies in the textile and consumer electronics industries have opted for outside sourcing, especially in Korea and Taiwan, and have instead concentrated on domestic marketing operations.

The Corporate Restructuring Objective. This objective refers to restructuring the corporate mission and definition, entailing issues related to divestiture and diversification. Especially in cases where the corporate retrenchment objective is not effectively reached and a worsening financial picture exists, a divestment strategy needs to be considered. In cases where management feels a redefinition of the business can make the firm profitable but where the funds required for such a move are unavailable, a merger may be particularly appropriate. Selling the firm to another business organization represents another possibility, although the market and intrinsic value of a company with an unsatisfactory margin and return would be relatively low. If all else fails and financial conditions further deteriorate, the liquidation procedures of assignment or bankruptcy may be the only recourse. For example, a number of small breweries have been acquired by larger breweries in the face of increased competition and declining market shares. In the process, Heilemann has become the third largest brewery after Anheuser-Busch and Miller Brewing Company. Similarly, a number of famous retailers such as A&P and Korvettes have been sold to foreign concerns.

If a firm is careful and engages in strategic planning, it is possible for it to initiate a diversification strategy early enough to revitalize itself from impending financial disaster, especially if a high level of financial reserves still exist. Here, the firm can (1) acquire other business organizations or (2) reallocate resources from one group of products to another group that will facilitate movement to its desired position in the marketplace. For example, several years ago Gould Inc. decided to diversify its business from industrial batteries to industrial electronics by acquiring another company. On the other hand, Zenith Corporation has successfully reallocated resources to make a partial switch from consumer electronics to business microprocessors. Perhaps the best example of what looks like a very successful diversification program is the recent acquisition of Dean Witter (a financial brokerage firm) and Coldwell Bankers (a real estate firm) by Sears to position itself in the emerging financial services industry.

Discussion and Implications

In our view, the margin-return model serves many useful functions in strategic market planning. First, it clearly subordinates all other functional goals and objectives such as market share, productivity and growth to the more fundamental and essential corporate financial goals. Since companies must be financially viable to survive and grow, this model reflects the concerns and philosophies of top management.

Second, the model enables the management to rank its strategic objectives and consequent marketing strategies based on the company's financial performance. For example, the model clearly discourages a company with poor reserves from engaging in market expansion programs.

Third, the model recommends short-term and long-term objectives and strategies for each financial situation with a clear emphasis that the short-term objectives should be sought first. For example, attempts to achieve market entrenchment within quadrant one should be made before seeking the market expansion objective.

Fourth, it stresses the appropriate role of marketing strategies for the business organization. Marketing is but one resource and function of the firm; therefore, marketing strategies should be examined only within the context of corporate financial goals and processes designed to achieve them. Unless specific marketing strategies are directly linked to the financial goals of the firm, it is likely that their relevance and importance can go unappreciated in the organization. Furthermore, without this direct link, specific marketing strategies may result in a suboptimization of corporate goals and objectives.

Fifth, the model strongly suggests that the role of strategic marketing is far more critical in the off-diagonal quadrants, where there is at least one form of financial leverage available to the company. By the same token, strategic marketing is less relevant when the company is in a poor financial condition and has to embark on a major corporate retrenchment and restructuring program.

Sixth, it is interesting to note that the traditional elements of the marketing mix (promotion-selling and distribution) are most appropriate when the company has a satisfactory margin but unsatisfactory return on investment. On the other hand, the other two elements of the marketing mix (product and price) are more appropriate when the firm is experiencing a satisfactory return but an unsatisfactory margin. Similarly, the role of selling and distribution (push-pull strategies) seems extremely critical at the early stages of the corporate life cycle. However, at the maturity stage, it is important to shift focus onto product-price elements of marketing. These are traditionally controlled by the manufacturing and accounting functions in a company.

Seventh, the model can be used for a competitive analysis. After placing each competitor in one of the four quadrants, a firm's management can forecast the competitive strategies they are likely to follow in the future.

Finally, the model is applicable to a portfolio analysis of a large, highly diversified, multi-business corporation such as Beatrice Foods.[4] Business units in quadrant one should have relatively high levels of excess funds and borrowing capacity and therefore would represent a major source of funds for units in the other quadrants. The model also provides clues as to what to do within each quadrant as well as how to allocate resources across the four quadrants. For example, it suggests how to plough back financial resources within the "star" businesses with the use of the market entrenchment objective.

The margin-return model can be extended in at least three different ways. First, the same general approach can be applied to nonprofit organizations. The main difference would be that the net profit margin criterion would be replaced by a "reserves" criterion, the difference in revenues a nonprofit organization receives versus the revenues that are spent. For example, at Blue Cross-Blue Shield maintaining targeted reserves (premiums received minus claims plus management costs) is the most commonly sought goal.

Second, the model needs to be expanded to include strategies that can be implemented by other functional areas to achieve the same organizational objectives. Certain functional areas would have relatively high prominence in certain quadrants. For example, marketing, finance and production are functions of dominant importance in quadrant two where revenues, turnover and leverage are important while, in quadrant three, marketing, purchasing and cost accounting are prominent where an increase in firm's net profit margin is important. By extending the model to include strategy development in other functional areas, the interdependence among the various functional areas of the firm could be more clearly identified.

Finally, in some cases it may be desirable or necessary to broaden the corporate perspectives beyond its financial performance. For example, employee satisfaction and social welfare may be added as additional corporate goals. Of course, this will complicate strategic analyses and planning. However, the analytic hierarchy approach recently developed by Saaty (1977) and Wind and Saaty (1980) can be particularly useful in evaluating such goals and deciding which strategies to implement when certain goals conflict.

We are hopeful that both practitioners and academic scholars will find the model sufficiently interesting to carry out experiments or field studies to test it empirically. No doubt additional refinement of the general model in terms of the recommended objectives and strategies within each quadrant would result from such efforts. Each objective and strategy must be developed in greater depth.

ENDNOTES

1. An alternative calculation of ROI, which breaks out its components in greater detail, is given below:

$$\text{Net Profit Margin} = \frac{\text{Net Profits}}{\text{Net Sales}}$$

$$\text{Asset Turnover} = \frac{\text{Net Sales}}{\text{Total Assets}}$$

$$\frac{\text{Net Profits}}{\text{Net Sales}} \times \frac{\text{Net Sales}}{\text{Total Assets}} = \frac{\text{Return on Assets}}{} \times \frac{\text{Total Assets}}{\text{Net Worth}}$$

$$= \frac{\text{Return on Assets}}{} \times \frac{\text{Leverage Ratio}}{} = \frac{\text{Return on Investment}}{}$$

2. At first glance, one may expect net profit margin and return to be highly correlated because the former is used in calculating the latter. However, in many cases they will not be highly correlated, if at all. The return measure also reflects assets management and financial management considerations. It will be heavily influenced by factors such as depreciation schedules that do not influence the net profit margin. As stressed earlier, a firm's return reflects the *effectiveness* (direction) of its overall strategic plan while its margin reflects its *efficiency* (operations)

in carrying out the plan. Most importantly, the model in Table 1 is not based on absolute levels of margin and return but on how they compare to targeted levels.
3. Contrary to the modern definition of marketing, most companies still organize their operations separately for each element of the marketing mix. For example, the product variable is often associated with manufacturing and engineering, price with the cost accounting function and place with the distribution function, with only promotion linked to the sales or marketing group. In that sense, our discussion is related to most operations within the firm.
4. Care must be taken in making return on investment comparisons across divisions or business units within a corporation. Transfer pricing, varying depreciation schedules and industry conditions, the book value of assets, projects requiring heavy investments with long gestation periods in certain units, and a variety of other factors can make one unit's return look very different from the returns of other units in the corporation (Weston and Brigham 1972).

REFERENCES

Abell, Derek and John Hammond (1979), *Strategic Marketing Planning,* Englewood Cliffs, NJ: Prentice-Hall Inc.

Day, George (1977), "Diagnosing the Product Portfolio," *Journal of Marketing*, 41 (April), 29–38.

Kotler, Philip (1980), *Marketing Management*, 4th ed., Englewood Cliffs, NJ: Prentice-Hall, Inc.

Montgomery, David and Charles Weinberg (1979), "Toward Strategic Intelligence Systems," *Journal of Marketing*, 43 (Fall), 41–52.

Porter, Michael (1980), *Competitive Strategy*, New York: The Free Press.

Rappaport, Alfred (1981), "Selecting Strategies That Create Shareholder Value," *Harvard Business Review*, 81 (May–June), 139–149.

Saaty, Thomas (1977), "A Scaling Method for Priorities in Hierarchical Structures," *Journal of Mathematical Psychology*, 15 (June), 234–81.

Stern, Louis and Adel El-Ansary (1977), *Marketing Channels*, Englewood Cliffs, NJ: Prentice-Hall, Inc.

Wensley, Robin (1981), "Strategic Marketing: Betas, Boxes, or Basics," *Journal of Marketing*, 45 (Summer), 173–82.

Weston, J. Fred and Eugene Brigham (1972), *Managerial Finance*, 4th ed., New York: Holt, Rinehart and Winston, Inc.

Wind, Yoram and Thomas Saaty (1980), "Marketing Applications of the Analytic Hierarchy Process," *Management Science*, 26 (July), 641–58.

SECTION C
Marketing Programs and Controls

Marketing programs and controls refer to the strategy and structure issues in marketing. There are three areas of interest and understanding. First, what specific marketing programs, including product, price, promotion, and place decisions, should the organization make to generate or correct demand in the marketplace? This defines the marketing program for each product or brand and includes strategies of market stimulation, market development, and market conversion.

Second, what should be the organizational structure for marketing? There are generally four types of marketing organizations. The first is a functional organization, in which marketing is functionally divided into advertising, sales, market research, sales promotion, and so on, with all reporting to the marketing manager. A second approach is a territorial or market organization, in which the markets are divided geographically and each regional manager reports to the headquarters. This is most common in the international markets, in which there is a marketing manager for each country. The third organizational structure is product management, in which each product or brand becomes the focus of specialization. Then, various brands or products are grouped together into units with profit responsibility. However, other functions, such as sales and advertising, are kept separate. Finally, there is a divisional structure in which each division has its own marketing responsibilities.

It is not clear which organizational structure is appropriate for a given company because organizational structure depends on the product-market scope, as represented in the following diagram:

		Product Single	*Product* Multiple
Market	Single	Functional Organization	Product Organization
	Multiple	Territorial Organization	Division Organization

The last area of understanding relates to marketing controls and marketing efficiency. It is important to get productivity measures of marketing, both internal and external to the organization, for each resource allocation. The most common approach is to measure each marketing expense as a percent of sales and to use both external and internal benchmarks or targets to be achieved by marketing. There is very limited research on marketing controls and productivity. It would appear that there is more expertise among the marketing practitioners than the marketing academics in this area.

8. The Major Tasks of Marketing Management

Philip Kotler

Reprinted from the *Journal of Marketing*, published by the American Marketing Association, Vol. 37 (October 1973), pp. 42–49. Reprinted by permission.

The popular image of the marketer is that he is a professional whose job is to *create* and *maintain* demand for something. Unfortunately, this is too limited a view of the range of marketing challenges he faces. In fact, it covers only two of eight important and distinct marketing tasks. Each task calls for a special type of problem-solving behavior and a specific blend of marketing concepts.

Marketing management may be viewed generically as the *problem of regulating the level, timing, and character of demand for one or more products of an organization.* The organization is assumed to form an idea of a desired level of demand based on profit maximization, sales maximization subject to a profit constraint, satisficing, the current or desired level of supply, or some other type of analysis. The *current demand level* may be below, equal to, or above the *desired demand level*. Four specific demand states make up *underdemand*: negative demand, no demand, latent demand, and faltering demand. Two specific demand states make up *adequate demand*: irregular demand and full demand. Finally, two demand states make up *overdemand*: overfull demand and unwholesome demand. These eight demand states are distinguished primarily with respect to the level of current demand in relation to desired demand; although two additional factors, the timing of demand (irregular demand) and the character of demand (unwholesome demand), are also important. The set of demand situations is fairly exhaustive and the order fairly continuous.

Each demand situation gives rise to the specific marketing task described in column 2 of Table 1. Negative demand results in attempts to disabuse it; no demand, in attempts to create demand; latent demand, in attempts to develop demand; and so on. Each of these tasks is given the more formal name shown in column 3.

All of these tasks require a managerial approach consisting of analysis, planning, implementation, organization, and control. Furthermore, they all utilize the two basic steps of marketing strategy development: defining the *target markets* and formulating a *marketing mix* out of the elements of product, price, promotion, and place. In these respects, all of marketing management has a unity, a core theory. At the same time, the eight tasks are not identical. They involve or emphasize different variables, different psychological theories, different managerial aptitudes. The eight tasks can give way to specialization. Some marketers may become especially skillful at developmental marketing, others at remarketing, others at maintenance marketing, and others at demarketing. Not all marketers are likely to be equally skilled at all tasks, which is one of the major points to be considered in assigning marketers to tasks.

A marketer in a given job may face all of these tasks as the product moves through its life cycle. At the beginning of the product's life, there may be only latent demand and the task is one of developmental marketing. In the stage of high growth, there may be overfull demand in relation to the firm's ability to produce, and some need for systematic demarketing. When facilities have been built up and demand reaches the maturity stage of the product life cycle, the task may be primarily one of maintenance marketing. When demand begins to decline or falter, it may be time to face some basic questions on reshaping it, or remarketing. Finally, the product may eventually fall into the category of being unwholesome either for the consumer or the company, and someone may undertake steps to destroy demand by countermarketing.

Thus the task of marketing management is not simply to build demand but rather to regulate the level, timing, and character of demand for the organization's products in terms of its objectives at the time. This view applies to all organizations. In the discussion that follows, each of the basic marketing tasks is developed and illustrated with examples drawn from profit and nonprofit organizations.

NEGATIVE DEMAND

Negative demand might be defined as *a state in which all or most of the important segments of the potential market dislike the product and in fact might conceivably pay a price to avoid it*. Negative demand is worse than no demand. In the case of no demand, the potential market has no particu-

TABLE 1. The Basic Marketing Tasks

Demand State	Marketing Task	Formal Name
I. Negative demand	Disabuse demand	Conversional marketing
II. No demand	Create demand	Stimulational marketing
III. Latent demand	Develop demand	Developmental marketing
IV. Faltering demand	Revitalize demand	Remarketing
V. Irregular demand	Synchronize demand	Synchromarketing
VI. Full demand	Maintain demand	Maintenance marketing
VII. Overfull demand	Reduce demand	Demarketing
VIII. Unwholesome demand	Destroy demand	Countermarketing

lar feelings about the product one way or another. In the case of negative demand, they actively dislike the product and take steps to avoid it.

Negative demand, far from being a rare condition, applies to a rather large number of products and services. Vegetarians feel negative demand for meats of all kinds. Some Jews and Arabs feel negative demand for pork. Many Americans feel negative demand for kidneys and sweetbreads. People have a negative demand for vaccinations, dental work, vasectomies, and gall bladder operations. A large number of travelers have a negative demand for air travel, and many others have a negative demand for rail travel. Places such as the North Pole and desert wastelands are in negative demand by travelers. Atheism, ex-convicts, military service, and even work are in negative demand by various groups.

The challenge of negative demand to marketing management, especially in the face of a positive supply, is to develop a plan that will cause demand to rise from negative to positive and eventually equal the positive supply level. We call this marketing task that of *conversional marketing*. Conversional marketing is one of the two most difficult marketing tasks a marketer might face (the other is countermarketing). The marketer faces a market that dislikes the object. His chief task is to analyze the sources of the market's resistance; whether they lie largely in the area of *beliefs* about the object, in the *values* touched upon by the object, in the raw *feelings* engendered by the object, or in the *cost* of acquiring the object. If the beliefs are misfounded, they can be clarified through a communication program. If the person's values militate against the object, the object can be put in the framework of other possible values that are positive for the person. If negative feelings are aroused, they may be modifiable through group processes[1] or behavioral therapy.[2] If the costs of acquisition are too high, the marketer can take steps to bring down the real costs. The marketer will want to consider the cost of reducing resistance and whether some other marketing opportunity might be more attractive and less difficult.

NO DEMAND

There is a whole range of objects and services for which there is no demand. Instead of people having negative or positive feelings about the object, they are indifferent or uninterested. *No demand* is *a state in which all or important segments of a potential market are uninterested or indifferent to a particular object*.

Three different categories of objects are characterized by no demand. First, there are those familiar objects that are perceived as having no value. Examples would be urban junk such as disposable coke bottles, old barbed wire, and political buttons right after an election. Second, there are those familiar objects that are recognized to have value but not in the particular market. Examples would include boats in areas not near any water, snowmobiles in areas where it never snows, and burglar alarms in areas where there is no crime. Third, there are those unfamiliar objects which are innovated and face a situation of no demand because the relevant market has no knowledge of the object. Examples include trinkets of all kinds that people might buy if exposed to but do not normally think about or desire.

The task of converting no demand into positive demand is called *stimulational marketing*. Stimulational marketing is a tough task because the marketer does not even start with a semblance of latent demand for the object. He can proceed in three ways. One is to try to connect the object with some existing need in the marketplace. Thus antique dealers can attempt to stimulate interest in old barbed wire on the part of those who have a general need to collect things. The second is to alter the environment so that the object becomes valued in that environment. Thus sellers of motor boats can attempt to stimulate interest in boats in a lakeless community by building an artificial lake. The third is to distribute information or the object itself in more places in the hope that people's lack of demand is really only a lack of exposure.

Stimulational marketing has drawn considerable attack from social critics. Since the consumer had no demand (not even latent demand), the marketer has intruded into his life as a manipulator, a propagandist, an exploiter. The target group had no interest in the object until the marketer, using the whole apparatus of modern marketing, "seduced" or "bamboozled" the consumer into a purchase.

Two things, however, must be said in defense of stimulational marketing. The buyer does not buy because he is forced or coerced by the seller. He buys because he sees the transaction as creating more value for him than avoiding it. The object, while he did not conceive of it on his own, is now seen as related to some need which he does have. The basic need is not manufactured by the marketer. At most, it is stimulated, activated, given a direction and object for expression. Social critics would also have to hold that it is not right for organizations to attempt to activate people's needs.

This nonintervention thesis becomes more difficult in light of the positive benefits that stimulational marketing can confer. Stimulational marketing applies to efforts to get villagers in developing nations to take immunization shots to protect them from dreadful diseases; farmers to adopt better means of farming; mothers to improve their child-rearing practices; and teenagers to improve their nutritional habits. Stimulational marketing is also responsible for accelerating the adoption of many material inventions for which there was no initial market interest. Altogether, a blanket condemnation of stimulational marketing would consign many positive developments, along with the negative ones, to a state of limbo.

LATENT DEMAND

A state of *latent demand* exists *when a substantial number of people share a strong need for something which does not exist in the form of an actual product*. The latent demand represents an opportunity for the marketing innovator to develop the product that people have been wanting.

Examples of products and services in latent demand abound. A great number of cigarette smokers would like a good-tasting cigarette that does not yield nicotine and tars damaging to health. Such a product breakthrough would be an instant success, just as the first filter-tip cigarette won a sizeable share of the market. Many people would like a car that promised substantially more safety and substantially less pollution than existing cars. There is a strong latent demand for fast city roads, efficient trains, uncrowded national parks, unpolluted major cities, safe streets, and good television programs. When such products are finally developed and properly marketed, their market is assured.

The latent demand situation might seem not so much a problem in demand management as one in supply management. Yet it is thoroughly a marketing problem because the latent need must be recognized, the right product developed, the right price chosen, the right channels of distribution put together, and adequate and convincing product information disseminated. Such products as electric dishwashers and air conditioners were adopted slowly at first because people were not convinced that these products could do the job or were worth the price.

The process for effectively converting latent demand into actual demand is that of *developmental marketing*. The marketer must be an expert in identifying the prospects for the product who have the strongest latent demand and in coordinating all the marketing functions so as to develop the market in an orderly way.

In contrast to the substantial social criticism directed at stimulational marketing, most observers feel that developmental marketing is not only natural but highly desirable from a social point of view. Latent demand is the situation for which "the marketing concept" is most appropriate. It is not a question of creating desire but rather of finding it and serving it. The buyers and sellers have complementary interests. There is, however, one important qualification that has come to the surface in recent years. The sheer existence of a personal need may not be sufficient to justify its being served and satisfied. There are needs that people have which, if satisfied, are harmful to others or themselves through the spillover effects of consumption. Satisfying those *needs* may hurt a lot of people's *interests*. Thus it is no longer sufficient for a developmental marketer to say that his new product is justified because there is a real need for it. He may have to show that the need is salutary and the product will not lead to more social harm than private good.

FALTERING DEMAND

All kinds of products, services, places, organizations, and ideas eventually experience declining or *faltering demand*. *Faltering demand is a state in which the demand for a product is less than its former level and where further decline is expected in the absence of remedial efforts to revise the target market, product, and/or marketing effort.*

For example, the natural fur industry is in deep trouble today as demand declines in the face of the trend toward more casual living, the emergence of artificial furs, and the attacks of ecologists who see the fur industry as preying on endangered species. Railway travel has been a service in steady decline for a number of years, and it is badly in need of imaginative remarketing. Many grand hotels have seen their clientele thin out in the face of competition from bright new hotels with the most modern, though somewhat aseptic, facilities. The downtown areas of many large cities are in need of remarketing. Many popular entertainers and political candidates lose their following and badly need remarketing.

The challenge of faltering demand is revitalization, and the marketing task involved is *remarketing*. Remarketing is based on the premise that it is possible in many cases to start a new life cycle for a declining product. Remarketing is the search for new marketing propositions for relating the product to its potential market.

Remarketing calls for a thorough reconsideration of the *target market*, *product features*, and *current marketing program*. The question of the appropriate *target market* is faced, for example, by a grand old hotel in Southern California whose clientele was formerly aristocratic and is now moving toward the comfortable middle class. Still, the hotel continues to try to attract its old clientele and to base its services and prices on this target market—an approach which neither attracts them back nor succeeds in building up the new clientele to its true potential.

The task of revising *product features* is faced by AMTRAK, the new semi-public corporation charged with the responsibility for revitalizing railway passenger travel. AMTRAK's initial temptation was to carry on a massive advertising campaign to get people to try the trains again. However, this would have been fatal because it would have shown people how really bad trains and train service have become. It is a marketing axiom that the fastest way to kill a bad product is to advertise it. This accelerates the rate of trial and the rate of negative word-of-mouth which finally puts the death knell on the product. AMTRAK wisely decided that mass advertising should come *after* product improvement. A sharp distinction must be drawn between *cosmetic marketing*, which tries to advertise a new image without revising the product, and *remarketing*, which calls for a thorough reconsideration and revision of all aspects of the product and market that may affect sales.

The task of overhauling the *marketing program* was faced by American Motors, whose auto sales sank to only three percent of the U.S. car market in 1967. A new management team undertook a major effort to overhaul the field marketing and sales organization and to prune out hundreds of low volume dealers. They also took a maverick approach to car warranties, product design, and advertising. These and other remarketing steps have reversed the decline in their sales.

Remarketing is similar to the physician's job of curing a sick patient. It calls for good diagnosis and a long-term plan to build up the patient's health. The marketing consultant who is good and experienced at remarketing is usually worth his fees because the organization has so much unshiftable capital tied up in the flagging business. In some ways, however, it might be charged that the skilled remarketer serves to slow down progress by trying to preserve the weaker species in the face of stronger competitors. There is some truth to this in that the product in faltering demand would probably disappear or stagnate in the absence of creative marketing respiration. In some situations, perhaps the organization simply should take steps to adjust the supply downward to match the demand. On the other hand, when the faltering demand is due to poor marketing premises and not to natural forces, able remarketing can make a major contribution to saving the organization's assets.

IRREGULAR DEMAND

Very often an organization might be satisfied with the average level of demand but quite unsatisfied with its temporal pattern. Some seasons are marked by demand surging far beyond the supply capacity of the organization, and other seasons are marked by a wasteful underutilization of the organization's supply capacity. *Irregular demand is defined as a state in which the current timing pattern of demand is marked by seasonal or volatile fluctuations that depart from the timing pattern of supply.*

Many examples of irregular demand can be cited. In mass transit, much of the equipment is idle during the off-hours and in insufficient supply during the peak hours. Hotels in Miami Beach are insufficiently booked during the off-seasons and overbooked during the peak seasons. Museums are undervisited during the week days and terribly overcrowded during the weekends. Hospital operating facilities are overbooked at the beginning of the week and under-utilized toward the end of the week to meet physician preferences.

A less common version of the irregular demand situation is where supply is also variable and in fact fluctuates in a perverse way in relation to demand. Imagine a kind of fruit which ripened in winter but which people yearned for in summer; or an animal species in which the mating instinct of the male peaked when the mating instinct of the female was at its nadir. Legal aid is more available to the poor in the summer (because of law students on vacations) but more in demand in the winter. Where demand and supply are both variable and move in opposite directions, the marketer has the option to attempt to (1) alter the supply pattern to fit the demand pattern, (2) alter the demand pattern to fit the natural supply pattern, or (3) alter both to some degree.

The marketing task of trying to resolve irregular demand is called *synchromarketing* because the effort is to bring the movements of demand and supply into better synchronization. Many marketing steps can be taken to alter the pattern of demand. For example, the marketer may promote new uses and desires for the product in the off-season, as can be seen in Kodak's efforts to show camera users that picture taking is fun on many occasions besides Christmas time and summer vacation. Or the marketer can charge a higher price in the peak season and a lower price in the off-season. This strategy is used in the sale of seasonal items such as air conditioners, boats, and ski equipment. Or the marketer can advertise more heavily in the off-season than in the peak season, although this is still not a common practice. In some cases, the pattern of demand will be readily reshaped through simple switches in incentives or promotion; in other cases, the reshaping may be achieved only after years of patient effort to alter habits and desires, if at all.

FULL DEMAND

The most desirable situation that a seller can face is that of full demand. *Full demand is a state in which the current level and timing of demand is equal to the desired level and timing of demand.* Various products and services achieve this condition from time to time. When this state is achieved, however, it is not a time for resting on one's laurels and doing simply automatic marketing. Market demand is subject to two erosive forces that might suddenly or gradually disrupt the equilibrium between demand and supply. One force is changing needs and tastes in the marketplace. The demand for barber services, engineering educations, and mass magazines have all undergone major declines because of changing market preferences. The other force is active competition. A condition of full demand is a signal inviting competitive attack. When a new product is doing well, new suppliers quickly move in and attempt to attract away some of the demand.

Thus the task of the marketer in the face of full demand is to maintain it. His job is *maintenance marketing*. This is essentially the task of the product manager whose product is highly successful. The task is not as challenging as other marketing tasks, such as conversional marketing or remarketing, in which creative new thinking must be given to the future of the product. However, maintenance marketing does call for maintaining efficiency in the carrying out of day-to-day marketing activities and eternal vigilance in monitoring possible new forces threatening demand erosion. The maintenance marketer is primarily concerned with tactical issues such as keeping the price right, keeping the sales force and dealers motivated, and keeping tight control over costs.

OVERFULL DEMAND

Sometimes the demand for a product substantially begins to outpace the supply. Known as *overfull demand*, it is defined as *a state in which demand exceeds the level at which the marketer feels able or motivated to supply it*. It is essentially the reverse of the situation described earlier as faltering demand.

The task of reducing overfull demand is called *demarketing*.[3] More formally, *demarketing deals with attempts to discourage customers in general or a certain class of customers in particular on either a temporary or permanent basis*.

There are two major types of demarketing situations: general demarketing and selective demarketing. *General demarketing* is undertaken by a seller when he wants to discourage overall demand for his product. This can arise for two quite different reasons. First, he may have a *temporary shortage* of goods and want to get buyers to reduce their orders. This situation was faced by Eastman Kodak when it introduced its Instamatic camera in the early 1960s and faced runaway demand; by Wilkinson Sword in the early 1960s when dealers besieged it for the new stainless steel blade; and by Anheuser-Busch in the late 1960s when it could not produce enough beer to satisfy demand. Second, the seller's product may suffer from *chronic overpopularity*, and he may want to discourage permanently some demand rather than increase the size of his plant. This situation is faced by some small restaurants that suddenly are "discovered" but the owners do not want to expand; by the John F. Kennedy Center of the Arts in Washington which draws larger crowds than it can handle resulting in vandalism, damage to the property, and high cleaning bills; by certain tourist places, such as Hawaii, where the number of tourists has become excessive in terms of the objective of achieving a restful vacation; and by the Golden Gate Bridge in San Francisco, where authorities are urging motorists to reduce their use of the bridge. The Chinese mainland is engaged today in demarketing pork, a meat product which is historically more popular than beef in China but is in chronically short supply. U.S. electric power companies are demarketing certain uses of electricity because of the growing shortage of power generation facilities. Several of the far Western states are actively demarketing themselves as places to live because they are becoming overcrowded.

Selective demarketing occurs when an organization does not wish to reduce everyone's demand but rather the demand coming from certain segments of the market. These segments or customer classes may be considered relatively unprofitable in themselves or undesirable in terms of their impact on other valued segments of the market. The seller may not be free to refuse sales outright, either as a matter of law or of public opinion, so he searches for other means to discourage demand from the unwanted customers.

Many examples could be cited. A luxury hotel which primarily caters to middle-aged, conservative tourists resorts to selective means to discourage young jet-setters. A renowned university wants to discourage marginal applicants because of all the paper work and the wish to avoid rejecting so many applicants and creating bad feelings. A prepaid medical group practice wants to discourage its hypochondriac patients from running to them with every minor ailment. A police department wants to discourage nuisance calls so that its limited resources can be devoted to major crime prevention.

Demarketing largely calls for marketing in reverse. Instead of encouraging customers, it calls for the art of discouraging them. Prices may be raised, and product quality, service, promotion, and convenience reduced. The demarketer must have a thick skin because he is not going to be popular with certain groups. Some of the steps will appear unfair ways to ration a product. Some of the groups who are discriminated against may have just cause for complaint. Demarketing may be highly justified in some situations and ethically dubious in others.

UNWHOLESOME DEMAND

There are many products for which the demand may be judged unwholesome from the viewpoint of the consumer's welfare, the public's welfare, or the supplier's welfare. *Unwholesome demand* is *a state in which any positive level of demand is felt to be excessive because of undesirable qualities associated with the product.*

The task of trying to destroy the demand for something is called *countermarketing* or *unselling*. Whereas demarketing tries to reduce the demand without impugning the product itself, countermarketing is an attempt to designate the product as intrinsically unwholesome. The product in question may be the organization's own product which it wishes to phase out, a competitor's product, or a third party's product which is regarded as socially undesirable.

Classic examples of unselling efforts have revolved around the so-called "vice" products: alcohol, cigarettes, and hard drugs. Various temperance groups mounted such an intense campaign that they succeeded in gaining the passage of the 18th Amendment banning the manufacture of alcoholic beverages. Antismoking groups managed to put enough pressure on the Surgeon General's office to get a law passed requiring cigarette manufacturers to add to each package the statement: "Warning: The Surgeon General Has Determined That Cigarette Smoking Is Dangerous To Your Health." They also sponsored many effective television commercials aimed at "unselling" the smoker. Later, they managed to get a law passed prohibiting cigarette advertising on television. Antidrug crusaders have sponsored advertising aimed at unselling the youth on the idea of drug usage.

Unselling appears in other contexts as well. Peace groups for years tried to unsell the Vietnam War. Population control groups have been trying to unsell the idea of large families. Nutrition groups have been trying to unsell the idea of eating pleasing but nutritionally poor foods. Environmental groups have been trying to unsell the idea of being careless with the environment as if it were inexhaustible. Many manufacturers engage in campaigns to unsell competitor products or brands, such as a natural gas company trying to unsell electric heating or a compact car manufacturer trying to unsell large, gas-eating automobiles.

Unselling is the effort to accomplish the opposite of innovation. Whereas innovation is largely the attempt to add new things to the cultural inventory, unselling is the attempt to eliminate cultural artifacts or habits. It is an attempt to bring about the discontinuance of something. Whereas innovation usually ends with the act of adoption, unselling seeks to produce the act of disadoption. In the perspective of innovation theory, unselling may be called the problem of *deinnovation*. Many of the concepts in innovation theory might be usable in reverse. The countermarketer attempts to identify the varying characteristics of the early, late, and laggard disadopters so that unselling effort can be aimed at them in this order. He also considers the characteristics of the product that will tend to facilitate unselling, such as relative disadvantage, incompatibility, complexity, indivisibility, and incommunicability.

At the same time, every effort to unsell something may also be viewed as an effort to sell something else. Those who attempt to unsell cigarette smoking are attempting to sell health; those who attempt to unsell large families are trying to sell small families; those who attempt to unsell the competitor's product are trying to increase the sales of their own product. In fact, it is usually easier to sell something else. For example, instead of trying to unsell young people on drugs, the marketers can try to sell them on another way of achieving whatever they are seeking through drugs.

Efforts to turn off the demand for something can profitably draw on certain concepts and theories in psychology. In general, the effort is largely one of deconditioning or habit extinction theory. Instead of trying to build up a taste for something, the marketer is trying to break down a taste for something. Learning and reinforcement theory are suggestive in this connection. The marketer is trying to associate disgust, fear, disagreeableness, or shame with the use of the unwholesome object. He is trying to arouse unpleasant feelings in the potential or actual users of the product.

In addition to these psychological steps, the marketer also attempts to load the other marketing variables against the use of the product. He tries to increase the real or perceived price. He tries to reduce the product's availability through reducing or destroying channels of distribution. He tries to find an alternative product which is wholesome and which can be substituted for the existing product.

Clearly unselling is one of the most difficult and challenging marketing tasks. Unselling is an attempt to intervene in the lives and tastes of others. Unselling campaigns often backfire, as witness the popularity of X-rated movies and drugs whose evils are publicized. In its defense, however, two things must be said. First, unselling relies on exchange and communication approaches to bring about legal and/or public opinion changes. It is an alternative to violent social action. Second, unselling has as much social justification in a democracy as does selling. To set up a double standard where selling—say of alcohol and cigarettes—is allowable but unselling by those who object is not allowable would compromise the rights of free speech and orderly legislative due process.

SUMMARY

The marketer is a professional whose basic interest and skill lies in regulating the level, timing, and character of demand for a product, service, place, or idea. He faces up to eight different types of demand situations and plans accordingly. If demand is negative, it must be disabused (conversional marketing); if nonexistent, it must be created (stimulational marketing); if latent, it must be developed (developmental marketing); if faltering, it must be revitalized (remarketing); if irregular, it must be synchronized (synchromarketing); if full, it must be maintained (maintenance marketing); if overfull, it must be reduced (demarketing); and finally, if unwholesome, it must be destroyed (countermarketing). Each demand situation calls for a particular set of psychological concepts and marketing strategies and may give rise to task specialization. Managerial marketing, rather than a singular effort to build or maintain sales, is a complex game with many scripts.

The author wishes to thank the many people who responded to preliminary presentations of this paper, including Professor Sidney J. Levy (Northwestern University), who suggested discussing irregular demand, and Ralph Gallay (New York University), who suggested discussing negative demand.

ENDNOTES

1. A classic discussion of alternative methods of trying to modify people's feelings is found in Kurt Lewin, "Group Decision and Social Change," in *Readings in Social Psychology*, Theodore M. Newcomb and Eugene L. Hartley, eds. (New York: Holt, Rinehart and Winston, Inc., 1952).
2. New behavioral therapies such as implosive therapy and systematic desensitization are discussed in Perry London, *Behavior Control* (New York: Harper and Row, 1969).
3. See Philip Kotler and Sidney J. Levy, "Demarketing, Yes, Demarketing," *Harvard Business Review*, Vol. 49 (November–December 1971), pp. 74–80.

9   How to Plan and Set Up Your Marketing Program

Edward S. McKay

Reprinted, by permission of the publisher, from *Blueprint for an Effective Marketing Program*, Marketing Series 91, by Edward S. McKay, pp. 3–15 © 1954 American Management Association, Inc. All rights reserved.

The subject of the program which I shall describe, as we are presenting it in our company, is "Marketing in *Your* Business." Since it deals with the basic problems of "How to Plan, Organize, and Operate," we believe that the concept to be explained applies to any business—large or small. As will be seen, this program suggests an approach, outlines a process, and offers a set of tools for establishing a high degree of *professional marketing management*.

The modern marketing concept calls for:

1. A factual marketing plan.
2. A functional organization structure.
3. A professionally managed operation.

These are the three fundamental requirements of the concept. They add up to this definition:

Professional marketing management is the planning, organizing, and carrying out, in an expert, scientific manner, of all the functions involved in planning and moving our products to the consumer with optimum sales volume and profits at minimum expense.

Now let's discuss each of the three requirements.

First, a *factual marketing plan*...

The modern marketing concept calls for a written, yet flexible, marketing plan for each business, developed in terms of specific short- and long-range objectives for profit and leadership, which assures that we will have available a product that people want, at a price they are willing to pay, where it is wanted, and when it is wanted. The marketing plan makes clear *what* is to be done, *when*, and *why*.

Second, a *functional organization structure*...

The modern marketing concept calls for an integrated company and distribution organization, designed to carry out this marketing plan, and all the required marketing functions, effectively, economically, and on time. The organization structure makes clear *who* is to do the various parts of the marketing job and *where*.

Third, a *professionally managed operation*...

The modern marketing concept calls for a unified, dynamic operation in which all the marketing functions are integrated, performance is carefully measured, and the best modern tools, methods, and procedures are used to carry out the plans and meet the established objectives of the business. The professionally managed operation assures that the organization carries out the plan *when* and *how* it is needed.

There we have the heart of this modern marketing concept: a factual plan, a functional organization, and a professionally managed operation. Now, with these working definitions as a background, let's consider the process and tools of each element.

MARKETING PLANNING PROCESS

The marketing planning process[...]starts and ends with the customer. Its base is careful research and sound forecasting. It keys all plans, programs, and activities to a master marketing plan and a master sales plan, thus providing a well-mapped road to planned profits.

Master Marketing Plan and Master Sales Plan

All sound planning starts with research. This process begins with *marketing research, analysis, and forecasting* to determine who and where the customer is; what he needs, wants, and will buy; where and how he will buy; and how much he will pay.

With this base of sound research, the *master marketing plan* is developed. You establish objectives for volume, position, profit, gross margins, and budgets. You determine the broad product line—the range of models or types, the quality level, the price range, and the permitted costs. You identify the markets—where they are, which to cultivate, and their size and potential. You select the sales channels to be used—direct, distributor, and any others. And you formulate policies—for sales, prices, distribution, advertising, service, and marketing personnel.

The master marketing plan is, of course, based upon general management's over-all plans for the business. It uses facts, ideas, and support from research and engineering, manufacturing, finance, law, employee and public relations—that is, from every management source.

The next step is to develop the *product plans and programs*—for specific models, time schedules, product size, capacity, range, style, and appearance; for quantity, prices, discounts, conditions, and terms.

Now you have a sound base for the *master sales plan*. This is the time to determine who will sell what, where, when, to whom, in what quantity—and how it will be sold.

Integrated Sales Programs

Out of the master sales plan stem the integrated functional plans and programs. Let's consider each of them separately for a moment before we bring them back together in integrated sales programs.

The *advertising and sales promotion plan* shows what products will be advertised, in what markets, utilizing what promotions, and at what cost. From this plan, you develop the specific advertising and sales promotion programs—by product, market, and channel of distribution—by media, national, local, and cooperative advertising.

The *sales training plan* shows who will be trained, in what functions, when, where, and by whom, utilizing what media, techniques, and tools. From this plan, you develop the specific sales training programs—by product, market, and channel of distribution—for headquarters, field, distributor, and dealer personnel.

The *product service plan* shows where the product will be serviced—when and by whom and in what manner. From this plan, you develop the specific product service programs—by product, market, and channel of distribution, including service training, operations, and manuals.

The *marketing personnel development plan* shows what personnel will be needed, where and when, to accomplish the objectives. From this plan, you establish the specific marketing personnel development programs—for management and supervisory development, for compensation, and for appraisal of personnel.

All these functional plans and programs are tied together in the *integrated sales programs*—by product, by market, and by channel of distribution—to make clear who will do what, where, when, and how... to assure effective execution of the plans and programs.

Plan of Action

The next step takes you out to the field sales organization with a plan of action for program execution—by man, by territory, and by customer—integrated to effect maximum effort on the right product, at the right place, at the right time.

Here your target is the customer if your sales are direct to him. If, however, the channels include distributors and dealers, the distributor plan of action must be integrated with company plans and programs and tailored to the distributor's own operating plans and programs for the market. Similarly, the dealer plan of action must be integrated with distributor plans and programs and tailored according to the dealer's own operation.

There you have the marketing planning process—an orderly method for making clear *what* is to be done, *when* and *why*, for everyone on the marketing team.

EXHIBIT A

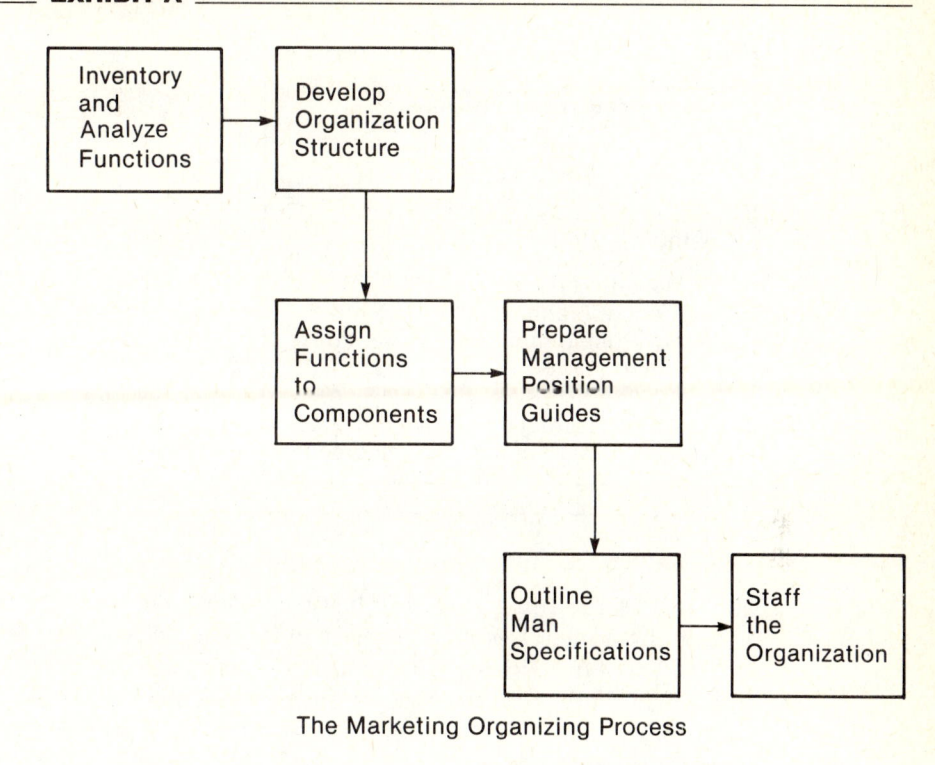

```
┌──────────┐      ┌──────────┐
│Inventory │      │Develop   │
│and       │─────▶│Organization│
│Analyze   │      │Structure │
│Functions │      │          │
└──────────┘      └────┬─────┘
                       │
                       ▼
                  ┌──────────┐      ┌──────────┐
                  │Assign    │      │Prepare   │
                  │Functions │─────▶│Management│
                  │to        │      │Position  │
                  │Components│      │Guides    │
                  └──────────┘      └────┬─────┘
                                         │
                                         ▼
                                    ┌──────────┐      ┌──────────┐
                                    │Outline   │      │Staff     │
                                    │Man       │─────▶│the       │
                                    │Specifications│  │Organization│
                                    └──────────┘      └──────────┘
```

The Marketing Organizing Process

MARKETING ORGANIZING PROCESS

Next, let's consider the second requirement of the modern marketing concept—the functional organization structure (Exhibit A).

The marketing organizing process consists of six steps: (1) You inventory and analyze functions; (2) you develop the organization structure; (3) you assign functions to components; (4) you prepare management position guides; (5) you outline man specifications; and (6) you staff the organization.

Functional Inventory and Analysis

The functional inventory and analysis is the key to the entire organizing process. It is important at this stage to make a clear distinction between *functions* and *organization*. While the two are closely related, they

EXHIBIT B

> **Marketing Functions**
>
> **MARKETING MANAGEMENT**
>
> Customer Relations
>
> 1. Marketing Research
> 2. Product Planning
> 3. Advertising and Sales Promotion
> 4. Sales
> 5. Product Service
> 6. Marketing Administrative Services
> 7. Marketing Personnel Development

aren't the same thing. For simplicity, let's say that *functions* means the work to be done. *Organization* refers to the people who do the work.

The list of functions given in Exhibit B represents the total work to be done in marketing. Since we see managing as a distinct kind of work, the inventory starts with the broad function of "marketing management." Next is "customer relations," an over-all function of marketing in every business.

Now we come to what we identify as the seven basic functions of marketing. These are:

1. Marketing research.
2. Product planning.
3. Advertising and sales promotion.
4. Sales.
5. Product service.
6. Marketing administrative services.
7. Marketing personnel development.

Set up on the basis of a careful and detailed functional inventory and a functional analysis in all our operations, these seven basic functions embrace all the work to be done in marketing.

Let's look now at the contents of each function.

Marketing management is leadership through planning, organizing, integrating, and measuring all marketing functions.

Customer relations in our business includes these activities:

- Creating, building, and maintaining good relations with customers, potential customers, and trade associations.
- Sales integration.
- Inspiring good customer relations practices.
- Personal contact and availability.
- Policy assistance.
- Interchange of information.
- District marketing councils.

Marketing research includes marketing studies and research (quantitative and qualitative) concerning:

- Size and location of markets.
- Attitudes, preferences, and needs regarding company products, product service, and marketing policies.
- Sales and distribution methods, channels, and territories.
- Price indexes, price trends, and product pricing.
- Sales and advertising programs.
- Industry sales forecasts.

In our business, marketing research is a continuous gathering, analyzing, and interpreting of facts and opinions concerning marketing. It is a function that serves all other functions of marketing.

Product planning includes:

- Control of products (lines and programs).
- Integrating, planning, and timing: additions, eliminations, and modifications.
- Formulation of pricing, discounts, conditions, terms, and permitted costs.
- Products' functions and quality level.
- Appearance, identification, cataloguing, and packaging.
- Simplification, standardization, and adaptation.
- Appraisals: competitive offerings, markets, buying motives, and plans vs. results.

Product planning is the function which makes certain that new products are added, old ones dropped, and dragging ones changed at the right time. It involves setting up clean-cut objectives for the complete line of products and adopting policies in line with these objectives.

Advertising and sales promotion includes:

- Creative advertising development.
- Media relations.

- Radio and television.
- Copy research.
- Sales promotion.
- Exhibits and displays.
- Product publicity.
- Advertising business procedures.
- Production and distribution.

This function plans, creates, and schedules all advertising and sales promotion. It conducts copy and media research and coordinates advertising with other marketing functions.

The *sales* function includes sales management, sales planning, and selling. Under sales management are:

- Sales analysis and control.
- Sales training.
- Management of headquarters and field sales organization.
- Operation and control of sales and distribution channels.
- Carrying out pricing, discounts, conditions, and terms.

Under sales planning are:

- Formulating sales objectives and policies.
- Product sales analysis.
- Planning and recommending sales and distribution channels.
- Formulating and recommending distribution policy.
- Analyzing needs and recommending on pricing, discounts, conditions, and terms.
- Planning sales and merchandising programs and methods.

And we include here the single large word *selling* because we are just old-fashioned enough to believe that even a sales manager ought to be able to sell.

The sales function plans, creates, and carries out both long- and short-range sales and merchandising plans, programs, and methods.

Product service includes:

- Establishing service objectives, policies, standards, plans, and programs.
- Service training programs.
- Management of headquarters and field product service organization.
- Warranties and protection plans.
- Service of products after sale.

- Repair parts (supply, inventory control).
- Service manuals and bulletins.

Product service is the function which makes certain that both moral and legal responsibilities with respect to product performance are properly fulfilled so that customer satisfaction and repeat business are obtained.

Marketing administrative services includes:

- Sales forecasting.
- Sales budgets.
- Sales records and statistics.
- Production scheduling to meet sales requirements.
- Control of finished goods inventory.
- Warehousing.
- Order service.
- Marketing office management (headquarters and field).
- Marketing expense budgets, analysis, and standards.

This function serves marketing management and all the other functions of marketing by providing the facts, tools, and procedures for effective and efficient operation and helps to free the marketing manager from administrative details and routines.

Marketing personnel development includes:

- Recruiting.
- Selection.
- Training.
- Placement.
- Development.
- Inventorying personnel.
- Marketing compensation.

The marketing personnel development function includes the over-all personnel administration work in marketing and serves all the other marketing functions on a professional counseling and development basis.

There you have in outline form an inventory of marketing work we find essential in our businesses. You have the seven basic functions of marketing and the over-all management function which leads and ties them together.

Development of Organization Structure

With the functional inventory completed, you are ready for the second step in the organizing process—development of the organization structure.

The structural organization chart shown in Exhibit C represents a typical operating department's marketing section. For simplicity, it indicates a unit for each of the seven basic marketing functions. This is done to show the relationship between functions (the work to be done) and the organization components (those who do the work). An organization component for a given business may consist of any number from one man to many. Functions, of course, can be combined as required by the size and other specific needs of the business.

There are many variations of this structure among our many operating businesses. Each is established in accordance with its specific requirements.

The principles recommended for developing the organization structure include these:

- Group like work.
- Deal first with the work to be done (the functions), not the people who are to manage or perform the work.
- Design a structure which will provide for effective integration of functions.
- Make sure all the functions required are provided for and properly assigned.

Assignment of Functions to Components

The structural chart, as the name suggests, merely indicates the *structure* of the organization. Now we come to the third step in the organizing process—the assignment of functions to components.

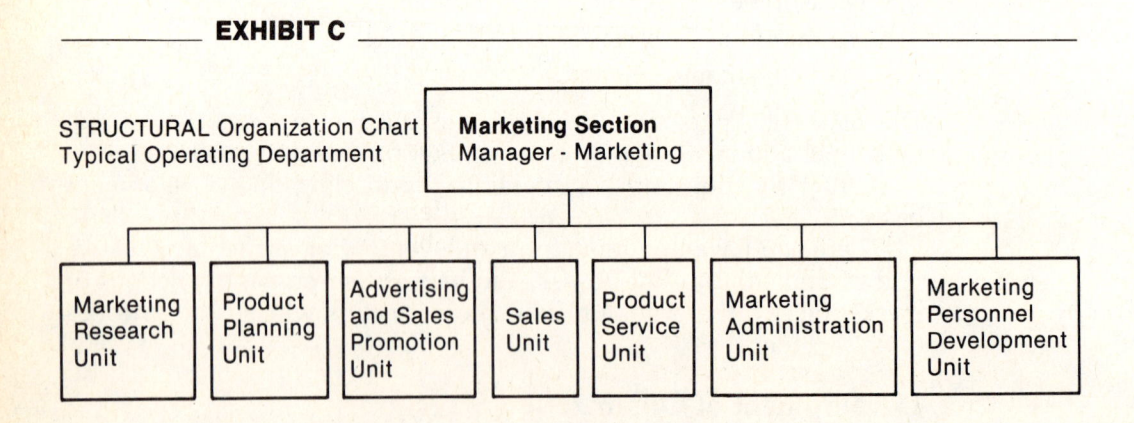

EXHIBIT C

STRUCTURAL Organization Chart
Typical Operating Department

Marketing Section
Manager - Marketing

- Marketing Research Unit
- Product Planning Unit
- Advertising and Sales Promotion Unit
- Sales Unit
- Product Service Unit
- Marketing Administration Unit
- Marketing Personnel Development Unit

9 — How to Plan and Set Up Your Marketing Program

EXHIBIT D

FUNCTIONAL Organization Chart
Typical Operating Department

Marketing Section
Manager - Marketing
Establish marketing objectives, policies, and plans
Organize marketing section
Integrate all marketing functions
Measure, review, and appraise all marketing activities
Create, build, and maintain good customer relations

Product Planning Unit
Control products — lines, and programs
Integrate, plan, and time: additions, eliminations, modifications
Formulate prices, discounts, and terms of sale
Appearance, identification, packaging
Appraise competitive offerings

Advertising and Sales Promotion Unit
Plan, develop, and place advertising and sales promotion
Media relations
Radio and television
Copy research
Exhibits and displays
Product publicity
Advertising business procedures
Production and distribution

Sales Unit
Sales Management:
 Sales analysis and control
 Sales training
 Manage sales organization
 Operate sales channels
Sales Planning:
 Formulate sales and distribution plans and policies
 Product sales analysis
 Plan sales and merchandising programs
Sell the Products

Exhibit D is a portion of the functional organization chart for the same marketing section. The chart shows the structure, the work to be done, and the assignment of the functions to the organization units.

Our experience with this program demonstrates that a good organization chart of this type can be a valuable management tool. Correctly planned and developed, it shows clearly the lines of authority and the delegation of responsibility.

Management Position Guides

The fourth step in the organizing process is the preparation of management position guides.

Closely related to the functional chart, the position guide is a document which contains a clear and comprehensive statement of:

- The basic function of the position, including its objective.
- The responsibilities and authority of the position.
- The important relationships of the position to other jobs.
- The accountability of the position.

The management position guide for the marketing manager is the base upon which all the jobs of the marketing section stand.

The box for each position on the functional organization chart is a summary of the complete description of the job contained in its corresponding management position guide.

Man Specifications Outline

In the fifth step in the organizing process, we use another related tool—the man specifications outline. This statement of the requirements for each job is almost as detailed as the management position guide. It states clearly what the man should *be*, what he should *know*, and what he should *do*. Along with the position guide, it provides a basis for sound manning of each job, in terms of its specific requirements, and serves as a tool for periodic rating.

Manning the Structure

The final step in the organizing process is manning or staffing the structure. This is where the entire process and all the tools which we have discussed are applied to establish the functional organization structure. Properly applied, this method makes clear *who* is to do the various parts of the marketing job and *where*.

A Professionally Managed Operation

The third fundamental requirement of the modern marketing concept, it will be recalled, is a professionally managed operation.

This approach recognizes the *professional* nature of management. It provides for management as a distinct kind of work, and it assigns to marketing broad responsibility and authority. Let's consider together for a moment each of these three aspects of professionally managed marketing.

The Implications

This approach requires an understanding that management is a distinct profession. It sees that progressive members of marketing management are rapidly acquiring all the time-honored characteristics of a profession: a body of special knowledge; high standards of ethics and performance; a responsibility to the public; and a concern with the development of qualified members of the profession.

This approach defines management as the science of establishing proper objectives and efficiently utilizing human, material, and time resources to achieve the objectives. It recognizes that the work of the modern marketing manager is leading by persuading, rather than by command, through planning, organizing, integrating, and measuring.

This approach requires that the marketing manager's job be wide in scope. His responsibility must be far greater than that assigned to the sales manager under older concepts of organization, and he must have authority over all the functions of the business which are essential to meeting this responsibility.

An Important Tool

Since this is the phase of management which emphasizes the integrating and measuring processes, we call attention here to an important tool for the over-all management of the marketing operation. This is a *master calendar* of major marketing events—a schedule which keeps all functions of the business informed on target dates for:

- Product introductions and changes.
- Field tests.
- Major sales activities.
- Advertising programs.
- Other marketing events.

Thus it serves to integrate all important activities in every functional area of marketing.

It is through the use of tools of this type that the professionally managed operation assures that the organization carries out the plan *when* and *how* it is needed.

A Simple Formula

This concept adds up to a rather simple formula for professional marketing management.

First, you *plan*. You conduct research. You set objectives. You develop the plans. And you establish programs. Second, you *organize*. You inventory functions. You develop the structure. You define positions. And you staff the structure. Third, you *manage*. You establish procedures. You integrate operations. You measure performance. And you carry out the plans.

This formula provides:

- A *philosophy* of professional management.

- A *process* of factual, orderly, continuous planning.
- A *method* for integrating operations and measuring peformance.
- A *set of tools* for making the marketing job easier and more effective.

This brings us back to the definition which we suggested early in this presentation. It should be clear now why we say that

Professional marketing management is the planning, organizing, and carrying out, in an expert, scientific manner, of all the functions involved in planning and moving our products to the consumer with optimum sales volume and profits at minimum expense.

In General Electric, we are finding that this approach gives us a simple, practical, sound way to manage the marketing aspects of any business—large or small. It

- Makes sure we know what and where our markets are.
- Sees that we have the right product, at the right place, at the right time, at the right price.
- Supports our products adequately with advertising and sales promotion.
- Sells to the greatest possible number of customers, through the most efficient and economical sales and distribution channels.
- Provides effective customer and product service.

And it keeps all marketing activities focused on the specific objectives for profit, volume, and position.

10 — Organizing the Marketing Function

Barton Weitz and Erin Anderson

Reprinted from the *Review of Marketing 1981*, published by the American Marketing Association, edited by B. Enis and K. Roering, pp. 134–142. Reprinted by permission.

Abstract

The effectiveness of a marketing organization is, in part, determined by the degree to which the organizational structure matches the environment in which it operates. In this article, the relationship between structural elements, environmental characteristics, and organizational characteristics is reviewed.

Introduction

Over the last thirty years, business firms have experienced enormous changes in the rate at which political, economic, social, and technological events occur. Not only is the environment rapidly changing, but business firms themselves are becoming more complex. Between 1949 and 1979, the majority of the Fortune 500 companies shifted from single-product-line firms to multiple-industry and even multi-national organizations (Rumelt 1974). This increasing complexity of both the business environment and the business organization has led to growing interest in strategic considerations, reflected in the composition of papers in this volume.

While there has been considerable discussion of models for making strategic decisions and key marketing variables related to long-term company performance, little attention has been directed toward another important strategic issue—the organization of the marketing effort. The structure and control mechanisms employed provide a framework through which an organization pursues a strategic direction and copes with its environment.

Many marketing plans fail because the planner did not consider the fact that the organization was not capable of implementing the plan. Short-range plans will require adaption to the existing organization, whereas long-range plans may require redesigning the organization.... The long-range planner must recognize that the organizational strategies may be the most critical part of the plan.

(Hughes 1978, 102–103)

For example, organizations structured for dealing efficiently with complex, rapidly changing, unpredictable markets typically will not be efficient in coping with simple, stable environments.

While there have been a number of conceptual articles (Ames 1971; Hanan 1974; Luck 1969; Luck and Nowak 1965; Dietz 1973), empirical research on organizational design issues has been restricted to surveys reporting the responsibilities of product managers in various industries (Buell 1975; Clewett and Stasch 1975; Hise and Kelly 1978; Lucas 1972), the influence mechanisms used by product managers as they undertake these responsibilities (Venkatesh and Wilemon 1976), and description of marketing organizations in various firms (Corey and Star 1971). Little research has been directed toward investigating factors related to the effectiveness of the organizational forms used in marketing organizations.

This paper examines the effectiveness of organizational structures such as functional departments, brand management, market management, and product divisions in performing marketing functions in various environments. A theoretical framework is presented, followed by specific propositions that relate organizational effectiveness, structure, environment, and tasks.

ORGANIZATION DESIGN IN MARKETING

The perspective adopted in this paper is that there is no one best organizational design for performing the marketing function. Certain organizational forms work in some situations and not in others. More specifically, the effectiveness of an organizational form is contingent upon the nature of the marketing tasks performed and the environment in which these tasks are performed. This contingency perspective has been adopted by modern organizational theorists (Lawrence and Lorsch 1976b; Miles 1980).

Trends in Marketing Organizations

Hughes (1978) suggests that the organizational design of marketing organizations has gone through three stages. Prior to the 1950s, marketing organizations typically were organized by functional departments. From the 1950s to 1970s, there was a shift to a brand management organizational structure.[1] During the 1970s, many firms adopted a market-oriented organizational structure, in which market managers are used to coordinate the activities of functional specialists or complete departments are established for each market.

In addition to the movement toward market-oriented organizational structures, there have been some changes occurring in the traditional brand management system. There is a trend toward emphasizing the role of the brand manager as a planner and coordinator and deemphasizing the decision-making responsibility and authority of the brand manager. Thus, people at higher levels of authority in the firm are making the key marketing and resource allocation decisions related to individual products and brands (Buell 1975).

Variations Across Companies

While there is some empirical evidence to support these broad developmental trends, numerous exceptions to the trend are reported. In particular, many companies may have abandoned the brand management organizational form [to] return to the traditional functional organization (*Business Week* 1973). In addition, there is wide variation across firms in terms of the organizational structure employed and the responsibilities assigned to key marketing personnel. A 1973 survey of national advertisers reported that 85% of consumer packaged goods companies had brand managers; however, 34% of other consumer goods companies and 55% of industrial goods companies used brand managers (Association of National Advertisers 1974). Surveys have shown wide variations in the responsibilities of consumer and industrial brand managers and between brand managers working for various manufacturers of consumer products. For example, 61% of brand managers have profit responsibility, while the remaining 39% occupy a coordinating role (Hise and Kelly 1978). Industrial brand managers typically have more contact with the market than consumer product managers. Only 22% of consumer brand managers have contact with customers, and 46% have contact with distribution channels. On the other hand, 76% of industrial brand managers have contact with customers and 66% have contact with distribution channels (Hise and Kelly 1978). Substantial differences between the activities performed by brand managers working for manufacturers of food packaged goods, packaged goods other than food, and health and beauty aid products were uncovered by Clewett and Stasch (1975).

Why do the structural forms of marketing organizations and the responsibilities of product managers vary so widely across companies? Why do some companies in the same industry adopt a functional form while others adopt a brand management form? While little empirical work in marketing has addressed these questions, research in macro organizational behavior provides an interesting framework for attacking these issues.

In the next section, the contingency model of organizational effectiveness is reviewed. The basic elements in the model—the characteristics of the environment and the organization—are discussed and related to the organizational design of marketing departments. The section concludes with a set of propositions relating characteristics of the marketing environment, the structure of the marketing organization, and the effectiveness of the marketing effort.

THE CONTINGENCY APPROACH TO ORGANIZATIONAL DESIGN

At one time, organizational theorists attempted to find the "one best way" to structure and manage all organizations. As with most attempts in the social sciences to uncover universal principles, these approaches failed to find organizational structures and management principles that are effective across a wide range of situations. Research demonstrated that certain organizational features work in some environments and not in others. This discovery led to the development of a contingency model of organizational effectiveness, illustrated in Figure 1.

The contingency model suggests that the effectiveness of an organizational structure depends upon the environment faced by the organization and the production technology employed by the organization. Most of the recent research has examined the moderating effects of the environment rather than the production technology. The underlying theme of this research is summarized in the "law of requisite variety" (Ashby 1968). This principle states that the variety of an organization must match the variety of the environment in which it operates.

> In terms more meaningful to the organizational designer and manager, the law of requisite variety and its extensions means that, in a highly complex environment, a viable organization must possess a corresponding degree of complexity or differentiation in its own structure. In order to cope with uncertainty emanating from the external environment, the organization must create parts that match the attributes of environmental sectors.
>
> (Miles 1980, p. 250)

This contingency approach to organizational design is based on an information processing viewpoint. The principal objective of the organizational structure is to either reduce the level of information needed by a unit to make decisions or provide channels of communications for information to flow freely between units. There is a striking parallel between the perspectives of organizational theorists and marketing theorists. Organizational theorists view the environment as basically given, just as marketing theorists view the needs of customers as given. Thus the design of the organization must respond to the environment, just as a marketing program must respond to customer needs. The effectiveness of the organization is determined by the match between structure and environment, while the effectiveness of a marketing effort is determined by the match between the marketing program (product, price, promotion, and distribution) and customer needs. Dimensions of the marketing environment and organizational structure that impact on the effectiveness of a marketing effort are described in the next section.

Characteristics of the Marketing Environment

From an organization design perspective, the three most important characteristics of the environment are as follows: (1) the complexity of the environment, (2) the interconnectedness of key elements in the environment, and (3) the predictability of the environment. Duncan (1972) and Jurkovich (1974) provide a more complete discussion of organizational environments.

Environmental Complexity. This characteristic of the environment re-

FIGURE 1. Contingency Model of Organizational Effectiveness

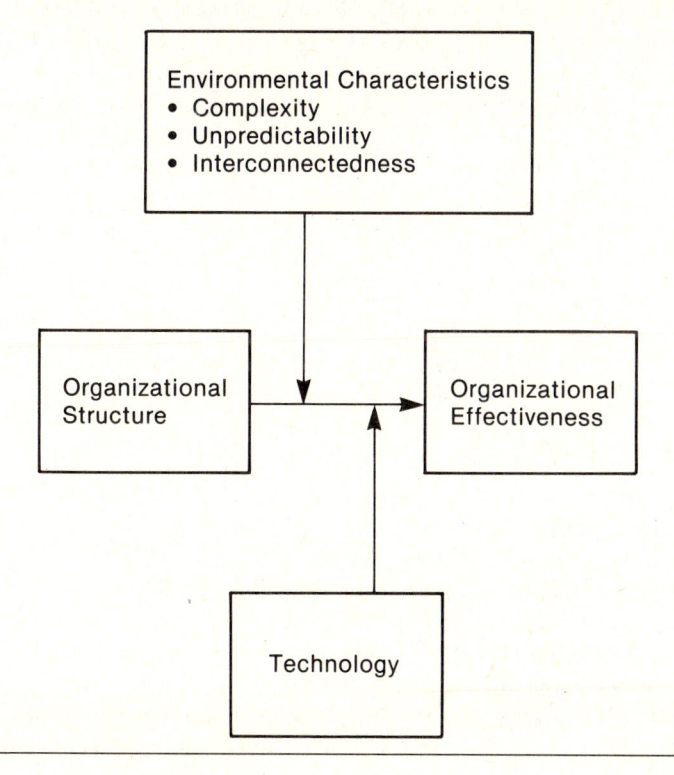

fers to the number of different organizationally relevant components in the environment. From a marketing perspective, the complexity of the environment is related to the number of product-markets that the company serves. When companies are active in a large number of product-markets, orderly and effective organizational functioning becomes more difficult.

> Organizations dealing with noncomplex environments have one advantage: there are fewer critical important information categories necessary for decision making. When environment sectors are essentially the same (the company faces an undifferentiated market), the range of their expected behavior, strategies and tactics, and formal goals is easier to account for.
> (Jukovich 1974, p. 382)

To some extent, marketing organizations are proactive in terms of increasing the level of environmental complexity when they attempt to differentiate their offerings (Levitt 1980). How can a marketing organization deal effectively with a complex environment? The law of requisite variety suggests that as the environment becomes more complex and differentiated, the organization, to be effective, needs to match the environment and become more complex and differentiated. In effect, the marketing organization needs to decentralize the marketing effort and create internal units that match the critical components in the markets. For example, by decentralizing the marketing organization into separate groups dealing with individual product-markets, the impact of environment complexity is reduced because each product-market group now deals with a relatively simple, homogeneous environment.

Environmental Interconnectedness. This characteristic refers to the degree to which key elements of components of the environment are organized and interrelated (Terreberry 1968). Environmental interconnectedness does not refer to linkages between the organization and environment, but linkages within the environment. An example of a highly interconnected environment is the market encountered by a manufacturer of commercial aircraft. There are a few customers (all large) for commercial aircraft, and the purchase decision made by each customer affects the decisions of other customers. A marketing environment would also be interconnected when a single distributor controls a channel servicing a number of product-markets or when a family brand is used for products sold to different segments. Most consumer markets do not displace a high degree of interconnectedness because consumers do not operate as a cohesive unit.

The marketing organization needs to respond to an interconnected environment by developing structural mechanisms for coordinating and integrating the activities within the marketing organization. Some commonly used methods for improving the level of integration are product managers, market managers, matrix organizational structures, temporary systems such as venture teams or new product development teams, and the development of organizational culture. Each of these methods is discussed in the next section.

Predictability of the Environment. The final characteristic of the environment is the degree to which variability in the environment is unstable and unpredictable. Some factors that contribute to unpredictability are the rate of change in the environment, the degree to which relationships with the environment are routinized, and the degree to which the organization has direct contact with the environment.

Environmental predictability is often viewed as part of the concept of uncertainty. However, attempts by organizational theorists to delineate and measure uncertainty have met with considerable difficulty (for a complete discussion, see Downey, Hellriegel and Slocum 1975). A significant stumbling block has been disagreement over whether perceived uncertainty (and if so, perceived by whom and at what level) or "objective" uncertainty is the construct of interest. Furthermore, theorists do not agree on the facets of uncertainty. Among major efforts, Child (1972) focuses on variability and unpredictability. Lawrence and Lorsch (1967a) emphasize lack of clear information, a long time span to definitive feedback, and general uncertainty of causal relationships. Duncan (1972) highlights lack of information on environmental factors relevant to decision making, ignorance about the consequences of decisions, and decision-maker confidence about his/her forecasted consequences. These three conceptualizations overlap but contain important differences.

Lawrence and Lorsch (1967a) and Duncan (1972) have developed measures of uncertainty. These have not fared well in validation tests, although Downey, Hellriegeal and Slocum (1975) point out that there is no reason to believe that the criterion measures used to validate are any better than the instruments being tested.

Typically, rapidly changing environments are less predictable than slowly changing environments. Some indications of a rapidly changing environment are the frequency with which products are introduced, the level of entry and exit of competitors, and length of the typical product life cycle. The predictability of the environment decreases as the organization must deal with more factors in reacting to its environment. Thus a company with long distribution channels faces a more unpredictable environment than a company with short channels.

One method of increasing the level of predictability is to develop a vertical marketing system. Another method for reducing the uncertainty in the environment is to routinize the relationship with the environment. For example, a company could attempt to develop long-term contractual relationships with customers. Arndt (1979) describes a number of situations in which companies form long-term relationships and thus decrease environmental uncertainty. A third method by which a marketing organization attempts to respond to an unpredictable, changing environment is by employing an adaptive organizational structure. Such organizational structures employ the same integrating mechanisms used to cope with an interconnected environment.

Characteristics of the Marketing Organization. Differentiation and integration are the basic concepts of understanding organizational structure. Differentiation refers to the distinctiveness of the cognitive and emotional orientations that result when employees are separated into different organization units. Integration refers to the method used to coordinate different structural elements (see Lawrence and Lorsch 1967c).

Differentiation. This term describes the extent to which an organization divides decision-making authority into units with different goals, time horizons, reward structures, and task specializations. An organization can be differentiated both vertically and horizontally.

Vertical differentiation is measured in terms of the number of management levels and differences in orientation between levels. For example, a market research department in which a number of researchers report to one department manager would exhibit little vertical differentiation. However, a sales department with unit, district, and regional managers would possess a high level of vertical differentiation, which would be accentuated if lower levels focused on short-term profits while higher levels focused on long-term profits.

Horizontal differentiation is the degree to which units at the same level differ from each other. Thus, a marketing organization consisting of specialists on particular products, markets, and marketing functions would have high horizontal differentiation.

Integration. Structural integration refers to the level of emphasis placed on integrating and controlling the units in an organization. In general, it is more difficult to control horizontal differentiation than vertical differentiation. This is because problems that arise due to vertical differentiation typically are resolved by the formal authority invested in the person occupying the higher level. For example, the national sales manager can largely control and coordinate with the activities of a regional sales manager by simply issuing directives. However, unique structural elements are frequently needed to deal with high levels of horizontal differentiation of the sort that might exist between a product manager and a regional sales manager.

Mechanisms used to provide integration can be divided into two categories: (1) conventional and (2) nonconventional (see Galbraith (1973) for a complete discussion). Conventional methods are the familiar coordinating and controlling techniques of plans, rules, policies, standard operating procedures, meetings, and the referral of problems to a superior. These integrating mechanisms are usually sufficient for organizations that are not highly differentiated. They usually do not require active management intervention and are the normal management approach to getting things done. However, these mechanisms are usually not sufficient for coordinating activities in highly differentiated organizations.

Coordination of highly differentiated organizations usually requires the use of more costly, nonconventional integrating mechanisms. Some of these non-conventional mechanisms are as follows: (1) individuals assigned to the task of integrating the efforts of functional specialist such as product or market managers, (2) temporary teams, such as venture teams or new product teams composed of specialists to complete a specific task, (3) simultaneous organizational structures such as the matrix organization and (4) the creation of integrated organizational culture.

To some extent, the identification of organizations as mechanistic or organic is related to the integration dimension. Mechanistic organizations are characterized by a rigid organizational structure with employees assigned to specific duties and controlled by rules and hierarchical authority. On the other hand, organic organizations are more flexible and adaptable. The roles and responsibilities of employees are not well defined. Organic organizations typically use nonconventional integrating mechanisms while mechanistic organizations rely on conventional mechanisms.

Matching the Marketing Organization to Its Environment

The contingency model of organizational effectiveness states that the effectiveness of an organization is contingent upon the match between the characteristics of the organizational structure and characteristics of the environment in which the organization operates. Specifically, highly differentiated organizations are most effective when facing complex environments, while organizations with low levels of differentiation are most effective when facing simple environments. Adaptive organizations employing nonconventional integrating mechanisms are most effective when facing rapidly changing, unpredictable environments. Less flexible organizations relying on conventional integrating mechanisms are most effective when facing stable, predictable environments. This basic model, illustrated in Figure 2, has been supported by a number of empirical studies in organizational behavior (Burns and Stalker 1961; Lawrence and Lorsch 1967a; Lorsch and Morse 1974).

In this model, the organization is characterized by the following three dimensions: (1) complexity, (2) interconnectedness, and (3) unpredictability. The organizational response to both increasing interconnectedness and unpredictability is to increase the level of coordination between organizational units. This increased coordination is achieved by employing more of the nonconventional integrating mechanisms mentioned earlier. Since the organizational response to interconnectedness and unpredictability is the same, these two dimensions are collapsed into the horizontal axis in Figure 2. The organizational response to increasing environmental complexity (the vertical dimension) is to increase the level of differentiation in the organization. In the remaining portion of this section, examples of marketing organizations related to each of the quadrants are discussed.

Simple, Predictable Environment—The Functional Organization

The simplest structure for a marketing organization is one person who organizes the marketing effort, and who performs all of the marketing functions (Quadrant III). Such an organization is completely undifferentiated. The addition of several employees sharing the marketing activities and reporting to a marketing manager generates vertical differentiation but avoids horizontal differentiation. These organizational forms are "simple" because they can be managed easily. Any problem that develops can be resolved by referring to the formal authority of the marketing manager. However, these simple forms are only appropriate for small organizations. As the size of the marketing organization in-

FIGURE 2. Structure-Environment Match

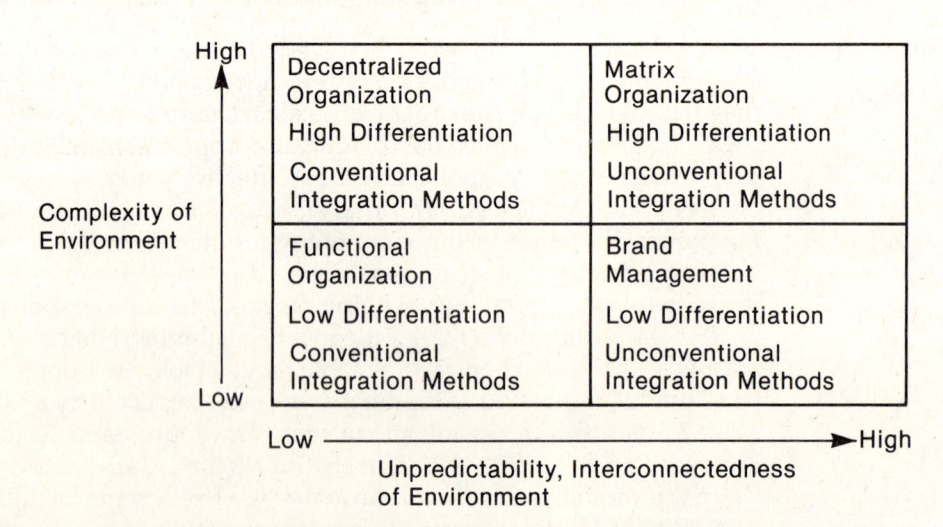

Complexity of Environment		
High	Decentralized Organization High Differentiation Conventional Integration Methods	Matrix Organization High Differentiation Unconventional Integration Methods
Low	Functional Organization Low Differentiation Conventional Integration Methods	Brand Management Low Differentiation Unconventional Integration Methods
	Low ⟶ High	
	Unpredictability, Interconnectedness of Environment	

FIGURE 3. Functional Organization

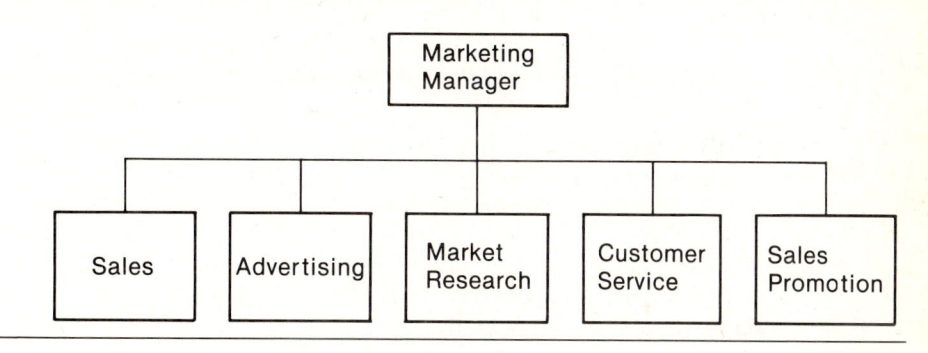

```
            Marketing
            Manager
    ┌──────┬─────┼─────┬──────┐
  Sales  Advertising  Market  Customer  Sales
                     Research  Service  Promotion
```

creases, it becomes possible to improve effectiveness through specialization.

The functional organization, shown in Figure 3, is the most common form of marketing organization. In this organizational form, horizontal differentiation arises when units specialize in terms of the marketing activities. The key strengths of the functional organization are that it facilitates the in-depth development of skills in performing specific marketing activities and that the communication network is simple. The marketing manager coordinates the work of the functional units and resolves disputes that arise.

Compared to the other organizational forms that are discussed in this section, the functional organization is relatively undifferentiated and employs a conventional, hierarchical integrating mechanism. Thus, this form is most efficient for the marketing departments that are operating in simple, predictable, and loosely connected environments.

The functional marketing organization is not effective when facing the complex environment encountered when a company participates in several product-markets. Each functional unit tends to identify more with the goals of its unit than the goals of the overall marketing organization. The sales department stresses the need for more salespeople, the advertising department promotes the need for larger advertising budgets, and the market research department emphasizes the importance of research studies. There is little effort directed toward developing plans to profitably exploit the array of product-markets in a complex environment. Product-markets that are not of interest to the functional specialists are ignored.

In addition, the functional form is ill-suited for coping with a rapidly changing, unpredictable environment. Since the principal method for integrating the functional activities is provided by the marketing manager, the functional organization is not able to respond quickly to a rapidly changing environment. Functional managers do not have the full range of information needed to make decisions concerning the organization's response to changing market needs. Thus, planning and coordination decisions must be made by the marketing manager, who quickly becomes overloaded in a dynamic and uncertain environment.

Complex, Predictable Environment—The Decentralized Organization

As the complexity of the marketing environment and the size of the marketing organization increases, decentralization of the marketing function offers an opportunity to increase effectiveness (Quadrant II). This decision to decentralize is referred to as the product versus function decision by organizational theorists (Walker and Lorsch 1968). Marketing organizations are typically decentralized on the basis of products, markets, or geography. An example of a marketing organization decentralized by product category is shown in Figure 4. In this organizational form, the increased level of complexity in the marketing environment is matched by an increased level of horizontal and vertical differentiation. Differentiation by product or market is added to the functional differentiation, resulting in a more complex organization.

Hanan (1974) describes the benefits of using market segments as a basis for decentralizing the marketing organization. This basis of decentralization, which he refers to as market centering, has been adopted by a number of companies, including General Foods, IBM and NCR. For example, problems with developing new products and with competitive brand proliferation caused General Foods to abandon its divisional structure based on previous acquisitions. General Foods replaced the process-oriented divisions—BirdsEye, Jell-O, Post, and Kool-Aid—with divisions focusing on the following markets: dessert foods, breakfast and beverages, and pet food.

Decentralization offers many benefits for coping with a complex multi-product-market environment. The unit managers can focus their entire efforts on a specific set of products and/or markets. They are task oriented versus function oriented. All of the resources to perform the marketing function are possessed by each decentralized unit. Thus, the need to compete for shared resources is eliminated. The unit managers in a decentralized organization assume some of the decision-making and coordination roles concentrated in the marketing manager of a functional organization. Thus, decisions are made more quickly. In effect, a complex environment has been divided up into a subset of simpler environments that can be effectively dealt with by the simple, functional organizational form.

The increase in effectiveness gained through decentralization is not costless. There is duplication of functional services across units and thus these specialized services may not be used to their full capacity. This duplication and potential under-utilization may lead to a deterioration of in-depth competence. It may be difficult, for example, to attract an advertising specialist to work in a product group as opposed to an advertising department.

Effects of Size. While there are problems with a decentralized organization, many organization theorists argue that the size of the organization dictates a need for decentralization, regardless of the level of complexity in the environment. Large size accentuates the problems of bureaucracies. As an organization grows in size, there are increases in employee alienation, opportunism (taking advantage of the organization), conservatism, and short-term orientations. The decline in the use of the functional form in business firms over the last 100 years has been attributed to increased size (Chandler 1966). The benefits of decentralized organiza-

FIGURE 4. Decentralized Organization

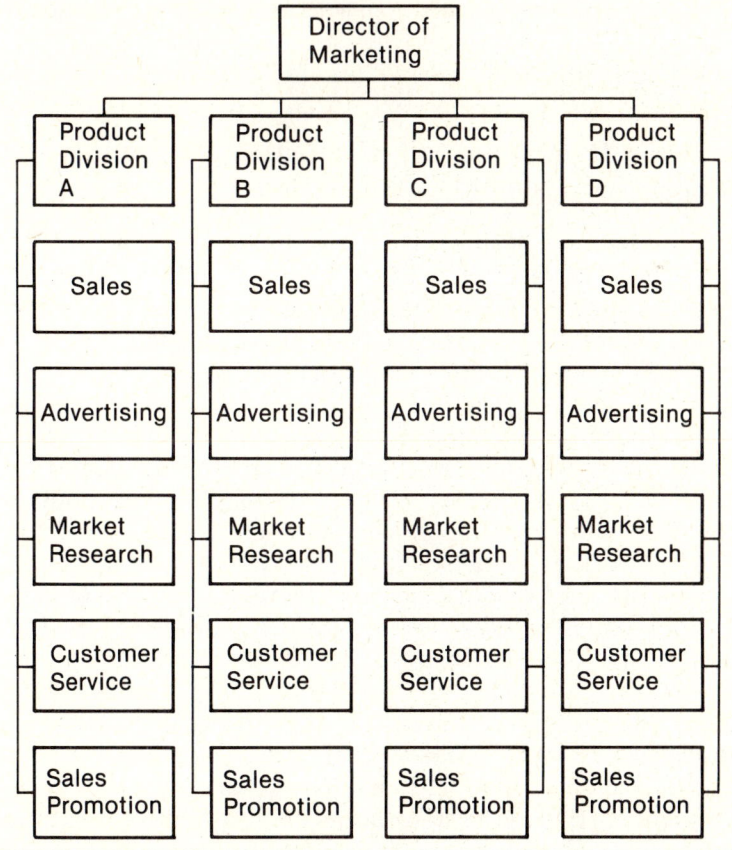

tions (M-form) over functional organizations (U-form) have been demonstrated empirically to vary as a function of size (Armour and Teece 1978; Burton and Obel 1980; and Steer and Cable 1978).

Need for Coordination. One major problem with decentralized marketing organizations is the difficulty of coordinating and integrating the activities of the units. Thus the decentralized form is only appropriate if the marketing activities of each unit are completely independent and can be self-contained within the unit. The units must be truly separable so that each unit has a clear measure of its own performance and thus can properly evaluate the effects of its decisions. Duncan (1979) has suggested that large, decentralized organizations need to become more independent in today's organizational environment, due to coordination needs arising from the regulatory environment, customer demands, technological changes, strategic considerations, and the scarcity of resources. The development of lateral relations is the principal method for improving coordination and integrating the marketing activities of different units, thus reducing the problems that arise from horizontal differentiation. In the next section, organizational forms that incorporate integrating mechanisms are discussed.

Simple, Interconnected, Unpredictable Environments—The Brand Management Organization

As the level of interconnectedness and unpredictability in the environment increases, conventional mechanisms (such as plans, procedures, and the use of a "shared boss") for integrating and coordinating the functional specialists within the marketing organization or decentralized unit become inadequate. A need for a formal integrative function develops (Quadrant IV). The most common marketing organizational form containing a formal integrative function is the brand management organization shown in Figure 5. While the brand manager is the most common integrative role in marketing organizations, market managers are more appropriate when a single brand or product is offered to several markets. When multiple brands are sold in multiple markets, both brand and market managers may be employed (Ames 1971).

Brand managers are responsible for coordinating the activities of the functional units with respect to their brand. While brand managers are responsible for the profitable promotion of their brands, they do not have either the staff or the authority over functional specialists who perform the work. The only authority of brand managers is provided through their assignments in brand plans. They exercise significant influence in the organization because of their access to information in the plan.

Variations in Responsibility of Integrators. A number of studies have documented the wide variation in responsibilities and duties of brand managers (Buell 1974: Clewett and Stasch 1975; Lucas 1972). In fact, Clewett and Stasch (1975) state that "...variations in the product managers' responsibilities and authority are the rule rather than the exception" (p. 69). They go on to suggest that this variation is due to the following factors:

1. The number of different products and the importance of the individual products to the company's success.
2. The number of management levels in the decision-making and plan-approval process.
3. The product manager's assignments relative to elements of the marketing mix and the use of internal or external functional organizations.
4. The degree to which resources are used in common between product managers.
5. The nature of the environment and the stage of the product life cycle.

FIGURE 5. Brand Management Organization

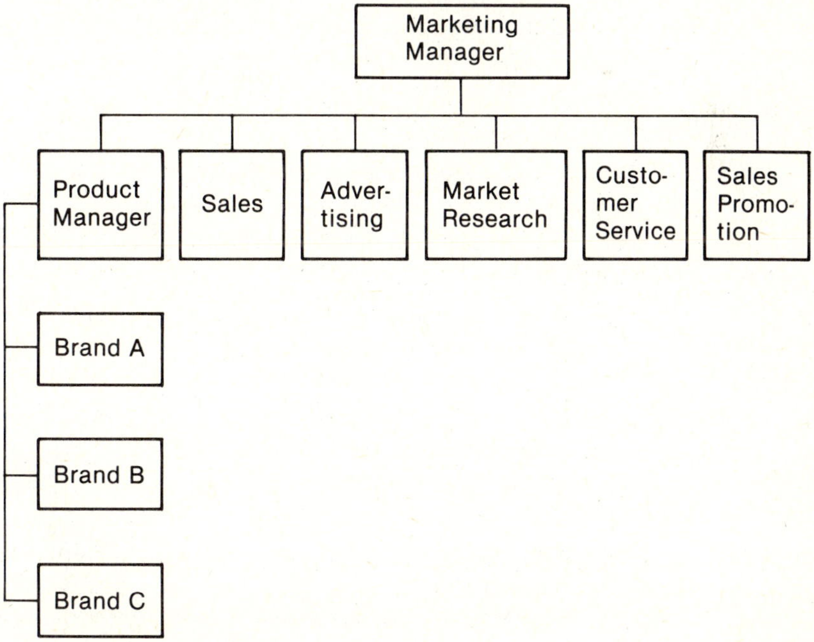

```
                    Marketing
                    Manager
        ┌──────┬──────┬──────┬──────┬──────┐
     Product  Sales  Adver-  Market  Custo-  Sales
     Manager        tising  Research mer    Promo-
                                    Service tion
       ├── Brand A
       ├── Brand B
       └── Brand C
```

The environment-structure contingency model presented in this paper suggests that the principal cause of variation is *differences in market environments*. The role of brand manager (or market manager) will be assigned more responsibility and will encompass more duties when the environment is highly interconnected, rapidly changing, and unpredictable. In a more stable environment, the responsibilities of the brand manager will be minimized.

This perspective is consistent with the perspective that the functions of a brand manager depend on the marketing environment reflected in the stage of the brand's product class life cycle (Clewett and Stasch 1975; Dietz 1973). Dietz described three forms of brand management: brand director, brand champion and brand coordinator. The brand director form assigns the most responsibility and authority to the brand manager and is appropriate for products in the development and introductory life cycle stages—the period of greatest environmental unpredictability. In the brand coordinator form, the brand manager has the least responsibility and authority. Thus, this form is most appropriate for stable environments encountered when products are in the late maturity and decline phases of the product life cycle. The implication of this contingency perspective is that the responsibility and authority of brand managers should vary within a marketing organization as a function of the environment faced by the brand.

Characteristics of Effective Integrators. The role of an integrator, a brand market manager, is particularly difficult because of the disparity between responsibility and formal authority. Research in organizational behavior has uncovered the following factors that enhance the effectiveness of integrators:

1. Maintaining a balanced orientation which recognizes the viewpoints of the various functional specialists whose activities they are coordinating and which understands the orientation and goals of the functional groups.
2. Rewarding integrators on the basis of their integrating performance. Thus, special rewards need to be established based on product or market performance.
3. Providing integrators with the information and the responsibility to resolve conflicts that develop between functional specialists. This involves development of conflict resolution skills by the integrator.
4. Using technical competence as a basis of influence rather than using the authority of their position. This involves broad technical training so that integrators understand the language of the specialists (Lawrence and Lorsch 1967b, 1967c).

To maintain a balanced perspective and develop technical competence, the frequent exchange of employees between integrator and functional specialist positions is necessary. In addition, Lawrence and Lorsch found that effective integrators had a high need for affiliation but there was no difference between effective and ineffective integrators in terms of their need for achievement or need for power.

While there is little research in marketing that has examined the behavior, personal characteristics, or responsibilities of effective brand or market managers, there is some support for the importance of relational and technical competence as a basis of influence. Consumer-good product managers report that, in order of declining importance, the most effective bases of influence for eliciting support from the staff and functional groups are as follows: human relations skill, expertise, respect for position, perceived authority, formal authority, indirect rewards, punishments, and direct rewards (Venkatesh and Wilemon 1976).

Complex, Interconnected, Unpredictable Environments— The Matrix Organization

The matrix or multidimensional organizational structure is a very complex organizational form which provides coordination in large, highly differentiated organizations. Thus, a matrix form is a method for dealing with a complex environment that is also unpredictable and interconnected (Quadrant I). The matrix form is commonly employed by high-technology and aerospace companies to integrate technologies with product-markets (Goggin 1974), and has been adopted in the marketing organizations of Citibank and AT&T.

The distinctive characteristic of a matrix structure is that it combines two or three dimensions of the organization simultaneously at the same hierarchical level. An example of a matrix for a marketing organization is shown in Figure 6. In this matrix, groups are formed on the basis of products and marketing functions. The consequence of this form is that the traditional organizational principle of unity of command is violated. The groups shown in Figure 6 report to both a product manager and a functional manager. Dow Corning employs a more complex, three-dimensional form based on functions, products and markets (Goggin 1974).

While the matrix form has the advantages of combining integration and differentiation (specialization), it is the most complicated and costly organization form to manage. The dual reporting relationship has an inherent potential for ambiguity and conflict. Special organizational and interpersonal skills are required to successfully implement this approach (Davis and Lawrence 1978; Duncan 1979; Galbraith 1971).

Additional Integrating Mechanisms

Temporary Structures. Temporary teams composed of staff and line personnel from various levels of the organization may be formed to handle a specific task. Frequently, such teams are formed to develop a new product, in which case they are called "venture teams." Venture teams are typically given responsibility for developing a product and bringing it to market. Von Hippel (1979) notes that the venture team concept aroused a flurry of interest in the 1970's and is now practiced routinely by many large corporations.

Von Hippel's exploratory study on venture teams concludes that they work well in a wide range of industries and may be successfully directed by "ordinary" managers (as opposed to managers screened for characteristics thought to be entrepreneurial). Von Hippel generates interesting hypotheses about what makes a successful venture team. He notes that the venture concept, while suffering its own problems, is nevertheless viewed by management as a way to bypass entrenched opposition to innovation within the organization. Ellis (1979), in discussing venture management at International Telephone and Telegraph, emphasizes the team's role in dampening serial communication distortion (due to the

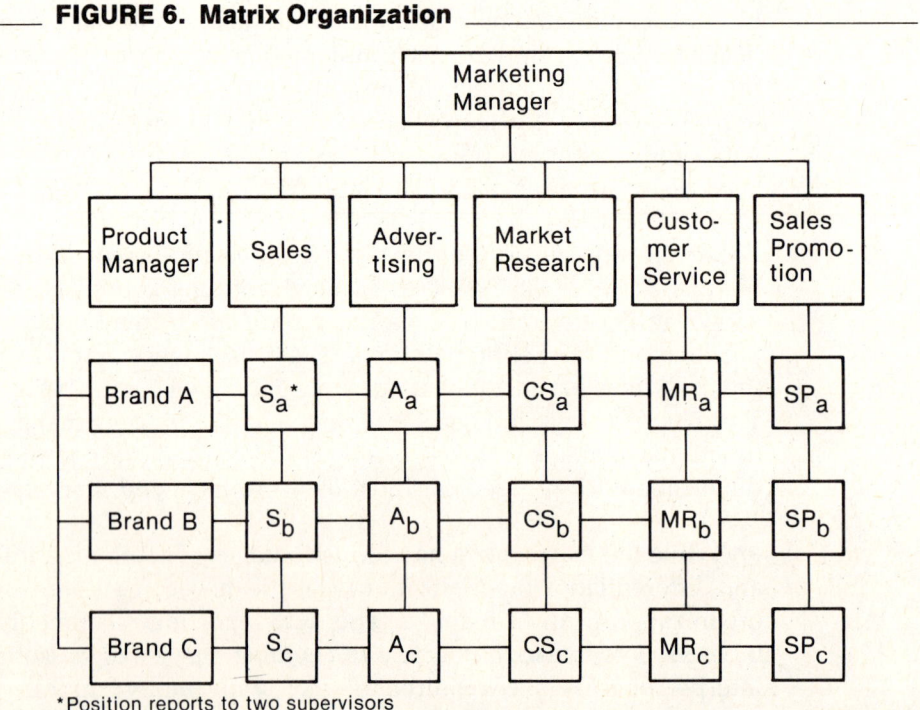

FIGURE 6. Matrix Organization

*Position reports to two supervisors

extremely large number of levels at ITT) and in facilitating personal, informal relationships within the organization.

Creation of Organizational Culture. Complex, interconnected, unpredictable environments put a heavy burden on bureaucratic control mechanisms, in part because it is difficult to specify appropriate rules and measures of performance. Thus, it is difficult to identify and reward performance, with attendant difficulty in motivating and controlling employees. One way to deal with such a problem is to abandon bureaucratic monitoring and rewards and to substitute an informal social structure, i.e., to develop organizational culture.

To develop organizational culture is to indicate a set of beliefs and values in all members of the organization. Such a value might be, "It is better to optimize corporate profit at the expense of my division than to optimize division profit at the expense of the corporation." At the extreme, an organization whose members have a commitment to it and a deep-seated sense of agreement about what constitutes proper behavior may be labelled a "clan" (Ouchi 1979). Clans are self-governing, without the need for elaborate audit and reward mechanisms. Perhaps the best-known example of a clan is the Japanese General Trading Firm; however, clan-type control mechanisms are also employed by U.S. companies such as IBM and Hewlett-Packard.

Ouchi (1979), notes that organization theorists have tended to treat clans as anomaly or as an epiphenomenon rather than as a subject central to organizational problems. He calls for the study of clans as an alternative control mechanism, with emphasis on how clans are created and sustained and in what situations they operate efficiently.

Propositions Concerning the Effectiveness of Organizational Structures for the Marketing Function

The following propositions are developed from the preceding discussion:

Proposition 1: The effectiveness of an organizational structure for a marketing department is a function of the degree to which the characteristics of the structure match the characteristics of the marketing environment in which the department operates.

Proposition 2: Highly differentiated organizations are needed to cope effectively with a complex environment consisting of many product-markets, or with large size.

Proposition 3: Strong integrating mechanisms (brand and/or market managers with increased authority and responsibility) are needed to cope effectively with an interconnected and unpredictable environment.

Conclusions

Organizational Effectiveness

The key question at this point is "so what?" What are the benefits of employing the appropriate organizational structure? What are the costs associated with using an inappropriate structure? While one can hypothesize that use of an inappropriate structure will make it more difficult for a marketing organization to achieve its goals, it could be very difficult to demonstrate this relationship empirically. There are substantial problems in developing measures of organizational effectiveness (Steers 1975). However, there are symptoms of an inappropriate organizational structure that can be readily observed. These symptoms are related to the information flow within the organization and role conflict and ambiguity experienced by the managers.

Some factors that might suggest an inappropriate organizational choice has been made are as follows:

1. An inability of decision makers to anticipate marketing problems before they occur: a tendency for reactive rather than proactive marketing plans.
2. A lack of needed information at the place in the organization where key decisions are to be made.
3. Slow reactions to changes in the marketing environment.
4. Poor prediction of trends in the marketing environment.
5. High levels of individual role conflict and role ambiguity in the marketing organization.

Directions for Future Research

In the preceding sections, a conceptual framework is presented for making a strategic organizational decision: the structure of the marketing department. This framework, and research in marketing and organization behavior, indicate that there is no one best way to organize. Neither the functional, brand management, market management, decentralized, nor matrix structure is most effective for organizing the marketing function. There is a set of circumstances under which each structure is most appropriate.

The key factor in determining the method for organizing and controlling the marketing function is the environment in which the marketing function is to be performed. The contingency framework suggests that the effectiveness of an organizational structure depends upon the complexity, unpredictability, and interconnectedness of the environment.

Most of the research on organizational issues in marketing has been descriptive in nature. Given the difficulty in undertaking cross-company research and the problems in developing a measure of organizational effectiveness, it seems appropriate to continue efforts to describe the prevalent methods for organizing the marketing function and the behavior of individuals performing in the various organizational forms. However, conceptual frameworks for approaching organizational issues are available. Thus, it is appropriate at this time to expand descriptive studies to include measures of the organizational environment in addition to the characteristics of the organization. Based on the conceptual frameworks, one would expect to find relationships between organizational characteristics and environments. Uncovering such relationships would provide a test of the frameworks and provide some guidance for management concerning the factors to consider when making organizational decisions.

ENDNOTES

1. When a company offers several brands within a product category, the person involved with the marketing effort for a specific brand is called a brand manager. However, a company that only offers one brand within a product category may refer to the person performing the same tasks as a product manager. Since the activities and responsibilities remain the same regardless of the title, the term "brand management" is used to indicate both product and brand management.

REFERENCES

Ames, B. Charles (1971), "The Dilemma of Product/Market Management," *Harvard Business Review*, 49 (March–April), 66–74.

——— (1963), "Payoff of Product Management," *Harvard Business Review*, 41 (November–December), 141–152.

Armour, Henry Ogden and David J. Teece (1978), "Organizational Structure and Economic Performance: A Test of the Multidivisional Hypothesis," *Bell Journal of Economics*, 9 (1), 106–22.

Arndt, Johan (1979), "Toward a Concept of Domesticated Markets," *Journal of Marketing*, 43 (Fall), 69–75.

Ashby, W. Ross (1968), "Variety, Constraint, and the Law of Requisite Variety," in Walter Buckley (ed.), *Modern Systems Research for the Behavioral Scientist: A Sourcebook*, Chicago: Aldine, 129–136.

Association of National Advertisers (1974), *Current Advertising Practices: Opinions as to Future Trends*, New York: Association of National Advertisers.

Buell, Victor P. (1975), "The Changing Role of the Product Manager in Consumer Goods Companies," *Journal of Marketing*, 39 (July), 3–11.

Burns, Tom, and G.M. Stalker (1971), *The Management of Innovation*, London, Tavistock.

Business Week, (1973), "The Brand Manager: No Longer King," *Business Week* (June 9), 58–66.

Burton, Richard M. and Borge Obel (1980), "A Computer Simulation Test of the M-form Hypothesis," *Administrative Science Quarterly*, 25 (September), 457–66.

Chander, Alfred D. (1966), *Strategy and Structure*, New York: Doubleday & Company, Inc., Anchor Books Edition.

Child, John (1972), "Organizational Structure, Environment, and Performance in the Role of Strategic Choice," *Sociology*, 6, 1–22.

Clewett, Richard M. and Stanley F. Stasch (1975), "Shifting Role of the Product Manager," *Harvard Business Review*, 53 (January–February), 65–73.

Corey, E. Raymond, and Steven H. Star (1971), *Organization Strategy: A Marketing Approach*, Boston: Division of Research, Graduate School of Business Administration, Harvard University.

Davis, Stanley M. and Paul R. Lawrence (1978), "Problems of Matrix Organizations," *Harvard Business Review*, 56 (May–June), 131–142.

Dietz, Stephen S. (1973), "Get More out of Your Brand Management," *Harvard Business Review*, 51 (July–August), 127–136.

Downey, M. Kirk, Don Hellriegel, and John W. Slocum, Jr. (1975), "Environmental Uncertainty: The Construct and Its Application," *Administrative Science Quarterly*, 20 (December), 613–29.

Duncan, Robert (1979), "What is the Right Organization Structure?" *Organizational Dynamics*, 8 (Winter), 59–80.

——— (1972), "Characteristics of Organizational Environments and Perceived Environmental Uncertainty," *Administrative Science Quarterly*, 17 (March), 313–27.

Ellis (1979), "Effective Use of Temporary Groups for New Product Development," *Research Management*, 22 (January), 31–34.

Galbraith, Jay R. (1973), *Designing Complex Organizations*, Reading, Mass.: Addison-Wesley.

——— (1971), "Matrix Organizational Designs," *Business Horizons*, 14 (February), 29–41.

Goggin, William (1974), "How the Multidimensional Structure Works at Dow Corning," *Harvard Business Review*, 52 (January–February), 54–55.

Hanan, Mack (1974), "Reorganize Your Company Around Its Markets," *Harvard Business Review*, 52 (November–December), 63–74.

Hise, Richard T. and J. Patrick Kelly (1978), "Product Management on Trial," *Journal of Marketing*, 42 (October), 28–33.

Hughes, G. David (1978), *Marketing Management: A Planning Approach*, Reading, Mass: Addison-Wesley.

Jurkovich, Ray (1974), "A Core Typology of Organizational Environments," *Administrative Science Quarterly*, 19 (June), 380–394.

Lawrence, Paul R. and Jay W. Lorsch (1967a), "Differentiation and Integration in Complex Organizations," *Administrative Science Quarterly*, 12 (March), 1–47.

——— (1967b), "New Management Job: The Integrator," *Harvard Business Review*, 45 (November–December), 142.

——— (1967c), *Organization and Environment: Managing Differentiation and Integration*, Homewood, Ill: Irwin.

Levitt, Theodore (1980), "Marketing Success Through Differentiation—of Anything," *Harvard Business Review*, 58 (January–February), 83–91.

Lorsch, Jay W. (1976), "Contingency Theory and Organizational Design: A Personal Odyssey," in Ralph H. Kilmann, Louis R. Pondy, and Dennis P. Slevin (eds.), *The*

Management of Organizational Design: Strategies and Implementation, Vol. 1, New York: North-Holland, 41–65.

———, and John J. Morse (1974), *Organizations and Their Members: A Contingency Approach*, New York: Harper and Row.

Lucas, Darrell (1972), "Product Managers in Advertising," *Journal of Advertising Research*, 12 (June), 41–44.

Luck, David J. (1969), "Interfaces of a Product Manager," *Journal of Marketing*, 33 (October), 32–36.

———, and Theodore Nowak (1965), "Product Management—Vision Unfulfilled," *Harvard Business Review*, 43 (May–June), 143–150.

Ouchi, William G. (1979), "A Conceptual Framework for the Design of Organizational Control Mechanisms," *Management Science*, 25 (September), 833–48.

Rumelt, Richard P. (1974), *Strategy, Structure, and Economic Performance*, Boston: Harvard Business School Division of Research

Steer, Peter, and John Cable (1978), "Internal Organization and Profit: An Empirical Analysis of Large U.K. Companies," *The Journal of Industrial Economics*, 27 (September), 833–48.

Steers, Richard M. (1975), "Problems in the Measurement of Organizational Effectiveness," *Administrative Science Quarterly*, 20 (December), 546–558.

Terreberry, Shirley (1968), "The Evaluation of Organizational Environments," *Administrative Science Quarterly*, 12 (December), 590–613.

Venkatesh, Alladi and Davis L. Wilemon (1976), "Interpersonal Influence in Product Management," *Journal of Marketing*, 40 (October), 33–40.

von Hippel, Eric (1979), "Successful and Failing Internal Corporate Ventures: An Empirical Analysis," *Industrial Marketing Management*, 6 (June), 163–174.

Walker, Arthur H. and Jay W. Lorsch (1968), "Organizational Choice: Product versus Function," *Harvard Business Review*, 48 (November–December), 129–138.

11 — The Marketing Audit Comes of Age

Philip Kotler, William Gregor, and William Rodgers

Reprinted from "The Marketing Audit Comes of Age," by Philip Kotler, William Gregor, and William Rodgers, SLOAN MANAGEMENT REVIEW, Vol. 18, No. 2 (Winter 1977), pp. 25–43, by permission of the publisher. Copyright © 1977 by the Sloan Management Review Association. All rights reserved.

Comparing the marketing strategies and tactics of business units today versus ten years ago, the most striking impression is one of marketing strategy obsolescence. Ten years ago U.S. automobile companies were gearing up for their second postwar race to produce the largest car with the highest horsepower. Today companies are selling increasing numbers of small and medium-sized cars and fuel economy is a major selling point. Ten years ago computer companies were introducing ever-more powerful hardware for more sophisticated uses. Today they emphasize mini- and micro-computers and software.

It is not even necessary to take a ten-year period to show the rapid obsolescence of marketing strategies. The growth economy of 1950–1970 has been superseded by a volatile economy which produces new strategic surprises almost monthly. Competitors launch new products, customers switch their business, distributors lose their effectiveness, advertising costs skyrocket, government regulations are announced, and consumer groups attack. These changes represent both opportunities and problems and may demand periodic reorientations of the company's marketing operations.

Many companies feel that their marketing operations need regular reviews and overhauls but do not know how to proceed. Some companies simply make many small changes that are economically and politically feasible, but fail to get to the heart of the matter. True, the company develops an annual marketing plan but management normally does not take a deep and objective look at the marketing strategies, policies, organizations, and operations on a recurrent basis. At the other extreme, companies install aggressive new top marketing management hoping to shake down the marketing cobwebs. In between there must be more orderly ways to reorient marketing operations to changed environments and opportunities.

ENTER THE MARKETING AUDIT

One hears more talk today about the *marketing audit* as being the answer to evaluating marketing practice just as the public accounting audit is the tool for evaluating company accounting practice. This might lead one to conclude that the marketing audit is a new idea and also a very distinct methodology. Neither of these conclusions is true.

The marketing audit as an idea dates back to the early fifties. Rudolph Dallmeyer, a former executive in Booz-Allen-Hamilton, remembers conducting marketing audits as early as 1952. Robert J. Lavidge, President of Elrick and Lavidge, dates his firm's performance of marketing audits to over two decades ago. In 1959, the American Management Associations published an excellent set of papers on the marketing audit under the title *Analyzing and Improving Marketing Performance*, Report No. 32, 1959. During the 1960s, the marketing audit received increasing mention in the lists of marketing services of management consulting firms. It was not until the turbulent seventies, however, that it began to penetrate management awareness as a possible answer to its needs.

As for whether the marketing audit has reached a high degree of methodological sophistication, the answer is generally no. Whereas two certified public accountants will handle an audit assignment using approximately the same methodology, two marketing auditors are likely to bring different conceptions of the auditing process to their task. However, a growing consensus on the major characteristics of a marketing audit is emerging and we can expect considerable progress to occur in the next few years.

In its fullest form and concept, a marketing audit has four basic characteristics. The first and most important is that it is *broad* rather than narrow in focus. The term "marketing audit" should be reserved for a *horizontal (or comprehensive) audit* covering the company's marketing environment, objectives, strategies, organization, and systems. In contrast, a *vertical (or in-depth) audit* occurs when management decides to take a deep look into some key marketing function, such as sales force management. A vertical audit should properly be called by the function that is being audited, such as a sales force audit, an advertising audit, or a pricing audit.

A second characteristic feature of a marketing audit is that it is conducted by someone who is *independent* of the operation that is being evaluated. There is some loose talk about self-audits, where a manager follows a checklist of questions concerning his own operation to make sure that he is touching all the bases.[1] Most experts would agree, however, that the self-audit, while it is always a useful step that a manager should take, does not constitute a *bona fide* audit because it lacks objectivity and independence. Independence can be achieved in two ways. The audit could be an *inside audit* conducted by a person or group inside the company but outside of the operation being evaluated. Or it could be an *outside audit* conducted by a management consulting firm or practitioner.

The third characteristic of a marketing audit is that it is *systematic*. The marketing auditor who decides to interview people inside and outside the firm at random, asking questions as they occur to him, is a "visceral" auditor without a method. This does not mean that he will not come up with very useful findings and recommendations; he may be very insightful. However, the effectiveness of the marketing audit will normally increase to the extent that it incorporates an orderly sequence of diagnostic steps, such as there are in the conduct of a public accounting audit.

A final characteristic that is less intrinsic to a marketing audit but nevertheless desirable is that it be conducted *periodically*. Typically, evaluations of company marketing effort are commissioned when sales have turned down sharply, sales force morale has fallen, or other problems have occurred at the company. The fact is, however, that companies are thrown into a crisis partly because they have failed to review their assumptions and to change them during good times. A marketing audit conducted when things are going well can often help make a good situation even better and also indicate changes needed to prevent things from turning sour.

The above ideas on a marketing audit can be brought together into a single definition:

> A marketing audit is a *comprehensive, systematic, independent*, and *periodic* examination of a company's — or business unit's — marketing environment, objectives, strategies, and activities with a view of determining problem areas and opportunities and recommending a plan of action to improve the company's marketing performance.

What Is the Marketing Audit Process?

How is a marketing audit performed? Marketing auditing follows the simple three-step procedure shown in Figure 1.

Setting the Objectives and Scope

The first step calls for a meeting between the company officer(s) and a potential auditor to explore the nature of the marketing operations and the potential value of a marketing audit. If the company officer is convinced of the potential benefits of a marketing audit, he and the auditor have to work out an agreement on the objectives, coverage, depth, data sources, report format, and the time period for the audit.

11 — The Marketing Audit Comes of Age 185

Consider the following actual case. A plumbing and heating supplies wholesaler with three branches invited a marketing consultant to prepare an audit of its overall marketing policies and operations. Four major objectives were set for the audit:

- Determine how the market views the company and its competitors.
- Recommend a pricing policy.
- Develop a product evaluation system.
- Determine how to improve the sales activity in terms of the deployment of the sales force, the level and type of compensation, the measurement of performance, and the addition of new salesmen.

Furthermore, the audit would cover the marketing operations of the company as a whole and the operations of each of the three branches, with particular attention to one of the branches. The audit would focus on the marketing operations but also include a review of the purchasing and inventory systems since they intimately affect marketing performance.

The company would furnish the auditor with published and private data on the industry. In addition, the auditor would contact suppliers of manufactured plumbing supplies for additional market data and contact wholesalers outside the company's market area to gain further information on wholesale plumbing and heating operations. The auditor would interview all the key corporate and branch management, sales and purchasing personnel, and would ride with several of those salesmen on their calls. Finally, the auditor would interview a sample of the major plumbing and heating contractor customers in the market areas of the two largest branches.

It was decided that the report format would consist of a draft report of conclusions and recommendations to be reviewed by the president and vice-president of marketing, and then delivered to the executive committee which included the three branch managers. Finally, it was decided

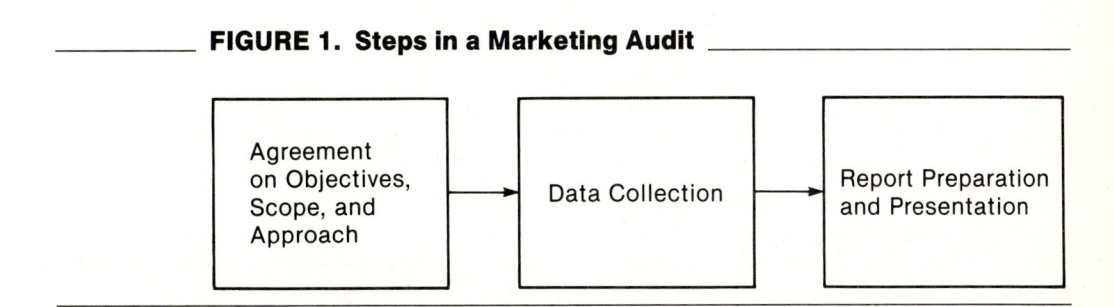

FIGURE 1. Steps in a Marketing Audit

Agreement on Objectives, Scope, and Approach → Data Collection → Report Preparation and Presentation

that the audit findings would be ready to present within six to eight weeks.

Gathering the Data

The bulk of an auditor's time is spent in gathering data. Although we talk of a single auditor, an auditing team is usually involved when the project is large. A detailed plan as to who is to be interviewed by whom, the questions to be asked, the time and place of contact, and so on, has to be carefully prepared so that auditing time and cost are kept to a minimum. Daily reports of the interviews are to be written up and reviewed so that the individual or team can spot new areas requiring exploration while data are still being gathered.

The cardinal rule in data collection is not to rely solely for data and opinion on those being audited. Customers often turn out to be the key group to interview. Many companies do not really understand how their customers see them and their competitors, nor do they fully understand customer needs. This is vividly demonstrated in Figure 2 which shows the results of asking end users, company salesmen, and company marketing personnel for their views of the importance of different factors affecting the user's selection of a manufacturer. According to the figure, customers look first and foremost at the quality of technical support services, followed by prompt delivery, followed by quick response to customer needs. Company salesmen think that company reputation, however, is the most important factor in customer choice, followed by quick response to customer needs and technical support services. Those who plan marketing strategy have a different opinion. They see company price and product quality as the two major factors in buyer choice, followed by quick response to customer needs. Clearly, there is lack of consonance between what buyers say they want, what company salesmen are responding to, and what company marketing planners are emphasizing. One of the major contributions of marketing auditors is to expose these discrepancies and suggest ways to improve marketing consensus.

Preparing and Presenting the Report

The marketing auditor will be developing tentative conclusions as the data comes in. It is a sound procedure for him to meet once or twice with the company officer before the data collection ends to outline some initial findings to see what reactions and suggestions they produce.

When the data gathering phase is over, the marketing auditor prepares notes for a visual and verbal presentation to the company officer or small group who hired him. The presentation consists of restating the objectives, showing the main findings, and presenting the major recommendations. Then, the auditor is ready to write the final report, which is largely a matter of putting the visual and verbal material into a good written communication. The company officer(s) will usually ask the auditor to present the report to other groups in the company. If the report calls for deep debate and action, the various groups hearing the report should organize into subcommittees to do follow-up work with another meeting to take place some weeks later. The most valuable part of the marketing audit often lies not so much in the auditor's specific recommendations but in the process that the managers of the company begin to go through to assimilate, debate, and develop their own concept of the needed marketing action.

MARKETING AUDIT PROCEDURES FOR AN INSIDE AUDIT

Companies that conduct internal marketing audits show interesting variations from the procedures just outlined. International Telephone and Telegraph, for example, has a history of forming corporate teams and sending them into weak divisions to do a complete business audit, with a heavy emphasis on the marketing component. Some teams stay on the job, often taking over the management.

General Electric's corporate consulting division offers help to various divisions on their marketing problems. One of its services is a marketing

FIGURE 2. Factors in the Selection of a Manufacturer*

Factor	All Users Rank	Company Salesmen Rank	Company Non-Sales Personnel Rank
Reputation	5	①	4
Extension of Credit	9	11	9
Sales Representatives	8	5	7
Technical Support Services	①	③	6
Literature and Manuals	11	10	11
Prompt Delivery	②	4	5
Quick Response to Customer Needs	③	②	③
Product Price	6	6	①
Personal Relationships	10	7	8
Complete Product Line	7	9	10
Product Quality	4	8	②

Marketing and Distribution Audit, A Service of Decision Sciences Corporation, p. 32. Used with the permission of the Decision Sciences Corporation.

audit in the sense of a broad, independent, systematic look at the marketing picture in a division. However, the corporate consulting division gets few requests for a marketing audit as such. Most of the requests are for specific marketing studies or problem-solving assistance.

The 3M Company uses a very interesting and unusual internal marketing plan audit procedure. A marketing plan audit office with a small staff is located at corporate headquarters. The main purpose of the 3M marketing plan audit is to help the divisional marketing manager improve the marketing planning function, as well as come up with better strategies and tactics. A divisional marketing manager phones the marketing plan audit office and invites an audit. There is an agreement that only he will see the results and it is up to him whether he wants wider distribution.

The audit centers around a marketing plan for a product or product line that the marketing manager is preparing for the coming year. This plan is reviewed at a personal presentation by a special team of six company marketing executives invited by the marketing plan audit office. A new team is formed for each new audit. An effort is made to seek out those persons within 3M (but not in the audited division) who can bring the best experience to bear on the particular plan's problems and opportunities. A team typically consists of a marketing manager from another division, a national sales manager, a marketing executive with a technical background, a few others close to the type of problems found in the audited plan, and another person who is totally unfamiliar with the market, the product, or the major marketing techniques being used in the plan. This person usually raises some important points others forget to raise, or do not ask because "everyone probably knows about that anyway."

The six auditors are supplied with a summary of the marketing manager's plan about ten days before an official meeting is held to review the plan. On the audit day, the six auditors, the head of the audit office, and the divisional marketing manager gather at 8:30 A.M. The marketing manager makes a presentation for about an hour describing the division's competitive situation, the long-run strategy, and the planned tactics. The auditors proceed to ask hard questions and debate certain points with the marketing manager and each other. Before the meeting ends that day, the auditors are each asked to fill out a marketing plan evaluation form consisting of questions that are accompanied by numerical rating scales and room for comments.

These evaluations are analyzed and summarized after the meeting. Then the head of the audit office arranges a meeting with the divisional marketing manager and presents the highlights of the auditor's findings and recommendations. It is then up to the marketing manager to take the next steps.

COMPONENTS OF THE MARKETING AUDIT

A major principle in marketing audits is to start with the marketplace first and explore the changes that are taking place and what they imply in the way of problems and opportunities. Then the auditor moves to examine the company's marketing objectives and strategies, organization, and systems. Finally he may move to examine one or two key functions in more detail that are central to the marketing performance of that company. However, some companies ask for less than the full range of auditing steps in order to obtain initial results before commissioning further work. The company may ask for a marketing environment audit, and if satisfied, then ask for a marketing strategy audit. Or it might ask for a marketing organization audit first, and later ask for a marketing environment audit.

We view a full marketing audit as having six major components, each having a semiautonomous status if a company wants less than a full marketing audit. The six components and their logical diagnostic sequence are discussed below. The major auditing questions connected with these components are gathered together in Appendix A at the end of this article.

Marketing Environment Audit

By marketing environment, we mean both the *macro-environment* surrounding the industry and the *task environment* in which the organization intimately operates. The macro-environment consists of the large scale forces and factors influencing the company's future over which the company has very little control. These forces are normally divided into economic-demographic factors, technological factors, political-legal factors, and social-cultural factors. The marketing auditor's task is to assess the key trends and their implications for company marketing action. However, if the company has a good long-range forecasting department, then there is less of a need for a macro-environment audit.

The marketing auditor may play a more critical role in auditing the company's task environment. The task environment consists of markets, customers, competitors, distributors and dealers, suppliers, and marketing facilitators. The marketing auditor can make a contribution by going out into the field and interviewing various parties to assess their current thinking and attitudes and bringing them to the attention of management.

Marketing Strategy Audit

The marketing auditor then proceeds to consider whether the company's marketing strategy is well-postured in the light of the opportunities and problems facing the company. The starting point for the marketing strategy audit is the corporate goals and objectives followed by the marketing objectives. The auditor may find the objectives to be poorly stated, or he may find them to be well-stated but inappropriate given the company's resources and opportunities. For example, a chemical company had set a sales growth objective for a particular product line at 15 percent. However, the total market showed no growth and competition was fierce. Here the auditor questioned the basic sales growth objective for that product line. He proposed that the product line be reconsidered for a maintenance or harvest objective at best and that the company should look for growth elsewhere.

Even when a growth objective is warranted, the auditor will want to consider whether management has chosen the best strategy to achieve that growth.

Marketing Organization Audit

A complete marketing audit would have to cover the question of the effectiveness of the marketing and sales organization, as well as the quality of interaction between marketing and other key management functions such as manufacturing, finance, purchasing, and research and development.

At critical times, a company's marketing organization must be revised to achieve greater effectiveness within the company and in the marketplace. Companies without product management systems will want to consider introducing them; companies with these systems may want to consider dropping them, or trying product teams instead. Companies may want to redefine the role concept of a product manager from being a promotional manager (concerned primarily with volume) to a business manager (concerned primarily with profit). There is the issue of whether decision-making responsibility should be moved up from the brand level to the product level. There is the perennial question of how to make the organization more market-responsive including the possibility of replacing product divisions with market-centered divisions. Finally, sales organizations often do not fully understand marketing. In the words of one vice-president of marketing: "It takes about five years for us to train sales managers to think marketing."

Marketing Systems Audit

A full marketing audit then turns to examine the various systems being used by marketing management to gather information, plan, and control the marketing operation. The issue is not the company's marketing strategy or organization per se but rather the procedures used in some or all of the following systems: sales forecasting, sales goal and quota setting, marketing planning, marketing control, inventory control, order processing, physical distribution, new products development, and product pruning.

The marketing audit may reveal that marketing is being carried on without adequate systems of planning, implementation, and control. An audit of a consumer products division of a large company revealed that decisions about which products to carry and which to eliminate were made by the head of the division on the basis of his intuitive feeling with little information or analysis to guide the decisions. The auditor recommended the introduction of a new product screening system for new products and an improved sales control system for existing products. He also observed that the division prepared budgets but did not carry out formal marketing planning and hardly any research into the market. He recommended that the division establish a formal marketing planning system as soon as possible.

Marketing Productivity Audit

A full marketing audit also includes an effort to examine key accounting data to determine where the company is making its real profits and what, if any, marketing costs could be trimmed. Decision Sciences Corporation, for example, starts its marketing audit by looking at the accounting figures on sales and associated costs of sales. Using marketing cost accounting principles,[2] it seeks to measure the marginal profit contribution of different products, end user segments, marketing channels, and sales territories.

We might argue that the firm's own controller or accountant should do the job of providing management with the results of marketing cost analysis. A handful of firms have created the job position of marketing controllers who report to financial controllers and spend their time looking at the productivity and validity of various marketing costs. Where an organization is doing a good job of marketing cost analysis, it does not need a marketing auditor to study the same. But most companies do not do careful marketing cost analysis. Here a marketing auditor can pay his way by simply exposing certain economic and cost relations which indicate waste or conceal unexploited marketing opportunities.

Zero-based budgeting[3] is another tool for investigating and improving marketing productivity. In normal budgeting, top management allots to each business unit a percentage increase (or decrease) of what it got last time. The question is not raised whether that basic budget level still makes sense. The manager of an operation should be asked what he would basically need if he started his operation from scratch and what it would cost. What would he need next and what would it cost? In this way, a budget is built from the ground up reflecting the true needs of the operation. When this was applied to a technical sales group within a large industrial goods company, it became clear that the company had three or four extra technical salesmen on its payroll. The manager admitted to the redundancy but argued that if a business upturn came, these men would be needed to tap the potential. In the meantime, they were carried on the payroll for two years in the expectation of a business upturn.

Marketing Function Audit

The work done to this point might begin to point to certain key marketing functions which are performing poorly. The auditor might spot, for example, sales force problems that go very deep. Or he might observe that advertising budgets are prepared in an arbitrary fashion and such things as advertising themes, media, and timing are not evaluated for their effectiveness. In these and other cases, the issue becomes one of notifying management of the desirability of one or more marketing function audits if management agrees.

WHICH COMPANIES CAN BENEFIT MOST FROM A MARKETING AUDIT?

All companies can benefit from a competent audit of their marketing operations. However, a marketing audit is likely to yield the highest payoff in the following companies and situations:

- *Production-Oriented and Technical-Oriented Companies.* Many manufacturing companies have their start in a love affair with a certain product. Further products are added that appeal to the technical interests of management, usually with insufficient attention paid to their market potential. The feeling in these companies is that marketing is paid to sell what the company decides to make. After some failures with its "better mousetraps," management starts getting interested in shifting to a market orientation. But this calls for more than a simple declaration by top management to study and serve the customer's needs. It calls for a great number of organizational and attitudinal changes that must be introduced carefully and convincingly. An auditor can perform an important service in recognizing that a company's problem lies in its production orientation, and in guiding management toward a market orientation.
- *Troubled Divisions.* Multidivision companies usually have some troubled divisions. Top management may decide to use an auditor to assess the situation in a troubled division rather than rely solely on the division management's interpretation of the problem.

- *High Performing Divisions.* Multidivision companies might want an audit of their top dollar divisions to make sure that they are reaching their highest potential, and are not on the verge of a sudden reversal. Such an audit may also yield insights into how to improve marketing in other divisions.
- *Young Companies.* Marketing audits of emerging small companies or young divisions of large companies can help to lay down a solid marketing approach at a time when management faces a great degree of market inexperience.
- *Nonprofit Organizations.* Administrators of colleges, museums, hospitals, social agencies, and churches are beginning to think in marketing terms, and the marketing audit can serve a useful educational as well as diagnostic purpose.

What Are the Problems and Pitfalls of Marketing Audits?

While the foregoing has stressed the positive aspects of marketing audits and their utility in a variety of situations, it is important to note some of the problems and pitfalls of the marketing audit process. Problems can occur in the objective-setting step, the data collection step, or the report presentation step.

Setting Objectives

When the marketing audit effort is being designed by the auditor and the company officer who commissioned the audit, several problems will be encountered. For one thing, the objectives set for the audit are based upon the company officer's and auditor's best *a priori* notions of what the key problem areas are for the audit to highlight. However, new problem areas may emerge once the auditor begins to learn more about the company. The original set of objectives should not constrain the auditor from shifting his priorities of investigation.

Similarly, it may be necessary for the auditor to use different sources of information than envisioned at the start of the audit. In some cases this may be because some information sources he had counted on became unavailable. In one marketing audit, the auditor had planned to speak to a sample of customers for the company's electro-mechanical devices, but the company officer who hired him would not permit him to do so. In other cases, a valuable new source of information may arise that was not recognized at the start of the audit. For example, the auditor for an air brake system manufacturer found as a valuable source of market intelligence a long-established manufacturers' representatives firm that approached the company after the audit had begun.

Another consideration at the objective-setting stage of the audit is that the management most affected by the audit must have full knowledge of the purposes and scope of the audit. Audits go much more smoothly when the executive who calls in the auditor either brings the affected management into the design stage, or at least has a general introductory meeting where the auditor explains his procedures and answers questions from the people in the affected business.

Data Collection

Despite reassurances by the auditor and the executive who brought him in, there will still be some managers in the affected business who will feel threatened by the auditor. The auditor must expect this, and realize that an individual's fears and biases may color his statements in an interview.

From the onset of the audit, the auditor must guarantee and maintain confidentiality of each individual's comments. In many audits, personnel in the company will see the audit as a vehicle for unloading their negative feelings about the company or other individuals. The auditor can learn a lot from these comments, but he must protect the individuals who make them. The auditor must question interviewees in a highly professional manner to build their confidence in him, or else they will not be entirely honest in their statements.

Another area of concern during the information collection step is the degree to which the company executive who brought in the auditor will try to guide the audit. It will be necessary for this officer and the auditor to strike a balance in which the executive provides some direction, but not too much. While overcontrol is the more likely excess of the executive, it is possible to undercontrol. When the auditor and the company executive do not have open and frequent lines of communication during the audit, it is possible that the auditor may place more emphasis on some areas and less on others than the executive might have desired. Therefore, it is the responsibility of both the auditor and the executive who brought him in to communicate frequently during the audit.

Report Presentation

One of the biggest problems in marketing auditing is that the executive who brings in the auditor, or the people in the business being audited, may have higher expectations about what the audit will do for the company than the actual report seems to offer. In only the most extreme circumstances will the auditor develop surprising panaceas or propose startling new opportunities for the company. More likely, the main value of his report will be that it places priorities on ideas and directions for the company, many of which have already been considered by some people within the audited organization. In most successful audits, the auditor, in his recommendations, makes a skillful combination of his general and technical marketing background (e.g., designs of salesman's compensation systems, his ability to measure the size and potential of markets) with some opportunistic ideas that people in the audited organization have already considered, but do not know how much importance to place upon them. However, it is only in the company's implementation of the recommendations that the payoff to the company will come.

Another problem at the conclusion of the audit stems from the fact that most audits seem to result in organizational changes. Organizational changes are a common outcome because the audit usually identifies new tasks to be accomplished and new tasks demand people to do them. One thing the auditor and the executive who brought him in must recognize, however, is that organizational promotions and demotions are exclusively the executive's decision. It is the executive who has to live with the changes once the auditor has gone, not the auditor. Therefore, the executive should not be lulled into thinking that organizational moves are any easier because the auditor may have recommended them.

The final problem, and this is one facing the auditor, is that important parts of an audit may be implemented incorrectly or not implemented at all, by the executive who commissioned the audit. Non-implementation of key parts of the audit undermines the whole effectiveness of the audit.

Summary

The marketing audit is one important answer to the problem of evaluating the marketing performance of a company or one of its business units. Marketing audits are distinguished from other marketing exercises in being *comprehensive*, *independent*, *systematic*, and *periodic*. A full marketing audit would cover the company's (or division's) external environment, objectives, strategies, organization, systems, and functions. If the audit covers only one function, such as sales management or advertising, it is best described as a marketing function audit rather than a marketing audit. If the exercise is to solve a current problem, such as entering a market, setting a price, or developing a package, then it is not an audit at all.

The marketing audit is carried out in three steps: developing an agreement as to objectives and scope; collecting the data; and presenting the report. The audit can be performed by a competent outside consultant or by a company auditing office at headquarters.

The possible findings of an audit include detecting unclear or inappropriate marketing objectives, inappropriate strategies, inappropriate levels of marketing expenditures, needed improvements in organization, and needed improvements in systems for marketing information, planning, and control. Companies that are most likely to benefit from a marketing audit include production-oriented companies, companies with troubled or highly vulnerable divisions, young companies, and nonprofit organizations.

Many companies today are finding that their premises for marketing strategy are growing obsolete in the face of a rapidly changing environment. This is happening to company giants such as General Motors and Sears as well as smaller firms that have not provided a mechanism for recycling their marketing strategy. The marketing audit is not the full answer to marketing strategy recycling but does offer one major mechanism for pursuing this desirable and necessary task.

APPENDIX A — COMPONENTS OF A MARKETING AUDIT

The Marketing Environment Audit

I. Macro-Environment

Economic-Demographic
1. What does the company expect in the way of inflation, material shortages, unemployment, and credit availability in the short run, intermediate run, and long run?
2. What effect will forecasted trends in the size, age distribution, and regional distribution of population have on the business?

Technology
1. What major changes are occurring in product technology? In process technology?
2. What are the major generic substitutes that might replace this product?

Political-Legal
1. What laws are being proposed that may affect marketing strategy and tactics?
2. What federal, state, and local agency actions should be watched? What is happening in the areas of pollution control, equal employment opportunity, product safety, advertising, price control, etc., that is relevant to marketing planning?

Social-Cultural
1. What attitudes is the public taking toward business and toward products such as those produced by the company?
2. What changes are occurring in consumer life styles and values that have a bearing on the company's target markets and marketing methods?

II. Task Environment

Markets
1. What is happening to market size, growth, geographical distribution, and profits?
2. What are the major market segments? What are their expected rates of growth? Which are high opportunity and low opportunity segments?

Customers
1. How do current customers and prospects rate the company and its competitors, particularly with respect to reputation, product quality, service, sales force, and price?
2. How do different classes of customers make their buying decisions?
3. What are the evolving needs and satisfactions being sought by the buyers in this market?

Competitors
1. Who are the major competitors? What are the objectives and strategy of each major competitor? What are their strengths and weaknesses? What are the sizes and trends in market shares?
2. What trends can be foreseen in future competition and substitutes for this product?

Distribution and Dealers
1. What are the main trade channels bringing products to customers?
2. What are the efficiency levels and growth potentials of the different trade channels?

Suppliers
1. What is the outlook for the availability of different key resources used in production?
2. What trends are occurring among suppliers in their pattern of selling?

Facilitators
1. What is the outlook for the cost and availability of transportation services?
2. What is the outlook for the cost and availability of warehousing facilities?
3. What is the outlook for the cost and availability of financial resources?
4. How effectively is the advertising agency performing? What trends are occurring in advertising agency services?

Marketing Strategy Audit

Marketing Objectives
1. Are the corporate objectives clearly stated and do they lead logically to the marketing objectives?
2. Are the marketing objectives stated in a clear form to guide marketing planning and subsequent performance measurement?
3. Are the marketing objectives appropriate, given the company's competitive position, resources, and opportunities? Is the appropriate strategic objective to build, hold, harvest, or terminate this business?

Strategy
1. What is the core marketing strategy for achieving the objectives? Is it a sound marketing strategy?
2. Are enough resources (or too much resources) budgeted to accomplish the marketing objectives?
3. Are the marketing resources allocated optimally to prime market segments, territories, and products of the organization?
4. Are the marketing resources allocated optimally to the major elements of the marketing mix, i.e., product quality, service, sales force, advertising, promotion, and distribution?

Marketing Organization Audit

Formal Structure
1. Is there a high level marketing officer with adequate authority and responsibility over those company activities that affect the customer's satisfaction?
2. Are the marketing responsibilities optimally structured along functional, product, end user, and territorial lines?

Functional Efficiency
1. Are there good communication and working relations between marketing and sales?
2. Is the product management system working effectively? Are the product managers able to plan profits or only sales volume?
3. Are there any groups in marketing that need more training, motivation, supervision, or evaluation?

Interface Efficiency
1. Are there any problems between marketing and manufacturing that need attention?
2. What about marketing and R&D?

3. What about marketing and financial management?
4. What about marketing and purchasing?

Marketing Systems Audit

Marketing Information System
1. Is the marketing intelligence system producing accurate, sufficient, and timely information about developments in the marketplace?
2. Is marketing research being adequately used by company decision makers?

Marketing Planning System
1. Is the marketing planning system well-conceived and effective?
2. Is sales forecasting and market potential measurement soundly carried out?
3. Are sales quotas set on a proper basis?

Marketing Control System
1. Are the control procedures (monthly, quarterly, etc.) adequate to insure that the annual plan objectives are being achieved?
2. Is provision made to analyze periodically the profitability of different products, markets, territories, and channels of distribution?
3. Is provision made to examine and validate periodically various marketing costs?

New Product Development System
1. Is the company well-organized to gather, generate, and screen new product ideas?
2. Does the company do adequate concept research and business analysis before investing heavily in a new idea?
3. Does the company carry out adequate product and market testing before launching a new product?

Marketing Productivity Audit

Profitability Analysis
1. What is the profitability of the company's different products, served markets, territories, and channels of distribution?
2. Should the company enter, expand, contract, or withdraw from any business segments and what would be the short- and long-run profit consequences?

Cost-Effectiveness Analysis
1. Do any marketing activities seem to have excessive costs? Are these costs valid? Can cost-reducing steps be taken?

Marketing Function Audits

Products
1. What are the product line objectives? Are these objectives sound? Is the current product line meeting these objectives?
2. Are there particular products that should be phased out?
3. Are there new products that are worth adding?
4. Are any products able to benefit from quality, feature, or style improvements?

Price
1. What are the pricing objectives, policies, strategies, and procedures? To what extent are prices set on sound cost, demand, and competitive criteria?
2. Do the customers see the company's prices as being in line or out of line with the perceived value of its offer?
3. Does the company use price promotions effectively?

Distribution
1. What are the distribution objectives and strategies?
2. Is there adequate market coverage and service?
3. Should the company consider changing its degree of reliance on distributors, sales reps, and direct selling?

Sales Force
1. What are the organization's sales force objectives?
2. Is the sales force large enough to accomplish the company's objectives?
3. Is the sales force organized along the proper principle(s) of specialization (territory, market, product)?
4. Does the sales force show high morale, ability, and effort? Are they sufficiently trained and incentivized?
5. Are the procedures adequate for setting quotas and evaluating performances?
6. How is the company's sales force perceived in relation to competitors' sales forces?

Advertising, Promotion, and Publicity
1. What are the organization's advertising objectives? Are they sound?

2. Is the right amount being spent on advertising? How is the budget determined?
3. Are the ad themes and copy effective? What do customers and the public think about the advertising?
4. Are the advertising media well chosen?
5. Is sales promotion used effectively?
6. Is there a well-conceived publicity program?

ENDNOTES

1. Many useful checklist questions for marketers are found in C. Eldridge, *The Management of the Marketing Function* (New York: Association of National Advertisers, 1967).
2. See P. Kotler, *Marketing Management Analysis, Planning and Control* (Englewood Cliffs, N.J.: Prentice-Hall, Inc., 1976), pp. 457–462.
3. See P. J. Stonich. "Zero-Base Planning—A Management Tool." *Managerial Planning*, July–August 1976, pp. 1–4.

SECTION D
Managing Market Information

Marketing planning and programs require information about the environmental forces, including customers, competitors, and regulation. This section is devoted to readings that address the issue of information gathering and information dissemination functions.

Although most organizations have access to market research information related to customers or competitors, it often is not organized around managerial marketing functions. The line management people feel frustrated and helpless despite availability of good information. It is, therefore, necessary to organize the market information in a way that will be directly relevant to managerial decisions. This is now referred to as the decision support system.

There are four types of marketing information needed to manage the various marketing functions. They are summarized in Figure 1.

The first type of marketing information is *diagnostic*. It requires taking the periodical or continuous pulse of the marketing environment, such as changing customer needs and composition or changing competitive structures. The most common research techniques are the digestion of public information and the use of syndicated services that monitor the marketplace.

The purpose of diagnostic information is to inform marketing managers of the emerging opportunities and threats created by environmental changes. For example, emergence of the dual-wage household, which has resulted in a time-poor, money-rich society, can become both an opportunity to introduce convenience products and services and a threat for time-consuming service industries, such as health care and financial services.

The second type of market information needed in the marketing organization is obtained by *testing*. Testing represents the feedback of preliminary ideas and concepts from the environment. Marketing managers plan to either capitalize on market opportunities or prepare themselves for emerging market threats. Testing includes research on new product concepts, new advertising campaigns, new pricing formulas, or new distribution arrangements.

Most testing research is experimental in nature and, therefore, requires experimental research techniques such as laboratory research, test panels, and test trials. The objective of test research is to narrow down large numbers of options to a manageable few for further strategy development. For example, there may be numerous color, shape, or size variations in designing a new product's packaging. Similarly, there may be several advertising copy and layout options that need to be reduced to a few manageable options for further development.

The third area of market information is *implementation*. It encompasses all the research activities associated with implementing new marketing programs and plans. These programs and plans include research on product quality control, regulatory requirements, physical distribution, service requirements, and sales and promotion budgets.

There is, unfortunately, only limited market research information related to this phase of strategic planning. Most of the research is either ad hoc or problem-solving in nature rather than ongoing. The research techniques most commonly useful for this are test markets and field tests.

The final marketing information relevant to managerial decisions is *tracking* information which is directly related to marketing control

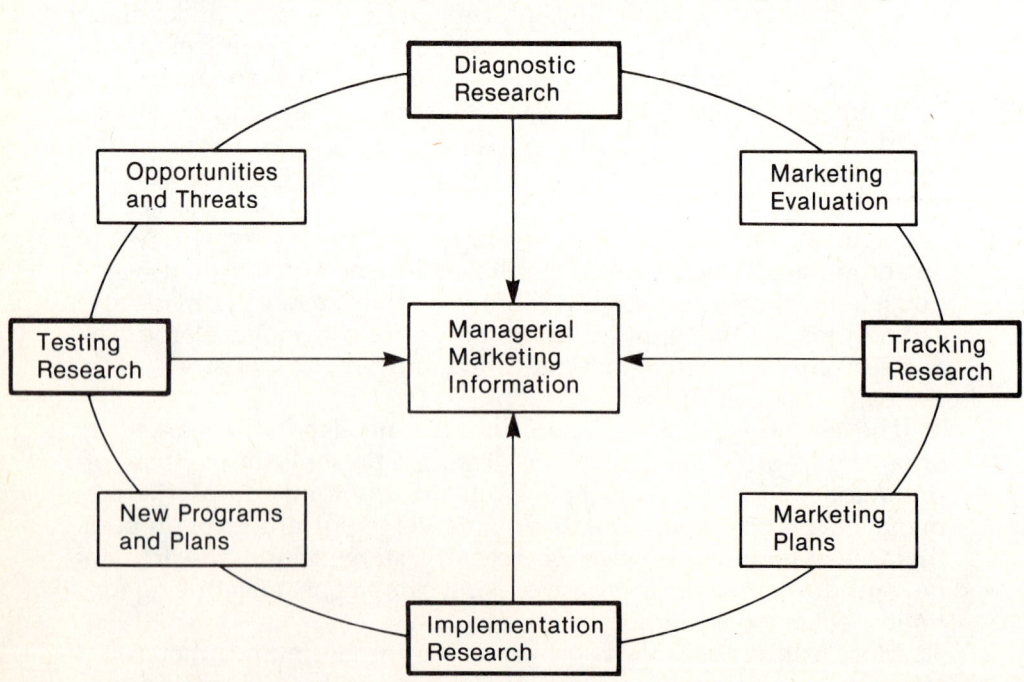

FIGURE 1. Marketing Information for Marketing Planning

and marketing productivity issues. It is often collected in order to assess how well the marketing organization is performing relative to expectations as well as competition. Tracking information is often used for sales compensation as well as executive compensation purposes.

Tracking research techniques include market surveys, competitive intelligence, and internal data analysis. Since tracking information is directly related to evaluating managerial performance, it is often numerical in nature. For example, most telephone companies survey their customers with respect to service changes, such as those for installing telephone lines or changing locations, by telephone calling on a statistical sampling basis. Customer perceptions about the way these services were performed becomes one of the bases for evaluating and rewarding the marketing services organization.

12 — Toward Strategic Intelligence Systems

*David B. Montgomery and
Charles B. Weinberg*

Reprinted from the *Journal of Marketing*, published by the American Marketing Association, Vol. 43 (Fall 1979), pp. 41–52. Reprinted by permission.

In the past 10 years, there has been a dramatic increase in the use of strategic planning tools such as BCG's growth/share matrix, AD Little's life cycle strategy, Shell's Directional Policy Matrix, and GE's stoplight strategy matrix. This has resulted from the much-needed perception by management that projecting yesteryear's trends into the future and then concentrating on day-to-day operating decisions is not enough for success. Strategic planning is rapidly being included in the definition of essential managerial tasks, and a tremendous amount of managerial interest has been focused on the techniques outlined above.

While this focus has been and should continue to be of great value, a critical point is often overlooked. *A strategic plan can be no better than the information on which it is based.* There has been little focus on strategic intelligence systems, the selection, gathering, and analysis of information needed for strategic planning. Yet it is obvious that without good market share information, a growth/share matrix will be unreliable, or that knowledge of a competitor's intentions can be the key determinant of a strategy.

This paper is designed first to present an overview of strategic intelligence systems (SIS) — their purpose and the kinds of information they gather. The second section discusses the collection of strategic intelligence. The final section provides a brief discussion of the analysis and processing of strategic intelligence.

Examples are provided describing different companies' approaches to SIS, based on a research project in which, in addition to an extensive literature review, more than 100 executives in over 30 companies were interviewed. Although corporate names need to be disguised, the firms interviewed come from a broad range of industries and in most cases had sales in excess of $100 million. These examples are not intended to add up to "the" one complete, integrated approach to be copied, but rather are illustrations and stimuli for thought.

STRATEGIC INTELLIGENCE SYSTEMS — AN OVERVIEW

Purposes

It is important that the design of a SIS consider the purposes for which it is intended. Some method is needed to avoid collecting vast quantities of meaningless data, while simultaneously preventing a focus so narrow that crucial information is missed. An understanding of the purposes of a SIS is helpful in achieving this aim.

Defensive intelligence is oriented towards avoiding surprises. A company plans and manages itself on the basis of certain implicit and explicit assumptions about the world. A properly designed SIS should monitor the world to make certain that these assumptions continue to hold and to send up a flag if a major change (usually a threat) occurs. In one company which desired to implement this mode of thinking, a policy was made that unanticipated "surprises" would not be accepted as a reason for not meeting a strategic business unit's (SBU) targets. The view taken was that if an event was potentially so important, the manager should have a SIS watching for it and would therefore be able to prepare contingency plans.

Passive intelligence is designed to provide benchmark data for objective evaluation. An example of this is Dayton-Hudson's gathering of competitive retailer performance in order to reward management performance on a basis relative to competition.

Offensive intelligence is designed to identify opportunities. Often opportunities that would not otherwise be discovered can be identified through a SIS. For example, one company's strategic intelligence indicated that a major competitor was laying off R&D people of a certain type during a recession. From this, the company knew that the competitor would be unable to respond on a timely basis to a certain class of research-generated product improvements. The company used this knowledge to justify current R&D expenditures which enabled it to capture market position when the competitor was weakest. Another example was when a company's intelligence system indicated that a competitor had a serious service problem. From its own previous experience, the company recognized this as an inventory investment problem and knew that it would take the competitor about two years to straighten out its problems. Armed with this knowledge, the company substantially increased its market share.

Areas of Focus

In order to accomplish the three purposes of defensive, passive, and offensive intelligence, a SIS should focus on the following environments.

Competitive

The competitive environment is of critical importance. However, a firm should not simply monitor its current competitors, but should scan the environment for potential competitors. The price of ignoring potential competitors and neglecting to take proactive steps to avoid or blunt their effect can be extremely high. For example, Scott Paper's preoccupation with acquisitions apparently diverted its attention from the threat posed by Procter & Gamble's potential and actual emergence as a substantial force in Scott's major paper markets (Hyatt and Coonly 1971).

Customers may also be potential competitors. One company which was heavily dependent upon a large customer analyzed that customer's incentives for backward integration. This analysis, triggered by an explicit requirement for contingency plans, suggested that, from the customer's viewpoint, backward integration was not in the customer's best interest. The next year, when the company's intelligence agents—its salespeople—learned about the customer's plans to integrate backward, the previous analysis was used to dissuade the customer from that course of action.

Technological

The technological environment is crucial not only because of its evolutionary impact on existing products but also because many innovations are introduced from outside a traditional industry—e.g., ball point pens, xerography, instant photography. Cooper and Schendel's (1976) study of 22 companies in seven industries (locomotives, vacuum receiving tubes, fountain pens, safety razors, fossil fuel boilers, propellers, and leather) found the first commercial introduction of an innovation occurred from outside the industry in four out of seven industries. The study further found that the old technologies did not decline immediately, but continued to expand in four out of the seven cases. In fact, it took anywhere from five to 14 years for the dollar volume of the new technology to exceed that of the old technology. The mode of penetration of the new technology tended to be the capturing of a series of submarkets. This study suggests that replacement technologies may emerge and develop even while companies engaged in the old technology are lulled into complacency by near term prosperity. From a strategic perspective, long-run survival requires at least a monitoring of emerging technology. In one company interviewed in our study, the corporate planning staff provides a list of emerging technologies and division managers then are required in their strategic plans to indicate the likely impact of these technologies upon their division. The purpose is not only to sensitize division managers, but the corporation as a whole to coming opportunities and threats.

Customer

Thorough analysis of a firm's customers and noncustomers is possibly the most valuable and most neglected area of strategic intelligence. Customer analysis means more than figuring out how to get Customer X to repeat or expand an order. Good customer and noncustomer analysis should reveal emerging technologies, competitive advantages and disadvantages, and new product ideas. Von Hippel's (1977) study of technological innovation in two industries found that in 74% of the 137 innovations studied, the source of the innovation was the supplier's customers. In these two industries, customers provided about three times as many new ideas as the company research departments.

Economic

The economic environment is of overriding importance to a company's future. Issues such as GNP, inflation, the money market, and interest rates are of obvious importance. Changes in the price of raw materials (e.g., oil) significantly affect most companies. It is also important to try to determine the secondary implications of these benchmark indicators. For example, a move towards balancing the federal budget may lower the amount of government-sponsored R&D forthcoming in a particular field. Government responses to continuing inflation, such as price and wage guidelines, should be anticipated and contingency plans prepared.

Examination of the effects of these issues on suppliers is also crucial. For example, many institutional food services on long-term, fixed price contracts have had profits severely hurt due to very sharp increases which their suppliers have imposed on certain products due to worldwide shortages.

Political and Regulatory

The political and regulatory environment is a difficult one as international companies are particularly aware. However, the increasing number of federal and state agencies which seek to impact on corporate policies, often with conflicting objectives, affects virtually all companies. In a recent survey of CEOs of the 1975 Fortune 500, government was cited as the number one area of concern (Burk 1976). Several companies such as Mobil and General Electric have adopted a proactive stance to try to improve the political climate within which private corporations must function (Ross 1976).

The fact that government agencies often do not correctly anticipate either the impact or the response to regulatory actions indicates the opportunity for a broadening of business/government contact. A recent example would be the FTC's de facto voiding (by unacceptable restrictions) the Bic purchase of American Safety Razor from Phillip Morris. The FTC rejected this acquisition on the grounds that it would be anticompetitive. This FTC action had been considered a remote possibility, and was apparently a surprise to the companies involved. Perhaps better intelligence would have identified the FTC as a potential major problem. Extensive advance briefing could have conceivably altered the outcome, or else the effort could have been abandoned before significant amounts of managerial time were expended.

Social

The final environment to be reviewed here relates to the rapidly changing social environment which has led to concerns with such issues as pollution control, conservation, and the rights of minorities. Again, appropriate intelligence may enable corporations to anticipate and react to such shifts in a more functional manner than has been typical of the past. As a case in point, GE claims that its environmental system led it to anticipate the emerging women's movement which enabled it to produce guidelines for women's employment one year ahead of the government (Wilson 1975). Anticipating social concerns generates a time advantage in which companies can provide positive, helpful input to government policy makers charged with establishing guidelines and regulations.

STRATEGIC INTELLIGENCE SYSTEMS IN THE STRATEGIC INTELLIGENCE CYCLE

Strategic intelligence systems can be seen as being part of the strategic intelligence cycle (see Figure 1). As mentioned above, most current work has been concerned with the latter stages of this cycle—processing and analysis, dissemination, and use. A SIS is essentially the feeder process to the analysis and use segments of the strategic intelligence cycle. The SIS performs two crucial functions, directing the intelligence function and collecting the information. This section will focus on these tasks.

Directing the Intelligence Function

This first stage of the intelligence cycle is concerned with establishing parameters for what information is needed, what priorities should be established, and what indicators should be monitored. Since a specific corporate application must account for idiosyncracies in the company's situation and its management style, the discussion in this section will not prescribe a formula, but rather will provide a broad outline of the issues and offer several specific illustrations.

Needs

There has been a substantial and praiseworthy increase in management's desires for environmental information. However, a word of caution is in order. The problem is not to generate data, but to determine what information is relevant and actionable. The emerging tools of strategic planning and analysis—product portfolios, competitive audits, etc.—provide a framework for ascertaining what information is needed and how it might be used if obtained. As the USE portion of the strategic intelligence cycle has become more sophisticated, the need for focused information also has increased.

A potentially useful framework for specifying information needs can be generated from the tripartite military paradigm of (1) areas of influence, (2) immediate zone, and (3) area of interest. The areas of influence would be the product/market segments in which the company is currently engaged. The immediate zone represents areas of competitive activity which are close to, but not directly competitive with, the company's current operations. The area of interest represents areas of potential opportunities or threats in the longer term. Generally there is less need for detail and a longer time horizon as the focus shifts outward from areas of influence.

Many companies fail to utilize available opportunities due to their exclusive concentration on their areas of influence and consequent lack of attention to their immediate zone and areas of interest. As an example of this kind of opportunity, Gillette noted that Bic, which had been a

FIGURE 1. The Intelligence Cycle

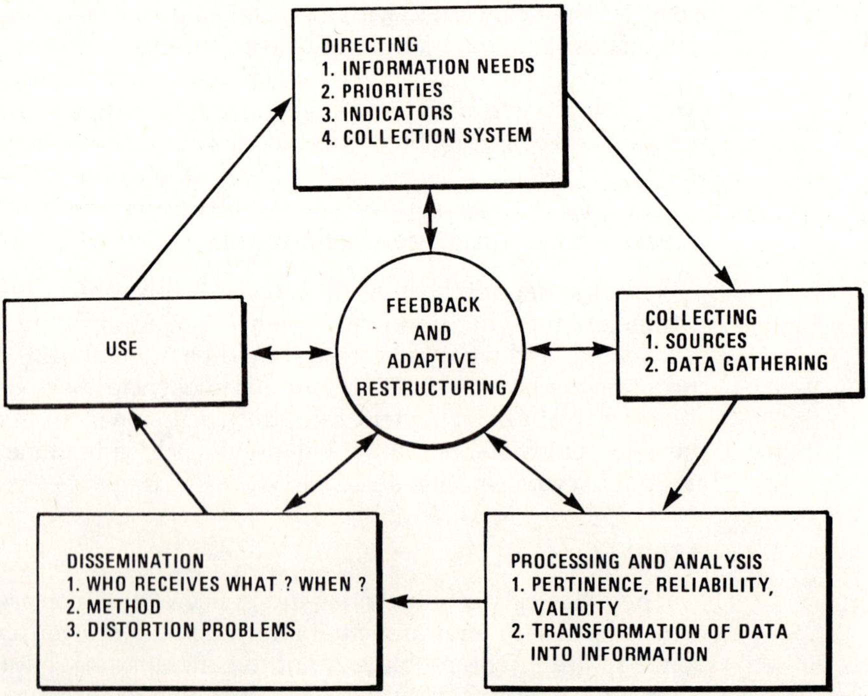

DIRECTING
1. INFORMATION NEEDS
2. PRIORITIES
3. INDICATORS
4. COLLECTION SYSTEM

USE

FEEDBACK AND ADAPTIVE RESTRUCTURING

COLLECTING
1. SOURCES
2. DATA GATHERING

DISSEMINATION
1. WHO RECEIVES WHAT? WHEN?
2. METHOD
3. DISTORTION PROBLEMS

PROCESSING AND ANALYSIS
1. PERTINENCE, RELIABILITY, VALIDITY
2. TRANSFORMATION OF DATA INTO INFORMATION

formidable competitor in the disposable lighter market, had pioneered disposable razors in Europe in 1975 (*Business Week*, Feb. 28, 1977). When Gillette learned that Bic had introduced the disposable razor in Canada in early 1976, it became clear that a major potential competitor was drawing near to the U.S. market. In response, Gillette rushed its "Good News" disposable razor into production and onto the national market in early 1976. Bic followed with U.S. test markets in mid-1976, but Gillette had apparently already paved the way for its dominance of this market. It is clear that by paying attention to its immediate zone and area of interest, Gillette was able to capitalize on an opportunity it would have lost had it only focused on its domestic markets.

Priorities

A useful conceptual approach to establishing priorities may be stated as follows:

$$\frac{\text{Importance of becoming}}{\text{aware of an event of interest}} = f(1. \text{ Importance of event to the organization.}$$
2. Speed with which the event can impact the organization.
3. Speed with which the organization can react to the event.)

Intelligence priorities should be established based upon (1) the importance of becoming aware of an event, (2) the likelihood the event will occur, and (3) the costs of anticipation and reaction. A SIS is justified if the costs of reacting to events exceed the costs of anticipating them and responding proactively. We believe that if companies were to carefully make such evaluations and trade-offs, then far more companies would attend to the development and nurturing of strategic intelligence systems.

Indicators

While a company might like to have some direct measures of a competitor's intentions, such measures are usually lacking. Hence firms must resort to using indicators or surrogate measures. For example, content analysis of corporate annual reports might be used in order to assess the extent to which a competitor's management is proactive or reactive in its approach to the world.

An indicator need not be unambiguous in its potential impact on the company. For example, if a competitor should make an unexpectedly low bid on a contract, this could be an indicator of one or more conditions such as: (1) the competitor's backlog is running dangerously low and he is getting desperate for work, (2) the persons in charge of the bid erred, or (3) the competitor has leap frogged existing technology. The indicator—an unusually low bid—may therefore relate to a variety of true states, each of which has substantially different strategic implications for the company.

Collecting Intelligence

Intelligence collection entails the notion of scanning the environments of a company in search of data which individually or collectively will provide decision relevant inputs to the firm.

Scanning can be subdivided into two subcomponents: surveillance and search. Surveillance is a viewing and monitoring function which does not focus upon a single target or objective, but rather observes multiple aspects of the environment being scanned in an effort to detect relevant changes. In contrast, search implies deliberate investigation and research. The detection of significant events in the environment by surveillance will often trigger a search for further answers. To illustrate, one of the companies interviewed learned, through its conventional competitive surveillance activities (e.g., attending to articles and announcements concerning competitors in the business press), that a major competitor had sold a particular manufacturing operation. Since the company knew from its own operations that this manufacturing activity was the most profitable portion of its own vertically integrated chain of activities, the question arose as to why the competitor had sold this operation. Two potential reasons seemed apparent: (1) the competitor, a closely held company, was in a serious cash bind and was forced to sell this profitable operation in order to improve its financial position or (2) the competitor had made a breakthrough that would render the sold technology either obsolete or at least substantially less valuable. Set against the background of data the company had, both answers seemed plausible. Learning the true answer had important strategic significance. If done for financial reasons, this could signal either competitor vulnerability or a reduction in his vulnerability depending upon the results of a further investigation. On the other hand, if the competitor had made some technological breakthroughs, then the company could no longer assume a stable environment. Clearly early resolution of these uncertainties was required. This example illustrates how a signal detected by the surveillance function of scanning can lead to questions which require search to answer.

There is some empirical evidence indicating that scanning can be beneficial. In his analysis of a contingency theory of strategy formulation, Miller (1975) concludes that successful firms tend to use more scanning. Or, to view the situation conversely, Schendel, Patten, and Riggs's (1976) study of corporate turn-around strategies in some 54 companies concluded that the original downturn typically resulted from the failure of the firm's scanning or management control procedure to identify more than one or two of the major problems confronting the firm. Thus, there can be both upscale reward and downside risk attached to environmental scanning. These results are consistent with Grinyer and Norburn's (1975) study which found that higher financial performance was positively associated with the use of more informal channels of communication and with the number of items of information used in reaching decisions.

Sources of Intelligence

Legitimate sources of intelligence are in abundant supply for the manager and company willing to apply imagination and effort in structuring a strategic intelligence system. Table 1 illustrates primary sources of intelligence along with selected examples of each. While it would be of doubtful value for any given company to pursue all sources on a continuing basis, a company should review a wide range of potential sources before choosing which one to use. The text will highlight some of the sources in Table 1 and examples of their use. Hopefully this will suggest the possibilities available to management.

Federal Government. A significant recent development has been the emergence of the federal government as a source of strategic intelligence.[1] While the government has long been a source of commercially relevant information, recent amendments to the Freedom of Information Act (FOIA) have greatly expanded the potential role of the government as an intelligence source. The 1966 FOIA was amended in 1974 in order to give it greater force. The amended Act provides that any person has the right of access to and can obtain copies of any document, file, or other record in the possession of any federal agency or department. To limit noncompliance by delay, the amended FOIA provides that requests must either be granted or denied within 10 working days in most cases. Nine specific discretionary exemptions are provided in the amended Act; exemption 4, which exempts "trade secrets and commercial or financial information obtained from a person and privileged or confidential," is of the greatest interest from the standpoint of corporate FOIA use.

It should be emphasized that the exemptions may be used at the discretion of the agency in question. Further, if the government is to use the exemptions to protect information, it must prove, if challenged, that the requested information is confidential and that its disclosure would result in substantial competitive injury to the company which originally supplied the information or would impair the agency's ability to obtain future information. Recent practice illustrates reluctance by some agencies to invoke the discretionary exemptions. For example, in response to FOIA requests, the Securities and Exchange Commission plans to release illegal or dubious payments information which had been volun-

TABLE 1. Sources of Intelligence

Source	Examples	Comment
Government	Freedom of Information Act Government Contract Administration	1974 amendments have led to accelerating use. Examination of competitor's bids and documentation may reveal competitor's technology and indicate his costs and bidding philosophy.
	Patent filings	Belgium and Italy publish patent applications shortly after they are filed. Some companies (e.g., pharmaceutical) patent their mistakes in order to confuse their competitors.
Competitors	Annual reports and 10Ks	FTC and SEC line of business reporting requirements will render this source more useful in the future.
	Speeches and public announcements of competitor's officers.	Reveal management philosophy, priorities, and self-evaluation systems.
	Products	Systematic analysis of a competitor's products via back engineering may reveal the competitor's technology and enable the company to monitor changes in the competitor's engineering and assembly operations. Forecasts of a competitor's sales may often be made from observing his serial numbers over time.
	Employment ads	May suggest the technical and marketing directions in which a competitor is headed.
	Consultants	For example, if a competitor has retained Boston Consulting, then portfolio management strategies become more likely.
Suppliers	Banks, advertising agencies, public relations firms, and direct mailers and catalogers, as well as hard goods suppliers.	Have a tendency to be more talkative than competitors since the information transmitted may enhance supplier's business. Can be effective sources of information on such items as competitor's equipment installations and on what retail competitors are already carrying certain product lines. Suppliers biases can usually be recognized.
	Purchasing Agents	Generally regarded as self serving. Low reliability as a source.
Customers	Customer engineers and corporate officers	Valued sources of intelligence. One company taught its salespersons to perform elementary service for customers in order to get the salespersons past the purchasing agent and on to the more valued sources of intelligence.
Professional Associations and Meetings	Scientific and technical society meetings, management association meetings	Examine competitor's products, research and development, and management approach as revealed in displays, brochures, scientific papers, and speeches.
Company Personnel	Executives, sales force, engineers and scientists, purchasing agents	Sensitize them to the need for intelligence and train them to recognize and transmit to the proper organizational location relevant intelligence which comes to their attention.
Other Sources	Consultants, management service companies, and the media	Wide variety of special purpose and syndicated reports available.

tarily supplied by companies after a promise of confidentiality. Another example of this tendency to release information is the FTC's decision to make material submitted by a defendant publicly available whenever hearings are held on proposed consent decrees in antitrust or consumer protection actions.

In the years since the FOIA amendments have taken effect, business has made increasing use of the FOIA as an intelligence source. The experience of Air Cruisers Co. illustrates both the threats and opportunities provided by the amended FOIA. In August 1975, Air Cruisers received Federal Aviation Administration (FAA) approval of its design for a 42-person inflatable life raft for commercial aircraft. As the largest raft ever to gain FAA approval, it constituted a substantial competitive advantage to Air Cruisers. Six months later, Air Cruisers learned that the FAA was about to release an 18-inch high stack of confidential technical documents to a competitor, Switlik Parachute Company, which had made an FOIA request for the documents. The material included results of performance tests and construction designs, which would enable Switlik to shortcut costly design, testing, and certification procedures. While Air Cruisers was able to block the FAA from releasing all of the data, it had to accept the release of some documents. This information helped Switlik design its own large raft with which it defeated Air Cruisers in a contest for an important European contract.

Additional examples abound. Consider the following which provide some notion of the breadth and type of competitive information potentially available from government agencies and departments under FOIA requests:

- A Washington, D.C. lawyer, presumably on behalf of a rival drug company, obtained an FDA inspector's report on conditions in the Midwestern plant of a large pharmaceutical company. It included such useful trade secrets as a description of proposed new products, manufacturing capabilities, and sterilization procedures at the inspected plant.
- Crown Zellerbach requested all FTC information on the Procter & Gamble announcement that "New White Cloud bathroom tissue is the softest bathroom tissue on earth. We have been called on to prove this claim by the United States Government and have."
- Westinghouse received from the Department of Commerce 10 reports which had been paid for and submitted by other corporations on how Japanese nontariff barriers hurt sales in Japan.
- Both Honeywell and Burroughs requested details of an $8 million Interior Department contract with Control Data Corporation.

Further evidence of substantial business use of FOIA may be found at the FTC and the FDA. In the nearly eight years between the July 1967 effective date of the original FOIA and the February 1975 effective date for the amendments, the FTC is estimated to have received less than 1,000 FOIA requests with 10% coming from business. Requests reached this same level, in the first 18 months after the amendments took effect, with almost 20% coming from business. To be sure, these figures understate total business use of FOIA because the original source of a request can often be masked by having attorneys and FOIA service companies make the direct request of a government agency. Nevertheless, the above usage data underscore the impact of the 1974 amendments on the functioning of the FOIA.

The agency with one of the largest volumes of FOIA requests and a substantial share from business is the FDA. In 1974, 2,000 FOIA requests were received by the FDA. The volume exploded to 13,052 in 1975, the year in which the amendments took effect, and doubled in 1976 to nearly 22,000. Over 70% of all requests were from industry or FOIA service companies. One reason for this rapid growth has been this agency's liberal interpretation of the FOIA.

While a substantial amount of business use has been made of the FOIA, the potential has just begun to be realized. Although corporate attorneys often claim that their managers know about the operation of the Act (usually because the attorneys had circulated a memo about it), field research indicated that only a tiny minority of managers were at all well informed about the Act and its managerial significance. Managers must be made aware of both the opportunities and inherent threats in the FOIA. The opportunities for learning about competitors are amply illustrated in the above examples. On the other hand, it is imperative that managers become aware of just how vulnerable their own confidential data are when in the hands of the government. Companies should plan in advance, as part of any submission of confidential data to the government, for the defense of such data against a FOIA request from a competitor for these data. Not to do so will increasingly expose a company to the prospect of meeting a 10 working day deadline in which it must convince an agency not to release the company's data. So whether for offensive or defensive purposes, companies must learn to live with and utilize the FOIA as a source of strategic intelligence.

The amended FOIA along with the Sunshine Laws which took effect in March 1977 have broader strategic implications than competitive intelligence. Together they have the potential to reduce the uncertainty which plagues business and government relations by more fully opening government decision processes to outside scrutiny. As discussed earlier, this potential is particularly important because the CEOs of Fortune's 500 indicated that government is their most troublesome area.

Competitors. A second major source of strategic intelligence is competitors themselves. Use of strategic planning tools such as one of the variants of product portfolio analysis helps management focus on critical strategy issues. Some of the most important of these issues relate to the incentives and opportunities facing various competitors and their financial and managerial capacities for carrying out alternative strategies. In a very real sense, the introduction of these strategic planning tools has raised a host of questions relating to competitive response and reaction. A variety of intelligence sources are available for addressing such questions. Annual reports and 10Ks may provide considerable insight into the philosophy and management capability of a competitor as well as his financial capabilities and technological and product plans. For example, GE was stimulated to take a careful look at solid state controls on washers and dryers as a result of having seen both Whirlpool and Hitachi mention these devices in their annual reports (Allen 1978). The FTC and SEC requirements for line of business reporting should greatly enrich annual reports and 10Ks as a source of intelligence. Further, a careful perusal of the footnote to a competitor's annual report may reveal, for example, pension obligations which will drastically impact the ability of a competitor to respond flexibly.

The priorities and self-evaluation systems of a competitor may also be revealed by public announcements and speeches as well as in 10Ks and annual reports. Presidents often cannot resist the opportunity to "brag," and in so doing may reveal much about the firm's growth objectives, investment strategy, trade-offs between long-term and short-term results, and product/market policies. The advantage of knowing a competitor's personality was underlined in the field study at one company. This company knew that one of its major competitors tended to be extremely inconsistent in its marketing activities. This knowledge enabled the company to avoid overreaction to any one of the competitor's scattered moves.

Much valuable competitive intelligence may be gleaned from scanning a competitor's personnel activities. For example, if technical personnel of a given type are being laid off, this can be indicative of the competitor's intentions and capabilities in that technical area. A company who observes a competitor taking such action may have an excellent opportunity to gain a technical and marketing edge on that competitor, as was discussed earlier. On the other hand, analysis of a competitor's employment ads may tell a great deal about that competitor's future plans. There is some evidence that such an approach may be valuable. In one case, an outside team was assigned to monitor the personnel ads of a company for one month. At the end of the month, the team reported on what they thought was going on. Not only were they accurate in most cases, but they spotted three problems in production and quality control which the firm's own top management didn't even know existed.

Own Personnel. A company's own personnel can be invaluable sources of intelligence if they have been trained to be receptive to intelligence and if they are encouraged to transmit the intelligence to appropriate organizational locations. Sales call reports which explicitly encourage reporting of intelligence and debriefing reports submitted by scientists and engineers upon return from professional meetings are two of the more common methods used. In many instances, a firm's purchasing agents may play a key role in intelligence acquisition. The key issue in tapping this internal source is to sensitize personnel to the need for intelligence, train them to recognize it, and reward them for transmitting it. In this area, the firm should bear in mind Pasteur's statement that "...chance favors the prepared mind."

In summary, most firms have a large number of potential intelligence sources. Some of these are common and widely used, such as trade association data, but others, such as studies of competitor's want ads, may be less so. The proper choice of intelligence sources depends not only upon the data that it provides, but also how it interrelates with other aspects of the company's strategic intelligence system.

ANALYSIS AND PROCESSING OF STRATEGIC INTELLIGENCE

A firm and its managers use a variety of approaches to combine, sort, and process the environmental *data* in order to produce timely and relevant *information* for forming, monitoring, evaluating, and modifying strategy. The strategic data management problem is complicated by the considerable emphasis placed on personal communications by senior managers. For example, Rohlf and Wish (1974) found that managers spend an average of six hours a day in personal or telephone communications. Further, the unstructured nature of many strategic decisions, especially in the problem finding state, increases the difficulty of transforming data into strategic information.

Despite these difficulties, the process of intelligence derivation is a critical one in the formulation of strategies. After data are generated or enter the system, they should be evaluated. The formal evaluation of data, although frequently carried out in military intelligence systems, appears to be rarely done by business.

Evaluation of Data

Evaluation includes determining the pertinence, reliability, and validity (accuracy) of data obtained. Evaluation of pertinence can include pertinence to a number of people in the organization and specifically determines if the data are relevant to the company, if needed immediately, and, if so, by whom.

Reliability is an evaluation of the source or agency by which the data are gathered or transmitted. The principal basis for judging reliability is previous experience with a source. This is particularly relevant for businesses which use such recurrent sources as the sales force, security analysts, and suppliers. Although it would seem that a "track record" of these sources can be built up over time, for example, to identify the biases of salesmen in reporting only certain events or in being overly optimistic, such practices were rarely observed in the field interviews. It should be noted that suppliers recognize that they are being used as a source of data and try to draw a line between "providing something of value, but not too much."

Validity or accuracy means the probable truth of the data itself. Methods for assessing validity include comparison with other data which may be available from other sources, searching for associated indicators, and face validity. For example, in a long-term policy study for the Environmental Protection Agency, 16 different futures studies were reviewed in a fixed format as one approach to convergent validity (Elgin, MacMichael, and Schwartz 1975).

Transformation of Data into Information

The six transformation functions—transmission, accumulation, aggregation, analysis, pattern recognition, and mixing—by which data can become information vary considerably in complexity (See Table 2). Although the six functions overlap, each has at its core a distinctive transformation. Obviously, the functions do not necessarily occur sequentially and can occur at several levels in an organization.

Transmission

Transmission, conceptually a very simple notion, is the movement of data from one point or person in the organization to another. Transmission can also occur simultaneously with some of the other processing functions. However, data which are received through many corporate entry points are often not communicated to those who can use them most effectively. In consequence, transmission should be at least conceptually considered as a separate function. Companies need to develop methods to facilitate ("force") the transmission of information by providing incentives for the reporting of certain types of information or by providing ways for a manager to know the information needs of others.

Accumulation

Accumulation is the storage of data in such a way that it can be retrieved by the managers in a company. A substantial data base provides a source from which the organization can learn about itself and its environment. This is particularly true when attempting to resolve un-

TABLE 2. Six Transformation Functions

Name	Description	Brief Examples
1. Transmission	1. Moving data from one point to another	1a) Manager in one company who receives information personally or by telephone from line managers and distributes information personally or by weekly newsletters 1b) Highly mechanized interactive computer system to make data base reachable by numerous managers
2. Accumulation	2. Storing data in one place; implies some notion of retrievability	2a) Corporate libraries or computer systems 2b) Not frequently observed in practice, managers tend to keep data in their heads or in individualized data bases ("little black book")
3. Aggregation	3. Many data points brought together into a smaller set which is usually more easily accessed.	3a) Use of computer program to reduce thick Nielsen reports to much shorter documents 3b) Page length limitation on planning documents
4. Analysis	4. The analysis, usually formal, of data in order to seek and measure relations	4a) Use of econometric consulting firms to provide forecasts of the economy 4b) Use of Shell's Directional Policy Matrix to locate businesses for a portfolio analysis
5. Mix	5. Passing of data around to a variety of managers looking for possible links. The data is often not well ordered	5a) CEO insists on plans which show multiple inputs at each phase 5b) Open planning meetings in which managers must give and defend plans before colleagues
6. Pattern Recognition	6. A more informal, less analytic process than analysis (4) in which patterns or relations are sought. Can be a result of the other five functions described	6a) Combining plant closing, financial and product change information to recognize a competitor is short of cash 6b) Special purpose competitor studies & role playing or the use of adversary teams

structured strategic problems, for which information needs are difficult to define beforehand.

The field interviews revealed limited amounts of accumulation of strategic environmental data. Several reasons explain why this accumulation does not take place. First, because the data often originate from the personal sources of a manager, the effort required to record it and enter it into a more formal and permanent system may not seem worthwhile, especially for "soft data." The remedies would seem to be easing the transmission process and increasing the rewards. In one company, the central collector receives data varying from rumors to documented facts by telephone or in person. The central collector then alerts line managers on an individual basis of particularly significant events, publishes a weekly newsletter, prepares special reports, and maintains files on competitors. There are substantial behavioral advantages to this system. The managers do not fill out forms, they input data verbally and are rewarded, in turn, by receiving pertinent information.

Second, information accumulation may not take place because managers do not think the system works well. For instance, computer-based systems often concentrate on the easily quantified factors in formats which reflect the needs of accounting systems rather than those of operating or strategy managers.

Third, managers may have incentives for not wanting others to have their full data set. In a corporate budgeting system, a manager may be able to present plans which maximize his or her capital allocation or limit his or her performance goals based on his or her unique knowledge of the data.

One consumer durables manufacturer has a particularly interesting central collection system based on a substantial disaggregated data base which includes such factors as factory shipments, survey data on consumer habits, and construction reports. The system is unique because rather than distribution of a large number of reports (as had been done in the past), the main way to use it is for managers to visit the central facility, which is located in the marketing department. The location was chosen to provide user access and the overall style is casual and user oriented to create an environment "painless and pleasant for the harried marketing executive" (from a company brochure).

Aggregation

Aggregation is the function in which many data points are collapsed into a smaller set of pertinent information. It is the first of the functions in which something is done to the data beyond making it available to managers. Summarization of environmental data occurs in virtually all companies, although with various degrees of care and attention. Given the massive amounts of data potentially available and a manager's limited time for reviewing information, aggregation is a vital function.

Corporate staff groups are often responsible for the summarization of economic trends. In a relatively smaller number of companies, social, political, and regulatory factors are summarized as well. Thus, on a macro or corporate level, summarization or aggregation of data takes place. However, only limited aggregation of environmental data, especially competitive data, was observed on a SBU or product-market basis except as part of the annual planning process or, in a few cases, when special purpose competitive assessment reports were made.

Analysis

The analysis of data is a formal process which attempts to find and measure relations among variables. Although at times it may draw heavily on mathematics and numeric procedures, it is a logical and not a mathematical process. A number of companies employ econometric consulting firms and others do similar work on their own. Many consumer goods companies employ analytical approaches to measure relationships between sales and marketing mix variables. In several companies, the main focus of analysis is on predicting industry capacity.

The level of analysis of environmental data varies extensively across companies. For example, in some companies, competitive balance sheets are used primarily as a benchmark or "scoreboard" to rate the company as compared to its competition. In others, it is used more aggressively to anticipate threats or provide opportunities. As an illustration, when one company noticed that a competitor was highly leveraged and consequently would be unable to finance new product development, it gained considerable market share by improving its own product.

Pattern Recognition

Pattern recognition, although not as structured or formal as the analysis process just discussed, also attempts to find patterns or relations among variables. Human abilities to perceive and determine patterns among disparate sets of information and data are the critical distinctive elements in the process of pattern recognition. Although computerized systems can be of great assistance, in strategic analysis the "lack of simple alpha-numeric indicators, combined with enormous textural complexity, suggests that [pattern recognition]...will not be trivial or automatic in the foreseeable future" (Webb 1969, p. 10). An example of pattern recognition occurred in one company when the information that a competitor was closing a plant and changing his product line was combined with balance sheet analysis to realize that the competitor was short of cash. This, of course, left the competitor vulnerable to a number of aggressive strategies. The generation and use of in-depth competitive assessment reports, the preparation of strategy documents from the viewpoint of a major competitor, and the formation of in-house competitor teams exemplify different organizational approaches to pattern recognition.

Mixing

The unstructured and often unstable nature of strategic problems requires that an additional transformation function be defined which brings together the apparently unrelated data spread throughout an organization in order to identify linkages. This function is termed "mixing."

A somewhat analogous notion is Cohen, March, and Olsen's (1972) garbage can model. In that conceptualization, an organization is conceived of as a collection of problems and solutions in which organizational members find ways either to enrich the collection of problems and solutions or to find links between the problems and solutions. The approach formulated here emphasizes two major factors. First, problems and solutions are viewed as being dynamic so that "windows" as to when linkages can be established are limited. Thus, problems and opportunities should be viewed as moving through a container rather than residing in a collection. Second, an active approach can be taken to ensure that problems and solutions are actively interchanged or mixed within an organization.

Companies appear to use a variety of techniques to force mixing including participative planning meetings across divisions and organizational levels, weekly senior executive sessions with invited presentations, and rejection of plans which do not reflect mixing. For example, in one company, the CEO rejected divisional plans out of hand because they did not show any evidence of interaction across divisions. In another, marketing managers were asked to write the finance plan, financial managers were asked to write the production plan, etc. In large companies, facing a broad variety of strategic options, mixing can help the company to become aware of the range of opportunities and threats facing it and to develop synergistic responses.

SUMMARY AND PERSPECTIVES

As more organizations implement strategic planning and management activities, there will be an increasing need for strategic intelligence systems which can help managers to learn about the important environments with which their organization interrelates and to become aware of threats and opportunities that are posed.

The construction of viable strategic intelligence systems is exceedingly complex because of the unstructured nature of strategic decisions, the difficulty of separating out important and relevant information from the vast amounts of data accessible to the manager, and the reliance of managers on personal information sources. As would be expected, in most of the companies interviewed tactical information systems were better articulated than strategic ones. On the other hand, a number of companies have developed effective means of learning about their environments and, most importantly, have implemented strategic decision systems which allow them to capitalize on opportunities and to defend themselves against threats. This article has developed a framework for examining intelligence systems which is sensitive to the character of the strategic process.

For a strategic intelligence system to be useful, a company must have a real commitment to strategic planning. Otherwise, the planning process, if carried out at all, becomes only an exercise and managers appear to place limited effort towards gathering and communicating accurate, relevant intelligence. There are a number of different organizational policies which can be utilized to promote the transformation of data into information and the utilization of this information. Elaboration on this issue is beyond the scope of this article. However, only in rare circumstances do effective intelligence systems emerge without organizational incentives to encourage their operation.

There appear to be a number of asymmetries in managers' perceptions about information collection. Four, in particular, stand out. (1) Companies tend to believe that their competitors nearly always detect and rapidly decide how to respond to company actions such as a price change. This perception persists in spite of knowledge of substantial delays in their own detection and response decision time in reacting to the competitors. This can lead a company to recind prematurely an effort to lead a price increase based upon a belief competitors won't follow, when in fact the lack of response by the competitor may merely be symptomatic of a poor and slow intelligence system. (2) The government is viewed as an extensive collector of information, but not as a source; the discussion of the FOIA indicated how companies could access data held by the government. (3) Conversely to the case of the government, suppliers are more often viewed as a source of information about competitors than as a source to the competitors. (4) Companies send engineers and managers to meetings with instructions to gather more information than they reveal; it would seem unlikely for this outcome to occur for all companies involved. These asymmetries, which obviously are not shared by all managers, suggest some of the potential available from a review of an organization's procedures to gather and process strategic data.

Information systems are a means to an end — decision making which leads to more profitable results. The concepts and structures for strategic intelligence systems discussed in this article are designed to help organizations make more profitable strategic decisions.

ENDNOTE

1. The following discussion of the Freedom of Information Act is based on Montgomery, Peters, and Weinberg (1978).

REFERENCES

Allen, Michael G. (1978), "Strategic Planning With a Competitive Focus," *The McKinsey Quarterly* (Autumn), 2–13.

Burk, Charles G. (1976), "A Group Profile of the Fortune 500 Chief Executives," *Fortune*, 19 (May), 173.

Business Week (1977), "Gillette: After the Diversification that Failed," (February 28), 58.

Cohen, Michael D., James G. March, and Johan P. Olsen (1972), "A Garbage Can Model of Organizational Choice," *Administrative Science Quarterly* (March), 1.

Cooper, A. C. and D. Schendel (1976), "Strategic Responses to Technological Threats," *Business Horizons*, 19 (February), 61.

Elgin, D. S., D. C. MacMichael, and P. Schwartz (1975), "Alternative Futures for Environmental Policy Planning: 1975–2000," Environmental Protection Agency (October).

Grinyer, P. H. and D. Norburn (1975), "Planning for Existing Markets: Perceptions of Executives and Financial Performance," *Journal of the Royal Statistical Society A*, 138 (Part 1), 70.

Hyatt, J. and J. Coonly (1971), "How Procter & Gamble Put the Big Squeeze on Scott Paper Company," *The Wall Street Journal* (October 20), 1.

Miller, D. (1975), "Toward a Contingency Theory of Strategy Formulation," paper presented at 35th annual Academy of Management Meeting (August).

Montgomery, David B., Anne H. Peters, and Charles B. Weinberg (1978), "The Freedom of Information Act: Strategic Opportunities and Threats," *Sloan Management Review*, 19 (Winter), 1–13.

Rohlf, J. and M. Wish (1974), "Analysis of Demand for Video Communication," Telecommunication Policy Research Conference, Airlie, Virginia (April 18).

Ross, I. (1976), "Public Relations Isn't Kid Gloves Stuff at Mobil," *Fortune*, 93 (September), 106.

Schendel, D. E., G. R. Patten, and J. Riggs (1976), "Corporate Turnaround Strategies: A Study of Profit, Decline, and Recovery," *Journal of General Management*, 3 (Spring), 3.

von Hippel, E. (1977), "Has a Customer Already Developed Your Next Product?" *Sloan Management Review*, 18 (Winter), 63.

Webb, Eugene J. (1969), "Individual and Organizational Forces Influencing the Interpretation of Indicators," unpublished working paper, Stanford: Graduate School of Business, Stanford University (April), 10.

Wilson, I. (1975), "Does GE Really Plan Better," *MBA*, 9 (November), 42.

13 — Decision Support Systems for Marketing Managers

John D. C. Little

Reprinted from the *Journal of Marketing*, published by the American Marketing Association, Vol. 43 (Summer 1979), pp. 9–26. Reprinted by permission.

The combination of large potential payoffs, highly motivated professional staffs, evolving OR/MS techniques, and rising computer power is making an impact on marketing management. A problem-solving technology is emerging that consists of people, knowledge, software, and hardware successfully wired into the management process. Following Gorry and Scott Morton (1971), we shall call the set of facilitating tools a decision support system or, more specifically a *Marketing Decision Support System* (MDSS). Intellectual contributions to MDSS have come from many disciplines: OR/MS, marketing research, computer science, behavioral science, and statistics, to name a few. We view the results collectively as an advance in management science or, more specifically marketing science. Our purpose is to define and illustrate the concept of an MDSS and show its effects on marketing practice.

What Is It? A Black Box View

A manager takes action with respect to an environment in order to achieve the objectives of his organization. To do this he must perceive and interpret the market, even if imperfectly. Then he must think up strategies, analyze them, and converge on one to put into practice. This process is conducted through a complicated system of people, paper, and machines. We call the inanimate part of this an MDSS. Figure 1, modified from Montgomery and Urban (1969), shows the MDSS and its components and traces their roles in interpreting and analyzing the environment.

Data Bank. A stream of information comes into the organization from the world at large in many ways: from members of the organization; from talking to people; from reading the *Wall Street Journal*; from purchasing market research; and especially from distilling the multitude of individual transactions of the business—orders, shipments, purchases, records of internal action, and much more. The data are stored in varied forms: on paper, in people's heads, and, most relevant for our present purposes, in large chunks on machine readable media. The amount of

FIGURE 1. A Manager Uses a Marketing Decision Support System (MDSS) to Learn About the Business Environment and Take Action with Respect to It

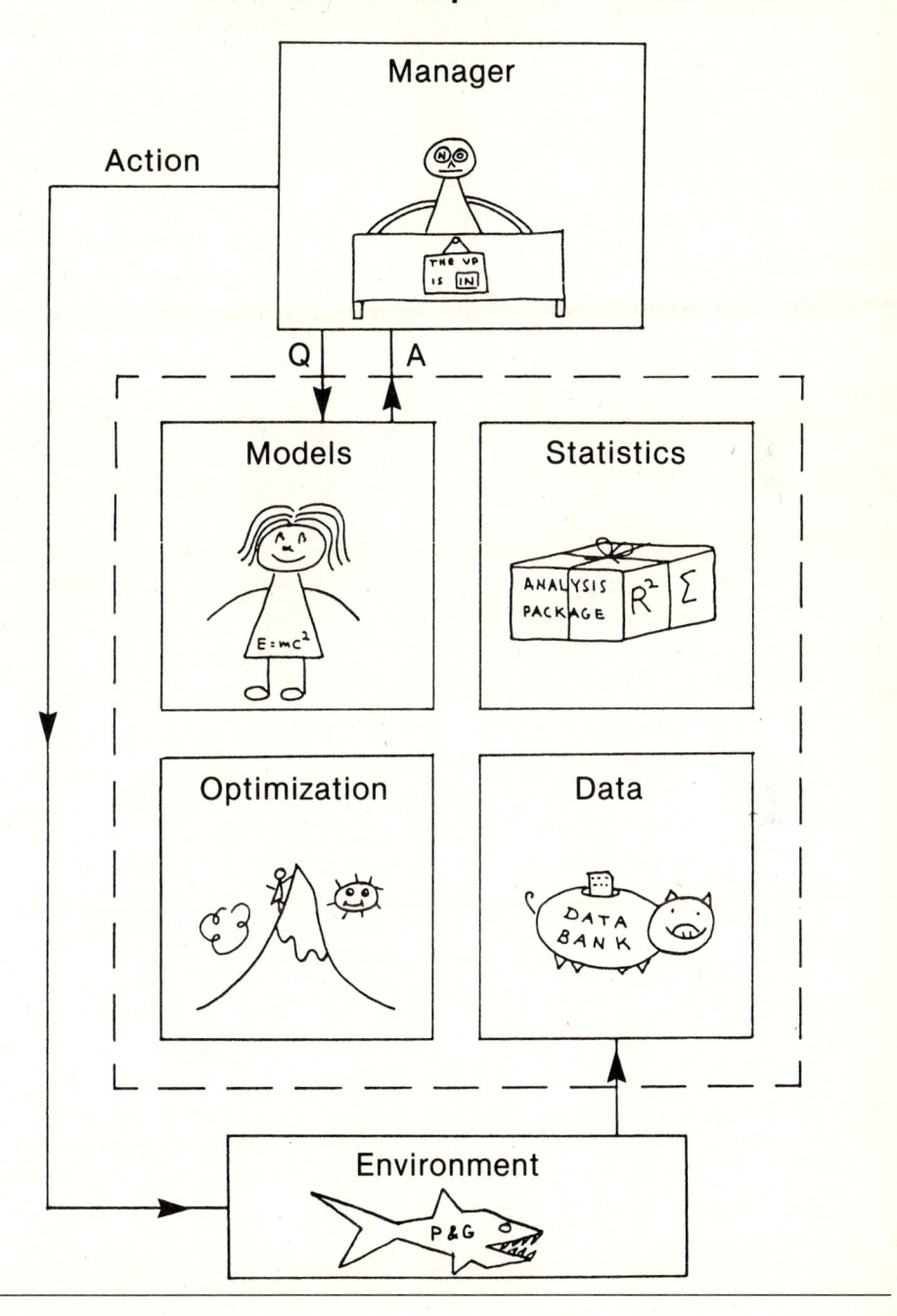

data handled by a large company is staggering. Business runs on numbers. Sales alone have vast detail, and might, for example, be broken out by time period, market area, brand, package size, salesperson, and customer. How did people get along before computers? (Quite well, thank you, but they missed many profit opportunities open to us now.)

Less obvious than the flood of data washing over companies is the information they do *not* have. Often they may have it in principle, but not in practice. For example, I recently asked a large and successful company for the following data, which they could not supply: product category sales by month and major market area, competitive advertising, and even more surprising, the company's own promotional spending by market area. At another company, I once sought advertising expenditures by month, but they could only be provided in terms of when the bills were paid, not when the advertising was run. This was not too helpful for marketing analysis. Certain data are simply not gathered, others are aggregated and the original detail lost or prohibitively costly to recover. Competitive data usually comes from syndicated services as hard copy which is inadequate for any, but the most aggregate analysis.

Clearly, a basic task of any MDSS is to capture major marketing variables such as sales, advertising, promotion, and price in reasonable detail and truly accessible form. Remarkably few companies do an adequate job today. The issue is cost and therefore value, since data for data's sake is a worthless luxury. It takes skillful analysis and effective coupling with management to provide the benefits that justify the cost, but the payback can be large.

Models. Whenever a manager (or anybody else) looks at data, he or she has a preconceived idea of how the world works and therefore of what is interesting and worthwhile in the data. We shall call such ideas *models*. Even a person who is browsing through tables has a set of constructs in mind that signal when a particular number is important and worth further consideration. Thus, a manager or management scientist uses theories to determine what aggregations or manipulations are meaningful for the decision at hand. The data user may want to confirm or disprove a hypothesis, guide an action, or learn the magnitude of a past number so as to judge the reasonableness of a current one. Manipulation of the numbers may cause an old theory to be discarded and a new one created to conform better to the facts.

Some models remain in people's heads, but the ones of most interest here are those that find explicit mathematical and computational representation. These aid planning, decision making, and many less publicized supporting tasks required for understanding and analyzing the market.

Statistics. We shall call the process of relating models to data *statistics*. The most important statistical operation is addition. This makes big important numbers out of small, trivial ones. Many sophisticated techniques also are available for model and hypothesis testing and they often prove useful. However, it is not widely realized, except by those with their hands on the data, that most frequent operations are basic ones like segregating numbers into groups, aggregating them, taking ratios, making comparisons, picking out exceptional cases, plotting, tabulating summaries, etc. These manipulations are required by such standard managerial models as proforma profit and loss statements, budgeting, and forecasting, to say nothing of more complicated models for new product tracking, marketing-mix planning, and the like.

Optimization. A manager constantly seeks to improve the performance of his organization. Abstractly this is optimization. The most frequent operations are deceptively simple: calculating two numbers and seeing which is larger, ranking a set of numbers, or sorting a set of alternatives into categories of effectiveness. In addition, there are many cases where formal OR/MS optimization methods such as linear programming and its extensions offer substantial payoffs.

Q/A. Finally, the manager and his or her staff must communicate with the system. Insofar as the required skills, talent, and information are distributed throughout the organization, communication involves the standard processes of meetings, studies, and reports. As the systems become formal and automated, some of the communication takes place through interactive time-shared computing. Individual tools are stored as computer programs. With the right software, data and files pass easily between analyses, and a management scientist or other person can perform a wide scope of analysis smoothly, quickly, and efficiently.

To summarize, a marketing decision support system is a coordinated collection of data, systems, tools, and techniques with supporting software and hardware by which an organization gathers and interprets relevant information from business and environment and turns it into a basis for marketing action.

THE CRITICS

We have described the concept, but what about the practice? Management science has its critics. Let's see what C. Jackson Grayson, Jr. (1973), says in the *Harvard Business Review*. Grayson, a Harvard DBA, author of a book applying decision analysis to oil drilling decisions, former dean of a business school, and currently head of a productivity institute, writes:

> Management Science has grown so remote from and unmindful of the conditions of "live" management that it has abdicated its usability.

We would like to dismiss this as an isolated complaint, not likely to be repeated. But wait, let's see what John D.C. Little (1970), professor of Operations Research and Management at M.I.T., says in *Management Science*:

> The big problem with management science models is that managers practically never use them.

This situation must be serious! On close examination, however, Grayson's article and mine are quite different in content and tone. Grayson reports that in the most important administrative role of his career (Chairman of the U.S. Price Commission), he found no use for his management science training. He goes on to describe managers generally as confused and dissatisfied with management science activities in their organizations and admonishes management scientists and managers to build bridges to each other. One can hardly advocate that they should not, but this proposal seems patronizing at best and indicates an ignorance of a great deal of useful work that has gone on.

My own paper, written three years earlier, sought to draw on a variety of practical experiences to describe "how-to-do-it" in building useful models. By 1970 much had been learned, sometimes by painful trial and error, about doing OR/MS successfully in business and government. Regrettably, good applications often lie concealed because little incentive exists for their revelation and, worse yet, strong forces favor secrecy. Fortunately, studies are beginning to appear more regularly. (See for example, the prize paper issues of *Interfaces*, Nigam, 1975, 1976, 1977.)

OR/MS practitioners and marketing researchers have continued to learn what works and what does not. This paper tries to report some of this.

———— How an MDSS Works. A True Story ————

The Marketing Manager, the Management Scientist and the MBA

Once upon a time (1973), an MBA student took a summer job with a large food manufacturer. He reported to a management scientist in the principal division of the company. The MBA was assigned to put key marketing information, basically store audit data, on a time-shared computer. The goal was an easy-to-use retrieval system, essentially the DATA box of Figure 1.

O.K. He did this.

By the end of the summer, word of the system had reached the marketing manager of the major product of the division who asked for a demonstration and so the three met. The MBA and the management scientist showed the marketing manager how simple, English-like commands could retrieve data items: sales, share, price, distribution level, etc., each by brand, package size, and month.

The marketing manager was impressed. "You must be fantastically smart," he told the MBA. "The people downstairs in MIS have been trying to do this for years and they haven't gotten anywhere. You did it in a summer."

It was hard for the MBA to reject this assessment out of hand, but he did acknowledge, and this is a key point, that the software world had changed. There are now high level analytic languages available on time-sharing that make it easy to bring up data and start working on it right away.

The MBA and the management scientist, flushed with success, now said to the marketing manager: "O.K. Ask us anything!" (Famous last words.)

The marketing manager thought a minute and said: "I'd like to know how much the competition's introduction of a 40 oz. package in Los Angeles cut into the sales of our 16 oz. package."

The MBA and the management scientist looked at each other in dismay. What they realized right away, and what you might too if you think about it, is that there isn't going to be any number in the machine for sales that *didn't* occur. This isn't a *retrieval* question at all, its an *analysis* question.

Here then is another point. The marketing manager had no idea the number would not be in the machine. To him it was just one more fact no different in his mind from other facts about the market. Notice also that the question is a reasonable one. One can visualize a whole string of managerial acts that might be triggered by the answer, possibly even culminating in the introduction of a new package by the company.

What is needed to answer the question is a *model*, probably a rather simple model. For example, one might extrapolate previous share and use it to estimate the sales that would have happened without the competitor's introduction. Then subtraction of actual sales would give the loss.

The three discussed possible assumptions for a few minutes and agreed on how to approach the problem. Then the management scientist typed in one line of high level commands. Out came the result, expressed in dollars, cases, and share points.

The marketing manager thought the answer was fine, a good demonstration. The MBA and the management scientist thought it was a miracle! They had responded to the question with a speed and accuracy unthinkable a few months earlier.

The story is simple but contains several important lessons. I see the same points coming up again and again in various organizations, although not always so neatly and concisely:

- *Managers ask for analysis not retrieval*. Sometimes retrieval questions come up of course, but most often the answers to important questions require nontrivial manipulation of stored data. Knowing this tells us much about the kind of software required for an MDSS. For example, a data base management system is not enough.
- *Good data are vital*. If you haven't done your homework and put key data on the system you are nowhere. Thus, a powerful analytic language alone is not enough.
- *You need models*. These are often simple, but not always. Some can be prepackaged. Many are ad hoc.
- *The management scientist is an intermediary*. He connects the manager to the MDSS. The manager does not use the system directly. The management scientist interprets questions, formulates problems in cooperation with the manager, creates models, and uses them to answer questions and analyze issues.
- *Quick, quick, quick*. If you can answer people's questions right away, you will affect their thinking. If you cannot, they will make their decisions without you and go on to something else.
- *Muscular software cuts out programmers*. New high-level languages on time-sharing permit a management scientist or recently trained MBA to bring up systems and do analyses singlehandedly. This makes for efficient problem-solving. Furthermore, the problem-solver identifies with and deals directly with marketing mangement so that his understanding and motivation are high. Time-sharing costs more than batch processing, but an army of programmers is eliminated and, far more important, problems get solved on time.

DECISION SUPPORT FOR THE PRODUCT LIFE CYCLE: CRADLE TO GRAVE CARE

Let's look at marketing per se. Over the past 10 or 15 years and continuing unabated, there has evolved from diverse origins a series of tools and techniques for support of the product life cycle.

By product life cycle we mean a sequence of conveniently defined stages that describe the history of a product from conception to possible demise. We do not imply that every product goes through every stage or that any stage lasts some prescribed length of time.

The product life cycle is illustrated in Figure 2. A product starts as someone's bright *idea*, thereby identifying a category. The idea then goes through a stage of concept and product *development and evaluation*, leading to a detailed design and market position. Development and evalua-

FIGURE 2. Marketing Scientists Have Developed Models and Measurements to Support Almost Every Stage of the Product Life Cycle

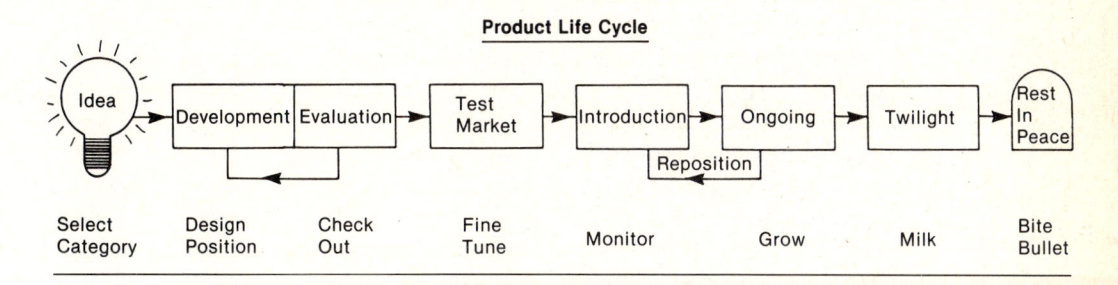

Product Life Cycle

Idea → Development | Evaluation → Test Market → Introduction → Ongoing → Twilight → Rest In Peace
                                                                  ← Reposition

| Select Category | Design Position | Check Out | Fine Tune | Monitor | Grow | Milk | Bite Bullet |

tion are closely linked; at various times during development, evaluations of greater or lesser depth will be made and the results fed back to refocus development.

The next step is usually *test market*, although an industrial product will not ordinarily have this step. Then comes national *introduction*. In the *ongoing* stage, the product becomes, one hopes, an established and profitable business. From time to time a product may go through a thorough revamping or "reintroduction." Many at some point go into a *twilight* of obsolescence (the slide rule and the mechanical watch seem headed this way). Finally many products including quite a few former household names, go out of existence entirely. The tombstone in Figure 2 might read: "Chrysler Imperial: 1926–1975, died at age 49 of sales starvation."

The mortality of new products has traditionally been notorious. For example, General Foods reported in *Business Week* (1973) a 15 year history in which 83% of new products did not get out of the idea stage. Of those that did, 60% never reached test market; of those entering test market, 59% failed; and even among those making it to national introduction, 25% were considered financial failures. At the same time, new product introduction is very expensive. For a typical package good of a major manufacturer, the development and evaluation stage might cost $150,000; a test market, $1 million; a national introduction, $5–10 million. A new industrial product would omit the test market expense, but might well spend an equivalent amount on development and evaluation.

Responding to the challenge of the heavy expenses and high profit aspirations of new products, marketing scientists have developed an array of methodologies and measurements to support decision making at various stages of the life cycle.

At the *idea and category selection* stage, systematic search procedures drawn from behavioral science supplement traditional inspiration. Focus groups (Cox, Higginbotham, and Burton 1976) probe customer feelings about needs and perceptions. "Synectics" (Prince 1972) is a technique where by a group of people seek to solve a problem in an organized way, e.g., conceive of a product to meet a specified set of customers' needs. As demonstrated by von Hippel (1978) customers themselves are an important source of industrial product ideas. Industrial and governmental data on potential markets suggest new product opportunities. Environmental scanning can turn up danger spots for existing products and needs for new ones.

The bulk of the new techniques, however, begins to come into play at the next stage: *development and evaluation*. Value-in-use analysis (Gross 1977) looks at a product from the customer's point of view and asks: "What advantages are there to the customer from using this product? What cost savings? What time savings? What investment would be required to achieve this savings?" By answering such questions for each potential market segment, an aggregate picture of volume versus price can be synthesized.

A particularly well-articulated description of a formal new product design, development, and positioning methodology is that of Hauser and Urban (1977). Their normative design process envisages first finding out the customer's words for talking about the product category. This might be done through focus groups. Then, customer words are developed into psychometric scales. Potential customers use these scales to rate new and existing products in the category. As customers do this, they also express preferences among the products and so generate data that can be analyzed to identify the customers' key utility dimensions. Such information permits the calibration of a model of new product share and sales. A feedback loop between model and manager facilitates the modification of the product and its market position.

Other tools fit in at this stage of the life cycle, some within the Hauser-Urban framework. These include mapping studies, conjoint measurement, and consumer choice models. Mapping is a general term to describe the visual representation of competitive products relative to each other in a space of consumer perceptual dimensions. Conjoint measurement (Green and Wind 1975) presents alternative product features to customers in order to obtain their trade-offs and build new products with high market potential. Consumer choice models (Shocker and Srinivasan 1977; Hauser 1978) relate choice to consumer utility or preference.

A particularly successful blend of models, measurements, and statistical techniques has emerged for *pretest market evaluation*. The best example is Silk and Urban's ASSESSOR (1978). In their method, people passing through a shopping mall are invited to participate in a marketing study. They view competing advertising commercials including one for the new product under test, and then have an opportunity to select a brand from a shelf display containing the new product. Data are taken by questionnaire during the process and later a telephone call-back determines the customer's likelihood of repurchasing. This type of careful orchestration of psychometric scaling, consumer choice models, trial-repeat purchase models, and statistical calibration has proven extremely useful to marketers of package goods and holds the promise of extension to new areas, e.g., pharmaceuticals and small durables.

As we move on to *test marketing* and *national introduction*, the techniques change. The principal tools become trial-repeat models calibrated by store audits, ad hoc surveys, and consumer diary panels. The task is to follow the buildup of consumer trial and repurchase and project to future sales and share. Parfitt and Collins (1968) provide a simple model and Urban (1970) in SPRINTER a comprehensive model for doing this. As pretest market evaluations increasingly eliminate costly failures, test marketing becomes more of a fine-tuning for the marketing mix than a go/no-go test. Therefore, new product tracking models that contain major control variables become most useful.

At the *established brand stage*, the picture changes again. Ongoing brands frequently take a back seat as new products consume managerial attention. Yet for many companies, this is a mistake since major profit opportunities often lie with the old breadwinners. Market response analyses assisted by marketing-mix models like Little's (1975) BRAND AID or Bloom and Stewart's (1977) MAPLAMOD harness major control variables such as price, promotion, and advertising for strategy planning and permit tracking predicted versus actual sales. Discrepancies lead to diagnosis of market problems. Econometric analysis of historical data (Parsons and Schultz 1976; Bass and Clarke 1972) can help calibrate such models. Consumer panel analyses like those of Ehrenberg (1972) can detect customer purchase shifts. Individual models of price, promotion, and advertising are frequently useful for specific tactical problems.

The basic information sources are also different in the ongoing stage since product management relies more heavily on continuing data: factory shipments; promotions reports; advertising expenses; and syndicated services such as store audits, warehouse withdrawals, and consumer panels. These services are well developed in consumer package goods, spotty in consumer durables, and almost absent in industrial markets.

The *twilight* or obsolescence stage also has attracted effort. For example, Hess (1967) discusses the pricing of new and old products when the new is destined to supplant the old. The final phasing out of a product from a product line is studied as part of product portfolio analyses (Day 1977).

Thus every part of the product life cycle has generated marketing science activity. Some efforts are more extensive and more successful than others in affecting practice, but it is clear that changes are afoot.

Marketing Science: Who Is Kidding Whom?

I like to use the term "marketing science." However, the phrase makes some people flinch and others stir restlessly. Is what we have described an advance in fundamental understanding or is it merely a series of commercial fads? Can we sensibly talk about science in a flamboyant field where the motivation and funding are so far from the usual domain of the natural philosopher? I shall argue that we are indeed engaged in science.

First, it should be observed that most of the actors on the marketing stage are *not* scientists. Many are skillful performing artists and very successful, but not scientists any more than, say, a sculptor is. But when a sculptor hammers a chisel into a piece of marble, he initiates a process that is well described by the laws of physics. In marketing we are not so far along.

Are we anywhere? Natural science is concerned with understanding how the world works. This means models and measurements, the twin engines of scientific advance. Models provide structure for describing phenomena and permit knowledge to be more than an encyclopedia of facts. Measurements separate good models from bad and allow good ones to be calibrated for practical application. It seems obvious that you can make a scientific study of any observable phenomenon and that we are certainly doing that on many occasions in marketing.

Whereas understanding is the province of science, application is the domain of technology. Common usage expands science to cover both. (Thus: "Science put men on the moon, why can't it cure the common cold?") The dividing line is blurred and we shall follow the common usage, but identify understanding as the essential ingredient of science.

Two characteristics of marketing practice tend to obscure accomplishments in fundamental understanding. First, application regularly oversteps knowledge, a situation that makes for confusion, since truths are often proclaimed that are not true. I used to read articles in the business press about marketing successes and marvel that people knew so much more about their markets than I was able to discover by analysis. Eventually I realized that the authors were using different standards of knowing. What was being written reflected the fact that businessmen often make good decisions with relatively poor information. As part of the process, they usually make assertive statements whether or not they possess firm knowledge. In any case, businessmen much prefer to have knowledge and would like us to give it to them wherever possible.

The second point is that, because so much marketing data collection, analysis, and model building is bent toward specific decisions, underlying discoveries are frequently the spinoff of the application, rather than the reverse. On the way to solving a practical problem, people often develop new understanding. This certainly isn't novel in science—probability, for example, was born at the gaming tables. Not all marketing studies produce scientific knowledge—most are not done nearly carefully enough—but the potential is there and sometimes the realization. The marketing papers appearing in *Management Science, Operations Research*, and *Journal of Marketing Research* over the past 15 years demonstrate the quality of the work and the vitality of the field.

Thus, we view marketing science as real. It is an applications-driven subject that is building a base of understanding about marketing processes.

Measurements

Measurements are contact points with reality, they generate the excitement of new discovery and practical payoff more often than models. Companies pay a great deal for measurements. Syndicated services in store audits, diary panels, media ratings, and the like constitute at least a $200 million industry per year in the United States. Ad hoc surveys, copy tests, etc., reach a comparable dollar magnitude.

Measurements motivated by theories and models are most valuable. For example, Figure 3 shows the results of an advertising test. Sales are plotted versus time before, during, and after a heavy-up of advertising.

The results are striking. Notice the rapid rise, leveling off, and slow decay. The data cry out for a theory—and more measurement. Why do sales go up quickly and down slowly? What would happen if the same test were repeated in the same areas a year later? Clearly Figure 3 has strong policy implications. It appears that much more profit was generated by removing the heavy advertising after six months than would have occurred by continuing it. This is because decay was so slow. However, to determine an optimal, or even a sensible, policy requires a theory of what is going on. This will expose the assumptions that must be made to turn these measurements into decisions. Clearly, there is no shortage of practical and scientific questions here.

The experiment just described was a project within a marketing decision support operation of a large package goods company. Management asked for the experiment because of concern over advertising budget levels. The sales data used were captured routinely from external syndicated sources and internal company records. Company management scientists analyzed the results using a high level language and wielding a variety of standard and nonstandard statistical tools.

Whenever new measurement technologies appear, they create special opportunities for learning how the world works. Figure 4 shows data of the type that are becoming available through automated checkout equipment in grocery stores. Shown is *daily* market share of two brands of a package good in a supermarket. The bumps are promotions. The speed and precision with which the promotion effect can be read are portentous. Here is an indicator of opportunities for new knowledge that will become possible in the near future.

Models

Models form the other half of the models and measurements team of natural science. They provide theories that seek to bring order to the chaos of collected facts. They are much less well understood by laypeople and, indeed, the word is used in enough different ways by professionals that its meaning is often unclear.

For present purposes, I shall define a model as a mathematical description of how something works. Once upon a time, in a simpler age, scientists thought they were discovering the laws of nature; thus in physics we find Ohm's law, Newton's laws, and the like. Unfortunately, as people subjected these laws to closer and closer examination, they often found unsettling imperfections. These frequently led not to outright rejection, but to deeper, more comprehensive theory. A famous

FIGURE 3. Sales Went up Quickly Under Increased Advertising, but Declined Slowly After It Was Removed. Sales Are Measured as the Ratio of Sales in Test Areas to Sales in Control Areas Not Receiving the Heavy Advertising

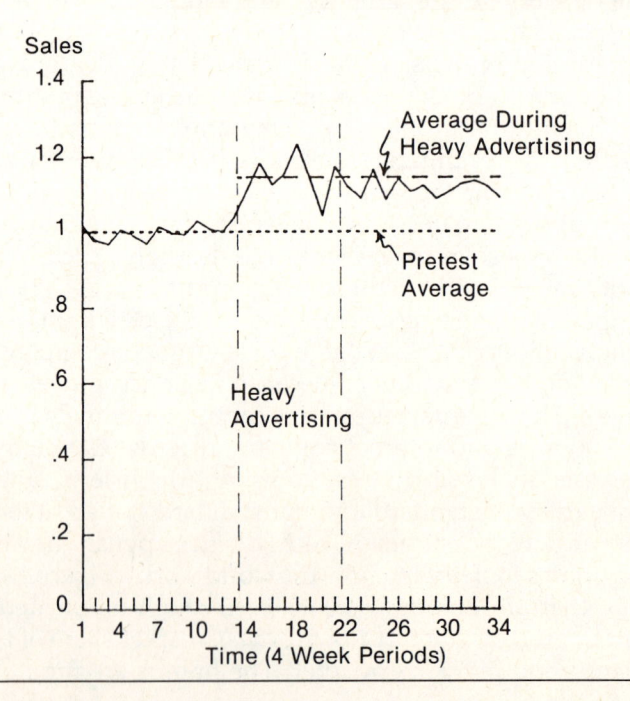

example is Einstein's generalization of Newtonian mechanics through relativity. However, after enough incidents like this, physical scientists became more cautious and often describe their theories as models. In more recent times, as social and management scientists have sought to develop mathematical understanding of their worlds, they have entertained few illusions about the exactness of their representations. Consequently, they have readily taken up the term.

There is an important practical advantage to the incompleteness implied by the word model. Consider the construction of a model to help solve a marketing problem. We would wish it to include all the important marketing phenomena required to analyze the problem, but, equally, we would wish it to exclude extraneous complication. This incompleteness

FIGURE 4. Daily Market Shares of Two National Brands in a Supermarket Chain Clearly Show the Effect of Store Specials. Data Was Collected on Electronic Checkout Equipment

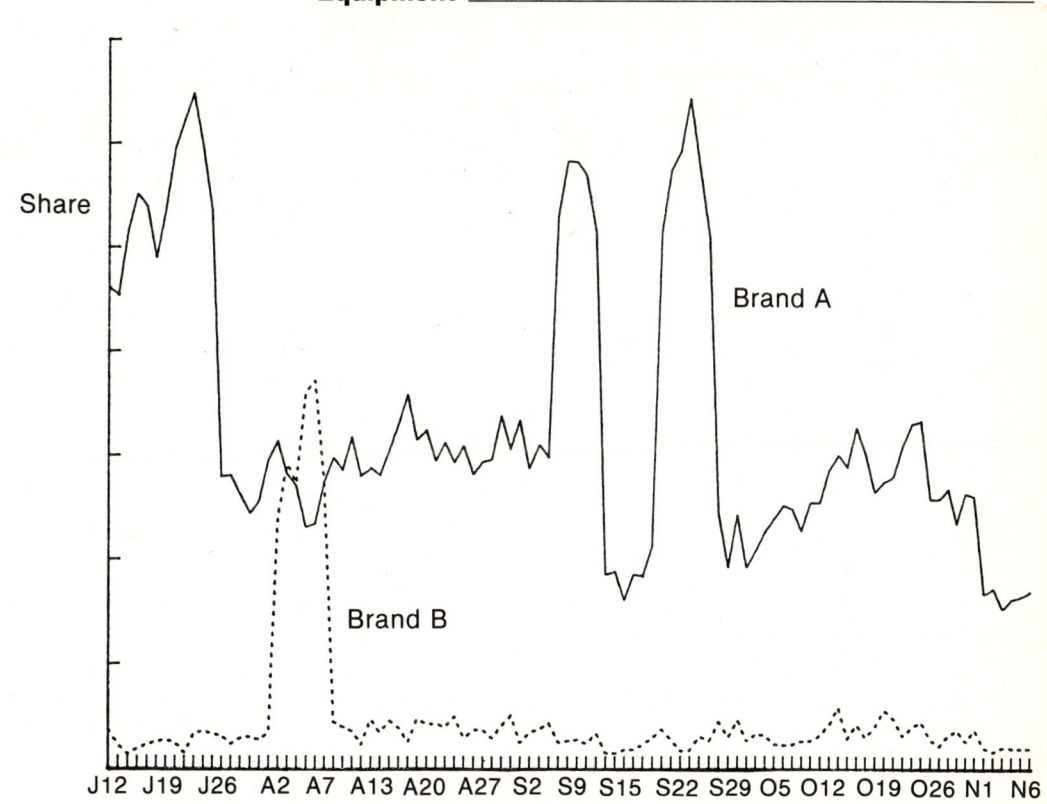

is important and desirable. Managers, however, are sometimes nervous about it; they conceive that science is exact (even though science and especially engineering abound with approximations). If a model is full of art, managers become wary. They say art is just what they were trying to get rid of by hiring expensive, overeducated terminal thumpers.

As something of a corroboration of this mind-set, we observe that consulting firms which say they have discovered "laws of marketing" have sometimes had remarkable success with high levels of management.

Managers use models all the time but without the name. Successful management scientists working with managers often deemphasize the word, using models as required for the job but communicating the results as ideas and phenomena, going into detail as requested. One important development in this direction should be noted by those complainers who say models are not used in practice. Management scientists imbed models into problem-solving systems where the models themselves are relatively inconspicuous because they are only a part of the final product. Silk and Urban's (1978) ASSESSOR for evaluating new products is a good example. It employs high technology consumer choice models and statistical calibration, yet the manager-client focuses on the output and its message for his product. A similar situation arises in the models used for audience exposure analysis of advertising media schedules (research and frequency studies). In such cases the client company should, and frequently does, treat the analytic system like any other industrial product and perform a technical evaluation of it before using it routinely.

I would like to distinguish between *model* and *procedure*. If you allocate the advertising budget to major markets proportional to last year's sales in those markets, you have specified a procedure. Implicit in the procedure may or may not be a model. For example, if you hypothesize that advertising response is proportional to last year's sales times a suitably chosen function of advertising dollars, then you can construct a model of market response that will yield as the optimal budget allocation the same results as the described procedure.

Thus a *procedure is a way of calculating a result; a model is a set of assumptions about how something works*. Managers frequently use procedures, usually based in part on implicit intuitive models. Management scientists devise procedures directly, but often try to develop and calibrate explicit models which will generate good procedures.

In my simple world, I like to distinguish between two types of models: good and bad. Bad models include those that are simply wrong. For example, a model with a linear relationship between sales and advertising has to be incorrect. Other models are vacuous. The symbols may not really be defined or the model may merely be a formalistic way of saying something obvious that is better said simply. Still other models are so extraordinarily elaborate that they collapse of their own weight as data and calibration requirements become so enormous that testing and calibration are infeasible.

We have lived through many bad marketing models and, if we are to continue to progress, we will have to live through many more. At least we have good models, too. Fortunately, it is a characteristic of science that once you discover something worthwhile you can use it from then on and make it a building block for continued progress.

Three types of good models are: (1) small models offering insight and structure for thinking, (2) general structures permitting the synthesis of a variety of phenomena, and (3) models of new phenomena. Without trying to cover the whole field, I shall illustrate each of these types.

Small Models Offering Insight. The customer flow model displayed in Figure 5 has very much affected people's thinking about new products in the past 15 years. Here is the basic proposition: A new product has some intended set of customers, called its target market. Suppose we have developed an inexpensive gyrocompass for recreational vehicles. Recreational vehicle owners are the *target population*. Before any of them can possibly buy the product they have to be *aware* of it. A company can inform people about the existence of a new product by advertising and, in fact, any advertising agency can produce a reasonable estimate of how much money it will take to do this. For some number of millions of dollars, for example, you can teach 20% of the American public your brand name.

But people cannot buy the product unless it is available. This is a distribution problem. Assuming a company is marketing somewhat similar goods, it will know the appropriate distribution channels and will be able to tell what kind of availability can be achieved for the product.

Once a person in the target market is aware of the product and has a place to buy it, the next question is will that person *try* the product, i.e., buy it once? Involved here is the success of advertising in communicating the product's attributes to the prospective customer and how the customer evaluates the desirability of those attributes. Reasonable estimates can usually be made of trial probability. In some categories of package goods, historical norms are now available. You can also make more refined estimates by taking field measurements with the actual product. Note, however, that even without this, and long before the product has even been made, estimates based on historical norms or managerial judgments will permit useful market calculations.

Given that a person has tried the product, the next question is whether he or she will *repeat* the purchase the next time such a product is needed. Alternatively the customer may *switch* to another brand. Provided that reasonable estimates of switching and repeating probabilities can be made, we can calculate the share of purchases going to the new product among people who try it once.

A straightforward calculation puts together the whole sequence: the number of people in the target market *times* the fraction who become aware of the product *times* the fraction who find it available *times* the fraction of those who try it *times* the share of purchases that triers devote to the new brand *times* the sales rate for the product class, determines the sales rate of the new product.

The notions of awareness, availability, trial, repeat, and switching are fundamental. These processes are obviously going on. The model can be

FIGURE 5. A Simple Customer Flow Model Provides a Mathematical Structure for Estimating Future Sales of a New Product

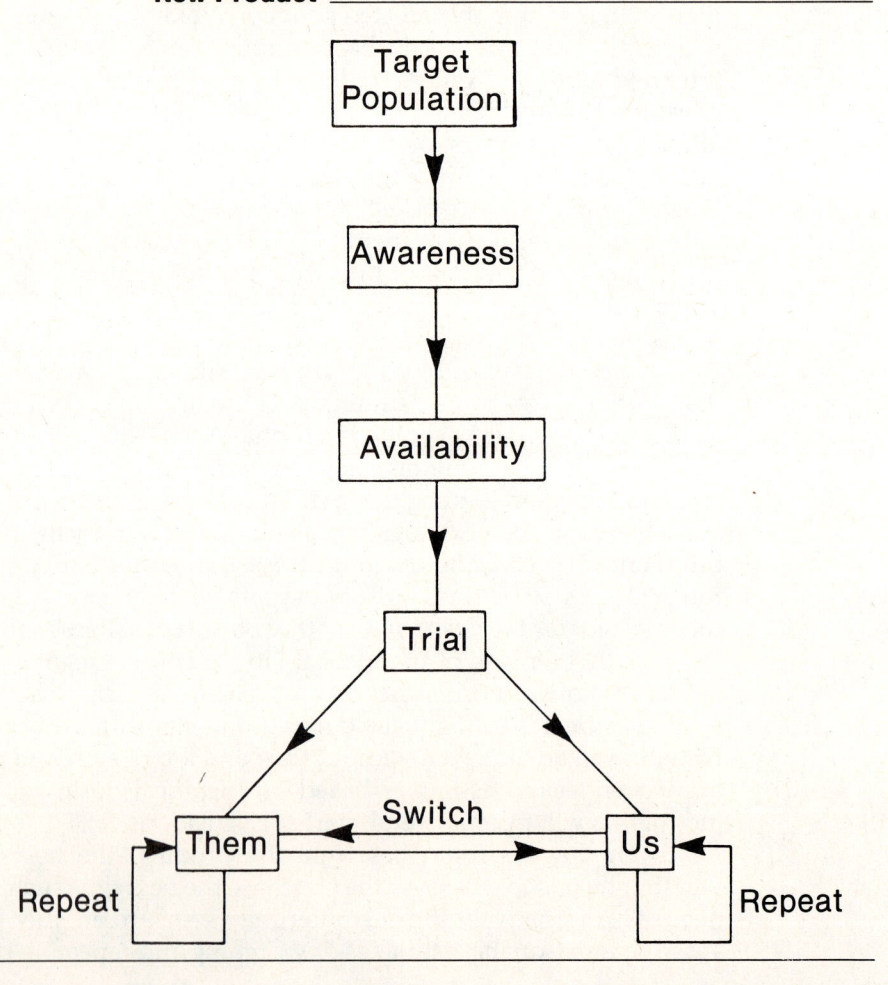

made very elaborate (see Urban 1970), but the basic conceptual structure and the process described above for calculating long-run sales rate are exceedingly simple.

The quality of that calculation will depend on the quality of the inputs, but just using sensible numbers helps keep the new product manager from becoming a total dreamer. Every new product manager is a wild advocate for his or her product. Probably this is necessary since most new products fail and somebody has to be a believer to keep from giving up before starting. The prehistoric way to estimate new product sales was to declare a final number in one judgmental swoop. Amazingly, the number usually turned out to be exactly that value which would justify continuing the development. The discipline of putting plausible numbers into the above calculation restricts answers to a believable range. Then, as the company goes through the new product development sequence, increasing investments in field measurements narrow the uncertainty in the final sales.

Models for Synthesis. Another useful type of model provides a structure for assembling measurements and phenomena from a variety of sources to solve a given problem. An example is the marketing-mix model BRANDAID (Little 1975). BRANDAID, when appropriately calibrated for a product of interest, relates brand sales and profit to major marketing control variables, competitive actions, and environmental influences. The structure is modular so that marketing effects can be added or deleted to suit the application. Each effect is a submodel which can be designed separately. Major control variables such as price, promotion, and advertising are premodeled, but custom versions can be substituted if desired. The number of geographic regions and competitors is flexible, from one to whatever patience will permit.

Model calibration makes the general structure specific to a particular application. Historical data, field experiments, econometric analysis, and whatever else may prove useful are used to develop values for model parameters so that the model becomes a suitable representation of a given market.

Usually a few key variables account for most of the effects on sales. Figures 6 and 7 show an application employing four submodels. The submodel outputs are plotted in Figure 6. These outputs multiply together to give the three-year retrospective tracking shown in Figure 7. Such a model is useful for brand planning and sometimes even more useful for generating an anticipated sales rate. This becomes a standard to be compared with actual sales. Discrepancies trigger diagnosis and feedback to management.

New Phenomena. It is always exciting to discover a new phenomenon and build a model of it. This does not happen often and, because of commercial secrecy, the news sometimes spreads rather slowly. An example that originated a number of years ago, but continues to have ramifications, deals with concentration of retail outlets. The original work was done on gasoline service stations. All the oil companies are familiar with it, but, as with many scientific phenomena, the principle is more general. In this case, it carries over into other franchise operations (e.g., branch banks and fast food outlets) and in these industries the idea is just beginning to take hold.

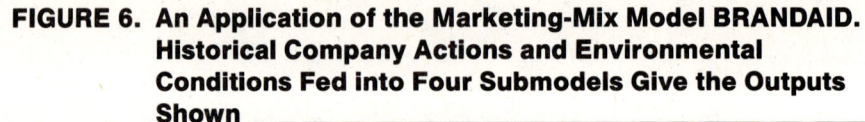

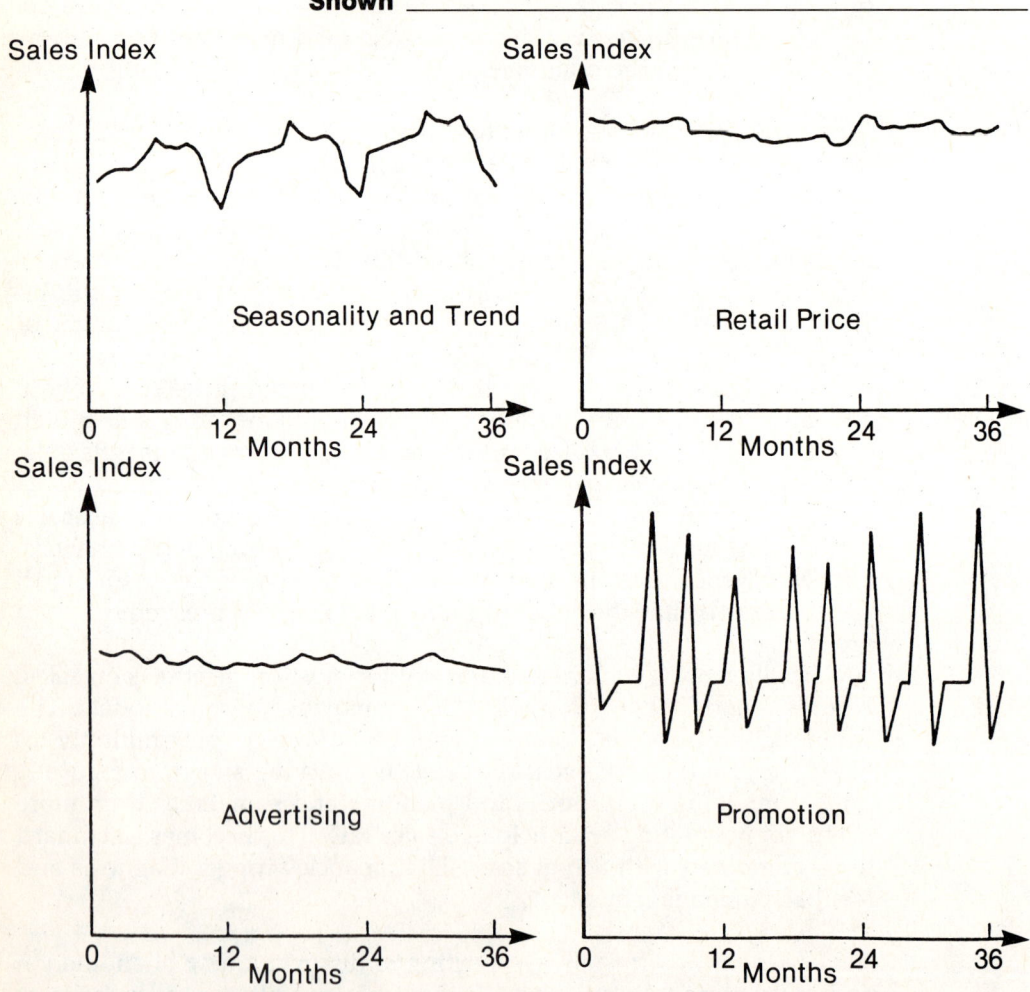

FIGURE 6. An Application of the Marketing-Mix Model BRANDAID. Historical Company Actions and Environmental Conditions Fed into Four Submodels Give the Outputs Shown

The phenomenon deals with competition between outlets in a given city. I recall sitting in the office of a marketing economist from a major oil company and discussing service station site location.

He said, "One thing you have to be careful about is putting two of our stations close together or putting too many stations in the same market. First of all, the dealers will scream, but, in addition, you start running into self-competition. If the company puts new stations in a market where it already has many, it is taking business away from itself."

This point of view is represented in Figure 8 by the curve marked "What people thought" and shows gallonage per station decreasing with number of outlets in a city.

What Hartung and Fisher (1965) and later Naert and Bultez (1975) did was to collect data, analyze it, and build a theory. After filtering out a variety of variables that confused the situation, they found that the curve actually goes *up*. In other words, up to a certain point, stations actually reinforce each other: the more stations the company has, the greater the gallonage *per station*.

To me this is quite surprising, although, once a fact is known, it is easy to offer explanations. For example, stations are outdoor advertise-

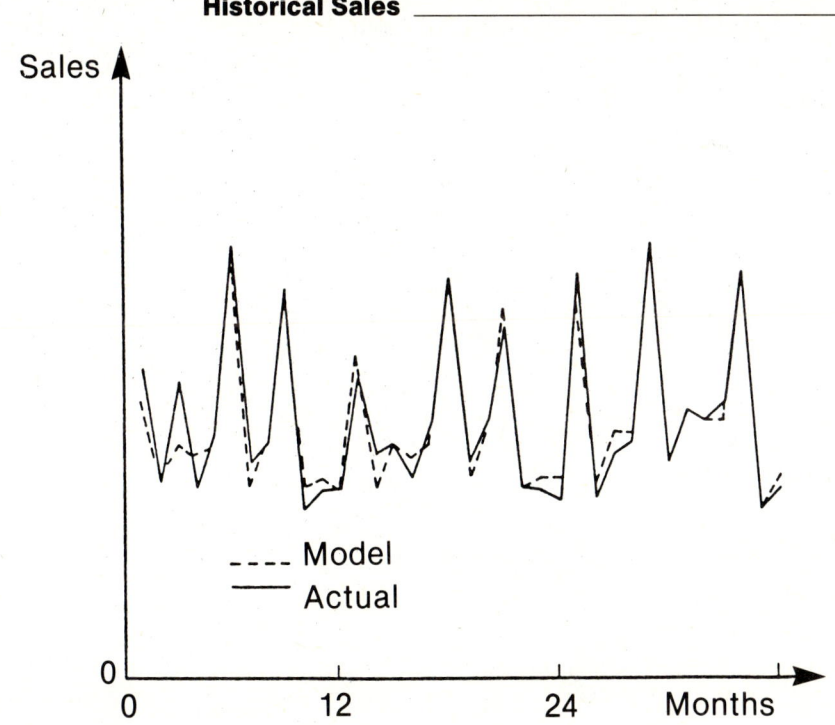

FIGURE 7. The BRANDAID Submodels Are Combined to Track Historical Sales

ments for the company; the more stations the more people become aware of the brand. In addition, media advertising which is hardly worthwhile for one or two stations in a market becomes economical if there are many. Credit cards become more useful to a customer if the brand has many stations and therefore will enhance total brand sales in the market. Everything makes sense—once you know the answer.

Figure 9 sketches the station reinforcement phenomenon as a plot of market share versus station share. If the effect did not exist, we would expect the diagonal straight line. With the effect, the company does worse than the straight line at low station share, then with increasing station share crosses over the diagonal, and finally bends over to unity as diminishing returns set in.

The strategy implications of the relationship are dramatic and quite opposite to the actions most oil companies were taking at the time. The curve tells a company to add stations where it is already strong, at least up to quite a high level, whereas most companies were trying to reach out geographically as fast as possible to become national companies with the widest possible markets. As we now see, this was not the best way to gain the most new business with new investment dollars. (Notice, incidentally, that the oil industry is characterized by strong regional marketers, a piece of empirical support for the underlying phenomenon.)

Later Lilien and Rao (1976) imbedded the reinforcement model into a financial model that takes into account laydown costs, competitive pricing conditions, building costs, total budget, etc. This provided marketing management with a tool to allocate service station investment dollars

FIGURE 8. Surprisingly, as the Number of Service Stations for a Brand in a City Increases, so Does the Gallonage per Station

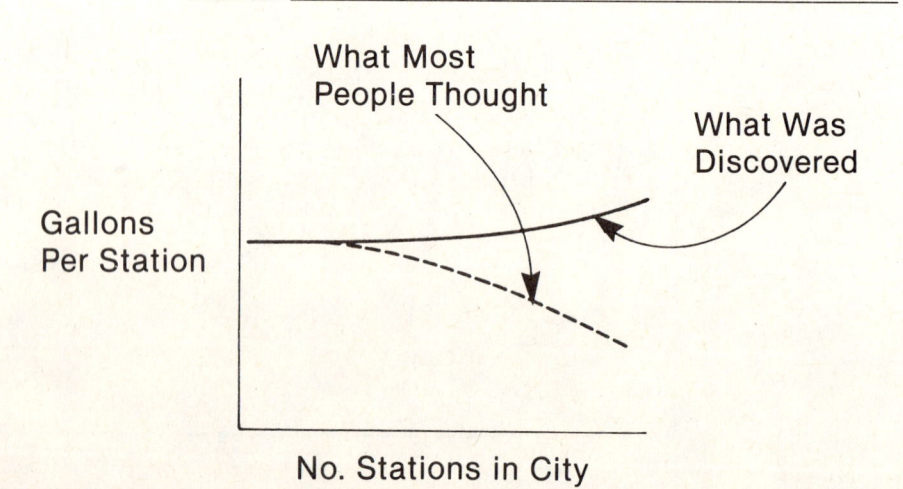

to maximize long-run return, thereby reaping the productivity of the basic discovery.

MDSS in Practice: The Bottom Line Is on Top

The best marketing decision support system I know of grew up over several years in the major division of a large package goods company. Although the first big data base came on stream in mid 1972, the system is still evolving. It has become an integral part of marketing operations and has materially affected management style in several ways.

A management science group of two or three professionals and a similar number of clerical and longtime company people run the activity. Their online data base contains internal company sales, records of marketing activities (e.g., advertising and promotion), and a sizeable block of syndicated data (e.g., panel and store audit information). As a rough estimate, 10^6 numbers are online and more can be available with a few days' notice.

The system software is a high level, analytic language which offers not only data base management, but powerful manipulative and statistical capabilities. Gradually, many small and large analytic routines and models have been written and incorporated into the system. The computer is in constant use; one or two people are logged in virtually all the time and overnight batch runs ordered online during the day are common.

FIGURE 9. The Resulting S-Shaped Relation Between Share of Market and Share of Stations Leads to Strong Regional Brands

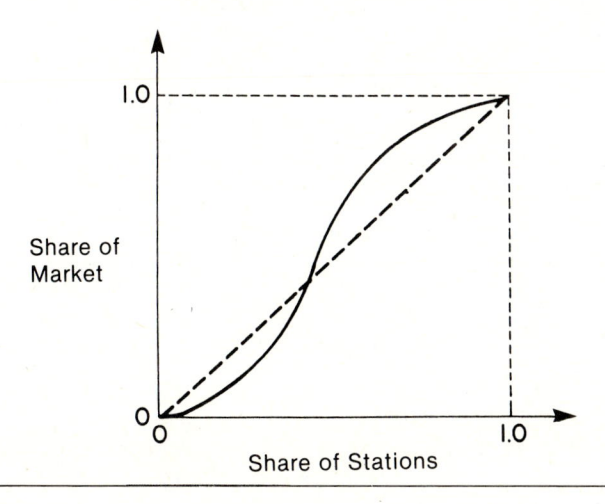

The bread and butter business of the MDSS consists of responding to a remarkable variety of small requests from brand managers and higher levels of marketing management. Rarely does raw data retrieval provide the answer. Almost always, data are manipulated and presented in a special way because of some issue at hand. Service is sufficiently good with such fast turnaround on short requests that, at one point, barriers had to be raised to reduce requests and maintain quality control on jobs performed. An important block of time goes into data base maintenance and updating.

Changes in Management Style

Two significant changes in marketing management style can be traced to the MDSS. Tendencies toward each had existed previously, but the MDSS permits them to emerge in a practical way.

The first is the growth of a "try and see" approach to new marketing programs. The marketing managers in the company are activists who want to introduce new ideas, but also want to know whether they really work. A miniexperiment program has evolved. The management science group has identified a bank of market areas appropriate for tests. The annual marketing plan includes a set of tests for the coming year. Extra tests can be put in the field quickly. Typical projects are new promotion ideas, packages, product line extensions, and changes in advertising media strategy, copy, or weight. The management science group has developed analytic and evaluative routines for reading the results quickly and efficiently. The detail, flexibility, and rapid turnaround of the MDSS along with the experience and skill of professional people make the operation possible.

The miniexperiment program is the invention of marketing management, not management scientists. This has important consequences. In the first place, the tests are sometimes not very precise. They are often done in single markets and, as any statistician will point out, it is difficult to estimate a standard error from one observation. Nevertheless, the program prospers. Although an individual test may be statistically weak, the whole collection screens a considerable number of new ideas. Real winners stand out. Run-of-the-mill improvements are hard to read but correspondingly less important. As has been shown by Gross (1972) in the case of advertising copy testing, significant gains accrue to creating multiple ideas and screening them, even if the precision is limited. It is doubtful that the management science department would ever have proposed the program on its own. The technical people would have proposed careful multiple market experiments that were more statistically defensible, but then costs would have prevented a really extensive program. As it is, marketing management, having invented the idea, is willing to absorb the uncertainties of the results.

Larger scale, multiple market experiments also are conducted. In fact, a carefully designed advertising weights test analyzed within the MDSS recently led to a major shift in advertising spending strategy.

The second managerial style change is a shift toward regional marketing. Anyone can think up regional strategies, but it is another matter to maintain management control over them and do follow-up evaluations. These are necessary to determine successes and failures and to adjust strategies to changing conditions. The MDSS has been critical in making this possible.

Market Response Reporting

Conventional reviews of brand and company performance stress *status* reporting, i.e., how things are. For example, what are sales, share, price, promotion, and advertising expenditures and what are their trends? Status reporting is characteristic both of standard market monitoring systems like SAMI and Nielsen and of internal company reporting.

A more action-oriented performance review is becoming possible with the evolution of MDSSs. This is market *response* reporting, i.e., how effective marketing actions are. For example, what is price elasticity, how do sales respond to promotion, and what effect will increased advertising have on sales?

The markets of this company have witnessed important competitive changes over the past few years. The historical events captured in company and syndicated data permit extensive analysis of various marketing tactics. Analytic methods have evolved not overnight, but over several years to permit estimates of market response to major changes in marketing actions. These response estimates are the subject of ongoing reviews similar to those conventionally made with static indicators and offer marketing management new and sharper information for decision making.

The market response information also permits projection of future performance by means of marketing-mix models. While this is done for certain purposes, a more important role of models has been in the historical analysis itself. A credible model of the effects of all major marketing variables is essential to performing the market response analysis.

Costs/Benefits

The cost of the MDSS in this company is large in dollars: several hundreds of thousands. As a fraction of sales, however, the cost of the system, the data, and the people who run it is small, perhaps 0.1%. This seems modest considering that marketing budgets run about 5% of sales and, more important, the decisions being affected influence sales and profit by much more. The cost of the system and its operation splits roughly equally among data, people, and computation.

The MDSS did not spring full blown from the marketing vice president's head nor did it evolve without controversy. Its growth has been incremental, moving from the first tentative beginnings and useful initial results, to further extensions, more results, and so on. This has brought certain inefficiencies ("If we'd known then, what we know now..."), but the idea of "best" at each evolutionary stage changes considerably by the time of the next one so that a flexible approach pays off.

The MDSS has used outside time-sharing services copiously and so has been a constant target for an inhouse data processing takeover. Yet the power, flexibility, and responsiveness of languages available on external time-sharing has not been duplicated inhouse. Marketing management has insisted on high and increasing levels of service which have only been available externally.

Some payoffs have been explicit. An analysis of promotion led to a strategy change with a profit increase in seven figures. Such incidents are obviously helpful and may well be essential for survival. However, my own feeling is that the largest benefits have come simply by facilitating good management. Bold changes of direction in a company are infrequent (which is probably good). For the most part management deals with a series of adjustments to conditions, no one adjustment being particularly spectacular nor uniquely traceable to any specific piece of data or analysis. Yet the collection of analyses adds up to influence, decision, and improved profit. Another usually unrecognized role is assistance in preventing disasters. The pressure for improvement in a company turns up fascinating proposals, some of which are bound to be bad. Analyses that lead to recommendations for inaction are not very exciting, but are sometimes more valuable than calls for revolution.

In summary, this particular company has developed an effective MDSS over a multiyear period. The process has been evolutionary with high costs, but higher benefits. Marketing management has become more innovative as it receives more and better feedback from "try and see" operations. The system has encouraged a shift from market status reporting to market response reporting. However, the main point to be made is that effective MDSSs are not "pie in the sky." They are here now.

PROBLEM SOLVING WITH INTERACTIVE SYSTEMS: THE GREY FLANNEL ROBOT

In the early days of time-shared computers, many people realized that a marvelous invention was at hand. A person could have convenient access to huge computers from any place with a telephone. Without too much difficulty, a computer could interrogate the user in a semblance of natural language, using words and phrases to ask for input and deliver output.

What People Thought

Clearly time-sharing was a breakthrough and the imaginations of the visionaries were stimulated. A new world was forecast in which managers would sit at terminals and formulate their problems. With the help of easy-to-use commands, they would put key assumptions and judgments into the computer. These would be incorporated into models relevant to the issues to be examined. The managers would ask "what if" questions and evaluate various strategies. New ones would be stimulated by the analysis. Finally the managers would select their best alternatives and go off to take action.

What People Found

Managers do not like terminals. They are impatient and busy. They do not formulate problems in model terms because that is not the way they naturally think. They want to think about strategy not analysis. They will propose actions to be analyzed, but they do not want to do it themselves.

Anecdotes to illustrate these points are many. I recall one excruciating incident in the early days of online models when the president of a very large corporation was invited to use the new toy hands-on. Unfortunately, he couldn't type—not even with a tolerable hunt and peck. The situation became embarrassing. Vice presidents fluttered about. Finally a data processing manager took over the keyboard. More fundamentally, however, managers do not go online because of their function and style. As Mintzberg (1973) has observed, the manager leads a high pressure, communications-intensive life which is much more try-and-see than think-and-analyze.

The notion of the hands-on manager is not dead, however. I have rather recently been told that a large computer manufacturer has sold an elaborate information system that will put video terminals on the desks of 10 bank vice presidents for constant use in running their departments. I am not optimistic about the ultimate level of use. We shall find an occasional top executive who is an avid hands-on analyst, but I feel quite confident the majority will not be for some time to come.

A New Role

All is not lost, however. Interactive systems are definitely the way to go. We need only recognize that managers work through human organizations in this as in most things they do. What we find happening is that individuals are emerging who can be described as *marketing science intermediaries*. They are typically OR/MS professionals or recent MBAs with good technical skills. They are first and foremost problem solvers. They convert managers' questions into models and analyses. They enter into dialogue with managers and others in the organization about what the problems really are. They provide answers to managers' questions and respond to the new questions that the answers provoke. They build portfolios of data bases, models, and systems to solve recurring problems. They do the homework managers lack the time to do. They want the manager's jobs in a few years. For the present they are the organizers and internal consultants who build knowledge and systems to support marketing operations.

Typically, marketing science intermediaries program and use models and systems personally, or with small staffs. However, they are not computer scientists and do not report to MIS. What makes their role possible are powerful new computer languages available on time-sharing.

Hardware and Software: Ready-to-Wear

Computers are impossible to work with, but are getting better. Advances in hardware and software are pushing the evolution of decision support systems. Hardware manufacturing costs are dropping and prices are following at a respectful distance. Some people forecast that hardware costs will eventually become negligible. I am not so sure because we are so good at thinking up big new jobs for computers. However, it is fair to predict that hardware cost will become a negligible part of the computations we are doing today. Software, on the other hand, continues to be expensive but has undergone advances in ways particularly relevant to us here.

The philosophy behind contemporary software is to let the computer solve its own problems. Why should users have to go through elaborate contortions to move data from a statistical package to a marketing model to a report generator? They shouldn't. Good software systems can solve these and many other machine problems, leaving the users free to concentrate on the essence of the analysis. High level commands permit easy plotting, tabling, array arithmetic, statistical analysis, optimization, report generation, and model building, all on the same data base.

As a user, I am most appreciative of "default" options. Thus, if SALES is a defined data variable, I can give a command like PLOT SALES and out comes a plot. It fits on an $8\frac{1}{2} \times 11$ inch page, the curve approximately fills the plot, the axes are labeled, a sensible grid has been selected that has round-number gradations, etc. The computer has finally become a moderately effective clerk. If I want something different from default specifications, I can override them, but most of the time, especially during exploratory work, the automated plot is fine. Furthermore the same commands will work on a dozen different terminals; it is only necessary to tell the computer which one is being used.

High level analytic languages that embody many of these features are increasing in number and scope. An early one with the emphasis on a concise and powerful mathematical notation is APL. A commercial system with a strong business orientation is EXPRESS. Somewhat similar are PROBE, TSAM, and XSIM. Some of the systems are easily extendable so that, for example, FORTRAN subroutines can be easily introduced as new commands. Why reinvent the wheel? Features and degree of power vary, but all of these languages try to let the analyst work an order of magnitude faster than a FORTRAN programmer on a bare-bones, time-sharing system.

Most of the observations just made about interactive systems extend well beyond the context of marketing (see for example, Keen and Scott Morton 1978).

IMPLEMENTATION: WHICH WAY IS UP?

Any attempt to install an MDSS has organizational ramifications. Will marketing management's antibodies reject the graft? Will the internal computer establishment gag?

Taking these issues in order, consider Argyris' view (1971) in *Management Science*:

> If management information systems achieve their designers' highest aspirations, they will tend to create conditions where executives will experience: (1) reduction of space of free movement, (2) psychological failure and double bind, (3) leadership based more on competence than formal power, (4) decreased feelings of essentiality. These experiences will tend to create genuine resistance to MIS.

Another hand-wringer. I do not agree and will argue otherwise, but first let me give an anecdote to favor Argyris' view. A marketing vice president I know refused to conduct a field experiment which would have sought to measure the effect of advertising on sales. He had various reasons for his position, but I suspect the real reason was that he had negotiated an increased advertising budget with the president. Therefore, if the experiment should confirm the increased budget, it would be redundant and, if not, he would look bad. So why do the experiment? To use Argyris' words, better information only restricted his space of free movement.

I believe that the executive was wrong and that by such actions his company could lose competitive advantage which would eventually reflect on him. However, this type of managerial reaction certainly exists.

A better style, in my opinion, is to view the advertising increase as an opportunity for measurement and further adaptation to the market.

Such examples notwithstanding, my main observation is that it takes a first class marketing manager to bring an MDSS into being in the first place and such people are not about to let their systems run them. On the contrary it gives them a feeling of power to act on moderately reliable information for a change.

Let's check other commentators on the MIS scene. Gruber and Niles (1976) write:

> Understanding what managers actually do and...organizing the information they currently use is the only way to build relevancy ...the biggest mistake in...current...work is that it...builds... products that serve some assumed decision making process which real managers do not carry out.

I agree in part, but we have gone past this stage. To support their point, I recall a director of marketing who was very impressed with computer technology and decided he wanted instant retrieval. His idea was to have a video terminal on his desk so that, if he wanted to know sales last month in Buffalo, he could press a button and, presto, the data would appear.

We told him, "It's not really retrieval you want but models," and explained why.

He said, "OK, you people are the experts, not me."

So we gave him models. It turned out that he wanted retrieval. We went back and gave him retrieval. Actually, what we gave him was retrieval plus analysis plus models, and even more important, he hired a marketing science intermediary. This particular marketing director was not about to push any buttons that did not have people on the other end of the wire.

Gruber and Niles' point about doing better and faster whatever is being done now is a good one and an excellent way to build credibility and support for an MDSS. However, we are well beyond that in many areas and have plenty of examples of new and useful analysis, measurements, and models. A variety of these have been discussed already.

A major issue for an MDSS is its relation to inhouse data processing and management information systems. The first 10 years of business applications of time-sharing have been dominated by external vendors. In this period, fixed costs of time-sharing have been high because of hardware, software, communication equipment, and marketing. Much of the marketing has really been low level applications consulting. The costs and required skills have deterred inhouse time-sharing in many organizations. Furthermore, inhouse data processing typically has had its hands full meeting its current operational commitments. As a result, most activities that look like MDSSs have been done on outside time-sharing. Yet, inhouse data processing departments, which typically live in an environment of repetitive batch jobs, frequently consider the cost of commercial time-sharing to be exorbitant. Marketing management, however, has not found the cost high relative to the value of the tasks performed and has preferred to pay an apparent premium rather than wait for specially programmed batch runs or, in some cases, deal with cumbersome, leanly serviced, inhouse time-sharing systems.

The scene continues to change with two rather different patterns now in evidence. On the one hand, central MIS is in some cases becoming a better time-sharing vendor, bringing in good operating systems and languages. It thus becomes a bigger supplier of computations, but one with less concern about the content of the computation, since the usage is decentralized. In our case, this would be done by a marketing science intermediary working for the marketing department.

Another and perhaps more significant development is the decentralization made possible by the increasing power of minicomputers. Small computers with high level analytic languages can be installed in the functional department and only interconnect with MIS to pick up or deposit data. Costs are moderate and technical support requirements manageable. If these machines and their software prove reasonably robust, the growth of decentralized MDSSs seems very likely.

SUMMARY: WHITHER DECISION SUPPORT?

The main thrust of this paper is to say that marketing management can, and should obtain better analytic help for its planning and operations. This can be done by a marketing decision support system that puts the new technology of computers and marketing science to work on increasing marketing productivity. An MDSS means hiring people with marketing science skills. It means organizing data bases and putting them in usable form. It means building a portfolio of models and analytic techniques directed at important company issues. It means integrating problem-solving and problem-finding within the marketing function using the marketing science intermediary to facilitate the process. A strong system does not spring up overnight. It takes two or three years of evolution and development, but it can lead to new styles of marketing management.

Let's look ahead. In the next five to 10 years, I foresee:

- *An order of magnitude increase in the amount of marketing data used*. Through MDSS development, the internal data of a company will finally become accessible on a rather detailed basis: sales, advertising, promotion, etc. Automatically collected point-of-sale information from the marketplace (e.g., Universal Product Code data from supermarkets) will replace most current store

audits. Much better longitudinal data on customers (e.g., panels) will be generally available and will include such currently missing information as media use. The monitoring of competitive advertising, promotion, and price will be vastly improved.
- *A similar tenfold increase in computer power available for marketing analysis*. The hardware is already built; it is out there and purchasable. The price is going to break. The only problem will be for marketing to absorb computer power in a useful way.
- *Widespread adoption of analytic computer languages*. These make data accessible and greatly facilitate analysis. Some exist now, more will be introduced, and all will improve.
- *A shift from market status reporting to market response reporting*. This is an important change. SAMI, Nielsen, and other market monitoring systems, including internal sales reporting, emphasize market status, i.e., how things are: what are sales, share, price, advertising, etc.?

    Tomorrow's systems will report response, i.e., how things react: what's price elasticity, advertising response, promotional effectiveness, etc.? Companies will even do a reasonably good job of monitoring competitor's market response.

    Much work lies ahead for marketing scientists in order for this to come to pass. We need well-designed data sources and many new tools. How do we handle eclectic data sources in developing and calibrating models? What are the best underlying models to represent marketing phenomena? We can expect a flowering of new work.
- *New methodology for supporting strategy development*. Marketing scientists will further advance our understanding of product-market boundaries. Better response measurements will expose more clearly the nature of competitive interaction and give rise to game theoretic strategy development.

And, finally, I foresee:

- *A shortage of marketing scientists*. You know what that means: higher salaries, more fun, exciting new toys. From this I conclude that marketing is the right field to be in.

REFERENCES

Argyris, Chris (1971), "Management Information Systems: The Challenge to Rationality and Emotionality," *Management Science*, 17 (February), B275–292.

Bass, F.M. and D.G. Clarke (1972), "Testing Distributive Lag Models of Advertising Effect," *Journal of Marketing Research*, 9 (August), 298–308.

Bloom, D. and M.J. Stewart (1977), "An Integrated Marketing Planning System," *Proceedings of ESOMAR Conference*, (February), 168–186.

Business Week (1973), "Ten Year Experience at General Foods," (August 25), 48–55.

Cox, K.K., J.B. Higginbotham, and J. Burton (1976), "Applications of Focus Group Interviews in Marketing," *Journal of Marketing*, 40 (January), 77–80.

Day, George S. (1977), "Diagnosing the Product Portfolio," *Journal of Marketing*, 41 (April), 29–38.

Ehrenberg, A.S.C. (1972), *Repeat Buying*, New York: American Elsevier.

Gorry, G. Anthony and Michael S. Scott Morton (1971), "A Framework for Management Information Systems," *Sloan Management Review*, 13 (Fall), 55–70.

Grayson, C. Jackson Jr. (1973), "Management Science and Business Practice," *Harvard Business Review*, 51 (July–August), 41–48.

Green, Paul E. and Yoram Wind (1975), "New Way to Measure Consumers' Judgments," *Harvard Business Review*, 53 (July–August), 107–117.

Gross, Irwin (1972), "The Creative Aspects of Advertising," *Sloan Management Review*, 14 (Fall), 83–109.

——— (1977), "The Value of 'Value-in-use,'" unpublished note, Wilmington, DE: DuPont Company.

Gruber, William H. and John S. Niles (1976), *The New Management*, New York: McGraw-Hill, 138–139.

Hartung, Philip H. and James L. Fisher (1965), "Brand Switching and Mathematical Programming in Market Expansion," *Management Science*, 11 (August), B231–243.

Hauser, John R. (1978), "Testing the Accuracy, Usefulness, and Significance of Probabilistic Choice Models: An Information Theoretic Approach," *Operations Research*, 26 (May–June), 406–421.

——— and Glen L. Urban (1977), "A Normative Methodology for Modeling Consumer Response in Innovation," *Operations Research*, 25 (July–August), 576–619.

Hess, Sidney W. (1967), "The Use of Models in Marketing Timing Decisions," *Operations Research*, 15 (July–August), 720–737.

von Hippel, Eric (1978), "Successful Industrial Products from Customer Ideas," *Journal of Marketing*, 42 (January), 39–49.

Keen, Peter G.W. and Michael S. Scott Morton (1978), *Decision Support Systems: An Organizational Perspective*, Reading MA: Addison-Wesley.

Lilien, Gary L. and Ambar G. Rao (1976), "A Model for Allocating Retail Outlet Building Resources Across Market Areas," *Operations Research*, 24 (January–February), 1–14.

Little, John D.C. (1970), "Models and Managers: The Concept of a Decision Calculus," *Management Science*, 16 (April), B466–485.

——— (1975), "BRANDAID: A Marketing-Mix Model, Parts 1 and 2," *Operations Research*, 23 (July–August), 628-673.

Mintzberg, Henry (1973), *The Nature of Managerial Work*, New York: Harper and Row.

Montgomery, David B. and Glen L. Urban (1969), *Management Science in Marketing*, Englewood Cliffs, NJ: Prentice-Hall, Inc.

Naert, Philippe A. and Alain V. Bultez (1975), "A Model of Distribution Network Aggregate Performance," *Management Science*, 21 (June), 1102–1112.

Nigam, A.K., ed. (1975, 76, 77), Special Issues on Practice, *Interfaces*, 6 (November), 7 (November), 8 (November), Part 2.

Parfitt, J.H. and B.J.K. Collins (1968), "Use of Consumer Panels for Brand-Share Prediction," *Journal of Marketing Research*, 5 (May), 131–145.

Parsons, Leonard J. and Randall L. Schultz (1976), *Marketing Models and Econometric Research*, Amsterdam: North Holland.

Prince, George M. (1972), *The Practice of Creativity*, New York: Macmillan.

Silk, Alvin J. and Glen L. Urban (1978), "Pre-Test Market Evaluation of New Packaged Goods: A Model and Measurement Methodology," *Journal of Marketing Research*, 15 (May), 171–191.

Shocker, A.D. and V. Srinivasan (1977), "Multiattribute Approaches for Concept Evaluation and Generation: A Critical Review," working paper no. 240 (October), Pittsburgh: Graduate School of Business, University of Pittsburgh.

Urban, Glen L. (1970), "SPRINTER Mod III: A Model for the Analysis of New Frequently Purchased Consumer Products," *Operations Research*, 18 (September–October), 805–854.

PART TWO
Marketing and the Environment

This section deals with the role of marketing in society. Fundamentally, there are two approaches: self-regulation and government regulation. There is considerable debate whether marketing can really regulate itself in view of the opportunities it enjoys and the power it exercises over customers.

Similarly, the question of how much government should regulate the marketing practice is also subject to debate. One extreme viewpoint even argues that it is good for the consumer not to rely on the government for protection because the consumer will always depend on someone else for what should be the basic functional skills of procurement, consumption, and disposition. Proponents of this view believe in the school of "hard knocks," in which the consumer learns by trial and error or by negative experiences in the marketplace. The other extreme view presumes that consumers are simply incapable of protecting themselves because they are helpless against the large corporations. Education and information are not sufficient to balance this power, and buying power also is not sufficient unless it is organized into group buying or cooperatives.

We believe that marketing and society will coexist partly through self-regulation and partly through government regulation. In our opinion, there is no room for self-regulation when it comes to product safety or other physically harmful side effects created by products and services. Government rules and regulations are essential in this area. On the other hand, in other areas of marketing practice such as pricing, promotion, and distribution, there is ample room for self-regulation and probably no real need for government regulation.

SECTION E
Social Responsibility

Social responsibility of marketing practice is an age-old issue. Its roots predate the Biblical age, in which merchants and traders were considered necessary evils of society. The malpractices of merchants and traders as well as the antisocial role of the commercial sector in the society even today have left a stigma with the marketing function, which is often equated with selling and trading.

It is, therefore, not unusual to find a sense of moral arrogance within the corporation among such other corporate functions as engineering, research and development, support services, and even human resources, in which they look down on marketing as a less-desirable and morally uncomfortable business function.

Worse yet, there are professionals who raise questions like: Would you allow your son or daughter to marry a marketer? In that regard, marketing's image within the society has been far less positive than that of medicine or the physical sciences.

The papers in this section attempt to clarify the social and moral issues involved in the marketing practice. Of course, there is no clear-cut answer. We believe that as marketing gets more and more separated from selling, there will be proportionately less and less concern about the social responsibility of marketing.

14   The Dangers of Social Responsibility

Theodore Levitt

Reprinted by permission of the Harvard Business Review. "The Dangers of Social Responsibility" by Theodore Levitt (September–October 1958). Copyright © 1958 by the President and Fellows of Harvard College; all rights reserved.

Concern with management's social responsibility has become more than a Philistinic form of self-flattery practiced at an occasional community chest banquet or at a news conference celebrating a "selfless example of corporate giving" to some undeserving little college in Podunk. It has become more than merely intoning the pious declarations of Christian brotherhood which some hotshot public relations man has pressed into the outstretched hands of the company president who is rushing from an executive committee meeting to a League of Women Voters luncheon. It has become a deadly serious occupation—the self-conscious, soul-searching preoccupation with the social responsibilities of business, with business statesmanship, employee welfare, public trust, and with all the other lofty causes that get such prominent play in the public press.

Contrary to what some uncharitable critics may say, this preoccupation is not an attitudinizing pose. Self-conscious dedication to social responsibility may have started as a purely defensive maneuver against strident attacks on big corporations and on the moral efficacy of the profit system. But defense alone no longer explains the motive.

THE NONPROFIT MOTIVE

When outnumbered by its critics at the polls, business launched a counterattack via the communications front. Without really listening to what the critics alleged, business simply denied all that they were saying. But a few executives did listen and began to take a second look at themselves. Perhaps this criticism was not all captious. And so they began to preach to their brethren.

Before long something new was added to the ideological stockpile of capitalism. "Social responsibility" was what business needed, its own leaders announced. It needed to take society more seriously. It needed to participate in community affairs—and not just to take from the community but to give to it. Gradually business became more concerned about the needs of its employees, about schools, hospitals, welfare agencies, and even aesthetics. Moreover, it became increasingly clear that if business and the local governments failed to provide some of the routine social-economic amenities which people seemed clearly intent on getting, then that Brobdingnagian freewheeling monster in far-off Washington would.

So what started out as the sincere personal viewpoints of a few selfless businessmen became the prevailing vogue for them all. Today pronouncements about social responsibility issue forth so abundantly from the corporations that it is hard for one to get a decent play in the press. Everybody is in on the act, and nearly all of them actually mean what they say! Dedication reverberates throughout the upper reaches of corporate officialdom.

Happy New Orthodoxy

This, it is widely felt, is good. Business will raise itself in the public's esteem and thereby scuttle the political attacks against it. If the public likes big business, nobody can make capital by attacking it. Thus social responsibility will prolong the lifetime of free enterprise. Meanwhile, the profit motive is compromised in both word and deed. It now shares its royal throne with a multitude of noncommercial motives that aspire to loftier and more satisfying values. Today's profits must be merely adequate, not maximum. If they are big, it is cause for apologetic rationalization (for example, that they are needed to expand the company's ability to "serve" the public even better) rather than for boastful celebration. It is not fashionable for the corporation to take gleeful pride in making money. What *is* fashionable is for the corporation to show that it is a great innovator; more specifically, a great public benefactor; and, very particularly, that it exists "to serve the public."

The mythical visitor from Mars would be astonished that such a happy tableau of cooperative enterprise can create such vast material abundance. "People's Capitalism" is a resounding success. The primitive principle of aggrandizing selfishness which the Marxists mistakenly contend activates capitalism does not count at all. What we have instead is a voluntary association of selfless entrepreneurs singularly dedicated to creating munificence for one and all—an almost spiritually blissful state of cooperative and responsible enterprise. We are approaching a jet-propelled utopia. And, unlike some other periods in the short and turbulent history of capitalism, today has its practicing philosophers. These are the men busily engaged in the canonistic exposition of a new orthodoxy—the era of "socially responsible enterprise."

A Lonely Crowd

Occasionally some big business representative does speak less sanctimoniously and more forthrightly about what capitalism is really all about. Occasionally somebody exhumes the apparently antique notion that the business of business is profits; that virtue lies in the vigorous, undiluted assertion of the corporation's profit-making function. But these people get no embossed invitations to speak at the big, prestigeful, and splashy business conferences — where social responsibility echoes as a new tyranny of fad and fancy.

About a year ago, Frank O. Prior, then president and now board chairman of Standard Oil Company (Indiana), made a speech that was in part reminiscent of the late but apparently unlamented tycoon:

> Without terminological pretensions, pseudodialectical profundity, or rhetorical subtlety, he called on his big business colleagues to run their businesses as they are intended to be run — for profit. Regarding people who publicly consider profit making a doubtful morality, he called on his colleagues to "move over to the offensive," "to stand up and fight," to talk about profits in terms of their central function, and to throw all sentiment to the wolves.
>
> His remarks must have sounded strange and harsh to people accustomed to a decade of viewing the corporation as a sort of miniature welfare state. Good human relations, he said, makes sense only when it "rests on a foundation of economic good sense and not just on sentiment. Sentiment has a tendency to evaporate whenever the heat is on. Economic good sense is durable."
>
> Then he said: "You aren't supposed to use language like that these times. You're supposed to talk about high ideals using high-flown words. You're expected to be mainly aware of what they call social responsibility.... This is fine, but I still say management's No. 1 problem is profits."

And where was this vigorous affirmation of no-nonsense capitalism made? Was it Chicago, the seat of Standard's home office and one of the few places where some think the old orthodoxy retains some semblance of primeval integrity? No. This was too unreconstructed a view even for Chicago, the city of broad shoulders. So the Chamber of Commerce of distant and isolated Casper, Wyoming, provided the platform. And even there Prior could not afford to let his forthright remarks stand as boldly as he started out. The corporation, he allowed, must develop "a fuller sense of responsibility and a much broader outlook on the facts of life" — and prices should be "fair."[1]

The fact is, the profit motive is simply not fashionable today among emancipated conferees of the Committee for Economic Development or even in the National Association of Manufacturers. It has been dying a lingering, unmourned death for ten years. Rarely can a big business leader eulogize it today without being snubbed by his self-consciously frowning peers.

Things have come to a remarkable pass. And if anyone doubts it, let him contemplate the spectacle of a recent NAM convention interrupting its urgent deliberations to hear Siobhan McKenna reading Yeats's poetry, presumably to set an appropriate tone of cultural emancipation and dedication. Can anybody picture this happening 25 years ago? Or the board chairman of Sears, Roebuck & Co., stating, as he did last year, that not only is business's first responsibility social but business executives, like Secretary Benson's farmers, should look less to their pocketbooks and more to their spirits? Not even his suggestion that the top brass are overpaid ruffled any managerial feathers.[2]

The Self-Persuaders

There is nothing mysterious about the social responsibility syndrome. It does not reflect a change in businessmen's nature or the decay of self-interest. Quite to the contrary, often it is viewed as a way of maximizing the lifetime of capitalism by taking the wind out of its critics' sails. Under direct questioning it will be confessed that activities such as supporting company intramural athletic programs, hiring a paid director for a company choral society, or underwriting employee dramatic performances (even on company time) are not charity. They are hardheaded tactics of survival against the onslaught of politicians and professional detractors. Moreover, they build morale, improve efficiency, and yield returns in hard cash.

In other words, it pays to play. If it does not pay, there is no game. For instance, when it comes to choosing between the small Arkansas supplier whose town would be ruined if orders stopped and the Minneapolis supplier who can make it cheaper, there is no doubt that even the most socially responsible corporation will take the latter. It can always fall back on responsibility to its employees, stockholders, or customers, and still pretend it is being fashionable.

In some respects, therefore, all this talk *is* merely talk. It stops at the pocketbook. How, then, can it be dangerous? I think the answer is very simple: what people say, they ultimately come to believe if they say it enough, and what they believe affects what they do. To illustrate how innocent talk, intended in some respects simply for show, can haunt and change the very people who make it, look at what has happened to the Republican Party in the last few years. The example is only too painfully obvious to many executives:

> For years the party fought the New Deal tooth and claw. Ultimately, in order to turn the Democrats out, it began matching the New Deal promise for promise. Republicans, it said, were not opposed to these measures; they simply wanted to do everything better and cheaper. The welfare state, it was emphasized, was lacking in sound business management.
>
> Having finally ascended to office and proposing to stay in, a

good many Republicans are now surprised to find themselves actually *doing* what they had promised during the election campaign. Some of the stalwarts who had lowered themselves to making expedient panegyric speeches about Modern Republicanism are now fighting a losing battle against its implementation.

The talk about social responsibility is already more than talk. It is leading into the believing stage; it has become a design for change. I hope to show why this change is likely to be for the worse, and why no man or institution can escape its debilitating consequences.

A New Feudalism

The function of business is to produce sustained high-level profits. The essence of free enterprise is to go after profit in any way that is consistent with its own survival as an economic system. The catch, someone will quickly say, is "consistent with." This is true. In addition, lack of profits is not the only thing that can destroy business. Bureaucratic ossification, hostile legislation, and revolution can do it much better. Let me examine the matter further. Capitalism as we like it can thrive only in an environment of political democracy and personal freedom. These require a pluralistic society—where there is division, not centralization, of power; variety, not unanimity, of opinion; and separation, not unification, of workaday economic, political, social, and spiritual functions.

We all fear an omnipotent state because it creates a dull and frightening conformity—a monolithic society. We do not want a society with one locus of power, one authority, one arbiter of propriety. We want and need variety, diversity, spontaneity, competition—in short, pluralism. We do not want our lives shaped by a single viewpoint or by a single way of doing things, even if the material consequences are bountiful and the intentions are honorable. Mussolini, Stalin, Hitler, Franco, Trujillo, Peron, all show what happens when power is consolidated into a single, unopposed, and unopposable force.

We are against the all-embracing welfare state not because we are against welfare but because we are against centralized power and the harsh social discipline it so ineluctably produces. We do not want a pervasive welfare state in government, and we do not want it in unions. And for the same reasons we should not want it in corporations.

Dangerous Power

But at the rate we are going there is more than a contingent probability that, with all its resounding good intentions, business statesmanship may create the corporate equivalent of the unitary state. Its proliferating employee welfare programs, its serpentine involvement in community, government, charitable, and educational affairs, its prodigious currying of political and public favor through hundreds of peripheral preoccupations, all these well-intended but insidious contrivances are greasing the rails for our collective descent into a social order that would be as repugnant to the corporations themselves as to their critics. The danger is that all these things will turn the corporation into a twentieth-century equivalent of the medieval Church. The corporation would eventually invest itself with all-embracing duties, obligations, and finally powers—ministering to the whole man and molding him and society in the image of the corporation's narrow ambitions and its essentially unsocial needs.

Now there is nothing wrong as such with the corporation's narrow ambitions or needs. Indeed, if there is anything wrong today, it is that the corporation conceives its ambitions and needs much too broadly. The trouble is not that it is too narrowly profit-oriented, but that it is not narrowly profit-oriented *enough*. In its guilt-driven urge to transcend the narrow limits of derived standards, the modern corporation is reshaping not simply the economic but also the institutional, social, cultural, and political topography of society.

And there's the rub. For while the corporation also transforms itself in the process, at bottom its outlook will always remain narrowly materialistic. What we have, then, is the frightening spectacle of a powerful economic functional group whose future and perception are shaped in a tight materialistic context of money and things but which imposes its narrow ideas about a broad spectrum of unrelated noneconomic subjects on the mass of man and society.

Even if its outlook were the purest kind of good will, that would not recommend the corporation as an arbiter of our lives. What is bad for this or any other country is for society to be consciously and aggressively shaped by a single functional group or a single ideology, whatever it may be.

If the corporation believes its long-run profitability to be strengthened by these peripheral involvements—if it believes that they are not charity but self-interest—then that much the worse. For, if this is so, it puts much more apparent justification and impulse behind activities which are essentially bad for man, bad for society, and ultimately bad for the corporation itself.

Example of Labor

The belief that one institution should encompass the complete lives of its members is by no means new to American society. One example can be taken from the history of unionism:

> In the latter part of the nineteenth century America's budding labor unions were shaken by a monumental internal struggle for

power. On the one side were the unctuous advocates for the "whole man" idea of the union's function. For them the union was to be an encompassing, social institution, operating on all conceivable fronts as the protector and spokesman of the workingman at large. In the process they acknowledged that the union would have to help shape and direct the aspirations, ideas, recreations, and even tastes—in short, the lives—of the members and the society in which they functioned.

Opposing this view were the more pragmatic "horny-handed sons of toil," the "bread and butter" unionists. All they wanted, in the words of Samuel Gompers, was "more, more, more." At the time it was widely believed that this made Gompers a dangerous man. Lots of pious heads shook on the sidelines as they viewed the stark contrast between the dedicated "uplifters" and Gompers' materialistic opportunism. Who would not side with the "uplifters"? Yet Gompers won, and happily so, for he put American unionism on the path of pure-and-simple on-the-job demands, free of the fanciful ideological projects and petty intellectualism that drain the vitality of European unions.

As late as the early 1930's the American Federation of Labor remained true to Gompers' narrow rules by opposing proposed Social Security legislation. And when, in the 1930's, the communists and the pseudo humanitarians pushed the "whole man" concept of unionism, they also lost. Today, however, without ideologically sustained or conscious direction, the more "progressive" unions have won the battle for what the nineteenth century ideologists lost. With all their vast might and organizational skill, these unions are now indeed ministering to the whole man:

- Walter Reuther's United Auto Workers runs night schools, "drop-in" centers for retired members, recreation halls; supports grocery cooperatives; publishes and broadcasts household hints, recipes, and fashion news; and runs dozens of social, recreational, political, and action programs that provide something for every member of the family every hour of the day.
- David Dubinsky's International Ladies' Garment Workers' Union has health centers, citizenship and hobby classes, low-cost apartment buildings, and a palatial summer resort in the Poconos.
- A Toledo union promotes "respectability" in clothes and hair styles among teenagers as a way of counteracting leather-jacketed, duck-tail rock-'n-roll delinquency.

Thus, the union is transformed in such cases from an important and desirable economic functional group into an all-knowing, all-doing, all-wise father on whom millions become directly dependent for womb-to-tomb ministration.

Toward a Monolithic Society

This is the kind of monolithic influence the corporation will eventually have if it becomes so preoccupied with its social burden, with employee welfare, and with the body politic. Only, when the corporation does this, it will do a much more thorough job than the union. For it is more protean and potentially more powerful than any democratic union ever dreamed of being. It is a self-made incubator and instrument of strength, more stable and better able to draw and hold a following than is the union. It creates its own capital and its own power by the sheer accident of doing what it is expected to do. (By contrast, the union can do nothing unless the corporation has done its job first. The union is essentially a luxury institution, not a necessity.)

I think it is significant that the right kinds of appeals to workers based on the corporation's materialistic self-interest are generally more successful than vague abstractions like "People's Capitalism." This is a truth the Soviet adherents to the materialistic philosophy stubbornly refused to learn as they tried with repeated failure to intrude ideological clack where only materialistic motives could work. Their denial of their own materialistic ideology finally surrendered to hard cash, first in the form of the "new economic policy," later through the system of "socialist competition," and now as industrial and agricultural decentralization.

If the corporate ministry of man turns out to be only half as pervasive as it seems destined to be, it will turn into a simonist enterprise of Byzantine proportions. There is a name for this kind of encircling business ministry, and it pains me to use it. The name is fascism. It may not be the insidious, amoral, surrealistic fascism over which we fought World War II, or the corrupt and aggrandizing Latin American version, but the consequence will be a monolithic society in which the essentially narrow ethos of the business corporation is malignantly extended over everyone and everything.

This feudalistic phantasmagoria may sound alarmist, farfetched, or even patently ridiculous. For one thing, it will be said, not all corporations see alike on all things. At the very least there will be the pluralism of differences arising out of corporate differences in productive functions and their differences as competitors. But look at it this way: When it comes to present-day corporate educational, recreational, welfare, political, social, and public relations programs, attitudes, ideas, promotions, and preferences, how much difference is there? Are they more alike or more unlike? Are they growing more similar or more dissimilar?

It may also be protested, "What is wrong with the corporate ideology, anyway? Who will deny the material abundance, the leisure, and even the aesthetic values it has created and fostered in the United States? Nobody!" But that is irrelevant. The point is: we do not want a monolithic society, even if its intentions are the best. Moreover, a group's behavior in the pluralistic, competitive past is no guarantee of its behavior once it reaches complete ascendance.

End of Capitalism

The power which the corporation gains as a sort of commercial demichurch it will lose as an agency of profit-motive capitalism. Indeed, as the profit motive becomes increasingly sublimated, capitalism will become only a shadow—the torpid remains of the creative dynamism which was and might have been. It will thrive in name only, at the convention rostrums and the chambers of commerce—a sort of verbal remains of the real thing, shakily sustained by pomp and ceremony. Like Rome, it will never know that when it believed itself at the height of its glory, it was undergoing its denouement. The incubus of the corporate ministry of man will be completely enthroned while capitalism withers away, a victim of its own haloed good intentions.

POWER INCORPORATED

The trouble with our society today is not that government is becoming a player rather than an umpire, or that it is a huge welfare colossus dipping into every nook and cranny of our lives. The trouble is, all major functional groups—business, labor, agriculture, *and* government—are each trying so piously to outdo the other in intruding themselves into what should be our private lives. Each is trying to mold the whole man into its own image according to its own needs and tastes. Each is seeking to extend its own narrow tyranny over the widest possible range of our institutions, people, ideas, values, and beliefs, and all for the purest motive—to do what it honestly believes is best for society.

And that is precisely what is wrong. It is this aspect of purity and service that is so nightmarish. It is perfectly legitimate for each group to fight for its survival by seeking to influence others. But somehow the past decade has produced a new twist: self-righteous, dedicated proselyte sustained by the mighty machinery of a powerful institution—particularly an economic institution. The reformer whose only aim is personal aggrandizement and whose tactics are a vulgar combination of compulsive demagoguery and opportunistic cynicism is much less dangerous than the social evangelist who, to borrow from Nietzsche, thinks of himself as "God's ventriloquist." As Greek tragedies show, there is nothing more corrupting than self-righteousness and nothing more intolerant than an ardent man who is convinced he is on the side of the angels.

When the spokesmen for such causes begin to make speeches and write books about their holy mission, to canonize their beliefs into faith, conviction, and doctrine, and to develop ways of thinking by which their particular institutional ambitions are ideologically sustained—that is the time for us to begin trembling. They will then have baptized their mission with a book—still the most powerful instrument of change devised by man.

American capitalism does not yet possess a dramatic ideological statement of the kind just described. But it is getting there. During the past decade business executives' bylines have appeared under an increasing number of book and article titles connoting a sense of mission, of reaching out—for example, *A Creed for Free Enterprise*,[3] "'Skyhooks' (With Special Implications for Monday Through Friday),"[4] *New Frontiers for Professional Managers*,[5] and "Business Leadership and a Creative Society."[6] That such titles should be chosen and that they should appeal to the management community are, I believe, significant signs of the times. There is no doubt that the sense of zeal and social responsibility is increasing.

So far the movement is a young and rather unassuming one. But when it really gathers momentum, when its forms become crystallized and its primal innocence becomes more professionalized, its success should amaze us. The corporation is not handicapped by the cumbersome authority that has always characterized the church and the state. It can make its authority sweet as honey by making itself the embodiment of material welfare, of unbounded security, of decorous comfort, amusing diversion, healthful recreation, and palatable ideology. It can far surpass even the medieval Church in efficiency and power.

It may have no intention of doing this (and I firmly believe that this is the last thing that the apostles of corporate humanity want), but what we get is seldom what we want. History is fortuitous. It does not move on tracks made by rational social engineers.

Separate Functions

Business wants to survive. It wants security from attack and restriction; it wants to minimize what it believes is its greatest potential enemy—the state. So it takes the steam out of the state's lumbering engines by employing numerous schemes to win its employees and the general public to its side. It is felt that these are the best possible investments it can make for its own survival. And that is precisely where the reasoning has gone wrong. These investments are only superficially *easy* solutions, not the best.

Welfare and society are not the corporation's business. Its business is making money, not sweet music. The same goes for unions. Their business is "bread and butter" and job rights. In a free enterprise system, welfare is supposed to be automatic; and where it is not, it becomes government's job. This is the concept of pluralism. Government's job is not business, and business's job is not government. And unless these functions are resolutely separated in all respects, they are eventually combined in every respect. In the end the danger is not that government will run business, or that business will run government, but rather that the two of them will coalesce, as we saw, into a single power, unopposed and unopposable.

The only political function of business, labor, and agriculture is to fight each other so that none becomes or remains dominant for long. When one does reach overwhelming power and control, at the very best the state will eventually take over on the pretense of protecting everybody else. At that point the big business executives, claiming possession of the tools of large-scale management, will come in, as they do in war, to become the bureaucrats who run the state.

The final victor then is neither government, as the representative of the people, nor the people, as represented by government. The new leviathan will be the professional corporate bureaucrat operating at a more engrossing and exalted level than the architects of capitalism ever dreamed possible.

The functions of the four main groups in our economy—government, business, labor, agriculture—must be kept separate and separable. As soon as they become amalgamated and indistinguishable, they likewise become monstrous and restrictive.

TENDING TO BUSINESS

If businessmen do not preach and practice social responsibility, welfare, and self-restraint, how can management effectively deal with its critics, the political attacks, the confining legislation—that is, the things which have induced it to create its own private welfare state? The answer is fairly simple: to perform its main task so well that critics cannot make their charges stick, and then to assert forthrightly its function and accomplishments with the same aroused spirit that made nineteenth-century capitalism as great as it was extreme.

Present Failures

It seems clear that today's practices fall far short of this prescription. When it comes to material things, the accomplishments of American capitalism are spectacular. But the slate is not clean. American capitalism also creates, fosters, and acquiesces in enormous social and economic cancers. Indeed, it fights against the achievement of certain forms of economic and social progress, pouring millions into campaigns against things which people have a right to expect from their government and which they seem to want their government to provide. For example:

- Business motives helped to create slums, and now business seems all too frequently to fight their abolition. The free operation of the profit motive has not abolished them. Indeed, it sustains them. But if abolishing slums is not a sound business proposition, business should cease its campaign against government doing a job which nobody in his right mind can deny should be done. If supporting state and federal efforts at urban renewal does not raise the public's esteem of business's good intentions, few things will. Certainly self-righteous claims of good intentions are not enough.

- The same is true of health insurance, pensions, school construction, and other proposals for activities which are best handled by government (for reasons of administration as well as of ability to meet the commitments) and are therefore logical government functions. Businessmen will simply have to accept the fact that the state can be a powerful auxiliary to the attainment of the good life. This is particularly so in a free enterprise economy where there is a natural division of social and economic functions, and where this division is fortified by countervailing institutional checks and balances.

Yet in both word and deed business constantly denies the potentially beneficial role of the state. Where it does not fight the public interest, it often adopts a placid air of indifference or a vapid neutrality. Its most shameful indifference is in matters of civil rights. Although business operates in a system where the guarantee of civil rights is the bedrock of its own effective existence, management seldom raises a voice in support of civil rights—whether the issue is legislation or protecting some anonymous Joe Doakes against a Congressional kangaroo-court committee supposedly developing information for legislation.

Business must learn to speak for Joe Doakes when civil rights are involved. In doing this it would actually be speaking for itself. Civil rights are a single cloth; they cannot be curtailed for some without being curtailed for everybody. Hence to speak for Joe Doakes is to act in one's self-interest—especially in management's case, for when civil rights are gone, business loses not only freedom but also money.

Sensible Welfare

I am not arguing that management should ignore its critics. Some of them have made a good case from time to time against business's social delinquencies and against its shortsightedness in fighting practically all of Washington's efforts to provide security. (Indeed, if business had not always fought federal welfare measures, perhaps the unions would not have demanded them from business itself.)

Nor am I arguing that management has no welfare obligations at all to society. Quite to the contrary. Corporate welfare makes good sense *if* it makes good economic sense—and not infrequently it does. But if something does not make economic sense, sentiment or idealism ought not let it in the door. Sentiment is a corrupting and debilitating influence in business. It fosters leniency, inefficiency, sluggishness, extravagance, and hardens the innovationary arteries. It can confuse the role of the businessman just as much as the profit motive could confuse the role of the government official. The governing rule in industry should be that *something is good only if it pays*. Otherwise it is alien and impermissible. This is the rule of capitalism.

No matter how much business protests that saying this is redundant because it is exactly the rule being practiced, the fact is that it is *seldom* followed. Businessmen only say they practice it because it is another one of those sacred articles of the capitalist faith that must be regularly reaffirmed in speech and print. Their words are belied by some of their most common policies, such as:

- *The growing constellation of employee welfare programs*—Do they really make good economic sense for the individual firm? I say they do not. Most company welfare measures—such as retirement, unemployment, and health benefits—are forms of mass insurance. They make economic sense only when operated on a compulsory national basis. The only conceivable basis on which it can be argued that they make economic sense when operated by individual companies is that they help attract and hold manpower. And that is seldom the primary motive. If there were adequate national mass insurance, the company that wants to attract and hold more and better manpower needs only to pay more. The whole thing would be cheaper and more efficient.
- *Stock purchase plans*—These plans, which are one of the sacred appurtenances of "People's Capitalism," are justifiable only if they provide direct incentives to differentially superior performance. They are a menace and a drag on the economy when (as is often the case) their real object is to let the corporate insiders in on some easy capital gains gravy, or to immobilize the labor market by tying people to a particular company.

If the public wants protection against the uneven consequences of all-out capitalism, let it run to its unions and to government. If business wants protection against unions and government, let it fight for its cause on the open battlefield of manful contention—on the front of economic and political pressures. We are not back in the age of the robber barons, with its uneven matching of economic and political functional groups. Business, government, and unions are now each big and powerful enough to take care of themselves. As Mao Tse-Tung once prescribed for China, "Let all flowers bloom together; let rival schools of thought contend."

Conclusion

Business will have a much better chance of surviving if there is no nonsense about its goals—that is, if long-run profit maximization is the one dominant objective in practice as well as in theory. Business should recognize what government's functions are and let it go at that, stopping only to fight government where government directly intrudes itself into business. It should let government take care of the general welfare so that business can take care of the more material aspects of welfare.

The results of any such single-minded devotion to profit should be invigorating. With none of the corrosive distractions and costly bureaucracies that now serve the pious cause of welfare, politics, society, and putting up a pleasant front, with none of these draining its vitality, management can shoot for the economic moon. It will be able to thrust ahead in whatever way seems consistent with its money-making goals. If laws and threats stand in its way, it should test and fight them, relenting only if the courts have ruled against it, and then probing again to test the limits of the rules. And when business fights, it should fight with uncompromising relish and self-assertiveness, instead of using all the rhetorical dodges and pious embellishments that are now so often its stock in trade.

Practicing self-restraint behind the cloak of the insipid dictum that "an ounce of prevention is worth a pound of cure" has only limited justification. Certainly it often pays not to squeeze the last dollar out of a market—especially when good will is a factor in the long-term outlook. But too often self-restraint masquerades for capitulation. Businessmen complain about legislative and other attacks on aggressive profit seeking but then lamely go forth to slay the dragon with speeches that simply concede business's function to be service. The critic quickly pounces on this admission with unconcealed relish—"Then why *don't* you serve?" But the fact is, no matter how much business "serves," it will never be enough for its critics.

The Strenuous Life

If the all-out competitive prescription sounds austere or harsh, that is only because we persist in judging things in terms of utopian standards. Altruism, self-denial, charity, and similar values are vital in certain walks of our life—areas which, because of that fact, are more important to the long-run future than business. But for the most part those virtues are alien to competitive economics.

If it sounds callous to hold such a view, and suicidal to publicize it, that is only because business has done nothing to prepare the community to agree with it. There is only one way to do that: to perform at top ability and to speak vigorously *for* (not in defense of) what business does.

Prior's stand on human relations, quoted earlier, is a good point of departure. But it is only a beginning.

In the end business has only two responsibilities—to obey the elementary canons of everyday face-to-face civility (honesty, good faith, and so on) and to seek material gain. The fact that it is the butt of demagogical critics is no reason for management to lose its nerve—to buckle under to reformers—lest more severe restrictions emerge to throttle business completely. Few people will man the barricades against capitalism if it is a good provider, minds its own business, and supports government in the things which are properly government's. Even today, most American critics want only to curb capitalism, not to destroy it. And curbing efforts will not destroy it if there is free and open discussion about its singular function.

To the extent that there is conflict, can it not be a good thing? Every book, every piece of history, even every religion testifies to the fact that conflict is and always has been the subject, origin, and life blood of society. Struggle helps to keep us alive, to give élan to life. We should try to make the most of it, not avoid it.

Lord Acton has said of the past that people sacrificed freedom by grasping at impossible justice. The contemporary school of business morality seems intent on adding its own caveat to that unhappy consequence. The gospel of tranquility is a soporific. Instead of fighting for its survival by means of a series of strategic retreats masquerading as industrial statesmanship, business must fight as if it were at war. And, like a good war, it should be fought gallantly, daringly, and, above all, *not* morally.

ENDNOTES

1. Speech delivered May 6, 1957.
2. Theodore V. Houser, 1957 McKinsey Foundation Lectures, reprinted as *Big Business and Human Values* (New York, McGraw-Hill Book Company, Inc., 1957).
3. Clarence B. Randall (Boston, Little, Brown and Company, 1952).
4. O.A. Ohmann, HBR May–June 1955, p. 41.
5. Ralph J. Cordiner (New York, McGraw-Hill Book Company, Inc., 1956).
6. Abram T. Collier, HBR January–February 1953, p. 29.

15 — Marketing: A Social Responsibility

*Thaddeus H. Spratlen**

Reprinted from the *AMA Combined Proceedings*, published by the American Management Association, Series No. 34 (1973), pp. 65–75. Reprinted by permission.

Social responsibility is a moral and philosophical issue of fundamental importance to a maturing management discipline and process. Its recognition as a possible standard for resource-use decisions reflects a consideration of values and value judgements as essential elements in the analysis of individual and organizational behavior.

In this paper an attempt is made to provide a "state of the art" assessment of social responsibility as it relates to marketing. The objectives and organization of the paper focus on reporting and interpreting the following aspects of the topic:

1. Background and definitions.
2. Rationale and role of management with respect to social responsibility.
3. Opposition to social responsibility.
4. Characteristics and topics associated with social responsibility in marketing.
5. Implementation and evaluation of social responsibility as social performance in the market system.
6. Implications of social responsibility for the future of marketing.

As an assessment, the paper is intended to be both a report and an interpretation of the current state of analysis, methodology, and practice in marketing with respect to social responsibility.[1]

BACKGROUND AND DEFINITIONS

Social responsibility refers to the expression in words and action of values and perspectives for considering the social consequences of individual and organizational behavior. Viewed in personal terms it is the individual's "obligation to evaluate in the decision-making process the effects of his personal and institutional decisions and actions on the whole social system."[2] It reflects a sense of obligation and accountability to those who are affected by the decisions and actions of individuals and groups. In practice, it involves meeting the expectations of those affected by the decisions and actions. In a more inclusive phrase, social responsibility in the context of managerial behavior is:

> "a modern amalgam of corporate good citizenship, enlightened self-interest, long-range planning, individual good citizenship, personal ethics, and rational management."[3]

Implicit in this statement is the notion that social obligations are fulfilled when management performance embodies the foregoing concepts and activities.

Whatever the wording of the definition, the essence of the meaning is that social responsibility is (1) a normative doctrine or concept of personal and social values; (2) a standard for judging what ought to be done with the power and resources which are utilized by individuals and institutions in society, and (3) a performance goal to be pursued by management through a balancing of the claims or expectations of several groups or alternative courses of action. Each facet of the term is associated with a desirable and beneficial response to the use of power, expression of social and moral concern, or other factors which determine the social content of individual and organizational behavior.

Social responsibility emerged as an important concept at a time when marketing people were preoccupied with adjusting to the rise of consumer behavior, quantitative methods, the marketing concept, and managerial marketing. This places its initial impact in the early 1950s.[4] The term was adopted as the theme of the Winter Conference of the American Marketing Association in 1961.[5] However, significant expression of concern for social responsibility in marketing did not occur until the mid-1960s. This is reflected in the number of articles published since 1965. But it should be noted that, even in 1972, the term has not achieved recognition as a standard index item in marketing textbooks. This may be seen as a lag between the journal and textbook literature as well as a reflection of the low priority given to value issues in marketing. Nevertheless, it has been widely discussed and debated as a basis for management decisions in marketing.

RATIONALE AND ROLE OF MANAGEMENT

A major difficulty in analyzing social responsibility is its incomplete or underdeveloped analytic and intellectual status as a concept or doctrine. As suggested by the preceding discussion, it is offered as an ethic or set of social values which can serve as guides to individual and group behavior. Yet, despite over a generation of discussion, it still lacks a coherent body of purposes, assumptions, and principles that can serve as yardsticks for judging its adequacy or acceptability in relation to an alternative ethic.[6] But it must compete with such a well developed ethic as profit-maximization in the traditional theory of the firm, or satisfying in the behavioral theory of the firm. What is urgently needed is a social value theory of the firm. Until there is such a clearly articulated theory, a crucial constraint on cumulative development of the social responsibility ethic will remain: the rule of contradiction which makes much that is inherent in social responsibility incompatible with the criteria, postulates, and other conceptual and analytic apparatus of the ruling ethic of enterprise—profit maximization. Although the present paper cannot address this issue, it is of crucial importance for advancing the conceptual as well as the operational side of social responsibility.

The current status of the social responsibility literature in marketing is suggested by the primary concerns expressed in various articles. The focus of analysis and discussion is presented as a continuum extending from conceptualization to empirical evaluation. This is summarized in Figure 1.

It seems to be appropriate to place most of the articles, papers, and speeches on the subject at the level of conceptualization and rationalization. As a further interpretation, the various premises or rationale which have been advanced to explain or justify fulfilling social responsibilities may be categorized under the following headings:

1. Power Thesis.
2. Mutual-Benefit Thesis.
3. Enlightened Self-Interest Thesis.
4. Enterprise-Defensive Thesis.
5. Ethical-Value or Eclectic Thesis.

Those who support the assumption of social responsibilities adopt the premises included in one or more of the above categories. In the first, power is equated with responsibility. Its premise is that whatever there is power over, there is responsibility for. It may take such diverse forms as influencing customer choices through merchandising, administering prices in oligopolistic markets, maintaining privilege through access to politicians and others who have power.

Second, it is argued that the expected benefits to be shared by various claimant groups establish the basis for management's social obligations. Thus, meeting responsibilities to consumers in the form of safe products and good product quality will, over time, result in such benefits as greater loyalty, favored image, and repeat business. Similar benefits may be associated with meeting responsibilities to other publics of the organization.

The third position holds that long-run organizational objectives are more likely to be realized when social responsibilities are assumed by management. Such action embodies a far-sighted view of anticipating

FIGURE 1. Focus of Analysis in the Social Responsibility Literature

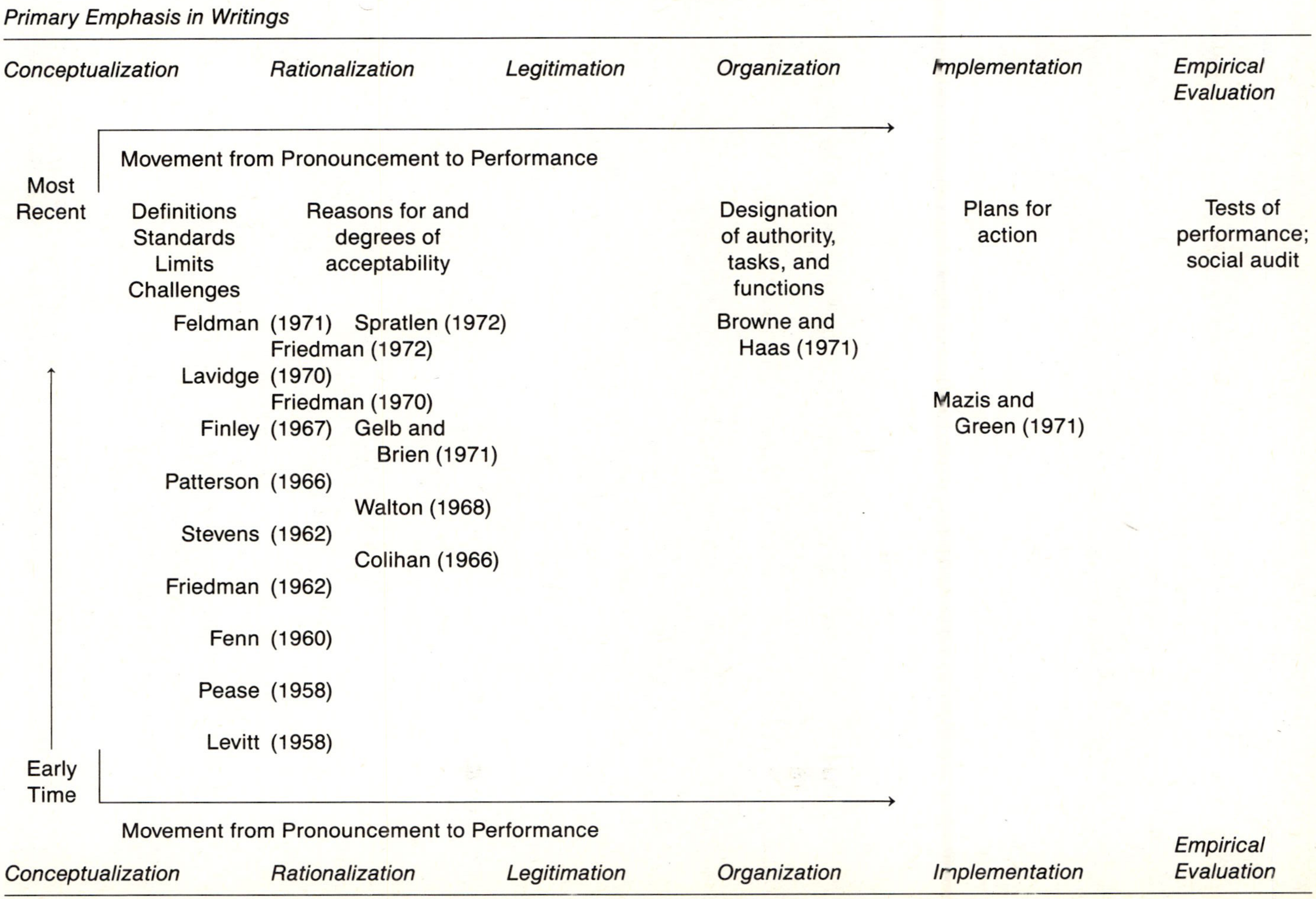

Primary Emphasis in Writings

Conceptualization	Rationalization	Legitimation	Organization	Implementation	Empirical Evaluation

Most Recent

↑ *Movement from Pronouncement to Performance*

Definitions Standards Limits Challenges	Reasons for and degrees of acceptability		Designation of authority, tasks, and functions	Plans for action	Tests of performance; social audit
Feldman (1971)	Spratlen (1972)		Browne and Haas (1971)	Mazis and Green (1971)	
Lavidge (1970)	Friedman (1972)				
Finley (1967)	Gelb and Brien (1971)				
Patterson (1966)	Walton (1968)				
Stevens (1962)	Colihan (1966)				
Friedman (1962)					
Fenn (1960)					
Pease (1958)					
Levitt (1958)					

Early Time

↑ *Movement from Pronouncement to Performance*

Conceptualization	Rationalization	Legitimation	Organization	Implementation	Empirical Evaluation

and meeting societal expectations. Thus, raising the standards of product quality may avoid the imposition of punitive and coercive measures of product liability legislation. More important, market opportunities may be realized through product adaptations associated with various social and ecological concerns.[7]

Fourth, a defensive posture is assumed in explaining social responsibility as a strategy to prevent coercion and regulation by government or the imposition of other forms of social control. Thus, fulfilling responsibilities preserves a wider area of discretion. It also protects the basis of initiative and freedom for management. As a negative threat, it is asserted that if business does not assume social responsibilities, then it will lose out to big government, big labor, or some other pressure or countervailing power group in the society. Put another way, the premise is that business should act before it is forced to act, since forced action is likely (1) to be more stringent, and (2) to result in lost political position or public image.

Finally, a variety of ethical or value positions may be used to explain the doctrine of social responsibility. They may be absolutist in reference to Biblical injunctions or other moral imperatives of social conscience. They may be relativist in relying on basic notions of situational ethics. They may be pragmatic or even humanistic.

Whether as moral imperatives based on utilitarianism, as personal convictions of individual executives, or as group judgment and consensus of corporate management, some system of ethical values can be applied. Not uncommonly, the basis of such judgments may not be explicitly stated. Under this heading it would be appropriate to place interpretations which are eclectic or which do not properly fall under either of the preceding rationales.

OPPOSITION TO SOCIAL RESPONSIBILITY

Limitations of the concept are discussed in this section. Thus, all criticisms are not to be interpreted as "opposition" statements.

Explanations of the limitations of social responsibility may also be summarized along the lines of identifiable premises. The various positions may be categorized under the following headings:

1. Classical Economic Thesis.
2. Ambiguity Thesis.
3. Radicals'–Cynics' Thesis.
4. Eclectic–Institutional Thesis.

The most rigorous opposition is associated with the views of economist Milton Friedman.[8] The foremost critic of social responsibility in marketing has been Theodore Levitt.[9] The essence of their position is that under profit-maximization criteria, management can accept or assume broader responsibilities, only on one condition—"if it pays." This position is supported by the classical tenets of economic theory.[10] Business responsibilities, then, are defined in relation to the enterprise as a technical, economic and legal instrument of production.[11] Business satisfies its social functions by simply fulfilling economic functions such as generating sales and profits.

A second thesis can be associated with the view that social responsibility defies measurement and the formulation of workable answers and operating rules. In calling attention to this limitation of the concept, James Patterson pointed out that there is "no specific, concrete guide to responsible action for marketing executives beyond a sort of 'watered-down' commercial version of the Golden Rule."[12] Given that the issues are complex and the standards vague or non-existent, management may well put them aside for workable guides which "help a marketing executive evaluate alternative courses of action in a specific concrete situation."[13] The substance of the position is that management has neither the competence nor the authority to define and assume social obligations. It is in essence a narrow and traditional view of the scope, purposes and functions of business enterprise.

Third, in a more cynical vein, it is sometimes suggested that businessmen seek respectability after abusing power, exploitation and other misdeeds. Thus, social responsibility is mostly rhetoric, a salve for the conscience. Its advocacy is a cover-up for inefficiency, lack of competition, inadequacy, or guilt.

Finally, numerous other points are encountered in discussions of the shortcomings of the social responsibility concept. In order to avoid an extended discussion, they are outlined below as a summary of the dangers of adopting social responsibility in business practice. It is stated that social responsibility:

a. Intensifies the concentration of corporate power through the transfer of economic means into diverse forms of control and influence.
b. Results in excessive discretion on the part of management by substituting personal preferences and political power for market-determined policies and programs.
c. Diverts the attention and preoccupation of management from efficiency, innovation, and other sources of growth and gain in business.
d. Reduces profits (in long-run and short-run) by adding burdens and expenditures without the assurance of commensurate returns.

e. Allows business to impose a tax through its arbitrary assignment of priorities and trade-offs of compensating one group and penalizing another.
f. Undermines the basis of the market economy and the free society through shifting values that subvert, diver, and otherwise weaken the impersonal, individualized forces of the market; and by overemphasizing collective, socially-oriented practices and standards to the neglect of the qualities which have made the U.S. economy the most affluent in all the world.

CHARACTERISTICS AND RELATIONSHIPS IN MARKETING

Because of the pervasive and public nature of marketing, it has many unique social dimensions. It is peculiarly identified with a societal interest. Marketing is pervasive because transaction behavior and activities in the marketplace exert an unavoidable impact on a wide range of relationships, institutions, and values in the society. It is public because there are numerous, complex, and diverse externalities associated with its role in the society.[14] From a technical point of view some of the interest in social responsibility stems from the recognition of its potential value in reducing negative externalities associated with marketing and consumption.

Aside from the characteristics of the social responsibility literature already mentioned, it seems appropriate to summarize briefly a few others.

Most of the literature is ethical rather than social in content and methods of analysis. It would appear that the research frameworks for analyzing social responsibility with reference to consumers and children are more sophisticated than the ones used with reference to managers.[15] To be sure, the task is considerably more difficult with reference to managers. But the potential gains would also appear to be much greater, given the influence of managers in the process of resource allocation.

Further, ideology and rhetoric continue to occupy a substantial portion of published statements. Understandably, the discussion lacks the compelling and appealing rigor of profitability or growth analysis and other guidelines for managerial behavior and performance.

In light of these and other characteristics, the remaining discussion in this section focuses on social responsibility as it relates to some of the recent controversies and challenges to marketing institutions and their management.

SOCIAL RESPONSIBILITY AND THE MARKETING CONCEPT

The basic orientation of marketing thought and practice since the early 1950s has been the marketing concept. However, its managerial focus has been essentially micro in scope. Cook provides an example of this point of view by stating that the basic function of marketing is "the building and maintaining of a consumer market for any product."[16] It has not explicitly encompassed the social, macro and value dimensions of marketing. Yet, these are fundamental elements of the doctrine of social responsibility. The essence of the dilemma is that the marketing concept stops with the satisfied customer, while marketing goes on beyond consumption to encompass externalities and social costs associated with the post-consumption consequences of resource-use decisions. The marketing concept, then, can be pursued as customer satisfaction through style, convenience, indulgence and many other attributes of personal appeal. Yet, social responsibility would subject such resource-use decisions to the constraints of safety, durability and social appeal. As Lavidge has phrased it, the questions would not be just 'can it be sold to a satisfied customer,' but 'should it be sold at all?'... "Is it worth its cost to society?"[17] Clearly, management performance which is socially responsible and consistent with serving larger long-run societal interests may often, if not generally, require an alteration in the marketing concept.[18]

RESPONSIBILITIES OF MARKETING MANAGEMENT

Social responsibilities for marketing management have been largely, if not formally, legitimized. The debate now centers on how many responsibilities there are and on which ones are to take precedence. It is not on whether they exist. It is on how and the extent to which they should be assumed.[19] Major attention centers on giving operational meaning to management responsibilities.[20]

At least three principal issues must be resolved: (1) what management is to be responsible for; (2) to whom management will be accountable; (3) how the responsibilities will be implemented or fulfilled; and (4) what methods of evaluation and measurement will be used.

On the first point, a number of lists have been presented. The following activities are illustrative:[21]

- increasing productivity or efficiency in distribution;
- improving innovation and performance in marketing;
- eliminating malpractices in the marketplace;
- making competition more workable;
- cooperating with government to increase consumer well-being through better information, products, etc.;
- increasing the social usefulness of advertising and sales promotion;
- supporting consumer education;

- meeting the needs of poor consumers;
- actively recruiting minorities in marketing;
- providing services to expand job opportunities for minorities, especially in marketing management;
- improving marketing in the inner-city;
- supporting the cause of social justice;
- extending marketing technology to low-income housing, new-town in-town planning, mass transit;
- contributing to pollution abatement;
- expanding conservation and recreational facilties;
- enhancing the quality of life;
- extending communications effectiveness in combatting racism; and
- orienting marketing policies towards societal and survival needs.

To whom will management be accountable? This question has not been dealt with adequately. Most writers are silent on this issue. After pointing out the inability of market constraints to ensure proper containment of corporate power, Browne and Haas[22] imply a blurring of distinctions between government and the large corporations and suggest the need to search for "mechanisms which would insure that corporate managers were accountable to the public in the same sense as are governmental representatives." More conventional solutions of countervailing power, competition, self-regulation, consumer organization and social action also form part of the mixture of arrangements for ensuring the accountability of marketing management. Given the power of the large corporations, enforceability seems likely to remain a highly uncertain element in the quest for management accountability to its publics.

The two other issues—implementation and measurement-evaluation—are considered to be important enough to warrant somewhat more analysis than the ones just discussed.

APPROACHES TO IMPLEMENTATION

A crucial test of socially responsible performance rests ultimately on the extent to which social responsibility is incorporated into marketing decisions and programs. Mazis and Green[23] stressed this point and suggested several alternatives. They emphasized the establishment of a Department of Social Affairs to manage the overall implementation of social responsibility programs. The basic requirements and alternatives for marketing have been outlined in Figure 2.

In applying the framework to a given organization and situation, consideration should be given to the level of commitment and to key

15 __ *Marketing: A Social Responsibility* 287

FIGURE 2. Requirements and Alternatives for Implementing Social Responsibility in Marketing

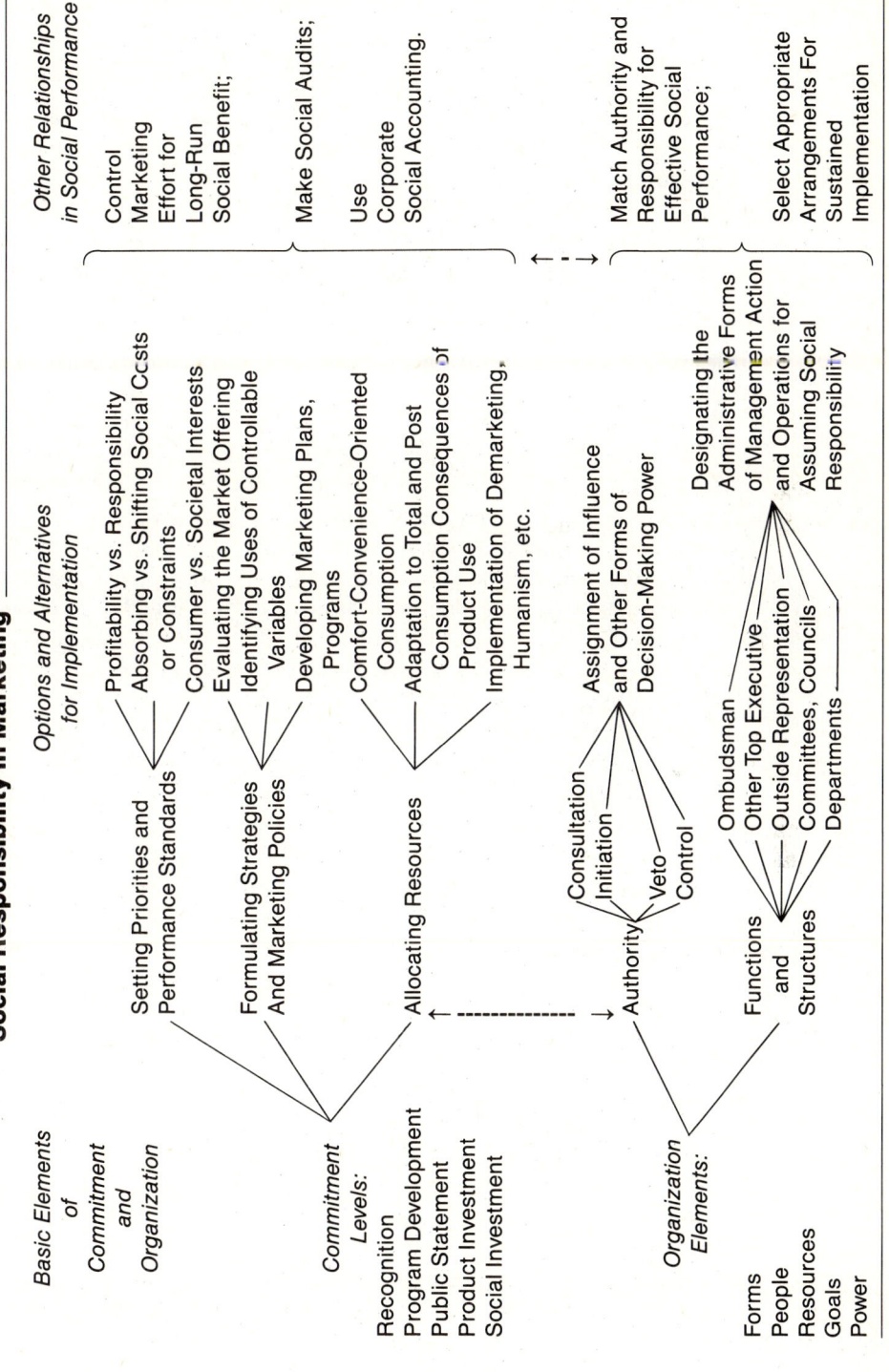

Basic Elements of Commitment and Organization

Options and Alternatives for Implementation

Other Relationships in Social Performance

Setting Priorities and Performance Standards
- Profitability vs. Responsibility
- Absorbing vs. Shifting Social Costs or Constraints

Formulating Strategies And Marketing Policies
- Consumer vs. Societal Interests
- Evaluating the Market Offering
- Identifying Uses of Controllable Variables

Allocating Resources
- Developing Marketing Plans, Programs
- Comfort-Convenience-Oriented Consumption
- Adaptation to Total and Post Consumption Consequences of Product Use
- Implementation of Demarketing, Humanism, etc.

Control Marketing Effort for Long-Run Social Benefit;

Make Social Audits;

Use Corporate Social Accounting.

Commitment Levels:
Recognition
Program Development
Public Statement
Product Investment
Social Investment

Authority
- Consultation
- Initiation
- Veto
- Control

Assignment of Influence and Other Forms of Decision-Making Power

Match Authority and Responsibility for Effective Social Performance;

Functions and Structures
- Ombudsman
- Other Top Executive
- Outside Representation
- Committees, Councils
- Departments

Designating the Administrative Forms of Management Action and Operations for Assuming Social Responsibility

Select Appropriate Arrangements For Sustained Implementation

Organization Elements:
Forms
People
Resources
Goals
Power

organizational elements. These factors establish the scope of social responsibility with respect to implementation. They can be combined with an assessment of external constraints and the related uncontrollable variable facing marketing management. Options and alternatives can then be weighed realistically. Various other relationships can then be analyzed for incorporation into social responsibility programs with the end result of (1) controlling marketing effort for long-run social benefit; (2) matching authority and responsibility for effective social performance; (3) selecting the appropriate arrangements for sustained implementation; and (4) measuring and evaluating overall performance results in terms of social responsibility.

Of course, it should be recognized that at the present time relatively little in the way of operational measurement has been conceptualized; and even less has been tested or used, based on the available literature.

Browne and Haas[24] identified some of the structural and power issues regarding social responsibility and market performance. Anderson and Cunningham[25] offered a "marketing concept" alternative—relate social responsibility to customer segmentation and satisfaction. But their analysis focused on characteristics of the socially responsible consumer, not the manager or the social consequences of resource-use decisions.

What is needed is a framework for evaluating social responsibility as social performance for both consumers and managers, but especially for the latter. As an initial step towards formulating such a framework, it is proposed that statistical indexing and scaling relationships be developed and applied. Some initial possibilities are outlined in Figure 3.

The methodology to be used would require initially that disinterested experts make judgments about the consumption and post consumption consequences of product use. Wherever possible non-expert or consumer judgments would also be included in the analysis. Several dimensions of performance impact would be identified. Ultimately, multi-dimensional scales would be constructed. Maps along with other graphical and statistical techniques would be designed for analyzing the combined or composite effects of marketing and consuming products.

The results could have several uses. The basis for prescriptive or corrective action would be established from the reasons given by experts for detrimental and beneficial effects of marketing performance. Taxation, investment or other allocation policies could be established in response to the results. Priority areas of social responsibility as social performance could be identified. Thus, those products which were uniformly placed at the negative end of the performance scales would call for special effort in both private and public action. As an example, −4 products would be taxed at a rate commensurate with their negative or detrimental effects. Likewise, to the maximum extent of feasibility, +4 products would be given quite favorable tax and investment consideration.

Besides providing additional information from which to assess the social consequences of consumption, it could provide some leverage for exposing undesirable practices and raising performance standards in industries. Evidence would also be obtained for legislative and regulatory controls as well as for social action by consumers, environmentalists and others.

Necessarily involved in the development and use of such a framework would be personnel from product testing organizations and universities as well as specialists from appropriate federal agencies. In this connection it is assumed that experts who are not primarily industry consultants would be relied upon most heavily. But if the approach is to be used effectively, the cooperation and participation of specialists from industry will be needed. Indeed, the extent of cooperation and participation would become one indicator of a firm's or industry's commitment to the implementation of social responsibility in the context of social performance criteria.

OUTLOOK AND IMPLICATIONS

The marketing literature referenced in this paper suggests that the boundaries and foundations of the discipline are being extended through the doctrine of social responsibility and related value changes in management and in the society. The outlook and implications for several changes are discussed briefly. Included in the discussion are consumerism, concern over environmental disruption, improving marketing in the inner-city, professionalism in management and education, extensions of the marketing concept, and the challenges of humanism.

Consumerism

If social responsibility were the standard for marketing practice, there would be no need for a consumerism movement. Consumer interests which are sustainable over the long-run would be served as part of serving societal or public interests.

Since the early 1960s, marketing management has been challenged to protect consumers and prevent the abuse of market power over consumers. Milestones along the way included President Kennedy's declaration of consumer rights (1962), Ralph Nader's emergence as a pro-consumer advocate and author with *Unsafe at Any Speed* (1965), the Fair Packaging and Labeling Act (1966), the Consumer Protection Credit Act (1968), the banning of radio and television cigarette advertising (1970) and issuance of proof of claim orders by the Federal Trade Commission (1972).[26] These and other actions have raised the standards of market performance and encouraged the adoption of more socially responsible marketing practice.

FIGURE 3. Performance Scales for Evaluating Social Responsibility in Marketing

Type of Scale	Criteria of Measurement	Measurement Units	Performance Impact Scales
			Highly *Highly* *Detrimental* *Beneficial* −5 −4 −3 −2 −1 0 +1 +2 +3 +4 +5 *Possible Product Examples*
Establishes the General Dimension of Performance of Results.	Identify Sources or Areas of Impact Associated with Performance.	Define the Bases of Quantifying Performance Results.	
1. Social Impact	Health, Safety, Poverty, etc.; User or Societal Well-Being.	Incidence of injury; Relationship of product consumption to illness or injury; Costs of injury or illness.	Cigarettes Penicillin
2. Environmental Impact	Pollution.	Volume of Pollutants; Costs of waste disposal; Costs of pollution abatement.	Automobiles High-phosphate detergents High-lead gasoline "Reusable" Containers
3. Aggregate Economic Impact	Resource Utilization; Economic Efficiency.	Rate of resource use; Costs of resources used; Costs of planned Obsolescence.	"Non-recycled" Containers Recycled Paper, Metals, Inc.

15 — Marketing: A Social Responsibility

			Petroleum Products	Textile Products
4. Power Concentration Impact	Maldistribution of Wealth; Concentration of Market Power.	Concentration ratios; Market shares; Social costs of concentration.		
5. Ethical Impact	Congruency or Conflict with Ethical Norms	Degree of conformity with ideal standards; Social costs of unethical behavior	Ads to increase cigarette consumption	Ads to increase cheese consumption
6. Cultural Impact	Congruency or Conflict with Cultural Norms and Values; Esthetic Qualities.	Degree of conformity with ideal standards; Social costs of cultural conflicts and pollution	Unsightly billboard and neon signs	Building plans to preserve natural surroundings
7. Product Distribution Impact a. Promotion b. Pricing c. Place d. Product e. Services	Social Efficiency in Distribution	Social and Market costs of distribution	a. Deceptive ads b. Brand drugs c. High costs to consumer d. Emphasis on appearance e. Partial disclosure of charges	Informative ads Generic drugs Low costs to consumer Emphasis on performance Full disclosure of charges

The full impact of social responsibility and its implementation in the consumer interest extends to such actions as the appointment of consumer ombudsmen, granting authority for corporate consumer affairs departments; "near-zero-defects" product quality standards, and generally imposing necessary constraints to serve consumer and societal interests.[27]

Concern over Environmental Disruption

Ecology, environmental quality, and pollution abatement suggest popular as well as technical terms in the search for ways to eliminate environmental disruption. Marketing occupies a central place in both the problems of pollution and their solution. Since product usage is a dominant factor in pollution, marketing bears special responsibility for its form and extent. Thus, as Zikmund and Stanton point out, a major part of recycling as a strategy for solid waste pollution abatement is a marketing rather than a production or technological problem.[28] A major challenge to marketers lies in the area of developing market opportunities in the process of contributing to pollution abatement and greater environmental quality.

Improving Marketing in the Inner City

By the late 1960s, special attention was focused on marketing management and its responsibilities regarding the ghetto marketplace. The Kerner Commission Report,[29] especially, dramatized and popularized the plight of the poor and minorities in the central city ghettos. The Report confirmed what David Caplovitz[30] had documented in the New York City area—the poor pay more. Although the findings were challenged and higher ghetto prices could be attributed to higher operating costs, the size and structure of ghetto business, and other factors, interest did shift to improving marketing in the ghetto as a social obligation of marketers.[31]

Professionalism in Management and Education

Marketing as a science and its practice as a profession are goals being pursued in the discipline. The extent to which they are achieved will be attributable in considerable degree to the influence of social responsibility. With respect to management it means internalizing a set of values which gives priority to the broader social purposes of resource use decisions. In education it calls for the expression of social concern and constraint in matters of acquiring and using marketing knowledge. Gelb and Brien have interpreted this aspect of challenge in the context of survival and social responsibility.[32]

Concept of Marketing

Social responsibility clearly requires a change in the marketing concept. This, in turn, necessitates an alteration of the concept of marketing. New boundaries are being defined. They are placing its technology in the service of broader social purposes. They are, thereby, expanding the social role of marketing and shifting its orientation closer to the requirements of social responsibility.

The Challenges of Humanism

Since the dominant philosophical theme in marketing is materialism the most fundamental changes in values center around the challenges of humanism. The implications for marketing extend to far more idealistic standards than have previously existed. Consistent with the essential meaning of social responsibility, performance standards and decisions are to be based on such ultimate measures of consequences as societal benefit, human welfare and long-run, sustainable outcomes.

To be sure, considerable doubt may be raised about the impact to data of these several challenges. However, value changes in the society seem to be shifting criteria and expectations of social institutions to adopt performance standards which are consistent with broader social purposes.

CONCLUSIONS

There is abundant evidence that social responsibility represents an idea whose time has come, whose place is secure in the search for higher-level performance standards in marketing and management. Support for this conclusion is indicated by the challenges, changes and responses to social performance standards.

However, the "state of the art" may be described as underdeveloped. Discussion is at the conceptualization-rationalization stage as primary concerns. Its content is more ethical than social in character. There is more evidence of pronouncements and proposals than plans and performance. Yet, the potential exists for the adoption of social responsibility as a standard for social performance. Whether the potential is realized depends on the policies and practices which are adopted in the future by marketing management. Both pressures and opportunities seem great enough to stimulate and accelerate the movement towards the adoption of social responsibility as a standard for social performance in marketing.

As for the future, the development of a coherent, theoretical framework and techniques for measurement and evaluation, will advance the study of social responsibility to a more sophisticated and systematic level. In this way, personal opinion about the subject will be replaced by empirical fact as a basis for its analysis and application as a standard of performance.

ENDNOTES

* Helpful comments on an earlier draft of the paper were received from Professors Edwin Epstein (University of California, Berkeley); David Luck (Southern Illinois University, Edwardsville); and John Wish (University of Oregon, Eugene).
1. It has been suggested by David Luck that there is an implicit advocacy of social responsibility in the paper. Scholarly neutrality has not been maintained. In reply I would submit that a balanced assessment has been attempted, subject to the constraint of an inherent value bias in any *interpretation* of social responsibility. A wide spectrum of opposing and supporting viewpoints has been presented. Of course, Professor Luck has correctly identified my philosophical and political position in the debate over the merits of fulfilling social responsibilities in marketing practice.
2. Keith Davis and Robert L. Blomstrom, *Business Society and Environment—Social Power and Social Response*, Second Edition (New York: McGraw-Hill Book Company, 1971), p. 85.
3. Dan H. Fenn, Jr., ed., *Business Responsibility in Action* (New York: McGraw-Hill Book Company, 1960), p. v.
4. Earlier titles include Harwood F. Merrill, ed. *The Responsibilities of Business Leadership*. (Cambridge, Mass., Harvard University, Graduate School of Business Administration, 1949); three years earlier, *Fortune* magazine featured the results of a poll in which special emphasis was given to the topic of corporate social responsibilities. In 1950, statements by Stuart Chase and others were published in *The Social Responsibility of Management* (New York: New York University, School of Commerce and Finance, 1950.) Perhaps most widely referred to is Howard R. Bowen, *Social Responsibilities of the Businessman* (New York: Harper and Row, 1953).
5. See William D. Stevens, ed., *The Social Responsibilities of Marketing*, Proceedings of the 1961 Winter Conference, Chicago: The American Marketing Association, 1962.
6. Criteria suggested by Eugene J. Meehan, *Value Judgment and Social Science—Structures and Processes* (Homewood, Illinois: The Dorsey Press, 1969), p. 138.
7. Harold H. Kasserjian, "Incorporating Ecology into Marketing Strategy: The Case of Air Pollution," *Journal of Marketing*, Vol. 35 (July, 1971), p. 65; Thomas Anderson, Jr. and William H. Cunningham, "The Socially Conscious Consumer," *Journal of Marketing*, Vol. 36 (July, 1972), pp. 30–31.
8. Milton Friedman, "The Social Responsibility of Business is to Increase Its Profits," *The New York Times Magazine* (September 13, 1970), pp. 32–33, 123; "Milton Friedman Responds," *Business and Society Review*, Vol. 1 (Spring, 1972), pp. 5–16; *Capitalism and Freedom* (Chicago: University of Chicago Press, 1962).
9. See his widely reprinted "Dangers of Social Responsibility," originally published in the September–October 1958 issue of *Harvard Business Review*. However, he does not categorically reject the notion that business has broader social respon-

sibilities, on the condition that their fulfillment is acceptable "if it pays." In a more sharply focused discussion for a trade audience, he suggested that "the cultural, spiritual, social, moral, etc., consequences of his (the businessman's actions) are none of his occupational concern. He is in business for his own personal edification—neither to save nor to ruin souls. His job is perfectly neutral on these matters." "Are Advertising and Marketing Corrupting Society? It's Not Your Worry," (p. 443 in C. H. Sandage and V. Fryburger, *The Role of Advertising* (Homewood, Illinois: R. D. Irwin, 1960), Reprinted from *Advertising Age*, October 6, 1958, pp. 89–92.

10. The firm is defined in terms of "property rights and contractual relationships." Francis X. Sutton, et al., *The American Business Creed* (New York: Schocken Books, 1962), p. 356. Responsibility is primarily or solely to owners and others within the confines of specific contractual commitments. By definition all others are "outsiders." This view is exemplified in *Capitalism and Freedom* (Chicago: University of Chicago Press, 1962) by Milton Friedman. He writes that the one and only social responsibility of business—profit-maximization—is to "use its resources and engage in activities designed to increase its profits so long as it stays within the rules of the game, which is to say, engages in open and free competition, without deception or fraud," (p. 133).

11. The thought here is that market behavior should be viewed in an exclusively amoral context—impersonally given conditions (automatic operation of market forces), self-interested, impersonal actions of individuals, with no obligation of social concern for others. See Arthur C. Kemp, "The Market Has No Morals," *The Intercollegiate Review*, Vol. 2 (October, 1965), pp. 139–142.

12. James M. Patterson, "What are the Social and Ethical Responsibilities of Marketing Executives?" *Journal of Marketing*, Vol. 30 (July, 1966), p. 12.

13. Same reference as footnote 12.

14. Briefly stated, externalities include all forms of favorable and unfavorable spillover effects on one or more individuals which are caused by the action(s) of another individual or individuals. Air pollution from automobiles, water pollution from high-phosphate detergents, noise pollution from inadequately insulated apartment walls are common illustrations of negative externalities associated with marketing (and consumption). Positive externalities include lower insurance rates resulting from better-trained, safety-conscious drivers and fewer accidents. Reduced negative externalities are based on shifting consumption away from products and activities which have adverse spillover effects, e.g., regular to low-lead gasoline, from automobile to public transportation, and so forth.

15. Compare references in footnote 7.

16. C. W. Cook, "The Social Values of Marketing," *The Conference Board Record*, Vol. 4 (February, 1967), p. 34.

17. Robert J. Lavidge, "The Growing Responsibilities of Marketing," *Journal of Marketing*, Vol. 34 (January, 1970), p. 27.

18. This is, of course, being recognized in the challenge for broadening and deepening of the marketing concept.

19. Influential sources including Editors of *Business Week* and *Fortune* along with a substantial number of marketists (educators, past and present American Marketing Association officials, etc.) as well as marketers (managers, retailers, etc.) take a decidedly supportive view towards the assumption of management's social responsibilities.

20. Betsy D. Gelb and Richard H. Brien, "Survival and Social Responsibility: Themes for Marketing Education and Management," *Journal of Marketing*, Vol. 35 (April, 1971), p. 3.
21. Same Reference as footnote 17; also, Committee for Economic Development, *Corporate Social Responsibilities*, (New York: The Committee, 1971), pp. 37–40.
22. Neil Browne and Paul F. Haas, "Social Responsibility and Market Performance," *MSU Business Topics*, Vol. 19 (Autumn, 1971) p. 10.
23. Michael Mazis and Robert Green, "Implementing Social Responsibility," *MSU Business Topics*, Vol. 19 (Winter, 1971), pp. 68–76.
24. Same reference as footnote 2.
25. Same reference as footnote 7.
26. These are intended to be illustrative of the momentum gained by the movement. The increased number and circulation of consumer oriented magazines, organized consumer protests and higher standards of information disclosure are other indicators which could be cited.
27. In a broader perspective, Kotler has identified the benefits of consumerism to marketers and marketing. See Philip Kotler, "What Consumerism Means for Marketers," *Harvard Business Review*, Vol. 50 (May–June, 1972), pp. 48–57.

    For some forecasts of the characteristics of the consumer environment of the 1970s, see William Lazer, John E. Smallwood and others, "Consumer Environments and Life Styles of the Seventies," *MSU Business Topics*, Vol. 20 (Spring, 1972), pp. 5–17.
28. William G. Zikmund and William J. Stanton, "Recycling Solid Wastes: A Channel-of-Distribution Problem," *Journal of Marketing*, Vol. 35 (July, 1971), pp. 34–39.
29. *Report of the National Advisory Commission on Civil Disorders* (New York: Bantam Books, Inc., 1968).
30. David Caplovitz, *The Poor Pay More* (New York: The Free Press, 1963).
31. Frederick D. Sturdivant, "Retailing in the Ghetto: Problems and Proposals," in *Marketing and the New Science of Planning*, Robert L. King, Ed. (Chicago: American Marketing Association, 1969), p. 532–534.

    See Alan Andreasen, Ed. *Improving Marketing in the Inner City* (Conference proceedings, in press, 1972).
32. Same reference as footnote 20.

SELECTED CLASSIFIED BIBLIOGRAPHY

The literature on marketing and social responsibility has been categorized under six headings. When articles or books overlap two or more of the categories, they are placed under the heading which best describes their main content. The category "Related Topics" identifies material which provides relevant background for interpreting marketing-social responsibility relationships, even though social responsibility may not be a specific concern of the author(s).

The categories used are as follows:

Marketing and Social Responsibility (including titles which provide an overview or interpretations of the meaning, rationale, and implications of social responsibility in marketing);

Social Responsibilities—Managerial Tasks and Relationships (including specific challenges and conceptions of the boundaries, social power and obligations of managerial roles and tasks associated with those who make decisions and policies in marketing organizations);

Ethical-Philosophical Perspectives in Marketing (including marketing ethics, suggested codes, sanctions, and standards of behavior for marketing people and organizations, and philosophical concepts as applied to marketing such as humanism, pragmatism, materialism, or other constructs from philosophy);

Social Values, Social Change, and Social Marketing (including social aspects of marketing, attitudes which shape marketing practices, marketing institutions as instruments of social change, and developments in the larger social system which influence marketing behavior);

General (references and chapters in marketing textbooks and related sources);

Related Topics (includes relevant material which provided ideas and insights for analyzing marketing and social responsibility).

Marketing and Social Responsibility

Browne, Neil and Paul F. Haas, "Social Responsibility and Market Performance." *MSU Business Topics*, Vol. 19 (Autumn, 1971), pp. 7–10.

Feldman, Lawrence P. "Social Adaptation: A New Challenge for Marketing." *Journal of Marketing*, Vol. 35 (July, 1971) pp. 54–60.

Gelb, Betsy D., and Brien, Richard H. "Survival and Social Responsibility: Themes for Marketing Education and Management." *Journal of Marketing*, Vol. 35 (April, 1971) pp. 3–9.

Lavidge, Robert J. "The Growing Responsibilities of Marketing." *Journal of Marketing*, Vol. 34 (January, 1970), pp. 25–28.

Social Responsibilities; Managerial Tasks and Relationships

Colihan, William J. Jr. "Marketers Must Help Educate Public." *Advertising Age*, Vol. 37 (December 12, 1966).

Patterson, James M. "What are the Social and Ethical Responsibilities of Marketing Executives?" *Journal of Marketing*, Vol. 30 (July, 1966), pp. 12–15.

Pease, Otis A. *"The Responsibilities of American Advertising." Private control and public influence, 1920–1940.* New Haven: Yale University Press, 1958.

Spratlen, Thaddeus H., "Social Responsibilities of Marketing Management," Paper presented to the 1972 Conference of the Southwestern Social Science Association, San Antonio, Texas, (March 31, 1972), Mimeo., 13 pages.

Ethical-Philosophical Perspectives In Marketing

Bartels, Robert. "Models for Ethics in Marketing." *Journal of Marketing*, Vol. 31 (January, 1967), pp. 20–26.

Clasen, Earl A. "Marketing Ethics and the Consumer." *Harvard Business Review*, Vol. 45 (January–February, 1967), pp. 79–86.

McMahon, Thomas F. "A Look at Marketing Ethics." *Atlanta Economic Review*, Vol. 18 (March, 1968), pp. 5–8.

Westing, J. Howard. "Some Thoughts on the Nature of Ethics in Marketing." *Changing Marketing Systems*, Chicago: American Marketing Association, 1967, pp. 161–163.

Social Values, Social Change, and Social Marketing

Atken, J. L. "Implications for Marketing in Current U. S. Social Trends." *Conference Board Record*, Vol. 71 (December, 1970), pp. 37–40.

Cook, C. W. "The Social Values of Marketing," *Conference Board Record*, Vol. 4 (February, 1967), pp. 32–37.

Cox, Reavis. "Changing Social Objectives in Marketing." *Emerging Concepts in Marketing*, Chicago: American Marketing Association, 1962. pp. 16–25.

Dixon, Donald F. "A Social Systems Approach to Marketing." *Southwestern Social Sciences Quarterly*, Vol. 48 (September, 1967), pp. 164–173.

Kotler, Philip and Zaltman, Gerald. "Social Marketing: An Approach to Planned Social Change." *Journal of Marketing*, Vol. 35 (July, 1971), pp. 3–12.

Lazer, William. "Marketing and Changing Social Relationships." *Journal of Marketing*, Vol. 33 (January, 1969), pp. 3–9.

Weiss, E. B. "Products with Shorter Life-Span will make it in Anti-Materialistic Society." *Advertising Age*, Vol. 42 (September 27, 1971), p. 73.

———. "Today's Consumer (and Tomorrow's) gets a New Look in our New Society." *Advertising Age*, Vol. 42 (February, 1971), p. 35.

General

Bowen, Howard R. *Social Responsibilities of the Businessman*. New York: Harper & Row Publishers, 1953.

Chase, Stuart and others. *The Social Responsibility of Management*. New York: School of Commerce, Accounts and Finance, New York University, 1950.

Fenn, Dan H., ed. *Business Responsibility in Action*. New York: McGraw-Hill Book Co., 1960.

Finley, Grace J. "Business Defines its Social Responsibilities." *Conference Board Record*, Vol. 4, (November, 1967), pp. 9–12.

"Fortune Magazine Poll." *Fortune*, March, 1946, pp. 197–198.

Mazis, Michael and Green, Robert. "Implementing Social Responsibility." *MSU Business Topics*, Vol. 19 (Winter, 1971), pp. 68–76.

Merrill, Harwood F. *Responsibilities of Business Leadership*. Cambridge, Mass.: Harvard University, Graduate School of Business Administration, 1949.

McDonald, Philip R. ed. *Marketing Involvement in Society and the Economy: 1969 Fall Conference Proceedings*. Cincinnati, Ohio, *American Marketing Association*, 1970, pp. 25–27.

Richman, Barry. *New Paths to Corporate Social Responsibility*. Los Angeles: University of California, Graduate School of Management. Paper series No. 2, (February, 1972) Mimeographed 65 pages. (Workshop Proceedings).

Stevens, William D., ed. *The Social Responsibilities of Marketing: 1961 Winter Conference Proceedings*. Chicago: American Marketing Association, 1962.

Walton, Clarence C. *Corporate Social Responsibilities*. Belmont: Wadsworth Publishing Company, 1968.

Related Topics

Berry, Leonard L. "Marketing Challenges in the Age of the People." *MSU Business Topics*, Vol. 20 (Winter, 1972), pp. 7–13.

———. "The Challenges of Marketing: A Field in Transition." *Southern Journal of Business*, (January, 1971), pp. 75–81.

Dixon, Donald F. "A Social Systems Approach to Marketing," *Southwestern Social Sciences Quarterly*. Vol. 48 (September, 1967).

Kassarjian, Harold H. "Incorporating Ecology into Marketing Strategy: The Case of Air Pollution," *Journal of Marketing*, Vol. 35 (July, 1971), pp. 61–65.

Kotler, Philip and Levy, Sidney J. "Broadening the Concept of Marketing." *Journal of Marketing*, Vol. 33 (January, 1969), pp. 10–15.

Kotler, Philip, and Levy, Sidney J. "Demarketing, Yes, Demarketing." *Harvard Business Review*, Vol. 49 (November–December, 1971), pp. 74–80.

16 Framework for Analyzing Marketing Ethics

Gene R. Laczniak

Journal of Macromarketing, Vol. 3 (Spring 1983), pp. 7–18. Reprinted by permission.

The issue of ethics in marketing continues to be a concern for marketing practitioners, educators, and researchers. Virtually every business manager would agree that ethical implications are often inherent in marketing decisions. Particularly perplexing are some of the "tough question" situations which can occur where the degree of moral culpability in a specific case is subject to debate. Capsuled below are a few illustrations of such situations, which will be analyzed later. The situations described in these scenarios deal with the areas of distribution/retailing, promotion, product management, pricing, and nonbusiness marketing. Thus, almost every area of marketing strategy can pose serious ethical questions.

Over the years, marketing writers have tried to address some of the ethical concerns stemming from the practice of marketing. A recent literature review on the topic of marketing ethics (Murphy and Laczniak 1981) identified and discussed nearly 100 articles, papers and books which include commentary related to specific ethical dimensions of marketing. Unfortunately, while the various writings contained many provocative suggestions, as well as some interesting insights, they were seldom based upon an underlying theory or framework of marketing ethics. Most often, the writings pointed out existing ethical abuses (e.g., Rudelius and Bucholz 1979), reported managerial perceptions of ethical behavior (e.g., Sturdivant and Cocanougher 1973; Ferrell and Weaver 1978) or provided some rudimentary suggestions for improving ethics (Kelley 1969; Kizelbach, et al. 1979). A few marketing academics have tried to take a more global approach to the ethics issue (see Table 1 for a summary), but even these writings, taken as a whole, have lacked sophisticated theoretical foundations. Normally, references to ethical theories or decision rules have been limited to the citation of simple ethical maxims. Typical of these thumbnail ethical maxims are the following:

- *The golden rule*: Act in the way you would expect others to act toward you.
- *The utilitarian principle*: Act in a way that results in the greatest good for the greatest number.
- *Kant's categorical imperative*: Act in such a way that the action taken

Marketing Scenarios Which Raise Ethical Questions[a]

Scenario 1
The Thrifty Supermarket Chain has 12 stores in the city of Gotham, U.S.A. The company's policy is to maintain the same prices for all items at all stores. However, the distribution manager knowingly sends the poorest cuts of meat and the lowest quality produce to the store located in the low-income section of town. He justifies this action based on the fact that this store has the highest overhead due to factors such as employee turnover, pilferage, and vandalism. *Is the distribution manager's economic rationale sufficient justification for his allocation method?*

Scenario 2
The Independent Chevy Dealers of Metropolis, U.S.A., have undertaken an advertising campaign headlined by the slogan: "Is your family's life worth 45 MPG?" The ads admit that while Chevy subcompacts are *not* as fuel efficient as foreign imports and cost more to maintain, they are safer according to government-sponsored crash tests. The ads implicitly ask if responsible parents, when purchasing a car, should trade off fuel efficiency for safety? *Is it ethical for the dealers association to use a fear appeal to offset an economic disadvantage?*

Scenario 3
A few recent studies have linked the presence of the artificial sweetener, subsurgural, to cancer in laboratory rats. While the validity of these findings has been hotly debated by medical experts, the Food and Drug Administration has ordered products containing the ingredient banned from sale in the U.S. The Jones Company sends all of its sugar-free J. C. Cola (which contains subsugural) to European supermarkets because the sweetener has not been banned there. *Is it acceptable for the Jones Company to send an arguably unsafe product to another market without waiting for further evidence?*

Scenario 4
The Acme Company sells industrial supplies through its own sales force, which calls on company purchasing agents. Acme has found that providing the purchasing agent with small gifts helps cement a cordial relationship and creates goodwill. Acme follows the policy that the bigger the order, the bigger the gift to the purchasing agent. The gifts range from a pair of tickets to a sporting event to outboard motors and snowmobiles. Acme does not give gifts to personnel at companies which they know have an explicit policy prohibiting the acceptance of such gifts. *Assuming no laws are violated, is Acme's policy of providing gifts to purchasing agents morally proper?*

Scenario 5
The Buy American Electronics Company has been selling its highly rated System X Color TV sets (21", 19", 12") for $700, $500 and $300 respectively. These prices have been relatively uncompetitive in the market. After some study, Buy American substitutes several cheaper components (which engineering says may reduce the quality of performance slightly) and passes on the savings to the consumer in the form of a $100 price reduction on each model. Buy American institutes a price-oriented promotional campaign which neglects to mention that the second generation System X sets are different from the first. *Is the company's competitive strategy ethical?*

Scenario 6
The Smith and Smith Advertising Agency has been struggling financially. Mr. Smith is approached by the representative of a small South American country which is on good terms with the U.S. Department of State. He wants S and S to create a multimillion dollar advertising and public relations campaign which will bolster the image of the country and increase the likelihood that it will receive U.S. foreign aid assistance and attract investment capital. Smith knows the country is a dictatorship which has been accused of numerous human rights violations. *Is it ethical for the Smith and Smith Agency to undertake the proposed campaign?*

[a]Adapted from Patrick E. Murphy and Gene R. Laczniak, 1981, p. 251.

TABLE 1. A Summary of Theoretical Commentaries on Marketing Ethics

Author/Year	Source[a]	Theme[b]
Walton (1961)	AMA Educator's Proceedings	Ethical standards of marketers are below par; however, society *in general* suffers from low moral standards.
Alderson (1964)	Report on Ethics to the AMA	Personal morality is constrained by organizational and ecological factors.
Patterson (1966)	Journal of Marketing	Operational guidelines are lacking for the ethical prescriptions postulated by organizations; more "checks and balances" needed.
McMahon (1967)	Atlanta Economic Review	A condemnation of "situational" ethics.
Farmer (1967)	Journal of Marketing	The public perceives the field of marketing as hucksterism.
Bartels (1967)	Journal of Marketing	Various external factors upon ethical behavior, such as culture and the given economic environment, are identified.
Westing (1967)	AMA Educator's Proceedings	Personal morality is the dominant factor in most ethical decisions; ethics exist above the law which regulates the lowest common denominator of expected behavior.
Colihan (1967)	AMA Educator's Proceedings	Consumer pressure will dictate marketing's ethics in years to come.
Pruden (1971)	Marketing and Social Issues (anthology)	Personal, organizational, and professional ethics interact to influence decision-making; sometimes they can conflict.
Steiner (1976)	Journal of Marketing	Marketers are perceived as unethical because of an inability of the public to perceive the value of the time, place, and possession utility provided by marketing.
Farmer (1977)	Journal of Marketing	Marketing will never be perceived as ethical because fundamentally it is persuasion.
Murphy, Laczniak, and Lusch (1978)	Journal of the Academy of Marketing Science	Organizational adjustments to insure ethical marketing are discussed.
Robin (1980)	AMA Theory Proceedings	The acceptance of relativist philosophy can alleviate ethical conflicts in marketing.

[a] For a full bibliographic citation, see References.
[b] For a more detailed discussion, see Murphy and Laczniak, 1981.

under the circumstances could be a universal law or rule of behavior.
- *The professional ethic*: Take only actions which would be viewed as proper by a disinterested panel of professional colleagues.
- *The TV test*: A manager should always ask: "Would I feel comfortable explaining to a national TV audience why I took this action?"

While not without value, these limited ethical frameworks have hampered the ethical analysis of marketing managers. They have also caused marketing educators some discomfort when discussing ethical issues in the classroom. In short, many marketing educators have shied away from lecturing on the topics of marketing ethics because of the perception that existing frameworks for analyzing marketing ethics are simplistic and lack theoretical rigor. The net result is that the seeming absence of theoretical frameworks for ethical decision-making has retarded the teaching, practice, and research of marketing ethics.

The purpose of this article is to present some existing ethical frameworks, which go beyond ethical maxims in their detail. These frameworks will likely be useful in (a) stimulating marketing ethics research, (b) establishing a background for discussion of ethical issues in the classroom, and (c) perhaps providing guidance for ethical decision-making by marketing managers. The frameworks discussed below hold within themselves no magical monopoly on moral propriety. Rather, they are presented with the hope that they might engender additional ethical sensitivity among marketing academics, students, researchers, and managers.

FRAMEWORKS VS. THEORIES

Some readers will undoubtedly be concerned whether the viewpoints reflecting ethics to be described below should properly be designated as theories, frameworks, propositions, or some other metaphysical specification. Rawls (1971), whose perspective will be examined, characterizes his own work as a theory and it is accepted as such by most moral philosophers. In contrast, if one uses the definition of theory utilized by Hunt (1976, p. 104), the work of Rawls might not qualify as a theory because of its normative nature and the fact that it is derived from an idealization which is not reflective of the real world.

Others, such as Fisk (1982, p. 5), view a framework as being broader than a theory and therefore more akin to a general paradigm which can accommodate several consistent or contrasting theories. For example, the life cycle *framework* has spawned a variety of life cycle inspired theories. On this basis, deeming the ethical viewpoints described below as frameworks would be incorrect because they are somewhat narrower in scope.

Since all marketers would fail to agree that the opinions expressed below about ethics are either frameworks or theories, the author is in a dilemma. Clearly the viewpoints below are at minimum "skeletal structures designed to support a perspective"—in this case, a perspective about ethics. Since this conforms to the dictionary definition of framework, I will use that terminology and offer my apologies in advance to those philosophers of science who subscribe to a lexicon more linguistically precise than my own.

RATIONALE FOR THE FRAMEWORKS

In the following pages, ethical frameworks developed by William David Ross, Thomas Garrett, and John Rawls are presented. Their paradigms have been selected because they are multidimensional, nonutilitarian in nature, and significant in some important fashion.

Multidimensional

One of the impediments that has limited the study of marketing ethics in the classroom is the perception by too many business educators that existing guidelines for ethical behavior are simplistic. This viewpoint has considerable validity. For example, what precisely is the value of the "golden rule" in assessing whether a firm should pay some bribe money in order to retain a lucrative foreign contract? Clearly, the usefulness of such a maxim is limited. One value of the three frameworks selected for presentation is that they illustrate that ethical frameworks do exist which go well beyond the frailty of a maxim in their sophistication. That is, there are ethical theories which attempt to specify multidimensional factors for consideration.

Nonutilitarian in Nature

In the main, much of the theoretical thinking about marketing ethics which has occurred has been implicitly based on utilitarian theory. Utilitarianism holds that actions should be judged primarily upon whether they produce "the greatest good for the greatest number." Utilitarianism, of course, is based historically on the well-known writings of Jeremy Bentham and John Stuart Mill. Many of the ethical defenses for the efficiency of the free market have also been rooted in utilitarianism. Typically, the argument revolves around showing how the unrestricted market allocates resources in a more beneficial manner to society than does a tightly controlled or regulated marketplace. In other words, free market capitalism benefits a greater number of persons than do controlled systems. There are many articulate, modern day spokesmen for utilitarianism (Sartorius 1975; Singer 1976). However, generally speaking, utilitarian analysis has been subjected to a large amount of criticism in recent years (Beauchamp and Bowie 1979). The crux of the objection to utilitarianism lies in the fact that a desirable *end* may come about because of an unjust *means*. Thus, in recent years, many moral philosophers have turned their attention to nonutilitarian theories which emphasize the *process* of arriving at outcomes as well as the *outcome* itself. Because of the relative familiarity of business managers with utilitarian thinking *and* the currency of examining other alternatives, the three frameworks highlighted below are nonutilitarian.

Significant

Each of the frameworks selected for explication is theoretically important for some reason. Ross was one of the first philosophers to try to specify a list of the major ethical responsibilities facing any person. In addition, Ross tried to create a paradigm which would be a supplement to rather than a replacement of utilitarian thinking. Garrett, in contrast, tried to take various streams of ethical thought and blend them in a fashion which would be useful to the practicing business manager. Thus, the major contribution of the Garrett work is its pragmatic orientation. Finally, the Rawls' theory is the most talked-about work on ethics in recent years. Rawls' writings have had an enormous influence on moral philosophy in the past decade and this impact is reflected in current writings on the topic of ethics.

With this general preface, attention is directed to the perspectives developed below.

THE PRIMA FACIE DUTIES FRAMEWORK

In his theory of moral philosophy, Englishman William David Ross tried to combine the underpinnings of utilitarianism with certain aspects of Kantian philosophical theory. The bulwark of the Ross (1930) model is the notion that there are several *prima facie* (at first sight) *duties* which, under most circumstances, constitute moral obligations. Ross contends that these prima facie duties are self-evident (1930, p. 29) in the sense that persons of sufficient mental maturity will recognize that there are certain acts they *ought to do*. Ross postulated six categories of prima facie duties:

(a) Duties of fidelity—*these stem from previous actions which have been taken*. Generally, this would include (to name a few) the duty to remain faithful to contracts, to keep promises, to tell the truth and to redress wrongful acts. In a marketing context, this might include conducting all the quality and safety testing which has been promised consumers, maintaining a rigorous warrantee/servicing program and refraining from deceptive or misleading promotional campaigns. For example, in Scenario 2, the dealers association may decide that the heavy handed fear appeal is in bad taste because of the implicit duty of fidelity they have to potential auto buyers.

(b) Duties of gratitude—*these are rooted in acts other persons have taken toward the person or organization under focus*. Generally, this means that a special obligation exists between relatives, friends, partners, cohorts, etc. In a marketing context, this might mean retaining an ad agency a while longer because it has rendered meritorious service for several years or extending extra credit to a historically "special customer" experiencing a cash flow problem. In Scenario 4, Acme management may conclude that the duty of gratitude would allow the provision of a small gift if such a practice is not explicitly forbidden by the client organization.

(c) Duties of justice—*these are based on the obligation to distribute rewards based upon merit*. The *justice* referred to here is justice beyond the letter of the law. For example, an organization using sealed-bid purchasing to secure services should award the contract according to procedure rather than allow the second or third lowest bidder to re-bid. Or in Scenario 1, the distribution manager might reason that the managerial problems caused by a few shoplifting or troublemaking customers is not a sufficient reason to discriminate against all of a store's buyers.

(d) Duties of beneficence—*these rest on the notion that actions taken can improve the intelligence, virtue or happiness of others*. Basically, this is the obligation to do good, if a person has the opportunity. In Scenario 6, this might mean that the Smith and Smith Agency turns down the public relations contract, albeit financially attractive, because of the duty to support the human rights of others.

(e) Duties of self improvement—*these reside in the concept that actions should be taken which improve our own virtue, intelligence or happiness*. This seems to represent a modified restatement of *moral egoism*—act in a way that will promote one's own self interest. In a marketing context, this might justify a manager attempting to maximize the ROI of his "profit center" because such performance may lead to pay increases and organizational promotion. In Scenario 6, this might mean that Smith and Smith undertakes the PR contract in order to survive; after all, the charges against the client country have not been proven and the

(f) Duties of nonmaleficence (noninjury)—*these consist of duties not to injure others*. In a marketing context, this might involve doing the utmost to insure product safety; providing adequate information to enable consumers to properly use the products they purchase; refraining from coercive tactics when managing a channel of distribution. For example, in Scenario 3, Jones Co. may decide against exporting the controversial soft drinks in order to maximize consumer safety, even though it believes the government's data to be invalid. (p. 21)

Several additional comments about these duties are now in order. First, Ross did not intend his six duties to constitute a comprehensive code of ethics. Rather, Ross believed that the list represented several moral obligations which persons incurred above and beyond the law. Thus, *if* a person recognized a prima facie duty, a moral obligation existed which might mandate specific ethical action.

But how does one recognize when a prima facie duty is present? Ross argues that the action required in many situations will be self-evident or obvious. Ross did not mean obvious in the sense of ingrained natural instinct, but rather self-evident in a way that reasonable men would acknowledge the probability that a moral duty is present. For example, in Scenario 1, the distribution manager might inherently accept the argument that the *duty of justice* compels a more equitable distribution of products to the "low income" store, regardless of its other managerial complications.

How does a person handle situations where there is a conflict among duties? For example, in Scenario 2, the Chevy dealer's highly emotional, fear-laden advertising may violate the implicit *duty of fidelity* the dealers have with consumers to refrain from manipulative promotion. On the other hand, if the crash test data is accurate, the dealers may feel that the *duty of self improvement* justifies implementing the campaign. How can such conflicts be resolved? Ross is clear, if not completely satisfying, on this point: "It may again be objected that...there are these various and often conflicting types of prima facie duty that leave us with no principle upon which to discern what is our actual duty in particular circumstances...for when we have to choose...the 'ideal utilitarian' theory can only fall back on an opinion...that one of the two duties is more urgent" (p. 23). Thus, conflicts among duties are resolved by our own opinion of how the general duties apply after carefully assessing the situation.

The discussion above may lead one to conclude that the Ross framework is rather arbitrary and incomplete. Certainly these are valid criticisms. However, the Ross framework interjects several important insights critical to the practice of ethical marketing. First, the Ross theory encourages managers to determine what their prima facie duties might be and to discharge them unless other such obligations take precedence. Thus, if a marketer knowingly misrepresents product quality to buyers, a *duty of fidelity* has been violated; if sales representatives are let go when their sales fall below quota, a *duty of gratitude* may be violated, and so on. Second, the Ross framework shifts attention in ethically sensitive situations away from *outcomes* (or ends) and toward a priori obligations. Put another way, the model emphasizes the constant moral obligations which *always* exist. It de-emphasizes the approach of attempting to predict results in morally sensitive situations. Such outcome-oriented approaches frequently are used to rationalize potentially unethical behavior. For instance (again alluding to the scenarios), if Jones Co. exports the subsugural laden soft drinks, they may speculate that consumers will not be hurt because the test data are invalid; *or* if Thrifty Supermarket continues its distribution policy, they may decide it is doubtful outsiders will ever know it. Thus, concern with outcomes may prohibit the examination of impending moral duties on the premise that no harm wil probably occur.

THE PROPORTIONALITY FRAMEWORK

Another multidimensional model of business ethics has been articulated by Garrett (1966). The framework is distinctive because it was specifically developed with the practicing business manager in mind. In addition, it attempts to combine the appealing utilitarian concern for outcomes ("the greatest good...") with the Kantian preoccupation with process or means. Garrett contends that ethical decisions consist of three components: intention, means, and end.

Intention has to do with the motivation behind a person's actions. Garrett believes that what is intended by a particular act is an important component of morality. For example, the organization that formulates a code of marketing ethics motivated solely by the belief that such a code will help sell its products to religious or sectarian organizations, has *not* acted ethically. Thus, purity of intention is a factor in evaluating the ethics of a specific situation.

Means refers to the process or method used to effect intention and bring about specific ends. For example, suppose a sales representative whose family has recently incurred some substantial medical expenses, begins to overstock his customers and pad his expense account. His intention, to relieve the financial distress of his family, is good; however, the means chosen to accomplish this goal is unethical.

Ends deal with outcomes, results, or consequences of actions. Utilitarian theory is based on the precept that the correctness of an action is determined by calculating the end "goodness" resulting from that action compared with the "goodness" produced by alternative actions that could have been taken. Garrett's view is that ends are properly evaluated by analyzing the intrinsic nature of the acts themselves rather than the consequences which these acts produce. Or, put another way, it will not allow permitting the end to justify the means. For example, suppose a brewing company announces that all the revenues from beer sales at a new hotel will be donated to charity. However, suppose the distribution rights at the hotel had been obtained by bribery. In this instance, the ends (a charitable contribution) do not justify the means (bribery).

The above three elements—combining concern for intent (or will), means, and ends—have been synthesized by Garrett (1966) into his *principle of proportionality* which states:

> I am responsible for whatever I will as a means or an end. If both the means and end I am willing are good, in and of themselves, I may ethically permit or risk the foreseen but unwilled side effects if, and only if, I have a proportionate reason for doing so. To put it another way: I am not responsible for unwilled side effects if I have sufficient reason for risking or permitting them, granted always that what I do will, as a means or an end, is good. (p. 8)

This principle raises a number of issues which require clarification. Most important, what is the nature of the side effects which are permitted? Garrett elaborates upon these issues with several amplifications.

(1) It is unethical to will, whether as a means or an end, a major evil to another. (p. 12)

By *major evil*, Garrett means the loss of a significant capacity that an entity (i.e., person, organization, etc.) needs to function. For example, in Scenario 3, suppose the substance subsugural had been linked to birth defects when consumed by pregnant women. Jones Co.'s strategy of exporting the product in order to avoid writing off a major financial loss (the end goal) would *not* be ethical because consumption of the Cola would have a reasonable probability of causing a major evil: a significant defect in a newborn.

(2) It is unethical to risk or permit a major evil to another without a proportional reason. (p. 14)

The concept of "proportionate reason" is the focus here. The principle of proportionality specifies that the risk of an unpleasant side effect is permitted if there is a satisfactory reason for allowing the risk. Or, put another way, a proportionate reason exists when the good willed as means or end equals or outweighs the harmful side effects which are *not* willed as either a means or end. For example, let's again examine the Scenario 3 situation. Suppose Jones Co. researchers knew for a fact that the government studies were invalid and that subsugural would soon be declared benign by the FDA. This would constitute proportionate reason for going ahead with the soft drink export.

(3) It is unethical to will, risk or permit a minor evil without a proportionate reason. (p. 14)

By *minor evil*, Garrett means a harm to physical goods or to some means that are useful but not necessary for an entity's operation. For instance, in Scenario 5, suppose the potential reduction of quality in the Buy American TV sets is such that, even if it occurred, the video and audio difference in the TVs could not be perceived by consumers. In this case, the minor evil (an unstated quality difference) would be justified by a proportionate reason (higher market share for Buy American and lower prices for consumers).

The above constitutes the essence of the proportionality framework. It must be acknowledged that certain dimensions of the model remain vague or at least subjective. For example, where does one draw the line between a major evil and a minor evil? Attempting to influence a purchasing agent with a pair of $10 sports tickets (Scenario 4) is probably a minor evil. However, if the company receives the contract because of the gift and the competing bidder goes bankrupt, does it become a major evil? Similarly, what constitutes a proportional reason? In Scenario 6, is it a proportionate reason for the financially ailing Smith and Smith agency to take the PR contract knowing that a demur will simply result in another reputable agency doing the work?

Despite these difficulties, the Garrett framework has much to recommend its use. Basically, it provides the marketing manager with a three-phase rough and ready battery of questions which can be used to analyze the ethics of a given situation:

Phase 1: Given the situation, what is willed as means and end? If a major evil is willed, the action is unethical and should not be taken.

Phase 2: Given the situation, what are the foreseen but unwilled side effects? If there is no proportionate reason for risking or allowing a major evil *or* willing a minor evil, the action is unethical and should not be taken.

Phase 3: Given the situation, what are the alternative actions? Is there an alternative to the end which would provide more good consequences and less evil consequences? Not to select this alternative would be unethical.

Notice that the three elements of any ethical decision—intent (will), means, and end—are incorporated into the framework. Moreover, the approach is consistent with the type of analysis many managers already conduct in their planning and forecasting efforts. That is, it involves attempting to predict outcomes of strategies and compare them with alternative options. This lends a dimension of familiarity to the model for planning-oriented managers. Finally, the principle of proportionality provides a flexible model of ethical decision-making; that is, it does not postulate specific trespasses. Rather, it provides general, universal, and applicable guidelines which can be applied to a wide variety of managerial situations.

THE SOCIAL JUSTICE FRAMEWORK

In intellectual circles, one of the most influential books of recent years has been John Rawls' *A Theory of Justice* (1971). Rawls, a Harvard University moral philosopher, proposed a detailed system of social ethics which attempted to maximize rewards to those most disadvantaged in a given social system. Rawls used deductive reasoning to arrive at his conception of social justice.

Central to the Rawls' thesis is the construction of an imaginary state of affairs called the "original position." This hypothetical situation would be somewhat analogous to the time frame *preceding* a game of chance. No participant knows in advance what the game of chance might hold—i.e., if they will be winners or losers. So, too, in the original position, no person knows what their place in society will be once the "game" of life begins. They do not know their social status, educational opportunities, class position, physical or intellectual abilities, etc. They might be king or pauper.

Why is the original position and the "veil of ignorance" it imposes so important? Rawls believes that hypothesizing such a state is the only way to reason to a "pure" system of justice. That is, one which is unblemished by the knowledge of the current state of affairs. For example, if a person knows that he has wealth in the society, that person will likely consider a system which heavily taxes the rich in order to provide for the poor, as unjust. Or, if a person is poor, he will probably feel the opposite. Therefore, what Rawls seeks to obtain from the original position is a vehicle which can be used to deduce an ideal system of justice—one which rational men would choose *if* they knew nothing of what their own station in life might be.

Rawls' entire treatise is devoted to specifying the conclusions or consequences that persons would arrive at for assigning rights and duties in a social system, given the original position. Rawls' arguments defy easy explanation, but basically he concludes that rational men (not knowing what their fortune will be) would utilize a *minimax* method of decision-making. That is, they would choose a system which minimizes the maximum loss which they could incur. In other words, they would opt for a system which seeks to avoid harsh losses (slavery? starvation?

indigence?) for those at the bottom of the scale, because conceivably this could be their position.

Rawls concludes that two principles of justice would be arrived at: the *liberty principle* and the *difference principle*.

> The liberty principle states that: *each person is to have an equal right to the most extensive basic liberty compatible with a similar liberty for others.*

> The difference principle states that: *social and economic inequalities are to be arranged so that they are both* (a) *to the greatest benefit of the least disadvantaged, and* (b) *attached to positions and offices open to all.* (p. 60)

These principles require some elaboration. The liberty principle guarantees equal opportunity as well as basic liberties such as the freedom of speech, the right to vote, the right to due process of the law, ownership of property, etc. In addition, the principle explicitly states that greater liberty should always be preferred to lesser liberty provided it can be attained without major social dysfunctions. For example, suppose a law specified that airline pilots should be between 40 and 60 years of age, but data showed that this job could be done with the proper training by anyone between 25 and 70; it would be a violation of the principle of liberty to accept the more restricted scheme. Holding that airline pilots must be between 40 and 60 would be unethical to those outside this age bracket who could perform the job. Similarly, an industry code which mandated that all bicycles should be built to withstand crashes with automobiles up to 55 MPH, would also likely violate the principle.

The difference principle specifies the conditions which must exist in order to properly act contrary to the liberty principle. In essence, inequality of economic goods or social position (i.e., the lessening of liberty) can be tolerated only when the practice which generates the inequality works to the advantage of every individual affected *or* to the advantage of those members of the system who are least well off. However, the basic liberties (e.g., the right to vote) can never be traded for economic goods or temporary social position. In this fashion, Rawls' system is a bold contrast to that of classical utilitarianism. Why? Utilitarians would permit some individuals to become worse off so long as a greater number of others become better off. The Rawls' framework claims to prohibit this. It is highly egalitarian in the sense that actions are never permitted which disadvantage the least well off; the tendency instead is a "drive to equality" (pp. 100–108) which over time should benefit those worse off in a particular system more than those better off.

What are the ramifications of the social justice theory upon marketing ethics? In all fairness, it should be emphasized that Rawls did not conceive his theory would be readily transferred to marketing or for that matter business ethics generally. However, the two guiding principles alone seem to suggest some enormous implications. The principle of liberty emphasizes the inherent right of individual persons to determine their own destiny and to always be treated equitably by others. This maximization of personal liberty, subject, of course, to the claims of others, would seem to underscore the consumer's right to safety, information, choice, and redress. Applied to a specific situation, for example Scenario 5, the liberty principle would seem to demand that Buy American Company inform consumers of the change in components and the possible reduction in quality of the second generation System X sets. Not to take this course of action would unfairly restrict the liberty of choice consumers have in this situation.

The difference principle holds an even more striking implication. It emphasizes the fact that it would be unethical to exploit one group for the benefit of others. A particularly severe violation of the principle would occur if a group that was relatively worse off were victimized in order to benefit a better-situated group. For example, in Scenario 6, the difference principle would probably suggest that the Smith and Smith Agency forego the public relations contract because its acceptance could add legitimacy to the ruling foreign government and further jeopardize the position of a worse-off group—the citizens of the totalitarian country. On a more general plane, Rawls' principles would seem to affirm the ethical validity of the marketing concept which formally incorporates the rights of a less powerful group (consumers) into the planning and goal setting of a more powerful group (business).

THE VALUE OF THE FRAMEWORKS

The potential contribution of these frameworks should be clearly stated. First, the purpose of the above perspectives is *not* to provide precise answers to specific ethical dilemmas. In fact, an attempt to apply more than one framework to a particular situation could lead to a conflicting conclusion. For example, in Scenario 1, the Rawlsian would undoubtedly conclude that Thrifty Supermarkets must cease and desist its practice of sending its lower-quality products to the economically inefficient retail store because this allocation scheme further discriminates against the already disadvantaged, low-income shopper. In contrast, one could argue using the Ross' *duty of gratitude* as a rationale, that Thrifty Supermarkets owes its loyal, up-scale customers a special status when it comes to the selection of their meats and produce.

If these frameworks do not answer "tough questions" dealing with marketing ethics, what is their value? Their major purpose is to be used as a pedagogical tool to sensitize managers to the factors that are important in coming to grips with ethical issues. There are few irrefutably "right" answers to these questions. But the fact that management has systematically considered the options along with their ethical ramifications is of ultimate importance. Thus, the contribution of such devices is to provide marketing managers with a philosophical mnemonic which serves to remind them of their ethical responsibilities. The perspectives provided by writers such as Ross, Garrett, and Rawls emphasize that the factors involved in reaching an ethical judgment are deeper than the jingoism of ethical maxims of the "Thou shalt be good" caliber.

Toward a Theory of Marketing Ethics

As noted earlier, there is nothing supernatural about the above frameworks. Their adoption will not automatically generate ethical behavior in marketing, no do these models explain or predict the incidence of unethical behavior which can occur in marketing. However, taken together, they introduce certain advantages to marketing educators, practitioners, and researchers.

For educators, the frameworks provide perspectives which go beyond the proverbial ethical maxim. The frameworks represent quasi-models of intermediate sophistication that suggest a rationale for why particular moral choices might be made. In this sense, the introduction of this material establishes a useful background for the classroom analysis of marketing cases having ethical implications. Explaining the models to students provides the educator with the opportunity to inject ethical considerations into the discussion of mainstream marketing strategy.

For practitioners, the frameworks suggest a list of possible factors which might be utilized to decide "tough question" situations regarding ethics. Some speculation about the possible application of these frameworks to real-world situations was discussed above. The following is a series of questions designed to determine, in general terms, whether action A constitutes an ethical or an unethical response in a given situation. If the answer to any of the following questions is yes, then action A is most probably unethical, and should be reconsidered; if every question truly can be answered negatively, then action A is probably ethical.

- Does action A violate the law?
- Does action A violate any general moral obligations:
    duties of fidelity?
    duties of gratitude?
    duties of justice?
    duties of beneficence?
    duties of self-improvement?
    duties of nonmaleficence?
- Does action A violate any special obligations stemming from the

type of marketing organization in question (e.g., the special duty of pharmaceutical firms to provide safe products)?
- Is the intent of action A evil?
- Are any major evils likely to result from or because of action A?
- Is a satisfactory alternative B, which produces equal or more good with less evil than A, being knowingly rejected?
- Does action A infringe on the inalienable rights of the consumer?
- Does action A leave another person or group less well off? Is this person or group already relatively underprivileged?

The questions need not be pursued in any lockstep fashion, but rather can be discussed in an order dictated by the situation.

For researchers, the frameworks may suggest some of the components necessary for the construction of a model describing ethical behavior in marketing. To be sure, such a model should: (a) specify appropriate standards of ethical action, (b) demarcate the factors, both internal and external, which influence the likelihood of ethical behavior, and (c) provide a listing of the organizational variables which might be adjusted to enhance the probability of ethical action. In this vein, the Ross framework identifies some fundamental duties or obligations which are incumbent upon managers and thereby would constitute several potential ethical standards. The Garrett framework, on the other hand, specifies three variables—intention, process (or means), and outcomes—which the researcher would have to analyze in order to have a relatively accurate picture of the ethics inherent in a particular action. It may very well be that different internal and external variables influence different dimensions of the ethical action. For example, the *attitude of top management* (an internal factor) may be a major influence upon the process or means a manager selects to handle an ethical question; in contrast, *professional standards* (an external variable) may be a major determinant of a manager's intent in a given situation. Thus, Garrett provides insight into the necessary requisites for empirically measuring the ethics of a given action. Finally, the Rawls' framework suggests some special considerations which could be introduced into an ethical evaluation. Namely, Rawls provides a justification for giving special ethical consideration to parties which are relatively worse off (i.e., socially disadvantaged). Rawls, in effect, sketches the moral equivalent of "affirmative action" ethics for marketing managers.

Assuming the frameworks of Ross, Garrett and Rawls could be integrated into one grand theory, it is still doubtful that the theory would constitute a satisfactory model of marketing ethics. Nevertheless, given the relevance of ethical questions in marketing, it is important that marketing academics continue to strive to develop a theory of marketing ethics.

On a more pragmatic level, the frameworks stimulate several suggestions concerning marketing ethics which could have a beneficial influence at the macro level. First, Garrett's concern with *major* and *minor* evils suggests that researchers should attempt to rank in terms of "severity," the various ethical abuses that regularly occur in the field of marketing. Since it is naive to believe that significant unethical conduct in marketing can be eliminated overnight, the resulting ranking could constitute a makeshift "hit list" which would then single out particular areas for concern and remedial action. For example, the recent passage of the Foreign Corrupt Practices Act forced most corporations operating overseas to reexamine the propriety of their selling practices. In publicizing areas of acute ethical concern, the marketing discipline could hopefully short circuit the necessity of legislation in order to engender ethical reform.

Second, Ross' compilation of prima facie duties, a listing formulated at the most general level, should motivate textbook writers in marketing to propose a listing of what they consider to be the minimum ethical responsibilities incumbent upon practicing marketing managers. While such specifications will undoubtedly cause some controversy and debate, the subsequent sifting and winnowing will spotlight the topic of ethics and should raise the moral sensitivities of students.

Third, Rawl's concern with the multifaceted impact of business policies upon various groups in society (especially the most disadvantaged) ideally should stimulate casewriters to incorporate ethical problems and analysis into the cases they author. The reason for this is that the case method is the best pedagogical tool for getting the student to visualize the influence of an organizational decision upon sundry stakeholders. Surely an inference which can be drawn from Rawls is that it is the duty of every discipline (including marketing) to foster mechanisms which will generate ethical introspection. The reputation of marketers may depend on it.

REFERENCES

Alderson, Wroe (1964), "Ethics, Ideologies and Sanctions," in *Report of the Committee on Ethical Standards and Professional Practices*, Chicago: American Marketing Association.

Bartels, Robert (1967), "A Model for Ethics in Marketing," *Journal of Marketing*, 31 (January), 20–26.

Beauchamp, Tom L., and Norman E. Bowie (1979), *Ethical Theory and Business*, Englewood Cliffs, NJ: Prentice-Hall.

Colihan, William J., Jr. (1967), "Ethics in Today's Marketing," in *Changing Marketing Systems*, Reed Moyers, ed., Chicago: American Marketing Association, 164–166.

Farmer, Richard N. (1967), "Would You Want Your Daughter to Marry a Marketing Man?" *Journal of Marketing*, 31 (January), 1–3.

⸺ (1977), "Would You Want Your Son to Marry a Marketing Lady?" *Journal of Marketing*, 41 (January), 15–18.

Ferrell, O. C., and K. Mark Weaver (1978), "Ethical Beliefs of Marketing Managers," *Journal of Marketing*, 42 (July), 69–73.

Fisk, George (1982), "Contributor's Guide for Choice of Topics for Papers," *Journal of Macromarketing*, 2 (Spring), 5–6.

Garrett, Thomas (1966), *Business Ethics*, Englewood Cliffs, NJ: Prentice-Hall.

Hunt, Shelby D. (1976), *Marketing Theory: Conceptual Foundations of Research in Marketing*, Columbus, OH: Grid.

Kelley, Eugene J. (1969), "Ethical Considerations for a Scientifically Oriented Marketing Management," in *Science in Marketing Management*, M. S. Mayer, ed., Toronto, Ontario: York University, 69–87.

Kizelbach, A. H., *et al.* (1979), "Social Auditing for Marketing Managers," *Industrial Marketing Management*, 8, 1–6.

McMahon, Thomas V. (1967), "A Look at Marketing Ethics," *Atlanta Economic Review*, 17 (March).

Murphy, Patrick E., and Gene R. Laczniak (1981), "Marketing Ethics: A Review With Implications for Managers, Educators and Researchers," in *Review of Marketing 1981*, B. Enis and K. Roering, eds., Chicago: American Marketing Association, 251–266.

⸺, ⸺, and Robert F. Lusch (1978), "Ethical Guidelines for Business and Social Marketing," *Journal of the Academy of Marketing Science*, 6 (Summer), 197–205.

Patterson, James M. (1966), "What Are the Social and Ethical Responsibilities of Marketing Executives?" *Journal of Marketing*, 30 (July), 12–15.

Pruden, Henry (1971), "Which Ethics for Marketers?" in *Marketing and Social Issues*, John R. Wish and Stephen H. Gamble, eds., New York: John Wiley and Sons, 98–104.

Rawls, John (1971), *A Theory of Justice*, Cambridge: Harvard University Press.

Robin, Donald P. (1980), "Value Issues in Marketing," in *Theoretical Developments in Marketing*, C. W. Lamb and P. M. Dunne, eds., Chicago: American Marketing Association, 142–145.

Ross, William David (1930), *The Right and the Good*, Oxford: Clarendon Press.

Rudelius, William, and Rogene A. Bucholz (1979), "Ethical Problems of Purchasing Managers," *Harvard Business Review*, 55 (March–April), 8, 12, 14.

Sartorius, Rolf E. (1975), *Individual Conduct and Social Norms: A Utilitarian Account of Social Union and Rule of Law*, Belmont, CA: Dickenson Publishing.

Singer, Peter (1976), "Freedoms and Utility in the Distribution of Health Care," in *Ethics and Health Policy*, R. Veatch and R. Branson, eds., Cambridge: Bellinger Publishing.

Steiner, John F. (1976), "The Prospect of Ethical Advisors for Business Corporation," *Business and Society* (Spring), 5–10.

Sturdivant, Frederick D., and A. Benton Cocanougher (1973), "What Are Ethical Marketing Practices?" *Harvard Business Review*, 51 (November–December), 10–12.

Walton, Clarence C. (1961), "Ethical Theory, Societal Expectations and Marketing

Practices," in *The Social Responsibilities of Marketing*, William D. Stevens, ed., Chicago: American Marketing Association, 8–24.

Westing, J. Howard (1967), "Some Thoughts on the Nature of Ethics in Marketing," in *Changing Marketing Systems*, Reed Moyer, ed., Chicago: American Marketing Association, 161–163.

17 — A Managerial Approach to Macromarketing

Jehiel Zif

Reprinted from the *Journal of Marketing*, published by the American Marketing Association, Vol. 44 (Winter 1980), pp. 36–45. Reprinted by permission.

The field of macromarketing is not new, but only recently have we found efforts to explore it systematically as a separate branch of study. Studies in this field have generally used the same approach used in macrosociology, the social facts approach (Bagozzi 1977). This approach attempts to emulate the natural sciences in that it seeks to account for observed changes through the analysis of facts that can be measured or inferred, not usually including the goals and decision processes of key actors. There are many examples of this approach in marketing studies of minority groups, social marketing, and channels of distribution (for example, see Bucklin 1977).

These studies have little in common with most micromarketing studies because their approach leaves no room for the concept of management, that is, purposeful action as the basis for change. The macro literature either ignores management or confines it to the administration of public policy. The use of the social facts approach derives from a view of macromarketing as essentially "unmanaged."[1]

In practice, however, there are many managers, in the United States and throughout the world, who direct the marketing of goods and services for complete sectors of the economy, such as agriculture, health care, transportation, and raw materials (Zif and Izraeli 1977, 1978a). The essentially passive social facts approach—which seeks to account for but not induce change, and which tends not to include managers' intentions among its explanatory factors—tells us little about the practices of these managers or about their effects on the economy and society.

The domain of macromarketing is a subject of some debate. Most attempts to distinguish between micro- and macromarketing do so along two dimensions: the level of aggregation (Bagozzi 1977; Hunt 1976) and the impact on society (Moyer 1972). Following Hunt (1977), I accept the notion that macromarketing is a multidimensional construct; a high level on either dimension would be considered macromarketing.[2]

I contend that macromarketing management is a viable concept that goes beyond public policy administration. Moreover, the primary variables used to study micromarketing management can be adapted to the macro context to become valuable tools for analysis. Unlike the more common social facts approach, the managerial approach accords a cen-

319

tral role to managers' behavior. An outline of this approach is presented here in the hope of stimulating scholarly debate. With further refinement and research, it may open avenues for the development of theory and the training and practice of macromarketing managers.

THE MANAGERIAL APPROACH

The managerial approach, most commonly used in studies of micromarketing, sees marketing as the "performance of business activities which direct the flow of goods from producer to consumer or user in order to satisfy customers and accomplish the company's objectives" (McCarthy 1968). Micromarketing is studied from the point of view of the manager who induces and guides changes.

Given the popularity of this approach, it is surprising to find it used so infrequently in macromarketing studies. Fisk (1967, 1976), Kotler and Zaltman (1971), and a study reported by Slater (1978) did recognize the role of purposeful action. This is the key to the use of the managerial approach in macromarketing: the assumption that macro changes can be managed, or at least guided; the assumption that managers' purposeful actions are major causes of change; and the intention to seek causal explanation, not only to understand macromarketing, but to influence it.

The major variables of the managerial approach are familiar from studies of micromarketing: (1) managerial responsibilities, (2) managerial objectives, (3) managerial orientations and strategies, and (4) decision making variables. With some adjustment and redefinition, these variables can be adopted to apply to macro phenomena. This is the task of the remainder of this paper, with a major focus on a dual concept of managerial orientations.

MANAGERIAL RESPONSIBILITIES

Classification of macromarketing managerial responsibilities can be aided by asking two questions: has a central marketing authority been established and is management responsible for directing the flow of goods and services. Figure 1 presents a classification of four managerial responsibilities based on answers to these questions. The four analytical categories attempt to capture what in the real world is frequently a continuum. Most examples of macromanagement fit neatly into one or another type, but there are exceptions. These managerial responsibilities are considered within the area of macromarketing, because of their significant impact on society, because of their high level of aggregation, or both.

Comprehensive Macromanagement

While central marketing authorities which direct the flow of goods and services are familiar in communist countries, it is important to recognize that comparable institutions also are widespread in Western countries. Even the United States, despite its general commitment to private enterprise, has established central marketing authorities—for example, Amtrak. In most other Western countries, even more sectors of the economy are controlled by central marketing institutions with no direct domestic competition. Common targets for complete government control are such major sectors as natural resources, transportation, and defense industries. Central marketing authorities also exist in the form of trade marketing boards, which are cooperative bodies sanctioned by the government to control the production and marketing of key agricultural crops. These boards are found in the United Kingdom, most countries of the former British Empire, and some other Western and developing countries (Abbott and Cruepelandt 1966; Izraeli and Zif 1977). Central marketing institutions of all these types have been established to assume responsibility for management of marketing on a macro level that has significant societal consequences.

It is possible that de facto macromarketing management is even more widespread in Western economies than the de jure marketing boards would suggest. Galbraith (1967, pp. 166, 343, 393) contends that mature corporations which depend on the state and identify with its goals, are becoming part of a large administrative complex associated with the government. Regardless of whether this assessment is accepted, the fact remains that large portions of Western economies are under comprehensive macromanagement. It is unfortunate that this phenomenon has so far received only limited attention in the literature.

Joint Micro/Macromanagement

When an organization is in charge of directing the flow of socially important goods or services and has achieved a near-monopoly position

FIGURE 1. Classification of Managerial Responsibilities

		Central Marketing Authority	
		Yes	No
Directing the Flow of Goods and Services	Yes	Comprehensive Macromanagement	Joint Micro/macro-Management
	No	Central Coordination and/or Regulation	Specialized Macromanagement

without central authority, a joint micro/macro responsibility exists. Many public service institutions—those that supply education, health care, mass communication, recreation, and so on—are the major source of a particular service for a target public. The managers of these institutions are responsible not only for micromanagement, but also for marketing activity that has significant impact on society.

Similarly, dominant business firms, because of their market position, create through their marketing activities significant societal consequences and thus have joint micro/macro responsibilities. While firms with limited market shares often do assume social responsibilities, these responsibilities are more limited and are, for the most part, optional. Most dominant firms have assumed macro responsibilities on their own, being aware that their freedom of action is restricted by their visibility and potential public action.

Discussions of the joint, and sometimes conflicting, responsibilities for business performance and social impact are numerous in the literature, but no conclusive guidance for managerial actions has yet resulted. However, there appears to be at least a general recognition of the public policy process as a source of goals for managerial activity not dictated by the market (Preston and Post 1975, p. 152).

Central Coordination and Regulation

In addition to comprehensive and joint micro/macro management, macromarketing responsibility encompasses central agencies set up or authorized by the government to coordinate and/or regulate marketing for a specific industry or agricultural branch. These agencies are not responsible for directing the flow of goods and services, and therefore, are not involved in selling or buying on behalf of their organizations. Nontrading agricultural marketing boards (Abbott and Cruepelandt 1966; Izraeli and Zif 1977), and the Civil Aeronautics Board are examples of this category.

Enterprises in this group were set up in order to introduce elements of macro planning and control and at the same time leave room for independent marketing action by micro participants. Balancing these two goals is frequently a difficult task. Performance depends not only on the organizational charter (which is frequently vague), but also on the changing orientations of government officials and agency executives. Some organizations in this group are very active in setting prices, regulating quantity, and negotiating transactions, similar to comprehensive macromanagement. Others, more conservative or passive, assume an advisory role or concentrate on regulating limited aspects of the marketing process. The deregulation process of domestic aviation in the United States is an example of a major change in the policy of a central agency.

Specialized Macromanagement

The fourth area of macromarketing responsibility involves managers in more specialized tasks. A manager is charged by the government, trade or consumer association with a limited reponsibility of influencing the market in a specific way, for example, setting quality or safety standards, enforcing regulations, protecting group interests, organizing group action, maintaining competition, negotiating interregional or international agreements, and so on.

Typically, these specialized macromarketing positions lack comprehensive coordination. Government actions often pull in different directions: antitrust enforcement, for instance, is intended to promote competition, but another agency's subsidies, exemptions, and differential treatment may undermine this goal. While one department is attempting to reduce consumption, another department is supporting growth — the case of tobacco is a good example. The USDA supports tobacco growth while HEW campaigns against consumption. These conflicts and inconsistencies are caused either by lack of a governing policy or by the inability to control, coordinate, or evaluate the activities of a large number of decentralized agencies.

In summary, there is evidence to suggest that macromarketing management activity of the types discussed here is a substantial and growing factor in Western economies. A strong tendency toward "unitary boards" (one industry, one board) can be observed in the large public enterprise sector of the United Kingdom (Corti 1979). Public service institutions in particular are among the largest and fastest growing segments of modern society (Drucker 1974, p. 130). The increasing role of governments in domestic business activity has spread to the international arena and is causing concern by executives of major private corporations (Caldwell 1979). Not only is a large number of managers involved in macromarketing, but they are responsible for some of the most important economic sectors in most countries.

MANAGERIAL OBJECTIVES

The aggregate marketing behavior and societal consequences of macromarketing require that management adopt multiple objectives. While this is not uncommon in business firms, there is little doubt that profit-related goals predominate in micromarketing and that societal goals, when stated, are often viewed more as constraints than as objectives. The situation is different when managers assume comprehensive responsibility on a macro level. In these cases, aggregate outcomes and societal consequences are *major* concerns and the importance of managing multiple objectives increases substantially

An examination of comprehensive macromanagement in agricultural marketing boards suggests that while specific objectives and their relative weights may vary from case to case, the main interests can be grouped into a few basic goal-areas: profitability, productivity, market development, social responsibility, and innovation (Zif and Izraeli 1978b). The same areas exist in micromarketing, but their content and scope are significantly enlarged at the macro level and their relative importance is different.

Profitability goals in macromarketing deal not only with levels of profit, but also with their distribution among the macro system participants. For example, the distribution of agricultural profits among farmers, wholesalers, and retailers is a major concern of agricultural marketing boards, while the distribution of oil profits was a central theme of the recent U.S. Senate debate over proposed energy legislation.

Social responsibility presents the greatest managerial challenge in macromarketing. It is rarely well defined; it consists of a dynamic and diffused set of economic and noneconomic subgoals, without clear-cut priorities. It is frequently a subject of public attention and is usually at variance with short-term profitability.

These five basic goal-areas represent a wide scope of societal interests, some of which are clearly conflicting. As a result, we may hypothesize that many macromarketing managers will avoid conflicts about operational definitions by stating goals and evaluating performances in very general terms. Also, they will frequently postpone the task of striking a clear balance among conflicting interests because of the more immediate political need of keeping the parties together. There is some empirical evidence to support this hypothesis (Zif and Izraeli 1978b). Additional insight into setting objectives and evaluating performance can be derived by analyzing managerial orientations.

MANAGERIAL ORIENTATIONS: A DUAL MACROMARKETING CONCEPT

Tasks

The generic job of marketing management is to bring about exchanges (Kotler 1972). When a comprehensive macromarketing responsibility is created, part of the exchange system is transferred from the marketplace to the political arena. The resulting two kinds of exchanges require two different tasks: managerial control in the product or services markets and cultivation of public support in political markets.[3]

Managerial control is concerned with the functional management of the enterprise. Its key elements are familiar from micromarketing: marketing organization, information systems, investment projects (including R&D), marketing-mix decisions, and product quantity decisions.

Public support can be divided into the public-at-large, political intermediaries (i.e., parties, government agents), and special interest groups. While there is interactive influence between the three, their positions and responses are not identical. Public support is essential in three common situations: when determining objectives and evaluating performance; when approval is required for capital investment or organizational or marketplace action; and when negotiated transactions, involving government representatives, replace competitive transactions. It is gained in response to a political "product mix" consisting of three kinds of elements: (1) operational objectives that reflect societal concerns, shared norms, and values (e.g., support of NASA); (2) utilitarian benefits, such as income, services, products, reciprocity of support, etc.; (3) power position and the potential or demonstrated ability to get results. Effectiveness in cultivating public support demands that the political "product mix" be supplemented by political promotion and public relations.

Framework

The strategic orientation of macromarketing is determined by the overall level of effort and its relative allocation to the tasks of managerial control and cultivating public support.[4] The level of effort indicates a position on a passive-active continuum, while the relative allocation of effort indicates a position on a managerial-political continuum. There is a trade-off relationship between the two tasks: a high degree of managerial control requires some independence from public interactions; a heavy involvement in cultivating public support leaves fewer resources and less time for managerial control. When skillfully performed, both tasks generate payoffs for the macromarketing organization, and clearly exhibit an interaction effect. The tasks can be used as the two dimensions of a matrix for classifying four basic managerial orientations in macromarketing (Figure 2).

A *passive* orientation—characterized by low levels of both managerial control and cultivation of public support—is unfortunately quite common. In some countries, this can be explained by historical and cultural factors; in others, it is a response to economic and political conditions. When the competitive market test is eliminated, the organization can survive without a high level of managerial control. When, at the same time, there is a serious political conflict over objectives, uninvolved neutrality can be the safest route. A manager has a strong temptation to maintain a passive orientation when there is no public interest in his activities or when any change from the status quo elicits strong opposition. This orientation is not usually conducive to societal progress.

A *political* orientation—characterized by a high level of cultivation of public support and a low level of managerial control—is prevalent under two sets of circumstances. In many countries, an executive position in a large public enterprise is a political patronage prize. The manager knows why he got the job and what orientation will help him keep it. Also, he is frequently an aspiring politician who gives his long-term interests priority. Another basis for a political orientation exists when the government dominates the economic payoff with contracts and foreign trade agreements or with special subsidies and taxes. Farmers' organizations and agricultural marketing boards frequently concentrate on cultivating political support in order to achieve their aims. An excessive preoccupation with political interactions can sometimes generate payoffs for the manager or the organization, but is rarely productive from a societal perspective.

A *business* orientation—characterized by a high level of managerial control and a low level of cultivation of public support—is typical of private firms that have grown to assume macro responsibility and of individuals with a career background in private business. Many executives of large American corporations find the transition from purely micro to a joint micro/macro responsibility difficult and tend to continue with their familiar orientations. A business orientation is usually efficient in achieving a narrow set of profit-related goals, which can lead to some independence from political pressures. However, it is less successful in dealing with multiple macro objectives. As a result, the organization is frequently subject to public criticism and attempts at government regulation.

The *social performance* orientation—high levels of both managerial control and cultivation of public support—can be very desirable from a societal point of view.[5] Cultivating public support is an interactive activity, especially when conducted at a high level. This means that management is not only trying to obtain support for its actions, but is also

FIGURE 2. Managerial Orientations: A Dual Macromarketing Concept

		Managerial Control	
		High	Low
Cultivating Public Support	High	Social Performance Orientation	Political Orientation
	Low	Business Orientation	Passive Orientation

responding by tailoring its objectives and plans to societal needs. In combination with a high level of managerial control, this orientation implies an intensive effort to achieve multiple objectives. It is relatively rare in practice, although some macro organizations appear to practice an orientation quite close to social performance, at least for a limited period of time. A possible example is the Japanese Ministry of International Trade and Industry, the government's central agency for implementing the successful post-war industrial strategy. The strategy was not only well defined in terms of general objectives and specific plans for key industries, it was also based on a consensus-seeking process of "eagerly searching out the views of the private sector and incorporating them into programs" (Yoshino 1976, pp. 10–11).

It is difficult to achieve a high level of activity in the two major tasks simultaneously. Nevertheless, while there is a trade-off between the efforts that are allocated to the two tasks, positive results on both counts are mutually reinforcing. High performances on multiple, socially desirable objectives generate public support, which simplifies the task of managerial control.

Measurement

The position of an organization in the conceptual framework of Figure 2 can be estimated in a number of ways. At this stage, a definitive statement about a preferred measurement methodology is premature. But it could be useful to explore how the dual concept can be operationalized and what problems might be encountered.

The task of measurement is to estimate the level of effort devoted to managerial control and the cultivation of public support. A straightforward, but unsophisticated way will be to ask senior managers to assess, based on subjective perceptions and in comparison with other organizations, the level of effort devoted to each task. The same scale should be used for both tasks to simplify comparisons.

For each organization studied, a point is recorded in a space generated by two axes corresponding to the two tasks. When a sample of organizations is available, interpretation can be based on the relative positions of each organization in the space and aided by multivariate analysis. Although it is expected that clusters of organizations would be formed based on the classification of the dual concept, some organizations will probably represent a mixture of more than one orientation. The measurement task must take into account at least four complicating factors: (1) operational definition of the level of effort, (2) response bias, (3) task separations, and (4) subjective differences among managers.

An operational definition of the level of effort can be based on all relevant expenses in monetary terms as a percentage of sales. Expenses such as promotion, personal sales, and managerial time are included.

This comprehensive coverage creates problems of estimation, and differences among industries with respect to spending levels can spoil interindustry comparisons. Alternatively, one could consider only managerial time, multiplied by salaries, as a percentage of sales. This would be simpler to estimate and would relate more directly to managerial orientations, but is based on partial effort. A desirable addition would be to assess quality (as a multiplier) in addition to quantity of effort. Quality, however, would have to be estimated subjectively from sources outside the organization.

Asking managers to estimate their level of effort is likely to generate an upward response bias. There is no problem if all managers have the same bias, but this is unlikely. An alternative approach will be to ask managers to estimate only the relative allocation of effort and to assess the overall level by an independent evaluation of a knowledgeable panel outside the organization. This approach is more cumbersome, but can probably produce more reliable results and take quality (or effectiveness) considerations into account. A comparison between the internal and external points of view should be of interest to management as well as the researcher.

When a specific act increases both managerial control and public support, it will be difficult to separate the effort allocated to each. This is not uncommon. For example, an advertising campaign announcing a price reduction can serve both functions. In these cases, it is necessary to consider the intended impact of the act on each count in order to properly assign efforts.

Subjective estimates of effort allocation from managers are likely to generate some disagreements since different managers view their enterprise from different perspectives. Minor disagreements can be handled by averaging responses. Serious disagreements may be indicative of an organization in a state of transition or disarray with no common orientation. It is also possible, particularly in large and geographically scattered organizations, that different management groups have different orientations. The subjective elements in the estimates can partially be eliminated by an objective study of the allocation of managerial time and funds to the two tasks. But even here, a subjective interpretation is frequently necessary to assess the intended effect of each effort.

Implications

The dual concept provides an important dimension, beyond type of industry and objective conditions, to explain marketing behavior. The following section explores selected implications of the dual concept as opening hypotheses for empirical research.

Marketing Goals and Behavior. The multiple objectives of the enterprise are given different weights with different orientations. As a result, different marketing goals are expected, although these may not be expressed formally in order to avoid political criticism. They can be interpreted, however, by analyzing behavior and performance.

In a passive orientation, a defensive strategy emphasizing sales stability and low risk is expected. Efforts to maintain market share will utilize limited public support to block competition rather than to initiate innovative responses.

More than any other orientation, the political is likely to emphasize a wide array of national interests although specific goals will depend on the political base which the firm cultivates. With a political orientation, we can expect relative instability from frequent shifts in priorities following the political mood. Considering, however, the interest of most governments to keep employment up and inflation down, managers are likely to stress volume objectives based on relatively low prices. Long-term profitability is not likely to be highlighted, as the marketing function is frequently dominated by the political need for visible short-term results and demonstration projects. In the socially-oriented European democracies, where one would expect political orientations in macro organizations to be quite common, the largest state-owned enterprises have generally experienced a high rate of sales growth and low, unstable profitability over the period 1968 to 1977 (Monsen and Walters 1979).

The managerial orientation is influenced by a desire to run a macromarketing enterprise free of political intervention. Since a major dependence on public support is financial (Aharoni 1979), the managerial orientation is likely to stress profitability, cash flow, and market diversification goals in order to reduce dependence on government. By increasing profitability and cash flow, there is less need to turn to government for funds. By decreasing reliance on a single product or market, management can increase its discretion in crisis periods.

Marketing goals of enterprises with a social performance orientation are likely to be more aggressive than the passive orientation, more focused on long-term goals than the political orientation, and less narrow than the managerial orientation. The enterprises in this category are likely to concentrate on developing new markets, new services, or new products which public opinion considers to be important. Since societal needs shift with time, management response under this orientation is also dynamic and open to change.

Strategy over Time. While the managerial and political orientations are based on imbalances between managerial control and cultivation of public support, both tasks are needed, particularly when new initiatives are contemplated. These two orientations are associated with two different strategies of balancing the two tasks over time.

In a political orientation, and to a lesser extent in a social performance orientation, management tends to cultivate public support for a new policy prior to action. If political backing by powerful parties cannot be mobilized, action is postponed. As a result of the diffusion of power and the bureaucratic nature of most democracies, action is frequently delayed until outside events force government and management to act. The enterprise and society pay a price for this reaction-time lag.

A managerial orientation is more likely to favor a strategy in which action is initiated first and support is cultivated during or after implementation. This strategy is considered an effective approach to achieve results with limited political intervention. At times, however, the strategy can backfire, such as when political opposition forces management to withdraw or to significantly alter plans.

Multinational Marketing. In recent years, an increasing number of state-owned enterprises, with macro responsibilities at home, are participating in international trade. The behavior of these enterprises is frequently different from that of private multinational firms.

Following national interests at home, a political orientation would lead management to push exports in order to earn foreign exchange and increase employment. Since profitability is not the major concern, a low price is a likely strategy particularly in periods of declining demand. As with product-line planning utilizing a loss-leader, macromanagement is willing to accept a loss in one enterprise provided the whole system is better-off. (An example: Following a long public debate, the tourist ministry in Israel was able to convince the government that low-priced charter flights would bring more tourists to the country and more than compensate for the loss of earnings of the national airline, El Al.) Foreign investment abroad, a favorable strategy of private firms, will usually be shunned in order to avoid opposition by labor leaders and others.

A different approach to multinational trade is likely to be followed by enterprises with a managerial orientation. Foreign expansion frequently provides an attractive opportunity to disengage from the restrictions of politicians at home. By seeking cooperative ventures with foreign partners, dependence on public support can be reduced. Operating abroad has the added advantage of circumventing various control procedures (e.g., foreign exchange) at home (Aharoni 1979). Enterprises in this category are also likely likely to cut prices sharply, since both profitability and multinational relations are important to the firm.

With a passive orientation, management will usually decline to initiate aggressive expansion into unfamiliar territories. When foreign trade is developed, probably by foreign initiative, it is likely to be a limited exporting effort.

Multinational marketing of enterprises with a social performance orientation is expected to combine a national point of view with a recognition of the long-term benefits from cooperation with foreign partners. As a result, exports will be emphasized, but foreign investments will also be initiated, provided macro benefits at home can be demonstrated.

Similar implications of the dual concept can be developed with respect to the behavior of regulation and coordination bodies. If the major implications of the dual concept are supported by empirical research, and if managerial orientations can be predicted based on the background of managers, organizational environment, and political climate, a managerial theory of macromarketing will be developed.

DECISION MAKING IN MACROMARKETING

In comparison with micromarketing, most macromarketing situations show a significant decrease in direct competition and an increase in cooperation in the regulation of consumption and in product-line planning.[6] The concept of the marketing manager as a strategist competing against adversaries shifts to that of an integrator concerned with the development of a whole market, working with a centralized data bank, and affected only by indirect competition. A comparison of major marketing factors affecting the decision making in micro and macro-marketing appears in Table 1.

An example of the cooperative opportunities in macromarketing is the case of milk advertising. Most marketing managers of milk-processing firms have refrained from advertising because they estimated that promotional elasticity for branded milk was very low. The situation changed when the American Dairy Association in cooperation with the U.S. Department of Agriculture (1965) took a macromarketing approach by concentrating on the promotion of generic milk demand. In a carefully designed two-year experiment, they tested the economic effects of nonbrand advertising and demonstrated that it can be very profitable.

While there are many dimensions of cooperative macromarketing action, one should not conclude that macromarketing managers are unconcerned about competition. Two sources of indirect competition create an outside threat: suppliers of substitutable products and services and suppliers of similar products and services outside the territory of the macromarketing organization. Indirect competition can strengthen the cooperative content of marketing decision making.

Once cooperative efforts have been initiated, by government sanction or voluntary process, keeping the parties together is a major organizational task. Organizational units have a tendency to enjoy the benefits of cooperative action, yet maintain freedom of independent action for themselves. Such difficulties are common, for example, in marketing boards and other forms of cooperative agricultural marketing. Maintaining the links among cooperative members can be aided by cultivating public support.

Decision making in cultivating public support has received only limited attention in the literature. The dual concept of macromarketing implies that this task deserves much more attention. There is a potential here for combining concepts from marketing, political science, and sociology to develop analytical models and practical guidelines.

CONCLUSION

This paper has introduced and discussed the idea of macromarketing management and the dual concept of macromarketing.

The scope of macromarketing management is not limited to the administration of public policy. A large number of managers throughout the world—many of them working in important growth segments of modern society—have macrosocietal responsibilities. The key variables of the managerial approach can be applied, with some modification, to the developing area of macromarketing.

The dual macromarketing concept is founded on the idea that two tasks, managerial control and cultivating public support, based on sepa-

TABLE 1. Comparison of Marketing Factors Affecting Decision Making in Micro and Macromarketing

Marketing Variable	Micromarketing	Macromarketing
Price determination	Response of customers as well as direct and indirect competitors	Response of customers, indirect competitors, and public opinion
Marketing channels	Dependence and interaction with marketing channels	Possibility for control of marketing channels
Advertising and promotion	Advertising for an increase of total market as well as market share	Possibility for nonbrand advertising to regulate consumption
Product policy	New product development devoted extensively to product differentiation	Potential for cooperative product-line planning and R & D
Production quantity	Based on the firm's marketing plan and forecast	Based on the need to guarantee employment and an adequate supply of product at reasonable prices
Marketing organization	Optimal structure to implement strategy and respond to marketplace conditions	Special emphasis on maintaining the links among cooperating parties
Marketing information system	Information confidential and primarily by brand	Centralized data bank for the industry

rate exchange relationships, must be performed in macromarketing.[7] Each organization needs to strike a strategic balance between the two tasks. The way this is done is indicative of the organizational orientation and behavior. The concept helps, therefore, to classify macromarketing organizations and provides a basis for explaining behavior and formulating testable hypotheses. It can also serve a normative function by helping managers to analyze their position relative to other managers and other organizations, thereby creating a more productive balance.

Although the managerial approach makes it possible and interesting to apply familiar concepts to new expanded problems, the most immediate research needs, however, are probably related to the dual concept: How do managers allocate their efforts between cultivating public support and managerial control? What are the relations between these allocation strategies, environmental conditions, and macro consequences? What can be done to achieve a balanced social-performance orientation? Other high-priority research topics should include exploration of other variables of the managerial approach not covered here: alternatives of performance evaluation with possible applications of decision theory with multiple and conflicting objectives, communication networks and information systems in cultivating public support, managing collective action, and micro versus macro organization and implementation.

ENDNOTES

1. Bartels and Jenkins (1977, p. 19) share the assessment that macromarketing has usually been thought of as unmanaged, but they propose that the concept of macromarketing management be limited to "the administration of public policy enforcement of laws,... and regulation of micromarketing behavior."
2. A consensus definition of macromarketing emerging from the third macromarketing seminar was: *Macromarketing is the study of exchange activities and exchange systems from a societal perspective* (Shawver and Nickels 1979).
3. A fifth P—Politics—has been proposed as an addition to the four Ps of the marketing mix by Arndt (1979) in his discussion of administered or domesticated markets.
4. This section is adapted from Etzioni's classification of societies (1970, pp. 137–140).
5. Cultivating public support with a focus on the needs of the enterprise, rather than the needs of the public, may not be socially desirable.
6. This section is based on prior work by Izraeli, Zif, and Izraeli (1976).
7. The concept is useful beyond macromarketing and particularly with domesticated markets and nonprofit enterprises.

REFERENCES

Abbott, J.C. and H.C. Cruepelandt (1966), *Agricultural Marketing Boards Their Establishment and Operation*, Rome: Food and Agricultural Organization of the United Nations, 2–4.

Aharoni, Y. (1979), "Managerial Discretion in State-Owned Enterprises," paper presented at the State-Owned Enterprises Conference, Harvard Business School, March 26–28.

Arndt, Johan (1979), "Toward a Theory of Domesticated Markets," *Journal of Marketing*, 43 (Fall), 69–82.

Bagozzi, Richard P. (1977), "Marketing at the Societal Level: Theoretical Issues and Problems," in *Macro-Marketing: Distributive Processes from a Societal Perspective*, P.D. White and C.C. Slater, ed., Business Research Division, University of Colorado, 8–44.

Bartels, Robert and Robert L. Jenkins (1977), "Macromarketing," *Journal of Marketing*, 41 (October), 17–20.

Bucklin, Louis P. (1977), "Structure, Conduct and Productivity in Distribution," in *Strategy and Structure = Performance*, Hans B. Thorelli, ed., Bloomington: Indiana University Press, 219–236.

Caldwell, Philip (1979), "Getting Our Share," *Newsweek* (April 16), 16.

Corti, B. (1979), "Public Corporations," paper presented at the State-Owned Enterprises Conference, Harvard Business School, March 26–28.

Drucker, Peter (1974), *Management Tasks Responsibilities Practices*, New York: Harper and Row.

Etzioni, Amitai (1970), "Toward a Macrosociology," in *Macrosociology Research and Theory*, James S. Coleman, Amitai Etzioni, and John Porter, eds., Boston: Allyn and Bacon.

Fisk, George (1967), *Marketing Systems*, New York: Harper International.

——— (1976) *Marketing and Social Priorities*, Chicago: American Marketing Association.

Galbraith, John K. (1967), *The New Industrial State*, Boston: Houghton-Mifflin.

Hunt, Shelby D. (1976), "The Nature and Scope of Marketing," *Journal of Marketing*, 40 (July), 20.

——— (1977), "The Three Dichotomies Model of Marketing: An Elaboration of Issues," in *Macro-Marketing: Distributive Processes from a Societal Perspective*, P.D. White and C.C. Slater, ed., Business Research Division, University of Colorado, 55–56.

Izraeli, D. and J. Zif (1977), *Societal Marketing Boards*, New York: John Wiley and Sons and Israel Universities Press.

———, ———, and D. Izraeli (1976), "Marketing Boards and Societal Marketing," *Journal of Rural Cooperation*, IV, 2.

Kotler, Philip (1972), "A Generic Concept of Marketing," *Journal of Marketing*, 36 (April), 53.

———, and Gerald Zaltman (1971), "Social Marketing: An Approach to Planned Social Change," *Journal of Marketing*, 35 (July), 3–12.

McCarthy, Jerome (1968), *Basic Marketing*, Homewood, IL: Richard D. Irwin, 9.

Monsen, Joseph R. and Kenneth D. Walters (1979), "A Theory of the State-Owned Firm in a Democracy," paper presented at the State-Owned Enterprises Conference, Harvard Business School, March 26–28.

Moyer, Reed (1972), *Macro-Marketing—A Social Perspective*, New York: John Wiley and Sons, vi-vii.

Preston, Lee E. and James E. Post (1975), *Private Management and Public Policy*, Englewood Cliffs, NJ: Prentice-Hall, Inc.

Shawver, Donald L. and William G. Nickels (1979), "A Rationalization for Macromarketing Concepts and Definitions," in *Macro-Marketing: New Steps on the Learning Curve*, G. Fisk and R.W. Nason, eds., Business Research Division, University of Colorado, 41.

Slater, C.C. (1978), "A Market Process Theory," in *Macro-Marketing: Distributive Processes from a Societal Perspective, An Elaboration of Issues*, P.D. White and C.C. Slater, eds., Business Research Division, University of Colorado.

U.S. Department of Agriculture (1965), *The Effects of Different Levels of Promotional Expenditures on Sales of Fluid Milk*, Washington, D.C.: Economic Research Service, ERS-259.

Yoshino, M.Y. (1976), *Japan's Multinational Enterprises*, Cambridge, MA: Harvard University Press.

Zif, J. and D. Izraeli (1977), "A Central Marketing Authority—The Case of Israeli Marketing Boards," in *Macro-Marketing: Distributive Processes from a Societal Perspective*, P.D. White and C.C. Slater, ed., Business Research Division, University of Colorado, 238–247.

———, and ——— (1978a), "Management of Quantity—A Study in Agricultural Macro-Marketing," in *Macro-Marketing: Distributive Processes from a Societal Perspective, an Elaboration of Issues*, P.D. White and C.C. Slater, eds., Business Research Division, University of Colorado, 151–165.

———, and ——— (1978b), "Objectives And Performance Evaluation of Marketing Boards," *European Journal of Marketing*, 12, 6.

SECTION F
Regulation of Marketing

Unfortunately, the role of regulation in marketing usually does not receive the amount of attention in most marketing management textbooks that it legitimately deserves. The reason for this paucity of analysis is that marketing managers and scholars typically focus the majority of their energies on the needs of consumers and the actions of competitors rather than on the activities of regulators. While marketing practitioners must understand their customers and competitors, their success in the marketplace will be limited unless they also appreciate the impact that regulation may have on their marketing plans. To correct this deficiency for future marketing managers, this readings book includes the following special section, which is devoted entirely to regulation of the marketing function.

Many marketing practitioners tend to perceive regulation as a constraint that impedes their marketing efforts and reduces their profitability. For this reason, marketers often complain about the supposedly trivial restrictions that frustrate their activities and the large number of government forms that they must complete to show evidence of their compliance with the regulations. Similarly, government officials responsible for enforcing regulations sometimes feel that marketers are trying to deviously skirt regulations to maximize their short-term profits. Thus, it is hardly surprising that the interaction between marketing practitioners and government regulators is commonly adversarial rather than cooperative.

This adversarial attitude is regrettable, because a certain degree of regulation of the marketing function is necessary to ensure the general welfare of the greater society. The challenge for future marketing managers is to become actively involved in the regulatory process so that their viewpoints can be adequately represented as new regulations are constructed. In the past, consumer activists have generally been more vocal and active than marketers in ensuring that their particular interests are heard. After their views are presented and these regulations are enacted, marketers must respond positively to the existence of the regulations and fashion their marketing strategies accordingly.

In addition, marketing practitioners must be prepared to modify their strategies as regulations are revised. An integral facet of regulatory decision making by the federal and state governments in the United States is its high degree of volatility. As new representatives and administrations are elected every few years, the focus of regulatory attention may also shift dramatically. For example, the Carter administration, following the precedent established by the Kennedy administration, was generally perceived to advocate greater federal control over business practices, while the present Reagan administration apparently favors increased delegation of regulatory power to the states. Thus, during Reagan's tenure there has been a considerable weakening of federal agencies such as the Federal Communications Commission and Federal Trade Commission. Also, there is now a trend toward deregulation of certain major industries, like the airlines and telephone industries. The general attitude of the current administration is that market forces, rather than government regulation, should play a more prominent role in dictating business practices.

The one dominant fact that students of marketing should appreciate is that the regulation of marketing is pervasive. That is, all areas of the marketing mix are affected to a certain degree by regulations. Although many fine articles have been written in recent years regarding the regulation of business, the following four articles were selected specifically because they demonstrate the breadth of regulatory influence in the marketing arena.

18 — Reasonable Rules and Rules of Reason: Vertical Restrictions on Distributors

John F. Cady

Reprinted from the *Journal of Marketing*, published by the American Marketing Association, Vol. 46 (Summer 1982), pp. 27–37. Reprinted by permission.

INTRODUCTION

Vertical restrictions on distributors (VRD) are restraints imposed by a firm at one level of the distribution system (usually the manufacturer) on the activities of a firm or firms at another level of the distribution system. Although the imposition of VRD by a manufacturer involves inevitable costs, in many situations these restrictions are an attractive and even necessary element of distribution strategy.

For the second time in 14 years the Supreme Court has declared the need for the development of an analysis of VRD that would provide guidance to those courts that must balance the costs associated with restricted intrabrand competition against the benefits of increased interbrand competition. Interbrand competition refers to the rivalry that exists among distributors with respect to the sale of the branded products of competing manufacturers. An example of interbrand competition would be that which exists between distributors of Ford automobiles and Chevrolet automobiles for the purchases of consumers who might buy either brand. Intrabrand competition refers to the rivalry that exists among distributors of any single manufacturer's branded product. An example of intrabrand competition would be that which exists among distributors of Ford automobiles for the purchases of consumers who might buy Fords. The FTC has echoed this declaration of the Court in a major appeal decision that relied heavily on ad hoc economic analysis as a means of determining the net social benefit of VRD in the soft drink industry (In the Matter of the Coca-Cola Company 1978).

This article develops an analysis of VRD that will result in several guidelines to structure the application of a rule of reason to these distribution restrictions. The criterion driving the guidelines is the minimization of total social costs related to VRD. The term *social costs* used in this article refers to the level of costs borne by the public associated with reductions in intrabrand competition among distributors contrasted to the level of costs without VRD. Costs may take the form of the purchase price paid by customers, but costs may also be incurred through unavailability of products or inadequacy of service. The guidelines may be used as an analytical framework by administrative agencies and courts, and as benchmarks against which firms may measure the desirability of establishing or maintaining VRD.

This article is divided into three main sections. Following a brief description of various typical forms of VRD, the first section examines the treatment of VRD by the courts and demonstrates the necessity for the development of legal guidelines. The second section explores the implementation of VRD, their effects on manufacturers, distributors and customers. The third section provides several specific guidelines for the application of a rule of reason that balances the needs of firms, consumer welfare and a public policy of fostering competition.

VERTICAL RESTRICTIONS ON DISTRIBUTORS

Vertical restrictions on distributors (VRD) are policies initiated by a manufacturer that attempt to reduce or restrict the degree of intrabrand competition among its distributors. VRD take various forms and each differs in the degree of its impact on intrabrand competition. The most familiar types of VRD are (1) territorial sales restrictions, (2) location clauses, (3) areas of primary responsibility and (4) customer restrictions. This paper will not consider vertical restrictions on price or vertical restrictions on product policy, both of which require analysis quite different from that developed in this article. All vertical restrictions on price have been considered per se illegal since the passage of the Consumer Goods Pricing Act in 1976, which overturned all existing state resale maintenance or "fair trade" laws. Tying arrangements and other product restrictions are also frequently judged under a per se rule.

1. Territorial sales restrictions limit a distributor to sales within a designated geographic territory. These restrictions are often coupled with a reciprocal agreement by the manufacturer not to allow any other distributor to sell within the designated territory. By granting exclusive rights to sell in a territory, the manufacturer completely eliminates intrabrand competition. Soft drink bottlers have historically operated within exclusive territories.

2. Location clauses restrict distributor's resale operations to a specified physical site. A location clause may reduce but does not eliminate intrabrand competition since customers can travel to any location they desire. Automobile dealerships, for example, are operated using location clauses, and GTE Sylvania utilized location clauses in the sale of its television sets.

3. Areas of primary responsibility are also territories assigned to a distributor. Within the territory the distributor must represent

the manufacturer to the latter's satisfaction. The degree of performance is frequently quantified through a territorial sales quota. If the distributor fails to perform to the manufacturer's satisfaction, it may lose the distributorship. Areas of primary responsibility are frequently coupled with profit-passover arrangements that require any distributor making a sale outside its designated territory to compensate the distributor in whose territory the sale is made. The manufacturer may set the amount of compensation to offset a portion of the presale or promotional costs of the distributor in whose territory the sale is made.

4. Customer restrictions are analogous to territorial restrictions in that they limit distributors in their choice of customers and thus reduce intrabrand competition. Perhaps the most common type of customer restriction is a house account or major account program. This type of restriction identifies customer accounts that are serviced and sold by the manufacturer's sales force. Manufacturers may initiate a major account program when, for example, a customer is national in scope and distributors are regional or local. A national customer may request or require that its purchasing be coordinated across all of its geographic units. In order to facilitate coordination in purchasing the manufacturer coordinates the selling activities. Major accounts may also develop as a result of other factors such as customers who require servicing or technical assistance that cannot be effectively provided by distributors.

The Legal Treatment of Vertical Restrictions on Distributors

Vertical restrictions on distributors fall under Section 1 of the Sherman Act, which prohibits "[e]very contract, combination... or conspiracy in restraint of trade...." The application of Section 1 to VRD has taken several turns since the Sherman Act was enacted. A brief review serves to point out the problems that competing theories of the effects of VRD have posed for the courts. In turn, inconsistent enforcement patterns and judicial rulings resulting from the rise and fall of those theories have served to increase private and societal costs.

A Legal Perspective on VRD

From 1890 to 1948 the Antitrust Division of the Justice Department did not challenge the legality of territorial restrictions, and the few courts that reviewed these restrictions generally found them to be legal. However, in 1948 the Division reversed its historic position and began to challenge territorial restrictions as per se violations of the Sherman Act.

The Antitrust Division was successful in negotiating consent decrees with most alleged violators until 1963, when *White Motor* became the first case involving vertical restrictions to reach the Supreme Court. But the Court refused to take a firm position, stating that it needed to "know more... about the actual impact of these arrangements on competition." The Court remanded the case back to the lower court.

In the *Schwinn* case (1966), the Supreme Court abandoned this cautious approach and adopted a per se rule for proscribing exclusive territorial restraints. Instead of analyzing the actual impact of these arrangements on competition, the Court disregarded the economic arguments put forward on both sides and based its per se rule on an entirely different element of antitrust law—the concern for the freedom of independent business units to sell their goods according to their own best business judgment.

The Schwinn decision provoked criticism which continued for 10 years (Robinson 1972). During that time, lower courts carved out exceptions and qualifications that allowed them to avoid the strict application of the Schwinn rule of per se illegality.

The *Sealy* decision of 1967 (*U.S. v. Sealy*) dealt with franchise agreements. The case differed from Schwinn in that it contained both horizontal and vertical restraints. In this case the Supreme Court held that the exclusive territorial restrictions were per se illegal but only when they constituted a horizontal division of the market and were characterized by price fixing agreements. Five years later the Supreme Court broadened the *Sealy* decision in the *Topco* case (*U.S. v. Topco Associates 1972*). In this decision the Court held that territorial exclusivity could be a per se violation even when no price fixing was involved.

Events in this legal arena took another turn in 1977 when the Supreme Court examined distributor restrictions for yet another time and, in *Continental TV., Inc. v. GTE Sylvania*, expressly overturned the Schwinn decision and required distributor restraints to be judged under the rule of reason. The case generated considerable excitement among legal commentators and managers because the decision relied heavily on economic analysis and because the opinion expressed a very favorable view of the justifications for VRD. In addition, the Court gave little recognition to possible drawbacks of VRD despite its statement that particular applications of these restrictions might justify per se treatment.

Although the *Sylvania* opinion requires that VRD be judged under the rule of reason, the Court provided little guidance as to the content of such an inquiry. This is a significant omission since the rule of reason is not actually a rule in the sense of being a well-understood legal standard. It is more accurate to describe the rule of reason as an invitation for a court to examine the purpose, history, nature and results of a challenged practice and to decide on the importance and reasonableness of that practice. The rule of reason, when applied to VRD, requires the court to weigh the reduction in intrabrand competition against any increase in interbrand competition and to determine whether or not the restraints are necessary to facilitate an efficient or effective system of distribution.

Given such formlessness, it is not surprising that the first major case decided under the *Sylvania* approach resulted in a decision that seems at odds with the favorable view of VRD expressed in *Sylvania*. In deciding the legality of territorial restrictions in the soft drink bottling industry, the FTC ruled that the restraints were illegal except for beverages sold in returnable bottles (In the Matter of the Coca-Cola Company 1978). The Commission stressed the restrictions' suppression of intrabrand competition and could find no redeeming virtues—such as the encouragement of investment by dealers, facilitation of the manufacturer's quality control, inducement of dealer advertising, or enhanced market penetration—to justify the restraints. The Commission allowed territorial restrictions to remain for soft drinks sold in returnable bottles because there was no efficient distribution alternative to solve the problem of assuring bottlers a steady supply of their own bottles.

The Effects of Inconsistent Legal Treatment of VRD

The confusing and sometimes contradictory treatment of VRD has resulted in the imposition of considerable costs both on manufacturers who attempt to develop effective distribution systems and on society at large.

Under a per se treatment where all vertical restrictions limiting intrabrand competition are regarded as illegal, there are virtually no litigation transaction costs and there may be only minimal monitoring costs incurred by enforcement agencies. However, two potentially significant costs may be incurred in the process. First, manufacturers cannot obtain the benefits (nor can consumers) of restrictions. These are basically private costs borne by the respective individuals. Second, the market system can suffer from a reduction in overall efficiency. This macro loss in efficiency occurs if VRD can ever, on balance, be pro-competitive. A per se treatment precludes the effects of any pro-competitive restrictions from being felt in the market. As developed later in this article, there are clearly situations in which VRD can have beneficial effects on competition and consumers. Thus, the per se treatment of VRD imposes higher than optimal costs on individuals and society.

On the other hand, an ill-defined rule of reason treatment will generally increase litigation transactions costs and enforcement monitoring costs substantially over those incurred under a per se treatment. Balancing these costs, the rule of reason approach enhances the socially desirable outcome of proscribing noncompetitive vertical restrictions but not discouraging pro-competitive restrictions entirely. Even a rule of reason treatment may not have the socially optimal outcome of eliminating all non-competitive vertical restrictions (given some level of enforcement and litigation costs), however. Unless very clear guidelines for management are laid down or emerge, the degree of uncertainty as to which vertical restrictions are illegal will probably be regarded as large. Management will refrain from using vertical restrictions in those cases where the expected costs of litigation and disrupted distribution programs exceed the expected benefits. Unfortunately, this situation may pose the most serious problem for new firms desiring to enter into well-developed markets. As explained later in this discussion, use by new entrants is one condition where VRD are quite likely to have a pro-competitive effect. On the other hand, an ill-defined rule of reason may actually encourage non-competitive use of VRD by some management on the premise that some court may find them legal at some time and for some noneconomic reason.

Reducing the uncertainty of whether litigation (*and* the associated costs and outcome) is to be expected from the imposition of vertical restrictions is desirable because it encourages those restrictions that are both publicly and privately efficient and discourages those that may be privately efficient but publicly noncompetitive and costly. Reducing uncertainty and obtaining the desired results requires more than the ability to distinguish pro-competitive from noncompetitive vertical restrictions. It requires the communication of rather specific guidelines to management and a policy of consistent enforcement. Such guidelines are currently lacking under the Supreme Court's *GTE Sylvania* ruling and/or under the FTC's Coca-Cola ruling. Table 1 shows a comparison of those two cases and reflects the economic arguments cited in the respective opinions. In neither case was a priority placed on any of the characteristics, a condition that leads to conjecture as to what was, in fact, decided concerning VRD.

Manufacturers and the Use of VRD

The Costs

Most manufacturers distribute their products without restrictions on intrabrand competition. They find that unrestricted competition among distributors results in the lowest competitive distributor selling price; this in turn results in expanded sales volume and higher profitability. VRD, which prevent price competition from driving down distributor margins, therefore, have inherent costs for a manufacturer (Posner 1975).

1. When protected from intrabrand competition, a distributor has an incentive to raise price above the competitive level. This higher distribution margin will raise the price of the product, thus reducing the units sold and the manufacturer's revenues.
2. In the case of territorial restrictions, the size of distributors protected from intrabrand competition will tend to be less than efficient unless the manufacturer can duplicate the effect of the competitive process by constantly readjusting the size of territories.
3. Manufacturers must bear the costs of policing the system of restrictions. Manufacturers must determine the optimal size for distributor territories, find optimal locations, screen and select distributors, monitor the development of new customers, supervise distributor compliance and arbitrate disputes among distributors.

The Benefits

Despite such inevitable costs, manufacturers impose VRD in the distribution of various types of products from consumer convenience goods, such as soft drinks to major appliances, industrial components and farm implements. Such varied application of these restrictions indicates that there are situations in which the benefits of these restrictions to the manufacturer more than offset the costs. In particular, there are four

TABLE 1. A Comparison of GTE Sylvania and Coca-Cola*

	GTE-Sylvania	Coca-Cola
Ruling	legal	illegal
Restriction		
—Type of restriction	location clause	exclusive territories
—Degree of intrabrand competition foreclosed	partial	total
—Degree of interbrand competition foreclosed	strong (?)	weak
Market Characteristics		
—Distributor concentration	low	high
—Producer concentration	high	high
Firm Characteristics		
—Market share	2–5%	21%
—Industry position	"faltering"	"dominant"
Product Characteristics		
—Convenience/shopping	shopping/specialty	convenience

*Source: Supreme Court decision in *Continential T.V. Inc.* v. *GTE Sylvania, Inc.* (1977) and Federal Trade Commission decision, In the Matter of the Coca-Cola Company et al. (1978).

situations in which manufacturers find the use of VRD cost efficient: inducing higher levels of distributor services, developing and marketing new products in new markets, increasing market coverage and market penetration, and providing incentives to promote a full product line to a full range of customers.

Distributor Services and the Free Rider Problem. Product demand may be heavily dependent on the level and quality of distributor's presale or post-sale services. Such services may include a wide range of distributor activities such as personal selling, demonstration, product promotion, field engineering, maintaining comfortable showrooms, training sales personnel and product installation and servicing. The provision of such services will generally increase the demand for a manufacturer's product more than enough to offset any reduction in demand resulting from the higher distribution margin necessary to compensate for them. If the services do not increase demand in such a way, they generally will not be provided.

When a manufacturer uses VRD to stimulate the provision of services, its interest is equated to that of the consumer (Bork 1966). A manufacturer has no incentive to provide service for which the utility to the consumer does not equal or exceed the cost of providing it, since to do so would simply reduce demand for the manufacturer's product. If a manufacturer miscalculates and induces too high a level of service (i.e., the service costs more than its value to the consumer), demand falls and the manufacturer's revenues are reduced. Revenues are also reduced if miscalculation leads a manufacturer to induce too low a level of service from distributors (the value of the service to customers is greater than the cost of providing it). By imposing VRD, a manufacturer seeks to restrict distributor profits to the competitive level by providing, through distribution, that level of service that results in marginal cost equalling marginal utility. This outcome is the socially optimal result for distribution performance, and this argument has led to the conclusion by some observers that all manufacturer-imposed vertical restrictions should be presumed legal (Bork 1966).

It has been argued, however, that VRD are not necessary to stimulate service provision: If consumer demand for additional service exceeds the cost of service provision, then distributors have sufficient incentive without any intervention on the part of the manufacturer. Each distributor could simply charge a higher price to cover the cost of providing valued additional services. Alternatively, products and services could be priced separately (Comanor 1968). Therefore, one additional element is necessary in order to explain fully why manufacturers must utilize VRD to stimulate service provision. The argument that VRD are unnecessary to stimulate service provision ignores the competition among distributors that raises the free rider problem (Bork 1966). A distributor will prefer, whenever possible, not to provide the optimal level of services if it can make sales by taking a free ride on the services provided by other distributors. Since free riding distributors do not incur the full costs of providing services, they can offer a lower price than distributors who do provide services. Eventually, under such conditions all distributors cease to provide services. This situation reduces consumer welfare since desired services cannot be obtained. It reduces manufacturers' welfare because sales revenue and profit are reduced. The alternative of charging separate prices for product and service is frequently unworkable. In many cases the "product" is "augmented" and includes a basic service level that is not subject to unbundling for pricing purposes. It seems unreasonable, for example, to suggest that if a distributor maintains a minimum inventory level in order to be able to fill 95% of all orders within three days, the distributor should charge some of its customers for this service but not others. In general, it seems equally implausible to suggest that a distributor train its sales force to make well-informed presentations to potential customers and then charge separately for the presentations. The purpose of providing many services, such as product inventory assortment and availability and sales and technical support, is to increase product sales; with some exceptions (such as repairs) there is no separable demand for the service apart from the product (Buzzell 1980).

New Products and New Markets: Another Form of Free Riding. Distribution of some products may require large investments in initial promotion and market development. A distributor undertaking initial market development may be faced with the prospect of a start-up period of unprofitable operations before reaching a normal return on investment. A distributor will refrain from making the required initial investment if there is a reasonable probability that a competitor can benefit from its market development activities before the costs of undertaking those efforts have been recouped and normal returns obtained.

In such a situation the absence of protection from intrabrand competition results in distributors engaging in a standoff: There is a potential market for the product but none of the distributors will make the expenditures necessary to develop it. The manufacturer (who may or may not be a new market entrant) may lack the resources, the requisite marketing skills or the knowledge of local markets to develop market potential. Without restrictions on intrabrand competition, potential demand would go unfilled.

Under such circumstances distributors must be provided some protection from intrabrand competition. From the manufacturer's standpoint, however, such restrictions are beneficial so long as they are limited to a time period no longer than necessary to allow the distributor to recoup that part of the initial investment that succeeding distributors do not need to make. Although the ability of manufacturers to determine accurately the amount of time appropriate to the use of VRD may be difficult, this problem should not be insurmountable. In a later section, the incentives for a manufacturer to develop restrictions that are limited in time are discussed. If a second or subsequent distributor must make all the same investments and incur all the same costs, then vertical restrictions may not benefit the manufacturer because there can be no free riding on the initial distributor's efforts.

There is one scenario that could conceivably reduce the strength of the argument that VRD may be necessary for the introduction of new products or the development of new markets. The market tends, in general, to reward innovative distributors through the ability to skim the market for any high margin accounts and, potentially, to become established and preferred by customers before competitors. Even if such abilities and conditions exist, however, a risk premium in the form of a restriction on intrabrand competition may still be initially warranted. The existence of high margin accounts can only be estimated; the benefits of early establishment in the market are uncertain. The success of an initial distributor unequivocally reduces the uncertainty of subsequent distributors who, therefore, require no similar risk premium.

Market Coverage and Market Penetration. In contrast to industrial or consumer products requiring extensive services for sales stimulation, the sales volume of consumer convenience products is often directly related to the number of distribution points at which these products are available. Consumers shopping for convenience products, such as dry groceries or common nonprescription drugs that are well-known and frequently purchased, rarely shop at a number of retail outlets. Rather, they purchase from some conveniently located retailer. For this reason, a manufacturer of convenience products desires to have its product available in a large number of appropriate outlets.

In attempting to gain widespread distribution, however, a manufacturer may face a dilemma: Increasing distribution coverage may increase the average costs of distribution as the manufacturer expands to smaller, less efficient or less effective distributors. There, costs will be reflected in the price that must be charged for the product. An increased level of demand that results from an expansion in distribution must be weighed against the reduced level of demand that results from the higher costs and prices. A manufacturer will attempt to expand distribution as long as the marginal cost of the expansion is less than the marginal revenue gained from the expansion, and no longer. Without vertical restrictions a product will be available in all outlets where the consumer is willing to pay the cost of getting it there, reflected in the product's price. There is no incentive to a manufacturer, distributor or consumer to have distribution expanded to too many outlets. In a competitive situation the degree of distribution coverage reflects the manufacturer's evaluation of the trade-off between distribution coverage and distribution cost.

The Role of Market Power in Obtaining Market Coverage. In the competitive situation described above, it is clear that VRD will not increase market coverage for a product. Even the complete elimination of intrabrand competition will not provide a distributor with any incentive to increase distribution costs that cannot be recovered from a buyer in the form of higher prices.

VRD may be an effective means of obtaining market coverage, however, for products facing imperfect interbrand competition, i.e., for products for which buyers have developed specific brand preferences. Such preferences will develop whenever one brand has different preferred product attributes (or higher quality attributes) as perceived by buyers (Lancaster 1966, Ratchford 1975). In such a situation a buyer is willing to pay a premium price for the preferred brand in order to obtain the preferred attributes. The amount of the sustained price premium buyers are willing to pay for a preferred brand is one measure of the brand's market power. Market power may be evidenced in other ways as well. Buyers might be willing to go out of their way to purchase the preferred brand, or might purchase it in preference to equally convenient and similarly priced brands.

Much product differentiation is socially useful in and of itself. Product differentiation based on inherent differences in the product itself shows the range of consumer choice and allows variations in consumer needs to be met. Differences in the size and performance of automobiles can benefit consumers by providing a wider choice. Even differences in styling are not wasteful if utility is measured in terms of the consumer's willingness to pay for those differences in the face of meaningful alternatives. Branded grocery products may be physically identical to unbranded products, but they also offer, in return for a higher price, the assurance of a certain quality level. Such assurance may be important to some or all consumers for products whose characteristics (such as flavor) are not readily apparent on prepurchase inspection. Although the discussion that follows is applicable regardless of the consumer utility of the differentiation, the guidelines proposed must either distinguish between socially useful and socially wasteful differentiation, or determine the degree of market power that society will tolerate regardless of its potentially useful nature. The latter approach has been used here, which avoids the debate over real vs. imagined consumer needs and also avoids dealing with the trivial and generally beneficial forms of differentiation discussed above.

The market power of a differentiated brand results in changes in the economics of distribution. Prices may be set at a level somewhat above competitors and profits may be increased. Distributors find that some customers are potentially more profitable to them because they are easily reached or because they are particularly attracted to the brand. From the distributor's standpoint such customers might be termed low-cost buyers. On the other hand, some customers may be harder to sell to because they are more costly to reach or because they are more price sensitive. These customers might be termed high-cost buyers. The revenue and profit maximizing strategy for a manufacturer in such a situation involves two steps: raising the price to the distributor (which is then passed on to buyers) above the market level, and finding a means by which distributors can extract higher profits from low-cost buyers without losing sales to the high-cost buyers (Comanor 1968). A manufacturer will take the first step regardless of whether VRD are available or not. The second step, however, is made possible by VRD.

Although some customers are potentially more profitable for distributors since these customers will pay a higher price or will purchase the product in less convenient outlets, this extra profit cannot be extracted if there is unrestricted intrabrand competition. Competition among distributors will prevent any one of them from making a more than competitive profit on its sales. If one distributor attempts to reap extra profits from sales to low-cost purchasers, other distributors will undersell it until the price again reaches the competitive level. This competition is desirable from a manufacturer's point of view. The manufacturer has no desire to see distributors earn higher than competitive profits, since such profits at the distributor level tend to reduce manufacturer profits. A more desirable situation from the manufacturer's standpoint would be for distributors to earn high profits from low-cost buyers and then use a portion of those profits to subsidize additional selling efforts to high-cost buyers. Distributors would earn competitive returns since the profit from sales to low-cost buyers would be spent on otherwise unprofitable selling efforts to high-cost buyers. The principal benefits accrue to the manufacturer. Sales of the product are expanded without reducing the manufacturer's selling price or increasing its selling expenses, and profits are increased.

VRD can enable a manufacturer to use available market power to increase sales and profits. The situation is unusual in that the manufacturer with market power increases profits by expanding output rather than restricting it. Previous analyses of VRD have typically focused on output reduction and resulting resource misallocation as the principal outcome that antitrust law seeks to avoid. Nevertheless, manufacturer's profits that result from output restriction or from output expansion coupled with VRD both have the undesirable effect of reducing consumer welfare and misallocating resources.

The use of VRD to expand market coverage has been accepted as desirable by many economists and viewed favorably by the Supreme Court on the basis that this use of VRD promotes interbrand competition and increases consumer choice. However, this tolerant view does not address an essential point: The increase in competitors and choice is costly relative to the benefits. VRD imposed in order to expand market coverage for brands with substantial market power inevitably reduce consumer welfare by misallocating resources. This is accomplished by inducing distributors to make the product available to those who would not buy it if they were charged the full costs of the additional distribution necessary to reach them. In effect, low-cost buyers subsidize high-cost buyers and pay the cost for the additional resources devoted to distribution activity. Without VRD intrabrand competition causes distributors to expand market coverage only as long as marginal revenues exceed marginal costs. This is the optimal solution in terms of efficient resource allocation. Any movement from this point reduces consumer welfare by misallocating resources.

The manufacturer of convenience products would not normally be expected to favor restrictions on distribution that increase the price to the consumer more than they increase the value of the product to the consumer. This situation is considerably different when the manufacturer possesses some substantial market power. Such a manufacturer might prefer more costly and inefficient distribution when such distribution increases product demand. When protected from intrabrand competition, distributors can charge higher prices to all buyers (and obtain higher profits) without fear that another distributor will undercut price. The distributors can then use these profits to subsidize sales efforts to high-cost marginal buyers. Though these buyers too must pay higher prices, the prices to them are not increased to offset fully the added costs of reaching them. These customers bear only a part of the added costs of distribution that are spread evenly over all buyers. The restraints benefit some buyers through increased availability but result in higher prices for all.

Market Penetration: Promoting a Full Product Line to a Full Range of Customers. Within a given broadly defined product market there are frequently a number of market niches to which a manufacturer's product or product line can be sold if the distributor makes the sales efforts appropriate to each niche. Within such a market there are considerable variations in the purchasing requirements of potential customers. Because of the characteristics of the product and a particular distributor's sales strategy, sales to some customers will be more easily and more profitably made than sales to others. The profits a distributor can earn by selling additional customers will diminish as the distributor expands efforts. These diminishing returns encourage a distributor to limit sales efforts to the more profitable customers or products. The situation is similar to the manufacturer's use of territorial restraints to expand market coverage. The manufacturer would like to see distributors earn extra profits on sales to that part of the market most easily reached, if those extra profits are used to subsidize sales efforts to less profitable customers or sales of less profitable products in the manufacturer's product line. When VRD are necessary to protect such profits from being driven away through distributor competition, the effects on consumer welfare are negative.

GUIDELINES FOR A RULE OF REASON ANALYSIS OF VERTICAL RESTRICTIONS ON DISTRIBUTORS

Based on the analysis of the effects of the various uses of VRD and the need for the development of guidelines for an appropriate, predictable and consistent rule of reason, the following three rules are proposed.

- VRD implemented to stimulate the provision of services subject to free riding are presumptively legal;
- VRD implemented to gain distributors for new products or to enter a market are presumptively legal;
- VRD implemented to increase market coverage or market penetration are presumptively legal in the absence of significant market power.

The underlying rationale for these rules is noted in the preceding section of this article. Specifically, it was argued that when services are subjected to free rider problems, manufacturers and consumers are penalized when VRD are illegal and, hence, unavailable to stimulate service provision. This outcome is unaffected either by market power that is possessed by manufacturers or by the potential market power that manufacturers might gain as a result of distributor service differentiation. Market power that exists in the absence of or prior to the implementation of VRD is, by definition, a separate issue and can be treated as such under the antitrust laws. If VRD could be used to increase market power temporarily, then the availability of VRD to all manufacturers potentially reduces the long run advantage of such restrictions to a single firm. Only when VRD would be coupled with exclusive distribution arrangements could market power be increased and maintained. However, it is the exclusivity of such an arrangement that gives rise to the market power rather than the VRD, and the standards for exclusive distribution arrangements are well articulated in antitrust law (Peterman 1975, Preston 1965).

Market power, however, is a critical distinguishing characteristic, should VRD be implemented to achieve increased market coverage or market penetration. As described above, in competitive markets increased coverage or penetration must be weighed against increased costs and reduced demand. This will be the case for such firms regardless of whether or not they use VRD since VRD will only reduce intrabrand competition; interbrand competition will still negate any attempts by distributors to raise price to low-cost buyers to provide funds to increase coverage or penetration. In fact, firms without market power should seldom, if ever, be observed implementing VRD merely to increase market coverage or market penetration. Without another reason, such as presale service provision, there appears to be no benefit for these firms from the use of VRD.

Firms with appreciable market power, however, will be able to utilize VRD to subsidize distributors' efforts to increase market coverage or penetration. Distribution margins can be raised in the absence of effective interbrand competition or intrabrand competition so that sales to low cost buyers subsidize sales to high-cost buyers. In the soft drink industry it has been noted that most franchise agreements required that the bottler service all retail outlets in its area regardless of whether the outlet was profitable (Cresap, McCormick and Paget 1972).

Firms entering new markets or developing new products have generally been allowed the use of VRD even during periods when such restrictions were viewed critically by the courts. The usual rationale is that in such circumstances, the manufacturer is faced with a form of the free rider problem noted earlier, and by definition, the manufacturer has no market power in a market it has yet to enter. It appears that the most likely use of VRD for new products would occur for specialty and shopping products that require pre- or post-sale services, or which would be viewed as somehow risky by final consumers (high cost video projection systems, for example). Similarly, entry into new markets may require VRD where market knowledge or acceptance of the technology embodied in the product is low.

In most situations it is expected that VRD would be discontinued after market entry or initial product acceptance takes place. If services subject to free riding are required to maintain market position, VRD will also be maintained. This phenomenon poses no competitive or legal problem.

However, in the case of the use of VRD for new product introduction two characteristics may simultaneously arise that do pose potential competitive problems. First, initial investment in service or free riding-prone promotion may become unnecessary as the product moves through the product life cycle. Second, market power may develop for the manufacturer of the innovative product. Such a combination may stimulate the manufacturer to expand market coverage or penetration further through the continued use of VRD with or without ancillary service provisions. Following the analysis developed earlier, the result of such further market expansion would be injurious to consumer welfare. Thus it becomes important to distinguish both the existence of appreciable market power and the types of services generally subject to free riding.

Market Power

In an earlier section it was noted that each brand of a differentiated product has some degree of market power because it possesses different product attributes. This merely reflects basic differences in preferences for attributes among consumers of the product and results in unequal market shares among brands. The question arises as to what degree of inequality of market shares among brands signals the presence of substantial market power.

The proposed rule clearly focuses the analysis required of the rule of reason approach to the issue of substantial market power. There are two types of benefits that result from this focusing. First, it provides a crude guideline to management as to whether its use of VRD is likely to be viewed as legally justifiable. Judge Hand in the *Alcoa* case, for example, made distinctions in market shares above which a monopoly position was a virtual certainty and below which was unlikely (*U.S.* v. *Aluminum Company of America* 1945). More recent cases have echoed such guidelines concerning indicia of monopoly power (*Berkey Photo, Inc.* v. *Eastman Kodak* 1978). Regardless of how imprecise the line determining significant market power, the proposed rules have the desirable characteristic of focusing on a central litigable factor. This focusing gives rise to the second type of benefit. A focused set of issues for litigation may substantially streamline the litigation process. As noted earlier in this discussion, the ad hoc manner in which cases dealing with VRD have been handled has led to lengthy trials characterized by, among other things, considerable argument over which issues were to be litigated and which case factors were relevant. Although the judicial determination of the degree of market power is probably the second most debated question in antitrust (the first being the determination of the "relevant market"), the debate is a familiar one. Over time, economists, marketers and the courts have developed a number of measures of market power. Generally, there are three indirect measures of market power: market share requirements (absolute market share and relative market share), profitability requirements (returns on investment, equity and assets relative to industry levels), and barriers to entry or effective competition (patents, economies of scale, absolute costs). In addition, there are two direct measures of substantial market power: the ability to control prices and the power to exclude competitors. None of these measures alone is sufficient to show the existence of appreciable market power, but each is indicative of the degree of market power possessed by the firm. Courts have generally found such measures sufficient to judge the presence or absence of appreciable market power, and the development of these measures in litigation is generally manageable.

Free Riding Services

As noted earlier, VRD used to promote services subject to free riding should be presumed legal regardless of the market power possessed by the manufacturer imposing them. The only reason for attempting to distinguish services prone to free riding from those not prone to free riding is to ensure that a manufacturer with appreciable market power could not require restricted distributors to provide nominal and unnecessary services in order to expand market coverage or penetration.

The line between services that are subject to free riding and thus appropriate to the use of VRD, and those that are not and hence not appropriate to the use of VRD, is frequently fine. However, some reasonably clear distinctions can be made. A first distinction is between services promoted by VRD and those that would be provided without them. These latter services benefit distributors directly and cannot be used by buyers who purchase the product elsewhere. Examples of such services are delivery, acceptance of noncash payment, trade-ins, distributor-specific return and exchange, and distributor set-up. A second type of service not requiring VRD is that which may be charged for separately from the basic product. Repair service is an example of this type of service.

The principal types of services prone to free riding appear to be the provision of information and distributor assistance in the customer buying process. Distributor advertising is less subject to free riding than personal selling due to the ability of the manufacturer to offset the distributor's cost of point-of-sale promotion or advertising. However, manufacturers cannot generally offset the sales lost when customers see advertising paid for by one distributor but purchase the product from another distributor. On the other hand, however, distributor assistance in the customer buying decision may not be provided without some form of VRD. Such assistance is clearly subject to free riding, since customers can make their product choice on the basis of product information and demonstration provided by one distributor and then purchase the product at a lower price from a dealer who provides no presale service. VRD used in conjunction with products where the customer's buying decision is perceived as a relatively important one, requiring information and distributor service, should therefore, be allowed.

POSSIBLE EXTERNALITIES OF THE PROPOSED RULE OF REASON FOR VRD

The analysis preceding the development of guidelines for the application of the rule of reason to VRD stressed the minimization of total social costs as a stimulus for that development. The guidelines presented

TABLE 2. Forward Vertical Integration, Market Share, and Return on Investment—Manufacturing Businesses[*]

Market Share of Reporting PIMS Business Unit[a]	Extent of Forward Vertical Integration by Company—Relative to Competitors[b]		
	Average Return on Investment[c]		
	Less	Same	More
Under 15%	17%	14%	11%
15–30%	24	21	15
Over 30%	32	30	28

[*]Source: Buzzell 1980. PIMS (Profit Impact of Market Strategies) database included 1,084 business units covering 2,467 overlapping 4-year periods, 1970–76.
[a]Market share is the share of the served market (defined as the total value of sales in the market actively served by the business unit) employed by the business unit.
[b]For each business unit, the extent of vertical integration within the unit or through separate business units belonging to the same parent company is compared with the extent of vertical integration by major, direct competitors.
[c]Pre-tax, pre-interest operating profit as a percentage of long-term investment (equity plus long-term debt).

here are somewhat stricter than a number of authorities have suggested, and because of this it is appropriate to inquire into the existence of any externalities that these guidelines might create.

One such possibility is vertical integration. Manufacturers finding several types of VRD foreclosed may also find incentives to integrate into wholesale or retail distribution. Although not all manufacturers who now employ vertical restrictions would find it advantageous to integrate forward, taking into account all of the costs and benefits of such a strategy, some undoubtedly would. For example, following the 1967 decision that its vertical restrictions were illegal, Schwinn did proceed to set up factory-owned distributorships (Buzzell 1980).

If, then, some manufacturers could and would adopt a strategy of vertical integration in lieu of VRD, it is interesting to ask which ones would be most likely to succeed. The available evidence suggests that vertical integration is more likely to be feasible for business units that enjoy large shares of their markets. Table 2 summarizes this evidence, based on data drawn from the PIMS (Profit Impact of Market Strategies) research program. These data show relationships between profitability and relative degrees of forward vertical integration for manufacturing businesses in three groups, classified by their market shares.

The data suggest that, on average, forward vertical integration tends to be unprofitable, i.e., it tends to be associated with a lower average rate of return regardless of market share. Insofar as the forward integration represented by the data concerns integration into wholesale or retail distribution, a reduction in average ROI is not surprising; wholesaling and retailing, as sectors of the economy, are generally less profitable than manufacturing.

The more important point suggested in Table 2, however, is that the penalty of forward vertical integration is less, proportionally speaking, for large share businesses than it is for those with smaller market shares. Presumably the reason for this is that there are some economies of scale in distribution. There are, for example, significant fixed costs associated with operating a regional wholesale sales branch. For a manufacturer with a small market share, these fixed costs may be prohibitively high relative to its sales in a given regional market area. Since vertical integration is more feasible for businesses with large market shares, a rule of reason that focuses in part on market power may result in higher levels of industry concentration.

Available data compiled by the FTC do not allow a complete examination that would answer the question of whether there is a relatively greater number of vertical mergers into distribution during periods of strict enforcement of VRD (1948–63, 1967–77). The data do show a decline in the proportion of vertical mergers involving large manufacturers since 1948, but that pattern could conceivably mask a trend toward any specific form of vertical merger (Federal Trade Commission 1977).

Although this type of externality may potentially reduce the benefits of the proposed rule of reason guidelines, it seems unlikely. For one thing, firms for which it is relatively profitable to integrate vertically will do so regardless of the legal status of VRD. In addition, it would seem that manufacturers in need of provision of distributor services subject to free riding would have the greatest incentive to integrate vertically without VRD. Since the analysis presented here specifically identifies those services as appropriate to a presumption of legality, vertical integration among such firms should not be affected by the proposed guidelines.

REFERENCES

Berkey Photo, Inc. v. Eastman Kodak Company (1978), 73 Civ. 424.
Bork, Robert (1966), "The Rule of Reason and Per Se Concept: Price Fixing and Market Division II," *Yale Law Journal*, 75 (January), 373.
Buzzell, Robert D. (1980), "Vertical Restrictions on Distributors: A Marketing Viewpoint," Conference Board conference on antitrust (Spring).
Comanor, William (1968), "Vertical Territorial and Customer Restrictions: White Motor and Its Aftermath," *Harvard Law Review*, 81 (May), 1419.
Continental T.V. Inc. v. GTE Sylvania, Inc. (1977), 433 U.S. 33.
Cresap, McCormick and Paget, Inc. (1972), "A Study of the Soft Drink Bottling and Canning Industry and the Impact of the FTC Complaint on the Industry's Future," in *Hearings on Exclusive Territorial Allocation Legislation*, U.S. Senate, 92nd

Congress, 2nd Session, 331, Committee on the Judiciary, Subcommittee on Antitrust and Monopoly.

Federal Trade Commission (1977), *Annual Report*, Bureau of Economics.

In the Matter of the Coca-Cola Company et al. (1978), Docket Number 8855.

Lancaster, Kalvin (1966), "A New Approach to Consumer Theory," *Journal of Political Economy*, 74 (April), 132.

Peterman, John L. (1975), "The Federal Trade Commission v. Brown Shoe Company," *Journal of Law and Economics*, 18 (April), 93–106.

Posner, Richard (1975), "Antitrust Policy and the Supreme Court: An Analysis of Restricted Distribution, Horizontal Merger and Potential Competition Decisions," *Columbia Law Review*, 75 (March), 283–85.

Preston, Lee E. (1965), "Restrictive Distribution Arrangements: Economic Analysis and Public Policy Standards," *Law and Contemporary Problems*, 30 (Summer), 506.

Ratchford, Brian T. (1975), "The New Economic Theory of Consumer Behavior: An Interpretive Essay," *Journal of Consumer Research*, 2 (September), 65.

Robinson, L. (1972), "Note. Territorial Restrictions and Per Se Rules—A Reevaluation of the Schwinn and Sealy Doctrines," *Michigan Law Review*, 70 (Winter), 616.

Sherman Antitrust Act (1890), Chap. 647 26 Stat. 209, as amended, 15 U.S. Code (1964).

United States v. *Aluminum Company of America* (1945), 148 F 2nd 416.

United States v. *Arnold, Schwinn and Co.* (1966), 388 U.S. 365.

United States v. *Sealy* (1967), 388 U.S. 350.

United States v. *Topco Associates* (1972), 405 U.S. 596.

White Motor Co. v. *United States* (1963), 372 U.S. 253.

19 Marketing and Product Liability: A Review and Update

Fred W. Morgan

Reprinted from the *Journal of Marketing*, published by the American Marketing Association, Vol. 46 (Summer 1982), pp. 69–78. Reprinted by permission.

INTRODUCTION

The controversy over the impact of product liability developments on business practices continues unabated (*Business Week* 1979, 1980, 1981; Johnson 1978). Marketers, like others within the corporation, have demonstrated an interest in product liability, although with apparent minimal information regarding the extent of the so-called liability problem. Furthermore, little has been written about the marketer's role in preventing the company from being a party to a product liability claim or lawsuit.

This article begins to correct these shortcomings by synthesizing existing data and legal cases relating marketing activities with product liability. First, an overview of the product liability situation in the United States is presented, with an emphasis whenever possible on a marketing perspective. Second, relevant legal cases are cited in order to outline the impact of specific marketing communications and distribution practices in establishing a consumer plaintiff's lawsuit. Finally, the implications of these trends for marketing practitioners are discussed. By taking several suggested steps, practitioners should be able to minimize their company's product liability vulnerability.

AN OVERVIEW OF THE PRODUCT LIABILITY "PROBLEM"

It is not hard to find conflicting evidence regarding the seriousness of the total product liability problem. For example, while product liability insurance premiums for manufacturers and retailers climbed from $1.3 billion in 1975 to $2.75 billion in 1978 (*Business Week* 1979), these premiums amount to less than 1% of sales dollars for the majority of firms (McKinsey & Company 1977). The average bodily injury settlement rose from $6,800 to $19,500 between 1972 and 1974 (McKinsey & Company 1977), although the average judgment for all product liability claims increased 100% from 1965–69 to 1970–75, not at all an alarming rate considering the length of time and the inflation in health care costs (The Research Group 1977).

Other inconsistent data can be offered, but one point has been clearly established: The product liability problem is a complex one and can be measured by several criteria including insurance premiums, settlements, claims administration costs, legal fees and number of claims filed. Depending on the criteria selected, the extent of the liability problem varies. Most experts seem to agree that the increase in insurance premiums experienced by many firms is an indication that insurance companies had not anticipated the increase in number of filed claims and settlement sizes in the late 1960s and early 1970s. Thus drastic premium increases were enforced in a short period of time, mainly 1974 to 1977, rather than experiencing a gradual increase beginning earlier.

From a marketing perspective, the product liability situation has been even less clearly described. Most product liability insurance is sold as a part of a firm's general liability coverage; therefore, many firms do not have detailed records (*Final Report* 1978), except perhaps for the last two or three years. There is also a time lag between the filing of a liability claim and the eventual settling of the case (Perham 1977) making existing data somewhat outdated. In addition, no data exist that correlate substantive product liability doctrines with the number and size of settlements (Johnson 1978).

Despite the paucity of information, implications for marketers can be extracted from three major studies of the product liability field (Alliance 1980, *Final Report* 1978, Insurance Services 1977), along with related follow-up reports (Gordon Associates 1977, McKinsey & Company 1977, *Selected Papers* 1978, The Research Group 1977, *Uniform Product Liability Law* 1979). Several conclusions of these studies are relevant for marketing practitioners.

Table 1 shows categories of injured persons for both bodily injury and property damage settlements, with the former accounting for more than 85% of total payments to injured parties (Insurance Services 1977). Generally, industrial workers (employees) suffered fewer losses than purchasers or users of consumer products; however, for large loss claims (awards larger than $100,000) two-thirds of the claims were filed by employees (Alliance 1980, "Can Monstrous Product..." 1980). Injuries to workers often involve machinery, which can cause very serious disabling injuries (Insurance Services 1977).

Users of products average three (for bodily injury) to four (for property damage) times larger settlements than purchasers of products. Nearly 50% of the people reimbursed for bodily injuries are nonwage earners (Insurance Services 1977). Organizations can suffer property damage losses but not bodily injury. While two-thirds of the parties receiving property damage settlements are individuals, nearly three-fourths of these payments go to organizations. Most expensive machinery that is damaged is likely to belong to corporations or other organizations (Insurance Services 1977).

More than 87% of total product liability payments are based on claims against manufacturers (Insurance Services 1977), compared with 85% for large loss claims (Alliance 1980). Thus the producer of an item is much more likely to be involved in a settlement than a distibutor (only 4.6% and 4.1% of total payments on behalf of wholesalers and retailers in the ISO and AAI studies).

Finally, food items generate the most bodily injury claims, while most property damage claims result from automobile related goods (auto service and repair, auto parts and tires) (Insurance Services 1977). Automobile parts, prescription drugs, and valves are responsible for most payments for bodily injury claims; however, valves, clothing and miscellaneous services account for the largest per-incident bodily injury settlements (Insurance Services 1977). Increasing product liability costs seem to be oppressive in only a few industries such as industrial machinery, industrial chemicals, automotive components and pharmaceuticals (Alliance 1980, McKinsey & Company 1977).

Several conclusions for marketers can be drawn from this data:

- Industrial goods manufacturers face considerably fewer, but potentially much more damaging, claims/lawsuits for both bodily injury and property damage than consumer goods manufacturers.
- Consumer goods manufacturers should warn users other than purchasers ("bystanders" in a legal context) as well as buyers of products.

TABLE 1. Status of Injured Persons/Parties

Liability Category	Injured Party	# of Persons with Payment	% of Persons with Payment	% of Total Payment	Average Payment
Bodily injury:	Employee	875	10.6%	42.0%	$97,884
	Purchaser	5,562	67.5	28.7	10,544
	User (not purchaser)	1,441	17.5	22.5	31,836
	Other	364	4.4	6.8	38,016
	Total	8,242	100.0%	100.0%	$24,752
Property damage:	Employee	12	0.2%	0.0%	$ 325
	Purchaser	3,928	78.7	64.3	5,466
	User (not purchaser)	359	7.2	22.8	21,185
	Other	695	3.9	12.9	6,176
	Total	4,994	100.0%	100.0%	$ 6,682

Source: Insurance Services 1977, p. 60, 63.

- Organizations, primarily corporations, receive much larger but many fewer property damage payments than individuals.
- Manufacturers are much more vulnerable to product liability claims than are resellers (wholesalers and retailers).
- Markets for automobile parts, chemicals, pharmaceuticals, clothing and industrial machinery are the most dangerous from the standpoint of exposure to very large product liability claims.

These conclusions present a general picture of the prevailing product liability situation; however, a more detailed review is required if marketing managers are to understand how specific marketing practices can lead to liability. The next section looks at lawsuits involving marketing activities (or omissions) from the perspective of different product liability theories.

CASE LAW TRENDS

Based on case law decisions, the marketing activities that could result in a company being party to a lawsuit include: (1) statements and actions of salespersons and other sales personnel, (2) print or broadcast advertisements, (3) labeling and written instructions, (4) retailers' actions and (5) wholesalers' actions. Thus the manufacturer's communications mix and distribution system are the critical elements to monitor if marketing-based liability for personal injury or property damage is to be avoided.

The marketing activities that could lead to liability are discussed in the context of the four major theories of product liability: negligence, breach of warranty, strict liability and misrepresentation. Each liability theory is described briefly; a full treatment of technical differences among the theories is beyond the scope of this article.

Negligence

Negligence is generally defined as a violation of the duty to use ordinary care under given circumstances (*American Jurisprudence 2d* 1971). If a person of ordinary prudence would not have performed the act, it is a negligent act. Negligence is, therefore, a breach of duty of reasonable care under the circumstances on the part of the seller (marketer).

The duty to exercise reasonable care extends to all parts of the production and distribution process (Kimble and Lesher 1979). Salespersons can be negligent in the way in which they present a product to a client (*Incollingo* v. *Ewing* 1971, *Love* v. *Wolf* 1967). In *Stevens* v. *Parke, Davis* (1973) salespersons overpromoted a drug product to the extent of causing physicians to pay little attention to warning circulars. When one user of the drug died as a result of a complication described in the warning circular, the manufacturer who did not provide adequate warning was found to be negligent because of its selling tactics.

Advertisements have been found to be actionably negligent acts in several cases (Morgan 1979). Plaintiffs must be able to convince the court that they relied upon the advertisement and that negligence in advertising caused the injury or harm (Hursh and Bailey 1974). Advertisements extolling product safety have led to liability for negligent design (*Texas Bitulithic* v. *Caterpillar* 1962). Specific advertised claims may create certain responsibilities for extra care in manufacturing (*W.H. Elliott* v. *King* 1961). The advertised slogan, "ready-to-serve boned chicken," required the defendant to exercise such care as to permit users to trust with reasonable certainty that bones had been removed from the product (*Bryer* v. *Rath* 1959).

Negligence claims regarding deficient labels have been upheld on behalf of an 18-month-old child (*Jonescue* v. *Jewel* 1974) and two semiliterate laborers (*Dougherty* v. *Hooker* 1976). In *Harrison* v. *Flota* (1978) a worker was severely injured when he inhaled fumes while cleaning up a chemical spill. The court found that the defendant had negligently failed to provide a reasonable and adequate warning label covering the chemical's dangerous properties. The word *prolonged*, as used on the label, was deemed vague; moreover, the label contained no information about how to clean up a spill. The fact that none of the plaintiffs in these cases had read the warning labels did not bar their recovery.

If a manufacturer, as a part of its marketing program, relies on certain retailers to inspect the product or to perform other activities, the manufacturer could be held negligently liable if the retailers are lax. Ford Motor Company was found negligent when one of its dealers failed to replace brake fluid at the appropriate inspection interval, resulting in a serious automobile accident (*Hasson* v. *Ford* 1977). By following prudent inspection procedures, the retailer could have prevented Ford from being held liable because the accident would not have occurred.

Retailers are ordinarily not chargeable for negligence relating to the manufacture of a product (*Product Liability Reporter* 1974). If the retailer is responsible for assembling the product or preparing it for sale to the consumer, the retailer can be found negligent for improper workmanship (*Parisi* v. *Bush* 1949). Retailers have been found negligent for breach of duty to inspect and test the manufacturers' products, even though the manufacturer is reputable and the product defect is not obvious. If retailers should have discovered the defect by exercising reasonable care, given their special product knowledge, they can be found negligent (*Finger* v. *Dobbs* 1978, *Hunt* v. *Ford* 1977).

Retailers have a duty to warn, verbally or through labels or instructions, whenever they have knowledge about a product's dangerous condition and when it appears that the consumer will not discover the danger (*Stapinski* v. *Walsh* 1978, *Westerman* v. *Sears* 1978). The jury questions of whether a warning should have been given and, if given, whether it was sufficient, are difficult ones.

Any institution in the distribution channel can be negligent simply by selling certain products. Examples include selling firearms to minors, drugs to obviously intoxicated persons and gasoline in unlabeled containers (*Product Liability Reporter* 1974).

By labeling a product as their own, retailers shift the burden of liability to themselves from the manufacturers (*Bigham* v. *J.C. Penney* 1978, *Moody* v. *Sears* 1971, *Spiller* v. *Ward* 1974). This status as "imputed manufacturer" (*Restatement* 1965) holds, even if the retailer could not possibly have discovered the defect after taking delivery of the item (Kimble and Lesher 1979).

Wholesalers technically owe duties to inspect, test and warn product users; however, since they neither manufacture the product nor sell it to final consumers, wholesalers are often merely "innocent" redistributors of packaged goods. The wholesaler generally has no obligation to inspect products in sealed packages (*Gobin* v. *Avenue* 1960), especially if the manufacturer is reputable (Kimble and Lesher 1979). As a result, very few cases based on negligence have been brought against wholesalers (Frumer and Friedman 1980).

The wholesaler must warn, however, when its channel position makes it more knowledgeable about the product than the retailer (*Blasing* v. *Hardenburgh* 1975, *Mehochko* v. *Gold Seal* 1966, *Starr* v. *Koppers* 1966). A dynamite wholesaler, dealing with hardware and implement retailers, was judged negligent for failing to instruct the retailers about proper fuse lengths (*Cooley* v. *Quick* 1974). When one customer of a retailer was severely injured, the wholesaler was found negligent for not checking to see whether the retailers were giving instruction pamphlets and verbal directions to dynamite buyers.

Warranty

In contrast to negligence, a tort action, warranty is a contractual theory of recovery governed by principles of sales (Kimble and Lesher 1979). A warranty is a representation by the manufacturer/seller about the product's qualities or characteristics.

Express warranties are described in detail in the *Uniform Commercial Code* (1972). A central issue in determining the existence of an express warranty is the extent of allowable seller puffing. General statements or affirmations that are nothing more than the seller's opinions about the product do not create an express warranty. Of course, distinguishing between express warranties and puffing is often left to the jury.

An implied warranty may exist as a matter of law even when no express warranty is stated. An implied warranty of merchantability is part of a sales contract, unless explicitly modified or negated, whenever the seller regularly offers the product in question for sale (*Uniform Commercial Code* 1972). Thus the occasional seller, such as a student selling a used book, is excluded from consideration here. This implied warranty means that the item is of average quality and can be used for the purposes for which such a product typically is used. The implied warranty of merchantability is established by the mere fact that a transaction takes place.

By contrast, an implied warranty of fitness arises when the buyer relies on the seller for advice regarding the suitability of the product for the buyer's intended purposes. To recover for breach of an implied warranty of fitness, the buyer must be able to demonstrate this reliance and that the seller knew or had reason to know of the buyer's specific needs. Even the occasional seller can establish an implied warranty of fitness.

Salespersons can readily establish express warranties during conversations with prospects (*A. L. Bell* v. *Harrington* 1975, *Griffin* v. *Wheeler-Leonard* 1976) as well as implied warranties of fitness, if the salesperson makes specific performance promises with regard to the prospect's intended use of the product (*Chemco* v. *DuPont* 1973). In three cases in which cattle were the victims, salespersons' statements about specific levels of milk production and weight gain were considered to be express warranties. When these promises were not met, the livestock owners recovered (*Boehm* v. *Fox* 1973, *D. L. Heil* v. *Standard* 1974, *Shotkoski* v. *Standard* 1975).

Whenever salespersons are clearly overstating the product's capabilities, the statements are likely to be considered puffing. If the salesperson obviously has superior product knowledge compared with the buyer, the salesperson's statements even if somewhat exaggerated are more likely to be interpreted by the courts as warranties (Morgan and Bodecker 1980). Further, total misrepresentation by the salesperson, though done unintentionally, might be taken as a warranty if the buyer is deceived (*American Jurisprudence 2d* 1973).

Advertising may easily be the basis for an express warranty. Consider the following statement from a widely distributed product liability reference (Frumer and Friedman 1980, paragraph 16.04):

> Manufacturers constantly extol and represent the quality of their products on labels, on billboards, on radio and T.V., newspapers and magazines, in brochures made available for dealers who are expected to disseminate them to prospective purchasers, . . . an increasing number of cases are holding or recognizing that under such circumstances a consumer can recover for breach of an express warranty. . . .

In *Scheuler* v. *Aamco* (1977) the substantial advertising support provided by Aamco to one of its franchised dealers was noted by the court as linking Aamco with a guarantee the dealer gave to its customers. The advertisements also mentioned Aamco's "coast-to-coast ironclad guarantee." Thus the advertisements did not warrant against product failure, but they did establish the tie between Aamco and the written guarantee.

Catalog statements have been interpreted as advertised express warranties when products have failed to perform as stated (*Community* v. *Dresser* 1977). Occasionally an implied warranty can arise out of advertised statements. Advertising and labels can create certain reasonable expectations in consumer's minds which, if not fulfilled, could lead to breach of implied warranty. When the plaintiff relied on televised advertising about the conditioning and revitalizing effects of a hair treatment, she recovered when her hair became brittle and had to be cut off (*West* v. *Alberto Culver* 1973).

In a labeling case, an implied warranty of fitness was also breached (*Wilson* v. *E-Z Flo* 1972a). The label on a chemical product specified that the product would perform in a certain manner if used according to instructions stated in an accompanying manual. Though noticing that the manual was missing, the retailer sold some of the chemical to the plaintiff, who recovered from the retailer (*Wilson* v. *E-Z Flo* 1972b).

A diagram was determined to be an express warranty to a child that a product could be used safely (*Tirino* v. *Kenner* 1973). The diagram apparently led a seven-year-old boy to apply the product to his face, supposedly causing his face to glow in the dark. The child recovered when the product dripped into his eyes, resulting in considerable irritation.

Usually the express warranty of a manufacturer does not bind the retailer (*Henry* v. *Don Wood* 1974) or wholesaler (*L. A. Green* v. *Williams* 1969) who sells the product when there is no evidence that either reseller has adopted the warranty. But the retailer's conduct may indicate to the court that it has adopted the manufacturer's warranty (*Wilson* v. *E-Z Flo* 1972b). If the manufacturer is at fault, the *Uniform Commercial Code* (1972) allows the retailer to "vouch in" the manufacturer, thereby assigning the defense to the latter; likewise, the wholesaler may vouch in the manufacturer.

The same implied warranties of the manufacturer are basically applicable to all nonmanufacturing sellers (Hursh and Bailey 1974), that is, to both retailers and wholesalers. Retailers of food products (*Huebner* v. *Hunter* 1978), beverages (*Demars* v. *Natchitoches* 1977), drugs (*Bichler* v. *Willing* 1977), and cosmetics (*Carpenter* v. *Alberto Culver* 1971) have to exercise greater care regarding implied warranties of fitness or wholesomeness.

Strict Liability

Strict tort liability is a relatively new doctrine and has been associated with the influx of product liability litigation in the U.S. in the past 20 years (*Product Liability Reporter* 1974). Strict liability developed as a response to a complex, consumer oriented economy in which buyers and users acquire products from manufacturers through a series of intermediate sellers.

Strict liability has eliminated some of the burdensome elements of both negligence and warranty actions. On the other hand, strict liability is not absolute liability. The plaintiff must prove that the product was defective when it left the defendant's control and that the product in question caused the plaintiff's injury. Thus strict liability represents a melding of warranty and negligence principles and introduces no concepts that were not already known and applied earlier (Kimble and Lesher 1979).

In a strict liability action, the quality of the product is questioned, not the possible breach of duty of reasonable care by the defendant (Weinstein et al. 1978). The basic statement of strict liability is set forth in *Restatement* (1965, section 402A):

(1) One who sells any product in a defective condition unreasonably dangerous to the user or consumer or to his property is subject to liability for physical harm thereby caused to the ultimate user or consumer, or to his property, if
   (a) The seller is engaged in the business of selling such a product, and
   (b) it is expected to and does reach the user or consumer without substantial change in the condition in which it is sold.
(2) The rule stated in Subsection (1) applies although
   (a) the seller has exercised all possible care in the preparation and sale of his product and
   (b) the user and consumer has not bought the product from or entered into any contractual relation with the seller.

Since the quality of the product is the key issue in strict liability pleadings, actions of salespersons are generally irrelevant. In transcripts of strict liability lawsuits, salespersons are occasionally mentioned but only because they may have sold the faulty products to the plaintiffs. Likewise, advertising has been only briefly mentioned in strict liability cases. In one case in which the seller of a defective tire was held strictly liable, the trial court referred to "sustained and vigorous advertising campaigns" (*McCann* v. *Atlas* 1971, p. 704). The judge implied that advertisements increased consumers' expectations regarding product performance. Thus societal legal standards could be altered by advertising programs.

Both statements by salespersons and advertised claims are discussed in greater detail with regard to tort liability in the next section. Section 402B (*Restatement* 1965) contains the rule of strict liability for misrepresentation which, for marketers, is especially relevant for selling and advertising activities.

Labels and printed warnings have been determined to be insufficient, thereby creating defective products in several cases (*Baker* v. *St. Agnes* 1979), *Bituminous* v. *Black* 1974, *Nissen* v. *Terre Haute* 1975, *Ortho* v. *Chapman* 1979). A lathe operator recovered from the manufacturer of safety glasses when they shattered during use, resulting in an eye injury (*American* v. *Weidenhamer* 1980). Prominently displayed on the box in which the glasses were delivered were the phrases *safety glasses, Sure Guard* and *surest protection*. A small warning was wrapped around the nosepiece of the glasses stating that they were not unbreakable and that they should be checked for pitting and scratching. Another person had removed this warning tag before giving the glasses to the plaintiff. The court decided that the warning was "dramatically smaller" in terms of print size than the above printed phrases, and the warning was ruled insufficient. Because of this ruling, the fact that the warning had been removed from the plaintiff's glasses by someone else was inconsequential.

Under strict liability the content and meaning of the label and accompanying warnings are examined in a different fashion in comparison with negligence and warranty actions. In a strict liability case the issues are likely to be presence or absence of appropriate labels, the size of print or the location of certain statements with regard to sales slogans.

Retailers can be brought within the scope of liability under section 402A (*Restatement* 1965), even if they do not deal exclusively or even primarily with the offending products (*Product Liability Reporter* 1974, paragraph 4160; *Sochanski* v. *Sears* 1979). Several reasons are commonly cited for holding retailers strictly liable: they are engaged in distributing their goods to the public and should therefore be held accountable for faulty goods; often they are the only visible parties to whom injured consumers can turn for redress; and they often play a major role in ensuring that the product is safe or they may pressure manufacturers for this purpose (*Corpus Juris Secundum* 1975). In *Chappius* v. *Sears* (1977) Sears was found stictly liable for not warning about the possible dangers of using a chipped hammer. The manufacturer from whom Sears purchased and labeled the hammer had also failed to include such a warning and was held liable. The court noted that Sears should have known about this danger because of its size, merchandising skills and power to control the quality of its products.

Courts have been reluctant to hold wholesalers strictly liable in all cases in which they have handled defective products, but under 402A (*Restatement* 1965) and its application, liability could attach even though wholesalers have never transacted with ultimate users of products (*Product Liability Reporter* 1974). A distributor of an aluminum coating machine was strictly liable when a workman using the machine was injured (*Rabadi* v. *Price* 1980). The court even mentioned that the distributor was not the principal defendant and that it was quite unlikely that the jury could conclude that the distributor manufactured the machine.

Conversely, a brokerage firm that arranged the sale of a drug proven to be the cause of death of a child was found not liable (*Lyons* v. *Premo* 1979). The brokerage firm was ruled to have had a passive role in the sale of the product, unlike the drug manufacturers who controlled the product and its quality.

Misrepresentation

The common thread uniting theories of negligence, warranty and strict liability is the defective product. Without a product defect, recovery is not allowed under any of these theories (*Corpus Juris Secondum* 1975). There is, however, the special case of misrepresentation, where the item is manufactured exactly according to non-negligent standards. Misrepresentation is covered in section 402B of the *Restatement* (1965), which permits a tort recovery:

> One engaged in the business of selling chattels who, by advertising, labels, or otherwise, makes to the public a misrepresentation of material fact concerning the character or quality of a chattel sold by him is subject to liability for physical harm to a consumer of the chattel caused by justifiable reliance upon the misrepresentation, even though
> (a) it is not made fraudulently or negligently, and
> (b) the consumer has not bought the chattel from or entered into any contractual relation with the seller.

Thus liability could attach if someone is injured who relied on false representations, even if they are made honestly based on laboratory or consumer research. The product itself is not defective but unrealistic performance claims were made about it. Misrepresentation under this section can occur without privity of contract or any statutory violation regardless of any dishonesty, bad faith, negligence or other fault (Kimble and Lesher 1979). Section 402B is another example of society's reacting to the influence of marketing practices, especially mass advertising, on consumer purchasing. Despite the ominous implications, the section has rarely been invoked (*Product Liability Reporter* 1974).

The leading case involving statements by salespersons resulting in misrepresentational liability is *Crocker* v. *Winthrop* (1974). Drug salespersons overpromoted a product to physicians and, according to the court, caused physicians to pay little attention to printed warnings about the drug. When one patient died as a result of drug addiction, a side effect that the salespersons specifically mentioned could not occur, the drug manufacturer was liable under section 402B. The salespersons' claims, apparently made in good faith and based on laboratory research, were critical in establishing the liability claim.

Advertising has also been cited as a marketing practice that led to a misrepresentation finding. In *Klages* v. *General* (1976) advertising brochures and other promotional materials contained claims that a Mace spray would totally and instantly subdue an assailant. A motel clerk was seriously injured by a burglar who was not immediately overcome by the spray. The manufacturer of the spray was found liable over its claims that the brochures amounted only to seller's puffing, a common defense in such a case (*Hoffman* v. *Chance* 1972).

In *Winkler* v. *American* (1979) a helmet was depicted on a carton as being used by a motorcyclist. Seeing this carton, an experienced police officer purchased the helmet for use while riding his motorcycle on duty. The helmet was not intended to be used as a motorcycle safety helmet, despite the carton diagrams. The helmet was also available to the general public at sporting goods stores. The court determined that the carton diagram had indeed been viewed by the public and could easily have been interpreted to mean that motorcyclists could safely use the helmet. Misrepresentation under section 402B therefore followed directly.

In *Hauter* v. *Zogarts* (1975) a teenage boy was injured while using a golf-training device. The label on the shipping carton and the cover of the instruction booklet both contained the statement, *Completely safe. Ball will not hit player.* The court viewed this statement as a false yet innocent misrepresentation, not seller's puffery. So either symbols or words can misrepresent the capabilities of a product, leading to manufacturer liability.

Though retailers have been parties to misrepresentation pleadings (*Klages* v. *General* 1976), they have generally been able to secure indemnification from manufacturers. Wholesalers have typically not been involved in misrepresentation lawsuits. It is quite conceivable, however, that both retailers and wholesalers could be held liable for the misrepresentations of their salespersons or of advertised statements.

Being the most recently developed and least used theory of liability in cases involving marketing activities, misrepresentation is still evolving in the courts. At this time, two issues that affect marketing have yet to be resolved. First, misrepresentation has been applied only when statements or disclosures have been alleged to be incorrect or misleading. Whether non-disclosure of relevant information constitutes misrepresentation remains undetermined (Kimble and Lesher 1979). Second, misrepresentation has been charged only in regard to communications to large numbers of product purchasers, not in the case of one or two individuals or nonconsuming buyers (*Product Liability Reporter* 1974). Liability due to marketing communications could readily be expanded if nondisclosures of important data to nonconsumers or to a single user are judged to be misrepresentations.

Conclusions Drawn from Case Law Trends

The cases discussed above illustrate current legal thought regarding the kinds of marketing practices that result in liability for personal injury or property damage because of faulty or improperly handled products. It should be clear from the descriptions of these cases that, for a given set of marketing activities, a company could be sued under several theories of product liability. Since the plaintiff will attempt to establish liability under each theory, the firm must be prepared to counter each of the accusations. For example, by refuting a charge of negligent labeling and packaging, the firm has not, as a matter of law, precluded a jury finding of strict liability for inadequate labeling. Every charge must be overcome, if the defendant company is to prevail.

The key cases with which marketing managers should become familiar are cross-referenced in Table 2 according to marketing activity involved and relevant legal theory. By studying these cases, the manager will be in a much stronger position to develop communications and distribution programs that do not implicate the company in product liability actions.

Since every case presents the court with a unique fact situation to consider, generalizations that hold across a strong majority of product liability cases and also lead to specific managerial implications are difficult to state. Nevertheless, given the discussion of the cases above, several broad conclusions can be suggested:

- Companies can be held liable for damages under negligence and warranty pleadings due to marketing communications—statements by salespersons, advertised messages, and packaging and labeling.
- Marketing communications can result in liability due to innocent misrepresentation of facts.
- Since strict liability is based on a product defect, advertising and personal selling activities are generally irrelevant in a strict liability pleading.
- Courts have interpreted defective labels, warnings and packaging as defective products, thereby establishing strict liability actions.
- Distributors—retailers and wholesalers—are generally not liable for the misrepresentations of manufacturers. Distributors' communications to customers can, however, misrepresent the product.
- Distributors are less likely to be found liable for product-related damages than manufacturers because the former are often able to assign the defense to the latter.
- Distributors who brand products as their own are treated as

manufacturers, thereby exposing themselves to manufacturers' liability under all theories of liability.
- One channel member's warranty generally does not bind another channel member unless the latter, either explicitly or through its actions, has adopted the warranty.
- The negligent acts of one channel member can result in other channel members being held liable if they should have ancipated the negligent act.

IMPLICATIONS

Marketing managers should keep abreast of product liability trends. To do this, the marketer must keep in close communication with the

TABLE 2. Product Liability for Marketing Activities Under Different Theories of Liability: Selected Cases

Marketing Activities	Legal Theory			
	Negligence	*Warranty*	*Strict Liability*	*Misrepresentation*
Selling	Stevens v. Parke, Davis (1973)	Shotkoski v. Standard (1975)	—	Crocker v. Winthrop (1974)
	Incollingo v. Ewing (1971)	Griffin v. Wheeler-Leonard (1976)		
Advertising	Texas Bitulithic v. Caterpillar (1962)	Scheuler v. Aamco (1977)	McCann v. Atlas (1971)	Klages v. General (1976)
	W. H. Elliott v. King (1961)	West v. Alberto Culver (1973)		Hoffman v. Chance (1972)
Labeling and Packaging	Harrison v. Flota (1978)	Tirino v. Kenner (1973)	American v. Weidenhamer (1980)	Winkler v. American (1979)
	Jonescue v. Jewel (1974)	Wilson v. E-Z Flo (1972b)	Baker v. St. Agnes (1979)	Hauter v. Zogarts (1975)
Retailing	Hasson v. Ford (1977)	Henry v. Don Wood (1974)	Chappius v. Sears (1977)	—
	Moody v. Sears (1971)	Huebner v. Hunter (1978)	Sochanski v. Sears (1979)	
	Stapinski v. Walsh (1978)			
Wholesaling	Cooley v. Quick (1974)	L. A. Green v. Williams (1969)	Lyons v. Premo (1979)	—
	Blasing v. Hardenburgh (1975)		Rabadi v. Price (1980)	

company's legal counsel and liability insurers. Both court decisions and insurance settlements are vital sources of information. Court decisions reflect current thought regarding the acceptability of business practices and often provide a measure of the cost to corporations of product liability claims. The vast majority of claims, 96% for bodily injury and 97% for property damage (*Insurance Services* 1977) are settled without a court verdict. Marketing managers must also assist their departments in developing a product safety attitude. Since manufacturing and engineering departments tend to be the focus of most product liability claims (*Insurance Services* 1977), marketers may develop a complacent attitude with regard to minimizing liability. This would be unfortunate because many departments within the firm must act responsibly to prevent product liability claims (Chandran and Linneman 1978, Perham 1977).

Liability prevention programs should be written for the entire corporation (Keeton, Owen and Montgomery 1980, Ross and Foley 1979), and the program for the marketing department should be consistent with organizational goals regarding liability prevention. These prevention programs should try to anticipate future problems (Gray et al. 1975). By providing each employee in the marketing department with practical guidelines, product safety will become a legitimate concern within the department.

Finally, consumer education programs should be instituted to narrow the gap between what consumers know and what they should know about product safety (Gray et al. 1975). Marketing activities are especially useful here. Televised advertisements can illustrate visually the safe and correct use of products. Salespersons can perform a reminder function by encouraging buyers to read instructional and safety pamphlets. Retailers can double-check the manufacturers' assembling and packaging procedures. Informed consumers may ultimately be the company's best insurance against product liability due to improper marketing practices.

REFERENCES

A. L. Bell v. *Harrington Manufacturing Company* (1975), 219 S.E.2d 906 (S.Ct. S.C.)
Alliance of American Insurers (1980), *A Survey of Large-Loss Product Liability Claims*, Chicago: Alliance of American Insurers.
American Jurisprudence 2d, Negligence (1971), 57.
American Jurisprudence 2d, Sales (1973), 67.
American Optical Company v. *Weidenhamer* (1980), CCH Prod.Liab.Rep. para. 8670 (C.A.4 Ind.).
Baker v. *St. Agnes Hospital* (1979), CCH Prod.Liab.Rep. para. 8563 (N.Y. Sup.Ct. App.Div.).
Bichler v. *Willing* (1977), 58 App.Div.2d 331, 397 N.Y.2d 57.

Bigham v. *J. C. Penney Co.* (1978), 268 N.W.2d 892, CCH Prod.Liab.Rep. para. 8196 (Minn.).

Bituminous Casualty Corp. v. *Black and Decker Manufacturing Co.* (1974), CCH Prod.Liab.Rep. para. 7445, 518 S.W.2d 868 (Tex.Cir.App.).

Blasing v. *P. R. L. Hardenburgh Co.* (1975), 226 N.W.2d 110, CCH Prod.Liab.Rep. para. 7394 (S.Ct. Minn.).

Boehm v. *Fox* (1973), CCH Prod.Liab.Rep. para. 6894 (C.A. 10 Kan.).

Bryer v. *Rath Packing Co.* (1957), 221 Md. 105, 156 A.2d 442, 77 A.L.R.2d 1.

Business Week (1979), "The Devils in the Product Liability Laws," (February 12), 72–78.

—— (1980), "A Product Liability Bill Has Insurers Uptight," (March 31), 43.

—— (1981), "More Punitive Damage Awards," (January 12), 86.

"Can Monstrous Product Liability Claims Be Contained?" (1980), *Journal of American Insurance*, 56 (Fall), 20–22.

Carpenter v. *Alberto Culver Co.*, 28 Mich.App. 399, 184 N.W.2d 547 (1971).

Chandran, Rajan and Robert Linneman (1978), "Planning to Minimize Product Liability," *Sloan Management Review*, 30 (Fall), 33–45.

Chappius v. *Sears, Roebuck & Co.* (1977), 349 So.2d 963 (La.App. 1st Cir.).

Chemco Industrial Applicators Co. v. *E. I. DuPont de Nemours & Co.* (1973), 366 F.Supp. 278, CCH Prod.Liab.Rep. para. 7122 (U.S.D.C. E.D.Mo.).

Community Television Services, Inc. v. *Dresser Industries, Inc.* (1977), 435 F.Supp. 214 (D.C. S.D.), aff'd 586 F.2d 637 (C.A.8 1978).

Cooley v. *Quick Supply Company* (1974), 221 N.W.2d 763 (S.Ct. Ia.).

Corpus Juris Secondum, Supplement, Products Liability (1975), 72.

Crocker v. *Winthrop Laboratories, Division of Sterling Drug, Inc.* (1974), 514 S.W.2d 429 (Tex.).

D. L. Heil v. *Standard Chemical Manufacturing Company* (1974), 223 N.W.2d 37 (S.Ct. Minn.).

Demars v. *Natchitoches Coca-Cola Bottling Co.* (1977), 353 So.2d 433, cert. den. 354 So.2d 1384 (La. 1977).

Dougherty v. *Hooker Chemical Corp.* (1976), 540 F.2d 174 (3rd Cir.).

Final Report (1978), *Interagency Task Force on Product Liability*, U.S. Department of Commerce, Washington, DC: U.S. Government Printing Office.

Finger v. *Dobbs* (1978), CCH Prod. Liab. Rep. para. 8138 (C.A. Tenn.).

Frumer, Louis R. and Melvin I. Friedman (1980), *Products Liability*, New York: Mathew Bender.

Gobin v. *Avenue Food Mart* (1960), 178 Cal.App.2d 345, 2 Cal. Rptr. 822.

Gordon Associates, Inc. (1977), *Interagency Task Force on Product Liability; Final Report of the Industry Study*, Springfield, VA: National Technical Information Service.

Gray, Irwin, Albert L. Bases, Charles H. Martin and Alexander Sternberg (1975), *Product Liability: A Management Response*, New York: AMACOM.

Griffin v. *Wheeler-Leonard Co., Inc.* (1976), 290 N.C. 185, 225 S.E.2d 557.

Harrison v. *Flota Mercante Grancolombi, ANA, S.A.* (1978), CCH Prod. Liab. Rep. para. 8350 (C.A.5).

Hasson v. *Ford Motor Company* (1977), 564 P.2d 857, 138 Cal. Rptr. 705.

Hauter v. *Zogarts* (1975), 14 Cal.3d 104, 120 Cal. Rptr. 681, 534 P.2d 377.

Henry v. *Don Wood Volkswagen, Inc.* (1974), 562 S.W.2d 483, CCH Prod. Liab. Rep. para., 7364 (C.A. Tenn.).

Hoffman v. *A. B. Chance Co.* (1972), 339 F.Supp. 1385 (D.C. Pa.).
Huebner v. *Hunter Packing Co.* (1978), 59 Ill.App.3rd 563, 16 Ill.Dec. 766, 375 N.E.2d 873.
Hunt v. *Ford Motor, Co.* (1977), CCH Prod. Liab. Rep. para. 7929 (C.A. La.).
Hursh, Robert D. and Henry J. Bailey (1974), *American Law of Product Liability,* 2d edition, Rochester NY: The Lawyers Co-operative Publishing Co.
Incollingo v. *Ewing* (1971), 444 Pa. 263, 282 A.2d 206.
Insurance Services Office (1977), *Product Liability Closed Claim Survey: A Technical Analysis of Survey Results,* New York: Insurance Services Office.
Johnson, Anita (1978), "Behind the Hype on Product Liability," *The Forum*, 14 (Fall), 317–326.
Jonescue v. *Jewel Home Shopping Service* (1974), 306 N.E.2d 312.
Keeton, W. Page, David G. Owen and John E. Montgomery (1980), *Products Liability and Safety: Cases and Materials,* Mineola, NY: Foundation Press.
Kimble, William and Robert O. Lesher (1979), *Products Liability*, St. Paul, MN: West Publishing Company.
Klages v. *General Ordnance Equipment Corp.* (1976), 367 A.2d 304 (Pa.Sup.Ct.).
L. A. Green Seed Co. v. *Williams* (1969), 246 Ark. 463, 438 S.W.2d 717.
Love v. *Wolf* (1967), 249 Cal.App.2d 822, 58 Cal. Rptr. 42.
Lyons v. *Premo Pharmaceutical Labs, Inc.* (1979), CCH Prod.Liab.Rep. para. 8547 (Super.Ct. N.J.).
McCann v. *Atlas Supply Company* (1971), 325 F.Supp. 701 (D.C. Pa.).
McKinsey & Company, Inc. (1977), *Interagency Task Force on Product Liability; Final Report of the Insurance Study,* Springfield, VA: National Technical Information Service.
Mehochko v. *Gold Seal Company* (1966), 213 N.E.2d 581 (C.A.5 Ill.).
Moody v. *Sears, Roebuck & Co.* (1971), 324 F.Supp. 844 (D.C. Ga.).
Morgan, Fred W. (1979), "The Products Liability Consequences of Advertising," *Journal of Advertising*, 8 (Fall), 30–37.
———and Karl A. Boedecker (1980), "The Role of Personal Selling in Products Liability Litigation," *Journal of Personal Selling & Sales Management*, 1 (Fall-Winter), 34–40.
Nissen Trampoline Co. v. *Terre Haute First National Bank* (1975), CCH Prod. Liab. Rep. para. 7800, 332 N.E.2d 820 (Ind.App.), rev'd on other grounds, 358 N.E.2d 974 (1976).
Ortho Pharmaceutical Corp. v. *Chapman* (1979), CCH Prod. Liab. Rep. para. 8450, 388 N.E.2d 541 (Ind.App.).
Parisi v. *Carl W. Bush Co.* (1949), 67 A.2d 875, 4 N.J.Super. 472.
Perham, John C. (1977), "The Dilemma in Product Liability," *Dun's Review*, 109 (January), 48–50, 76.
Product Liability Reporter (1974), New York: Commerce Clearing House.
Rabadi v. *Price Sales & Engineering, Inc.* (1980), CCH Prod.Liab.Rep. para. 8620 (D.C. N.Y.).
Restatement (Second) of Torts (1965), American Law Institute.
Ross, Kenneth and Martin J. Foley (1979), *Product Liability of Manufacturers: Prevention and Defense*, NY: Practicing Law Institute.
Scheuler v. *Aamco Transmissions, Inc.* (1977), 1 Kan.App.2d 525, 571 P.2d 48.
Selected Papers (1978), *Interagency Task Force on Product Liability,* U.S. Department of Commerce, Washington, DC: U.S. Government Printing Office.

Shotkoski v. *Standard Chemical Manufacturing Company* (1975), 237 N.W.2d 92 (Neb.).
Sochanski v. *Sears, Roebuck & Co.* (1979), 477 F.Supp. 320 (E.D. Pa.), CCH Prod. Liab. Rep. para. 8674 (C.A.3 1980).
Spiller v. *Montgomery Ward & Co.* (1974), 294 So.2d 803 (La.).
Stapinski v. *Walsh Construction Co., Inc.* (1978), CCH Prod. Liab. Rep. para. 8341 (C.A. Ind.).
Starr v. *Koppers Company* (1966), 398 S.W.2d 827, CCH Prod. Liab. Rep. para. 5506 (C.A. Tex.).
Stevens v. *Parke, Davis & Co.* (1973), 9 Cal.3d 51, 107 Cal.Rptr. 45, 507 P.2d 653, 94 A.L.R.3d 1059.
Texas Bitulithic Co. v. *Caterpillar Tractor Co.* (1962), 357 S.W.2d 406 (Tex. Civ. App.).
The Research Group, Inc. (1977), *Interagency Task Force on Product Liability; Final Report of the Legal Study.* Springfield, VA: National Technical Information Service.
Tirino v. *Kenner Products Company* (1973), 72 Misc.2d 1094, 341 N.Y.S.2d 61, CCH Prod. Liab. Rep. para. 6950.
Uniform Commercial Code (1972), American Law Institute. "Uniform Product Liability Law" (1979), Interagency Task Force on Product Liability Draft, *Federal Register*, 44 (January 12), 2996–3019.
W. H. Elliott & Sons, Inc. v. *E. & F. King & Co., Inc.* (1961), 291 F.2d 79 (C.A.1).
Weinstein, Alvin S., Aaron D. Twerski, Henry R. Piehler and William A. Donaher (1978), *Products Liability and the Reasonably Safe Product: A Guide for Management, Design, and Marketing*, New York: John Wiley & Sons, Inc.
West v. *Alberto Culver Co.* (1973), 486 F.2d 459 (C.A.10 Colo.).
Westerman v. *Sears, Roebuck & Co.* (1978), CCH Prod. Liab.Rep. para. 8416, 577 F.2d 873 (C.A.5 Fla.).
Wilson v. *E-Z Flo Chem. Co.* (1972a), 13 N.C.App. 610, 186 S.E.2d 679.
———(1972b), 281 N.C. 506, 189 S.E.2d 221.
Winkler v. *American Safety Equipment Corp.* (1979), CCH Prod. Liab. Rep. para. 8601 (C.A. Colo.).

20. Regulation in Advertising

S. Watson Dunn

Research in Marketing, Vol. 4, pp. 117–141.
Copyright 1981 by JAI Press, Inc.
Reprinted by permission.

Practitioners in advertising and marketing today are forced to operate under much more stringent regulations than their counterparts of but a few years ago. The proliferation of controls has caused some business people to complain that government regulators and such nongovernmental bodies as consumer groups are trying to take over the advertising industry. Certain critics, however, complain that the controls are still too lenient and too easy to circumvent. Researchers generally claim that both the regulators and the regulated make all too little use of modern research methodology.

In this chapter we shall look first at what problems are most subject to control in advertising, then at the methods which are used to cope with those problems, some of them informal and voluntary, others strictly legal or administrative. We shall then attempt to determine what the proper role of research should be in today's highly charged regulatory climate.

I. TYPES OF PROBLEMS WHICH ARE REGULATED

Most of the regulatory activity in advertising involves problems of the content of the advertising message, the type of product or service which is to be promoted, the proportion of advertising vs. nonadvertising material to be accepted by the media, fairness of advertising allowances, labeling, and the "fairness" of presenting all sides of a controversial matter (especially in the broadcast media).

A. Content of the Advertising Message

1. Deception. Much of the attention of those who regulate advertising focuses on what is communicated either intentionally or unintentionally in an advertisement. The problem of defining what is and what is not deceptive has long been a troublesome one for both advertising practitioners and for regulators. Yet it is a problem which must be faced realistically if advertising is to enjoy the confidence of consumers so that it can perform its communication job effectively.

To determine what such terms as "deception" and "truth" really mean we must look at what the Federal Trade Commission (the principal U.S. agency involved in regulation of avertising) and the various courts have to say about deception. According to Dunn and Barban [1] the following are the principal FTC criteria:

1. It is necessary only to establish the tendency or capacity of an advertisement to deceive, not actually deception itself.
2. Misrepresentation of fact is considered deceptive.
3. A totally false statement cannot be qualified or modified.
4. A statement may be deceptive even though, literally or technically, it is not construed to be misrepresentation.
5. In making product performance claims, substantial test data are needed to support claims.
6. Products must be "reasonably related" to the size of the containers in which they are needed to support claims.
7. There must be a "reasonable basis" for making product claims.
8. Ambiguous statements that are susceptible to both misleading and truthful interpretations will be construed against the advertiser.
9. Failure to disclose material fact where the effect is to deceive a substantial segment of the public is equivalent to deception.

Judged by these criteria most of the advertisements checked each year by the FTC are not deceptive. In a normal year the FTC issues about 270 complaints against "deceptive practices" in labeling and advertising. Less than one fourth of these require action. Both the courts and the FTC change their interpretation of when an advertisement is deceptive from time to time.

Some critics of advertising would include "puffery" as a part of deception. This is a description of a product or service which exaggerates its good qualities but is not necessarily deceptive under present interpretations of that word. For example, Preston [2] calls puffery "soft-core" deception; and comments on it as follows in one of his books:

> Puffery affects people's purchasing decisions by burdening them with untrue beliefs, but our regulators say it does no such thing except to the out-of-step individual who acts unreasonably and therefore deserves no protection. Puffery deceives, and regulations which have made it legal are thoroughly unjustified. There are many varieties of puffery and they account for a huge proportion of the claims made by sellers and advertisers in the marketplace.

Some critics regard as deceptive any advertisement that claims a brand contains a particular ingredient unless that ingredient was unique or unless the advertisement contains a statement disclosing the fact that it was *not* unique. However, Levitt [3] contends that advertising involves expected benefits rather than a literal interpretation of the truth. He notes the following:

> In a world where so many things are either commonplace or standardized, it makes no sense to refer to the rest as false, fraudulent, frivolous or immaterial. The world works according to the aspirations and needs of its actors, not according to the arcane or moralizing logic of detached critics who pine for another age.

Cunningham and Cunningham [4] presented a series of advertising statements (e.g., "A radial tire has at least eight belts of steel radial cord" and "Micro-encapsulated means that the particles in a pill are separately encapsulated") to a sample of 2,200 residents of a medium-sized Texas city. The percentage of incorrect responses ranged from a low of more than 19 percent to a high of more than 80 percent. They suggest that it is not possible for the government to attempt to protect the citizenry by requiring that all commercials be understood by "the least reasonable man." They suggest that only the "reasonable man" and not the "unreasonable man" should be protected by the FTC. For example, words like "micro-encapsulated" would not be permitted since they are not understood by vast numbers of the public. They suggest also that the FTC be given funds to establish a mechanism to test terms for their comprehension by the public. They believe that the latter mechanism would be particularly useful to firms which use technical words or expressions in their advertising copy.

Another suggestion comes from Gardner [5] who recommends that norms be set for each class of product. These would state what the average consumer believed about the product class. Extensive research among prospective consumers would be needed to determine whether an advertisement was or was not deceptive. This leads to serious difficulty, however, when one attempts to define both "class of product" and "average consumer." With the changing uses people make of products and the continuing avalanche of new products coming on the market, research in this area would be exceptionally complex.

Some practitioners contend that deception will be self-regulating in that consumers will turn against a product or service that does not live up to its claims. This is often true in the case of advertisements which contain information which is easily verifiable by consumers, such as price or physical characteristics of the product. However, we have all too little research on just how often such verifiable situations occur and how likely consumers are to check performance against advertising claims. We also do not know under what conditions deceptive advertising is any more effective than nondescriptive advertising in stimulating sales of a product. It is assumed by many critics of advertising that consumers take quite literally what they see or hear in advertising messages, and we know this is not necessarily the case.

The effect of advertising on children has been a special worry to many consumer groups. Although the areas of advertising's influence on children has been widely researched, the findings tend to contradict each other in certain important respects. For example, Scott Ward [6] provides the following summary of the effect of television advertising on children:

1. Between second and fourth grades children not only begin to discriminate between programs and commercials but also begin to understand the intent of the commercials.
2. By the sixth grade, children have relatively well-developed attitudes toward commercials.
3. Children do not "tune-in" to commercials (i.e., increase their attention to them relative to program fare).
4. Children do form positive and negative attitudes toward advertisements (i.e., adolescents are generally quite cynical toward advertising claims).
5. Television advertising is neither the sole nor necessarily the most influential determinant of children's wants and purchasing behavior.
6. Adolescents acquire consumer attitudes and skills from television advertising.
7. Black and white adolescents do not differ markedly in their responses to television advertising.
8. Intelligence is a better predictor of recall of commercial themes and slogans than exposure to television advertising (i.e., the higher the intelligence the greater the recall).

A somewhat contrary view has been presented by the FTC staff which has requested rulemaking hearings to consider serious reform of children's television advertising. In a document entitled *FTC Staff Report on Television Advertising to Children* [7] and released in February 1978, the staff attempted to summarize the result of research studies it has examined and make suggestions for correction of what it viewed as abuses. The staff was convinced that younger children are helpless before commercials directed to them. They were also convinced that there is danger in promoting heavily sugared foods to children on television. The proposed remedies included the curtailing of all advertising in children's programming for "sugar-laden" foods and all commercials aimed at young children. The FTC, as well as the business representatives, was seriously concerned about the welfare of children. They differed seriously in how children can best be protected—in the case of business much confidence was vested in the play of competitive forces, in the case of the FTC much more confidence in the power of the government to regulate competition.

The first director of the National Advertising Division of the Council of Better Business Bureaus, Emilie Griffin [8], cites the difficulty her unit—the first business-sponsored unit set up for regulation of children's advertising—has had in determining standards of deception among children. She contends that research should be directed more at what children perceive in advertisements, less on what they think about different types of advertising and advertised products.

2. Obscenity and Bad Taste. A second area in which problems of content arise is that of obscenity and bad taste. These terms cause considerable trouble for regulators since both involve subjective standards and concepts of each have changed drastically over time. The U.S. Supreme Court, for example, has tried to apply "community standards" to the interpretation of obscenity (which is illegal) and to bad taste (which is not) [1, p. 103]:

1. whether the average person applying contemporary community standards would find that the work, taken as a whole, appeals to prurient interests;
2. whether the work depicts or describes in a patently offensive way sexual conduct specifically defined by the applicable standards; and
3. whether the work—if it appeals to prurient interest and is patently offensive—lacks serious literary, artistic, political or scientific value.

Standards may change drastically over time. Within a few years nude pictures were accepted as not offensive in many leading magazines as standards changed. In many cases advertising which is acceptable in magazine advertising (e.g., live models demonstrating the virtues of women's underwear) is not deemed acceptable by those who regulate television advertising. An advertising message or illustration which is not considered offensive by the publishers of *Playboy* or *Penthouse* may be turned down by *Reader's Digest*.

3. Lotteries. Although more and more states now allow lotteries and other forms of gambling within their borders, these are still illegal in *interstate* commerce. This is an important distinction since most advertisements are considered illegal if three elements are present in the offer: prize, consideration, and chance. If any one of these is absent the offer does not constitute a lottery. For example, the matter of "consideration" is often a nebulous one and a frequent cause of confusion. In some states a contest that requires one to visit a certain store to qualify for a contest is illegal, because this requirement constitutes a "consideration."

4. Right of Privacy. An increasingly troublesome area in advertising is the extent to which a person has the right to be left alone. In the case of advertising the legal doctrine of right of privacy prohibits the use of the name or picture of a living person without consent and thus makes it necessary to get a signed release even from a professional model. It is sometimes argued that professional actors or celebrities of any kind are so much in the public eye that they have no real right of privacy. However, the courts have generally ruled that they cannot be featured in any commercial publicity without their consent. Nor can one use a "lookalike" model which the public might confuse with the celebrity.

With the increased focus on people's right to be left alone and the post-Watergate fears of too much government surveillance, privacy questions are likely to increase. At the same time both straight testimonial advertisements and advertising featuring celebrity spokesmen or spokeswomen have been on the increase. According to trade magazine reports, those firms using such celebrities as Joe Namath and Farrah Fawcett-Majors have enjoyed sizable sales increases. There is, however, little research to indicate whether it is the attention value of the celebrity which accounts for the impact of the advertisements or whether the consumer believes that the celebrity actually uses and endorses the product. We also do not know how soon the effect of such celebrity ads wears out.

5. Trademarks and Copyrights. According to the Lanham Trademark Act the term "trademark" includes "any word, name, symbol or device or any combination thereof adopted and used by a manufacturer or merchant to identify his goods or distinguish them from those manufactured or sold by others." In earlier times trademarks were used as means of policing the output of guilds or other organizations. Today the trademark is the symbol the advertiser uses to identify his products and make it easier for consumers to select them. Consequently the trademark is an important company asset and the seller will make great effort to protect it. Under present law not only a distinctive mark but names, symbols, titles, designations, slogans, character names and distinctive features emphasized in advertising are specifically protected. Such slogans as the Schlitz "The beer that made Milwaukee Famous" and Colonel Sanders (as spokesman for fried chicken) are protected.

Copyright protection, on the other hand, is used to cover creative works. For example, one may not copyright an idea but one may be protected on the way that idea is expressed in an advertisement. Copyright protection was extended through a new U.S. law which went into effect at the beginning of 1978.

B. Type of Product Advertised

Since January 1, 1971, it has been illegal in the United States to advertise cigarettes on the broadcast media. Many other countries of the world also prohibit such advertising, often in print as well as broadcast media. However, cigarettes can still be sold legally in most countries. This is a particularly interesting case of a product that can be sold legally being prohibited from being promoted, regardless of the type of advertising used. This has established a precedent which may well be extended to other products which many people consider harmful. For example, some countries prohibit advertising of alcoholic liquor although there is no such legal prohibition in the United States. On the other hand, the broadcast media have attempted to prevent members of their association from accepting liquor advertising on the basis that it might bring on great public pressure to curtail independence of broadcasting stations. Other groups would like to prohibit advertising of any product which might pollute the air, patent medicines, certain types of breakfast cereals, pornographic films, and many other types of products.

C. Excessive Amounts of Advertising

A troublesome problem for the advertisers and the managers of the advertising media is the decision as to how much advertising is too much (i.e., at what point do people rebel at the overuse of advertising). Most people have objected at one time to the pyramiding of commercials on radio or television programs. A great many people have protested at the excessive numbers of billboards on certain highways. Most newspapers and magazines contain more advertising than nonadvertising material but the managers of these media normally try for a certain ratio between the two which they attempt to maintain over time. Only in the case of the broadcast media have specific amounts of allowable advertising time been set, and these have been determined by the industry itself, rather than by law or administrative fiat. The broadcasting industry has long felt that excessive amounts of advertising need to be controlled more during the prime evening television hours when people presumably devote closer attention to what they are seeing on their television screen. Even in the case of television, however, research evidence regarding the threshold at which people rebel at advertising excesses is sadly lacking.

D. Advertising Allowances

This is a problem with which both business and government regulators have struggled for many years. The problem is that advertising allowances provided by manufacturers to dealers often constitute a hidden discount, particularly when they are offered to very large buyers, such as the chain stores. As such, they are considered illegal under the Robinson-Patman Act, since they constitute price discrimination. If, on the other hand, such advertising allowances are offered on an equitable basis to all dealers and they are actually used as an encouragement for advertising at the local level, there is not necessarily any legal problem.

In cases such as these, the only problem is one of control by the manufacturer so that he makes sure the quality is consistent with his national advertising and that the products which he wants featured in the advertising are actually featured by the local dealer.

An additional problem comes up in the case of collusion between the local advertising medium and the local retailer. In several cases the practice of "double billing" has resulted in action taken against media and loss of licenses by some radio stations. Under this practice, one bill is submitted to the retailer which he will in turn submit to the national manufacturer to collect his share of the space or time which he bought. Another bill (much lower) is submitted to the local retailer for actual payment.

E. Labeling

If we consider labeling as a form of advertising we run into another whole group of problems regarding what may or may not be said about products. This is a particularly troublesome problem in the case of the marketing of foods, drugs and cosmetics, for which specifications are set forth in the Food, Drug and Cosmetic Act. In the eyes of the regulatory bodies such products are worthy of special attention because of the danger that misuse of them may pose to the health of consumers. What is *not* included on a label, such as instructions on when to use or not to use the product, may be just as important as what is included. The regulatory authorities have in the late 1970s been giving considerably more attention to labeling than in previous years.

F. Fairness of Presentation

This is a problem that is of special importance to the managers of radio and television stations who are required under the First Amendment to give equal time to all sides of any controversial issue. Political and public relations ads are the ones that advertisers and stations must police with particular care. These are usually about services and people rather than products. For example, much advertising around election time involves the promotion of one candidate as compared with another. However, advertising for products may also fall under the "Fairness Doctrine." In 1967, before cigarette advertising was banned on television, the Federal Communications Commission decided that such advertising was controversial and that stations carrying it must give opponents of cigarette smoking the chance to air their views. Like truth, "fairness" is a nebulous concept and its exact interpretation by consumers is not particularly clear. For example, certain groups feel that radio and television stations should once again be required to include anti-cigarette-smoking commercials even though they are not allowed by law to carry those promoting smoking. This would seem, however, to be a dubious application of the fairness doctrine, since it would mean that only the opponents would have a chance to get their viewpoints across to the public. This is especially dubious in view of the fact that several state courts and the U.S. Supreme Court both reaffirmed in late 1976 that advertising is covered by the First Amendment to the Constitution. Up to this time, the exact nature of its coverage had been somewhat in doubt. The case which brought this to a head was one in Virginia involving rights of lawyers to advertise when a state statute prohibited such advertising [1]. In several states, laws have been passed to prohibit such professionals from advertising their wares in the public media. It remains to be seen whether people will be better informed about the comparative costs of such services as the proponents have claimed. The opponents had justified such curtailment of advertising on the basis that allowing professionals to advertise would denigrate the quality of service and lead to cutthroat price competition. There is no evidence at this point that such is the case.

II. Types of Control over Advertising

Consumers often think of controls only in terms of those who are given specific statutory power over advertising. In practice, controls come in many forms, some direct, some indirect, some long range, some short range. In general it is perhaps best to consider controls in two broad categories—those which are informal or voluntary, and those which are legal or administrative. Of the informal or voluntary controls, the more important are perhaps those by business itself, instituted in an attempt to regulate its own house. We should, however, also consider the controls by consumers, particularly since these have, during the late 1960s and early 1970s, exerted considerable pressure on advertising in almost every country of the world.

A. Control by Business

Business and marketing executives generally praise self-regulation as a responsible reaction to public demand for advertising to clean its own house. There are, however, some questions raised about it, such as the following [1, p. 11]: (1) Is it likely to conflict with the right of each firm to conduct its business freely as it sees fit? (2) Does it violate antitrust laws which are designed to encourage free and open competition? (3) Does it usurp the function of the government? (4) Is it a good idea to publish negative findings as a punitive technique? (5) Does vigorous promotion of complaint facilities elicit valid complaints or merely multiply frivolous ones? (6) Should self-regulation be conducted by practicing advertisers or by hired administrators?

Studies conducted in 1962 and 1971 [9] indicated that U.S. business executives were increasingly skeptical of management's abilities to enforce a code of advertising ethics, while they had increasing confidence in "a group of executives plus other members of the community" and in "a government agency" as regulators. More than half the respondents said that "if advertising cannot keep its house in order the government will have to."

Despite the pessimism, self-regulation has prospered in most countries during the 1970s [11]. This is a far cry from earlier times when, as Sandage, Fryburger and Rotzoll [10] point out:

> Prior to the 1970s it can be fairly asserted that the performance had not been meritorious. Simple disinterest, underfinancing, an absence of first-rate talent and an unwillingness to submit judgment of potential competitors have all led to an overall lackluster performance. That the mechanisms were not always carefully conceived can be suggested by the fact that many emerged only during periods of outside agitation with the wolf close to the door if not inside the house.

Self-regulation has taken many forms with some organizations such as the National Advertising Review Board representing all segments of the industry; at the same time various associations and individual advertising agencies, advertisers, media have all set up their own regulatory mechanisms.

1. National Advertising Review Board. This Board is the focal point of a three-tiered system which involves local Better Business Bureaus, the National Advertising Division of the nationwide Council of Better Business Bureaus, and the National Advertising Review Board. Complaints are forwarded by the local Better Business Bureau to the National Advertising Division of the Council. A complaint does not go to the NARB until it has been completely evaluated by the NAD and the advertiser has had full opportunity to defend his advertising. Since its beginning in 1971, the NARB has received praise from the advertising industry but some skepticism from leaders of the consumer movement. There is, however, considerable evidence to indicate that it has been the most successful of the advertising industry's regulatory efforts in the United States and that it has been able to overcome some of the difficulties that have beset previous industry-wide efforts.

The NARB consists of 50 members, 30 representing national advertisers, 10 representing advertising agencies and 10 representing the public or the nonindustry sector. Complaints about advertising are referred to this Board which may receive them from the public, from other businessmen, or from other sources. The NAD evaluates the complaints, and if it seems justified confers with the advertiser or its agency in an attempt to seek changes in the advertising. If this attempt is not successful the complaint is appealed to the NARB which appoints five-member panels of three advertisers, one agency person, and one public representative to review complaints and the findings of the NAD staff up to that point. If the panel upholds the staff decision the advertiser is again asked to change or withdraw the advertising in question. If this is unsuccessful, either the NARB publicly identifies the advertisers, the nature of the complaint and the Board's findings, or the case is referred to the appropriate government agency (in most cases the Federal Trade Commission). Since the NARB and NAD were established in 1971 an average of 200 cases per year have been submitted to the NAD for review, most of these having come from complaints or monitoring by the local Better Business Bureau. The proportion of complaints from consumer groups have decreased as these groups have found a more receptive climate in the government agencies.

In a comprehensive study in which he attempted to evaluate the efforts of the NARB, Zanot [12] found that, in 1976, 36 percent of the cases were substantiated, 35 percent led to modifications, 28 percent were closed administratively, and only 1 pecent reached the NARB panel level. He found that 52 percent were initiated as a result of monitoring by the National Advertising Division of the National Better Business Bureau, 26 percent by competitors and only 1 percent by consumer groups.

2. *Better Business Bureaus.* The local bureaus are financed by business firms which want to stamp out unfair competition in a particular locality. Complaints to these bureaus come from individuals or businesses, in most instances; for example, an advertising message in a local newspaper or a local radio station may offer a late-model used car at a very low price. When someone checks with the dealer and finds out that this car has been sold and an attempt is made to sell a higher-priced model, this is a typical example of what the BBB calls "bait" advertising. If the bureau finds out that this is, indeed, a misleading advertisement, it tries to persuade the advertiser to change his ways. If he does not stop, publicity may be used as a weapon to stop him. If the publicity does not work, legal action, probably under the laws of the particular state, will be taken.

There were, in 1976, 150 separate BBBs under the general supervision of the Council of Better Business Bureaus in New York City. They were supported by more than 100,000 membership firms whose total membership dues were in excess of $6.5 million per year. Each bureau is organized as an independent nonprofit corporation usually supported by a diversity of business interests in the community. The board of directors of each local bureau appoints a manager and authorizes the addition of needed staff members.

3. *Advertising Agencies.* Advertising agencies, both individually and cooperatively through the American Association of Advertising Agencies, attempt to exercise control over the advertising they plan and prepare for their clients. Individual agencies do much self-policing in an attempt to prevent either bad publicity or some sort of legal action. Such efforts by agencies are likely to increase since in recent years they have been held legally liable along with clients for misleading or fraudulent claims in their advertisements. Until recent years, liability had been judged to rest exclusively with the client which hired the agency and supposedly exercised careful surveillance over what was said in the advertising messages.

Most agencies have in-house legal counsel. Some will refuse to handle advertising for certain products, such as cigarettes, or proprietary medicines. Agencies are in a particularly good position to exercise even more control since most of the large ones have sophisticated researchers as well as lawyers on their staff and they are equipped to hire and work with outside research counsel.

What is needed in the agency field is the focusing of research efforts more on regulatory problems and perhaps less on problems of management of the advertising budget or on creative or media strategy per se.

4. *Advertising Media.* Almost all the major media carry on extensive regulation of the advertising they carry, both individually and through the associations of which they are members. For example, many newspapers have become famous for their refusal to accept questionable advertising. The *New York Times* has for more than fifty years had a strict set of standards administered by its own Advertising Acceptability Department. This department will not accept superlatives or claims which it feels might be misleading. It was decided in late 1977 to refuse advertising for movie theaters which promoted "X-rated" movies. Another comprehensive code is that of the Detroit News which bans advertisements for introductions to members of the opposite sex, those offering homework for pay, and those selling habit-forming drugs.

The fleeting nature of radio and television messages makes them especially difficult to police. In fact, many of them are never written at all but are merely ad-libbed by a studio announcer. However, many stations are quite selective about what they will or will not accept. Since they are government-licensed media, they must be particularly careful about what kind of advertising they carry since illegal advertising or even advertising in bad taste may constitute a black mark against them when their license comes up for renewal. Consequently, they rely more heavily than print media on advertising codes and are particularly concerned about techniques of presentation which may be misleading or offensive.

Some stations and networks have self-regulatory machinery for continuity acceptance departments which pass on all proposed advertising. Much of the regulation, however, is geared to the Television Review Board of the National Association of Broadcasters. This TV code, in effect since 1952, has gone through many revisions. However, it is quite specific in discouraging certain types of advertising as being not acceptable for television. Examples are: "bait" advertising, advertising for tip sheets, race track publications, fortune tellers, and astrologers. Advertising of liquor is banned with the exception of beer and wine. The TV code also limits the amount of broadcast time that may be devoted to commercials at different periods of the day. For example, in prime time the maximum allowed is nine and a half minutes and in nonprime time, sixteen minutes.

In the case of magazines, there is no industry-wide advertising code but many publishers have their own stringent rules. For example, management of *Good Housekeeping* claims it has a staff of 100 technicians and spends more than $1 million a year testing in the Good Housekeeping Institute products which advertise in its pages in order that advertising claims may be checked. It guarantees a refund for any product that does not live up to the advertised claim.

Almost all other media have an association which provide guidance in the policing of advertising carried by its members. For example, the Direct Marketing Association bans sending through the mail unsolicited merchandise, vulgar or immoral matter, and gambling devices. The Outdoor Advertising Association of America adopts a code of acceptable practice which is concerned especially with tasteful design and construction of display and placement of billboards.

The advertising industry has within it, groups which focus on various regulatory problems in its field. The leading publication in the field, *Advertising Age*, wages a consistent battle for more truthful and tasteful advertising and has carried on campaigns against violations of good taste and truth by professionals.

At least three major advertising associations—the American Advertising Federation, American Association of Advertising Agencies, and the Association of National Advertisers—have helped in the regulation of advertising. For example, the AAF, which is a federation of advertising organizations, helped establish the FTC and the BBB grew out of its own early "vigilance committees." Because most local advertising clubs belong to the AAF it is in a particularly good position to influence local advertisers.

The AAAA exercises control over member agencies through its ability to deny membership to agencies which prepare false or misleading statements or testimonials which do not reflect the real choice of competent witnesses. Since almost all large national agencies belong to the AAAA it is in a position to exert considerable pressure.

The ANA is an organization representing most of the major manufacturers in the United States. It also has a code and attempts by working through its members and its member agencies to exert pressure for more truthful advertising.

B. Controls by Consumers

The rise of the consumer movement during the middle and latter part of the twentieth century has exerted strong pressure on advertising practices. In the 1950s and 1960s the advertising professionals were subjected to searching criticism. Laws were proposed to tax advertising, to increase the police powers of federal agencies, to restrict the placing of billboards along highways, and to prohibit subliminal advertising in the broadcast media. By the late 1960s the consumer movement was so well organized and had gained so much power that a new word (consumerism) was created to describe it.

Consumerism is much more complex than past consumer movements and it stems from a variety of causes. Among these have been the rise of technology, mass-produced and often unreliable products, soaring medical and dental costs, and pollution of air and water. Problems of the consumer have been dramatized by books such as Rachel Carson's *Silent Spring* and Ralph Nader's *Unsafe at Any Speed*. The educational and sophistication level of the American consumer has been higher than in past periods. There is evidence that advertisers were slow to realize the upgrading of mass tastes and that they underestimated consumer discontent, particularly among some of the better educated people who have served as leaders in the consumer movement.

Consumerism had both an indirect and a direct effect on the practice of advertising. Perhaps its most direct effect has been alerting advertisers to be more conscious of the claims they make, especially in advertisements directed to children or when the product advertised uses resources such as energy. An effect has been the growth of consumer organizations and government regulatory agencies. Consumerism is an effective control over advertising only where advertisers have adequate information on which to base their decision. Professor James Engel [13] has suggested that consumerism will result in more sophisticated consumer research in order that business can find out what consumers are really thinking and when they are likely to act. Many, but not all advertisers, cooperate with consumerist leaders in efforts to bring about more enlightened buying by consumers. Some advertisers look upon the rise of consumerism as an opportunity for growth and profit, rather than as a straitjacket. For example, studies by Greyser and Diamond [14] indicated that business people see consumerism as "an ally, a tool through which profits can be generated.... Eighty-six percent agree that company investment in consumer services and satisfaction will usually pay for itself."

Consumers have found several formal channels through which they can express loudly and clearly their opinions on advertising and marketing. Among the most important are the Consumer Federation of America and the National Consumer League. The CFA was formed in 1968 by representatives of 44 consumer organizations and 12 supporting groups. By 1976 it consisted of over 200 national, state and local groups, labor unions, and electric cooperatives, along with such organizations as The National Council of Senior Citizens and the National Board of the Y.M.C.A.

The National Consumer League was founded in 1899 to work for better labor conditions through public pressure. In recent years it has concentrated more on consumer issues.

A second type of channel for consumers is the private, nonprofit testing organization, such as Consumers Union and Consumers' Research. The latter which was founded as an outgrowth of the publication *Your Money's Worth* by Stewart Chase and F. J. Schlink, both early consumerists. Consumers' Research rates products and issues its findings monthly in *Consumer Bulletin*. Still another nonprofit organization, Underwriters Laboratory, tests products for safety and publishes lists of products it has found acceptable.

C. Controls Over Advertising by the Government

The most stringent and apparent controls over advertising are those based on laws passed by Congress, state legislatures, or local municipal authorities. Enforcement is up to government administrators who must decide what the laws really mean and take appropriate actions which are subject to challenge in the courts. The legislators, the judges and administrators are constantly changing, so it is not surprising that advertising people must consult lawyers. More and more they are also consulting researchers to find evidence of what consumers perceive in an advertisement or of its effect in the marketplace.

1. Federal Controls. Although controls are exercised at state and local levels, by far the most important is that at the Federal level. Federal control has evolved primarily through attempts to cope with such problems as unfair competition, deceptive practices, protection of brand names and literary rights. The Federal Trade Commission Act, which established the agency most active in control of advertising, was passed in 1914 to eliminate unfair competition and it originally contained no statement about advertising. Focus on advertising came later.

a. Federal Trade Commission. To most advertising professionals the FTC symbolizes regulation of national advertising. In 1916 the FTC decided that advertising of products falsely took unfair advantage of a competitor and therefore was illegal under the provisions of the Act which set up that body. The U.S. Supreme Court upheld this interpretation in 1922, confirming the FTC's right to regulate false labeling and advertising as unfair methods of competition. The Wheeler-Lea Amendments of 1938 significantly extended FTC powers and clarified its authority to regulate advertising.

Although the FTC clearly has the power to cover all phases of "unfair competition" it had decided by the early 1970s according to one of its top officers, to give its highest priority to the enforcement of laws regarding advertising. One of the reasons given for this emphasis was the increasing amount of advertising and the decreasing tolerance of consumers for questionable advertising, as indicated by complaints of individual consumers and consumer groups as well as their Congressmen to the FTC. Because of the tremendous volume of advertising which had to be monitored by the late 1970s, the FTC set up a liaison with the Federal Communications Commission under which the FTC was provided with copies of complaints and orders involving broadcasters or broadcast advertising. The two agencies have extended the cooperation by making it possible for personnel of each to have access to confidential files of the other. The agencies also have agreed to inform each other when they obtain investigation leads of mutual interest.

The FTC is also responsible for administering such laws as the Fur Product Labeling Act and the Robinson-Patman Act of 1936. The former protects advertising and labeling of fur products and the latter protects the small retailers against large outlets who because of their size gain a substantial price advantage.

When a complaint is issued by the FTC the respondent has thirty days to reply. In cases where litigation is involved, hearings are held before a trial examiner employed by the FTC, but not under its discipline. His initial decision can be appealed to the FTC by either side. The FTC affirms or modifies the order, or the case may be dismissed. However, the decisions of the FTC, like any other government regulatory agency, are appealable to any Federal Court of Appeals.

During the 1970s the FTC has extended its influence in areas which were once considered outside its province. For example, it has contended that agencies as well as clients are liable for false or misleading advertising which they place. It has required automobile manufacturers to show documentation for specific claims made in their advertising. Among these are such claims as mileage, price and safety. It has insisted that pesticides should provide warnings.

The FTC has also mapped out new regulations such as the following: (1) unfairness doctrine (power to deal with what the FTC considers "unfair" practices), even these practices have no relation to monopolies or competition; (2) substantive rule-making power (making rules for procedure to be followed in questionable areas such as children's advertising on television); (3) ad substantiation (programs to educate the public on ways of substantiating claims); (4) unreasonable basis tests (emphasizing the point that advertisers must have substantiating data to back up any "unreasonable basis" for claims they make in advertising);

(5) corrective advertising (ordered by FTC to advertisers who are deemed to have so deceived consumers that they must devote a certain percentage of future ads to removal of "residual consumer deception").

The definition of "residual consumer deception" has been a troublesome one for both the regulators and the regulated. The FTC has attempted to determine how much deception might be lingering in the minds of prospective consumers, since this is the basis for requiring a certain percentage of future advertisements to remove this residue. There is a serious need for more research in this area.

In 1976, somewhat to the dismay of the U.S. Patent and Trademark Office, an FTC administrative judge decided that Borden should be required to license other companies to make Realemon (reconstituted lemon juice). This was the first attempt by a government agency or a court to require licensing of a trademark. The Department of Commerce disagreed with this decision of an administrative judge.

b. Food and Drug Administration. The Federal Food, Drug and Cosmetic Act of 1938 represented an attempt to eliminate some of the weaknesses and ambiguities of the original legislation setting up the Food and Drug Administration. The most important contributions were that it made failure to reveal material facts on a label an element of misbranding and thus a misdemeanor.

c. Federal Communications Commission. This Commission is empowered to operate our telecommunications system in "the public interest, convenience and necessity." These are the main criteria for awarding operating licenses for television and radio stations and for renewing them. Thus the FCC wields indirect control over the advertising because certain types of advertising and advertising practice are not considered to be in the public interest, convenience and necessity. In 1967 the FCC decided to apply the fairness doctrine to cigarette commercials with the rule that broadcasters must carry anticigarette announcements to counterbalance the cigarette commercials presently carried. The "counter ads" for cigarettes have been cited by various social-action groups who want such ads as warning against drugs, automobiles and a host of other "controversial" products carried on TV stations. Also concerns of the FCC are length of commercials, number of commercials, piling up of commercials, middle commercials in a program, sponsor vs. sustaining programs, lotteries.

The FCC has no power of censorship and does not act on individual programs or commercials, per se, unless it has received complaints. Instead, each station is required to keep a complete log of all programs and commercials it transmits and these may be examined when the license renewal is due. In several cases false or misleading advertising has been cited as a reason for failure of the FCC to renew a license or to provide a present licensee with additional stations.

d. The United States Postal Service. The Postal Service controls advertising through the mails mainly in the areas of obscenity, lottery, and fraud. In order to exercise control over advertising that is not legally obscene but may shock the families who receive it, a law has been passed that is designed to curb "pandering" advertisements. Anyone receiving such an ad now has the authority to ask that no more mail be forwarded from that sender. An advertisement is "pandering" if in the opinion of the receiver it is "erotically arousing or sexually provocative." The Postmaster General has the authority to withhold mail which he deems to constitute a lottery.

The Postal Service also has indirect authority to regulate advertising through granting or withholding the Second Class Mailing privilege to periodicals. The Supreme Court has, however, limited its powers in this sphere by deciding that it cannot deny a Second Class permit on the grounds of taste or morals. Although revocation of a Second Class permit is a potentially powerful sanction, the revocation proposed by the judiciary and the reluctance on the part of the Post Office to impose this restriction have made a minimal effectiveness in advertising regulation.

e. Alcohol and Tobacco Tax Division. In 1935 the Federal Alcohol and Tobacco Tax Administration was created as a division of the Treasury Department, to control practices, including advertisements, in the brewing and liquor industry. This unit is now the Alcohol and Tobacco Tax Division of the Revenue Service of the Treasury Department. At present, not only can the agency take action against deceptive practices but can also require inclusion of certain types of information on labels and advertising as well as prohibiting other types of information. The unit has worked out an elaborate classification system regulating what can and cannot be said about alcoholic content, presence of neutral spirits and so on in both labels and ads. For example, ads may not contain curative or therapeutic claims, reference to the American flag, or such terms as "pure" and "double distilled."

f. Patent Office. Anyone who wants to protect a slogan or brand name from infringement by competitors must make his application to the U.S. Patent Office. These include any words, names, similar device, or combination thereof adopted and used by a manufacturer or merchant to identify his goods and distinguish them from those manufactured and sold by others. The mark identifying the product need not be physically affixed. The Lanham Act also protects service marks used to distinguish services rather than products, certification marks used by persons other than the owners to signify geographical origin, grade or quality and collective marks used to indicate membership in an organization. In 1976 there were 34,573 applications for trademark registration at the Patent Office. Registrations were issued to 33,931.

Since the modern marketer often has no direct contact with the ultimate consumer, he will look for some sign that indicates that the product came from a reliable firm. Often products are so similar in outward appearance that it is important that a distinctive mark be used to connote high quality. This is particularly important in the case of products which are sold on a self-service basis. Because of the increasing importance of identification marks, more and more court cases have been focused on the problem of whether a particular variation of existing brand name or identification is likely to confuse large numbers of people. This is obviously an important, though difficult, area for the courts, and lawyers and judges have consequently depended more and more on researchers to provide evidence of whether confusion is actually caused.

g. Library of Congress. The Library of Congress enforces the copyright laws which give authors and other creators a monopoly over their use for a certain period of time. Most advertising lawyers will suggest that advertisements be copyrighted and they qualify for the easiest kind of copyright notice in that all that is required is a © and the name of the advertiser. The copyrighting of the periodical in which an ad appears does not necessarily protect an ad from paraphrasing or from variations of that advertising message, only from direct quotation.

h. Office of Consumer Protection. In 1971 President Nixon created the Office of Consumer Protection. Among the publications issued by this office are a monthly newsletter, "Consumer Education Guidelines," and a column on consumer services that is distributed to 4,500 weekly newspapers.

2. State Controls. Most advertising falls in the category of interstate commerce and thus is subject to Federal regulation. However, any activities that are primarily intrastate are regulated by the states themselves. Consequently, many states have passed variations of the *Printers Ink* "Model Statute," designed to make advertising more truthful. The statute, suggested by the advertising magazine, *Printers Ink*, said that any person who placed before the public an announcement that "contains any assertion, representation or statement of fact which is untrue, deceptive or misleading shall be guilty of a misdemeanor." This statute or some variation of it has been passed by all but three states; however, it is not stringently enforced because it is a criminal, not a civil, law and prosecutors know it is hard to get juries to convict under a criminal statute. Many states have also enacted laws that regulate lotteries, cosmetics, securities, bait and switch advertising, and advertising by special groups.

3. Municipal Control. Some municipal authorities have moved into the area of advertising control and into consumerism. For example, a former "Miss America," Bess Myerson, helped enforce New York City's Consumer Protection Act and helped in passing a regulation requiring New York City merchants to stamp the price per measure (unit measure) on supplies. She also backed strongly "open dating" on perishables which indicates the last day of acceptable use. Miss Myerson was succeeded by another well-known consumerist, Miss Betty Furness.

D. Control by the Courts

In practice, much advertising is controlled by court decision. When someone contests a law which is made by a regulatory agency, the court must render judgment. For example, in the Virginia State Board of Pharmacy *vs.* the Virginia Citizens Consumer Council, in 1976, the U.S. Supreme Court determined that advertising was, "contrary to previous decisions," protected by the First Amendment to the U.S. Constitution [1]. The law at issue was a Virginia statute, that a pharmacist would be "guilty of unprofessional conduct" and liable to discipline if he advertised or publicized or published the prices of discount terms for prescription drugs which he sold. The statute was attacked and suit was instituted by prescription drug users who argued that the First Amendment entitled users to receive such information from pharmacists. The courts decided the Statute was unconstitutional. This was a landmark decision because it held that advertising was protected under the First Amendment (as is nonadvertising material) as long as it is not misleading or does not promote an illegal product.

Many court battles have hinged on brand names and trademarks; for example, a Wisconsin court stopped Heileman from using "Light" for its beer on the basis that it infringed on Miller Brewing, which produces "lite" low-calorie beer. The judges decided that the critical question was the term "lite," which was descriptive or suggestive. If a word provides some direct information about a product it is descriptive; if the word stands for an idea that requires some imagination to associate it with the product it is suggestive. The judge decided that words like "lite" were suggestive and thus valid and protected as trademarks. Few beer drinkers, according to this judge, seriously believe that beer would actually cause them to weigh less. The other legal question was whether consumers would be confused. On this basis also the judge decided that Miller should be protected because "lite" and "light" are alike in sound and cannot easily be distinguished in conversation or oral communication or radio advertising.

III. Future of Research in the Regulation of Advertising

The dilemma of the regulators came into sharp focus when the Federal Trade Commission in 1971 required the makers of Profile Bread to "correct" or remove "residual consumer deception" by running commercials that corrected false impressions implanted by earlier commercials. This was the first example of "corrective advertising." This commercial, narrated by Julia Mead, began in the following manner:

> I'd like to clear up any misunderstanding you may have about Profile Bread or even from its name....

In early 1978 the Federal Trade Commission and the STP Corporation concluded an agreement that STP would purchase approximately $700,000 worth of advertising in national media to tell consumers that certain of its advertising claims may have been deceptive. FTC had little research on which to base this agreement but it stated that the settlement was designed to send businessmen a message that the agency henceforth seeks stronger enforcement measures against those accused of deceptive advertising. The corporation maintained that its claims that STP reduced automobile oil consumption were based on "defective oil consumption tests," but that these defective tests did not mean claims were untrue. The corrective advertisement pointed out that the company was carrying out an agreed-upon settlement with the Federal Trade Commission. As the *Wall Street Journal* pointed out at the time of the settlement, how many consumers would understand what such a statement was all about?

As we have seen, regulation lies in the hands of four primary groups: advertising professionals, government regulators, the courts, and the consumers themselves. These groups seem to agree only in very general terms. For example, most studies indicate that all favor better-informed consumers. However, when it comes to the specifics of how much information consumers need, how consumers perceive the claims they read or hear in advertisements, whether special provisions should be made for such special groups as children and many others, there seems to be wide disagreement. This disagreement seems to concentrate on three general areas: the value of research to policy makers, standards which can be used to interpret and compare findings, and the amount of interaction there should be between researchers and users.

A. Disagreement on Value of Research

During the 1970s most research publications in advertising and marketing have urged their readers to use research methodology to shed light on the various problems that so frequently trouble both the regulators and the regulated. They have been encouraged by increasing acceptance of research findings in court litigation—particularly in disputed trademark cases. There is, however, still far too little acceptance of research approaches by consumer advocates. For example, a study by Professor Steven Permut [15] in 1977 indicated only token acceptance of research by 89 executives in Federal and state regulatory agencies and in leading national consumer organizations. These conclusions emerged from his study:

1. Respondents in the public sector expressed little support for more research dealing with consumer information needs.
2. All respondents expressed skepticism regarding the contribution of research on information disclosure issues, primarily because such research is perceived as lacking recommendations as to specific actions to be taken.
3. Respondents in all groups view their own group (but not others) as being most capable of judging the real information needs of the consumer.

It is worth some examination as to why so many policy makers are so skeptical of research. Permut [15] has suggested that it is their background as lawyers and economists which leads them to believe that these approaches are more useful than the unfamiliar world of the behaviorist. There is undoubtedly some validity to this argument. Although the opinions of professional marketers was not included in this study, there is some reason to believe they would be more receptive than government regulators to research data. However, there is also reason to believe their superiors (the chief executive officers of corporations which are the largest advertisers) are less trustful of research. Most recent studies show that a financial or accounting executive is more likely to be the chief executive of a U.S. corporation than a marketing specialist.

Another reason for this skepticism may well be that the policymakers do not really like what they hear from researchers. For example, six separate studies of consumers' use of nutrition information available to these consumers indicated that "the vast majority of consumers neither acquire such information when making a purchase decision nor comprehend most nutritional information once they do receive it [16]." This lack of use may be the result of poor methods of communication by the marketers. There is, however, some suspicion that large numbers of consumers are simply not anxious to be burdened with great amounts of information pro and con regarding a prospective purchase—and such a conclusion goes counter to the basic philosophy of most consumer advocates.

An additional reason for this skepticism is the complexity of the perception process. Even the most zealous researchers would certainly not claim that modern research methodology can provide definitive answers to such questions as how consumers perceive (or misperceive) advertising messages and how much information they can process when they can read these messages. Most people have the experience from time to time of reading a book and receiving an impression quite different from that of someone else who read that same book. One person exposed to a mass of stimuli from a message will select certain ones and reject others, while another reader may make an entirely different selection from these same stimuli.

Perception is a complex process in which people manipulate the incoming information and select certain stimuli, reject others. People are, for example, influenced by their own existing motives and predispositions. They will see or hear communications that are favorable to their own point of view and reject those that are unfavorable. They may even perceive a neutral message as conforming with what they happen to believe.

In spite of the complexity of the processes studied, however, research is still a much better guide for the regulators or for those trying to avoid undue regulation than the "seat-of-the-pants" opinion so often relied on by lawyers, economists and would-be communicators.

B. Need for Standards for Comparing Research Findings

A major problem in the use of research by government regulators, judges, business people and consumer advocates is the complexity of so many research reports. Most are not schooled in either statistics or research methodology and their most objective and sincere efforts to understand the research reports may be very frustrating. And it is true that many researchers have great difficulty—as do many lawyers and economists—in expressing what they mean in good clear English sentences. Others are overly afraid of not properly qualifying their findings and end up by giving the impression that they have not really found out anything at all.

What is to be done? One helpful step would be agreement between the researchers and the regulators on certain standards. For example, how much of a standard error would be acceptable in probability sampling? Such agreement might allay some of the widespread suspicion that samples are not really representative of the opinions or actions of consumers. Some agreement might also be possible on how far supervisors would be required to go in minimizing nonsampling errors.

Agreement might also be possible as to what topical areas should be included in each "audit" or "research study" of consumer perception. A parallel might be found in the broadcast audience field where there is wide agreement that program ratings, sets-in-use data, average audience, total audience and certain other types of data are useful guides as to audience reaction to the program fare offered by programmers. It is true that sophisticated researchers complain about the looseness of some of these concepts and the errors which often creep into implementing them. Yet few would throw them out and go back to the early days of radio when no one had much idea at all of audience reaction. In the case of the broadcasting industry these data have been generated by the nervousness of executives who know the riskiness of long-term television commitments and their obvious need for some guidance in minimizing this risk. There is riskiness also in the area of advertising regulation and both regulator and the regulated should be working on setting standards for data they need on a regular basis.

C. Need for Interaction Between Researchers and Users of Research

There is little doubt that greater interaction between the researchers and those who decide on policy would result in better policies. For example, there is a great deal more information on consumer behavior and perception already available than most policymakers seem to realize. There are several stumbling blocks which seem to inhibit this interaction.

One stumbling block is the complexity of the whole communication process and the lack of clearcut findings or guides for action that come out of much of our present day research. It is not surprising that many of the government and business executives in their search for clear-cut answers become disenchanted with research. This feeling comes at least in part from the fear of the unfamiliar in that most of these administrators do not have training in research.

Another problem is the orientation of many researchers to theory rather than to the solving of problems. More problem orientation on the part of researchers and better communication to nontechnical readers would improve their interaction between researchers and users. One need only to go through some of our marketing and advertising journals to see how many research articles are written to communicate to other researchers and not to the policymakers.

A third problem is the lack of background on the part of researchers in the legal framework in which regulators have to operate. A stronger effort should be made to school researchers in legalistic approaches and the problems faced by policy makers. This should continue on a regular basis with meetings or institutes set up to bring researchers and policymakers together on a regular basis.

There have been some encouraging steps in the direction of improving interaction between researchers and regulators. One was a series of hearings the first of which was held in 1973 at which leading researchers and advertising professionals attempted to explain to FTC commissioners and some of their staff what they have found out about how advertising works and how it influences consumers. The conferences helped the commissioners understand the extent to which large corporations, advertising agencies, independent research firms and advertising media are researching the communication process. They also found out how creative people translate these findings into television commercials and print advertisements. The conference resulted in heightened interest on the part of commissioners in behavioral research, in some effort to bring academic researchers to the FTC on a temporary basis, to add behavioral scientists to their staffs, in inviting marketing professors to spend a semester or two in Washington working with them and in greater acceptance in general of behavioral findings.

There is evidence also that policymakers are more interested in the wealth of research that has become available in the middle and later 1970s on "consumer information processing." Some of these studies have been summarized in an excellent monograph by Wilkie [17], published by the government.

IV. Conclusion

The mechanism for the regulation of advertising is a complicated, cumbersome, often slow-moving one. It is not surprising that both the regulators and the regulated at times become impatient with its slowness and the often ambiguous resolution of so many regulatory problems. However, self-regulatory groups are certainly improving in efficiency and in stature in the eyes of fellow business people—especially the NARB. The consumer groups are militant but not particularly well organized, and certainly the most reluctant of all groups to use research in any meaningful way. All too often they are suspicious of it.

It is encouraging to see the Federal Trade Commission dip a tentative toe into the eddies of behavioral science, although it is clear that there is still much suspicion around the corridors of the Federal Trade Commission Building in Washington. It is encouraging also to find that courts are more and more open to research data and that consumer researchers are so much in demand as expert witnesses at court proceedings.

Complicated as it is to make real progress today in advertising regulation, certain approaches do hold out some promise for improvement. One is an organized effort to educate both the regulators and the regulated as to what we can expect from research and how it can if wisely used make regulation more efficient and more equitable for all. Another is the development of certain standards for comparing advertising and consumer behavior on a continuing basis. A third is the organization of a mechanism for continuing and fairly frequent interaction between the researchers and the regulators.

REFERENCES

1. Dunn, S. Watson, and Barban, Arnold M. *Advertising: Its Role in Modern Marketing*, 4th edition. Hinsdale, Ill: Dryden Press, 1978, p. 84.
2. Preston, Ivan L. *The Great American Blow-Up*. Madison, Wisc.: University of Wisconsin Press, 1975, p. 4.
3. Levitt, Theodore. "The Morality of Advertising." *Harvard Business Review*, July–August 1970.
4. Cunningham, Isabella C. M. and Cunningham, William H. "Standards for Advertising Regulation." *Journal of Marketing*, October 1977.
5. Gardner, David M. "Deception in Advertising: A Received-Channel Approach to Understanding." *Journal of Advertising*, Fall 1976, pp. 5–11.
6. Ward, Scott. "Effects of Television Advertising on Children." Boston: Marketing Science Institute, 1971, pp. 16–19; and "Children and Promotion." Boston, Mass.: Marketing Science Institute, 1972, pp. 9–13.
7. *FTC Staff Report on Television Advertising to Children*. Washington, D.C.: FTC, February 1978.
8. Griffin, Emilie. "What's Fair to Children? The Policy Need for New Research on Children's Perception of Advertising Content." *Journal of Advertising*, Spring 1976.
9. Greyser, Stephen A., and Reece, Bonnie B. "Businessmen Look Hard at Advertising." *Harvard Business Review*, May–June 1971, pp. 9–10; and S. Watson Dunn and David A. Yorke, "European Executives Look at Advertising." *Columbia Journal of World Business*, Winter 1974, pp. 54–60.
10. Stridsberg, Albert B. *Progress in Effective Advertising Self-Regulation*. New York: International Advertising Association, 1976.
11. Sandage, C. H., Fryburger, Vernon, and Rotzall, Kim. *Advertising Theory and Practice*. 10th edition. Homewood, Ill.: Richard D. Irwin, 1979, pp. 656–657.
12. Zanot, Eric J. "The National Advertising Review Board: Precedents, Premises and Performance." Unpublished doctoral dissertation. University of Illinois, 1977, p. 202.
13. Engel, James F. "Advertising and the Consumer." *Journal of Advertising*, Summer 1974.
14. Greyser, Stephen A., and Diamond, Steven L. "Business Is Adapting to Consumerism." *Harvard Business Review*, September–October 1974, p. 9.
15. Permut, Steven E. "Research on Consumer Information: Public Sector Perspectives." Paper delivered at International Symposium on Consumer Information, sponsored by the European Research Association for Consumer Affairs, and the Commission of the European Communities. Brussels, Belgium, November 23–25, 1977.
16. Jacoby, Jacob, Chestnut, Robert W., and Silverman, William. "Consumer Use and Comprehension of Nutrition Information." Purdue Papers in Consumer Psychology 163, 1976.
17. Wilkie, William L. *Assessment of Consumer Information Processing Research in Relation to Public Policy Needs*. Washington, D.C.: Government Printing Office, 1975.

21 The Concerns of the Rich/Poor Consumer

Lee E. Preston and Paul N. Bloom

© 1983 by the Regents of the University of California. Reprinted from *California Management Review*, Vol. 26, No. 1, pp. 100–119 by permission of the Regents.

The contemporary consumer environment is turbulent. Familiar necessities like heating fuel, food, and medical care have risen dramatically in price, while unfamiliar luxuries like video games, portable headphone-stereos, and designer clothes have suddenly become commonplace. Middle income families, stunned by inflation and an abrupt reduction in lifestyle expectations, have become intensely concerned with pocketbook issues, while young "up-scale" professionals plunge into condominium ownership and health-club contracts without reading the fine print. The structure of consumer interests and issues that evolved over the past two decades has become fragmented and diffused, and established approaches and programs in both government and business are being reviewed, revised, or abandoned.

There is, however, no indication that either the number or the urgency of consumer concerns has declined. Quite the contrary, persistent stagflation and sudden changes in relative prices and incomes have intensified some old problems and also given rise to new ones. Even while the Reagan Administration attempts to implement its claimed mandate to deregulate the economy, polls continue to show a clear majority of the general public concerned about "business exploitation of consumers" and in favor of strong consumer protection regulation.[1] The agenda of consumer policy issues confronting business and government—and the consumer organizations as well—remains long and compelling. This agenda is, however, different—both in overall structure and in specific detail—from what it has been in the past, and both the appropriate modes of policy formation and the content of effective policy responses will prove to be different as well.

This essay seeks to review and formulate the consumer policy agenda as a guide to policy making, both private and public, in the light of the changed environment of the 1980s and the likely outlook for the rest of the century. This new formulation is based upon our own observations and on the proceedings of two conferences involving some two hundred leading analysts, executives, policy makers, and consumer advocates.[2] We have drawn freely upon the viewpoints expressed at these sessions, synthesizing and interpreting them in ways that may not be clearly recognizable to their original authors.

We focus here on *policy issues*—i.e., matters that responsible persons may reasonably be expected to *do* something about—rather than simply on trends, basic social conflicts, or continuing differences of opinion. Neither trends (the aging population, the communications revolution) nor attitudinal differences (hedonism vs. asceticism; individualism vs. communitarianism) are policy issues in themselves, although they may give rise to issues and may have impact on the range and effectiveness of possible policy responses. Our focus here is on *consumer* policy—that is, policy issues associated with the consumption of goods and services by domestic households, and defined and viewed from *their* perspective.

The Old Agenda: Rights Through Regulation

Consumer policy from 1960 to 1980 centered on the achievement of the four elements of the Consumer Bill of Rights outlined initially by President John F. Kennedy in his Message to Congress of March 15, 1962:

- The right to safety.
- The right to be informed.
- The right to choose.
- The right to be heard.

These general objectives were more or less endorsed by both Presidents Johnson and Nixon. President Gerald Ford added a fifth:

- The right to consumer education.

Professor E. Scott Maynes has more recently distilled from the literature two more:

- The right to representation and participation in policy-making bodies (as distinct from the "right to be heard" in private sector decision-making).
- The right to recourse and redress.[3]

An underlying "right to consume" was apparently taken for granted in all of these formulations, leaving unaddressed the possibility that this more fundamental "right" might be abridged by inadequate purchasing power and/or by measures taken in pursuit of some of the other "rights" themselves.[4]

Consumer policy in the 1960's was intended to achieve these proclaimed "rights" primarily through regulation, and with the principal initiative coming from the federal government. Two different regulatory approaches were utilized. In some instances, business was required to perform specified functions directly for consumers (as in Truth-in-Lending and Truth-in-Packaging) or to modify its behavior in other ways (e.g.,

FTC affirmative disclosure requirements). In other instances, business was required to conform to specific government-set standards and reporting requirements (as in auto safety and emissions standards). The latter approach involved considerably more initiative and activity by government and made use of the power of large government purchases to influence compliance. Both approaches required extensive compliance effort and expense on the part of business.

The pursuit of rights through regulation was not without its successes. Product safety and health protections were improved in a number of specific instances (lawnmowers, toys, water and air pollution), and the general emphasis on safety probably had economy-wide effects. On the other hand, prescribed product quality standards in many instances increased costs and eliminated alternatives preferred by some buyers. New procedural safeguards were alleged to discourage new product development (as in the case of prescription drugs). In case after case, an operational definition of "safety" eluded common sense. The Delaney amendment banned cancer-causing food *additives*, not cancer-causing foods or tobacco. An appropriate trade-off between the hazards, costs, and benefits of new vs. old technologies and products proved difficult to make. Indeed, attempts to introduce economic rationality into such decisions ran up against the realities of political rationality (as in the case of seat-belt interlocks), and cost-benefit methodology generated its own cadre of disillusioned, and highly sophisticated, critics.[5]

The related rights "to be informed" and "to consumer education" generated noticeable amounts of activity, but the results were even less clear. Drug package inserts, Truth-in-Lending documents, and product warning labels littered the landscape, but much of the "information" contained in these materials did not appear to be used, or even useable, by consumers.

The "right to be heard" has probably been most importantly expanded by a voluntary increase in complaint-handling efforts (consumer hot-lines and other quick-response techniques) on the part of business. Consumer affairs offices, both public and private, have made the stimulation of these services one of their principal activities. Some businesses have also given their consumer offices a role to play in the design of products and services, the review of advertising claims, and the provision of marketing research data. However, the influence of most offices in these areas has been limited.

All of these informational and service efforts for consumers undoubtedly expand their "right to choose" in the sense that choices may be better informed and dependable. In addition, some de-regulatory initiatives, antitrust enforcement, and support of specific competition-expanding policies (such as generic drug identification) have clearly contributed to some widening of the range of consumer choice in the marketplace.

In spite of the adversary atmosphere that the regulatory approach generated, one surviving theme from the 1960s era is a widespread recognition of the *mutual interest* of business, government, and consumers in the identification of consumer concerns and the development of appropriate responses. Denial ("There isn't any jug, and anyway it isn't broken.") is no longer a viable business response to widespread consumer dissatisfaction. Nor is easy resolution through government directive ("We'll *make* them do it.") an effective response for bureaucrats. Both a long-run marketing perspective and a self-serving desire to attract customers while avoiding product liability suits account for the widespread perception that "consumer protection is business protection."[6] The stage may be set for the development of new modes of consumer policy formation, as well as new substantive responses, to the problems and challenges posed by a new environment.

THE NEW ENVIRONMENT: SCARCITY AND ABUNDANCE

> We are gathered here today not merely to dedicate a shopping mall but to rededicate ourselves, mind and body, to the spirit of consumerism, and to seek an ever more deeply indebted relationship to the process of purchasing merchandise.
>
> *"Congressman Bob Forehead"*
> in WASHINGTOON, The Village Voice

The world wide consumer movement of the 1960s and early 1970s took place primarily within an environment of increasing production and productivity. Consumerism was a "baby of prosperity."[7] However, as Scherf has noted, consumerism "was not born out of the gratitude of consumers for their good fortune...but out of a desire for 'more.'"[8] And, even more surprisingly, the demands for "more" focused not on continued increases in the quantity of goods and services available (indeed, a counter-trend toward "voluntary simplicity" emerged in some quarters), but on "more satisfaction" through a reduction in hazards and problems and an improvement in the overall quality of life. "Consumer policy," in the sense of collective action that might affect *general* consumer interests, became a topic of widespread discussion, and not only in the U.S. The OECD Committee on Consumer Policy issued a major factual compendium on member countries in 1972, and annual reports from 1974 onward. In 1977, the *Journal of Consumer Policy* was established in Germany with an international list of editors and contributors, and the material appearing there attested clearly to the substance and seriousness of worldwide interest in the subject.

In all of this activity it was implicitly assumed that increased consumer well-being, along with environmental protection and an improved quality of working life, was among the social benefits made possible by continuing prosperity and productivity gains. However, by the mid-1970s it began to become apparent—at least in the U.S.—that this assumption was no longer valid. Instead, critical shortages and rapidly increasing prices occurred in one sector of the economy after another, and instability in major industries undermined established patterns of income and employment. At the same time—while cheap energy became a thing of the past and the cost of a single-family dwelling rose beyond the reach of a major share of households—startling new products otherwise associated with affluence became commonplace and the demand for more from the entertainment industry—including professional sports—increased enormously.

This turbulent environment is the habitat of the rich/poor consumer. Economy-wide inflation is an important part of the picture, but the more significant phenomena are the changes in *relative* prices and incomes, and the consequent shifts in status and lifestyle, that occur within the great secular inflation wave. This turbulence will probably continue, perhaps even increase, during the transitional years of the eighties and when (and if) it subsides, the shape of the economic landscape will be quite different from what it was before.

Several different, but closely related, processes are going on at once. The permanent underclass of the disadvantaged is growing with the addition of an aging population and the casualties of economic decline in the older industrial sectors and regions. External forces (e.g., changes in job locations and skill requirements), the growing mass of the underclass, and cut-backs in government assistance programs increase the difficulty of returning to the economic and social mainstream. Distinctions between lifestyles and expectations associated with "comfort" and "need" have become sharpened and entrenched. And, as a result of changing *relative* prices and incomes, households well above the poverty line are beginning to feel and act "poor," even while they are constantly confronted with, and occasionally adopt, the consumption opportunities of contemporary affluence. Indeed, since all but the direst poverty is clearly relative, even families in very low economic brackets occasionally sample the smorgasbords of the rich. Thus, the great mass of U.S. consumers are both "rich" and "poor" at once, and policies for dealing with their problems need to reflect this new complexity.

DEALING WITH SCARCITY

"Sometimes I have to shoplift packages of beef stew for my son and me. You just pray you're not going to get caught."
Divorced mother with a $230 part-time job, whose welfare payments were reduced to $172 a month,
The Wall Street Journal

Contemporary consumers are affected by three distinct forms of scarcity. One is *traditional scarcity* associated with inadequate levels of household income. This familiar condition has been aggravated both by economy-wide inflation and recession and by industrial change. These have increased substantially the number of vulnerable households and significantly altered their consumption patterns, even though many of the new "have nots" remain well above the poverty level. The second contemporary form of scarcity is associated with periodic *specific shortages* of critical basic commodities—gasoline, sugar, etc. These shortages have been largely due to external developments, although the extent to which they have been or could be affected by domestic policies and actions is debatable. Finally, there is the problem of *induced scarcity*: those shortages and price increases that result from deliberate policies of government, often with the strong collaboration of affected business and labor. These three types of scarcity require different kinds of policy responses.

Traditional Scarcity

Consumer goods and services are always scarce in households with inadequate income. The development of an underclass consisting of such households has been a well-observed phenomenon of the post-war decades. In spite of the inflationary boom of the late sixties, massive expenditures for maintaining subsistence, and the "War on Poverty," this persisting underclass has been a major domestic policy disappointment. There is, unfortunately, nothing new about the existence of this "other America," nor is there any sign that its situation will be significantly altered in the near future. What *is* new at the present time, however, is the massive shift of formerly middle class families from "have" into "have not" status as a result of the loss of purchasing power due to general inflation and loss of income and employment caused by recession and industrial change.[9] These families are distinguished from the hardcore underclass by their accumulated assets (and debts) and their established consumption patterns and lifestyles. They are not acclimated to the culture of poverty, but they are in straitened circumstances. With reduced incomes and the need to consume out of savings, they are prime targets for low-price merchandising in all its forms. In particular, they are willing to substitute time and inconvenience for money by pumping their own gas, bagging their own groceries, performing do-it-yourself repairs and services, and searching for basic bargain models of household durables.

From the business perspective, the important point is that these families constitute a substantial and growing market. Effective business response involves an emphasis on "pocketbook consumerism"—discount pricing, providing "no-frills" versions of products and services, and offering information clearly designed to guide consumers toward "best buys." Special efforts to meet the needs of highly vulnerable consumers—such as Giant Food's recent program to *give* the poor edible but unsaleable items like dented cans and wilted produce—may also yield substantial public relations benefits.

On the government and philanthropic side, a wide assortment of actions can help alleviate the plight of the "have not" consumers. Continued or increased subsidization—in the form of food stamps, free cheese, health insurance, discounted mass transit, and low-interest mortgages and loans—can help many people. Innovative approaches—such as schemes that enable older people to extract a portion of the equity of their homes for living expenses, while continuing to live in them as long as they are able to do so—can respond to problems of imbalance between assets and income. Consumer education and direct assistance (e.g., "meals on wheels") efforts make an important contribution, and broader initiatives such as the establishment of weekly "farmers markets" in urban neighborhoods can widen the range of choice for both producers and consumers. All responsible groups can be vigilant in monitoring "bargain" offers aimed at vulnerable groups so as to assure their legitimacy and appropriateness.

Specific Shortages

Periodic shortages and associated rapid price increases for individual products pose quite different problems. Although, like most other social ills, these developments usually have their greatest impact on low income groups, policy response to the shortage of individual products necessarily involves the consuming public as a whole. Assuming that the shortage itself cannot be forestalled or rapidly eliminated, the policy response has two main dimensions: anticipation and adjustment. Responses in both dimensions were conspicuously inadequate during the commodities shocks of the seventies.

A major problem with devising better responses to this type of scarcity is that many of the superficially appealing schemes—those involving rationing, taxes, and subsidies—are immensely complicated and costly. They inevitably generate negative side effects, such as black markets, which may simply worsen the situation. Therefore, a preferable policy response from both business and government involves developing alternatives wherever possible and facilitating reductions in consumption. Examples of this are the carpooling programs generated by employers, unions, and local governments during the gasoline shortage and the energy-saving practices being urged more recently by electric power companies. The coming environment will probably provide many more opportunities for various forms of de-marketing, either market-wide or for specific types of users. To some extent, the use of de-marketing strategies is a complement to an emphasis on "best buy" products. The elimination of products or product attributes *not* offering favorable values may become an innovative, although perhaps dangerous, marketing strategy for the eighties. Such a strategy might involve removal of non-nutritious foods or potentially hazardous products from the market, or a reduction in color, style, or performance options on durable goods.

Induced Scarcities

With respect to induced scarcities, the obvious proposal that they should not be induced in the first place is, unfortunately, wrong. The fact is that deliberate business and government policies to induce scarcity and increase prices are adopted for clear and compelling reasons; and the mere allegation that these will result in harm to consumers is unlikely to cause them to be reversed. However, it is important that the consumer impact of deliberate scarcity policies be recognized and taken into account in public discussion. The Russian Wheat Deal of 1973, although not specifically designed to have domestic market impact, resulted in a doubling of wheat prices and transferred $1 billion from consumers to farmers.[10] Current "voluntary quotas" on imports of Japanese automobiles have already raised domestic auto prices by almost $2000 per car, and proposed "local content" legislation would result in even greater increases.[11]

DEALING WITH ABUNDANCE

> "Fifty thousand dollars a year. What can you do with it really? Just eat and sleep and make a down payment on a home. These days it's just a decent wage."
> *$12,000-a-year security guard, father of eight, and first winner of Washington, D.C. $1 million lottery ($50,000-a-year for 20 years),* The Washington Post

The classic focus of the contemporary consumer movement has been on dealing with abundance. Making wise choices among a wide range of products, evaluating individual product features, and understanding the trade-offs among performance alternatives have been conventional goals. The proclaimed rights "to be informed" and "to choose" are essential in our rich and varied market environment.

Paradoxically, the goals of adequate information and wise choice are made more difficult, not easier, by the contemporary explosion of new technologies and products. As Daniel Bell has pointed out, the very wealth of the post-industrial environment has created new kinds of scarcities, particularly of *information* and *time*:

When there's so much [knowledge] we have to have better judgment...and more guides to tell us what's relevant and what's not....The growth of knowledge means...we have more problems in dealing with it....Time is an absolute standard....You can't build a stock of time the way you can build a stock of capital....In an industrial society the producer was basically the economist....[But] in a post-industrial era, it's the consumer who becomes the economist, calculating cost-benefit, opportunity cost and trade-offs, in his allocation of time, information and money.[12]

It has been widely believed, or at least been desired, that the contemporary innovations in communications and electronics would greatly increase the amount of consumer information available and decrease search costs. Experience to date suggests precisely the opposite. Consumers are confronted with a mystifying array of new product and service alternatives—home computers, video games, health maintenance plans, telephone contact systems, energy-conservation devices, money market funds, etc.—many of which have totally unfamiliar performance features. The costs (including installation and routine operation) and benefits of many of these items are genuinely difficult to understand and estimate. Maintenance and enhancement features are not readily comprehended by the inexperienced. (Consider the state of common knowledge of the automobile, after half a century of widespread use.) It is no exaggeration to say that the "communications revolution" and its related technologies have, at least to date, exacerbated rather than mitigated the informational and choice problems of consumers.

The two areas of consumption currently presenting the greatest dilemmas of abundance are financial services and health care. The media are filled with ads featuring interest-bearing bank accounts, 24-hour teller locations, new insurance protections (and limitations), and personal financial services. Many of these offerings are genuinely new. Some are competitive alternatives made possible by changing government regulations; others are new options created in response to changing financial needs and life-styles. Similarly, increasing health care costs and expenditures have spawned an incredible array of service alternatives and pre-payment plans. Major employers are now sponsoring a range of options with a wide variety of contributory, deduction, and service features. Consumers are genuinely baffled by the range of choice available in both of these areas. Unlike the equally perplexing range of computer options, both financial services and health care are purchased as necessities by the great mass of consumers. The two areas share many common features: both are services rather than goods, and hence involve some descriptive ambiguity as well as considerable case-by-case variability; both involve complex combinations of features, for which trade-offs are hard to analyze and evaluate; and finally, criteria for "good value" and "best buy" vary greatly depending upon the particular characteristics of the consuming household and on future developments that cannot be anticipated.

Policy proposals for dealing with this new abundance move in two different directions. One is an informational approach which attempts to develop sets of performance criteria for new and unfamiliar products and devise means for describing and rating them for convenient reference and comparison by both producers and consumers. This could be done by government agencies, trade associations, individual companies, or other organizations. The various energy-conservation ratings now in use (e.g., EPA mileage ratings) are examples. Unfortunately, conscientious attempts to provide more comprehensive information in complex product/service areas—such as the large matrices of data provided by *Washington Checkbook*—often convey little more to the consumer than the fact that "this is even more complicated than I thought."

The other and more controversial policy approach involves organizing and channeling the flow of consumer information already passing, or available for transmission, through new communications systems. The new communications environment is incredibly "noisy." Relevant pieces of data are fluid and fugitive within an electronic system subject to abuse through manipulation and drown-out. (How many commercials did you see during the last television station break? What products do you remember? Why?) Although any restriction or selectivity in the information flow (e.g., Sears' proposal to transmit information over its own cable TV channel) raises issues of both monopoly and free speech. The notion that all additions to the number and volume of signals being sent constitute "increasing information" is clearly preposterous; in fact, they are more nearly the opposite. Some combination of reducing the communications "noise" and organizing the large volume of data (as, for example, in "classified" advertising) could clearly increase the amount of useable information available.

PROCESS ISSUES AND RESPONSES

In twenty years of political brawling, I have from time to time been disconcerted to recognize decent (though benighted) impulses lurking in adversary's breast. And a small voice occasionally breaks through the rhetoric of combat to urge that true problem solving means bridging controversy, achieving empathy with adversaries, seeking common ground, compromise and accommodation, not polarization.

Michael Pertschuk, Revolt Against Regulation

Up to this point we have focused primarily on the *substance* of consumer policy issues. Now we turn attention to the *processes* that might be used to achieve various objectives and to issues involving consumption-related processes themselves without regard to specific application. Process issues will become increasingly prominent and controversial over the coming decade, largely because the tendency of both government and business to fall back on inappropriate but conventional processes (regulation, advertising) to deal with new and emerging situations will prove increasingly unsatisfactory.

The processes used by governments to respond to consumer concerns fall into four categories:

- *formal regulation,* in which government is primarily responsible both for articulating specific goals and bringing about corrective actions;
- *private litigation* within a framework established by government authority;
- *subsidization*, both to needy individuals and needy business; and
- *facilitation*, including education and information, but with a new emphasis on participative and conciliatory activity among groups with diverse interests.

Although these four policy alternatives appear quite distinct in principle, in practice they tend to overlap and intertwine. They also involve a variety of responses and initiatives from the private sector.

Regulation

We noted earlier that the main thrust of the consumer movement for the past two decades was the achievement of "rights" through regulation.[13] As compared to prior eras, policy shifted first toward greater reliance on formal governmental authority and second—within the regulatory process itself—toward primary reliance on federal, rather than state and local, responsibility. Many factors account for this direction of development and some of them continue to have considerable validity even in the greatly changed regulatory environment of the eighties.

Two fundamental considerations underlie the support for government regulation. One is that since at least some consumer damage is very difficult to correct or recompense, regulatory action that prevents damage from occurring in the first place is desirable and very probably cost-effective. The entire history of health and safety regulation in both the workplace and the consumption environment is predicated on this proposition. The other consideration favoring a regulatory approach is the imbalance of resources and power between individual consumers and consumer groups, on the one hand, and individual producers and producer groups, on the other. Even if consumers suffer merely economic harm—so that financial restitution could in principle make the damaged party whole again—the time and expense involved in pursuing solutions through private action suggests an unequal battle.

Forces underlying the emphasis on federal, rather than state and local, authority were similar. Consumer problems were rarely differentiated by state boundaries, and producers and merchants were typically multi-state in their operations. Consumer groups were better organized and probably had greater clout at the national level and national policy action assured that malefactors did not escape behind the walls of state authority.

Given the continuing validity of these considerations and the considerable structure of regulatory activity that has been erected upon them, the current anti-regulatory climate may seem hard to understand. Yet, as part of the general disillusionment with activist government, there is widespread dissatisfaction with the federal regulatory approach to many consumer problems. The contrast with environmental protection, which apparently is receiving increasing public support and business acceptance, is instructive. The environmental protection movement can point to some notable successes which were achieved primarily through rule-making and enforcement proceedings ("continuous" regulation). Case-by-case compliance procedures have actually involved only a small number of firms, local governments, and other sources of environmental impact. By contrast, the successes of consumer protection are harder to identify when even the most conspicuous (drug safety, flammable fabrics) seem to involve only small fractions of the population and isolated items in the giant consumption cornucopia. Moreover, the bulk of consumer protection activity has been ad hoc and complaint-focused. Remedial actions are not confined to remote sources but affect the mass of consumers in ways that often seem costly, intrusive, and conducive to new dissatisfactions. The saga of auto safety devices provides the classic illustration.

Perceived dissatisfaction with federal regulation has generated two policy adjustments: de-regulation and devolution (i.e., the return of regulatory control to the states). De-regulation activity has already brought about major changes in particular industries (e.g., transportation, banking, and communications). A significant rollback in federal regulatory control over advertising and product safety seems to be in the offing. The issue of where and how much to de-regulate—and where to *re*-regulate—will remain the focus of considerable debate. Dissatisfaction with the results of de-regulation (from communities that have lost all airline service, for example) will inevitably emerge, just as complaints about regulation itself did in the past. Calls for continued or renewed regulatory activity will become more frequent. The confusion many consumers experience in dealing with the new abundance of specialized airline fares, financial services, and communications devices may spur demand for the creation of a simpler, if less exciting, regulated environment. Cases like the Tylenol poisonings highlight the security promised by a stricter regulatory regime.

Calls for maintaining or increasing federal regulatory activity could also emerge from those members of the business community who are concerned about the problems created by devolution and the growth of state and local regulatory activity. De-regulation has not, as yet, taken hold on the state and local level. Between 1980 and 1981, the number of proposed state regulations actually doubled, rising to a total of 50,000. Within the business community this activity created concern about "regulatory Balkanization" and stimulated interest in new federal pre-emptive legislation. State level "bottle bills," franchise-protection laws, deceptive advertising rules, and the like are proving to be thorns in the sides of many businesses. This situation seems likely to continue, since consumer activism apparently maintains its greatest strength at the grassroots level. While national consumer groups struggle for dollars and attention, many grassroots organizations are able to maintain their funding and activity levels, which then allows them to continue to pressure legislatures, attorney generals, and consumer policy officials for more vigorous consumer protection action. For example, the New York State Public Interest Research Group (a Ralph Nader affiliate) now has a $2.5 million budget and 180 full-time staff members.[15]

Private Litigation

Private litigation of consumer issues has increased dramatically in recent years. The huge number of product liability suits—and the large awards and settlements that have resulted from them—have probably helped to accelerate the recall or removal of products after defects are discovered (as in the case of Procter and Gamble's Rely tampon) and may have deterred marketing of many unsafe and hazardous products. To a much lesser extent, private antitrust actions have helped consumers by increasing freedom of choice in certain markets (e.g., *Berkey Photo vs. Kodak*; MCI's challenge to AT&T before the FCC).

Increased reliance on private litigation as a consumer protection process seems more likely in the future, particularly if formal regulation continues to be reduced. However, private litigation has at least two features that limit its effectiveness for policy-development. One is the problem of nuisance suits. Laws and rules of procedure may have to be modified to avoid clogging the courts with suits filed by eager lawyers willing to take on almost anything on a contingency fee basis. The second, and far more serious, problem associated with private litigation has to do with the imbalance of financial resources that typically exists between the defending business firms and the complaining parties. Class-action suits in which numerous less well-off parties band together against wealthier defendants create the possibility of enormous judgments and may generate corrective behavior or restitution as well as deter anti-consumer behavior. Although consumer class actions have not had great success in the past, recent proceedings in Cleveland led to a settlement in which three supermarkets will distribute more than $20 million in merchandise to citizens over a five year period.

Subsidization

Governments do not treat all individuals and organizations equally. Some individuals are entitled to food stamps, cheaper mortgages, or free health care, while some businesses are entitled to cheaper loans, special tax breaks, or tariff protection. While the consequences of these various forms of subsidy for the general consumer have typically been overlooked—both in discussion of the subsidies themselves and in consideration of consumer policy issues—we anticipate growing concern about the economy-wide effects of the great number and variety of current subsidy programs. This concern will increase, in part, because processes of economic change now underway are rapidly expanding the number of people and firms entitled to receive subsidies.

Facilitation and Conciliation

Many consumer problems can be made less severe without the use of regulations, lawsuits, or subsidies, and thus without the conflict and controversy often associated with these techniques. Governments can employ processes that rely less on coercion and confrontation, and more on cooperation and hard work. The establishment of an Office of Consumer Affairs in the White House—and now in hundreds of local and state governments—is an obvious example. Another example is found in the "consumer advocacy" programs of the FTC, in which the entire Commission, or a single Commissioner and/or staff unit, can intervene in federal regulatory processes on behalf of competitive and consumer considerations.[16] Consumer education and information programs would also fall under this rubric, as would programs designed to bring potentially hostile parties together to propose voluntary actions that might be taken to deal with consumer problems. A recent Consumer Product Safety Commission initiative to develop new voluntary safety standards for electric blankets provides an example, as does the U.S. Office of Consumer Affairs' effort to set up consumer mediation panels designed to settle consumer-seller disputes in certain industries (e.g., automobiles). Most of these new types of initiatives are still in the very early stages and both their costs and effectiveness are difficult to predict. Experimentation with such policy processes is a priority item on the current consumer agenda for both business and government.

Private Sector Initiatives

All of the government policy regimes mentioned imply, of course, a corresponding response from the private sector. Active compliance can make regulation less burdensome and more effective; recalcitrance can make it both costly and useless. Litigation opportunities and subsidy programs can be either appropriately pursued or abused. Non-adversarial initiatives are made fruitful by cooperation, useless by its opposite.

In addition to these responses to government initiatives, the private sector also has displayed significant process initiatives of its own. A major development of the past couple of decades has been the growth of the corporate consumer affairs function and the establishment of formal Consumer Affairs Offices within major business firms.[17] The number of such offices now exceeds 600; and membership in the Society of Consumer Affairs Professionals, which provides a meeting ground for both government and business personnel working in this area, has grown to 1200. Under the stimulus of these professionals, consumer advisory boards have been established in some firms—most conspicuously the consumer boards connected with local public utilities—and other new avenues for the expression of consumer concerns, including more broadly-focused consumer market surveys, have been developed. A related trend has been the publication by many firms of formal "Codes of Conduct," which include standards for dealing with consumers as well as with employees and others. This approach has been strongly emphasized in Great Britain, where it is particularly encouraged by trade associations under the sponsorship of the Office of Fair Trading.[18] The most notable example of industry self-regulation in the U.S. is the nationwide advertising review procedure operated by the Council of Better Business Bureaus. Finally, there are a few other examples of non-adversarial and conciliatory approaches to common problems arising entirely from the private sector and modeled on the joint business-environmental effort that became the National Coal Policy Project.[19]

THE SPECIAL PROBLEM OF PUBLIC SERVICES

The annual expenditures of all levels of government are more than half as great as total consumer expenditures for goods and services ($1.1 trillion and $2 trillion respectively, in 1982). Although about 15% of total government spending is for defense, the remainder—consisting primarily of transfer payments, costs of government programs, and direct provision of goods and services—has a wide range of direct and indirect impacts on consumers. An international forecast of consumer issues conducted for Nestlé notes the widespread perception that the state is the "biggest firm" with which consumers deal and anticipates increasing consumer pressure in this area.[20]

Contemporary attention to the consumer impact of government activity as a *general* matter (not simply with respect to isolated issues) was initially raised in Roland McKean's presidential address to the Southern Economic Association in 1973,[21] and has now become a well-recognized topic in the literature. Although McKean's initial coverage was very broad indeed, Dennis R. Young has emphasized the need to separate macro-societal policies and those with only indirect impact from policies involving direct government contact with the individual consumers and households.[22] Even with respect to the latter, there is a great difference between contacts involving access to income maintenance programs, at one extreme, and those involving individual use of specific services (transport, postal) on the other; somewhere in between are the basic services of fire and police protection. Public education seems to raise the complete range of public service consumption issues.

Young notes that the individual consumer faces four kinds of problems in dealing with this whole range of offerings:

- *Disappointing goods and services*—those that fail to meet consumer expectations;
- *Awareness and coping*—knowledge of the availability of public services and the means of obtaining them;
- *Preference-matching*—inability to get less, more, or different quality services than those provided by a particular political jurisdiction;
- *Access and location*—availability of and access to specific service within a jurisdiction (e.g., the need to move to obtain better public schools, or to purchase transport in order to use public health care).

Although all of these kinds of problems have their parallels in the private marketplace, their importance in the public sector is heightened by the monopoly position of government (either de jure or de facto) in many types of services and locations and the weak connection between the "tax-price" (tax charge per unit of service rendered) and actual costs, benefits, or consumption decisions.

Consumption of public services in all forms raises complex issues of scarcity, abundance, and process. Leaving aside the problems of adequacy and access to income maintenance programs, and the indirect effects of McKean's list of "anti-consumer public goods (and bads)" such as tariffs, price supports, subsidies and perverse regulations, many direct consumption concerns remain. Increased demand for public payment for medical care, intense pressures on public transportation systems, etc., reflect the scarcity impacts of rising costs and falling incomes.

Simultaneously, increasing needs for conventional services—police and fire protection, refuse collection, civic facilities—and interest in increased public support for education, the arts, and cultural activities reflect increasing affluence. The Tiebout hypothesis holds that individuals will locate so as to create homogeneous clusters, in each of which an optimal (for its residents) array of public services will be offered.[23] Complete reliance on this process to balance the supply and demand for public services neglects the fact that such moves are often costly (and involve many considerations other than public service availability) and also overlooks the impact of the clustering itself on the cost and availability of local amenities. Moreover, in the larger environment where services are "globally public," there may be no way to escape or "exit," and therefore individual "voice" and public protest become the only real alternative. For example, the Center for Auto Safety, an organization originally established by Ralph Nader but now independent, has recently brought suit against the Federal Highway Administration charging that the highway system is not being maintained and that the routes have become "killers from end to end" because of inadequate repair.[24]

The fact that the citizen consumer is himself a part of the government machinery may make process issues even more complex and difficult in the public sector than in the private market. The government as watchdog is, of course, entirely missing (except, of course, for the state surveillance of municipalities, federal of states, etc.). The overt political character of public service production decisions would seem to increase the openness and participative character of the decision process. However, the large scope of the issues, the remoteness of the ballot box from the committee room, and the gap between the tax payment and the receipt of services all result in powerlessness and anonymity. An informal survey of public agencies by Enis and Yarwood "indicated that dissatisfied consumers of public services had no recourse."[25]

Increased attention to the consumer perspective on public services should be a high priority concern at every level of government. It seems likely that there will be lessons to be learned from the private sector about the technical efficiency of customer service operations; as well as about the provision of appropriate levels of variety; and about the adaptation of both quality and quantity offerings over time. The use of voucher systems to allocate both students and funds among alternative public schools is a process experiment with wide implications and potential.

CONCLUDING REMARKS

Consumer policy in both business and government has come a long way since President Kennedy proclaimed his "Consumer Bill of Rights" in 1962. Indeed, one might say that it has come full circle. The consumer affairs function is now well established in leading corporations. Ralph Nader has declared the U.S. Office of Consumer Affairs to be a fraud and asked that it be abolished.[26] It seems clear that the era of "rights through regulation" has come to an end, and that a new environment has come into being which gives rise to new issues and requires new types of policy responses. Consumer policy must shift from an ex post orientation focused on complaints and pre-existing problems to an ex ante and anticipatory approach focused on the distinctive attributes of different types of consumption situations.[27]

This new environment is the world of the rich/poor consumer. Although highly vulnerable economic and social groups continue to require special consideration, the great mass of American consumers are both rich and poor at the same time. They encounter different kinds of problems, which in turn give rise to different kinds of policy needs in different consumption situations. The distinction between the problems arising from scarcity (particularly in conventional consumption areas) and those arising from abundance (particularly with respect to new technologies, products, and services) offers a basis for re-formulating the consumer policy agenda. Process issues take on a new importance in the new high-communication, anti-regulation environment. Concerns involving the quality, availability, and cost of public services become more and more pressing as consumers come to rely increasingly on the public sector for essential daily needs (e.g., transportation).

Will consumer policy remain a significant agenda item for both business and government over the coming decade? It is clear that "consumerism" as a social movement is in, at the very least, what former FTC Chairman Michael Pertschuk has called a "pause."[28] Like most social movements, "consumerism" arose from a widespread public discontent—in this case discontent with the commercial product environment and a perception of corrupting and exploitative behavior on the part of business. The fact that this discontent developed in a setting of unprecedented affluence may appear paradoxical, but that does not reduce its reality. And as with other social movements, consumer concerns became focused through organizations, principally the Nader groups and their local and specialized variants.

Both the underlying sense of consumer unease and the organizations built upon it are still largely present. Indeed, both have become increasingly institutionalized within both business and government. Thus, it would appear that the basic theme of "consumerism"—and hence a continuing search for appropriate consumer policies—will continue, even if the strident rhetoric and activist flavor of the movement vanishes entirely. Moreover, as Pertschuk has emphasized, many consumer concerns are "unifying issues among disparate groups...[and] tend not to be broadly divisive."[29] It seems entirely possible that busi-

EXHIBIT 1. Consumer Policy Agenda

Scarcity Issues

- Meeting the basic needs of the poor.
- Responding to emerging needs of the "new" poor.
- Identifying economy values and "best buys."
- Protecting vulnerable consumers against scams and deceptions.
- Using self-service and limited selection to hold down costs.
- Allocating short supplies among uses and users.
- Developing reserve stocks and potential substitution possibilities in advance.
- Bringing the consumer impact of supply-limiting policies into explicit consideration in the policy process.

Abundance Issues

- Developing appropriate product/service descriptors and corresponding information in areas of important innovation and change—particularly: communications and electronics, financial services, and health care.
- Helping consumers to cut through the volume and variety of available information (and misinformation) to isolate relevant alternatives.
- Highlighting the long-term cost implications of new product/service offerings and lifestyles.

Process Issues

- Monitoring the cost and effectiveness of regulation; minimizing its restrictive impact on both business and consumers.
- Seeking optimal combinations of state/federal authority and responsibility.
- Assessing the need and impact of subsidies for both production and consumption.
- Reducing the unnecessary use, length and cost of private litigation of consumer problems.
- Seeking non-adversarial methods of identifying and resolving consumer issues.
- Encouraging more business initiative in developing innovative responses to consumer concerns.
- Making more effective use of consumer education and information programs.
- Increasing two-way communication and participation in consumer policy decisions in both business and government.

Public Services Issues

- Mitigating effects of government monopoly on service provision and pricing.
- Maintaining and/or improving service quality, controlling cost, and adapting activity to community needs.
- Experimenting with innovative approaches and consumer-oriented operating modes.

ness, government, and consumers themselves will come to see consumer policy issues less as major sources of conflict than as opportunities for consensus-seeking and socially constructive innovation.

REFERENCES

1. Louis Harris and Associates, *Consumerism in the Eighties* (Study No. 822047, conducted for Atlantic Richfield Company, February 1983); see also, Paul N. Bloom and Stephen A. Greyser, "Exploring the Future of Consumerism" (Marketing Science Institute, 1981).
2. Frank E. McLaughlin, ed., *The Future of Consumerisim*, (Center for Business and Public Policy, University of Maryland, 1981); Paul N. Bloom, ed., *Consumerism and Beyond*, (Marketing Science Institute, 1982). See also: H. B. Thorelli, "Consumer Rights and Consumer Policy: Setting the Stage," *Journal of Contemporary Business 7* (1979): 3–16; E. Scott Maynes, "Consumer Protection: The Issues" and "Consumer Protection: Corrective Measures," *Zeitschrift Für Verbraucherpolitik* [Journal of Consumer Policy] *3* (1979):97–109, 191–212; and R. Rock, B. Biervert, and W. F. Fischer-Winklemann, "A Critique of Some Fundamental Theoretical and Practical Tenets of Present Consumer Policy," ibid., 4 (1980):93–101.
3. Maynes, op. cit., p. 99.
4. The logical priority of "freedom to consume" is stressed by H. B. Thorelli and S. V. Thorelli, *Consumer Information Systems and Consumer Policy* (Ballinger, 1977), p. 35. These authors formulate a three-fold consumer policy agenda: education, information, and protection.
5. Steven Kelman, "Cost-Benefit Analysis, An Ethical Critique," *Regulation* (January/February 1981): 33–40; Lester B. Lave, *The Strategy of Social Regulation*, (Brookings, 1981).
6. Lee H. Bloom, "Corporations and Consumerism: Compatible Goals?" in Frank McLaughlin, op. cit., p. 24.
7. Business International, *Europe's Consumer Movement, Key Issues and Corporate Responses* (1980), p. 2.
8. G. W. H. Scherf, "Consumer Dissatisfaction—Search for Causes and Alleviation Outside the Marketplace," *Zeitschrift Für Verbraucherpolitik* [Journal of Consumer Policy] *1* (1977): 101–108.
9. For a comprehensive update on relevant data, see "Sharing the Wealth: The Gap Between Rich and Poor Grows Wider," *National Journal* (23 October 1982), pp. 1788–1795.
10. David L. Blond, "External Effects and United States Wheat Prices," *Business Economics* (September 1976), pp. 70–80.
11. *Domestic Content Legislation*, (Harbridge House, 1982).
12. Daniel Bell, "The Frameworks of the Future" (*Proceedings of the MSI 20th Anniversary Conference*, May 1982), pp. 41–42.
13. For an excellent review of major regulatory issues and a report on recent Canadian experience, see D. T. Scheffman and E. Appelbaum, *Social Regulation in Markets for Consumer Goods and Services* (Ontario Economic Council, 1982).

14. "Business Mobilizes as States Begin to Move into the Regulatory Vacuum," *National Journal* (31 July 1982), p. 1340.
15. Juan Williams, "Return from the Nadir," *The Washington Post Magazine* (23 May 1982), pp. 6–15.
16. U.S. Federal Trade Commission, "Competition and Consumer Advocacy Policy Review Session" (24 May 1982).
17. Claes Fornell, *Consumer Input for Marketing Decisions* (Praeger, 1976).
18. Jeremy Mitchell, "Government-Approved Codes of Practice: A New Approach to Reducing Friction Between Business and Consumers," *Zeitschrift Für Verbraucherpolitik* [Journal of Consumer Policy] 2 (1978): 144–58.
19. "Doing It Without the Government," *National Journal* (25 October 1980), p. 1806.
20. *Business International*, op. cit. p. III–34.
21. Roland N. McKean, "Government and the Consumer," *Southern Economic Journal 39* (1973): 481–89.
22. Dennis R. Young, "Consumer Problems in the Public Sector: A Framework for Research," *Zeitschrift Für Verbraucherpolitik* [Journal of Consumer Policy] 1 (1977): 205–206, with subsequent comments and a reply by Young, ibid., 2 (1978): 265–77.
23. C. Tiebout, "A Pure Theory of Local Expenditures," *Journal of Political Economy 64* (1956): 416–24.
24. *Washington Post*, (5 October 1982).
25. Ben M. Enis and Dean L. Yarwood, "Governments as Marketers: Consumerism Issues," in McLaughlin, op. cit., pp. 104–107.
26. Letter, Ralph Nader to President Ronald Reagan, 6 August 1982; *Washington Post*, (7 August 1982).
27. Rock et al., op. cit.
28. Michael Pertschuk, *Revolt Against Regulation, The Rise and Pause of the Consumer Movement*, (University of California Press, 1982); see also, "The Consumer Movement in the 80s—A Sleeping Giant Stirs," Keynote Address to the 1983 CFA Consumer Assembly. For an analysis of the current status of the consumer movement, see Paul N. Bloom and Stephen A. Greyser, "The Maturing of Consumerism," *Harvard Business Review 59* (November/December 1981): 130–39.
29. Pertschuk, op. cit., pp. 134–35.

PART THREE
Managing the Marketing Mix

There are several concepts in marketing that often define managerial marketing.

The first is the concept of the four *P*s of marketing: product, price, place, and promotion. This refers to the components of value–price relationships offered to the customers in the marketplace. For example, product provides a functional or a nonfunctional value, place provides time and location values, and promotion provides perception values. All these values can be obtained for a price, which is the fourth *P* of marketing. Of course, there is considerable disagreement regarding whether components of marketing practice are limited to these four *P*s or there are other *P*s of marketing, such as politics and power. Others have argued that the four *P*s of marketing reflect less marketing practice or philosophy and more marketing's functional organization. In any case, it is the most commonly recognized element of marketing practice.

The second most popular concept in marketing practice is the marketing mix, or the recipe of market success. The recipe of market success deals with the optimal combination of the ingredients of the marketing mix needed to create a very palatable meal for the customers in the marketplace. The marketing concept clearly points out the *interdependence* of various elements of marketing practice, such as product, price, and promotion and, therefore, the need to integrate them in the proper balance called for by the recipe. Unfortunately, the fundamental propositions of the marketing mix (interdependence and integration) often are not practiced by functional specialists, who tend to be focused on one of the ingredients and not on the total recipe.

The third most popular concept of marketing is the combination of market segmentation and product differentiation. The concept is fundamentally tied to the argument that marketing should offer an alternative to price competition. This can be achieved by two distinct mechanisms. The first is differentiation of your product or service relative to competitive offerings in terms of either technical or psychological differentiation. It is hoped that this differentiation principle will motivate customers to be less price conscious and more brand loyal.

The second mechanism is segmentation of the market based on customer needs, wants, or resources and modification of the marketing mix (product, promotion, place) to customize for each market segment. The greater the degree of customization of marketing toward a specific market segment, the less the propensity to switch due to price competition.

In this part we have included readings on product, price, distribution, and promotion issues facing the marketing manager.

SECTION G
Managing the Product from Birth to Death

Product is probably the most important element of the marketing mix. The old adage about building a better mousetrap is generally valid, as proven by the recent Japanese conquest of consumer electronics and automobile industries on a worldwide basis.

Product management deals with four generic issues. First, how should a product or brand name be positioned in the marketplace? The same product without proper positioning fails to emphasize its strengths relative to competing alternatives and, therefore, becomes a loser. There are numerous examples of wrong or right positionings. The issue, however, is how to identify or create the right position for your brand name. As we develop more sophisticated positioning and mapping techniques, perhaps there will be more right than wrong positions of new products and services.

The second issue is the product life cycle. There is considerable controversy whether there is a life cycle to a product or brand. Opponents of the life-cycle concept contend that often a product has an eternal life cycle and, therefore, the concept of aging or declining is self-defeating. Others argue that we don't know the specific shape of the life cycle often suggested in the literature. Proponents of the life cycle, on the other hand, provide an overwhelming amount of historical data based on the diffusion of innovations, which suggests that there is a fairly regular and consistent life cycle pattern to most new products and technologies.

We believe that this controversy is mostly based on the confusion between the product and the brand life cycle. It appears that a product class has a definite pattern of life but a brand seems to have no definite pattern of life.

The third issue in product management is revitalization of mature products or brand names. What strategies can the product manager use to maintain or increase the growth rate of a mature product? The diagram on the next page provides some generic strategies.

Each generic strategy can lead to many specific strategies. For example, market entrenchment can be achieved by market segmentation or by specialty markets. Market expansion can be achieved by going international or by mandatory consumption imposed through

	Same Market	New Market
Same Use	Market Entrenchment	Market Expansion
New Use	Usage Expansion	Repositioning

government rules and regulations. Usage expansion can be achieved by new uses or by new situations. Finally, repositioning can be achieved by redefining the market or by repositioning in the same market.

The final issue in product management is exit strategies of products or brands. A company may want to divest a product for several reasons. First, it may be forced to do so due to lack of profits and growth. Second, the product may not fit in the newly defined mission of the corporation. Third, there may be a strong acquisition desire by other companies in the business, which makes the offer very attractive. Finally, the company may want to use the cash flow for other research and development efforts.

Whatever the reasons, the product manager must select from several strategies of exit. The most common exit strategy is milking the product. Another strategy is to integrate the product with other products. A third is to divest the product.

22 — Market Segmentation: A Tactical Approach

Frederick W. Winter

Business Horizons, Vol. 27 (January–February 1984), pp. 57–63. Copyright 1984 by the Foundation for the School of Business at Indiana University. Reprinted by permission.

Marketers have long recognized that a market is not really made up of customers and prospects with identical needs and wants. It has become commonplace to refer to segments, such as the senior citizen segment; the moist, dry, and semi-moist dog food segments; or the frequent long-distance caller segment. And yet these three seemingly routine applications of market segmentation are really misapplications of a concept simple in nature but difficult in practice. Although segmentation has great value in formulating marketing strategy,[1] it is difficult to translate theory into practice for one- to three-year horizon tactical decisions.

DEFINITIONS OF SEGMENTATION

The origins of segmentation go back to Robinson, but the acknowledged father of the concept was really Wendell Smith who defined segmentation this way: "segmentation is *disaggregative* in its effect and tends to bring about recognition of several demand schedules where only one was recognized before... market segmentation... consists of viewing a heterogeneous market (one characterized by divergent demand) as a number of smaller homogeneous markets in response to differing product preferences among important market segments. It is attributable to the desires of consumers for their varying wants."[2]

When Smith referred to the disaggregation of demand he really meant demand schedules (or responses of the market to variables such as price, advertising, or product features). As such the definition is still valid today. Unfortunately, for many years market segmentation was synonymous with the search for identifying characteristics of the "heavy half," those with a higher demand level. But defining bases by the demand level is not as appropriate, or as useful, as looking at the priority of price, special features, service offered, and so forth in the buying decision.

A more recent definition embodies the concept of "cost-benefit segmentation:"[3]

"Market segmentation is the recognition that groups or subsegments differ with respect to properties which suggest that different marketing mixes might be used to appeal to the different groups. These subsegments may then be aggregated if the reduction in cost exceeds the reduction in benefits (revenues). This aggregation is based on the fact that both subsegments respond most to the same marketing mix."

The point of cost-benefit segmentation is that unless different marketing mixes would be offered to different subgroups, there can be no benefit associated with segmenting the market. Although benefits (for example, revenues) increase as more marketing mixes are offered, multiple marketing mixes also mean higher inventory, administrative, promotion, and production costs. Eventually, appealing to different, and smaller, markets becomes so expensive that the costs make it unprofitable. As will be shown, grouping potential customers on the basis of similar ideal marketing mixes is not only theoretically sound, but also practical.

MISAPPLICATIONS OF SEGMENTATION

Before exploring useful applications of market segmentation, it is worthwhile to examine three common misapplications of market segmentation: overconcern with demand level, needless searching for identification, and myopic views of product forms.

CONCERN WITH DEMAND LEVEL

Smith's original concept of divergent demand forming a basis for segmentation was misinterpreted as divergent demand levels. Thus a typical practice was to put heavy users in one segment and contrast them to light users. The implication was that the marketer would be more efficient if he or she targeted efforts toward heavy users.

By concentrating only on the heavy user, the marketer ignores the potential for increased usage by the light user or the non-user. Although it may take some effort to convert the light user, sometimes the market share enjoyed in this forgotten part of the market may be particularly high. Honda in their initial entry into the motorcycle market concentrated on the non-user, leaving the current user to Harley-Davidson. The market share of Honda was exceptionally high within this new segment, and it was this segment which has experienced significant growth.

The heavy user segment can, however, be attractive depending on whether the market share is changeable. The key is, of course, response or *changeability*.

SEARCHING FOR IDENTIFICATION

After defining segments by demand level, the standard next step was to try to "identify" segments formed; this generally translated into developing demographic profiles of the alternative segments. The hope was that if the demographic profiles were significantly different, the marketing program could be "targeted" to a specific segment.

Identification based on demographics suffers from three fallacies:

- Finding differences among population groups is not necessary for effective segmentation. Assume that a target (a prospect for a specialized expensive camera) is no different from a non-target. We still would consider offering this specialized camera at a price suited for the prospect, perhaps using special distribution outlets. Lack of identifiability simply means that we must use a mass marketing promotional strategy—a shotgun approach instead of a rifle approach. Granted, promotional costs associated with advertising in the national edition of *Time* will be higher than in the southwest edition of *Popular Photography*, but the revenues associated with offering the product this way may offset these costs (cost-benefit segmentation considers this issue).

- Demographics can be misleading because of omitted variables. It is interesting that the X-rated movie goer happens to fit nicely with the demographic profile of Salt Lake City. Omitted variables having to do with religious convictions and interests are all important in this case. The problem is, of course, that demographics are rarely the cause of the behavior—they simply help to define some obvious constraints, at best. Demographics should be used for nothing more than reducing the set of feasible alternatives. For example, the X-rated movie exhibitor can select twenty alternative sites for his three new movie theaters from a possible set of 500 cities using demographic matching techniques. Next he should do an on-site survey or analysis to reduce the twenty choices to three. The same should be done for media selection: screen out inappropriate media using demographics, and then use direct measurement of media exposure of the target population.[4]

- Demographics are not particularly actionable. If, for example, you know that your target segment is middle class, with an average of 2.2 children, living in a city of 50,000 population, of what value is this? Actionable bases of segmentation are generally product or situation specific.

Often the preoccupation with demographics was so great that segments were not just identified, but were also formed using demograph-

FIGURE 1. Product Form Segmentation: Dog Food Market

Dry	25 lbs. and over
	under 25 lbs.
Semi-moist	— —
Moist	— —

ics. The "youth market," the "senior-citizen segment," and the "low-income group" are but three examples of this approach. Again we have the same three problems as before: weak relationships, no underlying causal base, and a lack of actionability.

CONCERN WITH PRODUCT FORM INSTEAD OF NEED

Figure 1 shows segments recognized by a major manufacturer of dog food. On the surface it seems that any new entrant should position itself on the basis of one of three types of dog food. To define markets on the basis of what people have done in the past, however, says nothing about the motivation for their actions and the appropriate marketing mixes to capture the segments. For example, the dry segment may buy dry dog food because it is cheaper, less messy, available in bulk, more nutritious, the only brand available, or recommended by the veterinarian. Which of these reasons was the motivating factor should drastically alter the marketing tactic to be used to attack or retain this market. It is possible to imagine a nutritious, semi-moist dog food that could compete for the segment of the dry dog food market which buys on the basis of nutrition or convenience. If market segments are formed on the basis of needs or motives rather than on behavior, the marketing mix strategy to appeal to the segments becomes more obvious; similarly, segments to be avoided are also obvious.

The light beer market segment of Figure 2 can be meaningfully separated into three motivation segments: those who are calorie-conscious, those who prefer less alcohol, and those who prefer a lighter taste. In fact, it is possible for one person to consume light beer on three separate occasions for three different reasons. The situation may dictate the segment the consumer falls into.

SEGMENT TREES: A METHOD TO CLASSIFY

Decision trees are routinely used to show alternative decisions available, and the tree method is helpful to illustrate alternative types of customers. For example, contrast the usefulness of a demographic-based segmentation of the lawn fertilizer (homeowner) market in Figure 3 with that of Figure 4. This specification of alternative types of consumers before data collection is referred to as *a priori* segmentation, and is probably the easiest to implement.

Construction of the segmentation tree requires some market insights and cannot be put in textbook form. Nevertheless, the following principles are helpful to keep in mind:

- Branches can reflect the degree of marketing effort—major effort, secondary or maintenance effort, "write offs" (no effort), or even avoids (negative value)—based on the value or desirability of the segment. Useful variables include potential expenditures (amount of dog food used, size of lawn), brand loyalty, likelihood of purchase, or profitability of the account.
- Branches can reflect the marketing mix. Thus the variables used to split the market should be actionable and should relate to some promotion, price, distribution, or product combination. Variables useful for segmentation include media habits, price awareness, distribution outlets frequented, and choice criteria. Some of the more recent marketing research techniques can be helpful in deriving the responses unobtrusively.
- It is often meaningful to distinguish between the product use decision and the brand choice decision. Users of the product should be differentiated from non-users; then, within the non-users group it will be useful to distinguish between potential users and non-potential users (no dogs, no lawns). Finally the potential users can be segmented on the basis of inhibiting fac-

FIGURE 2. Product Form Segmentation: Beer Market

Imported Beer	— —
Domestic Beer	Regular Beer
	Light Beer

tors such as unawareness of product, attitudinal misconceptions, or barriers to purchase.
- Variables helpful to segment a new (or underexposed) product or brand include aware versus unaware, information versus no information versus misinformation, and trial versus no trial.
- For some products it is critical to segment between buyers who choose the brand and buyers who choose the distribution outlet (for example, a buyer who goes to a particular television store and selects from among the brands there). If a significant proportion buys the distribution first and the brand second, then segmentation of retailers and distributors will be worthwhile.
- It is important not to be overly concerned with the large number of eventual "branches"; these will subsequently be reduced for one of two reasons. Some of the segments will be so small they can be "written off" or ignored (for example, 5 percent of the population); also, several of the subsegments may be captured with one marketing mix.

Returning to the tree in Figure 4, it is easy to see not only variables

FIGURE 3. Lawn Fertilizer Usage—Demographic Segmentation Plan

Heavy Users	High Income	Central City
		Suburban
		Rural
	Low Income	Central City
		Suburban
		Rural
Light Users	High Income	Central City
		Suburban
		Rural
	Low Income	Central City
		Suburban
		Rural
Non-Users	High Income	Central City
		Suburban
		Rural
	Low Income	Central City
		Suburban
		Rural

that need to be measured in the data base which form the basis for our segmentation scheme, but also the tactics that follow from the assessment. Some of the 16 segments, for example, can be written off. Both segments 2 and 15 would not be cost effective; the effort required to have an impact would probably be too large. Furthermore segment 16 is probably not worth considering here with the current product form since the homeowner is not the decision-maker; landscape-gardeners buy in bulk and are a different market needing their own segmentation plan.

Segment 1 may need a lesser effort to simply achieve a maintenance strategy.

Segment 3, 4, and 5 members, who select the retailer, are best reached with a "push" strategy, using heavy middleman allowance,

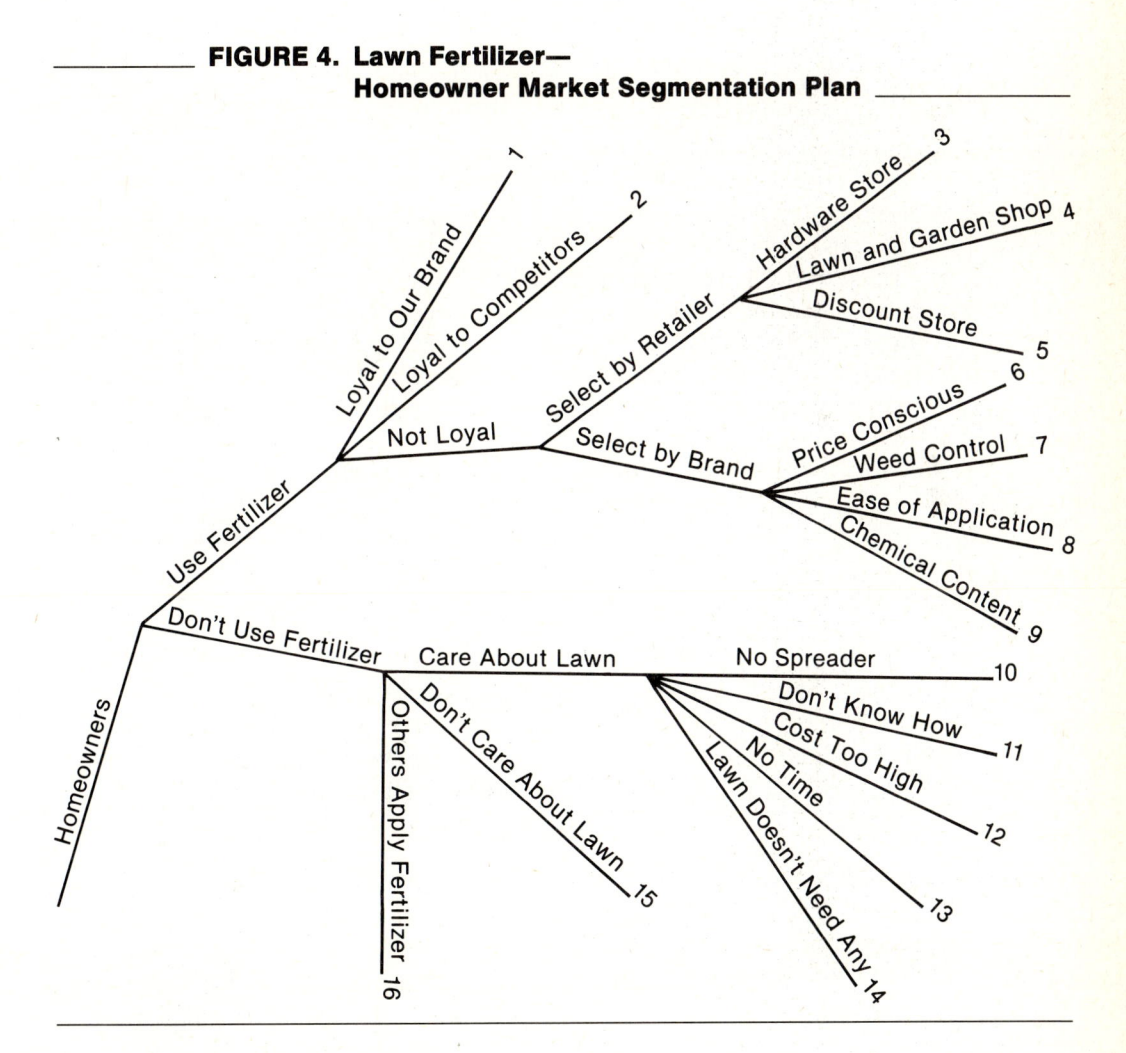

FIGURE 4. Lawn Fertilizer—Homeowner Market Segmentation Plan

point of purchase displays, and intensive distribution. It will be more effective to have segments 6 to 9, who select by brand, "pull" the product through the distribution channels. Mass advertising, deals, and new product development are but a few of the tactics to be employed. A selective distribution policy (fewer distribution outlets) could be used if necessary for these segments, particularly if brand buyers are many and retailer buyers largely use only one type of retailer.

It will be cost effective to try to group segments whenever possible. For example, advertising may be able to stress the "weed control" and "ease of application" of Brand X if segments 7 and 8 read the same media.

Segments 10 to 14 represent an attempt to increase the primary demand among those who care about lawns. Note that only a major market share firm would undertake going after segments 11 and 14. These education efforts will boost sales for all fertilizer markets, so they are worthwhile only if you expect a significant share of the increase. It may be possible to manipulate market share and product purchase together as in the case of segment 10: "with every purchase of X fertilizer get the use of a spreader free!"

Note that practically every variable used as a basis for forming segments is actionable and can be directly translated into a change in the marketing mix.

Segments 3 to 14 all represent opportunities whose effort and mix are determined by empirical as well as subjective means. Very small segments can be ignored if the purchase potential per consumer unit is also small. In addition, the firm may choose not to compete in various segments because of its limitations, competitor's strengths, or technological infeasibilities. For example, a firm with limited distribution and limited prospects to increase distribution would find it more worthwhile to compete in Segments 6 to 9.

A bank that was engaged primarily in retail transactions found the tree in Figure 5 useful. From this they were able to make the following observations:

- Turnover into the area is high (27.3 percent of the profitable market has been in the area two years or less).
- The bank is serving customers well. Of the profitable accounts who are customers of the bank, the ratio of satisfied to dissatisfied is 25.5:1. For competitors the ratio is 2.1:1.
- The majority of dissatisfied non-customers are not aware of the bank.

The tree of Figure 5 was "pruned" to the tree of Figure 6, which shows clearly the tactic to be used in dealing with the various segments. Note that other than continued good service for the "maintain" segment, intensive marketing effort is warranted for only the "encourage action" and "inform" segments, just 16.9 percent of the entire market. Thus large scale demand stimulation does not appear to be justifiable. The presence of an "avoid" segment indicated that non-targeted marketing efforts could have an undesirable impact on the firm. A search for differences in terms of needs, services, and problems among the "encourage action," "inform," and "avoid" groups was undertaken. The only difference of consequence was that "avoids" were more switchable on the basis of lower checking/service fees by a ratio of almost 2 to 1. Because of potential lost revenue from already satisfied and profitable customers and the great response by "avoids," a lower service fee was deemed undesirable. Currently, new incentives to acquire profitable accounts are under review. Management will attempt to find something that profitable accounts respond to that unprofitable accounts do not. Such a program, if enacted, would take place during summer months when new families tend to move into the area.

FIGURE 5. Initial Segmentation by Retail Bank

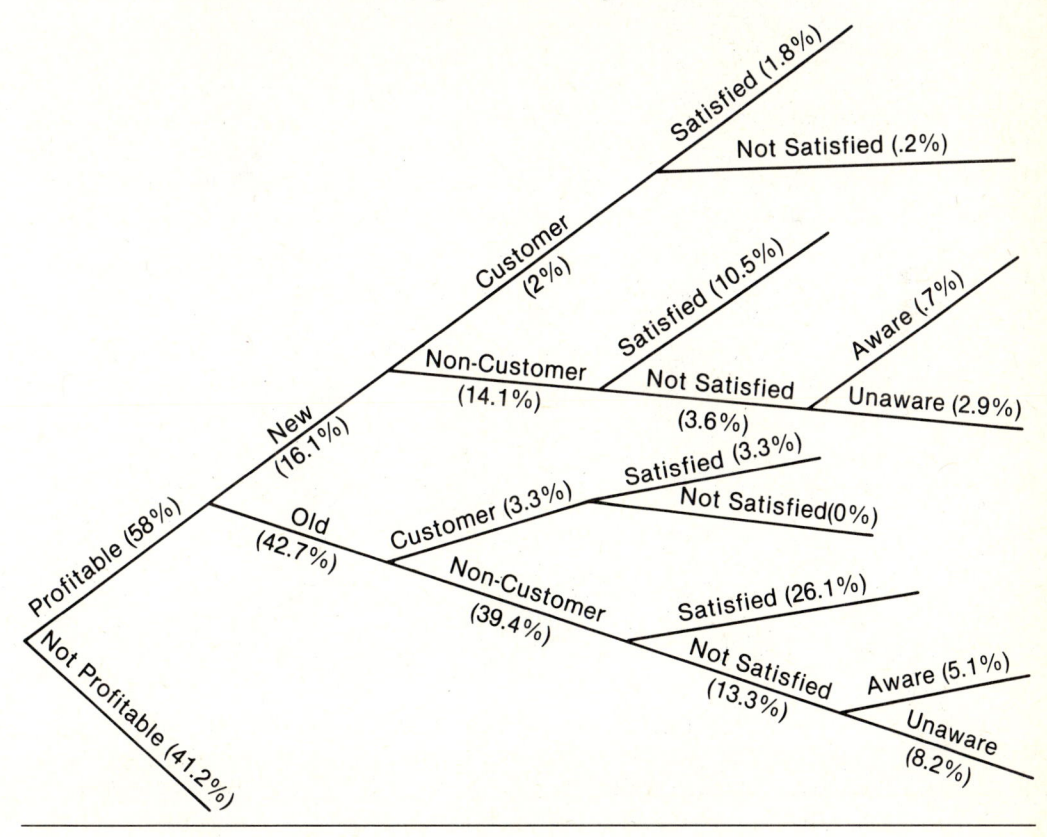

- Profitable (58%)
  - New (16.1%)
    - Customer (2%)
      - Satisfied (1.8%)
      - Not Satisfied (.2%)
    - Non-Customer (14.1%)
      - Satisfied (10.5%)
      - Not Satisfied (3.6%)
        - Aware (.7%)
        - Unaware (2.9%)
  - Old (42.7%)
    - Customer (3.3%)
      - Satisfied (3.3%)
      - Not Satisfied (0%)
    - Non-Customer (39.4%)
      - Satisfied (26.1%)
      - Not Satisfied (13.3%)
        - Aware (5.1%)
        - Unaware (8.2%)
- Not Profitable (41.2%)

DATA COLLECTION

The advantage of the recommended approach to tactical segmentation is that the data collection needs logically follow. For most consumer products the easiest approach will be a standard market survey, perhaps using an existing panel. In most cases the cost will not exceed $10,000. Industrial marketers will generally have to resort to more complicated sampling plans in conjunction with surveys: the problem is more difficult because of the presence of multiple influences in the purchase process, and the cost of the interviewing will be substantially higher.

It is recommended that the data be collected periodically—once every two years for most products. This will allow the manager to track the growth, and therefore the rising importance, of key segments.

It is possible to view each segment as a separate battle being fought with different competitors for market share. Thus, market share tracking

FIGURE 6. Action Oriented Segmentation by Retail Bank

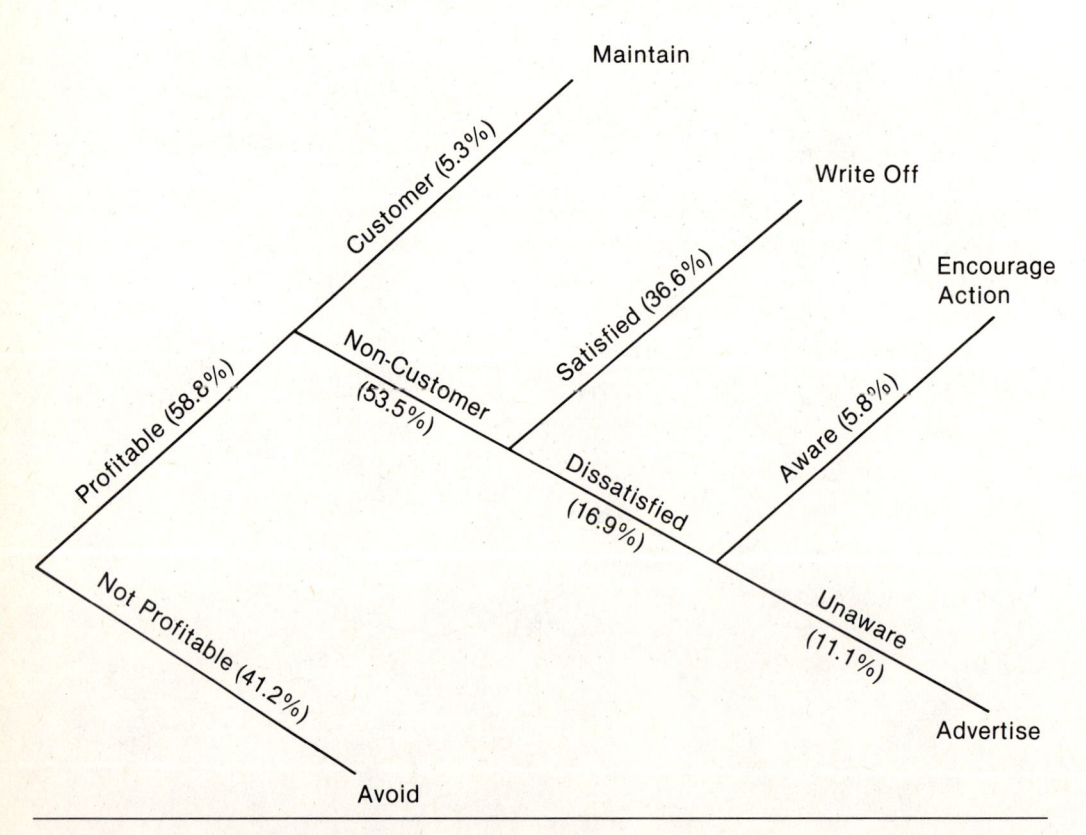

by segments may be helpful for decision-making. To insure accuracy, a purchase diary should probably be used for respondents.

The number of segments targeted must be responsive to the heterogeneity of the market. For this reason, a tree approach to a priori segmentation is most appropriate, and decisions based on this issue should not be made without the aid of some market research or some reasonably confident assumptions of the market.

Other factors critical to the number and nature of targets have to do with the costs of going after the segments, the ability to combine segments and reach with one overall strategy (taking into account the accompanying revenue falloff), and the resource constraints—capital, manpower, and institutional—of the firm. This clearly indicates the importance of integrated marketing, production, and financial decision making.

ENDNOTES

1. For example, market segmentation is a remedy for a low market share and/or a position in a low growth market. Segmentation, simply put, redefines the market such that a marketer's market share may now be dominant in a smaller niche; alternatively, certain segments of a low growth market may be growing.
2. Wendell Smith, "Product Differentiation and Market Segmentation as Alternative Strategies," *Journal of Marketing*, July 1956: 3–8.
3. Frederick Winter, "A Cost-Benefit Approach to Market Segmentation," *Journal of Marketing*, Fall 1979: 103–111.
4. Frederick Winter, "Match Target Markets to Media Audiences," *Journal of Advertising Research*, February 1980: 61–66.

23 New Product Models for Test Market Data[1]

*Chakravarthi Narasimhan and
Subrata K. Sen*

Reprinted from the *Journal of Marketing*, published by the American Marketing Association, Vol. 47 (Winter 1983), pp. 11–24. Reprinted by permission.

INTRODUCTION

In recent years several models have been proposed to evaluate the performance of a new product introduced in a test market (see, for example, Blattberg and Golanty 1978, Parfitt and Collins 1968, and Pringle, Wilson and Brody 1982). These models are all designed to study the performance of a new brand in an inexpensive, frequently purchased product category. However, the models vary greatly in their complexity and in their applicability to different aspects of new product evaluation, e.g., sales forecasting or the evaluation of alternative marketing mixes for the new product. Consequently, it would be valuable to review and evaluate the various models to determine which model (or models) is most appropriate for a specific objective (e.g., forecasting the sales of the new product).

Such reviews are available in varying degrees in several new product texts that have been published recently (see Midgley 1977, pp. 248–77; Urban and Hauser 1980, pp. 418–48; and Wind 1982, pp. 435–61). However, some of the reviews are limited to just a small subset of the models presented in the literature (e.g., Midgley 1977), while others are not sufficiently detailed (e.g., Urban and Hauser 1980 and Wind 1982). In contrast, this paper provides a detailed review and evaluation of the nine test market models that are cited most frequently in the marketing literature.

In order to position test market models correctly, we start by providing an outline of the new product introduction process. We then describe the dimensions on which the various models are evaluated. This is followed by an evaluation of each model in terms of these dimensions. The paper concludes with a discussion of future directions of research in the area of test market models.

THE NEW PRODUCT INTRODUCTION PROCESS

The introduction of a new product is preceded by a series of important steps:[2] market definition and evaluation (see, for example, Day,

Shocker and Srivastava 1979), idea generation and screening (Urban and Hauser 1980, pp. 122–50), concept evaluation (Hauser and Urban 1977, Shocker and Srinivasan 1979), pretest market evaluation (Robinson 1981, Silk and Urban 1978) and test marketing. Test markets are used for two purposes: validation of the sales forecasts made at the pretest market stage and evaluation of alternative marketing mixes for the new product (Achenbaum 1974; Klompmaker, Hughes and Haley 1976; Wind 1982, pp. 398–434).

This paper provides a critical review of several models that have been proposed to evaluate test market results. Some of the models reviewed focus only on sales prediction while others (generally, the newer models) emphasize both sales prediction and the impact of marketing mix variables. The nine models reviewed in this paper are listed in Table 1. These particular models were chosen for review because they are the most frequently cited test market models in the marketing literature.

It should be noted that new product diffusion models are not reviewed in this paper because most diffusion models deal only with the *first* purchase of the new product (Mahajan and Muller 1979). Consequently, they are primarily applicable for durables and are not applicable for frequently purchased products where repeat purchasing is very important. At best they might be useful in modeling the first stage (the "Penetration" stage) of the test market models reviewed in this paper (see Midgley 1976, for example). Even for this purpose, their applicability is not entirely clear since the first purchase diffusion models typically refer to a product class and not to a brand in a product category. Some diffusion models (most notably Dodson and Muller 1978) have tried to model the repeat purchase phenomenon that characterizes the purchase of inexpensive, frequently purchased products. However, these diffusion models focus primarily on issues such as word-of-mouth recommendations which, though very important for the purchase of durables, are unlikely to be important for inexpensive, frequently purchased products. The consumer can purchase and experience several alternative brands in such product classes at a relatively low cost, which would appear to be a more efficient way of acquiring information about such products than seeking word-of mouth recommendations. It appears, therefore, that diffusion models are really not appropriate for the types of products most test market models are intended for.

DIMENSIONS FOR MODEL EVALUATION

In this section we briefly describe the dimensions on which the various models are evaluated. The next section provides an evaluation of each model in terms of these dimensions.

TABLE 1. Classification of Test Market Models

Model	Model Objective	Level of Model Complexity	Quality of Modeling	Type of Sales Data Required	Diagnostics	Degree of Commercial Acceptance
Fourt and Woodlock (1960)	sales	low	unsatisfactory	panel	low	low
Parfitt and Collins (1968)	brand share	low	unsatisfactory	panel	low	high
STEAM (Massy 1969)	sales	high	unsatisfactory	panel	low	low
SPRINTER (Urban 1970)	sales	high	good	panel, store audit	high	medium
Eskin (1973)	sales	medium	unsatisfactory	panel	low	medium
Nakanishi (1973)	sales	high	unsatisfactory	panel	medium	low
NEWPROD (Assmus 1975)	brand share	medium	satisfactory	survey	medium	low
TRACKER (Blattberg and Golanty 1978)	sales	medium	good	survey	high	high
NEWS (Pringle, Wilson and Brody 1982)	sales	medium	good	survey	high	high

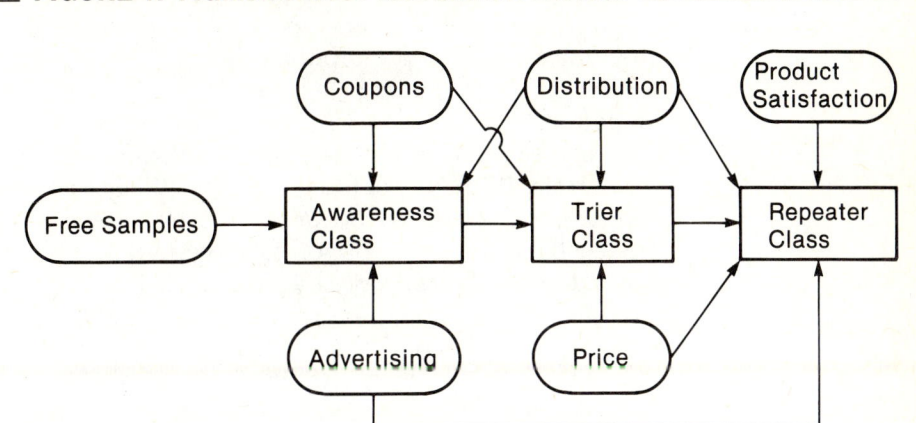

FIGURE 1. Framework for Test Market Models

Model Objective

The first dimension deals with the criterion variable that must be estimated from test market data. Equilibrium sales forecast, market share forecast and some measure of profitability are likely candidates for the criterion measure. Profitability is clearly the best criterion, but unlike the other criteria, it requires cost as well as sales data.

Modeling Aspects

There are three main aspects to this dimension: consideration of the different stages of new product acceptance, the mathematical structure of the model for each stage, and issues related to the estimation of the model's parameters.

Stages Considered. The three main stages through which a consumer becomes a new brand customer are indicated in the square blocks in Figure 1. The three stages consist of the awareness class, the trier class and the repeater class. The awareness class includes consumers who have become aware of the new brand through the firm's promotional activities. The trier class includes consumers who have made one purchase of the new brand, and the repeater class includes consumers who have purchased the new brand more than once.[3]

We now discuss this Awareness-Trial-Repeat process in more detail.

1. *Different ways of becoming aware and their effects on trial probability:* When a new brand is introduced in an established product class, the consumer must first be informed of the product's existence. The firm's marketing mix variables (such as use of advertising,

free samples and coupons) play an important role in informing the consumer of the existence of the new product. Even after being informed about the product, the consumer is likely to be uncertain about its quality, i.e., how the new brand compares with its substitutes in the product class. However, the consumer who becomes aware of the new product through a free sample can ascertain the quality of the product relatively easily by using the sample. Similarly, the consumer whose awareness was stimulated by the receipt of a coupon can ascertain the quality of the new product at a "lower" price by purchasing it with the coupon. In contrast, the consumer who becomes aware of the new product through the receipt of an advertising message can determine the quality of the product only by purchasing it at its market price. Therefore, it is reasonable to hypothesize that consumer segments that become aware through a free sample or a coupon are likely to have a higher probability of trial compared to consumers who become aware of the new product through advertising.

2. *Time of becoming aware and its effect on trial probability:* Next, the trial probability at time t, for a consumer who was informed about the product at time t, is likely to be higher than for someone who was informed about the product at some earlier time period (assuming that price and other marketing mix variables are held constant) because an informed consumer is most likely to try the new product within his/her next purchase cycle (assuming that there is not a large inventory of the product on hand). If this is not done, it is probably because the consumer does not like the product (if a free sample were used), does not like the information in the product's advertising, or because the new product's price (relative to the prices of existing brands) is too high. This would imply that the trial probability for trying in future periods given that the consumer is informed in the current period and has not tried the product, will be lower. Thus, in modeling the trial process, one should be concerned with different ways of becoming aware and the time of becoming aware, since these factors affect the trial probability.

3. *Time of becoming a trier and its effect on repeat purchase probability:* Consumers who tried the brand very soon after its introduction are likely to have a higher repeat purchase rate (see Parfitt and Collins 1968 for empirical support of this statement). This occurs because early triers usually are consumers who are favorably disposed towards the new brand. In addition, early triers tend to be heavy buyers—they try early and repeat more often because they are in the market more frequently.

4. *Depth of repeat and its effect on repeat purchase probability:* After trying the new product, the consumer may or may not repurchase the brand, depending on his/her usage satisfaction. A priori we would expect that the longer the brand has been used the more likely the consumer is to repurchase. Thus it may be necessary to analyze consumers in terms of the number of times they have repurchased the brand. This issue can become critical. Suppose one ignores the issue completely, and based on preliminary test market results, tries to project year-end repeat purchase fractions. Then due to aggregation bias (aggregating across different repeat levels) the projected repeat purchase fraction is likely to be erroneous. This would obviously be reflected in a poor estimate of the projected sales.[4]

In conclusion, the modeling of the new product adoption process should explicitly consider the issues we have highlighted in the above discussion.

Mathematical Models for Each Stage. The main issue here is the extent to which the models consider the effects of marketing mix variables. This issue is examined in Figure 1 where the oval blocks represent the marketing variables that effect a consumer's movement from one stage to another. Figure 1 indicates that free samples, coupons, advertising and distribution make the consumer aware of the new brand. The consumer's awareness level, along with coupons and the new brand's price and distribution, determine whether the consumer will try the product. The trial experience, positive or negative, along with distribution, price and advertising, will affect the consumer's decision to repeat purchase the brand.[5]

It is also important to consider whether the *appropriate* marketing mix variables are incorporated in the models for each stage. For example, a trial probability model that includes distribution but not price does not include the appropriate marketing mix variables. The models should also incorporate competitive marketing variables because the success of a firm's marketing mix depends on competitive reactions as well.

In the above discussion we have highlighted some key issues that should be considered while building a test market model. However, we are aware that increased sophistication at the modeling stage is not costless if the model is to be adopted and implemented by marketing managers. A model that is theoretically sound may be intractable in terms of its mathematical formulation, data requirements and estimation procedures. The model builder should be aware of these issues and any trade-offs that become necessary should be made with sound managerial judgment regarding costs, ease of estimation and model tractability.

Estimation Issues. Regarding estimation, we examine whether the model description reports specific methods of estimating the model's parameters and values of the estimated parameters.

Sales Data Requirements

To gather sales data in the test market, one could use either diary panel data or survey data. Panel data are likely to be more accurate (Wind and Learner 1979) but are more expensive than survey data. The survey method also permits the researcher to design questions to infer consumers' awareness, brand preferences, etc., an advantage not obtainable from diary panel data. This advantage is important for generating diagnostic information from the model.

Note that this dimension deals only with the source of *sales* data. A given model will obviously use a variety of other data such as data on media expenditures.

Diagnostic Aid

Apart from providing a sales forecast or a forecast of brand share, a test market model must aid the user in generating useful diagnostic information on the effectiveness of the various marketing mix variables. If the sales of a well-designed new product are low, management would like to know why the product is not performing better. For example, the awareness level for the new brand could be low, suggesting that the firm's advertising, couponing or distribution of free samples has been ineffective. Or, the trial rate may be low, suggesting probable bottlenecks in distribution or too high a price. Whatever the problem, it is necessary to isolate and identify it so that suitable corrective action can be taken. Even for a successful introduction, the firm is interested in knowing the relative effectiveness of its marketing instruments. It is clear, therefore, that to be an effective diagnostic aid, a model must explicitly incorporate the effect of marketing mix variables in modeling the various stages of new product acceptance.

Degree of Commercial Acceptance

The final dimension for evaluating the various test market models is the degree to which these models have been used commercially. Clearly, this is a difficult factor to assess. However, because it is an important issue for managers, we have tried to assess it by using information obtained from a variety of sources such as the developers of the models and executives of diary panel firms such as the Market Research Corporation of America.

CRITICAL EVALUATION OF THE MODELS

In this section we provide a critical evaluation of the nine models in terms of the dimensions described in the preceding section. Our evaluation compares the different models on each evaluative dimension. The highlights of this comparison are presented in Table 1.

Model Objectives

Table 1 reports the different criterion measures (e.g., sales, brand share) that are forecasted by the various models.[6] All the models predict the sales or the market share of the new brand.

Modeling Aspects

This dimension deals with a series of criteria that relate to the structure of the model and the mathematical and estimation details provided in each model's writeup. Our evaluation of the nine models on these criteria is summarized in Table 2. A "yes" indicates that the model considers the particular issue or reports the particular model or parameter estimate. A "no" indicates that it does not. "Partial" indicates that the issue is only partially dealt with. For example, the Parfitt/Collins model describes a specific mathematical model for trial but does not provide a specific model for repeat purchases. Consequently, Table 2 shows an entry of "partial" for the Parfitt/Collins model in the column titled "Report of Specific Models."

Table 2 provides a summary evaluation of the models on the "Modeling Aspects" dimension. The remainder of this section provides a critical evaluation of each model in terms of the criteria listed in Table 2.

Fourt and Woodlock (1960). This is a very simple model but suffers from the following shortcomings:

1. The awareness stage is not modeled. Thus, the effect on the probability of trial of (a) different ways of becoming aware and (b) the time of becoming aware cannot be studied.
2. The time of entry into the trial class and its impact on repeat purchase probability is not considered.
3. Marketing mix variables are totally ignored, making it extremely difficult for management to assess the effectiveness of the marketing tools under its control. However, to be fair to the authors, it was never their objective to evaluate the effects of marketing mix variables.
4. Accurate calculation of the various repeat purchase probabilities requires very large samples.

Parfitt and Collins (1968). The main contributions of the model are:

1. It is a simple model that appears to predict a new brand's market share accurately. In addition, it provides some useful diagnostic

TABLE 2. Modeling Details

Model	Stages Modeled	Details Regarding Each Stage — Awareness: Different Ways of Becoming Aware and Trial Probability	Awareness: Time of Becoming Aware and Trial Probability	Trial: Time of Becoming a Trier and Repeat Purchase Probability	Repeat: Depth of Repeat and Repeat Purchase Probability	Mathematical Models for Each Stage — Report of Specific Models	Marketing Mix Variables Considered	Inclusion of Appropriate Marketing Mix Variables	Estimation Issues — Report of Estimation Methods	Report of Parameter Estimates
Fourt and Woodlock (1960)	trial, repeat	—[a]	—	no	yes	yes	none	—	no	no
Parfitt and Collins (1968)	trial, repeat	—	—	yes	no	partial	none	—	partial	no
STEAM (Massy 1969)	trial, repeat	—	—	yes	yes	yes	none	—	yes	no
SPRINTER (Urban 1970)	awareness, trial, repeat	yes	yes	no	yes	yes	advertising, price, promotion, distribution	yes	yes	no
Eskin (1973)	trial, repeat	—	—	yes	yes	yes	none	—	yes	yes
Nakanishi (1973)	trial, repeat	—	—	yes	no	yes	advertising, promotion	no	yes	no
NEWPROD (Assmus 1975)	awareness, trial, repeat	yes	yes	no	no	partial	advertising, promotion	no	no	no
TRACKER (Blattberg and Golanty 1978)	awareness, trial, repeat	no	yes	no	yes	yes	advertising, price	yes	yes	yes
NEWS (Pringle, Wilson and Brody 1982)	awareness, trial, repeat	yes	yes	yes	yes	yes	advertising, promotion, distribution	no	yes	yes

[a] —: indicates that the particular column detail is inappropriate to the model. For example, since the Fourt and Woodlock model does not consider the awareness stage, one cannot comment on the details regarding the awareness stage for this model.

information if the brand's predicted market share is very low. If market share is low because trial is low while the repeat purchase rate is at an acceptable level, the marketing mix for the product should be altered to induce greater trial. If, on the other hand trial is high but repeat rates are low, the product should be withdrawn or reformulated because triers of the brand do not appear to like it.

2. It was clearly demonstrated that the repeat purchase rates were different for customers entering at different times after the new product was introduced. This difference is important in estimating the equilibrium repeat purchase rate.
3. The authors show that promotions such as temporary price cuts guarantee increased trial but not necessarily a higher repeat purchase rate. The increase in repeat purchase rate may be nominal, which may not warrant the cost of the promotion.

The model's shortcomings consist of:

1. The awareness stage is not modeled.
2. The impact of depth of repeat on repeat purchase probability is not considered.
3. The absence of marketing mix variables makes it impossible to assess the effects of advertising, sampling or couponing. Again, the authors never did intend to study the effects of marketing mix variables.
4. The subjective estimation of the equilibrium repeat purchase rate may create problems. Not only is the method ad hoc, but it also does not provide us with an estimate of the forecast error.
5. The model has been criticized in terms of the small sample sizes of the panels used to estimate the model's parameters. Shoemaker and Staelin (1976) show that the panel sizes that are typically used to estimate the parameters of the model are often too small to allow us to place much confidence on the forecasted brand share. This occurs mainly because the equilibrium repeat purchase rate cannot be estimated precisely.

STEAM (Massy 1969). This model is extremely complex, both mathematically and from the viewpoint of estimation. It suffers from the following problems:

1. It does not model the awareness stage.
2. It does not consider the effects of marketing mix variables (however, Massy, Montgomery and Morrison 1970, pp. 428–35, briefly discuss how marketing mix variables could be incorporated into STEAM).

3. Large sample sizes are required to estimate the model's parameters. The application reported in the paper uses a panel of about 6000 households. Given that sufficient observations are required for each depth of trial class in order to obtain reliable estimates, one would suspect that it is necessary to have extremely large sample sizes. This clearly increases the cost of implementing the model.

SPRINTER (Urban 1970). On the positive side, SPRINTER traces out the consumer adoption process carefully and considers the effects of marketing mix variables explicitly. However, the model can be criticized on the following grounds:

1. Time of entry into the trial class and its impact on repeat purchase probability is not modeled.
2. Due to the complexity of the model (it consists of approximately 500 equations), data requirements are very formidable. However, the model is designed to be used in a modular fashion, allowing simpler versions of the model to be used for individual applications (Urban and Karash 1971).

Eskin (1973). This model is positioned between the Parfitt/Collins model and the STEAM model. Thus, it is more complex than the former (i.e., the purchase process is modeled in greater detail), but is computationally less burdensome than the latter. The model suffers from the following shortcomings:

1. It does not model the awareness stage.
2. The effect of marketing mix variables is not modeled explicitly. Thus, any kind of diagnostic information on the effectiveness of these tools is not obtainable from the model.

Nakanishi (1973). This model represents an interesting early effort at building marketing response functions into a stochastic brand choice model. The problems with the model are as follows:

1. Even though Nakanishi mentions a "pretrial" stage when the consumer becomes aware of the new product, the awareness stage is not modeled explicitly. However, in a somewhat related paper (Nakanishi 1971) he does present explicit models for awareness.
2. The impact of depth of repeat on repeat purchase probability is not considered.
3. The trial and repeat models do incorporate the effects of marketing mix variables. However, the trial model does not consider the

appropriate marketing mix variables since it ignores the effect of relative price on trial.

NEWPROD (Assmus 1975). On the positive side, the model examines the effect of marketing mix variables in determining consumer acceptance of a new brand. However, NEWPROD can be criticized on the following grounds:

1. The impact of time of entry into the trier class on repeat purchase probability is not modeled.
2. The effect of depth of repeat on repeat purchase probability is ignored.
3. Relative price is not included in the trial model.
4. In general the details of the model are provided in a very sketchy manner, making it difficult to comment on the quality of the modeling.

TRACKER (Blattberg and Golanty 1978). This model has the following advantages:

1. Since marketing mix variables are incorporated in the model, TRACKER generates useful diagnostic information about the new product.
2. Since it uses only survey data, it is considerably cheaper than models that use diary panel data. Yet, TRACKER provides forecasts of comparable accuracy.

Some of the weaknesses of the model are:

1. Though TRACKER models all three stages of the adoption process, it does not consider all the details of the awareness and trial stages.
2. The model does not explicitly consider the distribution of free samples and coupons. The authors state that when a new product is sampled heavily, the effect of sampling can be taken into account by making suitable modifications to the model. However, these modifications are not described.
3. The assumption that all brands in a product class are equally responsive to marketing instruments is unappealing. For example, in determining the parameters of the awareness model, all brands are pooled and a single set of response parameters is estimated. Though data limitations force the authors to proceed in this manner, some of the unsatisfactory results in the awareness model's predictions may stem from the assumption of parameter homogeneity across brands. If one looks at the "Absolute Error" column in Table 4, p. 196, of Blattberg and Golanty

(1978), one observes some extremely large errors even though we are looking at the same data that were used to estimate the model's parameters.

4. In the projection model, most of the estimates are subjectively determined. Further, the assumption that the repeat rate, r, does not vary with time of entry into the market is contrary to empirical evidence (Parfitt and Collins 1968). Since the model seems to predict well, it appears that it is not very sensitive to such parameters except the d_is (which are defined in Figure 2).

NEWS (Pringle, Wilson and Brody 1982). NEWS is available in two versions: a pretest market version called NEWS/Planner and a test market version called NEWS/Market. The two versions are structurally identical. However, the nature of the data required to estimate the model's parameters is different for NEWS/Planner relative to NEWS/Market. Our comments on the model's estimation procedures refer only to NEWS/Market.

NEWS is a comprehensive model that represents the consumer adoption process carefully. On the positive side, NEWS is the only model that considers all four aspects related to modeling awareness, trial and repeat stages (see Table 2). It considers advertising, coupons, free samples and distribution as the key marketing mix variables.

The weaknesses of the model consist of the following:

1. In the trial model the relative price of the new brand is not considered explicitly. This important omitted variable is likely to lead to a biased estimate of the awareness to trial coefficient.

2. Several of the model's parameters are estimated judgmentally using company experience. Other parameters are estimated by means of an iterative numerical search procedure using two to four observations (see Pringle, Wilson and Brody 1982, p. 21, Table 3). The number of available observations is so small because NEWS uses data that relate *only* to the specific new product for which the model is being used.

    This approach to parameter estimation is in marked contrast to the approach used in TRACKER, where observations on several "similar" products are pooled to estimate the model's parameters. The approach used in TRACKER results in a relatively large number of observations. However, the developers of NEWS maintain that data on "similar" products may not be applicable for a specific new product. Hence, they prefer to use judgmental estimates or data based *only* on the current new product to estimate the model's parameters.

    There is clearly merit to this argument. However, it is likely that parameters estimated using a very small number of obser-

vations will tend to be unstable in general. In addition, much of the detailed mathematical modeling of the trial and repeat process in NEWS is made less valuable by the frequent use of judgmental parameter estimates. In spite of our reservations about the pooling procedure used in TRACKER, on balance we believe that statistical parameter estimation based on many observations (obtained, if necessary, from a judiciously selected set of "similar" products) is a superior approach to estimating a model's parameters.
3. Finally, because of the nature of the numerical search estimation procedure, it is not possible to compute standard errors for the NEWS parameter estimates.

The model evaluations made in Table 2 are summarized in Table 1 in the two columns labeled "Level of Model Complexity" and "Quality of Modeling." Level of Model Complexity refers to the complexity of the model structure (the number of variables, the number of equations, etc.) as well as the complexity of the analytical and estimation techniques used in the model. Our overall evaluation of each model's complexity is indicated in Table 1 in terms of three levels: low, medium and high. The Fourt/Woodlock and Parfitt/Collins models are simple models, while the STEAM, SPRINTER and Nakanishi models are very complex. The other four models have a medium level of complexity.

The Quality of Modeling criterion is based on two main aspects: the degree to which the various stages of the new product adoption process are modeled, and the extent to which appropriate marketing mix variables are incorporated in these models. In general, if all three stages are modeled and appropriate marketing mix variables are considered for each model, the Quality of Modeling rating is "good" in Table 1. The rating is "satisfactory" if the model considers all three stages and incorporates the effects of marketing mix variables, even though some of the marketing variables are not considered in an appropriate manner. The rating in Table 1 on this criterion is "unsatisfactory" if the model does not consider all three stages or totally ignores the effect of marketing mix variables. Based on these criteria, the "Quality of Modeling" is "good" only for SPRINTER, NEWS and TRACKER. It is "satisfactory" for NEW-PROD and is "unsatisfactory" for the remaining models.

It should be noted, however, that some of these models (e.g., Parfitt and Collins 1968) were not designed to evaluate the effects of marketing mix variables. Consequently, it may be somewhat unfair to give these models an unsatisfactory rating for "Quality of Modeling" simply because they did not consider marketing mix variables in their development.

Finally, none of the models do a good job of explicitly considering competitive marketing mix variables.

Type of Sales Data Required

As indicated in Table 1, most of the models require diary panel sales data. SPRINTER requires store audit data in addition to panel data. Only the NEWS, NEWPROD and TRACKER models use survey data. Consequently, they are likely to be cheaper than the other models listed in Table 1.

Diagnostic Aid

To be an effective diagnostic aid, a model must explicitly incorporate the effects of marketing mix variables. Our evaluation of the diagnostic capabilities of each model is summarized in Table 1. SPRINTER, NEWS and TRACKER clearly have high diagnostic capabilities. NEWPROD and Nakanishi's model have some diagnostic capabilities, while the four remaining models are weak on this dimension.

Degree of Commercial Acceptance

The Parfitt/Collins model has essentially superseded the Fourt/Woodlock model. According to executives of the Market Research Corporation of America (MRCA), the Parfitt/Collins model has gained wide acceptance in the United States and Britain. The Parfitt/Collins model has been applied to product categories such as toothpaste, dishwashing liquid, toilet tissue, butter, instant coffee and floor polish. Most of the applications reported in Parfitt and Collins (1968) appear to consist of predictions that were later validated by actual sales. The Fourt/Woodlock model has been applied to products such as cake mix, cereals, margarine, detergents, pet foods, canned fruits and scouring pads.

The development of STEAM was funded by diary panel companies such as MRCA. However, there is no evidence that it is currently being used by any company. The full-blown SPRINTER model has not been used very much, but there have been many applications of a simplified version of the model (Glen Urban, personal communication, 1981). Eskin's model was developed for the Pillsbury Company and is presumably being used by Pillsbury. The Nakanishi model was applied to the tomato catsup product category by the author. However, there is no evidence that this model is used commercially. The NEWPROD model was developed for a specific unnamed corporation, but it is not clear to what extent the model is used by the company.

The TRACKER model was developed for the Leo Burnett advertising agency. As reported in Blattberg and Golanty (1978), there is ample evidence of its use by clients of Leo Burnett. Specific products for which TRACKER has been used are cat food, cereal, candy, beer, scouring pads and medicinal products (Robert Blattberg, personal communication, 1981). Finally, the NEWS model (developed for BBDO's clients) has been applied to 85 brands in 41 product categories. Some of the products for which NEWS has been used are ball-point pens, bar soap, car wax, cat food, cigarettes, dog food, gasoline additive, margarine, shampoo, toilet tissue and toothpaste (Pringle, Wilson and Brody 1982, p. 3, Table 1).

Our overall evaluation of the degree of commercial acceptance of these models is summarized in the last column of Table 1. NEWS, TRACKER and the Parfitt/Collins model appear to have gained the greatest commercial acceptance.

Our evaluations of commercial acceptance are consistent with the results reported by Larréché and Montgomery (1977), who used a Delphi procedure to assess the likelihood that a given model would be accepted by marketing managers. NEWS, SPRINTER and STEAM are the only three models evaluated both in this paper and by Larréché and Montgomery (1977). Like us, they rank NEWS, SPRINTER and STEAM in descending order in terms of their likelihood of acceptance by marketing managers.

OVERALL EVALUATION

There appear to be two important objectives for the various test market models: sales prediction for the new brand and evaluation of the new product's marketing mix. If sales prediction is the principal concern, the Parfitt/Collins model is clearly the model to use. It is very simple to understand and explain to managers and is essentially a do-it-yourself model. It provides accurate predictions and has a record of extensive use, both in the U.S. and Britain.

If the test market model is expected to evaluate the new product's marketing mix in addition to providing a sales forecast, the TRACKER and NEWS models appear to be the preferred choices. Both models are complete in terms of modeling all stages and including marketing mix variables. Yet, they are not so complex that they are difficult and costly to implement. Both models provide good diagnostics, predict well and appear to enjoy a high degree of commercial acceptance.

SPRINTER comes close to TRACKER and NEWS for this purpose. However, the full-blown SPRINTER model described in Urban (1970) is too complex and costly in terms of data inputs to compete with TRACKER and NEWS. However, a simpler version of SPRINTER is likely to be a reasonable alternative if the total cost of implementation is competitive with that for TRACKER and NEWS.

The Parfitt/Collins, NEWS and TRACKER models are described in the Appendix. They appear to be the best of those models reviewed in this paper, and we feel it is pertinent to include a brief description of these models.

Conclusions and Future Directions of Research

In this paper we have reviewed a number of test market models that have appeared in the literature. These models vary markedly in terms of model design, complexity and data requirements. Many of the models claim excellent fit to the data, questioning the value of building very sophisticated models and using powerful estimation techniques. It would be interesting to apply a subset of these models to the same data set(s) and examine their comparative performance.

As experience with these models increases, both in the number of applications and in the number of different product classes where the models have been applied, we believe that managers will gain sufficient insights into the ranges of the model's parameter values. This experience should enable the manager to use these models for planning purposes in a pretest market sense for future new products. In other words, the model could be used to simulate the sales that would be generated by alternative marketing programs for the new brand. Thus, the simulations would enable the firm to choose the best marketing mix for the brand. This "planning" aspect is stressed in the publication describing TRACKER. In addition, pretest market versions of NEWS and the test market model by Eskin (1973) are already available (see Eskin and Malec 1976 for an early description of this model).

The state of the art for building test market models appears to be in an advanced state for frequently purchased products. On the other hand, the evaluation of test market data for infrequently purchased durables has not been tackled by marketing model builders (however, see Hauser and Urban 1982). For this purpose, the first purchase diffusion models (Mahajan and Muller 1979) or the ideas behind the diffusion models that incorporate repeat purchasing (see, for example, Dodson and Muller 1978) are likely to be useful. Of course, such models should also incorporate the effects of marketing mix variables such as price and advertising.

Appendix
Model Descriptions

Parfitt and Collins (1968)

Model Structure. The model's objective is to predict S, the long run share of the new brand, T, in the test market:

$$S = PRB$$

where

P = ultimate cumulative trial rate for the brand,
R = ultimate repeat purchase rate for the brand,

B = the buying rate factor that models the differences in purchase volume between buyers of the new brand and buyers of the product class in general. B is equal to 1.0 if buyers of the new brand buy it at the same rate as the rest of the product class buyers.[7]

Data Requirements. This model uses diary panel data.

Estimation. To estimate P, the authors use a growth rate model given by

$$K(t) = P(1 - e^{-at})$$

where

$K(t)$ = cumulative trial rate at time t
a = the rate of growth parameter.

P and a are estimated by discounted least squares procedures. To estimate R, the authors seem to use subjective extrapolation of the early test market data rather than a statistical model (see Shoemaker and Staelin 1976, for a specific statistical model to estimate R). B is the ratio of the amount of the product class bought by users of brand T to the amount of the product class bought by all buyers of the product class.

Finally, it is interesting to note that Jeuland (1978) shows how the Penetration and Repeat Purchase relationships of the Parfitt/Collins model can be derived by aggregating a simple first order stochastic choice model specified at the level of an individual consumer.

TRACKER (Blattberg and Golanty 1978)

The model's goal is to forecast year-end sales for the new product three months after it has been introduced in the test market. The sales forecast is based on three models, one for each of the three stages of new product acceptance: awareness, trial and repeat.

Awareness Model. The awareness model consists of the following relationship:

$$\ln\left(\frac{1 - A_t}{1 - A_{t-1}}\right) = a - b\text{GRP}_t$$

where a and b are parameters to be estimated, GRP_t is the gross rating points obtained by advertising, and A_t is the cumulative proportion aware of the brand in time period t. Note that the above relationship captures decreasing marginal returns to advertising.

Trial Model. In the trial model, two types of triers are considered: those who become aware in the current period and those who were aware in the previous periods but had not yet tried the product. Thus, the following model is proposed:

$$\Delta T_t = (T_t - T_{t-1}) = \alpha(A_t - A_{t-1}) + \beta(A_{t-1} - T_{t-1})$$

where α and β are parameters to be estimated, T_t is the cumulative proportion of triers of the new brand in period t, and A_t is the cumulative proportion of potential triers of the new product who are aware of the new product in period t. This model reflects the notion that newly aware potential triers have a probability of trial higher than that of those potential triers who were aware in the past but have not yet tried. In other words, the parameter α is expected to be larger than β (where α and β are both constrained to be between 0 and 1).

The above model of trial assumes that the new brand's price is the same as the average price in the product class. To allow for differential brand prices, the trial model is amended as follows:[8]

$$\Delta T_t^* = \frac{\Delta T_t}{\bar{P}_t^\gamma}$$

where

ΔT_t^* = observed price adjusted by incremental trial,

$\bar{P}_t$ = relative price, i.e., the price of the new brand divided by the average price of the product class,

γ = a parameter to be estimated ($\gamma > 0$).

If the new brand's price is greater than the average industry price, $\bar{P}_t > 1$ and $\Delta T_t^* < \Delta T_t$ (as expected). Similarly, $\Delta T_t^* > \Delta T_t$ if $\bar{P}_t < 1$ while $\Delta T_t^* = \Delta T_t$ if $\bar{P}_t = 1$.

Repeat Model. Given incremental trial, trial usage rate (TU), repeat usage rate (RU) and repeater proportions (r and $1 - d_i$), TRACKER computes sales for any period using the Projection model. The Projection model is illustrated in Figure 2 for period 4. Total sales in period 4, TS(4), could come from new triers in period 4 or from consumers who had tried the product in either period 1, 2 or 3 and who are repeating in period 4. The model estimates the percentage of consumers in each stage of repeat and computes each period's sales by aggregating the sales from each repeater class and the new trier class for that period. Year-end sales are obtained by summing the sales for each period.

Data Requirements. This model uses survey data that are collected by administering questionnaires to potential users of the product (sample sizes range between 500 and 1000) in three waves scheduled every four weeks following the introduction of the new product (though this timing could vary depending on the average purchase cycle for the product).

23 — New Product Models for Test Market Data

Estimation. The model's parameters are estimated by pooling observations for different brands in a product category and assuming homogeneity of the parameters across the brands. The authors are forced to do this because they have only three observations per brand and estimating the parameters for the test brand would be impossible if only the data for the test brand were to be used. The awareness model's parameters are estimated by ordinary least squares and the authors report R^2 values of 0.732 and 0.652 for two different product categories. In both product categories the signs of the parameters match intuitive expectations. The trial model is estimated by a nonlinear least squares method. Again, the parameter estimates appear to have reasonable signs and magnitudes. In the projection model, TU is set equal to 1 (because triers are likely to buy only one unit of the product), and the d(i) (see Figure 2 for a definition) are estimated subjectively, while r and RU are estimated through the telephone surveys. The authors report that the subjective estimate of r in

FIGURE 2. TRACKER: The Sales Projection Model for Period 4

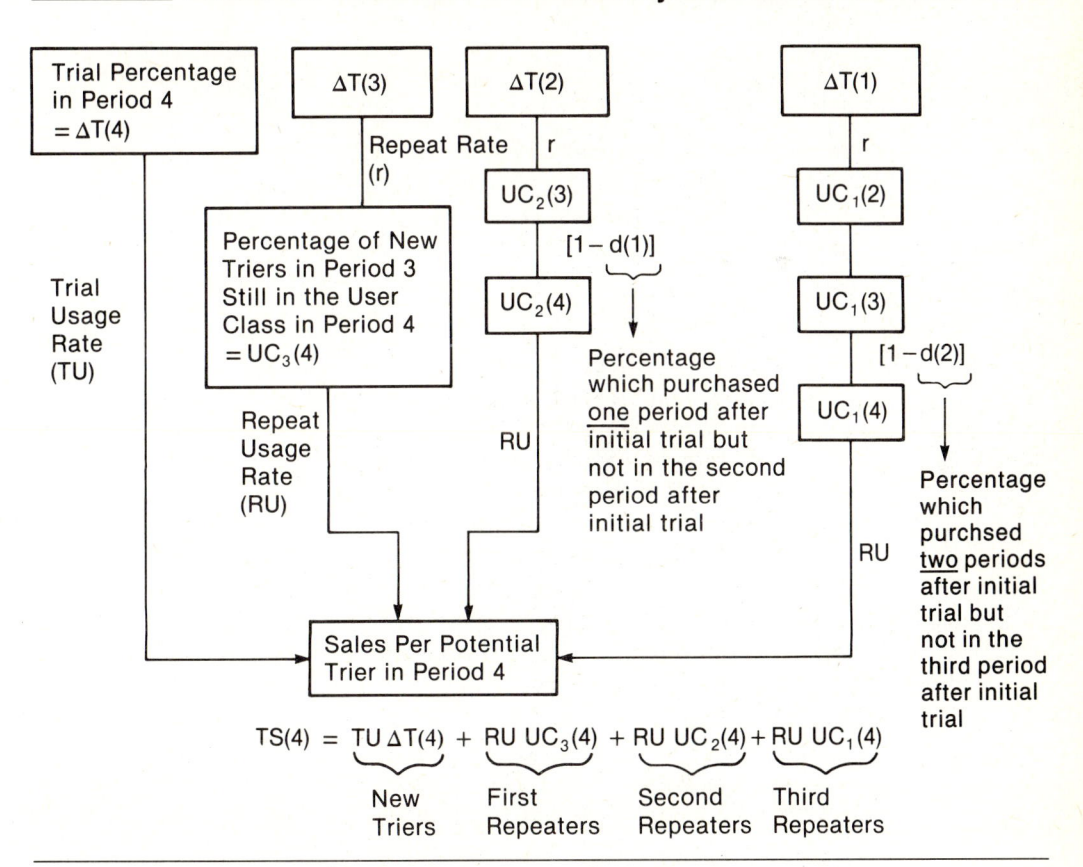

$$TS(4) = TU\,\Delta T(4) + RU\,UC_3(4) + RU\,UC_2(4) + RU\,UC_1(4)$$

- $TU\,\Delta T(4)$: New Triers
- $RU\,UC_3(4)$: First Repeaters
- $RU\,UC_2(4)$: Second Repeaters
- $RU\,UC_1(4)$: Third Repeaters

Components of the diagram:
- Trial Percentage in Period 4 = $\Delta T(4)$
- Trial Usage Rate (TU)
- Repeat Rate (r)
- Repeat Usage Rate (RU)
- Percentage of New Triers in Period 3 Still in the User Class in Period 4 = $UC_3(4)$
- $UC_2(3) \xrightarrow{[1-d(1)]} UC_2(4)$: Percentage which purchased one period after initial trial but not in the second period after initial trial
- $UC_1(2) \to UC_1(3) \xrightarrow{[1-d(2)]} UC_1(4)$: Percentage which purchsed two periods after initial trial but not in the third period after initial trial
- Sales Per Potential Trier in Period 4

the first period agrees closely with the latter estimates. Therefore, an average value of r is used in the model. As far as d(i) is concerned, a simulation conducted by the authors demonstrated that the predictions were sensitive to estimates of d(i).

NEWS (Pringle, Wilson and Brody 1982)

The New Product Early Warning System (NEWS) model developed by BBDO is an outgrowth of their earlier DEMON model (Learner 1968). Unpublished descriptions of the model have been available for many years (see BBDO 1975, for example). The objective of NEWS is to predict levels of awareness, trial, repeat, users and sales of a new product. NEWS explicitly considers the awareness-trial-repeat links.

Awareness Model. Awareness is generated by advertising and promotional efforts, viz. free samples and coupons.

AV_t, cumulative brand awareness in period t due to advertising only, is decomposed as follows:

$$AV_t = AR_t + AE_t + AN_t$$

where

AR_t = previously aware consumers who, though not exposed to the current period's advertising, retain their awareness.
AE_t = previously aware consumers who, by exposure to the current period's advertising, retain their awareness,
AN_t = previously unaware consumers who became aware due to the current period's advertising.

AN_t is computed by applying the learning operator $(1 - e^{-\alpha G_t})$ (where G_t is proportional to advertising expenditures at time t) to the previously unaware prospects. AE_t is computed in a similar manner by applying the learning operator to those who were aware last period, net of initial awareness, A_0. AR_t is the sum of A_0 and a quantity obtained by multiplying $(A_{t-1} - A_0 - AE_t)$ by the "retention rate" κ where A_{t-1} is total awareness at $(t-1)$. An assumption in the above computations is that those who are initially aware continue to retain their awareness without the aid of any advertising.

Incremental awareness due to promotion is computed as a fraction of those who are unaware. Thus, A_t, the total awareness at time t is given by:

$$A_t = AV_t + AP_t(A^* - AV_t)$$

where AP_t is the fraction aware due to promotion and A^* represents a ceiling awareness level.

Trial Model. T_t, the cumulative trial (proportion of the target population that has bought the brand one or more times prior to time t) at period t, is given by

$$T_t = TV_t + TP_t + T_{t-1}$$

where

TV_t = new trial induced by advertising, and
TP_t = incremental trial due to promotion.
$TV_t = TV'_t + TV''_t$

where

TV'_t = current period's newly aware consumers who now try the product, and
TV''_t = last period's newly aware consumers who now try the product.
$TV'_t = \tau\, AN_t D_t$

where τ is the awareness-trial rate (i.e., the fraction of the target population that will move from a state of new awareness to one of trial in a single purchase cycle) and D_t captures the effect of distribution. TV''_t is computed in a similar manner after netting out those who could have tried due to promotional efforts in the last period. Care is also taken to give a lower probability of trial to those who became aware last period but who try only in the current period.

Promotion generated trial, TP_t, is computed by partitioning consumers into six classes depending on how they became aware and which form of promotion (free samples or coupons) induced trial. Each group has a different probability of trial and is assumed to be equally likely to make a trial purchase in the current period or the next period. Thus, TP_t is defined as:

$$TP_t = \frac{1}{2} D_t \sum_{i=1}^{6} (TP_{i,t} + TP_{i,t-1})$$

$$TP_{i,t} = \tau_i AP_{i,t}$$

where τ_i is the awareness to trial coefficient for the *i*th promotion-generated trial class.

Repeat Model. First, consider cumulative first repeat, R_t. This can be broken down as

$$R_t = R_{t-1} + R'_t + R''_t$$

where

R'_t = new triers from the previous period who are now making their first repeat purchase, and

R''_t = new triers from the period before last who are now making their first repeat purchase.

R'_t is related to $(T_{t-1}-T_{t-2})$ through a trial to repeat coefficient, ω. R'_t is adjusted downwards for low levels of product availability. R''_t is computed similarly from $(T_{t-2}-T_{t-3})$. Those who had an occasion to make a first repeat last period but did not do so have a lower probability of repeating in the current period.

Next, U_t, the total proportion of users in any period, is computed as the sum of new triers, new first repeaters and ongoing repeaters. Ongoing repeat at time t is determined by applying a continued repeat purchase rate to the different new first repeaters (R_2-R_1), (R_3-R_2), etc.

Sales at any period t is the sum of the trial sales and repeat sales and is expressed as

$$\text{Sales} = (T_t - T_{t-1})TV + [U_t - (T_t - T_{t-1})]UV$$

where

TV = number of units bought by a trier,
UV = usage volume.

Data Requirements. NEWS uses data from secondary sources, BBDO's experiences with related products and telephone surveys. To estimate some of the parameters of NEWS/Market, approximately two to four specifically designed surveys are administered during the first three months of the test market. The number of respondents typically varies between 200 and 1000 per consumer survey.

Estimation. There are several parameters that have to be estimated. These are the learning operator α in the awareness model, the awareness to trial rate τ, the retention rate κ, the promotion trial rates τ_i, $i=1,\ldots 6$, the trial to repeat coefficient ω, and certain loyalty parameters (see Pringle, Wilson and Brody 1982, pp. 19–22 for details).

Several of these parameters (e.g., κ and τ_i) are estimated on the basis of company experience and secondary data. However, α, τ, ω and the loyalty parameters for NEWS/Market are estimated using a numerical search procedure. In contrast to TRACKER, the parameters for a given product are estimated using survey data for *that product only*. Thus, about two to four observations are generally available for estimation (e.g., Pringle, Wilson and Brody 1982, p. 21, Table 3). The authors report estimation results for two products. The estimated values of the parameters for these two products are reasonable and the reported fits are very good.

ENDNOTES

1. An earlier version of this paper appeared in a book of readings edited by Wind, Mahajan and Cardozo (see Narasimhan and Sen 1981). The authors would like to thank the many individuals who commented on earlier drafts of this paper. The comments of Gert Assmus, Edward Brody, Dan Horsky, Vijay Mahajan, Dov Pekelman, Alvin Silk, V. Srinivasan and Glen Urban were particularly valuable.
2. For a more detailed discussion of the new product introduction process, see, for example, Urban and Hauser (1980, pp. 31–40).
3. It might be argued that the models should also explicitly consider changes in the sales of the *product class*. However, if the new brand is introduced in an established product class, one could probably ignore the effect on primary demand and assume that the potential trier class for the new brand is fixed.
4. Though it is theoretically desirable to model different classes of repeaters separately, some recent empirical work by Kalwani and Silk (1980) appears to indicate that it is adequate to model explicitly the first repeaters only.
5. Actually, all the marketing mix variables listed in Figure 1 will affect each of the three stages in varying degrees. We have attempted to isolate the most important effects in Figure 1. In addition, other factors could influence the consumer to move from one stage to another. For example, a consumer who is aware of the new product may choose to buy it out of curiosity or in seeking variety without being unduly affected by the product's price. We have elected to omit such factors because they are difficult to model and none of the models reviewed explicitly take such factors into account.
6. Table 1 lists only the ultimate measure of interest, ignoring intermediate measures forecasted by some of the models. For example, models such as NEWS, SPRINTER and TRACKER can provide forecasts of intermediate measures such as brand awareness and trial probability.
7. In passing, we should mention a minor variation of the Parfitt/Collins model due to Ahl (1970). Ahl combines the P and B terms into a single term, the ultimate volume trial rate.
8. The notation in the equation that follows is slightly different from the notation in Blattberg and Golanty (1978).

REFERENCES

Achenbaum, Alvin (1974), "Market Testing: Using the Marketplace as a Laboratory," in *Handbook of Marketing Research*, Robert Ferber, ed., New York: McGraw-Hill Book Co., 4:31–4:54.

Ahl, David H. (1970), "New Product Forecasting Using Consumer Panels," *Journal of Marketing Research*, 7 (May), 160–67.

Assmus, Gert (1975), "NEWPROD: The Design and Implementation of a New Product Model," *Journal of Marketing*, 39 (January), 16–23.

BBDO, Inc. (1975), "The NEWS Model: A Technical Description," unpublished working paper.

Blattberg, Robert (1981), personal communication.

———— and John Golanty (1978), "TRACKER: An Early Test-Market Forecasting and

Diagnostic Model for New Product Planning," *Journal of Marketing Research*, 15 (May), 192–202.

Day, George S., Allan D. Shocker and Rajendra K. Srivastava (1979), "Customer-Oriented Approaches to Identifying Product Markets," *Journal of Marketing*, 43 (Fall), 8–19.

Dodson, Jr., Joe A. and Eitan Muller (1978), "Models of New Product Diffusion through Advertising and Word-of-Mouth," *Management Science*, 24 (November), 1568–78.

Eskin, Gerald J. (1973), "Dynamic Forecasts of New Product Demand Using a Depth of Repeat Model," *Journal of Marketing Research*, 10 (May), 115–29.

—— and John Malec (1976), "A Model for Estimating Sales Potential Prior to the Test Market," *Proceedings of the American Marketing Association*, Chicago: American Marketing Association, 220–33.

Fourt, Louis A. and Joseph W. Woodlock (1960), "Early Prediction of Market Success for New Grocery Products," *Journal of Marketing*, 25 (October), 31–38.

Hauser, John R. and Glen L. Urban (1977), "A Normative Methodology for Modeling Consumer Response to Innovation," *Operations Research*, 25 (July–August), 579–619.

—— and —— (1982), "Prelaunch Forecasting of New Consumer Durables: Ideas on a Consumer Value-Priority Model," working paper, Sloan School of Management, M.I.T.

Jeuland, Abel (1978), "Brand Choice Inertia and the Behavior of New Product Introduction Statistics," working paper, Graduate School of Business, University of Chicago.

Kalwani, Manohar U. and Alvin J. Silk (1980), "Structure of Repeat Buying for New Packaged Goods," *Journal of Marketing Research*, 17 (August), 316–22.

Klompmaker, Jay E., G. David Hughes and Russell I. Haley (1976), "Test Marketing in New Product Development," *Harvard Business Review*, 54 (May/June), 128–38.

Larréché, Jean-Claude and David B. Montgomery (1977), "A Framework for the Comparison of Marketing Models: A Delphi Study," *Journal of Marketing Research*, 14 (November), 487–98.

Learner, David B. (1968), "Profit Maximization through New Product Marketing Planning and Control," in *Applications of the Sciences in Marketing Management*, Frank M. Bass, Charles W. King and Edgar A. Pessemier, eds., New York: John Wiley & Sons, Inc., 151–67.

Mahajan, Vijay and Eitan Muller (1979), "Innovation Diffusion and New Product Growth Models in Marketing," *Journal of Marketing*, 43 (Fall), 55–68.

Massy, William F. (1969), "Forecasting the Demand for New Convenience Products," *Journal of Marketing Research*, 6 (November), 405–12.

——, David B. Montgomery and Donald G. Morrison (1970), *Stochastic Models of Buying Behavior*, Cambridge, MA: The MIT Press.

Midgley, David F. (1976), "A Simple Mathematical Theory of Innovative Behavior," *Journal of Consumer Research*, 3 (1976), 31–41.

—— (1977), *Innovation and New Product Marketing*, London: Croom Helm, Ltd.

Nakanishi, Masao (1971), "Consumer Learning in Awareness and Trial of New Products," in *Proceedings of the Second Annual Conference of the Association for Consumer Research*, David M. Gardner, ed., College Park, MD: Association for Consumer Research, Inc., 186–96.

——— (1973), "Advertising and Promotion Effects on Consumer Response to New Products," *Journal of Marketing Research*, 10 (August), 242–49.

Narasimhan, Chakravarthi and Subrata K. Sen (1981), "Test-Market Models for New Product Introduction," in *New Product Forecasting: Models and Applications*, Yoram Wind, Vijay Mahajan and Richard Cardozo, eds., Lexington, MA: Lexington Press, 293–321.

Parfitt, J. H. and B. J. K. Collins (1968), "Use of Consumer Panels for Brand Share Prediction," *Journal of Marketing Research*, 5 (May), 131–45.

Pringle, Lewis G., R. Dale Wilson and Edward I. Brody (1982), "NEWS: A Decision-Oriented Model for New Product Analysis and Forecasting," *Marketing Science*, 1 (Winter), 1–29.

Robinson, Patrick J. (1981), "Comparison of Pretest Market New Product Forecasting Models," in *New Product Forecasting: Models and Applications*, Yoram Wind, Vijay Mahajan and Richard Cardozo, eds., Lexington, MA: Loxington Proce, 181–204.

Shocker, Allan D. and V. Srinivasan (1979), "Multiattribute Approaches for Product Concept Evaluation and Generation: A Critical Review," *Journal of Marketing Research*, 16 (May), 159–80.

Shoemaker, Robert and Richard Staelin (1976), "The Effects of Sampling Variation on Sales Forecasts for New Consumer Products," *Journal of Marketing Research*, 13 (May), 138–43.

Silk, Alvin J. and Glen L. Urban (1978), "Pretest Market Evaluation of New Packaged Goods: A Model and Measurement Methodology," *Journal of Marketing Research*, 15 (May), 171–91.

Urban, Glen (1970), "Sprinter Mod III: A Model for the Analysis of New Frequently Purchased Consumer Products," *Operations Research*, 18 (September–October), 805–54.

——— (1981), personal communication.

——— and John R. Hauser (1980), *Design and Marketing of New Products*, Englewood Cliffs, NJ: Prentice-Hall, Inc.

——— and Richard Karash (1971), "Evolutionary Model Building," *Journal of Marketing Research*, 8 (February), 62–66.

Wind, Yoram (1982), *Product Policy*, Reading, MA: Addison-Wesley Publishing Company, Inc.

——— and David Learner (1979), "On the Measurement of Purchase Data: Surveys versus Purchase Diaries," *Journal of Marketing Research*, 16 (February), 39–47.

24 Positioning Your Product

David A. Aaker and J. Gary Shansby

Business Horizons, Vol. 25 (May–June 1982), pp. 56–62. Copyright 1982 by the Foundation for the School of Business at Indiana University. Reprinted by permission.

How should a new brand be positioned? Can a problem brand be revived by a repositioning strategy? Most marketing managers have addressed these and other positioning questions; however, "positioning" means different things to different people. To some, it means the segmentation decision. To others it is an image question. To still others it means selecting which product features to emphasize. Few managers consider all of these alternatives. Further, the positioning decision is often made ad hoc, and is based upon flashes of insight, even though systematic, research-based approaches to the positioning decision are now available. An understanding of these approaches should lead to more sophisticated analysis in which positioning alternatives are more fully identified and evaluated.

A product or organization has many associations which combine to form a total impression. The positioning decision often means selecting those associations which are to be built upon and emphasized and those associations which are to be removed or de-emphasized. The term "position" differs from the older term "image" in that it implies a frame of reference, the reference point usually being the competition. Thus, when the Bank of California positions itself as being small and friendly, it is explicitly, or perhaps implicitly, positioning itself with respect to Bank of America.

The positioning decision is often the crucial strategic decision for a company or brand because the position can be central to customers' perception and choice decisions. Further, since all elements of the marketing program can potentially affect the position, it is usually necessary to use a positioning strategy as a focus for the development of the marketing program. A clear positioning strategy can insure that the elements of the marketing program are consistent and supportive.

What alternative positioning strategies are available? How can positioning strategies be identified and selected? Each of these questions will be addressed in turn.

POSITIONING STRATEGIES

A first step in understanding the scope of positioning alternatives is to consider some of the ways that a positioning strategy can be conceived and implemented. In the following, six approaches to positioning strategy will be illustrated and discussed: positioning by (1) attribute, (2) price-quality, (3) use or applications, (4) product-user, (5) the product-class, and (6) the competitor.

POSITIONING BY ATTRIBUTE

Probably the most frequently used positioning strategy is associating a product with an attribute, a product feature, or customer benefit. Consider imported automobiles. Datsun and Toyota have emphasized economy and reliability. Volkswagen has used a "value for the money" association. Volvo has stressed durability, showing commercials of "crash tests" and citing statistics on the long average life of their cars. Fiat, in contrast, has made a distinct effort to position itself as a European car with "European craftsmanship." BMW has emphasized handling and engineering efficiency, using the tag line, "the ultimate driving machine" and showing BMWs demonstrating their performance capabilities at a race track.

A new product can upon occasion be positioned with respect to an attribute that competitors have ignored. Paper towels had emphasized absorbency until Viva stressed durability, using demonstrations supporting the claim that Viva "keeps on working."

Sometimes a product will attempt to position itself along two or more attributes simultaneously. In the toothpaste market, Crest became a dominant brand by positioning itself as a cavity fighter, a position supported by a medical group endorsement. However, Aim achieved a 10 percent market share by positioning along two attributes, good taste and cavity prevention. More recently, Aqua-fresh has been introduced by Beecham as a gel paste that offers both cavity-fighting and breath-freshening benefits.

It is always tempting to try to position along several attributes. However, positioning strategies that involve too many attributes can be most difficult to implement. The result can often be a fuzzy, confused image.

POSITIONING BY PRICE/QUALITY

The price/quality attribute dimension is so useful and pervasive that it is appropriate to consider it separately. In many product categories, some brands offer more in terms of service, features, or performance and a higher price serves to signal this higher quality to the customer. Conversely, other brands emphasize price and value.

In general merchandise stores, for example, the department stores are at the top end of the price/quality scale. Neiman-Marcus, Bloomingdale's, and Saks Fifth Avenue are near the top, followed by Macy's, Robinson's, Bullock's, Rich's, Filene's, Dayton's, Hudson's, and so on. Stores such as Sears, Montgomery Ward, and J.C. Penney are positioned below the department stores but above the discount stores like K-Mart. Sears' efforts to create a more upbeat fashion image was thought to have hurt their "value" position and caused some share declines.[1] Sears' recent five-year plan details a firm return to a positioning as a family, middle-class store offering top value. Sears is just one company that has faced the very tricky positioning task of retaining the image of low price and upgrading their quality image. There is always the risk that the quality message will blunt the basic "low-price," "value" position.

Positioning with Respect to Use or Application

Another positioning strategy is associating the product with a use or application. Campbell's Soup for many years was positioned for use at lunch time and advertised extensively over noontime radio. The telephone company more recently has associated long distance calling with communicating with loved ones in their "reach out and touch someone" campaign. Industrial products often rely upon application associations.

Products can, of course, have multiple positioning strategies, although increasing the number involves obvious difficulties and risks. Often a positioning-by-use strategy represents a second or third position designed to expand the market. Thus, Gatorade, introduced as a summer beverage for athletes who need to replace body fluids, has attempted to develop a winter positioning strategy as the beverage to drink when the doctor recommends drinking plenty of fluids. Similarly, Quaker Oats has attempted to position a breakfast food product as a natural whole-grain ingredient for recipes. Arm & Hammer baking soda has successfully positioned their product as an odor-destroying agent in refrigerators.

POSITIONING BY THE PRODUCT USER

Another positioning approach is associating a product with a user or a class of users. Thus, many cosmetic companies have used a model or personality, such as Brut's Joe Namath, to position their product. Revlon's Charlie cosmetic line has been positioned by associating it with a specific lifestyle profile. Johnson & Johnson saw market share move from 3 percent to 14 percent when they repositioned their shampoo from a product used for babies to one used by people who wash their hair frequently and therefore need a mild shampoo.

In 1970, Miller High Life was the "champagne of bottled beers," was purchased by the upper class, and had an image of being a woman's beer. Phillip Morris repositioned it as a beer for the heavy beer drinking, blue-collar working man. Miller's Lite beer, introduced in 1975, used convincing beer-drinking personalities to position itself as a beer for the heavy beer drinker who dislikes that filled-up feeling. In contrast, earlier efforts to introduce low-calorie beers positioned with respect to the low-calorie attribute were dismal failures. One even claimed its beer had fewer calories than skim milk, and another featured a trim personality. Miller's positioning strategies are in part why its market share has grown from 3.4 percent in 1970 to 24.5 percent in 1979.[2]

POSITIONING WITH RESPECT TO A PRODUCT CLASS

Some critical positioning decisions involve product-class associations. For example, Maxim freeze-dried coffee needed to position itself with respect to regular and instant coffee. Some margarines position themselves with respect to butter. Dried milk makers came out with instant breakfast positioned as a breakfast substitute and a virtually identical product positioned as a dietary meal substitute. The hand soap "Caress" by Lever Brothers positioned itself as a bath oil product rather than a soap.

The soft drink 7-Up was for a long time positioned as a beverage with a "fresh clean taste" that was "thirst-quenching." However, research discovered that most people regarded 7-Up as a mix rather than a soft drink. The successful "un-cola" campaign was then developed to position 7-Up as a soft drink, with a better taste than the "colas."

POSITIONING WITH RESPECT TO A COMPETITOR

In most positioning strategies, an explicit or implicit frame of reference is the competition. There are two reasons for making the reference competitor(s) the dominant aspect of the positioning strategy. First, a well established competitor's image can be exploited to help communicate another image referenced to it. In giving directions to an address, for example, it's easier to say, it is next to the Bank of America building than it is to detail streets, distances, and turns. Second, sometimes it's not important how good customers think you are; it is just important that they believe you are better (or as good as) a given competitor.

Perhaps the most famous positioning strategy of this type was the Avis "We're number two, so we try harder" campaign. The strategy was to position Avis with Hertz as a major car rental agency and away from National, which at the time was a close third to Avis.

Positioning explicitly with respect to a competitor can be an excellent way to create a position with respect to an attribute, especially the price/quality attribute pair. Thus, products difficult to evaluate, like liquor products, will often be compared with an established competitor to help the positioning task. For example, Sabroso, a coffee liqueur, positioned itself with the established brand, Kahlua, with respect to quality and also with respect to the type of liqueur.

Positioning with respect to a competitor can be aided by comparative advertising, advertising in which a competitor is explicitly named and compared on one or more attributes. Pontiac has used this approach to position some of their cars as being comparable in gas mileage and price to leading import cars. By comparing Pontiac to a competitor that has a well-defined economy image, like a Volkswagen Rabbit, and using factual information such as EPA gas ratings, the communication task becomes easier.

On Determining the Positioning Strategy

What should be our positioning strategy? The identification and selection of a positioning strategy can draw upon a set of concepts and procedures that have been developed and refined over the last few years. The process of developing a positioning strategy involves six steps:

1. Identify the competitors.
2. Determine how the competitors are perceived and evaluated.
3. Determine the competitors' positions.
4. Analyze the customers.
5. Select the position.
6. Monitor the position.

In each of these steps one can employ marketing research techniques to provide needed information. Sometimes the marketing research approach provides a conceptualization that can be helpful even if the research is not conducted. Each of these steps will be discussed in turn.

Identify the Competitors

This first step is not as simple as it might seem. Tab might define its competitors in a number of ways, including:

a. other diet cola drinks
b. all cola drinks
c. all soft drinks
d. nonalcoholic beverages
e. all beverages

A Triumph convertible might define its market in several ways:

a. two-passenger, low-priced, imported, sports car convertibles

b. two-passenger, low-priced, imported sports cars
c. two-passenger, low- or medium-priced, imported sports cars
d. low- or medium-priced sports cars
e. low- or medium-priced imported cars

In most cases, there will be a primary group of competitors and one or more secondary competitors. Thus, Tab will compete primarily with other diet colas, but other colas and all soft drinks could be important as secondary competitors.

A knowledge of various ways to identify such groupings will be of conceptual as well as practical value. One approach is to determine from product buyers which brands they considered. For example, a sample of Triumph convertible buyers could be asked what other cars they considered and perhaps what other showrooms they actually visited. A Tab buyer could be asked what brand [he/she] would have purchased had Tab been out of stock. The resulting analysis will identify the primary and secondary groups of competitive products. Instead of customers, retailers or others knowledgeable about customers could provide the information.

Another approach is the development of associations of products with use situations.[3] Twenty or so respondents might be asked to recall the use contexts for Tab. For each use context, such as an afternoon snack, respondents are then asked to identify all appropriate beverages. For each beverage so identified respondents are then asked to identify appropriate use contexts. This process would continue until a large list of use contexts and beverages resulted. Another respondent group would then be asked to make judgments as to how appropriate each beverage would be for each use situation. Groups of beverages could then be clustered based upon their similarity of appropriate use situations. If Tab was regarded as appropriate with snacks, then it would compete primarily with other beverages regarded as appropriate for snack occasions. The same approach would work with an industrial product such as computers, which might be used in several rather distinct applications.

The concepts of alternatives from which customers choose and appropriateness to a use context can provide a basis for identifying competitors even when market research is not employed. A management team or a group of experts, such as retailers, could employ one or both of these conceptual bases to identify competitive groupings.

DETERMINE HOW THE COMPETITORS ARE PERCEIVED AND EVALUATED

The challenge is to identify those product associations used by buyers as they perceive and evaluate competitors. The product associations will include product attributes, product user groups and use contexts. Even simple objects such as beer can evoke a host of physical attributes like container, after-taste, and price, and relevant associations like "appropriate for use while dining at a good restaurant" or "used by working men." The task is to identify a list of product associations, to remove redundancies from the list, and then to select those that are most useful and relevant in describing brand images.

One research-based approach to product association list generation is to ask respondents to identify the two most similar brands from a set of three competing brands and to describe why those two brands are similar and different from the third. As a variant, respondents could be asked which of two brands is preferred and why. The result will be a rather long list of product associations, perhaps over a hundred. The next step is to remove redundancy from the list using logic and judgment or factor analysis. The final step is to identify the most relevant product associations by determining which is correlated highest with overall brand attitudes or by asking respondents to indicate which are the most important to them.

DETERMINE THE COMPETITORS' POSITIONS

The next step is to determine how competitors (including our own entry) are positioned with respect to the relevant product associations and with respect to each other. Although such judgments can be made subjectively, research-based approaches are available. Such research is termed multidimensional scaling because its goal is to scale objects on several dimensions (or product associations). Multidimensional scaling can be based upon either product associations data or similarities data.

Product-Association-Based Multidimensional Scaling

The most direct approach is simply to ask a sample of the target segment to scale the various objects on the product association dimensions. For example, the respondent could be asked to express his or her agreement or disagreement on a seven-point scale with statements regarding the Chevette:

"With respect to its class I would consider the Chevette to be:

- sporty
- roomy
- economical
- good handling."

Alternatively, perceptions of a brand's users or use contexts could be obtained:

"I would expect the typical Chevette owner to be:

- older
- wealthy
- independent
- intelligent."

"The Chevette is most appropriate for:

- short neighborhood trips
- commuting
- cross country sightseeing."

In generating such measures there are several potential problems and considerations (in addition to generating a relevant product association list) of which one should be aware:

1. The validity of the task. Can a respondent actually position cars on a "sporty" dimension? There could be several problems. One, a possible unfamiliarity with one or more of the brands, can be handled by asking the respondent to evaluate only familiar brands. Another is the respondent's ability to understand operationally what "sporty" means or how to evaluate a brand on this dimension.
2. Differences among respondents. Subgroups within the population could hold very different perceptions with respect to one or more of the objects. Such diffused images can have important strategic implications. The task of sharpening a diffused image is much different from the task of changing a very tight, established one.
3. Are the differences between objects significant and meaningful? If the differences are not statistically significant, then the sample size may be too small to make any managerial judgments. At the same time, a small difference of no practical consequence may be statistically significant if the sample size is large enough.
4. Which product associations are not only important but also serve to distinguish objects? Thus, airline safety may be an important attribute, but all airlines may be perceived to be equally safe.

Similarities-Based Multidimensional Scaling

Product-association approaches have several conceptual disadvantages. A complete, valid, and relevant product association list is not easy to generate. Further, an object may be perceived or evaluated as a whole that is not really decomposable in terms of product associations. These disadvantages lead us to the use of non-attribute data—namely, similarity data.

Similarity measures simply reflect the perceived similarity of two objects. For example, respondents may be asked to rate the degree of similarity of assorted object pairs without a product association list which implicitly suggests criteria to be included or excluded. The result, when averaged over all respondents, is a similarity rating for each object pair. A multidimensional scaling program then attempts to locate objects in a two-, three- (or more if necessary) dimensional space termed a perceptual map. The program attempts to construct the perceptual map such that the two objects with the highest similarity are separated by the shortest distance, the object pair with the second highest similarity are separated by the second shortest distance, and so on. A disadvantage of the similarity-based approach is that the interpretation of the dimensions does not have the product associations as a guide.

ANALYZING THE CUSTOMERS

A basic understanding of the customer and how the market is segmented will help in selecting a positioning strategy. How is the market segmented? What role does the product class play in the customer's lifestyle? What really motivates the customer? What habits and behavior patterns are relevant?

The segmentation question is, of course, critical. One of the most useful segmentation approaches is benefit segmentation which focuses upon the benefits or, more generally, the product associations that a segment believes to be important. The identity of important product associations can be done directly by asking customers to rate product associations as to their importance or by asking them to make trade-off judgments between product associations[4] or by asking them to conceptualize and profile "ideal brands." An ideal brand would be a combination of all the customer's preferred product associations. Customers are then grouped into segments defined by product associations considered important by customers. Thus, for toothpaste there could be a decay preventative segment, a fresh breath segment, a price segment, and so on. The segment's relative size and commitment to the product association will be of intererst.

It is often useful to go beyond product association lists to get a deeper understanding of consumer perceptions. A good illustration is the development of positioning objectives for Betty Crocker by the Needham, Harper & Steers advertising agency.[5] They conducted research involving more than 3,000 women, and found that Betty Crocker was viewed as a company that is:

- honest and dependable
- friendly and concerned about consumers
- a specialist in baked goods but
- out of date, old, and traditional
- a manufacturer of "old standby" products
- not particularly contemporary or innovative.

The conclusion was that the Betty Crocker image needed to be strengthened and to become more modern and innovative and less old and stodgy.

To improve the Betty Crocker image, it was felt that an understanding was needed of the needs and lifestyle of today's women and how these relate to desserts. Thus, the research study was directed to basic questions about desserts. Why are they served? Who serves them? The answers were illuminating. Dessert users tend to be busy, active mothers who are devoted to their families. The primary reasons for serving dessert tend to be psychological and revolve around the family.

- Dessert is a way to show others you care.
- Dessert preparation is viewed as an important duty of a good wife and mother.
- Desserts are associated with and help to create happy family moments.

Clearly, family bonds, love, and good times are associated with desserts. As a result, the Betty Crocker positioning objective was to associate Betty Crocker uniquely with the positive aspects of today's families and their feelings about dessert. Contemporary, emotionally involving advertising was used to associate Betty Crocker with desserts that contribute to happy family moments.

MAKING THE POSITIONING DECISION

The four steps or exercises just described should be conducted prior to making the actual positioning decision. The exercises can be done subjectively by the involved managers if necessary, although marketing research, if feasible and justifiable, will be more definitive. However, even with that background, it is still not possible to generate a cookbook solution to the positioning questions. However, some guidelines or checkpoints can be offered.

1. Positioning Usually Implies a Segmentation Commitment

Positioning usually means that an overt decision is being made to concentrate only on certain segments. Such an approach requires commitment and discipline because it's not easy to turn your back on potential buyers. Yet, the effect of generating a distinct, meaningful position is to focus on the target segments and not be constrained by the reaction of other segments.

Sometimes the creation of a "diffuse image," an image that will mean different things to different people, is a way to attract a variety of diverse segments. Such an approach is risky and difficult to implement and usually would be used only by a large brand. The implementation could involve projecting a range of advantages while avoiding being identified with any one. Alternatively, there could be a conscious effort to avoid associations which create positions. Pictures of bottles of Coca-Cola with the words "It's the real thing" superimposed on them, or Budweiser's claim that "Bud is the king of beers," illustrate such a strategy.

2. An Economic Analysis Should Guide the Decision

The success of any positioning strategy basically depends upon two factors: the potential market size $\times$ the penetration probability. Unless both of these factors are favorable, success will be unlikely. One implication of this simple structure is that a positioning strategy should attract a sizeable segment. If customers are to be attracted from other brands, those brands should have a worthwhile market share to begin with. If new buyers are to be attracted to the product class, a reasonable assessment should be made of the potential size of that growth area. The penetration probability indicates that there needs to be a competitive weakness to attack or a competitive advantage to exploit to generate a reasonable market penetration probability. Further, the highest payoff will often come from retaining existing customers, so this alternative should also be considered.

3. If the Advertising is Working, Stick with It

An advertiser will often get tired of a positioning strategy and the advertising used to implement it and will consider making a change. However, the personality or image of a brand, like that of a person, evolves over many years, and the value of consistency through time cannot be overestimated. Some of the very successful, big-budget campaigns have run for ten, twenty, or even thirty years.

4. Don't Try to Be Something You Are Not

It is tempting but naive — and usually fatal — to decide on a positioning strategy that exploits a market need or opportunity but assumes that your product is something it is not. Before positioning a product, it is important to conduct blind taste tests or in-home or in-office use tests to make sure that the product can deliver what it promises and that is compatible with a proposed image.

Consider Hamburger Helper, successfully introduced in 1970 as an add-to-meat product that would generate a good-tasting, economical, skillet dinner.[6] In the mid-1970s, sales suffered when homemakers switched to more exotic, expensive foods. An effort to react by repositioning Hamburger Helper as a base for casseroles failed because the product, at least in the consumers' mind, could not deliver. Consumers perceived it as an economical, reliable, convenience food and further felt that they did not need help in making casseroles. In a personality test, where women were asked to describe the product as if it were a person, the most prevalent characteristic ascribed to the product was "helpful." The result was a revised campaign to position the product as being "helpful."

MONITORING THE POSITION

A positioning objective, like any marketing objective, should be measurable. To evaluate the positioning and to generate diagnostic information about future positioning strategies, it is necessary to monitor the position over time. A variety of techniques can be employed to make this measurement. Hamburger Helper used a "personality test," for example. However, usually one of the more structured techniques of multidimensional scaling is applied.

A variety of positioning strategies is available to the advertiser. An object can be positioned:

1. by attributes—eg., Crest is a cavity fighter.
2. by price/quality—eg., Sears is a "value" store.
3. by competitor—eg., Avis positions itself with Hertz.
4. by application—eg., Gatorade is for flu attacks.
5. by product user—eg., Miller is for the blue-collar, heavy beer drinker.
6. by product class—eg., Carnation Instant Breakfast is a breakfast food.

The selection of a positioning strategy involves identifying competitors, relevant attributes, competitor positions, and market segments. Research based approaches can help in each of these steps by providing conceptualization even if the subjective judgments of managers are used to provide the actual input information to the positioning decision.

ENDNOTES

1. "Sears' New 5-year Plan: To Serve Middle America," *Advertising Age*, December 4, 1978.
2. "A-B, Miller Brews Continue to Barrel Ahead," *Advertising Age*, August 4, 1980: 4.
3. George S. Day, Alan D. Shocker, and Rajendra K. Srivasta, "Customer-Oriented Approaches to Identify Product Markets," *Journal of Marketing*, Fall 1979: 8–19.
4. Paul E. Green and Yoram Wind, "New Ways to Measure Consumers' Judgments," *Harvard Business Review*, July–August 1975: 107–115.
5. Keth Reinhard, "How We Make Advertising" (presented to the Federal Trade Commission, May 11, 1979): 22–25.
6. Reinhard: 29.

25 Product Life Cycle Research: A Literature Review

David R. Rink and John E. Swan

Reprinted by permission of the publisher from "Product Life Cycle Research: A Literature Review," by David R. Rink and John E. Swan, *Journal of Business Research*, Vol. 7 (September 1979), pp. 219-242. Copyright 1979 by Elsevier Science Publishing Co., Inc.

Since the introduction of the idea of a product life cycle (PLC) almost 30 years ago [27, 28], a great deal has been written on the subject and several empirical studies have appeared. Numerous managerial-oriented articles and books have discussed the PLC. Yet the question remains: What is the scope of empirical evidence relevant to the PLC?

The amount of empirical research in the PLC field is both meager and concentrated. Researchers have focused almost exclusively on validating the existence of the PLC concept. Nondurable consumer goods have represented the primary products studied.

THE PRODUCT LIFE CYCLE CONCEPT

The PLC represents the unit sales curve for some product, extending from the time it is first placed on the market until it is removed [10, p. 50]. In portraying "the evolution of product attributes and market characteristics through time, (the PLC concept can be)...used prescriptively in the selection of marketing actions and planning" [58, p. 67].

Schematically, the PLC may be approximated by a bell-shaped curve (type I, Figure 1) that is divided into several stages [62]. Although the number of phases suggested in the PLC literature varies between four and six, a four-stage cycle—introduction, growth, maturity, and decline—is adopted.

The theoretical rationale behind the PLC concept emanates from the theory of diffusion and adoption of innovations [61]. That is, unit sales are low in introduction, because few consumers are aware of the new good (or service). With consumer recognition and acceptance, unit sales begin to increase at an increasing rate. This signals the start of the growth stage. However, the rate of growth in unit sales will subside as more competitors enter the industry and the market becomes smaller. Eventually, unit sales reach a plateau, and the product is in the maturity stage. Most of the mass market has already purchased the item. As consumers

FIGURE 1. Types of Product Life Cycle Patterns

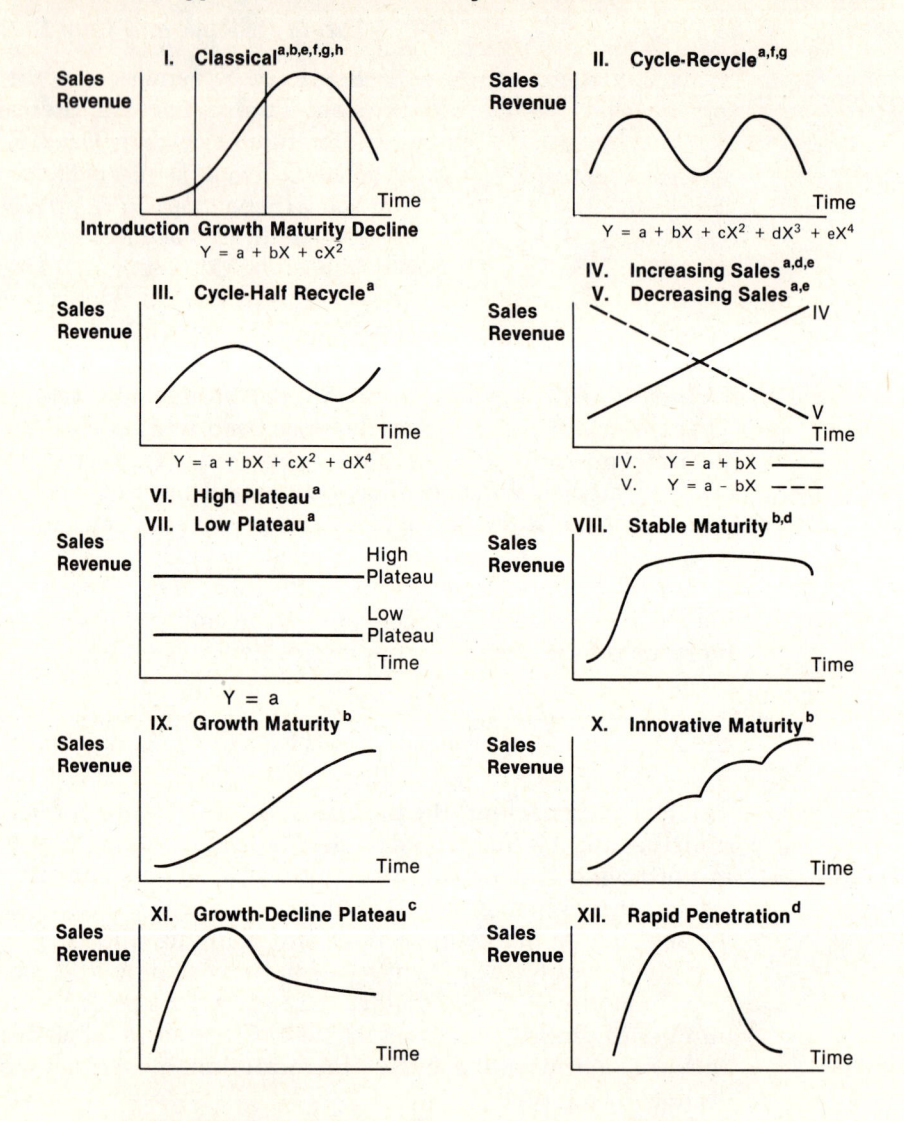

I. Classical[a,b,e,f,g,h]

Sales Revenue vs Time

Introduction | Growth | Maturity | Decline
$Y = a + bX + cX^2$

II. Cycle-Recycle[a,f,g]

Sales Revenue vs Time

$Y = a + bX + cX^2 + dX^3 + eX^4$

III. Cycle-Half Recycle[a]

Sales Revenue vs Time

$Y = a + bX + cX^2 + dX^4$

IV. Increasing Sales[a,d,e]
V. Decreasing Sales[a,e]

Sales Revenue vs Time

IV. $Y = a + bX$ ———
V. $Y = a - bX$ ---

VI. High Plateau[a]
VII. Low Plateau[a]

Sales Revenue vs Time

High Plateau
Low Plateau

$Y = a$

VIII. Stable Maturity[b,d]

Sales Revenue vs Time

IX. Growth Maturity[b]

Sales Revenue vs Time

X. Innovative Maturity[b]

Sales Revenue vs Time

XI. Growth-Decline Plateau[c]

Sales Revenue vs Time

XII. Rapid Penetration[d]

Sales Revenue vs Time

[a] Adapted from Cox [21, 22].
[b] Adapted from Buzzell [10].
[c] Adapted from Headen [40].
[d] Adapted from Frederixon [39].
[e] Adapted from Buzzell and Nourse [12].
[f] Adapted from Hinkle [41].
[g] Adapted from Cunningham [24].
[h] Adapted from Poli [58], Belville [5], Patton [57], Brockhoff [9], Branti [8], May [54], Kovac and Dague [46], Buzzell and Cook [59], Dean and Sengupta [26], Albach [1], Stobaugh [66], and Balachandran and Jain [2].

increasingly forsake the product for its newer counterparts, unit sales will decline rapidly. Removal from the market is imminent.

The PLC theory *per se* is directly analogous to other concepts that typify a more or less predictable pattern across time. Such notions represent a summary of a number of forces that determine some outcome of interest. As an example, a seasonal sales pattern for a product may be determined by a large number of factors, including changes in temperature across the seasons, social customs, and conventions, demand stimulation by business firms, and so on. The concept of seasonal sales has been very useful because of the fundamental fact that many products do have sales that vary by season and such variation is predictable enough to be useful for planning purposes. What can be said about the PLC based on empirical studies? What has been the scope of PLC studies? How much confidence can we have in conclusions about the PLC based on the number of studies that are relevant to a specific question about the PLC?

PURPOSE

The major purpose is to review research on the PLC in order to see what conclusions can be drawn as answers to the following fundamental questions and to assess the weight of evidence that is pertinent to each question:

1. Do recognizable PLC patterns across time in fact occur, and on what sample of industries and products is our knowledge of the PLC based?
2. Can PLC stages be forecasted?
3. Do we know how economic conditions or characteristics of the firm may affect the PLC?
4. To what extent is the PLC used in strategy planning?
5. What are the gaps in our knowledge of the PLC that future research could concentrate on?

A second purpose is to stimulate more extensive and diverse research. This will be accomplished by first, reviewing the scope of PLC studies that have been conducted; second, highlighting areas requiring empirical investigation; and third, providing guidelines for subsequent researchers.

EVIDENCE RELEVANT TO VALIDATING PLC PATTERNS

Types of PLC Patterns

The classical PLC shape (type I, Figure 1) has been only one of 12 types of PLC patterns discovered by investigators. Research on the different patterns shown in Figure 1 has been quite uneven.

Some 15 different studies of consumer nondurables and durables, as well as four studies of industrial goods, provide quite a bit of evidence that some products have validated the classical PLC curve (Figure 1). On the other hand, the cycle-recycle pattern has been found in four studies, including drugs [21], food products, household products [41], and industrial fluid measuring devices [24]. An increasing sales pattern was uncovered in three studies [12, 21, 39]. Although two studies support the decreasing sales pattern [12, 21], two other studies found a stable maturity pattern [10, 40]. The remaining PLC types of cycle-half-recycle, growth maturity, innovative maturity, high and low plateau, growth-decline plateau, and rapid penetration are the result of a single study. In summary, with the exception of the classical pattern, more research is needed to substantiate the remaining PLC patterns.

Reasons for Shape of Product Life Cycle Curve

While the studies previously mentioned have documented the general shape of the PLC curve, only a few researchers have extended their analysis to empirically ascertain why the curve assumes this shape. Although Belville concentrated on the initial PLC stages of color televisions, he found that seven factors were significant in triggering the takeoff point: price; volume of network color programming; public exposure to color; obsolescence of black-and-white sets; color quality; clarity of black-and-white pictures; and attitude of major set makers [5, p. 82]. Using unit sales data from 11 different automobile models, Brockhoff found that the PLC curve depended both upon time and sales of closely related products manufactured by the firm [9]. Other researchers and writers cite the common reasons of changing market and economic conditions, as well as reactions to competitors, as major factors determining the shape of the PLC curve [31, 43]. To date, however, these have not been empirically confirmed. Additionally, research should be conducted to ascertain whether management can influence these factors that affect the shape of the PLC. If so, what is the extent to which management can alter these factors, and, hence, influence the form of the curve?

THE SCOPE OF INDUSTRIES AND PRODUCTS INCLUDED IN PLC STUDIES

As shown in Table 1, 12 different studies of consumer nondurable goods have been the major focus of PLC research, followed by nine studies of consumer durable items. Only four studies of industrial goods were discovered by the authors.[1] The most obvious gap in knowledge of the PLC, therefore, involves industrial goods. As to why academic

TABLE 1. Industries and Products Included in PLC Studies

Industry (Number of Studies)	Product Category: Researcher(s) and Number of Products/Brands
Consumer durable goods (9)	Major appliances: Polli [58] 22; Buzzell and Cook [11] 50[a] Color television: Belville [5] 1 Black and white television: Patton [57] NA Refrigerators: Cunningham [24] NA Minor appliances: Polli [58] 28; Buzzell and Cook [11] 50[a] Automobiles: Brockhoff [9] 11; Brantl [8] 3; May [54] 1 Automobile tires: Kovac and Dague [46] 1
Consumer non-durable goods (12)	Drugs: Cox [21, 22] 258 Food: Hinkle [41] 275[b]; Polli [58] 56; Buzzell and Cook [11] 40; Cunningham [24] NA; Polli and Cook [59] 56; Dean and Sengupta [26] NA; Buzzell [10] 9; Buzzell and Nourse [12] 100; Headen [40] NA; Albach [1] 2 Household products/supplies: Hinkle [41] 275[b]; Polli [58] 45 Nonfood grocery items: Buzzell and Cook [11] 93 Health and beauty aids: Hinkle [41] 275[b]; Polli [58] 40; Polli and Cook [59] 51; Cunningham [24] Cigarettes: May [54] 4; Polli and Cook [59] 33
Industrial durable goods (2)	General engineering and fluid measuring devices: Cunningham [24] NA Automobile components: Cunningham [24] NA Established durable: Balachandran and Jain [2] NA
Industrial non-durable goods (2)	Petro-chemicals: Stobaugh [66] 9 Chemicals: Frederixon [39] 27

[a] Total only; unable to segregate by major versus minor household appliances.
[b] Total only; unable to segregate by food products, household products/supplies, and health and beauty aids.
NA = Not available in published research report.

researchers have been loathe to relate the PLC concept to industrial goods, two explanations may be offered. First, with industrial goods, "the time span tends to be extended and the market more conservative and slower to respond due to the historical inertia" [24, p. 34]. Second, since most industries lack records of product introduction, the development of PLC models requires

> ...a compilation of new product introductions. The difficulty of preparing such a compilation is perhaps the most serious obstacle to the widespread development of product life cycles for a variety of industries and products [22, p. 376].

Frequency of studies by type of customer—consumer versus industrial—can be misleading. Scrutinizing the type of goods utilized in consumer studies, not only do nondurable items outdistance durable ones

FIGURE 2. Classification of Consumer Products by Purchase Frequency, Price, Distribution, and Supply

		Price Level	Distribution: Intensive, Low	Distribution: Intensive, High	Distribution: Limited, Low	Distribution: Limited, High
Purchase Frequency	High	Low	1	2	3	4
	High	High	5	6	7	8
	Low	Low	9	10	11	12
	Low	High	13	14	15	16

by almost a 2:1 margin, but food products were overwhelmingly preferred (Table 1). Also, previous PLC researchers focused primarily upon those consumer products that were frequently purchased, low-priced, widely distributed, and not subject to wide variations on the supply side [58, p. 219]. The reasons investigators preferred nondurable consumer items were

> ...durables sales data, regardless of adjustment procedures, do not distinguish between adoption and replacement and therefore do not accurately measure the level of market acceptance. In addition, durable sales are heavily influenced by availability of materials (as during war years), income level changes, and consumer expectations.... These problems are not severe in nondurables [11, pp. 29, 35].

One investigator censured early PLC writers for generalizing "from a small and often biased sample of experiences" [58, p. 42]. This criticism is still appropriate as well as justified from the content and focus of relatively recent research. This conclusion can be substantiated by examining all possible combinations of four variables for consumer products, which were outlined by Polli [58, p. 39]: purchase frequency; price level; degree of distribution; and supply variations (Figure 2). Of the resulting 16 cells, researchers have concentrated almost exclusively on the first cell.

Before the PLC notion can become a theory in the strict scientific sense, extensive empirical observations and descriptions are mandatory.

For consumer goods, this can be accomplished by conducting research in each of the remaining 15 cells of Figure 2. The next step would entail replication of these empirical findings.

With industrial goods, the situation is slightly different. Not enough empirical studies have been performed for a theory to be developed. Hence, more industrial situations and products must be examined in order to establish that the PLC theory is applicable. Once this task is completed and a proposition developed, then researchers can attempt to fill the literature gaps by following a scheme similar to Figure 2, but for industrial goods. Replication would then follow.

DIFFERENT PRODUCT CONCEPTS ANALYZED IN PLC RESEARCH

Here the basic question is: To what extent have PLC studies covered different concepts of a new product and different levels of product aggregation?

Level of Product Aggregation

Typically, there are three levels of product aggregation—class, form, and brand. Product class represents items that are substitutes for the same want (e.g., cigarettes, cigars, and pipes). Product form is a finer classification of a product class (e.g., king-sized cigarettes, regulars, menthol cigarettes, etc.). Brand, on the other hand, is unique (e.g., Camels, Kools, etc.).

A major problem with previous, and sometimes current, PLC studies has been: What level of product aggregation was used? It is vital that these levels be differentiated because the PLC notion has a different degree of applicability in these three cases. That is, product classes possess the longest sales curves. Product forms probably exhibit the standard PLC histories. Product brands have very erratic sales trends [45, p. 431].

Most writers have accepted the idea that product forms are the most appropriate level of product aggregation to utilize in PLC research. However, this point requires more investigation as only one study has addressed this question. Based upon the sales histories of nonfood grocery product forms, Polli found no substantive evidence concerning the level of product aggregation that should be adopted by researchers interested in products other than nonfood grocery items [58, pp. 232-233]. Hence, more PLC research is needed utilizing various consumer and industrial goods to determine which product aggregation level should be adopted.

Definition of New Product

A difficulty in PLC studies has been: What is a new product? Does a variation in an established product represent a new product or part of the mother product? For example, should color television sets be considered as a separate product with their own PLC curve or as a part of black-and-white television's unit sales curve? Far from being resolved, this issue continues to plague PLC researchers. One author lamented that this question involves the "most complex element to untangle in understanding the life-cycle concept" [57, pp. 68–69].

A possible solution to the definitional quagmire surrounding the question, "What is a new product?" is to segregate new products into several degrees of newness. According to one writer, this can be accomplished, because "there appear to be a few universally recognized characteristics distinguishing the new product from an improved variation of an old one" [57, p. 69]. Continuing, this writer presented a four-way classification of new products: the unquestionably new product; the partially new product; the major product change; and the minor product change. This delineation, and others like it [12, p. 22], can be instrumental in alleviating the difficulty inherent with determining whether a new product is simply a variation of an old one or is a completely new item.

By integrating some of the previously mentioned variables, such as degree of perishability, customer type, degree of newness, and level of product aggregation, areas for future research can be easily identified. By taking all reasonable combinations of these four variables, the result is a possible 48-cell classification (Figure 3).

The major focus of consumer goods research (durable and nondurable) has been on minor product change—form with some emphasis on minor product change—class and brand. What little research has been directed at both major product change and partially new product has concentrated primarily on class and form. Brand has been almost totally ignored in this case. Other combinations suggested by Figure 3 represent potential areas for additional or new research.

In the industrial goods area (durable and nondurable), most of the studies have focused on minor product change—class and form. To the best of the authors' knowledge, no empirical research has been performed on the other cells of this group. Hence, these cells signify relatively untapped areas for future examination.

LEVELS OF MEASUREMENT

In the material previously reviewed and summarized in Figures 2 and 3, some potentially continuous variables, such as price level, have been treated as ordinal or nominal variables. This was done to simplify the

FIGURE 3. Classification of Goods by Newness, Customer, Product Aggregation, and Perishability

		Degree of Perishability	Level of Product Aggregation			Degree of Newness[a]			
			Class	Form	Brand	UNP	PNP	MPC	MIPC
Type of Customer	Consumer	Nondurable	1	2	3				
		Durable	4	5	6				
	Industrial	Nondurable	7	8	9				
		Durable	10	11	12				

[a]Columns are coded as follows: UNP = unquestionably new product; PNP = partially new product; MPC = major product change; MIPC = minor product change.

material and present a clear overview of some of the types of products and markets that have been the focus of PLC research. However, a basic question that should be addressed is: What level of measurement would be appropriate for such variables? This would depend upon the analytical use of such variables in PLC research. The variables may be used either to explain phenomena of interest concerning the PLC or to specify that part of the real world that a particular PLC model is applicable to. As explanatory variables, it would generally be best to retain continuous variables as continuous variables because a wider range of more powerful quantitative tools is available for continuous, interval level variables than is applicable to nominal or ordinal measures. As an example, if a researcher wished to test the idea that the lower the price of a new product, the shorter the introduction and growth stages of the PLC, then price measured as a continuous variable would be appropriate.

The second problem concerns specifying the limits of the application of PLC models. As previously noted, it has been felt that the classical PLC does apply to frequently purchased consumer nondurables. If the objective of a research study was to see if the classical curve could be generalized to infrequently purchased consumer nondurables, then only an ordinal measure of frequency of purchase would be necessary so that two classes of goods—frequently and infrequently purchased—could be contrasted. An initial study should probably contrast very frequently with very infrequently purchased products. Unfortunately, current knowledge of the PLC does not provide precise guidance for cutoff points to determine what is frequent compared to infrequent purchase. This could be an area for future research.

RESEARCH ON PLC STAGES

Forecasting Stage Transition

The main application suggested for the PLC has been to plan changes in marketing strategy as the product moves from stage to stage. It follows that the PLC would be more useful in strategy planning if one could more accurately forecast the time when a product changed PLC phases. To what extent can stages be predicted?

Two of the early researchers used initial data points in the PLC to predict the entire curve or next stage. Utilizing semilog paper to plot annual color set sales and number of color television-equipped households, as well as difference analysis relative to color set saturation, Belville identified the take-off point in color television sales, or the transition from introduction to growth stage [5, pp. 26–29]. Polli and Cook examined the percentage change in a product's real sales from year t to year $t+1$. Plotting these changes as a normal distribution with mean zero, they determined that if a product had a percentage change less than $½σ$, it was in the decline phase. A product with the percentage change exceeding $½σ$, was in the growth stage. In the range $±½σ$, the product was considered to be stable [59, pp. 390–391].

Other researchers have developed new product models that forecast the growth and maturity phases of a new item on the basis of either test market data [3, 4, 23, 36, 42, 47, 53, 68] or pretest research [17]. However, these models are unable to accurately predict the second half of the PLC curve. (This is similar to the problem encountered by various growth curves, e.g., Gompertz and logistics, except that they cannot estimate beyond the sales plateau.) For example, if one of the more accepted new product models [4] were permitted to forecast the remainder of the sales trend, it would predict "a very short maturity phase going into decline much faster than does the actual PLC" [20, p. 374].

In a different direction, researchers have discovered various leading indicators of the timing of the maturity phase, such as declining proportion of new triers versus replacement sales, declining profits, overcapacity in industry, appearance of new replacement products, decline in elasticity of advertising coupled with increasing price elasticity, present users' consumption rate, and style changes [70]. By incorporating these indicators into either technological forecasts, similar product analyses, or epidemiological models, a sales forecast for the maturity stage may be derived [4, 16]. In addition to its ex post facto nature, an obvious problem with this technique is that the initial PLC stages are ignored.

Another group of researchers has prescribed a different set of forecasting techniques for each PLC stage, because management must make different decisions at each phase, and "they require different kinds of information as a base" [15, pp. 51–52]. These recommendations, however, are grounded on limited empirical evidence, in particular, two products of Corning Glass Works—glass components for color TV tubes and cookware. But, the major difficulty with this approach is that the user must know the PLC stage the product is in before he can adopt the corresponding set of forecasting devices. Hence, the original problem of forecasting phase transition is encountered.

The forecasting aspect of the PLC concept requires estimation of two items: magnitude of the unit sales increase and length of the cycle. The new product models resolve half of this dilemma by predicting the magnitude and timing of the growth and maturity phases using data from the introduction stage. The problem, therefore, is

> ...reduced to one of predicting the length of the maturity phase and the rate of decline of the decay phase resulting in a prediction for the entire PLC from the early data points [20, p. 374].

This latter problem has been attacked by two researchers, who developed a computer program (LIFER) that uses early data points—known or estimated—to forecast the remainder of the PLC. Assuming that the PLC model "is a continuous real valued function of continuous time, the boundaries of the...(various) phases can be determined using techniques of elementary differential calculus" [20, p. 375]. The result is a multiplicative model of the following form

$$Y(t) = C_1 t^{C_2} \exp(C_3 t + C_4 t^2) e(t) t^{C_2} \geq 0$$

where

$Y(t)$ = recorded sales during period $(t-1, t)$,
$e(t)$ = multiplicative random component for period t,
C_1, C_2, C_3, C_4 are parameters to be estimated from available sales data.

Although this model includes "no exogenous variables and a limited number of parameters," it was tested using annual sales data for cigarettes, automobiles, various types of appliances, beer, wine, and ethical drugs and found to possess "the requisite flexibility to fit most (PLC) situations, in particular those involving extended decline phases, as well as a recycle" [20, pp. 374 and 377].

The subsequent step for investigators is to complicate the LIFER model by adding exogenous variables and more parameters. As one researcher stated

> stage identification is difficult because the sales curve is not a function of time alone. External environmental factors and control-

lable marketing instruments determine the shape of the sales response curve [55, p. 476].

Also, more diverse and varied products should be used in testing the universality of the LIFER model. Another researchable avenue is to examine the possibility of applying the recently acclaimed Box-Jenkins approach to PLC analysis.

Length and Sequence of Product Life Cycle Stages

Do PLCs follow the proposed sequence of four phases—introduction, growth, maturity, and decline? Also, what is the length of each phase? Only a few researchers have empirically examined these two issues. Cox, for example, discovered that the length of the phases for a typical ethical drug was 1 month, 6 months, 15 months, and over 22 months for the introduction, growth, maturity, and decline stages, respectively [22]. Another investigator examined the stability of the PLC phases, as well as the proportion of time various consumer nondurables spent in each stage [58, p. 67]. Dean, the purported Father of the PLC Theory [5, pp. 84–85], maintains that the length of the PLC phases is a function of the rate of technical change, rate of market acceptance, and ease of competitive entry [27, pp. 45–46]. Information concerning these two variables, especially length of PLC stages for a typical product in some industry, would assist managers in more effective management of a product's life cycle. Researchers, therefore, should focus their empirical endeavors on the length and sequence of PLC phases for numerous products and industries.

Economic Conditions

Because the PLC concept was born in the early 1950s, it is basically a theory that describes the unit sales trend for some product during either normal economic conditions or a boom period. Consequently, the PLC notion cannot (nor does it) reflect some product's unit sales history during nonnormal economic circumstances, such as recession or depression.

Economic events of the mid-1970s, however, have substantially increased the need for relating the PLC to an economic downturn. One group of writers has provided a general conceptualization of the impact of a nonnormal domestic economy upon products in various stages of the PLC. In the introduction stage, the product will probably be killed. A product in the growth stage, on the other hand, stands the best chance of resisting

> ...the adverse effect of a significant downturn in the general economy.... It is possible, with proper modifications, for market expansion to continue during this period [65, p. 229].

These modifications include adjusting product form, reducing price, and increasing promotional expenditures. This strategy was employed by electric refrigerator manufacturers during the depression of the 1930s and explains why their sales continued to increase relative to the sales of other appliances [7, p. 277]. Products in the maturity stage will "tend to rise and fall with changes in the general level of business activity because of the postponable nature of such products" [65, p. 229]. Smallwood observed this phenomenon among annual factory shipments of two big-ticket consumer durables, e.g., color televisions and portable dishwashers, during the minirecessions of 1966–67 and 1969–70 [63, p. 32]. Finally, a quicker exit from the market is generally expected for products in the decline phase [65, p. 229].

Future researchers must empirically examine the feasibility of this conceptualization. Completion of this task will stimulate additional research along these lines. The end result will be several PLC theories capable of handling all possible economic conditions

IS THE CONCEPT OF PLC STAGES HINDERING PLC THEORY DEVELOPMENT?

The concept of PLC stages may be hindering PLC research by diverting attention from other issues concerning product life cycles.[2] Are PLC stages worth the effort that they have received? The authors feel that PLC stages are quite worthwhile, because managerial use of the PLC concept readily flows from the stage notion. Without stages, the PLC concept would be rather difficult to apply to marketing problems. Ideas about stages are somewhat arbitrary, and work is needed to determine the value of different stage concepts for different managerial or conceptual problems. As an example, the decline stage is a critical stage for product abandonment decisions. In fact, for planning purposes, it may be fruitful to subdivide the decline stage into more detailed categories. To illustrate this point, suppose it was found that when half of the brands at the start of the decline stage have exited the market, price declines tend to stabilize and the market moves toward oligopoly. Some firms may find it very useful to try and predict the price stability stage, since the squeeze on profit margins may be less and staying in the market increases in value when that stage is reached.

The stage concept, when understood as a way to organize knowledge and observations about the PLC and to help forecast future developments, is very helpful. Armchair arguments about the exact number or sequence of stages, without an explicit consideration of how the resulting classification will be used, are not likely to be fruitful.

THE FIRM AND THE PLC

The size of the firm and the product lines marketed by the firm could influence the PLC. However, little research has been done on either of these issues.

Type of Firm

The magnitude of resources available to a large firm relative to its smaller counterpart would seem to infer two differently shaped PLC curves—even if their products were basically the same. Ambiguity concerning the size of firms examined precludes testing this and related hypotheses.

Likewise, none of the empirical studies distinguished between one-product and multiproduct firms. Allocation of scarce resources among several products may reduce the multiproduct firm's effectiveness in the market, as measured by unit sales, compared to the one-product firm, which can concentrate its efforts on one item. Again, this point has not been elaborated upon in past research.

Product Lines

When discussing product lines, marketing authors are quick to warn managers to be cognizant of the interactions and interrelationships between various products of a line. The axiom is: The sum of the individual products of a product line equals more than the product line itself. If this is true, then would not the PLC curves of products in a line be affected in some way as a result of these interrelationships? Excluding Brockhoff [9], researchers have not addressed themselves to this point.

A critical problem for a multiproduct firm is to determine how its limited resources will be allocated among various products in an optimum fashion. Numerous models have been developed for handling this question. One academician posited that the PLC concept could serve as "a superior basis for optimizing the allocation of the firm's resources" [22].

In managing its product line, the diversified firm will be confronted with multiple PLC curves [63]. To be successful, the firm must maintain a balance among its products in terms of their corresponding life-cycle positions, because such variables as risk and investment requirements vary across the PLC [65, pp. 240–241]. Although Smallwood and Marvin [52] were among the first researchers to conceptualize a balanced product portfolio, no one has empirically examined whether firms do indeed maintain such balanced portfolios. Such investigations would seem to be requisite for product development and planning purposes, formulation of marketing strategy, market segmentation, and eventual product-market positioning and realignment. Moreover, these studies should be segregated according to industry and product types.

USE OF THE PLC IN STRATEGY PLANNING

Several academicians have either hypothesized which variable(s) of the marketing mix is (are) most relevant or asserted the nature of the marketing mix to be employed by PLC phase [10, 18, 19, 27, 28, 34, 35, 45, pp. 434–437, 659–660, 48, 49, pp. 183–188, 50, pp. 345–348, 527–528, 670–672, 55, pp. 87–89, 57, 62, 64, pp. 166–182, 67, 69, pp. 247–248]. Other writers have also theorized the application of the PLC concept to their functional areas of interest in terms of strategy formulation, such as finance [37], purchasing [6], logistics [25, pp. 222–225], and sales management [30].

As observed by Wind and Claycamp, however,

> these recommendations have usually been vague, nonoperational, not empirically supported, and conceptually questionable, since they imply that strategies can be developed with little concern for the product's profitability and market share position.[3] ... Traditional (PLC) analysis ... ignores the competitive setting of the product, the relevant profit considerations, and the fact that product sales are a function of the marketing effort of the firm and other environmental forces [71, pp. 2 and 8].[4]

Excluding one researcher's study, no one has investigated empirically whether practitioners actually utilize academicians' PLC-strategy theories. The apparent underlying explanation for this complacency is that most academicians accept the PLC concept as a useful model for planning appropriate strategies. The empirical validity of the PLC theory is simply asserted [51, p. 39]. Interviewing industrial purchasing executives, however, Rink found that most were intuitively using Berenson's PLC-purchasing strategy (PS) model in formulating their firm's purchasing strategy across the PLC [60]. But this is an empirical test of only one of the PLC-strategy theories. Others beg examination. Such studies will determine which strategy models are appropriate for the practitioner to consider, as well as when and in what situations. Modifications may be required in some of these basic theories.[5]

Although Mickwitz [55, pp. 87–89] posited that the demand elasticities of the marketing mix variables change over the PLC, the literature provides almost no empirical evidence to substantiate this theory. Reportedly, one packaged goods company measured the advertising elasticities for a wide range of its products at their various PLC phases. The firm found that advertising elasticity tended to decrease as the product progressed through its PLC [44].

In examining the domestic sales and advertising for a household cleanser, Parsons found empirical support for Mickwitz's proposition, at least in the case of advertising. He recommended

> Future research should be directed toward confirming this exploratory find. In addition, marketing mix models should be examined to determine whether there are differential rates of change among the various elasticities. Finally, but most importantly, the elasticities should be expressed as functions of external environmental variables, and controllable marketing instruments instead of explicit functions of time alone [56, p. 480].

MAJOR RESEARCH NEEDS INVOLVING THE PLC

In critically appraising various facets of PLC research, numerous avenues for future study have been highlighted. Although these fertile areas have been discussed and some of the major points summarized, integrating the research possibilities into one table may be useful (see Table 2). This may underscore the need for a multidimensional approach to conceptualizing future PLC research.

For ease of reference, the 23 variables have been segregated into three groups: variables internal to the firm; variables external to the firm but internal to the industry; and macroenvironmental variables.

The 23 variables comprising Table 2 are not intended to be an exhaustive enumeration. At best, this table represents the starting point for further conceptualization. Some variables, for example, industry structure and industry type, may be too similar to segregate. In another case, product type, most researchers agree that commodity products do not exhibit the general PLC shape. Perhaps this should be examined more thoroughly. Finally, concerning market reach, an often-used strategy of multinational firms involves transferring a product that has transpired its PLC among highly industrialized countries to markets frequented by less industrialized countries. This permits the firm to reinitiate the PLC of its product, but with substantial cost economies via the experience curve phenomenon.

Additional work is needed in developing, refining, and crystalizing this list of 23 variables. However, the multidimensional approach epitomized in Table 2 will enrich, as well as stimulate, more extensive and diverse empirical PLC research as investigators examine feasible combinations of these variables.

CONCLUSIONS AND SUMMARY

Some tentative conclusions can be advanced on the basis of the empirical studies reviewed here. Unfortunately, there is little evidence

TABLE 2. Multidimensional Approach for Conceptualizing Future Product Life Cycle Research

Variables internal to the firm
  Type of customer
    Consumer
    Industrial
  Degree of perishability
    Durable
    Nondurable
  Degree of tangibility
    Good
    Service
  Degree of Newness
    Unquestionably new
    Partially new
    Major change
    Minor change
    Established
  Type of firm, such as
    Manufacturer
    Wholesaler
    Retailer
  Firm size in terms of either assets, sales, etc.
    Large
    Medium
    Small
  Function, such as
    Marketing
    Finance
    Purchasing
    Logistics
    Etc.
  Level of aggregation
    Class
    Form
    Brand
  Price level
    High
    Medium
    Low
  Degree of distribution
    Intensive
    Extensive
    Limited
  Number of product lines
    One
    Two or more
      Related
      Unrelated
  Product type
    Commodity
    Noncommodity

  Market reach
    Local
    Regional
    National
    International
  Degree of promotion
    High
    Medium
    Low
  Length and sequence of PLC stages
  Market share
    Small
    Average
    Dominant

Variables external to firm but internal to industry
  Industry type, such as
    Automobile
    Electrical appliance
    Home construction
    Electronic components
    Etc.
  Supply variations
    High
    Average
    Low
  Industry (or market) structure
    Pure competition
    Oligopoly
    Monopoly
    Monopolistic competition
  State of industry technology
    Volatile, ever-changing
    Changes periodically
    Stable
  Purchase Frequency
    High
    Medium
    Low

Macroenvironmental variables
  Domestic economy
    Boom
    Bust, e.g., recession, inflation, shortages, depression, etc.
  International economy (optional)
    Boom
    Bust

on which to base most of the following conclusions, so the need for additional research is the main conclusion of this report.

PLC Curves

Evidence for the existence of the classical bell-shaped PLC curve is strong, as a number of studies have found such a pattern. At least three studies have found other curves, including cycle-recycle, stable maturity, decreasing, and increasing patterns. Some half-dozen other life-cycle patterns have been found, but by only one or two studies. The weight of evidence suggests that the most common curve is the classical, but it is not the only PLC. Only two studies have been conducted that sought to test factors that may cause PLC patterns.

Industries/Products Analyzed

Most of the research on the PLC has been based on either consumer nondurables (12 studies) or consumer durables (nine studies). Only four studies have covered industrial goods. Thus, the confidence that we may have in generalizing about the PLC across types of goods is at least fair within consumer nondurables, but meager for industrial items. Furthermore, with consumer products, researchers have focused on items that are frequently purchased, low-priced, widely distributed, and not subject to wide variations on the supply side. Hence, our ability to generalize the PLC across consumer goods is also limited.

Product Concepts Investigated

A number of combinations can be formed in terms of levels of product aggregation and degree of product newness, specifically class (e.g., tobacco smoking products), form (e.g., cigarettes), brand (e.g., Camels), unquestionably new product (e.g., black-and-white television when it was introduced), partially new product, major product change (e.g., small, portable black-and-white television sets), and minor product change. However, researchers have concentrated mainly on minor product changes for product classes and forms. Brands have been largely ignored.

Forecasting PLC Stages

Some success has been claimed for methods designed to forecast the transition from one PLC stage to another. But these methods typically use data from a current stage to forecast the timing of the next stage. Thus, accurate long-range forecasting is not likely. Little is known about the length and sequence of PLC stages.

The Impact of Economic Conditions on the PLC

Very limited evidence suggests that the usual PLC concept applies to periods of either economic stability or growth. How recessions may influence the PLC is questionable.

Characteristics of the Firm and the PLC

Almost no research has been reported on how different characteristics of the firm may influence the PLC.

Use of the PLC in Business Planning

While much has been written on how the PLC could be used in business planning, the use of the PLC by business planners has only been investigated by one study.

ENDNOTES

1. These numbers result from counting each researcher's study only once under each of the three categories. On the other hand, if counting were with replacement, the corresponding numbers would be 20, 14, and 5 studies for consumer nondurable goods, consumer durable items, and industrial goods, respectively.
2. The authors are grateful to a *JBR* reviewer for suggesting this point.
3. Other interesting theoretical articles and rejoinders that focus on PLC and market share are reviewed in Catry, et al. [13, 14] and Fildes, et al. [33].
4. Other writers concur with the point that PLC is a dependent variable determined by marketing actions rather than an independent variable to which firms adapt their marketing programs [29, p. 105, 31, pp. 3–4, 32, p. 48, 33, p. 59].
5. On the basis of discussions with 45 purchasing executives, Fox and Rink [38] expanded Berenson's PLC-PS model [6] to include almost 100 purchasing strategies and tactics.

REFERENCES

1. Albach, H., *Zur Theorie des wachsenden Unternehmens, Schriften des Vereins für Socialpolitik*, *34NS*, Duncker and Humblot, Berlin, 1965.
2. Balachandran, V., and Jain, Subhash, A Predictive Model for Monitoring Product Life Cycle, in *Relevance in Marketing/Marketing in Motion*, Fred Allvine, ed., American Marketing Association, Chicago, 1972.
3. Barclay, William, A Probability Model for Early Prediction of New Product Market Success, *J. Marketing* 27 (January, 1963): 63–68.
4. Bass, Frank, A New Product Growth Model for Consumer Durables, *Man. Sci.* 15 (January, 1969): 215–227.
5. Belville, Hugh Jr., The Product Life Cycle Theory Applied to Color Television, Masters thesis, New York University, New York City, 1966.

6. Berenson, Conrad, The Purchasing Executive's Adaptation to the Product Life Cycle, *J. Purchasing* 3 (May, 1967): 52–68.
7. Borden, Neil, *Advertising in Our Economy*, Richard D. Irwin, Homewood, Ill., 1945.
8. Brantl, C., American Motors Corporation: An Empirical Study of the Firm, Ph.D. dissertation, Fordham University, New York City, 1963.
9. Brockhoff, Klaus, A Test for the Product Life Cycle, *Econometrica* 35 (July–October, 1967): 472–484.
10. Buzzell, Robert, Competitive Behavior and Product Life Cycles, in *New Ideas for Successful Marketing*, John Wright and Jac Goldstucker, eds., American Marketing Association, Chicago, 1966.
11. Buzzell, Robert, and Cook, Victor, *Product Life Cycles*, Marketing Science Institute, Cambridge, 1969.
12. Buzzell, Robert, and Nourse, Robert, *Product Innovation in Food Processing: 1954–1964*, Division of Research, Harvard Business School, Boston, 1967.
13. Catry, Bernard, and Chevalier, Michel, Market Share Strategy and the Product Life Cycle, *J. Marketing* 38 (October, 1974): 29–34.
14. Catry, Bernard, and Chevalier, Michel, Market Share Strategy: The Concept and the Evidence, *J. Marketing* 39 (October, 1975): 59–60.
15. Chambers, John, Mullick, Satinder, and Smith, Donald, How to Choose the Right Forecasting Technique, *Harvard Bus Rev.* 49 (July–August, 1971): 45–74.
16. Chambers, John, Mullick, Satinder, and Smith, Donald, *An Executive's Guide to Forecasting*, John Wiley and Sons, Inc., New York, 1974.
17. Claycamp, Henry, and Liddy, Lucien, Prediction of New Product Performance: An Analytical Approach, *J. Market. Res.* 6 (November, 1969): 414–420.
18. Clifford, Jr., Donald, Leverage in the Product Life Cycle, *Dun's Rev. Modern Industry* 85 (May, 1965): 62–70.
19. Clifford, Jr., Donald, Managing the Product Life Cycle, *Man. Rev.* 54 (June, 1965): 34–38.
20. Cooke, Ernest, and Edmondson, Ben, Computer Aided Product Investment Decisions, in *Increasing Marketing Productivity and Conceptual and Methodological Foundations of Marketing*, Thomas Greer, ed., American Marketing Association, Chicago, 1973.
21. Cox, Jr., William, Product Life Cycles and Promotional Strategy in the Ethical Drug Industry, Ph.D. dissertation, University of Michigan, 1963.
22. Cox, Jr., William, Product Life Cycles as Marketing Models, *J. Bus.* 40 (October, 1967): 375–384.
23. Crawford, C. Merle, The Trajectory Theory of Goal Setting for New Products, *J. Market. Res.* 3 (May, 1966): 117–126.
24. Cunningham, M. T., The Application of Product Life Cycles to Corporate Strategy: Some Research Findings, *Brit. J. Market.* (Spring, 1969): 32–44.
25. Davis, Grant, and Brown, Stephen, *Logistics Management*, D.C. Heath and Company, Lexington, 1974.
26. Dean, B., and Sengupta, S., On a Method for Determining Corporate Research Development Budgets, in Churchman and Verhulst, eds. *Management Science, Models and Techniques*, 2nd ed., Oxford University Press, London, 1960.
27. Dean, Joel, Pricing Policies for New Products, *Harvard Bus. Rev.* 28 (November–December, 1950): 45–53.
28. Dean, Joel, *Managerial Economics*, Prentice-Hall, Inc., Englewood Cliffs, 1951.

29. Dhalla, Nariman, and Yuspeh, Sonia, Forget the Product Life Cycle Concept! *Harvard Bus. Rev.* 54 (January–February, 1976): 102–112.
30. Dodge, H. Robert, and Rink, David, Phasing Sales Strategies and Tactics in Accordance with the Product Life Cycle Dimension Rather Than Calendar Periods, in *Research Frontiers in Marketing: Dialogues and Directions*, Subhash Jain, ed., American Marketing Association, Chicago, 1978.
31. Doyle, Peter, The Realities of the Product Life Cycle, *Q. Rev. Marketing* (Summer, 1976): 1–6.
32. Enis, Ben, LaGarce, Raymond, and Prell, Arthur, Extending the Product Life Cycle, *Bus. Horizons* 20 (June, 1977): 46–56.
33. Fildes, Robert, and Lofthouse, Stephen, Market Share Strategy and the Product Life Cycle: A Comment, *J. Marketing* 39 (October, 1975): 57–59.
34. Forrester, Jay, Industrial Dynamics, *Harvard Bus. Rev.* 36 (July–August, 1958): 37–66.
35. Forrester, Jay, Advertising: A Problem in Industrial Dynamics, *Harvard Bus. Rev.* 37 (March–April, 1959): 103–111.
36. Fourt, Louis, and Woodlock, Joseph, Early Prediction of Market Success for New Grocery Products, *J. Marketing* 25 (October, 1960): 31–38.
37. Fox, Harold, Product Life Cycle—An Aid to Financial Administration, *Fin. Executive* 41 (April, 1973): 28–34.
38. Fox, Harold, and Rink, David, Coordination of Purchasing with Sales Trends, *J. Purchasing* 13 (Winter, 1977): 10–18.
39. Frederixon, Martin, An Investigation of the Product Life Cycle Concept and Its Application to New Product Proposal Evaluation within the Chemical Industry, Ph.D. dissertation, Michigan State University, 1969.
40. Headen, Robert, The Introductory Phases of the Life Cycle for New Grocery Products: Consumer Acceptance and Competitive Behavior, Ph. D. dissertation, Harvard University, Cambridge, 1966.
41. Hinkle, Joel, *Life Cycles*, Nielsen, New York, 1966.
42. King, William, Early Prediction of New Product Success, *J. Adv. Res.* 6 (June, 1966): 8–13.
43. Kotler, Philip, Phasing Out Weak Products, *Harvard Bus. Rev.* 43 (March–April, 1965): 107–118.
44. Kotler, Philip, *Marketing Decision Making: A Model Building Approach*, Holt, Rinehart, and Winston, New York, 1971.
45. Kotler, Philip, *Marketing Management: Analysis, Planning, and Control*, 2nd ed., Prentice-Hall, Englewood Cliffs, N.J., 1972.
46. Kovac, F., and Dague, M., Forecasting by Product Life Cycle Analysis, *Res. Man.* 15 (July, 1972): 66–72.
47. Learner, David, Profit Maximization Through New Product Marketing Planning and Control, in *Applications of the Sciences in Marketing Management*, Frank Bass, Charles King, and Edgar Pessemier, eds., Wiley, New York, 1968.
48. Levitt, Theodore, Exploit the Product Life Cycle, *Harvard Bus. Rev.* 43 (November–December, 1965): 81–94.
49. Luck, David, and Prell, Arthur, *Market Strategy*, Appleton-Century-Crofts, New York, 1968.
50. McCarthy, E. Jerome, *Basic Marketing: A Managerial Approach*, 4th ed., Richard D. Irwin, Homewood, Ill., 1971.

51. Marple, Gary, and Wissman, Harry, eds., *Grocery Manufacturing in the United States*, Praeger, New York, 1968.
52. Marvin, P., Developing a Balanced Product Portfolio, *Man. Rev.* 48 (April, 1959): 20–26.
53. Massy, William, Forecasting the Demand for New Convenience Products, *J. Market. Res.* 6 (November, 1969): 405–413.
54. May, Charles, Planning the Marketing Program Throughout the Product Life Cycle, Ph.D. dissertation, Columbia University, New York City, 1961.
55. Mickwitz, Gösta, *Marketing and Competition*, Centraltryckeriet, Helsingfors, 1959.
56. Parsons, Leonard, The Product Life Cycle and Time-Varying Advertising Elasticities, *J. Market. Res.* 12 (November, 1975): 476–480.
57. Patton, Arch, Stretch Your Product's Earning Years: Top Management's Stake in the Product Life Cycle, *Man. Rev.* 48 (June, 1959): 9–14, 67–79.
58. Polli, Rolando, *A Test of the Classical Product Life Cycle by Means of Actual Sales Histories*, Ph.D. dissertation, University of Pennsylvania, 1968.
59. Polli, Rolando, and Cook, Victor, Validity of the Product Life Cycle, *J. Bus.* 42 (October, 1969): 385–400.
60. Rink, David, The Product Life Cycle in Formulating Purchasing Strategy, *Industr. Market. Man.* 5 (August, 1976): 231–242.
61. Rogers, Everett, *The Diffusion of Innovations*, The Free Press, New York, 1962.
62. Scheuing, Eberhard, The Product Life Cycle as an Aid in Strategy Decisions, *Man. Int. Rev.* 9 (1969): 111–124.
63. Smallwood, John, The Product Life Cycle: A Key to Strategic Marketing Planning, *MSU Bus. Topics* 21 (Winter, 1973): 29–35.
64. Staudt, Thomas, and Taylor, Donald, *A Managerial Introduction to Marketing*, 2nd ed., Prentice-Hall, Englewood Cliffs, N.J., 1970.
65. Staudt, Thomas, Taylor, Donald, and Bowersox, Donald, *A Managerial Introduction to Marketing*, 3rd ed., Prentice-Hall, Englewood Cliffs, N.J., 1976.
66. Stobaugh, Robert Jr., The Product Life Cycle, U.S. Exports, and International Investments, Ph.D. dissertation, Harvard Business School, Cambridge, 1968.
67. Thorelli, Hans, Market Strategy Over the Market Life Cycle, *Bull. Bureau Market Res.* 26 (September, 1967): 10–22.
68. Urban, Glen, A New Product Analysis and Decision Model, *Man. Sci.* 14 (April, 1968): 490–517.
69. Wasson, Chester, *Dynamic Competitive Strategy and Product Life Cycles*, Revised ed., Challenge Books, St. Charles, 1974.
70. Wilson, Aubrey, Industrial Marketing Research in Britain, *J. Market Res.* 6 (February, 1969): 15–28.
71. Wind, Yoram, and Claycamp, Henry, Planning Product Line Strategy: A Matrix Approach, *J. Marketing* 40 (January, 1976): 2–9.

26 The Death and Burial of "Sick" Products

R. S. Alexander

Reprinted from the *Journal of Marketing*, published by the American Marketing Association, Vol. 28 (April 1964), pp. 1–7. Reprinted by permission.

Euthanasia applied to human beings is criminal; but aging products enjoy or suffer no such legal protection. This is a sad fact of business life.

The word "product" is used here not in its broad economic sense of anything produced—such as wheat, coal, a car, or a chair—but in its narrower meaning of an article made to distinct specifications and intended for sale under a separate brand or catalogue number. In the broader sense of the word, certain products may last as long as industrial civilization endures; in the narrow sense, most of them are playthings of change.

Much has been written about managing the development and marketing of new products, but business literature is largely devoid of material on product deletion.

This is not surprising. New products have glamor. Their management is fraught with great risks. Their successful introduction promises growth in sales and profits that may be fantastic.

But putting products to death—or letting them die—is a drab business, and often engenders much of the sadness of a final parting with old and tried friends. "The portable 6-sided, pretzel polisher was the first product The Company ever made. Our line will no longer be our line without it."

But while deletion is an uninspiring and depressing process, in a changing market it is almost as vital as the addition of new products. The old product that is a "football" of competition or has lost much of its market appeal is likely to generate more than its share of small unprofitable orders; to make necessary short, costly production runs; to demand an exorbitant amount of executive attention; and to tie up capital that could be used more profitably in other ventures.

Just as a crust of barnacles on the hold of a ship retards the vessel's movement, so do a number of worn-out items in a company's product mix affect the company's progress.

Most of the costs that result from the lack of an effective deletion system are hidden and become apparent only after careful analysis. As a result, management often overlooks them. The need for examining the product line to discover outworn members, and for analysis to arrive at intelligent decisions to discard or to keep them, very rarely assumes the

501

urgency of a crisis. Too often, management thinks of this as something that should be done but that can wait until tomorrow.

This is why a definite procedure for deletion of products should be set up, and why the authority and responsibility for the various activities involved should be clearly and definitely assigned. This is especially important because this work usually requires the cooperation of several functional groups within the business firm, including at least marketing, production, finance, and sometimes personnel.

Definite responsibility should be assigned for at least the following activities involved in the process: (1) selecting products which are candidates for elimination; (2) gathering information about them and analyzing the information; (3) making decisions about elimination; and (4) if necessary, removing the doomed products from the line.

SELECTION OF PRODUCTS FOR POSSIBLE ELIMINATION

As a first step, we are not seeking the factors on which the final decision to delete or to retain turns, but merely those which indicate that the product's continuation in the product mix should be considered carefully with elimination as a possibility. Although removal from the product line may seem to be the prime aim, the result is not inevitably deletion from the line; instead, careful analysis may lead to changes in the product itself or in the methods of making or marketing it.

Sales Trend. If the trend of a product's sales is downward over a time period that is significant in relation to the normal life of others like it, its continuation in the mix deserves careful examination. There may be many reasons for such a decline that in no way point toward deletion; but when decline continues over a period of time the situation needs to be studied.

Price Trend. A downward trend in the price of a new product may be expected if the firm introducing it pursues a skimming-price policy, or if all firms making it realize substantial cost savings as a result of volume production and increased processing know-how. But when the price of an established product whose competitive pattern has been relatively stabilized shows a downward trend over a significant period of time, the future of that product should receive attention.

Profit Trend. A declining profit either in dollars or as a percent of sales or investment should raise questions about a product's continued place in the product line. Such a trend usually is the result of a price-factory cost squeeze, although it may be the outcome of a loss in market appeal or a change in the method of customer purchase which forces higher marketing expenditures.

Substitute Products. When a substitute article appears on the market, especially if it represents an improvement over an old product, management must face the question of whether to retain or discard the old product. This is true regardless of who introduces the substitute. The problem is especially difficult when the new product serves the same general purpose as the old one but is not an exact substitute for it.

Product Effectiveness. Certain products may lose some of their effectiveness for the purposes they serve. For example, disease germs may develop strains that are resistant to a certain antibiotic. When this happens, the question of whether to keep or delete the drug involves issues not only of the interests of the firm but of the public welfare.

Executive Time. A possible tipoff as to the location of "illness" in a product mix lies in a study of the amount of executive time and attention devoted to each of the items in the product line. Sick products, like sick people, demand a lot of care; but one must be careful to distinguish the "growing pains" of a new product from the more serious disorders of one that has matured and is now declining.

The six indicators mentioned do not of themselves provide evidence justifying deletion. But they can help management to single out from a line of products those upon which it can profitably spend time and money in analyzing them, with elimination from the line as a *possibility*.

ANALYSIS AND DECISION MAKING ABOUT "SICK" PRODUCTS

Although the work of analyzing a sick or decrepit product is usually done by people other than the management executives who decide what to do about it, the two processes are interdependent. Unless the right factors are chosen for analysis and unless the work is properly done, the decision is not likely to be an intelligent one. Accordingly, these two factors will be discussed together.

What information does a decision-maker need about a product, and what sort of analysis of it should he have in order to render a sound verdict as to its future? The deletion decision should not turn on the sole issue of profitability. Profit is the most important objective of a business; but individual firms often seek to achieve both long-run and short-run objectives other than profit.

So, in any individual case the critical factors and the weights assigned them in making a decision must be chosen in the light of the situation of the firm and the management objectives.

Profits

Profit management in a firm with a multi-product line (the usual situation in our economy) is not the simple operation generally contemplated in economic theory. Such a firm usually has in its product mix (1) items in various stages of introduction and development, some of which may be fantastically profitable and others deep "in the red"; (2) items which are mature but not "superannuated," whose profit rate is likely to be satisfactory; and (3) declining items which may yield a net profit somewhat less than adequate or may show heavy losses.

The task is to manage the whole line or mix so that it will show a satisfactory profit for the company. In this process, two questions are vital; What is a profit? How much profit is satisfactory?

Operating-statement accounting makes it possible to determine with reasonable accuracy the total amount of net profit a company earns on an overall basis. But when the management of a multi-product firm seeks to determine how much of this total is generated by its activities in making and marketing each product in its mix, the process is almost incredibly complex; and the results are almost certain to be conditioned on a tissue of assumptions which are so debatable that no management can feel entirely comfortable in basing decisions on them.

This is because such a large portion of the costs of the average multi-product firm are or behave like overhead or joint expense. Almost inevitably several of the items in the product mix are made of common materials, with the same equipment, and by manpower which is interchangeable. Most of the company's marketing efforts and expenses are devoted to selling and distributing the mix or a line within the mix, rather than individual items.

In general, the more varied the product mix of a firm, the greater is the portion of its total expense that must be classified as joint or overhead. In such a company, many types of cost which ordinarily can be considered direct tend to behave like overhead or joint expenses. This is particularly true of marketing costs such as advertising that does not feature specific items; personal selling; order handling; and delivery.

This means that a large part of a company's costs must be assigned to products on some arbitrary basis and that however logical this basis may be, it is subject to considerable reasonable doubt in specific cases. It also means that if one product is removed from the mix, many of these costs remain to be reassigned to the items that stay in the line. As a result, any attempt to "prune" the product mix entirely on the basis of the profit contribution, or lack of it, of specific items is almost certain to be disappointing and in some cases disastrous.

But if a multi-product firm could allocate costs to individual items in the mix on some basis recognized as sound and thus compute product-profit accurately, what standard of profit should be set up, the failure to meet which would justify deletion?

Probably most managements either formally or unconsciously set overall company profit targets. Such targets may be expressed in terms of dollars, although to be most useful in product management they usually must be translated into percentages on investment, or money used. As an example, a company may have as its profit target 15% on investment before taxes.

Certainly *every* product in the mix should not be required to achieve the target, which really amounts to an average. To do so would be to deny the inevitable variations in profit potential among products.

Probably a practical minimum standard can be worked out, below which a product should be eliminated unless other considerations demand its retention. Such a standard can be derived from a balancing out of the profit rates among products in the mix, so as to arrive at the overall company target as an average. The minimum standard then represents a figure that would tip the balance enough to endanger the overall target.

What role, then, should considerations of product profit play in managerial decisions as to deletion or retention?

1. Management probably will be wise to recognize an overall company target profit in dollars or rate on investment, and to set in relation to it a minimum below which the profit on an individual product should not fall without marking that item for deletion (unless other special considerations demand its retention).
2. Management should cast a "bilious eye" on all arguments that a questionable product be kept in the mix because it helps to defray overhead and joint costs. Down that road, at the end of a series of decisions to retain such products, lies a mix entirely or largely composed of items each busily "sopping up" overhead, but few or none contributing anything to net profit.
3. This does not mean that management should ignore the effect of a product deletion on overhead or joint costs. Decision-makers must be keenly aware of the fact that the total of such costs borne by a sick product must, after it is deleted, be reallocated to other products, and with the result that they may become of doubtful profitability. A detailed examination of the joint or overhead costs charged against an ailing product may indicate that some of them can be eliminated in whole or in part if it is eliminated. Such costs are notoriously "sticky" and difficult to get rid of; but every pretext should be used to try to find ways to reduce them.
4. If a deletion decision involves a product or a group of products responsible for a significant portion of a firm's total sales volume,

decision-makers can assess the effects of overhead and joint costs on the problem, by compiling an estimated company operating statement after the deletion and comparing it with the current one. Such a forecasted statement should include expected net income from the use of the capital and facilities released by deletion if an opportunity for their use is ready at hand. Surviving joint and overhead expenses can even be reallocated to the remaining products, in order to arrive at an estimate of the effect that deletion might have, not only on the total company net income but on the profitability of each of the remaining products as well. Obviously such a cost analysis is likely to be expensive, and so is not justified unless the sales volume stakes are high.

Financial Considerations

Deletion is likely not only to affect the profit performance of a firm but to modify its financial structure as well.

To make and sell a product, a company must invest some of its capital. In considering its deletion, the decision-makers must estimate what will happen to the capital funds presently used in making and marketing it.

When a product is dropped from the mix, most or all of the circulating capital invested in it—such as inventories of materials, goods in process, and finished goods and accounts receivable—should drain back into the cash account; and if carried out in an orderly fashion, deletion will not disturb this part of the capital structure except to increase the ratio of cash to other assets.

This will be true, unless the deletion decision is deferred until product deterioration has gone so far that the decision assumes the aspect of a crisis and its execution that of a catastrophe.

The funds invested in the equipment and other facilities needed to make and market the "sick" product are a different matter. If the equipment is versatile and standard, it may be diverted to other uses. If the firm has no need of it and if the equipment has been properly depreciated, management may find a market for it at a price approaching or even exceeding its book value.

In either case, the capital structure of the company is not disturbed except by a shift from equipment to cash in the case of sale. In such a case management would be wise, before making a deletion decision, to determine how much cash this action promises to release as well as the chances for its reinvestment.

If the equipment is suited for only one purpose, it is highly unlikely that management can either find another use for it or sell it on favorable terms. If it is old and almost completely depreciated, it can probably be scrapped and its remaining value "written off" without serious impairment of the firm's capital structure.

But if it is only partly depreciated, the decision-makers must weigh the relative desirability of two possible courses of action: (1) to delete immediately, hoping that the ensuing improvement in the firm's operating results will more than offset the impairment in capital structure that deletion will cause; or (2) to seek to recapture as much as possible of its value, by continuing to make and market the product as long as its price is enough to cover out-of-pocket costs and leave something over to apply to depreciation.

This choice depends largely on two things: the relation between the amount of fixed and circulating capital that is involved; and the opportunities available to use the funds, executive abilities, manpower, and transferable facilities released by deletion for making profits in other ventures.

This matter of opportunity costs is a factor in every deletion decision. The dropping of a product is almost certain to release some capital, facilities, manpower skills, and executive abilities. If opportunities can be found in which these assets can be invested without undue risk and with promise of attractive profits, it may be good management to absorb considerable immediate loss in deleting a sick product.

If no such opportunities can be found, it is probably wise to retain the product so long as the cash inflow from its sales covers out-of-pocket costs and contributes something to depreciation and other overhead expenses. In such a case, however, it is the part of good management to seek actively for new ventures which promise satisfactory profits, and to be ready to delete promptly when such an opportunity is found.

Employee Relations

The effect which product elimination may have on the employees of a firm is often an important factor in decisions either to drop or to retain products.

This is not likely to be a deciding factor if new product projects are under development to which the people employed in making and marketing the doubtful product can be transferred, unless such transfer would deprive them of the earning power of special skills. But when deletion of a product means discharging or transferring unionized employees, the decision-makers must give careful thought to the effect their action is likely to have on company-union relations.

Even in the absence of union pressure, management usually feels a strong sense of responsibility for the people in its employ. Just how far management can go in conserving specific jobs at the expense of deferring or foregoing necessary deletions before it endangers the livelihood of all the employees of the firm is a nice question of balance.

Marketing Factors

Many multi-product firms retain in their marketing mixes one or more items which, on the basis of profits and the company financial structure, should be deleted. To continue to make and market a losing product is no managerial crime. It is reprehensible only when management does not know the product is a losing one or, knowing the facts, does not have sound reasons for retaining it. Such reasons are very likely to lie in the marketing area.

Deletions of products are often deferred or neglected because of management's desire to carry a "full line," whatever that means. This desire may be grounded on sound reasons of consumer patronage or on a dubious yearning for the "prestige" that a full line is supposed to engender. But there is no magic about a full line or the prestige that is supposed to flow from it. Both should be evaluated on the basis of their effects on the firm's sales volume, profits, and capacity to survive and grow.

Products are often associated in the marketing process. The sale of one is helped by the presence of another in the product mix.

When elimination of a product forces a customer who buys all or a large part of his requirements of a group of profitable items from the firm to turn to another supplier for his needs of the dropped product, he might shift some or all of his other patronage as well. Accordingly, it is sometimes wise for management to retain in its mix a no-profit item, in order to hold sales volume of highly profitable products. But this should not be done blindly without analysis.

Rarely can management tell ahead of time exactly how much other business will be lost by deleting a product, or in what proportions the losses will fall among the remaining items. But in many cases the amount of sales volume can be computed that will be *hazarded* by such action; what other products will be subject to that hazard; and what portion of their volume will be involved. When this marketing interdependence exists in a deletion problem, the decision-makers should seek to discover the customers who buy the sick product; what other items in the mix they buy; in what quantities; and how much profit they contribute.

The firm using direct marketing channels can do this with precision and at relatively little cost. The firm marketing through indirect channels will find it more difficult, and the information will be less exact; but it still may be worth-while. If the stakes are high enough, marketing research may be conducted to discover the extent to which the customer purchases of profitable items actually are associated with that of the sick product. Although the results may not be precise, they may supply an order-of-magnitude idea of the interlocking patronage situation.

Product interrelationships in marketing constitute a significant factor in making deletion decisions, but should never be accepted as the deciding factor without careful study to disclose at least the extent of the hazards they involve.

Other Possibilities

The fact that a product's market is declining or that its profit performance is substandard does not mean that deletion is the *only* remedy.

Profits can be made in a shrinking market. There are things other than elimination of a product that can be done about deteriorating profit performance. They tend to fall into four categories.

1. *Costs.* A careful study may uncover ways of reducing factory costs. This may result from improved processes that either eliminate manpower or equipment time or else increase yield; or from the elimination of forms or features that once were necessary or worth-while but are no longer needed. The natural first recourse of allocating joint and overhead costs on a basis that is "kinder" to the doubtful product is not to be viewed with enthusiasm. After reallocation, these costs still remain in the business; and the general profit picture has not been improved in the least.
2. *Marketing.* Before deleting a product, management will be wise to examine the methods of marketing it, to see if they can be changed to improve its profit picture.

    Can advertising and sales effort be reduced without serious loss of volume? A holding operation requires much less effort and money than a promotional one.

    Are services being given that the product no longer needs?

    Can savings be made in order handling and delivery, even at some loss of customer satisfaction? For example, customers may be buying the product in small orders that are expensive to handle.

    On the other hand, by spending more marketing effort, can volume be increased so as to bring about a reduction in factory cost greater than the added marketing expense? In this attempt, an unexpected "assist" may come from competitors who delete the product and leave more of the field to the firm.

    By remodeling the product, "dressing it up," and using a new marketing approach, can it be brought back to a state of health and profit? Here the decision-makers must be careful not to use funds and facilities that could be more profitably invested in developing and marketing new products.
3. *Price.* It is natural to assume that the price of a failing product cannot be raised. At least in part, its plight is probably due to the fact that it is "kicked around" by competition, and thus that competition will not allow any increases.

    But competitors may be tired of the game, too. One company

that tried increasing prices found that wholesalers and retailers did not resent a larger cost-of-goods-sold base on which to apply their customary gross profit rates, and that consumers continued to buy and competitors soon followed suit.

Although a price rise will not usually add to the sum total of user happiness, it may not subtract materially from total purchases. The decision-makers should not ignore the possibility of using a price reduction to gain enough physical volume to bring about a more-than-offsetting decline in unit costs, although at this stage the success of such a gambit is not likely.

4. *Cross Production.* In the materials field, when small production runs make costs prohibitive, arrangements may sometimes be made for Firm A to make the *entire* supply of Product X for itself and Competitor B. Then B reciprocates with another similar product. Such "trades," for instance, are to be found in the chemical business.

Summation for Decision

In solving deletion problems, the decision-makers must draw together into a single pattern the results of the analysis of all the factors bearing on the matter. Although this is probably most often done on an intangible, subjective basis, some firms have experimented with the formula method.

For example, a manufacturer of electric motors included in its formula the following factors:

- Profitability
- Position on growth curve
- Product leadership
- Market position
- Marketing dependence of other products

Each factor was assigned a weight in terms of possible "counts" against the product. For instance, if the doubtful item promised no profits for the next three years, it had a count of 50 points against it, while more promising prospects were assigned lesser counts. A critical total for all factors was set in advance which would automatically doom a product. Such a system can include other factors—such as recapturability of invested capital, alternate available uses of facilities, effects on labor force, or other variables peculiar to the individual case.

The use of a formula lends an aura of precision to the act of decision-making and assures a degree of uniformity in it. But obviously the weights assigned to different factors cannot be the same in all cases. For example, if the deletion of a doubtful product endangers a large volume of sales of other highly profitable items, that alone should probably decide the matter.

The same thing is true if deletion will force so heavy a writeoff of invested funds as to impair the firm's capital structure. Certainly this will be true if all or most of the investment can be recaptured by the depreciation route if the product stays in the mix.

This kind of decision requires that the factors be weighted differently in each case. But when managers are given a formula, they may tend to quit thinking and do too much "weighing."

THE DELETION OF A PRODUCT

Once the decision to eliminate a product is made, plans must be drawn for its death and burial with the least disturbance of customer relations and of the other operations of the firm.

Such plans must deal with a variety of detailed problems. Probably the most important fall into four categories: timing; parts and replacements; stocks; and holdover demand.

- *Timing.* It is desirable that deletion be timed so as to dovetail with the financial, manpower, and facilities needs for new products. As manpower and facilities are released from the dying product and as the capital devoted to it flows back into the cash account, it is ideal if these can be immediately used in a new venture. Although this can never be completely achieved, it may be approximated.

    The death of a product should be timed so as to cause the least disturbance to customers. They should be informed about the elimination of the product far enough in advance so they can make arrangements for replacement, if any are available, but not so far in advance so they will switch to new suppliers before the deleting firm's inventories of the product are sold. Deletion at the beginning of a selling season or in the middle of it probably will create maximum customer inconvenience, whereas at the end of the season it will be the least disturbing.

- *Parts and replacements.* If the product to be killed off is a durable one, probably the deleting firm will find it necessary to maintain stocks of repair parts for about the expected life of the units most recently sold. The firm that leaves a trail of uncared-for "orphan" products cannot expect to engender much good will from dealers or users. Provision for the care and maintenance of the orphan is a necessary cost of deletion.

    This problem is much more widespread than is commonly understood. The woman who buys a set of china or silverware

and finds that she cannot replace broken or lost pieces does not entertain an affectionate regard for the maker. The same sort of thing is true if she installs draperies and later, when one of them is damaged, finds that the pattern is no longer available.
- *Stocks.* The deletion plan should provide for clearing out the stocks of the dying product and materials used in its production, so as to recover the maximum amount of the working capital invested in it. This is very largely a matter of timing—the tapering off of purchase, production, and selling activities. However, this objective may conflict with those of minimizing inconvenience to customers and servicing the orphan units in use after deletion.
- *Holdover demand.* However much the demand for a product may decline, it probably will retain some following of devoted users. They are bound to be disturbed by its deletion and are likely to be vocal about it; and usually there is little that management can do to mitigate this situation.

Sometimes a firm can avoid all these difficulties by finding another firm to purchase the product. This should usually be tried before any other deletion steps are taken. A product with a volume too small for a big firm to handle profitably may be a money-maker for a smaller one with less overhead and more flexibility.

Neglect or Action?

The process of product deletion is important. The more dynamic the business, the more important it is.

But it is something that most company executives prefer not to do; and therefore it will not get done unless management establishes definite, clearcut policies to guide it, sets up carefully articulated procedures for doing it, and makes a positive and unmistakable assignment of authority and responsibility for it.

Exactly what these policies should be, what form these procedures should take, and to whom the job should be assigned are matters that must vary with the structure and operating methods of the firm and with its position in the industry and the market.

In any case, though, the need for managerial attention, planning, and supervision of the deletion function cannot be overemphasized. Many business firms are paying dearly for their neglect of this problem, but unfortunately do not realize how much this is costing them.

SECTION H
Pricing Perspectives: Managerial Versus Consumer

Although pricing is one of the most important elements of the marketing mix, it is probably the least understood. There are several reasons for this situation.

First, pricing decisions often are not a part of marketing decisions. Instead, they are a part of either manufacturing or finance decisions. Therefore, pricing expertise rests outside the marketing arena.

Second, most of our pricing knowledge and research have been limited to the economic approach to price setting and price behavior. This approach has resulted in pricing policies based on cost or competition rather than the customer's willingness to pay.

There are, however, several relevant areas of pricing for marketing managers. For example, what is the role of price in determining the perception of quality of the product? Is there a price-quality relationship? If so, how does it work?

Similarly, we need to understand price perceptions and especially the concept of price distortion. For example, most consumers feel that the price of the long-distance calls charged by AT&T is higher than permitted by law, whereas the prices charged by MCI are lower than their true prices. What factors create price distortion in the minds of the customers?

Finally, we also need to understand the prices of substitutes and their impact on the demand for our products. What is the price differential beyond which the customer is likely to switch to a substitute product or technology?

27 Techniques for Pricing New Products and Services

Joel Dean

Handbook of Modern Marketing, edited by Victor Buell (New York: McGraw-Hill Book Company, 1970), pp. 5-51–5-61. Copyright 1970 by the McGraw-Hill Book Company. Reprinted with permission.

Pricing a new product or service is one of the most important and puzzling of marketing problems. The high proportion of new products which fail in the marketplace is partly due to the difficulty of pricing them correctly.

A *new* product (or service)[1] is here defined as one which incorporates a major innovation. It is new to the world, not just new to the company. This means that its market is, at the outset, ill defined. Potential applications cannot be foreseen with precision. Pricing decisions usually have to be made with little knowledge and with wide margins of error in the forecasts of demand, cost, and competitors' capabilities.

This section deals with the price level, not the price structure; e.g., the average price per ton-mile of air freight, not the structure of price differentials by size of shipment, density, distance, etc.

The difficulty of pricing new products is enhanced by the dynamic deterioration of the competitive status of most new products, which is speeded by today's high rate of innovation. This makes the evolution of a new product's economic status a strategic consideration in practical pricing.

DYNAMIC COMPETITIVE SETTING

A product which is new to the world, as opposed to being merely new to the company, passes through distinctive competitive stages in its life cycle. The appropriate pricing policy is likely to be different for each stage.

New products have a protected distinctiveness which is doomed to progressive degeneration from competitive inroads. As new competitors enter the field and innovations narrow the gap of distinctiveness between the product and its substitutes, the seller's zone of pricing discretion narrows. His distinctive "specialty" fades into a pedestrian "commodity" which is so little differentiated from other products that the seller has limited independence in pricing, even if rivals are few.

Throughout the cycle, continual changes occur in promotional and price elasticity and in costs of production and distribution. These changes call for adjustments in price policy.

Appropriate pricing over the cycle depends on the development of three different aspects of maturity which usually move in approximately parallel time paths: (1) *technical maturity*, indicated by declining rate of product development, increasing uniformity of competing brands, and increasing stability of manufacturing processes and knowledge about them; (2) *market maturity*, indicated by consumer acceptance of the basic service idea, by widespread belief that the products of most manufacturers will perform satisfactorily, and by enough familiarity and sophistication to permit consumers to compare brands competently; and (3) *competitive maturity*, indicated by increasing stability of market shares and price structures.

The rate at which the cycle of degeneration progresses varies widely among products. What are the factors that set its pace? An overriding determinant is technical—the extent to which the economic environment must be reorganized to use the innovation effectively. The scale of plant investment and technical reaction called forth by the telephone, electric power, the automobile, or the jet airplane makes for a long gestation period as compared with even such major innovations as cellophane or frozen foods. Development comes fastest when the new gadget fills a new vacuum.

Monopoly Pricing

New product pricing, if the product is truly novel, is in essence monopoly pricing. Stark monopoly pricing, which is the core of new product pricing, considers only what the traffic will bear—the price which will maximize profits, taking into account the price sensitivity of demand and the incremental promotional and production cost of the seller. What the product is worth to the buyer, not what it costs the seller, is the controlling consideration.

The competitive setting of the new product has, however, peculiar features that modify monopoly pricing. The monopoly power of the new product is (1) restricted (i.e., buyers have alternatives in the form of products that compete indirectly), (2) ephemeral (i.e., subject to inevitable erosion by imitation and obsolescence), and (3) controllable (i.e., capable of some degree of expansion and prolongation by actions of the seller).

For example, Quanta Welding's new diffusion bonding system, based on a millisecond-shaped power pulse, is a patented monopoly. But its pricing power is restricted by alternatives. For supersonic aircraft, these are resistance-welding or riveting, which are candidate pricing benchmarks. The market power of Quanta's superior metals-joining process will be eventually eroded. Solid-state devices may make obsolete the mercury vapor tube that supplies the controllable massive pulses of electrical energy on which the process depends. Penetration pricing might discourage this competitive entry.

These peculiarities of the new-product monopoly introduce dynamism and uncertainty which call for dynamic modifications of monopoly pricing. Examples include:

1. Substitute ways to get the service. These set limits on the market power of a new product and hence serve as benchmarks for pricing it.
2. The perishability of the new product's wanted distinctiveness. This makes the timing of price, promotion, and capacity competition crucial (e.g., choice between skimming and penetration pricing).
3. The ability to influence the amount and the durability of the new product's market power in some degree by specially planned pricing and promotion actions. This gives added weight to the effect of today's pricing upon tomorrow's demand.

DEMAND: SENSITIVITY OF VOLUME TO PRICE

Profitable monopoly pricing of a new product, even with these dynamic competitive modifications, requires an estimate of how price will affect sales. This relationship can be explored in two steps, by (1) finding what range of price will make the product economically attractive to buyers, and (2) estimating what sales volumes can be expected at various points in this price range.

Price Range

The price range is determined by the indirect competition of substitutes, which sets limits to the monopoly power of the new product. In this sense, no product is really new; the most novel product merely plugs an abnormally large gap in the chain of substitutes. This gap marks out the potential range of its price.

For industrial products, a relatively quick and cheap way to find this range is to "pick the brains" of professionals experienced in looking at comparative product performance in terms of buyers' costs and requirements—for example, distributors, prime contractors, and consulting engineers, as well as purchasing analysts and engineers of prospect companies.

For consumers' goods, different methods are needed. In guessing the price range of a radically novel product of small unit value, the concept of barter equivalent can be useful. For example, a manufacturer of paper specialties tested a dramatic new product this way: A wide variety of consumer products totally unlike the new product were purchased and spread out on a big table. Consumers selected the products they would swap for the new product.

Price-Volume Relationship

The effect of the price of the new product upon its volume of sales is the most important and most difficult estimate in pricing. We know in general that the lower the price, the greater the volume of sales and the faster its rate of growth. The air-freight growth rate is about 18 percent; priced higher, it will grow more slowly. But to know the precise position and shape of the price-quantity demand schedule or how much faster sales will grow if the price is 20 percent lower is not possible. But we must estimate.

The best way to predict the effect of price on sales volume for a new product is by controlled experiments: offering it at several different prices in comparable test markets under realistic sales conditions. For example, frozen orange juice was thus tested at three prices. When test marketing is not feasible, another method is to broaden the study of the cost of buyers' alternatives and include forecasts of the sales volume of substitutes (and other indications of the volume to customers of different categories). This approach is most promising for industrial customers, because performance comparisons are more explicit and measurable and economics more completely controls purchases. When buyers' alternatives differ widely in service value, the difficulty of translating this disparity into superiority premiums adds to the imprecision of this method of estimating price-volume relationships.

PRICING BENCHMARKS

The buyers' viewpoint should be controlling in pricing. For every new product there are alternatives. Buyers' best alternatives are usually products already tested in the marketplace. The new product will, presumably, supply a superior solution to the problem of some categories of buyers. The superiority differential over existing products differs widely among new products. The degree of superiority of any one new product over its substitutes usually also differs widely as viewed by different buyers.

Buyers' Alternatives

The prospective buyer of any new product does have alternatives. These indirectly competitive products are the benchmark for his appraisal of the price-performance package of a new product. This comparison with existing products determines its relative attractiveness to potential buyers. Such an analysis of demand can be made in the following steps:

1. Determine the major uses for the new product. For each application, determine the product's performance characteristics.
2. For each important usage area, specify the products that are the buyer's best alternative to the new product. Determine the performance characteristics and requirements which buyers view as crucial in determining their product selection.
3. For each major use, determine how well the product's performance characteristics meet the requirements of customers compared with the performance of these buyers' alternative products.
4. Forecast the prices of alternative products in terms of transaction prices, adjusted for the impact of the new product and translated into units of use. Estimate from the prices of these benchmark substitutes the alternative costs to the buyer per unit of the new product. Real transactions prices (after all discounts), rather than list prices, should be the benchmark in order to reflect marketplace realities. Prices should be predicted, after the introduction of the new product, so as to reflect probable competitive adaptation to the new product. Where eventual displacement of existing substitutes appears likely, short-run incremental cost supplies a Jeremiah forecast of defender's pricing retaliation.
5. Estimate the superiority premium; i.e., price the performance differential in terms of what the superior solution supplied by the new product is worth to buyers of various categories.
6. Figure a "parity price" for the product relative to the buyer's best alternative product in each use, and do this for major categories of customers. Parity is a price which encompasses the premium a customer would be willing to pay for comparative superiority in performance characteristics.

Pricing the Superiority Differential

Determining this price premium over benchmark products which the new product's superiority will most profitably warrant is the most intricate and challenging problem of new-product pricing.

The value to the customer of the innovational superiority of the new product is surrounded by uncertainties: whether the product will work, whether it will attain its designed superiorities, what its reliability and durability performance will be, and how soon it in turn will become obsolete. These uncertainties influence the price a customer would pay and the promotional outlay that would be required to persuade him to buy. Thus, customers' uncertainties will cost the seller something, either in price or promotion.

In essence, the superiority premium requires translation of differential performance characteristics into dollars, based on value analysis from the buyer's viewpoint. The premium will differ among uses, among alternative products, and among categories of customers. For some, it will be negative. Unless it proves practical to segment the market by application and to have widely discriminatory prices, the new product is likely to be priced out of some markets.

A simplistic, single-point premium reflecting "what the product can command in the marketplace" will not do. The customer-response pattern that is needed is the relationship between (1) a series of prospective superiority premiums and (2) the corresponding potential volumes.

What matters is superiority as *buyers* value it, not superiority as calibrated by technicians' measurements or by the sellers' costs. This means that more and better promotion can raise the premium-volume schedule and make a higher superiority premium achieve the same sales volume or rate of sales growth as would a lower premium without the promotion. This premium-volume schedule will be kicked about by retaliatory pricing of displaceable substitutes as well as by the imitative and innovative new-product competition of rivals.

The optimizing premium—i.e., the price that would maximize profits in any specified time period—will depend upon future costs as well as upon the hazy and dynamic demand schedule. It will be hard to find. Uncertainty about the future thus makes the appropriate pricing strategy for the long run a matter of sophisticated judgment.

RATE-OF-RETURN PRICING

Application of the principles of economic pricing is illustrated by rate-of-return pricing of new capital equipment. Industrial goods are sold to businessmen in their capacity as profit-makers. The technique is different for a producer's good (e.g., a truck) than for a consumer's good (e.g., a sports car).

The difference is caused by the fact that the essential service purchased if a product is a producer's good is added profits. A product represents an investment by the customer. The test of whether or not this investment is a desirable one should be its profitability to the customer. The pricing guide that this suggests is rate of return on the capital a customer ties up by his investment in a product.

Rate of Return on Customer's Investment

Rate-of-return pricing looks at a price through the investment eyes of the customer. It recognizes that the upper limit is the price which will produce the minimum acceptable rate of return on the customer's investment. The added profits obtainable from the use of equipment differ among customers and among applications for the same customer.

Cutoff criteria of required return also differ, so prospective customers differ in the rate of return which will induce them to invest in a given product. Thus, the rate-of-return approach opens up a new kind of demand analysis for industrial goods. This analysis consists of inquiry into (a) the costs to buyers from displaceable alternative ways to do the job; (b) the cost-saving and profit-producing capability of equipment in different applications and for different prospects; and (c) the capital budgeting policies of customers, with particular emphasis on their cost-of-capital and their minimum rate-of-return requirements.

The rate-of-return analysis just outlined is particularly useful in the pioneering stages of new products when the competition consists of only obsolescent ways of doing the job. At more mature stages in the life cycle of a new product, competitive imitation improves prospective customers' alternatives. These rival investment alternatives must then be taken explicitly into the analysis.

One way is to use a competitor's product as the benchmark in measuring the rate of return which a given product will produce for specified categories of prospects. The profitability from the product is measured in terms of its superiority over the best alternative new equipment offered by rivals rather than by its superiority over the customer's old equipment. Rate-of-return pricing translates this competitive superiority into dollars of added profit for the customer and relates this added profit to the added investment. In effect, one would say: "To be sure, buying my competitor's product will give you a 25 percent rate of return, and that is better than keeping your old equipment; but buying *my* product will give you a 30 percent rate of return." For each customer category, rate-of-return analysis reveals a price for a given product that makes it an irresistibly good investment to the customer in view of his alternatives and at the same time extracts from the customer all that can safely be demanded.

Investigation of (1) the productivity of the buyers' capital invested in your new product and (2) the required rate of return of prospective customers has proven a practical way to predict the demand for industrial goods. It must be coupled with forecasts of costs to find the immediately most profitable price, and with considerations of competitive strategy for the longer run.

The Role of Cost

To get maximum practical use from costs in new product pricing, three questions of theory must be answered: (1) Whose cost? (2) Which cost? and (3) What role? As to whose cost, three classes of costs are important: (1) those of prospective buyers, (2) those of existent and potential competitors, and (3) those of the producer of the new product. Cost should play a different role for each of the three, and the pertinent concept of cost will differ accordingly.

Buyers' Cost

How should costs of prospective customers be used in setting the price of a new product? By applying value analysis to prices and performance of alternative products to find the superiority premium that will make the new product attractive from an economic standpoint to buyers of specified categories. Rate-of-return pricing of capital goods illustrates this buyer's-cost approach, which is applicable in principle to all new products.

Competitors' Costs

Competitors' costs are usually the crucial estimate in appraisal of competitors' capabilities.

Costs of two kinds of competitive products can be helpful. The first kind are products already in the marketplace. The objectives are to estimate (1) their staying power and (2) the floor of retaliation pricing. For the first objective, the pertinent cost concept is the competitor's long-run incremental cost. For the second, his short-run incremental cost.

The second kind is the unborn competing product that could blight a new product's future or eventually displace it. Forecasts of competitors' costs for such products can help assess this crucial dimension of capability of prospective competitors and estimate the effectiveness of a strategy of pricing the new product so as to discourage entry. For this purpose, the cost behavior to forecast is the relationship between unit production cost and plant size as the new producer and his rivals move from pilot plant to small-scale test production plant to large-scale mass production. The cost forecasts should take into account technological progress and should be spotted on a time scale that reflects the potential head-start cost advantages that could be attained under a policy of penetration pricing and under skimming pricing.

Estimates of cost of unborn competitive products are necessarily rough, but evaluation of major differences between competitors' costs and the new producer's costs can nevertheless be useful. Thus cost estimates can help forecast a defending product's retaliation pricing and an invading product's conquest pricing.

Producer's Costs

The cost of the producer plays several roles in pricing a new product. The first is birth control. A new product must be prepriced provisionally early in the R&D stage and then again periodically as it progresses toward market. Forecasts of production and promotional costs at matching stages should play the role of forecasting its economic feasibility in determining whether to continue product development and ultimately to commercialize. The concept of cost relevant for this birth-control role is a prediction of full cost at a series of prospective volumes and corresponding technologies, and encompassing imputed cost of capital on intangible as well as tangible investment.

A second role is to establish a price floor which is also the threshold for selecting from candidate prices that which will maximize return on a new product investment over the long run.

For both jobs, the relevant concept is future costs, forecast over a range of volume, production technologies, and promotional outlays in the marketing plan.

Two categories of cost require separate forecasts and have quite different impacts on new-product pricing: (1) Production costs (including physical distribution), and (2) Persuasion costs, which are discretionary and rivalrous with price.

The production costs that matter are the future costs over the long run that will be added by making this product on the predicted scale (or scales) versus not making it. The added investment necessary to manufacture and distribute the new product should be estimated. Investment should include intangibles such as R&D, promotion, and launching outlays as well as increased working capital. Then the added costs of manufacturing and selling the product at various possible sales volumes should be estimated. It is important to calculate total costs (rather than unit costs) with and without the new product. The difference can then be assigned to the new product. Present overhead that will be the same whether or not the addition to the product line is adopted should be ignored. Future additions to overhead caused by the new product are alone relevant in pricing it. Two sets of cost and investment figures must be built up—one showing the situation *without* the new product and the other showing the situation *with* the new product added to the line, and at several possible volumes. High costs of pilot-plant production and of early small-scale production plants should be viewed as intangible capital investment rather than as the current operating costs. The losses of a break-in period are part of the investment on which a satisfactory return should be made.

Long-run future incremental costs, including costs of equity capital (i.e., satisfactory return on the added investment), supply the base line above which contribution profits of a new product should be maximized—not an impenetrable floor, but a calculation benchmark for optimization.

STRATEGY CHOICES

A major strategy decision in pricing a new product is the choice between (1) skimming pricing and (2) penetration pricing. There are intermediate positions, but the issues are made clearer by comparing the two extremes.

Skimming Pricing

Some products represent drastic improvements upon accepted ways of performing a service or filling a demand. For these products a strategy of high prices with large promotional expenditure in the early stages of market development (and lower prices at later stages) has frequently proved successful. This can be termed a "skimming-price" policy. There are four main reasons for its success:

1. Sales of the product are likely to be less sensitive to price in the early stages than when the product is "full-grown" and competitive imitations have appeared. In the early stages, the product usually has so few close rivals that cross elasticity of demand is low. Promotional sensitivity is, on the other hand, quite high, particularly for products with high unit prices, since it is difficult for the customer to value the service of the product.

2. Launching a new product with a high price is an efficient device for breaking the market up into segments that differ in price elasticity of demand. The initial high price serves to skim the cream of the market that is relatively insensitive to price. Subsequent price reductions tap successively more elastic sectors of the market. This pricing strategy is exemplified by the systematic succession of editions of a book, sometimes starting with a $50 limited personal edition and ending up with a 75-cent paperback book.

3. A skimming policy is safer, or at least it appears so. Facing an unknown elasticity of demand, a high initial price serves as a "refusal" price during the stage of exploration. How much costs can be reduced as the market expands and as the design of the product is improved by increasing production efficiency with new techniques is difficult to predict.

4. High prices frequently produce a greater dollar volume of sales in the early stages of market development than are produced by low initial prices. When this is the case, skimming pricing will provide funds to finance expansion into the larger volume sectors of a given market.

Penetration Pricing

Despite its many advantages, a skimming-price policy is not appropriate for all new product problems. Although high initial prices may maximize profits during the early stages of product introduction, they may also prevent sales to many of the buyers upon whom you must rely for a mass market. The alternative is to use low prices as an entering wedge to get into mass markets early. This may be termed penetration pricing. Such an approach is likely to be desirable under any of these conditions:

First, when sales volume of the product is very sensitive to price, even in the early stages of introduction.

Second, when it is possible to achieve substantial economies in unit cost of manufacturing and distributing the product by operating at large volume.

Third, when a product faces threats of strong potential competition very soon after introduction.

Fourth, when there is no "elite" market—that is, no class of buyers willing to pay a higher price to obtain the newest and the best.

While a penetration pricing policy can be adopted at any stage in the product's life cycle, this pricing strategy should always be examined before a new product is marketed at all. Its possibility should be explored again as soon as the product has established an elite market. Sometimes a product can be rescued from premature death by adoption of a penetration price after the cream of the market has been skimmed.

One important consideration in the choice between skimming and penetration pricing at the time a new product is introduced is the ease and speed with which competitors can bring out substitute products. If you decide to set your initial price low enough, your large competitor may not feel it worthwhile to make a big investment for slim profit margins. The speed with which your product loses its uniqueness and sinks from its sheltered status to the level of just another competitive product depends on several factors:

1. Its total sales potential. A big potential market entices competitive imitation.
2. The investment required for rivals to manufacture and distribute the product. A big investment barrier deters invasion.
3. The strength of patent and know-how protection.
4. The alertness and power of competitors.

Although competitive imitation is almost inevitable, the company that introduces a new product can use price to discourage or delay the introduction of competitive products. Keep-out prices can be achieved quickly by penetration pricing.

Pricing in Maturity

To price appropriately for later stages in the cycle of competitive maturity, it is important to be able to tell when a product is approaching maturity. When the new product is about to slip into the commodity category, it is sometimes desirable to reduce real prices promptly as soon as symptoms of deterioration appear. Some of the symptoms of degeneration of competitive status toward the commodity level are:

1. Weakening in brand preference. This may be evidenced by a higher cross elasticity of demand among leading products, the leading brand not being able to continue demanding as much price premium as initially without losing position.
2. Narrowing physical variation among products as the best designs are developed and standardized. This has been dramatically demonstrated in automobiles and is still in process in television receivers.
3. The entry in force of private-label competitors. This is exemplified by the mail-order houses' sale of own-label refrigerators and paint sprayers.
4. Market saturation. The ratio of replacement sales to new-equipment sales serves as an indicator of the competitive degeneration of durable goods, but in general it must be kept in mind that both market size and degree of saturation are hard to define (e.g., saturation of the radio market, which was initially thought to be one radio per home and later had to be expanded to one radio per room).
5. The stabilization of production methods, indicated by slow rate of technological advance, high average age of equipment, and great uniformity among competitors' introduction technology.

PROMOTION AND DISTRIBUTION

Promotion

Closely related to pricing is promotional strategy. An innovator must not only sell his product, but frequently he must also make people recognize their need for a new *kind* of product. The problem is one of "creating a market."

Initial promotion outlays are an investment in the product that cannot be recovered until some kind of market has been established. The innovator shoulders the burden of educating consumers to the existence and uses of the product. Later imitators will never have to do this job; so if the innovator does not want to be simply a benefactor to his future competitors, he must make pricing plans to earn a return on all his initial outlays before his pricing discretion evaporates.

The basic strategic problem is to find the right mixture of price and promotion to maximize long-run profits. A relatively high price may be chosen in pioneering stages, together with large advertising and dealer discounts, and the plan may be to get the promotion investment back early; or low prices and lean margins may be used from the very outset in order to discourage potential competition when the barriers of patents and investment in production capacity, distribution channels, or production techniques become inadequate.

Channels of Distribution

Choice of channels of distribution should be consistent with strategy for initial pricing and for promotional outlays. Penetration pricing and explosive promotion call for distribution channels that promptly make the product broadly available. Otherwise advertising is wasted or mass-market pricing stymied. Distribution policy also concerns the role the dealer is to play in pushing a given product, the margins he must be paid to induce this action, and the amount of protection of territory and of inventory required to do so.

Estimation of the costs of moving the new product through the channels of distribution to the final consumer must enter into the pricing procedure, since these costs govern the factory price that will result in a specified final price. Distributive margins are partly pure promotional costs and partly physical distribution costs. Margins must at least cover the distributors' costs of warehousing, handling, and order taking. These costs are similar to factory production costs in being related to physical capacity and its utilization; i.e., fluctuations in production or sales volume. Hence these set a floor to trade-channel discounts. But distributors usually also contribute promotional effort—in point-of-sale pushing, local advertising, and display—when it is made worth their while. These pure promotional costs are more optional.

Distributors' margins are best determined by study of distributors' alternatives. This does not mean that the distributor gross margin on a given product must be the same as that of rival products. It should instead produce a competitive rate of return on the distributors' investment (in inventory, shelf space and sales capacity).

SUMMARY

Pricing new products is an art. The important determinants in economic pricing of pioneering innovations are complex, interrelated, and hard to forecast. Experienced judgment is required in pricing and repricing the product to fit its changing competitive environment. This judgment may possibly be improved by some pricing precepts suggested by the preceding analysis:

1. Corporate goals must be clearly defined. Pricing a new product is an occasion for rethinking them. This chapter has assumed that the overriding corporate goal is long-run profit maximization; e.g., making the stock worth the most by maximizing the present worth, at the corporation's cost of capital, of its per-share earnings.
2. Pricing a new product should begin long before its birth. Prospective prices, coupled with forecast costs, should play the decisive role in product birth control.
3. Pricing a new product should be a continuing process of bracketing the truth by successive approximations. Rough estimates of the relevant concepts are preferable to precise knowledge of historical irrelevancies.
4. Costs can supply useful guidance in new-product pricing, but not by the conventional wisdom; i.e., cost-plus pricing. Three categories of costs are pertinent: those of the buyer, those of the seller, and those of the seller's rivals. The role of cost differs among the three, as does the concept of cost that is pertinent to that role: different costs for different purposes.
5. The role of cost is to set a reference base for picking the most profitable price. For this job the only costs that are pertinent to pricing a new product on the verge of commercialization (i.e., already developed and tested) are incremental costs; the added costs of going ahead at different plant scales. Costs of R&D and of market testing are now sunk and hence irrelevant.
6. The pricing implications of the changing economic status and competitive environment of a product must be recognized as it passes through its life cycle from birth to obsolescence. This cycle, and the plans that are made to influence it, are of paramount importance for pricing policy.
7. The product should be seen through the eyes of the customer and priced just low enough to make it an irresistible investment in view of his alternatives as he sees them. To estimate successfully how much a given product is worth to the prospect is never easy, but it is usually rewarding.
8. Customers' rate of return should be the main consideration in pricing novel capital goods. Buyers' cost savings (and other earnings) expressed as a return on his investment in the new product are the key to predicting the price sensitivity of demand and to pricing profitably.

9. The strategic choice between skimming and penetration pricing should be based on economics. The skimming policy—i.e., relatively high prices in the pioneering stage, cascading downward thereafter—is particularly appropriate for products whose sales initially are comparatively unresponsive to price but quite responsive to education. A policy of penetration pricing—i.e., relatively low prices in the pioneering stage in anticipation of the cost savings resulting from an expanding market—is best when scale economies are big, demand is price sensitive, and invasion is threatened. Low starting prices sacrifice short-run profits for long-run profits and discourage potential competitors.

ENDNOTE

1. Hereafter, the term "new product" will encompass new services as well.

SELECTIVE BIBLIOGRAPHY

Dean, Joel, *Managerial Economics*, Prentice-Hall, Englewood Cliffs, N.J., 1951 (especially pp. 419–424).

Harper, Donald, *Price Policy and Procedure*, Harcourt, Brace & World, New York, 1966.

Mulvihill, D. F., and S. Paranka, *Price Policies and Practices: A Source Book in Readings*, Wiley, New York, 1967.

Thompson, G. Clark and M. M. MacDonald, "Pricing New Products," *Conference Board Record*, National Industrial Conference Board, New York, 1964.

28   Buyers' Subjective Perceptions of Price

Kent B. Monroe

Reprinted from the *Journal of Marketing Research*, published by the American Marketing Association, Vol. X (February 1973), pp. 70–80. Reprinted by permission.

INTRODUCTION

In recent years there has been a growing awareness of the complex role of price as a determinant of a purchase decision. Recent behavioral research indicates there is no simple explanation of how price influences individual buyers' purchase decisions. In some situations a change in price produces behavioral responses consistent with the assumptions of Marshallian demand theory; in other situations these responses are not consistent with this theory. This article reviews the research on individual response to price and organizes the knowledge obtained from these studies.

The response of interest is individual's perception of price. However, price is only one aspect of the product stimulus confronting a buyer; i.e., the buyer responds to brand name, color, package, size, label, as well as price. The organization of these information cues as purchase decision inputs depends on the perceptual process an individual uses to give meaning to the raw material provided by the external world.

PSYCHOLOGICAL PRICING: TRADITIONAL VIEW

Many basic marketing textbooks provide examples indicating greater demand at particular price points, suggesting that demand falls at prices just above and below the critical price points. Depending on the situation, these psychological prices are referred to as customary prices, odd prices, or price lines. Theoretically, this phenomenon indicates that the consumer is perceptually sensitive to certain prices, and departure from these prices in either direction results in a decrease in demand.

Customary pricing excludes all price alternatives except a single price point. The traditional example has been the five-cent candy bar or package of gum. With customary prices, sellers adapt to changes in costs and market conditions by adjusting product size or quality, assuming the buyer would consider paying only one price.

Odd pricing assumes that prices ending with an odd number (e.g., 1,

3, 5, 7, 9), or just under a round number (e.g., 99, 98) increase consumer sensitivity. Evidence justifying such prices has largely been of an anecdotal nature. However, Ginzberg [28] imposed experimental patterns of odd and even prices on selected items in regional editions of a large mail-order catalog. Taking account of all variables influencing demand, he could not discern any generalizable result of the study. More recently, Gabor and Granger [21] concluded that the dominance of pricing below the round figure in some markets may be largely an artifact. That is, if sellers use odd pricing, then some buyers will consider the odd price as the real price and the round figure price as incorrect and respond accordingly. Again, there was no significant evidence supporting the psychological explanation of increased perceptual sensitivity.

Psychological Pricing: A Partial Explanation

Although the research of Ginzberg and Gabor and Granger suggests that buyers tend to expect certain prices after being exposed to them over a period of time, Friedman [19], noting a general consistency in grocery stores' and in suppliers' pricing patterns, offers reasons why certain psychological prices may have their roots in tradition:

1. Multiples of 12 are the most popular number of selling units packed in a case accounting for 74.5% of all test items.
2. Prices ending in 9 or 5 account for as much as 80% of retail food prices.
3. There was extensive multiple-unit pricing with the multiples never dividing evenly into the price.

However, using only odd prices in multiple-unit pricing is inconvenient to the buyer intent on comparing prices. As a recent *Progressive Grocer* study showed, if the multiple is too complicated, the buyer will buy only in quantities most easily calculated [30]. This *Progressive Grocer* finding suggests some discriminating process being applied by the buyer, but only if the comparative method used leads to a conclusion vis-a-vis the particular product offer. Otherwise, the buyer apparently withdraws from the complicated pricing situation.

4. Nearly 50% of all special off-price promotions were in multiples of 5, even-number discounts were more predominant, one-cent discounts were not found, with two-cent and nine-cent discounts very rare.

These findings imply the need to reduce price sufficiently to allow the buyer to perceive a price difference compared to the old price. Given earlier findings on odd number pricing and the rule of 9 and 5, the even-number discounts and the rarity of nine-cent discounts are easily understood.

Ad hoc explanations of traditional pricing practices suggesting critical prices or magical numbers have not been supported by the limited research available. Perhaps there are some logical explanations for these pricing practices based on traditional distribution practices. But retailers have found some pricing practices work better than others, thereby suggesting there are some buyer behavioral phenomena underlying the observed response patterns.

PRICE-CONSCIOUSNESS

According to economic theory, price is assumed to influence buyer choice because price serves as an indicator of purchase cost. That is, assuming the buyer has perfect information concerning prices and wants satisfaction of comparable product alternatives, he can determine a product mix that maximizes his satisfaction for a given budget constraint. However, the extent that buyers are conscious of the prices they pay influences the way prices are perceived and the role price plays in buyer choice.

Using three measures of price-consciousness, Gabor and Granger [20] surveyed 640 housewives to determine their awareness of grocery prices last paid. The first measure was simply the percentage of prices remembered (82%) irrespective of the correctness of the price named. The researchers also discovered that price-consciousness was inversely correlated with social class (income) with the exception of the poor, and that price-consciousness was lower for branded items. Second, 57% of the prices were named correctly, with the same general relationship with social class and branded goods. Finally, for a subsample of 184 incorrectly named prices, 52% of the prices differed from the correct price by not more than 10%.

Progressive Grocer also found that price-consciousness varied over products [31]. For 60 advertised and price-competitive brand items, the percentage of correct prices named varied from 86% for Coca-Cola to 2% for shortening, and for these items 91% and 34% of the named prices were within 5% of the correct prices.

Explicitly, no research evidence has linked price-consciousness with price perception, although these studies did assume that some recollection of the price paid can be taken as evidence of conscious concern for the price of a given item [20, p. 177]. However, Wells and LoSciuto [76], using direct observation, found that concern for price was exhibited by 13%, 17%, and 25% of shoppers purchasing cereal, candy, and detergent respectively.

Similar to Wells, Brown [4, 5] hypothesized that shopping behavior would be a better indicator of the ability to perceive price differences than conscious concern for price. His study was based on market basket price indices for 80 items in 27 supermarkets in 5 cities and personal interviews covering price perceptions of supermarkets, store patronage behavior, and patronage motives.

Analysis of the data revealed that shopping variables (number of stores shopped, concern for price, use of a shopping list) were the best discriminators of perceptual validity, which was measured by comparing shoppers' ordinal rankings of stores' price levels with the stores' market basket price indices. Further, price-consciousness was a better discriminator of perceptual validity than was price level of the store patronized; very price-conscious shoppers were more valid perceivers of price than non-price-conscious shoppers, but for intermediate levels of price-consciousness no generalizations were possible. In contrast to Gabor and Granger, Brown was unable to establish significant relationships between perceptual validity and socioeconomic variables.

Brown's findings partially corroborate Gabor and Granger's assumption of a positive relationship between price-consciousness and price perception. Both Gabor and Granger and the *Progressive Grocer* study found that for some items the brand influence exhibited dominance over price, thereby suggesting (as Wells did) that price is not of sufficient universal importance to be the primary determinant of choice. Evidence of an inverse relationship between socioeconomic standing and price perception validity found in the Gabor and Granger study was not found by Brown. Further complicating this relationship is the emerging tendency to find positive relationship between socioeconomic variables and use of unit price [50]. Who uses price and when is not well documented by research.

THE PRICE-QUALITY RELATIONSHIP

Finding some degree of price-consciousness among buyers does not necessarily imply that price is used solely as a measure of purchase cost. As Scitovsky [62] has noted, the buyer generally does not have complete information about the quality of alternative product offerings, yet he forms perceptions from the information available. When price information is available, and when the buyer is uncertain about product quality, it would seem reasonable to use price as a criterion for assessing quality.

The process of converting explicit and subjective information into perceptions is affected by the buyer's dispositions and his prior experience with the product. Another parameter of the perceptual situation is the symbolic value of the product—its capacity to evoke reactions relevant to a state of affairs it represents [7]. As the Bruner studies [6, 7] have shown, symbolic value leads to perceptual accentuation, i.e., subjectively magnified. Thus, the perceived value of a product may produce an accentuation in the assessed quality of the product, either positive or negative, and the direction and magnitude of the accentuation will depend on the particular prices and needs involved. Hence, as a criterion for assessing quality, or value, price may serve either to make the product more or less attractive.

Single-Cue Studies

Originally, price-quality studies considered situations where the only differential information available to respondents was price. Initiating these studies, Leavitt [37] asked 30 Air Force officers and 30 male and female graduate students to choose between two differentially priced, lettered, imaginary brands, for four products (moth flakes, cooking sherry, razor blades, and floor wax) and then indicate the "degree of satisfaction" with their choice. Subjects tended to be less satisfied when choosing lower-priced brands and also tended to choose the higher-priced brand when (1) price was the only differential information; (2) the products were perceived to be heterogeneous in quality; and (3) the price difference was large. Tull, et al. [73] replicated Leavitt's experiment using table salt, aspirin, floor wax, and liquid shampoo and found that the respondents tended to choose the higher-priced brands of products perceived to be heterogeneous.

Distinguishing between the effects of price as an indicator of quality on the perception of product attractiveness or on the perception of purchase offer attractiveness, Ölander [53] experimentally tested the effect of price for household textiles on more than 100 young women's perceptions of product attractiveness. When consequences were related to pairwise choices, similar towels were more often preferred when assigned a high price than when assigned a low price.

McConnell [38, 39, 40, 41] tested the hypothesis that product quality perception is a function of price. Sixty married students in each of 24 trials chose one bottle of an identical beer differing only in brand name and price. Analysis revealed that perceived quality was significantly and positively related to price. In an extensive experiment, Shapiro [64] found that for 600 women (1) price was generally an indicator of quality; (2) price could not overcome product preferences; (3) the use of price to judge quality was a generalized attitude; and (4) price reliance varied over products, but was more significant in situations of high risk, low self-confidence, and absence of other cues. Lambert [35, 36] found that for 200 undergraduates the frequency of choosing high-priced brands was positively correlated with perceived variations in product quality and perceived ability to judge quality. Finally, Newman and Becknell [52] found an apparent positive price-quality relationship for ratings of different models of a durable product.

Multicue Studies

A frequent criticism of the single-cue studies is that when price is the only information available, subjects naturally associate price and quality. Although this criticism applies directly to the Leavitt and Tull studies, the other studies cited included other experimentally controlled information, such as actual product samples or promotional information. Generally, when price was the only differential information, a positive price-quality relationship was observed which was enhanced when the products were perceived to be heterogeneous in quality and when the comparative price differences were accentuated.

To overcome the criticism of the single-cue studies, other price-quality studies have experimentally varied other cues in addition to price. Three experiments specifically tested the single-cue, price-quality relationship as a part of the overall experimental design. Using home economics students, housewives, carpet buyers, and salesmen, Enis and Stafford [16, 17] discovered that perception of the quality of carpeting was directly related to price. Although store information did not significantly affect perception of carpet quality, the interactive effect of price and store information was significant. Jacoby, et al. [32] asked 136 adult male beer drinkers to taste and rate four test beers. By experimentally manipulating price, composition differences, and brand image, it was determined that price, except when considered in isolation, did not have a significant effect on quality perception, whereas brand image did. Gardner [27] also found a brand-quality relationship replacing the price-quality relationship in an experiment testing students' perceptions of toothpaste, men's shirts, and men's suits. Moreover, in an earlier experiment using the same product categories, Gardner [26] could find no significant relationship between perceived quality and frequency of purchase or time spent shopping for the test products.

Although these three studies provide evidence of a positive price-quality relationship, their results do imply that price may not be the dominant cue in quality perception. Unfortunately, this diminished saliency of the price cue has not been a generalized finding in other multicue studies. Andrews and Valenzi [3] asked 50 female students to rate the quality of sweaters and shoes. Quality ratings for each product were obtained first for each cue presented separately (price, store name, brand name), then for all 27 variable combinations. The results indicated that the lower the price the greater the influence of brand names, but in combined quality judgments price was clearly the dominant cue.

Rao [59, 60], using 144 graduate students, experimentally tested the role of price in quality perceptions for electric razors and razor blades. Using the multidimensional model of individual differences, he discovered that after accounting for prior product knowledge, personality variables, and brand display, price did not significantly affect perception of product quality. Both prior product knowledge and consumer test information produced significant effects on quality perceptions.

Smith and Broome [67, 68] experimentally tested the effects of price and market standing information on brand preference using 196 student wives and toothpaste, aspirin, green peas, and coffee. Their findings suggest that price and market standing information influence preference of unknown brands, but neither influences preference for known brands. Della Bitta [13] experimentally determined that students used price as an indicator of product attractiveness for table and pocket radios. Moreover, a positive relation between an evaluator's uncertainty about ability to assess product attractiveness and the use of price as an evaluative criterion was discovered.

Finally, using coffee, fabric softener, and spray cologne, Monroe [48] discovered that when housewives had prior differential purchase or use experience, brand attitude overcame the price influence, implying less use of price as a preference decision cue. Departing from previous studies, Monroe disaggregated the data and discovered that when price was the only differential information, the respondents found it very difficult to decide which brand to prefer. In contrast to most previous studies, respondents were permitted to indicate no brand preference for any test situation, and when price was the only differential information, nearly 25% of all responses indicated indifference even when comparative prices were more than 40% apart.

Determining the specific effect price has on buyers' perceptions of quality is complicated by the multitude of research designs and products tested. But throughout the findings surveyed here emerges the suggestion that brand name is important and possibly dominates price for relatively inexpensive grocery products and beverages. For clothing there is an apparent increasing concern with price, although price may not always dominate the influence of brand name. Perhaps one major disadvantage of experimental research in this area is the difficulty of presenting a wide range of prices to obtain individuals' perceptions of product quality. Only Andrews and Valenzi and Monroe offered a systematic range of prices to the experimental respondents. Also, as suggested in the research reported in the section on differential price thresholds, the range of stimuli (prices) presented does affect respondents' perceptions.

Functional Form of the Price-Quality Relationship

As Gardner [27] has suggested, the research evidence precludes any generalization about a price-quality relationship. The single-cue studies unanimously observed a price-quality relationship, but the multicue studies often found little direct price-quality relations. In those studies where brand names were a part of the manipulations, the brand influence seemingly dominated the price influence, a result consistent with the price-consciousness studies.

Apart from the issue of generalizability, some of the studies produced evidence on the functional form of the price-quality relationship. McConnell [38, 39] observed a nonlinear relationship—the $1.30 and $1.20 brands of beer were separated by a greater perceptual distance than were the $1.20 and $0.99 brands. Also, Rao [59] observed: (1) that the price-quality relationship was not unidirectional and (2) that brand quality was exponentially related to price.

Noting the implied nonlinear or even discontinuous relationships in some of the previous studies, Peterson [58] estimated the price-quality functional form and discovered a parabolic relationship of the form:

$$\bar{Q}_i = a + bX_i - cX_i^2, \tag{1}$$

where $\bar{Q}_i$ is mean quality rating at the ith price level, X_i is the ith price level, $i = 1, 2, \ldots, n$, and a, b, c are parameters. It should also be noted that the general form of the relationship found by Peterson can also be represented by the exponential form suggested by Rao, except that the exponential form will asymptotically approach an upper limit.

Related to the functional form of the price-quality relationship is the implied demand curve resulting from such a relationship. Although none of these studies specifically examined the price-quality demand relationship, the evidence cited infers that, at least over some range of prices, demand is greater for higher prices, and the demand curve has a positive slope. Other than for such unique situations as inferior and "snob-appeal" goods, economists are understandably reluctant to accept such a possibility, since the positively sloping demand curve for a price-quality relationship is an inference without empirical evidence.

Price-Quality Mapping

How people use price to evaluate quality is suggested by a paradigm developed by Emery [14] in which buyers are hypothesized to categorize the product's price, categorize the assessed quality, and then judge whether the assessed quality is equivalent to the expected quality for the categorized price. His model is shown in the figure.

Mapping (a) to (b) and (c) to (d) is done simultaneously. Matching (b) and (c) depends on prior purchase experience with the product. If the line linking (b) and (c) has a negative slope, the item will be judged as high-priced relative to assessed quality, while a positive slope would provide a low price judgment. In either situation, if the value of the slope is perceived to be relatively large, the buyer may refrain from comparing his "standard" price-quality relationship against the one observed.

Subjective Mapping of Price and Quality

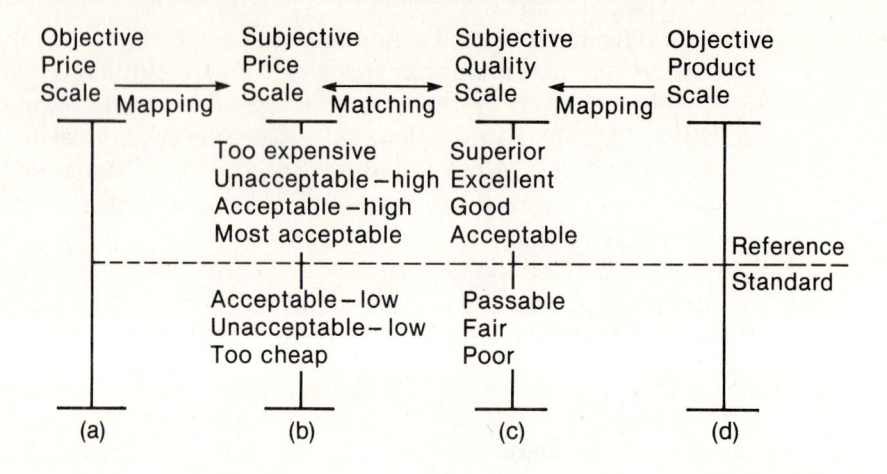

```
Objective          Subjective           Subjective           Objective
Price              Price                Quality              Product
Scale              Scale                Scale                Scale
       Mapping            Matching            Mapping
```

	Subjective Price	Subjective Quality	
	Too expensive Unacceptable – high Acceptable – high Most acceptable	Superior Excellent Good Acceptable	Reference Standard
	Acceptable – low Unacceptable – low Too cheap	Passable Fair Poor	
(a)	(b)	(c)	(d)

Source: [14, p. 104]; price categories adapted from [46].

ABSOLUTE PRICE THRESHOLDS

Research evidence reviewed so far has been directed toward the questions of whether buyers are aware of prices they pay and whether price is used as an indicator of quality without relating price perception to the perceptual process per se. But it is necessary to determine whether certain perceptual phenomena relating sensory processes to physical stimuli are analogous to price perception. In this section and the next, attention is directed to two perceptual phenomena: absolute and differential thresholds.

Every human sensory process has an upper and lower limit of responsiveness to a stimulus—*absolute thresholds* that mark the transition between response and no response. Within the stimulus set in which responsiveness occurs the *differential threshold* is the minimum amount of change in a stimulus necessary to produce "just noticeable difference" or JND. In a pricing situation, we are interested in the buyer's ability to discriminate between various product choices (stimuli). Therefore, two questions arise: (1) Do buyers have upper and lower price limits? and (2) Given differentially priced products, how do buyers discriminate among choices?

Theoretical Framework

The hypothesis that a buyer has lower and upper price limits for a contemplated purchase has foundation in psychophysics, the study of quantitative relationships between physical objects and corresponding psychological events. Originating much of the interest in threshold research was Weber's law which suggests that small, equally perceptible increments in a response correspond to proportional increments in the stimulus:

$$(2) \quad \Delta S/S = K$$

where S is the magnitude of the stimulus, ΔS is the increment in S corresponding to a defined unitary change in response, and K is a constant.

In judging differences between two intensities of a stimulus Weber's law holds only over limited ranges of stimulus intensity. In particular, when stimuli values approach the lower threshold, K may become considerably higher, and it also may increase for high stimuli values. Fechner argued that subjective sensation must be measured indirectly by using differential increments and derived the Weber-Fechner law (see [47] for a complete derivation):

$$(3) \quad R = k \log S + a$$

where R is the magnitude of response, S the magnitude of the stimulus, k a constant of proportionality, and a the constant of integration.

The Weber-Fechner law provides a means of experimentally determining the absolute threshold because a least squares regression relating R to $\log S$ can be fitted from the data. Then the threshold is operationally defined as the stimulus value with a probability of producing a response 50% of the time [12]. The importance of the Weber-Fechner law to pricing is it produces the hypothesis that the relationship between price and an operationally defined response is logarithmic.

Empirical Evidence for Absolute Price Thresholds

The hypothesis of lower and upper price thresholds implies the existence of a range of acceptable prices where some prices greater than $0 are unacceptable because they are considered too low. Stoetzel [70] demonstrated the existence of a range of prices buyers are willing to pay for a radio. Adam [1] then developed a technique for quantifying buyers' attitudes toward price. Interviewing over 6,000 people Adam determined upper and lower price thresholds for nylon stockings, an underwear item, children's shoes, men's dress shirts, a gas lighter, and refrigerators.

Fouilhé [18] extended the work of Stoetzel and Adam to include two household products and package soup and confirmed evidence for a range of acceptable prices. Fouilhé's methodology differed from Stoetzel and Adam in that he actually showed the products to each respondent, including brand name for two of them, and found that the known products had a distinctly narrower acceptable price range.

Gabor and Granger [22, 23] interviewed over 3,000 housewives to determine acceptable price ranges for a carpet, nylon stockings, food, and 2 household products. Gabor and Granger not only confirmed the acceptable price range hypothesis, but also found that the range shifted downward as income fell. Moreover, as income fell, the upper price threshold dropped less than the lower one, implying that low price was a more potent deterrent to the higher-income groups than was high price to lower-income groups.

Investigating social categorization as a function of acceptance and series range, Sherif [65] found price thresholds for a winter coat using 334 high school white and Indian students to be distinctly lower for the Indian students, particularly as the price stimulus set was lengthened to include higher prices. Monroe and Venkatesan [51] adapted psychophysical experimental methodology using college students, and upper and lower price limits were determined for a variety of clothing and personal care items. In a second experiment replicating Sherif's study using high school students, Monroe [46] determined price limits for a sport coat and dress shoes.

Alexis, et al. [2] asked 150 housewives to indicate the perceived importance of specific physical attributes and price for five articles of clothing and concluded that "the consumer goes shopping with a 'target' price in mind around which there is an acceptable deviation" [2, p. 28].

Functional Form of the Buy-Response Function

One implication of the price threshold concept is that the probability distribution a buyer will find an acceptable price is bell-shaped (the buy-response function) [23, 45]. Thus, if a buyer's perception follows the normal law, the cumulative response function is an S-shaped curve. Further, as hypothesized by the Weber-Fechner law, if equal increments in cumulative responses are produced only when price is increased by a constant proportion, then plotting the logarithm of price against cumulative response to show a uniform response increase will produce a symmetrical ogive.

Adam [1] proposed the logarithmic response function by suggesting that the size of the acceptable price range is proportional to the reference price:

(4) $$\Delta P/P = K$$

where ΔP is the acceptable price range, P is the reference price, and K is the constant of proportionality—essentially Weber's law. As indicated earlier, the logarithmic hypothesis is easily derived from this proportional relationship. In addition, Adam tested for a logarithmic relationship and concluded that the psychological scale of prices followed a logarithmic scale. Fouilhé [18] found that the logarithmic scale "appears to be well established, at least within the limits of the prices shown" [18, p. 90], as did Gabor and Granger [23].

Independently of these efforts, Cooper [10, 11] tested the relationship:

(5) $$Q = K \log P$$

where Q is perceived quality, P is price, and K is the constant of proportionality. Testing four products, he found a cumulative S-shaped function (ogive) and concluded, "judgments of value... when compared to objective cash scales follow a relatively stable logarithmic form" [10, p. 119]. In addition, he observed that the value of K varies with the magnitude of price, but is constant for a given product. Finally, Monroe [49] also found logarithmic relationships provided good fits in his psychophysical experiments.

DIFFERENTIAL PRICE THRESHOLDS

Usually a buyer has several choices for a contemplated purchase whose prices may provide cues that facilitate the discriminating process. However, even if the numerical prices are different, it cannot be assumed that the prices are perceived to be different. Hence, the problem becomes one of determining the effect of perceived price differences on buyer choice; and the major concern is when and under what circumstances are differentially priced but similar products perceived as different offers? Very little research has been reported on differential thresholds in pricing. This lack of research is surprising because of its practical implications for product line and sale pricing. Thus, the research to be reviewed comes primarily from psychological studies, with pricing implications drawn by analogy.

Weber's Law

Weber's law has often been cited as the basis for inferences about perceived price differences [15, 33, 43, 61, 75], but most writers have ignored other important variables affecting perception of price differences and simply assumed K to be constant for an individual over all price comparisons. But just as K varies over different physical stimuli and as stimuli values approach minimal or high intensity, so should K vary over different products (similarly priced) and over divergent price levels.

Uhl [74] postulated that behavioral response to price changes depends on exposure to and perception of a price change and motivation to alter behavior as a result of it. Further, the perception of a retail price change depends on the magnitude of the price change—in (2) the magnitude of ΔS. In the Uhl study, 74% of the experimental price changes were correctly identified, with the 5% deviations correctly identified 64% of the time, and the 15% deviations 84% of the time. Uhl interpreted the data to mean that the larger price changes exceeded the differential price thresholds of greater numbers of respondents.

Uhl also attempted a modified test of Weber's law during the study hypothesizing that, for example, a 15% change in the price of a 15¢ product should be perceived by more consumers than a 15% change for a 55¢ product. However, the respondents perceived the 15% price deviations better on the higher-priced items.

Finally, Uhl indicated that while perception of price changes was independent of their direction, the dominance of reaction thresholds made respondents more sensitive to price increases. Moreover, 26% perceptual errors due to differential price thresholds and directional errors suggested a significant portion of the respondents were perceptually limited in responding to price changes.

Although not directly concerned with measuring price change perception, Pessemier [55, 56] in his market simulation studies also found price sensitivity to be different for price increases as compared to price decreases. And in a later field experiment he observed that a price change for a specific brand had little short-run effect on demand [57].

As (5) indicates, Cooper [10, 11] tested the Weber-Fechner law relating perceived quality to price. In addition to his findings on the shape of the response function, Cooper found that the value of K varied for different products. The immediate implication is that consumers will be more sensitive to price changes for some products, i.e., have lower differential price thresholds. In other words, for some products a price increase or decrease may not be perceived, suggesting these products have a relatively high K value, using (2).

Recently Kamen and Toman [33, 34] criticized the attempt of marketing textbook writers to infer analogically that Weber's Law can be applied to a variety of marketing situations. Using a mail survey, they obtained buyer preferences for 36 pairs of gasoline prices and concluded that their data contradicted Weber's Law and, therefore, Weber's Law had been invalidated. Later, Stapel [69] supported Kamen and Toman and suggested that everybody can notice even a one-cent price difference. However, Monroe [47], and Gabor, Granger and Sowter [25] have indicated there is ample evidence to support the plausibility of Weber's Law applying within a pricing context, particularly when a buyer perceives the entire purchase offer as different. *There is still no valid test of the applicability of Weber's Law to pricing.*

Adaptation-Level Theory

Various researchers have suggested that one determinant of price perception is the price "last paid," or the buyers' notion of a "fair price," relative to the present price level, actual or perceived. This price perception hypothesis has theoretical foundation in Helson's adaptation-level theory [29].

Classical psychophysics provided the concept that judgments of stimulus differences are dependent on the magnitude of the standard against which the judgments are made. However, this notion considers the differential threshold to be dependent only on the standard or reference stimulus. Adaptation-level theory provides for a changing zero point from which behavioral responses are made and provides an explicit statement of the frame of reference to which behavior is relative.

According to Helson, an individual's behavioral response to stimuli represents modes of adaptation to environmental and organismic forces. These forces are not random, but rather impinge on organisms already adapted to past stimuli, internal as well as external. The pooled effect of three classes of stimuli—focal, contextual, and organic—determines the adjustment or adaptation level, (AL), underlying all forms of behavior. In price perception, focal stimuli are those the individual is directly responding to, and contextual or background stimuli are all other stimuli in the behavioral situation providing the context within which the focal stimuli are operative. Adaptation processes result in behavioral responses that are commonly expressed along a continuum ranging from rejection to acceptance with a neutral zone or point of indifference in the transitional region(s).

Perceptual judgment of a stimulus depends on the relationship between the physical value of that stimulus and the physical value of the current AL. In a pricing context, adaptation-level theory suggests that price perception depends on the actual price and the individual's reference price or AL.

Emery [14] has noted some important implications of adaptation-level theory on price perception:

1. Price perceptions are relative to other prices and to associated use-values.
2. This is a standard price for each discernible quality level for each product category.
3. The standard price serves as an anchor for judgments of other prices.
4. There is a region of indifference about a standard price such that changes in price within this region produce no change in perception.
5. The standard price will be some average of the prices for similar products.
6. Buyers do not judge each price singly, but rather each price is compared with the standard price and the other prices in the price range.

7. The standard price need not correspond with any actual price nor the price of the leading brand.

Evidence of a Standard Price

Although the hypothesis of a standard price serving as an AL for price judgments has not been directly tested, evidence does support the plausibility of this hypothesis. Initially Scitovsky [62] suggested that buyers consider traditional past prices as a product's fair price. When fair and actual prices differ, the judgment of cheap or expensive may be applied. Similarly, Shapiro [63] suggests that price does not indicate quality without a perceptible difference in price from the fair price. Gabor and Granger [22, 23, 24] indicate a buyer will probably decide to purchase if the product's price falls within an acceptable price range whose limits are related to prevailing market prices and the price of the product normally purchased. Data available to Ölander [53] also suggested that a buyer's price judgment is influenced by his perception of prevailing market prices and his perception of the price most frequently charged. McConnell [38, 40, 41], explaining the nonlinearity of perceptual distance between the high-, middle-, and low-priced brands, found evidence that subjects used the high-priced brand as a frame of reference.

Explaining the respondents' lack of success in identifying the price last paid, Uhl [74] observed that in judging a price change consumers use the range of prices last paid as a reference point. Moreover, consumer perception of price changes was related to the importance of the product in the budget and the frequency of product purchase (contextual variables in the AL paradigm). Kamen and Toman [33] advanced the notion consumers have a fair price for a given item. Respondents in Cooper's research [11] believed the standard price provided above average value; average value was judged for products priced 20–30% below current market prices (standard price). Alexis [2] discovered that the consumer goes shopping with a "target price" in mind around which there is an acceptable deviation. Finally, Peterson [58] found that the perceived quality ratings for some subjects appeared to result from an interaction between price and product frame of reference.

Assimilation-Contrast Effects

Several of the pricing studies cited suggest that the prevailing range of prices affects the standard or reference price. Since the stimulus range is affected by the extreme or end stimuli values, to explore the influence of price range on perception attention could be centered on the end prices. In particular, what happens to perceptions when the end prices are varied? Stimuli values used by individuals to make perceptual judgments (AL, end values) are called anchoring stimuli. When an anchor is introduced at or near the end of the stimulus series, the judgment scale is displaced toward the anchor and the new reference point is assimilated into the series. However, when the end reference point is too remote, displacement is away from the anchor and the end point is perceived as belonging to another scale (category)—the contrast effect [66].

Evidence of assimilation-contrast in a pricing context is meager, but if applicable the implications are profound. First, the high and low prices in a definable product offering may be more noticeable to a buyer and thus influence his perceptions. These end prices [44], along with the standard price, may accentuate the perceived value for a given product (a bargain) or may diminish the perceived value (too expensive), depending where the product's price lies in the price range. In addition, if either or both end prices are outside the acceptable price range, the reference price cues may increase the ambiguity of the price stimuli.

Second, the perception of a sale price may depend on its position in the price range. Positioning it below other offerings may lead to the perception of a bargain (assimilation effect) or to a disbelief that the sale price is a reduction from the advertised original (contrast effect) [42].

A third consideration is the effect of reducing the range of stimuli by shifting one or both end values toward the stimulus center. Available evidence indicates that respondents then have greater difficulty in discriminating among stimuli, and that this increase in ambiguity leads to assimilation [7, 9, 71, 72]. Thus, as the range of alternative prices narrows, buyers may have greater difficulty in discriminating between choices, leading to a judgment of no price differences (assimilation effect); in these cases it can be expected that other cues (e.g., brand name) will dominate the decision process.

Compounding the selection of an appropriate hypothesis is that concomitant with the price series is a value series (perceived quality), and as has already been observed, the price and value series may vary concurrently. Value is not a physical stimulus, although it is an important attribute, and efficient discrimination between stimuli in terms of differences in value usually is more important than discrimination in terms of price. Accentuation of price differences may lead to a greater accentuation of perceived value differences [6, 8, 71, 72]. The resultant purchase response in terms of current phenomenology is not predictable.

Sherif's work [65] is the only research evidence available directly testing the assimilation-contrast hypothesis in a pricing context [62, p. 155]:

> When a (price) range exceeded the latitude of acceptance (range of acceptable prices), higher values were assimilated into acceptable categories; but at the same time, a contrast effect occurred, as revealed in the tendency to lump together highly discrepant values into a broad objectionable category.... As a result of the interac-

tion between internal anchor and stimulus range, subjects discriminated most keenly among the acceptable values when they were not faced with numerous objectionable items.... The results indicate that the range of stimulus values presented for judgment is an important variable in determining whether effects of internal anchors will be detected at all.

Summary and Conclusions

The purpose of this article has been to organize existing research on buyer's subjective perceptions of price, contrasting existing research knowledge and current pricing practices with the unknown knowledge on buyer's price perceptions, and to shake the belief that the inverse price-demand relationship is "one of the best substantiated findings in economics" [54, p. 26]. Although Palda [54] argues that departures from the inverse price-demand relationship—for example, a positive relationship due to quality connotations—are caused by buyers' perceptual changes, the evidence suggests that the perceptual mechanism need not change to infer a positive price-demand relationship.

Findings on the price-quality relationship are mixed, although there are indications that a positive relationship exists, at least over some range of prices for some product categories. Implications of the price-quality relationship on the shape of the demand curve are inconclusive and must be explored directly through empirical studies. There appears to be a general lack of awareness of prices paid for recent purchases. And when buyers do compare prices, the range of prices offered, the reference price, and the end prices may affect judgment and, therefore, buyers' responses. If the price range and the end prices do affect judgment, the extent that the competitive environment leads to little price variation within alternative purchase choices decreases the likelihood of consumer awareness of prices paid and increases the likelihood that price changes within the narrow price range are not perceived.

Despite the evidence available from specific effect of price on choice studies, the evidence available from the absolute and differential price threshold research suggests we know very little about how price affects a buyer's perceptions of alternative purchase offers, and how these perceptions affect his response. Perception is one intervening variable between a stimulus and a response, and as suggested by adaptation-level theory, the stimulus context is indeed an important variable affecting perception. To direct research only to the focus variable (price) and ignore or assume constant the context variables is indeed a grave error. Because of the seemingly heavy reliance on the inverse price-demand function by price setters, it should be realized that a number of psychological and other contextual factors may lead to a perception of price by the buyer that is different from the perception assumed by the price setter.

REFERENCES

1. Adam, Daniel. *Les réactions du consummateur devant le prix.* Paris: SEDES, 1958.
2. Alexis, Marcus, George Haines, Jr., and Leonard Simon. "A Study of the Validity of Experimental Approaches to the Collection of Price and Product Preference Data," paper presented at 17th International Meeting of the Institute of Management Sciences, 1970.
3. Andrews, P. R. and E. R. Valenzi. "Combining Price, Brand, and Store Cues to Form an Impression of Product Quality," paper presented at Conference of the American Psychological Association, 1971.
4. Brown, F. E. "Price Perception and Store Patronage," *Proceedings.* Fall Conference, American Marketing Association, 1968, 371–6.
5. ———. "Who Perceives Supermarket Prices Most Validly?" *Journal of Marketing Research*, 8 (February 1971), 110–3.
6. Bruner, Jerome and Cecile Goodman. "Value and Need as Organizing Factors in Perception," *Journal of Abnormal and Social Psychology*, 42 (January 1947), 33–44.
7. Bruner, Jerome and A. Leigh Minturn. "Perceptual Identification and Perceptual Organization," *Journal of General Psychology*, 53 (July 1955), 21–8.
8. Bruner, Jerome and Leo Postman. "Symbolic Value as an Organizing Factor in Perception," *Journal of Social Psychology*, 27 (February 1948), 203–8.
9. Campbell, Donald, William Hunt, and Nan Lewis. "The Effects of Assimilation and Contrast in Judgments of Clinical Materials," *American Journal of Psychology*, 70 (September 1957), 347–60.
10. Cooper, Peter. "Subjective Economics: Factors in a Psychology of Spending," in Bernard Taylor and Gordon Wills, eds., *Pricing Strateg*. Princeton, N.J.: Brandon/Systems Press, 1970, 112–21.
11. ———. "The Begrudging Index and the Subjective Value of Money," in Bernard Taylor and Gordon Wills, eds., *Pricing Strategy*. Princeton, N.J.: Brandon/Systems Press, 1970, 122–31.
12. Corso, John. "A Theoretic-Historical Review of the Threshold Concept," *Psychological Bulletin*, 60 (July 1963), 346–70.
13. Della Bitta, Albert. "An Experimental Examination of Conditions Which May Foster the Use of Price as an Indicator of Relative Product Attractiveness," unpublished doctoral dissertation, University of Massachusetts, 1971.
14. Emery, Fred. "Some Psychological Aspects of Price," in Bernard Taylor and Gordon Wills, eds., *Pricing Strategy*. Princeton, N.J.: Brandon/Systems Press, 1970, 98–111.
15. Engel, James, David Kollat, and Roger Blackwell. *Consumer Behavior*. New York: Holt, Rinehart and Winston, 1968.
16. Enis, Ben and James Stafford. "Consumers' Perception of Product Quality as a Function of Various Information Inputs," *Proceedings*. Fall Conference, American Marketing Association, 1969, 340–4.

17. ———. "The Price-Quality Relationship: An Extension," *Journal of Marketing Research*, 6 (November 1969), 256–8.
18. Fouilhé, Pierre. "The Subjective Evaluation of Price: Methodological Aspects," in Bernard Taylor and Gordon Wills, eds., *Pricing Strategy*. Princeton, N.J.: Brandon/Systems Press, 1970, 89–97.
19. Friedman, Lawrence. "Psychological Pricing in the Food Industry," in Almarin Phillips and Oliver Williamson, eds., *Prices: Issues in Theory, Practice, and Public Policy*. Philadelphia: University of Pennsylvania Press, 1967, 187–201.
20. Gabor, André and Clive Granger. "On the Price Consciousness of Consumers," *Applied Statistics*, 10 (November 1961), 170–88.
21. ———. "Price Sensitivity of the Consumer," *Journal of Advertising Research*, 4 (December 1964), 40–4.
22. ———. "The Pricing of New Products," *Scientific Business*, 3 (August 1965), 141–50.
23. ———. "Price as an Indicator of Quality, Report on an Enquiry," *Economica*, 46 (February 1966), 43–70.
24. ———. "The Attitude of the Consumer to Price," in Bernard Taylor and Gordon Wills, eds., *Pricing Strategy*. Princeton, N.J.: Brandon/Systems Press, 1970, 132–51.
25. ———, and Anthony Sowter. "Comments on 'Psychophysics of Prices,'" *Journal of Marketing Research*, 8 (May 1971), 251–2.
26. Gardner, David. "An Experimental Investigation of the Price-Quality Relationship," *Journal of Retailing*, 46 (Fall 1970), 25–41.
27. ———. "Is There a Generalized Price-Quality Relationship?" *Journal of Marketing Research*, 8 (May 1971), 241–3.
28. Ginzberg, Eli. "Customary Prices," *American Economic Review*, 26 (June 1936), 296.
29. Helson, Harry, *Adaptation-Level Theory*. New York: Harper & Row, 1964.
30. "How Multiple-Unit Pricing Helps—and Hurts," *Progressive Grocer*, 50 (June 1971), 52–8.
31. "How Much Do Customers Know About Retail Prices?" *Progressive Grocer*, 43 (February 1964), C104–6.
32. Jacoby, Jacob, Jerry Olson, and Rafael Haddock. "Price, Brand Name, and Product Composition Characteristics as Determinants of Perceived Quality," *Journal of Applied Psychology*, 55 (December 1971), 470–9.
33. Kamen, Joseph and Robert Toman. "Psychophysics of Prices," *Journal of Marketing Research*, 7 (February 1970), 27–35.
34. ———. "'Psychophysics of Prices': A Reaffirmation," *Journal of Marketing Research*, 8 (May 1971), 252–7.
35. Lambert, Zarrel. "Price and Choice Behavior," *Journal of Marketing Research*, 9 (February 1972), 35–40.
36. ———. "Product Perception: An Important Variable in Price Strategy," *Journal of Marketing*, 34 (October 1970), 68–71.
37. Leavitt, Harold. "A Note on Some Experimental Findings About the Meaning of Price," *Journal of Business*, 27 (July 1954), 205–10.
38. McConnell, J. Douglas. "An Experimental Examination of the Price-Quality Relationship," *Journal of Business*, 41 (October 1968), 439–44.
39. ———. "The Development of Brand Loyalty: An Experimental Study," *Journal of Marketing Research*, 5 (February 1968), 13–9.

40. ———. "Effects of Pricing on Perception of Product Quality." *Journal of Applied Psychology*, 52 (August 1968), 313–4.
41. ———. "The Price-Quality Relationship in an Experimental Setting," *Journal of Marketing Research*, 5 (August 1968), 300–3.
42. McDougall, Gordon. "Credibility of Price-offs in Retail Advertising," unpublished doctoral dissertation proposal, University of Western Ontario, 1970.
43. Miller, Richard. "Dr. Weber and the Consumer," *Journal of Marketing*, 26 (January 1962), 57–61.
44. Monroe, Kent. "A Method for Determining Product Line Prices with End-Price Constraints," unpublished doctoral dissertation, University of Illinois, 1968.
45. ———. "The Information Content of Prices: A Preliminary Model for Estimating Buyer Response," *Management Science*, 17 (April 1971), B 519–32.
46. ———. "Measuring Price Thresholds by Psychophysics and Latitudes of Acceptance," *Journal of Marketing Research*, 8 (November 1971), 400–4.
47. ———. "'Psychophysics of Prices': A Reappraisal," *Journal of Marketing Research*, 8 (May 1971), 248–50.
48. ———, "The Influence of Price and the Cognitive Dimension on Brand Attitudes and Brand Preferences," paper presented at Attitude Research and Consumer Behavior Workshop, 1970.
49. ———. "Some Findings on Estimating Buyers' Response Functions for Acceptable Price Thresholds," *Proceedings*. Northeast Conference, the American Institute for Decision Sciences, 1972, in press.
50. ——— and Peter LaPlaca. "What Are the Benefits of Unit Pricing?" *Journal of Marketing*, 36 (July 1972), 16–22.
51. Monroe, Kent and M. Venkatesan. "The Concept of Price Limits and Psychophysical Measurement: A Laboratory Experiment," *Proceedings*. Fall Conference, American Marketing Association, 1969, 345–51.
52. Newman, Diane and James Becknell. "The Price-Quality Relationship as a Tool in Consumer Research," *Proceedings*. 78th Annual Conference, American Psychological Association, 1970, 729–30.
53. Ölander, Folke. "The Influence of Price on the Consumer's Evaluation of Products and Purchases," in Bernard Taylor and Gordon Wills, eds., *Pricing Strategy*. Princeton, N.J.: Brandon/Systems Press, 1970, 50–69.
54. Palda, Kristian. *Pricing Decisions and Marketing Policy*. Englewood Cliffs, N.J.: Prentice-Hall, 1971.
55. Pessemier, Edgar. "An Experimental Method for Estimating Demand," *Journal of Business*, 33 (October 1960), 373–83.
56. ———. *Experimental Methods of Analyzing Demand for Branded Consumer Goods*. Economic and Business Study No. 39, Pullman, Wa.: Washington State University Press, 1963.
57. ——— and Richard Teach. "Pricing Experiments, Scaling Consumer Preferences, and Predicting Purchase Behavior," *Proceedings*. Fall Conference, American Marketing Association, 1966, 541–57.
58. Peterson, Robert. "The Price-Perceived Quality Relationship: Experimental Evidence," *Journal of Marketing Research*, 7 (November 1970), 525–8.
59. Rao, Vithala. "The Salience of Price in the Perception and Evaluation of Product Quality: A Multidimensional Measurement Model and Experimental Test," unpublished doctoral dissertation, University of Pennsylvania, 1970.
60. ———. "Salience of Price in the Perception of Product Quality: A Multidimen-

sional Measurement Approach," *Proceedings*. Fall Conference, American Marketing Association, 1971, 571–7.
61. Roth, Elmer. "How to Increase Room Revenue," *Hotel Management*, 67 (March 1955), 52ff.
62. Scitovsky, Tibor. "Some Consequences of the Habit of Judging Quality By Price," *Review of Economic Studies*, 12 (1944–45), 100–5.
63. Shapiro, Benson. "The Psychology of Pricing," *Harvard Business Review*, 46 (July–August 1968), 14–8, 20, 22, 24–5, 160.
64. ———. "Price as a Communicator of Quality: An Experiment," unpublished doctoral dissertation, Harvard University, 1970.
65. Sherif, Carolyn. "Social Categorization as a Function of Latitude of Acceptance and Series Range," *Journal of Abnormal and Social Psychology*, 67 (August 1963), 148–56.
66. Sherif, Muzafer and Carl Hovland. "Judgmental Phenomena and Scales of Attitude Measurement: Placement of Items with Individual Choice of Number of Categories," *Journal of Abnormal and Social Psychology*, 48 (January 1953), 135–41.
67. Smith, Edward and Charles Broome. "A Laboratory Experiment for Establishing Indifference Prices Between Brands of Consumer Products," *Proceedings*. Fall Conference, American Marketing Association, 1966, 511–9.
68. ———. "Experimental Determination of the Effect of Price and Market-Standing Information on Consumers' Brand Preferences," *Proceedings*. Fall Conference, American Marketing Assocation, 1966, 520–31.
69. Stapel, Jan. " 'Fair' or 'Psychological' Pricing?" *Journal of Marketing Research*, 9 (February 1972), 109–10.
70. Stoetzel, Jean. "Psychological/Sociological Aspects of Price," in Bernard Taylor and Gordon Wills, eds., *Pricing Strategy*. Princeton, N.J.: Brandon/System Press, 1970, 70–4.
71. Tajfel, H. "Value and the Perceptual Judgment of Magnitude," *Psychological Review*, 64 (May 1957), 192–204.
72. ———. "Quantitative Judgment in Social Perception," *British Journal of Psychology*, 50 (February 1959), 16–29.
73. Tull, Donald, R. A. Boring, and M. H. Gonsior. "A Note on the Relationship of Price and Imputed Quality," *Journal of Business*, 37 (April 1964) 186–91.
74. Uhl, Joseph. "Consumer Perception of Retail Food Price Changes," paper presented at First Annual Meeting of the Association for Consumer Research, 1970.
75. Webb, Eugene. "Weber's Law and Consumer Prices," *American Psychologist*, 16 (July 1961), 450.
76. Wells, William and Leonard LoSciuto. "Direct Observation of Purchasing Behavior," *Journal of Marketing Research*, 3 (August 1966), 227–33.

29 Economic Foundations for Pricing

Thomas Nagle

Journal of Business, Vol. 57, No. 1, Pt. 2 (January 1984), pp. S3–S26. ©1984 by The University of Chicago. All rights reserved. Reprinted by permission.

INTRODUCTION

Pricing, like most business decisions, is an art. This is not, however, a justification for basing pricing decisions purely on the "hunch" of a talented manager. Art is beyond neither critical judgment nor scientific analysis. And talent is rarely by itself sufficient for artistic success. An architect's exceptional creativity, for example, could hardly compensate for an ignorance of structural engineering. No less important are the principles of economics to the successful study and practice of the art of pricing.

Yet, if one approaches economics expecting too much, one may well come away with too little. Economic models are not designed to describe realistically the way firms make pricing decisions or the way consumers respond to those decisions.[1] Economic models are abstractions; they hold constant many real variables that are not germane to their theoretical objectives. Consequently, they rarely provide practical algorithms for implementing pricing strategies.[2] But marketing academicians and practitioners, whose goal is to help firms make better pricing decisions, can little afford to ignore the interrelationships between price and other marketing variables that economists hold constant. Consequently, they are soon disillusioned if they look to economics for practical solutions to pricing problems.

Still, it would be shortsighted to label the theoretical models of economics irrelevant to practical pricing problems. Economic models may be weak in specific prescriptions for individual action, but they are strong in useful heuristics for understanding the consequences of action. To draw on an earlier analogy, no one rejects structural engineering as irrelevant because it "fails" to show architects how to design buildings. Likewise, the role of economics is not to price products, but to explain the economic principles to which successful pricing strategies will conform. Pricing products—including the development and testing of practical pricing procedures—is appropriately the task of marketing. If, however, economists are doing their job well—that is, if the principles they identify in theory have actual counterparts in reality—the marketer's task should prove less strenuous when he stands on a sound foundation of economic theory.

Economics is not, of course, the only useful foundation for research in marketing. Psychology, sociology, and even biology may also serve the marketer's purpose. Our premise here is simply that research with a theoretical base is more likely to be productive than ad hoc research and that economic theory provides a particularly sound basis for pricing research. Our goal in this paper will be to review those areas of economics that offer the most promise for practical application to pricing. Before proceeding with that review, however, a brief example, illustrating how pricing research can benefit from a foundation in economic theory, seems in order.

Dealing—that is, temporary price cutting—is an important element of pricing strategy for many frequently purchased, packaged goods. Marketers have long wondered whether consumers who responded to such deals were simply a cross-section of regular buyers or were a clearly identifiable segment. If the latter, marketers wanted to know how to identify that segment so as to target dealing where it would be most effective. Numerous statistical studies (e.g., Webster 1965; Montgomery 1971) that approached the problem without a theoretical foundation found little or no correlation between deal proneness and the demographic, socioeconomic, and personality characteristics the authors considered (Frank, Massey, and Wind 1972, p. 124). It appeared that deal proneness was simply randomly distributed among consumers.

That conclusion proved too hasty, however, when Blattberg et al. (1978) took a new look at deal proneness from the perspective of a newly developed branch of economic theory: the economics of the family. Economists in this area (primarily Gary Becker and his students) had characterized the family as a production unit, optimally allocating its resources (money, time, and talents) by making economic trade-offs.[3] Blattberg et al. hypothesized that deal proneness might be explicable as the result of such an optimal allocation. The advantage of this theoretical starting point was that it allowed the authors to select variables that should influence deal proneness and to hypothesize about their expected effect.

If the economics of the family characterized some aspect of purchase decisions among the families in the authors' sample, then families with a lower opportunity cost of buying on deal should have been more deal prone. Consequently, the authors hypothesized that

1. families that own homes and cars should be more deal prone because they generally have more storage space (i.e., lower inventory holding costs) and lower costs of transporting extra purchases of products on deal; and

2. families that have preschool children at home, a working wife, or high incomes should be less deal prone because of the high value of alternative demands on their time.

Without a theoretical foundation, one would not intuitively have suspected (and earlier authors apparently did not suspect) that variables such as auto ownership, or preschool children might influence a family's propensity to buy aluminum foil on deal. Yet the authors found that those variables did influence deal proneness for aluminum foil, as well as for waxed paper, headache remedies, liquid detergent, and facial tissue. With economic theory as a guide, they were able to identify a market segment that could not be identified by earlier empirical studies lacking an underlying theoretical structure.

A complete review of all economic theory with potential application to pricing is impossible within the confines of one paper. We will instead review topics in economic theory that (1) offer particularly fertile ground for the future growth of pricing theory and practice, and (2) have not yet been integrated into marketing.[4] Three general areas of economic theory that meet these criteria are the economics of information, the economics of spatial competition, and the economics of segmented pricing. Our discussions of them will necessarily be selective, since entire volumes could be written on each of these subjects. In addition, we will review individual papers that are not part of developing paradigms in economics but that are by themselves noteworthy in pricing research. In all cases, we will focus on the current and potential usefulness of the theories as a foundation for practical application rather than on their technical details.

The Economics of Information

George Stigler's seminal article (1961) precipitated an explosion of theoretical research on the economics of information. In that article, Stigler noted that economists traditionally ignored problems of information and, in doing so, failed to appreciate much that falls within the purview of marketing. Yet, in the years following, the economics profession has more than made up for lost time. Two subsets of that literature are of particular importance to pricing: one dealing with asymmetric information, the other with consumer information acquisition.

Pricing and Asymmetric Information

An exchange involves asymmetric information when one party to the exchange has more information than does the other. For example, a seller may know the quality of the goods he sells, but buyers do not know the quality until after they have purchased the product. If buyers cannot identify a seller's product quality, they must rely on some average quality as a guide to purchase. That leads to a clear problem for products above the average quality, which may be most products in the market. Uninformed buyers will be unwilling to pay an above-average price, forcing sellers of superior quality either to depreciate it, to withdraw from the market, or to accept a price that does not accurately reflect their products' value.

The study of this problem began with a paper by George Akerlof (1970), who cited the used car market as an example. The price that a seller can get for a used car, even one of the current model year, is usually substantially below the new car price adjusted for depreciation. A commonly heard rule of thumb is that a new car loses 10% of its value the moment it leaves the showroom and becomes "used." Akerlof rejected the contention that the price difference reflected simply the pure joy of owning a "new" car. Instead he explained it as a symptom of asymmetric information.

Among new cars, he argued, there are always some "lemons" that prove less reliable than the average car of its brand. For a new car purchase, there is some probability of getting a lemon, but neither the dealer nor the buyer knows whether or not the particular new car being sold will be one. For new cars, therefore, there is no problem of asymmetric information. For used cars, however, the problem is different. The previous owner, who is the seller of the used car, has learned from experience whether or not his car is atypically unreliable.

Those first owners who have lemons—and large repair bills—have an incentive to sell their cars sooner than those who are lucky enough to get more reliable cars. They do not, however, have the incentive to share that information honestly with buyers. Consequently, the used car market has proportionately more lemons than the new car market, though buyers still cannot distinguish them from more reliable cars. Recognizing this asymmetry of information between sellers and themselves, buyers demand a substantial discount on a used car before they are willing to risk getting a lemon. The pricing problem is that sellers who know that their cars are not lemons, and so worth more, are unable to price them accordingly.

Were this just a problem with automobiles, it would be of little interest to marketers. In fact, it is a general marketing problem occurring any time that sellers know more about their products' quality than do buyers, who then use average quality in determining the price they will pay. The problem has never been completely solved by restaurants in locations where there is little repeat business; consequently they rarely offer exceptional quality. The problem is also a common one for innovative manufactured products because, if an early entrant's product is a lemon, it can sour the market for later entrants whom buyers will view more skeptically. But, as Akerlof suggests, branding is a common solution to this problem, since brand names with which buyers have had past experience can signal quality above the average in a product class, enabling a firm to charge an above-average price.[5]

But how much more can a firm charge because its product is branded? Can it get just enough to cover the cost of its higher quality, or can it get a premium? Klein and Leffler (1981) attempt to answer these questions in a way that provides much insight into the relationship between branding and pricing. They show that in product classes characterized by asymmetric information about product quality a seller whose product quality is above average would not have the incentive to maintain it unless his price more than reflected his extra costs. A seller whose price just reflected the extra cost of high quality would have an incentive to reduce his quality (and production costs), thus earning extra profits until buyers learned about the reduction through disappointing purchases. Consequently, the price of a high-quality product "must not only compensate the firm for the increased average production costs incurred when [high quality] is produced, but must also yield a normal rate of return on the forgone gains from exploiting consumers' ignorance" (Klein and Leffler 1981, p. 624).

This analysis has important implications for pricing strategy. It implies that buyers who desire high quality in a market with asymmetric information will be influenced by the familiar "price-quality effect" even for repeat purchases.[6] The reason is that the higher the price, the greater the seller's incentive to establish and maintain high quality. If buyers recognize this effect, price competition should be less effective in markets with asymmetric information. Competitors who claim to offer high quality at lower prices should simply be less credible than those who claim to offer the same quality for a higher price.

Moreover, the Klein-Leffler paper implies that branding will be more valuable, that is, yield a higher price premium, for some products than for others, an important implication for a firm seeking to diversify. According to this theory, consumers should pay more of a premium for a high-quality brand (1) the more they think an opportunistic seller could depreciate quality without prepurchase detection and (2) the fewer the expected number of repeat purchases. Either of these effects raises the gains from cheating relative to those from repeat sales, requiring a high-price premium for quality maintenance.

Finally, the theory's most interesting implication is that, other things such as market size held equal, producing quality is particularly profitable. Marketers have often maintained this proposition on empirical grounds (e.g., Schoeffler, Buzzell, and Heany 1974), but heretofore without a theoretical explanation. The relative profitability of producing high quality may, under certain circumstances, be maintained even after competition has driven profits to their long-run equilibrium level. The reason is that because price cutting is an ineffective way to attract customers, competition necessarily takes the form of investments in "nonsalvageable capital" such as advertising or attractive places of business. If some firms have a cost advantage in making such investments (perhaps because of scale or experience economies), then they can earn profits (or more correctly "rents") that cannot be competed away by the entry of higher cost firms.

The Klein-Leffler paper is just one example of an idea in information theory that Telser (1980) formalized and titled "self-enforcing agreements." No one in the Klein-Leffler model must force the seller to supply the product quality he promises; he does so because, at the price he sets for that quality, it is in his interest to do so. There are numerous other applications of the theory of self-enforcing contracts that either have been, or could be, used to explain and prescribe pricing strategies. In one of the most interesting, Klein, Crawford, and Alchian (1978) use the idea to explain, among other things, why a successful pricing strategy for some products will involve primarily outright sales, while for others it will involve primarily leasing.

In the analysis of oligopolistic price competition, the self-enforcing agreement becomes a self-enforcing threat. Each firm attempts to deter its current or potential competitors from encroaching on its market share by threatening to cut price as low as necessary to maintain its intended sales level.[7] But how can it make such a threat credible? Spence (1977), Salop (1979), and Dixit (1980) argue that irrevocable investment in fixed assets, often at a rate faster than market growth would otherwise justify, can make the threat credible. By creating a cost structure with high sunk costs, the firm increases the losses it would suffer if it failed to attain its expected sales level because of new competition.[8] By boxing itself into one strategic option—to fulfill its threat to defend its market—the firm discourages competitive challenges and precludes the need to make good on the threat.

Pricing and Consumer Information Acquisition

The most fundamental concept in pricing is that of price elasticity, which measures the percentage sales loss (gain) from a certain percentage price increase (decrease). A firm may lose sales because buyers are willing to do without the product at a higher price or because they change suppliers. Since changing suppliers is generally less painful than doing without, buyers' willingness and ability to substitute one brand for another is, for most products, the dominant factor determining a brand's price elasticity.

Prior to their study of information, economists assumed that the importance of interbrand price competition, inducing consumers to substitute one brand for another, depended on the number of brands available and on their similarity. But Philip Nelson (1970) pointed out the error in that reasoning. In a world of imperfect information, what really determines price sensitivity is not the number and similarity of substitutes in the marketplace, but the number and similarity about which a typical consumer is aware.[9] That distinction is important, Nelson argued, because the cost of such information differs predictably depending upon the nature of a product's characteristics. Consequently, one can make a priori predictions, based on an analysis of product attributes, about the importance of price in interbrand competition.

Nelson classified product attributes into two types depending on how buyers learn about them.[10]

Search attributes are those that a buyer can readily evaluate prior to purchase. He may judge them from observation—as he would the style of a dress or the scheduled departure time of an airline—or with the aid of a simple test—as he would the purity of an industrial chemical. He therefore knows what he is buying before he makes a purchase decision.

Experience attributes are those that a buyer can evaluate only after consuming the product. He therefore does not know exactly what he is getting the first time he buys it. After having purchased once, however, he can repeat purchase the product in the future, having a good estimate of its attributes based on knowledge from past experience. The taste of a packaged food, the effectiveness of a dishwashing detergent, or the durability of a paint are examples of experience attributes.

Darby and Karni (1973) quickly followed Nelson's article with one of their own noting a third category:

Credence attributes are those that a buyer cannot confidently evaluate even after one purchase. He therefore must rely heavily on the product's reputation with respect to those attributes, even for repeat purchases. A buyer normally cannot, for example, evaluate a doctor's competence after one visit for the treatment of one complaint. In fact, such an evaluation may require a more controlled experiment and a larger sample than is achievable even over a single patient's lifetime.

The importance of these classifications lies in their relationship to the cost of consumer information acquisition. Information about price itself can be obtained directly for all types of products. But as one moves from the search to the experience and on to the credence category, information about brands' differentiating attributes becomes more costly. The greater the cost of information, the less of it people try to obtain. Consequently, other things equal, consumers should choose to inform themselves about the differentiating characteristics of fewer brands, and inform themselves less completely, in categories with high costs of collecting such information.[11]

The fewer brands about which buyers are informed, according to Nelson, the less price sensitive they will be to the price of any one brand. As a result, the effectiveness of price competition is reduced as is the ability of new competitors to enter the market with a strategy of low, penetration pricing. Nelson formally tested this proposition by classifying goods into search and experience categories and comparing the degree to which output is concentrated in a few competitors. He found markets for experience goods significantly more concentrated than those for search goods. Moreover, casual observation seems to confirm the value of this distinction as an analytical marketing tool. For example, the attributes differentiating brands of airline travel—time of departure, type of planes, airports used—are primarily search attributes and price competition for air travel is intense. Those differentiating brands of dishwashing liquids are primarily experience attributes and price competition is less intense. Those differentiating brands of photographic film are primarily credence attributes (at least for the casual photographer) and price competition in that market is notably ineffective.[12]

The literature on the economics of information is rich in its implications for pricing.[13] Moreover, it complements the work being done by marketers specializing in consumer behavior (e.g., Bettman 1979). In the hands of marketing researchers, the economics of information could aid in explaining even more marketing phenomena.

The Economics of Spatial Competiton

In the analysis of product positioning, current research in economics has a structure very similar to that in marketing. Known as the economics of spatial competition, this work analyzes the effect on price competition of a brand's location in physical space. The spatial location of brands serves in economics, as it does in marketing, as a metaphorical representation of product variety in any product attribute that is measurable and, therefore, spatially representable.[14] Models of spatial competition have a long history in economics beginning with Hotelling (1929) and Smithies (1941). Recently, however, the models have developed to a point that they have become useful tools for analyzing realistic positioning strategies and their effect on pricing. They now offer the potential to advance substantially our understanding of the relationship between product variety and interbrand price competition.

Though each author structures his model differently, I will attempt to illustrate the basic principles of spatial competition using one simple model adapted from Hay (1976). Assume that consumer preferences—what marketers call "ideal points"—are uniformly located along a straight line measuring some dimension of product variety. An individual consumer's demand depends both on the brand's price and on its closeness to his ideal point. All consumers have the same demand function; they differ only in the location of their ideal points.[15] Figure 1 illustrates the position of the first brand, A, in the market. Brand A's

29 — Economic Foundations for Pricing

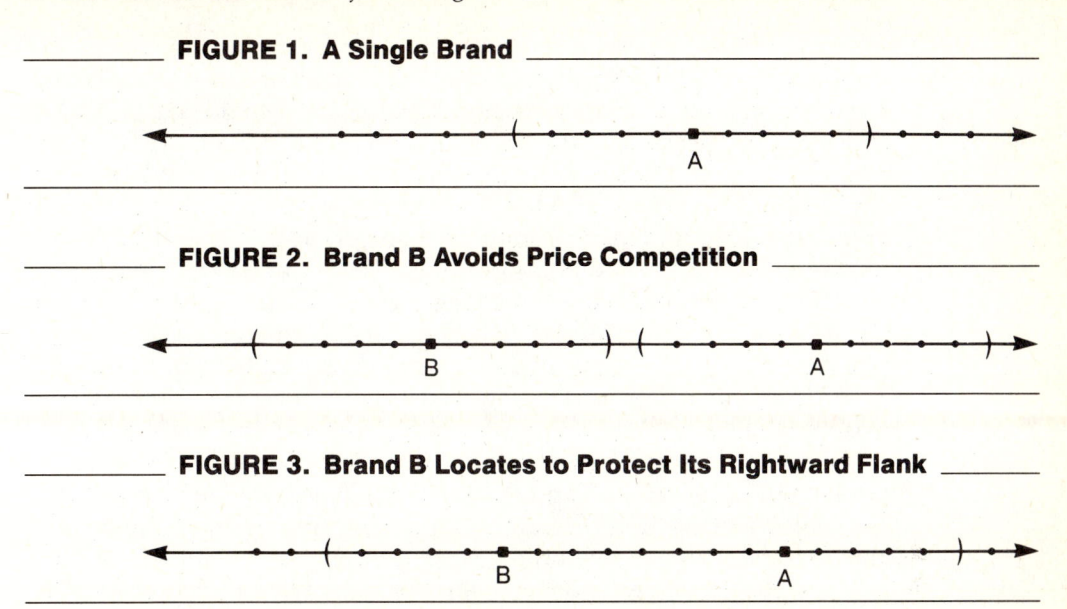

FIGURE 1. A Single Brand

◄———·—·—·—·—·—(—·—·—·—·—■—·—·—·—·—)—·—·—·—·—►
                                A

FIGURE 2. Brand B Avoids Price Competition

◄———(—·—·—·—■—·—·—·—)—(—·—·—·—·—■—·—·—·—·—)—►
              B   A

FIGURE 3. Brand B Locates to Protect Its Rightward Flank

◄———·—·—(—·—·—·—■—·—·—·—·—·—·—■—·—·—·—·—)—·—►
                 B   A

market area, the range of ideal points for which it is close enough to attract some sales, extends five units in each direction. Now, how should firms locate additional brands along this line in order to minimize price competition and, thus, maximize their long-run profitability?[16]

Hay (1976) shows that a new entrant can maximize his prices and profits in the short run by locating so as to avoid any overlaps (and thus any price competition) between his market area and the market area of A (fig. 2).[17] But that is not a good long-run strategy. To maximize long run profits, B need consider not only potential price competition with A, but also with potential entrants. To maximize long-run profitability, B must locate closer to A, suffering some price competition in the short run but precluding even more intense competition in the long run.

For example, if at current prices a later entrant would need to serve a market area of at least four units (two in each direction), then B could preclude new entry on its right flank by locating less than eight units from A (fig. 3). No entrant would try to squeeze between A and B, because it would achieve only slightly less than its minimum market share (four units) after sharing the market with B on its left flank and A on its right (fig. 3).[18] Both B and A pay a cost for this preemption, a bit more than one unit each on their shared flank, but they insure no further erosion of profitability in the long run. Moreover, if the new entrant anticipated that A and B would cut prices in response to its entry between them, it would anticipate the need to have a market area even longer than four units to survive. In that case, B could leave even more than eight units between itself and A while still precluding new entry between them.

There are also options that A could use to protect itself from B's encroachment. Richard Schmalensee (1978), in an analysis of the breakfast cereal market, showed how brand proliferation could be a profitable entry-deterring strategy when there are shared costs among brands of the same firm. For example, if the producer of A could produce other brands that could be profitable with market areas of only three units (as opposed to four for a new entrant with one brand), he might profitably preempt emerging market opportunities. His lower costs would enable each brand to be profitable while keeping a potential new entrant from finding a viable market for its first brand.[19] Eaton and Lipsey (1979) show that such a preemptive proliferation strategy is profitable even if established firms have no cost advantages when introducing new brands. The reason is that an established firm can reduce the negative effect of its new brands on the sales of its already established brands when selecting prices and locations. Rao and Rutenberg (1980) develop dynamic decision rules for the optimal timing of preemption, given expectations about rivals' actions based on past experiences.

Marketers are already using spatial representations of product positions and have techniques (called multidimensional scaling) for spatially representing actual markets. They use them to find "holes" for new product entries and to evaluate competitive interactions. A useful next step would be to incorporate the strategic principles from the economics of spatial competition into the analysis of product positioning, identifying not only where a firm might introduce a brand to maximize market potential, but also where it might introduce one to minimize potential competition from later entrants.[20]

THE ECONOMICS OF SEGMENTED PRICING

Though the "marketing concept" may be the essence of marketing theory, the guiding principle of marketing practice is "market segmentation." In fact, the process of segmenting buyers by designing marketing strategies more consistent with their diverse preferences is arguably the marketing concept's operational counterpart. In the last decade, marketing academicians have produced an abundance of research on segmenting markets for product and promotional targeting, (see Frank et al. 1972; Blattenberg and Sen 1974; Mahajan and Jain 1978) but research on segmenting for pricing has been notably small.[21] Fortunately, market segmentation for pricing has a long history in economic research. Since the economics literature on segmented pricing arose from attempts to explain specific pricing strategies, often to lawyers rather than to other economists, it is also usually accessible and directly applicable.

Segmented pricing is the policy of pricing differently to different groups of buyers. It may involve "price discrimination:" the offering of different prices for the same product, usually in the form of discounts to more price-sensitive buyers. More often it involves offering the same prices to all buyers, but with a structure of prices for different points in time, places of purchase, or product types[22] that results in some buyers' paying more relative to marginal cost than do other buyers who are more price sensitive. Airlines, for example, segment buyers by time of flight (weekend and evening versus weekday flights) and by product type (regular tickets allowing flexible scheduling versus discount tickets with scheduling restrictions; first class versus coach seating).

Ralph Cassady (1946a, 1964b) reviewed and illustrated the basic techniques of segmented pricing in two classic (though much neglected) articles that are as valid today as they were when written.[23] I will not repeat what is said there. Instead, I will review those advances in our understanding of segmented pricing that have occurred since then.

Segmenting by Tie-Ins and Metering

Segmentation by metering or tie-ins is often extremely important for the pricing of assets. The reason is that buyers generally value an asset more the more intensely they use it. The buyer of a photocopying machine who makes 20,000 copies a month will value it more than the buyer who makes just 5,000 copies. And food processors canning fruit year round in California will value canning machines more than will fish packers in Alaska who can salmon only a few months each year. In such cases, tactics that segment buyers by use intensity can substantially improve the effectiveness of a pricing strategy.

Before the Clayton Antitrust Act of 1914, a common method of monitoring use was the tie-in sale. Along with the purchase or lease of a machine, a buyer contractually agreed to purchase a commodity used with the machine exclusively from the seller. Thus, the Heaton Peninsular Company sold its shoemaking machines with the provision that buyers buy only Heaton Peninsular buttons. The A. B. Dick Company sold its mimeograph equipment with the provision the buyers buy paper, stencils, and ink only from the A. B. Dick Company. The Morgan Envelope Company sold its bathroom tissue dispensers with the provision that they forever dispense only Morgan's own brand (see *Morgan Envelope Co. v. Albany Perforated Paper Co.* [1893]; *Heaton Peninsular v. Eureka Specialty Co.* [1896]; *Henry v. A. B. Dick* [1912]). While the courts actually supported tying arrangements in these cases, they completely reversed themselves after 1914, claiming that tying arrangements were an illegal attempt to extend monopoly power from one product to the next. In the words of the Supreme Court "the illegality in tying arrangements is the wielding of monopolistic leverage; a seller exploits his dominant position in one market to expand his empire into the next" (*Times-Picayune Publishing v. United States* [1953]).

Economists were naturally skeptical of this argument because if an individual buyer must pay more for the tied good than he would have to pay elsewhere, that simply reduces the amount that he is willing to pay for the tying asset. Consequently, "extension of monopoly" would make sense only if it enabled the firm actually to increase the monopoly restriction—and thus the equilibrium market price—for the tied good. But, in almost all cases, the tying arrangements give the seller an insignificant amount of the market for the tied good. Consequently, the extension of monopoly argument seems highly implausible.

Economists instead explained tying as an effective device for price discrimination. Bowman (1957) and Burstein (1960*a*, 1960*b*) studied numerous tying cases in detail and found that, in each case, the asset itself was sold for a very low explicit price, close to the incremental cost of production. The tied commodity, however, was sold for a premium price. Thus, the true cost of the asset was its low explicit price plus the sum of the price premiums paid for the tied commodity. Since buyers who used the asset more intensely bought more of the tied commodity, they effectively paid more for the asset. The tied commodity was effectively a device for measuring a buyer's value of the asset and automatically charging for each incremental unit of value received.

Since the passage of the Clayton Act, the courts have refused to allow tying contracts in most cases.[24] In 1917, the Supreme Court refused to enforce a sales contract for a motion picture projector requiring that it be used to show only films produced by or under license from the seller. In 1922, United Shoe Machinery Corporation was ordered to cease the same tying policy that had been approved earlier for Heaton Peninsular. Later, IBM was ordered to stop tying computer punch cards in the leases for its machines (*Motion Picture Patents Co. v. Universal Film Manufacturing Co.* [1917]; *United Shoe Machinery Corp. v. United States* [1922]; *International Business Machines Corp. v. United States* [1936]).

Nevertheless, many tying opportunities without contracts still exist. Replacement parts and maintenance service are natural devices for measuring use intensity and for pricing accordingly. So also is food consumed in a theater or amusement park. Razor manufacturers design unique shaving technologies that naturally tie blades to razors. In the 1970s, a lower court did order Kodak to introduce no unique camera designs without first revealing the film's technology to its competitors, but that ruling was overturned on appeal (see *Berky Photo v. Eastman Kodak Co.* [1979]). It seems clear that, even without explicit contracts, the tie-in sale is still an important pricing tactic, and the literature in economics provides unusually explicit direction for its use.

The courts have nevertheless severely limited tying arrangements in precisely the cases where it is most dramatically effective. Their rulings challenge sellers to monitor use without restricting competition. In modern times, that challenge has frequently been met by renting assets rather than selling them outright, with the rental fee determined by a simple metering device. Xerox, for example, traditionally rented its copiers for a fixed fee plus so much per copy made.

As a final note, the tactic of monitoring use intensity is not limited to machines and may not involve an actual physical counting device. Nationally syndicated newspaper columns are sold to local papers at prices based on use intensity. The monitoring device is simply the paper's circulation figures. Film distributors rent movies at prices based on the number of seats in the theater. And franchisors lease their brand names and reputations to franchisees not for a fixed fee but for a percentage of sales. No matter how intangible the asset, monitoring use can be an important part of its pricing.

Segmenting by Product Bundling

Product bundling is perhaps the most widely used tactic to achieve segmented pricing, though its rationale often goes unnoticed. Retailers bundle "free" parking with a purchase in their stores. Grocery stores bundle trading stamps or chances in games with purchase of their groceries. Newspapers with morning and evening editions bundle advertising space in both of them. Restaurants bundle foods into fixed price dinners, generally a cheaper alternative to ordering the same items à la carte. And symphony orchestras bundle diverse concerts into season subscription tickets. These are but a small fraction of the goods sold in bundles, but they illustrate the breadth of the practice, from commodities to services and from necessities to entertainment. The question all these examples raise is "under what conditions does it pay to bundle goods for pricing?"

George Stigler (1963) answered that question in an article explaining the bundling of first-run movies, a practice known as block booking. The movie industry at the time would not rent individual films to theaters, but required they rent a block of films. As an example, Stigler cited the blocking together of *Gone with the Wind* and *Getting Gertie's Garter*. Why, he asked, would it make sense to require a theater to buy both films together? It cannot be that the distributors simply used their good films to force junk films on theaters, since a theater would not pay more for the two films together than the sum of what it would pay for the two separately.

Stigler explained this pricing strategy with the aid of the following illustration. Suppose that the dollar amounts that two theaters A and B would pay for the films is given by the following table:

	Gone with the Wind	Getting Gertie's Garter
Theater A	8,000	2,500
Theater B	7,000	3,000

The owners of both theaters would pay substantially more to show *Gone with the Wind* than *Getting Gertie's Garter*. The key to an effective bundling strategy, however, is the reversal in the relative valuations of the two films. *Gone with the Wind* is more valuable to theater A than to theater B, while the reverse is true for *Getting Gertie's Garter*.

To rent the films separately to both theater A and theater B at fixed prices, the movie distributor could have charged no more than $7,000 for *Gone with the Wind* and $2,500 for *Getting Gerie's Garter*, for a total of $9,500 for the pair. But theater A values the pair at $10,500 and theater B at $10,000. Thus by selling the films as a block for $10,000, the distributor can charge $500 more for the pair than if he sold them separately. Why is this segmented pricing? Because each theater pays the difference between the price of the films when sold separately ($9,500) and the price when sold together ($10,000) for different products. Theater A pays the extra $500 for *Gone with the Wind* while theater B pays it for *Getting Gertie's Garter*. Consequently, by charging a single price for an indivisible bundle, the distributor can effectively charge different prices for the components.

Adams and Yellen (1976) explain the conditions for bundling more formally and explicitly. In doing so, they show why products are not generally sold in indivisible bundles only. Most firms follow the tactic of "mixed bundling," whereby the individual products can be bought separately, but at prices exceeding their cost if bought together in the bundle. Mixed bundling is more profitable than indivisible bundling whenever some buyers value one of the items in the bundle very highly but value the other less than it costs to produce. Schmalensee (1982) shows that mixed bundling can be profitable even for a single-product monopolist who buys a competitively produced product from other firms to bundle with his own. Schmalensee (1984) formally derives the explicit conditions that make a bundling strategy profitable.[25]

Focusing on the pure theory and the obvious examples, one could easily underestimate the importance of bundling to pricing strategy. Most bundling opportunities are in fact quite subtle, but the principle of bundling is ubiquitously applied in both consumer and industrial markets. The marketing researcher who understood the principle could no doubt use it to explain many more applications; the marketing practitioner could no doubt find new applications not thought of heretofore.

ECONOMIC ANALYSES OF SPECIFIC PRICING PROBLEMS

In addition to the general areas of economic theory just reviewed, the economics literature of recent years contains a number of more narrowly focused papers analyzing specific pricing problems. These papers offer perspectives that could be immediately applied in marketing theory and practice.

Pricing Through a Distribution Channel

Managing a product through channels of distribution is a problem of growing interest to marketers (Stern and El-Ansary 1977). Part of that problem involves pricing to the channel, a topic that economic theorists have studied with some success.

Machlup and Taber (1960) have shown that when the uniqueness of a manufacturer's product gives a retailer some "monopoly power" over price, the retailer will set his resale price too high and sell too little to maximize the total channel (manufacturer plus retailer) profits. To avoid this problem, they show how the manufacturer can couple his wholesale pricing with maximum resale prices (which may be enforced merely by advertising a suggested retail price), minimum retail sales requirements, or a more complicated two-part pricing strategy.

Telser (1960) explains the conditions that make it profitable for a manufacturer to impose minimum resale prices. Essentially, his argument rests on the need to reward retailers for offering promotional and maintenance services that positively influence a product's demand. Officials in the current Justice Department have recently recognized this argument and are now committed to changing the courts' negative view of resale price maintenance ("Big Shift in Antitrust Policy" 1981).

The most ambitious study of the relationship between pricing and distribution channels is Porter's (1976) *Interbrand Choice, Strategy, and Bilateral Market Power*. Marketers often write about the "bargaining power" of various channel members. Porter seeks to identify the causes and effects of such power, relying not just on traditional economic concepts such as concentration, but also upon applications of the economics of information. In particular, he argues that bargaining power over margins shifts for manufacturers toward retailers the more buyers rely on retailers for the information they need to make interbrand choices. Adopting this same approach, a number of marketing researchers have recently begun to analyze the effect of channel relationships on pricing and have developed suggestions for favorably controlling those relationships (Farris and Albion 1980; McGuire and Staelin 1981; Zusman and Etgar 1981; Jeuland and Shugan 1982). This work is reviewed in part by Rao (1984).

Pricing Unique Durable Goods

Coase (1972) raised the problem of pricing a unique durable good. He noted that a rational buyer would not pay a monopoly price for a good, even though he valued it by more than the price, if he expected the price to come down. Consequently, a "skimming strategy" of progressively lower prices should fail to the extent that buyers recognize the seller's incentive to cut price and expand his market. Stokey (1981) shows, however, that a skimming strategy is theoretically viable, even if buyers have perfectly accurate expectations, to the extent that the adjustment to a new price level takes time. The reason is that the more highly a buyer values the services of the durable good, the higher is his cost of waiting. Thus, the longer the adjustment period that buyers anticipate, the less problematic are their anticipations of future price reductions.[26] Stokey's work also complements the theoretical research on price declines due to the "experience effect" (Robinson and Lakhani 1975; Dolan and Jeuland 1981; Kalish, in press), which is reviewed in Rao (1984).

Pricing for Peak Loads

Pricing strategy frequently must accommodate predictable variations in demand without the luxury of a storable product. In order to accommodate temporary peaks in demand, the firm must build production capacity that is excessive at other times. Economists have analyzed this problem of peak-load pricing in great detail (Houthakker 1951; Steiner 1957; Hirshleifer 1958; Williamson 1966; Symposium on Peak-Load Pricing 1976) and have shown how to allocate capacity costs in order to select profit maximizing prices and sales levels.[27] Unfortunately, because these analyses are almost always in the context of large public enterprises, their broad applicability is generally unappreciated. The principles of peak-load pricing are in fact equally applicable to such private enterprises as hotels, restaurants, health clubs, airlines, theaters, and to some degree most retail establishments. The economic literature in this area is ripe for profitable application.

Pricing by Priority

Harris and Raviv (1981) show that whenever a product is fixed in supply and has demand that potentially exceeds supply, a (monopolistic) seller can increase his profits by "priority pricing." The seller sets a schedule of prices for the product and then serves first those buyers who elect to pay the highest price, second those buyers who elect to pay the next highest price, and so forth until the supply is exhausted. Buyers who elect to pay higher prices increase the probability that they will be able to buy before the product is sold out. The authors' conclusion that this is a superior pricing scheme for products in fixed supply seems consistent with standard practice. They note that priority pricing is used for such obvious cases as antiques and oil leases, as well as for discontinued styles of consumer products that are sold at progressively increasing discounts.

Pricing in Two Parts

Two-part pricing is an important strategy in a large number of industries. Health clubs, amusement parks, auto rental agencies, and the telephone company all charge fixed fees plus variable usage charges for their products.[28] The seller's motivation for two-part pricing is to capture some of the consumer's surplus (excess of value over price for all but the last unit purchased). A number of authors (Hotelling 1938; Gabor 1955; Burstein 1960) analyzed two-part pricing for the case where buyers are homogeneous or where a unique two-part pricing schedule can be implemented for each buyer. They showed that two-part pricing in these cases could capture all consumer surplus for the seller. It was not however, until Oi (1971) that anyone dealt with the more realistic, and complicated, case of calculating a single two-part schedule for a population with demands of more than one type. Oi showed that with two types of buyers, the optimal variable fee must be higher and the fixed fee lower relative to the case of homogeneous buyers.[29] This substantially reduces the efficiency of two-part pricing, leaving some buyers with much of their surplus. Schmalensee (1982) provides the first completely general analysis of two-part pricing schedules, allowing for buyers with completely heterogeneous demand curves, for income effects (from which previous authors abstracted), and for sales to competitive firms whose derived demands depend on the selling prices of their own goods.

Pricing when Facing a Used Product Market

The effect of a resale market on the prices of new durable goods poses a problem that many durable good manufacturers face. Each unit a manufacturer sells today will add to the used market tomorrow, increasing competition with new units. The manufacturer must decide whether to encourage the used market, as do the automobile companies and some office equipment manufacturers, or to discourage it, as do textbook publishers. The rationale for encouraging the used market is that a high resale value will raise the prices buyers will pay for new goods. The rationale for discouraging the used market is that a smaller used market reduces competition with new product sales. Benjamin and Kormendi (1974) show that either strategy may be profit maximizing depending upon the substitutability of used for new products, the marginal cost of production, and the degree of competition in the industry.

Pricing Superstars

One recent and unique article in the literature of economics is "The Economics of Superstars" by Sherwin Rosen (1981). It has important, intuitively appealing implications for product pricing. The phenomenon that Rosen attempts to explain is the disproportionately high profits that the highest quality products—superstars—can earn in some markets. He cites, for example, the services of outstanding lawyers and physicians, performances by outstanding musicians, and copies of textbooks that are outstanding in their fields as examples of the superstar phenomenon. His explanation rests on the simple observation that, for some products, "quality" is not perfectly additive. No number of concerts by mediocre pianists can effectively substitute for an evening with Horowitz; no number of obtusely written textbooks can effectively substitute for one that makes the subject perfectly clear. This is not true for all products. Larger quantities of a mediocre detergent, for example, can give the same cleaning power as the highest quality brand. Thus, when pricing a high-quality product (or when deciding whether to produce one), an important factor to consider is the ability of more mediocre alternatives to compete with it by substituting quantity for quality.

CONCLUSION

Understanding the economic environment in which pricing decisions are made is a first step toward making them effectively. While economics traditionally offered a basic understanding of that environment, advances in the last two decades have significantly refined it. Economic theory now has much more to say about the roles of information, competition, and market segmentation in pricing strategy. Economic theorists have also analyzed specific pricing problems and opportunities in ways that shed much light on pricing practice.

Still, economic theory is just that—theory. No economic model captures the full richness of a practical pricing problem or sets out a complete prescription for solving it. Even with an understanding of economic theory, marketers are still left with the problem of how to price products. But they are left also with insights and perspectives that should make solutions more attainable and effective.

ENDNOTES

*I am indebted for helpful comments to Mark Albion, Terry Elrod, Abel Jeuland, Roger Kormendi, Chakravarthi Narasimhan, Kenneth Novak, Ram Rao, Subrata Sen, and to an anonymous reviewer.

1. Because of this lack of realism, some marketers approach economics with hostility. They, in effect, judge economics by the standards of good psychology, which it is not. Economic theorists do not claim to describe the processes by which people actually make decisions; they claim rather to explain why certain decisions persist. Economic theory assumes that persistent and widespread behavior, whatever the underlying psychological process leading to it, must

somehow be reinforced by success at furthering economic well-being. Such reinforcement encourages people, on average, to act "as if" they understood and responded "rationally" to the economic process that rewards their behavior (Alchian 1950; Friedman 1953).

2. For example, the fundamental economic principle, that current profit is maximized when marginal revenue equals marginal cost is neither a practical nor "optimal" prescription for action when demand is uncertain and when tomorrow's demand, cost, and competition are affected by today's pricing decision (see Alchian 1950; Dean 1951; Robinson and Lakhani 1975; Dolan and Jeuland 1981).

3. See Becker (1981) for a comprehensive statement of this work and for references to earlier contributions. For a critique of this literature that would be of particular interest to marketers applying it to practical problems, see Mack and Leighland (1982).

4. One important topic in economic theory that has been partially integrated into marketing is the hedonic theory (sometimes called the "New Theory") of consumer choice. According to this theory, consumers do not value a good holistically. Instead, they value it as the sum of the values of its individual characteristics. For a review of this literature that emphasizes marketing application, see Ratchford (1975).

5. For an interesting study of the "lemons" problem in the Soviet Union where branding is restricted, see Goldman (1960).

6. Charles Wilson (1980) offers another rationale for a price-quality effect with asymmetric information: that a higher price enables the buyer to draw from a distribution of products with a higher mean quality.

7. Threats are only one way to deter entry. In the sec. below on spatial competition, we will examine others.

8. See Porter (1980, pp. 335–40) for factors to consider before making such investments in a growing market.

9. Tibor Scitovsky (1950) actually pointed out this effect long before there was an "economics of information," but with little effect on economists' thinking about these problems.

10. Actually, Nelson did his early analysis based on search and experience goods rather than attributes. See Nelson (1978, 1980) and Wilde (1980) for reformulations based directly on attributes.

11. The cost of collecting information may, of course, differ across buyers. Assuming such a difference, Salop and Stiglitz (1977) explain the persistence of high- and low-priced stores for the same products. In their model, high-priced stores cater to buyers with a high cost of information collection.

12. One might object that the lack of price competition for photographic film is due to a lack of competitors. But the lack of competitors is a symptom of the information problem, because when new firms have tried to enter by undercutting Kodak's prices, they have failed to attract buyers (see "Kodak Fights Back" 1982).

13. See Wilde (1980) for a review of the development of this literature.

14. In contrast, however, to the multidimensional product maps generated by marketers, economic theorists usually assume that brands vary along a single product dimension (Eaton and Lipsey [1976] is an exception), which they represent spatially as distance along a line (with or without finite length) or around the perimeter of a circle. This simply reflects economists' predilection for tractable

models at the expense of descriptive realism. The principles of spatial competition they derive are nonetheless conceptually applicable to the multidimensional case (Baumol 1967; Lancaster 1975). These models have also been used to analyze the positioning of political candidates (see, e.g., Riker and Ordeshook 1973).

15. See Hay (1976) for a more specific and complete listing of assumptions. Eaton and Lipsey (1978) show the implications of changes in the standard assumptions.
16. Eaton and Lipsey (1978) prove formally that some spatial locations can maintain long-run profitability.
17. Assuming that sufficient room exists between A's market area and the end points of the market to enable B to gain an equally large market area without encroaching on A.
18. Of course, a new entrant would never even try to squeeze between competitors unless other more open areas were already filled. In addition, the model assumes that because of sunk capital expenditures, his entry will not prompt A and B to spread out further giving him more room.
19. A new entrant could, of course, enter with multiple brands. Schmalensee argues, however, that the cost of finding multiple attractive entry opportunities all at the same time generates a barrier to entry (1978, pp. 317–18). Schmalensee also argues that brand introduction by established firms may involve less uncertainty than by new entrants, reinforcing the tendency toward brand proliferation (p. 317).
20. Porter (1980, pp. 335–38) has begun to bring preemptive investment to the attention of practitioners.
21. Marketers do universally acknowledge the need for segmented pricing as part of an overall segmented marketing strategy, but research on strategies for price segmentation has not kept pace with that for product and promotional segmentation. Notable exceptions are Frank and Massy (1965), Elrod and Winer (1982), and Narasimhan (1982).
22. Eli Clemens (1951) shows that there is conceptually no difference between the pricing of different products produced with the same resources and the pricing of identical products for different market segments.
23. See also Joan Robinson (1936), for the seminal analysis of price discrimination, and Fritz Machlup (1955). Nagle (1983) discusses the implications of segmented pricing for the marketing practitioner.
24. The exceptions are tying contracts for service on new, highly technical products where it can be proven essential to maintain the product's performance and therefore its reputation. See *United States v. Jerrold Electronics Co.* (1961).
25. An interesting discovery of this paper is that the preference reversal, which Stigler and others have used to demonstrate the value of bundling, is neither strictly necessary nor sufficient.
26. Consequently, a firm attempting skim pricing might rationally commit itself not to cut price for a certain length of time.
27. Essentially, the optimal solution is to allocate that portion of capacity costs to the peak demand periods that is not covered by positive marginal revenues at other times.
28. In fact, the tie-in sale discussed above is, in theory, a two-part pricing strategy for the *services* of the asset.

29. Murphy (1977) presents a more intuitive discussion and relates the two-part pricing to other tactics.

REFERENCES

Adams, William James, and Yellen, Janet T. 1976. Commodity bundling and the burden of monopoly. *Quarterly Journal of Economics* 40 (May): 475–98.

Akerlof, George. 1970. The market for "lemons": Quality uncertainty and the market mechanism. *Quarterly Journal of Economics* 84, no. 3 (August): 488–500.

Alchian, Armen A. 1950. Uncertainty, evolution, and economic theory. *Journal of Political Economy* 58:211–21. Reprinted 1958 in R. Heflebower and G. Stocking (eds.), *A.E.A. Readings in Industrial Organization and Public Policy*. Homewood, Ill.: Irwin.

Baumol, William J. 1967. Calculation of optimal product and retailer characteristics: The abstract product approach. *Journal of Political Economy* 75 (October): 674–85.

Becker, Gary. 1981. *A Treatise on the Family.* Cambridge, Mass.: Harvard University Press.

Benjamin, Daniel K., and Kormendi, Roger C. 1974. The interrelationship between markets for new and used durable goods. *Journal of Law and Economics* 17 (October): 381–402.

Berky Photo v. Eastman Kodak Co. 603 F.2d 263 (2d Cir. 1979).

Bettman, James R. 1979. *An Information Processing Theory of Consumer Choice.* Reading, Mass.: Addison-Wesley.

Big shift in antitrust policy. 1981. *Dun's Review* 111, no. 2 (August): 39–40.

Blattberg, Robert and Sen, Subrata. 1974. Market segmentation using models of multidimensional purchasing behavior. *Journal of Marketing* 38 (October): 17–28.

Blattberg, Robert; Buesing, Thomas; Peacock, Peter; and Sen, Subrata. 1978. Identifying the deal-prone segment. *Journal of Marketing Research* 15 (August): 369–77.

Bowman, Ward S. 1957. Tying arrangements and the leverage problem. *Yale Law Journal* 67 (November): 19–36.

Burstein, M. L. 1960a. The economics of tie-in sales. *Review of Economics and Statistics* 27 (February): 68–73.

Burstein, M. L. 1960b. A theory of full line forcing. *Northwestern University Law Review* 55 (March–April): 62–95.

Cassady, Ralph. 1946a. Some economic aspects of price discrimination under non-perfect market conditions. *Journal of Marketing* 11 (July): 7–20.

Cassady, Ralph. 1946b. Techniques and purposes of price discrimination. *Journal of Marketing* 11 (July): 135–50.

Clemens, Eli. 1951. Price discrimination and the multiproduct firm. *Review of Economic Studies* 19:1–11. Reprinted 1958 in R. Heflebower and G. Stocking (eds.), *A.E.A. Readings in Industrial Organization and Public Policy*. Homewood, Ill.: Irwin.

Coase, Ronald H. 1972. Durability and monopoly. *Journal of Law and Economics* 15 (April): 143–50.

Darby, Michael R., and Karni, Edi. 1973. Free competition and the optimal amount of fraud. *Journal of Law and Economics* 16 (April): 67–88.

Dean, Joel. 1951. *Managerial Economics.* New York: Prentice-Hall.

Dixit, Avinash D. 1980. The role of investment in entry-deterrence. *Economic Journal* 90 (March): 95–106.

Dolan, Robert, and Jeuland, Abel. 1981. Experience curves and dynamic demand models: Implications for optimal pricing strategies. *Journal of Marketing* 45 (Winter): 52–62.

Eaton, C. Curtis, and Lipsey, Richard G. 1976. The non-uniqueness of equilibrium in the Löschian location model. *American Economic Review* 66 (March): 71–93.

Eaton, C. Curtis, and Lipsey, Richard G. 1978. Freedom of entry and the existence of pure profit. *Economic Journal* 88 (September): 455–69.

Eaton, C. Curtis, and Lipsey, Richard G. 1979. The theory of market pre-emption: The persistence of excess capacity and monopoly in growing spatial markets. *Economica* 46 (May): 149–58.

Elrod, Terry, and Winer, Russell S. 1982. An empirical evaluation of aggregation approaches for developing market segments. *Journal of Marketing* 46 (Fall): 65–74.

Farris, Paul W., and Albion, Mark. 1980. The impact of advertising on the price of consumer products. *Journal of Marketing* 44 (Summer): 17–35.

Frank, Ronald E., and Massy, William. 1965. Market segmentation and the effectiveness of a brand's price and dealing policies. *Journal of Business* 38 (April): 186–200.

Frank, Ronald E.; Massy, William; and Wind, Yoram. 1972. *Market Segmentation.* Englewood Cliffs, N.J.: Prentice-Hall.

Friedman, Milton. 1953. The methodology of positive economics. In *Essays in Positive Economics.* Chicago: University of Chicago Press.

Gabor, Andre. 1955. A note on block tariffs. *Review of Economic Studies* 23:32–41.

Goldman, Marshall I. 1960. Product differentiation and advertising: Some lessons from Soviet experience. *Journal of Political Economy* 68 (August): 346–57.

Harris, Milton, and Raviv, Arthur. 1981. A theory of monopoly pricing schemes with demand uncertainty. *American Economic Review* 71 (June): 347–65.

Hay, D. A. 1976. Sequential entry and entry-deterring strategies in spatial competition. *Oxford Economic Papers* 28 (July): 240–57.

Heaton Peninsular v. Eureka Specialty Co., 77 F.2d 288 (6th Cir. 1896).

Henry v. A. B. Dick, 224 U.S. 1 (1912).

Hirshleifer, Jack. 1958. Peak loads and efficient pricing: Comment. *Quarterly Journal of Economics* 72 (August): 451–62.

Hotelling, Harold. 1929. Stability in competition. *Economic Journal* 39:41–57. Reprinted 1952 in George Stigler and Kenneth Boulding (eds.), *A.E.A. Readings in Price Theory.* Homewood, Ill.: Irwin.

Hotelling, Harold. 1938. The general welfare in relation to problems of taxation and of railway and utility rates. *Econometrica* 6 (July): 242–69. Reprinted 1959 in R. A. Musgrave and C. S. Shoup (eds.), *Readings in the Economics of Taxation.* Homewood, Ill.: Irwin.

Houthakker, Hendrik. 1951. Electricity tariffs in theory and practice. *Economic Journal* 61 (March): 1–25.

International Business Machines Corp. v. United States, 298 U.S. 131 (Sup. Ct. 1936).

Jeuland, Abel P., and Shugan, Steven M. 1982. Managing channel profits. Working Paper. Chicago: University of Chicago, Center for Research in Marketing.

Kalish, Shlomo. In press. Monopolist pricing with dynamic demand and production cost. *Marketing Science*.

Klein, Benjamin; Crawford, Robert G.; and Alchian, Armen A. 1978. Vertical integration, appropriable rents, and the competitive contracting process. *Journal of Law and Economics* 21 (October): 297–326.

Klein, Benjamin, and Leffler, Keith B. 1981. The role of market forces in assuring contractual performance. *Journal of Political Economy* 89, no. 4 (August): 615–42.

Kodak fights back. 1982. *Business Week*, February 1, pp. 48–54.

Lancaster, Kelvin J. 1975. Socially optimal product differentiation. *American Economic Review* 65 (September): 567–85.

McGuire, T. W., and Staelin, Richard. 1981. An industry equilibrium analysis of downstream vertical integration. Working Paper. Pittsburgh: Carnegie Mellon University.

Machlup, Fritz. 1955. Characteristics and types of price discrimination. In *Business Concentration and Public Policy*. Princeton, N.J.: Princeton University Press (for National Bureau of Economic Research).

Machlup, Fritz, and Taber, Martha. 1960. Bilateral monopoly, successive monopoly, and vertical integration. *Economica* 27 (May): 101–19.

Mack, Ruth P., and Leighland, T. James. 1982. Optimizing in households: Toward a behavioral theory. *American Economic Review* 72, no. 2 (May): 103–8.

Mahajan, Vijay, and Jain, Arun K. 1978. An approach to normative segmentation. *Journal of Marketing Research* 15 (August): 338–45.

Montgomery, David. 1971. Consumer characteristics associated with dealing: An empirical example. *Journal of Marketing* 8 (February): 118–20.

Morgan Envelope Co. v. Albany Perforated Paper Co., 152 U.S. 425 (1893).

Motion Picture Patents Co. v. Universal Film Mfg. Co., 243 U.S. 502 (1917).

Murphy, Michael M. 1977. Price discrimination, market separation, and the multi-part tariff. *Economic Inquiry* 15 (October): 587–99.

Nagle, Thomas T. 1983. Pricing as creative marketing. *Business Horizons* 26 (July/August): 14–19.

Narasimhan, Chakravarthi. 1982. Coupons as price discrimination devices—a theoretical perspective and empirical analysis. Working Paper. Chicago: University of Chicago, Center for Research in Marketing.

Nelson, Philip. 1970. Information and consumer behavior. *Journal of Political Economy* 78 (March/April): 311–29.

Nelson, Philip. 1978. Advertising as information once more. In D. Tverck (ed.), *Issues in Advertising*. Washington, D.C.: American Enterprise Institute.

Nelson, Philip. 1980. Comments on "The economics of consumer information acquisition." *Journal of Business* 53, no. 3 (July): S163–S165.

Oi, Walter Y. 1971. A Disneyland dilemma: Two-part tariffs for a Mickey Mouse monopoly. *Quarterly Journal of Economics* 85 (February): 77–96.

Porter, Michael E. 1976. *Interbrand Choice, Strategy, and Bilateral Market Power*. Cambridge, Mass.: Harvard University Press.

Porter, Michael E. 1980. *Competitive Strategy: Techniques for Analyzing Industries and Competitors.* New York: Free Press.

Rao, Ram C., and Rutenberg, David P. 1979. Preempting an alert rival: Strategic timing of the first plant by analysis of sophisticated rivalry. *Bell Journal of Economics* 10 (Autumn): 412–28.

Rao, Vithala R. 1984. Pricing research in marketing: The state of the art. In this issue.

Ratchford, Brian T. 1975. The new economic theory of consumer behavior: An interpretive essay. *Journal of Consumer Research* 2 (September): 65–75.

Riker, William H., and Ordeshook, Peter C. 1973. *An Introduction to Positive Political Theory*. Englewood Cliffs, N.J.: Prentice-Hall.

Robinson, Bruce, and Lakhani, Chet. 1975. Dynamic price models for new product planning. *Management Science* 21 (June): 1113–22.

Robinson, Joan. 1936. *The Economics of Imperfect Competition*. London: Macmillan.

Rosen, Sherwin. 1981. The economics of superstars. *American Economic Review* 71 (December): 845–58.

Salop, Steven C. 1979. Strategic entry deterrence. *American Economic Review* 69:335–38.

Salop, Steven C., and Stiglitz, Joseph. 1977. Bargains and ripoffs: A model of monopolistically competitive price dispersion. *Review of Economics and Statistics* 54 (December): 493–510.

Schoeffler, Sidney; Buzzell, Robert D.; and Heany, D. F. 1974. Impact of strategic planning on profit performance. *Harvard Business Review* 52 (March): 137–45.

Schmalensee, Richard. 1978. Entry deterrence in the ready-to-eat breakfast cereal industry. *Bell Journal of Economics* 9 (Autumn): 305–27.

Schmalensee, Richard. 1982. Commodity bundling by single-product monopolies,. *Journal of Law and Economics* 25 (April): 67–72.

Schmalensee, Richard. 1984. Gaussian demand and commodity bundling. In this issue.

Scitovsky, Tibor. 1950. Ignorance as the source of oligopoly power. *American Economic Review* 40 (May): 48–53.

Smithies, Arthur. 1941. Optimal location in spatial competition. *Journal of Political Economy* 44:423–39. Reprinted 1952 in *A.E.A. Readings in Price Theory*. Homewood, Ill.: Irwin.

Spence, Michael. 1977. Entry, investment, and oligopolistic pricing. *Bell Journal of Economics* 8 (Autumn): 534–44.

Steiner, Peter O. 1957. Peak loads and efficient pricing. *Quarterly Journal of Economics* 71 (November): 585–610.

Stern, Louis W., and El-Ansary, Abel I. 1977. *Marketing Channels*. Englewood Cliffs, N.J.: Prentice-Hall.

Stigler, George. 1961. The economics of information. *Journal of Political Economy* 69, no. 3 (June): 213–25.

Stigler, George. 1963. United States v. Loew's Inc.: A note on block-booking. *Supreme Court Review*, pp. 152–57.

Stokey, Nancy L. 1981. Rational expectations and durable goods pricing. *Bell Journal of Economics* 12 (Spring): 112–28.

Symposium on peak-load pricing. 1976. *Bell Journal of Economics* 7 (Spring): 197–250.

Telser, Lester G. 1960. Why should manufacturers want fair trade? *Journal of Law and Economics* 3 (October): 86–104.

Telser, Lester G. 1980. A theory of self-enforcing agreements. *Journal of Business* 53, no. 1 (January): 27–44.

Times-Picayune Publishing v. United States, 345 U.S. 594, 611 (1953).

United Shoe Machinery Corp. v. United States 258 U.S. 451 (Sup. Ct. 1922).
United States v. Jerrold Electronics Co., 365 U.S. 567 (1961).
Webster, Frederick E. 1965. The "deal-prone" consumer. *Journal of Marketing Research* 2 (May): 186–89.
Wilde, Louis. 1980. The economics of consumer information acquisition. *Journal of Business* 53, no. 3 (July): S143–S158.
Williamson, Oliver E. 1966. Peak-load pricing and optimal capacity under indivisibility constraints. *American Economic Review* 56 (September): 810–27.
Wilson, Charles. 1980. The nature of equilibrium in markets with adverse selection. *Bell Journal of Economics* 11 (Spring): 108–30.
Zusman, Pinhas, and Etgar, Michael. 1981. The marketing channel as an equilibrium set of contracts. *Management Science* (March), pp. 284–302.

30 Pricing Research in Marketing: The State of the Art*

Vithala R. Rao

Journal of Business, Vol. 57, No. 1, Pt. 2 (January 1984), pp. S39–S60. ©1984 by The University of Chicago. All rights reserved. Reprinted by permission.

I. INTRODUCTION

Price is the only marketing mix variable that generates revenues; all others involve expenditures (or possibly investments) of funds. The effects of price changes more immediate and direct, and appeals based on price are the easiest to communicate to prospective buyers. However, competitors can react more easily to appeals based on price than to those based on product benefits and imagery. It can be argued that the price decision is perhaps the most significant among the decisions of the marketing mix (strategy) for a branded product. Conventional wisdom suggests that the price decision should be made in consonance with those of other elements of marketing strategy.

Despite the high importance of price, academic research on pricing issues in marketing has been modest at best. This has been true for various reasons: researchers have emphasized financial and cost analyses used to reach price decisions within a corporation, there has been greater support for and growth of advertising and product research, research in marketing has relied on behavioral science methodologies, data on pricing decisions within a corporation have not been available to academics, and methods needed for analyzing complex matters on pricing have not existed. At an aggregate level (e.g., industry or economy), pricing research has been the forte of economists.

Even though theoretical research on price setting is sparse, there does not seem to be a dearth of advice given to practitioners. The literature on such prescriptions seems to originate from the seminal articles by Dean published in 1950 (and reprinted in 1976) and 1969, and subsequently by Oxenfeldt (1960, 1966, 1973). They present a systematic approach to price setting that takes into account the factors of cost, market segmentation, consumer response, target market, and integration with other elements of the marketing mix. There appear to be two major strategic alternatives for a new product: skimming price and penetration price. Dean's articles emphasize that pricing remains an art, and that the price decision for new products requires sound judgment. These ideas have had a profound impact on practice, and it is only recently that they have been the subject of systematic theoretical research. Some recently published ways in which managers are advised to set prices for their products include setting prices according to customers' perceptions of product benefits and costs (Shapiro and Jackson 1978); setting prices to achieve a predefined target rate of return (Brooks 1975); and setting prices taking into account bargaining, buyer's and seller's strengths and weaknesses (Jain and Laric 1979). These ideas are too general, lack theoretical foundation, and are hard to implement.

Fortunately, the historical perspective depicted above has changed somewhat in recent years. Marketing academicians—notably those with some background in economics and related disciplines—are incorporating some useful concepts into research on pricing. Three categories of recent developments in marketing appear to have had an impact on current pricing research: cost-related developments, individual choice, and the dynamics of choice.

Cost-Related Developments

The most significant idea on costs comes from the empirical evidence published by the Boston Consulting Group (1968) that the marginal cost per unit declines with accumulated volume according to a power function. This has come to be known as the experience curve.

Individual Choice

A great majority of recent research in marketing has focused on how individual consumers choose among a set of alternatives. Some ideas significant to pricing research are listed below:

a) Brands can be described as multiattributed alternatives; the perceived positions of brands on these attributes are related to marketing activities of brands.

b) Consumers differ in the way they utilize various attributes (perceptions) in evaluating the brands.

c) Perceptions of brands on attributes enter into the formation of utility scores for the brands.

d) For any choice situation, only a subset of all possible alternatives may be considered by the consumer. This set is sometimes called the evoked set.

e) Price of an item enters either as an attribute in the evaluation stage of the choice process or as a constraint in the ultimate choice.

f) Ultimate choice is a function of the utility scores obtained in *c* subject to *e*; these functions are empirically derivable.

Dynamics of Choice

Considerable evidence suggests any population's adoption of an innovation is distributed over time. This idea has contributed much to research on pricing strategies over time for new products. A related idea for frequently purchased products is that there is a large stochastic component in the probabilities of choice for various brands in a given category. This aspect becomes relevant when one evaluates the effects of price promotions for frequently purchased products.

Against the background of these ideas, this paper will attempt to review recently published research in marketing on pricing issues. Some caveats on this review are in order here. First, it will focus on the literature appearing essentially in journals relating to marketing and management science (and not economics) during the last 5 years or so.[1] Second, the review is intended to be selective rather than exhaustive in terms of the topics covered.[2] The focus will be on six topics: pricing models for single periods, dynamic pricing models, price discount decisions, behavioral aspects of pricing, interactions of price and other elements of the marketing mix, and a miscellany of other topics such as pricing in a channel and organizational aspects. Third, the focus will be on decision making on price rather than a consideration of welfare and regulatory aspects resulting from corporate decisions on prices. Readers may wish to refer to a previous review on pricing decisions by Monroe and Della Bitta (1978), since this paper essentially will cover material published since that date.

The rest of the paper is organized as follows. Section II presents a formal statement of the pricing decision faced by a manager (management) of a firm. This section will indicate the kind of data that need to be considered in setting prices. Sections III–VIII will review selected articles along with a critique in each of the six topics indicated above.[3] Finally, Section IX will present some directions for future research.

II. A Framework for Price Decisions

Assume that a firm is about to launch a new product for which pricing decisions need to be made for a period of time. It is common practice to consider this decision as part of the overall marketing strategy for the product. Figure 1 lays out a framework adapted from Cravens (1982, p. 294) that managers are advised to follow in reaching these interdependent decisions. The factors of cost, competition, and the particular decisions for other elements of the marketing mix tend to interact with the decisions on price. The figure requires little elaboration.

The decision process is undoubtedly quite complex. To reach a final decision on the marketing mix for the new product (including price), the firm needs information on cost functions, anticipated marketing mixes of competing products, and consumer decision processes with respect to the firm's own product in light of competition. Two sets of price decisions may be differentiated from the firm's point of view: (1) the long-term pricing strategy which will determine the base price of the new product over time (or planning horizon), and (2) the structure of discounts (quantity based or temporary deals) which are of a tactical nature (within any particular time period of the planning horizon). Further, the intra-period decisions may be subsumed in the elements of the other (than price) elements of the marketing mix for the product. An initial formalization of this problem is shown in the Appendix.

While various formal models for setting optimal prices in various market structures exist, their application to practical problems is considerably impeded by various measurement problems (e.g., estimation of the demand and cost functions).[4] Thus, the methods by which practical decisions on prices are made in firms do not necessarily conform to

FIGURE 1. Price Decision Process for a New Product

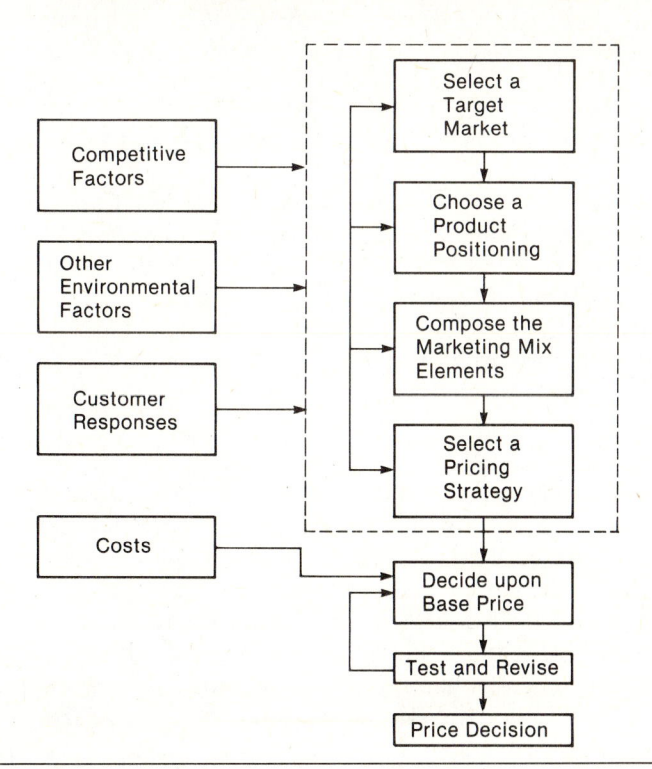

normative rules. A stream of research has attempted to develop descriptive models for the decision process for price decisions in various situations; the paper by Hulbert (1981) provides an overview of this research. Typically, the attempt here is to develop a flowchart that shows how various relevant factors are included in the decision process; the flowchart also lays out the criteria for evaluating a change in the price decision (base price or price off) and the operational procedures employed in an organization for the decision. The papers by Howard and Morgenroth (1968); Farley, Howard, and Hulbert (1971); Howard, Hulbert, and Farley (1975); Capon and Hulbert (1975); and Farley, Hulbert, and Weinstein (1980) report specific applications of this descriptive modeling approach.

The scheme for price-cost planning presented by Fogg and Kohnken (1978) systematically links elements of marketing strategy with manufacturing cost-reduction plans. It may be deemed a simplified version of the model shown in the Appendix. The cost reductions are largely the result of gains due to experience effects as volume of production increases over time. The procedure requires various statistical data on historical prices, historical costs, sales forecasts, and assumptions about competitive behavior. The usefulness of price forecasting for strategic planning is well illustrated for the case of petrochemicals by Stobaugh and Townsend (1975). See also Capon, Farley, and Hulbert (1975) for a descriptive model for pricing and forecasting in an oligopoly situation.

III. Static Models of Price Setting

The optimal price in a given period for a product can be derived for any case by solving the general condition that marginal revenue should equal marginal cost. Several problems occur in defining and measuring the revenue (demand) and cost (supply) functions in a particular situation. When applied to the case of monopoly (e.g., a new product), this condition yields the rule for optimal price, P^*, as

$$P^* = \frac{\epsilon_p}{1+\epsilon_p} \cdot MC, \qquad (1)$$

where ϵ_p is the price elasticity of demand (and is less than -1) and MC is the marginal cost per unit. This rule is for one period. Presumably, price changes should follow this rule as conditions change over time. Various factors relevant in the marketing environment for a brand are ignored by this rule. These factors include consideration of the competing set of products for the brand in question, variation of these competing sets across individual consumers, and interaction of price effects with those of other elements of the marketing mix (e.g., advertising, channels used), cost and demand dependencies, and dynamics over time.

This section will focus on two efforts in the literature that incorporate the factors of consumer choice process, competition, and channel-related issues in setting prices at one point in time: the problem of price setting can be more generally thought of as changing prices for the next time period. (We will postpone consideration of dynamics to a later section.) These are due to Mesak and Clelland (1979) and Little and Shapiro (1980). Both of these papers deal with frequently purchased, low-priced consumer products.

Mesak and Clelland address the problem of predicting the impact of simultaneous changes in prices for a set of competing brands on the sales of a given brand. Their competitive pricing model is specific to a given geographic market, and it uses data collected from a sample of consumers in that market. Using three postulates on the consumer decision process, they develop an equation for estimating expected percentage sales gain or loss for a given brand due to price changes in the total set of brands. This model was empirically tested against a competing model based on a regression of market share on price. Mesak and Clelland conclude that the model they proposed fared better. While their model suffers from the lack of strict validity tests, the approach is impressive on two grounds: first, it is a microlevel model, and second, it incorporates acceptable behavioral premises at the individual level. This approach should be useful in determining specific geographical areas and how much to raise (or reduce) prices for brands.

The Little-Shapiro paper develops a two-stage theory of price setting that postulates maximizing behavior on the part of customers and stores. In their model, once in the store, customers purchase goods to maximize utility; this process determines the short-run response to prices. The store's problem then is to maximize short-run profit subject to a constraint that a given level of customer utility be delivered. The utility level becomes a policy parameter for the store which, in part, determines the long-run attractiveness of the store to the customers. Their model is quite comprehensive in dealing with the customer-store interaction and is a stepping stone to a theory of pricing a bundle of goods at the level of a supermarket, which includes interactions among various products. Little and Shapiro comment on the measurement issues involved in estimating the cross-elasticities and anticipate progress on this front with the advent of scanner data. While the approach offers promise, the empirical issues can be quite formidable. Nevertheless, this paper presents a theory of pricing goods using accepted principles of economic behavior. The theory does not include such important phenomena as customers' desire to seek variety in shopping and stores' stocking behavior with regard to new products.

IV. Dynamic Models of Pricing

Recent years have witnessed an intense amount of activity on models for pricing products over time. Almost invariably this research relates to new products since dynamic issues are more important in that area. The existing knowledge on life cycle, experience curves, and consumer processes of adoption and diffusion has been integrated into this stream of research.

The issue of how price elasticities vary over the life cycle of the product has been studied empirically by Simon (1979). Based on an extensive analysis of West German data on sales and prices for three consumer products and 43 brands, Simon (1979) concludes that typical changes occur in price elasticities (ϵ) for brands as they go through their life cycles (i.e., $\epsilon_{\text{introduction}} \geqslant \epsilon_{\text{growth}} \geqslant \epsilon_{\text{maturity}} \leqslant \epsilon_{\text{decline}}$). Based on this analysis, Simon arrives at an optimal price behavior for a new brand which involves the myopic price and some adjustments due to changes in price elasticities. In particular, he concludes that the markup factor in the corresponding optimal price strategy—that is, $\epsilon_p/(1+\epsilon_p)$ when $\epsilon_p \leqslant -1$—is relatively smaller at the introduction and growth stages, relatively greater at the maturity stage, and decreases during the decline stage. Further, he concludes that his analysis lends support to a penetration strategy over time. This work has not incorporated all of the dynamics of the marketplace, as the studies reviewed below demonstrate.

We will start our review of dynamic pricing research by building a chronology of this research stream. Robinson and Lakhani (1975) may be credited with opening this area for further research. Their paper set up a mathematical model that incorporates the two concepts of declining costs over time and the evolution of demand for a new durable good according to the epidemic model applied by Bass in 1969. They tackled the problem of pricing a new product using dynamic programming. Subsequent contributions to this research have been made by Bass (1980), Dolan and Jeuland (1981), Jeuland and Dolan (1982), and Kalish (1983). These papers present either generalizations or solutions using different methodologies or empirical applications.

To get a flavor of this model-building effort, we will summarize the main results obtained by Jeuland and Dolan (1982), who also considered the case of nondurable goods. The authors portray purchasing behavior (applicable to any type of good) by three parameters: (1) innovative trial, α; (2) imitative trial, β; and (3) repeat buying, b. Note that for durable goods during the planning period of interest (when the new product has a monopoly), b is essentially equal to zero. Let m be the market potential for the product. They derive the time path for optimal price over the planning horizon to consist of two parts, one that represents the optimal price, $p_m(t)$, that would maximize short-term profits (i.e., for a myopic strategy) and the other that represents an adjustment, $\Delta p(t)$, due to the endogenous dynamics of the demand system. Thus, the optimal price, $p^*(t)$, is given by

$$p^*(t) = p_m(t) + \Delta p(t). \tag{2}$$

Their substantive results are:

1. For the case of undiscounted profits, the optimal price path for a durable good (i.e., $b=0$), is *low* introductory price and prices to peak and then decline (i.e., penetration strategy followed by skimming strategy) if the imitation effects are important (i.e., $\beta m > \alpha$) and *high* introductory and declines over time (i.e., skimming strategy) when imitation effects are *unimportant* (i.e., $\beta m < \alpha$).
2. In the case of undiscounted profits for a nondurable good with frequent repeat purchase (i.e., $b>0$), the optimal path is a low introductory price followed by continuous price increases (i.e., penetration strategy).
3. For a positive discount rate, results 1 and 2 are generally encountered.
4. As the discount rate becomes large, the adjustment becomes less important and the optimal strategy looks like the myopic strategy.

Also, Jeuland (1981) presents a set of parsimonious models of diffusion of innovation for a new product that incorporates price. The models utilize principles of rational consumer choice under uncertainty and the diffusion of innovations; these principles postulate that a consumer chooses a product only if its value exceeds its price (i.e., the reservation price concept) and that the consumer perceives that there is some uncertainty with regard to the value of the new product. He analyzes various situations and concludes that the earlier results of lower introductory price are still valid for some reasonable circumstances.

Kalish (1983) has demonstrated that the results obtained by Jeuland and Dolan using specific functional forms for cost and demand for durable goods generally hold for general functional forms. In addition, he has developed the conditions of demand and discount rates under which a penetration pricing policy would still be optimal for a myopic monopolist. See also Bass and Bultez (1982) for a comparison of profit implications of optimal pricing strategy over time versus myopic pricing strategy for technological innovations when the demand is expressed as a power function in price shifted by a time-dependent diffusion effect. Based on simulation studies, their conclusion is that discounted profits under myopic pricing are only slightly less than those under optimal multiperiod strategy.

While the above models deal with the issue of pricing a new product during the period of its monopoly power, the effects of competitive entry and subsequent dynamics in the market are ignored. The issue of competitive entry is studied by Eliashberg and Jeuland (1982) using game theory and by Clarke and Dolan (1984) using simulation methods. The theoretical results of Eliashberg and Jeuland indicate that the pricing strategy during the duopoly period (after entry by a competitor) may be quite different from that during the monopoly period. The simulation results of Clarke and Dolan identify conditions under which an innovative firm may follow skimming and penetration pricing strategies in response to a competitive entry; no generalizations can be derived except that competitive entry is a variable to be reckoned with in addition to the other variables identified above. The work of Thompson and Teng (1981) perhaps represents the state of the art on the use of non-zero-sum differential games for deriving optimal policies of pricing and advertising under oligopoly situations; they present numerical algorithms for finding solutions for the tripoly situation. The paper by Lieber and Barnea (1977) constructs the optimal price trajectory for a monopoly with a finite level of resources (a supply constraint) and competition induced by monopolistic selling price (a demand constraint). Using the game-theoretic approach, they find that optimal price path will initially decrease and eventually increase. Despite these several efforts, the topic of the effects of competition offers enormous opportunities for further research.

One item in the literature that applies dynamic models to pricing and production is by Lodish (1980). He tackles the problem of pricing and production decisions for products or services whose value to the consumer may be changing over time. Examples include pricing for broadcast spots on television. He develops a dynamic programming formulation for this problem and solves it using a simple computer program. His results are empirically validated for television spot prices.

We conclude this section with two specific comments. First, the theoretical research on pricing new products is at a fairly sophisticated stage and includes several relevant factors. It seems quite appropriate for practitioners to begin to depend on these results after ensuring that their decision situations fit the particular assumptions made in these models. Second, the theoretical results need to be empirically validated; such validation efforts would show opportunities for advancing the existing theories and perhaps would test the seriousness of assumptions made.

V. PRICE PROMOTION DECISIONS

Price promotion—or, more generally, offering a temporary price reduction in cash or kind—is a common marketing tool for increasing sales on a temporary basis. The literature contains several models that attempt to optimally determine the amount of price off (or deal), duration of price off, number of times such price off should be offered, and determination of long-term effects of price promotions. The context for this work typically is that of frequently purchased consumer goods. Some references in this stream of research are the articles by Kuehn and Rohloff (1967), Goodman and Moody (1970), Rao and Shakun (1972), Rao and Thomas (1973), Aaker (1973), Lilien (1974), Kinberg, Rao, and Shakun (1974), Kinberg and Rao (1975), and Blattberg et al. (1978). Reviews of this literature can be found in Monroe and Della Bitta (1978) and Rao and Sabavala (1980).

In their paper, Rao and Sabavala treat the decision problem of price promotion as an allocation of a marketing budget to advertising and promotion. Their model takes into account the peculiar feature of price promotions—that is, the effects on sales via temporary price change and the fact that the cost of the promotion is, in practice, allocated from a marketing budget. They derive optimal conditions for the regular price and temporary price reductions and argue for differentiating between short-term price elasticity and long-term price elasticity in the decisions on price promotions.

A typical approach for determining the effect of a price promotion is to evaluate the gain due to increased sales during the period of promotion against losses due to reductions in sales subsequent to withdrawal of the price deal (commonly known as the "stocking up" effect); see Rao and Thomas (1973). The sales increases or reductions have been modeled in various ways using such concepts as trade-off between opportunity costs of forgone sales and holding costs of excess inventories, consumer choice process of brands with increased quality-price relationships due to price promotion, game theory, and stochastic models of consumer choice. The modeling has typically been at the aggregate level. In general, this research has sought predictions of the phenomena rather than cogent explanations.

Recently, however, Blattberg, Eppen, and Lieberman (1981) have presented an explanation for dealing of storable products based on the idea of transferring carrying costs from the retailer to the consumer. They propose two models: one for the retailer and one for the consumer. The retailer seeks to balance fixed cost, inventory cost, and loss from deal to maximize profits, while the consumer seeks to balance holding cost and gain from the deal to maximize profits. A juxtaposition of these two models results in a necessary condition for dealing to be profitable: holding costs to certain consumers for the product category must be less than one-half those of the retailer. However, this paper ignores competition at the retail level. This paper is perhaps the first in the spirit of offering a cogent theoretical explanation for deals and then presenting empirical evidence. Jeuland and Narasimhan (1982) presented a similar model in which retailers are *not* assumed to be less efficient, but face a downward sloped demand curve, and consumers are heterogeneous in their preferences, and derived a sufficient condition for deals to occur. Work is necessary to compare these explanations using inventory theory with other explanations such as the one using quality-price evaluations.

The bargain value model (BVM) proposed and tested by Keon (1980) presents a procedure for modeling consumer brand choice which considers brand prices and offers a different explanation for consumer behavior under price promotions. Specifically, the BVM is based on the construct of bargain value defined as the ratio of monetary worth of a brand and its price and the premise that a consumer chooses that brand with the highest bargain value among the evoked set of brands. The implication of this model is that the effect of price promotions is not to create new brand loyalty but to keep loyal customers. Not enough empirical evidence is presented in this paper, but the underlying premises of the model are worth further investigation.

Narasimhan (1982) worked from the premises of a price-theoretic model (Rosen 1974) to explain the use of coupons by consumers. He has shown that users of coupons are more price elastic than nonusers of coupons and that the opportunity cost of time and other household resources are variables that determine the decision to use coupons. Various implications of his model are tested using diary panel data.

Another direction for price promotion research is the one being pursued by Thaler (1982) in which prospect theory (Kahneman and Tversky 1979) is employed to conceptualize the purchasing behavior under price changes. Thaler hypothesizes that individuals maintain a system of mental accounts that are adjusted on a transaction-by-transaction basis and postulates a process by which outcomes of transactions are coded (separately or as a package). His work has some implications in the way price promotions are presented (e.g., percent off or dollars off) and for the use of rebates. However, this research is still in a preliminary stage.

VI. Behavioral Aspects of Pricing

This section will consider research on the role played by price in the consumer choice process. Two distinct roles for price may be identified: an allocative role and a nonallocative (informative) role. The economic theory of consumer behavior and the stream of research on hedonic prices (which treats price as an indicator of opportunity costs) consider the allocative role of price (see Griliches 1971).[5]

The fact that price may convey some information on quality has been acknowledged by Scitovsky (1944). Empirical research on the topic of a link between price and quality has been undertaken in marketing since 1964. A review of studies prior to 1976 appears in Gardner (1977). Some of the recently published research on behavioral issues of price includes Monroe (1976), Wheatley and Chiu (1977), Hagerty (1978), Park and Winter (1979), Riesz (1980), and Etgar and Malhotra (1981).

In general, these studies have enumerated conditions specific to product and choice context where the informative role of price appears either to operate or not to operate. Generally speaking, the presence of additional information about the product or the purchase context diminishes the strength of the price-perceived quality link (see Rao 1971). In a recently published paper, Etgar and Malhotra (1981) conclude, on the basis of a series of experiments, that no uniform price-quality relationship exists and that the derived importance of price is not uniform across the various quality aspects of products evaluated by the subjects.

In conclusion, this research is not based on sound theory, and it tends to be largely descriptive. The results obtained are usually based on experiments conducted by the authors with no attempt to build a logically consistent story. Bowbrick (1980) makes this point rather strongly.

The basic issue of how price enters the choice process still remains to be resolved. Using certain assumptions on utility function, Srinivasan (1982) shows that there is a high degree of congruity between the two roles—informative and allocative—played by price. However, the fact that price has some informational role need not be contested. Research toward developing appropriate demand models that incorporate the informative role of price is needed to help us better understand the formation process at the individual level. An attempt in this direction is made by Rao and Gautschi (1982), who propose a construct that they term "evoked price" and show how the choice process may be modeled as a set of simultaneous equations. They are at a stage of empirically testing and validating the proposed models.

VII. Price and Other Elements of the Marketing Mix

While the issue of how price and other elements of the marketing mix interact is critical in making practical marketing decisions, the topic has been severely underresearched. Two aspects of this interrelationship will be reviewed here: the relationship between price and product characteristics, investigated by Hauser and Simmie (1981), and that between price and advertising, examined by Benham (1972), Eskin and Baron (1977), Wittink (1977), and Albion and Farris (1981). The first is a theoretical paper, and the last four are empirical studies. I shall review them all briefly.

Hauser and Simmie investigate the problem of positioning a product (or selecting features and price for the product) so as to maximize the firm's profit. Their theory attempts to integrate the available knowledge on how consumers process information (as developed in psychometrics) with the economic model of Lancaster (1971). They incorporate concepts of mapping product features and psychosocial cues into a perceptual space; consumers vary in their preference toward competing objects and the way they perceive products. Various measurement issues for implementing this theory have been addressed with respect to some new items in the communications market. Some assumptions with regard to scaling of the characteristics may not be easily satisfied. Nevertheless, it is a good attempt at integrating various elements of previous research.

The question of how advertising and prices interact is very interesting because of its managerial and social implications. On the basis of an econometric analysis of the eyeglasses market as of 1963, Benham (1972) concluded that prices were substantially lower in the states of the United States which allowed advertising of eyeglasses. A similar conclusion was arrived at by Albion and Farris (1981) based on an analysis of advertising and retail margin data for 51 product categories and 488 individual brands sold in supermarkets; they concluded that advertised brands are sold at lower retail margins than unadvertised brands. They further showed that this relationship is independent of the effect of advertising on unit sales. These empirical findings have implications such as potential necessity to alter retail or wholesale prices when advertising budgets are changed and potential underestimation of the long-term contribution of advertising to sales and profits.

Based on a series of four test market experiments for three food products and one household cleaning product, Eskin and Baron (1977) conclude that increases in advertising expenditures increase sales and that such increases are greater under low price conditions than under high price conditions; thus, there appears to be a negative price-advertising interaction. A similar finding that advertising may serve to increase price sensitivity is reported by Wittink (1977). Farris and Albion (1980) review arguments on the question of how advertising affects prices and review empirical research till that date. Ferguson's (1982) comments on the 1980 article and the reply by its authors (Farris and Albion 1982) are worth noting to indicate the lack of definiteness of the advertising-price relationship. Thus it appears that this area offers significant opportunities for both theoretical and empirical research.

VIII. A Miscellany of Topics

This section will briefly comment on a set of selected and somewhat unrelated topics.

The effects of delegating pricing authority to the sales force have been examined by Stephenson, Cron, and Frazier (1979). Based on data collected from a sample of 108 member firms of the American Surgical Trade Association, they found that those firms giving the highest degree of pricing authority to the sales force generated the lowest sales and profit performance. This study raises questions on the ideal location (sales force or management) for control for setting (and changing) prices in an organization and argues for placing relatively little pricing latitude in the hands of the salespeople.

The paper by Burt and Boyett (1979) reports on the effect of introducing competition into the supply sources for various items procured under the bidding process. Their study of 356 items which had been priced under sole source and then under competitive conditions showed that the introduction of competition is associated with a reduction in unit price of between 10.8% and 17.5%, depending on the size of the order.

The issues of pricing along the distribution channel and optimal quantity discounts have not received much attention in the literature. Beginnings of some work in the area of channels can be found in Jeuland and Shugan (1981) and McGuire and Staelin (1983). In their unpublished paper, Jeuland and Shugan (1981) explore how several mechanisms to achieve cooperation affect the total profits of all members of the channel and find that profit sharing can be implemented with quantity discounts. McGuire and Staelin (1983) develop a simple game-theoretic model of two manufacturers selling their competing products through retail outlets and draw various conclusions on the industry equilibrium; one conclusion of interest is that, if the manufacturers behave cooperatively, profits are greater and retail prices are lower with a pure company-store system than with privately owned dealers. The paper by Zusman and Etgar (1981), who analyze the marketing channel using the theory of dyadic contracts, is also relevant for the issue of determining optimal pricing policies along a distribution channel. In another unpublished paper, Dolan (1980) considers the role of quantity discounts as a means of coordinating the inventory policies of independent members of the distribution channel to achieve the goal of cost minimization of the whole system. These research efforts should form the basis for an intensive examination of the implications for pricing across a distribution channel.

Although the problem of pricing a line of interrelated products is managerially important, the marketing literature pays to it only a cursory attention. Loss leader pricing is one illustration of how firms utilize the concept of demand interdependencies in practice. The literature in economics presents theoretical solutions to the problem of pricing interrelated goods; for example, see Oren, Smith, and Wilson (1982, 1984). Little and Shapiro (1980) also propose pricing solutions to a product line. Monroe and Della Bitta (1978) derive a model which explicitly considers the demand and cost dependencies.

Equation (1) for optimal price ignores any effects of interdependence (of demand and costs) of the product with others. Assuming only one other product, B, in the line and no cost dependencies, the optimal price, P^*_A, for a product A (assuming that the sales are in the elastic portion of the demand curve) can be shown to be

$$P^*_A = \frac{\epsilon_A}{1+\epsilon_A} \cdot MC_A - \left(\frac{\eta_{AB}}{1+\epsilon_A}\right) \cdot \frac{Q_B(P_B - MC_B)}{Q_A} \tag{3}$$

where ϵ_A and η_{AB} are self- and cross-price elasticities for product A, Q_A and Q_B are sales quantities of A and B, and MC_A and MC_B are marginal cost functions of A and B, respectively. A and B are substitutes if η_{AB} is positive and complements if η_{AB} is negative. The extension of (3) to a set of B-type products is quite immediate. Implementation of this result presents several empirical problems for estimating the required elasticities and the problem of allocation of joint costs. (See Demski [1981] for a recent discussion on cost allocation.) Mahajan et al. (1982) show how the conjoint analysis can be used for this purpose. Reibstein and Gatignon (1982) report another empirical effort in which econometric methods are used to measure self- and cross-elasticities for eggs of different sizes using sales data at the store level; they also discuss how optimal prices for the line of eggs may be set using these estimates. The paper by Monroe and Zoltners (1979) presents a simpler approach to the product line pricing problem particularly when the firm faces resource constraints; they argue for the use of the criterion of contribution per resource unit as opposed to gross margin.

IX. SOME DIRECTIONS FOR FUTURE RESEARCH

The preceding review, although selective, indicates the state of the art of pricing research in marketing. It points out that recent research on pricing is somewhat disjointed and has not reached the same degree of comprehensiveness as other topics in marketing such as advertising. Various areas covered in the review require further work from both a theoretical and an empirical point of view. Some of these ideas are indicated below. These include an extensive study on how pricing decisions are made in practice, product line pricing, studies on the role of price in consumer choice, validation of dynamic models for pricing new products, and competitive pricing.

Practice of Determining Prices. Benefits of knowing more about the decision processes of how industry managers go about determining (and changing) prices for their products (see Hulbert 1981) are quite apparent. However, issues such as discount structures, variation of prices across different levels of channels, and reactions to competitive price moves do call for further empirical investigation; such studies could also determine the degree to which current economic theories or models available in the literature are being employed by practitioners and the role of market forces in setting prices of products. Such a study should also attempt to look at issues of price setting for one product as well as a line of related products and at various levels of the distribution channel; attention also has to be paid to the problems and procedures relating to the implementation of price policies. A good description of practice should lead to improved theoretical work. Thus, one essential research step would be to undertake a comprehensive study of price setting in selected industries. In a sense, research along the lines suggested would update an earlier case-oriented study by Kaplan, Dirlam, and Lanzillotti (1958).

Role of Price in Consumer Choice. As pointed out, behavioral research on prices has suffered from a lack of theoretical perspective. In order to obtain a better understanding of how price information is used by consumers in making brand choices, richer constructs are needed in this research. Constructs such as reservation price, evoked price, fair price, price willing to pay, and price paid will have to be differentiated and their predictive role in brand choice ascertained. Further, consumers' perceptions of price changes, rebates, and price discounts could also be examined. This stream of research should be of great value not only in setting prices but also in determining discounts or rebates.

Pricing for New Products. The models derived in the literature for setting optimal prices for new products need empirical validation. Further, these models should incorporate richer processes of consumer choice originating from disaggregated levels (e.g., inclusion of an appropriate set of items with which a new product might compete for the consumer's budget). Additionally, the applications of hedonic pricing in determining price structures for new products should be explored.

Product Line Pricing. It is obvious that extensive research is called for in the area of pricing a product line. In addition to resolving empirical issues in estimating the parameters of these models, the effects of portfolio analyses at various levels of the organization on product line pricing will need to be investigated.

Competitive Pricing Behavior. Various research issues remain to be investigated in the area of competitive pricing. These questions include: When would a competitor react to a price change by a rival firm? How large a price change will be implemented by a competitor in reaction to a price change by a rival? How would the reactions be when there is more than one rival in the industry? What roles do various factors (e.g., management culture, inflation, profit expectations) play in the competitive pricing behavior? What are the dynamics of competitive behavior? It appears that existing techniques of analysis (e.g., game theory, semi-Markov chains, reaction curves) may naturally be utilized in this research effort. Further, model validation may not present much difficulty since data on competitive price movements are generally in the public domain or are easily collected.

APPENDIX: A MATHEMATICAL FORMULATION OF PRICING PROBLEM FOR A NEW PRODUCT

In this Appendix, the decision of pricing a new product over time is presented as a mathematical programming problem. Various concepts are described using the following notation. Let

T	= number of periods in the planning horizon (numbered 0, 1, 2, ..., T);
$A_1(t)$	= set of products in the marketplace that compete with the new product B during period t;
$A_2(t)$	= set of products which have joint costs (manufacturing or marketing) with B within the firm;
$M(t)$	= marketing mix decisions (other than price) for product B during the period t;
$MX[A_1(t), t]$	= set of marketing mix decisions (including price) for all the products that compete with B during period t;
$P(t)$	= price of one unit of B during time t;
$c(t)$	= production cost per unit of B during time t;
$r(t)$	= rate of discount applicable to the firm for period t;
$CM(t)$	= cost of the marketing mix decisions for B in time period t;
$QA(t)$	= production in some comparable units of the items in set A_2 at time t;
$Q(t)$	= expected number of units sold of B at time t given $M(t)$ and $P(t)$;
$Z(t)$	= contribution to profit from B during time t; and
$V(0)$	= present value of the $Z(t)$ stream during the planning horizon.

We can now write the decision problem for the firm in setting the prices for B over the planning horizon. The problem is to choose $\{P(t); t=0, 1, 2, \ldots, T\}$ so as to maximize $V = \sum_{t=0}^{T} Z(t) / \prod_{k=0}^{t}(1+r_k)$ where $Z(t) = [P(t) - C(t)]Q(t) - CM(t)$. The functions that describe $Q(t)$ and $C(t)$ can be written as $C(t) = f_1[Q(t), C(t-1), QA(t)]$ and $Q(t) = f_2[P(t), Q(t-1), M(t), MX(A_1(t), t)]$. This formalization expresses the notions of interdependence and the interactive nature of the decision process. The function for $Q(t)$ may also be developed in terms of the choice processes of potential consumers in the marketplace. We may also note that this problem calls for a significant amount of data on market dynamics, market structure, competitive behavior, and cost behavior. In practice, the problem needs to be simplified so that a reasonable solution (strategy) can be derived. However, the formalization should help in thinking about the nature of questions that should be considered while tackling the pricing decision by a firm and the kinds of measurements necessary for the decision.

ENDNOTES

* I thank Sharon McCarthy for her assistance in this research and Darius Sabavala, Subrata Sen, and an anonymous reviewer for their comments on an earlier draft of this paper. This work was partially supported by the Summer Research Fund of the Graduate School of Business and Public Administration, Cornell University.

1. The reader is referred to the paper by Nagle (1984) in this issue which reviews relevant economics literature on pricing. A sample of such articles includes Newberry (1978), Schmalensee (1981, 1982), Stokey (1981), and Sherman and Visscher (1982).
2. The literature on market share models that utilize price information and competitive structures has not been included in this review. Undoubtedly, the way a market structure for a given product is defined will (or should) have an impact on the pricing decision.
3. The reference list to this paper contains various other items in the literature, even though they are not reviewed in the paper.
4. Recent developments in marketing research—notably using conjoint analysis—contributed much to the ability of researchers to measure utility functions at the individual level. See Hauser and Urban (1977) and Green and Srinivasan (1978). Mahajan, Green, and Goldberg (1982) report an application of conjoint analysis for measuring self- and cross-price/demand relationships. This review will not cover the measurement issues.
5. See Agarwal and Ratchford (1980) for a comprehensive empirical application of Rosen's (1974) model of consumer choice to the case of automobiles. See also the comment by Nelson (1982) and reply by Ratchford and Agarwal (1982). See Brown and Rosen (1982) for econometric issues of hedonic price models.

REFERENCES

Aaker, D. A. 1973. Toward a normative model of promotional decision making. *Management Science* 19 (February): 593–603.

Agarwal, M. K., and Ratchford, B. T. 1980. Estimating demand functions for product characteristics: The case of automobiles. *Journal of Consumer Research* 7 (December): 249–62.

Albion, M. S., and Farris, P. W. 1981. The effect of manufacturer advertising on retail pricing. Report no. 81-105. Cambridge, Mass.: Marketing Science Institute, December.

Bass, F. M. 1969. A new product growth model for consumer durables. *Management Science* 15 (January): 215–27.

Bass, FM. 1980. The relationship between diffusion rates, experience curves, and demand elasticities for consumer durable technological innovations. *Journal of Business* 53 (July): S51–S67.

Bass, F. M., and Bultez, A. V. 1982. A note on optimal strategic pricing of technological innovations. *Marketing Science* 1 (Fall): 371–78.

Benham, L. 1972. The effect of advertising on the price of eyeglasses. *Journal of Law and Economics* 15 (October): 337–52.

Blattberg, R.; Buesing, T.; Peacock, P.; and Sen, S. 1978. Identifying the deal-prone segment. *Journal of Marketing Research* 15 (August): 369–77.

Blattberg, R. C.; Eppen, G. D.; and Lieberman, J. 1981. A theoretical and empirical evaluation of price deals for consumer nondurables. *Journal of Marketing* 45 (Winter): 116–29.

Boston Consulting Group. 1968. *Perspectives on Experience*. Boston: Boston Consulting Group.

Bowbrick, P. 1980. Pseudo research in marketing: The case of the price/perceived quality relationship. *European Journal of Marketing* 14 (8): 466–70.

Brooks, D. G. 1975. Cost-oriented pricing: A realistic solution to a complicated problem. *Journal of Marketing* 39 (April): 72–74.

Brown, J. N., and Rosen, H. S. 1982. On the estimation of structural hedonic price models. *Econometrica* 50 (May): 765–74.

Burt, D. N., and Boyett, J. E. 1979. Reduction in selling price after the introduction of competition. *Journal of Marketing Research* 16 (May): 275–79.

Capon, N., and Hulbert, J. 1975. Decision systems analysis in industrial marketing. *Industrial Marketing Management* 4 (June): 143–60.

Capon, N.; Farley, J. U.; and Hulbert, J. 1975. Pricing and forecasting in an oligopoly firm. *Journal of Management Studies* 12 (May): 133–56.

Clarke, D. G., and Dolan, R. J. 1984. A simulation model for the evaluation of pricing strategies in a dynamic environment. *Journal of Business*. In this issue.

Cravens, D. W. 1982. *Strategic Marketing*. Homewood, Ill.: Irwin.

Dean, J. 1969. Pricing pioneering products. *Journal of Industrial Economics* 17 (July): 165–79.

Dean, J. 1976. Pricing policies for new products. *Harvard Business Review* 54 (November/December): 141–53. (Originally published, *HBR*, November 1950).

Demski, J. 1981. Cost allocation games. In Moriarity, S. (ed.), Joint Cost Allocations: Proceedings of the University of Oklahoma Conference on Joint Cost Allocations. Norman, Okla.: Center for Economic and Management Research.

Dolan, R. J. 1980. Determination of optimal quantity discount schedules. Working Paper. Chicago: University of Chicago, Graduate School of Business, January.

Dolan, R. J., and Jeuland, A. P. 1981. Experience curves and dynamic demand models: Implications for optimal pricing strategies. *Journal of Marketing* 45 (Winter): 52–73.

Eliashberg, J., and Jeuland, A. P. 1982. New product pricing strategies over time in a developing market: How does entry affect prices? Working Paper no. 82-021. Chicago: University of Chicago, Center for Research in Marketing, August.

Eskin, G. J., and Baron, P. H. 1977. Effects of price and advertising in test-market experiments. *Journal of Marketing Research* 14 (November): 499–508.

Etgar, M., and Malhotra, N. K. 1981. Determinants of price dependency: Personal and perceptual factors. *Journal of Consumer Research* 8 (September): 217–22.

Farley, J. U.; Howard, J. A.; and Hulbert, J. 1971. An organizational approach to industrial marketing information systems. *Sloan Management Review* 13 (Fall): 35–54.

Farley, J. U.; Hulbert, J. M.; and Weinstein, D. 1980. Price setting and volume planning by two European industrial companies: A study and comparison of decision processes. *Journal of Marketing* 44 (Winter): 46–54.

Farris, P. W., and Albion, M. S. 1980. The impact of advertising on the price of consumer products. *Journal of Marketing* 44 (Summer): 17–35.

Farris, P. W., and Albion, M. S. 1982. Reply to comments on "The impact of advertising on the price of consumer products." *Journal of Marketing* 46 (Winter): 106–107.

Ferguson, J. M. 1982. Comments on "The impact of advertising on the price of consumer products." *Journal of Marketing* 46 (Winter): 102–105.

Fogg, C. D., and Kohnken, K. H. 1978. Price-cost planning. *Journal of Marketing* 42 (April): 97–106.

Gardner, D. M. 1977. The role of price in consumer choice. *Selected Aspects of Consumer Behavior*. NSF/RA 77-0013. Washington, D.C.: Government Printing Office.

Goodman, D. A., and Moody, K. W. 1970. Determining optimum price promotion quantities. *Journal of Marketing* 34 (October): 31–39.

Green, P. E., and Srinivasan, V. 1978. Conjoint analysis on consumer research: Issues and outlook. *Journal of Consumer Research* 5 (September): 103–23.

Griliches, Z. 1971. *Price Indices and Quality Change*. Cambridge, Mass.: Harvard University Press.

Hagerty, M. 1978. Model testing techniques and price-quality tradeoffs. *Journal of Consumer Research* 5 (December): 194–205.

Hauser, J. R., and Simmie, P. 1981. Profit maximizing perceptual positions: An integrated theory for the selection of product features and price. *Management Science* 27 (January): 33–56.

Hauser, J. R., and Urban, G. L. 1977. A normative methodology for modeling consumer response to innovation. *Operations Research* 25 (July/August): 579–619.

Howard, J. A., and Morgenroth, W. M. 1968. Information processing model for executive decisions. *Management Science* 14 (March): 416–28.

Howard, J. A.; Hulbert, J.; and Farley, J. U. 1975. Organizational analysis and information systems design: A decision process perspective. *Journal of Business Research* 3 (April): 133–48.

Hulbert, J. 1981. Descriptive models of marketing decisions. In Randall L. Schultz and Andris A. Zoltners (eds.), *Marketing Decision Models*. New York: North-Holland.

Jain, S., and Laric, M. 1979. A framework for strategic industrial pricing. *Industrial Marketing Management* 8 (January): 75–80.

Jeuland, A. P. 1981. Parsimonious models of diffusion and innovation. Part B. Incorporating the variable of price. Working Paper. Chicago: University of Chicago, Center for Research in Marketing. July.

Jeuland, A. P., and Dolan, R. J. 1982. An aspect of new product planning: Dynamic pricing. In A. A. Zoltners (ed.), *Marketing Planning Models*. TIMS Studies in the Management Sciences, vol. 18. New York: North-Holland.

Jeuland, A. P., and Narasimhan, C. 1982. Why do some consumers buy on deal and retailers offer deals? Working Paper. Chicago: University of Chicago Graduate School of Business, September.

Jeuland, A. P., and Shugan, S. M. 1981. Managing channel profits. Working Paper. Chicago: University of Chicago, Graduate School of Business, October.

Kahneman, D., and Tversky, A. 1979. Prospect theory: An analysis of decision under risk. *Econometrica* 47 (March): 263–91.

Kalish, S. 1983. Monopolist pricing with dynamic demand and production costs. *Marketing Science* 2 (Spring): 135–60.

Kaplan, A. D. H.; Dirlam, J. B.; and Lanzillotti, R. F. 1958. *Pricing in Big Business: A Case Approach*. Washington, D.C.: Brookings Institution.

Keon, J. N. 1980. The bargain value model and a comparison of managerial implications with the linear learning model. *Management Science* 26 (November): 1117–30.

Kinberg, Y., and Rao, A. G. 1975. Stochastic models of a price promotion. *Management Science* 21 (April): 897–907.

Kinberg, Y.; Rao, A. G.; and Shakun, M. 1974. A mathematical model for price promotions. *Management Science* 20 (February): 948–59.

Kuehn, A. A., and Rohloff, A. C. 1967. *Consumer Response to Promotions. II. Promotional Decisions Using Mathematical Models*. Boston: Allyn & Bacon.

Lancaster, K. 1971. *Consumer Demand: A New Approach*. New York: Columbia University Press.

Lieber, Z., and Barnea, A. 1977. Dynamic optimal pricing to deter entry under constrained supply. *Operations Research* 25 (July/August): 696–705.

Lilien, G. L. 1974. Application of a modified linear learning model of buyer behavior. *Journal of Marketing Research* 11 (August): 279–85.

Little, J. D. C., and Shapiro, J. F. 1980. A theory for pricing non-featured products in supermarkets. *Journal of Business* 53 (July): S199–S209.

Lodish, L. M. 1980. Applied dynamic pricing and production models with specific application to broadcast spot pricing. *Journal of Marketing Research* 17 (May): 203–11.

McGuire, T. W., and Staelin, R. 1983. The industry equilibrium analysis of downstream vertical integration. *Marketing Science* 3 (Spring): 161–92.

Mahajan, V.; Green, P. E.; and Goldberg, S. M. 1982. A conjoint model for measuring self- and cross-price/demand relationships. *Journal of Marketing Research* 19 (August): 334–42.

Mesak, H., and Clelland, R. C. 1979. A competitive pricing model. *Management Science* 25 (November): 1057–68.

Monroe, K. B. 1976. The influence of price difference and brand familiarity on brand preferences. *Journal of Consumer Research* 3 (June): 42–49.

Monroe, K. B., and Della Bitta, A. J. 1978. Models for pricing decisions. *Journal of Marketing Research* 15 (August): 413–28.

Monroe, K. B., and Zoltners, A. 1979. Pricing the product line during periods of scarcity. *Journal of Marketing* 43 (Summer): 49–59.

Nagle, T. 1984. Economic foundations of pricing. *Journal of Business*. In this issue.

Narasimhan, C. 1982. Coupons as price discrimination devices: A theoretical perspective and empirical evidence. Working Paper. Chicago: University of Chicago, Graduate School of Business, July.

Nelson, J. P. 1982. Estimating demand functions for product characteristics: Comment. *Journal of Consumer Research* 9 (September): 219–20.

Newbery, D. M. G. 1978. Stochastic limit pricing. *Bell Journal of Economics* 10 (Spring): 260–69.

Oren, S. S.; Smith, S. A.; and Wilson, R. B. 1982. Nonlinear pricing in markets with interdependent demand. *Marketing Science* 1 (Summer): 287–313.

Oren, S. S.; Smith, S. A.; and Wilson, R. B. 1984. Pricing a product line. *Journal of Business*. In this issue.

Oxenfeldt, A. R. 1960. A multi-stage approach to pricing. *Harvard Business Review* 38 (July/August): 125–33.

Oxenfeldt, A. R. 1966. Product line pricing. *Harvard Business Review* 44 (July): 137–44.

Oxenfeldt, A. R. 1973. A decision-making structure for price decisions. *Journal of Marketing* 37 (January): 48–53.

Park, W., and Winter, F. 1979. Product quality judgments: Information processing approach. *Journal of the Market Research Society* 21 (July): 211–17.

Rao, A. G., and Shakun, M. F. 1972. Quasi game theory approach to pricing. *Management Science* 18 (January): 110–23.

Rao, V. R. 1971. Salience of price in the perception of product quality: A multidimensional measurement approach. *Marketing in Motion/Relevance in Marketing*. Chicago: American Marketing Association.

Rao, V. R., and Gautschi, D. A. 1982. The role of price in individual utility judgments: Development and empirical validation of alternative models. *Choice Models for Buyer Behavior*. Greenwich, Conn.: JAI.

Rao, V. R., and Sabavala, D. J. 1980. Allocation of marketing resources: The role of price promotions. In R. L. Leone (ed.), *Proceedings of the Second Market Measurement Conference*, Providence, R.I.: TIMS College of Marketing and the Institute of Managment Sciences.

Rao, V. R., and Thomas, L. J. 1973. Dynamic models for sales promotion policies. *Operational Research Quarterly* 24 (March): 403–17.

Ratchford, B. T., and Agarwal, M. K. 1982. Estimating demand functions for product characteristics: Reply. *Journal of Consumer Research* 9 (September): 221–24.

Reibstein, D. J., and Gatignon, H. 1982. Optimal product line pricing: The influence of elasticities and cross-elasticities. Working Paper. Philadelphia: University of Pennsylvania, Wharton School, November.

Riesz, P. C. 1980. A major price-perceived quality study re-examined. *Journal of Marketing Research* 17 (May): 259–62.

Robinson, B., and Lakhani, C. 1975. Dynamic pricing models for new product pricing. *Management Science* 21 (June): 1113–22.

Rosen, S. 1974. Hedonic prices and implicit markets: Product differentiation in pure competition. *Journal of Political Economy* 82 (January/February): 34–55.

Schmalensee, R. 1981. Monopolistic two-part pricing arrangements. *Bell Journal of Economics* 12 (Autumn): 445–66.

Schmalensee, R. 1982. Commodity bundling by single-product monopolies. *Journal of Law and Economics* 25 (April): 67–72.

Scitovsky, T. 1944–45. Some consequences of the habit of judging quality by price. *Review of Economic Studies* 12:100–105.

Shapiro, B. P., and Jackson, B. B. 1978. Industrial pricing. *Harvard Business Review* 56 (November/December): 119–27.

Sherman, R., and Visscher, M. 1982. Nonprice rationing and monopoly price structures when demand is stochastic. *Bell Journal of Economics* 13 (Spring): 254–62.

Simon, H. 1979. Dynamics of price elasticity and brand life cycles: An empirical study. *Journal of Marketing Research* 16 (November): 439–52.

Srinivasan, V. 1982. Comments on the role of price in individual utility judgements. *Choice Models for Buyer Behavior*. Greenwich, Conn.: JAI.

Stephenson, R. P.; Cron, W. L.; and Frazier, G. L. 1979. Delegating pricing authority to the sales force: The effects on sales and profit performance. *Journal of Marketing* 43 (Spring): 21–28.

Stobaugh, R. B., and Townsend, P. L. 1975. Price forecasting and strategic planning: The case of petrochemicals. *Journal of Marketing Research* 12 (February): 19–29.

Stokey, N. L. 1981. Rational expectations and durable goods pricing. *Bell Journal of Economics* 12 (Spring): 112–28.

Thaler, R. 1982. Using mental accounting in a theory of purchasing behavior. Working Paper no. 82-16. Ithaca, N.Y.: Cornell University, Graduate School of Business and Public Administration, April.

Thompson, G. L., and Teng, J. T. 1981. Optimal pricing and advertising policies for new product oligopoly models. Working Paper. Pittsburgh: Carnegie-Mellon University, Graduate School of Industrial Administration, August.

Wheatley, J., and Chiu, J. S. 1977. The effects of price, store image and product and respondent characteristics on perceptions of quality. *Journal of Marketing Research* 14 (May): 181–87.

Wittink, D. R. 1977. Exploring territorial differences in the relationship between marketing variables. *Journal of Marketing Research* 14 (May): 145–55.

Zusman, P., and Etgar, M. 1981. The marketing channel as an equilibrium set of contracts. *Management Science* 27 (March): 284–302.

SECTION I
Management of the Distribution Function

Distribution has also been a neglected area of emphasis and importance in marketing. This is partly explained by the fact that physical distribution and logistics have become highly specialized and automated functions that require a separate department. It is also partly due to the fact that there is far more third-party distribution and selling than direct dealing with the end users. Marketing has tended to focus on the channels of distribution, including the issues of channel selection, channel conflict, and channel power.

In our opinion, the third *P* of marketing, namely place, includes more than channel arrangements and channel relationships. In particular, marketing practitioners must pay attention to the following aspects of place.

First, it is becoming increasingly important to bridge the time gap between customer order and order fulfillment. For example, in a time-driven society, customers are less willing to wait than they were. This means "just in time" delivery systems must be created. For example, credit approval and verification should be almost instantaneous, rather than taking several minutes, hours, or in some cases, days. It also means that the customer should not wait for weeks to get his or her medical appointments. Finally, it means the use of electronic shopping and direct shipment to the customer's doorstep.

Second, it is also important to realize that no sale is final. It is, therefore, not sufficient to think that the distribution function is fulfilled with the delivery of the product or service. All the necessary post-sale services must be provided by the distribution channel, including proper installation, maintenance, reporting, or instructions necessary for consumption of the product or service.

Finally, it is the responsibility of the distribution channel, whether direct or indirect, to become the listening post of consumer complaints and concerns. The greater the distance between the producer and the consumer, the greater the need to create a listening post.

31 Get Leverage from Logistics

Roy D. Shapiro

Reprinted by permission of the *Harvard Business Review*. "Get Leverage from Logistics" by Roy D. Shapiro (May–June 1984). Copyright © 1984 by the President and Fellows of Harvard College; all rights reserved.

- After watching both its competitive position and profits erode steadily for several years, a manufacturer of consumer durables restructured its logistics system. This restructuring included a consolidation of distribution centers, a 50% reduction of investment in finished goods inventory, a centralization of the purchasing and materials management functions, a switch to intermodal truck and rail transport combinations, and a change in pricing policy to encourage customers to order full truckload shipments.

    These changes prompted a shift in the company's customer base from dealers who ordered in small quantities and required "when needed" delivery to dealers for whom larger orders at lower cost made sense. At first, market share decreased as short-term profits rose. Within two years, however, increased order volumes started to raise market share while profits remained strong.

- During the mid-1970s, a multifacility metals service center came under mounting competitive pressure from smaller local companies as well as from a large outfit that served the entire region with a narrow product line from one central site. Reacting aggressively, the multifacility center achieved a better record of on-time deliveries by boosting its number of branch warehouses and the level of finished goods inventory while cutting the market area served by each warehouse. In addition, the company extended its product lines to ensure full-line availability to its customers.

    These logistics choices were expensive, but they led to a higher market share among those customers who ordered frequently and in small quantities and who were willing to pay premium prices because the steel they ordered was a small percentage of their costs.

- Also in the mid-1970s, a broad-line producer of disposable medical supplies like catheters began to fall behind the industry's rapid growth. Product proliferation and waning control over its far-flung network of more than 20 distribution centers lay at the heart of the company's problem. Excess inventories played havoc with margins, and frequent stockouts pushed irate customers into the arms of competitors. Management consolidated operations in four distribution centers, an action that cut both total finished goods inventory and the likelihood of future stockouts. Simultaneously, management turned to air freight for most deliveries so as to ensure rapid response to customer orders.

Management viewed this consolidation not only as a way of reducing costs and gaining efficiency but also as a way of gaining control over a rapidly changing product line in a market characterized by fluctuating demand. Customers agreed. Growth got quickly back on track.

Each of these companies used its logistics system to gain competitive advantage, yet each chose a different way of doing so—by designing its logistics system and operating policies to fit carefully a chosen competitive strategy. That "fit" is the subject of this article.

Much as with Wickham Skinner's notion of the "focused factory," no single logistics system can do everything well.[1] Trade-offs are inevitable, for example, among considerations of low cost, range of services, and flexibility to changes in product specifications, volume, and customer preferences. Thus, the crucial question for managers is, "What must *our* logistics system do particularly well?"

These important logistical tasks, where a little effort can generate a lot of return, create opportunities for leverage. Identifying such key leverage points is, of course, part and parcel of the broader effort to fit logistics systems to a company's competitive strategy. The choice of an overall competitive focus—product innovation, for example, or superior customer service or cost leadership—sets logistical requirements that, if not explicitly considered in designing the system's trade-offs, can do much to undercut the prior choice of competitive focus. There is, then, much to be gained from successfully applying leverage through logistics—and much to be lost from applying that leverage incorrectly.

PRODUCT INNOVATION

An innovation-based strategy puts a premium on avoiding market saturation and on serving high-income markets with a flow of new, different, and high-performance products. Such a strategy need not be limited to companies in high-technology industries, as the success of consumer goods companies like Gillette or Procter & Gamble attests. What matters is the ability of management to develop the market—first by creating an awareness of the product among potential customers and then by ensuring product availability. The newer the product, the more important it is for customers to have a favorable first experience with it.

As a result, well-run distribution systems, especially those for consumer goods, become critical. If the product is not available, customers cannot make that crucial first purchase. At the same time, of course, retailers and wholesalers invest cautiously in new stock. Their typical orders are small and erratic, and this preference for thin stocks increases the demand for rapid delivery and so puts further strain on the distribution system.

To meet these requirements, a logistics system must ensure continuity of supply from vendors; keep high safety stocks to prevent stockouts; rely on air freight, where possible, to guarantee rapid and consistent delivery; and be able to handle small orders and erratic order frequencies. An innovation-based strategy, however, also entails rapid product change, uncertainty about volumes, low density of demand, and possible shifts in customer preferences. These requirements argue for flexibility in supplier contracts (because raw material specifications may change) and for low levels of investment in inventory (to minimize obsolescence) and in bricks and mortar (at least until stable demand patterns evolve).

Setting inventory policy in this strategic context is especially difficult. Concern for product availability and rapid delivery argues that large stocks be kept near the customer, but rapid product change and fear of obsolescence argue for minimizing inventories. Not surprisingly, this tension necessitates a compromise appropriate to the particular characteristics of both industry and product. The hard part is defining the compromise correctly.

Consider, for example, the phonograph record industry, in which all companies compete through innovation in products with built-in obsolescence. Only one new release in 50 is successful, yet in so fragmented and competitive an industry, product availability is truly essential. Because stockouts during the short period when a record is "hot" can spell failure, most record companies view obsolescence as an unavoidable cost of doing business and provide high safety-stock coverage during the time a release is being heavily promoted.

Exhibit I outlines the policy implications of the most important determinants of such inventory compromises—rate of product change and level of competitive intensity. As described previously, the record industry belongs in the upper right-hand quadrant. In the early 1960s, Xerox—to cite a different example—faced rapid product change yet enjoyed a patent position in its basic technology that guaranteed high entry barriers. Its centralized inventory policy for spare parts fits well in the lower right-hand quadrant. As the expiration of its patent in 1973 approached, however, Xerox foresaw increasing competition. Consequently, it rapidly

31 — Get Leverage from Logistics

EXHIBIT I. Inventory Policies

	Rate of Product Change: Low	Rate of Product Change: High
Competitive Intensity: High	Risk of obsolescence low Need for favorable customer impression high Safety stocks high Some regional or local stocks of finished goods likely, probably at leased or public warehouses to retain maximum flexibility	Risk of obsolescence high Shifts in customer preferences likely "Availability and when needed" delivery can strengthen competitive position Choices depend on specific product characteristics, market needs, and competitors' responses
Competitive Intensity: Low	Risk of obsolescence low Lack of competition lowers buyers' power to demand short lead times Some safety stocks can be carried to cover demand fluctuations Safety stocks will be carried centrally — for low value-added items, most likely in finished goods; for high value-added items, more likely in raw materials or work-in-process	Risk of obsolescence high Shifts in customer preferences likely Limited need for using short lead times to gain and maintain competitive advantage Either produce to order or carry limited inventory centrally (e.g., at the plant)

started to expand its local and regional warehouses in order to build an unassailable nationwide service network.

Recall, if you will, the case of the manufacturer of medical supplies described at the beginning of this article. Management viewed product innovation as the key to success in a high-growth and hotly competitive industry. In an attempt to get its new disposable catheters quickly to a nationwide customer base, the company had established more than 20 warehouses, but new product proliferation and demand uncertainty turned this network of warehouses into a corporate millstone. Inventory carrying costs grew in part due to unanticipated product obsolescence. Nonetheless, demand fluctuations created stockouts that could be filled only by disrupting the plant's production schedule so often that effective capacity plummeted and shipments fell further and further behind.

At last, management realized that fast transport by air could guarantee timely delivery. Local inventories were unnecessary in all markets; in fact, when the dust had settled, only four warehouses remained. Reduced inventory carrying costs more than offset increases in transport costs, and both obsolescence and local demand fluctuations became easier to handle.

Far too often, managers think an effective logistics system can provide benefits only through cost cutting. For companies following a strategy of innovation, however, other factors are often more important than straight cost reduction. Still, in their preoccupation with R&D, marketing and sales, and production—"getting the product out the door" once orders come in—managers commonly forget the real leverage in logistics. Worse, they approach logistics in a purely tactical, cost-minimizing fashion.

Listen, instead, to what Daniel T. Carroll, then president of Gould, told a 1978 meeting of the company's division general managers:

"If [you] really want to get scared, . . . remember that we spen[d] $12 million a year on new product R&D. Do you know the easiest way to bomb a new product? Poor materials management—you can't get the right materials or the quality is off or you can't get the product through the factory or you can't coordinate transportation and distribution to get the product into the hands of the customer. I would be willing to bet that substantially greater than half of all new product failures are not because the technology or market strategy is deficient, they're because people don't pay enough attention to materials management."[2]

CUSTOMER SERVICE

All differentiation-based strategies involve providing the market with a bundle of products and related services that is—or appears to the market—unique. One common differentiation strategy, followed by Coca-Cola and Colgate-Palmolive, relies on heavy advertising and other marketing expenditures to develop brand identification. Another, followed by Braun in small appliances and Mercedes-Benz in automobiles, emphasizes product performance. A third, exemplified by Xerox's response to the approaching expiration of its patent, uses logistics to provide superior customer service.

In practice, of course, the problem is that service can mean many different things. Before managers can answer the question, "What does our logistics system have to do especially well?" they must first decide what service is to be delivered—short delivery lead times, for example, or broad-line availability or consistent performance or responsiveness and flexibility to buyer needs.

How can managers use the structure and operating policies of a logistics system to support the needs of their customers? In the first place, they can do business with suppliers who themselves provide consistent delivery, product availability, and fast response. They can also employ local inventories (for example, by using public warehouses) to provide market presence and rapid delivery, even though such inventories need not imply excessive investment in an elaborate network of facilities. And they can establish a two- or three-tiered transport system, with short-haul arrangements for transport from local warehouses to customers, long-haul arrangements (in efficient full truckload or carload quantities) for restocking the local warehouses from regional or national facilities, and a network for emergency shipments.

Rather than pay the price for such a wide range of logistics-based services, many companies choose to focus their differentiation strategies on a more cost-effective subset of services. One key choice of focus is that between providing full-line availability and quick, consistent delivery. As illustrated schematically by *Exhibit II*, this choice has major implications for both inventory and product line policy.

Dimensions of Service

The vertical axis of *Exhibit II* captures where in the logistics pipeline inventory is to be carried. In general, the spectrum of approaches included here involves different degrees of "postponement" (make to order) and "speculation" (make to stock). The horizontal axis speaks to product-line breadth: Do we focus our resources on a narrow line or serve the entire market with a full line? All too commonly, managers decide on a product line or inventory location policy without paying adequate attention to how the interaction of the two is crucial to the effectiveness of a logistics system.

That interaction gives rise to the four generic modes of operation illustrated by *Exhibit II*:

Full Service. Two factors combine to drive costs here above those in any other quadrant: one, a broad product line requires more frequent changeovers and shorter production runs, both of which raise production costs; and two, higher levels of finished goods inventory, especially when coupled with product proliferation, boost inventory carrying costs. Still, for companies following a full-service strategy, these are necessary costs of doing business.

As an executive of a major appliance manufacturer observed, "Think about the emergency replacement market [for refrigerators]. If your refrigerator goes, you need a new one, and you need it *now*. And, if your kitchen is done in flamingo decor, you want a flamingo refrigerator. If we don't have one, you'll go somewhere else."

Low Cost. A strategy of offering neither product customization nor rapid delivery is, obviously, inappropriate for a company wishing to differentiate itself or its product in terms of service. It is, however, appropriate when the strategy is to be the low-cost producer, where differentiation of other than service dimensions is possible (for example, providing applications engineering consultation). It is also appropriate

EXHIBIT II. Where in the Logistics Pipeline Is Inventory Carried?

Increasing degree of "speculation" (vertical axis, top):
- Decentralized stocks of finished goods
- Centralized stocks of finished goods
- Inventory carried as work-in-process
- Raw materials stocked in quantity at the plant(s)
- Raw materials held by suppliers
- No inventory carried by channel

Increasing degree of "postponement" (vertical axis, bottom).

Increasing breadth of product lines (horizontal axis): Narrow line → Broad line

	Narrow line	Broad line
(top)	**Narrow line short lead time** Low production costs High inventory costs Service provided: Short delivery lead times Consistent delivery	**Full service** High production costs High inventory costs Service provided: Quick, consistent delivery Availability "One-stop" shopping
(bottom)	**Low cost** Low production costs Low inventory costs Service provided: Neither choice nor short lead times Rarely appropriate for the company that competes through customer services	**Full line long lead time** High production costs Low inventory costs Service provided: Availability "One-stop" shopping

where—as in the old days of the telephone industry—the intensity of competition is sufficiently low and barriers to entry sufficiently high that offering limited service does not provoke fear of retaliation.

Narrow Line. Companies following a low-cost strategy rely much less on logistics systems than on efficient production for competitive leverage. Those following a strategy of focused service, however, usually seek a moderate cost position while emphasizing a particular aspect of service. A narrow-line strategy trades off product-line breadth for low cost and rapid delivery, much as Ford rather emphatically did with the Model T in the early 1920s.

A less extreme example of this strategy is provided by the sound profitability and fast growth of Martin-Brower, now the third largest food distributor in the United States. Unlike most food distributors, which compete on the basis of full-line service and rapid delivery, Martin-Brower has restricted its customer list to eight large fast-food chains and stocks only their narrow product lines.

Full Line. By contrast, some companies choose to sacrifice quick delivery capability for product customization. Good examples here are mail-order operations like that of Sears and highly customized job shop operations like Avery Label's custom-printing business, National Lead's oil well products and services, and the commercial telephone systems industry.

Some batch manufacturers follow an important variant of this strategy. Rather than incur the exorbitant costs associated with production of each order as it comes in, these companies will often batch incoming orders (by model, size, or type) until enough have accumulated to warrant an efficient production run. This approach requires some inventory of raw materials. Alternatively, a company may carry standardized work-in-process inventory "upstream"—as U.S. automakers have done for years—and wait until orders come before assembling components into customized end products.

The metals service center described earlier successfully used logistics to pursue a strategy based on customer service. In the mid-1970s, McKinley Metals (not its real name) served a ten-state region of the western United States with four warehouses. Its largest competitor served the same region with a narrow line from a single large warehouse. Competition also came from several small local centers, each operating a single facility serving a single metropolitan area. McKinley was caught in the middle: its logistics system could not achieve the cost position of its prime competitor, nor could it boast the market presence or rapid delivery of the local centers.

McKinley acted to differentiate itself by providing *both* rapid delivery and broad-line availability—that is, by placing itself firmly in the "full-service" quadrant of *Exhibit II*. It opened four additional warehouses to make overnight deliveries possible for a larger part of its market and expanded its product line. Because a logistics system of this sort was expensive, McKinley aimed its services at end-users, especially those in high-tech industries, for whom steel was a small percentage of overall costs. The company kept costs in line by centralizing procurement and carefully coordinating its transport fleet.

The strategy worked. During the recession of 1981–1982, McKinley prospered while its major competitor suffered losses and several of the local service centers went under. With interest rates breaking 20%, steel users cut both inventories and order sizes. A company able to cope with frequent small orders and the need for immediate delivery was in great demand. McKinley had built its logistics system so that it was such a company.

COST LEADERSHIP

From the mid-1970s on, soaring costs of energy, raw materials, transportation, and capital have made an overall strategy of cost leadership increasingly attractive. As a result, managers have turned to logistics in the fight against eroding margins. And rightly so—on average, logistics costs eat up more than 21¢ of every U.S. sales dollar.

How can a company design its logistics system and associated operating policies to minimize cost while keeping service at an acceptable level? Most obviously, by making use of scale economies that arise from high production volumes, volume discounts in purchasing, and shipping full truckloads or rail carloads of goods. One major carmaker, for example, has established 14 centers across the United States to consolidate small shipments of raw materials and components from its more than 2,000 suppliers into full truckloads or carloads for transport to its various assembly plants.

Then, too, companies can centralize inventories as much as possible, especially for low-volume items, in a manner that is consistent with required levels of service. Montgomery Ward recognized that nationwide inventory reductions could be achieved by consolidating all slower moving items into one central warehouse seven miles from Chicago's O'Hare Airport. Lower carrying costs far outweigh higher transport charges from airfreighting items when rapid delivery is essential.

Another relevant tactic is to strive for the lowest cost routing of products from plants to warehouses to customers. This tactic is often of great importance to large companies late in their life cycles, when service has grown spotty and geographic expansion and multiple levels of warehouses have created a logistics nightmare.

In 1978 International Paper had 20 million acres of woodland and operated 124 manufacturing facilities and some 100 storage and transfer facilities in North America, France, Italy, and Brazil. Its network of raw materials suppliers and customers was world-wide in scope. An optimization-based system allowed it to rationalize this multifacility operational structure to ensure cost-efficiency—a task that would have been impossible without such a logistics-based decision aid.

Finally, companies can automate materials handling and order processing as much as is consistent with customer needs and the physical characteristics of the product.

True, the kind of cost-efficient system just detailed is rationalized, centralized, tightly coordinated, and inflexible. But since the choice of a low-cost strategy position is typically made late in a product's life cycle, customer preferences and product specifications have stabilized, and there is little uncertainty about overall volumes or demand patterns. Flexibility is, therefore, of less value than it would be earlier in the life cycle.

As the consumer durables manufacturer discussed earlier matured, it failed to become cost effective in a market where sophisticated buyers increasingly demanded lower prices. Management had tried to achieve a low-cost position by integrating vertically into metal fabrication and plastic-injection molding and by automating much of its production process. The resulting high quality and lower production costs should have given the company a competitive advantage, but its distribution system, which had been designed to provide short lead times, no longer suited a market that now prized low cost.

Market share and profitability continued to erode, as larger dealers, for whom cost was important, took their business elsewhere. With a manufacturing system and a distribution system pulling in different directions—the first toward a position of cost leadership, the second toward excellent, but high-cost, service—conditions rapidly deteriorated. As described earlier, management finally restructured the logistics system to achieve as low a cost as possible at a "reasonable" level of service. This new, coherent strategy paid off.

For logistics systems designed to support a strategy of overall cost leadership, the key management task is not just to get the elements of the system right. It is also to locate logistics planning in the appropriate organizational context. A low-cost strategy, for example, requires that such planning be designed, controlled, and administered as a centralized staff function. By contrast, innovation- and differentiation-based strategies, for which cost minimization is not a primary goal, require that line management be involved in the design and administration of the logistics system.

THE RIGHT FIT

In the preceding pages I have tried to show how a company might gain leverage by ensuring a good fit between its logistics system and its

EXHIBIT III. Leverage Through Logistics

Chosen Modes of Competition	Product Innovation	Customer Service	Cost Leadership
Goals of logistics system	Availability Flexibility to volume shifts Flexibility to product changes Ability to handle small orders Ability to handle erratic order frequencies	Rapid delivery Consistent delivery Availability Flexibility to customer changes	Minimum cost with an "acceptable" service level
Locus of planning			Staff
Procurement	Line management Seek vendors who can ensure: Supply continuity Quality Flexibility to changes in specifications	Line management Seek vendors who can ensure: Consistent delivery Full-line availability Responsiveness	Make maximum use of volume purchase economies Centralized purchasing organization Seek vendors offering low prices
Inventory policy	Tension between the need for high safety stocks kept locally to ensure availability and the need to keep inventories low to retain flexibility and guard against obsolescence: a compromise between these two extremes is required; the form of that compromise will depend on a variety of technological, physical, economic and competitive factors; most important are pace of product change and competitive intensity	For the company that produces to inventory, local inventories will be required for "market presence" and rapid, consistent delivery	Investment in inventory at minimal levels that ensure "acceptable" service
Transport policy	Premium, rapid transport (air freight if sensible) Use of common carrier rather than investment in private fleet LTL* shipments common	For normal supply, a mix of short-haul LTL* (for customer delivery) and long-haul TL** or CL† (for warehouse restocking) Emergency shipment network planned and available when needed Private fleet may be necessary for service (especially short-haul)	Low-cost transport (rail and/or piggyback) High utilization (full TL** or rail carload shipments) Volume discounts to encourage direct-from-the-plant, full-carload shipments Private fleet may be desirable for better control, lower transport costs
Facilities network	Almost nonexistent in most cases—delivery from plant to customer When warehouses required, public or leased warehouses used	For the company that produces to inventory, a multiechelon system (plant or national warehouses, regional warehouses, local warehouses) will be likely	Centralized Consolidated (minimize number of local facilities) Rationalized (number, size, scale) and sourcing decisions made to minimize costs Automated as much as is sensible

*LTL = less-than-truckload **TL = truckload †CL = carload

competitive strategy. *Exhibit III* summarizes the operational details of that fit. The three major examples cited illustrate the practical value such leverage can have.

But these companies are the successes. For much of U.S. industry, logistics remains a second-class citizen and a logistics strategy at best an afterthought. In today's competitive environment, such neglect is no longer tolerable. As Bernard LaLonde of Ohio State University has remarked, "American management's philosophy has typically been: 'If you're smart enough to make it, aggressive enough to sell it — then any dummy can get it there!' And now we're paying for [that philosophy]."[3]

ENDNOTES

1. See Wickham Skinner, "The Focused Factory," *HBR* May–June 1974, p. 113.
2. See Gould (A), Harvard Business School Case Services, 9-678-184 (Boston, Mass.: 1978), p. 1.
3. As quoted by James C. Johnson and Donald F. Wood, in *Contemporary Physical Distribution and Logistics* (Tulsa, Okla.: Pennwell Books, 1982), p. 3.

32 — Perspectives for Distribution Programming

Bert C. McCammon, Jr.

Vertical Marketing Systems, edited by L. Bucklin (Glenview, IL: Scott, Foresman and Company, 1970), pp. 32–50. Reprinted by permission.

Manufacturing executives tend to view distribution programming—the development of a comprehensive set of policies for the promotion of a product through the channel—as a secondary or tertiary area of decision making. The result is that many "programs" consist of hastily improvised trade deals, uninspired dealer contests, and unexamined discount structures. A variety of factors suggests that this traditional attitude toward distribution programming is a luxury that no longer can be easily afforded.

Two interconnected developments are particularly relevant in this regard. First, the structure of intermediate markets has undergone a series of remarkable transformations in recent years. Second, there has been an increasing pressure upon profits in these markets. When these factors are combined with the emergence of more manufacturing firms in many industries with competitive technological, production, and promotional expertise, the need for more skillful distribution programming appears. For the manufacturer, complete reliance upon traditional strategies involving product innovations, manufacturing efficiencies, and differentiated advertising campaigns to maintain satisfactory profit levels is no longer possible. Increasing weight must be shifted to distribution programming, yet the changes occurring in the distributive sector require enlightened planning to elicit the cooperation required.

The primary purpose of this paper is to discuss relevant perspectives for distribution decisions, with particular emphasis upon the manufacturer's relationships with its retailers. More precisely, the initial section of this paper will explore a general framework which may be used by the manufacturer to outline the factors he must consider in developing policy. The second and third sections will examine the economic and structural changes occurring in the distributive trades and creative reactions to these developments.

THE FORMULATION OF DISTRIBUTION POLICIES

The executive responsible for formulating distribution policies must consider the firm's marketing goals, its channel requirements, and re-

EXHIBIT 1. A Frame of Reference for Distribution Programming

Manufacturer's Marketing Goals

Based on a careful analysis of:
- corporate capability
- competition
- demand
- cost-volume relationships
- legal considerations
- reseller capability

and stated in terms of:
- sales (dollars and units)
- market share
- contribution to overhead
- rate of return on investment
- customer attitude, preference and "readiness-to-buy" indices

Manufacturer's Channel Requirements

Reseller support needed to achieve marketing goals (stated in terms of):
- coverage ratio
- amount and location of display space
- level and composition of inventory investment
- service capability and standards
- advertising, sales promotion, and personal selling support
- market development activities

Retailer's Requirements

"Compensation" expected for required support (stated in terms of):
- managerial aspirations
- trade preferences
- financial goals
    - rate of inventory turnover
    - rate of return on investment
    - gross margin (dollars and percent)
    - contribution to overhead (dollars and percent)
    - gross margin and contribution to overhead per dollar invested in inventory
    - gross margin and contribution to overhead per unit of space
- nonfinancial goals

Distribution Policies
- "Price" concessions
- Financial assistance
- Protective provisions

---

tailer expectations. The relationship between these factors is schematically diagrammed in Exhibit 1.

A growing number of firms have accepted the premise that all marketing activities should be designed to achieve carefully identified and precisely stated goals. These objectives—stated in terms of target market share, desired sales volume, expected rate of return on investment, and other criteria of corporate performance—should be realistically based on a detailed analysis of the company's strengths and weaknesses, prevailing demand patterns, competitive conditions, cost-volume relationships, and retailer capability. Having delineated appropriate goals, the executive must then identify: (1) the amount of trade support needed to achieve them, and (2) the "compensation" expected by retailers for providing this support. More specifically, the executive must determine the firm's channel requirements and the payment expected by retailers for satisfying these requirements. It is within this context that distribution policies are meaningful, since they are designed to produce a pattern of behavior in the distribution network that simultaneously satisfies supplier and trade objectives.

Manufacturer's Channel Requirements

The basic issues in this area revolve around questions such as the following:

1. What percentage and which types of outlets in a given line of trade are required to achieve a specified level of brand sales?
2. How much retail display space is needed to produce a stipulated share of industry sales and where should such space be located in stocking outlets?
3. What is the optimal relationship between trade inventories (in dollar and units) and total product category volume?
4. How much local advertising, sales promotion, and personal selling is needed to produce an optimal cost-volume relationship for a specified brand?

Answers to issues such as these provide the basis for precisely specifying the amount of trade support needed to achieve selected marketing goals. Without such data it is difficult to determine which distribution alternatives are most appropriate. The lack of much published research on these questions, and similar ones, suggests again the lack of depth that has historically plagued distribution programs.

Retailer's Requirements

Retailers carry a product line or brand because it satisfies their operating objectives. Furthermore, they support those lines or brands that produce the most attractive results. The decision-making process underlying these choices is a fairly complicated one, but there are at least four variables that are particularly relevant from the manufacturer's point of view.

First, there is the question of entrepreneurial aspirations. An impressive number of studies indicate that small retailers in particular have relatively static expectations. They apparently strive to achieve and maintain a given level of sales and profits, and once this scale is reached, they are relatively uninterested in expansion. Such entrepreneurs *are* interested in simplifying their operations, however, and they are likely to give preferential treatment to suppliers that have easy-to-administer distribution programs. Suppliers with such programs often increase their market share, even though the retailers involved are uninterested in expansions per se. Other retailers are growth-oriented, of course, and thus their frame of reference parallels that of most marketing executives in manufacturing concerns.

Second, the executive responsible for policy decisions should be aware of deeply entrenched trade preferences for certain distribution policies as opposed to others. Ready-to-wear retailers, for example, are almost unanimously opposed to any kind of net pricing program. They much prefer to receive a standard trade discount and an "inflated" cash discount of eight percent, since the latter is perceived to be a cushion against buying mistakes as well as an important source of profits. Thus, ready-to-wear retailers resist any pricing scheme that would incorporate trade and cash discounts in a net price quotation, even though the resulting net price is equivalent to the combined discounts currently received. In similar fashion many carpet retailers prefer to receive volume rebates on an annual rather than on a quarterly basis, because they apparently enjoy receiving one sizable check rather than several smaller ones throughout the year. Franchised car dealers are strongly in favor of the holdback discount programs initiated in the automobile industry several years ago. Dealers argue that these programs tend to stabilize retail prices and partially guarantee profits. Thus they oppose any plan in which all discounts are given immediately rather than reserving some of them for distribution at the end of the accounting period. From an "outsider's" point of view, these trade positions appear to be somewhat illogical, but they exist, they are strongly held, and it would probably be fruitless for a single supplier to attempt to change them. Manufacturer distribution policies should therefore be based on an awareness of what appear to be idiosyncratic trade preferences.

Third, the executive responsible for formulating distribution policies should be intimately acquainted with the retailer's financial objectives, the peculiarities of his accounting system, and the criteria he uses to guide decisions. A growing number of retailers are establishing financial goals for major product categories that are stated in terms of target rates of inventory turnover, desired gross margins (in dollars and percent) and other "profitability" criteria. Significantly, such criteria are becoming more sophisticated from an analytical point of view, and suppliers marketing product lines producing substandard results are experiencing increased difficulty in obtaining even minimum trade support. Furthermore, it now appears that relatively small firms will soon have "affordable" access to computer programs which will provide detailed information on product flow and item profitability. Thus distribution policies designed to satisfy trade expectations will be even more important in the future than they are today.

Fourth, manufacturer distribution policies should be based on an awareness of the retailer's nonfinancial objectives. Many retailers, as an illustration, promote an "unprofitable" product line if it contributes to the firm's fashion image, generates customer traffic, facilitates an even distribution of traffic throughout the store, or otherwise contributes to the achievement of goals that are essentially nonfinancial in nature, but important to the firm's long-run survival. Thus, distribution programs may succeed, despite their limited profit potential, if they contribute to the solution of important merchandising problems.

Developing Trade Support

Distribution policies are exclusively and explicitly designed to secure the quantity and quality of trade support needed to market a manufacturer's product line. From the manufacturer's point of view, distribution policies involve trade "concessions" that are required to insure the performance of necessary marketing functions. Retailers are equally interested in manufacturer distribution policies because they affect the merchant's revenue and cost structure.

Distribution policies vary widely between and within industries because they are frequently used by manufacturers to gain a differential advantage over their competitors. Despite the diversity of policy alternatives, they can be divided into three categories—price concessions, financial assistance, and protective provisions—which are schematically diagrammed in Exhibit 2.

First, manufacturers may attempt to secure trade support by offering *price concessions* to retailers that take the form of discounts or discount substitutes. The former affect the retailer's cost of goods sold and gross margin, while the latter affect his operating expenses. For example, a distribution programmer might increase his company's trade discount by five percentage points to secure greater retailer cooperation, or he might grant equivalent concessions by partially underwriting local advertising programs, by paying in-store demonstrators' salaries, or by agreeing to premark merchandise. In the first instance the retailer's cost of goods sold would decline, and in the second instance his operating expenses would decrease, with both types of concessions having the same effect on profitability. Thus, discount substitutes may be viewed as a price concession that affects the retailer's operating expenses rather than his cost of goods sold.

Second, manufacturers can secure trade cooperation by providing *financial assistance* in the form of conventional lending arrangements or extended dating. In either case the manufacturer partially finances the retailer's operation which presumably results in stronger trade support and heavier field inventories.

EXHIBIT 2. Selected Distribution Policy Alternatives

I. "Price" Concessions
   A. Discount Structure:
       trade (functional) discounts
       quantity discounts
       cash discounts
       anticipation allowances
       free goods
       prepaid freight
       new product, display, and advertising allowances (without performance requirements)
       seasonal discounts
       mixed carload privilege
       drop shipping privilege
       trade deals
   B. Discount Substitutes:
       display materials
       premarked merchandise
       inventory control programs
       catalogs and sales promotion literature
       training programs
       shelf-stocking programs
       advertising matrices
       management consulting services
       merchandising programs
       sales "spiffs"
       technical assistance
       payment of sales personnel and demonstrator salaries
       promotional and advertising allowances (with performance requirements)

II. Financial Assistance
   A. Conventional Lending Arrangements:
       term loans
       inventory floor plans
       notes payable financing
       accounts payable financing
       installment financing of fixtures and equipment
       lease and note guarantee programs
       accounts receivable financing
   B. Extended Dating:
       E.O.M. dating
       seasonal dating
       R.O.G. dating
       "extra" dating
       post dating

III. Protective Provisions
   A. Price Protection:
       premarked merchandise
       fair trade
       "franchise" pricing
       agency agreements
   B. Inventory Protection:
       consignment selling
       memorandum selling
       liberal returns allowances
       rebate programs
       reorder guarantees
       guaranteed support of sales events
       maintenance of "spot" stocks and fast delivery
   C. Territorial Protection:
       selective distribution
       exclusive distribution

Third, manufacturers can strengthen their relationship with the trade by *protecting retailers against the risks of doing business*. Lines distributed on a selective basis are given preferential treatment by many retailers, and inventory and price protection programs are often equally well received. In effect, such concessions make the retailer's profits more certain and are attractive to the trade for this reason. How these various policies may be applied in the development of successful distribution programs may now be considered in the light of the economic and structural changes affecting the intermediate markets.

THE CHANGING ECONOMICS OF RETAILING

The changing economics of retailing can be effectively analyzed in the context of the accountant's long-run profit model, the principal components of which are as follows:

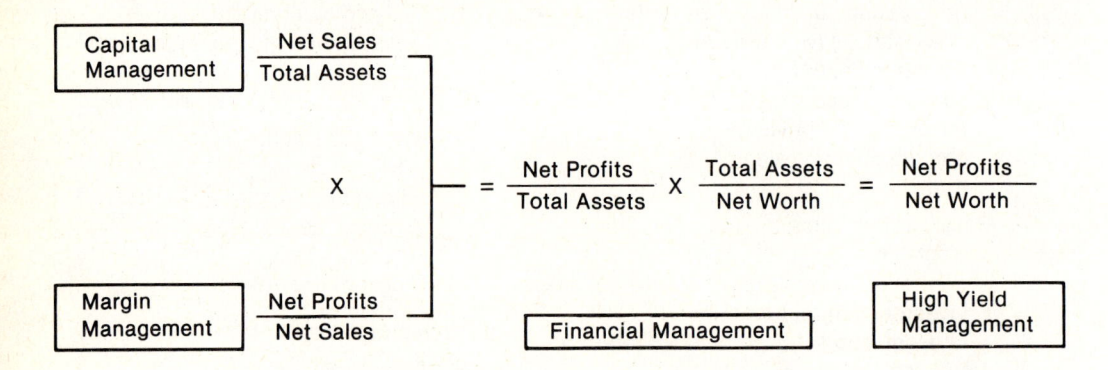

$$\text{Capital Management}: \frac{\text{Net Sales}}{\text{Total Assets}} \times \frac{\text{Net Profits}}{\text{Net Sales}} \text{ (Margin Management)} = \frac{\text{Net Profits}}{\text{Total Assets}} \times \frac{\text{Total Assets}}{\text{Net Worth}} \text{ (Financial Management)} = \frac{\text{Net Profits}}{\text{Net Worth}} \text{ (High Yield Management)}$$

The long-run profit model has four important managerial purposes:

1. The model specifies that a firm's principal financial objective is to earn an adequate or target rate of return on net worth.
2. The model identifies the three "profit paths" available to an enterprise. That is, a firm with an inadequate rate of return on net worth can improve its performance by accelerating its rate of asset turnover, by increasing its profit margin, or by leveraging its operations more highly.
3. The model dramatizes the principal areas of decision-making within the firm, namely, capital management, margin management, and financial management. Furthermore, firms interrelating their capital, margin, and financial plans effectively may be described as engaged in the practice of high-yield management.

EXHIBIT 3. Strategic Profit Model for Winn-Dixie Stores, Inc. 1967

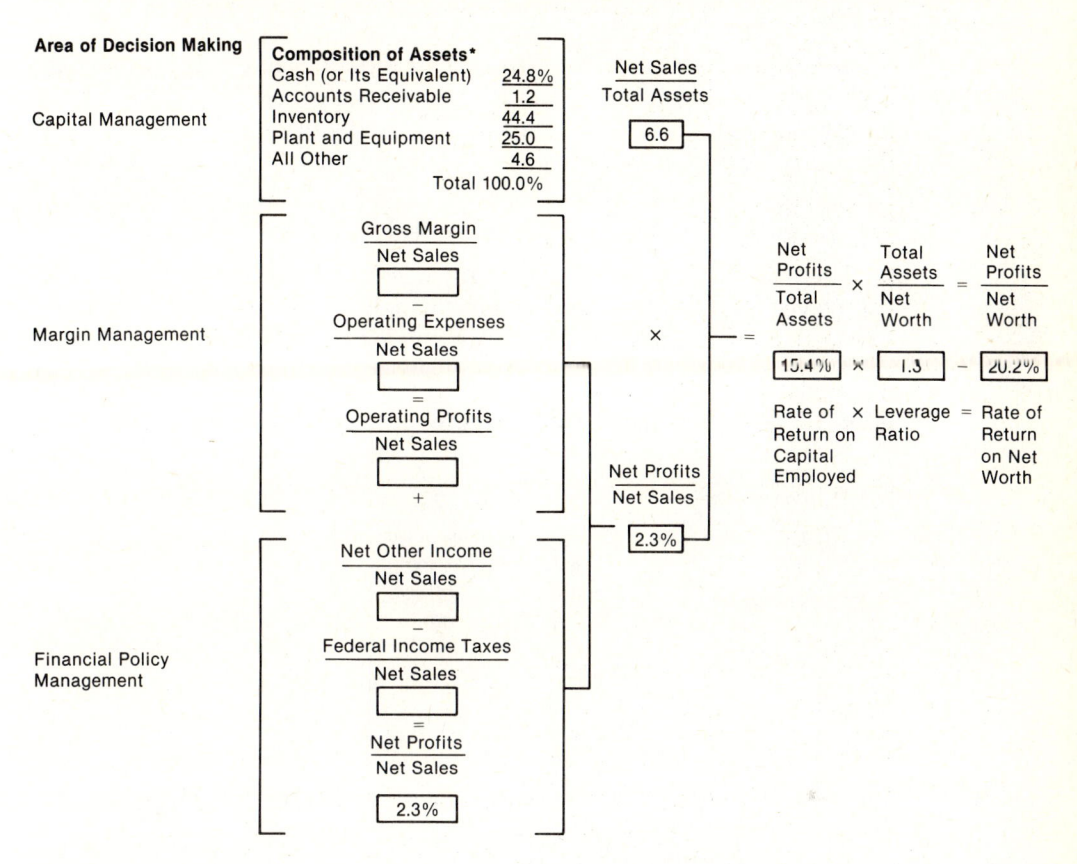

Area of Decision Making		
Capital Management	**Composition of Assets***	
	Cash (or Its Equivalent)	24.8%
	Accounts Receivable	1.2
	Inventory	44.4
	Plant and Equipment	25.0
	All Other	4.6
	Total	100.0%

$$\frac{\text{Net Sales}}{\text{Total Assets}} = 6.6$$

Margin Management:

$$\frac{\text{Gross Margin}}{\text{Net Sales}} - \frac{\text{Operating Expenses}}{\text{Net Sales}} = \frac{\text{Operating Profits}}{\text{Net Sales}}$$

Financial Policy Management:

$$+ \frac{\text{Net Other Income}}{\text{Net Sales}} - \frac{\text{Federal Income Taxes}}{\text{Net Sales}} = \frac{\text{Net Profits}}{\text{Net Sales}} = 2.3\%$$

$$\frac{\text{Net Profits}}{\text{Net Sales}} = 2.3\%$$

$$\frac{\text{Net Profits}}{\text{Total Assets}} \times \frac{\text{Total Assets}}{\text{Net Worth}} = \frac{\text{Net Profits}}{\text{Net Worth}}$$

$$15.4\% \times 1.3 = 20.2\%$$

Rate of Return on Capital Employed × Leverage Ratio = Rate of Return on Net Worth

*Profit model excludes leased equipment, fixtures, and facilities. The model also excludes the capital structure of nonconsolidated subsidiaries.

4. The model provides a useful perspective for appraising the financial strategies used by different organizations to achieve target rates of return on net worth. As indicated in Exhibits 3 and 4, Lucky's and Winn-Dixie, two high-yield food chains, achieve comparable rates of return on net worth.

Their strategies for achieving this goal, however, are quite dissimilar. Winn-Dixie is conservatively financed and thus must rely on a high-asset turnover rate and a high-profit margin to achieve a rate of return on net worth in excess of 20 percent. Lucky's, on the other hand, uses a discount merchandising format to achieve target results and therefore programs its operation to spin off a relatively narrow profit margin, which is offset by an adventuresome leverage ratio.

In sum, the accountant's long-run profit model is a versatile, analytical device for programming retail operations and for evaluating the results achieved. More importantly, this model will be used as a basis for evaluating the changing economics of retailing in the paragraphs that follow.

Financial Performance of Retailing Corporations

The "profit squeeze" in retailing has been widely discussed and extensively deplored by merchants and analysts alike. Certainly, Internal Revenue Service data provide support for this widespread concern.

EXHIBIT 4. Strategic Profit Model for Lucky Stores, Inc. 1967

Area of Decision Making

Capital Management

Composition of Assets*
Cash (or Its Equivalent)	10.9%
Accounts Receivable	2.4
Inventory	30.1
Plant and Equipment	25.4
All Other	31.2
Total	100.0%

$\dfrac{\text{Net Sales}}{\text{Total Assets}} = 5.2$

Margin Management

$\dfrac{\text{Gross Margin}}{\text{Net Sales}}$

$-$

$\dfrac{\text{Operating Expenses}}{\text{Net Sales}}$

$=$

$\dfrac{\text{Operating Profits}}{\text{Net Sales}}$

$+$

Financial Policy Management

$\dfrac{\text{Net Other Income}}{\text{Net Sales}}$

$-$

$\dfrac{\text{Federal Income Taxes}}{\text{Net Sales}}$

$=$

$\dfrac{\text{Net Profits}}{\text{Net Sales}} = 1.8\%$

$\dfrac{\text{Net Profits}}{\text{Net Sales}} = 1.8\%$

$\dfrac{\text{Net Profits}}{\text{Total Assets}} \times \dfrac{\text{Total Assets}}{\text{Net Worth}} = \dfrac{\text{Net Profits}}{\text{Net Worth}}$

$9.5\% \times 2.8 = 26.4$

Rate of Return on Capital Employed × Leverage Ratio = Rate of Return on Net Worth

*Profit model excludes leased equipment, fixtures, and facilities. The model also excludes the capital structure of nonconsolidated subsidiaries.

More specifically, Internal Revenue Service data indicate that after-tax profits for all retail corporations plummeted from 2.84 percent of sales in 1950 to 1.15 percent of sales in 1964, which represents a decline in profit margins of 59.5 percent during the most recent fifteen-year period for which comprehensive data are available. A variety of factors was responsible for this disquieting erosion in profit margins, including increased taxes, liberalized depreciation allowances, and escalating media costs. A careful analysis of available data indicates, however, that declining gross margin percentages, rising payroll expense ratios, and increased occupancy costs were primarily responsible for the profit squeeze.

Retailers confronted by the spectre of declining profit margins and operating—at least intuitively—on a high-yield basis, attempted to maintain their rates of return on net worth by increasing their rates of asset turnover and/or by leveraging their operations more highly. Internal Revenue Service data indicate that these attempts were partially successful.

The rate of asset turnover for all retail corporations climbed from 2.65 times per year in 1950 to 2.77 times per year in 1964. Similarly, the ratio of total assets to net worth for all retail corporations rose from 1.57 times per year in 1950 to an unprecedented 2.06 times per year in 1964, which represents a 31.9 percent increase in this important leverage ratio during the past fifteen years.

Although a separate and complex subject, the growing importance of financial leverage in the structure of retailing deserves comment. Since 1950, retailers have expanded their operations at an unprecedented rate. New and significantly larger stores have been opened in outlying areas, smaller facilities abandoned, existing outlets simultaneously remodeled and expanded, and inventory assortments increased dramatically. Parenthetically, a rising proportion of the capital required to finance this expansion has been obtained from outside sources of funds with trade creditors being particularly important sources of short- and long-term capital. As a result, suppliers have become major financial institutions—the implications of which deserve careful study.

Unfortunately, these financial strategies did not completely offset the erosion in profit margins that occurred between 1950 and 1964. More specifically, neither the increases achieved in asset turnover rates nor the higher leverage ratios were sufficient to fully compensate for the decline experienced in profit margins. Consequently, rates of return on net worth for retail corporations decreased sharply between 1950 and 1964.

Internal Revenue Service data indicate that the after-tax rate of return on net worth for all retail corporations declined from 11.82 percent in 1950 to 6.57 percent in 1964, which is well below the minimum acceptable level of 10.0 percent recommended by Dun and Bradstreet and security analysts.

More recent data suggest that retail profit margins will continue to be exposed to pressure throughout the foreseeable future. Specifically, profit margin percentages will continue to decline as competitive pressures intensify and payroll and occupancy expenses continue to rise. Consider, for example, the following recent developments with respect to gross margin percentages. Appliance dealers in 1967 operated on a composite gross margin of 25.63 percent of sales, which represents a twenty-year low in this important performance measurement; food chains reported a lower gross margin percentage in 1967 than during any of the preceding six years; and drug chains have experienced eroding gross margins over the last decade, in large part because of mounting discount department-store competition.

As a result of these and other trends, retailers will have to experiment aggressively and innovate relentlessly in order to maintain relatively slender profit margins. Higher rates of return on net worth are most likely to be achieved by firms that accelerate their rates of asset turnover and/or leverage their operations more highly. Stated alternatively, capital management has become a decisive management arena in many lines of retail trade.

Internal Revenue Service statistics indicate that retail corporations deployed their assets in the following manner during 1964:

Cash	8.42%
Accounts receivable	23.63
Inventory	32.97
Plant and equipment	21.85
Outside investments and all other assets	13.13
Total Assets	100.00%

Assuming for the moment that retailers cannot reduce their relative cash balances and that they have automated or mechanized their credit function, it is apparent that improved capital management is virtually synonymous with improved inventory management and more intensive utilization of physical facilities. The significance of this is that inventory and space management have become critically important decision-making areas to retailers in achieving satisfactory rates of return on net worth.

THE CHANGING STRUCTURE OF RETAILING

Retailing was in a state of continuous ferment in the last two decades. Shopping centers proliferated during the early 1950s; discount department stores emerged as a significant competitive reality several years later; and scrambled merchandising programs increased in relative importance in many lines of trade particularly during the early 1960s. These and other trends have been extensively chronicled in professional journals and in trade papers. They constitute the *visible* terrain of change.

The purpose of this section is to explore several significant changes in the structure of retailing that have received less attention. More specifically, ensuing paragraphs examine three developments that could have a decisive impact on distribution programing, namely the ascendancy of the planned vertical marketing systems, the growing fragmentation of the structure of retailing, and the increasing polarity of retail trade.

The Ascendancy of Planned Marketing Systems

Goods and services in the American economy have historically been distributed through highly fragmented networks in which *loosely* aligned manufacturers, wholesalers, and retailers have bargained with each other at arm's length, negotiated aggressively over terms of sale, and otherwise behaved autonomously. For the most part, the firms participating in these provisional coalitions have traditionally operated on a relatively small scale and performed a conventionally defined set of marketing functions.

Each of these organizational characteristics is actually or potentially a source of diseconomies. The autonomy of operating units in conventional marketing channels frequently results in duplicative programming, scheduling inefficiencies, and high selling costs. Similarly, the persistence of small units results in the sacrifice of scale economies.

Finally, and perhaps most importantly, the functional rigidity characteristic of most conventional marketing channels ignores the economies that can be achieved by realigning activities within the network. As a result of these factors, conventional marketing channels tend to be relatively inefficient and highly vulnerable distribution mechanisms.

Consequently, it is not surprising to observe that planned vertical marketing systems are rapidly displacing conventional marketing channels as the dominant mode of distribution in the American economy. Planned systems are professionally managed and centrally programmed networks, pre-engineered to achieve operating economies and maximum market impact. Stated alternatively, these vertical marketing systems are rationalized and capital-intensive networks designed to achieve technological, managerial, and promotional economies through the integration, coordination, and synchronization of marketing flows from points of production to points of ultimate use. Exhibit 5 provides a more detailed analysis of the distinctions between planned vertical marketing systems and conventional marketing channels.

The economies inherent in vertical marketing systems have been frequently identified and classified but seldom measured. A careful analysis of the literature suggests that the following types of economies are most important in explaining the emergence and growth of vertical

EXHIBIT 5. Salient Characteristics of Competing Distribution Networks

Network Characteristic	Conventional Marketing Channel	Integrated Marketing System
Composition of network	Network composed of isolated and autonomous units, each of which performs a conventionally defined set of marketing functions. Coordination primarily achieved through bargaining and negotiation.	Network composed of interconnected units, each of which performs an optimum combination of marketing functions. Coordination achieved through the use of detailed plans and comprehensive programs.
Economic capability of member units	Operating units frequently unable to achieve systemic economies.	Operating units *programmed* to achieve systemic economies.
Organizational stability	Open network with low index of member loyalty and relative ease of entry. Network therefore tends to be unstable.	Open network but entry rigorously controlled by the system's requirements and by market conditions. Membership loyalty assured through the use of ownership or contractual agreements. As a result, network tends to be relatively stable.
Number and composition of decision makers	Large number of strategists supported by a slightly larger number of operating executives.	Limited number of strategists supported by a *significantly* larger number of staff and operating executives.
Analytical focus of strategic decision makers	Strategists preoccupied with cost, volume, and investment relationships at a *single* stage of the marketing process.	Strategists preoccupied with cost, volume, and investment relationships at *all* stages of the marketing process. Corresponding emphasis on the "total cost" concept accompanied by a continuous search for favorable economic trade-offs.
Underlying decision-making process	Heavy reliance on judgmental decisions made by generalists.	Heavy reliance of "scientific" decisions made by specialists or committees of specialists.
Institutional loyalties of decision makers	Decision makers emotionally committed to traditional forms of distribution.	Decision makers *analytically* committed to marketing concept and viable institutions.

marketing systems: (1) repositioning economies; (2) scheduling/synchronization economies; (3) simplification economies; (4) access economies; and (5) scale economies. Irrespective of the measurement problems involved, it is apparent that these economies, individually and collectively, generate substantial savings for constituent organizations in vertical marketing systems.

In point of fact, three types of these planned systems—corporate, contractual, and administered—currently compete for differential advantage in the American economy. As their title implies, *corporate systems* achieve operating economies and market impact by combining successive stages of production and distribution under a single ownership. Vertically integrated corporations have existed in the American economy for an extended period of time. Their growth has been particularly rapid in recent years, however, as is suggested by the following statistics and corporate vignettes:

1. Firms operating eleven or more stores increased their share of total retail sales from 18.1 percent in 1953 to at least 26.6 percent in 1967. Most of the firms in this size category have the capacity to operate partially integrated networks, and some are gradually evolving into self-supply systems.
2. Federal Trade Commission data indicate that 22.5 percent of all mergers consummated between 1948 and 1965 involved vertical acquisitions. Many of the conglomerate mergers—particularly those involving product and market extensions—also resulted in the achievement of vertical economies.
3. At the corporate level, Sherwin-Williams currently owns and operates over 2000 retail outlets; Hart, Schaffner, and Marx operates over 200 stores, and Eagle generates 30 percent of its volume from captive locations. Many large food chains obtain 15 to 20 percent of their requirements from company-owned processing facilities, and Sears reportedly obtains 50 percent of its throughput from manufacturing facilities in which it has an equity interest. Similarly, Holiday Inns is evolving into a self-supply network that includes a carpet mill, a furniture manufacturing plant, and numerous captive redistribution facilities. In short, these and other organizations are massive, vertically integrated systems. To describe them as "retailers," "manufacturers," or "motel operators" oversimplifies their operating complexities and ignores the realities of the marketplace.

Administered systems are operationally more complex and analytically more interesting than their corporate counterparts. In an administered system, coordination of marketing activities is achieved through the use of programs developed by one or a limited number of firms. Stated alternatively, administrative strategies and the exercise of economic and political power are relied upon to achieve systemic economies. Manufacturing organizations, for example, have historically relied on administrative expertise to coordinate reseller marketing efforts. Suppliers with dominant brands have predictably experienced the least difficulty in securing strong trade support, but many manufacturers with "fringe" items have been able to elicit reseller cooperation through the use of liberal distribution policies that take the form of attractive discounts (or discount substitutes), financial assistance, and various types of concessions that protect resellers from one or more of the risks of doing business. Consequently, administrative strategies of both a formal and informal nature can be, and have been, used to coordinate marketing activities and to reduce friction within the network. When this condition prevails, the resulting network may be designated as an administered system.

Finally, and most significantly, vertical coordination of marketing activities can be achieved through the use of contractual agreements. That is, independent firms at different levels in the distribution network can integrate their programs on a contractual basis to obtain systemic economies and market impact that could not be achieved through individual action. *Contractual systems* have expanded more rapidly in recent years than their corporate or administered counterparts, and this development in retrospect may be one of the most significant trends to emerge during the 1950–1968 period.

Contractual integration is an unusually flexible economic device, and thus there is a variety of affiliations from which individual firms may choose. Despite this diversity, the principal types of contractual systems involve voluntary, cooperative, or franchise forms of organization. Each type tends to have a different operating profile. The economic rationale of these networks is identical, however, with the result that they achieve comparable cost savings and market impact. Available data suggest that retailers affiliated with voluntary, cooperative, and franchise systems generated aggregate sales of 117.6 billion dollars in 1967. Consequently, firms participating in the most comprehensive forms of contractual systems obtained 37.5 percent of total retail sales during this year.

Furthermore, the "total" for voluntary, cooperative, and franchise groups represents only a part of the sales generated by contractually linked enterprises. Retailers belonging to programmed groups, procuring merchandise on a contractual basis, or participating in programs sponsored by resident buying offices obviously generate a significant, though indeterminate, fraction of total retail volume, which suggests that the role of contractually linked enterprises in the structure of distribution is considerably greater than the above "total" indicates.

In sum, it appears that vertically integrated networks—of a corporate, administered, and contractual nature—have already emerged as the preferred mode of distribution in the consumer goods sector of the American economy. As indicated above, corporate chains—many of which are vertically integrated—currently account for approximately 26.6 percent of total retail sales, and firms aligned with voluntary, cooperative, and franchise systems generate an additional 37.5 percent of aggregate retail volume. Consequently, retail outlets affiliated with vertical marketing systems have already "captured" 64.1 percent of the available market.

The explosive growth of vertical marketing systems has widespread implications for distribution programmers. To an increasing extent, durable and programmed linkages between suppliers and retailers are replacing the opportunistic and ad hoc linkages that have historically prevailed in many lines of trade. As this trend accelerates, many firms operating outside of existing systems will experience growing difficulty in achieving adequate sales and rates of return on investment.

Fragmentation of the Structure of Retailing

Disposable personal income and discretionary spending power rose uninterruptedly between 1950 and 1968. Consumers confronted by this new affluence and liberated from historically prescribed shopping habits became increasingly reluctant to accept the compromises inherent in purchasing mass-produced and mass-distributed goods. Instead, they began to scour the marketplace for goods and services that *precisely* satisfied their aesthetic, psychological, and functional requirements. As a result of these and related factors, relatively homogeneous mass markets quickly disintegrated into a series of identifiable and potentially profitable demand segments.

The growing diversity of consumer markets resulted in parallel diversity at the retail level. Housewares, for example, are currently sold in over 250,000 retail outlets, including supermarkets, discount department stores, drug stores, garden supply stores, and other nontraditional distribution points. Similarly, automotive parts, accessories, and chemicals are merchandised in at least 400,000 different outlets—many of which entered the market for the first time in the early 1960s—and numerous hardware lines enjoy equally widespread distribution in traditional and nontraditional outlets. This increase in the number and diversity of outlets competing within a given product category suggests that the structure of retailing is becoming more and more fragmented. Manufacturers interested in maintaining and achieving a dominant position in the *total* market must therefore develop multiple distribution programs to satisfy the economic requirements of multiple retail and consumer groups.

Manufacturers are currently using a variety of techniques to distribute closely related product lines through different types of retail outlets. Available data suggest that the following techniques have been most successful:

Derivative Model Programs. These are essentially confined distribution programs in which special models (or style numbers) are selectively distributed through a limited number of outlets. Appliance manufacturers, in particular, tend to be vigorous proponents of derivative model programs with the result that many department stores and other outlets interested in insulating themselves from the rigors of competition obtain 70 percent or more of their appliance sales from "exclusive" models. Equivalent programs are also endemic in the carpet industry, the ready-to-wear industry, and other industries in which manufacturers need the support of diverse retail organizations to reach their sales goals.

Multiple Brand Programs. The traditional dichotomy of national versus private brands oversimplifies the complexities of the marketplace. The leading rubber companies, for example, currently market a diversity of national brands, associate brands, private brands, and so-called private labels. Thus, these firms have differentiated product lines and distribution programs for each type of outlet they serve. Stated alternatively, Goodyear with its multiple brand programs obtains effective distribution through discount department stores, tire, battery and accessory dealers, service stations, independent garages, food chains, conventional department stores, and other equally dissimilar outlets.

Similarly, Sunbeam with its *Vista* program obtains distribution through "prestige" stores while simultaneously serving mass merchandising outlets with its regular line. Proctor is even more adventuresome in this regard, since it markets six family brands, each of which is supported by a distribution program tailored to the economic requirements of a particular type of outlet.

Multiple Franchising Programs. This approach to distribution involves the development of *total* merchandising programs to support entire product lines. Consequently, multiple franchising programs are a logical extension of the multiple brand concept.

Baumritter Corporation is currently one of the most vigorous proponents of the multiple franchising approach to distribution. More specifically, Baumritter has developed a complete franchise program to support both its *Ethan Allen* and *Kling* lines. Franchisers participating in either of these programs receive a full array of supporting services, including financial assistance, operating manuals, professionally prepared advertising programs, inventory control systems, accounting systems, and the like. As a result of its multiple franchising approach, Baumritter is able to effect a deeper penetration of local markets through more outlets than would be the case if the company concentrated on a single program.

Programmed Merchandising Agreements. Manufacturers embracing the programmed merchandising concept develop specialized merchandising plans for each type of outlet they serve. More accurately, programmed merchandising is a "joint venture" in which a specific retail account and a supplier develop a comprehensive merchandising plan to market the supplier's product line. These plans normally cover a six-month period but some are of longer duration. More importantly, they involve joint programming of the following activities for each brand and for each store included in the agreement:

1. Merchandising Goals
    a. Planned sales
    b. Planned initial markup percentage
    c. Planned reductions, including planned markdowns, shortages, and discounts
    d. Planned gross margin
    e. Planned expense ratio (optional)
    f. Planned profit margin (optional)
2. Inventory Plan
    a. Planned rate of inventory turnover
    b. Planned merchandise assortments, including basic or model stock plans
    c. Formalized "never out" lists
    d. Desired mix of promotional versus regular merchandise
3. Merchandise Presentation Plan
    a. Recommended store fixtures
    b. Space allocation plan
    c. Visual merchandising plan
    d. Needed promotional materials, including point-of-purchase displays, consumer literature, and price signs
4. Personal Selling Plan
    a. Recommended sales presentations
    b. Sales training plan
    c. Special incentive arrangements, including "spiffs," salesmen's contests, and related activities
5. Advertising and Sales Promotion Plan
    a. Advertising and sales promotion budget
    b. Media schedule
    c. Copy themes for major campaigns and promotions
    d. Special sales events
6. Responsibilities and Due Dates
    a. Supplier's responsibilities in connection with the plan
    b. Retailer's responsibilities in connection with the plan

Programmed merchandising agreements are fairly widespread in the following product categories: garden supplies, major appliances, traffic appliances, bedding, sportswear, cosmetics, and housewares. Manufacturing organizations currently engaged in programmed merchandising activities include: General Electric (on major and traffic appliances); Baumritter (on its *Ethan Allen* furniture line in nonfranchised outlets); Sealy (on its *Posturepedic* line of mattresses); Scott (on its lawncare products); and Villager (on its dress and sportswear lines).

These and related examples of high-yield distribution programs reinforce the vertical marketing system theme developed above. Clearly, programmed and durable linkages are rapidly replacing opportunistic and ad hoc linkages as the basic coordinating mechanism in a growing number of distribution networks.

The Polarity of Retail Trade

The structure of retailing may be viewed as a spectrum of operating methods, ranging from mass merchandising organizations at one end of the spectrum to professionally managed specialty stores at the other. Available data suggest that retail enterprises operating at either end of the spectrum obtain higher rates of return on net worth than firms positioned in the middle. Stated alternatively, firms operating in the middle of the spectrum lack the merchandising capability to compete effectively on a price basis against mass merchandisers or on a nonprice basis against enlightened specialty store operators. Consequently, conventionally managed and relatively undifferentiated enterprises in the middle of the spectrum are becoming increasingly vulnerable.

Traditional hardware stores, for example, are ill-equipped to offset the strategic inroads being made in their markets by discount department stores, garden supply stores, cash-and-carry lumber yards, and other organizations operating at the extremities of the retail spectrum. Consequently, it appears that a rising number of lines of trade will be characterized by a growing polarity in which mass merchandising organizations and enlightened specialty store operators dominate the market. In point of fact, this development has already manifested itself as evidenced by the following examples: The Tandy Corporation plans to expand its Radio Shack network to 1000 units by 1972; Eugene Ferkhauf, one of the pioneers of the discount department store movement, recently announced that he plans to open a nationwide chain of high-fashion, decorative home accessories stores; Alexander's, a well-established promotional department store chain, is currently experimenting with free-standing ready-to-wear boutiques; Zayre's, the fourth largest discount department store chain in the country, is opening specialized fabric shops at a rapid rate; and Federated Department Stores recently announced its intention to develop a chain of hardgoods discount outlets.

Thus, a variety of high-yield retail organizations are simultaneously extending their mass merchandising and specialty store capability with the result that conventional outlets will experience growing operating difficulties.

The simultaneous ascendancy of mass merchandising organizations and specialty stores creates distribution "problems" for suppliers. Clearly, suppliers must ultimately align themselves with high-growth outlets. At the same time, they must maintain volume through conventional networks in order to achieve adequate rates of return on investment. Consequently, the decade ahead will probably be a period of transitional programming in which suppliers structure their policies to simultaneously accommodate the requirements of conventional outlets as well as those that are in the early stages of their institutional life cycle.

Other Developments

Distribution programmers should also be aware of several other important changes in the structure of retailing. First, concentration ratios are increasing in many lines of trade. In 1967, the twenty leading chains in their respective categories accounted for 18.1 percent of total drug store sales; 30.4 percent of total grocery store sales; 44.1 percent of total discount department store sales; and 47.6 percent of total conventional department store sales. These ratios, high by historical standards, will probably increase further during the decade ahead.

Second, free-form corporations, as suggested by the above paragraphs, are emerging as a major competitive reality in many retail categories. Consider, for example, the growing and diverse capability of Household Finance, Gamble-Skogmo, the Dayton Company, Dolly Madison, L. S. Ayres, Federated Department Stores, and other conglomerate organizations.

Third, and finally, professional executives are rapidly displacing proprietary managers as the dominant strategists in most lines of retail trade. Unlike their more traditional counterparts, professional executives tend to be vigorous proponents of the management-by-objectives philosophy and of the high-yield approach to doing business. More compellingly perhaps—from a vendor's point of view—many professional executives are almost evangelical in their perceived need to develop and implement integrated management information systems, the output of which will provide a continuing basis for evaluating and appraising vendor performance.

In sum, the structure of retailing is currently undergoing a series of transformations that are as profound in their impact as those that occurred in manufacturing industries during the eighteenth century, which suggests that distribution programming will become an increasingly critical area of decision making in the future.

33 An Integrative Model of the Channel Decision Process

J. Taylor Sims, Herbert E. Brown, and Arch G. Woodside

Foundations of Marketing Channels, edited by Woodside, et al. (Austin, TX: Lone Star Publishers, Inc., 1978), pp. 47–65. Reprinted by permission.

A review of the literature involving the study of marketing channels reveals four major areas of inquiry: (1) channel structure; (2) channel relationships; (3) channel models; and (4) channel management.[1] The first area includes numerous studies involving channel selection and design.[2] The second includes reports and observations of channel power, conflict, and cooperation.[3] The third area involves the application of operations research techniques, decision theory, and quantitative analyses to channel evaluation decisions.[4] The fourth area includes books, articles, and papers which examine the interaction of the total marketing mix and the effects of the environmental change on the channel management process.[5] This chapter is an attempt to reconcile and integrate this knowledge into a comprehensive model that will both identify and classify the primary variables utilized in channel decision making.

A Description of the Channel Decision Process

An integrative model of the channel decision process is illustrated in Figure 1. The decision areas outlined in the model are (1) mission of the organization (integrate with definition of market targets and strategic opportunity assessment), (2) the development of marketing strategy, (3) interaction of channel decisions in the marketing mix, (4) the identification of channel activities, (5) the development of channel objectives (integrate with identification of market targets and tactical opportunity assessment), (6) channel coverage, (7) channel cooperation and control, (8) channel structure and design, (9) determination of the market offer, and (10) definition of market targets (integrate with mission of the organization and strategic opportunity assessment). A discussion of each area and its decision implications follows.

Mission of the Organization

The channel decision process begins with an understanding of the mission of the organization. A clear definition of market targets based

FIGURE 1. An Integrative Model of the Channel Decision Process

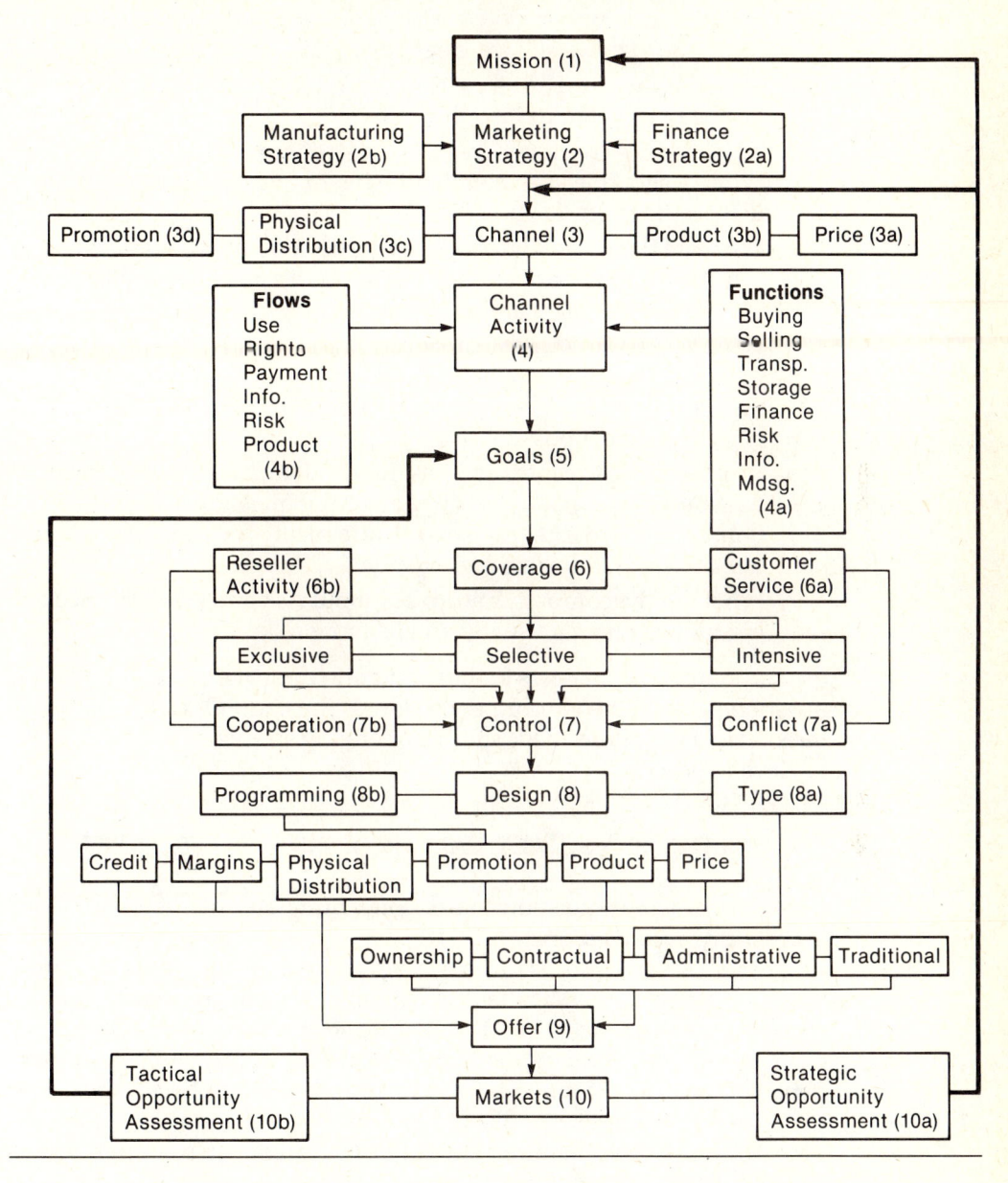

upon the strategic opportunity assessments of the organization is the major input. Perhaps the process of mission determination can best be explained by identifying several of the broad question areas often asked of the organization. Such questions include:

1. What business is the company in? (A functional approach can be useful at this point: Do we make automobiles or provide transportation? Do we sell ice cream or fun?)
2. Who are the company's customers? What are their needs? Why do they buy from us?
3. What are the company's resources, strengths, and weaknesses? What assets does the company have in terms of people, products, reputation, facilities, etc.?
4. What are the company's major opportunities and threats? Where can the company apply its resources most profitably? What are the most vulnerable areas?
5. What rate of growth appears best for the company? This should include a clear delineation of specific numbers with regard to the rate of growth in sales, profits, and return on investment (zero growth is also a possibility).
6. What share of the market is best for the company? This opens up the question of market position; i.e., the question of whether to dominate the market, whether to be a secure second, or whether to be small but flexible and creative.
7. What are the company's attitudes about risk and stability? Seeking higher returns usually entails more risk.

The sum of the answers to these and other pertinent market oriented questions equals the corporate mission of the firm. Once the corporate mission is clearly identified, specific operating strategies and tactics may be developed.

STRATEGIC VS. TACTICAL OPPORTUNITY ASSESSMENT

A fundamental question to ask concerning any marketing decision process involves its scope:

Is the decision process of a *strategic* nature or of a *tactical* nature? Strategy planning establishes the broad direction in which the firm wishes to go. The tactics are the specific steps needed to get there. For example, if company strategy dictates that the firm will be price competitive and a close competitor runs a special sale at a lower price, then the price competitive firm will have to tactically respond with a like price. Strategic marketing planning should be comprehensive enough to provide marketing management with a substantial operational range of tactical responses.

Identifying the marketing decision as being either strategic or tactical is crucial to the basic marketing planning process. The alternatives and the decision processes associated with each are basically different. A strategic decision requires the examination of and/or the adjustment of the company's basic goals, objectives, and operating policy. The resolution of strategic decision problems is the task of top-level management. On the other hand, tactical decisions can generally be handled at the mid-management levels.

The Development of Marketing Strategy

The mission of the organization is a general guideline to the development of an operating marketing strategy. The financial capacity and objectives of the organization set the upper limits of the marketing program as well as for the manufacturing strategy that will support it.

The marketing strategy objectives should be specific and measurable whenever possible. The topics that should be considered for planning are:

1. *Profits*. Pre-tax or after-tax; amount each year; growth rate (high profits are not always desirable. Too much profit may invite both the threat of aggressive competition and the intervention of the government).
2. *Profitability*. Return on investment (total capital or stockholder's equity for the whole company or by division); gross margins; earnings per dollar of sales; earnings per share.
3. *Sales*. (In units or dollars.) Prices; sales by division, product line, or geographic regions. Sales growth: internal or by acquisition (in related or unrelated business).
4. *Markets*. Share of market; balance between consumer/industrial or foreign/domestic; distribution techniques.
5. *Products*. Expand, reduce, or phase out certain lines; create or acquire new products.
6. *Research and Development*. Basic research; creating new products; copying successful products.
7. *Production*. Efficiency, costs, facilities (add, improve, sell); inventory policies.
8. *Finance*. Needs and timing; sources; cash flow; dividend policy; earnings-per-share goals.
9. *Organizational structure*. Add or strengthen a division; reorganize.
10. *Personnel*. Development programs; hiring new people; salaries, wages, and benefits; labor relations.
11. *Social responsibility*. Donations; time off to employees for social programs; public relations; environmental concerns.

INTERACTION OF CHANNEL DECISIONS IN THE MARKETING MIX

The marketing organization must consider five major elements in order to develop and integrate a successful marketing program. These are (1) price, (2) product, (3) channels, (4) physical distribution (logistics), and (5) promotion. These elements make up the decision variables of the marketing mix.

The selection of market targets and the strategic opportunity assessment necessary to reach them culminates in the organization's marketing mix. The elements of the marketing mix interact and are interdependent. The type of product developed and the promotion and distribution program utilized will influence the price of the product in the market place.[6] The channels and physical distribution program should be developed to deliver the right product to the right place at the right time and at the lowest cost that will achieve required customer service levels for the various market targets. If these objectives are not met, sales and customers will be lost. For example, if a consumer goes to a department store with the intention of buying a pair of shoes and the right size is not available, he may go to another store. If he goes to another store, finds the right size, and purchases the shoes, the first store has lost the revenue from the missed sale, and, possibly, any future business from that customer. Such stock-outs may become a serious problem in industries where repeat purchases are one of the primary objectives of marketing strategy.[7]

Another significant factor is the impact of the promotional program on the distribution activities of the organization. A promotional program that is not carefully coordinated with distribution support may result in unfulfilled product demand. If production has not coordinated its efforts to demand levels developed by a particular promotion program, the results may well be a disruption in production schedules, rush orders from suppliers, premium transportation costs, and strained manufacturer-channel relationships. On the other hand, if a product is forced into full distribution without adequate promotional support, excess inventories may result, with a possible final effect of losing wholesale and retail channel support entirely.[8]

In the long run the price of a product must cover all costs associated with its production and marketing program. This means, among other things, that any waste in distribution effort must ultimately be passed on to the consumer in the form of either a higher price or poor product quality. If the organization cannot control distribution costs, profits will be impaired in the short run, and survival may be threatened in the long run.[9]

Effective control of distribution costs can give an organization an advantage. Reduced prices can be passed on to the consumer if the firm can lower its distribution costs, and funds may be released for market expansion purposes. However, a major portion of final product price is composed of distribution costs. This, in itself, makes price vulnerable to any upward or downward movement in such cost and will directly influence the firm's marketing mix.[10]

THE IDENTIFICATION OF CHANNEL ACTIVITIES

The ultimate objective of all corporate marketing effort, whether strategic or tactical, is the creation, unambiguous presentation, and efficient delivery of a problem solving product or service to relevant markets. In sum, totality of all organizational marketing activity is what is termed the offer to sell. The channel component of the market offer is usually a critical element of the offering. Channel is also the delivery system for the satisfactions customers derive from their acceptance of the offer. Thus, the channel becomes the unit of analysis and planning in marketing. Ideally, then, such analysis and planning should *not* be done by and for a single level in the channel, but simultaneously for all levels and participants. The most basic decision involving the manufacturer and/or other intermediaries is which of the functions of marketing will be performed by themselves and which will be delegated to other channel intermediaries.

A marketing channel is identified as involving a series of relationships among organizations and final users to whom marketing effort is directed. These organizations are grouped together in various combinations linking producing units with particular using units. Flows of physical possession, ownership and title transfer, negotiation, financing, information, risk taking, ordering, and payment are, thus, identified. The channel of distribution, then, can be thought of as the sequence of agencies through which one or more of these flows move, and, in which functions necessary to move them are performed.[11]

The basic functions depicted in Point 4 of Figure 1 cannot be avoided or eliminated. Their performance by marketing organizations along with their interactions through channels of distribution make up the total network of marketing systems. If a manufacturer bypasses some middleman in the distributive process, he only eliminates the middleman, not the functions he performed. These functions must now be assumed by the manufacturer, who may or may not be able to reduce the cost of their performance.

The question of cost reduction in marketing relates to efficient performance. If an efficient middleman, say wholesaler, is performing the function of storage for the manufacturer, the elimination of his performance of this function would reduce costs only if someone else (manufacturer) could perform this function more efficiently.

The main effort to reduce marketing costs should not be on eliminating middlemen but rather on the means of obtaining more efficient performance of the marketing functions. This increased efficiency can sometimes be obtained by the elimination of the middleman, but in other cases it can come through the introduction of a new middleman specializing in particular marketing tasks.

Marketing functions may be performed numerous times in the marketing of a given product. Buying and selling, for example, is performed each time the title to a product changes hands—for example, manufacturer to wholesaler, wholesaler to retailer to ultimate consumer. Storage may also be performed at each of these levels, as may financing, risk taking, and all other functions.

THE DEVELOPMENT OF CHANNEL OBJECTIVES

A systematic approach to marketing channel management identifies marketing objectives that are consistent with and supportive of the firm's overall goals. Once this has been accomplished, specific activities that will contribute to the accomplishment of the objectives can be identified. This should culminate into an effective marketing plan.[12]

The marketing channel system must efficiently implement marketing planning involving specific market target groups. The manufacturer may find it necessary to use different tactics for different market segments, which necessitates a series of subplans that reflect the heterogeneous nature of the market. All tactical elements of the marketing mix may be involved, including the product and its availability, promotional appeals, channel sales effort, physical distribution, and the level of consumer service. A likely objective of the manufacturer would be to establish a channel system that would yield the optimum marketing program in each market segment, resulting in the generation of the maximum potential profit. The system should reach its optimal level somewhere between profit maximization and functional performance.

The use of different channels to be used for each identified market segment or target group is usual. The use of different channels for each segment might be necessitated by: (1) the need for accomplishing different segment marketing strategies, (2) the availability, willingness, and ability of channel members to serve particular segments, and (3) the compensation required by channel members if they are to perform the desired functions.

The actual channel selection process requires an in-depth knowledge of available middlemen and their capacity to perform the needed marketing functions. Specific decisions must be made on the market coverage needed and the degree of market control desired.

CHANNEL COVERAGE

The question of market coverage involves two decision points: (1) the type of outlet which should handle the product, and (2) the intensity of distribution needed.

Type of Outlet Required

In order for the manufacturer to determine the type of outlets best suited to sell his product, he must know the caliber of each of the potentially suitable outlets. If his product requires a relatively large investment in inventory, the potential number of available outlets may be immediately reduced. If a specialized environment is needed, for example, to sell luxury items such as silverware and china, the number of outlets capable of meeting market requirements is limited. Other factors, such as the need for credit or the availability of service, may also restrict the number of available outlets.

The Intensity of Distribution

The intensity of distribution is clearly related to the objectives of the organization, the nature of the product, and the structure of the market. Three degrees of intensity can be identified: (1) intensive, (2) selective, and (3) exclusive.

Intensive distribution has three different facets. First, it can refer to the total marketing area over which distribution is desired such as local, regional, or national distribution. Second, it can refer to the objective of gaining market exposure in all outlets in which buyers are willing to purchase a product. Third, it may refer to the number of outlets, regardless of type. For example, cigarettes are offered for sale in just about every kind of outlet that will handle it. Most low-unit-value-high-frequency-of-purchase products require at least some variation of intensive distribution.

Selective distribution is most often used to distribute shopping goods. Such products as clothing, microwave ovens, refrigerators, and furniture are normally identified as shopping goods, and, as such are selectively distributed. The number of outlets is restricted or selective because these products require an outlet that can provide specific services or environment in order to achieve desired sales volume. To market the shopping good product in just any outlet might damage the product's prestige. The cost of inventory would, in most cases, make prohibitive the marketing of such products through intensive channels.

Exclusive distribution is actually a special type of selective distribution. A single outlet is given an exclusive franchise to handle the product in a prescribed territory. Products which exhibit a high degree of brand loyalty are often distributed in this manner. For example, the consumer desiring to purchase an expensive Rolex wristwatch, and no other brand, will seek out the specific outlet that handles this particular brand.

CHANNEL COOPERATION AND CONTROL

The typical pattern in the establishment of channels of distribution is that there is an initiator who may structure the relationship and hold the channel together. This "channel captain" controls relationships either through a command or cooperation relationship.[13]

We have implied (perhaps too strongly) that the manufacturer is the channel captain and that the various middlemen are channel followers. In fact, the channel selection process may involve a mutual seeking-out process on the parts of the manufacturer and middlemen. Channel intermediaries often seek out manufacturers. For example, a sales representative from a wholesaling firm may call on a manufacturer and attempt to sell the virtues of his organization over those of his competitors. On the other hand, the manufacturer and his product may be relatively unknown, in which case the primary selling job through the channel system may rest with him. In this case, he will have to convince various channel intermediaries that the product has a substantial potential market and that distribution would be profitable for them.

Thus, the very process of exchange may be a source of conflict between channel members.[14] For example, it is quite natural for the seller in an exchange to want a higher price than the buyer. Wholesalers may be unwilling to carry the manufacturer's products under the manufacturer's designated pricing system. Under these conditions, the manufacturer has two alternatives: (1) he may perform the channel functions himself, or (2) he may offer higher margins in an attempt to persuade the wholesaler to cooperate. If these tactics are rejected, then the manufacturer may have to alter his marketing strategy and repeat the channel selection process.

There are other sources of power and conflict in the pricing area that can be illustrated. A manufacturer may try to dictate the resale price of his merchandise, or change the price of merchandise in the channel without warning. Texas Instruments, Inc., has been guilty of this latter practice in reducing drastically the price of its hand calculators without informing wholesale and retail channel members.[15] The result has been substantial losses by middlemen on existing inventories purchased at higher prices.

Channel conflict may also arise in other areas of the marketing program. A manufacturer may wish to promote a product in a certain manner that retailers oppose; or the manufacturer may wish to distribute his product extensively, but his wholesalers and/or retailers may demand exclusives.

One possible source of channel conflict may arise if there is a difference in the business philosophy of channel members. The large dynamic manufacturer may find it hard to contend with the small conservative retailer. The growth strategies of the manufacturer, such as broadening the line of merchandise and developing extensive advertising and promotion campaign, may conflict with the rather static objectives of the small retailer who is satisfied with a "good living" no-growth policy.[16]

Despite these and other potential power and conflict factors, channel members generally have more common interests than conflicting ones. The major common interest is the sale of the product. In this they have a single goal to reach and must cooperate as a marketing team in order to do it. In this objective channel members must compromise their own private motives in order to reach the overall channel goals. The goal is to minimize conflict and maximize cooperation.[17]

The power factor of the channel captain, whether manufacturer or wholesaler, may be enhanced by doing certain things for its resellers. For example, the manufacturer may provide missionary salesmen to aid the sales of channel members. Helping retailers to set quotas, studying market potential for them and aiding in their inventory planning and protection are other examples of consolidating aids. The large manufacturer can often act as a general management consultant within its channel system offering assistance in accounting, financing, buying, site selection, and promotion.

In conclusion, all members of the channel must finally agree to coordinate their efforts if the channel's basic objective of selling specific products and services is to be met. This mutuality of interest stresses a philosophy of cooperation.

CHANNEL STRUCTURE AND DESIGN

After the channel objectives have been determined, detailed facility decisions must be made. Agreement must be reached on the number, size, and location of each type of middlemen.

Types of Channels

The traditional marketing channel (manufacturer to wholesaler to retailer to consumer) is finding increasing competition from corporate, administered, and contractual channels. A *Corporate Channel* is a centrally owned and operated vertical marketing system that combines successive stages of production and distribution under a single ownership. These centralized systems, arising primarily through mergers or internal expansion, now operate manufacturing facilities, warehousing units, and retail outlets. In other words, the principal stages of production and distribution have been combined under one roof, which affords much greater control than traditional channel systems. Sherwin-Williams, for example, operates over 2,000 paint stores. Sears maintains equity in producing companies that supply over thirty percent of the company's inventory requirements.

An *Administered Channel* is one in which an organization is able to exercise administrative control over a vertical system through sheer economic power. For example, Kraftco and Mead Paper Corporation are examples of companies that have developed a controlled pipeline from raw materials to finished products and enjoy space management privileges in their respective outlets to administer their end point marketing mix.

A *Contractual Channel* is one in which independent firms have joined together on a contractual basis to achieve buying and selling power through combination. Examples of contractual channels include voluntary retail associations and franchise organizations.

The important point to remember in the channel selection process is the emerging differences in structure which point to increasing channel competition in terms of alternative vertical marketing structures, rather than just the competition between loosely linked independent firms such as wholesalers or retailers.[18]

CHANNEL PROGRAMMING (AND SELECTION)

The functions that must be performed by an organization's channel system are derived from the needs of buyers and the organization's objectives. In order to determine these functions and their relative importance it is vital to analyze in detail the characteristics of the product, the market, and the manufacturer, keeping in mind the types of channel structures that can perform the various activities necessary for the marketing task. Space limitations prohibit examining each of these factors in detail. Here they are simply identified and left to the reader for examination in more depth.

Product Characteristics

1. *Unit value.* Where the unit value is high, the tendency is toward direct channels. When the unit value is low, there is a tendency toward intensive coverage.
2. *Bulk.* The value of the product relative to its weight is an important consideration in channel design and structure. If it has a

high value per unit weight, the extent of market coverage is not usually limited. If the unit value is low, the cost of movement may restrict the market to a regional area close to that of the production site.

3. *Perishability.* Perishable goods tend to be handled through the shorter channels. In this case speed of movement through the channels is essential.
4. *Product technicality.* The more technical the product the more apt it is to require a direct channel. In this case, the possibility of a constant need for product adjustment after the sale necessitates a large measure of channel control.
5. *Breadth of the line.* Products that are complementary in use and purchase are usually sold to a single market. In this case, the broader line allows for high average sale size. This high sales volume offsets low unit value so that a broad product line of low-unit-value products can be intensively distributed by direct methods. The Campbell Soup Company, for example, distributes its broad lines directly to retail outlets from its own distribution centers.
6. *Seasonality.* Whenever production and consumption schedules do not balance, a storage problem is created. Since most middlemen are not willing to hold inventory for long periods of time, the manufacturers must do it. This may force a more direct distribution system than would normally be used because of the necessity to integrate logistics functions.
7. *Degree of market acceptance.* New products generally require a high level of aggressive selling. Thus, the first channel used may be a direct one. As a product achieves acceptance, a switch to more indirect channels may be made.

Market Characteristics

1. *Users of the product.* The users must be identified (market segments) before channel design and structure can be determined. Each user group may require a different channel system.
2. *Size of the market.* The size of the market determines the complexity of the distribution network required and the number of activities that can be performed at the manufacturer level. A small market, for example, may dictate a shift of functions to available middlemen, because of the scarcity of available funds.
3. *Geographic concentration/dispersion.* The more concentrated the market, the lower the cost of distribution per unit and the greater the feasibility of using direct distribution channels. A dispersed market increases the cost of distribution per unit because of high

transportation and storage costs. Indirect distribution with many middlemen is often most feasible in this case.
4. *Frequency of purchase.* The selection of the channel system must take into account the customer's frequency of purchase. Heavy industrial machinery with a purchase frequency of once every ten years may lend itself to direct distribution because of the low sales call cost. On the other hand, a product with a purchase frequency of once per week would more than likely prohibit nationwide direct sales by the manufacturer. The sales calls could run into the thousands.

Manufacturer Characteristics

1. *Financial capacity.* A direct relationship exists between financial capacity and the amount of control that a manufacturer may exercise over his distribution system. In general, the higher the financial worth of the manufacturer, the more marketing functions he can perform for himself, thus exercising more direct control.
2. *Manufacturer reputation.* A direct relationship exists between the manufacturer's general reputation and his ability to contract with the best channel system for his products. The better known the manufacturer the higher the likelihood of attracting top distributors.
3. *Policies of the manufacturer.* Policies with respect to sales, service, price, and promotion influence the type of channel system used. For example, a high-price, limited market policy, which skims the cream from the market, may afford margins large enough for expensive channels to be used. In contrast, a low-price, mass market policy which attempts to penetrate every market in depth usually calls for an intensive distribution policy.

THE MARKET OFFER

In selecting a channel of distribution it is important to consider the needs and desires of consumers, the mission and objectives of the marketing organization, and the availability of efficient channel members to perform the required functions. The characteristics of the product, market, and manufacturer is critical to this determination.

After assessing the functional needs of the market, consideration should be given to the cost and revenue results of alternative channels. Based upon all of these assessments, a specific channel system may be selected and programmed. Assuming that other marketing mix elements have been similarly programmed and integrated with the channel decision, a clear and unambiguous offer to sell can be presented to the market. Care taken to this point should result in a channel mix component which is a good fit with customer requirements. But because the environment is dynamic, the passage of time will create the necessity for change in either channel strategies or tactics or both. Management, therefore, must monitor the market place for the appearance of both strategic and tactical opportunities and threats. The model thus provides a strategic opportunity/threat feedback loop to marketing strategy and objectives and a tactical opportunity/threat feedback loop to channel objectives.

IMPLICATIONS FOR CHANNEL RESEARCH

There are several implications for channel research evolving from the integrative model described above.

First, the variables of the model all lend themselves to quantification. By operationalizing the variables it should be possible to develop meaningful computer simulations to aid in the channel decision process.

Second, a systematic examination of the power positions of various channel members involved in the distribution system is inherent to meaningful analysis of the model.

Third, it is important in developing any research base for channel decisions that the process of conflict resolution and its impact on the operation of the channel be understood and analyzed.

Finally, most channel decisions involve many subjective as well as objective decision variables. Techniques need to be developed and integrated that will synthesize these types of data into meaningful decision criteria.

ENDNOTES

1. For a comprehensive list of references, see Ronald D. Michman, Myron Gable, and J. Taylor Sims, *Marketing Channel Strategy: A Selected and Annotated Bibliography* (Chicago: American Marketing Association, 1976).
2. F. E. Balderston, "Design of Marketing Channels," in Reavis Cox, Wroe Alderson, Stanley Shapiro (eds.), *Theory in Marketing* (Homewood, Illinois: Richard D. Irwin, Second Series, 1964), pp. 163–75.
   Roland Artle and S. Berglund, "A Note on Manufacturers' Choice of Distribution Channel," *Management Science* (July, 1959), pp. 460–71.
   Thomas L. Berg, "Designing the Distribution System," in W. D. Stevens (ed.), *The Social Responsibilities of Marketing* (Chicago: American Marketing Association, 1962), pp. 481–490.
   Hakan Hakasson and Bjorn Wootz, "Supplier Selection in an International En-

vironment: An Experimental Study," *Journal of Marketing Research*, Vol. XII, (February, 1975), pp. 46–51.

Louis Bucklin, "Postponement, Speculation, and the Structure of Distribution Channels," *Journal of Marketing Research*, Vol. II (February, 1965), pp. 26–31.

E. W. Lambert, Jr., "Financial Considerations in Choosing a Marketing Channel," *MSU Business Topics* (Winter, 1966), pp. 17–26.

Louis P. Bucklin and James M. Carman, "Vertical Market Structure Theory and the Health Care Delivery System," in Jagdish N. Sheth and Peter L. Wright (eds.), *Marketing Analysis for Societal Problems* (Urbana, Illinois: University of Illinois Bureau of Economic and Business Research, 1974), pp. 7–21.

Bruce E. Mallen, "Functional Spin-Off: A Key to Anticipating Change in Distribution Structure," *Journal of Marketing*, Vol. 37 (July, 1973), pp. 18–25.

William R. Davidson, "Channels of Distribution—One Aspect of Marketing Strategy," *Business Horizons* (February, 1961), pp. 84–90.

Phillip McVey, "Are Channels of Distribution What the Textbooks Say?" *Journal of Marketing*, Vol. 24 (January, 1960), pp. 61–65.

3. Louis P. Bucklin, "A Theory of Channel Control," *Journal of Marketing* (January, 1973), pp. 39–47.

David W. Cravens, Robert B. Woodruff, and Joe C. Stamper, "An Analytic Approach for Evaluating Sales Territory Performance," *Journal of Marketing* (January, 1972), pp. 31–37.

William R. Davidson, "Changes in Distributive Institutions," *Journal of Marketing* (January, 1970), pp. 7–10.

Adel I. El-Ansary and Robert A. Robicheaux, "A Theory of Channel Control: Revisited," *Journal of Marketing* (January, 1974), pp. 2–7.

Adel I. El-Ansary and Louis W. Stern, "Power Measurement in the Distribution Channel," *Journal of Marketing Research* (February, 1972) pp. 47–52.

Michael Etgar, "Channel Domination and Countervoiling Power in Distributive Channels," *Journal of Marketing Research* (August, 1976), pp. 254–62.

J. Robert Foster and F. Kelly Shuptrine, "Using Retailers' Perceptions of Channel Performance to Detect Potential Conflict," *1973 Combined Proceedings* (American Marketing Association), pp. 118–23.

Shelby B. Hunt and John R. Nevin, "Power in Channels of Distribution: Sources and Consequences," *Journal of Marketing Research* (May, 1974), pp. 186–93.

Robert W. Little, "The Marketing Channel: Who Should Lead this Extra-Corporate Organization?" *Journal of Marketing* (January, 1970) pp. 31–38.

Joseph Barry Mason, "Power and Channel Conflicts in Shopping Center Development," *Journal of Marketing* (April, 1975), pp. 28–35.

Mel S. Mayer and Neil M. Whitmore, "An Appraisal of the Marketing Channels for Automobiles," *Journal of Marketing* (July, 1976) pp. 35–40.

Louis W. Stern, Brian Sternthal, and C. Samuel Craig, "Managing Conflict in Distribution Channels: A Laboratory Study," *Journal of Marketing Research* (May, 1973), pp. 169–79.

Larry J. Rosenberg and Louis W. Stern, "Conflict Measurement in the Distribution Channel," *Journal of Marketing Research* (November, 1971), pp. 437–442.

Larry J. Rosenberg and Louis W. Stern, "Toward the Analysis of Conflict in

Distribution Channels: A Descriptive Model," *Journal of Marketing* (October, 1970), pp. 40–46.

Bert Rosenbloom, "Conflict and Channel Efficiency: Some Conceptual Models for the Decision Maker," *Journal of Marketing* (July, 1973), pp. 26–30.

4. Frederick Balderston and Austin Hoggatt, "Simulation of Market Processes," in Bruce E. Mallen, *The Marketing Channel* (New York: John Wiley and Sons, Inc., 1967), pp. 178–91.

Wroe Alderson and Paul E. Green, "Bayesian Decision Theory in Channel Selection," in Bruce Mallen, *The Marketing Channel* (New York: John Wiley and Sons, Inc., 1967), pp. 199–203.

Helmy H. Baligh, "A Theoretical Framework for Channel Choice," in Peter D. Bennett, *Economic Growth, Competition, and World Markets* (Chicago: American Marketing Association, 1965), pp. 631–54.

Robert E. Weigand, "The Accountant and Marketing Channels," *The Accounting Review*, Vol. 38 (July, 1963), pp. 584–90.

George Schwartz, "Breyer Study: Quantitative Systemic Analysis and Control," in *Development of Marketing Theory* (Cincinnati: Southwestern Publishing Co., 1963), pp. 121–25.

David L. Huff, "A Probabilistic Analysis of Consumer Spatial Behavior," in William S. Decker, (ed.), *Emerging Concepts in Marketing* (Chicago: American Marketing Association, 1963), pp. 443–61.

Phillip Kotler, "Distribution Decision Models," in *Marketing Decision Making: A Models Building Approach* (New York: Holt, Rinehart, Winston, 1971), Chapter 11, pp. 287–333.

Helmy H. Baligh and Leon E. Richartz, *Vertical Market Structures* (Boston: Allyn and Bacon, Inc., 1967).

5. Johan Arndt, "Temporal Lags in Comparative Retailing," *Journal of Marketing* (October, 1972), pp. 40–45.

David J. Bowersox, "Planning Physical Distribution Operations with Dynamic Simulation," *Journal of Marketing* (January, 1972), pp. 17–25.

"J. C. Penney: Getting More from the Same Space," *Business Week* (August 18, 1975).

"The Retail Push to Keep Inventories Down," *Business Week* (March 24, 1975), pp. 100–102.

"Retailers Try a Junior Size," *Business Week* (June 9, 1975), pp. 62–64.

"When Food and Soft Drinks Talk Different Codes," *Business Week* (March 30, 1974), pp. 64–66.

Ronald C. Curhan, "Shelf Space Allocation and Profit Maximization in Mass Retailing," *Journal of Marketing* (July, 1973) pp. 54–60.

M. S. Mayer, "Management Science in Retailing," *Journal of Marketing* (January, 1972), pp. 17–25.

David B. McKay, "A Microanalytic Approach to Store Location Analysis," *Journal of Marketing Research* (May, 1972), pp. 134–140.

Ross Pirasteh, "Prevent Blunders in Supply and Distribution," *Harvard Business Review* (March–April, 1969).

William D. Perreault, Jr., and Frederick A. Russ, "Physical Distribution Service and Industrial Purchase Decision," *Journal of Marketing* (April, 1976), pp. 53–62.

Daniel J. Sweeney, "Improving the Profitability of Retail Merchandising Decisions," *Journal of Marketing* (January, 1973), pp. 60–68.

C. K. Walter and John R. Grabner, "Stackout Cast Models: Empirical Tests in a Retail Situation," *Journal of Marketing* (July, 1975), pp. 56–60.

"Cramping the Style of Franchisers," *Business Week* (June 16, 1975), pp. 82–84.

Shelby D. Hunt and John R. Nevin, "Full Disclosure Laws in Franchising: An Empirical Investigation," *Journal of Marketing* (April, 1976), pp. 53–62.

Shelby D. Hunt and John R. Nevin, "Tying Agreements in Franchising," *Journal of Marketing* (July, 1975), pp. 20–26.

William G. Zikmund and William J. Stanton, "Recycling Solid Wastes: A Channels of Distribution Problem," *Journal of Marketing* (July, 1971), pp. 34–39.

6. A. J. Alton, "Pricing Practices and Channel Control," in William G. Moller, Jr., and David L. Wilemon (eds.), *Marketing Channels: A Systems Viewpoint* (Homewood: Richard D. Irwin, Inc., 1971), pp. 233–39.

7. See Burr W. Hupp, "Inventory Policy Is A Top Management Responsibility," in Donald L. Bowersox (ed.), *Readings in Physical Distribution Management* (New York: Macmillan Company, 1969), pp. 179–84.

8. For an interesting analysis of the importance of timing and of cooperation among channel participants, see John M. Brion, "Marketing Through the Wholesale/Distributor Channel," in Bruce E. Mallen (ed.), *The Marketing Channel* (New York: John Wiley and Sons, Inc., 1967), pp. 270–72.

9. Ronald J. Lewis, "Strengthening Control of Physical Distribution Costs," in Donald J. Bowersox (ed.), *Readings in Physical Distribution Management* (New York: Macmillan Company, 1969), pp. 316–30.

10. Marvin Flaks, "Total Cost Approach to Physical Distribution," in Bowersox, *Ibid.*, pp. 224–34.

11. J. Taylor Sims, J. Robert Foster, and Arch G. Woodside, *Marketing Channels: Systems and Strategies* (New York: Harper and Row Publishers, Inc., 1977), p. 3.

12. Mark E. Stern, *Marketing Planning* (New York: McGraw-Hill Book Company, 1966), Chapter 1.

13. Bruce Mallen, "Conflict and Cooperation in Marketing Channels" in L. George Smith, *Reflections on Progress in Marketing* (Chicago: American Marketing Association, 1964), pp. 65–85.

14. See Jagdish N. Sheth, "Buyer-Seller Interaction: A Conceptual Framework," in Beverlee B. Anderson, *Advances in Consumer Research* (proceedings of Association of Consumer Research, 6th Annual Conference, 1976), pp. 382–86.

15. "Texas Instruments: Pushing Hard into the Consumer Markets," *Business Week* (Austin, 1974), pp. 39–42.

16. See Warren J. Wittreich, "Misunderstanding the Retailer," *Harvard Business Review* (May–June, 1962), p. 149.

17. Valentine F. Ridgeway, "Administration of Manufacturer-Dealer Systems," in *Managerial Marketing*, rev. ed., Wm. Lazwe and Eugene J. Kelley (eds.) (Homewood: Richard D. Irwin, Inc., 1962), p. 480.

18. See Bert C. McCammon, Jr., and Albert D. Bates, "The Emergence and Growth of Contractually Integrated Channels in the American Economy," in Peter Bennett, ed., *Economic Growth, Competition and World Markets* (Chicago: American Marketing Association, 1965). pp. 496–515.

34 — Distributor Portfolio Analysis and the Channel Dependence Matrix: New Techniques for Understanding and Managing the Channel

Peter R. Dickson

Reprinted from the *Journal of Marketing*, published by the American Marketing Association, Vol. 47 (Summer 1983), pp. 35–44. Reprinted by permission.

There is a movement of strategic influence in marketing management which, if underrated, may have serious consequences for manufacturers. Increasingly, distributors have become arbiters of what products will enter the marketplace and thus often control a product's destiny. If the trend continues, marketing in the 1990s may well be taught from the distributor's rather than manufacturer's perspective. The evidence of and reasons for this shift of power are many and varied. First and foremost, there has been the growth in private branding and now generic or nonbranding (*Business Week* 1981). Even where the manufacturers are maintaining some control and influence through brand advertising and promotion, a substantial amount of that expenditure is dependent on distributors' goodwill. Some 60% of the total advertising and sales promotion budgets of leading U.S. manufacturers of consumer package goods is spent on sales promotions that require substantial retailer cooperation (Inouye 1979).

The collapse of resale price maintenance has undermined manufacturer's ability to prescribe the retail price. Discretionary pricing has been a boon to the aggressive retailer and a conspicuous signal to the weaker distributor as to the real locus of channel power. The damage done to a manufacturer's investment in brand image by a retailer's discounting and loss leader pricing is another consequence of this loss of control that is seldom considered. Several other channel management practices traditionally used by manufacturers and regarded as the legitimate exercise of power have been successfully challenged in the courts in recent years.

The boom and bust economic conditions of the last 30 years have also contributed to the weakening of manufacturer control. Some retailers have caught a wave and become very powerful marketing organizations. Others such as auto dealers have been trapped with dead stock and unattractive contracts. Their trust in manufacturer judgment has been shaken, with a resultant loss in manufacturer's credibility and power. Chronic inflation has produced a preoccupation with price that has eroded margins, retailer goodwill and manufacturer discretion. Structurally, there has been a trend towards fewer but more powerful retailers controlling an ever-growing percentage of retail sales (Tillman 1971). Strong trade associations and buying groups have also emerged to give the weak retailers collective strength.

Finally, even technological changes have affected channel power relations in favor of the retailer. Containerization and other new forms of packing and transportation have often led retailers to prescribe what are for them the most convenient methods of transportation and warehousing. The Universal Product Code information system will enable retailers to evaluate new products and promotions cheaply and quickly, which is bound to increase the retailers' information power over the manufacturer. The very introduction of UPC is itself an example of retailers' collective power. Having obtained manufacturers' cooperation in labelling there is every indication that retailers will withhold the understood quid pro quo of free market information. Looking a little further into the future, it can be forecast that, unless manufacturers dramatically increase their mail order operations, interactive cable TV marketing will be dominated by retailers. It is not improbable that a general merchandiser like Sears will have its own TV selling channel that will supersede or complement its catalogs. If this occurs, manufacturers' new product TV campaigns may become even more dependent on retailers' willingness to run parallel promotions, particularly on their direct selling TV channels.

If ever there were an era when the manufacturer generally dominated the market channel, it is now clearly over. The situation, however, may be retrievable. There are ways of aggressively countering the distributors' increasing influence. One of the first and most basic steps a manufacturer can take is to develop a better insight into the *true* trading relationships it has with distributors and consequently improve management and control of these individual customer accounts. This article offers two simple frameworks for such strategic management of relations with distributors. The first, Distributor Portfolio Analysis (DPA), monitors the attractiveness of customer accounts as cost-profit centers and identifies tomorrow's traders that should be followed and today's millstones that should be dropped. Overall, Distributor Portfolio Analysis can reveal the strategic vulnerability of a manufacturer. It is based on the portfolio concept, which has been widely adopted in product management. The second framework, the Channel Dependence Matrix (CDM), offers a basis for understanding channel influence and the dynamic effects of disturbing market share and the balance of power.

PRODUCT PORTFOLIO ANALYSIS

The portfolio approach to marketing management is most widely used in the strategic planning of the product line. It is a refined identification of yesterday's, today's and tomorrow's breadwinners. The use of product portfolio diagnosis (Day 1977) or some other form of matrix approach to product evaluation (Wind and Claycamp 1976) provides an ordered framework for evaluating products and balancing cash flow investment. An important advantage of such integrated analysis is the effect of seeing the product line as a whole rather than evaluating products separately. The dimensions used in such analysis are commonly market share, sales or sales growth and profitability. Other dimensions have been used that consider risk and externalities such as regulatory control. This has led some analysts to suggest that two composite evaluative dimensions should be used, such as market attractiveness and business position (Hussey 1978). The weakness of a more general framework is that product performance is, in the main, evaluated subjectively and as a result can become, under the direction of the evaluator, a self-fulfilling prophecy.

Although widely acclaimed and used, the product portfolio approach does have its problems (Day 1977). Its theoretical rationale (i.e., that relative market share is a surrogate for production and marketing skills, and consequently for profitability), may be true for some products, but it is a suspect assumption in markets where there are many brands or products with short life cycles, constant technological innovation, cannibalization and volatile consumer demand. There are problems in defining the market and in evaluating a product that may be positioned as a "dog" but is a necessary complementary product to a "star." The strategic ramifications are also not as straightforward as some glibly describe. An enterprise first and foremost needs to cover overhead. The labelling of a product as a dog does not automatically mean it should be "canned"; some income generating substitute that makes a better contribution to overhead recovery must first be found.

In short, labelling and structure are not a substitute for creative strategic thinking and are in some cases a positive barrier to it. Competitors' likely reactions must also be considered. In some circumstances, it might be better to expand market share in a product line that is on the downside of the life cycle, if everyone else is quitting. The low cost of picking up the abandoned market share may make such an action a most attractive short-term cash flow investment.

Used sensibly and in combination with other planning aids, product portfolio analysis is a very useful aid for strategic marketing. If nothing else, the approach often explodes myths and outdated or misconceived loyalties.

CHANNEL MANAGEMENT

One of the weaknesses of a product management orientation is that a manufacturer's marketing to a retailer or wholesaler account is diffused across a number of product plans. The product planning approach can result in a lack of coordination and control of the allocation of total company resources directed at getting all of the company's products down the channel (Pommerening 1979). In such circumstances an enterprising distributor may chisel concessions on each product purchase. When considered collectively, these may represent an unreasonable investment in goodwill by the manufacturer, an investment that could be better spent in developing other distributor relationships.

According to Bowersox et al. (1980), the development of a channel strategy involves four considerations. The first is evaluation of the relative power (and hence negotiating position) of the various parties. Second is the arrangement of channel commitments and the formulation of evaluation procedures. The third consideration is accurate measurement of channel performance. The final consideration is evaluation of change potential and the management of this change. This last stage is claimed to be the culmination of effective channel strategy planning.

Most changes involve replacing a channel member by another of the same type. Presumably, the replacement of a channel member requires a comparison of performance, yet it was found in one study of distribution channel decisions that only one of the companies surveyed conducted a profitability analysis by customer (Lambert 1978). Even this analysis involved the arbitrary allocation of distribution costs on the basis of sales rather than customer location. It appears that much channel strategy pays only lip service to the formulation of sensible evaluation procedures and to the accurate measurement of channel performance. It is also hard to see how the power or negotiating position in a channel can be assessed without information that describes the distributors as sales, cost and profit centers.

The two techniques described in this paper address all four of the above considerations. They are designed to help the manufacturer measure bottom line channel member performance, evaluate the relative power and negotiating positions of the parties, identify new channel trading opportunities, and evaluate the likely and actual effect of changes in channel strategy. From a business policy perspective, DPA and CDM analyses provide information about three of the four criteria Porter (1980) suggests should be used as a framework for buyer/distributor selection and strategy: growth potential, structural bargaining power and the cost of servicing. In fact, the approaches offer an opportunity to extend Porter's criteria by identifying the percentage gross profitability and profit contribution of particular channels and each channel's unique role in an overall channel portfolio. Porter's fourth criterion requires the separate evaluation of the match between the manufacturer's offering and the distributor's special needs.

DISTRIBUTOR PORTFOLIO ANALYSIS

Key customer account profitability analysis has been proposed by Pommerening (1979) to help manufacturers market to distributors. The total net sales, discounts, gross profit, trade promotion expenses, sales force costs, distribution costs and trading profit are calculated for each key account. Distributor Portfolio Analysis is an extension of this approach and is illustrated in Figure 1. Major distributor accounts are plotted on two axes. The vertical axis measures the distributor's rate of sales growth after adjusting for inflation. This dimension indicates whether the distributor is expanding or contracting its total sales volume of all products that it sells. The horizontal axis measures the manufacturer's share of distributor's sales of a particular product or group of products. The area of each circle is proportional to the manufacturer's sales of the product or product group to each distributor.[1] A distributor who is currently not being supplied should be represented as a point on the vertical axis.[2] Each sales circle or cake is divided into direct manufacturing costs and gross profit. The latter segment is itself divided into sections representing various direct costs incurred in selling to the particular distributor and overhead recovery. Only three such costs are represented in Figure 1, but the marketing costs that can be illustrated include (in addition to volume discounts, cooperative advertising subsidies and physical distribution allowances) direct sales force costs, return allowance costs, promotion and handling allowance costs, push money costs and credit costs.

DPA quickly identifies the aggressive, rapid growth distributor. All other things being equal, the company should seek to expand its market share of such an operator's sales and to expand its total sales through this operator by increasing his/her total allowances. Such an aggressive investment strategy may require the deliberate sacrifice of short-term trading profitability in exchange for long-term sales. Distributor A in Figure 1 is clearly a candidate for such treatment; conversely, distributor E appears to be struggling. If his/her position worsens or there are other current symptoms of operating problems such as the taking of extended credit, then every effort should be made by the manufacturer to withdraw allowances and tighten credit. This must be done carefully, as any dramatic action may precipitate the collapse of the distributor. The movement desired in Figure 1 is for this circle to shrink in relative size and move to the left. The ultimate strategic decision is to abandon trading with such a distributor.

The four basic strategies involved are offensive investment, defensive entrenchment, strategic retreat and abandonment. Defensive entrenchment is a trading strategy used with a distributor who is growing and who currently has a substantial trading relationship with the company.

In Figure 1 distributor B is a candidate for such a strategy. The manufacturer must keep a close watch on competitors' trading tactics with this distributor so as to match their offers. Distributor B is today's breadwinner, so it is necessary to attempt to maximize net profit from total sales to this trader rather than to expand or contract sales and market share. What is required is a special mix of allowances that generates the most goodwill for the manufacturer at the least cost.

The visual presentation is also a very useful aid for comparative cost and profit analysis. The manufacturing gross profit on sales to distributor D is higher than the manufacturing gross profit on sales to other distributors because the mix of product sales to that distributor produced a higher overall manufacturing gross profit. In such circumstances it may

FIGURE 1. Distributor Portfolio Analysis

MC - Manufacturing costs
OR - Overhead recovery
D - Deals and discounts
P - Promotion allowances
F - Freight allowances

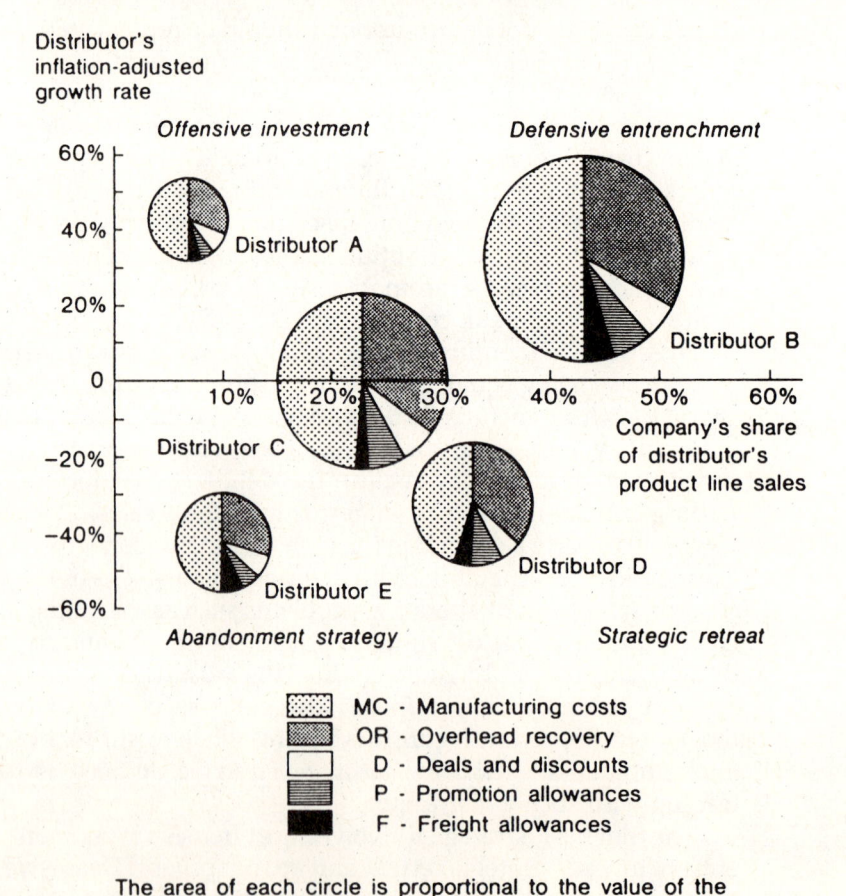

The area of each circle is proportional to the value of the distributor's purchases

be worthwhile to examine whether a similar sales mix can be achieved with other distributors.

Extraordinarily high selling costs to distributors are also immediately obvious. Some of these costs such as transport may be readily explained. Other unusually high expenses may not be so easily understood and indicate a need for special attention and control.

Distributor Portfolio Analysis suggests where a company should invest its allowances and hence goodwill in the channel. It recognizes that at any time a company may be investing, entrenching and strategically retreating in its channel dealings. In addition DPA identifies unique profit and cost features. It provides an evaluation framework that allows the accurate measurement of certain channel performance criteria and assists in the evaluation of change potential and the management of change.

The management of channel strategy must, of course, be undertaken with an eye on the fair trade laws. Allowances and discounts cannot be offered on a purely discretionary basis (see Trombetta and Page 1978). A distributor may attempt to use fair trade legislation to defend against a manufacturer's attempt to retreat or abandon the relationship because of the cost and risk of doing business with the distributor. DPA reveals but does not create the inequities in trading relations. It is up to the marketing manager to decide whether he/she can justify such inequities personally or to a court of law. Refusing to monitor channel trading relations on the grounds that the illegal favoring of particular distributors may be exposed is a dangerous head-in-the-sand option. If a manufacturer does not use DPA to justify its channel management, it may find a government body using DPA to justify an antitrust suit.

THE LEVEL OF ANALYSIS QUESTION

Distributor Portfolio Analysis can be undertaken at the brand specific level or at a more general product group level. At the brand specific level, the horizontal axis measures the brand's market share of each distributor's sales in the specific product line. The circle sizes represent the relative contributions that sales of the brand to each distributor make to total turnover. At this level of analysis, which is of most interest to the brand manager, it might be better to measure the distributor's real growth in sales of the specific product line on the vertical axis, rather than the distributor's growth in sales across all product lines. This dimension would then measure product specific rather than general sales momentum.

At the most aggregate level of analysis the horizontal axis measures the manufacturer's share of distributor sales of all the products that the manufacturer produces. In this most general DPA, the size of the circle represents the contribution of the distributor to total company sales. This type of DPA is of most interest to the sales or marketing manager, as it addresses overall trading relation issues.

The choice of unit of analysis will depend on the brand or product specificity of the strategic planning and the managerial responsibility of the executive. A manufacturer may find it most useful to undertake DPA for groups of products under the control of particular managers as well as a general DPA of the company's entire line of products. A brand or product subgroup DPA may identify a weak distributor who, at the more general DPA level, is a valued trading partner and vice versa. Identification of such disparities may help identify distributors who are pruning or expanding particular product lines and changing their trading image.

Data Sources

Some of the data for DPA are fairly readily obtainable. However, surrogate measures or estimates may have to be used for data that are difficult to obtain. The growth rate of a distributor can be obtained from its annual shareholders' report or from information (such as the 10-K form) that is supplied to the SEC. Trade associations collect industry sales information that is often available on request and can provide comparative growth performance information.

A company's relative market share of individual distributor or types of distributor sales can be obtained from market research firms such as A.C. Nielsen or, in the future, from UPC information. It may be difficult to obtain data on market share of a specific product group, but in some situations market share of total distributor sales may be sufficient. When sales and market share information are obtained directly from individual distributors, they should be carefully evaluated and, where possible, cross checked. This is because it is often to the distributor's advantage to overstate (or on occasions even understate) such information when negotiating with a manufacturer.

The manufacturer's accounting system has to provide the information for comparative analysis of total sales, manufacturing cost, trading costs and contribution to joint costs and overhead. With ever-improving hardware and software technology, it is inevitable that most companies' accounting systems will be updated in the near future. Consequently, modular data bases where costs and invoices are coded by function, product and customer are likely to become the norm rather than, as at present, the exception. This type of accounting data base is able to provide revenue and cost information by function, product and customer (Mossman, Fischer and Crissy 1974).

Every effort should be made to capture the *direct* costs of trading with a customer. The alternative arbitrary allocation of marketing costs to distributor accounts in budgeting or profitability analysis (e.g., allocation based on sales volume) defeats the whole intent of the comparative analysis. In general, many accountants believe that the allocation of any joint costs such as overhead and depreciation of shared assets serves no useful purpose (Kaplan 1977). Other accountants believe that the value of allocating costs arbitrarily depends on the objective of the exercise, and in certain circumstances the allocation of costs, even if arbitrary, can be used for controlling and motivating managers (Zimmerman 1979). It would appear that the arbitrary allocation of costs serves no useful purpose in the evaluation of distributors and therefore should not be undertaken in Distributor Portfolio Analysis. However, the growth of nonallocated trading and manufacturing costs must still be watched. They may grow as direct allocated costs shrink, either because of changes in the marketing approach or perhaps even as a result of some surreptitious transferring of direct costs to joint cost or overhead accounts.

An Actual Illustration of DPA

A DPA for a medium size manufacturer of drink mixes and flavorings is presented in Figure 2.[3] The vertical axis presents the growth rates of five major supermarket chains for the 1979–80 year. The horizontal axis measures the manufacturer's share of each supermarket's total sales. It appears that one operator (Y) has suffered a trading setback. Unfortunately the share of each supermarket's sales of drink mixes and flavorings could not be obtained. Consequently the horizontal axis does not indicate the distributor's dependence on the manufacturer for the supply of the product group of interest, but it does provide a measure of the relative importance of the manufacturer, as a supplier, to the supermarket. Figure 2 reveals that the manufacturer is a relatively less important supplier of supermarket Y. The size of the circles indicates, however, that this operator is the second biggest buyer of the company's products. There is another reason why the manufacturer should be concerned about relations with this particular operator. What had not been so starkly apparent until the DPA was the relatively low contribution to overhead recovery of each dollar of sales to this distributor. Proportionately supermarket chain Y has been given or has extracted more concessions from the manufacturer than any of the other chains.

From the evidence of this DPA it appears that the manufacturer should attempt to channel more sales through supermarket chains V, W and particularly X. Not only is supermarket chain X growing faster than the other distributors but it is also purchasing an assortment of company products whose weighted average manufacturing cost is lowest. Expanding trade with supermarket chain Z at the expense of Y could be a dangerous strategy. It may be desirable to create a more balanced trading portfolio by reducing dependency on Z and developing more trade with V, W and X.

Before embarking on major changes in distributor relations, however, a number of important questions need to be answered. Has supermarket chain Y suffered only a temporary setback or is it really going under? Should trading be continued for other reasons (e.g., distributor's importance in a particular market or personal loyalties)? How did this chain manage to extract such favorable trading concessions? Why does supermarket chain X purchase an assortment of products that produces a lower weighted average manufacturing cost? Is this operator a rising star or simply bouncing back from a poor trading performance the year

FIGURE 2. Actual DPA for a Drink Mix Manufacturer

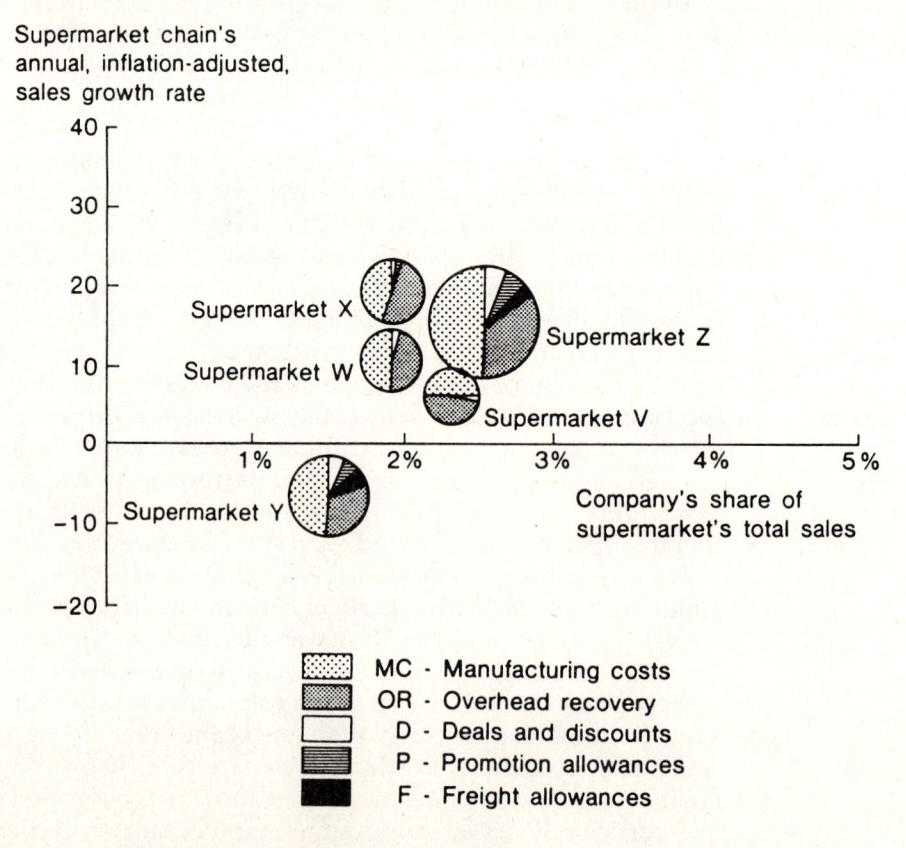

MC - Manufacturing costs
OR - Overhead recovery
D - Deals and discounts
P - Promotion allowances
F - Freight allowances

The area of each circle is proportional to the value of the distributor's purchases

before? A sequence of annual DPAs may be required to answer this question. In summary, this example points out that DPA by itself is certainly not a complete diagnostic tool but, at the least, it does help ensure that important questions are asked and answered.

POWER RELATIONSHIPS

The evaluation of the relative power or negotiating position of the manufacturer and distributor has received much less attention than the study of methods of creating or exercising power. Most researchers of channel behavior have studied power tactics using French and Raven's (1968) bases (see Stern and Beier 1969). For example, Hunt and Nevin (1974) came to the conclusion that a franchisor's power or influence over a franchisee is directly related to the franchisor's ability to reward or punish the franchisee. It would have been surprising if it were otherwise. There is some evidence that nonpecuniary services are more influential power tactics when dealers are relatively independent than financial rewards or penalties (Etgar 1976). However, the same researcher in a later study (Etgar 1978) concluded that economic rewards and penalties, such as the offering or withdrawal of various discounts or allowances, have distinct advantages over power tactics that are based on legitimacy, expertise and identification. A frequent problem with this research is that it has relied on a single executive's subjective assessment of the influence of a manufacturer on distributor decisions. Such assessments may be suspect because the executive is either too close or too far from the decisions.

The distributor portfolio circle segments provide a display of the manufacturer's use of economic power tactics on various distributors. However, the allowances and discounts illustrated in DPA can also be viewed in another way. They have been extracted from the manufacturer by the distributor and consequently reflect the power of the distributor over the manufacturer, rather than the manufacturer's power tactics. Power is often the result of subjective perceptions and therefore based on impression management. Distributor Portfolio Analysis enables an appraisal of whether the power of a distributor, as measured by its success in extracting economic allowances, is consistent with what its power or influence should be, based on current sales, market share, growth potential, profitability or cooperation in launching new products, undertaking special projects or supplying market information. In the example of DPA presented in Figure 2 it appears that, based on its ability to extract economic allowances, supermarket chain Y's power over the manufacturer is inconsistent with this distributor's contribution to current sales and overhead recovery and its current growth potential.

Previous researchers' conceptualizations of the source of power of a supplier over a distributor usually have been conceived in terms of direct dependency rather than relative dependency (see El-Ansary and Stern 1972, Stern and Beier 1969). They have postulated that the greater the dependency of the supplier on a distributor, the less power the supplier has over the distributor. It seems, however, to make intuitive sense to define the power of one party over another as a function of *relative* dependency or interdependency. A supplier's ability to exercise influence over a distributor depends not only on the supplier's dependency on the distributor but also on the distributor's dependency on the supplier. In functional form, it is suggested that $P_{ij} = f(d_{ji}/d_{ij})$, where P_{ij} is the power of i over j, d_{ij} is the dependency of i on j and d_{ji} is the dependency of j on i.[4] Etgar (1976) partially recognized this relationship by using Galbraith's concept of countervailing power as a moderator in his model, but he did not conceptualize power and countervailing power in terms of relative dependency. El-Ansary and Robicheaux (1974), in criticizing Bucklin's (1973) unidirectional definition of authority, also recognized that the power dependency model should be defined and measured in terms of a two-way dyadic relationship.

Theoretically it seems reasonable to assume that the tolerance or ability of a distributor to resist the demands of a manufacturer (and vice versa) ultimately depends on the relative trading alternatives that are available to the distributor and manufacturer. The more trading alternatives a distributor has, the less dependent it is on the manufacturer. A manufacturer will be able to exercise a considerable amount of power if a distributor cannot readily find another source of supply and the manufacturer can find another buyer. If, on the other hand, the distributor can choke the manufacturer by readily switching its source of supply, then the manufacturer's power is weakened. Etgar (1976) has noted that a distributor's acceptance of control depends on the nature of the trading activity and the number of suppliers currently used by the distributor, suggesting that power relations can be studied by looking at the options available to the parties. For instance, it can be seen readily in Figure 2 that the company is heavily dependent on sales to supermarket Z. The desire to exploit this distributor by treating it as a cash cow must be tempered by a concern over alienating it, unless the company has other alternative distributors waiting to pick up the sales revenue that may be lost.

THE CHANNEL DEPENDENCE MATRIX

One way to look at the alternatives available to channel members and appreciate the related concept of positional power is to examine the channel members' shares of each others' sales by the use of a Channel Dependence Matrix (illustrated in Table 1). Each cell in the matrix presents the market share of a particular manufacturer-distributor channel.

TABLE 1. A Channel Dependence Matrix

Manufacturer's Market Share	Distributor's/Retailer's Market Share					
	A	B	C	D	E	
X	20	20	5	0	5	50%
Y	20	0	5	5	0	30%
Z	10	0	0	5	5	20%
	50%	20%	10%	10%	10%	100%

The manufacturer-by-distributor market shares are spread across the matrix with the row marginal totals indicating each manufacturer's overall market share and the column marginal totals indicating each distributor's overall market share. For example, manufacturer X has a 50% overall market share. Its sales are produced by the X-A and X-B channels that each move 20% of total market sales and X-C and X-E channels that each move 5% of total market sales. Similarly, distributor A has a 50% share of retail sales made up of 20% from the X-A channel, 20% from the Y-A channel and 10% from the Z-A channel. The percentages in the cells should always total 100%. The private label market share in consumer product markets can be represented by presenting two percentages in each manufacturer-distributor cell of the matrix. In the upper left the overall market share of the channel is presented. In addition, the percentage of private branded sales in each channel can be displayed in the lower right corner of the cell. This additional information may be critical in drawing inferences about relative power relationships from the CDM.

The CDM can be used in a number of ways to complement DPA. First, a comparison within the marginals indicates the extent of market concentration at the two levels of the channel. The comparison between the row and column marginal totals provides some insight into the extent of bilateral oligopoly (see Hefflebower 1957) and whether the big sellers are balanced by big buyers with so called countervailing power (Galbraith 1956). Second, the dependence matrix can be used to examine channel imbalance. A perfectly balanced channel is one in which each manufacturer's market share of each distributor's sales is equal to the manufacturer's overall market share, and vice versa. All distributors have the same buying relationship with each manufacturer. A balanced dependence matrix is presented in Table 2. Such a channel trading pattern is highly unlikely in practice. The more probable imbalanced matrix occurs when a manufacturer's market share of a particular distributor's sales (or when a distributor's market share of a manufacturer's sales) is greater or less than its overall market share. Such imbalances have definite power and influence ramifications. The CDM helps assess the relative dependency of one party on another in terms of current sales or supply and the

TABLE 2. A Balanced Channel Dependence Matrix

Manufacturer's Market Share	Distributor's/Retailer's Market Share					
	A	B	C	D	E	
X	25	10	5	5	5	50%
Y	15	6	3	3	3	30%
Z	10	4	2	2	2	20%
	50%	20%	10%	10%	10%	100%

realistic channel alternatives that are available. For example, manufacturer X in Table 1 is in a position to exercise powerful influence over distributor B because while X has a diversified distributor portfolio, the distributor has not spread its purchasing across a portfolio of suppliers. It may be relatively easy for a distributor to switch his/her source of supply, but it is more likely that a considerable investment would be required to establish the distribution link with a new manufacturer. The abandoning of consumer goodwill linked exclusively with the previous manufacturer and the cost of building new goodwill leaves the distributor with little alternative, and consequently a high tolerance threshold. The other distributors have links with at least two manufacturers and consequently can force manufacturers to compete against each other. Manufacturer Y is relatively more dependent than the others on distributor A, who is supplied by all three manufacturers. It might be expected that distributor A will extract more concessions from manufacturer Y. The smallest manufacturer may not be in such a weak situation with distributor A as might first appear because if it developed B and C as additional outlets, the other two manufacturers, particularly X, might be reluctant to pick up the Z-A market share, as this would increase their sales dependence on the major distributor.

If trading relations are going to be disturbed, then, ignoring the issue of market growth, a change in one manufacturer-distributor's market share will have repercussions throughout the matrix. The reaction of other channel members to this disturbance must be anticipated. The channel dependence matrix can assist in predicting likely reactions. For example, an attempt by manufacturer Y to sell to distributor E may well be seen by manufacturer Z as threatening its sales to that distributor. The retaliatory action could be the establishment of a trading relationship between Z and C. The net effect could be that Y-E acquires 2% market share and Y-C drops to a 3% share. The overall manufacturer and distributor market shares remain the same. However, the two manufacturers and two distributors involved in the swapping of market share may still prefer the new channel dependency matrix and consider the market development exercise worthwhile. The manufacturers have spread their distributor portfolios and the distributors have spread their supply portfolios. Both have reduced dependency and vulnerability. On the other hand, the result may lead to a dissipation of effort and may be regarded by the participants as an internecine market share war that should not have been initiated by manufacturer Y. Indeed it might not have been initiated if the manufacturer had had the foresight and assistance of CDM analysis.

The Channel Dependence Matrix may also enable a more useful conceptualization of bilateral oligopoly, market leadership and countervailing power. These concepts have been described traditionally in terms of the overall market shares of the set of manufacturers and the set of distributors. Each cell in the matrix represents the outcome of a unique trading dyad with a unique power-dependency relationship. The size and distribution of the market shares in these cells, rather than just the overall marginal row and column market shares, can be used to describe countervailing power and bilateral oligopoly, allowing the identification and study of many types of competitive structures. Such a framework may, indeed be useful in examining *inter*brand versus *intra*brand competitive trade-offs in supplier-distributor antitrust cases.

Finally, power is a complex phenomenon and a CDM analysis is only one of several ways of studying power relationships. Other factors that must be taken into consideration include personal loyalties between executives across the channel, legally binding contracts, the uniqueness of each manufacturer's offering and each distributor's service, and the cost in goodwill and management resources of tampering with the status quo.

CONCLUSION

For two decades product management has dominated marketing strategy. It is not suggested that this will change. Product managers using their planning and analytical techniques will continue to play a crucial role in marketing. It is likely, however, that channel management will become a more important concern in the future, particularly if the locus of channel power continues to swing away from the manufacturer towards the distributor and retailer. Analytical aids for channel management are in somewhat short supply. Distributor Portfolio Analysis complements product portfolio analysis. It assists in planning the long-term channel distribution mix and helps to develop and control overall channel trading tractics. DPA basically keeps tabs on the highly aggressive distributor and the potential millstone and monitors channel market share growth and slippage. It also incorporates a comparative analysis across the distributor cost centers. DPA can provide the manufacturer with market power by specifying the true nature of its trading relationships with its distributors.

The technique, of course, has its limitations. Some of the criticisms of the product portfolio approach also apply to DPA: The evaluative dimensions do not acknowledge the value of a distributor in terms of its trendsetting or status image, its willingness to assist in new product development and other projects and its role as a source of market information (see Stern and El-Ansary 1982, Chapter 11, for other channel performance criteria). Care must also be taken not to fall into the label trap of rushing to a judgment on a distributor and having the judgment become, by the company's actions, a self-fulfilling prophecy. There are several possible reasons why a distributor may suffer a slump in total sales turnover. The distributor may be retrenching so as to emerge a stronger trader in a smaller range of product lines, including the product group of interest. This illustrates the importance of understanding the reasons behind growth and market share performance. DPA is a signalling device rather than an explanatory tool. At best, the technique is essentially an aid to convergent thinking, planning and control. It is a descriptive rather than a prescriptive tool and is of little assistance in promoting the divergent thinking needed to develop creative channel strategy. The data needed to undertake DPA may also not be readily available, and this is probably the biggest stumbling block to the application of DPA. However, reasonable surrogates can be found or intelligent estimates made. New information systems becoming available to the manufacturer will be able to provide the desired statistics. Distributor Portfolio Analysis is explicitly designed to help the manufacturer examine lower channel levels. The view up the channel from the retailer is not considered, although a technique similar to DPA might be used by distributors to evaluate suppliers. Both of these perspectives tend to understate the interdependency between manufacturer and supplier. The CDM analysis was developed to help examine interdependency.

It should be recalled that the above techniques were developed to help manufacturers regain some of their control over the channel, but gathering such information and undertaking such analysis is only the first and perhaps the easiest step along a difficult path. Unquestionably the tried and proven method of dominating a channel is to build a consumer franchise (through advertising superior branded products) that pulls the product through the channel. If a product lacks a strong brand image or a unique and genuine selling feature, then it is likely to require many promotional concessions to push it down the channel. An interesting strategic question is whether manufacturers are currently spending too little on new product research and development and too much on promotional concessions to the trade.

Distributor Portfolio Analysis, when coupled with the Channel Dependence Matrix, also provides new insight into channel relationships.

Clearly the two techniques together do not consider all of the variables that produce the very complex interdependencies found in channels. They do, however, portray the bottom line concerns of market share, growth, cost and profitability. Etgar (1977) has observed that channel leadership and power relationships become more important in distribution channels when the channel faces a threatening economic environment. These techniques would therefore appear to be particularly relevant at present, as there are few marketing channels today that do not feel threatened.

ENDNOTES

1. In his product portfolio article, Day (1977) made the diameter rather than the area of the circle proportional to the product's contribution to total company sales. This results in a significant likelihood of misinterpretation of the contribution of products with higher sales volume.
2. I am indebted to Fred Sturdivant who made this suggestion.
3. The author wishes to acknowledge the generous cooperation he received from John Mahoney who gave permission to publish this DPA and also Jenny Collingwood who collected the data. For obvious reasons the supermarkets are not identified. The analysis presented was for the 1979/80 trading year.
4. Whether relative dependency should be conceptualized as a ratio or a difference is an interesting theoretical and measurement question. The ratio or difference may also have to be weighted by $(d_{ij} + d_{ji})$ which represents in a sense the importance of the relationship. If the power-dependency relationship is linear and generalizable and if $P_{ij} = \beta(d_{ji}/d_{ij})$, $P_{ji} = \beta(d_{ij}/d_{ji})$ and $P_{ij} = 0$ if $d_{ji}/d_{ij} = 0$, then $P_{ij} \cdot P_{ji} = \beta^2$, where β is the power of each party when they are equally dependent on each other. These issues and relationships raise some interesting and testable theoretical propositions beyond the scope of this paper.

REFERENCES

Bowersox, Donald J., M. Bixby Cooper, Douglas M. Lambert and Donald A. Taylor (1980), *Management in Marketing Channels*, New York: McGraw-Hill.

Bucklin, Louis P. (1973), "A Theory of Channel Control," *Journal of Marketing*, 37 (January), 39–47.

Business Week (1981), "No-Frills Food, New Power for the Supermarkets," (March 23), 70–80.

Day, George S. (1977), "Diagnosing the Product Portfolio," *Journal of Marketing*, 41 (April), 29–38.

El-Ansary, Adel I. and Robert A. Robicheaux (1974), "A Theory of Channel Control: Revisited," *Journal of Marketing*, 38 (January), 2–7.

———and Louis W. Stern (1972), "Power Measurement in the Distribution Channel," *Journal of Marketing Research*, 9 (February), 47–52.

Etgar, Michael (1976), "Channel Domination and Countervailing Power in Distribution Channels," *Journal of Marketing Research*, 13 (August), 254–62.

———(1977), "Channel Environment and Channel Leadership," *Journal of Marketing Research*, 16 (February), 69–76.

———(1978), "Selection of an Effective Channel Control Mix," *Journal of Marketing Research*, 14 (February), 69–76.

French, John R. P. and Bertram Raven (1968), "The Bases of Social Power," in *Group Dynamics: Research and Theory*, Dorwin Cartwright and Alvin Zander, eds., New York: Harper and Row.

Galbraith, John K. (1956), *American Capitalism*, Boston: Houghton Mifflin Co.

Hefflebower, Richard B. (1957), "Mass Distribution: A Phase of Bilateral Oligopoly or of Competition," *American Economic Review*, 57 (May), 274–85.

Hunt, Shelby D. and John R. Nevin (1974), "Power in a Channel of Distribution: Sources and Consequences," *Journal of Marketing Research*, 11 (May), 186–93.

Hussey, David E. (1978), "Portfolio Analysis: Practical Experience with the Directional Policy Matrix," *Long Range Planning*, 11 (August), 2–8.

Inouye, David (1979), *Second Annual Survey of Promotion Practices*, Stamford, CT: Donnelly Marketing.

Kaplan, R. (1977), Application of Quantitative Models in Managerial Accounting: A State of the Art Survey," in *Management Accounting—State of the Art*, Madison: University of Wisconsin Press, 30–71.

Lambert, Douglas, M. (1978), "The Distribution Channels Decision," New York: The National Association of Accountants; Hamilton, Ontario: The Society of Management Accountants of Canada, working paper.

Mossman, Frank H., Paul M. Fischer and W. J. E. Crissy (1974), "New Approaches to Analyzing Marketing Profitability," *Journal of Marketing*, 38 (April), 43–48.

Pommerening, Dieter J. (1979), "Brand Marketing: Fresh Thinking Needed," in *Marketing Trends: An International Review*, Northbrook, IL: A.C. Nielsen Company, 1, 7–9.

Porter, Michael E. (1980), *Competitive Strategy: Techniques for Analyzing Industries and Competitors*, New York: The Free Press.

Stern, Louis W. and F. J. Beier (1969), "Power in the Distribution Channel," in *Distribution Channels: Behavioral Dimensions*, Louis W. Stern, ed., Boston: Houghton Mifflin.

———and Adel I. El-Ansary (1982), *Marketing Channels*, Englewood Cliffs, NJ: Prentice-Hall.

Tillman, R. (1971), "Rise of the Conglomerchant," *Harvard Business Review*, 49 (November-December), 44–51.

Trombetta, William L. and Albert L. Page (1978), "The Channel Control Issue under Scrutiny," *Journal of Retailing*, 54 (no. 2), 43–59.

Wind, Yoram and Henry J. Claycamp (1976), "Planning Product Line Strategy: A Matrix Approach," *Journal of Marketing*, 40 (January), 2–9.

Zimmerman, Jerold C. (1979), "The Costs and Benefits of Cost Allocations," *The Accounting Review*, 54 (July), 504–21.

SECTION J
Special Topics in Promotion

Promotion, including selling and advertising, has received the greatest attention in marketing practice and research. This is largely because we still think of marketing as selling. There are several emerging issues in promotion management.

First, there is a growing belief that a company needs integrated communication across all channels, such as selling, advertising, sales promotion, and public relations. Unfortunately, this integration has been lacking in the past, with consequent inconsistency in the brand, product, or corporate positioning.

Second, there is also a growing interest in electronic shopping and selling and their impact on the promotion function. For the first time, it seems possible to bring the producer and the consumer closer to each other on a direct and real-time basis through telemarketing and videotex technologies. This impacts traditional approaches to advertising and personal selling.

Third, there is a concern with the issue of productivity of promotion management. This *P* of marketing has been least amenable to measurement, and top management is raising questions of accountability and justification for promotion programs. It would appear that we must create productivity measurements for promotion tools as soon as possible so that marketing can become respectable in the organization.

35 New Ways to Reach Your Customers

Benson P. Shapiro and John Wyman

Reprinted by permission of the Harvard Business Review. "New Ways to Reach Your Customers" by Benson P. Shapiro and John Wyman (July–August 1981). Copyright © 1981 by the President and Fellows of Harvard College; all rights reserved.

From farther back than any of us can remember, personal selling, advertising, and sales promotion have been the essential marketing approaches. But these tested and proved methods for reaching customers also have their limitations, particularly in the light of two significant changes that have taken place in the business picture over the past decade:

1. The costs of communication climbed radically. Media costs skyrocketed. And the cost of a sales call, as estimated by McGraw-Hill, rose from $49 in 1969 to $137 in 1979.
2. A new set of options evolved, giving marketers a wider array of communications tools.

These developments mean that the marketing manager can make the best use of the newer methods, as well as the older ones, to respond to increasing top management demand for efficient and effective communication. In particular, the evolving options offer opportunities to improve the precision and impact of the marketing program, sometimes at great cost savings over the traditional methods.

There is no need for us to belabor the all too familiar change in communications costs. On the other hand, little note has been made of the newer options. Thus, in the first section of this article, we will focus on them. Then, in the second section, we will provide a four-step approach for developing a marketing program that makes the best use of both the newer and the older communications tools.

EVOLVING OPTIONS

In the past, the marketer's primary communications tools were *media advertising, direct mail advertising, telephone selling, trade shows,* and *face-to-face selling*. These traditional methods differed in impact and cost per message, with media advertising at the low end and personal selling at the high end. Telephone and personal selling offered flexibility in tailoring the message to the target prospect and in having two-way contact but at a substantial cost, particularly for the field sales force. Trade shows added the excitement and impact of product demonstration but were competitive and temporary in nature.

Whereas the opportunities to "mix and match" the five traditional approaches into a coherent, synergistic marketing program were limited, we believe that the increase in the number of available tools gives the marketing manager the ability to develop a more integrated, tailored, and cost-effective communications program than was previously possible.

The newer tools include *national account management, demonstration centers, industrial stores, telemarketing,* and new forms of *catalog selling*. These tools, used together and with the traditional methods, are leading to a new economics of selling. Let us look first at these five evolving options individually and then at the opportunities they offer when combined with the traditional methods.

National Account Management

A few large accounts comprise a disproportionately large percentage of almost any company's sales (industrial as well as consumer goods and services). National account management can often be applied (a) if these large accounts are geographically or organizationally dispersed, (b) if the selling company has many interactions with the buying company's operating units, and (c) if the product and selling process are complex. National account management thus is an extension, improvement, and outgrowth of personal selling. In essence, this method is the ultimate form of both personal selling and management of the personal selling process.

National account management responds to the needs of the customer for a coordinated communications approach while giving the seller a method of coordinating the costs, activities, and objectives of the sales function for its most important accounts. It is expensive, but the value to customer and seller alike is high if the situation is appropriate and the concept well executed.

Many people and companies use other names for this approach. Banks (as well as some other companies) call it *relationship management* because it draws attention to the primary objective of creating and developing an enduring relationship between the selling and buying companies. Others call it *corporate account management* because the accounts are managed at the corporate level, although the customers buy from several divisions in a multidivisional corporation. Yet others prefer the term *international account management* because the relationships transcend national boundaries. We prefer to use *national account management* because it appears to be the most popular and descriptive term.

National account management programs share certain characteristics, depending on the sales situation:

- First, the accounts managed are large relative to the rest of the company's accounts, sometimes generating more than $50 million each.
- Second, the national account manager is often responsible for coordinating people who work in other divisions of the selling company or in other functional areas. (This raises a great many issues of conflicting objectives and priorities.)
- Third, the national account manager often has responsibility for a team that includes support and operations people.
- Finally, the manager calls on many people in the buying company in addition to those in the formal buying function (e.g., engineering, manufacturing, finance) and often gets involved in highly conceptual, financially oriented systems sales.

The first issue that confronts companies considering national account management is how many accounts to involve. At this point the marketing managers need to understand the difference between "special handling" for a few select accounts and a real national account management program. Almost any company can develop a way to give special attention to a few accounts. But a full-blown national account management program requires fundamental changes in selling philosophy, sales management, and sales organization. Often the special handling of a few select accounts by top-level sales and marketing managers will lead to a formal program because the managers involved cannot find enough time for both the accounts and their regular duties.

Once the program begins, the selection of national accounts is an important phase. American Can Co., for example, found that careful account selection helped to define the nature of the program and to ease its implementation. Many companies, including IBM, separate their programs into different account categories depending on size, geographical dispersion, and servicing needs.

National accounts need special support, as do the managers responsible for them. All of the standard issues of sales management arise: selection, training, supervision, and compensation. The job requires people with both selling and administrative skills. Training and supervision must be keyed to the need for both depth and breadth in skills. And compensation—both amount and form (salary, commission, or both)—becomes important.

But often the most sensitive matter is how to organize. Some companies organize their national account managers with line authority over a large, dispersed sales and support team. Some go so far as to create separate manufacturing operations for each account, and the account team becomes a profit center. Other companies prefer to view the national account managers as coordinators of salespeople who report to different profit centers or divisions. There is a myriad of choices between these two extremes.

Demonstration Centers

Specially designed showrooms, or demonstration centers, allow customers to observe and usually to try out complex industrial equipment. The approach supplements personal selling and works best when the equipment being demonstrated is complex and not portable. Demonstration centers have been used in many industries including telecommunications, data processing, electronic test gear, and machine tools. A variant of the approach is a traveling demonstration center in which the equipment (or process) for sale is mounted in a trailer truck or bus. Rank Xerox, for example, once used a railroad train to demonstrate its equipment all over Europe.

The demonstration center also supplements trade shows, with three major differences between them:

1. The demonstration center is permanent and thus can more easily be fitted in a company's marketing and sales schedule. Trade shows, on the other hand, are temporary and are not scheduled for the convenience of any single company.
2. The company can determine the location of the demonstration center, unlike trade shows.
3. Demonstration centers are designed to provide a competition-free environment for the selling process. Trade shows, of course, are filled with competitors.

But the primary benefit to the seller comes from demonstration—often to high-level executives who are unavailable for standard sales presentations. Demonstration centers in some situations, furthermore, replace months of regular field selling. The economic trade-off then becomes partially a comparison of the cost of the center versus the cost of traveling salespeople. Demonstrating equipment or processes often has more impact than describing them. The most effective demonstration centers relate directly to the customer's needs and include a custom-designed demonstration.

An outstanding example of the concept involved the use of trailer-mounted, demonstration-sized versions of Union Carbide's UNOX wastewater treatment system by the company's Linde division. In the early 1970s, Linde used these models (costing $100,000 each) to demonstrate that its system could handle the wastewater of an industrial plant or even a particular municipality.

Linde had available to it all of the traditional communications approaches. UNOX sales, however, had been slow and difficult. After carefully considering the time and effort involved in selling, Linde executives decided that the demonstration units would speed sales, generate some sales that otherwise would be lost, and save the substantial expense of traditional approaches. And the demonstration units in fact accomplished all these objectives.

Industrial Stores

This approach also involves a demonstration of equipment or a process with the emphasis generally on cost reduction, not the creation of seller benefits. Stores are permanent, but the same concept is used by companies that present customer seminars and demonstrations in hotels, trade shows, or other temporary facilities. Here too the idea is to bring the customer to the salesperson. Boeing Computer Services, for example, has used hotel room demonstrations effectively in selling structural analysis computer time-sharing services to engineering firms. The store approach works well when:

- The sale is too small to justify sales calls. A substantial percentage (often as high as two-thirds) of industrial salespeople's time is spent traveling and waiting to see customers. If the sale is small, personal selling is not economical. One way around the problem is to ask the prospect to do the traveling. Thus, the customer comes to the salesperson's location, not vice versa.
- The product or process is complex and lends itself to demonstration.
- The company does not sell many products to the same customer. (If, on the other hand, the company has a large, active account with the same customer, the cost of a sales call can be amortized over the sale of many products.)

The store approach has been successful in the small business computer industry, where Digital Equipment has more than 20 stores in operation and development. IBM uses a similar approach but promotes it differently, using office space instead of retail space and encouraging appointments instead of drop-ins. In November 1980, however, IBM announced a commitment to develop stores more along the evolving concept used by Digital and other competitors. Xerox has made stores a major part of its marketing strategy.

Industrial stores vary widely according to product lines offered and approach used to attract people to visit. Xerox carries a wide variety of items, including many *not* made by Xerox; other stores offer limited lines produced only by the owners. Some, especially those in prime retail locations, can generate walk-in traffic. Others are in more office-oriented settings. For management, the stores certainly raise retail-oriented questions—location, fixtures, sales staffing—concerning their operations. In addition to display and sales service, stores can also provide physical distribution and service facilities to customers.

Economics has played a large part in the development of the store concept. As selling and travel costs escalate, the use of stores will become even more popular.

Telemarketing

Telephone marketing is an important emerging trend that companies can exploit in five ways—as a less costly substitute for personal selling, a supplement to personal selling, a higher-impact substitute for direct-mail and media advertising, a supplement to direct mail and other media, and a replacement for other slower, less convenient communications techniques.

Cost Savings. Telephone selling has traditionally provided a highly customized means of two-way communication. Greater sophistication in telecommunications equipment and services, new marketing approaches, and broader applications have turned telephone selling into telemarketing. It still does not provide the quality of a personal visit but is much cheaper. While a commercial or industrial salesperson might average perhaps 5 or 6 fast personal sales calls per day, he or she can average perhaps 30 long telephone calls. The costs are much lower because of the lack of travel. Personal sales calls tend to cost upward of $100 each, while normal-length telephone calls cost generally under $10 each.

The cost advantage makes telemarketing a good substitute for visits to small accounts. Fieldcrest, for example, has been using telemarketing in conjunction with catalogs to introduce and sell bed and bath fashions to stores in sparsely settled areas.

Supplement to Personal Visits. Some selling situations require periodic sales visits. Often the cost of the required call frequency is greater than the sales volume justifies and, in these cases, telephone calls can supplement personal visits. The visits might be made two to four times per year and the telephone calls eight to ten times per year for a total frequency of one per month—but at a cost substantially lower than twelve visits. Personal visits would be used for the opening presentation of, say, a new line of apparel or furniture or the sale of equipment, while telephone calls would be used for fill-in orders or supply sales.

Substitute for Direct Mail. Some insurance salespeople who wish to keep in touch with their customers have switched from using direct mail to the telephone, which gives greater impact—at an admittedly higher cost. For the economics to work well, the person called must be either an existing customer or a good prospect, not just a random name from the phone book. Telemarketing has been successful in selling subscription renewals and other continuity sales and could also aid sales of large consumer durables such as automobiles, swimming pools, and appliances. A Cadillac salesperson might, for example, telephone owners of Lincoln Continentals or Mercedes that are a few years old.

As a Supplement. Telemarketing can add to as well as replace direct mail and media advertising. Many companies have effectively used 800 telephone numbers in direct mail, television, and print media advertising. Such a program has three advantages over mail replies: (1) the prospect can make an immediate commitment to purchase while the idea is fresh and the desire for action greatest—and, perhaps more important, he or she can get an immediate reply; (2) it is easier for most people to telephone than to fill in a coupon and mail it; (3) the selling company can become actively involved in supplying product information to aid the customer's decision making, and the customer can also express concerns to be responded to by the telephone salespeople in the future media communication or even in later product development.

The combined media/telemarketing approach has been successful for a variety of products, including specialty coffees, smokeless tobacco, books, and records. AT&T uses the approach to sell many of its products and services. An additional advantage is the quick generation of data about media effectiveness. Within a few days a company or its advertising agency can determine the effectiveness of a new advertising campaign. With mail response, the time lag slows the analysis so that a compaign is generally run longer before review.

Customer-Company Coordination. Finally, the telephone can be used as a part of a communications program to tie companies to their constituencies. The responsiveness and convenience of the telephone, combined with its two-way message content, make it particularly appropriate for this use. A dissatisfied customer, for example, can get a quick response to a problem.[1]

Confused customers who need product information can get it when they need it most, thus preventing product misuse and abuse. O.M. Scott & Sons Co. uses this approach to good advantage in its lawn and garden care business. Problems with the product or its distribution become clear to the seller and can be rectified quickly without much loss of the expensive time of dealers and salespeople. A manufacturer can use the telephone to gather information from salespeople or dealers to find, for example, whether a new product is selling well or whether competitors met a price increase.

The use of the telephone in marketing can create junk phone calls much like junk mail in direct mail advertising. For both economic and customer relations reasons, we advocate the use of selective telemarketing, showing good judgment and good taste. Otherwise, the attention-getting quality of the telephone in uncontrolled situations can irritate consumers.

The telephone's particular mix of benefits and growing cost-effectiveness versus other media make it an increasingly important part of the communications mix. Ongoing telephone contact with customers or prospects can produce important information through close communication. And once the line is open, there are ever-increasing opportunities to creatively cross sell complementary products and services.

Catalog Selling

An old approach in the consumer goods market, catalog selling is an evolving method in industrial and commercial markets. Companies active in the office- and computer-supply businesses have found catalogs to be an efficient way of generating the relatively small dollar sales typical of their businesses. The Drawing Board, an office supply company in Dallas, apparently relies solely on its catalog for communication with customers.

Wright Line, Inc., a $50 million vendor of computer-related supplies and capital equipment for computer rooms, programmers and analysts, and small businesses, has developed an elaborate communications system that includes personal selling, telemarketing, and catalogs. The 140-person sales force makes visits for the larger capital equipment sales and for developing systems sales. The quarterly catalog generates both fill-in sales of capital equipment and supplies for already-sold systems, as well as orders from customers whose size would not justify a personal call. Customers can place orders by mail, through the salespeople, or by telephone. Most orders come in by telephone and mail. The catalog—a new approach at Wright Line—has improved sales volume more than Wright Line executives had expected.

Wright Line's integrated approach developed through a combination of careful analysis and trial-and-error testing. Management has been willing and able to try new approaches, carefully analyze the results, and commit resources to the successful experiments.

Other industries have also used catalogs, particularly in conjunction with telephone order centers or telemarketing centers. Sigma Chemical Co., for example, uses a catalog to sell enzymes for laboratory use, although competitors generally use sales forces. Other catalog applications include electronic components and industrial supplies. The approach is highly cost-effective in transmitting a great deal of information to selected prospects and customers in a usable, inexpensive format.

It is interesting to relate the development of the five evolving options to the more traditional approaches. Personal selling led to national account management. Demonstration centers and industrial stores are variations on the trade show. Telemarketing developed from telephone selling and the early inside order desks of industrial distributors. And industrial stores and catalog selling are based on retail stores and consumer catalogs, such as those used by Sears, Roebuck and Co., that date from the nineteenth century.

Economics and technology are driving the evolution, and the need for more precise communications programs is encouraging it.

CREATING A PROGRAM

The newer ways of selling, when combined with the traditional communications approaches, enable marketers to make precise choices in developing their communications programs. Four major steps are necessary for developing an effective program:

- Analyze the communications costs.
- Specify the communications needs.
- Formulate a coherent program.
- Monitor the total system.

Analyze Current Costs

The basic device for understanding marketing costs is a marketing-oriented income statement that divides all costs into three primary categories—manufacturing, physical distribution, and communication—and two generally smaller categories—nondivisible overhead and profit (see Exhibit 1).

This income statement differs from the company's income statement. To be useful, it should begin with the price the customer pays. Distributor discounts are allocated to communications cost (the value of the retail and/or wholesale salespeople, display, advertising, trade show attendance) and physical distribution cost (order processing, inventory carrying, transportation). If the distributor customizes the product in the field (e.g., adds accessories, cuts to shape, mixes), the cost of doing so should be allocated to the manufacturing task.

The well-designed marketing-oriented income statement helps marketers determine the role of each set of costs (manufacturing, distribution, and communication) in their businesses. Marketers can then ask questions such as:

- Where should I concentrate my cost-cutting activities?
- What do I get and, more important perhaps, what does my customer get from each of the three functions?

EXHIBIT I. A Marketing-Oriented Income Statement

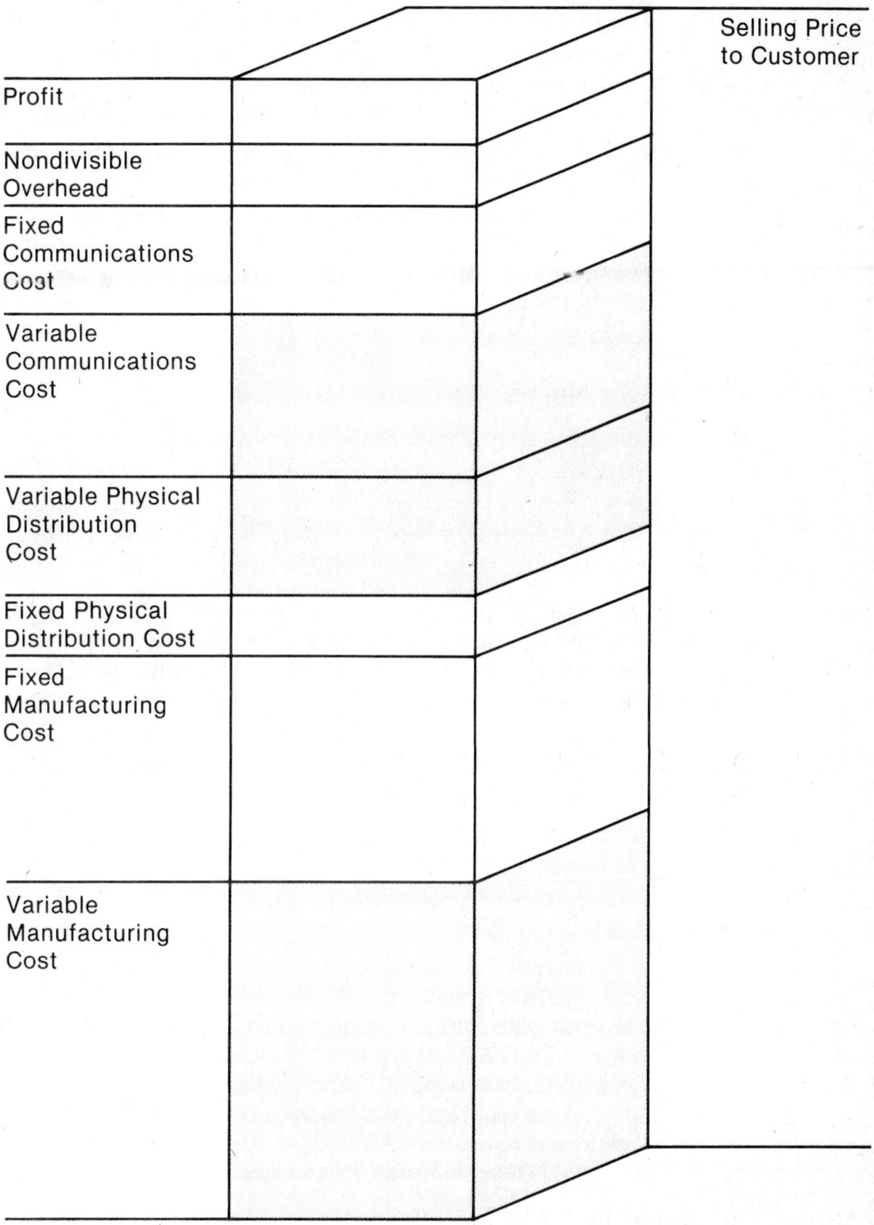

- Selling Price to Customer
- Profit
- Nondivisible Overhead
- Fixed Communications Cost
- Variable Communications Cost
- Variable Physical Distribution Cost
- Fixed Physical Distribution Cost
- Fixed Manufacturing Cost
- Variable Manufacturing Cost

- Do the benefits provided by each function justify the costs?

Marketing executives can thus categorize their businesses as communications intensive, distribution intensive, or manufacturing intensive and can then analyze competitors from the same viewpoints. Avon Products, for example, trades off higher physical distribution costs (sending its cosmetics and toiletries in small packages to its several hundred thousand salespeople) against the higher communications costs of its competitors, which place more emphasis on advertising but use more efficient distribution methods (large sales to supermarket and drug chains that depend on the customer to pick up the order and transport it home).

The marketing-oriented income statement helps to analyze communications costs at a strategic, but not a tactical, level. We cannot consider the detailed costs without first specifying marketers' communications needs or objectives.

Specify Needs

Marketing executives must state precisely the objectives of the communications program and also understand the costs of achieving each objective. There are many different types of communication between a company and its marketing constituencies. Companies may wish to strive for four major goals in specifying their needs:

1. *Persuasive impact.* Two-way communication is more effective than one-way communication. Media advertising by itself, for example, tends to be one way—from the seller to the buyer—while methods such as telemarketing allow a two-way dialogue.
2. *Customization.* Different people, even within the same buying unit, desire different information, and opportunities for customization vary. Two-way communication, of course, enables the seller to tailor a message to the precise needs of a specific customer at a given moment.
3. *Speed.* Some information is much more time sensitive than others. An order to a commodities broker, for example, is urgent. And because we live in an era that stresses instant gratification, many consumers want to obtain the product as soon as possible after making their choice, even if they have labored over that choice for weeks, months, or even years.
4. *Convenience.* Almost everybody, from a professional purchasing agent to a child buying a stick of bubble gum, wants convenience in making purchases.

Formulate a Program

Marketers can create the most effective communications program only with a complete understanding of the relationships among both the old and the evolving options. Perhaps even more important than the media on their own is their potential for integration into a synergistic system that uses each to its best advantage. Exhibit II shows the evolving and traditional options and their varying impact and cost per message.

Combinations are especially powerful because each medium has a different mix of benefits and economics. It is easy to envision a communications system that uses all 10 of the media and combinations listed in Exhibit II. To illustrate, media advertising gives broad coverage at a low cost. Direct mail can be used for a somewhat focused message to a specific group of people at a very reasonable cost. Catalog selling provides a great deal of information, particularly for a wide product assortment, to a focused audience. Telemarketing increases the cost relative to options below it but adds a two-way personalized message, convenience, speed, and the best timing.

The combination of catalogs and telemarketing mixes good economics, much information transmittal, and the advantages of the telephone. Industrial stores and trade shows offer the benefits of personal selling with the cost advantages of a stationary sales force. Of course, customer convenience suffers.

Again, personal selling provides important advantages at a high cost. The addition of a demonstration center increases the cost but provides important benefits in major sales. And, finally, national account management provides the ultimate communications medium at the highest cost.

Different approaches can be used for different customers, products, situations, and communications needs. Companies that market many products to many different types of customers will generally need a wider variety of communications modes than companies having a narrower product and customer mix. It should be no surprise that companies such as Digital Equipment and AT&T, with their many products, many types of customers, and new technologies to sell, have been at the forefront of the new approaches. They had little choice.

Time is an important dimension in the development of a synergistic communications program for three major reasons:

- First, marketers must plan each communications program with regard to the events of the product's life cycle. The planned introduction of a variation in a product, for example, might require an equally carefully planned change in the communications mix—perhaps to emphasize a new use or a new set of users. Customer knowledge moves through its own life cycle. At some points in a product's life, developing brand awareness among prospects might be particularly important, while at other times the primary emphasis would be on reassuring existing customers.

EXHIBIT II. Comparing the Evolving and Traditional Options

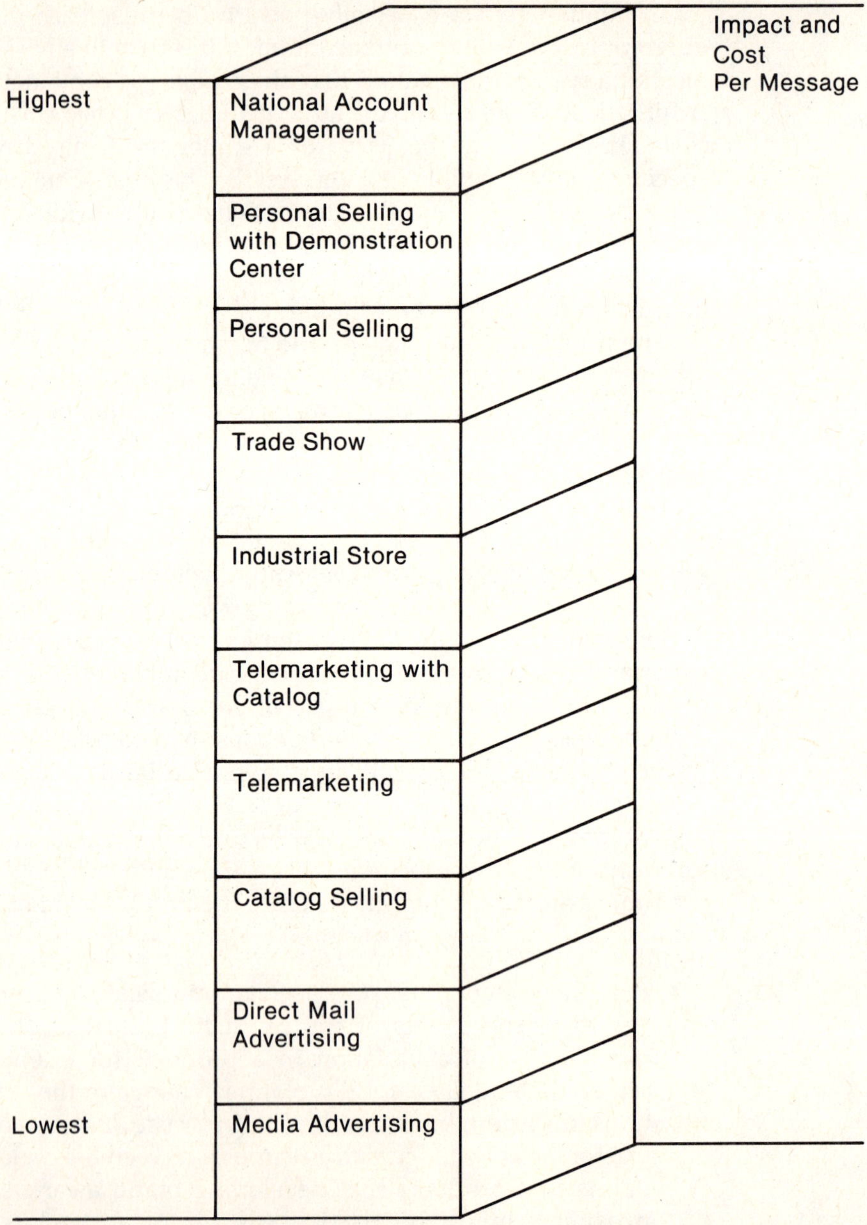

Impact and Cost Per Message

Highest
- National Account Management
- Personal Selling with Demonstration Center
- Personal Selling
- Trade Show
- Industrial Store
- Telemarketing with Catalog
- Telemarketing
- Catalog Selling
- Direct Mail Advertising
- Media Advertising

Lowest

- Second, it takes a long time to implement communications programs. The progression from initial start-up to effective operation of a national account program, for example, can take four to five years. The same is true, but to a lesser extent, of the other media shown in Exhibit II. It can take a year to develop, test, and carefully execute a good media advertising or catalog sales program. In general, the communications methods with greater impact and higher cost per message in Exhibit II require more time to implement than those lower in the hierarchy.
- Third, careful planning over time involves the raison d'être of all marketing activities—the customer. Customers remember. Thus, frequently changing communications programs is ineffective, inefficient, and confusing. Customers used to sales calls will not immediately embrace an industrial store or a telemarketing program. All communications programs must reflect a concern for the customer's memory.

The mix-and-match process of developing a program from a set of communications media alternatives has four integral dimensions: market segments, products, media, and time. A lack of concern for any of these elements weakens the whole program.

Monitor the Total System

In some communications-intensive companies the cost of communication can be upward of one-fourth of total sales. Obviously, such expenditures warrant careful control.

Wherever possible, managers should gather and analyze all the data related to the communications process. Executives who use industrial stores will have to think as retailers do about such things as traffic (flow of people into the store) and accessibility.

For example, they should monitor the number of visitors to an industrial store, the source of their initial communication, the percentage of "qualified" prospects, and the percentage of sales. Catalog marketers and telemarketers, of course, can monitor such factors as the average size of an order by customer type, the types of products purchased, and frequency of order.

EFFECTIVENESS & EFFICIENCY

This article began by discussing reasons for the evolution of newer communications options which, in essence, developed because of cost pressures and the need to accomplish new tasks. The evolving options save costs in three ways:

1. *Greater impact.* A demonstration center, for example, replaces a great deal of traditional personal selling effort. The concept that a smaller amount of high-impact media is more effective than a larger amount of low-impact media is behind a good deal of the evolving options.
2. *Time saving.* Marketers can save time either through the use of the medium with the greatest impact (as in the demonstration center) or through less travel (as in the case of industrial stores, telemarketing, or catalogs).
3. *Greater coordination and closer control.* Marketers can also eliminate waste through greater coordination, as in national account management, or through the closer control possible in industrial stores, telemarketing centers, and catalog operations than in a traditional field sales force.

In summary, then, careful cost analysis, precise needs specification, creative program formulation, and meticulous monitoring will lead to more effective and efficient communication with greater customer impact and lower costs.

ENDNOTES

1. For an example of this application, see "Good Listener: At Procter & Gamble Success Is Largely Due to Heeding Customer," *Wall Street Journal*, April 29, 1980.

36 Effectiveness in Sales Interactions: A Contingency Framework

Barton A. Weitz

Reprinted from the *Journal of Marketing*, published by the American Marketing Association, Vol. 45 (Winter 1981), pp. 85–103. Reprinted by permission.

In 1978, the average expenditure for training each industrial salesperson was over $15,000 (*Sales and Marketing Management* 1979). Even though annual sales training expenses are well over one billion dollars, there is only limited knowledge about which selling behaviors are most effective in customer interactions. A conceptual framework for exploring this issue is presented in this paper.

To demonstrate the focus of this framework, a scheme for classifying variables related to salesperson performance is shown in Figure 1. The initial classification is based on whether the variable relates to the salesperson's macroenvironment or microenvironment. Macroenvironmental variables include territorial characteristics such as potential and workload and the level of effort expended by the salesperson in covering the territory. However, the objective of the framework presented in this paper is to delineate factors related to the effectiveness of salespeople in influencing customers during interpersonal interactions. Thus, the framework focuses on the effectiveness of sales behaviors in the microenvironment of the sales interaction.

Variables related to effectiveness in the microenvironment are further classified into those related to the sales situation and those related to the salesperson. Variables related to the salesperson's effort during customer interactions are not treated in the framework. Thus, the framework focuses on the shaded areas in Figure 1.

The fundamental idea behind the framework is that effectiveness in sales interactions can be understood best by examining the interactions between sales behaviors, resources of the salesperson, the nature of the customer's buying task, and characteristics of the salesperson-customer relationship. This framework provides a mechanism for integrating previous research and a direction for future research.

In the next section, the shortcomings of prior research on effectiveness in sales interactions are discussed. These shortcomings suggest the need for a contingency approach. After presenting the nature and applications of a contingency approach, the approach is expanded into a framework. The basic postulate of the framework is stated, constructs in the framework are defined, and a set of propositions is developed. These propositions are supported by research in leadership, bargaining, social psychology, and personal selling. Further research is needed to complete the framework; however, the portions of the framework presented in this paper suggest a potentially fruitful direction for studying effectiveness in sales interactions. The paper concludes with a discussion of a research program to explore this new direction.

RESEARCH ON EFFECTIVENESS IN SALES INTERACTIONS

Research concerning effectiveness in sales interactions has concentrated on uncovering salesperson behaviors, behavioral predispositions,

FIGURE 1. Variables Related to Salesperson Performance

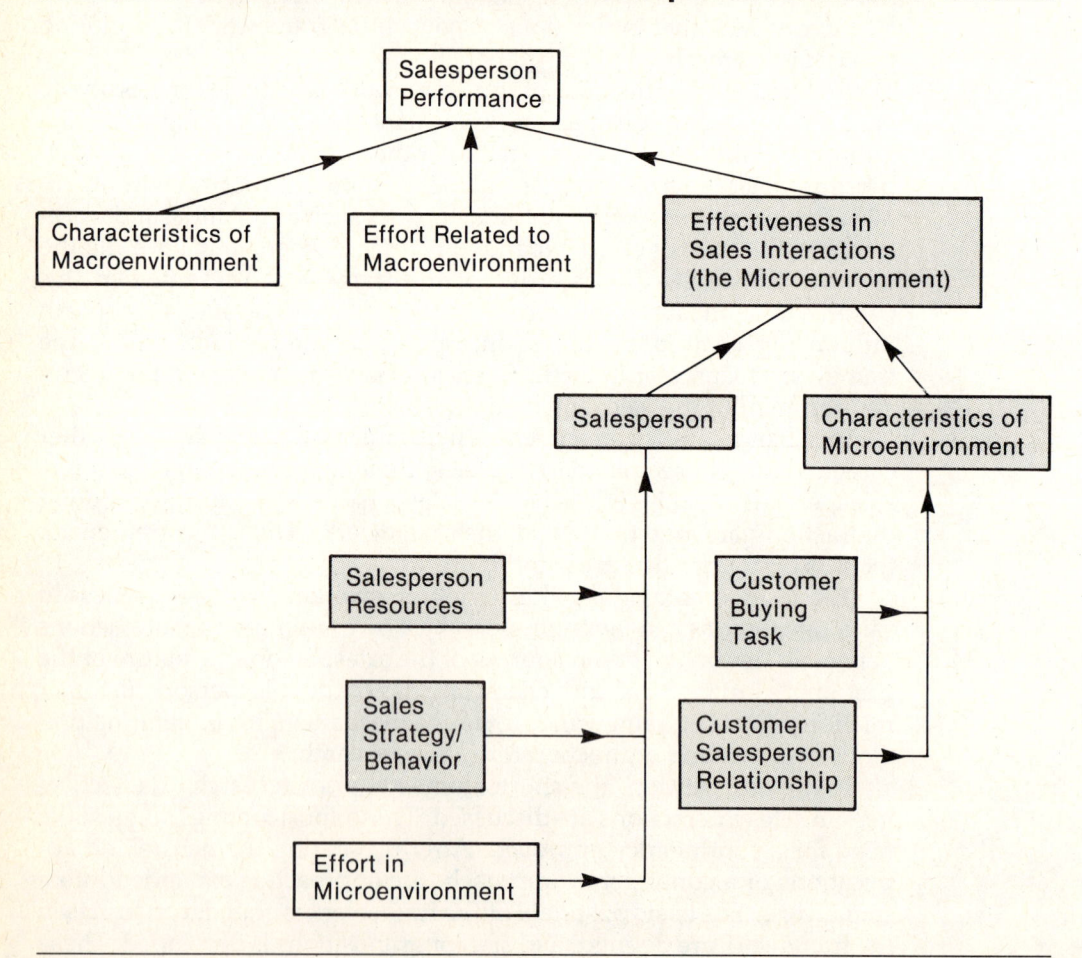

and capabilities related to performance. Each of these research streams is reviewed below. (See Weitz 1979 for a more detailed review.)

Sales Behaviors and Behavioral Predispositions

The study of sales behaviors has been limited to experimental studies examining the effectiveness of different types of messages delivered by salespeople.[1] These studies have found little difference in effectiveness across message types. Levitt (1965) found that a "good presentation" was more effective than a "poor presentation." Jolson (1975) reported that a "canned" presentation generated more purchase intention than an "extemporaneous" presentation but the universality of this finding has been questioned (Reed 1976). There were no significant differences in the effectiveness of a product-oriented versus a personal-oriented message (Farley & Swinth 1967); "hard sell," emotional appeals versus "soft-sell," rational appeals (Reizenstein 1971); and six different sales appeals based on Bales Interaction Process Analysis categories (Capon 1975). Thus, experimental studies have failed to uncover influence strategies consistently related to effectiveness in an interaction.

Correlational studies have attempted to uncover relationships between personality traits/behavioral predispositions and performance. The results of these studies are summarized in Table 1.[2] This summary demonstrates that the relationship between these personality traits and performance is equivocal. Characteristics associated with forcefulness were significantly related to performance in ten studies but were not significantly related to performance in four studies. Social orientation was significant in two studies and insignificant in six studies.

Capability and Resources of Salespeople

A second stream of research has examined relationships between performance and the salesperson's resources and capabilities. Several studies have examined the relationship between performance and specific abilities conceptually related to interpersonal persuasion. These studies indicate that effectiveness in sales interactions is related to the salesperson's ability to develop accurate impressions of customer beliefs about product performance (Weitz 1978); the salesperson's ability to use these impressions in selecting influence strategies (Weitz 1978), and the salesperson's ability to detect the impact of influence strategies and make adaptations (Grikscheit and Crissey 1973).

The results of studies that have examined more general measures of capabilities are summarized in Table 2. This summary indicates that the relationship between capabilities and performance, like the relationship between performance and behavioral predispositions, is quite *inconsistent*, and in some cases, even *contradictory*. In some cases these inconsistencies may be due to variations in methodology across studies. However, several studies have used the same methodology across different sales forces and reported inconsistent results (Dunnette and Kirchner 1960; Howells 1968; Mattheiss et al. 1977; Scheibelhut and Albaum 1973). Even variables that can be assessed with high accuracy and reliability, such as age, education, and sales experience, are related to performance in some studies and unrelated in others.

Customer Characteristics—The Dyadic Approach

The disappointing results from prior research on sales behaviors, behavioral predispositions, and general salesperson capabilities have led to a growing interest in dyadic research approaches. While there are a wide variety of studies associated with the dyadic approach, the unifying theme of these studies is that characteristics of the customer as well as those of the salesperson are considered. This approach is consistent with a contingency approach because it suggests that effectiveness in sales interations is moderated by or dependent upon characteristics of both the salesperson and the customer.

Dyadic similarity studies have not demonstrated a meaningful rela-

татLE 1. Behavioral Predispositions and Performance

Significantly Related to Performance	Not Significantly Related to Performance
Forcefulness	
oil company (Harrell 1960)	oil company (Miner 1962)
life insurance (Merenda & Clarke 1959, Greenberg & Mayer 1964)	life insurance (Zdep & Weaver 1967)
retail/trade (Howells 1968)	retail (Howells 1968)
technical rep (Howells 1968)	stockbroker (Ghiselli 1973)
commodities (Howells 1968)	
mutual fund (Greenberg & Mayer 1964)	
automobile (Greenberg & Mayer 1964)	
trade (Dunnette & Kirchner 1960)	
stockbroker (Ghiselli 1973)	
food, appliance wholesaler (Mattheiss et al. 1977)	
Sociability	
life insurance (Merenda & Clarke 1959)	oil company (Miner 1962, Harrell 1960)
technical rep (Howells 1968)	industrial (Pruden & Peterson 1971)
retail (Howells 1968)	real estate (Scheibelhut & Albaum 1973)
retail/trade food (Howells 1968)	utility (Scheibelhut & Albaum 1973)
	industrial (Bagozzi 1978)
	food, appliance wholesaler (Mattheiss et al. 1977)

tionship between similarity and effectiveness. Several correlational studies have either not supported the relationship (Doreen, Emery, and Sweitzer 1979) or found similarity explains a low percentage of the variance (Churchill, Collins, and Strang 1975). In addition, the correlation studies (Churchill et al. 1975; Evans 1963; Riordan, Oliver and Donnelly 1977) have not controlled for the plausible rival hypothesis that customers who made purchases perceived that they were more similar to the salespeople than customers who did not make purchases (Davis and

TABLE 2. Salesperson Capabilities and Performance

Significantly Related to Performance	Not Significantly Related to Performance
Age	
industrial (Kirchner et al. 1960)	household durable (Cotham 1969)
retail (Mosel 1952, Weaver 1969)	life insurance (Tanofsky et al. 1969; Merenda and Clarke 1959)
	industrial (Lamont & Lundstrom 1977)
	retail (French 1960)
Education	
life insurance (Merenda & Clarke 1959)	specialty food manufacturer (Baehr & Williams 1968)
retail (Mosel 1952, Weaver 1969)	insurance (Tanofsky et al. 1969)
	industrial (Lamont & Lundstrom 1977)
	household durable (Cotham 1969)
	retail (French 1960)
Sales Related Knowledge, Sales Experience, Product Knowledge, Training	
Life insurance (Baier & Dugan 1957)	life insurance (Tanofsky et al. 1969, Merenda & Clarke 1959)
	specialty food manufacturer (Baehr & Williams 1968)
	household durable (Cotham 1969)
	retail (French 1960)
Intelligence	
stockbroker (Ghiselli 1973)	oil company (Harrell 1960)
oil company (Miner 1962, Harrell 1960)	trade (Dunnette & Kirchner 1960)
industrial (Bagozzi 1978)*	appliance wholesaler (Mattheiss et al. 1977)
Empathy	
new automobile (Tobolski & Kerr 1952)	used automobile (Tobolski & Kerr 1952)
automobile (Greenberg & Mayer 1964)	industrial (Lamont & Lundstrom 1977)
life insurance (Greenberg & Mayer 1964)	
mutual fund (Greenberg & Mayer 1964)	

*significant but negatively related.

Silk 1972). While experimental studies found that similarity is a significant factor in determining sales performance, it has not been as important as expertise (Bambic 1978; Busch and Wilson 1976; Woodside and Davenport 1974).[3]

Research exploring the effectiveness of dyadic similarity has not provided the new approach needed for studying effectiveness in sales interactions. These dyadic studies have focused on a single, static property and have not considered the interaction between sales behaviors and dyadic characteristics. The contingency framework presented in this paper expands upon the dyadic approach by describing the relationship between effectiveness, sales behaviors, and a variety of salesperson and customer characteristics.

CONTINGENCY FACTORS AND PERSONAL SELLING EFFECTIVENESS

Past research efforts have attempted to uncover universal characteristics or behaviors that enable salespeople to perform successfully across a wide range of situations. Interactions between sales behaviors and aspects of the sales situation have not been considered. This research has ignored the unique advantage of personal selling in a company's marketing communication mix. Salespeople have the opportunity to match their behavior to the specific customer and situation they encounter. They can consider each interaction individually and present themselves and their product so as to be maximally effective in that interaction. In some interactions salespeople might find it more advantageous to present themselves as similar to their customers, while in other interactions salespeople might find it more advantageous to be perceived as an expert.

Prior Considerations of Contingency Factors

The impact and managerial significance of examining the interaction between sales behaviors and sales environment is not a novel idea. Thompson (1973, p. 8) states that "every contact a salesman has... involves different human problems or situations. In brief, *there is no one sales situation and no one way to sell.*" Gwinner (1968) proposed that four traditional approaches to selling have advantages and drawbacks that make each suitable in particular selling environments. In addition, it has been suggested that different approaches and salesperson characteristics are needed to be effective in selling new business versus selling to established customers (Kahn and Shuchman 1961), selling to purchase-oriented versus salesperson-oriented customers (Blake and Mouton 1970), and selling to customers who vary on the dimensions of dominance-submissive and hostile-warm (Buzzota, Lefton, and Sherberg 1972).[4]

Although little empirical research has explicitly considered interactions between environmental variables and sales behaviors, several researchers have demonstrated empirically that the relationship between performance and behavioral predispositions varies across sales circumstances. Differences in the relationship between personality traits and effectiveness have been found for industrial/trade salespeople and retail sales clerks (Ghiselli 1969), trade and industrial salespeople (Dunnette and Kirchner 1960; Howells 1968), real estate and private utility salespeople (Scheibelhut and Albaum 1973), and new and used car salespeople (Tobolski and Kerr 1952). Chapple and Donald (1947) found that the relationships between communication styles and performance differed across retail selling situations. For example, speech initiation behavior was related to the performance of salespeople operating in an open floor environment but not related to salespeople working behind a counter.

Contingency Factors in Leadership Research

The leadership research illustrates the benefits to be gained by considering interactions between behaviors and moderating variables. The analogy between personal selling and leadership is particularly appropriate due to the similarity in behaviors considered and the similarity in historical development. Personal selling can be defined as the process by which a salesperson attempts to influence a customer to purchase his/her product, while leadership is defined as the "process whereby one person exerts social influence over the members of a group" (Filley, House, and Kerr 1976, p. 211). Thus, the salesperson directs influence behaviors toward customers just as the leader directs influence behaviors toward group members.

Three approaches have been used to study leadership effectiveness (Filley et al. 1976). The first approach looked for personality traits that differentiate effective and ineffective leadership. These studies were followed by attempts to identify behavior patterns associated with effective leadership. The inability to find universally effective behaviors has led researchers over the past twenty years to direct their attention toward studying the interaction between leader characteristics, leader behaviors, and characteristics of the work situation (Filley et al. 1976). Theories based on these interactions are referred to as contingency theories since the relationship between performance and leader behavior is contingent upon or moderated by characteristics of the leader, the subordinates, and the work situation.

A contingency approach also provides a promising framework for studying the effectiveness of interpersonal influence behaviors in sales situations. Such a framework is developed in the next section. After stating a basic postulate, each construct is defined and propositions describing the relationship between the constructs are presented.

A Contingency Framework for Sales Effectiveness Across Interactions

A contingency framework for investigating the effectiveness of sales behaviors across interactions is shown in Figure 2. The basic elements of the framework are (a) the behavior of the salesperson in customer interactions, (b) the salesperson's resources, (c) the customer's buying task, and (d) the customer-salesperson relationship. The following basic postulate describes the interrelationship of these elements:

> Basic Postulate The effectiveness of sales behaviors across customer interactions is contingent upon or moderated by (a) the salesperson's resources, (b) the nature of the customer's buying task, (c) the customer-salesperson relationship and interactions among (a), (b), and (c).

This framework for personal selling specifies that effectiveness is related to the first-order interaction between behaviors and characteristics associated with the salesperson, the customer, and the dyad. Potential higher-order interactions are anticipated in the basic postulate. Based on this postulate it is not surprising that previous research on personal selling has failed to find consistent, main effect relationships between performance and individual elements such as behavioral tendencies (forceful or sociable personality traits), behaviors (hard sell versus soft sell or establishing referent versus expertise influence bases), salesperson resources (intelligence, empathy), and characteristics of customer-salesperson relationships (dyadic similarity).

Each of the constructs associated with the framework is discussed in the next section, followed by some propositions derived from past research. The elements and propositions discussed in this paper were selected on the basis of past research in personal selling and leadership. They are not intended to exploit completely the potential set of propositions that can be developed from the framework.

Constructs in a Contingency Framework

Salesperson Effectiveness

Effectiveness is defined from the perspective of the salesperson rather than the salesperson-customer dyad. This perspective differs from a conceptualization of the salesperson-customer interaction as a problem solving activity in which two parties attempt to reach a mutually beneficial solution (Willett and Pennington 1966). The problem solving perspective is not used because it does not consider the inherent advocacy nature of the salesperson's activities. While salespeople are somewhat interested in searching for a solution to the customer's problem that maximizes customer satisfaction, they and their managers strongly prefer solutions that incorporate the purchase of the products or services they are selling.

Consistent with the salesperson and sales management perspective, effectiveness in sales interactions is defined by the degree in which the "preferred solutions" of salespeople are realized *across their customer interactions*.[5] This definition of effectiveness incorporates the fundamental interest of management in the performance of salespeople and selling

FIGURE 2. A Contingency Model of Salesperson Effectiveness

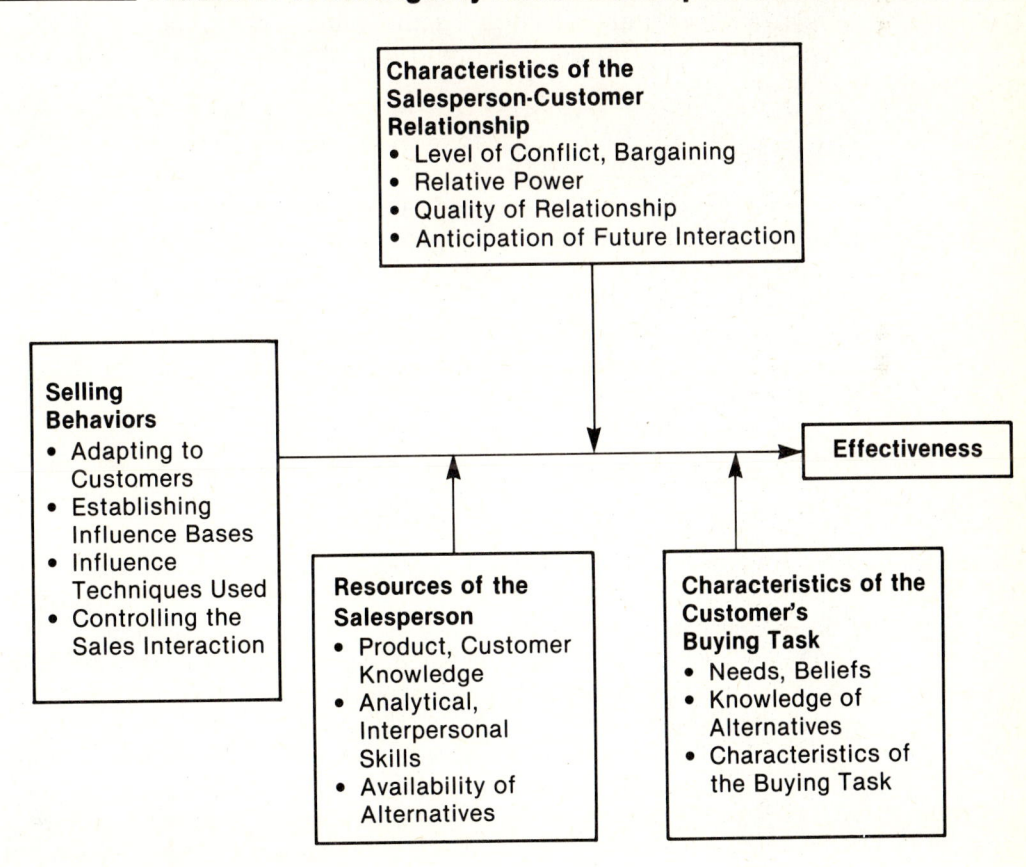

Characteristics of the Salesperson-Customer Relationship
- Level of Conflict, Bargaining
- Relative Power
- Quality of Relationship
- Anticipation of Future Interaction

Selling Behaviors
- Adapting to Customers
- Establishing Influence Bases
- Influence Techniques Used
- Controlling the Sales Interaction

Resources of the Salesperson
- Product, Customer Knowledge
- Analytical, Interpersonal Skills
- Availability of Alternatives

Characteristics of the Customer's Buying Task
- Needs, Beliefs
- Knowledge of Alternatives
- Characteristics of the Buying Task

Effectiveness

behaviors across the entire set of interactions in which salespeople engage. The outcome of a specific interaction is of secondary interest.[6]

Even though this definition of effectiveness does not explicitly consider customer satisfaction, customer satisfaction is considered implicitly because effectiveness is defined across customer interactions. The following illustration demonstrates the implications associated with an effectiveness measure based on performance across interactions rather than during one interaction. Suppose a salesperson made a sale by using a deceptive influence strategy. From the salesperson's perspective, this influence strategy would have been effective in the interaction. However, the customer might not be satisfied with the product, and realizing the deception, would not buy products from the salesperson in the future. Thus, the use of deceptive influence strategies would not be effective for the salesperson across interactions with the customer, even though it was effective in one specific interaction.

Adopting a salesperson perspective does not mean that the customer's characteristics and needs are not considered. Customer characteristics and needs are considered in the framework, but only in terms of their moderating influence on the effectiveness of a salesperson's behavior.

Salesperson Behaviors

While marketers have described salesperson orientations (Blake and Mouton 1970) or general sales approaches (Gwinner 1968), most empirical research on salesperson behaviors have considered microbehaviors such as the effectiveness of specific sales messages. Little though has been directed toward identifying underlying dimensions in which a salesperson's behavior can be assessed. In the remaining portion of this section, some of these dimensions are discussed.

Adapting to the Customer. The behavior of salespeople can be characterized by the degree to which they adapt their behavior to the interaction. At one extreme, salespeople are nonadaptive when they deliver the same "canned" presentation (Jolson 1975) to all customers. In contrast to this nonadaptive behavior, salespeople can engage in a unique behavior pattern oriented to each customer.

Dimensions on which sales behavior can be adapted are discussed in following sections. It seems reasonable to assume that the effectiveness of influence bases, influence techniques, specific messages and formats, and the degree of control exerted varies across a salesperson's customers. Thus a salesperson could increase effectiveness in a specific interaction by altering behavior along the above mentioned dimensions (Weitz 1980).

Measures of adaptivity in sales behavior have not been developed;

however, there are some personality measures that indicate a predisposition to engage in adaptive behaviors. For example, one would expect dogmatism and authoritarianism to be negatively related to adaptivity while tolerance for ambiguity would be positively related to adaptivity. A dispositional measure that appears to be closely related to adaptive behavior is self-monitoring. Snyder (1974) has developed a scale to measure the degree to which people monitor their environment and use these environmental cues to alter their behavior. One would expect that high self-monitors would be more adaptive in sales situations.

Establishing a Base of Influence. Another dimension of salesperson behavior is attempting to establish a base of influence. Wilson (1975) suggests that salespeople need to develop source credibility and legitimacy during the initial stages of an interaction. Without such a base of influence, salespeople cannot effectively influence their customers.

In a review of the use of influence bases in organizational setting, McCall (1979) concluded that "the relevance of a given power base, the appropriateness of various tactics, and the likely impacts of power use are intimately linked with each other and with the situation at hand." (p. 205) Thus, given a set of possible influence bases (French and Raven 1959), salespeople need guidance as to which bases are most effective in specific circumstances. Propositions concerning variables that moderate the effectiveness of these influence bases are presented in the next section.

Influence Techniques Used. Salesperson behaviors can be classified in terms of the influence techniques used. Several studies have been directed toward defining and analyzing a wide variety of influence techniques (Capon and Swasy 1977; Falbo 1977; Spiro and Perreault 1979). These studies suggest that influence techniques can be classified using the following dimensions: (a) open/direct v. closed/indirect and (b) business/product-related v. emotional/person-related. When open/direct influence attempts are used, the purpose of the influence attempt is not hidden. Closed influence techniques involve the use of deception and hidden purposes. (See Yalch 1979 for a discussion of closed sales techniques used in finalizing a sale.)

Product-related influence techniques are defined as business or task oriented messages—information messages directed toward the product and the purchase decision. In contrast, emotional messages are directed toward the customer with the intent of appealing to psychological needs and improving customer-salesperson relations. Emotional messages attempt to reduce risks associated with the social consequences of the purchase decision, while product messages attempt to reduce risks associated with product performance (Newton 1967).

Influence techniques can also be classified by the target and format of the messages delivered. The target can be defined as the specific cognitive element, belief, or value toward which the message is directed. Message formats include comparative v. noncomparative messages and one-sided v. two-sided appeals.

Controlling the Interaction. The final dimension of sales behavior to be considered is the extent to which the salesperson controls the sales interaction. This behavioral dimension is closely related to the dominant-submissive dimension proposed by Buzzotta, Lefton, and Sherberg (1972), the salesperson-oriented dimension proposed by Blake and Mouton (1970), and the traditional salesperson behavior of using high or low pressure. The use of control or pressure is a method of aggressively directing the flow of the interaction toward making a sale. Several researchers have attempted to assess the degree of control exercised by salespeople by analyzing recordings of sales interactions (Willett and Pennington 1966, Olshavsky 1973).

Some insights into control behaviors of salespeople can be gained by examining leader control behaviors. Autocratic and "initiating structure" leader behaviors are associated with a high degree of leader control. In the context of a sales interaction, autocratic behavior is related to the use of high pressure tactics. Initiating structure behavior is related to the salesperson aggressively structuring the customer's problem so that the solution involves purchasing the salesperson's product.

Moderating Variables

A wide variety of moderating variables are suggested by personal selling and leadership research. In the contingency framework shown in Figure 2 moderating variables are organized into the following three categories: (a) the customer's buying task, (b) the salesperson's resources, and (c) the customer-salesperson relationship. These categories parallel the following moderating variables used in Fiedler's leadership studies (Fiedler and Chemers 1974): the structure of the group's task, the leader's resources (positive power), and the leader-member relations.

Customer's Buying Task. Several researchers have suggested that sales behaviors should vary depending on the buying task confronting the customer. Robinson, Farris, and Wind (1967) defined three types of buying tasks—new buy, modified rebuy, and straight rebuy. The new buy task begins as an ill-structured problem that the customer has confronted in the past, while the straight rebuy is a highly structured, routinized decision. Since these tasks differ in amount of information needed and the level of uncertainty or risk associated with the purchase decision, one would expect that different sales behaviors would be appropriate for each situation. The different sales behaviors required in these situations have led Kahn and Shuchman (1961) to suggest that salespeople should specialize in either selling new customers (new buy or modified rebuy situations) or existing customers (straight rebuy situations).

Hakansson, Johanson, and Wootz (1977) and Newton (1967) have classified purchase decision in terms of the risk associated with decision outcomes. They have defined specific types of risks and suggested appropriate sales behaviors for each risk type. While the Robinson et al. (1967) classification scheme has received wide acceptance in the marketing literature, measures of the underlying dimensions have not been developed. In Fiedler's leadership research, task structure is also an important moderating variable. Task structure is operationalized by examining the following task characteristics: (a) goal clarity, (b) goal path multiplicity, (c) decision verifiability, and (d) decision specificity. These characteristics in a buying task context represent the degree to which the product requirements are known by the customer, the degree to which a variety of products could satisfy the customer's needs, and the degree to which the customer is able to evaluate the performance of the product after the sale.

The Salesperson's Resources. The salesperson enters a customer interaction with a set of skills or abilities, a level of knowledge about the products and the customer, and a range of alternatives that can be offered to the customers. These factors can amplify the effectiveness and/or constrain the range of behaviors in which the salesperson can act effectively. The inclusion of salesperson resources as moderating variables is related to the notion that salespeople should "lead from strength." It is reasonable to assume that salespeople are more effective when they engage in behaviors related to the skills, abilities, and personal characteristics they possess. For example, a highly trained salesperson would be more effective at establishing an expert base on influence and delivering highly informational communications.

In addition to personal resources, the company which the salesperson represents provides resources that can moderate the effectiveness of sales behaviors. Some of these company-provided resources are company reputation, the range of alternatives the salesperson can offer, and the degree to which the salesperson can alter characteristics of the extended product (price, delivery, terms, etc.) to satisfy customer needs. Levitt (1965) demonstrated that the effectiveness of the quality of a sales presentation is moderated by the reputation of the salesperson's company. Saxe (1979) found that the effectiveness of customer-oriented sales behaviors (assessing customer needs, offering products that will satisfy those needs, describing products accurately, avoiding high pressure, etc.) is moderated by the salesperson's ability to help the customer. Ability to help was operationalized as the match between the salesperson's products and the customer needs, the time available to the salesperson, and the support provided by the salesperson's company.

The Customer-Salesperson Relationship. As mentioned previously, dyadic similarity is the only variable associated with the customer-salesperson relationship that has been considered in sales effectiveness research. This research, reviewed above, indicates that the dyadic similarity is, at best, weakly related to effectiveness.[7]

Two characteristics of the customer-salesperson relationship that have not been considered in sales effectiveness research are the relative power and the level of conflict between the members of the dyad. Both power and conflict have received considerable attention in social psychology (Raven and Rubin 1976), organizational behavior (McCall 1979; Thomas 1976) and channels of distribution (Reve and Stern 1979).

Relative power can be defined in terms of dependency (Emerson 1962). The relative power of a salesperson over a customer is related to the degree to which the salesperson mediates the customer's achievement of a goal and the importance the customer places on achieving the goal. Thus, a salesperson possessing unique information concerning a solution to a customer's problem would have power over the customer. The more important the problem is to the customer, the more power the salesperson possesses. Conversely, if the salesperson's rewards (income) are dependent upon the customer's business, the customer has power over the salesperson. Thus, the relative power in an interaction could be measured in terms of the importance of each party's goals related to the purchase decision and the degree to which each party affects the other party's achievement of those goals.

Conflict, like relative power, has not been considered in personal selling research. Conflict includes a wide variety of phenomena such as:

> (1) *Antecedent conditions* (for example, scarcity of resources, policy differences) of conflict behavior, (2) *affective states* (e.g., stress, tension, hostility, anxiety) etc., (3) *cognitive states* of individuals (i.e., their perception of awareness of conflict situations), and (4) *conflictful behavior*, ranging from passive resistance to overt aggression (Pondy 1967, p. 268).

In a salesperson-customer relationship, the level of conflict is reflected in the quality of the relationship, the amount of negotiating or bargaining associated with making a sale, the level of competition the salesperson faces, and the degree to which the salesperson's offerings can satisfy the customer's needs.

In addition to relative power and conflict, the *nature of the present customer-salesperson relationship* and the *anticipation of future interactions* can moderate the effectiveness of sales behaviors. One important aspect of the salesperson-customer relationship is whether the salesperson represents an "in" or an "out" supplier. An "in" salesperson is presently selling the product to the customer, while an "out" salesperson is attempting to make an initial sale. Both Kahn and Shuchman (1961) and Robinson et al. (1967) have suggested that "in" and "out" salespeople need to perform different functions. Thus, one would expect that different sales behaviors would be appropriate in each situation.

A final characteristic of the customer-salesperson relationship is the anticipation of future interactions. Research has shown that this characteristic influences the bargaining behavior undertaken by two parties (Rubin and Brown 1975) and presumably the effectiveness of sales behaviors. For example, one would expect that effective retail and industrial salespeople typically engage in different behaviors because industrial salespeople typically have continuing relationships with customers, while the retail salespeople do not.

CONTINGENCY PROPOSITIONS

Some propositions incorporating the previously defined constructs are presented in this section. These propositions are stated so that testable hypotheses can be derived to direct future research efforts.

Propositions Concerning Adaptive Behavior

Proposition 1: Engaging in adaptive sales behaviors across interactions is positively related to effectiveness in the following circumstances:

- Salesperson resources — the salesperson has the resources, both personal abilities and product alternatives, to engage in adaptive sales behaviors.
- Customer buying tasks — the salesperson's customers typically are engaged in complex buying tasks that could result in large orders.
- Customer-salesperson relationship — the salesperson has a good relationship with the customer characterized by a low level of conflict and the salesperson anticipates future relationships with the customer.

In general, the salesperson who adapts his/her behavior to the specific interaction situation will be better at presenting a product as a solution to the customer's problem. Thus, one would expect the degree of adaptive behavior to be positively related to effectiveness in a specific interaction.

However, a salesperson's effectiveness across a series of interactions may not be positively related to adaptiveness because there is a cost associated with adaptive sales behavior. The salesperson must spend time during the interaction to collect information from the customer. This information is used to adapt the sales presentation to the specific customer. The time spent collecting information about the customer is not directly related to the salesperson's effectiveness across customers. The salesperson's effectiveness might be higher if more time were spent selling the customer or calling on other customers.

Thus, one would hypothesize that adaptive sales behavior is positively related to sales performance when the benefits outweigh the costs of adapting. Such circumstances are likely to occur when the benefits of adapting are high (large potential orders, opportunity to use information in anticipated future interaction, high probability of securing an order because of a wide range of alternatives that can be offered) or the costs of adapting are low (low expected cost of collecting information due to good relationships with customers.) In contrast, one would hypothesize no relationship between adaptivity and performance when the costs typically equal or outweigh the benefits. This circumstance is likely to occur when the expected benefits are low (small orders with no potential for future orders) or the expected costs are high (a conflicting relationship that makes it difficult to collect information.) Some empirical support for this proposition is provided by Saxe (1979). He found that a salesperson's resources in terms of capabilities in satisfying customer needs moderated the relationship between effectiveness and the practice of customer-oriented, adaptive behaviors.

Support for these contingency hypotheses concerning adaptive behavior also can be found in the various sales approaches used in industry. Gwinner (1968) indicates that highly qualified and paid salespeople are needed to implement adaptive approaches like problem solution and need satisfaction. These approaches are typically used in industrial sales situations. The least adaptive approach, stimulus response, is limited to "very simple selling situations (low product complexity), to very low-priced products, or to buyer-seller relationships wherein time is an important factor" (Gwinner 1968, p. 39). Thus the stimulus-response approach has been used primarily in door-to-door selling of household products. The mental states approach, a more adaptive approach, is used "in those situations where the product or service is complicated and difficult to understand. In addition, this strategy may be employed when repeat calls on a long-run basis are required. A salesman representing a multiproduct line can effectively use this strategy since the method allows him to vary his sales presentation within the framework of an established plan" (Gwinner 1968, p. 40).

Propositions Concerning the Establishment of an Influence Base

Proposition 2: Attempting to establish an expertise base of influence is positively related to effectiveness in the following circumstances:

- Salesperson resources—the salesperson has a high level of knowledge about the product and the customer's applications.
- Customer buying tasks—the salesperson's customers typically are engaged in high risk, complex buying tasks.
- Customer-salesperson relationship—the salesperson is typically an "out" supplier.

To establish an expertise base of influence or social power, salespeople need to create the impression that they possess superior skills or knowledge related to the purchase decision. It is reasonable to assume that salespeople who actually possess greater knowledge will be more effective in assuming the role of an expert.

The effectiveness of an expertise base of influence is related to the customer's need to make a correct decision. Thus, this base of influence will be more appropriate when customers are engaged in complex, high risk purchase decisions (new buy or modified rebuy tasks). In these purchase decisions, customers have a great need for information that will help in making a good decision. Salespeople who are perceived as experts or as possessing unique skills at reducing the risks associated with the customer's decision will be able to exert substantial influence on the customer's decision.

Wilson (1975) has suggested that the initial stage of customer encounters should be devoted to establishing "credibility and legitimation. Unless this basic acceptability is developed, further communication is likely to become quite ineffective if not impossible" (p. 394). Thus, establishing credibility by creating the impression of expertise would be most effective when an "out" salesperson makes initial contact with a customer.

Proposition 3: Attempting to establish similarities with a customer as a base of influence is positively related to effectiveness in the following circumstances:

- Salesperson resources—the salesperson is actually similar to the customer in terms of characteristics related to the purchase decision.
- Customer-buying task—the salesperson's customers typically are engaged in simple, low risk purchase decisions or in purchase decisions with high psychological or social risks.
- Customer-salesperson relationship—the salesperson is typically an "in" supplier.

Wilson and Ghingold (1980) found that salespeople feel establishing rapport with customers is a critical aspect of effectiveness in sales interactions. One method for establishing rapport is for the salesperson to create a link with the customer by identifying similarities—characteristics they have in common. Establishing similarities may increase the trustworthiness of salespeople, facilitate the exchange of information about salespeople and customers, and lead customers to feel their needs and problems are well understood. Salespeople who actually are similar to their customer will be in a better position to establish this base of influence.

When customers are making simple purchase decisions, their information needs are not great. In these situations, an influence base associated with getting the customers to identify with the salesperson will be more effective than an expertise base of influence. Capon and Swasy (1977) provides some support for this proposition. In a role playing situation, students felt that messages directed at establishing a similarity influence base would be more effective when selling to consumers as opposed to purchasing agents. Presumably consumers typically engage in simpler decision processes with higher psychological risks than purchasing agents.

It may be particularly important for the "in" salesperson to maintain good relations with a customer over a long time period by establishing a similarity base of influence. In support of this proposition, Bambic (1978) found that purchasing agents indicate the greatest preference for an attitudinally similar salesperson when the salesperson represents a qualified "in" supplier.

Proposition Concerning the Use of Influence Techniques

Proposition 4: The use of closed as opposed to open influence techniques is more effective under the following circumstances:

- Customer-salesperson relationships —
  a) The salesperson typically is more powerful than his/her customers.
  b) The level of conflict between the customers and the salesperson is high.
  c) The salesperson typically does not anticipate future interactions with the customer.

The use of closed influence techniques suggests that salespeople are willing to sacrifice a customer's long-term satisfaction so that they can make an immediate sale. This type of behavior would be most effective when customers do not have the opportunity to sanction the salesperson if they discover that they have been manipulated or deceived. If the customers will not be encountering the salesperson in the future, they will not have the opportunity to invoke sanctions such as not considering the salesperson's products in future applications. If the salespeople are more powerful than the customers, the customers will have to forego invoking sanctions because the salespeople control the degree to which the customers can satisfy their needs.

Salespeople might decide to sacrifice future sales to make an immediate sale. This would occur if the immediate sale is very large, larger than potential future sales. In this circumstance, salespeople would risk the long-term consequences associated with closed influence techniques to seek a short-term benefit.

Spiro and Perreault (1979) found that salespeople use closed influence techniques when engaging in difficult sales situations—situations characterized by poor customer-salesperson relationships, low customer interest, and routine purchase decisions involving undifferentiated products. Open influence tactics were used when there was a high level of buyer/seller involvement—situations characterized by good customer-salesperson relationships and purchase decisions that were important to both parties. Assuming that, on average, salespeople engage in appropriate sales behaviors, these findings indicate that closed influence tactics are more effective in high involvement situations.

Proposition Concerning Control of the Sales Interactions

Proposition 5: Attempting to exert control over the sales interaction is related to effectiveness in the following circumstances:

- Customer's buying task—customers are engaged in ambiguous purchase decisons.
- Customer salesperson relationship—
  a) future interactions between customers and the salesperson are not anticipated.
  b) the salespeople typically are more powerful than the customers.

Salespeople who exert a high level of control in a sales interaction frequently direct the interaction toward an outcome that is more compatible with the needs of the salespeople than the needs of the customers. This behavior would be most effective when the customers are confronting an ambiguous problem and do not have adequate information to solve the problem. Since the exertion of control might sacrifice customer satisfaction, this behavior would be more effective when the salesperson has a goal of making an immediate sale. When future interactions with a customer are anticipated, the salesperson's long-term effectiveness will be more closely related to satisfying the customer's needs. Under these circumstances, salespeople might be less effective when they control the interaction towards an outcome desired by them. These conclusions are consistent with Bursk's (1947) description of situations in which low pressure selling is more effective than high pressure selling. Bursk suggests that low pressure selling (low control of the sales interaction) is most appropriate when the customer is knowledgeable and when continued goodwill is at stake.

The leadership research also provides support for this proposition. This research indicates that autocratic, "initiating structure" behaviors (high control behaviors) are most appropriate when the group is engaged in an ambiguous, stressful, and nonroutine task. In addition, the more the group members perceive that they possess the abilities to accomplish a task, the less willing they are to accept directive or coaching behavior from their leader (Filley et al. 1976, p. 255). Supportive, participative, consideration leader behaviors (low control behaviors) are most effective when group members possess information about the task and when the task is routine. Based on these research findings, salespeople will be more effective if they attempt to control sales situations when customers are engaged in routine buying decisions (straight rebuys).

Since little personal selling research has considered the effect of moderating variables, the previously stated propositions are quite speculative. Little empirical support can be provided at this time. A research program for developing and testing contingency hypotheses follows.

Developing and Testing Contingency Propositions

In this section, a research program is outlined for developing and testing contingency hypotheses. The three stages of this program are hypothesis generation, hypothesis testing in a laboratory environment, and hypothesis testing in a field setting. These stages parallel the general framework suggested by Ray (1978) for examining communication phenomena.[8] In discussing the hypothesis testing stage, contingency research approaches are contrasted with the traditional research approach used in personal selling.

Generating Contingency Hypotheses

In the preceding section, a number of contingency propositions are presented. These propositions were developed by reviewing the limited amount of research in personal selling that has considered moderating variables and by translating relevant leadership research into a personal selling context. However, these propositions represent only a portion of the contingency "theories" used by salespeople in their customer interactions.

The everyday use of contingency influence strategies is illustrated in a recent study by Falbo and Peplau (1980). When asked to write open-ended essays on the topic "how I get my way," many subjects indicated that their power strategies varied depending on the target. Thus, the existence of contingency influence strategies arises naturally without prompting from researchers.

Methodologies for uncovering rules or "theories" employed by practitioners are reviewed in Zaltman, Lawther, and Heffring (1980). (See Wilson and Ghingold 1980 for an example of a "theories in use" approach used in a personal selling context.) These "theories in use" methodologies involve observing and questioning salespeople.

One approach for uncovering "theories in use" is to investigate how salespeople organize their knowledge and experience. A richer taxonomy of moderating variables can be developed by determining what characteristics salespeople use to classify customers and sales situations. (See Cantor and Mischel 1979 for a review of the research on social classification schemes used by people.)

Schank and Abelson (1977) proposed that part of knowledge is organized around hundreds of stereotypical situations and activities. The implications of these scripts (stereotypic-action sequences) have been empirically investigated by Bower, Black, and Turner (1979). Salespeople probably possess contingency selling scripts that guide their behavior in customer interactions. One might access these scripts by asking salespeople to describe their behavior in specific sales situations. The nature of the differences in scripts across sales situations should be useful in developing contingency propositions.

Theories in use also can be uncovered by using a cognitive response methodology. Salespeople can be asked to describe their thoughts during specific customer encounters. These thoughts can be collected directly after the encounter or during a replay of a recording of the encounter. A more structured format can be used to collect these cognitive responses by asking salespeople to indicate their thoughts when observing a standardized recording of a customer-sales encounter (Grikscheit 1971).

In contrast to these open-ended methods for collecting information, salespeople can be asked to answer questions concerning the appropriate behavior when confronting a sales scenario (Capon and Swasy 1977) or questions concerning their behavior during a specific past sales encounter (Spiro and Perreault 1979). Vroom and Yetton (1973) have developed a method for soliciting contingency leader responses and describing relevant situational variables.

Experimental Testing of Contingency Propositions

Having developed contingency hypotheses, the next step is to test these hypotheses in a laboratory environment using an experimental design. Laboratory experiments are quick and effective ways for testing behavioral propositions. The control achieved in a laboratory allows the researcher to determine causal relationships between variables and eliminate potential alternative explanations.

The experimental approach has been used in several studies previously reviewed; however, these studies have not been designed to examine contingency hypotheses. Only main effect relationships between effectiveness and salesperson characteristics or behavior were considered in these studies. For example, Woodside and Davenport (1974) manipulated two sales behaviors (establishing an expertise base of influence, and establishing a similarity base of influence) and tested whether differences in these behaviors had an effect on purchasing behavior.

In contrast to these past studies, contingency propositions are tested in an experimental setting by examining the interaction between a sales behavior and a moderating variable. Thus, the second part of proposition 2 would be tested by manipulating the level of expertise expressed by the salesperson and the complexity of the buying decision confronting the subject (customer), and testing for a significant interaction between these two factors.

Levitt's (1965) classic study on industrial selling is the only study in which the effectiveness of a behavior-sales circumstance interaction was investigated. In this study, a behavior (quality of presentation) and a resource of the salesperson (company reputation) were manipulated. Unfortunately, there were methodological problems in examining the contingency (interaction) hypotheses (Capon et al. 1972).

While laboratory experiments are an excellent method for testing theories and determining causality, there are two problems with laboratory experiments for testing hypotheses concerning personal selling. First, laboratory experiments typically sacrifice external validity to insure high internal validity. To insure homogeneous treatments, the salesperson frequently is removed from the experiment. In some experiments, the salesperson is replaced by a videotape (Busch and Wilson 1976), a film (Levitt 1965), or a paper and pencil description (Bambic 1978). In these experiments, the phenomenon under study is more closely related to impersonal, mass communication than interpersonal influence.

Second, laboratory experiments are most readily adapted to testing the effectiveness of sales behaviors in one-shot, selling situations. It is difficult to create laboratory situations that examine the effects of behaviors across sales interactions. This arises because some behaviors such as adaptation and the use of close influence techniques have "carry over" effects. Both adaptation and the close influence techniques can lead to increased effectiveness in one interaction but decreased effectiveness in subsequent interactions. These "carryover effects" are difficult to manipulate and measure in an experimental design. Due to this problem, some propositions can be tested only in field studies. In addition, field tests offer a method for assessing the impact of behavior across actual selling interactions.

FIGURE 3. Steps in Correlational Test of Contingency Hypotheses

```
┌─────────────────────┐         ┌─────────────────────┐
│ Develop measures of │         │ Develop measures of │
│ salesperson         │         │ typical sales       │
│ resources, customer │         │ behavior or         │
│ buying tasks, and   │         │ behavioral          │
│ customer-salesperson│         │ predispositions     │
│ relationships       │         └─────────────────────┘
│ associated with     │                   │
│ typical sales       │                   ▼
│ interactions        │         ┌─────────────────────┐
└─────────────────────┘         │ Administer measures │
           │                    │ to Salespeople      │
           ▼                    └─────────────────────┘
┌─────────────────────┐                   │
│ Administer measures │                   ▼
│ to either sales     │         ┌─────────────────────┐
│ managers or         │         │ Collect performance │
│ customers           │         │ measure for the     │
└─────────────────────┘         │ salespeople         │
           │                    └─────────────────────┘
           │         ┌──────────────────────────┐   │
           └────────▶│ Investigate the          │◀──┘
                     │ moderations effects of   │
                     │ sales situation measures │
                     │ on the behavior-         │
                     │ performance relationship │
                     └──────────────────────────┘
```

Field Testing of Contingency Hypotheses

The steps in testing contingency hypotheses in the field are shown in Figure 3. When contingency hypotheses are tested in the field across interactions, the first step is to develop reliable and valid measures of typical sales behaviors and sales situations (moderator variables) in which salespeople engage.

Few measures of sales behaviors exist; however there are paper and pencil measures to determine influence techniques typically used (Arch 1979), the degree to which a customer-oriented behavior is employed (Saxe 1979), and behavioral predispositions such as self-monitoring. Although studies have postulated moderating variables in the sales situation, no measures of circumstances encountered in sales situations have been developed. Thus, research must be directed toward developing measures of sales behaviors and moderating variables before contingency hypotheses can be tested in field settings.

When behavior and situation measures have been developed, contingency hypotheses can be tested by getting measures of typical behavior patterns from salespeople, typical situation measures from independent sources such as sales managers or customers, and then relating these measures to salesperson effectiveness using techniques for examining moderator variable relationships (Allison 1973; Zedeck 1971). While traditional measures of sales performance such as sales or sales to quota can be used as measures of effectiveness, care must be taken to control for sources of variance unrelated to effectiveness in sales interactions (see Figure 1).

The difference between testing contingency hypotheses in the field and traditional correlational studies of salesperson effectiveness is illustrated by the shaded areas in Figure 3. Traditional correlational studies have considered only the shaded steps. In these studies, measures of salesperson behavioral predispositions and performance are collected. No measures are made of the typical sales situations encountered by the salesperson. Hypotheses are tested by correlating performance with behavioral predispositions.

Contingency studies necessitate the inclusion of the unshaded steps—the collection of situational measures. In addition, the test of contingency hypotheses requires the use of moderator variable regressions so that interactions can be examined.

CONCLUSION

Most empirical research on salesperson performance has been based on the implicit assumption that a universal set of characteristics or behaviors is associated with successful sales performance across all sales situations. It is reasonable to investigate such parsimonious propositions in the early stages of studying a problem, but more complex propositions are warranted if simple propositions fail to explain the phenomenon of interest. The review of the research of personal selling effectiveness at the beginning of this paper illustrates the lack of support for simple universal propositions. These universal propositions have been of some value, but few have consistently explained a significant proposition of the variance in performance. Thus, it is appropriate, at this time, to investigate the more complex propositions in which circumstances of the sales situation moderate the relationship between the salesperson behavior and effectiveness.

To provide a direction for this research approach, some salesperson behaviors and moderating variables were defined and propositions suggested concerning the effectiveness of these behaviors in different sales interaction circumstances. The group of behaviors and moderating variables considered is intended to be suggestive rather than exhaustive. Little research has been directed toward developing a taxonomy of sales behaviors or characteristics of the salesperson-customer interaction. When descriptive research on classifying sales behaviors and interaction characteristics is more advanced, many additional and richer contingency propositions can be developed and tested.

Even though the propositions presented in this paper are limited, some new and potentially significant variables for understanding personal selling effectiveness have been introduced. Sales behaviors related to adapting to the customer and controlling the sales interaction have not been investigated empirically, even though practitioners view these behaviors as critical to sales effectiveness. Dyadic research has focused on similarity, a dyadic characteristic which appears to have little relationship to effectiveness. Characteristics of the customer-salesperson relationship such as relative power, level of conflict, and the anticipation of future interactions have played an important role in interpersonal influence research in social psychology and organizational behavior, but have been ignored in personal selling research. While this new research direction suggests more complex propositions and research designs, it is anticipated that the effort expended on this new approach will lead to a substantial improvement in our understanding of personal selling effectiveness.

ENDNOTES

1. Several descriptive studies (Olshavsky 1973; Pennington 1968; Taylor and Woodside 1968; Willett and Pennington 1966) have examined sales behavior but have not explicitly considered the effectiveness of sales behaviors.
2. In this table, personality traits indicating a predisposition toward forceful behavior in interpersonal relations (such as dominance, ego drive, achievement motivation, and aggressiveness) have been combined under sociability. To facilitate comparisons across studies, the performance measure used to report the results shown in Tables 1 and 2 is the most objective measure considered in the study. Thus, relationships with sales and sales to quota are reported rather than relationships to sales manager's evaluations.
3. The expertise conditions explained more variance than the similarity conditions. These differences may be due to the weaker relationship between similarity and effectiveness, but they may also be due to differences in the strengths of the manipulations.
4. While Blake and Mouton (1970) and Buzzotta et al. (1972) recognize that the effectiveness of sales behaviors varies across customers, their conceptualizations on personal selling are not contingency approaches of the type suggested in this

paper. Both of these conceptualizations contend that one sales behavior, either warm-dominant (Q4 type in Buzzotta et al.) or problem-solving oriented (9-9 type in Blake and Mouton), is most effective across all sales situations. A contingency approach is based on the notion that the most effective sales behavior varies across sales situations.
5. An interaction is defined as beginning when a salesperson first contacts a customer in an attempt to make a sale. The interaction concludes when the salesperson makes the sale or decides to discontinue efforts in this direction. An interaction may be concluded during one face-to-face encounter or may continue over a sequence of encounters.
6. This framework focuses on individual differences in effectiveness across interactions that are due to interpersonal influence behavior. However, traditional measures of performance across interactions such as sales or sales-to-quota incorporate other important sources of variance in effectiveness (see Figure 1). These factors must be controlled when testing propositions developed from this framework.
7. The lack of a meaningful relationship may be due to the definition of similarity used in the studies. In an extensive review on source credibility, Simons et al. (1970) concluded that only relevant similarities between the communicator and the recipient of the communications have significant impact on attitude change. Relevancy is defined in terms of beliefs or experiences pertaining to the object of the attitude. Thus, one would expect that only similarity of beliefs and experiences with respect to the product and the buying decision would influence effectiveness. Dyadic studies in personal selling have operationalized the similarities in terms of physical characteristics, demographics, and irrelevant attitudes.
8. The microtheoretical notions discussed by Ray (1978) are similar to the contingency propositions developed from the framework presented in this paper.

REFERENCES

Allison, P. D. (1973), "Testing for Interaction in Multiple Regression," *American Journal of Sociology*, 83 (July), 144–53.

Arch, David (1979), "The Development of Influence Strategy Scales in Buyer-Seller Interactions," in *1979 Educators' Conference Proceedings*, N. Beckwith et al., eds., Chicago: American Marketing Assocation.

Baehr, Melany E. and G. Williams (1968), "Prediction of Sales Success from Factorially Determined Dimensions of Personal Background Data," *Journal of Applied Psychology*, 52, (April), 98–103.

Bagozzi, Richard P. (1978), "Salesforce Performance and Satisfaction as a Function of Individual Difference, Interpersonal, and Situational Factors," *Journal of Marketing Research*, 15 (November), 517–31.

Baier, Donald and Robert D. Dugan (1957), "Factors in Sales Success," *Journal of Applied Psychology*, 41 (February), 37–40.

Bambic, Peter (1978), "An Interpersonal Influence Study of Source Acceptance in Industrial Buyer-Seller Exchange Process: An Experimental Approach," unpublished Ph.D. dissertation, Graduate School of Business, Pennsylvania State University.

Blake, Robert R. and J. S. Mouton (1970), *The Grid for Sales Excellence*, New York: McGraw-Hill Book Co.

Bower, Gordon H., John B. Black, and Terrence J. Turner (1979), "Scripts in Memory for Text," *Cognitive Psychology*, 11 (April), 177–220.

Boyd, Harper W., Michael L. Ray, and Edward C. Strong (1972), "An Attitudinal Framework for Advertising Strategy," *Journal of Marketing*, 36 (April), 27–33.

Brock, Timothy C. (1965), "Communicator-Recipient Similarity and Decision Change," *Journal of Personality and Social Psychology*, 1 (June), 650–54.

Bursk, Edward C. (1947), "Low Pressure Selling," *Harvard Business Review*, 25 (Winter), 227–42.

Busch, Paul and David T. Wilson (1976), "An Experimental Analysis of a Salesman's Expert and Referent Bases of Social Power in the Buyer-Seller Dyad," *Journal of Marketing Research*, 13 (February), 3–11.

Buzzotta, V. R., R. E. Lefton, and Manual Sherborg (1972), *Effective Selling Through Psychology*, New York: John Wiley & Sons.

Cantor, N. and W. Mischel (1979), "Prototypes in Person Perception," in *Advances in Experimental Social Psychology*, L. Berkowitz, ed., Vol. 12, New York: Academic Press, 3–52.

Capon, Noel (1975), "Persuasive Effects of Sales Messages Developed from Interaction Process Analysis," *Journal of Business Administration*, 60 (April), 238–44.

———, Morris Holbrook, and John Hulbert (1972), "Industrial Purchasing Behavior: A Reappraisal," *Journal of Business Administration*, 4, 69–77.

———, and John Swasy (1977), "An Exploratory Study of Compliance Gaining Techniques in Buyer Behavior," in *Contemporary Marketing Thought*, B. Greenberg and D. Bellenger, eds., Chicago: American Marketing Association.

Chapple, Eliot and Gordon Donald, Jr. (1947), "An Evaluation of Department Store Salespeople by the Interaction Chronograph," *Journal of Marketing*, 112 (October), 173–85.

Churchill, Gilbert A., Jr., Robert H. Collins, and William A. Strang (1975), "Should Retail Salespersons be Similar to Their Customers?" *Journal of Retailing*, 51 (Fall), 29–42+.

Cotham, James C., III (1969), "Using Personal History Information in Retail Salesman Selection," *Journal of Retailing*, 45 (Summer), 31–38+.

Davis, Harry L. and Alvin J. Silk (1972), "Interaction and Influence Processes in Personal Selling," *Sloan Management Review*, 13 (Winter), 56–76.

Doreen, Dale, Donald R. Emery, and Robert W. Sweitzer (1979), "Selling as a Dyadic Relationship Revisited." Paper presented at the 1979 AIDS Conference, New Orleans.

Dunnette, Marvin D. and Wayne K. Kirchner (1960), "Psychological Test Differences between Industrial Salesmen and Retail Salesmen," *Journal of Applied Psychology*, 44 (April), 121–25.

Emerson, Richard M. (1962), "Power-Dependence Relations," *American Sociological Review*, 27 (February), 31–41.

Evans, Franklin (1963), "Selling as a Dyadic Relationship—A New Approach," *American Behavioral Scientist*, 6 (May), 76.

Falbo, Toni (1977), "Multidimensional Scaling of Power Strategies," *Journal of Personality and Social Psychology*, 35 (August), 537–47.

———, and Letitia Peplau (1980), "Power Strategies in Intimate Relationships," *Journal of Personality and Social Psychology*, 38 (June), 618–28.

Farley, John and R. Swinth (1967), "Effects of Choice and Sales Message on Customer-Salesman Interaction," *Journal of Applied Psychology*, 51 (April), 107–110.

Fiedler, Fred E. and Martin M. Chemers (1974), *Leadership and Effective Management*, Glenview, Il: Scott, Foresman and Company.

Filley, Alan C., Robert J. House, and Steven Kerr (1976), *Managerial Process and Organizational Behavior*, 2nd ed., Glenview, Il.: Scott, Foresman and Company.

French, Cecil L. (1960), "Correlates of Success in Retail Selling," *American Journal of Sociology*, 66 (April), 128–34.

French, John R. P. and Bertram Raven (1959), "The Bases of Social Power," in *Studies in Social Power*, D. Cartright, ed., Ann Arbor: University of Michigan, Institute for Social Research, 150–67.

Gadel, M. S. (1964), "Concentration by Salesmen on Congenial Prospects," *Journal of Marketing*, 28 (April), 64–66.

Ghiselli, Edwin E. (1969), "Prediction of Success of Stockbrokers," *Personnel Psychology*, 22 (Summer), 125–30.

——— (1973), "The Validity of Aptitude Tests in Personnel Selection," *Personnel Psychology*, 26 (Winter), 461–77.

Greenberg, Herbert and David Mayer (1964), "A New Approach to the Scientific Selection of Successful Salesmen, *Journal of Psychology*, 57 (January), 113–23.

Grikscheit, Gary M. (1971), "An Investigation of the Ability of Salesmen to Monitor Feedback," Ph.D. dissertation, Michigan State University.

———, and William J. E. Crissy (1973), "Improving Interpersonal Communication Skill," *MSU Business Topics*, 21 (Autumn), 63–68.

Gwinner, Robert (1968), "Base Theory in the Formulation of Sales Strategy," *MSU Business Topics*, 16 (Autumn), 37–44.

Hakansson, Hakan, Jan Johanson, and Bjorn Wootz (1977), "Influence Tactics in Buyer-Seller Processes," *Industrial Marketing Management*, 5 (Fall), 319–32.

Harrell, Thomas W. (1960), "The Relation of Test Scores to Sales Criteria," *Personnel Psychology*, 13 (Spring), 65–69.

Howells, G. W. (1968), "The Successful Salesman: A Personality Analysis," *British Journal of Marketing*, 2, 13–23.

Jolson, Marvin A. (1975), "The Underestimated Potential of the Canned Sales Presentation," *Journal of Marketing*, 39 (January), 75–78.

Kahn, George N. and Abraham Shuchman (1961), "Specialize Your Salesmen!," *Harvard Business Review*, 39 (January/February), 90–98.

Kirchner, Wayne K., Carolyn S. McElwain, and Marvin D. Dunnette (1960), "A Note on the Relationship between Age and Sales Effectiveness," *Journal of Applied Psychology*, 44 (April), 92–93.

Lamont, Lawrence M. and William J. Lundstrom (1977), "Identifying Successful Industrial Salesmen by Personality and Personal Characteristics," *Journal of Marketing Research*, 14 (November), 517–29.

Levitt, Theodore (1965), *Industrial Purchasing Behavior: A Study in Communications Effects*, Boston, Ma: Division of Research, Harvard Business School.

McCall, Morgan, W., Jr. (1979), "Power, Authority, and Influence," in *Organizational Behavior*, S. Kerr, ed., Columbus, Oh: Grid Publishing Company, 185–206.

Mattheiss, T. H., Richard M. Durnad, Jan R. Muczyk, and Myron Gable (1977), "Personality and the Prediction of Salesmen's Success," in *Contemporary Marketing Thought*, B. Greenberg and D. Bellenger, eds., Chicago: American Marketing Association, pp. 499–502.

Merenda, Peter F., and Walter V. Clarke (1959), "Predictive Efficiency of Temperament Characteristics and Personal History Variables in Determining Success of Life Insurance Agents," *Journal of Applied Psychology*, 43 (December), 360–66.

Miner, John B. (1962), "Personality and Ability Factors in Sales Performance," *Journal of Applied Psychology*, 46 (February), 6–13.

Mosel, James N. (1952), "Prediction of Department Store Sales Performance from Personnel Data," *Journal of Applied Psychology*, 36 (February), 8–10.

Newton, Derek A. (1967), "A Marketing Communication Model for Sales Management," in *Risk Taking and Information Handling in Consumer Behavior*, Donald F. Cox, ed., Boston: Division of Research, Graduate School of Business Administration, Harvard University.

Olshavsky, Richard W. (1973), "Customer-Salesmen Interaction in Appliance Retailing," *Journal of Marketing Research*, 10 (May), 208–12.

Pasold, Peter W. (1975), "The Effectiveness of Various Modes of Sales Behavior in Different Markets," *Journal of Marketing Research*, 12 (May), 171–76.

Pennington, Alan (1968), "Customer-Salesmen Bargaining Behavior in Retail Transactions," *Journal of Marketing Research*, 8 (November), 501–504.

Pondy, Louis R. (1967), "Organizational Conflict: Concepts and Models," *Administrative Science Quarterly*, 12 (September), 296–320.

Pruden, Henry O. and Robert A. Peterson (1971), "Personality and Performance-Satisfaction of Industrial Salesmen," *Journal of Marketing Research*, 8 (November), 501–504.

Raven, B. H. and J. Z. Rubin (1976), *Social Psychology: People in Groups*, New York: John Wiley & Sons.

Ray, Michael L. (1978), "The Present and Potential Linkages between the Microtheoretical Notions of Behavioral Science and the Problems of Advertising: A Proposal for a Research System," in *Behavioral and Management Science in Marketing*, Harry L. Davis and Alvin Silk, eds., New York: Ronald Press, 99–141.

Reed, Jim D. (1976), "Comments on 'The Underestimated Potential of the Canned Sales Presentation,'" *Journal of Marketing*, 40 (January), 67–68.

Reizenstein, Richard C. (1971), "A Dissonance Approach to Measuring the Effectiveness of Two Personal Selling Techniques through Decision Reversal," *Proceedings*, Fall Conference, Chicago: American Marketing Association, 176–180.

Reve, T. and L. Stern (1979), "Interorganizational Relations in Marketing Channels," *Academy of Management Review*, 4 (July), 80–91.

Riordan, Edward A., Richard L. Oliver and James H. Donnelly, Jr. (1977) "The Unsold Prospect; Dyadic and Attitudinal Determinants," *Journal of Marketing Research*, 14 (November), 530–37.

Robinson, P. J., C. W. Farris, and Y. Wind (1967), *Industrial Buying and Creative Marketing*, Boston: Allyn and Bacon.

Rubin, Jeffrey Z. and Bert R. Brown (1975), *The Social Psychology of Bargaining and Negotiation*, New York: Academic Press.

Sales and Marketing Management (1979), "1979 Survey of Selling Costs," 124 (February 26).

Saxe, Robert (1979), "The Customer Orientational Salespeople," unpublished Ph.D. dissertation, Graduate School of Management, University of California at Los Angeles.

Schank, R. C. and R. P. Abelson (1977), *Scripts, Plans, Goals and Understanding*, Hillsdale, NJ: Lawrence Erlbaum Associates.

Scheibelhut, John H. and Gerald Albaum (1973), "Self-Other Orientations Among Salesmen and Non-Salesmen," *Journal of Marketing Research*, 10 (February), 97–99.

Simons, Herbert W., Nancy N. Berkowitz, and R. John Moyer (1970) "Similarity, Credibility and Attitude Change: A Review and A Theory," *Psychological Bulletin*, 73 (January), 1–16.

Snyder, Mark (1974), "The Self-Monitoring of Expressive Behavior," *Journal of Personality and Social Psychology*, 30 (October), 526–37.

Spiro, Rosann L. and William D. Perreault, Jr. (1979), "Influence Used by Industrial Salesmen: Influence Strategy Mixes and Situational Determinants," *Journal of Business*, 52 (July), 435–55.

Tanofsky, Robert, R. Ronald Shepps, and Paul J. O'Neill (1969), "Pattern Analysis of Biographical Predictors of Success as an Insurance Salesman," *Journal of Applied Psychology*, 53 (April), 136–39.

Taylor, James L. and Arch G. Woodside (1968), "Exchange Behavior Among Life Insurance Selling and Buyer Centers in Field Settings," Working paper no. 72, Center for Marketing Studies, Research Division, College of Business Administration, University of South Carolina.

Thomas, Kenneth W. (1976), "Conflict and Conflict Management," in *Handbook of Industrial and Organizational Psychology*, M. Dunnette, ed., Chicago: Rand McNally.

Thompson, Joseph W. (1973), *Selling: A Managerial and Behavioral Science Analysis*, New York: McGraw-Hill Book Co.

Tobolski, Francis P. and Willard A. Kerr (1952), "Predictive Value of the Empathy Test in Automobile Salesmanship," *Journal of Applied Psychology*, 36 (October), 310–11.

Vroom, V. H. and P. W. Yetton (1973), *Leadership and Decision Making*, Pittsburgh: University of Pittsburgh Press.

Walker, O. C., Jr., G. A. Churchill, and W. M. Ford (1977), "Motivation and Performance in Industrial Selling: Existing Knowledge and Needed Research," *Journal of Marketing Research*, 14 (May), 156–68.

Weaver, Charles N. (1969), "An Empirical Study to Aid in the Selection of Retail Salesclerks," *Journal of Retailing*, 45 (Fall), 22–26.

Weitz, Barton A. (1978), "The Relationship Between Salesperson Performance and Understanding of Customer Decision Making," *Journal of Marketing Research*, 15 (November), 501–16.

―――― (1979), "A Critical Review of Personal Selling Research: The Need for a Contingency Approach," in *Critical Issues in Sales Management: State-of-the-Art and Future Research Needs*, G. Albaum and G. Churchill, eds., Eugene, OR: University of Oregon, College of Business Administration.

―――― (1980), "Adaptive Selling Behavior for Effective Interpersonal Influence," paper presented at AMA Conference on Theoretical and Empirical Research on Buyer-Seller Interactions, Columbia, South Carolina.

Willett, Ronald P. and Alan L. Pennington (1966), "Customer and Salesman: The Anatomy of Choice and Influence in a Retail Setting," in *Science, Technology, and Marketing*, Raymond M. Hass, ed., Chicago: American Marketing Association, 598–616.

Wilson, David T. (1975), "Dyadic Interaction: An Exchange Process," in *Advances in*

Consumer Research, B. Anderson, ed., Cincinnati, OH: Association for Consumer Research, 394–97.

———, and Ghingold, Morry (1980), "Building Theory from Practice: A Theory-in-Use Approach," in *Theoretical Developments in Marketing*, C. Lamb, Jr. and P. Dunne, eds., Chicago: American Marketing Association, 236–39.

Woodside, Arch G. and William J. Davenport (1974), "The Effect of Salesman Similarity and Expertise on Consumer Purchasing Behavior," *Journal of Marketing Research*, 11 (May), 198–202.

Yalch, Richard F. (1979), "Closing Sales: Compliance-Gaining Strategies for Personal Selling," in *Sales Management: New Developments from Behavioral and Decision Model Research*, R. Bagozzi, ed., Cambridge, MA: Marketing Science Institute.

Zaltman, Gerald, Karen Lawther, and Michael Heffring (1980), *Theory Construction in Marketing*, New York: John Wiley & Sons Inc.

Zdep, S. M. and H. B. Weaver (1967), "The Graphoanalytic Approach to Selecting Life Insurance Salesmen," *Journal of Applied Psychology*, 51 (June), 295–99.

Zedeck, Sheldon (1971), "Problems with the Use of 'Moderator' Variables," *Psychological Bulletin*, 76 (October), 295–310.

37 Sales Force Management: Integrating Research Advances

Adrian B. Ryans and
Charles B. Weinberg

© 1981 by the Regents of the University of California. Reprinted from *California Management Review*, Vol. 24, No. 1, pp. 75–89 by permission of the Regents.

Nearly half of the marketing expenses of industrial marketing companies are direct selling expenses. For most of these firms, selling expenditures exceed 5 percent of sales revenues.[1] In spite of this heavy commitment of marketing resources to personal selling, researchers have only recently given this area the attention it warrants. The surge of research in this area has been accompanied by the development of a number of models to provide conceptual frameworks for the research. As might be expected, the variety of research approaches and perspectives has resulted in a plethora of specialized models, each being well suited to the needs of the particular researchers, but integrating poorly with the models and conceptual frameworks developed by others. Even the most general of these conceptual models, the one proposed by Orville Walker, Gilbert Churchill, and Neil Ford, appears to emphasize psychological elements at the expense of organizational and situational factors.[2]

This fragmentation makes it difficult to determine the state of knowledge in the personal selling area, to integrate different research efforts, and, perhaps most importantly, to identify where the major gaps in knowledge lie. The specialized nature of the models used in much sales force research, and the lack of managerial perspective in many of the models, calls into question, at least for managers, the relevance of many of the research results achieved. In addition, when a model provides low explanatory power because of the omission of some intuitively important variables, managers may be skeptical about the reasonableness of the results. A major objective of this article is to help managers understand and interrelate different research directions in sales force management.

A three-stage conceptual model of personal selling and the management of the personal selling function is proposed. This multilevel framework incorporates factors ranging from the specification of the role of personal selling in the marketing mix to individual salesperson factors such as role perceptions and motivation. The three stages of the framework reflect the major decision-making levels—strategic, tactical, and operational (or implementation)—in the management of the personal selling function.

Other decision-oriented models of personal selling are available (David Montgomery and Glen Urban's and Kenneth Davis and Frederick Webster's are two early examples).[3] However, we believe that the proposed model goes further than these by providing a means to integrate current empirical results, behavioral science theories, and marketing models into a decision-oriented framework.

Much of the empirical research to date has focused on the operational level and has not fully considered the impact of decisions at the strategic and tactical levels on the situation at the operational level. We will review carefully the types of decisions that are made at the two prior levels and the factors that are important in making these strategic and tactical decisions. As limited empirical evidence is available about these two levels, this review will be largely expository; relevant empirical research will be cited at all three levels.

THE THREE-LEVEL MODEL

Conceptually, a model of personal selling and the management of the personal selling function can be viewed as being comprised of the three stages shown in Figure 1: a strategic, a tactical, and an operational or implementation level. A multilevel model is appropriate because sales force and personal selling decisions are made at several different levels in the marketing organization. The decisions at each level are made within guidelines set by the levels above it in the organization. The results and feedback obtained from the lower levels in the organization provide one basis for modifying the policies and plans at higher levels. From a research strategy perspective, it is usually necessary to focus on one part of the sales management system at a time, otherwise the problems encountered in conducting research can become unmanageable.

Three stages are specified because this number seems to best capture the levels of sales force decision making, and the decisions at each stage tend to be the responsibility of, or to involve, different persons. At the strategic level, decisions are made by the top management of the company or business unit. At the tactical level, decisions are typically made by senior sales management but are frequently implemented by managers lower in the sales organization. At the operational or implementation level, the focus is on the salesperson, although many of the decisions are made or influenced by field sales management.

STRATEGIC LEVEL

The nature of a firm's personal selling program and the contribution it makes to the achievement of the firm's objectives are ultimately determined by the firm's or business unit's marketing strategy and the plans developed to implement this strategy. In the briefest possible terms, as Figure 2 indicates, a well-formulated marketing strategy is based on a thorough analysis and understanding of the company's internal and external environment. The analysis of the internal environment involves a careful review of the company's mission and objectives and a critical assessment of its resources and capabilities. The analysis of the external environment includes analyses of the company's customers, channel members, competitors and markets, and the likely impact of political, regulatory, economic, social, and technological trends on these groups and on the company. From the possible marketing strategies that might be adopted to achieve the company's objectives, top management selects the strategy that appears most likely to capitalize on the opportunities and solve the problems uncovered by these analyses. The marketing strategy selected can imply very different roles for personal selling. The role assigned to personal selling has two major dimensions: the emphasis on personal selling relative to the other elements of the marketing communication mix (advertising, sales promotion, and publicity); and the particular set of objectives that the personal selling function is expected to accomplish. This role of personal selling in the marketing strategy (the desired role) is the major influence on the tactical decisions made by senior managers in the sales force.

Researchers have recently begun to examine empirically the relationship of expenditures on personal selling activities to product-market characteristics and factors related to the firm's strategy. The ADVISOR project includes an analysis of the marketing budgeting practices of a number of major U.S. industrial marketers for a large number of products.[4] Two of the models estimated in the project provide some guidance

FIGURE 1. Structure of Conceptual Model

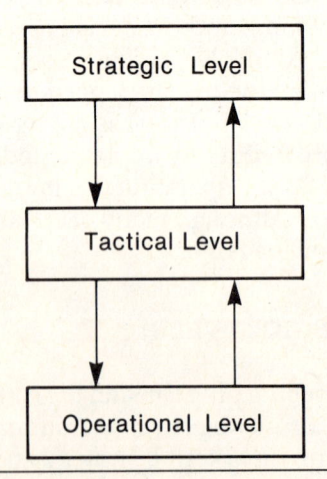

on the norms for marketing expenditures and the advertising/marketing expenditure ratio (and conversely some indication of the sales force/marketing expenditure ratio) given the characteristics of the product-market. Robert Buzzell and Paul Farris have also looked directly at the variables associated with the sales force/sales revenue ratio for three types of businesses using the PIMS data base.[5] While it is obviously difficult to infer a causal relationship for many of the independent variables, these models may be useful to managers charged with setting general levels for budgets for new or existing products given a particular strategy and particular market conditions.

TACTICAL LEVEL

Typically, the top sales executive in the company and his or her staff are responsible for developing an organization and a set of policies and procedures (the tactical decisions) so that the sales force can achieve its desired role in the company's marketing strategy. Figure 3 indicates the main decision areas that must be considered.

FIGURE 2. The Strategy Level

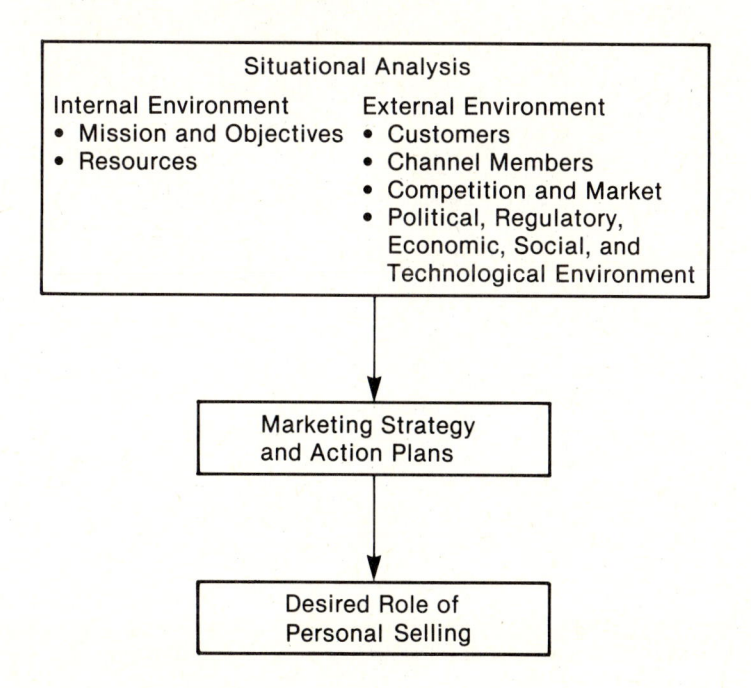

```
┌─────────────────────────────────────────────────┐
│              Situational Analysis               │
│                                                 │
│  Internal Environment     External Environment  │
│  • Mission and Objectives • Customers           │
│  • Resources              • Channel Members     │
│                           • Competition and Market │
│                           • Political, Regulatory, │
│                             Economic, Social, and  │
│                             Technological Environment │
└─────────────────────────────────────────────────┘
                          │
                          ▼
              ┌───────────────────────┐
              │  Marketing Strategy   │
              │   and Action Plans    │
              └───────────────────────┘
                          │
                          ▼
              ┌───────────────────────┐
              │   Desired Role of     │
              │   Personal Selling    │
              └───────────────────────┘
```

Organization

The major organizational decision is whether the sales force should be organized on a geographic, product, or market basis, or some combination of these. Many companies find it more effective to deal with their major or national accounts with a special sales force. Other organizational decisions include the number of levels of sales management, the number of people who will report to each type of manager (the span of each manager's control in the organization), and whether staff specialists, such as sales trainers, are needed.

Deployment of Personal Selling Resources

Once the basic sales organization is determined, decisions must next be made about how the sales resources of the company should be deployed. The issues include the assignment of accounts to salespersons—the territory design problem—and allocation of sales force time to accounts, product lines, and activities, such as opening new accounts versus servicing existing accounts. While a company's sales management usually develops general policy guidelines on deployment issues, the implementation of deployment policies is generally made by the field

FIGURE 3. The Tactical Level

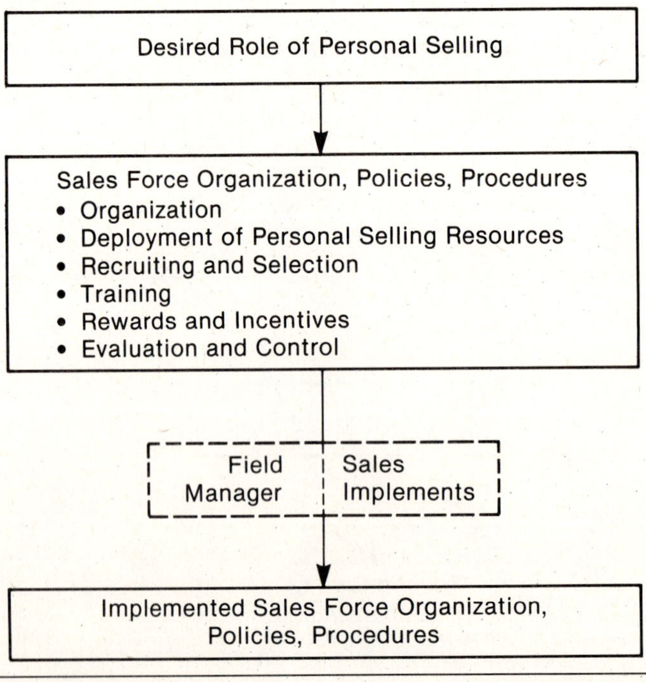

```
           Desired Role of Personal Selling
                        |
                        v
    Sales Force Organization, Policies, Procedures
      • Organization
      • Deployment of Personal Selling Resources
      • Recruiting and Selection
      • Training
      • Rewards and Incentives
      • Evaluation and Control
                        |
              Field   | Sales
              Manager | Implements
                        |
                        v
    Implemented Sales Force Organization,
              Policies, Procedures
```

sales manager and the salesperson. Deployment is one aspect of the management of the personal selling function that lends itself quite well to quantitative modeling. A number of models have been proposed and several have been used to deal with deployment problems. Thomas Glaze and Charles Weinberg, Sidney Hess and Stuart Samuels, Leonard Lodish, and Roy Shanker, Ronald Turner, and Andris Zoltners have all proposed models to help with the territory design problem.[6] Zoltners and Kathy Gardner have recently reviewed the available sales force decision models.[7]

Recruiting and Selection

The desired role of personal selling and the tasks the salesperson is expected to carry out help suggest the types of salespersons needed in the sales force, likely sources of these salespersons, and the criteria that should be used in the selection processs. For example, corporate resources, the size of the sales force, and job requirements often determine whether the company should try to hire experienced or inexperienced people.

Training

Almost all companies must do some training. For newly hired salespersons, training might provide selling skills, detailed understanding of the customers and their needs, extensive knowledge of products and services, and company policies and procedures. Besides this initial training, additional training for experienced salespersons is often needed in order to improve selling skills, to inform them about new products and policies, or to prepare them for new or more responsible positions within the sales organization.

Rewards and Incentives

Rewards and incentives include both financial and nonfinancial elements. Rewards can be subdivided into two main categories, intrinsic and extrinsic rewards. Intrinsic rewards, which are linked to the carrying out of the job, include such intangibles as feelings of competence, completion, and self-actualization. Managers and researchers are paying increasing attention to intrinsic rewards as part of the overall incentive system, but the relative importance and interrelationship of these rewards as compared to extrinsic ones are still controversial.[8]

Extrinsic rewards, tangible, external factors that are controlled by the organization, include financial and other benefits. The compensation systems should be designed to encourage the types of behavior desired by the company. The relative importance of salary, commissions, and bonuses can have a significant effect on the behavior and performance of the salesperson. A heavy emphasis on commissions often focuses the salesperson on the short term, sometimes causing him or her to pay insufficient attention to building long-term account relationships. Because a heavy emphasis on commissions lessens the roles of salary and bonuses, it also reduces the control the field sales manager has over the salespersons. The field sales manager usually has a good deal of influence over these latter forms of compensation and can use them to help guide the salesperson's efforts in directions that are important to the company's long-term needs. The compensation system also serves to attract and retain qualified people for the sales force.

Evaluation and Control

The evaluation and control procedures in a sales force allow the sales executives to monitor the performance of the individual salespersons and units in the sales force against certain standards. This information can then be fed back to the involved parties so that corrective action can be taken if it is necessary. The standards can be in the form of measures of input—such as the number of sales calls to be made, number of new accounts to be contacted, and level of salesperson's knowledge—or output—such as sales quotas, perhaps by product line. Performance against some of these standards can be measured quite objectively, while performance against others must often rely on the subjective judgment of the field sales manager. Clearly, a good evaluation and control system can be an important management tool providing the field sales manager and the salesperson with an opportunity to identify areas of strength and weakness and to develop programs to correct any deficiencies that are identified.

Field Sales Manager

Limited empirical research, along with much folklore, suggests that the first-level field sales manager is a major factor in the success of a sales force.[9] Figure 3 positions the field sales manager as the critically important implementer of the policies and procedures developed by the senior sales executive. The field sales manager's responsibilities can include the deployment of sales resources, the final selection of salespersons, salesperson training, the setting of salaries and bonuses, the setting of quotas, and the evaluation and motivation of the salespersons. He or she must also be skilled in dealing with problem salespersons, including dismissing them when necessary. In addition, the field sales manager is responsible for tailoring the personal selling program in response to the particular environmental factors that obtain in his or her territories. The role of the field sales manager as an implementer requires that in empirical studies of a sales force, measurement should be based on the

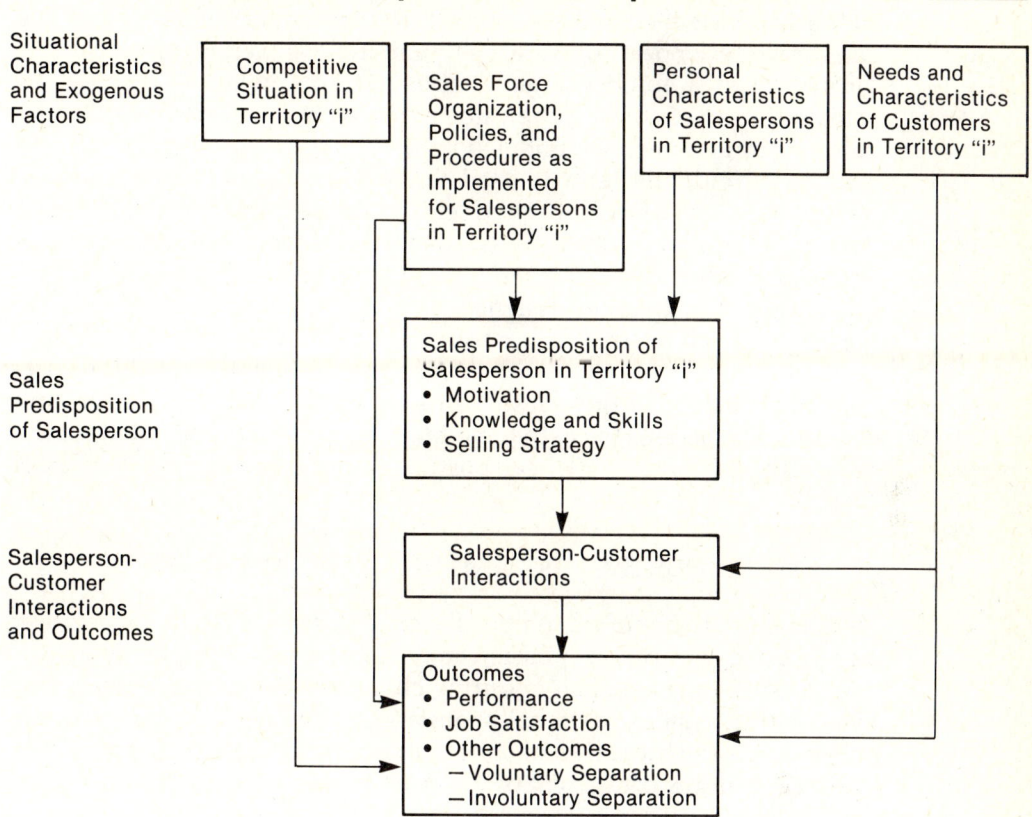

FIGURE 4. The Implementation or Operational Level

Situational Characteristics and Exogenous Factors

- Competitive Situation in Territory "i"
- Sales Force Organization, Policies, and Procedures as Implemented for Salespersons in Territory "i"
- Personal Characteristics of Salespersons in Territory "i"
- Needs and Characteristics of Customers in Territory "i"

Sales Predisposition of Salesperson

- Sales Predisposition of Salesperson in Territory "i"
  - Motivation
  - Knowledge and Skills
  - Selling Strategy

Salesperson-Customer Interactions and Outcomes

- Salesperson-Customer Interactions
- Outcomes
  - Performance
  - Job Satisfaction
  - Other Outcomes
    - Voluntary Separation
    - Involuntary Separation

---

value of variables as implemented by the manager, which are not necessarily the same as those suggested by senior sales management.

IMPLEMENTATION OR OPERATIONAL LEVEL

The model's third level, the implementation or operational level, focuses on the individual salesperson as the unit of analysis. As illustrated in Figure 4, this level consists of three types of constructs: situational characteristics and exogenous factors; the sales predisposition of the salesperson—motivation, knowledge and skills, and selling strategy; and salesperson-customer interactions and outcomes, including the salesperson's job performance and job satisfaction.

In developing the model at the salesperson level, we are using the term *implementation* in two senses. First, it represents the fact that we are examining the effect of exogenous variables as implemented by the field sales manager in particular and the company in general for that particular salesperson. To choose an obvious example, when examining the impact of span of control, the value to use is the one that the particular salesperson is supervised under, not the average for the organization as a whole. Second, the term is used to refer to whether (and how) the assigned selling tasks (the desired selling job) are carried out. In advertising, implementation concerns essentially cease once the advertisement is designed and placed in the media; however, a salesperson may not consistently carry out the assigned tasks and role. Does the salesperson allocate time across accounts, products, and selling activities in a manner consistent with the policies and procedures developed at the tactical level? The actions of the salespersons are influenced by the actual and anticipated reactions of customers. Most prior conceptualizations of the sales response model have been postulated at the individual salesperson level.[10]

Exogenous Factors and Situational Constructs

The four groups of exogenous factors and situational constructs are: sales force organization, policies, and procedures, as implemented for the salesperson; personal, enduring characteristics of the salesperson; competitive situation in the salesperson's territory; and characteristics of the customers in the salesperson's territory. The first group of variables is situational and is comprised of variables under the control of the company, whereas the last three groups are best regarded as exogenous, since the company has only very limited control over them in the short run. Thus, while the four groups are treated as exogenous with regard to analysis at the individual salesperson level, these variables are not necessarily exogenous at previous levels of the model.[11] For example, at the sales management level, the sales executive decides what the span of control will be. Furthermore, in the long run, the company's recruitment and selection programs will partially determine the personal characteristics of the salespersons, or at least the range of personal characteristics that are present in the sales force. The competitive situation in the territory can be most clearly classified as exogenous, but even here the company's actions with regard to territory design may influence the level of competitive activity encountered in any given territory. Similarly, the company's actions can influence which customers are actually served.

Personal Characteristics

This set of constructs includes all characteristics which are defined as being part of the individual and are not contingent on organization and other factors. We would include such variables as verbal intelligence and age as personal characteristics, but we would not include the salesperson's perceived role ambiguity because it is a consequence of organizational as well as personal factors. We would also exclude measures of the salesperson's motivation, since it can be modified as a result of such things as the firm's compensation plan. We think it is important to identify constructs that are both individual-specific and not contingent on organizational factors. As Walker, Churchill, and Ford point out, one of the major failings in models of salesperson performance is the failure to recognize that some "determinants are *not* independent; there are substantial interaction effects among them."[12] Our approach attempts to identify exogenous and contingent variables a priori and classify them separately.

Personal characteristics include:

- physical factors, such as physical appearance, posture, sex, and age;
- historical factors, such as educational background, previous occupations, and previous sales experience;
- personality factors, such as interpersonal style, social sensivity, locus of control and risk taking;
- mental factors, such as general intelligence, verbal ability, quantitative ability, and cognitive style.

In the past few years there has been a growing realization among personality researchers that situational factors are at least as important as personality traits in understanding why individuals behave the way they do.[13] Thus, relationships found in personal selling contexts may have only limited generalizability. Similarly, findings from other settings must be used with careful attention to the situational contingencies present in a personal selling situation. An individual who exhibits a certain style of risk-taking behavior in his or her personal life may exhibit a different pattern at work.

Organization, Policies, and Procedures

This set of constructs includes those variables which are set for the sales force as a whole at the sales management (or tactical) level, but which are implemented at the level of the individual salesperson. Some of these variables may be set uniformly for the sales force, while others may vary. A company may rigidly adhere to a certain span of control in the field sales organization while allowing wide variations in the market potential of the individual sales territories. Special focus needs to be placed on the implementation of the organizational, policy, and procedures variables for the individual salesperson, particularly, as transmitted by the field sales manager. The salesperson's understanding of the specific selling tasks to be performed is dependent on how well the field sales manager interprets and explains those tasks. This clearly raises some difficult measurement issues with regard to what the assigned tasks are and what the field sales manager communicates to the salesperson.

Among the constructs we would include here are span of control (the number of salespersons that report to the first-level sales manager); territory characteristics, including potential, concentration of potential among accounts, and geographic dispersion of customers; type and level of marketing support provided to the territory, including direct mail effort, marketing support personnel, and seminars and advertising; salesperson training programs; salesperson's assigned tasks; and the compensation program as implemented for the individual salespersons. Although many organizations have undoubtedly made formal or informal assessments of the impact of these factors on performance, only limited published, empirical research exists. The most well-developed literature concerns territory characteristics, where several studies have indicated the relationships between territory potential and sales performance.[14]

Competitive Situation

Depending on the nature of the market the company is in, the competitive variables of concern may vary. These variables can include product and service attributes, the competitive equivalent of any type of marketing support that the company can provide for its own sales force, and finally, the nature and intensity of the competitor's personal selling efforts.

Characteristics of Customer

This is again largely an exogenous set of variables. As will be discussed later, there is evidence in the personal selling literature that indicates that the performance outcomes from the salesperson-customer interaction depend on the characteristics of both members of the dyad.

SALES PREDISPOSITION OF THE SALESPERSON

The performance of an individual salesperson can be viewed as being a function of three classes of factors: motivation, knowledge and skills, and selling strategy.[15] This classification, while consistent with the one proposed by Walker, Churchill, and Ford in which motivation, aptitude, and role perceptions are used, is more general and can be used to incorporate and categorize more of the research that has been conducted on sales performance and its antecedents.[16]

As Figure 4 indicates, the sales predisposition of the salesperson is viewed as being largely a function of the enduring personal characteristics of the salesperson (which are in part a result of the organization's recruiting and selection policies), and the sales force organization, policies, and procedures. In contrast to the enduring personal characteristics, sales predisposition is mediated by the tactical levers under the control of sales management.

Motivation

Motivation in the personal selling context has been defined as "the amount of effort the salesman desires to expend on each of the activities and tasks associated with his job, such as calling on potential new accounts, planning sales presentations and filling out reports."[17] As Terence Mitchell has noted, theoretical research in motivation can be viewed as being focused on three problem areas: individual needs and motives, classification systems of needs and motives, and the motivational process itself.[18] Theories dealing with the first two of these areas are termed *content theories of motivation* since they are concerned with the factors that lead to motivational arousal. The third area involving process theories focuses directly on the mental processes underlying the behavioral choice—in the personal selling area, on the decision to devote effort to certain tasks.

Richard Bagozzi, in his study on sales force performance, approaches the motivational question largely from the first orientation using the theory of need for achievement.[19] Examples of the second orientation—the use of classification schemes in motivation research—includes Maslow's hierarchy of needs and the controversial dual factor theory of Frederick Herzberg, Bernard Mausner, and Barbara Snyderman, where potential organizational rewards are broken into two groups—the hygienes and the motivators.[20] Basically, Herzberg and his colleagues view the hygienes (monetary rewards and working conditions) as merely maintaining employees in a neutral state of satisfaction, whereas the motivators (advancement and recognition) can be used to generate high job satisfaction. While there appears to have been no formal research in the sales area on this theory, the approach has undoubtedly influenced the design of motivational policies in some sales organizations.

Process theories of motivation, as suggested above, are concerned with the process by which people decide to work hard and to allocate their efforts over the possible activities open to them. Expectancy theory has been the most widely used theoretical approach to motivation in personal selling research.[21] However, expectancy theory has been difficult to test in the personal selling area due to methodological problems. The results obtained to date, which are not particularly strong, have been summarized by Walker, Churchill, and Ford.[22]

Most managers would support the hypothesis that a salesperson's motivation is a function of both enduring personal characteristics and the full range of organizational, policy, and procedures factors. Span of control (an organizational factor), deployment policies, recruiting and selection policies, training, the evaluation and control system, and the incentive system all can clearly affect the motivation of a salesperson. The particular theoretical orientation to motivation adopted by the researcher would probably suggest a somewhat different emphasis on these factors if the motivational level of the salespersons is to be improved. For example, a need-for-achievement orientation might result in attention being paid to recruiting and selection policies and, to a lesser extent, training,[23] whereas other orientations might place greater emphasis on the incentive system. In spite of the obvious importance of motivation in sales performance, almost no empirical research has been conducted on how various organizational practices and sales force policies and procedures affect the motivation of salespersons.

Knowledge and Skills

The performance of a salesperson can be viewed as being a function of the following types of knowledge and skills:

- Product knowledge: this includes not only knowledge of the product line and its features, but knowledge of the benefits associated with each feature, the ability to handle common product-related objections, and a detailed understanding of the product line strengths and weaknesses relative to competitive products or services.
- Customer knowledge: this includes knowledge of the customer's business, how the product or service fits into the customer's operations, and a thorough understanding of the customer's decision-making process.
- Knowledge of company policy and procedures: this can be particularly critical in some industrial selling situations, where the salesperson's role is largely one of marshalling his or her company's resources and specialist talents to solve the customer's problems. It is essential to have a good in-depth knowledge of the company's organization and the location of specialist talent.
- Interpersonal and communication skills: this includes skills in establishing rapport with members of a customer decision-making unit, probing and questioning skills to uncover needs, communication and persuasion techniques, and skills in reading a customer's reactions to ideas and proposals. One persuasion technique that has received considerable attention is "foot-in-the-door": start with a small request (asking a retailer to place a

manufacturer's sign in his store window) before going on to the large request (asking the retailer to attend a sales presentation at the manufacturer's office).[24] A considerable amount of empirical research (largely in nonmarketing contexts) has been conducted on foot-in-the-door and other compliance-gaining techniques.[25] However, as Richard Yalch points out in his excellent review, "There has been no published research adequately evaluating what happens when an individual is involved in a series of compliance-gaining strategies."[26] Recent research is also beginning to clarify other situational contingencies under which these techniques are likely to be effective.[27]

The knowledge and skills of the salespersons are largely the result of the recruiting and selection policies of the sales organization and the types of training programs it offers to the salespersons. The span of control in the organization and the level of sales manager-salesperson interaction it encourages undoubtedly also indirectly influence the knowledge and skills of the salespersons.

Selling Strategy

Selling strategy subsumes the role perceptions component that plays a central role in the Walker, Churchill, and Ford model.[28] It involves: allocation of effort across the salesperson's accounts and products; a perception of the role the salesperson is to play; and a strategy for dealing with each individual account. The first and third elements of the selling strategy are expected to change over time as a result of the feedback the salesperson receives from his or her interactions with the individual customers.

Little is known about how salespersons decide to allocate effort (particularly time) across their accounts, yet this appears to be a very important decision and is closely related to the salesperson's performance. Lodish, who developed the CALLPLAN model to help allocate salesperson's time across customers and prospects,[29] has reported that a salesperson using the model had, on average, sales 8 percent higher than a matched colleague who did not have access to the model.[30] Some companies influence the time and effort allocations for their salespersons by establishing rigid call policies—a certain number of calls per day, or a required number of calls per effort period for each type or size of account.

Walker, Churchill, and Ford have developed the role perceptions component most fully in the personal selling area, and we follow their discussion of this component.[31] The role attached to the position of salesperson in any firm represents the set of activities or behaviors to be performed by any person occupying that position. This role is defined largely through the expectations, demands, and pressures communicated to the salesperson by his or her role partners—persons inside and outside the firm who have a vested interest in how the salesperson's job is performed, such as top management, the sales manager, customers, and family members. The salesperson's perceptions of these role partners' expectations and demands strongly influence his or her understanding of the job and the kinds of behavior necessary to perform it well.

It is clear from the above discussion that the elements of the role perceptions component are partly a function of the sales force organization, policies, and procedures. Training, in particular, can do a great deal to resolve issues of role accuracy and perceived role ambiguity. Recruiting and selection policies can also help seek out persons capable of handling the inevitable role conflict and who are less likely to experience serious perceived role ambiguity. While some research has been conducted on the relationship between aspects of role perceptions and such outcomes as job performance and job satisfaction,[32] only a very limited amount of research has been conducted on the antecedents of aspects of role perceptions. Walker, Churchill, and Ford found a significant negative relationship between salesperson experience and both role conflict and role ambiguity, and between both span of control and the salesperson's influence over supervisory standards and role ambiguity.[33]

The development of a strategy for dealing with the decision-making unit at each individual account is an important area that has received little research attention. Barton Weitz has done perhaps the most interesting and innovative research in this area.[34] He proposes a five-stage model of the sales process: developing an impression of the customer; formulating a strategy; transmitting the selected communication; evaluating the effect of the communication; and making appropriate adjustments in the strategy. While this five-step model clearly involves and requires the various types of knowledge and skills discussed in the earlier section, it requires more than them. It involves taking the information gathered, synthesizing and organizing it, developing alternative selling strategies for given situations, and selecting one, which must then be implemented. In many respects, effective interpersonal and communication skills of the type alluded to earlier are necessary, but not sufficient, skills in developing an effective strategy. In the empirical part of his study, Weitz demonstrated that there was a significant positive relationship between a salesperson's performance and understanding of the customer's choice decision process. Since Weitz only studies the first two stages of the model in a relatively simple selling environment (well-known product, single decision maker in the customer organization), much remains to be done in this area.

A salesperson's ability to develop effective strategies is likely to be largely the result of the salesperson's experience, the knowledge and skills he or she possesses to develop the necessary base of information about the customer, and the training the salesperson has received. A particularly important aspect of the training in more complicated selling situations where experiential learning may be very important is the coaching provided by the field sales manager. The degree to which this interaction can occur will be influenced by the span of control.

THE SALESPERSON AND THE CUSTOMER

The ultimate success of the strategic and tactical decision made with respect to a company's personal selling program depends on the individual interactions of salespersons and customers. The inputs to this interaction process can, to a large extent, be controlled, but the interaction process itself contains a significant set of uncontrollable elements as well. Researchers have attempted to probe aspects of this interaction process to gain a better understanding of what influences the productivity of a given salesperson-customer dyad. Early research by Franklin Evans and M. S. Gadel relates sales performance in a life insurance company to the similarity of the buyer-seller dyad.[35] However, a reanalysis of Evans's data by Noel Capon, Morris Holbrook, and James Hulbert suggests that given the number of variables studied, a significant correlation would be expected on a chance basis.[36] More recent research attempts to establish what types of similarity, or in more formal terms, bases of power in social exchanges, are the major sources of the relationship between similarity and performace.[37] The results to date have been inconclusive, and this research approach may not be as productive in the long term as research of the type conducted by Weitz.

The interrelationships between the various outcomes at the implementation level are only now beginning to receive attention from marketing scholars. It has been generally assumed that high job satisfaction leads to improved performance, but the relationship between the two constructs is proving to be a surprisingly weak one. Mitchell, in summarizing the industrial psychology literature on this point, reports that the average correlation between job satisfaction and peformance is about .15. Bagozzi, in a further analysis of the data in his 1978 paper (he omits the territory potential variable) concludes that performance is an antecedent of satisfaction.[38] Other research in industrial psychology, such as Edwin Locke's, tends to support this finding.[39] As might be expected, this relationship appears to be contingent on individual difference factors and other situational factors. Finally, the relationship between job satisfaction and other outcomes, such as turnover and absenteeism, while an intuitively appealing one which has received support in other occupational groups, has not yet received much empirical support in marketing. Again, any relationship is likely to be a highly contingent one.

UNANSWERED QUESTIONS

The conceptual model proposed in this article is not intended to be a general theory, but a framework sufficiently comprehensive so that the major research streams in personal selling can be interrelated. It also suggests areas which might be productively explored in future research. Particularly from the manager's perspective, the model links the research and researchable issues in personal selling with the levels of decision making in the sales force and the types of decisions that must be made at each level. We now turn to some of the unanswered questions that the three-level model suggests are important areas warranting further research.

At the strategic level, the ADVISOR and PIMS data bases are being used to address a critical sales management issue—the budgeting decision. Both data bases are not adequate for the task. The ADVISOR project is focused on advertising issues and only tangentially touches on the personal selling expenditure issue, and the PIMS project has a much broader strategic marketing focus. Both lack the specific sales force data necessary for a more complete examination of the strategic sales issues. In particular, major tactical variables, such as the type of sales organization, the span of control, and the compensation system, need to be investigated in models designed to explain the sales force expenditures/ sales ratio, the profitability of a product, and the like. This would begin to give some insight into the effectiveness of different tactical approaches in various product-market environments. A strategic issue that has received no attention in the literature to date is the decision to use manufacturers' representatives versus a direct sales force. The markets and hierarchies approach espoused by Oliver Williamson might suggest some useful hypotheses about when the use of sales representatives would be the most productive approach.[40]

Only limited empirical research has focused on the tactical levers available to sales management, probably because of the difficulties involved in conducting such research. Few of the relevant variables show any variation within a given sales force—compensation systems are usually uniform throughout the sales force.[41] This area does not lend itself well to laboratory experimentation and field experimentation will likely meet a great deal of managerial resistance given the risks involved and the difficulty of developing research designs with strong internal and external validity. Empirical research must usually follow one of two directions: cross-sectional studies involving a number of different sales forces; or longitudinal studies within one or more companies covering a period when a significant change in policies and procedures occurs. Even in the latter case, variables may be confounded since a change in one variable, such as the organization, frequently occurs simultaneously with a change in other variables, such as the compensation system. Despite the difficulties involved, quasi-experimental research may be the best hope for establishing the direction of causality which is so frequently ambiguous in observational studies in the personal selling area.[42] Rene Darmon's investigation of a change in sales compensation system in a company is one of the few examples of longitudinal research on these types of sales force policies.[43]

The operational level has received the most attention from marketing researchers. Much of the research has focused on the "selling knowledge and skills" and "salesperson-customer interactions" constructs included in Figure 4. As Capon, Holbrook, and Hulbert point out, a number of studies have implicitly or explicitly used the source-message-receiver model from mass communications to study the effects of the personal characteristics of the salesperson, the needs and characteristics of the customer, and the content of the message on some output measure of interest. As was pointed out earlier, few of these studies have viewed the salesperson and customer as an interacting dyad. Most of these studies do not explicitly recognize situational characteristics and exogenous factors on which the findings may be contingent. Furthermore, researchers have just begun to grapple with the fact that from a sales force perspective many customer decision-making units are multiperson and that many salesperson-customer interactions are part of an ongoing process, not a one-shot meeting. These raise important, but complex, research questions.

Other researchers have approached the study of the operational level differently. These researchers have shown less interest in the results of the individual interactions between salespersons and customers and have focused on long-run, aggregate outcome measures of sales performance and job satisfaction. This research has generally involved a more comprehensive set of the constructs from Figure 4 than do models that emphasize the interaction level. It is useful to distinguish two approaches that have been followed in this type of research.

Walker, Churchill, and Ford's work, which exemplifies such research, is an attempt to develop a theory of motivation and performance in the industrial sales force.[44] Much of their empirical research to date has involved the testing of hypotheses from their theory in a number of sales forces. As a result of this systematic program of research, an improved understanding of many of the links of their model is emerging. Because a great deal of their attention is devoted to psychological variables and the relationships between these variables, and because, to this point, their research has focused on dependent variables not closely related to sales performance (usually the variable of most direct managerial interest), the payoff in terms of results of high managerial relevance is likely to occur in the long run. Furthermore, as this research program proceeds and the contingent nature of many of the relationships in the model becomes apparent, their model will probably become more complex in order to incorporate these contingencies. In fact, this may already be occurring, as can be seen by comparing the model as originally conceived by Walker, Churchill, and Ford in 1977 with the 1978 version.[45]

The territory sales response models of Henry Lucas, Charles Weinberg, and Kenneth Clowes, Charles Beswick and David Cravens, Bagozzi, and Adrian Ryans and Charles Weinberg represent a second type of comprehensive model at the operational level.[46] Here, the focus has been on the relationship between an objective measure of sales performance and observable, readily measured factors that are believed to influence sales performance. These models, when set in the context of clear conceptual frameworks, can lead to greater understanding of the personal selling process through identification of important factors and measurement of their relationships. Moreover, such models can be tailored to the needs of, and readily estimated for, the individual sales force. In the four studies cited, the dependent variable is sales, which is the variable generally of most direct interest to sales management. This choice of dependent variable, combined with the operational nature of the independent variables, can have direct managerial impact.[47]

USING THE RESULTS

Although substantial gaps in knowledge exist, substantive findings of interest are available at all three levels of the model. However, a manager must be cautious in attempting to apply these findings to a specific setting for several reasons.

First, the research findings may have been developed in selling environments quite different from his or her own environment. As was pointed out above, much of the research on compliance-gaining strategies has been conducted in one-time selling situations. Even findings that seem quite robust, such as the foot-in-the-door strategy (demonstrated in field studies by Jacob Varella and Alice Tybout)[48] may not be effective if used on a continuing basis by a particular salesperson with a particular customer, or if the requested behavior is viewed as being very costly by the customer. As these findings are verified in richer, more externally valid settings (from the point of view of the individual manager), then the manager can have more confidence in applying the results.

Most importantly, as the three-stage model highlights, many relationships are likely to be contingent ones. The manager must try to determine if variables that were not considered in a particular study might not mediate the results. A general conceptual model such as the one proposed here provides the manager with a structure for reviewing these contingencies. If a manager finds it necessary to verify the relationships and findings for his or her own sales force, then the three-stage model will help to indicate which variables need to be studied. For example, the three-stage model can be used in conjunction with the emerging literature in the territory sales response area to provide a framework for developing such a function and to offer some guidelines on how particular variables might be put into operation.

Studies which rely heavily on attitudinal and other psychological variables will be difficult to verify in individual company settings. With increasing attention to invasion-of-privacy issues among the management of many companies, there may be serious concern about gathering much of this information.[49] Furthermore, for some variables, employees might be reluctant to give honest responses. Respondents who are asked for the valence of various rewards might attempt to "game" the researcher rather than provide honest responses. One potential tactical area where many of the findings from this stream of research might be valuable is the selection area, but it is in this area where it is difficult and expensive to demonstrate that psychological tests or other types of information do not unfairly discriminate against members of minority groups.[50]

One value of the three-stage model proposed here is that it provides a way for the manager to structure the different aspects of sales force decision making. The model emphasizes that the sales manager has a mix of tactical levers to implement a desired strategic sales force role, and that these levers should not be treated in isolation.

CONCLUSIONS

The three-stage sales force model developed in this article emphasizes the relationship between sales force management decision making and the empirical research being conducted in the personal selling area should not be underestimated. Moreover, the situational contingencies upon which research findings depend need to be specified clearly. Current research has provided a base of knowledge for researchers who wish to work in the field, but no area of personal selling is so well understood that further research is foreclosed. In conclusion, we believe that the conceptual model provided in this article provides a useful way to summarize present knowledge, to approach personal selling decisions, and to identify areas for further study.

REFERENCES

1. Sales and Marketing Management, "Survey of Selling Costs" (26 February 1979), p. 57.

2. Orville C. Walker, Jr., Gilbert A. Churchill, Jr., and Neil M. Ford, "Motivation and Performance in Industrial Selling: Present Knowledge and Needed Research." *Journal of Marketing Research*, Vol. 14 (May 1977), pp. 156–68.
3. David B. Montgomery and Glen L. Urban, *Management Science in Marketing* (Englewood Cliffs, New Jersey: Prentice-Hall, Inc., 1969); Kenneth R. Davis and Frederick E. Webster, Jr., *Sales Force Management* (New York: Ronald Press Company, 1968).
4. Gary L. Lilien, "ADVISOR 2: Modeling the Marketing Mix Decision for Industrial Products," *Management Science*, Vol. 25 (February 1979), pp. 191–204.
5. Robert D. Buzzell and Paul W. Farris, "Industrial Marketing Costs: An Analysis of Variations in Manufacturers' Marketing Expenditures." Report Number 76-118 (Cambridge, Massachusetts: Marketing Science Institute, 1976).
6. Thomas A. Glaze and Charles B. Weinberg, "A Sales Territory Alignment Program and Account Planning System," in Richard Bagozzi (ed.), *Sales Management: New Developments from Behavioral and Decision Model Research* (Cambridge, Massachusetts: Marketing Science Institute, 1979); Sidney W. Hess and Stuart A. Samuels, "Experiences with a Sales Districting Model: Criteria and Implementation," *Management Science*, Part II, Vol. 18 (December 1971), pp. 41–54; Leonard Lodish, "'Vaguely Right' Approach to Sales Force Allocation," *Harvard Business Review*, Vol. 52 (January–February 1974), pp. 119–24; Roy J. Shanker, Ronald E. Turner, and Andris A. Zoltners, "Sales Territory Design: An Integrated Approach," *Management Science*, Vol. 22 (November 1975), pp. 309–20.
7. Andris A. Zoltners and Kathy S. Gardner, "A Review of Salesforce Decision Models," unpublished working paper (Evanston, Illinois: Northwestern University, 1980).
8. Terence R. Mitchell, *People in Organizations: Understanding Their Behavior* (New York: McGraw-Hill, 1978).
9. Robert T. Davis, "Sales Management in the Field," *Harvard Business Review*, Vol. 36 (January–February 1958), pp. 91–98; idem, "A Sales Manager in Action," in H. W. Boyd, Jr., and R. T. Davis (eds.), *Readings in Sales Management* (Homewood, Illinois: Richard D. Irwin, 1970): J. S. Livingston, "Pygmalion in Management," *Harvard Business Review*, Vol 47 (July–August 1969), pp. 81–89.
10. Richard P. Bagozzi, "Towards a General Theory for the Explanation of the Performance of Salespeople," unpublished doctoral dissertation (Northwestern University, 1976); Adrian B. Ryans and Charles B. Weinberg, "Sales Territory Response," *Journal of Marketing Research*, Vol. 16 (November 1979), pp. 453–65; Walker, Churchill, and Ford, op. cit.
11. Researchers attempting to estimate the effect of exogenous and situational factors on outcomes such as performance or job satisfaction must be concerned about whether the implemented sales force organization, policies, and procedures have suppressed the effects of interest. If the sales force's management has a policy of assigning territories of equal potential, then it would make little sense to include this variable in a research study designed to relate territory sales performance to territory characteristics. However, it would be incorrect to assume that territory potential has no effect on sales performance.
12. Orville C. Walker, Jr., Gilbert A. Churchill, Jr., and Neil M. Ford, "Where Do We Go From Here?—Selected Conceptual and Empirical Issues Concerning the Moti-

vation and Peformance of the Industrial Sales Force," paper presented at the American Institute for Decision Sciences, St. Louis (1978), p. 4.
13. Mitchell, op. cit.
14. Adrian B. Ryans and Charles B. Weinberg, "Managerial Implications of Models of Territory Sales Response," in Neil Beckwith et al. (eds.), *1979 Educators' Conference Proceedings* (Chicago, Illinois: American Marketing Association, 1979), pp. 426–30; Ryans and Weinberg, op. cit.
15. This is similar to the conceptualization used by J. Richard Hackman and Charles G. Morris in their discussion of the performance of task groups. See J. Richard Hackman and Charles G. Morris, "Group Tasks, Group Interaction Process, and Group Performance Effectiveness," in L. Berkowitz (ed.), *Advances in Experimental Social Psychology*, Vol. 7 (New York: Academic Press, 1975).
16. Walker, Churchill, and Ford, "Motivation and Performance."
17. Ibid., p. 162.
18. Mitchell, op. cit.
19. Bagozzi, op. cit.
20. Frederick Herzberg, Bernard Mausner, and Barbara B. Snyderman, *The Motivation to Work* (New York: John Wiley and Sons, 1975).
21. Walker, Churchill, and Ford, "Motivation and Performance."
22. Walker, Churchill, and Ford, "Where Do We Go?"
23. David McClelland, the originator of the need-for-achievement theory, has reported some success in increasing the level of need for achievement in adults through training. See David C. McClelland, *The Achieving Society* (Princeton, New Jersey: Van Nostrand, 1961).
24. Alice M. Tybout, "The Relative Effectivenss of Three Behavioral Influence Strategies as Supplements to Persuasion in a Marketing Context," *Journal of Marketing Research*, Vol. 15 (May 1978), pp. 229–42; Jacob A. Varella, *Psychological Solutions to Social Problems* (New York: Academic Press, 1971).
25. William DeJong, "An Examination of Self-Perception Mediation of the Foot-in-the-Door Effect," *Journal of Personality and Social Psychology*, Vol. 37 (December 1979), pp. 2221–39; Richard F. Yalch, "Closing Sales: Compliance-Gaining Strategies for Personal Selling," in Bagozzi (ed.), op. cit. (Cambridge, Massachusetts: Marketing Science Institute, 1979).
26. Yalch, op. cit. p. 197.
27. Robert D. Foss and Carolyn B. Dempsey, "Blood Donation and the Foot-in-the-Door Technique: A Limiting Case," *Journal of Personality and Social Psychology*, Vol. 37 (1979), pp. 580–90; Yalch, op, cit.
28. Walker, Churchill, and Ford, "Motivation and Performance."
29. Leonard Lodish, "CALLPLAN: An Interactive Salesman's Call Planning System," *Management Science*, Part II, Vol. 18 (December 1971), pp. 25–40.
30. William K. Fudge and Leonard M. Lodish, "Evaluation of the Effectiveness of a Model Based Salesman's Call Planning System by Field Experimentation," *Interfaces*, Part II, Vol. 8 (November 1977), pp. 97–106.
31. Walker, Churchill, and Ford, "Motivation and Performance," and "Where Do We Go?"
32. Gilbert A. Churchill, Jr., Neil M. Ford, and Orville C. Walker, Jr., "Organizational Climate and Job Satisfaction in the Salesforce," *Journal of Marketing Research*, Vol. 13 (November 1976), pp. 323–32; and Bagozzi, op. cit.

33. Orville C. Walker, Jr., Gilbert A. Churchill, and Neil M. Ford, "Organizational Determinants of the Industrial Salesman's Role Conflict and Ambiguity," *Journal of Marketing*, Vol. 39 (January 1975), pp. 32–39.
34. Barton A. Weitz, "Relationship Between Salesperson Performance and Understanding of Customer Decision-Making," *Journal of Marketing Research*, Vol. 15 (November 1978), pp. 501–16.
35. Franklin Evans, "Selling as a Dyadic Relationship—A New Approach," *American Behavioral Scientist*, Vol. 6 (May 1963), pp. 76–79; M. S. Gadel, "Concentration by Salesmen on Congenial Prospects," *Journal of Marketing*, Vol. 28 (January 1964), pp. 64–66.
36. Noel Capon, Morris B. Holbrook, and James M. Hulbert, "Selling Processes and Buying Behavior: Theoretical Implications of Recent Research," in Arch G. Woodside, Jagdish N. Sheth, and Peter D. Bennett (eds.), *Consumer and Industrial Buying Behavior* (New York: Elsevier North-Holland, 1977), pp. 323–32.
37. Timothy C. Brock, "Communicator-Recipient Similarity and Decision Change," *Journal of Personality and Social Psychology*, Vol. 1 (June 1965), pp. 650–54; Paul Busch and David T. Wilson, "An Experimental Analysis of a Salesman's Expert and Referent Bases of Social Power in the Buyer-Seller Dyad," *Journal of Marketing Research*, Vol. 13 (February 1976), pp. 3–11.
38. Richard P. Bagozzi, "Salesperson Performance and Satisfaction as a Function of Individual Difference, Interpersonal, and Situational Factors," *Journal of Marketing Research*, Vol. 15 (November 1978), pp. 517–31; idem, "Performance and Satisfaction in an Industrial Sales Force: An Examination of their Antecedents and Simultaneity," *Journal of Marketing*, Vol. 44 (Spring 1980), pp. 65–77. The omission of territory potential from the Bagozzi 1980 model is surprising given the highly significant correlation between it and both performance and job satisfaction in his earlier paper. The framework proposed here emphasizes the need to include relevant precursors.
39. Edwin A. Locke, "The Nature and Causes of Job Satisfaction," in M. D. Dunnette (ed.), *Handbook of Industrial and Organizational Psychology* (Chicago, Illinois: Rand McNally, 1976), pp. 1297–1349.
40. Oliver E. Williamson, *Markets and Hierarchies: Analysis and Antitrust Implications* (New York: The Free Press, 1975).
41. However, considerable theoretical attention has been devoted to the design of optimal compensation systems under assumptions about the salesperson's objective function and constraints under which the salesperson operates. See John U. Farley, "Optimal Plan for Salesmen's Compensation," *Journal of Marketing Research*, Vol. 1 (May 1964), pp. 39–43; Venkataraman Srinivasan, "The Non-Optimality of Equal Commission Rates in Multi-Product Sales Force Compensation Schemes," Working Paper No. 529 (Stanford, California: Graduate School of Business, 1979); and Charles B. Weinberg, "Jointly Optimal Sales Commissions for Non-Income Maximizing Sales Force," *Management Science*, Vol. 24 (August 1978), pp. 1252–58.
42. Territory sales response models could be used in some situations to increase the statistical precision of the experiment.
43. Rene Y. Darmon, "Salesmen's Response to Financial Incentives: An Empirical Study," *Journal of Marketing Research*, Vol. 11 (November 1974), pp. 418–26.
44. Walker, Churchill, and Ford, "Motivation and Performance," and "Where Do We Go?"

45. Ibid.
46. Bagozzi's research can be viewed as straddling both types of models, as it, for example, also examines some motivational components. See Bagozzi, "Salesperson Performance"; Charles A. Beswick and David W. Cravens," A Multistage Decision Model for Sales Force Management," *Journal of Marketing Research*, Vol. 14 (May 1977); Henry C. Lucas, Jr., Charles B. Weinberg, and Kenneth Clowes, "Sales Response as a Function of Territorial Potential and Sales Representative Workload," *Journal of Marketing Research*, Vol. 12 (August 1975), pp. 298–305; and Ryans and Weinberg, "Sales Territory."
47. Ryans and Weinberg, "Managerial Implications."
48. Varella, op. cit.; Tybout, op. cit.
49. Frank T. Cary, "IBM's Guidelines to Employee Privacy," *Harvard Business Review*, Vol. 54 (September–October, 1976), pp. 82–90.
50. William C. Byham and Morton E. Spitzer, "Personal Testing: The Law and Its Implications," *Personnel*, Vol. 48 (September–October 1971), pp. 8–19.

38 — Today's Top Priority Advertising Research Questions

Diane H. Schmalensee

Journal of Advertising Research, Vol. 23 (April–May 1983), pp. 49–60. Reprinted from the Journal of Advertising Research © Copyright 1983, by the Advertising Research Foundation. Reprinted by permission.

ADVERTISING RESEARCH CONTROVERSY

Advertising research has matured in the past twenty years. Research suppliers have developed standardized measures of advertising effectiveness, such as Burke's Day After Recall, ASI's interest and brand preference scores, or Tele-Research's selling effectiveness. Advertising academics have developed many theories of how advertising works, such as the hierarchy-of-effects model by Lavidge and Steiner (1961) and later variations by Palda (1966), Ray (1973), and others. And practitioners have learned how to translate the test scores and theories into effective advertising executions.

Today, however, advertising research—and especially copy testing—is in danger of moving past the maturity phase of its life cycle. Perhaps because advertising has been extensively studied—probably more than any other aspect of marketing—and because of the diversity of researchers involved, the weaknesses in advertising research have become very apparent. Anyone involved in advertising cannot fail to be aware of the criticisms leveled at advertising research (*Marketing News*, 1982; Honomichl, 1981; *Ad Forum*, 1980). "... Few could argue about the desirability of using research to evaluate copy ideas and commercials, though many [continue to] argue about the relative merits of the great variety of techniques" Lipstein and Neelankavil, 1982).

Many people have devoted a great deal of time and effort to studying how advertising works and how its effects can be measured. For example, the Advertising Research Foundation's (ARF) Copy Research Validation Council and its Television Copy Research Council are charged with studying copy-research measures and methods, and the ARF has sponsored many conferences and published research reports on advertising measures. The American Association of Advertising Agencies (4As) and its members have frequently met to discuss advertising research issues and have tried to develop copy-testing principles ("21 Ad Agencies Copy Testing Principles," 1982). And many research suppliers have conducted validation and reliability studies on their techniques (ARS, 1979).

The Marketing Science Institute (MSI) has also become involved in the effort to increase our understanding of how advertising works for two reasons. First, MSI believes that the question of how advertising works is very important, as evidenced by the many studies published by MSI dealing with the impact of advertising on consumers (Clarke, 1977; Courtney, 1970; Greyser, 1973; McDonald, 1971; McNeill and Swinyard, 1980; Ray and Webb, 1978; Ray, 1973; Ray, Ward, and Reed, 1974; Silk and Vavra, 1974). Second, because MSI is an unbiased nonprofit research institute sponsored by leading corporations and agencies that wish to support scholarly research, MSI is unusual in being able to combine the expertise of the leading advertisers, agencies, and academics.

Given the current volume of criticism directed at advertising research today, MSI felt that it would be constructive to examine what is unknown, what needs to be known, and where the gaps in advertising research lie in order to initiate productive research in the future. Working with many leading advertising researchers and practitioners, including the ARF, the 4As, the Association of National Advertisers (ANA), MSI's sponsoring companies and agencies, and leading academics, MSI has developed a set of top priority researchable advertising questions. These questions were selected because they cover the most important, fundamental issues facing practitioners—such as how consumers respond to advertising and how to measure the effects of advertising—and because they appear to be researchable.

The purpose of this paper is to discuss these top priority advertising questions: how they were identified, why they are important, their implications, and suggestions for appropriate approaches to address the questions.

These are not the only questions worthy of research. Other organizations may have different priorities. But the questions are representative of the priorities of many of the interests involved in advertising research, and answers to the questions will help close the major gaps existing in our understanding of how advertising works.

How the Questions Were Identified

The process of identifying the top priority advertising questions took place over a two-year period and involved hundreds of people. In July 1980, MSI formed its Advertising Steering Group, which is composed of academics and practitioners from many of MSI's sponsoring companies, to help MSI identify advertising research topics deserving of MSI funding. At its first meeting, Joseph Plummer of Young & Rubicam and others suggested that MSI sponsor an industry-wide conference on the problems of advertising research.

The Ad Gaps conference, formally called "Closing the Gaps in Advertising Research," was held October 23 and 24, 1980. The attendees, who represented advertising agencies, advertisers, universities, research suppliers, as well as the ARF, ANA, and 4As, were charged with the task of identifying topics (1) that would be important in the future and (2) where the greatest gaps existed between what was known and what needed to be known about advertising. The conference was organized around five concurrent group sessions that used a Synectics brainstorming approach to identify the topics. At the end of each day, the small groups joined to share their ideas.

A summary of the conference topics then served as the basis for another meeting of MSI's Advertising Steering Group in September 1981, where the members set priorities on the topics. As the steering group discussed the topics, a number of issues emerged that the group unanimously agreed were top priority.

Finally, in May 1982, MSI's Trustees from its sponsoring companies—all of whom are senior marketing executives although not necessarily researchers—met to plan the direction of MSI's research program for the next few years. They discussed research topics dealing with all phases of marketing, including advertising research. The advertising research topics selected by MSI's steering group and the Ad Gaps conference were also voted top priority by MSI's trustees, confirming the importance of the issues.

TODAY'S TOP PRIORITY ADVERTISING RESEARCH QUESTIONS

The top priority advertising research topics fall into three categories (see Table 1):

I. Theory of Individual Consumer Response to Advertising;
II. Measures of Individual Consumer Response to Advertising;
III. Advertising Operating Issues.

Of the three, the first two appear to be the highest priority because they deal with the central issue of how consumers respond to advertising and how to measure that response. Only by understanding how advertising works and how to measure its effects can the operating questions facing advertising managers be answered satisfactorily.

I. THEORY OF INDIVIDUAL CONSUMER RESPONSE TO ADVERTISING

The debate over copy-testing methods has reached a point where even loyal users of traditional research methods are aware of the prob-

TABLE 1. Top Priority Advertising Research Questions and Suggested Approaches

I. *Theory of Individual Consumer Response to Advertising*
   A. Questions to Be Answered:
      1. How do consumers respond to advertising? Is there a link, and if so, what kind, between advertising and resultant consumer behavior?
      2. How does advertising affect consumers? And is there any evidence to support this?
      3. What factors affect consumers' response to advertising?
   B. Suggested Approaches:
      1. Define terms and build taxonomy
      2. Critically review existing theory
      3. Identify implicit theories
      4. Develop new theory

II. *Measures of Individual Consumer Response to Advertising*
   A. Questions to Be Answered:
      1. How should individual consumer response to advertising be measured?
      2. How do alternative measures compare with each other and with actual consumer behavior?
   B. Suggested Approaches:
      1. Analyze empirical interrelationships of measures and behavior
      2. Build shared advertising data bank

III. *Advertising Operating Concerns*
   A. Questions to Be Answered:
      1. What is the minimum number of repetitions required for impact? At what point does advertising wear out?
      2. What are the effects of nonverbal elements of advertising and how can the effects be measured?
      3. Under what conditions should which media (medium) be used, considering audience involvement and issues of media measurement?
      4. How can advertising concepts and whole advertising campaigns (as opposed to single commercials or executions) be measured?
      5. What consumer characteristics affect consumers' response to advertising?
      6. What is the ideal relationship between market share and share of voice?
      7. How should communications budgets be allocated over advertising, sales promotion, personal selling, and corporate communications?
      8. What are the uses for and impact of corporate communications?
   B. Suggested Approaches:
      1. Empirical work and experiments
      2. Review of how firms now make these decisions
      3. Critical review of existing research on corporate communications (including definition and taxonomy)

lems and willing to re-examine the theory underlying the measures. If the debate is to be resolved, this requires thinking about the basics, asking such questions as how advertising affects consumers in both the short and long run, how consumers make purchase decisions, and what is the relationship between advertising and the final objective—be it a sales or nonsales objective such as improving corporate image or increasing stock prices. More generally, the link between communication and the thoughts and behavior of consumers needs to be understood.

The question underlying the heated debates on advertising copy testing is: How do consumers respond to advertising? The debate about how to measure the effects of advertising is merely the symptom of the problem. The lack of consensus about how consumers respond to advertising is the cause.

Lavidge and Steiner's "Model for Predictive Measurement of Advertising Effectiveness" (1961), commonly known as the hierarchy-of-effects model, appeared for a time to answer these questions. Their model posited a progression from awareness, to knowledge, to liking, to preference, to conviction, to purchase. This model and others similar to it, such as Attention, Interest, Desire, Action (AIDA) and learning hierarchy models of Cognition, Affect, Conation, were widely hailed because they made intuitive and apparently logical sense. The consumer would learn about the product through advertising, develop an interest in it, be convinced it offered some desired qualities, and finally make a purchase.

However, the theories clearly did not work under all circumstances. Krugman (1965) suggested that the medium used for advertising could affect the process, and that television advertising might bypass the awareness and knowledge steps of the hierarchy simply because consumers absorbed the beliefs without being aware of it. Ray (1973) suggested that the progress from exposure to purchase was affected by the degree of involvement the consumer felt for the product class. For a low-involvement product, requiring little conscious thought by the consumer, the consumer might purchase even before being convinced of the product's superiority. He suggested that the traditional hierarchy of effects might apply more to high-involvement than to low-involvement products. Smith and Swinyard (1982) suggested that belief strength, or the probability that a consumer would associate a product with a given attribute, was a key link between advertising exposure and the formation of attitudes about a product. Park and Mittal (forthcoming) developed a theory to cover both high- and low-involvement products, which posited two types of affects or two types of attitudes toward a product. The lower-order affect, which is ephemeral, may occur after being exposed to advertising but before a trial of the product. After trial, the higher-order affect occurs because the consumer has had some experience with the product. Further, their theory is among the first to distinguish between trial and adoption of a product, so a single trial is not equated with loyal adoption of a product.

Variables such as medium, product class, involvement, and belief strength may mediate consumer response to advertising, but most theories do not account for the variables to everyone's satisfaction (Tauber, 1980). There is a need for theory, or at least a general set of principles, that can explain the effects of mediating variables as it describes how consumers respond to advertising.

There are many people who believe that the development of another theory of how consumers respond to advertising is busy work at best and counter-productive at worst. For instance, Leo Bogart (1982) has said, "The endless search for the Philosopher's Stone of advertising is really busy work that disguises the difficulty of making valid generalizations.... No matter how much we know or how much we learn about what makes an ad memorable or persuasive, the rules have to be bent or revised every time to accommodate the real article. There is no single truth in persuasion."

On the other hand, others argue that theory is a useful starting point for studying advertising. "Theory is a very useful guide in organizing a complicated world. It provides a basis for organizing observations and facts into a coherent structure. Events can be sequenced and structured into a rationalized and orderly world. One of the important derivatives of specifying a model is that it provides the basis for measurement" (Lipstein and Neelankavil, 1982). While a single, unified theory may not be possible, it is still important to aim for a set of limited theories or principles to offer guidance to practitioners and researchers.

Some specific questions that should be answered by the theory are:

1. How do consumers respond to advertising? Is there a link, and if so what kind, between advertising and resultant consumer behavior?
2. How does advertising affect consumers and is there any evidence to support this?
3. What factors affect consumers' response to advertising?

Four approaches to the study of the theory of consumer response to advertising have been suggested: (1) Define terms and build a taxonomy of variables relevant to consumers' response to advertising; (2) critically review existing theory; (3) identify implicit theories; and (4) develop new theory.

1. Define Terms and Build a Taxonomy

These definitions and taxonomy, or classification framework of factors affecting consumers' response to advertising, will serve as the foundation for any critical literature review or new theory development. They are the means to an end, rather than an end in themselves. They can be used to identify areas of overlap among past articles or publications and to suggest variables that might need to be considered in advertising theory.

The taxonomy should include all relevant independent and dependent advertising variables. As with any taxonomy, the objective is to include only those variables which mediate the effect of advertising on consumers. It may be best to include all possible variables in the beginning and gradually drop those that are proven to be irrelevant. The MSI Advertising Steering Group has informally developed a partial taxonomy (shown in Appendix A) that includes the nature of the advertised product, the medium used, the target audience, the intent of the advertising, the tone of the advertising, executional variables, the familiarity of the advertising, and the dependent measures used to evaluate the advertising. This listing may serve as a starting point for a more comprehensive taxonomy.

2. Critically Review Existing Theory

A thorough and critical review of the literature dealing with individual consumer response to advertising would be helpful to practitioners and academics alike. John D. C. Little's (1979) excellent review of the models dealing with macro-advertising or the relation of advertising spending to product sales, might serve as an illustration of what is desired in a survey of the micro-advertising issue of individual consumer response to advertising. The literature review should (1) develop a framework for classifying and relating theories to each other; (2) identify areas of agreement as general principles; (3) illuminate the areas of agreement as general principles; and (4) suggest future research that could narrow the areas of disagreement among the theories.

3. Identify Implicit Theories

Some advertising theory may be implicit rather than explicit. Behind each of the commonly used measures of advertising effectiveness may lie many implicit assumptions. For instance, some advertising agencies use different copy-testing techniques at different times, and it might be very revealing to learn what rules and assumptions underlie their decisions about which to use when.

One way to do this might be to hold a group discussion, similar to a focus group, or a series of one-on-one in-depth interviews with advertising researchers from agencies, advertisers, and research suppliers, as well as with advertising managers and creatives, to uncover the underlying theoretical assumptions they hold about copy-testing measures. Or, it might be helpful to collect a series of case histories of how various businesses conduct advertising research in order to develop rules of thumb about the rationale behind each method. For instance, the ARF study of copy-testing practices (Lipstein and Neelankavil, 1982) shows that the hierarchy-of-effects model is implied by many of the measurement systems used.

4. Develop New Advertising Theory

Since existing theories of individual consumer response to advertising are not universally accepted, work on new theories might be fruitful. For example, most advertising theories tend to discuss certain static states (the consumer is aware, persuaded, has tried a product, and so on). Perhaps a theory that is based on the *process* of consumer reaction to advertising would be more helpful than the more *static* approach. If so, then cognitive processing and other consumer theories may have some useful implications for advertising theory. The new theory might address such questions as: What happens to an individual upon exposure to advertising? Do individuals react in predictable ways? What variables mediate consumer response to advertising? What dependent measures of the effect of advertising would be appropriate, given the new advertising theory?

The process of theory development is as difficult to explain as creativity. However, Olson (1981) has suggested a number of techniques that might be helpful in building new theory. For example, theory could be borrowed from other disciplines and then adapted to advertising. Making implicit assumptions explicit may lead to the development of new theory. Counterintuitive theories which force the researcher to determine why they cannot be true may lead to theoretical breakthroughs, as may in-depth comparisons or competing theories or improving existing theories to apply more generally. Finally, researchers might try to develop theory that addresses aspects of consumer behavior more general than advertising alone.

II. MEASURES OF INDIVIDUAL CONSUMER RESPONSE TO ADVERTISING

Associated with the need to study advertising theory is the need to review the measures now used in copy testing and in assessing the effects of advertising. Copy-testing measures have been challenged on the grounds of uncertain reliability and validity for many years (Clancy and Ostlund, 1976; Bloom, Andrea, and Twyman, 1971; Honomichl, 1981), as well as for the interaction of measures with methods (*Ad Forum*, 1980; Yuspeh, 1979; Achenbaum, Haley, and Gatty, 1967; ARS Research Systems, 1979), and need to be studied carefully.

Each step in hierarchical advertising models has one or more measures associated with it. Each of the three learning-theory stages of cognition, affect, and conation has several measures that might be used.

- Cognition: Recall
  Recognition
  Belief strength
  Awareness
  Comprehension of main copy points
- Affect: Attitudes about a product's features
  Product preferences
  Extent of match of product with self-image
  Internalization of message
- Conation: Purchase intent
  Intent to try product (trial)
  Intent to adopt product (commitment)
  Actual purchase behavior

In addition to these measures, there are the measures of involuntary psychophysiological responses to advertising, such as electrodermal response, pulse rate, brain waves, and so on. Thus, even if a theory of advertising is developed, the choice of measure for determining the effect of advertising is still not obvious. For example, hypothetical Commercials A and B might vary in rank depending on whether recall or persuasion is used as the main dependent variable. Which measure should an advertiser rely on to find the most effective commercial? For another example, measures that may appear very similar often yield different results (Bagozzi and Silk, 1981; Krugman, 1977; Lucas, 1960; Wells, 1964; Haskins, 1964; and Young, 1972). If recall and recognition, for instance, do not measure the same thing even though both measures are associated with the cognition step in the learning model, what measure should be used and why? Or, when should 24-hour recall be used versus shorter or longer recall periods?

Any research evaluating the measures of advertising effectiveness is bound to be controversial because so many people have so much invested in a given copy-testing measure. However, it is precisely because this is such a financially important topic that it has been identified as a top priority. Ultimately, the purpose of the research on advertising measures should be to determine which measures are really measuring which consumer responses to advertising.

Specific questions that should be answered are:

1. How should individual consumer response to advertising be measured?
2. How do alternative measures compare with each other and with actual consumer behavior?

Two approaches are suggested for studying these measures: (a) analyze the empirical interrelationships between measures and behavior, and (b) build a shared advertising data bank.

1. Analyze Empirical Interrelationships of Measures and Behavior

An analysis of the interrelationships of advertising measures should answer such questions as: Are these measures getting at the same dimension of advertising or perhaps at several dimensions? Or, are they all unrelated? Are some measuring long-run effects while others are measuring short-run? If a battery of measures were collected from each individual consumer, would factor analysis yield only a few factors or many?

Ideally, the measures should be compared with each other and also with actual behavior. This should be done with a variety of measures for the same commercials, if possible, and might be tied in with the advertising data bank discussed next.

2. Build Shared Advertising Data Bank

Another possible approach involves building a shared advertising data bank, similar to the PIMS bank of marketing and profit data, so advertisers, agencies, and suppliers could share information, including advertising testing and development data. The purpose of this data bank would be to find a common ground for future research on advertising, to study the interrelationships between the measures of advertising effects and the variables mediating those effects, to empirically test advertising theory, and ultimately to answer such advertising operating issues as how often to run a commercial.

Ideally, the advertising data bank should include a wide range of products and services. Using an advertising taxonomy or classification system as a guide, shared information for each product might include copy-testing results, sales figures, classification of the advertising tested and actually run, and background on the product's market position. Initially, it might be limited to television advertising and then expanded to include all forms of advertising.

The first step in the development of such a shared advertising data bank could be to create a standardized reporting or taxonomic system and then to establish a central depository where confidentiality could be guaranteed. An academic or trade association, such as ARF or ANA, might be a logical coordinator of this data bank, with an administrator handling the data on a daily basis. Creatives and advertising managers should work with advertising researchers in the planning of the data bank in order to have a well-rounded program. Advertisers might contribute the background information on the product as well as the sales information. Advertising agencies might contribute information on advertising development and style. Research organizations might contribute copy-testing results. And organizations such as MSI, ARF, ANA, and the 4As might contribute the funding to get the data bank started.

III. ADVERTISING OPERATING CONCERNS

The term "operating concerns" is used to cover a group of everyday decisions facing all advertisers, such as the optimal frequency for running an ad or how to allocate communication spending over advertising, sales promotion, corporate communication, and personal selling. At bottom, all operating concerns deal with how to maximize the effectiveness of advertising spending. The operating concerns identified here have been studied repeatedly, but have not been definitively answered. Because of their important financial implications for advertisers, questions about these operating concerns are considered high priority, even though a final resolution may be distant.

However, the study of operating concerns is given lower priority than the study of advertising theory and advertising measures because the research on operating concerns depends to a great extent on what is believed about how consumers respond to advertising and how to measure their response. For example, tests of how often to run a television commercial must use some empirical measure of the commercial's effects, even though the debate about which measure of effectiveness should be used has not been resolved. Still, research on these operating concerns should go forward concurrently with research on theory and measures because the theory and measurement questions will probably not be answered in the near future.

1. Determine Optimal Repetition and Point of Wearout

The effects of advertising often vary with time. For instance, the cumulative effect of advertising may differ from its effect after only one exposure. The length of time between exposures to advertising can affect consumers' responses. Consumers who liked a commercial the first time they saw it may become bored or irritated after many repetitions, and so on.

Determining the optimal number of repetitions and the point at which advertising begins to wear out is important to advertisers because of the obvious cost implications. No advertiser wants to run advertising more than necessary, but no one has been able to satisfactorily answer the question of how much advertising is optimal. For example, Naples' (1979) review of frequency research asserts that the optimal effective range is three to ten effective exposures, but this is still quite a wide range.

The following are some of the important time-related questions that merit further study. What factors (such as product type, style of advertising, and target audience) reduce the average number of repetitions or impressions needed? How much repetition is not enough, just enough, or too much (the point of wearout)? What is advertising wearout and when does it occur? What criteria can be used to measure wearout or determine the optimal number of repetitions? What is the value of the continuity of an advertising message over time? In theory, response to advertising peaks after repeated exposures and then gradually drops. Is this always true, and if not, what factors affect it? What are the effects on optimal exposure and wearout decisions of using only one commercial in a campaign versus creating a campaign composed of several commercials?

Two approaches are suggested to study these issues. First is a critical review of the literature. In cases where two empirical studies have yielded different results, the researcher might pay particular attention to differences in methodology or situation that could be important mediating variables. Second is a review of the methods used today by advertisers and agencies to determine how often to run their advertising and when their advertising has worn out. Perhaps by studying the literature as well as how the decisions are made in practice, some underlying principles will emerge that can be empirically tested.

2. Study and Measure Nonverbal Communication

A great deal of what goes on in a commercial or an ad is nonverbal: the actors, the body language, the setting, the colors, the style or tone, the music and voices, and even the scents can affect the impressions imparted to the consumer by advertising. For instance, it is not difficult to think of an instance where the performer in a commercial or the design of a print ad made the advertising memorable even though the spoken words or body copy were rather ordinary.

And yet, when advertising is tested and studied, the research is usually limited only to the verbal aspects of the advertising, to what is said or written. Copy testing is just that, a testing of copy. It does not study feelings or images evoked by the nonverbal aspects of advertising. Thus, it would be useful to develop measures of the nonverbal aspects of advertising and to examine the relative importance and role of nonverbal versus verbal communication in advertising.

Related to the study of nonverbal communication is the study of emotional versus rational appeals in advertising. Rational appeals might be defined as the logical selling arguments or factual information about the product or service being advertised. Emotional appeals might be defined as everything else, from the use of exciting or glamorous visuals with few verbal elements to the focus on a heartwarming story. Do consumers respond differently to advertising that is primarily rational than to advertising that is primarily emotional? If so, how?

Two methods were suggested for this research. First, test television commercials without sound and print ads without body copy in order to determine what messages are being conveyed by the nonverbal elements of the advertising. Second, in order to compare effects of verbal versus nonverbal communication, consumers could be exposed to either the verbal or nonverbal elements and their reactions measured by common dependent measures such as long- and short-term recall, attitude shifts, and internalization.

3. Study Optimal Media Choices

The choice of advertising media is usually dictated by the identity of the target audience or the nature of the product. For instance, for a packaged good aimed at a broad audience, national television is commonly used. For theaters and restaurants, local newspapers are fairly standard. Billboards and radio are often used to reach commuters, and so on.

However, advertisers must select from several media that might all be effective in a given situation. In this case, advertisers would like answers to several questions about the media.

How does the medium interact with the advertiser's message? (Are some media more appropriate than others for introducing new, complex, infrequently-purchased, inessential, frivolous, or risky products? Are some media more appropriate than others for advertising appeals that are humorous, hard sell, emotional?)

What is the effect of the editorial or programming material in which the advertising is embedded? (Do programs with similar Nielsen ratings and audiences vary in their desirability because of the nature of audience involvement with the programs, as Television Audience Assessment's research suggests? Is an ad more effective placed in an op-ed or news page of a newspaper?)

When, if ever, is a coordinated media buy in several media more effective than the concentrated use of a single medium? (Would it be better for an advertiser to buy time on a single show, week after week, to buy time on a variety of shows, or to place the advertising on radio as well as television? Do combinations of television, radio, and newspaper ads produce more of the desired effect than the use of only one of the media?)

What is the effect of the changing media environment (caused by cable and VCRs, for example) on advertisers' choices?

These questions are asked routinely. While agencies and advertisers have developed many rules of thumb for dealing with these questions, scientific, empirical research on these questions would be valuable. Empirical tests and experiments, using split cable, test cities, and controlled media buys, have been suggested as the most logical methods to use to answer the questions.

4. Determine Ways to Test Concepts and Campaigns

Most advertising research focuses on individual ads or commercials. However, two of the most important aspects of advertising—the *concept* behind the advertising and the series of executions comprising a *campaign*—do not have standardized research methods.

An advertising *concept* could be defined as the developmental strategy or selling argument behind the advertising executions that consumers actually see. A concept could take many forms, from a simple statement of copy claims (Product X offers superior strength) to a fairly finished quasi-execution that shows the tone or style of the advertising as well as the main claims (Product X tastes good and the advertising promoting it is light, with youthful characters and humor.) Because an advertising concept may be the basis for millions of dollars of advertising and for several complete advertising campaigns over a long period of time, the selection of the best concept is of immense financial importance to advertisers.

However, concept research is not nearly as standardized or as highly developed today as copy research or research on a single advertisement. Many important questions remain unanswered about concept research. For instance, what techniques should be used to test concepts—could commercial- or product-testing methods be used? Do warm-up techniques (in which the consumers are introduced to the interviewer and the task at hand) matter, and, if so, how? What is the ideal degree of finish or development stage when testing a concept? Should the dependent variables in a concept test be purchase intent (similar to a mail-order test), liking, or something else? Can the concept be tested independently of the tone or style of the advertising?

An advertising *campaign* is typically composed of several executions of a single, common advertising theme. For example, several celebrities might be used in several commercials to present the same message, or the same selling point might be made in a variety of settings. Since much advertising is planned as a campaign—even though only a single execution may be tested as representative of the full campaign, for obvious financial reasons—the question is whether a single commercial test is truly representative of the full campaign? Is there some way to evaluate a full campaign for a reasonable cost? Single commercials are often tested in comparison with competitors' single commercials. Can campaigns be compared to competitors' campaigns in a similar fashion?

When studying campaigns, perhaps it would be fruitful to begin with empirical tests. One study might compare simple repetition of the same commercial with an equal number of different executions from the same campaign in order to determine which is more effective over time. Or, several executions from a campaign could be tested singly and compared to each other to determine whether they yield similar results and under what conditions a single commercial is representative of a full campaign.

5. Determine Mediating Consumer Traits

Certain consumer traits or characteristics may affect consumers' responses to advertising (Schlinger, 1982). Consumer traits, such as lifestyle (as measured by VALS and Monitor, for instance), demographics, cognitive structures, and especially purchasing behavior, would be of considerable interest to advertisers if they mediated the consumers' responses to advertising. For example, do some consumer segments require more exposure to advertising before they are motivated to purchase than others? Do some consumer segments respond better than others to executional elements such as music, humor, or superimpositions? Do some segments respond better to print than to broadcast advertising? If so, then answers to these questions would clearly affect advertisers' media selection, advertising strategy, and even their advertising testing methods.

No research methods emerged during the MSI topic review process as being especially appropriate for this topic, but large sample experimental studies, perhaps in conjunction with established copy-testing services, might be appropriate.

6. Study Relation between Share of Voice and Share of Market

Share of voice refers to a single brand's share of the advertising for its product category, when all relevant brands' advertising is considered. One might expect a brand's share of voice to be related to its share of the market, with the larger brands advertising more heavily. Some firms find, however, that the brands with the smaller market shares need to advertise at a much higher share of voice merely in order to maintain share of market. In other words, the largest-selling brands may require less share of voice than the small or new brands.

In order to answer the question of what a brand's share of voice should be, given its market share, researchers might study published data on advertising spending and market share for a variety of product categories. Another approach might be to work with advertisers to develop a new data base specifically for this research.

7. Study Communication Spending Allocation

The communication budget for a firm may be split among advertising (to consumers and distributors), sales promotion, corporate communications (issue-oriented communication designed to influence the environment), and personal selling. Since these communication functions are often performed by different departments or divisions within the firm, there is likely to be a great deal of interest in how the communication spending is allocated for each function. Further, the top marketing management must worry that it is allocating its spending for maximum impact.

The following are some of the most commonly asked questions about communication spending. What is the trade-off between advertising and sales promotion? Does this vary for new versus established products? How should spending be allocated between personal selling and advertising at various points in the product life cycle? How should communication spending be allocated over the channel of distribution? How does corporate communications interact with product advertising?

Researchers interested in this topic might approach the question from the empirical point of view of how firms currently make such decisions or try to build experiments or measure the trade-offs between the various types of spending.

8. Evaluate the Impact of Corporate Communications

Corporate communications differ from product advertising in topic and purpose. Corporate communications discuss issues rather than products and their purpose is to influence thinking rather than to directly increase sales of a certain product. While corporate communications may increase sales in the long run, as a secondary effect, their main purpose is to alter the external environment facing a firm (be it public opinion or regulators' opinions) in some way.

While many firms use corporate communications, many questions about how it works and what it does remain unanswered. For example, what are the effects of corporate advertising on the corporate image as seen by the public and regulators? What are the strategic uses for and impact of corporate communications? How can corporate communications be compared to advertising in terms of relative importance for a brand, and do the two interact?

A literature review might be a fruitful way to begin the study of these corporate communications questions. This review might examine what is known about the successful uses and effects of corporate communications.

WHAT HAPPENS NEXT?

Research on these top priority advertising questions may well involve a cooperative effort, with input from academics, advertising agency people, the advertiser and advertising research supplier committees, and associations such as the ARF, 4As, ANA, and MSI. Each of these communities has something important to bring to the research effort that may not be available from the others. For example, academics bring their impartiality and scholarly expertise, but they could benefit from the experience of practitioners who have access to proprietary data and informal rules of thumb. Advertising research suppliers have access to a great deal of data, but their research runs the danger of being seen as self-serving and biased if they work alone. Advertisers are needed to supply their resources, lending their advertising and information to experimental studies, for instance. But, since advertisers would clearly prefer not to share their information with competitors, a disinterested third party is needed to coordinate advertiser efforts and guarantee confidentiality. The advertising research advocated here would probably advance most rapidly if the various communities work together—perhaps coordinated by the ARF, 4As, ANA, MSI, or some other professional group.

APPENDIX A[1]: TAXONOMY OF ADVERTISING

A. *Product*
  1. Product life cycle
     a. unknown or new
     b. maturing
     c. mature
  2. Type of Product
     a. consumer nondurable
     b. consumer durable
     c. consumer service
     d. industrial product
     e. industrial service
     f. corporate (including issue and public service)
  3. Relative brand share of advertised product
     a. small
     b. average
     c. large
  4. Brand loyalty within product class
     a. extreme loyalty, low switching
     b. average
     c. low loyalty, high switching

B. *Medium*
   (Could also be expressed in terms of the senses of sight or sound that are involved)
   1. Television
   2. Radio
   3. Magazines
   4. Newspapers
   5. Other
C. *Target Audience*
   1. Demographics
   2. Usage of product or brand
   3. Benefit segment or psychographics
D. *Intent of Advertising*
   1. Inform of existence/build awareness (Existence) as, for example, mnemonics devices
   2. Inform of attributes (Attributes)
      a. comparative
      b. noncomparative
   3. Inform of what the product does for the viewer (Functional)
   4. Convince of desired associations (Associational) may associate viewer with situation or personalities desired
E. *Media Weight*
   1. Spending
   2. Shared Voice
F. *Tone of Advertising*
   1. Emotional (transformation, indirect sell) vs. informational (rational, direct sell). This could also be called the "Ombre" of commercial and may be a continuous variable.
   2. Humorous vs. nonhumorous tone
   3. Dramatic tension, surprise; surprise vs. straightforward
G. *Executional Variables*
   1. Format
      a. story/drama
      b. slice of life
      c. testimonial
      d. demonstration of product in use
      e. problem and solution
      f. analogy
   2. Music/dancing
      a. extravaganza
      b. major element
      c. used but not major element
      d. not used

3. Presenter
    a. celebrity
    b. authority
    c. ordinary person
    d. voice over vs. seen
    e. number of presenters
4. Visuals
    a. no product shown
    b. realistic
    c. fantasy or surreal visuals
    d. scenic beauty or personal beauty used
    e. graphic display of points (charts, graphs, etc.)
    f. cartoons or animation

H. *Familiarity of Advertisement*
   1. Does it use jingle or theme song used before
   2. Does it use presenters or characters used before
   3. Is it a new execution of an established campaign

I. *Measures Used*
   1. Commercial recall (24-hour, 48-hour, 72-hour)
   2. Recognition
   3. Purchase intent
   4. Brand preference and preference change (persuasion)
   5. Interest, believability, positive or negative impact of commercial
   6. Message playback

ENDNOTE

1. Developed by MSI's Advertising Steering Group.

REFERENCES

Achenbaum, Alvin A., Russell I. Haley and Ronald Gatty. "On-Air versus In-Home Testing of TV Commercials." *Journal of Advertising Research*, 7, 4 (1967): 15–19.

ARS. *Factors Affecting Measurements of Related Recall.* Evansville, Ind.: Advertising Research Systems Corporation, 1979.

Bagozzi, Richard P. and Alvin J. Silk. "Recall, Recognition, and the Measurement of Memory for Print Advertisements." Alfred P. Sloan School of Management Working Paper No. 1262, 1981.

Bloom, Derek, Andrea Jay and Tony Twyman. "The Validity of Advertising Pretests." *Journal of Advertising Research*, 17, 2 (April 1977): 7–16.

Bogart, Leo. "New Agenda for Advertising Research." Speech given at Advertising Research Foundation 28th Annual Conference, New York, N.Y., March 1982.

Clancy, Kevin J. and Lyman E. Ostlund. "Commercial Effectiveness Measures." *Journal of Advertising Research*, 16, 1 (February 1976): 29–34.

Clancy, Kevin J., Lyman E. Ostlund, and G. A. Wymer. "False Reporting of Magazine Readership." *Journal of Advertising Research*, 19, 5 (October 1979): 23–30.

Clarke, Darral G., ed. *Cumulative Advertising Effects: Sources and Implications*. Cambridge, Mass.: Marketing Science Institute, 1977.

"Copy Testing Critics Seek Better Techniques." *Ad Forum* (September 1980): 28.

Courtney, Alice E. *Practitioners' Conceptions of the Advertising Process*. Cambridge, Mass.: Marketing Science Institute, 1970.

Dunn, Theodore. Remarks from the Chairman of the Board at Advertising Research Foundation 28th Annual Conference, New York, N.Y., March 1982.

Greyser, Stephen A. *Irritation in Advertising*. Cambridge, Mass.: Marketing Science Institute, 1973.

Haskins, Jack B. "Recall as a Measurement of Advertising Effectiveness." *Journal of Advertising Research*, 4, 1 (1964): 2–8.

Honomichl, Jack J. "TV Copy Testing Flap: What to Do About It." *Advertising Age* (January 19, 1981): 59.

Krugman, Herbert E. "The Impact of Television Advertising: Learning without Involvement." *Public Opinion Quarterly*, 29, 3 (1965): 349–56.

———. "Memory without Recall, Exposure without Perception." *Journal of Advertising Research*, 17, 4 (August 1977): 7–12.

Lavidge, Robert J. and Gary A. Steiner. "A Model for Productive Measurements of Advertising Effectiveness." *Journal of Marketing*, 25 (October 1961): 59–62.

Lipstein, Benjamin and James Neelankavil. *Television Advertising Copy Research Practices Among Major Advertisers and Advertising Agencies*. New York: Advertising Research Foundation, 1982.

Little, John D. C. "Aggregate Advertising Models: The State of the Art." *Operations Research* 27 (July/August 1979): 629–67.

Lockwood, Thornton C. "Copy Testing Validation: Why Is It Important? Why Hasn't the Validation Been Resolved?" Speech to Advertising Research Copy Validation Workshop, New York, N.Y., November 1981.

Lucas, D. B. "The ABC's of ARF's PARM." *Journal of Marketing*, 25 (July 1960): 9.

McDonald, Colin, *What Is the Short Term Effect of Advertising?* Cambridge, Mass.: Marketing Science Institute, 1971.

McNeill, Dennis L. and William R. Swinyard. *Comparative Product Information and Its Interaction with Brand Name and Product Type*. Cambridge, Mass.: Marketing Science Institute, 1980.

Naples, Michael J. *Effective Frequency: The Relationship Between Frequency and Advertising Effectiveness*. New York: Association of National Advertisers, 1979.

Olson, Jerry C. "Presidential Address—1981: Toward a Science of Consumer Behavior." Speech given at Association for Consumer Research National Conference, St. Louis, Missouri, October 1981.

Palda, Kristian S. "The Hypothesis of a Hierarchy of Effects: A Partial Evaluation." *Journal of Marketing Research*, 3 (February 1966): 13–24.

Park, C. Whan and Banwari Mittal. "Role of Involvement in Consumer Behavior." G. Zaltman and M. Wallendar (eds.), *Consumer Behavior*, 2nd ed. (forthcoming).

Ray, Michael L. and Peter H. Webb. *Advertising Effectiveness in a Crowded Television Environment*. Cambridge, Mass.: Marketing Science Institute, 1978.

Ray, Michael L. *Marketing Communication and the Hierarchy of Effects*. Cambridge, Mass.: Marketing Science Institute, 1973.

Ray, Michael L. "Strategy by Situation." Speech given at Issues in Communications Symposium, sponsored by American Association of Advertising Agencies, New York, N.Y., March 1982.

Ray, Michael L., Scott Ward and Jerome B. Reed. *New Directions for Advertising Pretesting Research*. Cambridge, Mass.: Marketing Science Institute, 1974.

Schlinger, Mary Jane Rawlins. "Respondent Characteristics That Affect Copy-Test Attitude Scales." *Journal of Advertising Research*, 22, 1 (February/March 1982): 29–35.

Silk, Alvin J. and Terry Vavra. *Advertising's Affective Qualities and Consumer Response*. Cambridge, Mass.: Marketing Science Institute, 1974.

Smith, Robert E. and William R. Swinyard. "Information Response Models: An Integrated Approach." *Journal of Marketing*, 46 (Winter 1982): 81–93.

Swinyard, William R. and Michael L. Ray. "Advertising-Selling Interactions: An Attribution Theory Experiment." *Journal of Marketing Research* (November 1977): 509.

Tauber, Edward M. "Six Questionable Assumptions in Ad Research." *Marketing News* (September 19, 1980): 9.

"21 Ad Agencies Copy Testing Principles." *Marketing News* (February 19, 1982): 1.

Wells, William D. "Recognition, Recall, and Rating Scales." *Journal of Advertising Research*, 4, 3 (1964): 2–8.

Young, Shirley. "Copy Testing Without Magic Numbers." *Journal of Advertising Research*, 12, 1 (1972): 3–12.

Yuspeh, Sonia. "J. Walter Thompson's Program Environment Study." *Marketing News* (April 6, 1979).

39 — Marketing and Public Relations

Philip Kotler and William Mindak

Reprinted from the *Journal of Marketing*, published by the American Marketing Association, Vol. 42 (October 1978), pp. 13–20. Reprinted by permission.

One can sense growing confusion as to the future roles of marketing and public relations in the modern organization:

- **Marketing people** are increasingly interested in incorporating publicity as a tool within the marketing mix, although this tool has normally been controlled by public relations.
- **Public relations** people are growing increasingly concerned with their company's marketing practices, questioning whether they "square" with the company's social responsibility. They seek more influence over marketing and more of a counseling and policy-making role.
- At the same time, a new corporate function called **public affairs** has split off from public relations, causing some confusion as to the scope of public relations.

In nonprofit organizations particularly (e.g., hospitals, colleges, and museums), where public relations is a well-established function, marketing is emerging as a "hot" topic. Public relations people are beginning to worry that they won't be able to control this new function or, what is worse, will end up working for marketing.

Where does marketing end and public relations begin? Where does public relations end and public affairs begin? The increasingly fuzzy boundaries have led to conflict among these departments. Usually they choose either to operate independently with little teamwork or to bicker over resources and strategies.

Yet marketing and public relations *are the major external functions of the firm*. Both functions start their analysis and planning from the point of view of satisfying outside groups. Both are relative newcomers on the corporate scene. Both normally operate separately, at some loss in overall effectiveness.

RELATIVE LEVELS OF USE

Enterprises fall into four classes with respect to their use of marketing and public relations (Exhibit 1):

Class One enterprises barely use either function in a formal sense. An example would be small nonprofit organizations such as social service agencies. Their administrators do not recognize having marketing problems or tasks as such. Nor do they feel they have the budgets to support a formal public relations staff.

Class Two enterprises have a well-established public relations function but no marketing function. Almost every hospital and college has a public relations officer who takes responsibility for designing publications, attracting favorable press coverage, and counseling the president on the institution's image. On the other hand, hardly any hospitals and colleges have created a marketing position, although interest in the marketing function is growing rapidly.

Class Three enterprises operate a strong marketing or sales organization but a weak or nonexistent public relations function. For example, small manufacturing concerns are heavily involved in finding and serving customers, but they do little to cultivate other publics. They may not have any stockholders to please; they may have no community groups to appease. Public relations is run minimally in these enterprises.

EXHIBIT 1. Four Levels of Use of Marketing and Public Relations in Enterprises

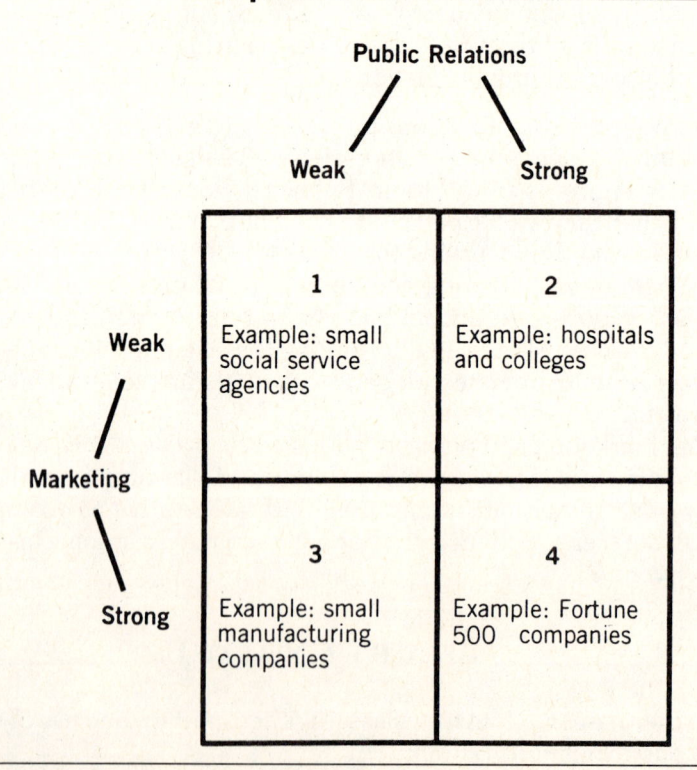

	Public Relations Weak	Public Relations Strong
Marketing Weak	1. Example: small social service agencies	2. Example: hospitals and colleges
Marketing Strong	3. Example: small manufacturing companies	4. Example: Fortune 500 companies

Class Four enterprises operate strong marketing and public relations departments. Typical are the large Fortune-500 corporations, whose marketing activities have impact on a large number of publics in a way that warrants sizeable public relations activities. In these organizations, the marketing and public relations departments normally operate independently under separate officers, both of whom report to top management. In a few cases, public relations is under marketing, but this is an exception to the rule. Marketing may have responsibility, however, for the part of public relations dealing with product publicity.

New Emphases

Some enterprises are currently moving to strengthen either marketing or public relations relative to the other. In the following two cases, marketing is being given increased influence relative to public relations:

> Financial institutions discovered public relations before they discovered marketing. Their thinking ran primarily along lines of publics, community relations, consumer education, and "imagery." Now banks and savings and loan associations are rapidly moving toward marketing thinking. They refer more to "markets," "profit centers," and "positioning." Their associations sponsor annual marketing conferences with rapidly growing attendance. The top marketing person is likely to have more power than the top public relations officer.
>
> Hospitals have long depended on public relations for communicating with their publics. But they gave little thought to marketing until recent years, when they began to experience low bed occupancy, loss of patients to newer hospitals, changing levels of demand for different services, and low utilization of hospital facilities during weekends. These problems have sparked a strong interest in marketing. The Evanston Hospital, Evanston, Illinois, appointed a fulltime marketing vice president, probably the world's first. Other hospitals are seeking to bring in marketing through establishing a marketing job position. Some hospitals have thought of adding marketing to the job responsibilities of the public relations director but are facing doubts about whether their public relations director has the skills and attitudes for effective marketing planning.

Other institutions, in contrast, are strengthening their public relations relative to marketing:

> "A major food company has set up a product review board. This group reviews the nutritional contribution of planned new products before they are brought to market and must be convinced of their nutritional validity before project approval is given. This pro-

cedure grew out of policy conceived by the public relations director. He is also head of the review board which has absolute authority in this area."[1]

"Exxon has announced the formation of a Public Affairs Department whose function is to identify issues and develop plans with full consideration for the audiences to be reached and the communication vehicles or means for reaching these audiences. The advertising emphasis has moved from marketing to corporate issues."[2]

These develoments pose a number of interesting questions for the management of any company:

- Are the company's marketing managers sufficiently sensitized to public issues when they develop their plans?
- Are the company's public relations people sufficiently trained to apply market-oriented reasoning to their own activities?
- Is the company allocating the proper budgets to marketing and public relations?
- Are the organizational arrangements optimal for taking advantage of the interdependence of marketing and public relations?

To deal with these issues, we will have to first analyze how these functions evolved.

THE EVOLUTION OF MARKETING

A widespread misconception prevails that marketing is a very old subject. The truth is that marketing is a relatively new subject. Modern marketing, as we know it today, evolved over many years through the five stages shown in Exhibit 2A.

Early Functions

Marketing's origins trace back to the ancient function known as *selling*, with which it is often confused. As soon as early man produced surpluses of certain goods, he began to look for trading opportunities, first on a barter basis, and later on a monetized basis. The fine art of finding buyers, displaying goods attractively, and negotiating effectively developed early in the history of civilization and continues to undergo refinements to this day.

In the late nineteenth century, with the development of national markets and mass communication, manufacturers began to recognize the value of regular *advertising* as a supplement to their sales force activities. Advertising expenditures could produce customer leads, generate customer awareness and interest, and reinforce loyalty. Companies hired their own advertising specialists and/or advertising agencies to perform this function.

The rapid growth of national markets in the twentieth century increased the need for *marketing information* on which company marketing management could base their planning. Sellers recognized that they could reduce their risk by spending money to find out what customers really wanted, how customers perceived the company and its products, and so on. The first marketing department was formally established by the Curtis Publishing Company in 1911, and the example was soon followed by U.S. Rubber (1916) and Swift & Co. (1917).

Coordination and Orientation

These three functions—sales, advertising, and marketing research—operated fairly independently of each other, although nominally they were supposed to be coordinated by the vice president of sales. But his heart lay in the sales force, and he tended to neglect the other two functions. This led to the fourth stage, when these functions—and others such as customer service, pricing, marketing planning—were finally combined into a *marketing department*. The purpose of a marketing department was to develop a balanced marketing program which coordinated all the marketing mix instruments and forces impinging on the customer. To head this department, a vice president of marketing was appointed.

The establishment of a marketing vice presidency did not automati-

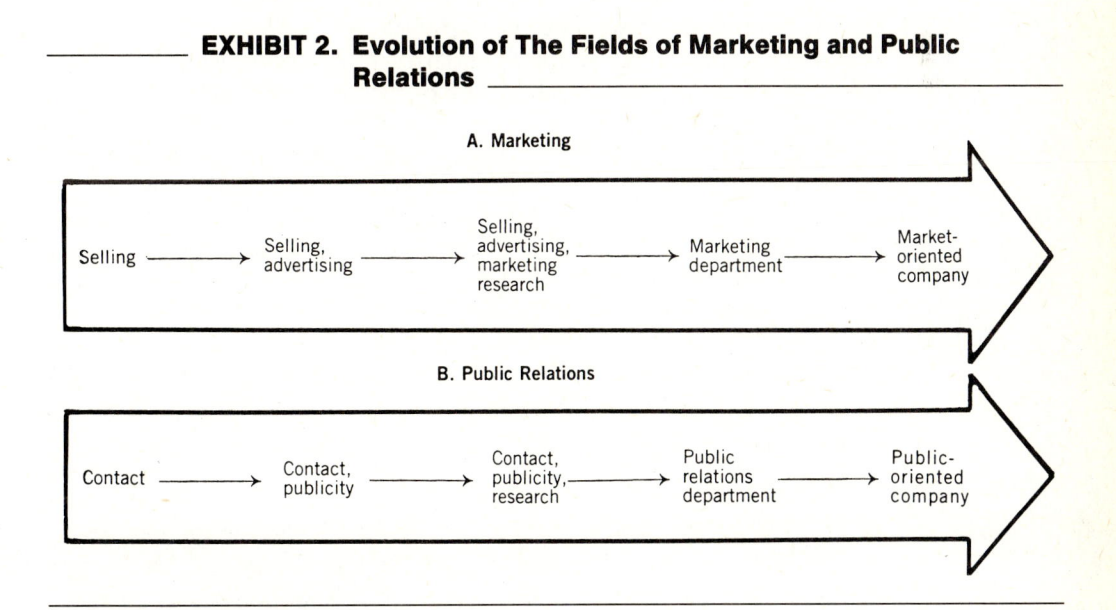

EXHIBIT 2. Evolution of The Fields of Marketing and Public Relations

A. Marketing

Selling → Selling, advertising → Selling, advertising, marketing research → Marketing department → Market-oriented company

B. Public Relations

Contact → Contact, publicity → Contact, publicity, research → Public relations department → Public-oriented company

cally insure that the company as a whole was *market oriented*. This stage only came about when the various departments of the company (purchasing, R & D, engineering, finance, manufacturing) all adopted and practiced a customer philosophy (i.e., they recognize that in the words of Peter Drucker, "the purpose of the company is to create a customer."[3]).

To some observers, even a market orientation is not enough. They call upon the firm to become public-oriented, to exhibit a greater concern over its impact on the environment, consumer's health and safety, and consumer pocketbooks. In short, they would place marketing under increased public relations control.

To complicate the matter further, the concept of marketing recently has been "broadened" to cover the problem of marketing any entity to any public, whether a product, service, place, person or idea.[4] Generic marketers argue that communicating with the public is not enough. Often the objective is to influence a public, and this is best done by considering the problem in terms of *exchange theory* and not simply *communication theory*.

Marketers may be in a better position to plan for achieving desired responses from target publics than public relations people. Extention of this argument to the limit suggests that marketers should take over the public relations function.

EVOLUTION OF PUBLIC RELATIONS

Public relations is also a relatively new corporate function although it, too, has its roots in ancient human activities.

Edward L. Bernays, one of the fathers of modern public relations, posited that the three main elements of public relations are as old as society: a) informing people, b) persuading people, and c) integrating people with people.[5] And he traced public relations from primitive society (in which leaders controlled by force, intimidation, and persuasion) to Babylonia (where kings commissioned historians to paint favorable images of them).

Historical Milestones

The Renaissance and Reformation freed men's minds from established dogmas, leading institutions to develop more subtle means to influence people. In America, historical milestones for "public relations" include:

- Samuel Adams' use of the press to unite the colonists against the British.
- The abolitionist movement's use of public relations as a political

tool to rally support for blacks in the North, including the publication of *Uncle Tom's Cabin*.
- P. T. Barnum's use of public relations to generate newsworthiness about an event—the arrival of his circus—by placing articles in newspapers.

Corporate public relations evolved more recently and passed through the five stages shown in Exhibit 2B. In the first stage, corporations established a *contact* function to influence legislators and newspapers to support positions favorable to business. The legislative contact function became known as *lobbying*, and the newspaper contact function became know as *press relations*. George Westinghouse is credited with the formal establishment of public relations when he hired two men in 1889 to fight the advocates of direct current electricity and to promote instead alternating current.[6]

The next stage occurred when companies began to recognize the positive value of planned *publicity* to create customer interest in the company and its products. Publicity entailed finding or creating events, preparing company or product-slanted news stories, and trying to interest the press in using them. Companies recognized that special skills are needed to develop publicity and began to add publicists to their ranks.

Somewhat later, public relations practitioners began to recognize the value of conducting *research* into public opinion prior to developing and launching public relations campaigns. The emerging sciences of public opinion measurement and mass communication theory permitted more sophistication in the conduct of public relations. Forward looking firms added specialists who could research public opinion.

P. R. Department

These functions—contact, publicity, and research—were typically ill-coordinated. For example, those doing government work had little to do with those arranging publicity; those developing publicity made little use of research. This finally led to the concept of a *public relations department* integrating all of the work going on to cultivate the goodwill of different publics of the company. Over time, the public relations department developed further subspecialties dealing with each public (stockholders, neighbors, employees, customers, government agencies) and each tool (conferences, publicity, graphics, etc.)

The presence of a modern public relations department did not insure that the company as a whole acted like a *public company*. The vice president of public relations had limited influence over other departments and needed the backing of top management to press for public-oriented actions by all the departments. Companies were facing formidable new challenges in the form of consumerism, environmentalism, energy con-

EXHIBIT 3. Models of the Possible Relationship Between Marketing and Public Relations

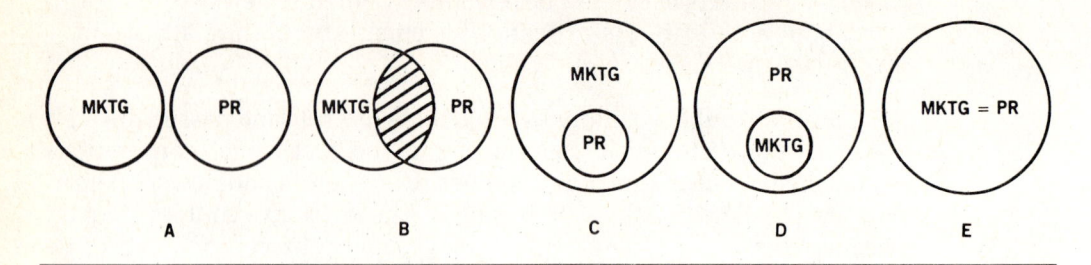

servation, inflation, shortages, employment discrimination, and safety. The public relations people wanted a more active role in counseling the company and its departments on how to act as public citizens.

ALTERNATIVE MODELS OF RELATIONSHIP

Marketing and public relations are both reaching maturity and seeking more policy making roles within the corporation. They deal with the external environment as their starting point for planning. One hopes to make the company more market-oriented while the other hopes to make the company more public-oriented—objectives which are not necessarily compatible. What relation should the two functions have to each other?

We can conceive of five different models for viewing the relationship between marketing and public relations (Exhibit 3):

Separate but Equal Functions (A)

The traditional view of the two functions is that they are quite different in their perspectives and capacities. Marketing exists to sense, serve, and satisfy customer needs at a profit. Public relations exists to produce goodwill in the company's various publics so that these publics do not interfere in the firm's profit-making ability.

The educational backgrounds of marketing and public relations practitioners differ considerably, producing almost two separate "cultures":

- **Marketers**, for the most part, are trained in business schools where they gain skills in economic, quantitative, and behavioral analysis. Trained to be profit-oriented in their planning activities, they normally get little exposure to the subject of communications and mass media.
- **Public relations practitioners**, on the other hand, come out of journalism schools where they are expected first to learn media

skills, be good spellers and grammarians, and learn how to write summary leads. Many journalists who do not find opportunities in journalism enter public relations as a second choice. They normally come with little training in political, economic or social analysis and some of them grew up with anti-business attitudes.

No wonder the two groups carry around denigrating stereotypes of each other. Marketing people often view public relations people as press agents, flacks, sponsors of pseudo-events (e.g., Miss "Pickle-Queen of 1977"). Public relations people view marketers as hucksters, "numbercrunchers," deodorant salesmen. Often each views the other's function in its narrowest perspective. Marketing really *is* sales; public relations really *is* publicity.

A public relations scholar recently articulated the traditional view when he said:

"The extension of the marketing concept to nonprofit agencies appears to me to be describing public relations under a new garb. I hold strongly that marketing men should confine themselves to the marketing field and use advertising and product publicity as part of the marketing mix. I don't think that most marketing oriented persons have the experience, aptitude or approach for sound public relations."[7]

Equal but Overlapping Functions (B)

Another school of thought says that while marketing and public relations are important and separate functions, they share some common terrain. The most obvious common group is product publicity. Carefully planned publicity can create great visibility and interest in a product or brand. How should publicity skill be supplied to, say, a product manager? The company can either locate product publicity in the marketing department or "borrow" it as needed from the public relations department. The more important product publicity is to product success, the better it is to locate it within the marketing department.

Another common ground is customer relations. Marketing is adept at selling customers and less adept at responding to customer complaints after the product is sold. Customer complaints tend to reach the public relations department. Public relations personnel try to salve the customer's wounds and get the marketing department to avoid practices that will lead to similar grievances in the future. A latent function of the public relations department is to "watchdog" the marketing department.

Marketing as the Dominant Function (C)

Some marketers advance the view that corporate public relations should be placed under the control of the corporate marketing department. They argue that public relations exists essentially to make it easier for the firm to market its goods. Public relations is not in the corporate picture simply to do good deeds. One of the most articulate spokesmen for this view is Howard Geltzer of Ries and Geltzer:

> "I grew up in the General Electric 'school,' which views public relations as a fundamental marketing tool. In every client situation, our public relations tactics are closely tied to the strategic marketing objectives. I view the role of public relations to support and further the overall marketing objectives. This occurs most successfully when public relations reinforces the impact of other marketing communication techniques, like promotion and advertising, by adding another voice to the overall position. In my opinion, public relations as a separate entity from marketing is outdated and no longer feasible in today's economic environment."[8]

Public relations does a poor job of measuring its contribution to profits, some criticize. Public relations practitioners measure impact in communicating terms: specifically, how many clippings or mentions they could count. A new measurement approach is needed that measures how well public relations contributes to moving the marketing objectives forward.

The "broadening of marketing" movement views public relations as a subset of marketing. The generic task of marketing is:

> "The analysis, planning, implementation, and control of carefully formulated programs designed to bring about voluntary exchanges of values with target markets for the purpose of achieving organizational objectives."[9]

Thus marketers can view any public as a "target market" if the problem is formulated as one of how to incentivize the voluntary exchange of valued resources between two parties. The valued resources include time, energy, attention, and goodwill, as well as money. Levy and Zaltman advanced the view "that all interactions may be interpreted from a marketing point of view."[10]

Public Relations as the Dominant Function (D)

It is also conceivable that in some quarters marketing will be viewed as a subfunction of public relations rather than the reverse. The argument would be made that the firm's future depends critically on how it is viewed by key publics, including stockholders, financial institutions, unions, employees, community leaders, as well as customers. The task of the firm is to satisfy these publics as much as possible. Satisfying the customers is one part of the task, the part called *marketing*. Satisfying the customers must be kept in balance with satisfying other groups. Marketing cannot be allowed to go its own way regardless of the consequences. Marketing should be put under public relations control to make sure that the goodwill of all key publics is maintained.

In for-profit firms, this view is implemented by transferring some power to approve or disapprove of certain practices of the marketing department to the public relations people. We saw earlier examples of a food company and an oil company creating greater public relations control over marketing.

Nonprofit organizations express this view in another way. The nonprofit organization normally has a public relations director before it ever recognizes a need for marketing. When marketing problems emerge, the administration may choose to expand the job responsibilities of the public relations officer to include some marketing work, rather than establish a separate job position for marketing. Or a marketing person might be hired and asked to report to the public relations director. The public relations director will go through the motions of learning about marketing concepts and tools. This is not always successful, and often marketing remains a stepchild of the public relations program.

Marketing and Public Relations as the Same Function (E)

Another way of viewing the two functions is as rapidly converging in concepts and methodologies. They both talk in terms of publics and markets; they both recognize the need for market segmentation; they both acknowledge the importance of market attitudes, perceptions, and images in formulating programs; and the primacy of a management process consisting of analysis, planning, implementation, and control. In some organizations, the two functions might be feasibly merged under a Vice President of Marketing and Public Relations. This person is in charge of planning and managing the external affairs of the company.

Exhibit 4 shows the planning methodology such a department would follow. The first step calls for auditing the present position of the firm and its major products in the eyes of target markets and publics. The audit would answer such questions as:

- How visible is the firm to different publics?
- How favorably is the firm seen by different key publics? What negatives exist in the current image?
- What factors cause the negative impressions?
- What threat power do these various publics have on the firm?

The second step calls for defining a desired position for the firm and its products vis-à-vis its competition:

- Does this position make marketing sense?
- Does it make public relations sense?

- Can it be achieved given the firm's resources?

The third step calls for developing a portfolio of products and services that is well-balanced cyclically, seasonally, and in terms of risks to reversals in public opinion. The firm should not rely too heavily on products that are vulnerable to public criticism and legislative action.

The fourth step calls for setting specific marketing and public relations objectives, policies, and strategies to guide conduct and performance in the market place and public arena. Strict marketing objectives and strategies should be tempered by such considerations as:

EXHIBIT 4. Joint Methodology of Marketing and Public Relations

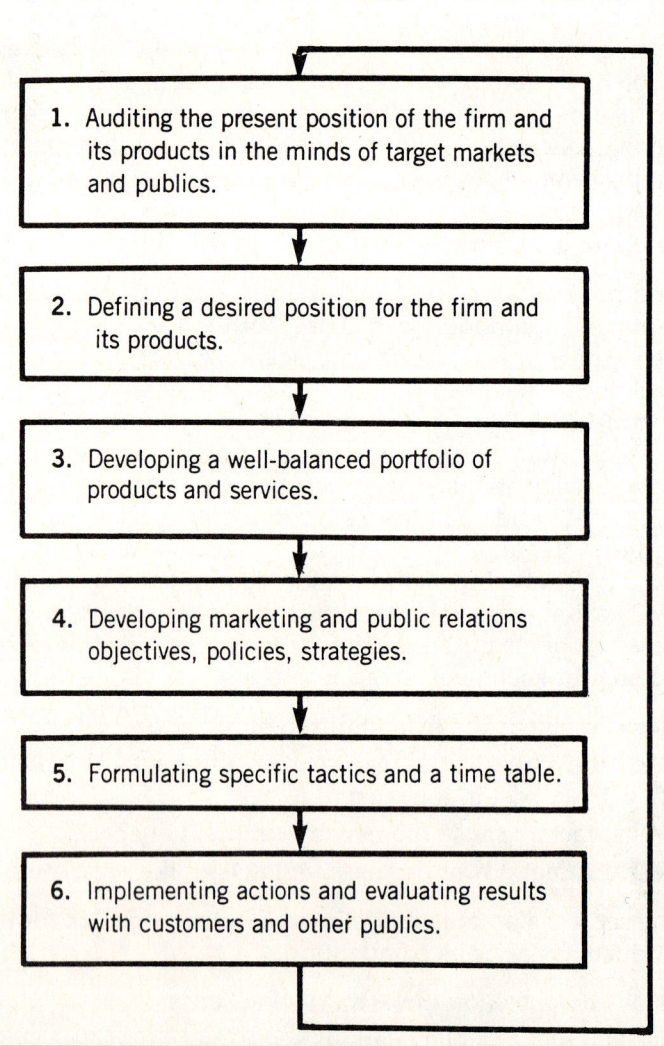

1. Auditing the present position of the firm and its products in the minds of target markets and publics.

2. Defining a desired position for the firm and its products.

3. Developing a well-balanced portfolio of products and services.

4. Developing marketing and public relations objectives, policies, strategies.

5. Formulating specific tactics and a time table.

6. Implementing actions and evaluating results with customers and other publics.

- Is the product healthful and safe?
- Is the pricing defensible?
- Is the environmental harm minimal?

The fifth step calls for developing specific tactics and a time table to implement marketing and public relations strategies. The implications of specific tactics should be reviewed for their potential in creating public relations backlash.

The sixth step calls for implementing planned actions and monitoring their impacts on customers and other key publics:

- Are plans being achieved?
- Are the publics responding in the expected way?
- Should strategies or tactics be changed?

What about this model? In principle, it synthesizes the two functions so as to reduce interdepartmental conflict and lack of coordination. It would hopefully avoid the difficulties recently experienced by two giant corporations when they failed to take a joint marketing/public relations programming of their marketing activities:

> "It has not been clearly established that General Motors deliberately misled many purchasers of Buicks, Oldsmobiles, and Pontiacs by delivering their cars with motors also used in Chevrolets or that New York Telephone intended to conceal existence of less expensive services from certain subscribers. However, because such customers of both companies have felt they were deceived, there have been scores of unfavorable media reports and further damage to the public reputation of business as a whole and additional anti-business regulation may result."[11]

LOOKING AHEAD

The neat and tidy divisions separating marketing and public relations are breaking down. It may be that the best way to solve a marketing problem would be through public relations activities. It also is possible that the best way to solve a public relations problem might be through the disciplined orientation that marketing provides.

Both marketing and public relations people want more of a voice in corporate policy making. To the extent that marketers incorporate sound public relations in their thinking, this will obviate the need for an expanded corporate public relations department. To the extent that they fail to do this, public relations people are going to press for more influence over marketing decisions.

Not all managements, however, are responsive to using corporate public relations practitioners as simply communication specialists. The president of a Fortune 500 food corporation told one of the authors:

> "I don't expect counsel from my public relations department about public issues or the stand my company should take about these issues. I consult issues 'experts' in product safety, government, and other areas. I then go to public relations to help effectively communicate our position to mass and selective audiences. I don't think public relations people have had the training or knowledge to give advice on 'issue positions.'"[12]

This company set up a separate public affairs department in which the real expertise on public issues is expected to lie. The growth of public affairs departments in recent time has removed some of the argument from public relations directors that they should provide a counseling as well as a communications function to top management.

On the other hand, viewing public relations as simply a communications function will lead a lot of chief executive officers to miss some of this function's potential value. It could even be counterproductive, according to Harry Dreiser, an experienced public relations practitioner:

> "Assuming the public relations director is a thoroughgoing professional, seasoned and skilled, this process wastes his talents and may give rise to real public relations problems. He ought to be in on the decision process early, and have a chance to affect it. He contributes his knowledge of the media and how they are likely to treat a corporate action, and his perception of the public and its attitudes. If he is to be fully effective he cannot be simply handed a decision and told to go out and sell it. He must know the bits and pieces of fact and opinion that went into the making of the decision, and if it is a decision with profound public relations implications he should have a chance to influence it as well."[13]

Educational Gap

The counseling potential of the public relations director depends on his being "a thoroughgoing professional, seasoned and skilled." This begs the question of what training a fully effective public relations director should have. The present arrangements for training public relations people leave a great deal to be desired. Public relations people receive their training for the most part in schools of journalism, which equip them to spell but hardly to understand economics and take a management point of view. Business schools still refuse to offer majors or even courses in public relations. Thus there is a serious educational gap.

Against great odds the professional public relations societies are trying to raise the quality of practitioners. One of the authors recently spoke to a chapter of the Public Relations Society of America arguing that the profession's future depended on its ability to provide counsel to top management on policy issues. The audience listened politely, but the question and answer session that followed became animated only when the failure of public relations neophytes to *spell correctly* was brought up as an issue.

Public relations and marketing have managed to establish themselves as essential corporate functions. As corporations undergo inceased regulation and pressure from interest groups and government agencies, new patterns of operation and interrelation can be expected to appear in these functions. No one model will be appropriate for all enterprises. The environmental pressures facing the individual enterprise, as well as its own history, will dictate whether to strengthen its marketing function or public relations function or even whether to start a new pattern of meeting and coping with external opportunities and threats.

ENDNOTES

1. Private correspondence from a public relations specialist.
2. Don E. Lee, Public Affairs Director, Carter Oil Company, Houston, in an address to the American Academy of Advertising, reproduced in their *Proceedings* of 1976 edited by C. Dennis Schick, 1977, 17–19.
3. Peter F. Drucker, *The Practice of Management* (New York: Harper & Row, 1954), 37.
4. See Philip Kotler and Sidney J. Levy, "Broadening the Concept of Marketing," *Journal of Marketing*, (January 1969), 10–15. Also see Philip Kotler, *Marketing for Nonprofit Organizations* (Englewood Cliffs, N.J.: Prentice-Hall Inc., 1975).
5. Edward L. Bernays, *Public Relations* (Norman, Oklahoma: University of Oklahoma Press, 1952).
6. Scott M. Cutlip, "The Beginning of PR Counseling," *Editor and Publisher*, (Nov. 26, 1960), 16.
7. Private note from an eminent professor of public relations at a leading university.
8. Private correspondence to the authors.
9. Philip Kotler, "A Generic Concept of Marketing," *Journal of Marketing*, (April 1972), 46–54.
10. Sidney J. Levy and Gerald Zaltman, *Marketing, Society and Conflict* (Englewood Cliffs, N.J.: Prentice-Hall, Inc., 1975), 6
11. Denny Griswold (ed.), *Public Relations News*, 32 (May 2, 1977), 1.
12. Private interview.
13. Private interview.

40 The Association Model of the Advertising Communication Process

Ivan L. Preston

Journal of Advertising, Vol. 11, No 2 (1982), pp. 3–15. Reprinted by permission.

INTRODUCTION

This article presents a new model of the advertising communication process. The purpose is to extend and improve upon the long tradition of such models, best exemplified by the famous AIDA formulation.

The principal reason for offering a new model is to incorporate all of the measures of research commonly used in advertising. If they are worth paying for and using, they should be adequately represented in any model that purports to be useful. No model to date has been related comprehensively to research, with identification of individual steps for each of the standard measures that are popularly used. In the new model each type of research measure is recognized by a designation of the distinct step of consumer response that it indexes.

THE ASSOCIATION MODEL

The Association Model is shown in Figure 1, the arrows indicating the flow of the process from step to step. In the following discussions of individual steps, the work of Fletcher & Bowers (9) has contributed much toward identification of the related research measures.

Distribution, Vehicle Exposure, and Ad Exposure

These steps are discussed together because the role of the first two is to serve as surrogate indicators for the third. In a strict sense the advertising process begins only with Ad Exposure, with the first two steps falling short of that. When ads are placed in media vehicles and the vehicles are successfully distributed (circulated if print, transmitted if broadcast), the vehicles will not necessarily be exposed to the intended consumers. And, when the vehicles are exposed, the ads will not necessarily be. Thus, some observers may feel, the first two steps are not part of the process of advertising because they involve no impact of the ad upon the consumer.

Although technically correct, such analysis does not recognize the practical problem of the research used to measure Ad Exposure. Only in the case of outdoor and point-of-purchase advertising can Ad Exposure be measured directly, because these vehicles are wholly ads and because consumers distribute themselves into their presence rather than the reverse. For other media the advertiser does not measure Ad Exposure directly but rather infers it from research on one of the two earlier steps.

In some cases the advertiser uses measures of audience (Vehicle Exposure). These are available on a year-round basis for network television (Nielsen) and for about 140 magazines and three nationally-circulated newspapers (Simmons). They are also available at certain times (sweeps periods) in many markets for local broadcast (Nielsen and Arbitron for television, Arbitron for radio). Custom surveys are available for other situations, but are not widely used. These measures of Vehicle Exposure are the closest the advertiser can come to Ad Exposure, so they serve as substitutes for the latter.

In other cases no measurement of Vehicle Exposure is available, so the advertiser must rely on measures of Distribution (circulation, transmission). This is the case for most newspapers, smaller magazines, radio networks, and those local stations not covered by Nielsen or Arbitron.

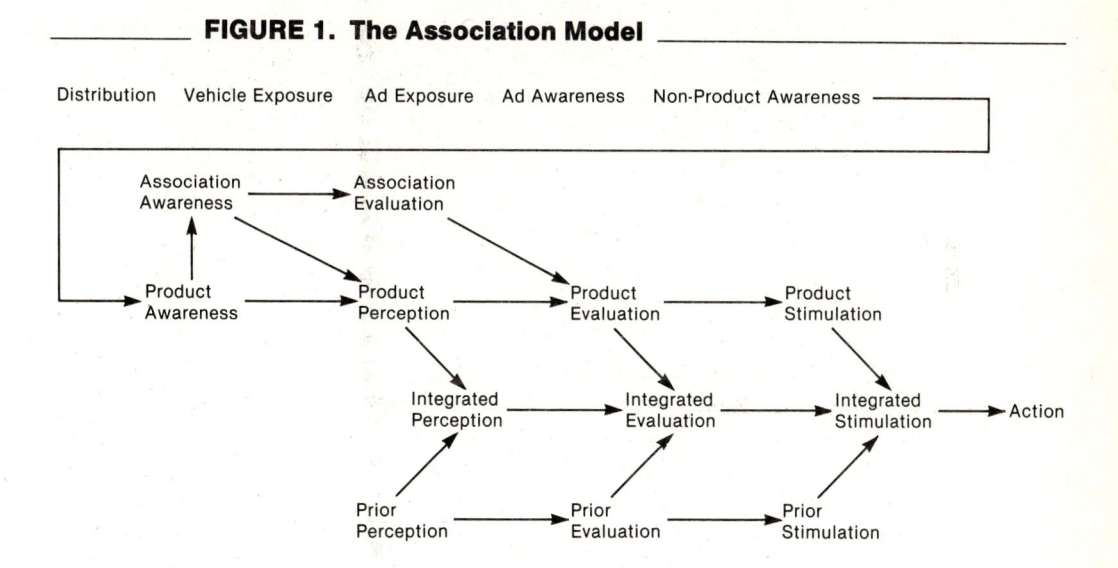

FIGURE 1. The Association Model

Thus, although the advertising process technically starts with Ad Exposure, most advertisers can "see" that factor only by measuring Vehicle Exposure if available, or Distribution if not, and estimating Ad Exposure therefrom. For these reasons it seems appropriate to designate all three steps rather than just one.

Another reason for recognizing all three is that advertisers appear to work consciously with these distinctions. They seek a wide Distribution for the vehicles carrying their ads, but they also seek the widest possible Vehicle Exposure within that Distribution, as well as the widest possible Ad Exposure within that Vehicle Exposure.

Ad Awareness

From Ad Exposure the Association Model moves to several steps of Awareness. This term is chosen instead of others for the following reasons. "Perception" is very good, particularly in expressing the active voice ("The consumer perceived") rather than the passive ("The consumer became aware"). But "Perception" can be applied to various steps, so is saved for later. "Attention" is a popular term, but can refer ambiguously to a state of mind necessary for awareness but not necessarily producing it. Those using "Attention" seem to treat it as meaning not merely that the consumer was attentive but that he actually became aware. Thus we speak here of Awareness.

The several steps of Awareness involve actual noticing by the consumer, which cannot be assumed from mere Ad Exposure. Ad Awareness involves noticing the ad itself, with no indication of differential noticing of any specific elements. The latter types of Awareness are indicated as subsequent steps of the model.

Because Ad Awareness is not an automatic result of Ad Exposure, advertisers research the proportion of exposed consumers who actually notice. The "Noted" measure of the Starch measurements of print ads reports the percentage who say "yes" when asked if they recognize the ad from seeing it previously. It is a measure of the ad as a whole, not of any part of it.

There are also standard recall measures which report Ad Awareness. Burke's "Claimed Recall" reports the percentage of consumers who recall seeing the ad after getting a product or brand cue. Burke's "Related Recall," along with Gallup & Robinson's "Proved Commercial Registration" and "Proved Name Registration," report the percentage who recall seeing the ad, after getting a product or brand cue, who can also describe accurately some specific elements of the ad. Possibly these methods produce only an approximate indication of Ad Awareness because they intermingle it with other types of Awareness discussed below.

Ad Elements Awareness

This step involves awareness of specific parts of an ad. Some of these elements, which depict or refer to the product or to things associated with the product, are important enough to be identified as separate steps below. For the most part the remaining elements are ones used by the advertiser for attention-getting purposes. The advertiser hopes the consumer who is attracted by these elements will then be directed toward the elements relating to the product. In addition there are extraneous elements included merely as filler content, or included by accident (as in illustrations that show people in the background); they represent no significant purpose on the advertiser's part.

Some ads may contain none of the these types of elements, and in general this step may be regarded as the least important in the entire model. In certain ads, however, it will importantly affect response to the overall ad.

Ad Elements Awareness is measured by Starch's scores for those individual elements that refer neither to the product nor to its associations. It may also be indicated by the verbatim statements collected by such researchers as Burke, Gallup & Robinson, ASI, and Starch's Reader Impression Studies (RIS).

Product Awareness

Product Awareness involves recognition of the specific item being advertised, usually a specific brand. It is possible to be aware of the ad as a whole, or of specific elements, without noticing what is advertised. Obviously the advertiser intends that the consumer accurately perceive the brand. For that reason the Association Model designates Product Awareness as a separate type of Awareness.

Starch's "Associated" score tells what percentage of consumers report previously seeing some part of the ad that named or pictured the product. The Burke and Gallup & Robinson recall measures mentioned earlier ask people whether they saw ads for such-and-such product. Thus they treat Product Awareness more as a stimulus for later responses rather than as a response on its own, which may appear to underrate the importance to the advertiser of this step. However, the respondents are next asked to describe the ad, and the advertiser can learn how many did so accurately and how many reflected misawareness by describing an ad for another brand.

Association Awareness

This is the step in which the product is described, its attributes identified, claims about it made, people using it depicted, benefits discussed—in short, associations established between the product and whatever items the advertiser chooses. These items may be the product's own physical or performance attributes, or anything apart from the product that the advertiser chooses to associate with it.

The Association Model is so named because of a conviction that choosing what to say about the product is the most critical step in the advertising process. Success in obtaining intended sales response occurs fundamentally because of the value of what the advertiser associates with the product. If the consumer sees the product differently than before, he likely will respond to it differently.

Simply because he places them in the ad, the advertiser is not guaranteed that consumers will see the associated items. Some consumers will see that the ad is for a given product, but will not see what is said about it. Others will inaccurately perceive what is said. For this reason the step of Association Awareness is separated from Product Awareness.

Starch reports percentages of consumers recognizing individual ad elements; for this step the elements that present product associations are pertinent. Burke's figures for "Sales Messages" and Gallup & Robinson's "Idea Communication" report percentages of accurate recall of sales points. Measures also are available from the verbatim statements supplied by Burke, G & R, ASI, and RIS.

Association Evaluation

When advertisers associate their products with various things, they intend that the consumer regard these things positively. That, however, is a decision for each individual. Some will recognize no evaluation, while others will feel negative or neutral rather than positive. Association Awareness is the step of making that decision.

There are two ways to do so. The first is based on the evaluation offered and urged by the ad. The consumer's response choice will parallel that for Association Awareness—he will see or not see an evaluation offered, and, if seeing one, will see it either as the advertiser intended or otherwise. The advertiser can research this step at the same time he measures Association Awareness, using the measures discussed under Association Awareness that involve verbatim responses to ads.

In current practice, the syndicated researchers do not make as much a point of reporting evaluations of associations as they do the associations themselves. This apparently is due to an assumption that any consumer aware of the association will be aware of how advertisers evaluate it. That may be reasonable inasmuch as advertisers predictably will place a strong positive evaluation on anything related to their products. Such assumption may be questioned, however, because of the second way that consumers decide about Association Evaluation.

The second way involves having an evaluation as a prior state of mind, based on earlier encounters with the associated item. In such cases the consumer ignores the ad's urgings and invokes this already-held evaluation when he sees the item linked with the product. The way to research this second way is to question consumers about things that have been or may be associated with the product. Such questions often are incorporated in product image studies (also called brand image, product usage, or tracking studies). This research involves no examination of ads, so some may not identify it as part of advertising research. It is highly relevant, however, because it helps the advertiser choose content and assess effects. Such effects could be assessed in copytesting, but the advertiser would be best off to know about negative items prior to choosing themes for copytesting.

Product image research does not appear to involve any standardized, syndicated measures, probably because variations in the nature of products require custom rather than standard measures. Many corporations do their own custom studies, and others order them from firms such as Market Facts, National Family Opinion, Opinion Research Corporation, and Burke.

It may be that Association Evaluations are not researched as much as they should be. Given the second way of forming them, advertisers should assume they will often not be positive. They should do research in advance to determine the actual evaluations held, then choose only those associated items that are valued positively.

Product Perception, Prior Perception, and Integrated Perception

Product Perception consists of the total picture of the product that the consumer acquires *from* the ad. It is cognitive, non-evaluative; evaluation is represented elsewhere. It is more than Product Awareness, which involves merely noticing that the product was a subject of the ad. It is close to being the sum of Association Awareness and Association Evaluation, but is more than just that. Those steps involve the consumer's separate responses to the separate associated items, however many there may be, whereas Product Perception represents an integrated summation of all those responses.

A reason for incorporating this total perception into the Association Model is as a lead-in to the related steps of Prior and Integrated Perception. Prior Perception represents a summation of all the consumer's perceptions of the product acquired prior to his present confrontation with the ad. They came from any and all past inputs, including personal experience and information from any sources, including other ads. Sometimes there may be no Prior Perception, but not often.

Will Product Perception and Prior Perception differ? Perhaps they will not, if the advertiser knows and approves of the prior state and aims his current ad at reinforcing it in the consumer's mind. A situation probably more frequent, however, is that the advertiser is dissatisfied with the Prior Perception and so strives to produce a Product Perception that will be different in a favorable way.

The consumer handles these differences by combining Product and Prior Perception into the Integrated Perception, which represents the overall picture of the product that he will use as a basis for further response. The past inputs are combined with the present to create the future. If the present is rejected, the future will only mimic the past. The advertiser's goal, of course, is to have the present dominate the past so as to create a new future.

It thus is not sufficient for the advertiser merely to establish a Product Perception. Rather, his goal must be a Product Perception influential in determining the Integrated Perception. The Product Perception reflects only what the consumer sees the ad *communicating*; the Integrated Perception indicates what he decides to *believe*. Moreover, today's Integrated Perception will become tomorrow's Prior Perception.

Research measures of Product Perception report the consumer's response to the immediate advertising input only, while measures of Prior Perception are based on prior inputs only and measures of Integrated Perception are based on those two sets of inputs combined. Available measures sometimes are ambiguous with respect to which of these is being reported.

Research measures of Product Perception may be obtained through methods similar to those discussed for Association Awareness and Association Evaluation. Research measures of Prior Perception typically come from product image studies, as discussed above, carried out prior to consumers' interaction with the current advertising. Measures of Integrated Perception are available from product image studies done after consumers have had a chance to be exposed to the current advertising.

Some advertisers may find little value in research data about Product Perception if they can just as easily examine the Integrated Perception. The latter, of course, should be the better for predicting future response. Knowledge of the former, however, may assist in explaining how and why the consumer arrived at the latter.

Product Evaluation, Prior Evaluation, and Integrated Evaluation

These steps parallel the threesome just discussed. Upon formulating a Product Perception the consumer also formulates his Product Evaluation, based on the immediate advertising input. He probably already holds a Prior Evaluation based on earlier inputs. He then creates his Integrated Evaluation by combining both sets of inputs. As stated for the steps of Perception, the Product Evaluation represents what the consumer sees the ad communicating to him about feeling, while the Integrated Evaluation represents how he decides to feel.

Standardized measures of Product Evaluation are not common; however, Gallup & Robinson's "Favorable Attitude" and Starch's RIS provide them. Many advertisers do custom studies in this area. Research measures of Prior and Integrated Evaluation may be obtained from the product image studies discussed earlier.

Product Stimulation, Prior Stimulation, and Integrated Stimulation

This final set of three related steps describes the process of acquiring an internal stimulus or motivation toward the final step of Action. The consumer develops a Product Stimulation based on the immediate advertising input, then combines it with his Prior Stimulation based on prior inputs to create an Integrated Stimulation based on all inputs. Depending on the impact of the Prior Stimulation, the Product Stimulation may or may not be echoed by the Integrated Stimulation. The advertiser's challenge, of course, is to produce a favorable Product Stimulation which will be emulated in the Integrated Stimulation.

The steps of Stimulation may not seem much different from the steps of Evaluation, since having an attitude toward a thing may seem virtually equivalent to having a desire to act toward it. They are separated here, however, because researchers tap them separately. In product image and other custom studies consumers may be asked "Do you intend to purchase this item?" along with being asked for evaluations. This reflects that consumer processing includes both a response to what has come before as well as a stimulus toward the Action to follow. It also reflects the fact well known to researchers that changes in evaluations are not necessarily paralleled by changes in stimulations.

Stimulation (intention to purchase) is often examined in theater studies, although the measures may be ambiguous with respect to the types of Stimulation. If ASI's theater test, for example, is interpreted as producing a measure of intention to purchase (literally, it's a simulated purchase requiring no expenditure), then it is uncertain whether the measure is tapping Product or Integrated Stimulation. The advertiser most wants to know about Integrated Stimulation, but the research setting may enhance the impact of the immediate advertising input and reduce the impact of prior inputs.

Perhaps better attuned to measuring Integrated Stimulation is the Competitive Environment Test of the Dancer-Fizgerald-Sample agency (48). Subjects are given simulated purchase choices and asked to allocate them among a number of brands both before and after seeing commercials for all in one viewing session. Each brand may be assigned none or any number of purchases, totalling to ten. The way in which the number changes for a given brand is taken to indicate effect on intent to purchase. A strength of the method is that response is made after seeing ads for several brands rather than just one.

Action

The Integrated Stimulation, positive or negative, weak or strong, now will prompt the final step of Action. Some may feel it is equivalent to Action, but comparisons of measures of intent to purchase to measures of actual purchase show that the penultimate does not necessarily imply the ultimate. The reason is that while measures of intention reflect inputs available at the time of research, the consumer often is responsive to additional inputs between then and the moment of the purchase decision.

Should intention to purchase be measured a split second prior to the purchase decision, it might predict that decision perfectly. But the time lag enables a variety of situational factors (3, 7), such as cash available at the moment of the purchase decision, to affect that decision. It is advisable, therefore, to treat Integrated Stimulation and Action as separate steps.

Action, which most typically means sales, generally is researched through market research measures such as Nielsen's which do not relate sales specifically to advertising. However, at least one syndicated research method, AdTel, measures comparative sales by sets of diary panelists that have seen different commercials. Of course the Association Model can be used to analyze noncommercial advertising goals, such as voting, giving to charities, and public opinion, equally as well as commercial goals.

Some may feel that sales Action should be broken into the separate steps of Trial and Adoption, and Adoption in turn divided into brand-switching and brand-loyal modes. These distinctions are not formally offered here, but the Model could easily incorporate them.

Summary

Figure 2 summarizes the research methods discussed under the various steps. The list is intended to illustrate that there is research activity at the various steps, but not to be complete, particularly not in acknowledging all "name brands" of research that are available. Figure 2 also compares the Association Model to previous models, as discussed next.

THE ASSOCIATION MODELS AND ITS PREDECESSORS

The Association Model is compared in Figure 2 to a chronological listing of previous models of advertising or communication processes. A debt is owed to Holbrook (10) for unearthing some references not frequently cited. All may be called "hierarchy of effects" models, a name originally applied by Palda (30) to the creation of Lavidge & Steiner (14).

Their prototype, AIDA (alternatively: AIDCA), was created in the 19th century. Sources mentioning it since the 1950s give it no attribution, apparently accepting it as a misty lost legend. According to Strong (46), the model was created by E. St. Elmo Lewis in 1898, and was sometimes used with the term "satisfaction" added at the end, the latter contributed by Sheldon (43). Strong also cited sources for using "conviction" either as a fifth term (AIDCA) or as a substitute for "desire" (AICA). Today it is presented most often with four steps, occasionally with the fifth. There is no record of further models being developed until the flurry of activity beginning in 1961.

A purpose in citing these past models is to show the debt that is owed; they clearly are the inspiration for the Association Model. Each of their steps is retained in the latter. There are only two instances in which separate steps of a past model are not treated as separate here. Rogers' "trial" and "adoption" are combined under Action as discussed earlier. Longman's "reading" and "comprehension" are combined because researchers do not appear to follow his distinction that "reading" involves "getting" the message while "comprehension" involves "understanding" it. The conclusion here thus is that what the consumer "gets" is the same as what he "understands."

A further purpose of Figure 2's review of previous models is to show that none has been comprehensive enough to accommodate all the types of consumer response and related research used regularly by advertisers. Each step of each previous model is listed opposite the step of the Association Model to which it is most closely related. A dash appears where the model has no counterpart in the Association Model and therefore fails to reflect the given type of research.

These designations may be disputable in a few cases in which the label for a step and the authors' discussion of it (if any) do not resolve ambiguity. Some steps may belong in other locations, and some might reasonably encompass two or more of the Association Model's steps. In particular "attention," "awareness," or "perception" may have been intended to cover two or more types of Awareness. Sandage & Fryburger's "integration" probably reflects Integrated Evaluation as much as Integrated Perception. "Retention" and "memory" are difficult to interpret, with "retention" meaning something different to McGuire than to Schwartz.

Despite such problems, the limited scope of the previous models remains evident. Were a certain step shifted to another location, there would still be as many dashes in Figure 2. Were a step expanded to cover two or more of the Association Model's steps, it would fail to distinguish among the various types of consumer response and related research.

Only five of the previous models mention steps prior to Awareness, and only ARF mentions Distribution and Vehicle Exposure. The various kinds of Awareness are not well recognized. Association Evaluation and

FIGURE 2. Relationships of Association Model to Research Measures and to Previous Advertising Models

Step of Assn. Model	Research Measures	AID(C)A (46)	Colley (5)	Lavidge & Steiner (14)	Advertising Research Foundation (1)	Industrial Conference Board (50)
Distribution	Audited counts by ABC, BPA, VAC for print; census data for broadcast	—	—	—	Vehicle Distribution	—
Vehicle Exp.	Nielsen, Arbitron, Simmons (SMRB)	—	—	—	Vehicle Exposure	—
Ad Exposure	Outdoor and p-o-p: local counts	—	—	—	Ad Exposure	—
Ad Awareness	Starch "Noted" scores; Burke's "Claimed Recall" and "Related Recall"; Gallup & Robinson's "Proved Commercial Registration" and "Proved Name Registration"	Attention	Awareness	—	Ad Perception	Awareness
Ad Elements Awareness	Starch scores for separate elements; content verbatims from Burke, G&R, ASI, and Starch's Reader Impression Studies (RIS)	—	—	—	—	—
Product Awareness	Starch "Associated" scores; Burke's "RR"; G&R's "PCR" and "PNR"	—	—	Awareness	—	—
Association Awareness	Starch scores for elements stating ass'ns; Burke's "Sales Messages"; G&R's "Idea Communication"; verbatims from Burke, G&R, ASI, RIS	—	Comprehension	Knowledge	Ad Communication (information)	—
Association Evaluation	Product image studies; verbatims used for Association Awareness	—	—	—	—	—
Product Perception	Measures used for Association Awareness and Association Evaluation	—	—	—	—	—
Prior Perception	Product image studies (before adv.)	—	—	—	—	—
Integrated Perception	Product image studies (after adv.)	—	—	—	—	—
Product Evaluation	G&R's "Favorable Attitude"; RIS	Interest	—	Liking	Ad Communication (attitude)	Acceptance
Prior Evaluation	Product image studies (before adv.)	—	—	—	—	—
Integrated Evaluation	Product image studies (after adv.)	—	—	Preference	—	Preference
Product Stimulation	Theater research such as ASI	Desire	—	—	—	—
Prior Stimulation	Product image studies (before adv.)	—	—	—	—	—
Integrated Stimulation	Product image studies (after adv.); Competitive Environment Test	(Conviction)	Conviction	Conviction	—	Intention
Action	Market data such as Nielsen's on sales and inventory; AdTel	Action	Action	Purchase	Sales	Sale

The Association Model of the Advertising Communication Process

Mendelsohn (23)	Rogers (38)	Aspinwall (2)	Sandage & Fryburger (41)	Howard & Sheth (11)	Schwartz (42)	McGuire (20,22)	Longman (15)	Holbrook (10)
—	—	—	—	—	—	—	—	—
—	—	—	—	—	—	—	—	—
—	—	—	Exposure	—	Exposure	Presentation	Exposure	—
Rudimentary response (recall)	—	—	Perception	Attention	Attention	Attention	Attention	Attention
—	—	—	—	—	—	—	—	—
—	Awareness	—	—	—	—	—	—	Perception
—	—	—	—	Comprehension	—	Comprehension	Reading; Comprehension	—
—	—	—	—	—	—	—	—	—
—	—	—	—	—	—	—	—	—
—	—	—	—	—	—	—	—	—
—	—	—	Integration	—	Retention	—	Belief	Memory
Emotional Response (affect)	Interest	Acceptance	—	Attitude	—	Yielding	—	Attitude
—	—	—	—	—	—	—	—	—
—	Evaluation	Preference	—	—	Attitude Change	Retention	—	—
—	—	—	—	—	—	—	—	—
—	—	—	—	—	—	—	—	—
—	—	Insistence	—	Intention	—	—	Motivation	Intention
Active Response	Trial, Adoption	—	Action	Purchase	Purchase	Behavior	Action	—

Product Perception are not recognized at all. Two models omit Action. The steps involving prior inputs are never recognized, nor is the notion of three parallel steps for each of Perception, Evaluation, and Stimulation. It is true there are steps relating to the integration of inputs, which may involve implicit recognition of the combining of present and prior inputs. Yet the powerful process of integration is recognized explicitly and expressed cogently only by Sandage & Fryburger. Although "integration" as they use it is spread unsatisfactorily over a number of processes, it is nonetheless a unique contribution.

This discussion should acknowledge that the past models were created for purposes specified by their authors, not necessarily including the research criterion emphasized here. No doubt they have excellently carried out their intended goals. In particular, we should recognize the value of such formulations in giving the advertising practitioner a frequent reminder of valuable procedures. To play this role, a model should be brief, simple, and memorable.

Surely the steps of the Association Model will never match the facility for rolling off the tongue that has enabled the four letters of AIDA to become lastingly memorable. A favorite mnemonic device begins with the most memorable television commercial of 1980 (47), featuring Pittsburgh Steeler defensive lineman Mean Joe Greene for Coca-Cola. Mean Joe's name in Italian, any sophisticate will realize, is Giuseppe Verdi. Verdi, of course, was the renowned composer of many grand operas, of which the grandest is "Aida." The letters of "Aida," naturally, stand for "attention, interest, desire, and action."

The above is recounted in dead seriousness to illustrate how advertising models typically have made their reputations. The merit of AIDA's alphabetical fortuity certainly has exceeded that of its descriptive exactitude in assuring its fame. There is no parallel hope that advertising people will develop a similar facility in mouthing the steps of the Association Model. The latter, therefore, is unlikely to make the sort of contribution that AIDA has achieved.

The situation is different, however, when advertising theory and research are seriously considered. AIDA leaves many things out. Each of the popular models omits things that others include. The growth and maturity of the advertising profession surely require that the facts of life be taken up in all their bewildering complexity. For research purposes, in other words, the criterion of brevity is no match against the criterion of sufficiency.

Further Justification for the Association Model

A new advertising model could improve on the old ones merely by combining their contributions into a total set of steps, adding nothing new. Obviously the Association Model does more than that; it includes new steps and new terminology. And it offers a rationale: the new steps are needed in order to indicate and differentiate the types of research methods used in advertising.

This section offers an additional rationale for certain of the new steps, focussing not at the level of steps but at the broader level of consumer response theories. The steps involved are Association Awareness and Association Evaluation, and also those indicating the various prior states, leading to combining present and prior input to create integrated input. Most of these are steps not seen in previous models; however, Association Awareness is not new but rather is a new name for what has been known by such terms as "claims," "facts," "knowledge," "information" and "communication."

Reflecting Consumer Information Processing (CIP)

A most important development of the recent era is the rise of the study of consumer information processing (CIP) (3). Its key role is that of interference with what the advertiser tries to achieve. The consumer, by using a variety of product-related content already present in his head, makes up his own mind about the advertiser's suggestion. Often this means rejecting that suggestion. Advertising models beginning with AIDA have reflected CIP, long in advance of the creation of its name, by stressing a series of internal processes prior to Action that help determine Action.

The recent models, however, including McGuire's which is labeled "an information-processing model," have not been detailed enough to inform users properly of the full role CIP can play. In particular, they do not make explicit the consumer's prior states of perception, evaluation, and stimulation that may override and eliminate the impact that an ad's present input might otherwise have. The Association Model specifies these prior states explicitly, and emphasizes the relationships that follow among present, prior, and integrated inputs.

Perhaps the previous models imply such processes. One could say, for example, that Lavidge & Steiner's "preference" and "conviction" represent the way prior states alter the impact that "liking" would otherwise have. However, because these prior states are explicitly studied and utilized by advertisers, it seems preferable to treat them openly.

The role of Association Evaluation can be interpreted in the same way. The consumer may invoke a prior evaluation of the associated item which interferes with the evaluation the advertisement tries to establish. Again, explicit treatment of the step seems advisable.

There is probably no situation in advertising that is not potentially subject to a range of CIP activity, with serious consequences for message effectiveness. Accordingly, the Association Model has been structured so as to alert its users to prior inputs and consumer decision-making rather than encouraging them to conceptualize an ad as being the sole determinant of its impact.

Reflecting the Traditional S-R Viewpoint Along With CIP

Because this section may appear to contradict the one above, the reader is cautioned that the differences are a matter of degree and a matter of effects that occur under varying conditions.

A significant characteristic of CIP is that it emphasizes the consumer's own decisions and choices. A central requirement for an advertising model, meanwhile, is that it sufficiently reflects the goal-oriented efforts of the advertiser to obtain a desired response. It should, in short, be primarily a model of advertising effectiveness, not of consumer choice-making.

Accordingly, it is important that a model's conceptualizing of the advertising process not fall too thoroughly into the CIP orbit. While the previous section argued that CIP should not be ignored, this section argues that it should not be all-encompassing.

McGuire (21) says the cognitive psychology that CIP reflects is fashionable and has replaced the older psychology known as S-R theory or behaviorism as "the dominant Establishment view." Be that as it may, those involved particularly with advertising should not forget that advertisers want to introduce messages that will have the ability to shape and control behavior. That is, they wish to use messages that will be followed by predicted responses just as reliably as those expected by the S-R psychologists.

Wilkie & Farris (49) recognize this need when they say the advertiser is interested in the stimulus (the ad) and the response it evokes, without particular concern for internal processing, while the CIP researcher is interested in the processing and response, without concern for any particular stimulus. That is natural, they point out, because the advertiser is interested in his own message and the preferred response to it, while CIP researchers are interested in whatever stimuli consumers are exposed to, or seek out, and whatever responses they make. In short, the advertiser wants to control the outcome while CIPers are interested mainly in observing it so as to describe and explain what produced it. Those devoted to advertising research rather than to CIP ought not to let this difference go unnoticed.

Of course the CIP viewpoint is correct in reminding that the advertiser often doesn't get what he wants. Determination of response is not the prerogative of the message sender alone; the consumer has much to say about the matter. It is possible, however, that recent theorizing has carried this point too far, leading to the equally inappropriate view that response is determined to an insignificant degree by the message.

The advertiser may not get his way often, but he gets it often enough. The proof of this claim (practical proof, if not strictly so) is simply that the advertising business continues to function. Nobody would play "Black" in chess if the rules gave "White" all the choices. Nor would they advertise unless the perceived probability of success, along with the perceived payoff, encouraged them to do so. What exists in advertising, in other words, must be some reasonable approximation of the parity that prompts people to continue playing chess.

There is, moreover, reason to believe the eclipsing of S-R by CIP is being reversed in at least one area pertinent to advertising—that of nonverbal messages. Recent research on consumer acquisition of pictorial associations suggests that nonverbal associations may be established in the consumer's mind more readily and automatically than verbal ones (4, 16, 39, 40).

What is needed, then, is an advertising model that reflects both S-R and CIP views and encourages partisan adherents to acknowledge that varying circumstances may allow either to dominate at different times. The following examines the way in which the Association Model accommodates these possibilities.

The relevant S-R paradigm is the classical conditioning model in which the stimulus of interest (conditioned stimulus, CS) is paired with another (unconditioned stimulus, US) toward which the subject possesses a reliable and therefore predictable response (UR). The expectation is that the subject will adopt a similar response (CR) toward the stimulus of interest. The nature of the subject does not intervene; rather, the determinant of response is the association of the second stimulus with the first:

$$US \rightarrow UR$$
$$\uparrow \qquad \uparrow$$
$$CS \leftarrow CR$$

This four-part model is embedded in the Association Model. Presentation of CS and US (often more than one US, in advertising) are seen in the steps of Product Awareness and Association Awareness. (This of course means the CS and US are what the consumer *sees* them to be, not necessarily what the advertiser intended. However, under many conditions they are likely to be the same or approximately so, as determinable by measures of Product Awareness and Association Awareness.) The UR is represented by Association Evaluation (again as determined by the consumer). The CR is indicated by the ultimate step of Action.

Of course to embed the classical conditioning model within the more complex model is to recognize a whole litany of problems that may upset its presumably automatic functioning. The ad may never be exposed to the consumer. An exposed ad may never get attention. An attentive consumer may see the ad but not notice the product therein, or perceive the wrong brand. He may see the product accurately but not notice the associated items. He may have responses toward the latter that spoil the advertiser's expectations. He may consequently acquire unanticipated perceptions and evaluations, and be stimulated negatively. Even if stimulated favorably by the ad, he may be ultimately compelled by prior perceptions and evaluations to be stimulated negatively overall.

If any of these things happen, the CIP viewpoint will be superior to the S-R. Still, the proper expectation is that such problems are only potential. They need not occur and frequently do not, at least not strongly enough to interfere with the advertiser's intended outcome. The adherent of CIP may accurately remind us that in such felicitous situations internal processing factors are not absent but merely benign. However, the adherent of S-R may argue that his view is equally accurate and much more parsimonious, therefore superior.

Recent support for this position is offered by the conclusion of Olshavsky & Granbois (27) that "A significant proportion of purchases may not be preceded by a decision process" and that "even when purchase behavior is preceded by a choice process, it is likely to be very limited." They cite Kassarjian (12) on the point.

Support is also offered by Nord & Peter's (26) assertion that marketing objectives often are accomplished by "simply studying environmental conditions and manipulating them to influence consumer behavior," and that "consumer behavior can be influenced through this external emphasis without a complete psychology of internal processes." Further, they say "there is a considerable evidence that the behavior of consumers is far more consistent with the principles of the BMP ["behavior modification perspective," which includes classical conditioning] than with traditional expectations."

Parenthetically, their reference to "traditional expectations" illustrates the degree to which the CIP perspective captures the thought of contemporary marketing researchers. It is an odd reversal, caused apparently by the lack of historical perspective in the training of researchers young enough that CIP research constitutes their understanding of tradition. S-R theory in reality has a prior and far longer tradition, which Nord & Peter wish to reinvigorate.

Owing to a similar desire to retain the S-R perspective, the present model is named the Association Model. Associating the product with selected items of value is the key process of S-R behavior. This explains why Association Evaluation is treated so prominently, and why Association Awareness is given its name. The latter has usually been called things such as "knowledge" or "information," but it seems useful to emphasize that an ad's critical role is not just the transmission of facts but rather the *linking* of them to the product—just as in classical conditioning. It is the values attributed to the product by this linkage which the advertiser hopes will motivate the consumer to treat the product more positively.

In short, the Association Model is so named because its ancestors traditionally were intended to serve the orientation of the advertiser primarily, not the CIP researcher primarily. There is no reason, however, why it cannot (nor excuse why it should not) reflect both S-R and CIP perspectives.

THE ASSOCIATION PROCESS IN THE RESEARCH LITERATURE

If advertising research has recently been "captured" by the CIP orientation, it may be because the topic of association has received little attention in the advertising literature. This article, therefore, concludes with a section on what literature exists, with the intent of suggesting that greater attention may be merited in the future.

The Process of Associating

This author long ago became impressed with the discussion by Osgood *et al.* (29) of the "sign-significate" process. People respond to a stimulus because it acts as a sign, signifying a significate or "thing signified." Evaluation of the significate then operates as a determinant of evaluation and subsequent response to the sign. At about the same time Mayer (19) offered his "added value theory," holding that "advertising, in addition to its purely informing function, adds a new value to the existing values of the product." The connection seeming propitious, this author (32) proceeded to discuss Mayer's theoretical point in the context of Osgood *et al.*'s terminology and science.

These ideas are incorporated in the Association Model as follows: An object (Product Awareness) is perceived to have certain attributes or other associations (Association Awareness) valued by the consumer (Association Evaluation), the evaluation rubbing off onto the object (Product Evaluation) and becoming a determinant of behavior (Action). The "added value" consists of the Association Evaluations linked to the product as a result of the ad.

This notion, over a context of years during which CIP developed, has largely lain dormant in advertising and consumer literature. However, Olson & Mitchell (28) and Mitchell & Olson (24) have worked in the area, grounding their ideas in Osgood *et al.*, as well as in Fishbein (8). Their discussion, reflecting classical conditioning and S-R theory, stresses the automatic nature of the eliciting of prior evaluations of associated attributes, and of the way in which these tend to determine the evaluation of the object. They also stress, following Fishbein, that there typically are multiple instances of what is here called Association Awareness, each with an independent Association Evaluation, and that the Product Evaluation will be a function of the combining of all Association Evaluations. The discussion of Rossiter and Percy (40) also is relevant.

Types of Associations in the Literature

Another line of research literature, stressing *types* of associated things rather than the process, was introduced by this author (32), taken up independently by Shimp (44), and continued in the collaboration of Shimp and Preston (45). It began with a typology of associated items (significates), as follows:

1. **Inherent associations** are tangible, physical features or performance attributes of the object advertised. They are an inherent part of it; they are really there.
2. **External associations** are noninherent in the object and are found in the life context surrounding it and its consumer. They may include such things as packaging and premiums, but the largest category is sociological associations. That is, the object signifies the numbers or types of people who use it, or its status or cultural meaning—i.e., the responses of society to the object.
3. **Internal associations** are noninherent and are located in the inner nature and personality of the consumer, including such motivating concepts as guilt or anxiety, or the need for such things as achievement or affiliation.

The distinction between external and internal associations may become blurred, as when an association with status seems difficult to distinguish from an association with internalized concern over status. Fortunately for the typology, there is more practical significance in how the combination of these two, which are jointly called noninherent associations, contrasts with inherent ones. The most important subset of noninherent associations has been labeled social-psychological associations (34, 44).

The literature has also discussed the dynamic whereby advertisers, particularly those with brands scarcely discriminable from competitors in inherent features, have turned to using noninherent associations in great quantity (44). The consequent lessened use of inherent associations (and thereby the lessening, some would say, of information) has also been chronicled (18, 37, 13, 31, 6). Consumer preference for inherent or noninherent associations has been examined (25), as has the potential for deception of the non-inherent (34, 45). There remain many questions about the impact of noninherent (especially social-psychological) associations.

Association in the Literature on Creativity

Another research area conferring attention on the association process is advertising creativity. Ability to be creative is held to be related to ability to associate ideas, because much of what copywriters do is try to produce in the consumer's mind associations of various items with the product (35, 36).

Linking the Association Model with Other Consumer Models

There has been no attempt thus far to interpret the Association Model outside the context of advertising models. Nonetheless it is intended to be consistent with and able to incorporate the characteristics of other consumer behavior models.

For example, in "expectancy-value" models such as Fishbein's (8), there is postulated a set of beliefs which amount to subjective perceptions of the probability of association between the object of interest and certain attributes. There are also the evaluations of each of these attributes. Finally, there is the summed combination of the evaluation of each attribute multiplied by the probability of its association. In the Association Model the beliefs are represented by the Integrated Perception (assuming that probability of association is determined in part by Prior Perception), the evaluations by Association Evaluation, and the summed combination by Integrated Evaluation.

A potential problem is that of processes such as low involvement which appear to require a fundamentally different ordering, such as specifying that steps such as Awareness and Evaluation occur after Action. We sympathize here with the suggestion of Wilkie and Farris (49:67) that such steps may actually precede Action in low involvement, although not becoming measurable until a time closer to the moment of purchasing than to that of encountering the ad—see a similar suggestion by Preston (33:294). Or, it may be that Awareness and Evaluation are measurable immediately after encountering the ad in low involvement situations provided methods appropriate to low involvement are used—e.g., recognition in place of recall.

As its predecessors, the Association Model is a "hierarchy of effects" and so a high involvement model. Low involvement threatens the ordering but not the validity of the steps themselves. Thus reordering if necessary can be accomplished without eliminating the Model's essential characteristics, nor obscuring the differences between it and previous models.

The Association Model in turn challenges low involvement conceptualizers, who typically do their reordering upon a model having only steps labeled "cognitive, affective, conative" ("learn, feel, do"). In present terms that involves only Association Awareness, Product Evaluation, and Action. What would be their ordering of a low involvement model incorporating all of the steps of the Association Model?

Summary

Although the literature on association is limited, it shows a potential for use in developing the S-R viewpoint in the analysis of consumer response to advertising. The Association Model offers the advertising researcher the opportunity to incorporate both S-R and CIP theorizing in the study of the advertiser's search for effectiveness.

REFERENCES

1. Advertising Research Foundation, Audience Concepts Committee. *Toward Better Media Comparisons*. New York: ARF, 1961.
2. Aspinwall, Leo V. "Consumer Acceptance Theory," in R. Cox, *et al.*, eds., *Theory in Marketing*, Homewood, Ill.: Richard D. Irwin, 1964.
3. Bettman, James R. *An Information Processing Theory of Consumer Choice*. Reading, MA: Addison-Wesley, 1979.
4. Bonoma, Thomas V., and L. C. Felder. "Nonverbal Communication in Marketing: Toward A Communication Analysis," *Journal of Marketing Research*, Vol. 14 (May, 1977), pp. 169–80.
5. Colley, Russell H. *Defining Advertising Goals for Measured Advertising Results*. New York: Association of National Advertisers, 1961.
6. Dowling, Grahame R. "Information Content in U.S. and Australian Television Advertising," *Journal of Marketing*, Vol. 44 (Fall, 1980), pp. 34–37.
7. Engel, James, David Kollat, and Roger Blackwell. *Consumer Behavior*. Hinsdale: Dryden, 3d ed., 1978.
8. Fishbein, Martin. "A Behavior Theory Approach to the Relations Between Beliefs About an Object and the Attitude Towards the Object," in M. Fishbein, ed., *Readings in Attitude Theory and Measurement*. New York: Wiley, 1967, pp. 389–400.
9. Fletcher, Alan D., and Thomas A. Bowers. *Fundamentals of Advertising Research*. Columbus: Grid, 1979.
10. Holbrook, Morris B. "A Review of Advertising Research," Appendix Two of John A. Howard and James Hulbert, *Advertising and the Public Interest*. Chicago: Crain, 1975.
11. Howard, John A., and Jagdish N. Sheth. *The Theory of Buyer Behavior*. New York: Wiley, 1969.
12. Kassarjian, Harold H. "Presidential Address," in H. Keith Hunt, ed., *Advances in Consumer Research*, Vol. 5. Ann Arbor: Association for Consumer Research, 1978, pp. xii–xiv.
13. Laczniak, Gene R. "Information Content in Print Advertising," *Journalism Quarterly*, Vol. 56 (Summer, 1979), pp. 324–27.
14. Lavidge, Robert J., and Gary A. Steiner. "A Model for Predictive Measurements of Advertising Effectiveness," *Journal of Marketing*, Vol. 25 (October, 1961), pp. 59–62.
15. Longman, Kenneth A. *Advertising*. New York: Harcourt Brace, 1971, p. 255.
16. Lutz, Kathy A., and Richard J. Lutz. "Imagery-Eliciting Strategies: Review and Implications of Research," in H. Keith Hunt, ed., *Advances in Consumer Re-

search, Vol. 5. Ann Arbor: Association for Consumer Research, 1978, pp. 611–20.
17. Lutz, Richard J., and John L. Swasy. "Integrating Cognitive Structure and Cognitive Response Approaches to Monitoring Communications Effects," in William D. Perrault, Jr., ed., *Advances in Consumer Research*, Vol. IV. Atlanta: Association for Consumer Research, 1977, pp. 363–71.
18. Marquez, F. T. "Advertising Content: Persuasion, Information or Intimidation?" *Journalism Quarterly*, Vol. 54 (Autumn, 1977), pp. 482–91.
19. Mayer, Martin, *Madison Avenue U.S.A.* New York: Harper, 1958. Ch. 19.
20. McGuire, William J. "An Information-Processing Model of Advertising Effectiveness." Paper presented to Symposium on Behavioral and Management Science in Marketing, University of Chicago, 1969.
21. McGuire, William J. "Psychological Factors Influencing Consumer Choice," in R. Ferber, ed., *Selected Aspects of Consumer Behavior*. Washington: National Science Foundation, 1977, p. 337.
22. McGuire, William J. "An Information-Processing Model of Advertising Effectiveness," in H. L. Davis and A. J. Silk, eds., *Behavioral and Management Science in Marketing*. New York: Ronald, 1978, pp. 156–80.
23. Mendelsohn, Harold. "Measuring the Process of Communications Effect," *Public Opinion Quarterly*, Vol. 26 (Fall, 1962), pp. 411–16.
24. Mitchell, Andrew A., and Jerry C. Olson. "Cognitive Effects of Advertising Repetition," in William D. Perrault, Jr., ed., *Advances in Consumer Research*, Vol. IV. Atlanta: Association for Consumer Research, 1977, pp. 213–20.
25. Mizerski, Richard W., and Robert B. Settle. "The Influence of Social Character on Preference for Social Versus Objective Information in Advertising," *Journal of Marketing Research*, Vol. 16 (November, 1979), pp. 552–58.
26. Nord, Walter R., and J. Paul Peter. "A Behavior Modification Perspective on Marketing," *Journal of Marketing*, Vol. 44 (Spring, 1980), pp. 36–47.
27. Olshavsky, Richard W., and Donald H. Granbois. "Consumer Decision Making—Fact or Fiction?" *Journal of Consumer Research*, Vol. 6 (September, 1979), pp. 93–100.
28. Olson, Jerry C., and Andrew A. Mitchell. "The Process of Attitude Acquisition: The Value of a Developmental Approach to Consumer Attitude Research," in Mary Jane Schlinger, ed., *Advances in Consumer Research*, Vol. 2. Cincinnati: Association for Consumer Research, 1975, pp. 249–64.
29. Osgood, Charles E., George J. Suci, and Percy H. Tannenbaum. *The Measurement of Meaning*. Urbana: University of Illinois, 1957, Ch. 1.
30. Palda, Christian S. "The Hypothesis of a Hierarchy of Effects: A Partial Evaluation," *Journal of Marketing Research*, Vol. 30 (February, 1966), pp. 13–24.
31. Pollay, Richard W., Judy Zaichkowsky, and Christina Fryer. "Regulation Hasn't Changed TV Ads Much," *Journalism Quarterly*, Vol. 57 (Autumn, 1980), pp. 438–46.
32. Preston, Ivan L. "Theories of Behavior and the Concept of Rationality in Advertising," *Journal of Communication*, Vol. 17 (September, 1967), pp. 211–22.
33. Preston, Ivan L. "A Reinterpretation of the Meaning of Involvement in Krugman's Models of Advertising Communication," *Journalism Quarterly*, Vol. 47 (Summer 1970), pp. 287–95.
34. Preston, Ivan L. *The Great American Blow-Up: Puffery in Advertising and Selling*. Madison: University of Wisconsin, 1975, Ch. 14.

35. Reid, Leonard N. "Factors Affecting Creativity in Generation of Advertising," *Journalism Quarterly*, Vol. 55 (Winter, 1978), pp. 781–85.
36. Reid, Leonard N., and Herbert J. Rotfeld. "Toward an Associative Model of Advertising Creativity," *Journal of Advertising*, Vol. 5 (No. 4, 1976), pp. 24–29.
37. Resnik, Alan, and Bruce L. Stern. "An Analysis of Information Content in Television Advertising," *Journal of Marketing*, Vol. 41 (January, 1977), pp. 50–53.
38. Rogers, Everett M. *Diffusion of Innovation*. New York: Free Press, 1962.
39. Rossiter, John R., and Larry Percy. "Visual Imaging Ability as a Mediator of Advertising Response," in H. Keith Hunt, ed., *Advances in Consumer Research*. Ann Arbor: Association for Consumer Research, Vol. 5, 1978, pp. 621–29.
40. Rossiter, John R., and Larry Percy. "Attitude Change Through Visual Imagery in Advertising," *Journal of Advertising*, Vol. 9, No. 2 (1980), pp. 10–16.
41. Sandage, Charles S., and Vernon F. Fryburger. *Advertising Theory and Practice*, 7th ed. New York: McGraw-Hill, 1967.
42. Schwartz, David A. "Measuring the Effectiveness of Your Company's Advertising," *Journal of Marketing*, Vol. 33 (April, 1969), pp. 20–25.
43. Sheldon, Arthur F. *Salesmanship*, a correspondence course, 1911.
44. Shimp, Terence A. "Social Psychological (Mis)Representations in Television Advertising," *Journal of Consumer Affairs*, Vol. 13 (Summer, 1979), pp. 28–40.
45. Shimp, Terence A., and Ivan L. Preston. "Deceptive and Nondeceptive Consequences of Evaluative Advertising," *Journal of Marketing*, Vol. 45 (Winter, 1981), pp. 22–32.
46. Strong, Edward K., Jr. *The Psychology of Selling and Advertising*. New York: McGraw-Hill, 1925.
47. Video Storyboards Tests, Inc. Survey. New York: 1980.
48. Weilbacher, William M. *Advertising*. New York: Macmillan, 1980, p. 488.
49. Wilkie, William L., and Paul W. Farris. *Consumer Information Processing: Perspectives and Implications for Advertising*. Cambridge: Marketing Science Institute, 1976, pp. 55, 61, 67.
50. Wolfe, H. D., J. K. Brown, and G. C. Thompson. *Measuring Advertising Results, Studies in Business Policy*, No. 2. New York: The National Industrial Conference Board, 1962.

PART FOUR
Broadening the Marketing Context

No other area of marketing has generated both the excitement and the criticism as broadening the marketing horizons from the marketing of tangible products for profit to the marketing of intangible, nonprofit services. There are several fundamental issues raised by this broadening of the marketing context.

First, is marketing a generic discipline applicable to all domains of market transactions or exchange? In other words, what are the boundaries of marketing? In particular, can marketing practice and principles be extended to such areas as intangible services, nonprofit organizations, and international markets?

There are, of course, two schools of thought on this issue. The first school of thought has strongly advocated that the basic principles of marketing (four *P*s, marketing mix, market segmentation, product differentiation, and customer satisfaction) are universal and, therefore, equally applicable to all contexts of marketing. In other words, there are no real differences between profit and nonprofit, consumer and industrial, domestic and international, and products and services marketing.

The second school of thought, on the other hand, strongly advocates that the context makes the difference and, therefore, one must create distinct marketing concepts and practices for each domain of marketing. In other words, the environmental forces (customer, competition, technology, and regulation) are so significantly different that it is not possible to adapt or adjust marketing concepts and practices predominantly generated for the packaged goods industry. Their contention is that understanding the context is more critical than application of marketing concepts and practices. Indeed, most mismarketing, or marketing blunders, can be easily attributed to blind extension of marketing concepts and practices to nontraditional areas of market behavior.

Second, if marketing is so universal as to explain all exchanges or transactions between two or more parties, what is the boundary of marketing as distinct from other social sciences, such as economics, social psychology, and sociology? How does marketing differ from these disciplines? In short, there is a danger of an identity crisis if marketing is broadened too much from its traditional roots in packaged goods.

Finally, if marketing should become relevant to a much broader context than originally intended, do we need to revise the basic concepts of the four *P*s, the marketing mix, market segmentation, product differentiation, and customer satisfaction? Are additional concepts needed to make marketing a more universal discipline or function?

SECTION K
Nonprofit and Social Marketing

Traditionally, nonprofit organizations in charge of public services have been expertise-driven rather than customer-driven. They have practiced the philosophy of "we do it our way" rather than the marketing philosophy of "we do it your way." As public alienation and criticism of nonprofit organizations has increased over the years, and furthermore, as competition has emerged, there is an increasing interest in applying marketing concepts and practices to services, including health care, financial, and recreation services.

It is, however, unfortunate that most nonprofit public service organizations think of marketing as either public relations or mass advertising. In other words, to them marketing means selling. It is, therefore, not surprising that the impact of marketing practice has been inconsistent. In some cases, it has worked wonders and in other cases, it has been disastrous for the organization.

A related problem of applying the marketing concepts and practices is the "corporate culture" of the nonprofit, regulated, or public service organization. Both employees and managers of these organizations have tremendous pride in their profession and expertise and believe that marketing either lowers public esteem or creates public harm. This corporate culture is most vivid in the health care industry, as demonstrated by the constant power struggles between physicians and hospital administrators.

This should not be surprising. After all, it is nothing more than a manifestation of resistance to change. Perhaps it will take a crisis of survival before marketing will be accepted as a legitimate function and a discipline in these organizations.

41 — The Marketing of Social Causes: The First 10 Years

Karen F. A. Fox and Philip Kotler

Reprinted from the *Journal of Marketing*, published by the American Marketing Association, Vol. 44 (Fall 1980), pp. 24–33. Reprinted by permission.

During the past decade the "territory" of marketing has expanded to include the marketing tasks of non-profit organizations and the marketing of worthwhile social causes. Kotler (1979) reviewed the accomplishments in the first area, describing how an increasing number of nonprofit organizations—particularly hospitals, colleges, social service agencies, and cultural organizations—are applying marketing concepts and techniques to improve the marketing of their services. Despite earlier controversy, few marketers dispute the relevance of marketing to the management of nonprofit organizations (Nickels 1974).

The time is now appropriate to evaluate the status of work in the area of social cause marketing—social marketing. Here the applicability of marketing is more hotly contested. Social marketing as a distinct application area for general marketing theory was advanced about a decade ago (Kotler and Zaltman 1971). Since then, various reform groups and government agencies have applied social marketing to such causes as family planning, energy conservation, improved nutrition, antismoking, prevention of alcohol and drug abuse, safer driving, and myriad other causes. Yet no review of these efforts and of the issues and problems connected with social marketing has been published. In fact, some recent articles—written by academic marketers rather than practitioners—question the appropriateness and ethics of social marketing just as it is being more widely adopted (e.g., Laczniak, Lusch, and Murphy 1979). G. D. Wiebe's (1951–52) question of 30 years ago, "why can't you sell brotherhood like you sell soap?", persists along with the newer question, "Should you be selling brotherhood?" Furthermore, the whole discussion is plagued by confusion about what social marketing is. As the technology of social marketing will shortly mark its first decade, an assessment of its nature, successes, limitation, and future is now warranted.

As background for such an assessment, we undertook an extensive review of the literature in marketing and in public health (where many of the applications of social marketing have been carried out). We interviewed key people in two leading social marketing firms to learn what problems they have tackled and what successes and frustrations they have encountered, and interviewed people in federal government agencies concerned with health and nutrition about their awareness of and experience with social marketing. Our findings are presented in the form of answers to the following questions.

- What is social marketing?
- What situations call for social marketing?
- What has social marketing accomplished?
- What are the major criticisms of social marketing?
- What are the hurdles in successful social marketing?
- What is the future of social marketing?

WHAT IS SOCIAL MARKETING?

Social marketing was originally defined as:

> ...the design, implementation, and control of programs calculated to influence the acceptability of social ideas and involving considerations of product planning, pricing, communications and marketing research (Kotler and Zaltman 1971, p. 5).

Thus social marketing was conceived to be application of marketing concepts and techniques to the marketing of various socially beneficial ideas and causes instead of products and services in the commercial sense. Synonymous terms might be "social cause marketing," "social idea marketing," or "public issue marketing."

The term "social marketing" unfortunately has been given different meanings by other writers. For example, Lazer and Kelley (1973) published *Social Marketing: Perspectives and Viewpoints* which includes articles on marketing's social responsibilities and social impacts, as well as the marketing of social ideas, under the term "social marketing." In a recent article entitled "Social Marketing: Its Ethical Dimensions," Laczniak, Lusch, and Murphy (1979) confuse social marketing with nonprofit organization marketing by improperly including the marketing of political candidates and urban police departments as examples of "social marketing." Our position is that social marketing should be distinguished from "societal marketing" on the one hand and "nonprofit organization marketing" on the other.

The Evolution of Social Marketing

One can best understand social marketing by seeing it in relationship to the major broad approaches to producing social change—the legal, technological, economic, and informational approaches. Consider how these approaches apply in inducing people to reduce their cigarette consumption. The *legal* approach is to pass laws that make cigarette smoking either illegal, costly, or difficult (e.g., prohibiting smoking in public places). The *technological* approach is to develop an innovation that will help people reduce their smoking or the harm thereof (e.g., an antismoking pill, a harmless cigarette). The *economic* approach is to raise the price or cost of smoking (e.g., higher cigarette taxes, higher insurance rates for smokers). Finally, the *informational* approach is to direct persuasive information at smokers about the risks of smoking and the advantages of not smoking (e.g., "Warning: The Surgeon General Has Determined That Smoking Is Dangerous to Your Health").

The roots of social marketing lie in the informational approach, in the form known as *social advertising*. Many cause groups, struck by the apparent effectiveness of commercial advertising, began to consider its potential for changing public attitudes and behavior. Family planning organizations in India, Sri Lanka, Mexico, and several other countries have sponsored major advertising campaigns attempting to sell people on the idea of having fewer children. Messages on billboards and over radio tell the public that they can have a higher standard of living with fewer children (India) or be happier (Sri Lanka). Nutrition groups have also used advertising extensively to encourage people to adopt better eating habits. The U.S. Department of Energy has plans for a multimillion-dollar advertising campaign to promote energy conservation to the American people.

Properly designed, these campaigns can influence attitudes and behavior. The problem is that all too often these campaigns are the only step taken to motivate new behavior and, by themselves, are usually inadequate. First, the message may be inadequately researched. For example, media campaigns to encourage people in developing countries to improve their diets miss the point that many people lack knowledge of which foods are more healthful, they may lack the money to buy these goods and, in remote areas, they may not find certain foods available. Second, many people screen out the message through selective perception, distortion, and forgetting. Mass communications have much less direct influence on behavior than has been thought, and much of their influence is mediated through the opinion leadership of other people. Third, many people do not know what to do after their exposure to the message. The message "Stop smoking—it might kill you" does not help the smoker know how to handle the urge to smoke or where to go for help.

As these limitations were recognized social advertising evolved into a broader approach known as *social communication*. Much of current social marketing has moved from a narrow advertising approach to a broad social communication/promotion approach to accomplish its objectives. Social communicators make greater use of personal selling and editorial support in addition to mass advertising. Thus, the family planning campaign in India utilizes a network of agents, including doctors, dentists, and barbers, to "talk up" family planning to people with whom they come in contact. Events such as "Family Planning Day" and family planning fairs, together with buttons, signs, and other media, get across the message.

Only recently has *social marketing* begun to replace social communication as a larger paradigm for effecting social change. Social marketing adds at least four elements that are missing from a pure social communication approach.

One element is sophisticated *marketing research* to learn about the market and the probable effectiveness of alternative marketing approaches. Social advertising amounts to "a shot in the dark" unless it is preceded by careful marketing research. Thus social marketers concerned with smoking would examine the size of the smoking market, the major market segments and the behavioral characteristics of each, and the benefit-cost impact of targeting different segments and designing appropriate campaigns for each.

The second element added by social marketing is *product development*. Faced with the problem of getting people to lower their thermostats in winter, a social advertiser or communicator will see the problem largely as one of exhorting people to lower the thermostat, using patriotic appeals, fuel-cost-saving appeals, or whatever seems appropriate. The social marketer, in addition, will consider existing or potential products that will make it easier for people to adopt the desired behavior, such as devices that automatically lower home heat during the middle of the night or that compute fuel cost savings at various temperature settings. In other words, whenever possible the social marketer does not stick with the existing product and try to sell it—a sales approach—but rather searches for the best product to meet the need—a marketing approach.

The third element added by social marketing is *the use of incentives*. Social communicators concentrate on composing messages dramatizing the benefits or dis-benefits of different kinds of behaviors. Social marketers go further and design specific incentives to increase the level of motivation. For example, social marketers have advised public health officials who are running immunization campaigns in remote villages to offer small gifts to people who show up for vaccinations. Some hospitals in South America run "price specials" on certain days whereby people who come in for health checkups pay less than the normal charge. The sales promotion area is rich with tools that the marketer can use to promote social causes.

The fourth element added by social marketing is *facilitation*. The marketer realizes that people wishing to change their behavior must invest time and effort, and considers ways to make it easier for them to adopt the new behavior. For example, smoking cessation classes must be conveniently located and conducted in a professional manner. Marketers are keenly aware of the need to develop convenient and attractive response channels to complement the communication channels. Thus they are concerned not only with getting people to adopt a new behavior, but also with finding ways to facilitate maintenance of the behavior.

Our discussion of how social marketing goes beyond social advertising and social communication can be summarized by saying that social marketing involves all "four P's," not just one. Social marketing involves coordinating product, price, place, and promotion factors to maximally motivate and facilitate desired forms of behavior. Furthermore, social marketing calls for marketing research and for preparation of a full marketing plan, strategy, and budget to get initial "sales" and to reinforce the new behavior over time.

What Situations Call for Social Marketing?

Social marketing potentially can be applied to a wide variety of social problems. It appears to be particularly appropriate in the following three situations.

When New Information and Practices Need to Be Disseminated

In many situations people need to be informed of an opportunity or practice that will improve their lives. In developing nations, social marketers have had to tackle such challenges as:

- Convincing people to boil their water and keep the water supply covered.
- Encouraging people to build and use latrines.
- Explaining to mothers the advantages of continuing to breastfeed their babies instead of switching them to less nourishing gruel at an early age.
- Encouraging people to buy and use iodized salt to prevent goiter.
- Showing parents a simple way to treat infant diarrhea at home — important because infant diarrhea is a major cause of infant mortality in less developed countries.

In industrialized nations the social marketer often must disseminate new information resulting from scientific research, including significant changes in high blood pressure treatment, in childhood immunization, in cancer detection and treatment, and in recommended diet.

Consider the changing concepts of what constitutes a good diet. In the early 1950s American elementary school children were taught about the seven basic food groups and were told to eat foods from each group daily. The 1969 USDA Yearbook entitled *Food For Us All* indicated that the American population was well fed and reported that "sugar or a sweet in some form is a daily necessity" (Mikesh and Nelson 1969, p. 232). Yet in 1979, the Surgeon General's Report on health promotion and disease prevention criticized the typical American diet, linking a diet high in fat, sugar, cholesterol, and salt and low in dietary fiber to heart disease, dental caries, high blood pressure, and colon cancer (U.S. Public Health Service 1979). These shifts in our knowledge of sound health practices suggest that we cannot simply relegate new health information to a slot in the elementary school curriculum, trusting that the next generation will be better informed and thus healthier than their parents. New information must be transmitted much more widely and more rapidly along with facilitation, price, and innovation steps to stimulate and reinforce new behavior.

When Countermarketing Is Needed

In various nations of the world, companies are promoting the consumption of products that are undesirable or potentially harmful—for example cigarettes, alcoholic beverages, and highly refined foods which contribute to lung and heart disease, liver damage, overweight, and other problems. The large promotional budgets behind these products tend to crowd out opposing views, because those who disagree are often too fragmented, too few in number, or have inadequate resources to present the counterposition. Social marketing is now viewed by many public interest groups and government agencies as a way to present the other side of the story and stimulate people to adopt more healthful behavior. Sweden, for example, has taken vigorous steps to countermarket alcohol consumption, including running ad campaigns stigmatizing drunk behavior, restricting the availability of alcoholic beverages, raising the prices of alcoholic beverages, establishing stiff penalties for drunken driving, and increasing anti-alcohol school education programs.

Another current example of countermarketing has come in response to the promotion of infant formula in Third World countries. Borden, Nestlé, and other infant formula manufacturers, faced with declining birth rates in developed countries, began aggressive marketing to mothers in Africa, Latin America, and other less developed regions characterized by poverty, illiteracy, lack of pure water, lack of facilities for sterilizing bottles, and lack of refrigeration for storing mixed formula (Post and Baer 1978). Social marketing campaigns have been carried out to counter such powerful slogans as "Give your baby love and Lactogen" and to inform mothers of the advantages of breastfeeding.

When Activation Is Needed

Often people know what they should do, but do not act accordingly. For example, nine out of 10 smokers interviewed in a 1975 government survey said they would like to quit, yet 57% expected to be smoking five years later (Fisher 1977). Likewise, many people "know" they should lose weight, get more exercise, floss their teeth, and do other things, but they do not do them. In part their inertia is related to the myriad alternatives they have and the countervailing media messages to enjoy life and maintain current habits ("Have a Coke and a smile" instead!). Furthermore, the benefits may be obtainable only by sustained effort, and the personal "payoff" over a lifetime may be exceedingly difficult to estimate. As one elderly man reportedly said, "If I had known I was going to live this long, I would have taken better care of my health" (*Forbes* 1979).

In such situations, the task of social marketing is to move people from intention to action. Marketers have studied the many factors that affect the readiness of people to act, and have developed several approaches to motivate and facilitate action. In the future, various national or local emergencies—such as water shortages, oil shortages, and epidemics—may increase the need for public agencies to know how to activate people quickly.

What Has Social Marketing Accomplished?

Although social marketing is an appealing social change approach in theory, to what extent has it been effective in practice? At this time, we can only review the accomplishments of social marketing on an impressionistic basis. The bona fide applications of social marketing—as distinguished from social advertising or social communication—are too few to provide a full data base. Moreover, because social marketing often has been carried out without experimental controls, it is difficult to know whether behavioral changes were due to social marketing efforts or to other factors.

We consider two major areas of application—family planning and motivating healthier life styles—and a sampling of other interventions which reflect elements of a social marketing approach.

Family Planning

Family planning has been a major focus of social marketing efforts, reflected in a growing literature. Roberto (1975) provides an excellent exposition of social marketing theory applied to the problem of family planning. The Population Information Program at The Johns Hopkins University recently published a detailed review of social marketing applications, including information on features of specific programs and their effectiveness (Population Information Program 1980). The report defines the basic goal of such programs as providing contraceptives "efficiently, economically, and conveniently to people who will use them" (p. J-395). The majority of campaigns to market family planning are government-sponsored, motivated by the availability of effective birth control products and by the growing awareness that economic and social gains can be wiped out by rapid population growth. Many of these social marketing campaigns have been successful, as the following cases show.

A successful social marketing campaign in Sri Lanka (formerly Ceylon) was based on principles of marketing research, brand packaging, distribution channel analysis, and marketing management and control. Consumer research prior to the campaign indicated widespread approval of the idea of family planning but little knowledge and use of contraception. The government, in cooperation with several agencies, centered its efforts on achieving widespread usage of condoms as a means of birth control. A brand was developed named "Preethi" (meaning happiness), and was sold in a three pack for four cents (U.S.), one of the lowest costs in the world. Preethi achieved distribution in more than 3,600 pharmacies, teahouses, grocery and general stores, as well as by direct mail. Literature and order forms for condoms were distributed by agricultural extension workers on their regular visits to farm families. The sale of condoms was supported through a mass media campaign, including newspaper and radio ads, films, and a booklet entitled "How to Have Children by Plan and Not by Chance." Distributors also received large point-of-purchase displays. As a result of this orchestrated marketing approach, Preethi sales grew from 300,000 per month (in mid-1974) to an average of 500,000 per month in 1977. It was estimated that 60,000 unwanted pregnancies were averted by this social marketing project (Population Services International 1977).

Similar campaigns have been successful in parts of India, Thailand, Bangladesh, and other countries. For example, in Bangladesh this type of campaign resulted in the monthly use of more than 1.5 million condoms and about 100,000 cycles of oral contraceptives, providing full contraceptive protection for approximately 400,000 couples at a yearly cost of about $4 per couple. In Thailand, the Community-Based Family Planning Services marketing program for promoting birth control includes some novel features. The agency stages contests with prizes to the person who inflates the biggest "balloon"—a condom—as a way to break down taboos about contraception. Contraceptives are accepted in rural villages, where villagers often ask local Buddhist monks to bless newly arrived shipments of contraceptives. The agency has recruited 5,000 rural distributors, including rice farmers, shopkeepers, village elders, and others who receive a one-day training course on selling condoms and keeping records, for which they receive a modest commission. The cost of all this effort is $3.50 per recipient per year, less than half of the cost of a similar government program in Thailand not using a marketing approach (Mathews 1976).

In Mexico, family planners face a tougher challenge because traditional values oppose the idea of family planning, as did past government policy designed to increase the population. Manhood and womanhood have traditionally been measured by the number of children produced. The dominant Catholic culture and widespread ignorance of birth control further hamper family planning efforts. Yet in 1974 the Mexican government established the National Population Council (NPC) to slow the country's galloping rate of population increase. The NPC adopted a classic social marketing approach with the following elements. All promotional materials feature a logo showing a mother, a father, and two children. The family planning messages are carried by posters, booklets, and radio and TV spots. Family planning commercials are broadcast virtually every half hour on the radio. Free contraceptives are available at about 950 hospitals and clinics operated by the Ministry of Health and at 930 clinics run by an affiliate of the International Planned Parenthood Foundation (Wille 1975).

The effectiveness of social marketing of family planning can be assessed by looking at sales data, distribution systems, changes in knowledge, attitudes, and practices of consumers, cost-effectiveness, and, at the macro level, changes in fertility and birth rates. The Population Information Program reports micro-level measures indicating positive results. Positive results also can be claimed at the macro level. Bogue and Tsui (1979), analyzing the effect of several different variables, found that family planning efforts explain much more of the birth rate reduction since 1968 than does any other factor, including changes in economic and social development which usually have been given most of the credit. According to their data, the recent decline in the world fertility rate has been primarily due to "the worldwide drive by Third World countries to introduce family planning as part of their national social-development services" (pp. 99–100).

Heart Disease Prevention

Coronary disease is a byproduct of "the good life." Though nearly nonexistent in most of the world, it has reached epidemic proportions in Western industrialized countries. Between 1972 and 1975 the Stanford Heart Disease Prevention Program carried out an interdisciplinary intervention to determine ways to reduce risk of coronary disease through long-term changes in health practices—decreasing dietary cholesterol consumption and cigarette use, and increasing exercise levels.

Though fundamentally a sophisticated use of social communication, carried out by public health and communications research specialists, the program embodied many of the elements of a social marketing approach. As in the case of family planning, the goal of long-term behavior change required carefully designed and implemented interventions. To facilitate evaluation, the program was carried out in three similar rural California communities: in one community a mass media campaign alone was used; in a second, a mass media campaign was combined with personal instruction for a sample of high-risk individuals; in the third, neither treatment was used.

The extensive media campaign in the first two communities consisted of radio and TV spots and minidramas; "doctor's columns" and columns on diet in local newspapers; printed items, including an information booklet, a heart health calendar, and a cookbook, mailed to all residents; and billboards and bus posters. Residents in the second community also received personal instruction utilizing modeling and reinforcement to encourage them to quit smoking, lose weight, and get more exercise. In each of the three communities a sample of people was selected and tested at the beginning of the program and followed up annually.

The mass media were used to teach specific behavioral skills whenever possible, rather than simply to exhort people to change. Maccoby and Alexander (1979) cite several other key features of the study which match marketing considerations, including:

- The establishment of specific objectives for each component of the campaign over time.
- Clearly defined audience segments.
- The creation of clear, useful, and salient messages through formative research and pretesting.
- Utilization of creative media scheduling to reach the audience with adequate frequency.
- Stimulation of interpersonal communication to encourage a synergistic effect of multiple channels.
- Promotion of clear and well-paced behavioral changes in messages.
- Use of feedback to evaluate the campaign's progress over time.
- The use of a long-term campaign to avoid threshold effect considerations.

The program demonstrated that long-term changes in habits and significant reduction in risk for heart disease could be assisted through communitywide interventions utilizing the mass media (Meyer and Maccoby 1978). Both interventions yielded a significant increase in knowledge of risk factors and of desirable practices and a significant reduction in overall risk, with the media-plus-direct instruction intervention producing the greater changes.

A social marketer might consider ways of extending the effectiveness of the Stanford Heart Program. For example, participants might be given special incentives or reinforcements for conforming to good health habits. Grocery stores might participate by highlighting healthful foods, as is now being done by Giant Food Stores in the Washington, D.C., area.

The direct support of local doctors and dentists could be enlisted because they are particularly likely to see high-risk individuals.

Other Applications of Social Marketing

A growing number of health improvement programs reflect or have been consciously developed with a social marketing approach:

1. The Cancer Information Office of the National Institutes of Health has produced and pilot-tested a "Helping Smokers Quit" kit to encourage physicians to use their influence with patients who smoke. The kit includes a brief guide for the doctor, patient education materials, and a followup letter and brochure to be sent to the patient after the office visit.
2. The U.S. Department of Agriculture is supporting a project to use mass media and other channels to improve children's eating habits. The project began with extensive consumer research—interviews with children about their food preferences and eating habits.
3. The American Hospital Association's Center for Health Promotion is working to encourage preventive health measures and healthy "life habits" through programs run by hospitals, businesses, and community organizations. The Center recently conducted a workshop for hospital decision makers on marketing health promotion programs to local industry.
4. When infant immunization levels in Missouri dropped to ominous levels, a marketing plan was designed on the basis of a statewide study of the social-psychological factors affecting the problem (Houston and Markland 1976). The market was segmented and promotional material was directed to parents and expectant parents, as well as to the staff of the Missouri Division of Health. The campaign spokesman, "Marcus Rabbit, M.D.," was created to link the program to children, but to appeal to adults.
5. Public health specialists are using new channels to provide diagnostic services. A team of homosexual male clinicians from the Denver Metro Health Clinic conducted weekly VD screening in one of Denver's three steam baths catering to homosexuals (Judson, Miller, and Schaffnit 1977).
6. The National Heart, Lung, and Blood Institute changed eating habits in a National Institutes of Health employee cafeteria through a "Food for Thought" game. Food information was presented on playing-card-like cards which employees received each time they went through the serving line. Small prizes were awarded to those who acquired sets of cards. An increase in

purchases of skim milk and decreases in purchases of bread and desserts and in total calories consumed were measured with the aid of the existing inventory control cash register system which automatically recorded every food item selected (Zifferblatt, Wilbur, and Pinsky 1980).

Although many of these campaigns are still to be evaluated, especially in terms of benefit/cost criteria and long-term effects, the use of conscious social marketing planning by cause organizations is clearly on the upswing.

What Are the Major Criticisms of Social Marketing?

Not surprisingly, the increasing application of social marketing has been accompanied by questions about its legitimacy and possible negative impacts. The following four classes of criticism have appeared.

Social Marketing Is Not Real Marketing

Some marketers still feel that marketing is largely a business discipline with little or no application to social causes. They believe that marketing is valid only where there are markets, transactions, and prices. As stated by Laczniak and Michie (1979), marketers should "take enough pride in the scope of traditional marketing."

Every discipline has its orthodox group which is content to ply familiar waters, believing either that their discipline has nothing to offer in the new territory or that, if it does, others will resent the intrusion. However, we believe that scholars and practitioners have a right, indeed, an obligation, to venture out and look freshly at phenomena from their discipline's perspective. Such ventures have produced such new fields as political sociology, economic anthropology, social psychology, and quantitative geography. If the new framework or findings are accepted, then the discipline has made a contribution.

Social Marketing Is Manipulative

Many of the issues in social marketing call for changing people's attitudes and behavior, urging them to give up or cut back on comfortable habits. In contrast, commercial marketing frequently supports and encourages present habits, including those that are potentially harmful. Given that commercial marketing is often accused of being manipulative (primarily in persuading people to buy more things or in convincing them that one brand will satisfy a given need better than another brand), it is not surprising that social marketing is charged with being even more manipulative. For example, Laczniak, Lusch, and Murphy (1979) believe that social marketing is potentially unethical in giving power to a group to influence public opinion on such contested issues as pornography and abortion.

The word "manipulative" is something of a red herring in this discussion. The word "manipulative" usually connotes hidden and unfair ends and/or means used in the influence process. We argue that if a cause is marketed openly with the purpose of influencing someone to change his or her behavior, then the process is not manipulative, any more than is the activity of a lawyer, religious leader, or politician trying to convince others. If the social marketer simply makes the strongest possible case in favor of a cause without distorting the facts, the approach is not manipulative. Social marketing, especially when used in countermarketing, can provide a voice for those with competing points of view.

Social Marketing Is Self-Serving

Some critics might be distressed that some social marketers who are promoting a cause are also making a profit in the process. Consider the following examples.

- Seat belt manufacturers are major supporters of auto safety legislation, partly because they stand to gain.
- Bottled water manufacturers in France have backed efforts to influence French citizens to reduce their alcohol consumption.
- Condom manufacturers have lent support to campaigns against VD because they stand to gain through greater use of condoms.
- Life insurance companies are encouraging people to jog, cut down on fats and sugar, install smoke alarms, and in other ways reduce illness, accidents, and premature deaths, thus cutting insurance claims and raising company profits.

Clearly commercial enterprises will increasingly support social marketing programs as they see financial benefits accruing to their companies while they also promote beneficial social change. This development appears to us to be desirable because it increases the incentive for commercial marketers to consider the best interests of consumers. Too often, social marketing efforts are undertaken by underfinanced cause organizations which run the risk of creating excessive demands on their limited resources when they achieve a major success, a phenomenon which Houston and Homans (1977) term "the failure of success."

A more troublesome issue is the use of tax money by government agencies to promote politically motivated efforts. For example, a booklet on energy conservation measures was delivered to every home in New England at the start of the 1979–80 heating season, paid for by the Department of Energy and private corporate contributions. Critics pointed to the "coincidence" of the upcoming New Hampshire primaries and President Carter's need to improve his image as an effective leader on conservation. In contrast, most government-sponsored social marketing efforts are likely to be fairly uncontroversial when used to increase the effectiveness of legislatively mandated social programs. Social marketing is already being applied in this way by several federal agencies.

Social Marketing Will Damage the Reputation of Marketing

Some marketers fear that applications of social marketing might arouse negative public sentiment toward marketing. Social marketing might acquire a bad name in two ways. First, it might be attacked for promoting unpopular causes, such as abortion or family planning. Second, it might influence people to accept a new behavior that turns out not to be in their best interest. The public might ultimately turn against social marketing and call for its curbing or regulation. Such attacks might strengthen present criticisms of commercial marketing and result in a setback to both.

There is some irony in this scenario because social marketing should, if anything, add luster rather than disrepute to marketing's image as the public sees marketing used to enhance the quality of their lives.

What Are the Real Hurdles to Successful Social Marketing?

The most devastating blow to social marketing would be to demonstrate that it is ineffective, that it does not change anything. Ineffective marketing is wasteful of resources and may lead people to expect results which cannot be produced. Novelli (1980) notes that managers and planners looking for a panacea for a "quick fix" may rush to embrace social marketing with inflated expectations: "When these quick solutions are not forthcoming, they are disappointed and view marketing as having failed." Some social issues are not likely to be affected by social marketing because the costs, although mainly nonmonetary, are too great and because the level of consumer involvement is either too low to overcome inertia—e.g., antilittering campaigns—or so high that producing behavior change will require great facilitation effort—e.g., antismoking campaigns (Rothschild 1979).

Social marketing practitioners are the first to admit that social marketing will have a different degree of effectiveness with different social causes, and that most social marketing problems will be more formidable than the typical marketing problems facing commercial marketers. William Novelli, a leading social marketing practitioner, admits, "It's a thousand times harder to do social marketing than to do package goods marketing." He and Paul Bloom recently reviewed the major hurdles faced by social marketers, and their observations are summarized hereafter (Bloom and Novelli 1979).

First, the market is usually harder to analyze. Social marketers have less good quality secondary data about their consumers. They have more difficulty in obtaining valid and reliable measures of salient consumer attributes, and in sorting out the relative influence of various determinants of consumer behavior. They have more difficulty getting consumer research studies funded, approved, and completed in a timely fashion.

Second, target market choice is more difficult. There is often public pressure to attempt to reach the whole market rather than to zero in on the best target groups. Thus a family planning campaign is restrained from focusing on the families who have the most children because of charges of racial or religious discrimination. When the relevant groups can be targeted, these groups are usually the most negatively predisposed to adopt the desired behavior, and thus success is harder to achieve.

Third, formulating product strategy is more difficult. The antismoking crusader should really invent a safe cigarette but this is not easy to do, and therefore the range of product innovation options is smaller. For many causes the reformer must get people to do something that is unpleasant rather than offering them something that would be even more pleasant than their present behavior.

Fourth, social marketers have fewer opportunities to use pricing and must rely more on other approaches that would increase or decrease the cost to consumers of certain behavior. Thus getting people to stop littering is not accomplished as well through a fine (very difficult to enforce) as by reducing the cost of not littering by providing more refuse containers in parks and on busy thoroughfares.

Fifth, channels of distribution may be harder to utilize and control. For example, a family planning organization may be able to get many retailers to carry condoms but has less control over how they will display them, price them, sell them, and replace them when out of stock.

Sixth, communication strategies may be more difficult to implement. Some groups may oppose the use of certain types of appeals that otherwise would be very effective. The particular cause may require a longer explanation than is available within the confines of a short message. The budget may be too low to permit pretesting the message or to ensure its wide distribution or the evaluation of its impact.

Seventh, cause organizations are often backward in their management and marketing sophistication. Many cause organizations are small, rely mainly on volunteers, and have little familiarity with marketing concepts or planning approaches. They may not be able to handle a large demand for their service, should it arise. The staff may not really be committed to solving the problem, especially if they will lose their jobs when they succeed.

Eighth, the results of social marketing efforts are often difficult to evaluate. For example, should the success of a family planning campaign be measured by total births averted or by births averted in high fertility groups? Or should the measure be the number of people who become aware of family planning, or who begin to show an interest in adopting it? Even after an appropriate measure is determined, the contribution of the marketing program to the final outcome is often difficult to estimate.

The resolution of these problems will depend in part on the accumulation of additional experience in applying and evaluating social marketing, on continuing efforts to integrate and disseminate findings from social marketing programs, and on theoretical and empirical work to improve our understanding of factors that can be used to increase the impact of such programs (Bloom 1980; Cook and Campbell 1979; Cook and McAnany 1979; Fine 1979; Fox 1980; Rothschild 1979).

What Is The Future of Social Marketing?

The 1980s outlook for social marketing is one of continued growth and application to an ever-widening range of issues. More and more cause organizations and government agencies will turn to social marketing in a search for increased effectiveness. Many will come to social marketing only by passing through the stages of social advertising and social communication first. Large and expensive advertising blitzes may be attempted, rather than integrated social marketing campaigns. The risk is that if such social advertising campaigns fail, critics may charge that marketing does not work when in fact it was not really tried.

Clearly there will be a need for more and better trained social marketers rather than simply social advertisers. The ideal training would have several components. Business marketing training which stresses market analysis, economic analysis, and management theory would be desirable. Because social marketers are involved in trying to change attitudes and behavior rather than simply to meet existing needs, they should study the social science disciplines, particularly sociology, psychology, and anthropology. They should also be trained in communication theory. In addition, social marketers will need to acquire a social problem-solving perspective which will lead them to search for possible technological solutions that may eventually replace present solutions based on self-denial, regulation, or economic incentives.

Social marketers working in multicultural contexts in the United States and in overseas development projects will need particular sensitivity to cultural differences, a knowledge of relevant aspects of the cultures in which they work, and facility in language or in working with persons who have the necessary language competence. It is no wonder that many social marketers now working on overseas projects have been Peace Corps volunteers or have studied or worked overseas for extended periods. Courses in language, history, and anthropology contribute to this preparation.

Though at present many social marketers are outside consultants, a look into the future suggests that organizations may attract or develop their own "in house" social marketers. These people may already be educators, public health specialists, policy analysts, and communications experts, for example. Or organizations may attract business-trained marketers who are able to cross over by gaining an understanding of the specific issues and tasks that confront a specific organization or field, such as health promotion. In effect, social marketers will be dual specialists who can apply marketing to specific social causes.

SUMMARY

What impact is social marketing likely to have on promoting beneficial social change in an effective manner? The evidence from the first decade of social marketing applications is promising. We have described social marketing as the application of marketing thinking and tools to the promotion of social causes, and have traced its evolution through social advertising and social communication. Cases from family planning, heart disease prevention, and other health areas are presented to illustrate the range and impact of social marketing applications, though we acknowledge that many are not fully elaborated examples of social marketing.

A growing number of cause organizations and government agencies are turning to social marketing. Groups that once relied on social advertising alone are now moving toward social communication and social marketing. Applications of social marketing have achieved some notable results and provide insights into the challenges confronting social marketers. We foresee that social marketing specialists, combining business marketing skills with additional training in the social sciences, will be working on a wider range of social causes with increasing sophistication. Advances in conceptualizing social marketing problems and in evaluating the impacts of social marketing programs will further enhance their effectiveness.

REFERENCES

Bloom, Paul N. (1980), "Evaluating Social Marketing Programs: Problems and Prospects," *1980 Educators Conference Proceedings*, Chicago: American Marketing Association.

―――― and William D. Novelli (1979), "Problems in Applying Conventional Marketing Wisdom to Social Marketing Programs," paper presented at American Marketing Association Workshop, "Exploring and Developing Government Marketing," Yale University.

Bogue, Donald J. and Amy Ong Tsui (1979), "Zero World Population Growth?" *The Public Interest*, 55 (Spring), 99–113.

Cook, Thomas D. and Donald T. Campbell (1979), *Quasi-Experimentation: Design and Analysis Issues for Field Settings*, Chicago: Rand McNally College Publishing.

―――― and Emile G. McAnany (1979), "Recent United States Experiences in Evaluation Research with Implications for Latin America," in *Evaluating the Impact of Nutrition and Health Programs*, Robert E. Klein et al., eds., New York: Plenum.

Fine, Seymour H. (1979), "Beyond Money: The Concept of Social Price," working paper, Rutgers University.

Fisher, Lucille (1977), "National Smoking Habits and Attitudes," American Lung Association.

Forbes (1979), 123 (September 17), 25.

Fox, Karen F. A. (1980), "Time as a Component of Price in Social Marketing, *1980 Educators Conference Proceedings*, Chicago: American Marketing Association.

Houston, Franklin S. and Richard E. Homans (1977), "Public Agency Marketing: Pitfalls and Problems," *MSU Business Topics*, 25 (Summer), 36–40.

―――― and Robert Markland (1976), "Public Agency Marketing—Improving the Adequacy of Infant Immunization," in *Proceedings*, American Institute for Decision Sciences, 461–3.

Judson, Franklyn N., Kenneth G. Miller, and Thomas R. Schaffnit (1977), "Screening for Gonorrhea and Syphilis in the Gay Baths—Denver, Colorado," *American Journal of Public Health*, 67 (August), 740–2.

Kotler, Philip (1979), "Strategies for Introducing Marketing into Nonprofit Organizations," *Journal of Marketing*, 43 (January), 37–44.

―――― and Gerald Zaltman (1971), "Social Marketing: An Approach to Planned Social Change," *Journal of Marketing*, 35 (July), 3–12.

Laczniak, Gene R., Robert F. Lusch, and Patrick E. Murphy (1979), "Social Marketing: Its Ethical Dimensions," *Journal of Marketing*, 43 (Spring), 29–36.

―――― and Donald A. Michie (1979), "The Social Disorder of the Broadened Concept of Marketing," *Journal of Marketing Science*, 7 (Summer), 214–31.

Lazer, William and Eugene J. Kelley (1973), *Social Marketing: Perspectives and Viewpoints*, Homewood, Illinois: Richard D. Irwin, Inc.

Maccoby, Nathan and Janet Alexander (1979), "Field Experimentation," in *Research in Social Contexts: Bringing about Change*, R. F. Munoz, L. R. Snowden, and J. G. Kelly, eds., San Francisco: Jossey-Bass.

Mathews, Linda (1976), "What Makes Mechai Run, or How to Curb the Births of a Nation," *Wall Street Journal* (January 15), 1.

Meyer, Anthony J. and Nathan Maccoby (1978), "The Role of Mass Media in Maintaining Health," in *Vestinnan Virtauksia*, Erja Erholn and Leif Aberg, eds, Keruu, Finland: Delfiinikirkat.

Mikesh, Verna A. and Leona S. Nelson (1969), "Sugar, Sweets Play Roles in Food Texture and Flavoring," in *Food for Us All*, 1969 Yearbook of the United States Department of Agriculture, Washington, D.C.; Government Printing Office, 232–6.

Nickels, William G. (1974), "Conceptual Conflicts in Marketing," *Journal of Economics and Business*, 27 (Winter), 140–3.

Novelli, William G. (1980), personal communication, January 3.

Population Information Program (1980), "Social Marketing: Does It Work?", *Population Reports*, Family Planning Programs, Series J, number 21, The Johns Hopkins University.

Population Services International (1977), "Preethi Project Transferred to Sri Lanka FPA," *PSI Newsletter* (November/December), 4.

Post, James E. and Edward Baer (1978), "Demarketing Infant Formula: Consumer Products in the Developing World," *Journal of Contemporary Business*, 7 (4) 17–35.

Roberto, Eduardo (1975), *Strategic Decision-Making in a Social Program: The Case of Family-Planning Diffusion*, Lexington, Massachusetts: Lexington Books.

Rothschild, Michael L. (1979), "Marketing Communication in Nonbusiness Situations: or Why It's So Hard to Sell Brotherhood Like Soap," *Journal of Marketing*, 43 (Spring), 11–20.

U.S. Public Health Service (1979), *Healthy People: The Surgeon General's Report on Health Promotion and Disease Prevention*, Washington, D.C.; Government Printing Office.

Wiebe, G. D. (1951–52), "Merchandising Commodities and Citizenship on Television," *Public Opinion Quarterly*, 15 (Winter), 679–91.

Wille, Lois (1975), "Mexico Battles the Baby Boom," *Chicago Daily News* (December 3), 5.

Zifferblatt, Steven M., Curtis S. Wilbur, and Joan L. Pinsky (1980), "Changing Cafeteria Eating Habits: A New Direction for Public Health Care," *Journal of the American Dietetic Association*, 76 (January), 15–20.

42 A Model of Strategy Mix Choice for Planned Social Change

Jagdish N. Sheth and Gary L. Frazier

Reprinted from the *Journal of Marketing*, published by the American Marketing Association, Vol. 46 (Winter 1982), pp. 15–26. Reprinted by permission.

PLANNED SOCIAL CHANGE

"A significant hallmark of mid-century America is the greatly accelerated growth of institutions that choose to—or are mandated to—bring about what they define as socially desirable attitudes and behaviors" (Andreasen 1981, p. 1). These social marketers include such organizations and/or groups as health maintenance organizations, Alcoholics Anonymous, the Office of Cancer Communications, and the United Way. Public sector agencies are often concerned with creating significant changes in consumption behavior and patterns in the marketplace (e.g., decrease alcohol and cigarette purchases, decrease food consumption among overweight people, increase the use of contraceptives). Fox and Kotler (1980) indicate that many of these organizations have recently discovered marketing as a potentially useful tool to help them achieve their objectives, which often deal with planned social change.

Zaltman (1974) defines social change as an alteration in the structure and functioning of a social unit or social system. Therefore, planned social change refers to active intervention by change agents (e.g., officials in public agencies) with a conscious policy objective to bring about a change in magnitude and/or direction of a particular social or consumption behavior by means of one or more strategies of change (Hornstein et al. 1971, Jones 1969, Lippitt, Watson, and Westley 1968, Niehoff 1966, Zaltman and Duncan 1977).[1] Planned social change consists of the following characteristics:

- The social behavior to be changed must be identified and well-defined.
- There should be a policy objective with respect to the magnitude and/or direction of social change.
- Some entity should be earmarked as the change agent and supplied with appropriate resources or powers.
- One or more strategies of change should be utilized.

This definition of planned social change, therefore, excludes the following types of social changes:

- Changes that are evolutionary, accidental, or random phenomena (Arensberg and Niehoff 1971, Bennis 1966, Lippitt, Watson, and Westley 1968).
- Changes that arise by the process of contagion as is so typical in the diffusion of innovations (Rogers and Shoemaker 1971, Zaltman 1974, Zaltman and Stiff 1973). The contagion process is merely a behavioral phenomenon (Bass 1969, Mansfield 1961). Of course it can be harnessed and utilized as a strategy by a change agent to achieve a policy objective in a given social change arena, but by itself it does not constitute planned social change as often implied in the diffusion of innovation literature.

Planned social change is, therefore, a *managerial rather than a behavioral task* that requires making decisions as to which strategies to use, in what combination, and for which target groups in order to achieve policy objectives related to bringing about a prespecified magnitude and/or direction of change in a given social or consumption behavior (Chin and Benne 1969, Zaltman 1974). As such, it must possess elements of strategic planning and decision making. Only after these decisions are made does planned social change become an implementation task for managers. If the managerial task stage is skipped or performed poorly, the chances of widespread social change in the direction desired by the change agent will be relatively low.

Problems in the Present Social Change Approach

Two major problems now exist in the way change agents attempt to motivate planned social change. First, very often only a single strategy is utilized in an attempt to bring about a planned social change at a given point in time and sometimes over a period of time. Different appeals for different population segments are typically not designed under this single strategy approach (Zaltman and Duncan 1977). In other words, change agents have practiced a universal approach as opposed to a segmentation approach toward planned social change.

Secondly, change agents have been primarily concerned with implementing specific strategies for specific programs. Little attention has been paid to developing a more global picture to predict when and where certain strategies may be relatively appropriate. At present, there is no theory of strategy mix but only an acknowledgement that efficient selection and application of varying strategies is highly complex. Zaltman (1974, p. 92) states, "Many factors affect the success of a particular strategy; not uncommonly factors favoring different strategies are simultaneously present and factors which contraindicate a particular strategy coexist with factors favoring its use." It seems that change agents believe in a particular strategy based on some ideological value system and utilize it universally without regard to allocating resources in an optimal manner among a mixture of strategies.

Purposes of This Study

This study presents a model of strategy mix choice for planned social change that will provide the change agent with a more global picture of the planned social change process. Based on the concept of attitude-behavior consistency/discrepancy, a model is proposed that provides insights to the change agent about different processes and objectives of planned social change. Later, (1) influence strategies that can be utilized by a change agent in facilitating a given process and attaining a given objective are identified, and (2) a consumer based methodology (based on the use of discriminant analysis) to help change agents decide which of the behavior-attitude processes they must facilitate in given social change situations is explained. The basic value of this method is to provide change agents with a starting point in strategy negotiations and selections within their organizations. While additional trade-off factors such as money, personal agendas, agency politics, other stakeholder attitudes, and time constraints must be considered and incorporated in the final choice of a specific mix of strategies, they are treated as ceteris paribus in our model.

This paper also highlights the importance of a consumer orientation (especially in regard to varying population segments with different needs, wants, attitudes, and behavior) within public agencies. A consumer orientation is often missing in public sector decision making and programs designed to change consumption patterns in the marketplace (Deshpande and Krishnan 1981, Fox and Kotler 1980).

A Model of Strategy Mix Choice

Attitudes and Behavior

A significant body of literature on the attitude-behavior relationship supports the general assumption that attitudes and behavior are, on the whole, positively related (cf. Engel, Warshaw, and Kinnear 1979, McGuire 1978). People often manifest behaviors towards which they have positive attitudes (contributions to charity) and avoid those behaviors towards which they have negative attitudes (deviant behavior). As such, attitude-behavior consistency generally holds in an aggregate analysis.

However, in a case by case analysis, attitude-behavior discrepancy also certainly exists (Belk 1981, Sheth and Horowitz 1977, Sheth and

TABLE 1. A Typology of Strategy Mix For Planned Social Change

	Attitude Positive	Attitude Negative
Engaged (Relevant Behavior)	**Cell 1** Reinforcement Process 1. Behavioral Reinforcement 2. Psychological Reinforcement	**Cell 2** Rationalization Process Attitude Change
Non-engaged	**Cell 4** Inducement Process Behavioral Change	**Cell 3** Confrontation Process 1. Behavioral Confrontation 2. Psychological Confrontation

Newman 1981, Sheth and Wong 1981). This construct implies that there are situations in which peoples' attitudes and behavior are at odds with each other. For example, many people possess positive attitudes toward wearing seat belts but they don't use them; conversely, some people may have negative attitudes toward going to church but still attend.[2]

Except in a very homogeneous society, it is not likely that everyone will manifest the same degree or direction of attitude-behavior consistency/discrepancy, especially toward socially relevant behaviors. For example, some couples practice birth control and have a positive attitude toward birth control (segment one), others avoid it because they have negative attitudes (segment two), still others practice birth control but more out of necessity (segment three), and finally some believe in birth control but do not practice it (segment four).[3]

Processes of Planned Social Change

The conceptual framework suggests that there are four major processes of planned social change, each one most appropriate for each of four combinations of attitude-behavior consistency/discrepancy, as summarized in Table 1. When attitudes and behavior are consistent as well as in the positive direction toward the relevant social behavior (cell one in Table 1), a *reinforcement process* seems most appropriate for sustaining the planned social change. It refers to rewarding people for engaging in a behavior they enjoy (like) and which the change agent wants to continue and sustain.

The general objective of the reinforcement process is to keep people in the positive attitude, engaged behavior cell. This can be accomplished through (1) reinforcing the behavior, (2) reinforcing the attitude, and/or (3) reinforcing both. Behavioral reinforcement involves providing economic rewards to the individual so as to strengthen the probability of future compliant behavior as suggested by operant conditioning (Nord and Peter 1980, Skinner 1953). On the other hand, psychological reinforcement centers on the attitude towards the behavior and is based on intrinsic rewards (e.g., encouragement, compliments) and logic (e.g., the "whys" behind the behavior) rather than on economic rewards. A carrot (rather than a stick) approach should be the basis for the reinforcement process for this segment, since people here are already performing the desired behavior and have a positive attitude toward it.

When people possess a positive attitude toward a desirable social behavior but do not or cannot presently engage in the concomitant behavior (cell four), an *inducement process* needs to be facilitated. It refers to minimizing or removing organizational, socioeconomic, time, and place constraints that intervene between the positive attitude and the consequent behavior (Howard and Sheth 1969, Sheth 1974). Behavioral change is the primary objective, given that a positive attitude already exists in this segment and, as such, movement of people from cell four to cell one (Table 1) is desired.

The *rationalization process* is most appropriate when people are currently engaged in a desirable social behavior but have a negative attitude toward it (cell two). Often, this may be due to lack of choice or due to a temporary situation. In each case, the behavior may only be temporary and may not lead to subsequent attitude change. Thus the primary objective of this process is to generate attitude change that will be consistent with the behavior and, therefore, may be more difficult to alter when the temporary situation is removed. Movement of people to cell one by the process of attitude change is desirable.

Finally, when both attitude and behavior are consistent but in the negative direction toward a desirable social behavior (cell three), a *confrontation process* may be necessary (Bennis et al. 1976). This is the most painful and difficult process of planned social change. The change agent must, therefore, decide whether it is worth the effort to change the social behavior in light of negative public opinion as well as the apparent high costs associated with this strategy.

Behavioral confrontation requires the change agent to utilize his/her power base to create blockades toward the existing, undesirable behavior and alter peoples' motivations toward performing the desirable social behavior. Psychological confrontation involves a direct attack on the existing attitudes that individuals have toward the planned social change. In each case, a stick approach appears to be necessary. Movement of people directly to cell one may be too radical a change in some situations. If so, the change agent can utilize a two-stage process in which he/she first moves people from cell three to either cell two or four and then eventually to cell one in Table 1.

STRATEGIES OF PLANNED SOCIAL CHANGE

Thus far only the processes of planned social change and their basic objectives have been discussed. To implement these processes and attain their objectives, influence or communication strategies must be selected and utilized by the change agent. The most basic implication of the model is that the change agent must use different types of influence strategies and/or change the orientation (tactics) of specific strategies across the different attitude-behavior consistency/discrepancy groups. While a particular strategy and tactic may be effective in facilitating one

TABLE 2. Strategies of Planned Social Change

1. *Informing and Education* (Chin and Benne 1969, Zaltman, Kotler, and Kaufman 1972). Objective information is disseminated to the population with no conclusions drawn within the communication; left to the recipient to process the objective information and make conclusions on his/her own.
2. *Persuasion and Propaganda* (Boyk 1973, Lee 1975, Rogers 1972). Conclusion drawing and dramatic statements of benefits or ill effects of performing or avoiding a certain behavior are stressed; may involve a biased presentation of facts and figures in an aggressive manner to impact and change attitude.
3. *Social Controls* (Hornstein et al. 1971, Smith 1973). Refer to group identification and norms, values, and pressures that peer groups bring to bear for both ensuring and sustaining social change; involve subtle or direct pressure and even implied punishments for nonconformity.
4. *Delivery Systems* (Spreke 1971, Zaltman 1974). The emphasis is to minimize the accessibility problems associated with the usage of many public services. This entails offering flexible time schedules, more delivery contact points, and, in general, making the public feel welcomed in making use of the public services associated with a specific planned social change.
5. *Economic Incentives* (Pohlman 1971, Rogers 1972, Zaltman 1974). Include not only cost reduction tactics (e.g., tax credits for home insulation) but also cash or other tangible incentives (e.g., cash payments for a vasectomy).
6. *Economic Disincentives* (Rogers 1973, Zaltman 1974). Involve tangible punishments for performing a certain behavior (e.g., adding extra duties, tariffs, surcharges, and taxes to the cost of a product or service).
7. *Clinical Counseling and Behavior Modification* (Hornstein et al. 1971). Involve the unlearning of socially undesirable behavior or learning of a socially desirable behavior among a hard core of individuals in a society; the psychiatric and psychoanalytic programs tailored for each deviant individual as well as small group therapy programs are examples of this strategy.
8. *Mandatory Rules and Regulations* (Jones 1969, Niehoff 1966, Zaltman, Duncan, and Holbek 1973). Legal restrictions on behavior are by definition involuntary and universal in nature; punitive measures can be utilized given noncompliance.

TABLE 3. Appropriateness of the Strategies in Facilitating the Processes of Planned Social Change

Strategies	Reinforcement Behavioral	Reinforcement Psychological	Inducement Behavioral	Rationalization Psychological	Confrontation Behavioral	Confrontation Psychological
Informing and Educating	No	Yes	No	Maybe	No	No
Persuasion and Propaganda	No	Maybe	No	Yes	No	Yes
Social Controls	No	Maybe	Yes	Yes	Maybe	Yes
Delivery Systems	Maybe	No	Yes	No	No	No
Economic Incentives	Yes	No	Yes	No	No	No
Economic Disincentives	No	No	Yes	No	Yes	No
Clinical Counseling and Behavior Modification	No	No	No	No	Yes	No
Mandatory Rules	Yes	No	Maybe	No	Yes	No

process or objective, it may not work well in facilitating each process or objective.

Given this viewpoint, it is vital that available influence strategies are linked to the processes of planned social change to aid the change agent in their implementation (cf. Zaltman 1974). Table 2 briefly describes eight categories of influence strategies available for use by change agents. An attempt to link these strategies and the processes of planned social change is exhibited in Table 3. Here, an evaluation of each strategy is presented in terms of its apparent appropriateness in facilitating each social change process. Where a reasonably high level of confidence does not exist concerning whether a given strategy is appropriate or inappropriate in facilitating a given process, a "maybe" prediction is included in the table.

The predictions within Table 3 are based on the character of each strategy, the nature of each process, and the logic that either attitude change, behavior change, or both must be attained within a given process. For example, to promote psychological reinforcement, the informing and educating strategy appears most effective (cf. Zaltman and Duncan 1977). Objective information on the situation and the value and benefits of the relevant social behavior will tend to be processed (not selectively screened) by consumers in this group and serve to remind them, in a nonpressurized way, why their current attitudes and behavior are justified (Engel, Warshaw, and Kinnear 1979). A detailed description of the logic behind each of the predictions in Table 3 is beyond the scope of this paper. However, three additional points must be stressed at this time:

- Several strategies appear to be appropriate in more than one cell. However, the specific character and orientation of a strategy may change across conditions. For example, use of persuasion and propaganda in the rationalization process might include information packaged in a biased way in favor of the desired behavior. Often this entails partial disclosure of facts, exaggeration of positive aspects in the given social behavior, and minimization of negative consequences. On the other hand, use of this strategy in the confrontation process appears to require a more direct, pressurized approach centering on fear appeals. Similar examples can be made for variations in social controls and mandatory rules across the processes.
- The stick approach recommended in the confrontation process is very risky. When people have negative attitudes and are not performing the behavior, pressurized measures may merely serve to alienate them. Defense mechanisms may arise, causing such an approach to fail (cf. Argyris 1970). However, use of other strategies or a more indirect approach appear even less effective here.
- The emphasis of certain strategies on either behavior or attitudes in the reinforcement and confrontation processes, from the viewpoint of the change agent, is to aid them in formulating specific social change plans for facilitating each process. Certainly, feedback effects from attitudes to behavior and from behavior to attitudes may result. For example, providing economic incentives to people as rewards in the behavioral reinforcement process directly centers on behavior. Subsequently, because more positive connotations surround the performance of the behavior, individuals' attitudes toward the behavior may become more positive.

The predictions within Table 3 must be considered tentative at this time. However, they should provide change agents with a greater understanding of the processes of planned social change and guidance in normatively evaluating the costs and benefits of the strategies identified in Table 2 and their applicability under varying attitude-behavior conditions.

ESTIMATING WHICH PROCESSES SHOULD BE FACILITATED

How to allocate resources among the alternative processes of planned social change and whether or not a single process will be sufficient or not depends, in large part, on the distribution of the general population in the four cells of the attitude behavior consistency/

discrepancy matrix. The larger the percentage of people exhibiting attitude-behavior consistency, the greater the need to implement reinforcement and confrontation processes (cells one and three in Table 1). On the other hand, the larger the percentage of people who exhibit attitude-behavior discrepancy (the lower the aggregate positive correlation between attitudes and behavior), the greater the need to implement inducement and rationalization processes (cells two and four in Table 1). The more heterogeneous the cultural and economic backgrounds of people in a society, the less likely it is that all of them will be concentrated in any one cell (cf. Okediji 1972). Therefore, in highly diverse and complex societies it appears necessary to utilize a mix of processes and strategies for an optimal achievement of planned social change.

Knowledge of the population distribution is necessary but not sufficient for determining which social change processes should be implemented. As suggested previously, there will likely be differential (1) coefficients of effectiveness, depending on the percentage of a target group that a strategy moves in the desired direction, (2) constraints, and (3) costs associated with facilitating each process through use of an influence strategy or a combination of strategies. Such considerations must be taken into account by the change agent along with information about the population distribution.

Two methods of estimating the population distribution within the attitude-behavior consistency/discrepancy matrix are now described.

A Simple Estimation Method

The simple method rests on the proposition that attitude is a unidimensional phenomenon and can be reliably measured in terms of like-dislike, enjoy-hate, good-bad, favorable-unfavorable, and other semantic differential rating scales (Fishbein 1967, Howard and Sheth 1969, Triandis 1971). Through distribution analysis, the sample can be divided into positive and negative attitude groups engaged or disengaged in that social behavior. This is a simple procedure but can be very useful as a first cut to understand whether there is a lopsided distribution in favor of a particular cell in the strategy mix matrix.

A More Complex Estimation Method

A more complex approach is to measure a person's evaluative beliefs (Sheth 1974) that underlie his/her attitudes toward a social behavior. It is a two-stage process. In the first stage, the cognitive structure underlying the attitudinal judgment is assessed by qualitative research on small groups of people who are engaged *and* disengaged in the behavior or by assessment of prior research findings. In the second stage, a multi-attribute profile of evaluative beliefs is generated from a large sample study to measure the composition of people's attitudes toward the specified behavior.

Given a multiattribute vector of attitudinal beliefs, it is now possible to perform a two-group discriminant analysis between those who are engaged and those who are disengaged in a given social behavior. The multiattribute attitudinal profile represents the predictor set of variables, and the dichotomous behavioral manifestation represents the criterion variable in the two-group discriminant analysis.

Since the objective in discriminant analysis is to maximize the correlation between group membership and the predictor variable profile, it is possible to measure the degree and direction of consistency or discrepancy between attitudes and behavior by the use of the classification procedures in the discriminant analysis. In other words, the proportion of people whose attitudes and behavior are consistent as well as those whose attitudes and behavior are inconsistent or discrepant in each direction can be estimated. For example, some people in the sample may have a negative attitude profile even though they are engaged in a given behavior. The discriminant analysis model will clearly classify them as people who should not be engaged in that behavior. Similarly, there may be other people whose attitude profile is positive, but they are not engaged in that behavior. The discriminant analysis model will classify them as people who should be engaged in that behavior even though they are not. In short, the correct classifications in the discriminant analysis reflect the attitude-behavior consistency and the misclassifications reflect the attitude-behavior discrepancy (Wind 1977).

CAR POOLING EXAMPLE

An operationalization of the simple and complex approaches just described is illustrated by a research study of van pooling or car pooling behavior (Sheth and Horowitz 1977). Despite powerful personal and societal advantages, car pooling has received very low acceptance in the U.S. It is estimated that less than 10% of commuters use car pooling as a mode of travel to work (Herman and Lam 1975, Zwanzig 1977). As such, it provides a useful scenario for estimating which processes of planned social change should be considered to promote this behavior better.

Collection of Data

A survey was conducted among residents of the Chicago metropolitan area contacted through their employers. Personnel departments of 43 firms, chosen randomly from a large list of companies employing at least 100 people, were first contacted and asked to contact roughly equal numbers of car poolers, solo drivers, and public transit users to answer a self-administered mail back questionnaire, which was hand delivered.

TABLE 4. Population Distribution on Overall Attitude Scale Toward Car Pooling

		Car Pooling Attitude		
		Positive	Negative	Behavior Totals
Behavior	Car Poolers	257 (73%)	66 (19%)	323
	Solo Drivers	97 (27%)	285 (81%)	382
	Attitude Totals	354	351	705

Of 2,000 questionnaires distributed, 1020 were returned. After eliminating those with relevant missing data, 822 questionnaires remained for analysis: 323 car poolers, 382 solo drivers, and 117 public transit users.

Because almost all car poolers in our sample owned at least one automobile while 75% of transit users did not, it was assumed that automobile ownership is a necessary condition for sharing a ride to work. For this reason, only data relating to car poolers and solo drivers were analyzed for this study.

Data and Analysis

The respondents indicated the degree to which they liked or disliked the idea of being a member of a car pool on a seven-point scale ranging from extreme like to extreme dislike. This item was used to represent their overall attitude toward car pooling. Table 4 presents the cross-tabulation of respondents with positive or negative attitudes toward car pooling and their actual commuting behavior. It represents the simple estimation method discussed earlier. As evident, the table reflects a reasonably high attitude-behavior consistency. Still, of those people with a positive attitude, 27% were solo drivers and of those with negative attitudes toward car pooling, 19% actually were car pooling, which suggests that there may be significant market niches where policy planners can utilize inducement and/or rationalization processes.

Figure 1 shows the specific evaluative beliefs utilized in operationalizing the complex method. They were developed based on past literature, in-depth interviews with a small group of car poolers, and our own thinking. It also shows the profiles of car poolers and solo drivers with respect to their attitudes toward car pooling. As can be seen from the profile, the attitudes toward car pooling between solo drivers and car

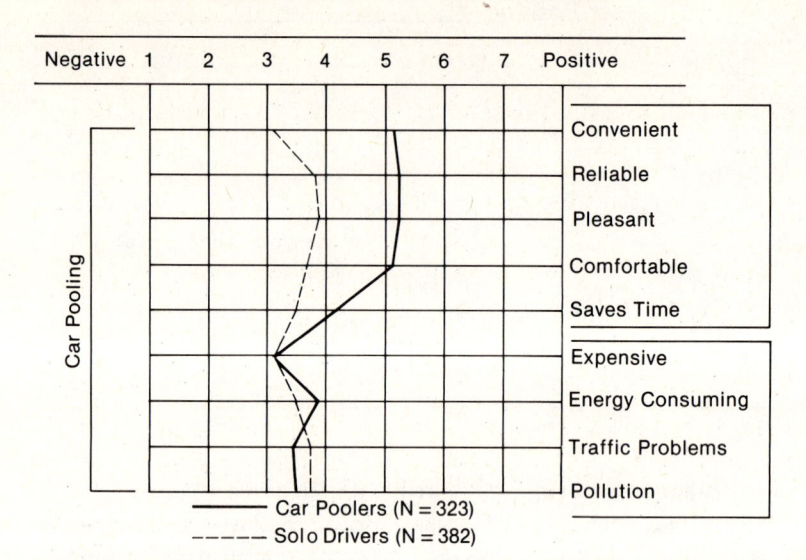

FIGURE 1. Evaluation of Car Pooling Profile

```
                Negative  1   2   3   4   5   6   7   Positive
                                              Convenient
                                              Reliable
                                              Pleasant
                                              Comfortable
   Car Pooling                                Saves Time
                                              Expensive
                                              Energy Consuming
                                              Traffic Problems
                                              Pollution
                ——— Car Poolers (N = 323)
                ----- Solo Drivers (N = 382)
```

poolers are similar with respect to expense, energy, traffic, and pollution problems. On the other hand, car poolers are far more positive than solo drivers toward car pooling with respect to convenience, reliability, comfort, pleasantness, and time saving. In other words, there are significant differences on personal experience attributes but virtually no differences on social and economic consequences of car pooling behavior between the two groups.

As suggested by the theory and its operationalization, a two-group discriminant analysis was performed utilizing the above evaluative beliefs as the predictor variables of car pooling behavior. The discriminant analysis results are summarized in Table 5a.[4] As would be expected, those beliefs on which there were significant differences between car poolers and solo drivers (convenient, reliable, pleasant, saves time) were retained in the discriminant function, and others were discarded as not relevant since they did not contribute toward maximizing the correlation between behavior and attitudes of two groups of commuters.

The classification matrix that results from the discriminant analysis is shown in Table 5b. First of all, notice that the population distribution in Table 5b is highly similar to the distribution in Table 4 that resulted from the simple method. This provides a predictive validity check on each of the methods. However, the multiattribute profile and the discriminant function go one step beyond and enable the policy planner not only to estimate the relative sizes of each segment but what specific beliefs to use in carrying out various processes such as inducement, reinforcement, confrontation, and rationalization processes.[5]

As can be seen from Table 5b, the vast majority of people with positive attitudes toward car pooling (70%) do actually engage in it. Similarly, a vast majority of people with negative attitudes toward car pooling actually engage in solo driving (77%). This suggests that primary approaches for increasing car pooling behavior should be a combination of the reinforcement and confrontation processes. Since our data with respect to car poolers versus solo drivers are not proportional to the population ratios, it will be necessary to estimate the population proportions of car poolers statistically. Since car pooling is practiced by less than 10% of the population, the dominant approach for increasing car pooling behavior appears to be the confrontation process.

However, as stated previously, the confrontation process is both very difficult and painful to implement since it requires fundamental changes in both the values and habits of people and may be accompanied by political risks and negative public opinion. As an alternative, perhaps the policy planner should lower his/her aspirations and attempt to make

TABLE 5.

a. Discriminant Analysis Between Solo Drivers and Car Poolers— Attitude Toward Car Pooling

i	Variable	F Value	d.f.	SOLO a_i	CP a_i
1	Convenient	197.6**	1;703	0.12	0.52
2	Reliable	38.9**	1;702	0.33	0.68
3	Pleasant	10.8**	1;701	0.43	0.64
4	Saves Time	4.1*	1;700	−0.11	−0.04
0	(Constant)	—	—	−13.60	−17.50
	F between groups	66.6**	4;700	—	—

b. Classification Matrix Results

		Car Pooling Attitude Positive	Car Pooling Attitude Negative	Behavior Totals
Behavior	Car Poolers	239 (70%)	84 (23%)	323
	Solo Drivers	102 (30%)	280 (77%)	382
	Attitude Totals	341	364	705

*: $p \leq 0.05$
**: $p \leq 0.001$

modest improvements in car pooling behavior by concentrating on those people with positive attitudes who do not presently car pool (30% of all those with positive attitudes), as well as on those who do car pool at present but have negative attitudes toward it (23%). The former group would require an emphasis on the inducement process involving such strategies as a change in work schedules, providing a vehicle exclusively for car pooling purposes, and facilitating the matching process of car poolers to minimize time and distance inconveniences. The latter group would require implementation of the rationalization process including the use of persuasive strategies involving propaganda leaflets, appeals to national pride, mass media campaigns to "hang in there," and special interpersonal support through pep talks and workshops.

If we presume that 75% of all commuters are solo drivers (the balance divided between car pooling and mass transit), then nearly 55% of all commuters would need more drastic measures underlying the confrontation process to motivate them to change to car pooling behavior. An additional 20% will need strategies involved with the inducement process, and the remaining 25% of all commuters will require a combination of strategies dealing with the reinforcement and rationalization processes. Looking at this from a different perspective, it suggests that with the adoption of strategies that foster the rationalization and inducement processes, the policy maker should be able to increase car pooling behavior to a level where combined with mass transit, it will have market share of approximately 45% of all commuters. In other words, solo driving and other modes of commuting to work can be brought to a more or less parity level without the utilization of more painful and politically risky strategies associated with the confrontation process. Furthermore, based on increased acceptability of car pooling, it may generate sufficiently strong pressures on the current solo drivers to encourage them to switch to car pooling, resulting in a snowball effect as suggested in diffusion research.

Discussion

Both the simple approach and the technique of discriminant analysis suggest something about the magnitude of attitude-behavior consistency/discrepancy and the consequent managerial decision as to which processes of planned social change should be facilitated. They involve a microlevel analysis which enables the change agent to identify people in each cell and target a specific mix of strategies to each of the four segments.

The primary use of discriminant analysis in the paper is to develop a predictive model to classify individuals as either car poolers or solo drivers. However, the multiattribute attitude profile also provides clues about the substantive elements to be included in each of the selected strategies. Let us illustrate this with an example. Suppose we find a group of people who engage in birth control and those who do not. We measure their attitudes on a multiattribute profile consisting of cost, convenience, accessibility, social taboo, and fear of side effects. Based on the two-group discriminant analysis, we find that the most significant discriminating attributes are fear of side effects and cost. We also find that there is a group of people who have fear of side effects and cost problems even though they are engaged in birth control. Implementation of the rationalization process might consist of a campaign stressing safety as well as lowering the cost of birth control targeted to this segment of the population.

On the other hand, there is another group of people who have a positive attitude with respect to side effects and cost of birth control, but they are not engaged in birth control practices. They need to be induced to manifest their positive attitudes into actual behavior. This can be achieved by strategies such as more efficient delivery systems (birth control devices practically available everywhere) as well as strong encouragement from social or organizational structures similar to the current physical fitness programs.

Finally, to reach those who do not practice birth control and have a fear of side effects as well as high cost perception, implementation of the confrontation process may be required. Clinical counseling, establishing mandatory product safety guidelines for the suppliers of birth control devices, and generating economic disincentives toward nonpractice of birth control are strategies that could be utilized.

It is relatively easy to identify the four segments of the total population on their socioeconomic and demographic profiles. In addition, it may be useful to collect data on their daily activities and interests (lifestyles) to pinpoint the role a particular social behavior plays in their daily life.

The change agent would now have sufficient information about the target segments to plan the process and strategy mix with respect to both resource allocation and substantive content for each strategy. He/she can now decide which processes and strategies to use based on the population distribution in the attitude-behavior consistency/discrepancy matrix and the normative evaluation of each strategy, what specific attributes should be emphasized in his/her strategy based on the discriminant coefficients of the attitude profile, whom to target a specific strategy mix element based on the demographic profile of each of the segments, and how to implement or communicate to each identified and targeted segment based on the lifestyle and value profile of each of the segments in the population.

AN EXTENDED MODEL

There are at least two improvements that can be made to the model presented herein. The first improvement relates to extending the model to a situation where people are distributed as positive, negative, or neutral in their attitudes. There are several examples in the area of planned social change where apathy is dominant and, therefore, people really don't care or they are truly indifferent toward alternative courses of behavior. For example, a large percentage of people are not concerned about nutrition in their diet. Secondly, the social behavior in question may not be a dichotomous phenomenon but a continuous phenomenon such as heavy versus light usage. For example, we may want to reduce the per capita consumption of cigarettes among smokers as well as encourage people to quit smoking. The challenge in developing such an extended model would be to determine which process or combination of processes would be most appropriate for each cell.

An extended attitude-behavior consistency/discrepancy model is presented in Table 6 with underlying processes of planned social change and examples of specific strategies that can be used to implement them identified in each cell. Two important differences concerning processes of planned social change are evident in this model in comparison with the simpler model presented in Table 1. First, for the rationalization, inducement, and confrontation processes, a distinction is made between moderate and radical processes; that is, in a given cell a change agent may face moderate difficulty in successfully implementing a certain process, while in another cell stiffer resistance may be encountered. For example, for a segment of people who have negative attitudes toward the use of contraceptives and currently don't use them, a radical confrontation process may need to be implemented with rather direct influence strategies such as mandatory rules. A moderate confrontation process appears appropriate in situations where a negative attitude toward use of contraceptives exists but where people use them on an infrequent basis. Less drastic strategies such as those dealing with economic disincentives may be more appropriate here.

Secondly, attitude enhancement and behavioral enhancement processes are identified in Table 6. Their implementation involves a less drastic approach in comparison with the implementation of the radical rationalization and moderate inducement processes. Thus important distinctions in degree of directness and difficulty of implementing a process in achieving desired objectives are made within the extended model which change agents must carefully consider and evaluate in attempts to motivate planned social change.

Operationalization of the extended model is straightforward if the simple method of measuring unidimensional attitudes is utilized. It will require generating a 3×3 matrix based on positive, neutral, or negative unidimensional attitudes and nonusers, light users, or heavy users of a particular social phenomenon. However, when we have multiattribute beliefs, it will be necessary to perform a three-group discriminant analysis. While the analysis is more complex in this case, the output in terms of the classification matrix is the same. The interpretation of multiple discriminant functions and individual variables is more complex but certainly manageable. A given belief is likely to be associated with a given discriminant function, especially after rotation. The sign of its weight will indicate how a change in that belief will change group membership as affected by the first discriminant axis. If a given belief is significantly loaded on two discriminant axes with opposite signs, this would mean that it will have opposite or differential impacts in various segments and, therefore, proper care must be undertaken in choosing and implementing specific strategies that will maintain "walls" around each group. In other words, a rifle versus shotgun approach will be needed.

A limitation of the extended model is that it is restricted to a binary choice of engaging or not engaging in social behavior. However, often the choice is not dichotomous but multichotomous in nature. For example, the choices of transportation modes for commuting purposes consist of driving, car pooling, trains, or the bus transit system in any metropolitan area. In other words, the change agent must pinpoint what the alternative options are and estimate the degree of cross-elasticity of a given

TABLE 6. An Extended Model of Strategy Mix Choices for Planned Social Change

		Attitude		
		Positive	Neutral	Negative
Relevant Behavior	Regular Users	Reinforcement Process (information)	Attitude Enhancement Process (education)	Radical Rationalization Process (persuasion and propaganda)
	Infrequent Users	Behavioral Enhancement Process (social controls)	Moderate Rationalization Process (social controls)	Moderate Confrontation Process (economic disincentives)
	Nonusers	Moderate Inducement Process (delivery systems)	Radical Inducement Process (economic incentives)	Radical Confrontation Process (mandatory rules, clinical counseling, and behavior modification)

planned social change with respect to the competing alternatives. Thus, if one wants to increase car pooling behavior, one must understand whether the change will come from people who now drive or from people who now take the train or bus. This is an important policy issue that needs to be addressed in future research.

One solution is to measure people's multiattribute attitude profiles toward the planned social behavior but sample them from each of the competing behavior domains. For example, we can ask people to express their attitudes toward car pooling although at present they are driving, taking the train, riding the bus, car pooling, or bicycling to work. It is now possible to extend the model by utilizing multiple group discriminant analysis. The classification table would be extended to all alternative options besides car pooling. An analysis of the classification matrix will then reveal those segments of the total population that are likely to be attracted toward car pooling behavior from each of the substitute modes of commuting.

SUMMARY

This article has attempted to offer a conceptual model of strategy mix choice for planned social change. The fundamental axiom on which the framework is developed is the attitude-behavior consistency/discrepancy with respect to a given social behavior. The model suggests that the change agent must not think in terms of a universal strategy approach but seriously consider segmenting the total population and utilize a mix of influence strategies on a selective basis from among those that facilitate reinforcement, inducement, rationalization, and confrontation processes.

It is evident that considerable work remains in investigating processes of planned social change and evaluating influence strategies that may be used in implementing these processes. This paper lays a basic foundation upon which others must build and provides change agents and researchers with insights into where future planning and research must proceed in analyzing the nature and effectiveness of planned social change.

ENDNOTES

1. The social change process is also important within and between formal organizations, but such an emphasis is beyond the scope of this paper. Andreasen (1981) considers this topic as he discusses varying strategies that social marketers can use in attempting to gain influence on the behavior of other organizations.

2. See Zaltman and Duncan (1977) for reasons why a conflict between attitudes and behaviors might exist.
3. Of course this situation can be considerably more complex if a husband and wife within one family unit lack congruence or agreement in their attitudes and behavior concerning birth control.
4. In view of the fact that the variance-covariance matrices for the solo drivers and car poolers were not equal ($\Sigma_1 \neq \Sigma_2$) in our sample, it was necessary to utilize the likelihood ratio criterion C (see Anderson 1958, p. 141–42) rather than the traditional discriminant function criterion to allow for the effects of unequal variance-covariances of the predictor variables between the two groups. This requires calculating separate linear combinations of each group (solo drivers and car poolers), utilizing each group's mean vector as deviation from the total sample, and dividing by its unique variance-covariance matrix estimated by the sample.
5. Multicolinearity among the variables did not appear to present serious problems. While multicolinearity could bias the impact that individual variables have on the discriminant function, given that the primary objective of this analysis is prediction (i.e., to attain a classification matrix of the sample), this would not present a serious problem in this study.

REFERENCES

Anderson, T. W. (1958), *An Introduction to Multivariate Statistical Analysis*, New York: Wiley.

Andreasen, Alan (1981), "Power Potential Channel Strategies in Social Marketing," working paper #743, Bureau of Economic and Business Research, University of Illinois.

Arensberg, Conrad M. and Arthur H. Niehoff (1971), *Introducing Social Change: A Manual for Community Development*, 2nd edition, Chicago: Aldine-Atherton.

Argyris, Chris (1970), *Intervention Theory and Method*, Reading, MA: Addison-Wesley.

Bass, Frank M. (1969), "A New Product Growth Model for Consumer Durables," *Management Science*, 15 (January), 215–17.

Belk, Russell (1981), "Theoretical Issues in the Intention-Behavior Discrepancy," paper presented at the American Psychological Association Convention (Division 23), Los Angeles.

Bennis, Warren (1966), *Changing Organization*, New York: McGraw-Hill.

———, Kenneth D. Benne, Robert Chin, and Kenneth E. Corey (1976), *The Planning of Change*, 3rd edition, New York: Holt, Rinehart, and Winston.

Boyk, J. (1973), "Research Report: Learning Performance in the Defensive Drive Course (DDC) and the DDC Self-Instruction Program," Washington, DC: National Safety Council Research Department, November.

Chin, Robert and Kenneth D. Benne (1969), "General Strategies for Effecting Changes in Human Systems," in *The Planning of Change*, W. G. Bennis, Kenneth D. Benne, and Robert Chin, eds., New York: Holt.

Deshpande, Rohit and S. Krishnan (1981), "A Consumer Based Approach for Establishing Priorities in Consumer Information Programs: Implications for Public Policy," in *Advances in Consumer Research*, Vol. VIII, K. B. Monroe, ed., 338–43.

Engel, James, Martin Warshaw, and Thomas Kinnear (1979), *Promotional Strategy*, Homewood, IL: Richard D. Irwin, Inc.

Fishbein, Martin, ed. (1967), *Readings in Attitude Theory and Measurement*, New York: John Wiley & Sons.

Fox, Karen and Philip Kotler (1980), "The Marketing of Social Causes; The First Ten Years," *Journal of Marketing*, 44 (Fall), 24–33.

Herman, R. and T. Lam (1975), "Carpools at Large Suburban Technical Center," *Transportation Engineering Journal*, 101 (May), 311–19.

Hornstein, Harvey A. et al. (1971), *Social Intervention: A Behavioral Approach*, New York: Free Press.

Howard, J. A. and J. N. Sheth (1969), *The Theory of Buyer Behavior*, New York: John Wiley & Sons.

Jones, Garth N. (1969), *Planned Organizational Change*, New York: Praeger.

Lee, Kam Han (1975), "Social Marketing Strategies and Nutrition Education," unpublished Ph.D. dissertation, Northwestern University.

Lippitt, R., Jeanne Watson, and Bruce Westley (1968), *The Dynamics of Planned Change*, New York: Harcourt.

Mansfield, Edwin (1961), "Technical Change and the Rate of Imitation," *Econometrica*, 29 (October), 741–66.

McGuire, William (1978), "Psychological Factors Influencing Consumer Choice," in *Selected Aspects of Consumer Behavior*, Robert Ferber, ed., Washington, DC: National Science Foundation.

Niehoff, Arthur (1966), *A Casebook of Social Change*, Chicago: Aldine-Atherton.

Nord, Walter and J. Paul Peter (1980), "A Behavior Modification Perspective on Marketing," *Journal of Marketing*, 44 (Spring), 36–47.

Okediji, Francis O. (1972), "Overcoming Social and Cultural Resistances," *International Journal of Health Education*, 15 (July–September), 3–10.

Pohlman, Edward (1971), "Incentives and Compensations in Birth Planning," Monograph 2, Durham: University of North Carolina, Carolina Population Center.

Rogers, E. M. (1972), "Field Experiments in Family Planning Incentives," Lansing: Michigan State University, Department of Communications.

——— (1973), "Effects of Incentives on the Diffusion of Innovations: The Case of Family Planning in Asia," in *Processes and Phenomena of Social Change*, Gerald Zaltman, ed., New York: Wiley Interscience.

——— and F. F. Shoemaker (1971), *The Communication of Innovations*, New York: Free Press.

Sheth, Jagdish N. (1974), "A Field Study of Attitude Structure and Attitude-Behavior Relationship," in *Models of Buyer Behavior*, J. N. Sheth, ed., New York: Harper and Row, 242–68.

——— and A. D. Horowitz (1977), "Strategies of Increasing Car Pooling Behavior Among Urban Commuters," in *Social Research*, Amsterdam: ESOMAR, 183–98.

——— and Bruce Newman (1981), "Determinants of Intention-Behavior Discrepancy in the 1980 National Elections," paper presented at the American Psychological Association Convention (Division 23), Los Angeles.

——— and John Wong (1981), "Impact of Unexpected Events on Intention-Behavior Consistency: An Experimental Study," faculty working paper, Bureau of Economic and Business Research, University of Illinois.

Skinner, B. F. (1953), *Science and Human Behavior*, New York: Macmillan.

Smith, Anthony D. (1973), *The Concept of Social Change*, London: Routledge and Kegan Paul.

Spreke, J. T. (1971), "Incentives in Family Planning Programs: Time for a New Look," working paper, U.S. Agency for International Development, Office of Population.

Triandis, Harry C. (1971), *Attitude and Attitude Change*, New York: John Wiley & Sons.

Wind, Yoram (1977), "Brand Loyalty and Vulnerability," in *Consumer and Industrial Buying Behavior*, Arch Woodside, Jagdish N. Sheth, and Peter Bennett, eds., New York: North Holland.

Zaltman, Gerald (1974), "Strategies for Diffusing Innovations," in *Marketing Analysis for Societal Problems*, Jagdish N. Sheth and Peter Wright, eds., Urbana: University of Illinois Press.

——— and Robert Duncan (1977), *Strategies for Planned Social Change*, New York: Wiley-Interscience.

———, ———, and Jonny Holbek (1973), *Innovations and Organizations*, New York: Wiley-Interscience.

——— Philip Kotler, and Ira Kaufman, eds. (1972), *Creating Social Change*, New York: Holt.

——— and Ronald Stiff (1973), "Theories of Diffusion," in *Consumer Behavior: Theoretical Sources*, S. Ward and T. Robertson, eds., Englewood Cliffs, NJ: Prentice-Hall.

Zwanzig, Francis R., ed. (1977), *Forecasting Passenger and Freight Travel*, (Transportation Research Record 637), Washington, DC: Transportation Research Board.

43 Strategies for Introducing Marketing into Nonprofit Organizations

Philip Kotler

Reprinted from the *Journal of Marketing*, published by the American Marketing Association, Vol. 43 (January 1979), pp. 37–44. Reprinted by permission.

In most societies of the world, economic activity is a function of the actions and interactions of a profit sector and a governmental sector. The American economy, however, contains an important third sector made up of tens of thousands of private, not-for-profit organizations ranging from The Society for the Preservation and Encouragement of Barber Shop Quartet Singing in America to major foundations, colleges, hospitals, museums, charities, social agencies, and churches.

This strong third sector constitutes a *middle way* for meeting social needs, without resorting to the profit motive on the one hand or government bureaucracy on the other. Third sector organizations tend to be socially responsive and service-oriented. They specialize in the delivery of social services that are not adequately provided by either business or government.

While Big Business is healthy and Big Government continues to grow, the third sector, unfortunately, is in trouble. Third sector organizations depend upon the support of private citizens and upon grants from the other two sectors. Many colleges, hospitals, churches, social agencies, performance groups, and museums are increasingly feeling the pinch of rising costs and stable or declining revenues. Consider the following:

- More than 170 private colleges have closed their doors since 1965, unable to get either enough students or funds or both. Tuition at Stanford and Yale is now over $6,000; if college costs continue to climb at the current rate, the parents of a child born today will have to put aside $82,830 to buy that child a bachelor's degree at one of the better private colleges (Pyke 1977).
- Hospital costs continue to soar, leading to daily room rates of $300 or more in some large hospitals; many hospitals are experiencing underutilization, particularly in the maternity and pediatrics sections. Some experts have predicted the closing of 1,400–1,500 hospitals in the next 10 years.
- The Catholic Church drew as many as 55% of all adult Catholics under 30 years of age to church in a typical week in 1966. By 1975

the figure had fallen to 39% and further declines in weekly attendance were expected.
- Many performance groups cannot attract large enough audiences. Even those which have seasonal sellouts, such as the Lyric Opera Company of Chicago, face huge operating deficits at the end of the year.
- Many third sector organizations that flourished in earlier years — the YMCA, Salvation Army, Girl Scouts, and Women's Christian Temperance Union — presently are reexamining their mission in an effort to reverse membership declines.

In a word, these third sector organizations have marketplace problems. Their administrators are struggling to keep them alive in the face of rapidly changing societal needs, increasing public and private competition, changing client attitudes, and diminishing financial resources. Board members and supporters are asking administrators tough questions about the organization's mission, opportunities, and strategies. Unfortunately, many administrators are mere "Monday-morning quarterbacks" when it comes to strategic planning. At a time when these organizations face uncertain prospects, the lack of management depth poses a serious threat to survival.

Let us examine a major requirement for such survival: third sector administrators must begin to think like marketers. Ten years ago, Sidney J. Levy and I advanced the thesis that marketing is not just a business function — it is a valid function for nonbusiness organizations as well — and that all organizations have marketing problems and all need to understand marketing (Kotler and Levy 1969). The article created considerable controversy. Many academic marketers attacked it, saying that marketing made sense only in profit-oriented enterprises. However other marketing professors found the idea stimulating and, without necessarily agreeing that it was valid, began to study and experiment with it. Initial interest was confined to academia. The issue was of little concern to businessmen, and was largely ignored by administrators of nonprofit institutions.

More articles followed in the 1970s, reporting applications of marketing technology to such areas as college recruiting, fund raising, membership development, population problems, public transportation, health services, religion, and arts organizations.[1] Benson Shapiro's article in the September-October 1973 issue of the *Harvard Business Review* elicited many favorable comments, published in the following issue of *HBR*. The only textbook on the subject, *Marketing for Nonprofit Organizations*, appeared in 1975 and has enjoyed a growing readership (Kotler 1975). Recently Gaedeke (1977) published a book of readings, Lovelock and Weinberg (1977) a book of cases, Lovelock (1977) a bibliography of over 100 cases, and Nickels (1978) a general marketing textbook giving equal attention to business and nonbusiness marketing. It appears that marketing for nonprofit organizations is an idea whose time has come.

How have administrators of nonprofit organizations responded? Are they interested or aware? Enthusiastic? Do they know how to use marketing? Is it making a difference anywhere? On this tenth anniversary of the idea's launching, we are in a position to supply some answers.

ENTER MARKETING

Of all the classic business functions, marketing has been the last to arrive on the nonprofit scene. Some years earlier, nonprofit managers began to get interested in accounting systems, financial management, personnel administration, and formal planning. Marketing lagged, except where the nonprofit institution experienced a decline in clients, members, or funds. As long as institutions operated in a sellers' market—as colleges and hospitals did throughout the 1960s—marketing was ignored, but as customers and/or resources grew scarce the word "marketing" was heard with increasing frequency, and organizations suddenly discovered marketing or reasonable facsimiles thereof.

Colleges

Colleges provide a good example of this development. By the mid-1970s, they were reading this grim scenario: (1) the annual number of high school graduates would decline from a peak of 3.2 million in 1977 to 2.8 million in 1982–83; (2) the proportion of high school students electing to go to college might decline; (3) a higher proportion of the college-bound students would elect to attend community colleges instead of four-year colleges; and (4) the absolute and relative future level of tuition would deter college-going in general and hurt private colleges in particular.[2]

What are college administrators doing about this? One group is doing nothing. Either enrollment hasn't slipped, or if it has, the administrators believe the decline is temporary. Many believe it is "unprofessional" to go out and "sell" their colleges.

A second group has responded with "marketing," which in too many cases means aggressive promotion unaccompanied by any real improvements in competitive positioning, teaching quality, or student services. For example:

- The admissions office at North Kentucky State University planned to release 103 balloons filled with scholarship offers.
- The admissions staff of one college passed out promotional frisbees to high school students vacationing on the beaches of Fort Lauderdale, Florida during the annual Easter break.

- St. Joseph's College in Rensselaer, Indiana achieved a 40% increase in freshmen admissions through advertising in *Seventeen* and on several Chicago and Indianapolis rock radio stations. The admissions office also planned to introduce tuition rebates for students who recruited new students ($100 finders fee), but this was cancelled.
- Bard College developed a same-day admission system for students who walk into their office and qualify.
- Worcester Polytechnic Institute offers negotiable admission in which credit is negotiated for previous study or work experience to shorten the degree period.
- The University of Richmond has spent $13,000 to create a 12-minute film for showings to high school students and other interested publics.
- Drake University advertised on a billboard near Chicago's O'Hare Airport that "Drake is only 40 minutes from Chicago" (if one flies).
- Duke University paid for a supplement in *The New York Times* to tell its story.

Promotional competition has not yet led to premiums given to students for enrollment (free radio, typewriter) or offers of "satisfaction guaranteed or your money back," but these may come.

In equating marketing with intensified promotion, there are several dangers. Aggressive promotion tends to produce strong negative reactions among the school's constituencies, especially the faculty, who regard hard selling as offensive. Also, such promotion may turn off as many prospective students and families as it turns on. Aggressive promotion can attract the wrong students to the college—students who drop out when they discover they don't have the qualifications to do the work or that the college is not what it was advertised to be. Finally, this kind of marketing creates the illusion that the college has undertaken sufficient response to declining enrollment—an illusion which slows down the needed work on product improvement—the basis of all good marketing.

Promotion alone doesn't always work. Briarcliff College, a long-established women's college, faced an enrollment drop from 688 in 1969 to 280 in 1973. The college president scrambled to find ways to "sell" Briarcliff to prospects, including advertising and more high school visits. He personally went on the road to talk up Briarcliff, managing to raise enrollment to 350. But his effort was too little and too late. Briarcliff's finances continued to deteriorate and the college finally closed its doors in 1977.[3]

A genuine marketing response has been undertaken by a relatively small number of colleges. Their approach is best described as *market-*

EXHIBIT 1. Issues in Market-Oriented Institutional Planning Facing Colleges and Universities

MARKET ANALYSIS

1. What important trends are affecting higher education? (Environmental analysis)
2. What is our primary market? (Market definition)
3. What are the major market segments in this market? (Market segmentation)
4. What are the needs of each market segment? (Need assessment)
5. How much awareness, knowledge, interest, and desire is there in each market segment concerning our college? (Market awareness and attitude)
6. How do key publics see us and our competitors? (Image analysis)
7. How do potential students learn about our college and make decisions to apply and enroll? (Consumer behavior)
8. How satisfied are current students? (Consumer satisfaction assessment)

RESOURCE ANALYSIS

1. What are our major strengths and weaknesses in faculty, programs, facilities, etc.? (Strengths/weaknesses analysis)
2. What opportunities are there to expand our financial resources? (Donor opportunity analysis)

MISSION ANALYSIS

1. What business are we in? (Business mission)
2. Who are our customers? (Customer definition)
3. Which needs are we trying to satisfy? (Needs targeting)
4. On which market segments do we want to focus? (Market targeting)
5. Who are our major competitors? (Competitor identification)
6. What competitive benefits do we want to offer to our target market? (Market positioning)

---

oriented institutional planning. In this approach, marketing is recognized as much more than mere promotion, and indeed, the issue of promotion cannot be settled in principle until more fundamental issues are resolved. These issues are shown in Exhibit 1. By doing its homework on market, resource, and missions analysis, a college is in a better position to make decisions that improve student and faculty recruitment and institutional fundraising.

As an example, the University of Houston recently completed an intensive institutional audit using several faculty task forces. The final report presented recommendations on the university's mission, strategy, and portfolio. The portfolio section recommended which components of the university's "product mix" (schools and departments) should be built, maintained, phased down, or phased out. The criteria included: (1) the centrality of that academic program to the mission of the university, (2) the program's academic quality, and (3) the program's marketing viability. Thus, a department of women's studies that is marginal to the mission of the school, of low national reputation, and unable to attract an adequate number of students, would be slated for phasing down or out. A few other schools such as New York University, Northwestern University, and Kent State University are taking marketing initiatives to bring strategic planning and marketing into their operating frameworks.

Hospitals

Hospitals are beginning to treat marketing as a "hot" topic. A few years ago, health professionals scorned the idea of marketing, imagining that it would lead to ads such as "This week's special—brain surgery, only $195." Hospital administrators also argued that patients didn't choose hospitals, their doctors did; so marketing, to be effective, would have to be directed to doctors.

Thus, it came as a surprise when a single and tentative session on marketing for hospital administrators, sandwiched between several other sessions during the 1975 convention of the American College of Hospital Administrators, drew about one-third of the 2,000 attendees. Perhaps they were tired of hearing panels on rising hospital costs and money collection problems, but more probably they were beginning to sense an opportunity, in marketing, to halt their declining occupancy rates.

As did many colleges, some hospitals rushed into marketing with more enthusiasm than understanding, believing it to consist of clever promotional gimmicks. For example:

- Sunrise Hospital in Las Vegas ran a large advertisement featuring the picture of a ship with the caption, "Introducing the Sunrise Cruise, Win a Once-in-a-Lifetime Cruise Simply by Entering Sunrise Hospital on any Friday or Saturday: Recuperative Mediterranean Cruise for Two."
- St. Luke's Hospital in Phoenix introduced nightly bingo games for all patients (except cardiac cases) producing immense patient interest as well as a net annual profit of $60,000.
- A Philadelphia hospital, in competing for maternity patients, let the public know that the parents of a newborn child would enjoy a steak and champagne candlelight dinner on the eve before the mother and child's departure from the hospital.
- A number of hospitals, in their competition to attract and retain physicians, have added "ego services," such as saunas, chauffeurs, and even private tennis courts.

Fortunately, some hospitals are now beginning to apply marketing to a broader set of problems. Where should the hospital locate a branch or ambulatory care unit? How can the hospital estimate whether a new service will draw enough patients? What should a hospital do with a maternity wing that is only 20% occupied? How can the hospital attract more consumers to preventive care services, such as annual medical checkups and cancer screening programs? How can a hospital successfully compete in the recruitment of more highly trained specialists who are in short supply? What marketing programs can attract nurses, build community goodwill, attract more contributions?

The marketing naivete of the typical hospital is well-illustrated by a hospital in southern Illinois that decided to establish an Adult Day Care Center as a solution to its underutilized space. It designed a whole floor to serve senior citizens who required personal care and services in an ambulatory setting during the day, but who would return home each evening. The cost was $16 a day and transportation was to be provided by the patient's relatives. About the only research that was done on this concept was to note that a lot of elderly people lived within a three-mile radius. The Center was opened with a capacity to handle thirty patients. Only two signed up!

Not all hospital administrators launch new services without research and testing of market size and interest. An increasing number are now attending marketing seminars to learn more about marketing research and new service development. The Evanston Hospital, Evanston, Illinois, a major 500-bed facility, appointed the world's first hospital vice president of marketing. Recently, MacStravic (1977) published an entire book devoted to hospital marketing, and many articles are now appearing on health care marketing.[4]

Other Institutions

In addition to colleges and hospitals, other institutions are paying more attention to marketing. The YMCA is taking a fresh look at its mission, services, and clients in order to develop new services and markets for the 1980s. Major charities like the Multiple Sclerosis Society, the American Heart Association, and the March of Dimes are investigating marketing ideas that go beyond selling and advertising. Marketing successes have been reported by arts institutions,[5] family planning associations (Roberto 1975), and energy conservation groups (Henion 1976). It is likely that within 10 years, much of the third sector will have some understanding and appreciation of the marketing concept.

IMPLEMENTING MARKETING

The interesting thing about marketing is that all organizations do it whether they know it or not. When this dawns on a nonprofit organization the response is much like Moliere's character in *Le Bourgeois Gen-*

EXHIBIT 2. Approaches to Introducing Marketing in a Nonprofit Institution

1. Appoint a Marketing Committee
2. Organize Task Forces to Carry out an Institutional Audit
3. Hire Marketing Specialist Firms as Needed
4. Hire a Marketing Consultant
5. Hire a Director of Marketing
6. Hire a Vice President of Marketing

tilhomme who utters: "Good Heavens! For more than forty years I have been speaking prose without knowing it." Colleges, for example, search for prospects (students), develop products (courses), price them (tuition and fees), distribute them (announce time and place), and promote them (college catalogs). Similarly, hospitals, social agencies, cultural groups, and other nonprofit organizations also practice marketing, wittingly or unwittingly; whether they do it well is a separate issue. For institutions which would like to improve their marketing effectiveness, I recommend consideration of the six steps shown in Exhibit 2. The "steps" really represent alternative approaches to the introduction of marketing into a nonprofit institution rather than a rigid sequence of steps.

Marketing Committee

As early as possible, the head of the institution should consider appointing a marketing committee to examine the institution's problems and look into the potentialities of marketing. In a college, for example, such a marketing committee might consist of the president, vice presidents of faculty and development, director of admissions, dean of students, and one or two school deans. The committee should also include a marketing professor and/or a marketing practitioner. The marketing committee's objectives are (1) to identify the marketing problems and opportunities facing the institution; (2) to identify the major needs of various administrative units for marketing services; and (3) to explore the institution's possible need for a full-time director of marketing.

Task Forces

The chief administrator should consider appointing task forces to carry out various phases of an institutional audit. The aim is to discover how the institution is seen by key publics, what its main constituencies want that institution to be, which programs are strong and which weak, and so on. The task force's reports should adduce a consensus on institutional goals, positioning, and strategies. Even when task forces fail to find dramatic solutions, the members usually gain a deeper appreciation and understanding of the institution's problems and the need to work together to solve them.

Marketing Specialist Firms

From time to time, the organization should engage the services of marketing specialist firms, such as marketing research firms, advertising agencies, direct mail consultants, and recruitment consultants. A marketing research firm might be hired to survey the needs, perceptions, preferences, and satisfaction of the client market. An advertising agency might be hired to develop a corporate identification program or an advertising campaign. High quality marketing specialist firms bring more than their specific services to the client; they take a total marketing viewpoint and raise important questions for the institution to consider concerning its mission, objectives, strategies, and opportunities.

Marketing Consultant

As a further step, the organization should seek a marketing consultant to carry out a comprehensive *marketing audit* on the problems and opportunities facing that organization. The marketing consultant could be someone affiliated with the institution—such as a marketing professor, or a board member who is a marketing specialist. However, volunteers tend to give less attention than is necessary to the project, and often lack objectivity. It is usually preferable to engage a professional marketing consultant, one who has experience in that nonprofit subsector of the economy. In education, for example, several consulting firms have emerged specializing in college marketing and management. Alternatively, the institution could seek the services of a general consulting firm. In any event, the institution should make an effort to invite at least three proposals from which to select the best consultant. A contract should be written which specifies the objectives, the time frame, the research plan, and the billing. A liaison person within the institution should be assigned to work with the consultant, arrange interviews, read and comment on the emerging reports, and make arrangements for the final presentation and implementation of proposals.

The marketing consultant will interview representative sets of people connected with the institution. In the case of a college, he or she will interview the president, members of the board of trustees, major vice presidents, directors of admissions and public relations, several school deans, several department chairmen, several professors, several students, representative alumni, and outside opinion leaders. The marketing consultant would seek to answer the following questions for each *academic program* studied:

- What is happening to student size and quality?

- How successful is the program in attracting qualified students?
- What are the main competitive programs and their positions in the market?
- What is the image and reputation of this program?
- What is the mission and what are the objectives of this program over the next five years?
- What budget is needed to accomplish these objectives?
- What fund raising potentials exist in the program?
- What marketing problems face the program and what marketing activities are being pursued?
- What useful services could a marketing director contribute to this program?

On the basis of this survey, the marketing consultant will develop and present a set of findings and recommendations regarding the institution's operations, opportunities, and needs in the marketing area. One of the recommendations will specifically deal with whether the institution is ready to effectively utilize a marketing director or vice president of marketing.

Marketing Director

Eventually the organization might become convinced of the need to appoint a director of marketing. This requires the development of a job description which specifies to whom this person reports, the scope of the position, the position concept, the functions, responsibilities, and major liaisons with others in the institution. Exhibit 3 presents a job description in a university context. The job is conceived as a middle management position, one in which the occupant primarily provides marketing services to others in the institution.

A major issue is where this person should be located in the organization and his or her relationships with kindred functions. Specifically, what is the marketing director's relationship to planning, public relations, and fund raising? A good case could be made for locating the marketing director within the planning office and therefore reporting to the vice president of planning. It would not make sense for the marketing director to report to public relations or fund raising because this would overspecialize the use made of marketing. The solution used by a large, eastern hospital consisted of appointing a vice president of institutional relations to whom directors of marketing, public relations, fund raising and planning reported.

Some public relations directors have been uncomfortable about the emergence of marketing directors, out of fear that they may eventually be reporting to the latter. Some public relations directors argue that marketing isn't needed, or that it is being done, or that they can do it. To the extent that marketing is thought to be aggressive promotion, public relations people feel they are best equipped to carry out this function. To the extent that marketing is seen to consist of market analysis, new services development, marketing strategy, product line evaluation, and so on, public relations personnel are not equipped insofar as their

---

EXHIBIT 3. Job Description: Director of Marketing for a University

POSITION TITLE: Director of Marketing

REPORTS TO: A vice president designated by the president

SCOPE: University-wide

POSITION CONCEPT: The director of marketing is responsible for providing marketing guidance and services to university officers, school deans, department chairmen, and other agents of the university.

FUNCTIONS: The director of marketing will:

1. Contribute a marketing perspective to the deliberations of the top administration in their planning of the university's future
2. Prepare data that might be needed by any officer of the university on a particular market's size, segments, trends, and behavioral dynamics
3. Conduct studies of the needs, perceptions, preferences, and satisfactions of particular markets
4. Assist in the planning, promotion, and launching of new programs
5. Assist in the development of communication and promotion campaigns and materials
6. Analyze and advise on pricing questions
7. Appraise the workability of new academic proposals from a marketing point of view
8. Advise on new student recruitment
9. Advise on current student satisfaction
10. Advise on university fundraising

RESPONSIBILITIES: The director of marketing will:

1. Contact individual officers and small groups at the university to explain services and to solicit problems
2. Prioritize the various requests for services according to their long run impact, cost saving potential, time requirements, ease of accomplishment, cost, and urgency
3. Select projects of high priority and set accomplishment goals for the year
4. Prepare a budget request to support the anticipated work
5. Prepare an annual report on the main accomplishments of the office

MAJOR LIAISONS: The director of marketing will:

1. Relate most closely with the president's office, admissions office, development office, planning office, and public relations department
2. Relate secondarily with the deans of various schools and chairmen of various departments

training is basically in the fields of journalism and communications, not economics and business analysis. However, public relations persons can, of course, take courses in marketing and attempt to promote the concept of a combined office of marketing and public relations.

Marketing Vice President

The ultimate solution is the establishment of a vice president of marketing position. This is an upper level management position which gives more scope, authority, and influence to marketing. A vice president of marketing not only coordinates and supplies analytical services but also has a strong voice in the determination of where the institution should be going in terms of its changing opportunities.

The vice president of marketing would be responsible for planning and managing relations with several publics. The person's title may be altered to that of vice president of institutional relations or external affairs to avoid unnecessary semantic opposition. Thus far, only a few nonprofit organizations have gone this route.

The top marketing job should be tailored to the specific institution. Consider the YMCA, often called "the General Electric of the social service business." The YMCA is in not one, but several "businesses": recreation, education, camps, physical fitness, hotels, and so on. Central headquarters must wrestle with decisions on where to build new facilities, what new programs to introduce, what programs to drop, how to promote membership, and dozens of other matters. Were a vice president of marketing appointed, this person would be responsible for defining better ways to serve various constituencies. Reporting to the vice president would be functional marketing specialists (marketing research, pricing, promotion, and planning), product managers (recreational programs, educational programs, camps) and market managers (teens, young marrieds, senior adults). These people would design programs and offer services to the various YMCA units throughout the country. There is no question that marketing decisions are being made all the time throughout the YMCA system but they are made, unfortunately, without professional marketing expertise.

Let us assume that an institution decides to hire a marketing vice president. This person's contribution will be carefully scrutinized. The new appointee will have to develop a strategy to make marketing visible and useful.

The marketing executive is not likely to be immediately swamped with requests for services, because many administrators initially will not understand marketing. The marketing executive should spend the first few months meeting various groups within the institution to learn about their problems. For example, Evanston Hospital's new marketing vice president arranged separate meetings with senior physicians, residents, interns, senior nurses, and others. At each meeting he described his job position, explained the nature of marketing, indicated the kinds of problems he could solve and services that he could offer, and then opened the meeting to discussion. He sought suggestions of projects that he might conduct. At the end of two months, he found more than enough useful projects. His problem, in fact, was to set priorities for the many projects, and he did so by rating each potential project using the following criteria (on five-point scales): (1) the importance or centrality of the project to the future of the institution; (2) the magnitude of the improved service or cost savings that it might effect; (3) its probable cost; (4) the difficulty of carrying it out; and (5) the length of time it would take to complete. An ideal project was one that was very important, would effect great cost savings, would cost little to do, could be easily carried out, and could be completed in a short time. It became clear which projects went to the top of the list, and he concentrated his efforts in the first year on these projects.

The marketing executive will be expected to prepare an annual marketing plan listing major projects and a required budget. Much of the budget will go toward buying the services of outside marketing research firms and advertising agencies for needed projects. At each year's end, the executive will prepare a report summarizing levels of accomplishment and savings. Eventually, the nature of this position will become well understood within the organization and easy to assess its contributions toward institutional survival and growth.

Conclusion

At the present time, the marketing idea is beginning to attract the interest of administrators in the third sector. This is evidenced by the growing literature on college, hospital, and other third sector marketing, as well as by increased attendance at specialized marketing conferences for nonprofit organizations. Interest is not likely to abate; indeed, it is likely to increase as more administrators come to see their institution's future in marketing terms. For an institution, marketing offers a much richer understanding of what is happening and throws light on new opportunities.

Despite the growing interest in marketing, however, many nonprofit organizations still resist it. Many groups within these organizations see marketing as a threat to their autonomy or power. Eventually, out of necessity, marketing ideas will filter into these organizations. Marketing will initially be viewed as advertising and promotion rather than as a revolutionary new way to view the institution and its purposes. A few institutions will lead the others in developing an advanced understanding of marketing. They will start performing better. Their competitors will be forced to learn their marketing. Within another decade, marketing will be a major and accepted function within the nonprofit sector.

The issue that frightens some observers is not that marketing will be ineffective but that it may be too effective. They see funds and clients flowing to institutions that are willing to spend the largest sums of money on advertising and promotion. They fear that large scale promotional warfare will ruin the smaller institutions that cannot afford marketing, and will create a competitive stalemate among the larger institutions. This fear is based, once again, on the fallacy of viewing marketing as primarily promotional.

The real contribution of marketing thinking is to lead each institution to search for a more meaningful position in the larger market. Instead of all hospitals offering the same services, marketing leads each hospital to shape distinct service mixes to serve specific market segments. Marketing competition, at its best, creates a pattern of varied institutions, each clear as to its mission, market coverage, need specialization, and service portfolio.

Administrators and businessmen who have a stake in the third sector are beginning to recognize the contributions that marketing thinking can make. Marketing will lead to a better understanding of the needs of different client segments; to a more careful shaping and launching of new services; to a pruning of weak services; to more effective methods of delivering services; to more flexible pricing approaches; and to higher levels of client satisfaction. Altogether, marketing offers a great potential to third sector organizations to survive, grow, and strengthen their contributions to the general welfare.

ENDNOTES

1. A relevant 43-page bibliography lists over 600 references. See Rothschild, Michael L. (1977), *An Incomplete Bibliography of Works Relating to Marketing for Public Sector and Nonprofit Organizations*, Second Edition, Boston, MA: Intercollegiate Case Clearing House 9-577-771.
2. See *A Role for Marketing in College Admissions*, New York: College Entrance Examination Board, 1976, 54 and elsewhere.
3. See "Rest in Peace," *Newsweek*, April 11, 1977, 96.
4. See, for example, the special issue on marketing of hospitals, *Journal of the American Hospital Association*, June 1, 1977.
5. See, Newman, Danny (1977), *Subscribe Now! Building Arts Audiences through Dynamic Subscription Promotion*, New York: Theatre Communications Group, Inc. This book deals primarily with the use of promotion as a marketing tool rather than with overall marketing strategy.

REFERENCES

Gaedeke, R. M. (1977, *Marketing in Private and Public Nonprofit Organizations: Perspectives and Illustrations*, Santa Monica, CA: Goodyear Publishing Co.

Henion, Karl E. (1976), *Ecological Marketing*, Columbus, Ohio: Grid, Inc.

Kotler, Philip (1975), *Marketing for Nonprofit Organizations*, Englewood Cliffs, NJ: Prentice-Hall, Inc.

────── and Levy, Sidney J. (1969), "Broadening the Concept of Marketing," *Journal of Marketing*, 33 (January), 10–15.

Lovelock, Christopher H., ed. (1977), *Nonbusiness Marketing Cases*, 8–378–001, Boston, MA: Intercollegiate Case Clearing House.

────── and Charles B. Weinberg (1977), *Cases in Public and Nonprofit Marketing*, Palo Alto, CA: The Scientific Press.

────── and Charles B. Weinberg (1978), "Public and Non-profit Marketing Comes of Age," in *Review of Marketing 1978*, Gerald Zaltman and T. Bonoma eds., Chicago, IL: American Marketing Association, 413–52.

MacStravic, Robin E. (1977), *Marketing Health Care*, Germantown, MD: Aspen Systems Corp.

Nickels, William G. (1978), *Marketing Principles*, Englewood Cliffs, NJ: Prentice-Hall, Inc.

Pyke, Donald L. (1977), "The Future of Higher Education: Will Private Institutions Disappear in the U.S.? *The Futurist* 374.

Roberto, Eduardo (1975), *Strategic Decision-Making in a Social Program: The Case of Family-Planning Diffusion*, Lexington, MA: Lexington Books.

Shapiro, Benson (1973), "Marketing for Nonprofit Organizations," *Harvard Business Review*, 51 (September–October), 123–32.

44 Strategic Management for Multiprogram Nonprofit Organizations

Robert E. Gruber and Mary Mohr

© 1982 by the Regents of the University of California. Reprinted from CALIFORNIA MANAGEMENT REVIEW, Vol. 24, No. 3, pp. 15-22 by permission of the Regents.

"Strategic planning," "strategic audits," "portfolio management," and "product line pruning" are familiar terms in the private sector, but they also have ready applicability for many nonprofit organizations. These business concepts can be particularly useful to nonprofit organizations that provide more than one service to their clientele. Examples of such institutions are numerous and include such diverse operations as human services, arts and culture, health maintenance, and religious organizations. These and many other groups operate a variety of programs, and, like their private sector, multiproduct counterparts, they are learning that maximum effectiveness can only be obtained if the collection of programs or services the organization offers—what we shall refer to as the agency's "program portfolio"—is managed as a totality.

The concept of managing a totality (say, managing a product line rather than merely concentrating on individual products within the line) stems principally from the work of the Boston Consulting Group in the early 1970s.[1] In its now well-known and accepted "product-portfolio" model, the group maintained that important interdependencies exist among products in a line. Particular products could not and should not be considered in isolation. It is the purpose of this article to demonstrate the utility of this seemingly simple idea in a nonprofit context by the presentation of a "program classification" model that facilitates strategic decisions.

INTERDEPENDENCIES AMONG PROGRAMS

Programs, like products, must not be considered in isolation since they often interact with one another. In the private sector, examples of interactions among products in a product line abound. The most common example is that of so-called complementary products, such as cameras and film. The demand for the camera, which is priced so as to yield little or no profit, can trigger demand for a fully priced, and hence highly profitable, film line. Obviously, it would be absurd for a manager to make any change in the camera line, such as a price increase, without considering the impact on the sale of film as well. So, too, can programs interact. For example, the social activities offered by religious groups may stimulate attendance at church services.

Further, programs, like products, should not be considered in isolation if for no other reason than that they compete with one another for the scarce resources of the organization. This competition requires that upper-level management make the long-term strategic decisions concerning which programs to emphasize, which to deemphasize, and which to discontinue. The model described below attempts to facilitate these important decision areas. It should prove helpful to administrators, to donors, to boards of directors, and to all those who oversee organizational functions by:

- encouraging strategic (long-range—what to do) as opposed to tactical (short-range—how to do it) thinking;
- encouraging a holistic, as opposed to an atomistic, viewpoint;
- identifying trade-offs to be considered by program-oriented personnel;
- identifying programs in need of redesign, candidates for expansion, or candidates for divestiture;
- suggesting the direction of cash flow among programs; and
- providing broad guidelines for assessing the overall health of an organization.

COST BENEFIT ANALYSIS

The model, described in the next section, provides a way of thinking about the kinds of programs offered by an organization. The scheme suggests that programs can be more readily evaluated if they are first classified in terms of the costs and benefits associated with them.

Cost/benefit analysis is commonly used in the private sector, perhaps because it is relatively easy to accomplish. One assesses the dollar costs and merely compares these to the benefits—which, in the usual case, are readily measurable profits, also denominated in dollars. This process is not as straightforward in the nonprofit case. The principal difficulty is that the benefits are social benefits, intangible and extremely difficult to quantify.[2] This issue is complicated because programs can be beneficial if they serve any social need, no matter how broadly defined. This complication can be avoided by more narrowly defining a program as producing a benefit, which we can refer to as a "relevant benefit," only if it contributes to the overall mission and purpose of the nonprofit organization, to the specific set of social goals the organization was set up to accomplish.

This evaluation is made difficult because benefits are usually multifaceted in nature. Programs can benefit the constituency being served in more than one way. Hot meals served at a senior citizen community center are beneficial from a nutritional and a social point of view. The social benefit may or may not outweigh the nutritional, but both must be taken into account when assessing the total benefits derived from a hot meal program.

Costs, like benefits, are multidimensional and include more than the money costs associated with the operation of a given program. Costs should be conceived of in terms of total resources—money, manpower, floor space—dedicated to a program. For simplicity, we will consider only operating costs, at first.

In many cases, costs are partially or completely defrayed by the fees received for the service. The next expenditure is what we are after, the difference between costs and fees. Where fees actually exceed costs, a rare but not impossible situation, we can say the program enjoys positive financial returns. In the more usual case, where costs are greater than fees, the program can be said to produce negative financial returns. How important are positive financial returns? That depends to a great extent on the financial situation of the nonprofit organization. Those organizations that are richly endowed, the recipients of a stream of gifts and grants, will obviously place a lower value upon net income derived from fees for service. Those that seek, to some extent, the goal of financial self-sufficiency will more highly value such income. As with social benefits, the degree to which positive financial returns are desirable is a function of the requirements and goals of the particular organization.

Conceptually, costs and revenues are more readily evaluated than benefits. However, as a practical matter, many nonprofit organizations suffer from the lack of an adequate accounting system. This important issue has been addressed elsewhere and is beyond the scope of this article.[3] In the sections that follow, a sound system of accrual accounting will be assumed.

THE MODEL

The program classification model described in this section is based upon the principles of cost/benefit analysis, discussed above. The idea is to consider each of the programs offered by the organization in turn and to decide that program A is, for example, high in benefits and provides positive financial returns, that program B is low in benefits and produces negative financial returns, and so forth.

Notwithstanding the difficulties of assessing benefits or accounting for costs, referred to in the preceding section, we will rely on the expert opinion of program-oriented personnel to dichotomize programs into

FIGURE 1. 4-Way Program Classification Model

	Low Benefits (Social Value)	High Benefits (Social Value)

Financial Returns Positive	**Sustaining** (Necessary evil?)
	Basic Strategy:
	  Maintenance
	Use of Funds:
	  Subsidize "Worthwhile" Programs
		Beneficial (Best of all possible worlds)
		Basic Strategy:
		  Cautious Expansion
		Use of Funds:
		  Trade-off — Plowback or Subsidize "Worthwhile" Programs

Financial Returns Negative	**Detrimental** (No redeeming qualities)
	Basic Strategy:
	  Pruning
	Use of Funds:
	  None Available
		Worthwile (Satisfying, good for society)
		Basic Strategy:
		  Careful Nurturing
		Use of Funds:
		  None Available

* Refers to internally generated funds.

those judged high in terms of relevant benefits as opposed to those thought of as low in this regard. We assume that programs exhibiting negative financial returns can be distinguished. This leads to the classification scheme illustrated in Figure 1. The four basic program types are described below. The names assigned to each category are primarily for convenient reference in the discussion that follows.

Beneficial Programs

Beneficial programs are those judged high in terms of the relevant social benefits provided. They are very beneficial to the constituency being served and contribute greatly to the social goals of the organization. Beneficial programs take in more in revenue than they pay out in expenses (positive financial returns) — and, hence, contribute to the survival of the organization in a very practical way. These highly desirable programs, the best of all possible worlds, may be hard to find but are not difficult to imagine. Consider an inexpensive cancer vaccine, where an easily affordable token fee exceeds the vaccine costs.

Worthwhile Programs

These programs are also rated high in terms of relevant social benefits, but they differ from the first category in that they are costly to operate — costs exceed fees. They exhibit negative financial returns and, therefore, are a drain upon the resources of the organization. Worthwhile programs serve important community needs. They are good for society, bad for the pocketbook. If the costs of the hypothetical cancer vaccine mentioned above exceeded the fee that could reasonably be charged, the program would be placed in the worthwhile category.

Sustaining Programs

Those programs judged to be low in terms of the social benefits they provide but which generate funds in excess of their operating costs are sustaining programs. They provide positive financial returns. One example is the operation by a hospital of a gift shop, which provides benefits in that it contributes, at least to a limited extent, to the physical and mental well-being of the patients, and which operates at a profit.

There are three very important aspects of sustaining programs that should be examined at the outset. First, why would a nonprofit organization wish to have such a program at all? The answer to this question has been discussed above: if the organization desires some degree of self-sufficiency, then sustaining programs must be included. Second, what about the tax consequences of sustaining programs? If related to the nonprofit organization's exempt purpose (the hospital gift shop qualifies), there is no problem. If unrelated, the potential problems range from having to pay a tax on the proceeds to actually losing tax exempt status (the latter is uncommon).[4] Third, and of particular interest in the context of this article, "The IRS considers how the funds derived from the activity are used as immaterial in determining whether the activity is related or unrelated."[5] The sustaining activity must be substantially related to the tax exempt purpose of the nonprofit organization even if the funds are used to subsidize worthwhile offerings, as will be suggested below.

Detrimental Programs

The last of our four categories, these programs are the worst of all possible worlds, low in terms of benefits and producing negative financial rewards. The hospital gift shop that is poorly managed, customarily out of the many items patients desire, and not being operated on a profitable basis is an example. A detrimental program has no redeeming features; it provides neither benefits nor financial returns.

IMPLICATIONS FOR STRATEGY

Using the scheme outlined above, the first step in program portfolio analysis is the classification of the organization's various offerings. Once programs are classified, the implications for strategy, resource allocation, and direction of cash flow will often be obvious. Indeed, in the usual case, the most straightforward implications are those that apply to the beneficial and detrimental categories. These will be considered first.

In the case of a detrimental program, the most direct response is to simply eliminate it. Programs of this type are detrimental to the organization because they fail to measure up in terms of either benefits or financial rewards. Thus, the basic strategy for a detrimental program is to prune it from the portfolio. As with all pruning, the underlying notion is to sacrifice a part for the good of the whole.[6] The implications for resource allocation are equally straightforward. Paraphrasing Peter Drucker, famed management consultant, good programs should be nourished and bad ones starved. If detrimental programs cannot be eliminated—and it is hard to think of compelling reasons why they should not be—then resource allocations should be reduced to a bare minimum so that they can be more gainfully employed elsewhere. A caveat: With reduced support, the already deficient service may become even more of a liability if allowed to deteriorate to the point where it can further degrade the image of the organization's other offerings. At this point, two responses are possible: the appropriate and courageous one—prune immediately; or the incorrect, yet prevalent, one—siphon off much-needed resources from more deserving programs to maintain the detrimental service at a minimally acceptable level.

The knee jerk response in the case of beneficial programs is "expansion," but first an additional dimension, the demand for the program, must be explicitly considered. If the program is known to be in great demand, then expansion may be justified. But expansion implies that more, or even most, of the organization's finite supply of resources be allocated to beneficial programs and that all "profits" be "plowed back," reserved for use in the beneficial program that generated them in the first place. The alternative possibility is to divert resources, including all or part of the financial rewards obtained from beneficial programs, to subsidize their worthwhile fellows. Funds should be diverted to those programs where the relevant benefits are greatest. This determination requires value judgments, which can only be made by those with intimate knowledge of the programmatic aspects and of the principal goals of the organization. Thus, the basic strategic response for beneficial programs can best be restated as "cautious expansion."

Sustaining programs generate funds in excess of their costs. Just as General Electric's mundane light bulb division helps to subsidize more esoteric and perhaps soul-satisfying corporate endeavors, so can sustaining programs provide sustenance to other, more socially desirable programs in the portfolio. Here is a perfect example of why programs should not be considered in isolation. If the sustaining program is considered alone, then one possible, but misguided, strategic response is to prune it. The sustaining program may not make an important, direct contribution to the attainment of the desired social goals of the organization, but its indirect contribution may be enormous, the providing of financial support for other, more socially desirable offerings. A more pragmatic view, and the basic strategy recommended here, is "maintenance" of these programs, followed by the use of their excess "profits" to subsidize their worthwhile fellows. By maintenance we mean that sufficient resources must be made available to sustaining programs on an ongoing basis so as to insure the viability of these bread-and-butter offerings. Obviously, the goal of self-sufficiency and the tax implications discussed above also play an important part in determining the strategies for sustaining programs.

Finally, consider the worthwhile programs. The greatest number of programs in any given portfolio probably fall into this category; they rate high in terms of benefits but produce negative financial returns. These important components of the portfolio must be handled with extreme care. Prudent management must resist the tendency towards undue expansion and proliferation of worthwhile programs to the point where available resources, spread thinly over many of these programs, are simply insufficient to insure effective implementation of any one of them. Pruning (of those highest in cost and lowest in benefits) may be abhorrent, but should be considered by courageous managers.

A worthwhile program may no longer provide the requisite benefits or may be too costly to operate. Perhaps it is being retained out of inertia or out of loyalty to some long-term, respected supporter of the organization. All alleged worthwhile programs (and all others, for that matter) should be periodically reviewed—on a "zero-base" or "sunset law" basis—and considered as candidates for pruning.

These caveats notwithstanding, the recommended basic strategy for worthwhile programs is "careful nurturing," the redirecting of funds obtained from money-making programs to their use. In this way, internally generated funds can supplement the more usual external sources of funds on which worthwhile programs depend. The term *careful nurturing* is intended to remind program managers of the dangers of proliferation, discussed above, and to suggest that these programs, collectively, be very carefully controlled, so that good intentions do not outrun cash flow.

PROGRAM REDESIGN

Since programs that rate highest in terms of benefits are preferred and since beneficial programs are the best of all possible worlds, wherever possible an attempt should be made to move programs toward worthwhile or beneficial status by redesigning program content or pricing.[7] Perhaps some socially redeeming feature can be added to a sustaining program—some state governments have attempted this by directing lottery proceeds be used to support schools and hospitals. Perhaps fees on a worthwhile program can be based on ability to pay and effectively be raised. Conceptually, even detrimental programs can be revitalized but only if the time and effort for redesign are kept at a bare minimum. The simplest and quickest modification may be to raise the fees drastically. If the program cannot quickly be converted to sustaining status, if it fails to attract clients at the new higher price, then it deserves to die.

When considering prices, other product line pricing concepts are relevant. In the commercial product context, prices should be set on individual products so as to maximize revenues or profits across the entire product line.[8] This focus on total monetary return is appropriate for sustaining as well as detrimental programs, since their only reason for being is to produce positive financial rewards. Specifically, sustaining programs in great demand can and should be priced high, high enough to be "profitable" when all costs are considered but not so high as to inhibit demand and reduce total revenues.[9] In the case of worthwhile and beneficial programs, where social goals are paramount, this narrow monetary view does not suffice. Yet setting fees too low in such programs may be myopic if higher prices (at least for some clients) can lead to a more viable (self-sufficient) organization, which can better serve all of its constituencies and thereby better accomplish its prime mission and goals.

ADDITION OF NEW PROGRAMS

Another strategic decision is whether or not the organization should attempt to inaugurate a new program. This decision is conceptually identical to the new product decision faced by private sector firms. Considering the product or program in isolation, there is one overriding condition that must be satisfied: Does the new program contribute to the accomplishment of the nonprofit organization's mission and purpose? Are its benefits relevant? A new program may fulfill many other conditions (be socially beneficial in a general sense, fulfill an unmet need of a client group), but if this condition is not satisfied, the new program probably should not be added. It is often all too easy to stray from one's main mission by falling into the trap of going where the funds are and this tendency must be resisted.

Consideration of a program's contribution to the overall mission, in isolation, is not enough. As this article suggests, the potential interdependencies among the new and existing programs are also of great importance and should be carefully examined. An appropriate question is, How will the new program fit in with others in the portfolio? How might the new offering be categorized in terms of our program classification model, and what, exactly, can we expect from it in terms of benefits and financial returns? If the new program falls into the worthwhile category, which resources (money, space, manpower—including volunteers) will it siphon off, and from where? Which existing programs will it complement? Which will it detract from or even cannibalize?

A further consideration is the overall manageability of the portfolio. Experience in the private sector indicates a tendency towards unnecessary product proliferation. The same tendencies can be observed in the nonprofit area. The question is whether or not an ever-increasing number of programs can be effectively implemented, administered, and controlled by the organization. This reinforces the notion that a new program must contribute substantially to the prime purpose of the nonprofit organization if it is to be added to the portfolio and suggests the possible applicability of the dictum, "Never add a new product until you drop an old (and presumably, worn-out) one."

An Illustration

The Jewish Community Center of Denver, Colorado is a forward-looking social service agency primarily serving the social, cultural, and athletic needs of the Jewish community in Denver.[10] The various services provided by the agency are also made available to the public at large. In terms of general scope of services offered, it is an organization like the Y.M.C.A., funded by such donor agencies as United Way and the Allied Jewish Federation. Some fraction of its income is generated by fees received for certain of its services. Although it is a local agency, the center is not unlike other Jewish community centers across the country.

The Denver Jewish Community Center is a good example because it provides many, diverse offerings, including programs for the elderly such as hot meals, programs for children (a day care center), athletic and health club services (saunas, exercise rooms, swimming), an extensive educational program (language instruction, dance, arts and crafts) for all age groups, and much more.

In line with the scheme described above, the Jewish Community Center's various programs can be classified along the dimensions of costs and benefits, where the multifaceted benefits which this organization provides can be conveniently subsumed under the label "Jewish values." An adult education program such as language instruction in Hebrew can be classified as worthwhile since it is high in Jewish values yet costly (the fees charged do not cover the cost of instruction). By contrast, swimming is sustaining, "profitable," but low in Jewish values. The health club is a good example of a beneficial program. It is financially rewarding, actually "profitable," and is perceived to be high in terms of value because it

TABLE 1. Partial Listing of JCC Programs

Adult Education (Jewish programs)	Rentals
Adult Education (non-Jewish programs)	Russian Resettlement
Art Classes	Senior Citizens
Art Exhibits	Singles
B'nai Brith	Skiing
Boys Camp	Swimming
Day Camp	Tennis
Early Childhood Education	Theatre (Jewish content)
Health Club	Theatre (no Jewish content)
Health and Physical Education	Volleyball
Holiday Programs	Young Judea
Jewish Art Shows	Youth Department
Jewish Performing Arts	Youth Programs

facilitates affiliation and sociability among the predominantly Jewish membership.

A partial listing of the center programs is presented in two ways. Table 1 contains a simple tabulation of these programs. Other than noting there are many programs and that efficient management of the agency is a formidable task, particular strategic implications cannot readily be seen. In Figure 2 the same listing is presented, classified in accordance with the model described above. Programs in heavy demand (now or based on future projections) are indicated by capital letters.

We hope you agree that merely placing these programs in categories is extremely helpful in assessing the Jewish Community Center's situation. Among the strategic questions that come to mind are:

- Why continue to offer skiing or the other six detrimental programs? Have they been classified correctly? Can any of them be easily converted to sustaining via an increased fee schedule, or should they all be seriously considered as candidates for pruning? (In actuality, the center does not have seven detrimental programs. Most of those shown have been intentionally misclassified for illustrative purposes.)

- Can the rather large number (twelve) of worthwhile programs be adequately managed? Are some less worthwhile than others? Should some be dropped or cut back? Could (or should) fees be raised on others so as to make them, at least, self-supporting?

- Are the "profits" from sustaining programs being correctly allocated? Are these services being properly maintained? Could one or more of them be expanded within IRS limitations, so as to provide increased cash inflows (say, health and physical education), or would such an expansion take much-needed resources

(such as floor space) from other, more socially deserving offerings?
- Should any of the beneficial programs be expanded? Could a cautiously expanded early childhood education program (the one in greatest demand) subsidize and thus contribute to the careful nurturing of its companion, worthwhile offering, day camp?

We might ask which of the programs can be considered as substitutes for one another. The adult education program competes with those of other institutions, its external competition. But how about competition among the center's own programs: Do folk dance, modern dance, and ballet compete one with the other for clients from a limited pool, and would one or more survivors be healthier if some judicious pruning were done? Is there a proper mix of programs? If not, in which direction must the organization move to bring its portfolio into balance?

Conclusion

The task of managing a multiprogram nonprofit organization can be arduous. Such organizations must manage their program portfolios in order to maximize effectiveness. Programs should not be considered in isolation from one another. The program classification model presented here allows nonprofit managers to view their programs with a holistic perspective.

FIGURE 2. Classification of JCC Programs

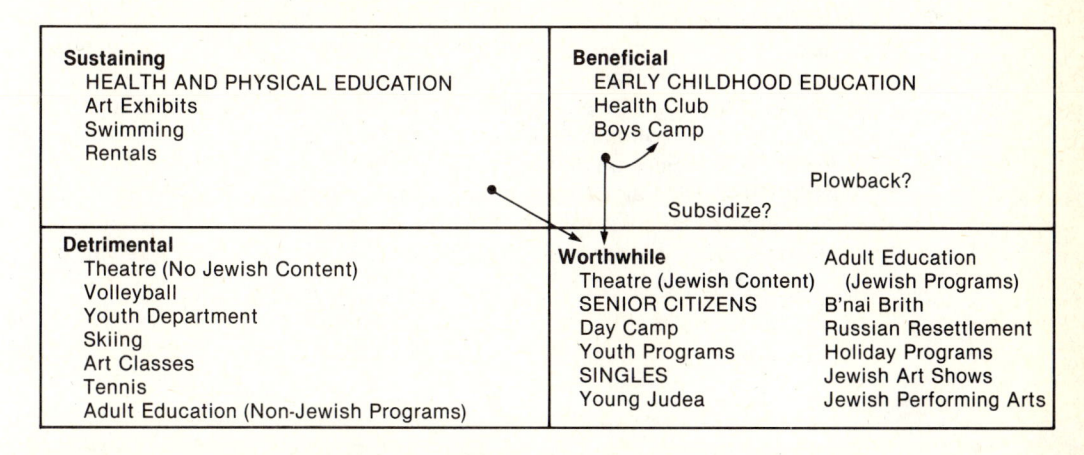

Sustaining	Beneficial
HEALTH AND PHYSICAL EDUCATION Art Exhibits Swimming Rentals	EARLY CHILDHOOD EDUCATION Health Club Boys Camp Plowback? Subsidize?
Detrimental	**Worthwhile**
Theatre (No Jewish Content) Volleyball Youth Department Skiing Art Classes Tennis Adult Education (Non-Jewish Programs)	Theatre (Jewish Content) Adult Education SENIOR CITIZENS (Jewish Programs) Day Camp B'nai Brith Youth Programs Russian Resettlement SINGLES Holiday Programs Young Judea Jewish Art Shows Jewish Performing Arts

Note: arrows represent use of internally generated funds.

There is a growing demand for accountability in a sophisticated donor community, motivated in part by the generally poor economic environment. This provides the impetus for the adoption of well-known business concepts so that nonprofit organizations may use their dwindling funds more effectively. Administrators and board directors of nonprofit organizations will be faced with increasingly severe competition for time, money, and management skills as the nonprofit sector becomes more cost conscious. Dedication must be accompanied by performance results, idealism tempered with pragmatism.[11]

REFERENCES

1. B. D. Henderson, "The Product Portfolio," pamphlet (Boston Consulting Group, 1970). Also see W. E. Cox, Jr., "Product Portfolio Strategy: An Analysis of the Boston Consulting Group Approach to Marketing Strategies," *Proceeds of the American Marketing Association* (1974).
2. Even in the private sector, firms often have objectives other than profits, such as reputation or market standing, changes in which are difficult to quantify.
3. See for example, R. Herzlinger, "Managing the Finances of Nonprofit Organizations," *California Management Review* (Spring 1979); and R. K. Macleod, "Program Budgeting Works in Nonprofit Institutions," *Harvard Business Review* (September/October 1971).
4. See G. N. Scrivner and Christopher T. Callahan, "A Path to Self-Sufficiency," *Philanthropy Monthly* (September 1980).
5. Ibid., p. 16.
6. See "The Product-Elimination Decision," in P. Kotler, *Marketing for Nonprofit Organizations* (Prentice-Hall, 1975), p. 173.
7. Ibid., p. 172.
8. Ibid., p. 178.
9. Ibid. The concept of price elasticity of demand is discussed on pp. 185–86.
10. One of the pioneering nonprofit organizations in the use of strategic planning as a way of providing an overview of their operations, the Jewish Community Center actually wrote a strategic plan for itself. It was among the first agencies of its kind to respond to an environmentally induced decline in demand by coordinating all "marketing" activities under a marketing manager (the junior author).
11. Another interesting article on the audit of program portfolios is D. B. Herron, "Developing a Marketing Audit for Social Service Organizations," in C. H. Lovelock and C. B. Weinberg (eds.), *Readings in Public and Nonprofit Marketing* (The Scientific Press, 1978), pp. 267–71.

SECTION L
International Marketing

The importance of international marketing is increasing as countries become more and more interdependent through international trade and direct investments. There are three issues facing international marketing.

First, can we extend the successful marketing mix developed for the domestic market to international markets? The general answer seems to be no and yes. It is no if the extension is for the total market, but it is yes if it is for a targeted segment such as teenagers, the affluent, or the elderly.

Second, while markets may or may not be global, there is no question that competition is becoming global through mergers and acquisitions. This condition is likely to generate internal conflicts related to the marketing practices of different domestic companies. We still don't know how to create a holistic, global corporation out of acquisitions that practice divergently.

Finally, international marketing is likely to impact on our values and ethics of marketing practice. For example, from a moral viewpoint, what is the difference between bribery, kickback, and reciprocity arrangements? Although they may be legal or illegal from country to country, they all ultimately result in a noncompetitive, favorable position for one company against others. In our opinion, international marketing is likely to broaden the horizons of marketing ethics just as international travel broadens the average citizen's horizons of the world.

45 Are Domestic and International Marketing Dissimilar?

Robert Bartels

Reprinted from the *Journal of Marketing*, published by the American Marketing Association, Vol. 32 (July 1968), pp. 56–61. Reprinted by permission.

As marketing managers become increasingly involved in international marketing, and as schools of business undertake to internationalize their programs, both have queried whether there are significant differences between domestic and international marketing, and have asked whether these differences prescribe dissimilar practices and programs. Experience in international markets has shown some marketers the inadvisability of projecting domestically successful marketing strategies into foreign situations. Yet, other companies operate successfully from the premise that the world is a market in which business principles have universal applicability. That such divergent experiences and convictions persist without theoretical resolution of their apparent inconsistencies is evidence that the concept of international marketing needs further clarification. As a practice, international trading is old; as a type of modern marketing, it is a relatively new idea.

In the internationalization of marketing, as in all substantial changes in marketing practice and thought, new ideas pass through three stages in becoming accepted and established. First, a stage of *identification*. When a new idea is perceived, even before its nature is fully recognized, it is often given a name to facilitate reference and communication concerning it. The designation may be a familiar term or one newly coined. It may have temporary or lasting usage. Second, a stage of *conceptualization*, in which definition occurs as the idea gains distinctive form and meaning. Third, a stage of *assimilation* and integration into the established body of thought. This is the process of the enlargement of thought or theory and its enrichment with new ideas.

The extension of marketing practice beyond national borders has in recent years initiated this process with respect to the terms "comparative" and "international" as applied to marketing. What had earlier been called "foreign trade" became *"international* marketing," as domestically originated techniques were applied to marketing outside the country. The arguments over the similarities and differences of marketing in the two realms have provided a degree of confusion as conceptualization progresses beyond the initial stage of identification of this broader field of marketing.

Likewise, the term *comparative* marketing has been used, designating not so much a practice of marketing but a type of analysis whereby nationally dissimilar marketing systems and practices can be compared—or more often, contrasted. The fruitlessness of simply comparing numerous differences soon became apparent and hinted at the need of a more conceptual view of the differences in marketing as practiced in different national environments. Thus, attention has turned to defining "comparative" as applied to marketing. Incorporation of the concepts, both "international" and "comparative," into marketing theory awaits further clarification of their meaning. Toward this end, the following conceptualization is offered for consideration.

WHAT IS MARKETING?

Before *"international* marketing" can have a meaning, the term *marketing* itself must be understood for "international" only qualifies the basic process. In general, marketing connotes a process of two-fold character: technical and social.

Technical Process

As a technical process, marketing consists of the application of principles, rules, or knowledge relating to the non-human elements of marketing. Non-human elements include factors such as products, price, profit, cost, and others listed in the left half of Figure 1. They include also categories such as channels, institutions, markets, buyers, and "economic man," which express economic concepts involving people, but which do not connote the full range of non-economic human behavior of the individuals occupying those roles.

Marketing has traditionally been regarded as a technical process, and marketing management as the utilization of technical means for the achievement of desired ends. Marketing technology, or marketing thought, has been elaborately developed, and the concepts and generalizations thereof have been held to have a universality transcending national boundaries and cultural differences. The technologies of turnover rates, of economies of large scale operations, of length of distribution channel, and of identification of products have generally been regarded as universal, without respect to time and place.

Recognizing this universality, or presuming it, marketers have with varying success applied this technology around the world, only to learn the limitations of its applicability under certain environmental circumstances.

Social Process

As a social process, marketing is a complex of interactions among individuals acting in role positions in the various systems involved in the distribution of goods and services.

This concept emphasizes the human element, the individual acting under the full range of influences, both economic and non-economic, which affiliation with the social institutions of his society imposes upon him. The categories of thought implicit in this concept of marketing are indicated in the right half of Figure 1.

As a social process, marketing in two nations may differ markedly. While the *roles* in which individuals interact may be identical, their *expectations* and *behavior patterns* in two societies may be quite different. Marketing strategies planned for another country may differ accordingly, and similarities could be expected only to the extent that the customs, values, attitudes, and motivations of two people are alike.

Business in general and marketing in particular thus are seen to consist of two complementary aspects: the technical and the social. Managerial generalizations concerning the former appear to be more universally valid than generalizations concerning behavior and interaction in the marketing process. Applications of even presumably universally valid theories, however, may vary with the environments, thus requiring an environmental concept of marketing.

What Is Environmentalism?

Environmentalism is a concept which relates marketing to the environment in which it is performed and holds it to be in large measure

FIGURE 1. Concepts of Marketing and Their Related Elements

Concepts of Marketing	
Technical (Nonhuman)	Social (Human)
Products	Social Systems
Price	Roles
Profits	Behavior
Costs	Interaction
Brands	Management
Differentiation	
Layouts	
Scales	
Channels	
Markets	
Institutions	
Flows	
Processes	

determined thereby. Marketing, of course, helps to shape the societal environment, but the environmental concept of marketing as a social process throws the emphasis in the other direction. Environmental interpretation of business is relatively new and is itself a product of the growing experience of businessmen in environments other than that of their home country. Heretofore, although marketers have always operated in a societal environment, this factor has generally been taken for granted. Patterns of behavior were learned as a part of maturation; all participants in business operated within the same legal and ethical framework; and basic uniformity characterized the diversity of the business world. This is not so in the foreign and international realms.

Merely to *perceive* environment, however, is one thing; to *conceptualize* it is another and is the essential second step in the groundwork leading to the construction of theory in international or comparative marketing. Toward this end, the abstract elements of environment—domestic and foreign—need to be identified as bases of the comparability of environments in different countries. Aid in the interpretation of environment as it affects marketing is found in several of the scholarly disciplines: geography, economics, sociology, anthropology, and psychology.

While recognizing the weakness of oversimplification, there seems to be tenability in the generalization that physical and economic environmental factors are primary determinants of the *technical* aspects of business, whereas cultural environmental factors tend to be the principal determinants of the *social* aspects of business. As suggested in Figure 2, such factors as size of country, dispersion or concentration of population, transportation and communication facilities, levels and distribution of income, and price levels are significant affectors of markets, channels, outlets, price lines, and promotion budgets. Marketing practices relating to these functions vary from country to country as the physical and economic circumstances differ.

The social aspects of marketing, on the other hand, are the more sensitive to the societal and social environments of the individuals engaged in marketing. The societal environment consists of the major institutional structure of the society and of its values on the highest level. Thus, the relationships and obligations within the family, the doctrines of the church, or the philosophy of the political regime would affect behavior of individuals as business participants. So, too, would the social environment, the influences within the lesser groups and organizations in which marketing participants act. Thus, pressures exerted through institutions which are common to all societies, but which differ in character among them, produce dissimilarities in marketing within different nations.

What Is Comparative?

Identification of marketing (1) as a dual technical and social activity and (2) as a consequence of environmental circumstances leads to the next question: What is *comparative* marketing? The term "comparative" has been used in the first stage of its definition to mean simply comparison. This has been a casual uncritical usage but one which has had acceptance because of the ease with which visual comparison or contrasts can be made by anyone observing two business systems. One country has smaller (perhaps family-oriented) retail establishments than another, buyers rather than sellers take initiative in market search and negotiation, or management decisions are made with either greater haste or greater deliberation—these facts have been cited as "comparative" evidence. The truth is that they are descriptive rather than comparative, as shown by the following illustration.

Assume that marketing and its environments are identified in two countries. As shown in Figure 3, let

- A represent the marketing process in the home country,
- B represent the marketing process in the foreign country,

FIGURE 2. Relation of Environmental Factors to Dependent Elements of Marketing

		Elements of Marketing	
		Technical	Social

National Environments / Physical and Economic	Size of:
	  Country
	  Population
	  GNP
	Level of Living
	Transportation System
	Etc.
		Products
		Price
		Profits
		Costs
		Brands
		Differentiation
		Layouts
		Scales
		Channels
		Markets
		Institutions
		Flows
		Processes	

National Environments / Societal and Social	Family School Church Economy Government Military Leisure		Social Systems Roles Behavior Interaction Management

- C represent the environment of the home country, and
- D represent the environment of the foreign country.

The *comparison* of marketing in two countries may be indicated by the symbols A : B. This is simply a descriptive statement, not an analytical one. So too is the relationship of C : D, which indicates a comparison of environments.

The relationships of A : C and of B : D, on the other hand, are statements of *environmentalism*. They indicate the orientation of each marketing system to its own environment, or rather to its particular complex of environments—physical, societal, social, economic, legal, and political. None of these sets of relationships, however, represents a truly comparative statement.

The *comparative* analysis in this illustration is suggested by the following equation:

$$A : C = B : D$$

This is to say that comparative study is not simply a description of either marketing or environmental differences but rather a *comparison of relationships between marketing and its environment in two or more countries*. In this context, differences which might be emphasized in simple comparisons may become similarities when related to an environmental frame of reference. It is in this sense that similarities—similarities of relationships, patterns, causes-and-effects—become more significant than bare differences to the seasoned international observer. To the extent that unexplainable differences can be replaced by explainable

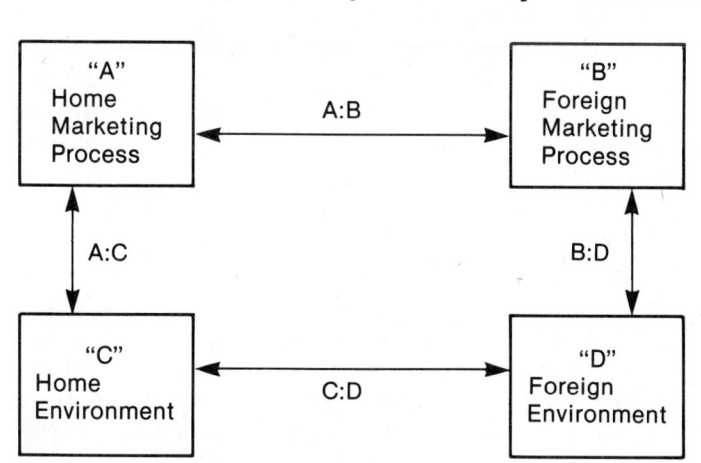

FIGURE 3. Model for Comparative Analysis

relationships, tentative generalizations can be postulated and theories constructed.

The translation of differences into such comparative patterns relates directly to the question of whether marketing in two countries is really "different," whether it should be organizationally segregated in the business enterprise and academically specialized in "international" functional courses contrasted with those for domestic business. An answer to this question is suggested in the distinctions here made. To the extent that either business managers or academicians *perceive* differences in foreign and domestic marketing, they will deal with them as distinct and different. To the extent that they perceive the inherent similarities, they will deal with them in more integrated marketing theory, business structure, and academic offering.

WHAT IS INTERNATIONAL?

The explanation of comparative analysis is intended to emphasize the actions and interactions of participants in the marketing process who act under the constraints of their respective societies. Their interactions constitute the business or marketing process and are generally private entrepreneurial undertakings. Cross-cultural private negotiations, however, are not the whole of international trade. In addition to the respective national environments, there is an identifiable international—or rather *inter-national*—environment affecting marketing and other business decisions. This is the environment in which trade and transactions are made *across* national borders, rather than *within* different national domains. It is created by national sovereignties on behalf of the collective interests of their nations. This inter-national environment presents still another factor to be considered in the question of whether domestic and international marketing are different or similar.

To illustrate the character of this environment and its distinction from the national environments previously discussed, the point might be made that greater environmental differences may be found within a country than between countries. For example, differences between Manhattan and Mississippi may be more significant for marketers than those between Manhattan and Madrid. Notwithstanding the similarities of environments *within two countries*, when the national interests of two nations are involved, a special environmental circumstance may arise. Within each nation there is usually a uniform national trade policy. Among nations, the respective interests of each make constraints upon marketers which are additional to those of the societal influences upon the market participants. These constraints may be exerted upon foreigners in international trade as well as upon citizens of the constraining nation.

As an example, the societal environments and business systems of three countries may be so similar that, in terms of comparative analysis, there would be little differences between their domestic and international marketing. On the other hand, while one nation may permit free trading across its borders, another, to protect its national interests, may restrict imports, impose tariffs, limit currency conversion, require trade registrations, set import quality standards, and so forth. Thus, while their *national* environments may produce similarities, the environment created *between* those nations, or the *inter*-national environment, makes for dissimilarities between domestic and international marketing. This fact concerning international marketing requires consideration in both business practices and academic curricula.

Conceptually represented, the international environment is depicted in Figure 4 as areas of influence in which the national or public interests of either home or host country governments influence the private commercial relations of both their own and foreign nationals. Normal marketing transactions, indicated at point A as private-private interactions, have already been explained as subject to the national environments of each participant. The international environment is identified by the interactions lettered, B, C, D, E, and F.

National interests affecting international marketing are expressed in part in relations of a government with *its own citizens* (B and C) through both encouragement and discouragement. Encouragement to exporting and direct foreign investment may be given through research, assistance, trade fairs, export credit insurance, and investment guarantees; discouragement may be given through import and export restrictions, investment restrictions, and antitrust regulation. Likewise, each country affects *foreign nationals* trading with its own citizens, as through import tariffs and other non-tariff regulations and other inducements to investment, joint venture restrictions, and the like. These relationships are denoted in blocks D and E. Finally, the international environment consists in part of the *interactions of governments* (F) which affect international marketing, as through the creation of common markets and free trade areas, consummation of commercial treaties, agreement on tariffs, or the unification of antitrust laws. Together these conditions constitute an environment quite apart from the foreign national environments of individuals with whom one may trade. It is truly an inter-national environment, and to the extent that it exists it increases the differences rather than the similarities between domestic and international marketing.

Conclusions

In relation to the question initially posed: "Are domestic and international marketing dissimilar?" the foregoing analysis leads to the following conclusions:

1. That marketing technology has universal validity and potential universal applicability.
2. That the applicability of marketing technology is dependent upon circumstances of the environments in which it is applied.
3. That the behavioral aspects of marketing, reflecting mainly cultural, societal, and social circumstances, indicate wide differences in marketing as it is carried on in different countries.
4. That notwithstanding particular behavior differences, the *relationships* between marketing practice and environment are susceptible to generalizations in analysis termed "comparative marketing."
5. That in addition to the national environmental influences upon marketing participants in different countries, nations' interests, individually and collectively, create an inter-national environ-

FIGURE 4. Relations of Private and Public Sectors in the International Environment

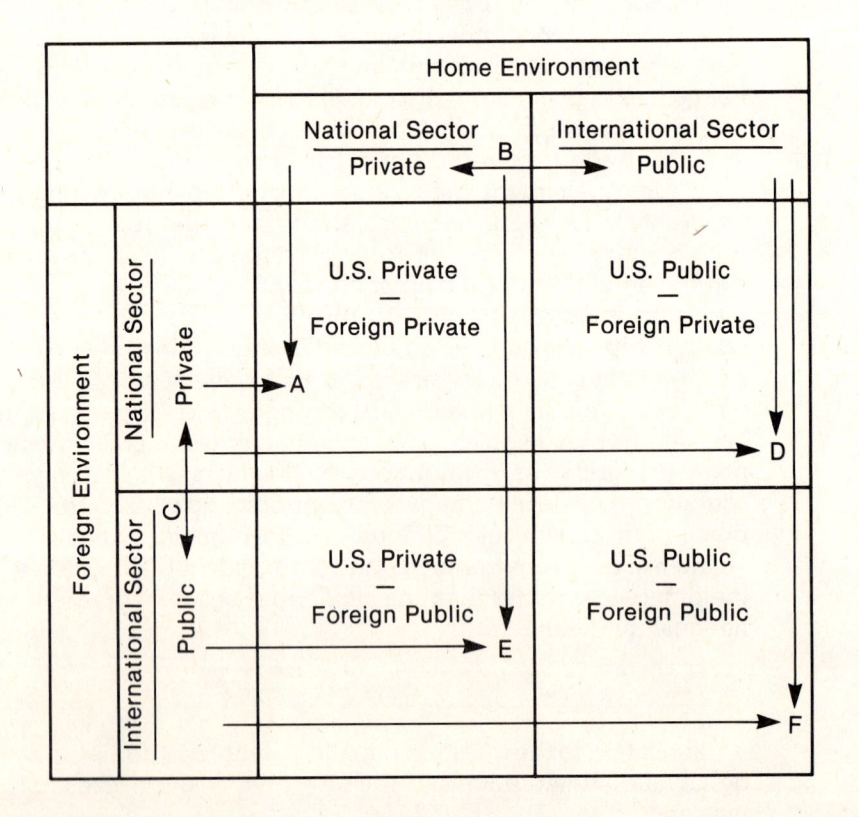

		Home Environment	
		National Sector Private	International Sector Public
Foreign Environment	National Sector Private	U.S. Private — Foreign Private	U.S. Public — Foreign Private
Foreign Environment	International Sector Public	U.S. Private — Foreign Public	U.S. Public — Foreign Public

ment in which the marketers operate. There is generally no equivalent to these factors within the national or domestic economy.
6. That marketing managers need to approach the international situation with expectation of both similarities and differences relative to domestic marketing, but with an understanding that both are embraced within a consistent body of marketing theory.
7. That academic marketing offerings should provide for thorough grounding in basic marketing technology, in environmental analysis both at home and abroad, and in those aspects of the international situation for which there is no equivalent in either country.

46 — The De-Americanization of Marketing Thought: In Search of a Universal Basis

Nikhilesh Dholakia, A. Fuat Firat, and Richard P. Bagozzi

Reprinted from *Theoretical Developments in Marketing*, published by the American Marketing Association, edited by Lamb and Dunne (1980), pp. 25–29. Reprinted by permission.

ABSTRACT

This paper argues that marketing thought is context-bound to the American industrial context. This has constrained the concepts in many important ways and retarded the development of globally valid analytical categories. A reconceptualization of the field, based on consumption needs is suggested.

INTRODUCTION

Theoretical exploration has become serious business in the field of marketing in recent years. It is possible today to discern paradigmatic diversity in the field (Bagozzi 1976), outlines of general theories (Bagozzi 1979, Bartels 1968, Hunt 1976), reflexive thinking (Bartels 1974) and even critical self-examination (Tucker 1974). These are vital signs in a field striving for theoretical depth and autonomy.

Surprisingly, the theoretical movement in marketing is bereft of any significant examination of the contextual character of marketing concepts. This paper explores the relationship between the contextual and conceptual bases of marketing. Specifically, it argues that:

1. Marketing concepts are a product of, and contextually bound to, the American industrial system.
2. This fact limits the spatial and temporal validity of marketing concepts.
3. The context boundedness inhibits the emergence of a universal conception of the nature and scope of marketing.
4. Specific biases and barriers are created in terms of theoretical development in the field.

5. Efforts are needed to de-contextualize, re-conceptualize and thereby universalize the analytical categories of marketing.

THE CONTEXT OF MARKETING THOUGHT

The history of the emergence and growth of marketing thought is well documented (Bartels 1962). Marketing as an academic field and distinct profession emerged in America at the turn of the century. Two questions are seldom asked: Why did this happen at the turn of the century? Why in America?

Timing of Marketing's Birth

Marketing activities like peddling, purveying, trading, bartering and hustling have existed throughout recorded history. Kotler (1980) is perceptive to recognize the paradox that "while marketing is one of man's newest action disciplines, it is also one of the world's oldest professions" (p. 3).

The formalization of marketing as a field of study in the early twentieth century, however, was no coincidence. Up to the late nineteenth century, capitalist industrialization was well underway but retained the broad character of classic atomistic competitive capitalism. However, with the development of mass-production and automation techniques the productive capabilities grew immensely. Local markets could no longer absorb this capacity, and distributive systems for widely dispersed markets were needed. Thus, the interest in distributive systems, and the movement of commodities through these, marked the beginnings of the marketing discipline, characterized by the commodity approach (Bartels 1962). As the commodity movements grew in size and quantity, recognition of different functions for smooth distribution and the organization, institutionalization and rationalization of these functions became a necessity, ushering in the functional and institutional approaches. Finally, growth and development in production techniques increased the supply capabilities to such an extent that effective demand was falling short of supply even when all possible markets were reached (Sweezy 1970). As a result, the managerial approach was developed to enable effective organization and orchestration of all the possible functions to regulate and promote demand (Kotler 1973).

Around the turn of the century, competitive capitalism—through a variety of centralizing mechanisms—transformed into monopoly capitalism (Sweezy 1970). Growth of marketing management organizations was further fostered by this concentration and centralization of capital, production and distribution. As Chandler (1966) observed, by the beginning of the twentieth century "most of the major industries had become dominated by a few large enterprises. These great industrial corporations no longer purchased and sold through agents, but they had their own nationwide buying and marketing organizations" (p. 110).

Thus, marketing developed hand-in-hand with two important trends: (i) growth of supply capabilities leaving effective demand behind creating a crisis of unused capital, and therefore, depression, and (ii) concentration of capital, leading to oligopolistic and monopolistic situations, changing the rules of competitive capitalism. These trends influenced the basic orientation of marketing thought. This orientation can be characterized by:

1. Marketing developed as a business activity, looking at the world and the markets from the perspective of the managers of business.
2. It developed as a technology of managing different elements of the marketing mix in order to regulate demand to meet supply capabilities.
3. It developed within capitalism, acquiring the characteristics of this system as its premise. Therefore, certain structural constraints specific to capitalism were assumed given.

The growth of monopoly capitalism as one of the structural constraints both enhanced marketing's development and gave it a certain character. In perfect competition the ability of individual firms to determine or influence price, product qualities, distribution structures, and information dissemination is minimal. Any real control over these elements necessitates some departure from perfect competition. Thus, the growth of techniques to influence consumer choice, rather than just study consumer preferences and inform consumers of potential alternatives, is directly related to imperfections in the competitive structure. As a matter of fact, one could say that there would be no need for formalized marketing in the pre-monopoly stage and monopoly capitalism could not survive without a highly developed managerial technology of marketing (Baran and Sweezy 1966, ch. 5). The concepts and methods of marketing have constantly adapted to the needs and demands of monopoly capitalism. Without being aware of the term, Baran and Sweezy correctly identify "the marketing concept" as an essential condition of the American economy in the 1950s and 1960s. They observe the "emergence of a condition in which the sales and production efforts interpenetrate each other to such an extent as to become virtually indistinguishable" (p. 131).

Although marketing concepts are still closely tied to the requirements of capitalism, it is possible to discern a trend from the late 1960s of treating marketing concepts as separate from the industrial-economic context. The broadening movement and the subsequent exchange–theoretical developments represent the first strivings for "disciplinarity" (as opposed to mere technical advance) in marketing.

Place of Marketing's Birth

Not only is marketing a product of capitalism, it is specifically an American product. Although America was not the leading capitalist country at the turn of the century, it had features that set it apart from other capitalisms: (a) acccumulation and growth occurred through internal colonization rather than external colonialism, (b) there was no significant feudal legacy to leave its imprint on industrial structures and methods, (c) immigration and expansion of frontiers created a geographically and demographically vast market, (d) centralization of capital occurred more through outright acquisitions and mergers than through holding companies or financial ties, as happened in Europe (Sweezy 1970, ch. 14).

In such an environment, demand creation and servicing tasks could not be handled by traditional European-type institutions such as holding companies, managing agencies and trading houses. Consequently, American capitalism invented a unique—and in retrospect highly successful—model of capital accumulation through demand management. This was the corporate marketing department, which over the years assumed increasing centrality in corporate as well as general economic affairs. Correspondingly, in the academic field, the conception of marketing moved from a peripheral sales-stimulative function to a central and strategic corporate function (Kotler 1980, ch. 1). It is significant to note that with the collapse of colonialism and the ravages of two world wars, European and Japanese capitalism found their traditional "marketing" models increasingly irrelevant. They started emulating the American model with the result that America became the fountainhead of marketing knowhow in the post-war years.

GLOBAL VALIDITY OF MARKETING CONCEPTS

The Dominant Paradigm

The dominant operational paradigm of marketing used throughout most of the world is the American one. The prototypical marketer is a large firm standing in competition against few other large firms. The marketer selects a strategic stance (product/market/competitive positioning) so as to maximize profit potential in a given business environment. The skeletal strategy is provided flesh in the form of a marketing plan based on an appropriate marketing mix. The formulation and execution of the marketing plan is carried out by a corporate marketing department with requisite informational support from market research.

This operational paradigm of marketing is used globally not because it is a valid representation of marketing reality worldwide but because of its spectacular success in the American business environment. The more remote a business environment is from the American one, the greater the likely irrelevance of the dominant paradigm.

Situations Repudiating the Dominant Paradigm

Many situations are observable in the world that do not fit the dominant paradigm in marketing. For example, in the socialist countries, regional, communal or societal planning mechanisms are used to satisfy demand. In practice this means that pricing and resource allocation decisions are made through a complex process of negotiations and adjustments. The point is that the quintessential marketing-like activities are *not* carried out in accordance with the marketing mix. Reforms (Lauter 1971) have been at times interpreted as a sign of convergence. This thesis is not borne out by facts. The adoption of Western managerial methods has been highly selective, not altering the basic character of socialist decision making (Gutman and Arkwright 1979).

Situations repudiating the marketing mix do not occur only in socialist countries. Third world countries that are by and large capitalist, but best characterized as dependent (Amin 1977; Wilber 1973), have little resemblance to "demand shortage" or "monopoly capitalism" situations in developed capitalist economies. Only a small sector in these third world countries, dominated by multinational companies, approximates American capitalism, and in this sector the dominant marketing paradigm finds some relevance and acceptance. When it comes to agricultural products, products of decentralized cottage industry, public sector industries, essential social services, etc., the marketing mix model offers little help to the decision makers of the third world. The marketing mix paradigm constantly recommended to these countries as part of the larger development assistant packages (Slater 1968), and as part of the dominant ideology, has been at times implemented by the decision makers in the third world with manifest counter-productivity (Illich 1973).

Finally, even in the developed capitalist countries one finds cases where the dominant marketing paradigm does not hold. In Japan, for example, prices, market segments, production level, etc., are planned and negotiated between industry and government representatives (Vogel 1978). In Scandinavia, consumer cooperatives act as members' buying agents, and negotiations replace the marketing mix model (Arndt 1979). Indeed, Arndt suggests that the marketing mix model be replaced with a newer one whose elements are negotiations, politics, administrative methods and conflict resolution techniques.

The main conclusions of the above arguments are that: (a) the dominant marketing paradigm is not valid or even relevant for large sections of the world system (b) even in the developed capitalist countries, as monopoly capitalism takes on newer forms, the relevance of the marketing mix diminishes.

CRISIS OF UNIVERSALITY

The global validity of the dominant marketing paradigm would not be a major problem were it not for the growth of a theoretical movement in the field which seeks a universal, disciplinary character for marketing concepts. If pragmatic ends are the only ends, American marketing technology can take an isolationist position and not be concerned with global issues. The growth of the field, however, has created a subjective need (for the researchers) to understand the nature of marketing and an objective need (for the field) to create more powerful conceptual frameworks. To use an analogy, alchemy continued as a basis of industry and medicine until the social conditions necessitated the emergence of modern physical science. In a similar way, the global social conditions today necessitate the creation of a universal social science of marketing. The lack of universality of marketing concepts manifests itself in the form of theoretical impasses discussed below.

Failure to Transcend Techno-Managerial Orientation

Although marketing emerged as a managerial technology to serve the requirements of American monopoly capitalism, it has grown to be a substantial body of knowledge concerned with a particular set of social phenomena, viz., how a society meets its consumption needs. As soon as one leaves the eclectic arena of definitions, however, and moves into the arena of substantive concepts, one finds that marketing has failed to develop any significant concepts that are explanatory rather than techno-managerial in orientation. Techniques and relationships in marketing are judged on the basis of how good a *predictor* these are of buying behavior or profitability rather than how well these *explain* the underlying social phenomena. This preoccupation with prediction and control has several consequences for theory development: (a) the process of inquiry rarely goes beyond the identification of regular patterns of (managerial) stimulus—(behavioral) response, (b) since predictive patterns hold within a given socioeconomic context, the generalizability of marketing concepts suffers, (c) only behavior of managerial interest (e.g., brand choice) rather than of wider social interest (e.g., consumption pattern formation and transformation) gets studied.

The techno-managerial orientation treats all phenomena which are not "manageable" as secondary, constituting an "uncontrolled" environment which must be tolerated and examined to the extent it affects manageable phenomena. Emergence of consumption patterns and cultures, public and collective consumption choices, institutionalization of consumption and marketing practices, etc., are ignored or peripherally treated by marketing researchers (Firat and Dholakia 1977).

Artificial Partialing of Behavioral Phenomena

As a subfield of marketing, consumer behavior has exhibited considerable theoretical depth in the study of behavioral phenomena. The inquiry into these behavioral phenomena, however, is truncated as soon as the behavior is outside the ambit of marketing mix influences. The focus, thus, is on buyer behavior rather than on the totality of consumption behavior. For example, consumption (and satisfaction of needs) may occur without antecedent buyer behavior as when a person grows his or her own food or shares things with fellow human beings. Such consumption behavior, however, would not find any research interest or support in the field of so-called consumer behavior. It is easy to imagine what other social sciences would be like if they focused only on instrumental behaviors: political science would study only voting behavior, economics would study only allocation processes, social psychology would study only influence strategies, etc.

The instrumental concerns in marketing and consumer behavior have resulted in real as well as opportunity losses in a theoretical sense. The real loss has been the high amount of unexplainable variance in brand choice models (Jacoby 1978). This is because brand buying is the unstable tip of the whole iceberg of consumption behavior and the explanation of brand buying may lie in the wider consumption context. The opportunity loss has been the failure of marketing scholars to study the social role of consumption, in spite of the favorable vantage point they have. This has meant the inability of marketing to contribute to social policies where consumption may have had an indirect but important influence.

Failure to Link Micro and Macro Concepts

Marketing concepts have been predominantly micro concepts, dealing with the buyer or the marketer. Very little work exists on marketing processes at a societal level (Bartels and Jenkins 1977). More disturbing, however, is the absence of any framework linking micro and macro concepts. Typically, marketing studies may focus on the effect of information load on choice behavior but not on social processes causing the information load, they may examine the relationship between personality and brand choice but not the formative aspects of personality or brand proliferation, they may investigate power relationships in a channel but not the wider power relationships in society of which these may be a part, and so on. It is not being suggested here that marketing expand its scope to include all social behavior. Nor is it necessary for each micro study to provide macro explanations of its terms and variables. What is required, however, is an overall conceptual framework which links micro and macro phenomena so that each study — micro, macro or mixed — can be related to the field as a whole and thereby contribute to its advance. In the absence of such framework, production of knowledge in marketing tends to be cumulative without being integrative.

IN SEARCH OF UNIVERSALITY

The quest for universality in marketing is not new; it is the normal striving for a field seeking autonomous professional status (Kuklick 1978). The broadening movement in marketing provided a decisive impetus to this quest for universality (Kotler and Levy 1969, Kotler 1972).

The broadening movement, however, chose precisely those concepts for generalization which were the products of a specific context and carried its birthmark. It generalized the dominant *operational* paradigm (marketing strategy and marketing mix) to non-traditional contexts, leaving the philosophical domain of marketing as restrictive as ever (Spratlen 1972). The broadening movement, thus, generalized the managerial paradigm of marketing but failed to universalize the theoretical basis of marketing.

The Universals of Marketing

What are the universals of marketing? Exchange has been proposed as the general (and by implication universal) basis on which a theory of marketing can be built (Bagozzi 1979). It is true that exchange is a generic concept which encompasses the transactional character of all marketing behavior and provides a powerful explanatory framework for such behavior. Exchange, however, is an instrumental concept—it can explain the *actions* of the participants in a marketing system but not the *ends* that marketing tries to achieve. Implicit in the earlier discussion on global validity of marketing was the notion that marketing is directed to the same ends globally—the satisfaction of consumption needs. The formation, transformation and satisfaction of consumption needs represent a global and universal set of social phenomena that could form the basis for an emergent social science of marketing.

The question of universality is in essence an epistemological and a topological one—what is the aim of the knowledge producing system in marketing and what boundaries does it want to operate within? If one is looking for a theory of *marketing action* mainly within the framework of commodity-exchange economies, then the exchange-theoretic approach is appropriate. If, however, one is interested in a larger theory of *marketing phenomena* (goals, structures, processes, actions, effects), then the basis of marketing thought should be the phenomena that are universally associated with marketing or marketing-like activities. Temporally as well as spatially, the formation, transformation and satisfaction of consumption needs represent such a set of universal phenomena.

Preface to a New Theory

It would be pretentious to claim that a comprehensive theory of marketing based on the formation, transformation and satisfaction of consumption needs is possible at this stage. It is possible, however, to outline some key features of such a theoretical paradigm. It may be useful to illustrate some of the ideas or *themes* that would require development as a part of such a theoretical approach.

A basic idea is that *consumption needs are social formations*. In case of organized consumers—corporations, institutions or families—this is a self-evident fact. Even in the case of individual human needs, there are social forms even though a few of these may have biological origins (Mennell 1979). For example, the basic hunger need of a baby soon takes on specific social forms—milk, cereal, meat, etc. It is easy to see that hunger would be expressed as a need for different food forms in different cultures. An important area of inquiry, therefore, concerns the *socialization processes* by which consumption needs are formed and the specific forms they take.

In a transitional period in a society, needs could get dramatically transformed. For example, Illich (1973) notes how thirst gets transformed into the need for a Coke as underdeveloped countries get integrated into the world market. Hence, *social change* would be an important theme for the new theoretical paradigm.

Broad consumption need-forms and corresponding satisfaction methods create *consumption patterns*. For example, transportation need in the American society has spawned a consumption pattern based on the private automobile and a system of highways. The emergence of specific consumption patterns is a social phenomenon in which political and economic factors play key roles. The *political economy of social choice* would have to be examined in detail to understand why different societies exhibit specific consumption patterns at particular stages (Carson 1978).

The consumption context for specific products and brands lies within given consumption patterns. The *structure of choice* would be a key variable in the study of choice behavior. The structure of choice is largely an outcome of the system of organizing the production in a society. Comparative marketing studies could contribute greatly by investigating the choice structures which different production systems create.

The *process of consumption* by which specific consumption choices are made would entail not only the study of learned behavior and influence processes but also the ways in which this process itself re-creates need-forms and related psychosocial orientations.

CONCLUSION

It is the weaving together of several such macro and micro themes which would make possible the emergence of a theoretical framework in marketing which is not context-bound and has universal validity. The research methodologies required for such theorizing already exist to a large measure as also a large supportive body of social science knowledge. What is most direly needed is a new philosophical orientation—to strive for understanding and comprehension and to remain critical of those tendencies which gloss over social reality in the name of one ideology or the other.

ENDNOTES

1. The term "monopoly capitalism" should not be confused with the term "monopoly." The latter refers to a single seller dominating a market. Monopoly capitalism (in contrast to competitive capitalism) refers to a stage in an economy when there is a high concentration of capital and control in a few firms.
2. The exchange theoretical work is an exception (Bagozzi 1979), but this work is more in the nature of a general theory of exchange rather than a general theory to explain the phenomena which marketing purports to explain.

REFERENCES

Amin, Samir (1977), *Imperialism and Unequal Development*, New York: Monthly Review, 1977.

Arndt, Johan (1979), "Toward a Concept of Domesticated Markets," *Journal of Marketing*, 43 (Fall), 69–75.

Bagozzi, Richard P. (1976), "Science, Politics and Social Construction of Marketing," in *Marketing: 1776–1976 and Beyond*, K. L. Bernhardt, ed., Chicago: AMA.

―――― (1979), "Toward a Formal Theory of Marketing Exchanges," AMA Special Conference on Marketing Theory, Feb. 7–9, 1979, Phoenix.

Baran, Paul A. and Paul M. Sweezy (1966), *Monopoly Capital: An Essay on the American Economic and Social Order*, New York: Monthly Review Press.

Bartels, Robert (1962), *The Development of Marketing Thought*, Homewood, IL: Irwin.

―――― (1968), "The General Theory of Marketing," *Journal of Marketing*, 32 (January), 29–33.

―――― (1974), "The Identity Crisis in Marketing," *Journal of Marketing*, 30 (October), 32–39.

―――― and Roger L. Jenkins (1977), "Macromarketing," *Journal of Marketing*, 41 (October), 17–20.

―――― (1973), "The Tasks of Marketing Management," *Journal of Marketing*, 37 (April), 42–44.

Chandler, Jr., Alfred D. (1966) "The Beginning of 'Big Business' in American History," in *Pivotal Interpretations of American History*, C. N. Degler, ed., New York: Macmillan.

Connerton, Paul (1976), "Introduction," in *Critical Sociology*, P. Connerton, ed., New York: Penguin.

Firat, A Fuat and Nikhilesh Dholakia (1977), "Consumption Patterns and Macromarketing: A Radical Perspective," *European Journal of Marketing*, 11 (September) 291–98.

Gutman, Patrick and Francis Arkwright (1979), "Multinationalization and the Countries of Eastern Europe," in *Transnational Corporations and World Order*, G. Modelski, ed., San Francisco: W. H. Freeman.

Hunt, Shelby D. (1976), "The Nature and Scope of Marketing," *Journal of Marketing*, 40 (July), 17–28.

Illich, Ivan (1973), "Outwitting the 'Developed' Countries," in *The Political Economy of Development*, C. K. Wilber, ed., New York: Random House.

Jacoby, Jacob (1978), "Consumer Research: A State of the Art Review," *Journal of Marketing*, 42 (April), 87–96.

Kotler, Philip (1972), "A Generic Concept of Marketing," *Journal of Marketing*, 36 (April), 46–54.

——— (1973), "The Tasks of Marketing Management," *Journal of Marketing*, 37 (April), 42–49.

——— (1980), *Marketing Management: Analysis Planning and Control*, 4th ed., Englewood Cliffs, NJ: Prentice-Hall.

——— and Sidney J. Levy (1969), "Broadening the Concept of Marketing," *Journal of Marketing*, 33 (January), 10–15.

Kuklick, Henrika (1978), "The Perils of Professionalism," *Social Science History*, 2 (Spring), 368–75.

Lange, Oskar and Fred M. Taylor (1938), *On the Economic Theory of Socialism*, New York: McGraw-Hill.

Lauter, G. Peter (1971), "The Changing Role of Marketing in the Eastern European Socialist Economies," *Journal of Marketing*, 35 (October), 16–20.

Mennell, Stephen (1979), "Theoretical Considerations on the Study of Cultural Needs," *Sociology*, 13 (May), 235–57.

Slater, Charles C. (1968), "Marketing Processes in Developing Latin American Societies," *Journal of Marketing*, 32 (July), 50–55.

Spratlen, Thaddeus H. (1972), "The Challenge of a Humanistic Value Orientation in Marketing" in *Society and Marketing*, N. Kangun, ed., New York: Harper and Row.

Sweezy, Paul M. (1970), *The Theory of Capitalist Development*, New York: Monthly Review Press.

Tucker, W. T. (1974), "Future Directions in Marketing Theory," *Journal of Marketing*, 38 (April), 30–35.

Vogel, Ezra F. (1978), "Guided Free Enterprise in Japan," *Harvard Business Review*, 56 (May–June), 161–70.

Wilber, Charles K., ed. (1973), *The Political Economy of Development and Underdevelopment*, New York: Random House.

47 The Globalization of Markets

Theodore Levitt

Reprinted by permission of the *Harvard Business Review*. "The Globalization of Markets" by Theodore Levitt (May–June 1983). Copyright © 1983 by the President and Fellows of Harvard College; all rights reserved.

A powerful force drives the world toward a converging commonality, and that force is technology. It has proletarianized communication, transport, and travel. It has made isolated places and impoverished peoples eager for modernity's allurements. Almost everyone everywhere wants all the things they have heard about, seen, or experienced via the new technologies.

The result is a new commercial reality—the emergence of global markets for standardized consumer products on a previously unimagined scale of magnitude. Corporations geared to this new reality benefit from enormous economies of scale in production, distribution, marketing, and management. By translating these benefits into reduced world prices, they can decimate competitors that still live in the disabling grip of old assumptions about how the world works.

Gone are accustomed differences in national or regional preference. Gone are the days when a company could sell last year's models—or lesser versions of advanced products—in the less-developed world. And gone are the days when prices, margins, and profits abroad were generally higher than at home.

The globalization of markets is at hand. With that, the multinational commercial world nears its end, and so does the multinational corporation.

The multinational and the global corporation are not the same thing. The multinational corporation operates in a number of countries, and adjusts its products and practices in each—at high relative costs. The global corporation operates with resolute constancy—at low relative cost—as if the entire world (or major regions of it) were a single entity; it sells the same things in the same way everywhere.

Which strategy is better is not a matter of opinion but of necessity. Worldwide communications carry everywhere the constant drumbeat of modern possibilities to lighten and enhance work, raise living standards, divert, and entertain. The same countries that ask the world to recognize and respect the individuality of their cultures insist on the wholesale transfer to them of modern goods, services, and technologies. Modernity is not just a wish but also a widespread practice among those who cling, with unyielding passion or religious fervor, to ancient attitudes and heritages.

Who can forget the televised scenes during the 1979 Iranian uprisings of young men in fashionable French-cut trousers and silky body shirts thirsting with raised modern weapons for blood in the name of Islamic fundamentalism?

In Brazil, thousands swarm daily from pre-industrial Bahian darkness into exploding coastal cities, there quickly to install television sets in crowded corrugated huts and, next to battered Volkswagens, make sacrificial offerings of fruit and fresh-killed chickens to Macumban spirits by candlelight.

During Biafra's fratricidal war against the Ibos, daily televised reports showed soldiers carrying bloodstained swords and listening to transistor radios while drinking Coca-Cola.

In the isolated Siberian city of Krasnoyarsk, with no paved streets and censored news, occasional Western travelers are stealthily propositioned for cigarettes, digital watches, and even the clothes off their backs.

The organized smuggling of electronic equipment, used automobiles, western clothing, cosmetics, and pirated movies into primitive places exceeds even the thriving underground trade in modern weapons and their military mercenaries.

A thousand suggestive ways attest to the ubiquity of the desire for the most advanced things that the world makes and sells — goods of the best quality and reliability at the lowest price. The world's needs and desires have been irrevocably homogenized. This makes the multinational corporation obsolete and the global corporation absolute.

LIVING IN THE REPUBLIC OF TECHNOLOGY

Daniel J. Boorstin, author of the monumental trilogy *The Americans*, characterized our age as driven by "the Republic of Technology [whose] supreme law... is convergence, the tendency for everything to become more like everything else."

In business, this trend has pushed markets toward global commonality. Corporations sell standardized products in the same way everywhere — autos, steel, chemicals, petroleum, cement, agricultural commodities and equipment, industrial and commercial construction, banking and insurance services, computers, semiconductors, transport, electronic instruments, pharmaceuticals, and telecommunications, to mention some of the obvious.

Nor is the sweeping gale of globalization confined to these raw material or high-tech products, where the universal language of customers and users facilitates standardization. The transforming winds whipped up by the proletarianization of communication and travel enter every crevice of life.

Commercially, nothing confirms this as much as the success of McDonald's from the Champs Elysées to the Ginza, of Coca-Cola in Bahrain and Pepsi-Cola in Moscow, and of rock music, Greek salad, Hollywood movies, Revlon cosmetics, Sony televisions, and Levi jeans everywhere. "High-touch" products are as ubiquitous as high-tech.

Starting from opposing sides, the high-tech and high-touch ends of the commercial spectrum gradually consume the undistributed middle in their cosmopolitan orbit. No one is exempt and nothing can stop the process. Everywhere everything gets more and more like everything else as the world's preference structure is relentlessly homogenized.

Consider the cases of Coca-Cola and Pepsi-Cola, which are globally standardized products sold everywhere and welcomed by everyone. Both successfully cross multitudes of national, regional, and ethnic taste buds trained to a variety of deeply ingrained local preferences of taste, flavor, consistency, effervescence, and aftertaste. Everywhere both sell well. Cigarettes, too, especially American-made, make year-to-year global inroads on territories previously held in the firm grip of other, mostly local, blends.

These are not exceptional examples. (Indeed their global reach would be even greater were it not for artificial trade barriers.) They exemplify a general drift toward the homogenization of the world and how companies distribute, finance, and price products.[1] Nothing is exempt. The products and methods of the industrialized world play a single tune for all the world, and all the world eagerly dances to it.

Ancient differences in national tastes or modes of doing business disappear. The commonality of preference leads inescapably to the standardization of products, manufacturing, and the institutions of trade and commerce. Small nation-based markets transmogrify and expand. Success in world competition turns on efficiency in production, distribution, marketing, and management, and inevitably becomes focused on price.

The most effective world competitors incorporate superior quality and reliability into their cost structures. They sell in all national markets the same kind of products sold at home or in their largest export market. They compete on the basis of appropriate value—the best combinations of price, quality, reliability, and delivery for products that are globally identical with respect to design, function, and even fashion.

That, and little else, explains the surging success of Japanese companies dealing worldwide in a vast variety of products—both tangible products like steel, cars, motorcycles, hi-fi equipment, farm machinery, robots, microprocessors, carbon fibers, and now even textiles, and intangibles like banking, shipping, general contracting, and soon computer software. Nor are high-quality and low-cost operations incompatible, as a host of consulting organizations and data engineers argue with vigorous vacuity. The reported data are incomplete, wrongly analyzed, and contradictory. The truth is that low-cost operations are the hallmark of corporate cultures that require and produce quality in all that they do. High quality and low costs are not opposing postures. They are compatible, twin identities of superior practice.[2]

To say that Japan's companies are not global because they export cars with left-side drives to the United States and the European continent, while those in Japan have right-side drives, or because they sell office machines through distributors in the United States but directly at home, or speak Portuguese in Brazil is to mistake a difference for a distinction. The same is true of Safeway and Southland retail chains operating effectively in the Middle East, and to not only native but also imported populations from Korea, the Philippines, Pakistan, India, Thailand, Britain, and the United States. National rules of the road differ, and so do distribution channels and languages. Japan's distinction is its unrelenting push for economy and value enhancement. That translates into a drive for standardization at high quality levels.

Vindication of the Model T

If a company forces costs and prices down and pushes quality and reliability up—while maintaining reasonable concern for suitability—customers will prefer its world-standardized products. The theory holds, at this stage in the evolution of globalization, no matter what conventional market research and even common sense may suggest about different national and regional tastes, preferences, needs, and institutions. The Japanese have repeatedly vindicated this theory, as did Henry Ford with the Model T. Most important, so have their imitators, including companies from South Korea (television sets and heavy construction), Malaysia (personal calculators and microcomputers), Brazil (auto parts and tools), Colombia (apparel), Singapore (optical equipment), and yes, even from the United States (office copiers, computers, bicycles, castings), Western Europe (automatic washing machines), Rumania (housewares), Hungary (apparel), Yugoslavia (furniture), and Israel (pagination equipment).

Of course, large companies operating in a single nation or even a single city don't standardize everything they make, sell, or do. They have product lines instead of a single product version, and multiple distribution channels. There are neighborhood, local, regional, ethnic, and institutional differences, even within metropolitan areas. But although companies customize products for particular market segments, they know that success in a world with homogenized demand requires a search for sales opportunities in similar segments across the globe in order to achieve the economies of scale necessary to compete.

Such a search works because a market segment in one country is seldom unique; it has close cousins everywhere precisely because technology has homogenized the globe. Even small local segments have their global equivalents everywhere and become subject to global competition, especially on price.

The global competitor will seek constantly to standardize his offering everywhere. He will digress from this standardization only after exhausting all possibilities to retain it, and he will push for reinstatement of standardization whenever digression and divergence have occurred. He will never assume that the customer is a king who knows his own wishes.

Trouble increasingly stalks companies that lack clarified global focus and remain inattentive to the economics of simplicity and standardization. The most endangered companies in the rapidly evolving world tend to be those that dominate rather small domestic markets with high value-added products for which there are smaller markets elsewhere. With transportation costs proportionately low, distant competitors will enter the now-sheltered markets of those companies with goods produced more cheaply under scale-efficient conditions. Global competition spells the end of domestic territoriality, no matter how diminutive the territory may be.

When the global producer offers his lower costs internationally, his patronage expands exponentially. He not only reaches into distant markets, but also attracts customers who previously held to local preferences and now capitulate to the attraction of lesser prices. The strategy of standardization not only responds to worldwide homogenized markets but also expands those markets with aggressive low pricing. The new technological juggernaut taps an ancient motivation—to make one's money go as far as possible. This is a universal—not simply a motivation but actually a need.

THE HEDGEHOG KNOWS

The difference between the hedgehog and the fox, wrote Sir Isaiah Berlin in distinguishing between Dostoevski and Tolstoy, is that the fox knows a lot about a great many things, but the hedgehog knows everything about one great thing. The multinational corporation knows a lot about a great many countries and congenially adapts to supposed differences. It willingly accepts vestigial national differences, not questioning the possibility of their transformation, not recognizing how the world is ready and eager for the benefit of modernity, especially when the price is right. The multinational corporation's accommodating mode to visible national differences is medieval.

By contrast, the global corporation knows everything about one great thing. It knows about the absolute need to be competitive on a worldwide basis as well as nationally and seeks constantly to drive down prices by standardizing what it sells and how it operates. It treats the world as composed of few standardized markets rather than many customized markets. It actively seeks and vigorously works toward global convergence. Its mission is modernity and its mode, price competition, even when it sells top-of-the-line, high-end products. It knows about the one great thing all nations and people have in common: scarcity.

Nobody takes scarcity lying down; everyone wants more. This in part explains division of labor and specialization of production. They enable people and nations to optimize their conditions through trade. The median is usually money.

Experience teaches that money has three special qualities: scarcity, difficulty of acquisition, and transience. People understandably treat it with respect. Everyone in the increasingly homogenized world market wants products and features that everybody else wants. If the price is low enough, they will take highly standardized world products, even if these aren't exactly what mother said was suitable, what immemorial custom decreed was right, or what market-research fabulists asserted was preferred.

The implacable truth of all modern production—whether of tangible or intangible goods—is that large-scale production of standardized items is generally cheaper within a wide range of volume than small-scale production. Some argue that CAD/CAM will allow companies to manufacture customized products on a small scale—but cheaply. But the argument misses the point. (For a more detailed discussion, see the insert, "Economies of Scope.") If a company treats the world as one or two distinctive product markets, it can serve the world more economically than if it treats it as three, four, or five product markets.

Why Remaining Differences?

Different cultural preferences, national tastes and standards, and business institutions are vestiges of the past. Some inheritances die gradually; others prosper and expand into mainstream global preferences. So-called ethnic markets are a good example. Chinese food, pita bread, country and western music, pizza, and jazz are everywhere. They are market segments that exist in worldwide proportions. They don't deny or contradict global homogenization but confirm it.

Many of today's differences among nations as to products and their features actually reflect the respectful accommodation of multinational corporations to what they believe are fixed local preferences. They *believe* preferences are fixed, not because they are but because of rigid habits of thinking about what actually is. Most executives in multinational corporations are thoughtlessly accommodating. They falsely presume that marketing means giving the customer what he says he wants rather than trying to understand exactly what he'd like. So they persist with high-cost, customized multinational products and practices instead of pressing hard and pressing properly for global standardization.

I do not advocate the systematic disregard of local or national differences. But a company's sensitivity to such differences does not require that it ignore the possibilities of doing things differently or better.

There are, for example, enormous differences among Middle Eastern countries. Some are socialist, some monarchies, some republics. Some take their legal heritage from the Napoleonic Code, some from the Ottoman Empire, and some from the British common law; except for Israel, all are influenced by Islam. Doing business means personalizing the business relationship in an obsessively intimate fashion. During the month of Ramadan, business discussions can start only after 10 o'clock at night, when people are tired and full of food after a day of fasting. A company must almost certainly have a local partner; a local lawyer is required (as, say, in New York), and irrevocable letters of credit are essential. Yet, as Coca-Cola's Senior Vice President Sam Ayoub noted, "Arabs are much more capable of making distinctions between cultural and religious purposes on the one hand and economic realities on the other than is generally assumed. Islam is compatible with science and modern times."

Barriers to globalization are not confined to the Middle East. The free transfer of technology and data across the boundaries of the European Common Market countries are hampered by legal and financial impedi-

Economies of Scope

One argument that opposes globalization says that flexible factory automation will enable plants of massive size to change products and product features quickly, without stopping the manufacturing process. These factories of the future could thus produce broad lines of customized products without sacrificing the scale economies that come from long production runs of standardized items. Computer-aided design and manufacturing (CAD/CAM), combined with robotics, will create a new equipment and process technology (EPT) that will make small plants located close to their markets as efficient as large ones located distantly. Economies of scale will not dominate, but rather economies of scope—the ability of either large or small plants to produce great varieties of relatively customized products at remarkably low costs. If that happens, customers will have no need to abandon special preferences.

I will not deny the power of these possibilities. But possibilities do not make probabilities. There is no conceivable way in which flexible factory automation can achieve the scale economies of a modernized plant dedicated to mass production of standardized lines. The new digitized equipment and process technologies are available to all. Manufacturers with minimal customization and narrow product-line breadth will have costs far below those with more customization and wider lines.

ments. And there is resistance to radio and television interference ("pollution") among neighboring European countries.

But the past is a good guide to the future. With persistence and appropriate means, barriers against superior technologies and economics have always fallen. There is no recorded exception where reasonable effort has been made to overcome them. It is very much a matter of time and effort.

A Failure in Global Imagination

Many companies have tried to standardize world practice by exporting domestic products and processes without accommodation or change—and have failed miserably. Their deficiencies have been seized on as evidence of bovine stupidity in the face of abject impossibility. Advocates of global standardization see them as examples of failures in execution.

In fact, poor execution is often an important cause. More important, however, is failure of nerve—failure of imagination.

Consider the case for the introduction of fully automatic home laundry equipment in Western Europe at a time when few homes had even semiautomatic machines. Hoover, Ltd., whose parent company was headquartered in North Canton, Ohio had a prominent presence in Britain as a producer of vacuum cleaners and washing machines. Due to insufficient demand in the home market and low exports to the European continent, the large washing machine plant in England operated far below capacity. The company needed to sell more of its semiautomatic or automatic machines.

Because it had a "proper" marketing orientation, Hoover conducted consumer preference studies in Britain and each major continental country. The results showed feature preferences clearly enough among several countries (see the *Exhibit*).

The incremental unit variable costs (in pounds sterling) of customizing to meet just a few of the national preferences were:

	£	s.	d.
Stainless steel vs. enamel drum	1	0	0
Porthole window		10	0
Spin speed of 800 rpm vs. 700 rpm		15	0
Water heater	2	15	0
6 vs. 5 kilos capacity	1	10	0
	£6	10s	0d

$18.20 at the exchange rate of that time.

Considerable plant investment was needed to meet other preferences. The lowest retail prices (in pounds sterling) of leading locally produced brands in the various countries were approximately:

U.K.	£110
France	114
West Germany	113
Sweden	134
Italy	57

Product customization in each country would have put Hoover in a poor competitive position on the basis of price, mostly due to the higher manufacturing costs incurred by short production runs for separate features. Because Common market tariff reduction programs were then incomplete, Hoover also paid tariff duties in each continental country.

How to Make a Creative Analysis

In the Hoover case, an imaginative analysis of automatic washing machine sales in each country would have revealed that:

EXHIBIT. Consumer Preferences as to Automatic Washing Machine Features in the 1960s

Features	Great Britain	Italy	West Germany	France	Sweden
Shell dimensions*	34" and narrow	Low and narrow	34" and wide	34" and narrow	34" and wide
Drum material	Enamel	Enamel	Stainless steel	Enamel	Stainless steel
Loading	Top	Front	Front	Front	Front
Front porthole	Yes/no	Yes	Yes	Yes	Yes
Capacity	5 kilos	4 kilos	6 kilos	5 kilos	6 kilos
Spin speed	700 rpm	400 rpm	850 rpm	600 rpm	800 rpm
Water-heating system	No†	Yes	Yes‡	Yes	No†
Washing action	Agitator	Tumble	Tumble	Agitator	Tumble
Styling features	Inconspicuous appearance	Brightly colored	Indestructible appearance	Elegant appearance	Strong appearance

* 34" height was (in the process of being adopted as) a standard work-surface height in Europe.
† Most British and Swedish homes had centrally heated hot water.
‡ West Germans preferred to launder at temperatures higher than generally provided centrally.

1. Italian automatics, small in capacity and size, low-powered, without built-in heaters, with porcelain enamel tubs, were priced aggressively low and were gaining large market shares in all countries, including West Germany.
2. The best-selling automatics in West Germany were heavily advertised (three times more than the next most promoted brand), were ideally suited to national tastes, and were also by far the highest priced machines available in that country.
3. Italy, with the lowest penetration of washing machines of any kind (manual, semiautomatic, or automatic) was rapidly going directly to automatics, skipping the pattern of first buying hand-wringer, manually assisted machines and then semiautomatics.
4. Detergent manufacturers were just beginning to promote the technique of cold-water and tepid-water laundering then used in the United States.

The growing success of small, low-powered, low-speed, low-capacity, low-priced Italian machines, even against the preferred but highly priced and highly promoted brand in West Germany, was significant. It contained a powerful message that was lost on managers confidently wedded to a distorted version of the marketing concept according to which you give the customer what he says he wants. In fact the customers *said* they wanted certain features, but their behavior demonstrated they'd take other features provided the price and the promotion were right.

In this case it was obvious that, under prevailing conditions, people preferred a low-priced automatic over any kind of manual or semi-automatic machine and certainly over higher priced automatics, even though the low-priced automatics failed to fulfill all their expressed preferences. The supposedly meticulous and demanding German consumers violated all expectations by buying the simple, low-priced Italian machines.

It was equally clear that people were profoundly influenced by promotions of automatic washers; in West Germany, the most heavily promoted ideal machine also had the largest market share despite its high price. Two things clearly influenced customers to buy: low price regardless of feature preferences and heavy promotion regardless of price. Both factors helped homemakers get what they most wanted — the superior benefits bestowed by fully automatic machines.

Hoover should have aggressively sold a simple, standardized high-quality machine at a low price (afforded by the 17% variable cost reduction that the elimination of £6-10-0 worth of extra features made possible). The suggested retail prices could have been somewhat less than £100. The extra funds "saved" by avoiding unnecessary plant modifications would have supported an extended service network and aggressive media promotions.

Hoover's media message should have been: *this* is the machine that you, the homemaker, *deserve* to have to reduce the repetitive heavy daily household burdens, so that *you* may have more constructive time to spend with your children and your husband. The promotion should also have targeted the husband to give him, preferably in the presence of his wife, a sense of obligation to provide an automatic washer for her even before he bought an automobile for himself. An aggressively low price, combined with heavy promotion of this kind, would have overcome previously expressed preferences for particular features.

The Hoover case illustrates how the perverse practice of the marketing concept and the absence of any kind of marketing imagination let multinational attitudes survive when customers actually want the benefits of global standardization. The whole project got off on the wrong foot. It asked people what features they wanted in a washing machine rather than what they wanted out of life. Selling a line of products individually tailored to each nation is thoughtless. Managers who took pride in practicing the marketing concept to the fullest did not, in fact, practice it at all. Hoover asked the wrong questions, then applied neither thought nor imagination to the answers. Such companies are like the ethnocentricists in the Middle Ages who saw with everyday clarity the sun revolving around the earth and offered it as Truth. With no additional data but a more searching mind, Copernicus, like the hedgehog, interpreted a more compelling and accurate reality. Data do not yield information except with the intervention of the mind. Information does not yield meaning except with the intervention of imagination.

Accepting the Inevitable

The global corporation accepts for better or for worse that technology drives consumers relentlessly toward the same common goals—alleviation of life's burdens and the expansion of discretionary time and spending power. Its role is profoundly different from what it has been for the ordinary corporation during its brief, turbulent, and remarkably protean history. It orchestrates the twin vectors of technology and globalization for the world's benefit. Neither fate, nor nature, nor God but rather the necessity of commerce created this role.

In the United States two industries became global long before they were consciously aware of it. After over a generation of persistent and acrimonious labor shutdowns, the United Steelworkers of America have not called an industrywide strike since 1959; the United Auto Workers have not shut down General Motors since 1970. Both unions realize that they have become global—shutting down all or most of U.S. manufacturing would not shut out U.S. customers. Overseas suppliers are there to supply the market.

Cracking the Code of Western Markets

Since the theory of the marketing concept emerged a quarter of a century ago, the more managerially advanced corporations have been eager to offer what customers clearly wanted rather than what was merely convenient. They have created marketing departments supported by professional market researchers of awesome and often costly proportions. And they have proliferated extraordinary numbers of operations and product lines—highly tailored products and delivery systems for many different markets, market segments, and nations.

Significantly, Japanese companies operate almost entirely without marketing departments or market research of the kind so prevalent in the West. Yet, in the colorful words of General Electric's chairman John F. Welch, Jr., the Japanese, coming from a small cluster of resource-poor islands, with an entirely alien culture and an almost impenetrably complex language, have cracked the code of Western markets. They have done it not by looking with mechanistic thoroughness at the way markets are different but rather by searching for meaning with a deeper wisdom. They have discovered the one great thing all markets have in common—an overwhelming desire for dependable, world-standard modernity in all things, at aggressively low prices. In response, they deliver irresistible value everywhere, attracting people with products that market-research technocrats described with superficial certainty as being unsuitable and uncompetitive.

The wider a company's global reach, the greater the number of regional and national preferences it will encounter for certain product features, distribution systems, or promotional media. There will always need to be some accommodation to differences. But the widely prevailing and often unthinking belief in the immutability of these differences is generally mistaken. Evidence of business failure because of lack of accommodation is often evidence of other shortcomings.

Take the case of Revlon in Japan. The company unnecessarily alienated retailers and confused customers by selling world-standardized cosmetics only in elite outlets; then it tried to recover with low-priced world-standardized products in broader distribution, followed by a change in the company president and cutbacks in distribution as costs rose faster than sales. The problem was not that Revlon didn't understand the Japanese market; it didn't do the job right, wavered in its programs, and was impatient to boot.

By contrast, the Outboard Marine Corporation, with imagination, push, and persistence, collapsed long-established three-tiered distribution channels in Europe into a more focused and controllable two-step system—and did so despite the vociferous warnings of local trade groups. It also reduced the number and types of retail outlets. The result was greater improvement in credit and product-installation service to customers, major cost reductions, and sales advances.

In its highly successful introduction of Contac 600 (the timed-release decongestant) into Japan, SmithKline Corporation used 35 wholesalers instead of the 1,000-plus that established practice required. Daily contacts with the wholesalers and key retailers, also in violation of established practice, supplemented the plan, and it worked.

Denied access to established distribution institutions in the United States, Komatsu, the Japanese manufacturer of lightweight farm machinery, entered the market through over-the-road construction equipment dealers in rural areas of the Sunbelt, where farms are smaller, the soil sandier and easier to work. Here inexperienced distributors were able to attract customers on the basis of Komatsu's product and price appropriateness.

In cases of successful challenge to prevailing institutions and practices, a combination of product reliability and quality, strong and sustained support systems, aggressively low prices, and sales-compensation packages, as well as audacity and implacability, circumvented, shattered, and transformed very different distribution systems. Instead of resentment, there was admiration.

Still, some differences between nations are unyielding, even in a world of microprocessors. In the United States almost all manufacturers of microprocessors check them for reliability through a so-called parallel system of testing. Japan prefers the totally different sequential testing system. So Teradyne Corporation, the world's largest producer of microprocessor test equipment, makes one line for the United States and one for Japan. That's easy.

What's not so easy for Teradyne is to know how best to organize and manage, in this instance, its marketing effort. Companies can organize by product, region, function, or by using some combination of these. A company can have separate marketing organizations for Japan and for the United States, or it can have separate product groups, one working largely in Japan and the other in the United States. A single manufacturing facility or marketing operation might service both markets, or a company might use separate marketing operations for each.

Questions arise if the company organizes by product. In the case of Teradyne, should the group handling the parallel system, whose major market is the United States, sell in Japan and compete with the group focused on the Japanese market? If the company organizes regionally, how do regional groups divide their efforts between promoting the parallel versus the sequential system? If the company organizes in terms of function, how does it get commitment in marketing, for example, for one line instead of the other?

There is no one reliably right answer—no one formula by which to get it. There isn't even a satisfactory contingent answer.[3] What works well for one company or one place may fail for another in precisely the same place, depending on the capabilities, histories, reputations, resources, and even the cultures of both.

THE EARTH IS FLAT

The differences that persist throughout the world despite its globalization affirm an ancient dictum of economics—that things are driven by what happens at the margin, not at the core. Thus, in ordinary competitive analysis, what's important is not the average price but the marginal price; what happens not in the usual case but at the interface of newly erupting conditions. What counts in commercial affairs is what happens at the cutting edge. What is most striking today is the underlying similarities of what is happening now to national preferences at the margin. These similarities at the cutting edge cumulatively form an overwhelming, predominant commonality everywhere.

To refer to the persistence of economic nationalism (protective and subsidized trade practices, special tax aids, or restrictions for home market producers) as a barrier to the globalization of markets is to make a valid point. Economic nationalism does have a powerful persistence. But, as with the present almost totally smooth internationalization of investment capital, the past alone does not shape or predict the future. (For reflections on the internationalization of capital, see the insert, "The Shortening of Japanese Horizons.")

Reality is not a fixed paradigm, dominated by immemorial customs and derived attitudes, heedless of powerful and abundant new forces. The world is becoming increasingly informed about the liberating and enhancing possibilities of modernity. The persistence of the inherited varieties of national preferences rests uneasily on increasing evidence of, and restlessness regarding, their inefficiency, costliness, and confinement. The historic past, and the national differences respecting commerce and industry it spawned and fostered everywhere, is now subject to relatively easy transformation.

Cosmopolitanism is no longer the monopoly of the intellectual and leisure classes; it is becoming the established property and defining characteristic of all sectors everywhere in the world. Gradually and irresistibly it breaks down the walls of economic insularity, nationalism, and chauvinism. What we see today as escalating commercial nationalism is simply the last violent death rattle of an obsolete institution.

Companies that adapt to and capitalize on economic convergence can still make distinctions and adjustments in different markets. Persistent differences in the world are consistent with fundamental underlying commonalities; they often complement rather than oppose each other—in business as they do in physics. There is, in physics, simultaneously matter and anti-matter working in symbiotic harmony.

The earth is round, but for most purposes it's sensible to treat it as flat. Space is curved, but not much for everyday life here on earth.

Divergence from established practice happens all the time. But the multinational mind, warped into circumspection and timidity by years of stumbles and transnational troubles, now rarely challenges existing overseas practices. More often it considers any departure from inherited domestic routines as mindless, disrespectful, or impossible. It is the mind of a bygone day.

The successful global corporation does not abjure customization or differentiation for the requirements of markets that differ in product preferences, spending patterns, shopping preferences, and institutional or legal arrangements. But the global corporation accepts and adjusts to these differences only reluctantly, only after relentlessly testing their immutability, after trying in various ways to circumvent and reshape them as we saw in the cases of Outboard Marine in Europe, SmithKline in Japan, and Komatsu in the United States.

There is only one significant respect in which a company's activities around the world are important, and this is in what it produces and how it sells. Everything else derives from, and is subsidiary to, these activities.

The purpose of business is to get and keep a customer. Or, to use Peter Drucker's more refined construction, to *create* and keep a customer.

The Shortening of Japanese Horizons

One of the most powerful yet least celebrated forces driving commerce toward global standardization is the monetary system, along with the international investment process.

Today money is simply electronic impulses. With the speed of light it moves effortlessly between distant centers (and even lesser places). A change of ten basis points in the price of a bond causes an instant and massive shift of money from London to Tokyo. The system has profound impact on the way companies operate throughout the world.

Take Japan, where high debt-to-equity balance sheets are "guaranteed" by various societal presumptions about the virtue of "a long view," or by government policy in other ways. Even here, upward shifts in interest rates in other parts of the world attract capital out of the country in powerful proportions. In recent years more and more Japanese global corporations have gone to the world's equity markets for funds. Debt is too remunerative in high-yielding countries to keep capital at home to feed the Japanese need. As interest rates rise, equity becomes a more attractive option for the issuer.

The long-term impact on Japanese enterprise will be transforming. As the equity proportion of Japanese corporate capitalization rises, companies will respond to the shorter-term investment horizons of the equity markets. Thus the much-vaunted Japanese corporate practice to taking the long view will gradually disappear.

A company must be wedded to the ideal of innovation—offering better or more preferred products in such combinations of ways, means, places, and at such prices that prospects *prefer* doing business with the company rather than with others.

Preferences are constantly shaped and reshaped. Within our global commonality enormous variety constantly asserts itself and thrives, as can be seen within the world's single largest domestic market, the United States. But in the process of world homogenization, modern markets expand to reach cost-reducing global proportions. With better and cheaper communication and transport, even small local market segments hitherto protected from distant competitors now feel the pressure of their presence. Nobody is safe from global reach and the irresistible economies of scale.

Two vectors shape the world—technology and globalization. The first helps determine human preferences; the second, economic realities. Regardless of how much preferences evolve and diverge, they also gradually converge and form markets where economies of scale lead to reduction of costs and prices.

The modern global corporation contrasts powerfully with the aging multinational corporation. Instead of adapting to superficial and even entrenched differences within and between nations, it will seek sensibly to force suitably standardized products and practices on the entire globe. They are exactly what the world will take, if they come also with low prices, high quality, and blessed reliability. The global company will operate, in this regard, precisely as Henry Kissinger wrote in *Years of Upheaval* about the continuing Japanese economic success—"voracious in its collection of information, impervious to pressure, and implacable in execution."

Given what is everywhere the purpose of commerce, the global company will shape the vectors of technology and globalization into its great strategic fecundity. It will systematically push these vectors toward their own convergence, offering everyone simultaneously high-quality, more or less standardized products at optimally low prices, thereby achieving for itself vastly expanded markets and profits. Companies that do not adapt to the new global realities will become victims of those that do.

ENDNOTES

1. In a landmark article, Robert D. Buzzell pointed out the rapidity with which barriers to standardization were falling. In all cases they succumbed to more and cheaper advanced ways of doing things. See "Can You Standardize Multinational Marketing?" *HBR* November–December 1968, p. 102.
2. There is powerful new evidence for this, even though the opposite has been urged

by analysts of PIMS data for nearly a decade. See "Product Quality, Cost Production and Business Performance—A Test of Some Key Hypotheses" by Lynn W. Phillips, Dae Chang and Robert D. Buzzell, Harvard Business School Working Paper No. 83-13.
3. For a discussion of multinational reorganization, see Christopher A. Bartlett, "MNCs: Get Off the Reorganization Merry-Go-Round," *HBR* March–April 1983, p. 138.

SECTION M
Industrial Marketing

There has been a recent resurgence of interest in industrial marketing as a separate and unique domain of marketing practice. It is argued that most marketing concepts and practices are less relevant to industrial marketing because they are based on the realities of consumer marketing.

Many marketers point out that selling a large mainframe computer system to an industrial account is not the same as selling toothpaste. While this is true, it must be also pointed out that selling a custom-built house to a consumer is also not the same as selling toothpaste. Conversely, selling office supplies such as paper clips and stationery is also not the same as selling the large mainframe computer system. Thus, there may be more commonality between office supplies and toothpaste in terms of product, price, distribution, and promotion practices. Similarly, there may be more similarities with respect to the marketing mix between installing a mainframe computer and building a custom house. In other words, there are more differences *within* industrial and consumer marketing than *between* them.

It is also not proven that industrial buyers are more rational than other consumers. The degree of rational versus nonrational buying behavior seems to be equally prevalent in both markets. If you do not believe this, it may be worth noticing the conspicuous consumption behavior among officer workers in such areas as office furniture, office size, dress, and other normative criteria provided for organizational stratification.

Finally, it is also not true that industrial markets tend to be commodity markets in which only price is the driver for market share. Both industrial and consumer markets tend to have price as well as nonprice competition.

It is our belief that the differences between industrial and consumer marketing are more imagined than real.

48. Fundamental Differences Between Industrial and Consumer Marketing

Industrial Marketing Committee Review Board*

Reprinted from the *Journal of Marketing,* published by the American Marketing Association, Vol. 19 (October 1954), pp. 152–58. Reprinted by permission.

INTRODUCTION

The subject of this monograph concerns modern marketing with its many ramifications, apparent cross currents, and obvious parallelisms. It is manifestly impossible to lay down "hard and fast" rules which encompass all of the fringe differences between industrial and consumer marketing. So many exceptions exist in most areas that these differences, as well as similarities, can only be stated in general terms.

There is, however, a definite need for "bench marks" to which the reader may return from time to time like a surveyor to check the accuracy of his work or to serve as a "point of departure" into other parts of the geography surrounding the bench marks.

For us, these fixed points will be definitions basic to the subject.

Marketing

Marketing includes those business activities involved in the flow of goods and services from production to consumption.[1]

Goods and services are of two types; consumer and industrial.

Consumer Goods

Goods destined for use by the individual ultimate consumer and in such form that they can be used by him without further commercial processing...[1] ...This is a portion of the definition prepared by the Committee on Definitions and the balance of the statement does not include consumer services such as hairdressing, window-washing, furnace-cleaning, laundry, etc., yet these are an integral part of the broad consumer marketing field.

Industrial Goods

Goods which are used in producing consumers' goods, other business or industrial goods, and services and/or in facilitating the operation of an enterprise, may include land and buildings for business purposes, equipment (installation and accessory), operating supplies, raw materials, fabricated materials.[2] Thomas A. Staudt of Indiana University boils this down to "Industrial goods are commonly defined as those goods used in the production of other goods and services." (This definition seems to omit industrial services which are playing an inceasingly important part in the operation of a number of industries such as acid-treatment for oil wells and prospecting services, aerial surveys, and the like.)

Even with these definitions there must be an awareness that in many instances a specific commodity may either be an industrial good or a consumer good, depending upon the use to which it is put. Two examples will suffice to illustrate the points:

1. A manufacturing company may buy the same kind of powdered soap for use in soap dispensers in lavoratories which the housewife buys in an identical package for use in her washing machine;
2. The typewriter used for making out production orders for machine tools, wire rope, office furniture or what-have-you, may be identical with the one purchased at the local office equipment store for occasional use in the home.

DIFFERENCES OWING TO THE NATURE OF THE MARKET OR THE BUYERS

1. A part of the demand for industrial goods is a derived demand from consumer goods and services and a part from government, defense, and war purchases. The apparent influence of the derived demand for various types of industrial goods is diluted rapidly as the chain of purchases recedes from the consumer product application.
2. Rational buying motives appear to predominate in the industrial field (as against emotional motives in the consumer field) but their influence declines with the increase in product similarity.
3. Industrial buyers usually purchase raw materials and component parts on a policy formulation basis expressed in quantity, price, and specification; capital production equipment on a projected cost analysis; and supplies from habit and availability. Consumer purchasing policies and methods are less well-defined.
4. The number of industrial buyers is much smaller than the number of consumer buyers. (In 1947 there were 240,881 man-

ufacturing plants as contrasted with the 1950 census population figure totaling 42,520,000 family units.) Some specialized industrial markets may comprise less than a dozen potential customers.

5. Industrial markets are likely to be much more concentrated geographically. For example, the 1947 Census of Manufacturers shows that the 53 metropolitan areas in the U.S. each having over 40,000 industrial wage earners had 59 percent of the total industrial wage earners but only 24 percent of the total U.S. population. The disparity is much more pronounced if the top ten industrial metropolitan areas are compared—37 percent of the wage earners but only 13 percent of the population.
6. Single unit or small volume purchases are characteristic in consumer marketing. Industrial buying covers not only single unit purchases but also a prevalence of volume purchasing of raw materials and component parts and may include volume purchasing of supplies.
7. Multiple-buying responsibility is commonplace in the industrial field in the purchase of major items of equipment and in the establishment of formulas for purchases of raw materials and component parts.
8. Successful development of "yardsticks" for industrial market determination from a sample depends on the individual product-market situation. Consumer buying can be measured more universally through sampling techniques, panels and inventory movement studies.
9. In the industrial market there is a higher degree of sensitivity to satisfactory product performance than there is in the consumer market because of the time lag through the longer trade channels usually found in the latter.
10. There is a greater fluctuation in the volume of industrial goods as a whole from the high to the low of the business cycle.
11. The need for and influence of *service* both before and after the sale is greater in industrial marketing.
12. Leasing and renting of equipment (with or without the option of purchase) is important for many industrial products because of the possibility of the production cost savings being used to liquidate the first cost. In consumer marketing instalment selling spreads the cost and brings immediate physical possession.

DIFFERENCES ARISING OUT OF THE CHARACTERISTICS OF THE PRODUCTS

1. Industrial products are usually marketed by giving the purchaser more factual and technical data than are consumer prod-

ucts, since the former generally are bought on a basis which requires *proof* of suitability for the particular use.

2. Prices of industrial goods are likely to fluctuate within narrower limits than consumer goods. "Loss leaders" and "clearance-mark-downs" are devices of consumer marketing.

3. Industrial goods are usually bought and sold on a more complete and usually more precise description or specification basis. (Mail order catalogs for consumer goods, although quite descriptive, are usually not as detailed as the specifications for industrial goods.) An important portion of industrial selling activity may be in influencing the preparation of specifications to favor the vendors' products.

4. Bids may or may not be submitted in marketing industrial goods. Bids are less prevalent in manufacturing industries than in government, leasing, construction procurement, or wherever the comparison of offers can be reduced to a common dollar denominator. In marketing to manufacturing industries, however, quotations or contracts, evaluated in terms of projected product performance, are more often the basis of purchase.

    Although there is much shopping in the consumer field, there is little formal bidding or negotiation.

5. The descriptions, specifications and acceptance tests for industrial goods are usually more precise than in the case of consumer goods. These are physical or chemical measurements, or both, rather than measurements of taste, flavor and style. (An example of the difference in preciseness might be the measurement of color—the industrial user of colors is likely to use the spectrophotometer to measure the precise shade of blue, whereas the consumer wants to "see it in daylight" to know if that shade of blue is suitable.)

6. Industrial goods are subject to greater standardization as the influence of obsolescence in industrial goods is largely in utility, while consumer goods suffer from the impact of fashion, style, and utility. The necessity of design changes for increased salability is more pronounced in the consumer field.

DIFFERENCES ARISING OUT OF ORGANIZATION OR OPERATIONAL SETUP

1. The channels of distribution for industrial goods are likely to be shorter than channels for consumer goods. There are fewer middlemen in the industrial distribution chain and a much

larger percentage of industrial goods is sold direct to the buyer in industrial marketing than the percentage sold direct to the consumer in consumer marketing.
2. The media used and the types of advertising copy (used in the broad sense) prepared to carry the message vary considerably between the two types of products. The industrial marketer usually reaches his prospects through the trade and business publications and the consumer marketer through the so-called "mass publications," radio and television.
3. Reciprocity, a factor of indeterminate importance in the industrial field, appears to be less prevalent in the consumer field.
4. In industrial marketing the seller commonly goes to the buyer — the reverse is the situation in the consumer field, with the exception of door-to-door selling.
5. Production for inventory is less widespread in the industrial field than in the consumer field, partially due to the shorter "pipe lines" of distribution.

Other Differences

1. Speed and dependability of delivery are important in the marketing of both types of goods. Consumer goods are more readily available to the buyer than are industrial goods (other than supplies), since consumers usually buy direct from local or nearby inventories.
2. Longer periods of salesman training are generally required for industrial marketing as compared with consumer marketing, often due to the technical nature of products sold to industrial goods manufacturers.
3. Sales promotion expense (including advertising but excluding direct selling) in relation to the selling price is likely to be much lower in industrial selling than in consumer marketing.
4. Industrial salesmen's compensation on raw materials and production equipment is likely to be in the form of salary or a combination of salary plus bonus; on smaller items and supplies it is more likely to be either salary plus a bonus or some form of drawing account plus commission to straight commission.
5. Major equipment items may be purchased only once every 10 or 20 years unless expansion or obsolescence is an overriding factor. In the case of fabricated parts, materials, and operating supplies, buying is often done on a contract basis.
6. The industrial marketer has a greater problem in keeping con-

tact with customers to avoid possible loss of orders and yet not incur needless sales expense.

7. The number of women who exert direct influence upon industrial purchases is very small compared to the number in buying positions throughout the trade channels for consumer goods. It is, of course, obvious that women exert a dominant influence in purchasing for the millions of family units in the country.

8. In the field of industrial marketing a large proportion of sales is in raw materials, semi-finished products and component parts, while in the consumer marketing field the largest proportion of sales is in finished products.

9. In measuring a majority of industrial markets through marketing research, it is essential that well-trained technical people do the basic interview work because of the technical problems involved and technical questions which may be asked during the interview. In the consumer field, however, interviewers with a less technical background may often be used, and in the case of much consumer marketing research housewives or others with no technical training may obtain valid answers.

10. The packaging of industrial products, often in much larger units than is required for consumer goods packaging, is both functional and serviceable, lacking the eye appeal or definite advertising or promotional slant. Containers for industrial goods are often designed for return to the manufacturer and reuse for the same purpose, whereas consumer goods are often placed in an attractive package which later serves the consumer in an entirely different way. (As an example, certain foods are packaged in glass or metal suitable for table use as glasses or with jar tops as coasters or ashtrays.)

SIMILARITIES BETWEEN INDUSTRIAL AND CONSUMER MARKETING

1. Industrial marketing and consumer marketing are both carried on under the following common objectives:
   a. To result in a profitable operation.
   b. To obtain a growing share of the market or at least to maintain the present share of the market.
   c. To achieve efficiency in the expenditure of all monies involved in the operation.
   d. To develop and use advertising and promotional efforts which will both find new customers and maintain current customers.

e. To market at all times the right product or products to meet customer needs or desires.
   f. To be alert to the development of new products in the same or related fields which will affect the marketing operation.
   g. To maintain the good name of the producer.
2. Where there is no distinguishable product difference there are marked similarities in buying motives and buying motivations.
   a. Habit, the universal resistance to change in buying patterns, is equally important in both industrial and consumer marketing fields.
   b. The personality of the salesman is important in both fields.
3. The use of contracts is characteristic in the marketing of both industrial and consumer goods. Industrial equipment, raw materials, component parts and even supplies may be purchased on this basis, an infrequent occurrence in the field of consumer marketing.
4. Well organized and highly skilled purchasing groups are found both among the customers of industrial marketers and the customers of consumer goods marketers.
5. In measuring the market for either industrial goods or consumer goods the manufacturer can obtain much basic data from his internal sales and production records. The marketer of industrial products, however, can place more reliance on his sales and production record information due to his much closer relationship with his customers than can the manufacturer of consumer goods in measuring his ultimate consumer market, since the trade channels are usually longer and in some cases rather devious.

Conclusions

Few rules can be formulated to portray the fundamental differences or similarities between industrial and consumer marketing.

Although both industrial marketing and consumer marketing have as a common goal the satisfaction of the wants and needs of the customer, the two are significantly different in many important respects. The differences can be attributed to a number of reasons, the most evident of which seems to be the difference in the products themselves.

Industrial goods move in a series of steps from the mine, forest, farm, air or ocean in which the raw materials originate through everything from a simple to a very complex set of manufacturing and marketing operations before reaching that final step where they are assembled into the end product, whether it be an industrial good or a consumer good.

Consumer goods as they leave the manufacturer and head into the channels of distribution, regardless of how complex the channels may be, are finished goods and usually require no further processing.

Every practitioner of marketing, whether it be industrial or consumer, should become, if he not already is, thoroughly conversant with the ramifications of those phases of marketing with which he is engaged and constantly be on the alert to visualize new relationships, new exceptions to his previously accepted theories, and new approaches to his chosen profession.

Every teacher of marketing who does not already do so should visualize our modern marketing machine as being at least as complex as an electronic computer. Each marketing teacher should teach the fundamental principles underlying the entire marketing setup, rather than the methodology by which the results are achieved. Students of marketing would thereby obtain not only a head full of rules with a magnificent array of exceptions but an ability to trace the right path or paths through the maze of this complicated distribution system which will result in his finding the right answer to the particular problem at hand. After all, teaching is lighting a lamp, not filling a bucket.

ENDNOTES

*This monograph has been prepared by the Review Board on Fundamental Differences Between Industrial and Consumer Marketing as part of the Industrial Marketing Committee's plan for the development of three industrial marketing subjects. This plan was presented to the Policy Staff Group of the Industrial Marketing Committee by Francis Juraschek following his appointment as chairman of the Industrial Marketing Committee. The purpose of the Review Board has been drawn from several communications to the chairman and might be stated as follows:

> "To produce a monograph that will be authoritative, that will clear away some very hazy ideas about the subject held by many people in all ranks of business and even in the teaching profession; a monograph which, in the final analysis, will be accepted by and be useful to both the practitioners of marketing and teachers of marketing, wherever they may be."

Members of the Review Board have drawn upon their own varied experience in marketing as well as on the source material submitted by local chapter task committees and published materials as listed in the bibliography. Members of the Board express their appreciation to all contributors of material incorporated in this monograph.

Review Board

Edward C. Cassel, Dept. of Business & Public Administration, Temple University, Philadelphia, Pa.

John A. Grove, Apparatus Sales Division, General Electric Company, Schenectady, N.Y.
Frank W. Hankins, F. W. Hankins Company, Philadelphia, Pa.
Harry Leopold, Jr., John A. Roebling's Sons Company, Trenton, N.J.
N. Dana Lovell, The Davison Chemical Company, Baltimore, Md.

1. Prepared by the Committee on Definitions of the National Association of Marketing Teachers: Professors R. S. Alexander of Columbia University, G. R. Collins and John W. Wingate of New York University, Robert F. Elder of Mass. Institute of Technology, and Charles E. Bellatty of Boston University.
2. Ibid.

BIBLIOGRAPHY

Panel: Fundamental Differences Between Industrial and Consumer Marketing presented at the American Marketing Association Summer Conference, Detroit, Mich., July 21, 1951.
> Introduction and Summary: Francis Juraschek, U.S. Steel Corp., Pittsburgh, Pa.
> Industrial Marketing: Frank Waldo, Columbia Chemicals Div., Pittsburgh Plate Glass Co.
> Major Factors in Marketing Consumer Goods as Compared to Industrial Goods: Harold P. Alspaugh, H. J. Heinz Co., Pittsburgh, Pa.
> A Dual Viewpoint: C. E. Skinner, Gulf Oil Corp., Pittsburgh, Pa.
> A Summation: Dr. A. E. Boer, University of Pittsburgh, Pittsburgh, Pa.

The Special Characteristics of Industrial Goods and Markets—a Foundation for an Industrial Marketing Course
> A paper presented to the 1950 Winter Conference of the American Marketing Association: Thomas A. Staudt, Indiana University

Differences in Measuring Industrial and Consumer Goods Markets
> An unpublished paper presented by O. F. Armstrong & J. A. Rafert of the General Electric Company at the Industrial Marketing Committee Meeting, American Marketing Association, Cleveland, Nov. 22, 1950.

Industrial Market Research—Introduction and Lecture 1
> Of a cooperatively organized comprehensive course on the subject presented in 1946 jointly by the University of Pittsburgh and the Sales Department of the Carnegie-Illinois Steel Corp., Pittsburgh, Pa.

Marketing Research from the Standpoint of the Industrial Buyer
> A paper read before the Chemical Marketing Research Association, March 30, 1950 by Howard T. Lewis, Harvard University, Cambridge, Mass.

Marketing by Manufacturers
> Editor: Charles F. Phillips, Bates College, published 1946, Richard D. Erwin, Inc., Chicago, Ill.

Outlines of Marketing
> Agnew Jenkins & Drury, 1st Ed., McGraw-Hill Book Co., Inc., 1936.

49 — The Industrial/Consumer Marketing Dichotomy: A Case of Insufficient Justification

Edward F. Fern and James R. Brown

Reprinted from the *Journal of Marketing*, published by the American Marketing Association, Vol. 48 (Spring 1984), pp. 68–77. Reprinted by permission.

Many marketing scholars make a distinction between industrial marketing and consumer marketing. This distinction is evident in academic course offerings, professional journals, marketing textbooks, and in professional organizations and meetings. This paper shows that this distinction is unjustified because: (1) it is neither based in theory nor empirically supported, (2) it establishes artificial intradisciplinary boundaries which inhibit the development of marketing theory, (3) it interferes with the collection and dissemination of marketing knowledge, and (4) it stifles creativity in developing effective marketing strategies. The industrial-consumer dichotomy will be challenged on three different grounds: the classification does not adequately partition marketing phenomena, counter-examples which point to the lack of differences are readily available, and the differences within industrial and consumer marketing are greater than the differences between them. However, before exploring this dichotomy further, a few concepts need to be defined.

Concept Definitions

Many of the characteristics which purportedly distinguish industrial from consumer marketing are product or market related. Therefore it is not surprising that accepted definitions of these two concepts deal with product and/or market differences. According to the Industrial Marketing Committee Review Board (1954), "Marketing includes those business activities involved in the flow of goods and services from production to consumption." Consumer goods are "goods destined for use by the individual ultimate consumer and in such form that they can be used by him without further commercial processing. . . ." On the other hand, industrial goods are characterized as "Goods which are used in producing consumers' goods, other business or industrial goods, and services and/or in facilitating the operation of an enterprise, may (sic) include land and buildings for business purposes, equipment (installation and accessory), operating supplies, raw materials, and fabricated materials."

The Board admitted "there must be an awareness that in many instances a specific commodity may either be an industrial good or a consumer good, depending upon the use to which it is put" (p. 153). It follows that consumer goods marketing includes those business activities involved in the flow of goods and services destined for use by the individual ultimate consumer in such form that they can be used by him/her without further processing. And industrial goods marketing includes business activities involved in the flow of goods and services used in producing consumer goods, other business or industrial goods, and/or in facilitating the operation of an enterprise. These definitions seem to capture the themes common to most definitions of consumer and industrial marketing (Corey 1976, Haas 1981, Hutt and Speh 1981, Kotler 1980b, Vinson and Sciglimpaglia 1975, and Webster 1979).

THE INDUSTRIAL/CONSUMER DICHOTOMY

The industrial/consumer dichotomy can be viewed from a buyer behavior perspective as well as from a marketing perspective. Several authors have noted the correspondence between industrial and household buying behavior. However, the parallels between industrial and consumer marketing have been largely ignored in the marketing literature.

Sheth (1974) implicitly recognizes the similarity between industrial and household buying behavior in his theory of family buying decisions. At the individual level, Zaltman and Wallendorf (1979) specify the similarities between consumer behavior and industrial buyer behavior as the cultural effects on purchase behavior, norms governing purchase behavior, and the role of others' expectations on purchase behavior. Additionally, "In the process of making a purchase, each gathers information about alternatives, processes this information, learns about available products, determines which alternative matches the perceived needs most closely, and carries through by making a purchase" (p. 9). Moreover, Zaltman and Wallendorf contend that families make group decisions on large or important purchases similarly to organizations. After presenting Nicosia's summary of his model of consumer behavior, Webster and Wind (1972) suggest "Change the words *consumer* to *organizational buyer* and *advertisement* to *any marketing input* in the above statement and you have a general structure of organizational buying behavior." However, they caution that going beyond this level is not operationally feasible. Finally in a classic article on segmentation, Wind (1978) acknowledges "the concept of segmentation and most of the segmentation research approaches are equally applicable to industrial market situations." He demonstrates this contention by discussing problems (in consumer as well as organization segmentation) in moving from individual to multiperson *buying centers* (i.e., all persons involved in the buying process).

Compared to the above, only two sources were found that look at the similarities between industrial and consumer marketing. As exemplified in Table 1, most sources point to the differences. The Industrial Marketing Committee Review Board (1954) delineated these differences as: the nature of the market or buyers, characteristics of the product, organizational or operational set-up, and other (unspecified) differences. In contrast to their discussion of the differences, the Board paid relatively little attention to the similarities; firms engaged in both consumer and industrial marketing were characterized as having common objectives, similar buying motives for similar products, the use of contracts, well-organized and highly skilled purchasing groups, and use of internal sales and production records as sources of market information.

On the other hand, one author has analyzed both the differences and similarities between marketing to industrial firms and households. Sheth (1979) has summarized the traditional differences between industrial and consumer marketing as relating to the purchase and decision-making processes, the mechanics of marketing management, and the nature of environmental influences. But he raises the question, "Is industrial marketing really unique?" and concludes that "there are more similarities between industrial marketing and household marketing than these differences." As an example, he points to the increased adoption of mass marketing strategies by industrial firms which includes the increased use of television advertising, price promotions, and direct mail. The position taken in this article both supports and elaborates Sheth's basic argument—industrial and consumer marketing are more similar than different.

In summary, several distinct bases have been presented in support of the notion that industrial and consumer marketing are different: (1) the type of goods being purchased (Corey 1976, IMCRB 1954); (2) the buyer's decision-making process (Sheth 1979); (3) characteristics of the product market (Corey 1976); (4) the nature of the selling firms' marketing activities (IMCRB 1954, Sheth 1979); and (5) the nature of environmental influences (Sheth 1979). Some of these differences are presented in greater detail in Table 1. It should be noted that the dimensions (i.e., the column headings) under which specific differences are listed were used by the IMCRB. However, the authors acknowledge that other more explicit dimensions could have been used (e.g., McCarthy's 4 Ps or McGary's 8 functions).

Although the differences noted by the IMCRB have persisted throughout marketing texts for over 20 years, few scholars have examined the similarities. A fundamental question raised in this paper is whether the importance or magnitude of these differences is sufficient to justify the commonly accepted industrial/consumer dichotomy. The first step toward answering this question is to evaluate the dichotomy as a classification scheme.

CLASSIFYING MARKETING PHENOMENA

Classification is important because organization of phenomena into groups is often a first step in the development of marketing theory and practice. However, as an end in itself, classification provides relatively little understanding. Therefore, it makes sense that stronger classification schemes may be more useful than weaker ones for the purpose of

TABLE 1. Dimensions of Commonly Held Differences Between Industrial and Consumer Marketing

Market	Product	Organization of Operational Set-Up	Others
Derived vs. primary demand (Kotler 1980b, McCarthy 1978, Stanton 1981)	Technical complexity (Webster 1979)	Channel length (Kotler 1980a, Stanton 1981)	Message appeal (Boone 1972)
Elasticity of demand (McCarthy 1978, Stanton 1981)	Purchase frequency (Stanton 1981)	Promotion mix (Corey 1976, McCarthy 1978, Stanton 1981)	Delivery importance (Stanton 1981)
Demand fluctuation (Kotler 1980a, Stanton 1981)	Classification (Kotler 1980a, McCarthy 1978)	Reciprocity (Kotler 1980b, Stanton 1981)	Sales force compensation (Stanton 1981)
Number of suppliers (Buell 1970)	Service requirement (Boone 1972, Stanton 1981)	Adequacy of supply (Stanton 1981)	Sales force training (Stanton 1981)
Number of buyers (Kotler 1980a, McCarthy 1978)	Amount of information search (Hughes 1978, Rosenberg 1977)	Degree of integration (Corey 1976)	Leasing (Boone 1972, Kotler 1980b, Rosenberg 1977)
Number of influencers (Kotler 1980a, McCarthy 1978)	Negotiated prices (Corey 1976, Stanton 1981)		
Geographic concentration (Kotler 1980a, McCarthy 1978)	Dollar volume (Kotler 1980a, Rosenberg 1977)		
Knowledgeability (Kotler 1980a, Stanton 1981)	Riskiness (Hughes 1978)		
Rationality (Kotler 1980a, McCarthy 1978)			

theory development. To determine the strength of the industrial/consumer dichotomy, Hunt's (1976) criteria for evaluating classification schemata will be used:

- adequacy for specifying the phenomenon
- adequacy of characteristics to be used in classifying
- mutual exclusiveness of categories
- collective exhaustiveness of categories
- usefulness of schema

According to Hunt (1976), a classification scheme should adequately specify the phenomenon that is to be classified. However, it is not apparent that marketing scholars are in agreement as to what is being classified. Depending on which source is consulted, the industrial/consumer dichotomy refers to differences between classes of goods, products, markets, and/or marketing strategies. Moreover, Table 1 provides a wide range (but not exhaustive list) of notions about how these two entities differ. Yet, there is relatively little agreement on any of these differences. Therefore, it is concluded that more thought could be devoted to specifying what it is that should be classified.

Effort spent in specification should also provide less ambiguous properties or characteristics to be used in classifying marketing phenomena. At present, a good's "intended use" seems to be the most widely accepted criterion for differentiating industrial goods from consumer goods. However, the usefulness of this approach is not at all clear, particularly when one attempts to partition other marketing functions into industrial and consumer segments. Moreover, this criterion may be intersubjectively ambiguous (i.e., providing low interjudge reliability). The intended use criterion does provide a convenient classification for goods that fit nicely into both categories, but it does not totally overcome a more fundamental flaw in the industrial/consumer dichotomy—the lack of mutual exclusiveness.

The primary reason for the intended use criterion was to overcome the lack of mutual exclusiveness in the existing categories. It is easy to think of goods which do not fit neatly into one or the other category (e.g., paint, lumber, and furniture). Traditionally, however, marketers have focused on extreme examples of goods to illustrate the differences and have ignored the large number of goods common to both industrial and consumer markets. Furthermore, the industrial/consumer scheme does not provide mutually exclusive categories for the other marketing mix variables.

A fourth criterion is the degree to which the categories are collectively exhaustive. Again, the industrial/consumer distinction falls short. One can point to several other categories into which marketing knowledge has been classified such as nonprofit marketing, social marketing, the marketing of services, health care marketing, and international marketing. A more useful scheme for classifying marketing phenomena might be developed around some dimension(s) common to all of these categories.

The final criterion to be considered is usefulness. According to Hunt, usefulness may outweigh all other criteria. Yet, on this dimension the dichotomy holds up no better than on the others. The purported utility of the industrial/consumer distinction is that it allows different marketing strategy to be formulated for the different segments. However, the authors' review of the marketing literature suggests that the number of similarities may exceed the number of differences. Moreover, the similarities may be more useful in formulating marketing strategy than the differences. More on this notion will be presented later.

In summary, the industrial/consumer dichotomy, as it now stands, does not do well under Hunt's criteria. Specifically, the dichotomy does not adequately specify or classify marketing phenomena, does not provide mutually exclusive or collectively exhaustive categories, and lacks utility for strategy development. Consequently, if it cannot be determined which category a phenomenon fits into, how can it be determined whether the marketing situation is industrial or consumer? Perhaps this argument can be strengthened by offering the skeptical reader a few counter-examples.

COUNTER-EXAMPLES

Many of the purported differences between industrial and consumer marketing are too general to be useful, too specific to be generalizable within consumer goods or industrial goods marketing, or they are not differences at all. It is not the purpose of this paper to analyze each of the purported differences in Table 1; however, it may be useful to illustrate their deficiencies by three examples.

The first dimension under *Market* in Table 1 was taken from the notion that demand for industrial goods is derived, while demand for consumer goods is primary. However, it can also be argued that demand for such consumer goods as flour, sugar, gifts and wrapping paper, lumber, and many other products is also derived. Demand for these goods is derived from the demand for baked goods, gift giving, and home improvements. Moreover, demand for typewriters, light bulbs, and many other products used by industrial organizations can be viewed as primary. That is, these products are needed for their inherent usefulness and not as inputs into other goods which are destined for the ultimate consumer. Therefore, the derived demand thesis does not seem to point to a unique facet of marketing by organizations, nor does primary demand exclusively describe the need for goods by individual consumers.

Another difference deals with negotiated pricing. It is commonly thought that price negotiation is more predominant in industrial marketing than consumer marketing. However, negotiated prices are frequently found in consumer marketing (e.g., automobiles, furniture, major appliances, and homes). Moreover, administered prices occur in industrial marketing (e.g., office supplies, office equipment, utilities, and in some situations, parts and raw materials). Obviously, pricing policy is not solely a function of the industrial/consumer dichotomy; other factors must be considered. The price of a good relative to the buyer's budget, the good's profit margin, the quantity being purchased, the nature of the buyer-seller relationship, and competitors' pricing policies are just a few of the factors that help determine whether or not a price is negotiable. These factors are common to both industrial and consumer markets and may be the determinant factors in accounting for existing pricing policies in both areas.

Finally, it is claimed that more people are involved in the organizational buying process than in consumer buying. This may be the case depending upon the size of the firm, the dollar amount to be committed, and the nature of the product. Yet, it is not difficult to think of situations where the whole family may be involved in purchase decisions. Several studies have looked at husband/wife joint buying situations (David 1971, Kelly and Egan 1969, Morgan 1961) and some have looked at the roles of still other family members in the purchase process (Wells 1966). Zaltman and Wallendorf (1979) summarize the authors' position nicely. In regards to group decisions, they contend that families make group decisions on large important purchases similarly to organizations. Conversely, organizational buyers autonomously purchase less important items in much the same way as consumers. Additionally, some of the same choice criteria are used such as price, time efficiency, and status enhancement. As previously mentioned, Webster and Wind (1972) noted the similarity between consumer buying behavior models and organizational buyer behavior models.

Although derived demand, negotiated pricing, and the number of individuals involved in the purchase decision were the only counter-examples presented, many others could have been discussed. Make or buy decisions, leasing versus purchasing, and frequent purchasing versus maintaining inventories are just a few. At this point the focus will move to a comparison of the differences between industrial and consumer marketing and the differences within each one.

WITHIN VERSUS BETWEEN GROUP VARIATION

An additional argument against the industrial/consumer marketing dichotomy will be presented in the form of an analysis of variance analogy. According to the traditional perspective, variations *between* the practice of marketing to organizations and marketing to consumers should be greater than the variation *within* the two classes of marketing practice. The perspective being presented in this paper argues just the opposite—the differences *within* industrial marketing and consumer marketing are greater than those that have long been recognized as distinguishing the two areas. If this latter perspective is reasonable, it should be possible to formulate principles of marketing that explicitly account for the *within group* variation and are generalizable across both areas of marketing. This can only be possible if the between group variation relative to the within group variation is insignificant. An example, using classification schemes for goods, may help clarify these notions.

GOODS CLASSIFICATION SCHEMES

Several typologies for goods and purchase situations have been developed for the industrial and consumer sectors (see Figure 1). For example, the degree to which a good enters the finished product has been offered as one means of classifying industrial products (Kotler 1972). Robinson, Faris, and Wind (1967) classified industrial goods according to the buying situation: straight rebuy, modified rebuy, or a new task. Yet, another classification system uses the degree of consumption to categorize industrial goods. In the consumer sector, routinized, limited, and extensive problem solving are categories in which products can be placed. Bucklin (1963) classified consumer goods according to patronage motive, while the AMA Committee on Marketing Definitions (1960) distinguished between services and the durability of tangible goods. Aspinwall (1962), in an ingenious attempt to differentiate between types of consumer goods, used colors to illustrate his categories.

All of the above typologies appear to be more useful in explaining product variations within each sector than between them. In short, the classification schemes in Figure 1 seem to explain some within group variation but virtually no between group variation. That is, each classification scheme seems to apply equally well to organizations and households (i.e., there is no main effect).[1] Moreover, it is expected that there will be no interaction effect (i.e., it is an additive model). Thus, the two levels of the between groups factor could be collapsed (or pooled) into a single level called *markets*. Then a classification scheme could be developed based on variations in product characteristics, usage behavior, and/or need satisfaction regardless of whether it is purchased by industrial organizations or households. However, this approach requires analysis of the commonalities between these two sectors rather than the differ-

the product, the more concerned the marketing managers should be with aiming their advertising at broad audiences. Others think that the greater the total market size, the more indirect intensive and multiple the channel system can be (Bucklin 1966; Cox, Goodman, and Fichandler 1965; Kotler 1980b; Rosenbloom 1978; Stern and El-Ansary 1977). These principles were used in the following proposition:

> P3: The greater the number of buyers in the market, the more continuous the supply of the offering should be and the more continuous the firm's communication with the market should be.

This principle suggests that market size and density determine the degree to which mass communications should be employed. Obvious economies through lower cost per targeted customer reached can be achieved by using network television and mass circulation magazines when the number of potential buyers is large. Efficiencies are also realized by intensively distributing the offering when the market is large.

Two examples may illustrate this proposition. The market for photocopying machines is fairly large since it includes not only large corporations but small businesses as well. These products are widely distributed through office supply firms as well as through the manufacturer's own sales branches. In large metropolitan areas with larger numbers of buyers, the intensity of distribution varies from intensive to selective, depending upon the brand. In less concentrated markets, the distribution intensity for photocopiers ranges from selective to intensive, again depending upon the particular brand. The use of mass media to advertise photocopiers is widespread, with Xerox and Canon relying heavily upon television.

McDonald's has also achieved intensive distribution. Moreover, they use television along with other media to reach their large target market. Regardless of whether the target is an organization or a consumer, intensive distribution and heavy use of the mass media will enable marketers to reach their markets, especially if they are large markets.

In summary, three general propositions were derived which appear to be applicable to both industrial and consumer marketing contexts. Examples, which point to the reasonableness of these propositions, were also presented. Now it is time to examine the implications of all that has been presented.

OBSERVATION AS COMPELLING EVIDENCE

Up to this point it has been argued that the industrial/consumer dichotomy has serious limitations for classifying marketing phenomena. Additionally a few counter-examples were presented to illustrate that the

frequently, and buyers accept substitute products (Michman 1974 and Woodside et al. 1978). Shopping and specialty products, unlike the more frequently purchased convenience goods, require more personal selling and service, command higher margins, and require more seller guarantees (Pessemier 1977, Sturdivant 1970). Finally, the higher the buying frequency, the more continuous the advertising should be (Aaker and Myers 1975). One general proposition that might be suggested by the above is:

P2: The more frequently the buyers purchase the product/service, the more continuous the availability of the offering and the communication associated with the offering should be.

This proposition suggests that for frequently purchased goods and services, a continuous supply should be readily available through intensive distribution. Also, continuous promotion of important product benefits and availability should be implemented to ensure awareness among potential buyers.

Many consumer goods could easily illustrate this proposition. Beer, for example, is heavily advertised during televised sporting events and is widely available, depending upon state laws, for consumers to purchase. Since many consumers of this product are frequent purchasers, continuous promotion is undertaken to remind them of their favorite brands or to entice them to switch brands. Wide availability of each brand provides an additional method for reducing the likelihood that a consumer will switch brands because his/her favorite is not stocked at convenient outlets. Thus, goods such as beer, bread, eggs, milk, cigarettes, and candy bars may be both intensively advertised and distributed.

Office supplies have similar characteristics; they are purchased frequently and often with a minimum amount of effort. Accordingly, the communication is continuous through the use of salespersons who may call on an individual account up to once every two weeks. In addition, buyers are usually encouraged to call the salesperson should their stocks need replenishing before the next sales call.[3] Buyers of office supplies are also assured of speedy delivery in that the delivery schedule can be altered by marketing-oriented office supply houses to meet the specific needs of the buyer. In fact, small items are sometimes hand-carried by the salesperson to fill an urgent order. Again, continuous availability and communication with the market characterize convenience-type goods, whether for consumer or organizational use.

A final example involves the number of buyers or the size of the potential market. According to some authors (Clewitt 1970; Cox, Goodman, and Fichandler 1965; Walters 1977), the more potential customers there are, the less personal selling is used (i.e., the longer the channel). Another source (Buell 1970) suggests that the more consumer oriented

quality. Another principle states that more direct and selective channels of distribution are called for when technical knowledge is required for the sale, installation, maintenance, and repair of products (Bucklin 1966; Buell 1970; Clewitt 1970; Cox, Goodman, and Fichandler 1965; Walters 1977; and Woodside et al. 1978). Additionally, when the product is technical in nature, the buyer is not knowledgeable, and much information is to be disseminated, the firm should rely on print media to raise the level of the buyer's knowledge (Aaker and Myers 1975).

From the three principles just reviewed, a more general proposition linking the market dimension dealing with a buyer's product knowledge to the selling firm's marketing activities was derived:

P1: The less knowledgeable the market is about a firm's market offering, particularly when the product is technically complex, the more direct the method of communication should be, given the firm's financial constraints.

This proposition implies that the requisite level of customer knowledge will dictate whether the firm uses its own sales force or uses intermediaries, whether intensive distribution or some degree of selective distribution will be used, and what influence source will be used, personal or impersonal. All of these alternatives represent different degrees or levels of direct communication. Of course, failure to communicate leaves the market free to use whatever information is available, and in some cases, this may be price.

An example may clarify the implications this proposition has for a firm developing its total market offering. Personal computers are fairly technical and, subsequently, potential buyers are likely to have only limited knowledge about these products. The proposition indicates that direct communication should be used. Thus, a personal computer manufacturer should use relatively direct and selective marketing channels which emphasize personal selling to reach its potential buyers. By selling directly only to dealers who have very strong in-house service capabilities and by providing them with extensive sales force training, Apple Computers is able to market to the buyer with no computer expertise. For Apple, this buyer may be a small businessperson or a novice hobbyist; the key factor in reaching either of these potential customers, however, is that buyer's knowledgeability, rather than whether the product is an industrial good or consumer good.

According to some authors, the more frequently purchases are made, the more feasible it is for a manufacturer to use direct distribution (Buell 1970, Clewitt 1970, Kotler 1980a, Walters 1977, and Woodside et al. 1978). Also, convenience goods and common raw materials are generally distributed intensively (Buell 1970; Kotler 1980b; Sims, Roster, and Woodside 1977; and Woodside 1975). Moreover, distribution saturation is attempted when the price is relatively low, buyers purchase the product

ences. These commonalities could provide the basis for formulating more general propositions of marketing.

GENERAL PROPOSITIONS OF MARKETING

A convenience sample of 20 general marketing texts was reviewed, which provided a list of 193 marketing principles. These principles ranged from those well-grounded in economic and psychological theory to those based on conjecture. The purpose of this section is to review several marketing principles, incorporate these principles into more general normative propositions (i.e., generalizable across industrial and consumer marketing),[2] and illustrate applications of the propositions.

The level of a buyer's knowledge has been related to pricing, channels of distribution, and promotion. Higher priced goods are often seen as "better," particularly when price is the only information available (Harper 1966, Monroe 1979, Oxenfeldt 1975, Palda 1971, and Sturdivant 1970). The implication is that when buyers lack information about a product or brand, price in some instances becomes a surrogate for

FIGURE 1. ANOVA Framework for Differences Between Industrial and Consumers' Markets

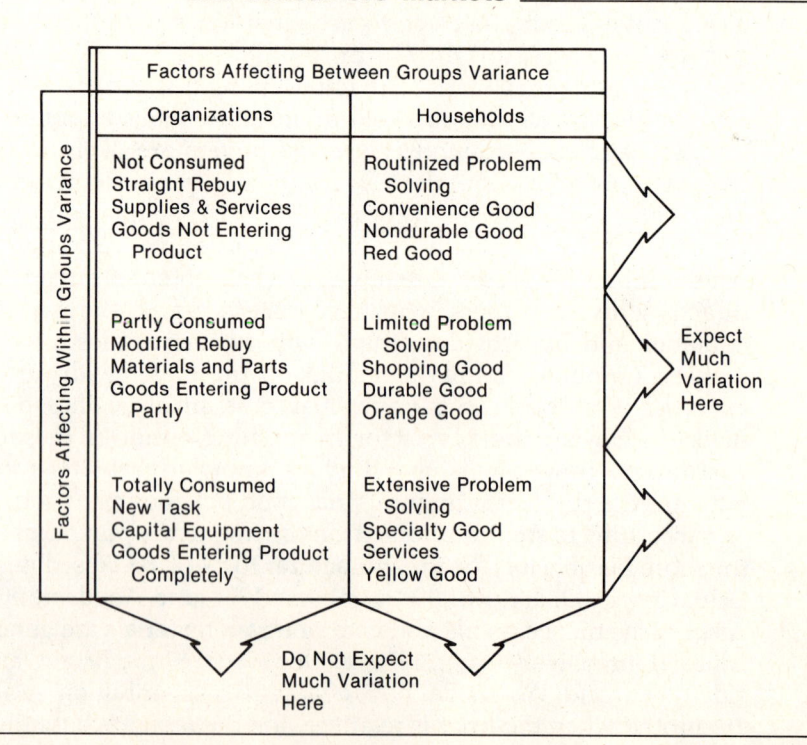

	Factors Affecting Between Groups Variance	
	Organizations	Households
Factors Affecting Within Groups Variance	Not Consumed Straight Rebuy Supplies & Services Goods Not Entering Product	Routinized Problem Solving Convenience Good Nondurable Good Red Good
	Partly Consumed Modified Rebuy Materials and Parts Goods Entering Product Partly	Limited Problem Solving Shopping Good Durable Good Orange Good
	Totally Consumed New Task Capital Equipment Goods Entering Product Completely	Extensive Problem Solving Specialty Good Services Yellow Good

Expect Much Variation Here →

Do Not Expect Much Variation Here ↓

traditionally accepted differences between these two categories—while making intuitive sense—may not be too meaningful in terms of advancing marketing thought or theory. Finally, an ANOVA analogy was presented, along with a set of general marketing propositions and examples. Moreover their potential applicability to marketing strategy formulation was discussed.

Yet it must be acknowledged that these ideas run contrary to popular beliefs and in the extreme may be viewed as heretical. The unconvinced reader can point to observed differences between the current practices of marketing to organizations and marketing to households. Observation provides rather compelling evidence that the two areas must indeed be different in some fundamental ways. For example, product specifications, purchase contracts, reciprocal buyer/seller relationships, and leasing contracts may be more prevalent in industrial marketing than in consumer marketing. Moreover, their reward and organizational structures differ dramatically. Additionally, since industrial goods are more subject to technical obsolescence than style obsolescence, there is less reliance on clearance sales and mark-downs to reduce inventories. Yet these observations merely indicate what is—not how it should be. Therefore, caution must be exercised in making normative inferences from these observations.

Sheth (1979) offers another criticism of observed differences. As he aptly points out, observations are often based on extreme examples while the full spectrum of examples is ignored. Consistent with the three propositions discussed earlier, a nuclear power plant might be marketed through direct sales, selective distribution, and intermittent advertising (see Figure 2). This marketing mix is typical of what many would call industrial marketing. But not all industrial goods are marketed to organizational buyers in this manner any more than all consumer goods are marketed through mass promotion, intensive distribution, and continuous advertising. Thus, extreme examples, although they do exist, tend to obscure the more basic similarities between industrial and consumer marketing.

UNRESOLVED ISSUES

The hypothesis proposed in this article is that industrial and consumer marketing are not significantly different. The widely accepted alternative hypothesis is that they are different. However, no empirical support has been offered for either position. Proponents of the dichotomy can argue that the burden of evidence is on those that reject the dichotomy. On the other hand, opponents can argue that no significant differences exist (i.e., the similarity hypothesis cannot be rejected) until empirical results can be provided to support the alternative hypothesis.

To date, supporting arguments for both positions are mainly anecdotal. Moreover, the anecdotes can be criticized as representing extreme positions on the issues. Although these issues can be rigorously debated, their ultimate resolution may be achieved by advancing logical normative arguments and theoretical propositions which can be tested empirically.

However, before research is conducted it must be determined which similarities and differences are being examined. At various points in this article discussion has focused on differences in industrial/consumer goods, industrial/consumer buyer behavior, industrial/consumer marketing, and industrial/consumer goods marketing. There is no doubt that vacillation in terminology leads to confusion about what is being classified. This confusion can only be reduced by more clearly defining these concepts and their interrelationships.

Finally, it must be acknowledged that although issues were raised concerning the industrial/consumer dichotomy, they were not resolved. By drawing attention to some of the problems surrounding the use of these concepts, it is hoped that marketing scholars will devote more thought and research effort to resolving the issues raised in this article.

SUMMARY AND IMPLICATIONS

Unfortunately, to date the observed differences between industrial and consumer marketing (1) have not been causally related to marketing practice or theory formulation, (2) have not been tested empirically, and (3) have not been justified on logical grounds. In short, the purported differences have not played an instrumental role in the development of marketing thought.

As an alternative approach, the reader is asked to consider the similarities between marketing to organizations and marketing to households. Perhaps these similarities provide a key to the development of marketing theory and practice. Perhaps it is time to back up a bit and

FIGURE 2. Industrial Goods Versus Consumer Goods Marketing

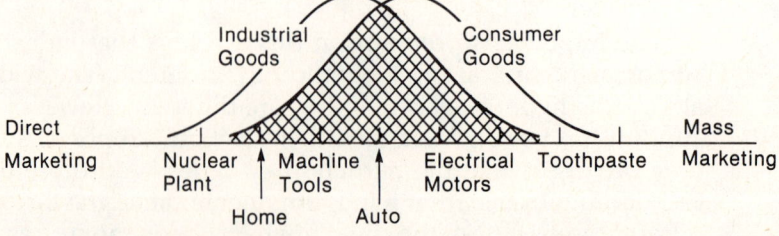

Source: Sheth (1979, p. 55)

examine the utility (or lack of utility) of commonly accepted classification schemes for marketing phenomena. If they cannot be supported logically, it may be time to start looking at other typologies. The industrial/consumer dichotomy requires theoretical development along two similar but separate paths. By removing this distinction and examining marketing phenomena for commonalities, dimensions should be identified (e.g., buying center size, buyer's knowledge, frequency of purchase, and market concentration) which provide the opportunity for developing a more general theory of marketing.

This latter approach to theory development poses the potential for greater efficiency in acquiring and disseminating marketing knowledge by eliminating duplication of research effort, redundancy among professional journals, and replication of academic course offerings under different titles. An additional benefit might be greater creativity or more innovative strategy development by practicing managers.

By considering only the inherent market characteristics in strategy formulation, managers will face the task of studying the interrelationships among common factors or dimensions. This is contrasted with the notion that some managers are engaged in doing industrial marketing (an area seen as underdeveloped by some authors) while trying to apply consumer marketing concepts. Managers well-trained in understanding fundamental marketing concepts, principles, and relationships should have an easier time developing appropriate strategies regardless of whether the buying center is an organization or a household.

ENDNOTES

1. It should be noted that the authors use consumers, individuals, families, and households interchangeably throughout the paper—technically they have different meanings.
2. The general propositions that follow assume ceteris paribus.
3. Note that although mass promotion might be appropriate here, other factors such as the size of the market, the width of the product line, etc. cause personal selling to be more useful. Also note that frequent sales calls and the use of telephone ordering can be effective substitutes for intensive advertising for products such as office supplies.

REFERENCES

Aaker, David A. and John G. Myers (1975), *Advertising Management*, Englewood Cliffs, NJ: Prentice-Hall.
American Marketing Association, Committee on Definitions (1960), *Marketing Defini-*

tions: A Glossary of Marketing Terms, Ralph S. Alexander, chairman, Chicago: The Association.

Aspinwall, Leo V. (1962), "The Characteristics of Goods Theory," in *Managerial Marketing: Perspectives and Viewpoints*, William Lazer and Eugene J. Kelley, eds., Homewood, IL: Irwin, 633–43.

Boone, Louis E. (1972), *Management Perspectives in Marketing*, Encino, CA: Dickension Publishing Co.

Bucklin, Louis P. (1963), "Retail Strategy and the Classification of Consumer Goods," *Journal of Marketing*, 27 (January), 50–55.

——— (1966), *A Theory of Distribution Channel Structure*, Berkeley, CA: Univ. of Calif., Institute of Business and Economic Research.

Buell, Victor P. (1970), *Handbook of Modern Marketing*, New York: McGraw-Hill.

Clewitt, Richard M. (1970), *Marketing Channels*, Chicago, IL: Irwin.

Corey, E. Raymond (1976), *Industrial Marketing*, Englewood Cliffs, NJ: Prentice-Hall.

Cox, Reavis, Charles S. Goodman, and Thomas C. Fichandler (1965), *Distribution in a High-Level Economy*, Englewood Cliffs, NJ: Prentice-Hall.

David, Harry L. (1971), "Measurement of Husband-Wife Influence in Consumer Purchase Decisions," *Journal of Marketing Research*, 8 (August), 305–12.

Haas, Robert W. (1981), *Industrial Marketing Management*, 2nd ed., Boston: Kent.

Harper, Donald V. (1966), *Price Policy and Procedure*, New York: Harcourt.

Hughes, G. David (1978), *Marketing Management: A Planning Approach*, Reading, MA: Addison-Wesley.

Hunt, Shelby D. (1976), *Marketing Theory*, Columbus, OH: Grid.

Hutt, Michael D. and Thomas W. Speh (1981), *Industrial Marketing Management*, Chicago: Dryden.

Industrial Marketing Committee Review Board (1954), "Fundamental Differences between Industrial and Consumer Marketing, *Journal of Marketing*, 19 (October), 152–58.

Kelly, Robert F. and Michael B. Egan (1969), "Husband and Wife Interaction in a Consumer Decision Process," in *Marketing and the New Science of Planning*, Robert L. King, ed., Chicago: American Marketing, 250–58.

Kotler, Philip (1972), *Marketing Management: Analysis, Planning, and Control*, Englewood Cliffs, NJ: Prentice-Hall.

——— (1980a), *Principles of Marketing*, Englewood Cliffs, NJ: Prentice-Hall.

——— (1980b), *Marketing Management: Analysis, Planning, and Control*, 4th ed., Englewood Cliffs, NJ: Prentice-Hall.

McCarthy, Jerome E. (1978), *Basic Marketing: A Managerial Approach*, Homewood, IL: Irwin.

Michman, Ronald (1974), *Marketing Channels,* Columbus, OH: Grid.

Monroe, Kent B. (1979), *Pricing: Making Profitable Decisions*, New York: McGraw-Hill.

Morgan, James N. (1961), "Household Decision Making," in *Household Decision Making*, Nelson Foote, ed., New York: New York University Press, 91.

Oxenfeldt, Alfred R. (1975), *Pricing Strategy*, New York: American Management.

Palda, Kristian S. (1971), *Pricing Decisions and Marketing Policy*, Englewood Cliffs, NJ: Prentice-Hall.

Pessemier, Edgar A. (1977), *Product Management Strategy and Organization*, Santa Barbara, CA: Wiley.

Robinson, Patrick J., Charles W. Faris, and Yoram Wind (1967), *Industrial Buying and Creative Marketing*, Boston: Allyn & Bacon.

Rosenberg, Larry J. (1977), *Marketing*, Englewood Cliffs, NJ: Prentice-Hall.

Rosenbloom, Bert (1978), *Marketing Channels: A Management View*, Hinsdale, IL: Dryden.

Sheth, Jagdish N. (1974), "A Theory of Family Buying Decisions," in *Models of Buyer Behavior*, Jagdish N. Sheth, New York: Harper, 17–33.

────── (1979), "The Specificity of Industrial Marketing, *P. U. Management Review*, 2 (January–December), 53–56.

Sims, J. Taylor, J. Robert Roster, and Arch G. Woodside (1977), *Marketing Channels: Systems and Strategies*, New York: Harper.

Stanton, William J. (1981), *Fundamentals of Marketing*, New York: McGraw-Hill.

Stern, Louis W., and Adel S. El-Ansary (1977), *Marketing Channels,* Englewood Cliffs, NJ: Prentice-Hall.

Sturdivant, Frederick D. (1970), *Managerial Analysis in Marketing*, Glenview, IL: Scott, Foresman.

Vinson, Donald E. and Donald Sciglimpaglia (1975), *The Environment of Industrial Marketing*, Columbus, OH: Grid.

Walters, Glenn C. (1977), *Marketing Channels*, Santa Monica, CA: Goodyear.

Webster, Frederick E., Jr. (1979), *Industrial Marketing Strategy*, New York: Wiley.

────── and Yoram Wind (1972), *Organizational Buying Behavior*, Englewood Cliffs, NJ: Prentice-Hall.

Wells, William D. (1966), "Children as Consumers," in *On Knowing the Consumer*, Joseph Newman, ed., New York: Wiley, 138–39.

Wind, Yoram (1978), "Issues and Advances in Segmentation Research," *Journal of Marketing Research*, 15 (August), 317–37.

Woodside, Arch G., J. Taylor Sims, Dale M. Lewison, and Ian F. Wilkinson (1978), *Foundations of Marketing Channels*, Austin, TX: Lone Star.

Zaltman, Gerald and Melanie Wallendorf (1979), *Consumer Behavior: Basic Findings and Management Implications*, New York: Wiley.

50 The Development of Buyer-Seller Relationships in Industrial Markets*

David Ford

European Journal of Marketing, Vol. 14, No. 5/6 (1980), pp. 339–53. Reprinted by permission.

It has frequently been noted that buyer-seller interdependence is a crucial characteristic of industrial marketing [1], i.e., that industrial firms establish buyer-seller relationships which are often close, complex and frequently long-term. Despite this, the nature of these relationships has, until recently, received scant attention in the literature [2]. Instead, marketing writers have been more concerned with analysis of the (albeit complex) process by which buying firms arrive at individual purchase decisions, and the ways in which the seller can influence this process in its favour.

This paper examines the nature of buyer-seller relationships in industrial markets by considering their development as a process through time. It is based on ideas generated from the IMP project [3] and is particularly concerned with the following factors:

What is it that makes a buyer establish and develop relationships with one or a few suppliers, as an alternative to "playing the market"?

How do the relationships between buying and selling firms change over time? What are the factors which aid or hinder the development of close relationships? Which of these are within the control of the two companies?

What are the implications of close buyer-seller relationships for the two organisations involved? What problems can they lead to? How are the day-to-day dealings between the companies affected by, and how do they affect, the overall relationship?

THEORETICAL BASIS

Buyer-seller relations can be examined with reference to the interaction approach as developed by the IMP group [4] as well as concepts drawn from the "New Institutionalists" within economics [5].

The Interaction Approach. This sees buyer-seller relationships taking place between two *active* parties. This is in contrast to the more traditional view of marketing which analyses the *reaction* of an aggregate market to a seller's offering. The interaction approach considers that either buyer or seller may take the initiative in seeking a partner. Further, both companies are likely to be involved in adaptations to their own process or product technologies to accommodate each other. Neither party is likely to be able to make unilateral changes in its activities as buyer or seller without consultation, or at least consideration, of the possible reactions of their individual opposite numbers. Thus, industrial marketing and purchasing can properly be described as the "management of buyer-seller relationships."

The Nature of Relationships

Not all of the dealings between industrial buying and selling firms take place within close relationships. There are clear differences between the supply of paper clips and automotive components, or lubricating oil and factory buildings. The product and process technologies of the two companies are important factors in determining the nature of buyer-seller relations. Also important are the buyer and seller market structures which exist and hence the availability of alternative buyers and sellers.

Companies will develop close relationships rather than play the market, where they can obtain benefits in the form of cost reduction or increased revenues. These benefits are achieved by tailoring their resources to dealing with a specific buyer or seller, i.e., by making "durable transaction specific investments" [6]. These investments mark major *adaptations* by a company to the relationship. By definition, they are not marketable, or at least their value in other transactions is less than in the specialised use for which they were intended. Therefore these adaptations mark a *commitment* by the buyer or seller to the relationship. They can be seen most clearly in such things as a supplier's development of a special product for a customer, a buyer's modification of a production process to accommodate a supplier's product or the joint establishment of a stock facility in a neutral warehouse. On the other hand, companies can be involved in "human capital investments" [7] i.e., alterations in procedures, special training, or allocation of managerial resources. These human adaptations produce savings by the familiarity and trust which they generate between the parties.

Overall Relationships and Individual Episodes

The complexity of buyer-seller relations and the importance of mutual adaptations means that the analysis of relationships must be separated between the overall relationship itself and the individual *episodes* which comprise it. Thus, each delivery of product, price negotiation or social meeting takes place within the context of the overall relationship.

Each episode is affected by the norms and procedures of the relationship as well as the atmosphere of co-operation or conflict which may have been established. Additionally, each episode affects the overall relationship and a single episode can change it radically, e.g., a relationship can be broken off "because" of a single failure in delivery. In fact, this failure is more likely to be the culminating episode in a worsening relationship. Thus, only a partial analysis of buyer-seller relations is achieved by researching individual episodes, e.g., a particular buying decision. On the other hand, an incomplete picture is obtained by examining the overall atmosphere of a relationship, for example in terms of power and dependency. Thus it is important to analyse both individual episodes and the overall relationship, as well as to understand the interaction between the two [8].

The Development of Buyer-Seller Relationships

This paper is less concerned with the reasons for the choice of buyer or seller partners (although this is acknowledged as a question of considerable importance!). Instead, it analyses the process of establishment and development of relationship over time by considering five stages in their evolution. We should also note that the process described here does not argue the inevitability of relationship development. Relationships can fail to develop or regress depending upon the actions of either party or of competing buyers or sellers. Throughout the examination, the bilateral nature of relationships will be stressed, particularly the similarity of the buyer's and seller's activities. The five stages are illustrated in Table I. Throughout the analysis we consider the variables of Experience, Uncertainty, Distance, Commitment and Adaptions.

Stage 1: The Pre-Relationship Stage

Previous authors have stressed the *inertia* of buying companies, when it comes to seeking new sources of supply [9]. Buyers may continue with existing sources with relatively little knowledge or evaluation of the wider supply markets available to them. We will take as our starting point the case of a company which has grown to rely on a main supplier for a particular product purchased on a regular basis, as in the case of equipment, or continuously as with a component.

In these circumstances a decision to evaluate a potential new supplier can be the result of a particular episode in an existing relationship. For example, a UK producer of consumer durables started to evaluate alternative suppliers following a major price increase by a company, which had until then supplied all its requirements for a certain product.

Other reasons which may cause evaluation of new potential suppliers include: a regular vendor analysis in which the performance and potential of existing suppliers is assessed; the efforts of a non-supplying

TABLE I. The Development of Buyer/Seller Relationships in Industrial Markets—Summary

1 The Pre-Relationship Stage	2 The Early Stage	3 The Development Stage	4 The Long-Term Stage	5 The Final Stage
Evaluation of new potential supplier	Negotiation of sample delivery	Contract signed or delivery build-up scale deliveries	After several major purchases or large	In long established stable markets
Evaluation initiated by:				
• particular episode in existing relationship	Experience • Low	• Increased	• High	
• general evaluation of existing supplier performance	Uncertainty • High	• Reduced	• Minimum development of institutional-isation	Extensive institutional-isation
• efforts of non-supplier	Distance • High	• Reduced	• Minimum	
• other information sources	Commitment Actual—Low	Actual—Increased	Actual—Maximum	Business based on Industry Codes of Practice
• overall policy decision	Perceived—Low	Perceived—Demonstrated by Informal Adaptations	Perceived—Reduced	
Evaluation conditioned by:				
• experience with previous supplier	Adaptation			
	High Investment of Management time. Few cost-savings.	Increasing formal and informal adaptations. Cost savings increase.	Extensive adaptations. Cost savings reduced by institutional-isation.	
• uncertainty about potential relationship				
• "Distance" from potential supplier				
Commitment • zero				

company to obtain business, perhaps based on a major change in its offering, e.g., a new product introduction; some change in requirements or market conditions experienced by the buyer, e.g., a UK car manufacturer began evaluating overseas sources for windscreens following the move towards tempered glass for which there was a European capacity shortage.

Alternatively, the evaluation of potential suppliers can be the result of a general policy. For example, widespread industrial troubles in the UK in 1974 ("the three day week") caused one manufacturer to adopt the policy of obtaining approximately 40 per cent of its components from overseas. It then started a search to find and evaluate potential sources of supply to carry out this policy.

A company's evaluation of a potential new supplier will take place without any commitment to that supplier at this stage. The evaluation will be conditioned by three factors; experience, uncertainty and distance. Experience in existing and previous relationships provides the criteria by which the potential and performance of a new partner will be judged — a partner of which the company has no experience. The buyer will face uncertainty about the potential costs and benefits which are likely to be involved in dealing with a new supplier. The costs can be separated into those involved in making a change to a particular partner, e.g., in a buyer modifying its own product to suit that of a new seller. Additionally, there are the opportunity costs involved in the continuing relationship, when compared with alternative partners, e.g., in a buyer having to accept less frequent deliveries.

The distance which is perceived to exist between buyer and seller has several aspects:

- *social distance*, being the extent to which both the individuals and organisations in a relationship are unfamiliar with each others' ways of working;
- *cultural distance*, being the degree to which the norms, values or working methods between two companies differ because of their separate national characteristics;
- *technological distance*, being the differences between the two companies' product and process technologies;
- *time distance*, being the time which must elapse between establishing contact or placing an order, and the actual transfer of the product or service involved;
- *geographical distance*, being the physical distance between the two companies' locations.

Technological distance is likely to be great in evaluations for the purchase of innovative products. Social distance will be considerable in all new relationships as the companies know little of each other. This is combined with large cultural and geographical distance when the companies are dealing across national boundaries [10]. Finally, the companies will be considering a purchase which is unlikely to take place for considerable time, with consequent apprehension that it will not come to fruition as desired.

We can now see the effects of these variables of Experience, Uncertainty, Distance and Commitment in the early stages of dealings between the companies.

Stage 2: The Early Stage

This is the time when *potential* suppliers are in contact with purchasers to negotiate or develop a specification for a capital goods purchase. This stage can also involve sample delivery for frequently purchased components or supplies. The stage can be characterised as follows.

Experience. At this early stage in their relationship, both buyer and seller are likely to have little experience of each other. They will only have a restricted view of what the other party requires of them, or even of what they hope to gain from the relationship themselves. No routine procedures will have been established to deal with issues as they arise, such as sample quality, design changes, etc. These issues can only be resolved by a considerable investment of management time at this stage. This investment of human resources is likely to precede any investment in physical plant.

Uncertainty. Human resource investment will be made at a time of considerable uncertainty, when the potential rewards from the relationship will be difficult to assess and the pattern of future costs is undetermined.

Distance. There will have been little opportunity to reduce the distance between the parties at this early stage in their dealings.

  Social Distance. There will be a lack of knowledge between buyer and seller companies as well as an absence of personal relationships between the individuals involved. This will mean that many of the judgements made of each company will be on their reputation, as a substitute for experience of their abilities.

  Geographical/Cultural Distance. Geographical distance is, of course, beyond the control of the seller except in so far as it can be reduced by the establishment of a local sales office or by sending staff out to the customer on a residential basis. Cultural differences can only be reduced by employment of local nationals. The lack of social relationships means that there is nothing to reduce the effects of geographical and particularly cultural distance. This can result in a lack of trust between the companies. For example, a supplier may believe that he is simply being used as a source of information and that the customer has no intention of placing major orders or building a relationship. Further, the distrust of an individual supplier can cause a purchaser to place emphasis on cultural stereotypes—e.g., a customer may attach importance to the alleged "discipline" of German suppliers, as opposed to a lack of faith in "undisciplined" British suppliers.

Technological Distance. Inexperience of a supplier's product will emphasise any differences which may exist between the product or process technologies of the two companies.

Time Distance. In the early stage of a relationship, companies are likely to be negotiating about agreements or transactions which may only come to fruition at some considerable time in the future. This maximises the buyer's concern about whether he will receive the product in the form specified and at the promised price and time. Similarly, the seller will be concerned as to whether orders being discussed will ever materialise in the way it expects.

Commitment. Both companies will be aware of the risks involved and will have little or no evidence on which to judge their partner's commitment to the relationship. In fact, it is likely that the actual commitment of both parties will be low at this time. Thus, perceptions of the likely commitment of the other company are strongly influenced by factors outside the relationship such as the number and importance of its other customers or suppliers.

The actions of seller and buyer in the future will be influenced by their initial assessment of the performance and potential of their partner. Their judgement of the place and importance of this relationship within the company's portfolio of suppliers or clients will also be important. Thus, a US engineering manufacturer clearly separates those "development suppliers" from others, very early in their dealings. It is these suppliers who receive the customer's investment of time, money and expertise to build the relationship. It may be that only one of the partners may seek to develop the relationship, while the other remains passive. Also, efforts at development may founder, either because of the unwillingness of the partner or the incompetence of the initiator in overcoming the problems inherent in the early stages of a relationship.

We can now consider the development of a relationship beyond the early stage in terms of the tasks of building experience, increasing commitment and the associated reduction in uncertainty and distance.

Stage 3: The Development Stage

The development stage of a relationship occurs as deliveries of continuously purchased products increase. Alternatively, it is the time after contract signing for major capital purchases. Staged deliveries may be being made or the supplier may have started work on the item. Both buyer and seller will be dealing with such aspects as integration of the purchased product into the customer's operations or pre-delivery training, etc.

Experience. The development stage is marked by increasing experience between the companies of the operations of each other's organisations. Additionally, the individuals involved will have acquired some knowledge of each other's norms and values.

Uncertainty. The uncertainties which exist for both parties in the relationship will have been reduced by experience. In particular, the adaptations required to meet the wishes of the partner company will have become more apparent and the costs involved in these adaptations will also become clearer. Each company will be better able to judge the adaptations to meet its own requirements. These include those made by itself and those which it should require from its partner.

Distance

Social Distance. This is reduced by the social exchange which takes place between the companies. As well as increasing their knowledge of each other, these personal relations establish trust between individuals. Nonetheless, this trust cannot be based upon social relationships alone. It also requires personal experience of the other company's satisfactory performance in exchange of product or services and finance.

Geographical and Cultural Distance. The reduction in social distance also contributes to a lessening of the effects of geographical and cultural distance. However, in a relationship between companies in different countries, it is possible that the seller company may reduce geographical and cultural distance through the establishment of a local office and employment of local nationals as business builds up.

Technological Distance. The adaptations which companies make to suit each other reduce the technological distance between them. Thus, their respective products, production and administrative processes become more closely matched with each other. This produces consequent savings for one or both parties.

Time Distance. The experience of transactions means that the time distance between negotiation and delivery is eliminated in the case of continually delivered products. However, in the case of irregular purchases of, for example, capital goods then each cycle of order and delivery can be marked by similar time distances. Nevertheless, the importance of this distance decreases as the companies' mutual experience and trust of each other builds up.

Commitment. Much of a company's evaluation of a supplier or customer during the development of their relationship will depend on perceptions of their commitment to its development. Efforts to reduce social distance are one way for the supplier to demonstrate commitment. Commitment can also be shown in other ways:

> It can be indicated by "adapting" to meet the needs of the other company, either by incurring costs or by management involvement. It is useful to separate these adaptations into *formal* adaptations which are contractually agreed between the companies and *informal* adaptations which may be arranged subsequently, to cope with particular issues which arise as the relationship develops. It is possible that the formal adaptations between companies may be dictated by the nature of the industry, e.g., that special products must always be developed for individual customers. On the other hand, a supplier's informal adaptations beyond the terms of a contract are often an important indicator of commitment [11]. For example, one large UK buying organisation lists a major criterion in assessing the commitment of suppliers to be their "flexibility," for example in arranging a rapid increase in supply to cope with a sudden demand change.
>
> In the international context, a company can demonstrate its commitment to a general market. This can be done by setting up a sales or buying office in that market. For example, a UK manufacturer and a French company had not progressed beyond the stage of exchanging "letters of intent" to buy. This was despite being in contact with each other for over two years. It was clear that the buyer doubted the supplier's commitment to it or the market, because of its unwillingness to establish a French office or assign specific personnel to the relationship during its development.
>
> Finally, a company can emphasise commitment to a relationship by the way it organises its contacts with its partner. This includes both the status of personnel involved and the frequency of contact. For example, a British buyer of packaging machinery formed an unfavourable impression of the commitment of a Swedish supplier because of the lack of seniority of the people with which it had to deal and their slow speed of response in their contacts.

The process of development of an inter-company relationship is associated with an increasing level of business between the companies. Over time, many of the difficulties existing in the early stages of a relationship are removed through the processes we have described in the development stage. However, development does not continue indefinitely. The relationship can be discontinued by either party on the basis of their assessment of its potential, the performance of the other party, or of the actions of outsiders. Even if this does not occur, the character of a relationship will change gradually. The changes which slowly develop are of vital significance to both buying and selling firms and we now turn to their description.

Stage 4: The Long-Term Stage

It is not possible to put a timetable on the process by which a relationship reaches the long-term stage. This stage is characterised by the companies' mutual importance to each other. It is reached after large-scale deliveries of continuously purchased products have occurred or after several purchases of major unit products [12].

Experience. The considerable experience of the two companies in dealing with each other leads to the establishment of standard operating procedures, trust, and norms of conduct. For example, a UK supplier of components to a German truck producer has arrangements for deliveries against three-month "firm" and six-month "tentative" orders. Prices are negotiated on an annual basis with an effective date of 1 January... "although we often don't get round to firming them up until well in the spring, so we just apply them retrospectively." Similarly, a UK producer of marine diesel engines will start construction of an individual unit costing up to £100,000 on the basis of a verbal order from a main customer. Formal orders often follow much later.

Uncertainty. Uncertainty about the process of dealing with a particular partner is reduced to a minimum in the long-term stage. Paradoxically, this reduction in uncertainty can create problems. It is possible that routine ways of dealing with the partner will cease to be questioned by this stage. This can be even though these routines may no longer relate well to either parties' requirements. We refer to this phenomenon as *institutionalisation*. For example, discount structures may have become unrelated to developing delivery patterns, product variety may involve increased production costs for the seller whilst the buyer may be able to use a much narrower range of product.

These institutionalised patterns of operation make it difficult for a company to assess its partner's real requirements and so it may appear less responsive or uncommitted to the relationship. Institutionalised practices may also allow a company to drift into overdependence on a partner or incur excessive costs in its dealings. One company may exploit the other's institutionalised practices and lack of awareness and hence reduce its own costs at the expense of the partner. Finally institutionalised practices of one relationship can affect a company's whole organisation and hence its development of other relationships. For example, a supplier of high grade alloys had become very heavily involved with a large domestic customer. It then attempted to transfer its experience with this customer to others in different market segments overseas. So many aspects and operations within this relationship had become institutionalised, or taken for granted that the supplier was unable to modify its procedures to suit new customers.

Distance

Social Distance. This is also minimised in the long-term stage. There are three particular features to the close relationship established by this stage.

Firstly, an extensive contact pattern will have developed between the companies. This may involve several functional areas and its aim will be to achieve an effective matching and adaptation of the systems and procedures of both supplier and customer. However, in the long-term stage the interactions by the different functions may become separated. For example, the technical problem solving between a supplier and its customers can become quite separate from the commercial transactions which take place. This can lead to problems of co-ordination and control if different departments are not to work in conflict with each other. For example, a German engineering company had 40 of its staff in constant contact with 12 people in a UK supplier. In view of this, the customer appointed a section head to "manage" the relationship. It was his responsibility to ensure that all of the separate interactions with the supplier were mutually compatible and in line with the overall policy of the buying company.

Secondly, strong personal relationships will have developed between individuals in the two companies. The strength of these can be seen by the extent of mutual problem solving and informal adaptations which occur. However, it may be difficult for an individual to separate these personal relationships from the business relation. Difficulties can arise when company interests are subordinated to those of the personal relationships. This has its most extreme form in the phenomenon of "side-changing" where individuals act in the interests of the other company and against their own, on the strength of their personal allegiances.

Thirdly, in the long-term stage, companies may become personified in an individual representative. Indeed, it may be the seller's policy to identify closely a relationship with the person of their local representative. This may be of value in establishing a presence in an overseas market. However it inevitably involves problems if this individual has to be replaced or acts in his own interests rather than those of the company. For example, a UK exporter of machinery had to re-negotiate spares prices charged to its main French customer. These had previously been fixed by the supplier's local representative at a very low level. This had been done because the representaive was greatly concerned about the effects of losing this business on his own position.

Technological Distance. Successive contracts and agreements between the companies lead to extensive formal adaptations. These closely integrate many aspects of the operations of the two companies. This close integration is motivated by cost reduction for both companies as well as increased control over either their supply or buyer markets. De Monthoux has emphasised the barriers to the entry of other companies to which this close integration leads [13].

Commitment. By the long-term stage, both seller and buyer companies' commitment to the relationship will have been demonstrated by the extensive formal and informal adaptations which have occurred. Nevertheless, the seller company faces two difficulties over commitment at this stage.

Firstly, it is likely to be difficult for a company to balance the need to demonstrate commitment to a client against the danger of becoming overly dependent on that client. This was expressed by a UK supplier faced with a major customer as follows: "We want them to think they are still important to us. At the same time we also want them to believe that they must work for our attention in competition with other customers."

Secondly, a customer's perception of a supplier's commitment to a relationship may differ from the actual level. This is because the required investment of resources has largely been incurred before the long-term stage is reached. It is also possible that the level of business between the companies has stabilised. Thus, paradoxically, when a supplier is at his most committed to a long-term and important client, he may *appear* less committed than during the development stage.

We have now come "full circle" in the description of relationship development. We have reached that stable situation before evaluation of potential new suppliers which was our starting point. In this, a company may continue with existing sources of supply or customers with little knowledge or evaluation of the available supply or customer markets. However, before concluding, it is worthwhile to mention a final stage which buyer-seller relationships may enter.

Stage 5: The Final Stage

This stage is reached in stable markets over long periods of time. It is marked by an extension of the institutionalisation process to a point where the conduct of business is based on industry codes of practice. These may have relatively little to do with commercial considerations, but correspond more to a "right way to do business," e.g., the avoidance of price cutting and restrictions on changes in the respective roles of buyer and seller. It is often the case that attempts to break out of institutionalised patterns of trading in the final stage will be met by sanctions from other trading partners or the company's fellow buyers or sellers [14].

MARKETING IMPLICATIONS

We have described how the development of buyer-seller relationships can be seen as a process in terms of:

- the increasing experience of the two companies;
- the reduction in their uncertainty and the distance between them;
- the growth of both actual and perceived commitment;
- their formal and informal adaptations to each other and the investments and savings involved.

We can now turn to some of the implications of this process for the marketing company. The most obvious implication is that a company cannot treat its market in some overall way. Not only must it segment that market according to the different requirements of companies, it must also see its potential market as a network of relationships. Each of these must be assessed according to the opportunity they represent and how the relationship can be developed. The company's marketing task then becomes the establishment, development and maintenance of these relationships, rather than the manipulation of a generalised marketing mix. Further, this management of relationships must take place with regard to the company's skills and the costs involved, as well as the allocation of its resources between different relationships according to the likely return.

Establishing Relationships

The existing relationships between buying and selling companies in an industrial market are a powerful barrier to the entry of another company. The barrier consists of the inertia in existing relationships, the uncertainties for the customer in any change of supplier, the distance which exists between buyer and a potential seller, and the lack of awareness or information about possible alternative partners. These factors are particularly significant in the case of overseas purchases [15], where buyers may form stereotypes of national characteristics.

The marketer should be involved in the following activities to overcome these problems:

Market Analysis. An analysis is required, which goes beyond determining which markets or sectors to enter. This analysis must examine the relationships held by potential customers and existing competitors. Customers may be categorised into those with long-established supplier relationships for the product, or those in the development or early stages. It is difficult to generalise at which stage relationships are easiest to break into, although different approaches will be required depending on the stage. Thus, a potential customer in the early stages of a relationship with a supplier may be facing problems which require considerable management involvement. This may mean that the company is in a position to evaluate alternatives and is aware of the inadequacies of its existing relationship. In contrast, a company which has begun to adapt and become committed to a supplier, may be unwilling to face further uncertainty by considering a change. Thus, in the case of a satisfactorily developing or long-term relationship, it is likely that a new supplier will only be considered if there is some failure or particular inadequacy in an existing supplier. For example, we have pointed out that a buyer's perception of a supplier's commitment can decrease in the long-term stage and that problems may arise through institutionalised practices.

The analysis we refer to will indicate the required approach to different potential customers. Breaking into existing, early-stage relationships may involve emphasis on a broad range of factors, e.g., product specification, prices and delivery. Also, the approach may be to the senior management which is likely to be involved at this stage. The approach to customers with more established relationships involves determining the *specific* problems they are facing. Also, the seller must examine whether an attempt to solve these problems is within its capabilities. The company must question whether the adaptations it must make will provide adequate returns. Finally, it must tailor its approach to the individuals within the customer who are in the areas of the relationship where problems have arisen.

Developing Relationships. We have discussed the importance of commitment and distance reduction in the development of relationships. Those involve a supplier in human and capital costs—in an overall market. It is worth noting that commitment to a market normally involves investment, in the form of local offices, etc., *before* business has developed. This contrasts with the attitudes of many industrial exporters who seem only prepared to invest in a sales or service operation *after* sales have been achieved.

The development of relationships can also be considered as a problem of strategy and organisation. We must distinguish between the "strategic management" of relationships and the "operational management" of a single relationship. Strategic management involves the assessment of any one relationship within the company's strategy in a particular market or markets. Further, strategic management covers a portfolio of relationships. It is concerned with the interplay between them, their respective importance and the consequent resource allocation between them. It is difficult for those people involved in detailed interaction with a customer to see that relationship in perspective or to see the possible effects of institutionalisation on it. It is because of this, that the strategic management function should be carried out by marketing staff who are not involved in the day-to-day operation of relationships.

A company's marketing structure should also follow from the nature of its relationships. A functional organisation within marketing may be appropriate for a firm with a large number of small clients. However, the complexity of the interaction with major clients emphasises the importance of co-ordination of all aspects of a company's dealings with a client. There is a clear role for a "relationship manager" as in the German buying company referred to earlier. This is someone of sufficient status to co-ordinate all aspects of the company's relationships with major clients at the operational level. This individual is the major "contact man" for the company. He takes overall reponsibility for the successful development of a relationship. This is based on his assessment of appropriate resource allocation to that relationship and his orchestration of the interactions between *all* functions — product development, production, sales, quality, and finance, etc. This requires more than the kind of authority usually given to an industrial salesman or "key account executive." In fact, the relationship manager should be independent of those departments which he co-ordinates in managing his portfolio of important relationships. Relationship management is most likely to be seen in operational form in industrial export marketing. Paradoxically, the limited resources often allocated by the seller company to export business mean that one man is involved directly or indirectly in all contacts — hence providing effective co-ordination. The relationship manager has a vital function in the case of irregularly purchased products, e.g., capital equipment. In this case, there is a clear need to *maintain* the relationship between purchase opportunities, either using sales staff or by his own contact.

Our research indicates that industrial companies are more likely to invest marketing resources at the operational than at the strategic level, perhaps because of their more immediately apparent results. This means that many companies are better staffed in the sales areas than under such designations as market planning or market development managers. Thus, staff are often pulled between the separate tasks of day-to-day operations and longer-term strategic planning. Under these circumstances it is not surprising that strategic planning is inadequately covered in the company.

Maintaining Relationships. We have noted that perhaps the most significant aspect of long-term relationships is the problem of institutionalisation. This can make a seller unresponsive to the changing requirements of its customers. The separation of operational and strategic management within the company's marketing is the key to reducing these problems. Strategic management includes a company's market analysis and points to differences in market sector and customer characteristics. Hence, it reduces the danger of transferring inappropriate marketing practices from one market to another. Strategic management involves a re-examination of the company's existing operations to see if they continue to be relevant to particular client relationships and market conditions. Finally, strategic management determines the resource allocation between different relationships according to their potential and stage of development. The over-emphasis on operational marketing within many companies means that they do not have the staff or the time to re-examine those activities which have been taken for granted in the company's long-term relationships.

Final Remarks

In conclusion, it is important to emphasise that companies should examine their existing relationships whether home or overseas to see which of the stages described here they fall into. This examination should be a preliminary to an assessment of each relationship, as follows:

1. What is the likely potential of this relationship?
2. What resources are required to fulfill this potential?
3. Where do the threats to this development come from?
4. Where does this relationship fit within the context of the company's overall operations and resource allocation in that market?
5. Are the current efforts devoted to the relationship appropriate to this overall strategy?
6. Are we over-committed to this customer?
7. Finally, are our ways of dealing with this customer appropriate both to its needs and our strategy or are they dealings based on habit or history?

ENDNOTES

*The author acknowledges the contribution of Anna Lawson who read earlier drafts of this paper.

REFERENCES

1. For example, Webster, F. E., *Industrial Marketing Strategy*, New York, John Wiley, 1979.
2. Exceptions include de Monthoux, P.B.L.G., "Organizational Mating and Industrial Marketing Conservation—Some Reasons why Industrial Marketing Managers Resist Marketing Theory," *Industrial Marketing Management*, Vol. 4, 1975, pp. 25–36; Blois, K. J., "Vertical Quasi-Integration," *Journal of Industrial Economics*, Vol. XX, July, 1972, pp. 253–72; Hakansson, H. and Wootz, B., "A Framework for Industrial Buying and Selling," *Industrial Marketing Management*, Vol. 3, 1979, pp. 28–39.
3. For details, see Cunningham, M. T., "International Marketing and Purchasing of Industrial Goods: Features of a European Research Project," *European Journal of Marketing*, this issue.
4. *Ibid*.
5. See, for example, Williamson, O. E., *Markets and Hierarchies: Analysis and Anti-Trust Implications*, New York, Free Press, 1975.
6. Williamson, O. E., "Transaction Cost Economics: The Governance of Contractual Relations," *Journal of Law and Economics*, Vol. 22 No. 2, October 1979, pp. 232–62.
7. *Ibid*.
8. For a discussion of the methodological implications of analysis of episodes and relationships see Ford, I. D., "A Methodology for the Study of Inter-Company Relations in Industrial Market Channels," *Journal of the Market Research Society*, Vol. 22 No. 1, 1980, 44–59.
9. See, for example, Cunningham, M. T. and White, J. G., "The Determinants of Choice of Supply," *Euorpean Journal of Marketing*, Vol. 7 No. 3, 1973, pp. 189–202.
10. For use of a similar concept of distance in international business, see Johansson, J. and Wiedersheim-Paul, F., "The Internationalisation of the Firm—Four Swedish Case Studies," *Journal of Management Studies*, October, 1975, pp. 305–22. For an attempt to analyse the effect of distance on purchase behaviour see, Hakansson, H. and Wootz, B., "Supplier Selection in an International Environment—An Experimental Study," *Journal of Marketing Research*, Vol. XII, 1975, pp. 46–51.
11. Suppliers' informal adaptations are often referred to in the purchasing literature as "Supplier Value Added."
12. This does not mean that a single supplier has been responsible for all of a customer's requirements of a continuously purchased product or every purchase of a major item.
13. de Monthoux, *op. cit*.

14. For further discussion of institutionalised practices in long established markets see Ford, I. D., "Stability Factors in Industrial Marketing Channels," *Industrial Marketing Management*, Vol. 7, 1978, pp. 410–27.
15. See Hakansson, H. and Wootz, B., "Supplier Selection in an International Environment," *Journal of Marketing Research*, Vol. XII, February 1975, pp. 46–51.

51   Situational Segmentation of Industrial Markets

Richard N. Cardozo

European Journal of Marketing, Vol. 14, No. 5/6 (1980), pp. 264/76. Reprinted by permission.

Organisational buying situations may be classified on four distinct dimensions. Individual dimensions and combinations of dimensions may be used to group industrial market transactions into separate segments. Segmentation based on buying situations can help marketers design and modify marketing programmes, and can assist marketers in predicting the response of particular segments to specified offerings. For example, Choffray and Lilien [5] have shown that knowledge about the composition of the decision-making unit (DMU) or buying centre in a specified situation helps marketers design or modify communication programmes, and concentrate attention on those market segments to which their competitive advantages are most meaningful.

Formal analysis of differences among organisational buying situations received its greatest impetus from Robinson, Faris and Wind [14] who in 1967 differentiated new tasks from modified rebuys from straight rebuys. Moriarity and Galper [11] and the *Scientific American* [15] have classified buying situations by product. Hakansson, Johanson and Wootz [8] and Luffman [10] differentiated situations on the basis of perceived risk. Other scholars have refined and expanded these classifications.

Interviews* with purchasing personnel and other members of DMUs, and with industrial marketing personnel, indicate that practitioners have adapted these classifications to suit their own needs and have in that process enriched the classification system. Specifically, practitioners differentiate buying situations on the bases of importance to the buying organisation, the source or origin of the buying process, and the level of funding approval needed.

Information from scholarly and practitioner sources may be combined to produce a four-dimensional classification system for industrial buying situations. These dimensions include:

(1) buyers' familiarity with the buying task (new or rebuy);
(2) product type;
(3) importance of the purchase to the buying organisation; and,
(4) principal type of uncertainty present in the purchase situation.

FAMILIARITY WITH THE BUYING TASK

One may classify buying tasks into "buyclasses" [14] on the basis of the familiarity of personnel in the buying organisation with the buying task. A "new task" is one with which members of the buying organisation have not dealt before, at least in their present organisation. A "straight rebuy" involves purchases of previously purchased items from suppliers already judged acceptable. "Modified rebuys" represent an intermediate residual category of purchases with which individuals in the buying organisation are familiar, but for which buyers may re-evaluate their buying objectives and will re-evaluate suppliers. In their analysis of organisational buying, Robinson, Faris and Wind [14] described modified rebuys as having some of the characteristics of new tasks and many of the characteristics of straight rebuys. Brand [1] follows this position and limits modified rebuys to changing of suppliers. But in a study of industrial marketing organisations Doyle, Woodside and Michell [6] found that new tasks and modified rebuys were quite similar, and that the two combined differed from straight rebuys. In contrast, professional purchasing personnel group buying tasks into "new" and "rebuy," without distinguishing between modified and straight rebuys.

Because empirical evidence suggests that the purchasing process does differ to some extent between modified and straight rebuys, and because that difference may enable marketers to develop useful strategies to deal with particular buying decisions, the three-category system remains useful. For particular analytical purposes, "modified rebuys" may be combined either with "new tasks" or with "straight rebuys," provided the definitions of each of the three classes is complete and unambiguous, and the basis for the combination reported fully. For purposes of managing either the marketing effort or the purchasing process, the combination may be justified on the basis of practical utility.

Both the individuals involved in the purchasing process and the process itself vary among new tasks, modified rebuys and straight rebuys. The three buyclasses vary with respect to the following stages of the purchase process:

- source of problem recognition
- formation of the DMU
- determination and description of the characteristics of the item(s) to be purchased
- search for and qualification of vendors
- analysis of alternatives
- evaluation of offers and negotiation
- order routines and performance evaluation.

TABLE I. Differences Among Buyclasses

Stage in Purchase Process	New Task	Modified Rebuy	Straight Rebuy
Source of problem/opportunity recognition	—New product development —Analysis of operations —Expansion of capacity	—Change in specifications or process for existing product —Expansion of operations —New offer from non-supplier —Dissatisfaction with current supplier(s) (Process resembles that for straight rebuys except for seeking bids from non-suppliers)	—Inventory control system —Production schedule —Sales forecast
Formation of decision-making unit	*New product* / *Operations change* / *Expansion*	*Expansion or change in specification or process* / *New product offered* / *New price offered*	
—Initiator	Senior management, marketing, engineering or research / Engineering / Senior management, engineering	Engineering / Engineering / Purchasing	Purchasing or using department
—Source of contact with supplier	line managers, technical specialists	Manufacturing, engineering and/or purchasing / Engineering, purchasing / Purchasing	Purchasing
—Size of DMU —Membership in DMU	3-6 members Senior management, functional managers, technical specialists from marketing, engineering, manufacturing; purchasing specialist / Line managers and technical specialists in engineering, manufacturing; purchasing specialist / Similar to "new product"	3-6 members Line managers, technical specialists, purchasing	2-3 members Purchasing, engineering, manufacturing

—Activity of DMU members	Senior management involved early as influencers; Technical specialists dominate early stages; purchasing assists in acquiring information and participates in qualifying suppliers; technical specialists dominate evaluation stage; purchasing influential in final supplier choice.	Senior management consulted if large expenditures or major resources involved; Buyer works with technical personnel to make decision; confirms with line managers.	Purchasing consults with staff specialists in using department
Determination and description of characteristics and quantity of item(s) to be purchased	Extensive requests for information and samples from vendors, informally and through formal request for quotation to determine specifications; forecasts to determine quantity for new product.	New specifications from engineering; quantities from sales and production forecasts.	Specifications available from prior purchases; quantities from sales and production forecasts; negligible information sought from suppliers.
Search for and qualification of sources	Intensive working sessions (perhaps including site visit) with suppliers who appear interested and capable; technical specialists interested in reducing number of prospective vendors; buyers, in increasing number.	Respond to non-supplier initiative; contact current vendors and perhaps other non-suppliers.	Contact current vendors, perhaps others considered capable.
Acquisition and analyses of proposals	Obtain and analyse formal quotations, samples, results of tests; refine specifications.	In some cases, seek new quotations from established suppliers; in others seek new information only from non-supplier involved	For annual/continuing supply agreement, seek quotations from vendors who have qualified; for individual purchases, draw against supply agreement.
Evaluation of offers, suppliers	Evaluation by technical personnel; senior management may add other considerations not directly related to value analysis.	Technical evaluation of non-supplier's offering.	Evaluate against pre-set criteria price and delivery offered; some organizations maintain multiple sources.
Negotiation	Much negotiation on specifications, performance and guarantee; some on delivery; little on price.	Negotiation emphasizes price and delivery	Minimum negotiation; emphasis on price, delivery and terms of sale.
Selection of order routine and performance evaluation	Routine for new task varies by organization; new vendors monitored closely at first.	Similar to new task for new vendor; to straight rebuy, for established supplier.	Order routine specified in supply agreement; in addition to regular informal contact, evaluation through formal vendor rating system; exception reports from using department.
Length of process	7–60 months	7–60 months	1 week to 7 months

In practice, these stages of the purchase process may overlap. Particularly in straight rebuy situations many stages may be dramatically compressed, and the entire process may be shorter [1].

A summary of differences among these buyclasses along these dimensions, based on previously published research [1, 6, 14, 15, 17] supplemented with data from interviews in a variety of buying organisations in the United States, appears in Table I. Note that the source of problem/opportunity recognition affects the formation of the decision-making unit, but has little impact on subsequent stages of the process.

Illustrative Marketing Implications

Marketers facing new task situations should attempt to become involved at the very beginning of the buying process with technical personnel or others who will play a key role in determining specifications and qualifying vendors. Marketers interested in obtaining business in new task situations must be prepared to invest the time necessary to co-operate with the customer as he works through all phases of the buying process.

Similar advice is appropriate for marketers facing modified rebuy situations that result from changes in specifications of one of the buying firm's products. Nonsuppliers should take initiative in cases in which buying organisations are dissatisfied with present suppliers, or are expanding output and interested in adding sources of supply; or in which non-suppliers have a measurably superior offering that current suppliers cannot likely match.

In straight rebuy situations, vendors currently supplying the buying organisation may minimise opportunities for non-suppliers by seeing to it that customers do not have cause for dissatisfaction and by adapting to the changing needs of present customers. Non-suppliers should attempt to persuade purchasing and technical personnel that re-evaluating suppliers will be worth the effort to take advantage of new technology, product features or opportunities for better value. In straight rebuy situations, non-supplier initiatives are likely to be more productive when major supply agreements come up for renewal than when the purchaser simply draws against an existing agreement.

PRODUCT TYPE

Most purchasers and analysts [2, 4, 9, 15, 16] agree that organisational buying activities vary among specific products purchased. This variation shows itself in the number and identity of departments represented in the DMU [12, 15]. Interview data suggest that the greater the number of departments and the higher the organisational levels represented, the longer the decision process and the more careful scrutiny each alternative receives. Principal dimensions of this variation appear to be product use and degree of standardisation.

Product use includes four categories:

1. products and services for maintenance, repair and operation (MRO);
2. components of the organisation's finished products;
3. materials to be used in the production process; and
4. equipment.

Applications for equipment include (a) replacement of existing equipment, (b) retrofit of new equipment into existing facilities and (c) placement of equipment in expanded or new facilities. Although real estate is not explicitly included in this classification scheme, those organisations that regularly expand or relocate facilities treat those decisions in a manner similar to capital equipment decisions.

Table II shows the extent to which each of four types of individuals (as designated by job titles) is involved in the purchase decision for each of these four categories of product in new task or modified rebuy situations. An "x" indicates significant involvement; a "–" negligible involvement. Job titles not listed may be significant participants in particular decisions, but not across a broad range of purchase decisions. Across all types of decisions, managers and technical specialists are most important in the early stages of the buying process, but they also are involved in evaluation of bids and negotiations. Purchasing personnel become influential principally in the later stages.

The length of the purchase process and care exercised by buyers in analysis of alternatives appear to increase from left to right across the categories in Table II. Purchases of MRO items are generally described as far quicker and less complicated than the other three; components, quicker and less painstaking than materials and equipment. Interviewees reported that equipment purchases typically, but by no means always, received longer and more careful analysis than materials purchases.

The degree of standardisation of the product or service being purchased also affects the composition and behaviour of the DMU. Products (services) may be defined as:

1. custom, i.e., a unique design for a particular customer;
2. modular, i.e., a unique combination of standard available components or materials; or
3. standard, i.e., a combination of ingredients that has been offered previously.

Custom and modular products may become standard over time as they are sold repeatedly to one customer or to a broader range of customers. A custom product first purchased as a new task could become a straight rebuy.

In the purchase of custom products, engineering personnel are frequently involved to a greater degree and earlier in the buying process than in purchase situations in which buying organisations select among standard alternatives. Frequently this involvement of technical specialists leads to exclusion of all but one or two vendors, whereas several vendors may be considered as sources for standard products.

Within any use category, custom products or services are likely to receive more careful analysis over a longer time period than are modular products or services. Standard products and services are likely to be purchased in less time and with less deliberation.

Illustrative Implications for Marketing

Knowledge of the different departments involved in a purchase decision suggests whom the marketer must contact throughout the marketing-purchase decision process for particular types of products. Information about the length of the purchase decision and depth of analysis performed in the buying organisation may help the marketer to estimate his marketing costs, and to determine whether the pursuit of a particular account or group of accounts appears worthwhile. Marketers should recognise that sale of custom or modular products, which may

TABLE II. Participation in Purchase Decisions

Position	MRO	Product Use Components	Materials	Equipment
Senior management	—	—	only for new products	x
Operating management	x	x	x	x
Design engineering	—	x	x	primarily for new materials or new products
Production engineering	—	primarily for changes in production process	primarily for changes in production process	x
Research	—	only for new products	primarily to set specifications	x
Purchasing	x	x	x	x

Note: "new products" means products that the buying organisation intends to manufacture and sell, but has not done so previously.

appear to offer a marketer a competitive advantage over standard products in some instances, typically requires longer and more intensive marketing effort than standard products. Finally, because many purchasing departments organise their buying activities into the four use categories, knowledge of the use or application of a particular product may help a marketer to identify quickly the appropriate contact within the purchasing department.

IMPORTANCE OF PURCHASE TO BUYING ORGANISATION

Importance refers to the degree of risk believed present in the purchase situation. Type of risk forms a separate category. Although both degree and type of risk have been discussed in organisational buying literature [12, 16], attempts to measure them reliably have met with limited success. Perception of risk varies among situations and individuals because of differences in perceptions of the exposure to loss, the uncertainty surrounding decisions and the individual's own risk tolerance and preference. Although individual differences lie beyond the scope of this paper, the two situational components of risk—exposure & uncertainty— can be differentiated here.

The exposure to loss in a particular purchase decision forms one useful dimension for defining the risk present in that situation. Exposure includes both the cost of the purchased products themselves and the total cost to the buying organisation if the purchased product should fail. The cost of purchased products themselves may be expressed in money volume involved and/or as a percentage of annual volume of purchases represented in a particular decision. For example, negotiation of an annual supply agreement for office supplies involves far more money than does the purchase of several reams of paper or of filing cabinets within that agreement. Although both decisions would be classified as straight rebuys of MRO items, the former is clearly more important than the latter. The total cost of purchasing a product which fails to perform as specified or is delivered late, may include costs of down time, product rejection and even recall. Such total costs can far exceed the costs of the purchased product itself. Most professional purchasers consider total cost rather than just the cost of the purchased units themselves in calculating exposure to loss [3, 7].

Some purchase situations may involve limited monetary exposure for the organisation, but substantial non-monetary exposure for the individuals involved in a particular decision. For example, a buyer and maintenance supervisor in a manufacturing complex considered the award of a cleaning contract for the executive and general office a highly important purchase even though the contract represented an insignificant sum and was classified as a routine maintenance purchase. The situation was important to the DMU members because substandard performance – dirty offices – would be highly visible, and would evoke executive criticism of both buyer and maintenance supervisor.

The other dimension useful for defining degree of risk in a purchase situation is the degree of uncertainty with respect to the outcome. That uncertainty may be defined as the difference between what would, in retrospect, have been the best buying decision and the decision actually made. That difference may be expressed in terms of percentage savings, or percentage improvement in performance or specifications for a set purchase price. In the office supplies example cited above, the differences in cost or performance of the items are likely to be small, and the degree of uncertainty therefore modest. In contrast, advance purchases of materials whose prices fluctuate widely, and for which no orderly hedging market exists, involve a great deal of uncertainty. Buying decisions that involve changes, such as adoption of an innovation or modification of a critical process in the organisation, ordinarily carry greater uncertainty than do decisions that do not require major changes. New tasks bear more uncertainty than do rebuys.

The two dimensions of exposure to loss and degree of uncertainty may be combined to form a simple graph of importance, as shown in Figure 1. If the two dimensions were equally powerful determinants of importance, the importance curve would be a straight line running from the upper left to the lower right position of the figure. But because interview data suggest that exposure is more influential (quite probably because it is easier to quantify) than uncertainty, the importance curve is convex to the origin.

Many organisations group the items they purchase into "A", "B" and "C" categories on the basis of importance to the organisation and, therefore, attention needed when purchasing. "A" items are ordinarily limited in number, involve high exposure and considerable uncertainty, and account for a high percentage of an organisation's purchase volume, "C" items typically include hundreds or thousands of items low in uncertainty and generally (but not always) low in annual purchase volume. Together, "C" items typically account for a small percentage of an organisation's purchase volume. "B" items form an intermediate class.

Importance directly influences the size and composition of the DMU, as well as its behaviour. In most instances in large organisations, the greater the importance, the larger the DMU, the higher the organisational levels involved and the more painstaking the buying process. Decisions involving large amounts of the organisation's resources ordinarily must pass through more organisational levels of funding approval than decisions involving limited exposure to loss. At each level, decisions considered uncertain will receive more careful analysis, including the search for information to reduce or at least to manage the uncertainty, than will decisions regarded as relatively sure. Important decisions in which extensive consultation or analysis appear unproductive or dysfunctional may be made by a very small DMU comprised of the top management of an organisation.

Although importance appears to affect the composition and behaviour of the DMU in a manner similar to product type, the two dimensions are conceptually distinct. Importance may vary within product type, and each of several types of products might be represented at any specified importance level.

Illustrative Marketing Implications

Because of the multiple organisational levels involved and the intensity of analysis on the part of the buying organisation, high-importance purchase situations ordinarily require longer and more extensive marketing efforts than do low-importance situations. When a large purchase is involved but uncertainty is low, marketers may simply have to ensure that they work with their principal contacts in the buying organisation to carry their proposal through the multiple levels of approval needed. Little more than routine selling activity may be needed at each level.

In high-uncertainty situations, marketers will probably have to spend considerable time at every level to provide assurance that their offering will indeed turn out to be the best decision. In such a situation explicit warranties may form an essential part of the offering.

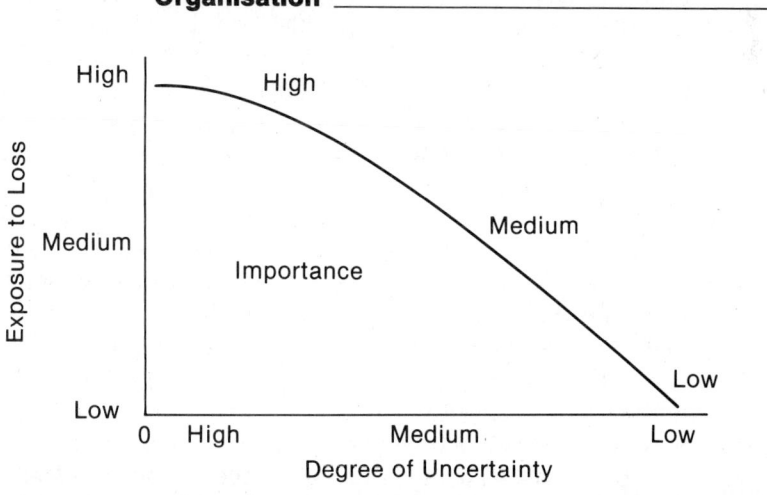

FIGURE 1. Importance of Purchase Decisions to Buying Organisation

Principal Type of Uncertainty in the Buying Situation

Studies by Lehmann and O'Shaughnessy [9], Hakansson, Johanson and Wootz [8] and Parket and Rabinowitz [13] enable us to identify five principal types of uncertainty in purchase situations. These five include:

1. need uncertainty,
2. technical uncertainty,
3. market uncertainty,
4. acceptance uncertainty, and
5. transaction uncertainty.

Need uncertainty [8] means that the buying organisation lacks a clear and unambiguous definition of the specifications for a product (and attendant services, if any) to be purchased. This type of uncertainty is most likely to appear in the early stages of the purchase process in new task situations and is unlikely to occur in straight rebuys. The buying behaviour reported by Hakansson, Johanson and Wootz [8] in the face of this type of uncertainty closely parallels that described by Robinson, Faris and Wind [14] and Brand [1] for new task situations in general. Hakansson, Johanson and Wootz add that purchasers prefer to deal with known vendors, or at least those who are "culturally close," to manage need uncertainty. This type of uncertainty could occur in any product category and at any importance level.

Technical uncertainty implies that the product may not perform properly in the buying organisation's environment. The cause of such failure, should it occur, might be failure of the product itself to meet specifications ("a performance problem" in Lehmann and O'Shaughnessy's [9] terms); or the lack of proper integration into the operating systems of the buying organisation (Lehmann and O'Shaughnessy's "procedural problem" [9]). Uncertainty with respect to the product itself is most likely to occur in new task situations, and more likely to occur in situations in which custom products are used than when standard products are purchased. Uncertainty related to integration of the product into the organisation could occur either in a new task, or in a modified rebuy situation in which the ability of a new vendor to provide post-purchase service support was untested. Technical uncertainty may occur in any type of product, but appears more likely to occur in the purchase of custom items than standard ones.

Market uncertainty [8] refers to the heterogeneity among offerings [13] and the rate of change in vendor's products and attendant services. Market uncertainty could occur in new tasks or rebuys of any type of product. Buying organisations facing market uncertainty in particular product classes typically maintain contacts with a large number of vendors and attach a high importance to purchases in that product class. Parket and Rabinowitz [13] found that buyers who perceived product classes as "generic" (i.e., homogeneous) purchased a higher percentage of their requirements from distributors than did those who perceived the product classes as "non-generic" (i.e., heterogeneous).

Acceptance uncertainty implies a reluctance to purchase a product because personnel in the buying organisation cannot agree on whether the purchase is appropriate, even though the need may be clearly defined. Acceptance uncertainty may arise from a resistance to change within the buying organisation, or from competition for funds within the buying organisation. (Lehmann and O'Shaughnessy [9] call the latter a "political problem".) Acceptance uncertainty typically arises in important new task situations. It is likely to appear more frequently in decisions to purchase capital equipment than to purchase other categories of products.

Transaction uncertainty [18] refers to uncertainty associated with delivery dates or terms of sale. Transaction uncertainty is likely to occur in dealing with a vendor unfamiliar to the buying organisation, and will therefore appear in many modified rebuy and new task situations. Transaction uncertainty may also arise in straight rebuys. Transaction uncertainty may occur in the purchase of any type of product at any level of importance.

Illustrative Marketing Implications

Marketers facing situations of high need uncertainty should stress their abilities as suppliers to help the customer define the need and solve the underlying problem (or capitalise on the underlying opportunity).

Technical uncertainty with respect to the product itself may be reduced through providing samples, test results, and reports from other users of the product. Technical uncertainty related to integration of the product into the buying organisation's operations may be reduced through firm and detailed offers of post-purchase installation and training services, and offers to modify delivery schedules and even product characteristics if necessary. Testimony from previous customers of a vendor new to a particular buying organisation would also serve to reduce technical uncertainty.

In situations buyers consider high in market uncertainty competition among vendors may focus on product characteristics and perhaps related services. Marketers should invest appropriately in product development and stress technical characteristics of the product. Marketers may be able to turn buyers' perceptions of market uncertainty to their own advantage by attempting to increase the amount of market uncertainty perceived in straight rebuy situations, in order to convert the situation to a modified rebuy [8]. This approach involves persuading buyers that all offerings are not the same (generic), and appears more likely to be profitable for manufacturers than for distributors.

Acceptance uncertainty based on resistance to change may require marketers to follow procedures similar to those for situations high in technical uncertainty. Acceptance uncertainty arising from competition for resources within the organisation may be addressed through multi-level selling emphasising return-on-investment concepts. No matter how well executed this approach may be, marketers should recognise that intra-organisation considerations unrelated to the benefits of a proposed purchase may prevent successful consummation of a sale.

Vendors new to a particular buying organisation may reduce transaction uncertainty through providing detailed post-purchase service agreements and testimony from previously satisfied customers. Suppliers with an established relationship with a buying organisation can minimise transaction uncertainty by reliably meeting delivery dates and terms of sale.

Conclusion

The four dimensions—familiarity, product type, importance and type of uncertainty—may be used separately or in combination to classify organisational buying situations. These classes of situations constitute market segments. Individual marketers may choose to vary their marketing programmes among situational segments, or may elect to concentrate their efforts on a particular segment [18].

The particular combination of situational dimensions which are used to form segments depends upon the marketing objective. The dimensions of familiarity and product type are most useful to identify DMU membership for purposes of determining what media to use for sales-support advertising. Tables I (familiarity) and II (product type) together provide more detail on DMU membership than does either one by itself. Knowledge type of uncertainty may be the single most useful dimension to decide what attributes to emphasise in communications about a particular product. The dimensions of importance and familiarity can usefully be applied within any product type to estimate marketing costs. These vary with the number of departments and levels in the buying organisation involved in the buying task, and with the intensity of analysis at each level.

Characteristics of buying situations, particularly when specified on multiple dimensions, appear to constitute a useful basis for segmenting industrial markets. Interview data suggest that the use of situational segmentation, when combined with segmentation based on such characteristics of buying organisations as size, industry classification, and the like, may significantly increase the ability of marketers to refine marketing programmes and select the most promising segments on which to focus their marketing activities.

ENDNOTES

*Extensive interviews were conducted over a period of several years with more than 30 organisations in the United States. These organisations varied with respect to products and services produced, geographical location and size.

REFERENCES

1. Brand, G. T., *The Industrial Buying Decision*, London, Cassell/Associated Business Programmes, 1972.
2. Buckner, H., *How British Industry Buys*, London, Hutchinson, 1967.
3. Cardozo, R. N., "Segmenting the Industrial Market," *Proceedings of the American Marketing Association Educators Conference*, 1968.
4. Cardozo, R. N. and Cagley, J. W., "An Experimental Study of Industrial Buyer Behaviour," *Journal of Marketing Research*, Vol. VIII, August, 1971.
5. Choffray, J. M., and Lilien, G. L., *A New Approach to Industrial Market Segmentation*, Working Paper WP977–78, Sloan School of Management, Massachusetts Institute of Technology, Cambridge, Mass.
6. Doyle, P., Woodside, A. R. and Michell, P., "Organizations' Buying in New Task and Rebuy Situations," *Industrial Marketing Management*, Vol. 8, 1979.
7. Feldman, W. and Cardozo, R. N., "The 'Industrial' Revolution & Models of Buyer Behaviour," *Journal of Purchasing*, November, 1969.
8. Hakansson, H., Johanson, J. and Wootz, B., "Influence Tactics in Buyer-seller Processes," *Industrial Marketing Management*, Vol. 5, 1977.
9. Lehmann, D. R. and O'Shaughnessy, J., "Difference in Attribute Importance for Different Industrial Products," *Journal of Marketing*, Vol. 38, April, 1974.
10. Luffman, G., "The Processing of Information by Industrial Buyers," *Industrial Marketing Management*, Vol. 3, 1974.
11. Moriarity, R. T. and Galper, M., *Organizational Buying Behaviour: A State-of-the-Art Review & Conceptualization*, Cambridge, Mass., Marketing Science Institute, 1978.
12. Newall, J., "Industrial Buyer Behaviour," *European Journal of Marketing*, Vol. 3, November, 1977.
13. Parket, I. R. and Rabinowitz, M., "The Influence of Product Class Perception on Industrial Buyers' Channel Source Choice," *Journal of Economics & Business*, Vol. 26, Spring, 1974.
14. Robinson, P. J., Faris, C. W. and Wind, Y., *Industrial Buying & Creative Marketing*, Boston, Allyn & Bacon, Inc., 1967.
15. Scientific American, *How Industry Buys/1970*, New York, The Scientific American, 1969.

16. Webster, F. E., Jr. and Wind, Y., *Organizational Buying Behaviour*, Englewood Cliffs, N.J., Prentice-Hall, Inc., 1972.
17. Wind, Y., "The Boundaries of Buying Decision Centers," *Journal of Purchasing & Materials Management*, Summer, 1978.
18. Wind, Y. and Cardozo, R. N., "Industrial Market Segmentation," *Industrial Marketing Management*, Vol. 3, 1974.

SECTION N
Services Marketing

Services marketing is becoming increasingly important as the economy shifts from an industrial society. A much larger share of the customer dollar is now spent on intangible services as compared to tangible products.

There are three major issues related to services marketing. First, services have no stored value. They are, therefore, highly perishable commodities. This suggests that all our knowledge and expertise related to perishable products, such as agricultural products, may be relevant to services marketing. This includes the monetary value of time, marginal pricing, and time-sensitive pricing policies.

Second, services are intangible and, therefore, abstract. It may be important to make services tangible by visual representation and symbolism. In other words, marketing promotion, including personal selling and advertising, becomes even more critical in services marketing, since the product itself is incapable of communicating its benefits.

Finally, in services marketing, the delivery agents become the surrogates or symbols of the quality of service. Since a large percentage of those agents are human beings, it becomes extremely important to use proper training and customer orientation to minimize individual differences inherent among human agents. Even then, it is impossible to fully standardize the quality of services as we can in the manufacturing of products. Perhaps with more mechanization of delivery systems, such as computerized reservations, education, and information, we may be able to achieve some standardization.

52 — Marketing Intangible Products and Product Intangibles

Theodore Levitt

Reprinted by permission of the Harvard Business Review. "Marketing Intangible Products and Product Intangibles" by Theodore Levitt (May–June 1981). Copyright © 1981 by the President and Fellows of Harvard College; all rights reserved.

Distinguishing between companies according to whether they market services or goods has only limited utility. A more useful way to make the same distinction is to change the words we use. Instead of speaking of *services* and *goods*, we should speak of *intangibles* and *tangibles*. Everybody sells intangibles in the marketplace, no matter what is produced in the factory.

The usefulness of the distinction becomes apparent when we consider the question of how the marketing of intangibles differs from the marketing of tangibles. While some of the differences might seem obvious, it is apparent that, along with their differences, there are important commonalities between the marketing of intangibles and tangibles.

Put in terms of our new vocabulary, a key area of similarity in the marketing of intangibles and tangibles revolves around the degree of intangibility inherent in both. Marketing is concerned with getting and keeping customers. The degree of product intangibility has its greatest effect in the process of trying to get customers. When it comes to holding on to customers—to keeping them—highly intangible products run into very special problems.

First, this article identifies aspects of intangibility that affect sales appeal of both intangible and tangible products. And, next, it considers the special difficulties sellers of intangibles face in retaining customers.

INTANGIBILITY OF ALL PRODUCTS

Intangible products—travel, freight forwarding, insurance, repair, consulting, computer software, investment banking, brokerage, education, health care, accounting—can seldom be tried out, inspected, or tested in advance. Prospective buyers are generally forced to depend on surrogates to assess what they're likely to get.

They can look at gloriously glossy pictures of elegant rooms in distant resort hotels set exotically by the shimmering sea. They can consult current users to see how well a software program performs and how well the investment banker or the oil well drilling contractor performs. Or they can ask experienced customers regarding engineering firms, trust companies, lobbyists, professors, surgeons, prep schools, hair stylists, consultants, repair shops, industrial maintenance firms, shippers, franchisers, general contractors, funeral directors, caterers, environmental management firms, construction companies, and on and on.

Tangible products differ in that they can usually, or to some degree, be directly experienced—seen, touched, smelled, or tasted, as well as tested. Often this can be done in advance of buying. You can test-drive a car, smell the perfume, work the numerical controls of a milling machine, inspect the seller's steam-generating installation, pretest an extruding machine.

In practice, though, even the most tangible of products can't be *reliably* tested or experienced in advance. To inspect a vendor's steam-generating plant or computer installation in advance at another location and to have thoroughly studied detailed proposals and designs are not enough. A great deal more is involved than product features and physical installation alone.

Though a customer may buy a product whose generic tangibility (like the computer or the steam plant) is as palpable as primeval rock—and though that customer may have agreed after great study and extensive negotiation to a cost that runs into millions of dollars—the process of getting it built on time, installed, and then running smoothly involves an awful lot more than the generic tangible product itself. Such intangibles can make or break the product's success, even with mature consumer goods like dishwashers, shampoos, and frozen pizza. If a shampoo is not used as prescribed, or a pizza not heated as intended, the results can be terrible.

Similarly, you commonly can't experience in advance moderate-to-low-priced consumer goods such as canned sardines or purchased detergents. To make buyers more comfortable and confident about tangibles that can't be pretested, companies go beyond the literal promises of specifications, advertisements, and labels to provide reassurance.

Packaging is one common tool. Pickles get put into reassuring see-through glass jars, cookies into cellophane-windowed boxes, canned goods get strong appetite-appealing pictures on the labels, architects make elaborately enticing renderings, and proposals to NASA get packaged in binders that match the craftsmanship of Tyrolean leatherworkers. In all cases, the idea is to provide reassuring tangible (in these examples, visual) surrogates for what's promised but can't be more directly experienced before the sale.

Hence, it's sensible to say that all products are in some important respects intangible, even giant turbine engines that weigh tons. No matter how diligently designed in advance and carefully constructed, they'll fail or disappoint if installed or used incorrectly. The significance of all this for marketing can be profound.

When prospective customers can't experience the product in advance, they are asked to buy what are essentially promises—promises of satisfaction. Even tangible, testable, feelable, smellable products are, before they're bought, largely just promises.

BUYING PROMISES

Satisfaction in consumption or use can seldom be quite the same as earlier in trial or promise. Some promises promise more than others, depending on product features, design, degree of tangibility, type of promotion, price, and differences in what customers hope to accomplish with what they buy.

Of some products less is expected than what is actually or symbolically promised. The right kind of eye shadow properly applied may promise to transform a woman into an irresistible tigress in the night. Not even the most eager buyer literally believes the metaphor. Yet the metaphor helps make the sale. Neither do you really expect the proposed new corporate headquarters, so artfully rendered by the winning architects, automatically to produce all those cheerfully productive employees lounging with casual elegance at lunch in the verdant courtyard. But the metaphor helps win the assignment.

Thus, when prospective customers can't properly try the promised product in advance, metaphorical reassurances become the amplified necessity of the marketing effort. Promises, being intangible, have to be "tangibilized" in their presentation—hence the tigress and the contented employees. Metaphors and similes become surrogates for the tangibility that cannot be provided or experienced in advance.

This same thinking accounts for the solid, somber Edwardian decor of downtown law offices, the prudentially elegant and orderly public offices of investment banking houses, the confidently articulate consultants in dark vested suits, engineering and project proposals in "executive" typeset and leather bindings, and the elaborate pictorial documentation of the performance virtuosity of newly offered machine controls. It explains why insurance companies pictorially offer "a piece of the rock," put you under a "blanket of protection" or an "umbrella," or place you in "good hands."

Not even tangible products are exempt from the necessity of using symbol and metaphor. A computer terminal has to look right. It has to be packaged to convey an impression of reliable modernity—based on the assumption that prospective buyers will translate appearance into confidence about performance. In that respect, the marketing ideas behind the packaging of a $1 million computer, a $2 million jet engine, and a $.5 million numerically controlled milling machine are scarcely different from the marketing ideas behind the packaging of a $50 electic shaver or a $2.50 tube of lipstick.

Importance of Impressions

Common sense tells us, and research confirms, that people use appearances to make judgments about realities. It matters little whether the products are high priced or low priced, whether they are technically complex or simple, whether the buyers are supremely sophisticated in the technology of what's being considered or just plain ignorant, or whether they buy for themselves or for their employers. Everybody always depends to some extent on both appearances and external impressions.

Nor do impressions affect only the generic product itself—that is, the technical offering, such as the speed, versatility, and precision of the lathe; the color and creaminess of the lipstick; or the appearance and dimensions of the lobster thermidor. Consider, for example, investment banking. No matter how thorough and persuasive a firm's recommendations and assurances about a proposed underwriting and no matter how pristine its reputation for integrity and performance, somehow the financial vice president of the billion-dollar client corporation would feel better had the bank's representative not been quite so youthfully apple-cheeked.

The product will be judged in part by who offers it—not just who the vendor corporation is but also who the corporation's representative is. The vendor and the vendor's representative are both inextricably and inevitably part of the "product" that prospects must judge before they buy. The less tangible the generic product, the more powerfully and persistently the judgment about it gets shaped by the packaging—how it's presented, who presents it, and what's implied by metaphor, simile, symbol, and other surrogates for reality.

So, too, with tangible products. The sales engineers assigned to work with an electric utility company asking for competitive bids on a $100 million steam boiler system for its new plant are as powerfully a part of the offered product (the promise) as is the investment banking firm's partner.

The reason is easy to see. In neither case is there a product until it's delivered. And you won't know how well it performs until it's put to work.

The Ties That Bind

In both investment banking and big boilers, becoming the designated vendor requires successful passage through several consecutive gates, or stages, in the sales process. It is not unlike courtship. Both "customers" know that a rocky courtship spells trouble ahead. If the groom is not sufficiently solicitous during the courtship—if he's insensitive to moods and needs, unresponsive or wavering during stress or adversity—there will be problems in the marriage.

But unlike a real marriage, investment banking and installed boiler systems allow no room for divorce. Once the deal is made, marriage and gestation have simultaneously begun. After that, things are often irreversible. Investment banking may require months of close work with the client organization before the underwriting can be launched—that is, before the baby is born. And the construction of an electric power plant takes years, through sickness and in health. As with babies, birth of any kind presents new problems. Babies have to be coddled to see them through early life. Illness or relapse has to be conscientiously avoided or quickly corrected. Similarly, stocks or bonds should not go quickly to deep discounts. The boiler should not suddenly malfunction after several weeks or months. If it does, it should be rapidly restored to full use. Understandably, the prospective customer will, in courtship, note every nuance carefully, judging always what kind of a husband and father the eager groom is likely to make.

The way the product is packaged (how the promise is presented in brochure, letter, design appearance), how it is personally presented, and by whom—all these become central to the product itself because they are elements of what the customer finally decides to buy or reject.

A product is more than a tangible thing, even a $100 million boiler system. From a buyer's viewpoint, the product is a promise, a cluster of value expectations of which its nontangible qualities are as integral as its tangible parts. Certain conditions must be satisfied before the prospect buys. If they are not satisfied, there is no sale. There would have been no sale in the cases of the investment banker and the boiler manufacturer if, during the prebidding (or courtship) stages of the relationship, their representatives had been improperly responsive to or insufficiently informed about the customers' special situations and problems.

In each case, the promised product—the whole product—would have been unsatisfactory. It is not that it would have been incomplete; it just would not have been right. Changing the salespeople in midstream probably would not have helped, since the selling organization would by then have already "said" the wrong thing about its "product." If, during the courtship, the prospective customer got the impression that there might be aftermarket problems—problems in execution, in timeliness, in the postsale support necessary for smooth and congenial relations—then the customer would have received a clear message that the delivered product would be faulty.

SPECIAL PROBLEMS FOR INTANGIBLES

So much, briefly, for making a sale—for getting a customer. *Keeping* a customer is quite another thing, and on that score more pervasively intangible products encounter some distinct difficulties.

These difficulties stem largely from the fact that intangible products are highly people-intensive in their production and delivery methods. Corporate financial services of banks are, in this respect, not so different from hairdressing or consulting. The more people-intensive a product, the more room there is for personal discretion, idiosyncracy, error, and delay. Once a customer for an intangible product is sold, the customer can easily be unsold as a consequence of the underfulfillment of his expectations. Repeat buying suffers. Conversely, a tangible product, manufactured under close supervision in a factory and delivered through a planned and orderly network, is much more likely than an intangible product to fulfill the promised expectation. Repeat buying is therefore less easily jeopardized.

A tangible product is usually developed by design professionals working under conditions of benign isolation after receiving guidance from market intelligence experts, scientists, and others. The product will be manufactured by another group of specialists under conditions of close supervision that facilitate reliable quality control. Even installation and use by the customer are determined by a relatively narrow range of possibilities dictated by the product itself.

Intangible products present an entirely different picture. Consider a computer software program. The programmer does the required research directly and generally on the customer's premises, trying to understand complex networks of interconnecting operations. Then that same person designs the system and the software, usually alone. The process of designing is, simultaneously, also the process of manufacturing. Design and manufacturing of intangible products are generally done by the same people—or by one person alone, like a craftsman at a bench.

Moreover, manufacturing an intangible product is generally indistinguishable from its actual delivery. In situations such as consulting, the delivery *is* the manufacturing from the client's viewpoint. Though the consulting study may have been excellent, if the delivery is poor, the study will be viewed as having been badly manufactured. It's a faulty product. So too with the work of all types of brokers, educators and trainers, accounting firms, engineering firms, architects, lawyers, transportation companies, hospitals and clinics, government agencies, banks, trust companies, mutual funds, car rental companies, insurance companies, repair and maintenance operations, and on and on. For each, delivery and production are virtually indistinguishable. The whole difference is nicely summarized by Professor John M. Rathwell of Cornell University: "Goods are produced, services are performed."[1]

Minimizing the Human Factor

Because companies making intangible products are highly people-intensive operations, they have an enormous quality control problem. Quality control on an automobile assembly line is built into the system. If a yellow door is hung on a red car, somebody on the line will quickly ask if that's what was intended. If the left front wheel is missing, the person next in line, whose task is to fasten the lug bolts, will stop the line. But if a commercial banker misses an important feature of a financing package or if he doesn't do it well, it may never be found—or found too late. If the ashtrays aren't cleaned on a rented car, that discovery will annoy or irritate the already committed customer. Repeat business gets jeopardized.

No matter how well trained or motivated they might be, people make mistakes, forget, commit indiscretions, and at times are uncongenial—hence the search for alternatives to dependence on people. Previously in HBR, I have suggested a variety of ways to reduce people dependence in the so-called service industries. I called it the *industrialization of service*, which means substituting hard, soft, or hybrid technologies for totally people-intensive activities:

- *Hard* technologies include automatic telephone dialing for operator-assisted dialing, credit cards for repetitive credit checking, and computerized monitoring of industrial processes. And the benefits are considerable. Automatic telephone switching is, for example, not only cheaper than manual switching but far more reliable.

- *Soft* technologies are the substitution of division of labor for one-person craftsmanship in production—as, for example, organizing the work force that cleans an office building so that each worker specializes in one or several limited tasks (dusting, waxing, vacuuming, window cleaning) rather than each person doing all these jobs alone. Insurance companies long ago went to extensive division of labor in their applications processing—registering, underwriting, performing actuarial functions, issuing policies.

- *Hybrid* technologies combine the soft and the hard. The floor is waxed by a machine rather than by hand. French fries are precut and portion packed in a factory for finishing in a fast-food restaurant in specially designed deep fryers that signal when the food is ready. A computer automatically calculates and makes all entries in an Internal Revenue Service form 1040 after a moderately trained clerk has entered the raw data on a console.

The Managerial Revolution. Industrializing helps control quality and cut costs. Instead of depending on people to work *better*, industrialization redesigns the work so that people work *differently*. Thus, the same modes of managerial rationality are applied to service—the production, creation, and delivery of largely intangible products—that were first applied to production of goods in the nineteenth century. The real significance of the nineteenth century is not the industrial revolution, with its shift from animal to machine power, but rather the managerial revolution, with its shift from the craftsman's functional independence to the manager's rational routines.

In successive waves, the mechanical harvester, the sewing machine, and then the automobile epitomized the genius of that century. Each was rationally designed to become an assembled rather than a constructed machine, a machine that depended not on the idiosyncratic artistry of a single craftsman but on simple, standardized tasks performed on routine specifications by unskilled workers. This required detailed managerial planning to ensure proper design, manufacture, and assembly of interchangeable parts so that the right number of people would be at the right places at the right times to do the right simple jobs in the right ways. Then, with massive output, distribution, and aftermarket training and service, managers had to create and maintain systems to justify the massive output.

ON BEING APPRECIATED

What's been largely missing in intangible goods production is the kind of managerial rationality that produced the industrial revolution. That is why the quality of intangibles tends to be less reliable than it might be, costs higher than they should be, and customer satisfaction lower than it need be.

While I have referred to the enormous progress that has in recent years been made on these matters, there is one characteristic of intangible products that requires special attention for holding customers. Unique to intangible products is the fact that the customer is seldom aware of being served well. This is especially so in the case of intangible products that have, for the duration of the contract, constant continuity—that is, you're buying or using or consuming them almost constantly. Such products include certain banking services, cleaning services, freight hauling, energy management, maintenance services, telephones, and the like.

Consider an international banking relationship, an insurance relationship, an industrial cleaning relationship. If all goes well, the customer is virtually oblivious to what he's getting. Only when things don't go well (or a competitor says they don't) does the customer become aware of the product's existence or nonexistence—when a letter of credit is incorrectly drawn, when a competitive bank proposes better arrangements, when the annual insurance premium notice arrives or when a claim is disputed, when the ashtrays aren't cleaned, or when a favorite penholder is missing.

The most important thing to know about intangible products is that the *customers usually don't know what they're getting until they don't get it*. Only then do they become aware of what they bargained for; only on dissatisfaction do they dwell. Satisfaction is, as it should be, mute. Its existence is affirmed only by its absence.

And that's dangerous—because the customers will be aware only of failure and of dissatisfaction, not of success or satisfaction. That makes them terribly vulnerable to the blandishments of competitive sellers. A competitor can always structure a more interesting corporate financing deal, always propose a more imaginative insurance program, always find dust on top of the framed picture in the office, always cite small visible failures that imply big hidden ones.

In getting customers for intangibles it is important to create surrogates, or metaphors, for tangibility—how we dress; how we articulate, write, design, and present proposals; how we work with prospects, respond to inquiries; and initiate ideas; and how well we show we understand the prospect's business. But in keeping customers for intangibles, it becomes important regularly to remind and show them what they're getting so that occasional failures fade in relative importance. If that's not done, the customers will not know. They'll only know when they're *not* getting what they bought, and that's all that's likely to count.

To keep customers for regularly delivered and consumed intangible products, again, they have to be reminded of what they're getting. Vendors must regularly reinstate the promises that were made to land the customer. Thus, when an insurance prospect finally gets "married," the subsequent silence and inattention can be deafening. Most customers seldom recall for long what kind of life insurance package they bought, often forgetting as well the name of both underwriter and agent. To be reminded a year later via a premium notice often brings to mind the contrast between the loving attention of courtship and the cold reality of marriage. No wonder the lapse rate in personal life insurance is so high!

Once a relationship is cemented, the seller has created equity. He has a customer. To help keep the customer, the seller must regularly enhance the equity in that relationship lest it decline and become jeopardized by competitors.

There are innumerable ways to do that strengthening, and some of these can be systematized, or industrialized. Periodic letters or phone calls that remind the customers of how well things are going cost little and are surprisingly powerful equity maintainers. Newsletters or regular visits suggesting new, better, or augmented product features are useful.

Even nonbusiness socializing has its value—as is affirmed by corporations struggling in recent years with the IRS about the deductibility of hunting lodges, yachts, clubs, and spouses attending conferences and customer meetings.

Here are some examples of how companies have strengthened their relationships with customers:

- An energy management company sends out a periodic "Update Report" on conspicuous yellow paper, advising clients how to discover and correct energy leaks; install improved monitors, and accomplish cost savings.
- A computer service bureau organizes its account managers for a two-week series of blitz customer callbacks to "explain casually" the installation of new central processing equipment that is expected to prevent cost increases next year while expanding the customers' interactive options.
- A long-distance hauler of high-value electronic equipment (computers, terminals, mail sorters, word processors, medical diagnostic instruments) has instituted quarterly performance reviews with its shippers, some of which include customers who are encouraged to talk about their experiences and expectations.
- An insurance company sends periodic one-page notices to policyholders *and* policy beneficiaries. These generally begin with a single-sentence congratulation that policy and coverage remain nicely intact and follow with brief views on recent tax rulings affecting insurance, new notions about personal financial planning, and special protection packages available with other types of insurance.

In all these ways, sellers of intangible products reinstate their presence and performance in the customers' minds, reminding them of their continuing presence and the value of what is constantly, and silently, being delivered.

MAKING TANGIBLE THE INTANGIBLE

It bears repeating that all products have elements of tangibility and intangibility. Companies that sell tangible products invariably promise more than the tangible products themselves. Indeed, enormous efforts often focus on the enhancement of the intangibles—promises of bountiful benefits conferred rather than on features offered. To the buyer of photographic film, Kodak promises with unremitting emphasis the satisfactions of enduring remembrance, of memories clearly preserved. Kodak says almost nothing about the superior luminescence of its pictures. The product is thus remembrance, not film or pictures.

The promoted products of the automobile, as everyone knows, are largely status, comfort, and power—intangible things of the mind, rather than tangible things from the factory. Auto dealers, on the other hand, assuming correctly that people's minds have already been reached by the manufacturers' ads, focus on other considerations: deals, availability, and postpurchase servicing. Neither the dealers nor the manufacturers sell the tangible cars themselves. Rather, they sell the intangible benefits that are bundled into the entire package.

If tangible products must be intangibilized to add customer-getting appeal, then intangible products must be tangibilized—what Professor Leonard L. Berry calls "managing the evidence."[2] Ideally, this should be done as a matter of routine on a systematic basis—that is, industrialized. For instance, hotels wrap their drinking glasses in fresh bags or film, put on the toilet seat a "sanitized" paper band, and neatly shape the end piece of the toilet tissue into a fresh-looking arrowhead. All these actions say with silent affirmative clarity that "the room has been specially cleaned for your use and comfort"—yet no words are spoken to say it. Words, in any case, would be less convincing, nor could employees be reliably depended on to say them each time or to say them convincingly. Hotels have thus not only tangibilized their promise, they've also industrialized its delivery.

Or take the instructive case of purchasing house insulation, which most home owners approach with understandable apprehension. Suppose you call two companies to bid on installing insulation in your house. The first insulation installer arrives in a car. After pacing once around the house with measured self-assurance and after quick calculations on the back of an envelope, there comes a confident quote of $2,400 for six-inch fiberglass—total satisfaction guaranteed.

Another drives up in a clean white truck with clipboard in hand and proceeds to scrupulously measure the house dimensions, count the windows, crawl the attic, and consult records from a source book on the area's seasonal temperature ranges and wind velocities. The installer then asks a host of questions, meanwhile recording everything with obvious diligence. There follows a promise to return in three days, which happens at the appointed hour, with a typed proposal for six-inch fiberglass insulation at $2,800—total satisfaction guaranteed. From which company will you buy?

The latter has tangibilized the intangible, made a promise into a credible expectation. Even more persuasive tangible evidence is provided by an insulation supplier whose representative types the relevant information into a portable intelligent printing terminal. The analysis and response are almost instant, causing one user to call it "the most powerful tool ever developed in the insulation industry." If the house owner is head of a project buying team of an electric utility company, the treasurer of a mighty corporation, the materials purchasing agent of a ready-mixed cement company, the transportation manager of a fertilizer manufacturer, or the data processing director of an insurance company, it's almost certain this person will make vendor decisions at work in the same way as around the house. Everybody requires the risk-reducing reassurances of tangibilized intangibles.

Managers can use the practice of providing reassuring ways to render tangible the intangible's promises—even when the generic product is itself tangible. Laundry detergents that claim special whitening capabilities lend credibility to the promise by using "blue whitener beads" that are clearly visible to the user. Procter & Gamble's new decaffeinated instant coffee, "High Point," reinforces the notion of real coffee with luminescent "milled flakes for hearty, robust flavor." You can *see* what the claims promise.

Keeping customers for an intangible product requires constant reselling efforts while things go well lest the customer get lost when things go badly. The reselling requires that tasks be industrialized. The relationship with the customer must be managed much more carefully and continuously in the case of intangibles than of tangible products, though it is vital in both. And it gets progressively more vital for tangible products that are new and especially complex. In such cases, "relationship management" becomes a special art—another topic all its own.

Meanwhile, the importance of what I've tried to say here is emphasized by one overriding fact: a customer is an asset usually more precious than the tangible assets on the balance sheet. Balance sheet assets can generally be bought. There are lots of willing sellers. Customers cannot so easily be bought. Lots of eager sellers are offering them many choices. Moreover, a customer is a double asset. First, the customer is the direct source of cash from the sale and, second, the existence of a solid customer can be used to raise cash from bankers and investors—cash that can be converted into tangible assets.

The old chestnut "nothing happens till you make a sale" is awfully close to an important truth. What it increasingly takes to make and keep that sale is to tangibilize the intangible, restate the benefit and source to the customer, and industrialize the processes.

ENDNOTES

1. John M. Rathwell, *Marketing in the Service Sector* (Cambridge, Mass.: Winthrop Publishers, 1974), p. 58.
2. Leonard L. Berry, "Service Marketing Is Different," *Business*, May–June 1980, p. 24.

53 Classifying Services to Gain Strategic Marketing Insights

Christopher H. Lovelock

Reprinted from the *Journal of Marketing*, published by the American Marketing Association, Vol. 47 (Summer 1983), pp. 9–20. Reprinted by permission.

INTRODUCTION

Developing professional skills in marketing management requires the ability to look across a broad cross-section of marketing situations, to understand their differences and commonalities, and to identify appropriate marketing strategies in each instance. In the manufacturing sector many experienced marketers have worked for a variety of companies in several different industries, often including both consumer goods and industrial firms. As a result, they have a perspective that transcends narrow industry boundaries.

But exposure to marketing problems and strategies in different industries is still quite rare among managers in the service sector. Not only is the concept of a formalized marketing function still relatively new to most service firms, but service industries have historically been somewhat inbred. The majority of railroad managers, for instance, have spent their entire working lives within the railroad industry—even within a single company. Most hoteliers have grown up in the hotel industry. And most hospital or college administrators have remained within the confines of health care or higher education, respectively. The net result of such narrow exposure is that it restricts a manager's ability to identify and learn from the experience of organizations facing parallel situations in other service industries—and, of course, from marketing experience in the manufacturing sector. Conversely, marketers from the manufacturing sector who take positions in service businesses often find that their past experience has not prepared them well for working on some of the problems that regularly challenge service marketers (Knisely 1979, Lovelock 1981, Shostack 1977).

This article argues that development of greater sophistication in services marketing will be aided if we can find new ways to group services other than by current industry classifications. A more useful approach may be to segment services into clusters that share certain relevant marketing characteristics—such as the nature of the relationship between the service organization and its customers or patterns of demand relative to supply — and then to examine the implications for marketing action.

After briefly reviewing the value of classification schemes in marketing, the article summarizes past proposals for classifying services. This is followed by presentation and discussion of five classification schemes based on past proposals or on clinical research. In each instance examples are given of how various services fall into similar or different categories, and an evaluation is made of the resulting marketing insights and what they imply for marketing strategy development.

THE VALUE OF CLASSIFICATION IN MARKETING

Hunt (1976) has emphasized the usefulness of classification schemes in marketing. Various attempts have been made in the past by marketing theorists to classify goods into different categories. One of the most famous and enduring is Copeland's (1923) classification of convenience, shopping and specialty goods. Not only did this help managers obtain a better understanding of consumer needs and behavior, it also provided insights into the management of retail distribution systems. Bucklin (1963) and others have revised and refined Copeland's original classification and thereby been able to provide important strategic guidelines for retailers. Another major classification has been between durable and nondurable goods. Durability is closely associated with purchase frequency, which has important implications for development of both distribution and communications strategy. Yet another classification is consumer goods versus industrial goods; this classification relates both to the type of goods purchased (although there is some overlap) and to product evaluation, purchasing procedures and usage behavior. Recognition of these distinctions by marketers has led to different types of marketing strategy being directed at each of these groups. Through such classifications the application of marketing management tools and strategies in manufacturing has become a professional skill that transcends industry divisions.

By contrast, service industries remain dominated by an operations orientation that insists that each industry is different. This mind set is often manifested in managerial attitudes that suggest, for example, that the marketing of airlines has nothing at all in common with that of banks, insurance, motels, hospitals or household movers. But if it can be shown that some of these services do share certain marketing relevant characteristics, then the stage may be set for some useful cross-fertilization of concepts and strategies.

How Might Services Be Classified?

Various attempts have been proposed in the past for classifying services and are outlined, with brief commentaries, in Table 1. But

TABLE 1. Summary of Previously Proposed Schemes for Classifying Services

Author	Proposed Classification Schemes	Comment
Judd (1964)	(1) Rented goods services (right to own and use a good for a defined time period) (2) Owned goods services (custom creation, repair or improvement of goods owned by the customer) (3) Nongoods services (personal experiences or "experiential possession")	First two are fairly specific, but third category is very broad and ignores services such as insurance, banking, legal advice and accounting.
Rathmell (1974)	(1) Type of seller (2) Type of buyer (3) Buying motives (4) Buying practice (5) Degree of regulation	No specific application to services—could apply equally well to goods.
Shostack (1977)[*] Sasser et al.[*] (1978)	Proportion of physical goods and intangible services contained within each product "package"	Offers opportunities for multiattribute modeling. Emphasizes that there are few pure goods or pure services.
Hill (1977)	(1) Services affecting persons vs. those affecting goods (2) Permanent vs. temporary effects of the service (3) Reversibility vs. nonreversibility of these effects (4) Physical effects vs. mental effects (5) Individual vs. collective services	Emphasizes nature of service benefits and (in 5), variations in the service delivery/consumption environment.

Thomas (1978)	(1) Primarily equipment based
	  (a) automated (e.g., car wash)
	  (b) monitored by unskilled operators (e.g., movie theater)
	  (c) operated by skilled personnel (e.g., airline)
	(2) Primarily people-based
	  (a) unskilled labor (e.g., lawn care)
	  (b) skilled labor (e.g., repair work)
	  (c) professional staff (e.g., lawyers, dentists)
		Although operational rather than marketing in orientation, provides a useful way of understanding product attributes.

Chase (1978)	Extent of customer contact required in service delivery
	  (a) high contact (e.g., health care, hotels, restaurants)
	  (b) low contact (e.g., postal service, wholesaling)
		Recognizes that product variability is harder to control in high contact services because customers exert more influence on timing of demand and service features, due to their greater involvement in the service process.

Kotler (1980)	(1) People-based vs. equipment-based (2) Extent to which client's presence is necessary (3) Meets personal needs vs. business needs (4) Public vs. private, for-profit vs. nonprofit	Synthesizes previous work, recognizes differences in purpose of service organization.

Lovelock (1980)	(1) Basic demand characteristics
	  —object served (persons vs. property)
	  —extent of demand/supply imbalances
	  —discrete vs. continuous relationships between customers and providers
	(2) Service content and benefits
	  —extent of physical goods content
	  —extent of personal service content
	  —single service vs. bundle of services
	  —timing and duration of benefits
	(3) Service delivery procedures
	  —multisite vs. single site delivery
	  —allocation of capacity (reservations vs. first come, first served)
	  —independent vs. collective consumption
	  —time defined vs. task defined transactions
	  —extent to which customers must be present during service delivery
		Synthesizes previous classifications and adds several new schemes. Proposes several categories within each classification. Concludes that defining object served is most fundamental classification scheme. Suggests that valuable marketing insights would come from combining two or more classification schemes in a matrix.

[*] These were two independent studies that drew broadly similar conclusions.

developing classification schemes is not enough. If they are to have managerial value, they must offer strategic insights. That is why it is important to develop ways of analyzing services that highlight the characteristics they have in common, and then to examine the implications for marketing management.

This article builds on past research by examining characteristics of services that transcend industry boundaries and are different in degree or kind from the categorization schemes traditionally applied to manufactured goods. Five classification schemes have been selected for presentation and discussion, reflecting their potential for affecting the way marketing management strategies are developed and implemented. Each represents an attempt to answer one of the following questions:

1. What is the nature of the service act?
2. What type of relationship does the service organization have with its customers?
3. How much room is there for customization and judgment on the part of the service provider?
4. What is the nature of demand and supply for the service?
5. How is the service delivered?

Each question will be examined on two dimensions, reflecting my conclusion in an earlier study (Lovelock 1980) that combining classification schemes in a matrix may yield better marketing insights than classifying service organizations on one variable at a time.

WHAT IS THE NATURE OF THE SERVICE ACT?

A service has been described as a "deed, act or performance" (Berry 1980). Two fundamental issues are at whom (or what) is the act directed, and is this act tangible or intangible in nature?

As shown in Figure 1, these two questions result in a four-way classification scheme involving (1) tangible actions to people's bodies, such as airline transportation, haircutting and surgery; (2) tangible actions to goods and other physical possessions, such as air freight, lawn mowing and janitorial services; (3) intangible actions directed at people's minds, such as broadcasting and education; and (4) intangible actions directed at people's intangible assets, such as insurance, investment banking and consulting.

Sometimes a service may seem to spill over into two or more categories. For instance, the delivery of educational, religious or entertainment services (directed primarily at the mind) often entails tangible actions such as being in a classroom, church or theater; the delivery of financial services may require a visit to a bank to transform intangible financial assets into hard cash; and the delivery of airline services may affect some travelers' states of mind as well as physically moving their bodies from one airport to another. But in most instances the core service act is confined to one of the four categories, although there may be secondary acts in another category.

Insights and Implications

Why is this categorization scheme useful to service marketers? Basically it helps answer the following questions:

1. Does the customer need to be *physically* present:
   a. throughout service delivery?
   b. only to initiate or terminate the service transaction (e.g., dropping off a car for repair and picking it up again afterwards)?
   c. not at all (the relationship with the service supplier can be at arm's length through the mails, telephone or other electronic media)?
2. Does the customer need to be *mentally* present during service delivery? Can mental presence be maintained across physical distances through mail or electronic communications?
3. In what ways is the target of the service act "modified" by receipt

FIGURE 1. Understanding the Nature of the Service Act

What Is the Nature of the Service Act?	Who or What Is the Direct Recipient of the Service?	
	People	Things
Tangible Actions	Services directed at people's bodies: • health care • passenger transportation • beauty salons • exercise clinics • restaurants • haircutting	Services directed at goods and other physical possessions: • freight transportation • industrial equipment repair and maintenance • janitorial services • laundry and dry cleaning • landscaping/lawn care • veterinary care
Intangible Actions	Services directed at people's minds: • education • broadcasting • information services • theaters • museums	Services directed at intangible assets: • banking • legal services • accounting • securities • insurance

of the service? And how does the customer benefit from these "modifications"?

It's not always obvious what the service is and what it does for the customer because services are ephemeral. By identifying the target of the service and then examining how it is "modified" or changed by receipt of the service act, we can develop a better understanding of the nature of the service product and the core benefits that it offers. For instance, a haircut leaves the recipient with shorter and presumably more appealingly styled hair, air freight gets the customer's goods speedily and safely between two points, a news radio broadcast updates the listener's mind about recent events, and life insurance protects the future value of the insured person's assets.

If customers need to be physically present during service delivery, then they must enter the service "factory" (whether it be a train, hairdressing salon, or a hospital at a particular location) and spend time there while the service is performed. Their satisfaction with the service will be influenced by the interactions they have with service personnel, the nature of the service facilities, and also perhaps by the characteristics of other customers using the same service. Questions of location and schedule convenience assume great importance when a customer has to be physically present or must appear in person to initiate and terminate the transaction.

Dealing with a service organization at arm's length, by contrast, may mean that a customer never sees the service facilities at all and may not even meet the service personnel face-to-face. In this sort of situation, the outcome of the service act remains very important, but the process of service delivery may be of little interest, since the customer never goes near the "factory." For instance, credit cards and many types of insurance can be obtained by mail or telephone.

For operational reasons it may be very desirable to get the customer out of the factory and to transform a "high-contact" service into a "low-contact" one (Chase 1978). The chances of success in such an endeavor will be enhanced when the new procedures also offer customers greater convenience. Many services directed at *things* rather than at people formerly required the customer's presence but are now delivered at arm's length. Certain financial services have long used the mails to save customers the inconvenience of personal visits to a specific office location. Today, new electronic distribution channels have made it possible to offer instantaneous delivery of financial services to a wide array of alternative locations. Retail banking provides a good example, with its growing use of such electronic delivery systems as automatic teller machines in airports or shopping centers, pay-by-phone bill paying, or on-line banking facilities in retail stores.

By thinking creatively about the nature of their services, managers of service organizations may be able to identify opportunities for alternative, more convenient forms of service delivery or even for transformation of the service into a manufactured good. For instance, services to the mind such as education do not necessarily require attendance in person since they can be delivered through the mails or electronic media (Britain's Open University, which makes extensive use of television and radio broadcasts, is a prime example). Two-way communication hook-ups can make it possible for a physically distant teacher and students to interact directly where this is necessary to the educational process (one recent Bell System advertisement featured a chamber music class in a small town being taught by an instructor several hundred miles away). Alternatively, lectures can be packaged and sold as books, records or videotapes. And programmed learning exercises can be developed in computerized form, with the terminal serving as a Socratic surrogate.

What Type of Relationship Does the Service Organization Have with Its Customers?

With very few exceptions, consumers buy manufactured goods at discrete intervals, paying for each purchase separately and rarely entering into a formal relationship with the manufacturer. (Industrial purchasers, by contrast, often enter into long-term relationships with suppliers and sometimes receive almost continuous delivery of certain supplies.)

In the service sector both household and institutional purchasers may enter into ongoing relationships with service suppliers and may receive service on a continuing basis. This offers a way of categorizing services. We can ask, does the service organization enter into a "membership" relationship with its customers—as in telephone subscriptions, banking and the family doctor—or is there no formal relationship? And is service delivered on a continuous basis—as in insurance, broadcasting and police protection—or is each transaction recorded and charged separately? Figure 2 shows the 2×2 matrix resulting from this categorization, with some additional examples in each category.

Insights and Implications

The advantage to the service organization of a membership relationship is that it knows who its current customers are and, usually, what use they make of the services offered. This can be valuable for segmentation purposes if good records are kept and the data are readily accessible in a format that lends itself to computerized analysis. Knowing the identities and addresses of current customers enables the organization to make effective use of direct mail, telephone selling and personal sales calls—all highly targeted marketing communication media.

The nature of service relationships also has important implications for pricing. In situations where service is offered on an ongoing basis, there is often just a single periodic charge covering all services contracted for. Most insurance policies fall in this category, as do tuition and board fees at a residential college. The big advantage of this package approach is its simplicity. Some memberships, however, entail a series of separate and identifiable transactions with the price paid being tied explicitly to the number and type of such transactions. While more complex to administer, such an approach is fairer to customers (whose usage patterns may vary widely) and may discourage wasteful use of what are perceived as "free" services. In such instances, members may be offered advantages over casual users, such as discounted rates (telephone subscribers pay less for long-distance calls made from their own phones than do pay phone users) or advance notification and priority reservations (as in theater subscriptions). Some membership services offer certain services (such as rental of equipment or connection to a public utility system) for a base fee and then make incremental charges for each separate transaction above a defined minimum.

Profitability and customer convenience are central issues in deciding how to price membership services. Will the organization generate greater long-term profits by tying payment explicitly to consumption, by charging a flat rate regardless of consumption, or by unbundling the components of the service and charging a flat rate for some and an

FIGURE 2. Relationships with Customers

Type of Relationship Between the Service Organization and Its Customers

Nature of Service Delivery	"Membership" Relationship	No Formal Relationship
Continuous Delivery of Service	insurance telephone subscription college enrollment banking American Automobile Association	radio station police protection lighthouse public highway
Discrete Transactions	long-distance phone calls theater series subscription commuter ticket or transit pass	car rental mail service toll highway pay phone movie theater public transportation restaurant

incremental rate for others? Telephone and electricity services, for instance, typically charge a base fee for connection to the system and rental of equipment, plus a variety of incremental charges for consumption above a defined minimum. On the other hand, Wide Area Telephone Service (WATS) offers the convenience of unlimited long-distance calling for a fixed fee. How important is it to customers to have the convenience of paying a single periodic fee that is known in advance? For instance, members of the American Automobile Association (AAA) can obtain information booklets, travel advice and certain types of emergency road services free of additional charges. Such a package offers elements of both insurance and convenience to customers who may not be able to predict their exact needs in advance.

Where no formal relationship exists between supplier and customer, continuous delivery of the product is normally found only among that class of services that economists term "public goods"—such as broadcasting, police and lighthouse services, and public highways—where no charge is made for use of service that is continuously available and financed from tax revenues. Discrete transactions, where each usage involves a payment to the service supplier by an essentially "anonymous" consumer, are exemplified by many transportation services, restaurants, movie theaters, shoe repairs and so forth. The problem of such services is that marketers tend to be much less well-informed about who their customers are and what use each customer makes of the service than their counterparts in membership organizations.

Membership relationships usually result in customer loyalty to a particular service supplier (sometimes there is no choice because the supplier has a monopoly). As a marketing strategy, many service businesses seek ways to develop formal, ongoing relations with customers in order to ensure repeat business and/or ongoing financial support. Public radio and television broadcasters, for instance, develop membership clubs for donors and offer monthly program guides in return; performing arts organizations sell subscription series; transit agencies offer monthly passes; airlines create clubs for high mileage fliers; and hotels develop "executive service plans" offering priority reservations and upgraded rooms for frequent guests. The marketing task here is to determine how it might be possible to build sales and revenues through such memberships but to avoid requiring membership when this would result in freezing out a large volume of desirable casual business.

How Much Room Is There for Customization and Judgment?

Relatively few consumer goods nowadays are built to special order; most are purchased "off the shelf." The same is true for a majority of

FIGURE 3. Customization and Judgment in Service Delivery

Extent to Which Customer Contact Personnel Exercise Judgment in Meeting Individual Customer Needs	Extent to Which Service Characteristics Are Customized	
	High	Low
High	legal services health care/surgery architectural design executive search firm real estate agency taxi service beautician plumber education (tutorials)	education (large classes) preventive health programs
Low	telephone service hotel services retail banking (excl. major loans) good restaurant	public transportation routine appliance repair fast food restaurant movie theater spectator sports

industrial goods, although by permutating options it's possible to give the impression of customization. Once they've purchased their goods, of course, customers are usually free to use them as they see fit.

The situation in the service sector, by contrast, is sharply different. Because services are created as they are consumed, and because the customer is often actually involved in the production process, there is far more scope for tailoring the service to meet the needs of individual customers. As shown in Figure 3, customization can proceed along at least two dimensions. The first concerns the extent to which the characteristics of the service and its delivery system lend themselves to customization; the second relates to how much judgment customer contact personnel are able to exercise in defining the nature of the service received by individual customers.

Some service concepts are quite standardized. Public transportation, for instance, runs over fixed routes on predetermined schedules. Routine appliance repairs typically involve a fixed charge, and the customer is responsible for dropping off the item at a given retail location and picking it up again afterwards. Fast food restaurants have a small, set menu; few offer the customer much choice in how the food will be cooked and served. Movies, entertainment and spectator sports place the audience in a relatively passive role, albeit a sometimes noisy one.

Other services offer customers a wide choice of options. Each telephone subscriber enjoys an individual number and can use the phone to obtain a broad array of different services—from receiving personal calls from a next-door neighbor to calling a business associate on the other side of the world, and from data transmission to dial-a-prayer. Retail bank accounts are also customized, with each check or bank card carrying the customer's name and personal code. Within the constraints set down by the bank, the customer enjoys considerable latitude in how and when the account is used and receives a personalized monthly statement. Good hotels and restaurants usually offer their customers an array of service options from which to choose, as well as considerable flexibility in how the service product is delivered to them.

But in each of these instances, the role of the customer contact personnel (if there are any) is somewhat constrained. Other than tailoring their personal manner to the customer and answering straightforward questions, contact personnel have relatively little discretion in altering the characteristics of the service they deliver: their role is basically that of operator or order taker. Judgment and discretion in customer dealings is usually reserved for managers or supervisors who will not normally become involved in service delivery unless a problem arises.

A third category of services gives the customer contact personnel wide latitude in how they deliver the service, yet these individuals do not significantly differentiate the characteristics of their service between one customer and another. For instance, educators who teach courses by lectures and give multiple choice, computer scored exams expose each of their students to a potentially similar experience, yet one professor may elect to teach a specific course in a very different way from a colleague at the same institution.

However, there is a class of services that not only involves a high degree of customization but also requires customer contact personnel to exercise judgment concerning the characteristics of the service and how it is delivered to each customer. Far from being reactive in their dealings with customers, these service personnel are often prescriptive: users (or clients) look to them for advice as well as for customized execution. In this category the locus of control shifts from the user to the supplier—a situation that some customers may find disconcerting. Consumers of surgical services literally place their lives in the surgeon's hands (the same, unfortunately, is also true of taxi services in many cities). Professional services such as law, medicine, accounting and architecture fall within this category. They are all white collar "knowledge industries," requiring extensive training to develop the requisite skills and judgment needed for satisfactory service delivery. Deliverers of such services as taxi drivers, beauticians and plumbers are also found in this category. Their work is customized to the situation at hand and in each instance, the customer purchases the expertise required to devise a tailor-made solution.

Insights and Implications

To a much greater degree than in the manufacturing sector, service products are "custom-made." Yet customization has its costs. Service management often represents an ongoing struggle between the desires of marketing managers to add value and the goals of operations managers to reduce costs through standardization. Resolving such disputes, a task that may require arbitration by the general manager, requires a good understanding of consumer choice criteria, particularly as these relate to price/value trade-offs and competitive positioning strategy. At the present time most senior managers in service businesses have come up through the operations route; hence, participation in executive education programs may be needed to give them the necessary perspective on marketing to make balanced decisions.

Customization is not necessarily important to success. As Levitt (1972, 1976) has pointed out, industrializing a service to take advantage of the economies of mass production may actually increase consumer satisfaction. Speed, consistency and price savings may be more important to many customers than customized service. In some instances, such as spectator sports and the performing arts, part of the product experience is sharing the service with many other people. In other instances the customer expects to share the service facilities with other consumers, as in hotels or airlines, yet still hopes for some individual recognition and custom treatment. Allowing customers to reserve specific rooms or seats in advance, having contact personnel address them by name (it's on their ticket or reservation slip), and providing some latitude for individual choice (room service and morning calls, drinks and meals) are all ways to create an image of customization.

Generally, customers like to know in advance what they are buying—what the product features are, what the service will do for them. Surprises and uncertainty are not normally popular. Yet when the nature of the service requires a judgment-based, customized solution, as in a professional service, it is not always clear to either the customer or the professional what the outcome will be. Frequently, an important dimension of the professional's role is diagnosing the nature of the situation, then designing a solution.

In such situations those responsible for developing marketing strategy would do well to recognize that customers may be uneasy concerning the prior lack of certainty about the outcome. Customer contact personnel in these instances are not only part of the product but also determine what that product should be.

One solution to this problem is to divide the product into two separate components, diagnosis and implementation of a solution, that are executed and paid for separately. The process of diagnosis can and should be explained to the customer in advance, since the outcome of the diagnosis cannot always be predicted accurately. However, once that diagnosis has been made, the customer need not proceed immediately with the proposed solution; indeed, there is always the option of seeking a second opinion. The solution "product," by contrast, can often be spelled out in detail beforehand, so that the customer has a reasonable idea of what to expect. Although there may still be some uncertainty, as in legal actions or medical treatment, the range of possibilities should be narrower by this point, and it may be feasible to assign probabilities to specified alternative outcomes.

Marketing efforts may need to focus on the process of client-provider interactions. It will help prospective clients make choices between alternative suppliers, especially where professionals are concerned, if they know something of the organization's (or individual's) approach to diagnosis and problem-solving, as well as client-relationship style. These are considerations that transcend mere statements of qualification in an advertisement or brochure. For instance, some pediatricians allow new parents time for a free interview before any commitments are made. Such a trial encounter has the advantage of allowing both parties to decide whether or not a good match exists.

WHAT IS THE NATURE OF DEMAND AND SUPPLY FOR THE SERVICE?

Manufacturing firms can inventory supplies of their products as a hedge against fluctuations in demand. This enables them to enjoy the economies derived from operating plants at a steady level of production. Service businesses can't do this because it's not possible to inventory the finished service. For instance, the potential income from an empty seat on an airline flight is lost forever once that flight takes off, and each hotel daily room vacancy is equally perishable. Likewise, the productive capacity of an auto repair shop is wasted if no one brings a car for servicing on a day when the shop is open. Conversely, if the demand for a service exceeds supply on a particular day, the excess business may be lost. Thus, if someone can't get a seat on one airline, another carrier gets the business or the trip is cancelled or postponed. If an accounting firm is too busy to accept tax and audit work from a prospective client, another firm will get the assignment.

But demand and supply imbalances are not found in all service situations. A useful way of categorizing services for this purpose is shown in Figure 4. The horizontal axis classifies organizations according to whether demand for the service fluctuates widely or narrowly over time; the vertical axis classifies them according to whether or not capacity is sufficient to meet peak demand.

Organizations in Box 1 could use increases in demand outside peak periods, those in Box 2 must decide whether to seek continued growth in demand and capacity or to continue the status quo, while those in Box 3 represent growing organizations that may need temporary demarketing until capacity can be increased to meet or exceed current demand levels. But service organizations in Box 4 face an ongoing problem of trying to smooth demand to match capacity, involving both stimulation and discouragement of demand.

Insights and Implications

Managing demand is a task faced by nearly all marketers, whether offering goods or services. Even where the fluctuations are sharp, and inventories cannot be used to act as a buffer between supply and demand, it may still be possible to manage capacity in a service business—for instance, by hiring part time employees or renting extra facilities at peak periods. But for a substantial group of service organizations, successfully managing demand fluctuations through marketing actions is the key to profitability.

To determine the most appropriate strategy in each instance, it's necessary to seek answers to some additional questions:

1. What is the typical cycle period of these demand fluctuations?
   - predictable (i.e., demand varies by hour of the day, day of the week or month, season of the year).
   - random (i.e., no apparent pattern to demand fluctuations).

FIGURE 4. What Is the Nature of Demand for the Service Relative to Supply?

Extent to Which Supply Is Constrained	Extent of Demand Fluctuations over Time	
	Wide	*Narrow*
Peak Demand Can Usually Be Met without a Major Delay	1 electricity natural gas telephone hospital maternity unit police and fire emergencies	2 insurance legal services banking laundry and dry cleaning
Peak Demand Regularly Exceeds Capacity	4 accounting and tax preparation passenger transportation hotels and motels restaurants theaters	3 services similar to those in 2 but which have insufficient capacity for their base level of business

2. What are the underlying causes of these demand fluctuations?
   - customer habits or preferences (could marketing efforts change these)?
   - actions by third parties (for instance, employers set working hours, hence marketing efforts might usefully be directed at those employers).
   - nonforecastable events, such as health symptoms, weather conditions, acts of God and so forth—marketing can do only a few things about these, such as offering priority services to members and disseminating information about alternative services to other people.

One way to smooth out the ups and downs of demand is through strategies that encourage customers to change their plans voluntarily, such as offering special discount prices or added product value during periods of low demand. Another approach is to ration demand through a reservation or queuing system (which basically inventories demand rather than supply). Alternatively, to generate demand in periods of excess capacity, new business development efforts might be targeted at prospective customers with a countercyclical demand pattern. For instance, an accounting firm with a surfeit of work at the end of each calendar year might seek new customers whose financial year ended on June 30 or September 30.

Determining what strategy is appropriate requires an understanding of who or what is the target of the service (as discussed in an earlier section of this article). If the service is delivered to customers in person, there are limits to how long a customer will wait in line; hence strategies to inventory or ration demand should focus on adoption of reservation systems (Sasser 1976). But if the service is delivered to goods or to intangible assets, then a strategy of inventorying demand should be more feasible (unless the good is a vital necessity such as a car, in which case reservations may be the best approach).

How Is the Service Delivered?

Understanding distribution issues in service marketing requires that two basic issues be addressed. The first relates to the method of delivery. Is it necessary for the customer to be in direct physical contact with the service organization (customers may have to go to the service organization, or the latter may come to the former), or can transactions be completed at arm's length? And does the service organization maintain just a single outlet or does it serve customers through multiple outlets at different sites? The outcome of this analysis can be seen in Figure 5, which consists of six different cells.

Insights and Implications

The convenience of receiving service is presumably lowest when a customer has to come to the service organization and must use a specific outlet. Offering service through several outlets increases the convenience of access for customers but may start to raise problems of quality control as convenience of access relates to the consistency of the service product delivered. For some types of services the organization will come to the customer. This is, of course, essential when the target of the service is some immovable physical item (such as a building that needs repairs or pest control treatment, or a garden that needs landscaping). But since it's usually more expensive to take service personnel and equipment to the customer than vice versa, the trend has been away from this approach to delivering consumer services (e.g., doctors no longer like to make house calls). In many instances, however, direct contact between customers and the service organization is not necessary; instead, transactions can be handled at arm's length by mail or electronic communications. Through the use of 800 numbers many service organizations have found that they can bring their services as close as the nearest telephone, yet obtain important economies from operating out of a single physical location.

Although not all services can be delivered through arm's length transactions, it may be possible to separate certain components of the service from the core product and to handle them separately. This suggests an additional classification scheme: categorizing services according to whether transactions such as obtaining information, making reservations and making payment can be broken out separately from delivery of the core service. If they can be separated, then the question is whether or not it is advantageous to the service firm to allow customers to make these peripheral transactions through an intermediary or broker.

FIGURE 5. Method of Service Delivery

Nature of Interaction Between Customer and Service Organization	Availability of Service Outlets	
	Single Site	Multiple Sites
Customer Goes to Service Organization	theater barbershop	bus service fast food chain
Service Organization Comes to Customer	lawn care service pest control service taxi	mail delivery AAA emergency repairs
Customer and Service Organization Transact at Arm's Length (mail or electronic communications)	credit card co. local TV station	broadcast network telephone co.

For instance, information about airline flights, reservations for such flights and purchases of tickets can all be made through a travel agent as well as directly through the airline. For those who prefer to visit in person, rather than conduct business by telephoning, this greatly increases the geographic coverage of distribution, since there are usually several travel agencies located more conveniently than the nearest airline office. Added value from using a travel agent comes from the "one-stop shopping" aspect of travel agents; the customer can inquire about several airlines and make car rental and hotel reservations during the same call. Insurance brokers and theater ticket agencies are also examples of specialist intermediaries that represent a number of different service organizations. Consumers sometimes perceive such intermediaries as more objective and more knowledgeable about alternatives than the various service suppliers they represent. The risk to the service firm of working through specialist intermediaries is, of course, that they may recommend use of a competitor's product!

DISCUSSION

Widespread interest in the marketing of services among both academics and practitioners is a relatively recent phenomenon. Possibly this reflects the fact that marketing expertise in the service sector has significantly lagged behind that in the manufacturing sector. Up to now most academic research and discussion has centered on the issue, "How do services differ from goods?" A number of authors including Shostack (1977), Bateson (1979) and Berry (1980) have argued that there are significant distinctions between the two and have proposed several generalizations for management practice. But others such as Enis and Roering (1981) remain unconvinced that these differences have meaningful strategic implications.

Rather than continue to debate the existence of this broad dichotomy, it seems more useful to get on with the task of helping managers in service businesses do a better job of developing and marketing their products. We need to recognize that the service sector, particularly in the United States, is becoming increasingly competitive (Langeard et al. 1981), reflecting such developments as the partial or complete deregulation of several major service industries in recent years, the removal of professional association restrictions on using marketing techniques (particularly advertising), the replacement (or absorption) of independent service units by franchise chains, and the growth of new electronic delivery systems. As competition intensifies within the service sector, the development of more effective marketing efforts becomes essential to survival.

The classification schemes proposed in this article can contribute usefully to management practice in two ways. First, by addressing each of the five questions posed earlier, marketing managers can obtain a better understanding of the nature of their product, of the types of relationships their service organizations have with customers, of the factors underlying any sharp variations in demand, and of the characteristics of their service delivery systems. This understanding should help them identify how these factors shape marketing problems and opportunities and thereby affect the nature of the marketing task. Second, by recognizing which characteristics their own service shares with other services, often in seemingly unrelated industries, managers will learn to look beyond their immediate competitors for new ideas as to how to resolve marketing problems that they share in common with firms in other service industries.

Recognizing that the products of service organizations previously considered as "different" actually face similar problems or share certain characteristics in common can yield valuable managerial insights. Innovation in marketing, after all, often reflects a manager's ability to seek out and learn from analogous situations in other contexts. These classification schemes should also be of value to researchers to whom they offer an alternative to either broad-brush research into services or an industry-by-industry approach. Instead, they suggest a variety of new ways of looking at service businesses, each of which may offer opportunities for focused research efforts. Undoubtedly there is also room for further refinement of the schemes proposed.

REFERENCES

Bateson, John E. G. (1979), "Why We Need Service Marketing," in *Conceptual and Theoretical Developments in Marketing*, O. C. Ferrell, S. W. Brown and C. W. Lamb, eds., Chicago, American Marketing Association, 131–46.

Berry, Leonard L. (1980), "Services Marketing Is Different," *Business Week* (May–June), 24–29.

Bucklin, Louis (1963), "Retail Strategy and the Classification of Consumer Goods," *Journal of Marketing*, 27 (January), 50.

Chase, Richard B. (1978), "Where Does the Customer Fit in a Service Operation?," *Harvard Business Review*, 56 (November–December), 137–42.

Copeland, Melvin T. (1923), "The Relation of Consumers' Buying Habits to Marketing Methods," *Harvard Business Review*, 1 (April), 282–9.

Enis, Ben M. and Kenneth J. Roering (1981), "Service Marketing: Different Products, Similar Strategies," in *Marketing of Services*, J. H. Donnelly and W. R. George, eds., Chicago: American Marketing Association.

Hill, T. P. (1977), "On Goods and Services," *Review of Income and Wealth*, 23 (December), 315–38.

Hunt, Shelby D. (1976), *Marketing Theory*, Columbus, OH: Grid.

Judd, Robert C. (1964), "The Case for Redefining Services," *Journal of Marketing*, 28 (January), 59.

Knisely, Gary (1979), "Marketing and the Services Industry," *Advertising Age* (January 15), 47–50; (February 19), 54–60; (March 19), 58–62; (May 15), 57–58.

Kotler, Philip (1980), *Principles of Marketing*, Englewood Cliffs, NJ: Prentice-Hall, Inc.

Langeard, Eric, John E. G. Bateson, Christopher H. Lovelock and Pierre Eiglier (1981), *Services Marketing: New Insights from Consumers and Managers*, Cambridge, MA: Marketing Science Institute.

Levitt, Theodore (1972), "Production Line Approach to Service," *Harvard Business Review*, 50 (September–October), 41.

―――― (1976), "The Industrialization of Service," *Harvard Business Review*, 54 (September–October), 63–74.

Lovelock, Christopher H. (1980), "Towards a Classification of Services," in *Theoretical Developments in Marketing*, C. W. Lamb and P. M. Dunne, eds., Chicago: American Marketing Association, 72–76.

―――― (1981), "Why Marketing Management Needs to Be Different for Services," in *Marketing of Services*, J. H. Donnelly and W. R. George, eds., Chicago, IL: American Marketing Association.

Rathmell, John M. (1974), *Marketing in the Service Sector*, Cambridge, MA: Winthrop.

Sasser, W. Earl, Jr. (1976), "Match Supply and Demand in Service Industries," *Harvard Business Review*, 54 (November–December), 133.

――――, R. Paul Olsen and D. Daryl Wyckoff (1978), *Management of Service Operations: Text and Cases*, Boston: Allyn & Bacon.

Shostack, G. Lynn (1977), "Breaking Free from Product Marketing," *Journal of Marketing*, 41 (April), 73–80.

Thomas, Dan R. E. (1978), "Strategy Is Different in Service Businesses," *Harvard Business Review*, 56 (July–August), 158–65.

54 The Marketing of Services
Why and How Is It Different?

Kenneth P. Uhl and Gregory D. Upah

Research in Marketing, Vol. 6, pp. 231–57.
Copyright 1983 by JAI Press, Inc.
Reprinted by permission.

I. INTRODUCTION

Services and the unique requirements for marketing them have received and continue to receive a good deal of attention from marketing practitioners and academicians. Indeed, it might be said that interest in service marketing has taken off over the past five years. In early 1980, the AMA sponsored its first service marketing conference. In a recent review of published research on service marketing, over 70% of the references cited were dated 1975–1980 inclusive (Uhl and Upah, 1980b). This increased interest in service marketing might be attributed to a variety of factors—e.g., the acceptance of major arguments put forth regarding the unique requirements for effective service marketing, recent regulatory decisions mandating marketing efforts which were heretofore banned in the professions (medicine, law, public accounting, and dentistry), and increases in service as compared to product expenditures in the United States—at least as has been determined by the categorizations and tabulations of consumption expenditures made by federal government agencies.

Regardless of the reason for the heightened interest, the fact remains that practitioners and academics are seeking to improve the existing marketing knowledge as it applies to the marketing of a variety of services in the public and private sector and in professional and commercial realms.

To date, there have been a number of useful articles and monographs written on the subject. However, it is our contention that whereas the growth in interest and the development of ideas has been rapid, the foundation on which much recent research is based is not altogether firm. The overall purpose of the present paper is to attempt to remedy this state of affairs with respect to service marketing theory. We will attempt to accomplish this objective by stating and reassessing the basic rationale for the separate area of study called service marketing. In addition, we will present in the form of propositions a set of positive and normative marketing implications of the unique characteristics of services.

Before discussing the specific objectives of the paper, the following brief review of the growing body of literature on service marketing is presented.

II. Relevant Literature

As noted above, the subarea of marketing referred to as service marketing is not without significant empirical and theoretical research input. Much of the writing in service marketing has been concerned with building the argument that services are different from products[1] and that these differences necessitate special marketing considerations (Eiglier et al., 1977; Judd, 1964; Rathmell, 1974; Uhl and Upah, 1978). The authors of this research went on to say that the concepts developed in marketing were biased toward product marketing and not necessarily applicable in the service realm.

Many of the assumptions made in the major initial and subsequent research on service marketing have come under criticism (Bonoma and Mills, 1979; Wyckham et al., 1975) — criticism we will discuss later. However, recent work in this area has dealt not so much with arguing the issues of product-service differences and resulting differences in marketing. Instead, many have accepted (or possibly avoided) the differences arguments and gone on to develop positive as well as normative theory for service marketing practice.

In the opinion of Ryans and Wittink (1977), arguments as to differences between products and services have ceased to be productive. Their suggestion is to move forward with the development of better strategic planning models to guide service marketers. In essence, they seem to suggest that services deserve special marketing consideration in the same way that certain categories of products do.

A. Marketing Intangible Offerings

Several authors have concerned themselves with the implications of the intangibility of services for advertising and otherwise marketing services. Some studies have dealt with the need for, and possible means of, emphasizing the tangible aspects of services in advertising (Shimp and Dyer, 1978; Shostack, 1977; Smith and Meyer, 1980). Others have dealt with the ecological/situational factors (e.g., physical surroundings) affecting consumer perceptions of the nature and quality of services (Berry, 1975; Eiglier and Langeard, 1977; Shostack, 1977). The importance of public contact personnel also has been stressed (Berry, 1975; George, 1977; Sasser and Arbeit, 1976).

Much of the focus on intangibility and the resulting importance of the tangible aspects of service firm capabilities has shifted from commercial services to professional services (Bloom, 1977; Shimp and Dyer, 1978;

Smith and Meyer, 1980; Uhl and Upah, 1980a). This movement has been accelerated by recent Federal Trade Commission lawsuits and by Supreme Court decisions which have effectively removed bans on advertising from the codes of ethics of virtually all of the professions while still allowing control over content of advertisements to remain in the hands of professional associations. The issues now faced deal not with the "should-professionals-advertise" question, but with the "how-should-they-advertise" question.

In our view, further progress in the area of the promotion-advertising of services of all types is hampered by the lack of a solid body of theory particularly relevant to the unique problems involved in marketing services. In addition, published empirical research support for the efficacy of those advertising/marketing strategies which have been proposed and used has been minimal. There are, however, exceptions to the latter point. There has been some research designed to assess the decision criteria used by consumers in selecting services and to relate these criteria to effective advertising strategy (e.g., Anderson et al., 1976; Shimp and Dyer, 1978).

B. Studies of Service Marketing Practice

A good deal of research has been directed toward describing and drawing normative implications from the marketing practices of firms in specific service industries. This research has, for instance, dealt with the particular marketing problems of, and response to those problems by, organizations providing accounting services (Kotler and Connor, 1977), professional services in general (Wilson, 1972), banking services (Berry, 1975; Rathmell, 1974; Shostack, 1977), retail services in general (Judd, 1968; George, 1977; Upah, 1980), transportation (Vaughn, 1979), and the performing arts (Currim et al., 1981).

C. Studies Dealing with Particular Marketing Problems in Various Service Industries

Other studies have dealt with the common service marketing challenges faced by firms across service industries. Sasser (1976) and Lovelock and Young (1977) deal with the need for, and procedures used to, more closely match supply and demand for services. Levitt (1972, 1976) discusses means by which service organizations can improve productivity through increased mechanization of service operations. Sasser and Arbeit (1976) then go on to discuss the potential problems in employee alienation as a result of the use of increased structure in, and mechanization of, service tasks.

Related to research on productivity are studies dealing with achieving production economies in the use of multisite service operations

(Chase, 1978; Upah, 1980) and improving the ability to realize economies in promotion when multisite operations are used (Upah, 1980). The distribution-channel-related issues surrounding service marketing also have been addressed by Donnelly (1976) and Stern and El-Ansary (1977).

D. Classification Schema for Services

Finally, some of the recent research emphasis in the area of service marketing has been the renewed interest in developing classification schema for services (Lovelock, 1980; Ryans and Wittink, 1977). The ultimate objective of this research is to begin to develop the strategic marketing implications of the categorization of a service along one or more dimensions of relevance to consumers (Lovelock, 1980).

What then, are the significant gaps, in this diverse and fairly substantial body of literature, which our paper seeks to address? First, it is our view that these papers cited above have made many useful, if fragmented, contributions. However, few of them have been based on a sufficiently comprehensive theoretical foundation and strong definitional base that clearly delineates between products and services. As a result, notions about product-service differences and the resulting marketing implications still reflect considerable disagreement (see, for example, Bonoma and Mills, 1979; Wyckham et al., 1975) and fragmentation. Second, where controversies have begun, there has been no effort to characterize, evaluate, and reconcile the competing arguments and draw conclusions from them.

Third, there are, in our opinion, still many miscomprehensions as to what market offerings should be termed services and which of these deserve special marketing consideration. This state of affairs has resulted from a failure to develop the criteria for making such classifications as well as for some economic accounting reasons (i.e., the federal government's classification of some goods as services, e.g., owned housing, for purposes of calculating GNP).

Finally, to summarize the above points, the major gap in existing research is the lack of any research effort which integrates the isolated and often conflicting notions of product-service differences and the major marketing implications of those differences.

Without a stronger theoretical foundation, further positive or normative research is likely to be even more fragmented and lacking in direction. In addition, without such a base, the subarea of service marketing itself is neither likely to be justified nor receive the more widespread recognition by marketing scholars and practitioners it deserves.

III. Purpose

The purpose of this paper then is to (a) identify and classify the major differences that exist between products and services; and (b) suggest a set of propositions for service marketing that reflect the implications of these differences. The ultimate objective of this paper is to provide a basis for the development of additional theories and research that will contribute to a better understanding and more effective management of service marketing.

In an earlier paper (Uhl and Upah, 1978), we began to set forth what we considered to be the key strategic management implications resulting from the unique marketing problems faced in the marketing of services. The present paper reflects the evolution in our thinking on these issues. However, it also involves an effort to "pull together" much of the useful work on service marketing presented by others.

As will be shown later, our view is that there are a small number of major differences between products and services. Furthermore, we would agree with Bonoma and Mills (1979), who suggest that differences between products and services and the resulting differences in marketing are "much more a matter of emphasis than nature or kind." Nevertheless, these differences between products and services do lead to a number of significant differences in the marketing strategies service organizations are and should be using.

IV. A Definition of Services

To facilitate exposition of these issues, a definition of services is offered. In addition, a discussion of criteria used to delineate between services and products is provided.

Two fairly broad definitions of services have been suggested dealing specifically with the intangibility of services. Judd (1964) defines a service as the object of a transaction which does not entail the transfer of ownership of a tangible commodity. Rathmell (1974) defines a service as any intangible product bought and sold in the marketplace. Although neither of these definitions wrongfully characterizes services, a more comprehensive definition is needed for further discussion. This definition emphasizes a number of the unique aspects of services which make them different from products:

> A service is any *task (work)* performed for another or the *provision of any facility, product*, or *activity* for another's *use and not ownership*, which arises from an exchange transaction. It is *intangible* and *incapable of being stored or transported*. There may be an accompanying sale of a product.

A. Meaning of Terms

Task or work means physical labor like repairing a car, cutting hair, or driving a bus. It also includes mental efforts such as the thought put into a case by a physician, accountant, or attorney.

Provision of a facility could be the rental of a house or motel room or admission to a swimming pool or amusement park.

Provision of a product could be the rental of power saw, a car, or a computer.

Provision of an activity could be the right to view a sporting event or an opera or to receive instruction at a university.

Use and not ownership means that an activity or a tangible object is available, with restricted use rights, to the buyer, but only for the duration specified in the exchange transaction. Further use calls for an additional exchange transaction.

Intangible means lacking physical properties. Services cannot be touched or felt. Some services, however, are translated in a tangible form—for example, a tax return or a consultant's report represent services. The services themselves are intangible. Electricity and natural gas have commonly been misclassified as services. They are tangible. They are products.

Incapable of being stored indicates that the user of a service is a recipient only as it is being produced. For example, a barber or a hotel has capacity to provide haircuts or lodging, but actually provides the services only as hair is being cut or someone has use of the room. Furthermore, the unused capacity of a service producer is lost forever. It cannot be recalled for use at some later time. Empty hotel rooms, seats on an airline flight, in a barber shop, or at an opera, or unused hours of an accountant's time cannot be stored and recalled for use in future periods of peak demand.

Incapable of being transported indicates that almost no services can be produced in one place and then shipped elsewhere for use. For example, haircuts and medical checkups cannot be produced in one place, accumulated, and shipped to customers elsewhere for later consumption. There are, however, some exceptions to the lack of transportability. Various innovations in electronics allow simultaneous provision of information or entertainment to customers at points far from the origin of the service activity.

V. INTERTWINING OF SERVICES AND PRODUCTS

Services and products have traditionally been tangled together both in the marketplace and in the thinking and writing of practitioners and scholars concerned with services. The first task of this article, therefore, is to delineate the various forms or roles of services in market offerings and to point out which ones present special marketing problems.

The total market offering to a customer almost always contains a service as well as a product component. In fact, few services occur without the sale of products and vice versa. Designation of a market offering as a service or product normally only indicates which is dominant—the tangible or the intangible element.

Shostack (1977) has proposed a "molecular" model to aid in classifying market offerings as products or services. Very simply, this model classifies a market offering as a product or a service according to the degree to which ownership of a tangible object is transferred from buyer to seller in the market transaction. A purchase of a package of salt in a grocery store is an example of a transaction where the exchange is almost totally dominated by a tangible object (i.e., a product). In contrast, an airline flight is almost totally devoid of any exchange of products (except food and drinks). In between those two extremes, however, are many market offerings which might be termed product-service hybrids.[2] Food served in restaurants, for example, has a considerable service component.

Indeed, services, as we have just suggested, may take on a variety of forms and roles as part of a total market offering. However, not all services are marketed differently from products. Services should be and are most often marketed like the products they are sold with when they are dominated by the product component of the market offering, or when they are of minor significance in a buying decision. For example, when services such as personal selling, credit, warranties, and delivery play only relatively minor roles in accompanying and facilitating the sale of a product, they are marketed as components of the product.

Services are usually marketed differently from products, or at least require special marketing consideration, when the services:

1. Are "pure"; or
2. Form part of a product-service hybrid in such a way that they:
   a. Dominate the service-product mix; and/or
   b. Strongly influence consumers involved in the buying process.

Legal, consulting, and other professional services are examples of "pure" or near-pure services. So are entertainment services, such as sporting events or concerts, and personal services such as hair care. Insurance, accounting, and similar services that are typically translated in the form of a policy, a statement, or a contract are virtually pure services. Illustrations of service-product mixes dominated by services would include dinner shows at dinner theatres and the repair and maintenance of electrical fixtures, shoes, and computers. Even when the relevant product components cost more than the services in such transactions, the supplier selection decision is typically based on the service, not the product component.

Some products have been misclassified as services. Natural gas and electricity are products. Natural gas satisfies virtually all of the product criteria. The only question for electricity concerns is storage capability. These two products are tangible, are produced prior to use, and can be transported. They may, however, be sufficiently intertwined with service components to be best marketed as services.

VI. Propositions for the Marketing of Services

The remainder of the paper focuses on the marketing meaning of four major differences between products and services. These differences relate to (1) tangibility; (2) ability to be stored; (3) ability to be transported, and (4) ability to be mass-marketed. A set of propositions is offered relating these differences to the special marketing efforts required to effectively market services. Following the statement of each proposition is a discussion of the logic, theory, and research-based justifications for the proposition.

VII. Managing Intangibility

Proposition 1: *In the marketing of services, tangible production "capabilities" are of major importance in attracting the attention of prospective users, suggesting the quality and the nature of the services, and providing support or evidence that benefits will be forthcoming.*

The applicability of this proposition can best be illustrated by reference to so-called pure services, i.e., market offerings involving virtually no exchange of tangible objects. Medical checkups, legal or business advice from attorneys, accountants, and consultants, as well as air travel and lodging are examples of such market offerings. What, then, do customers look to in order to assess the nature and quality of the services to be received? From a merely logical—deductive or inductive—point of view, we would suggest that customers evaluate what they can't see, i.e., the service itself, by what they can see—e.g., the location and decor of the office, the demeanor and appearance of the office staff and principal service providers. For such commercial services as lodging and air travel, the nature and quality of services may be gauged by evaluating the service firm's physical facilities (e.g., a hotel's outward appearance, room decor and recreational facilities) and/or equipment (e.g., aircraft, cabin appointments), as well as the key personnel involved in operating the facilities and equipment. Arguments as to the impact of these environmental or ecological factors on behavior are presented in research done in a variety of disciplines (Barker, 1968; Belk, 1975; Hall, 1959; Nord and Peter, 1980).

Factors such as facilities and personnel are relevant in purchases of products as well. However, for many purchases of products, the product itself may be evaluated with only slight dependence on the external cues of store decor or appearance of personnel. Many branded goods have sold well in discount stores because of price and the fact that expertise of sales help or store decor are rather unimportant. The product and its features provide enough evidence of probable satisfaction with the purchase. With pure services or services which are major components of a market offering (e.g., technical, programming services for a major computer system) the tangible cues of the seller's capability to deliver that service become more important.

Wyckham et al. (1975), who argue that service marketing is not materially different from product marketing, do not take issue with this point. Rather, they seek to minimize its significance. They argue that the presence of tangible products does not aid consumers in decision making. This state of affairs is attributed to (1) the immense variety of products and the high-level complexity of some products; and (2) the inability of consumers to effectively judge so many, and sometimes complex, products by merely assessing the physical characteristics of those products. On the contrary, we would argue that many consumers seem readily able to discriminate on the basis of physical characteristics. Many consumers are able to distinguish higher-quality fresh produce from poor-quality produce, badly made garments from well-made garments, and poorly constructed and finished furniture from well-constructed and finished furniture by inspecting the physical characteristics of these products—and not by merely looking to such cues as brand or store names. Furthermore, because televisions in operation can be watched, stereo sets heard, and calculators programmed, assessments based on physical characteristics are eminently possible, even if *not made* by some consumers seeking to purchase these products.

In spite of the arguments pertaining to the abilities of consumers to evaluate various types of products, the essential point is that sellers of services have virtually no choice but to point to their tangible capability as an indicator of the quality and nature of the service to be performed. In product transactions the buyer has the product to evaluate. In transactions for pure services, the focus of evaluation is directed more toward the tangible *evidence* of the seller's capability to provide the service plus any relevant and attendant environmental cues. Demonstrations are, of course, possible. Sports teams, performing arts programs, and recreational facilities may provide complimentary tickets to allow consumers to sample what they have to offer. Demonstrations seem less feasible in professional services, but are not impossible. Accountants and business consultants can outline their procedures.

Others (Berry, 1975; Eiglier and Langeard, 1977; George, 1977; Shostack, 1977) have alluded to the importance of situational characteristics in purchase decisions for services. Two major situational factors for service decisions are what Belk (1975) calls the physical (e.g., store decor, lighting, and location) and social surroundings (e.g., other persons present, their roles in providing/consuming the service) about the stimulus object. Our supposition is that due to absence of physical characteristics of the service itself, these situational factors have greater impact on consumer behavior for service purchases than on consumer behavior for product purchases. Shostack (1977, p. 78) puts it this way: "service reality is arrived at by the consumer mostly through a process of deduction, based on the total impression that the [tangible] evidence creates."

We are speaking of a difference of degree, not kind, between products and services in the promotion-advertising aspect and, as we will see, most other aspects of service marketing. Furthermore, we are not necessarily suggesting that most service marketers already subscribe to this belief and have adjusted their activities accordingly. What we are suggesting is that those who haven't should make the change in focus outlined above and that those who have are likely to have already benefitted from doing so.

> **Proposition 2:** *Four principal production capabilities are available to service organizations to attract customers. They are the facilities and equipment, people, methods, and overall organizational capabilities used to provide services.*

Different services and situations appear to call for the focus of marketing on different capabilities. Services like data processing, air travel, car and equipment rental, and lodging are dominated by physical facilities or equipment. The rendering of these services involves people, but the bulk of the service is based on the organizations' facilities or equipment.

Professional services such as dental and medical treatment and legal and accounting advice are dominated by people. This is also true for insurance, barbering, and advertising services. Some facilities and equipment are involved, but the services are heavily people-centered.

Banks, savings and loan associations, and other financial organizations have yet another orientation. They, like issuers of insurance, are obligated to their customers for large financial payments. These are organizations that depend on being entrusted with other peoples' savings or financial well-being. They may find facilities and people important, but a major determinant and indicator of their ability to provide services is their overall organizational capability in terms of financial stability, expertise, and resources.

> **Proposition 3:** *In the marketing of facility or equipment intensive services:*
>   a. *Facilities/equipment capabilities are featured when uniquely superior facilities or equipment are present.*

b. Person-facilities/equipment interaction capabilities are featured when the major facilities/equipment are less unique, but still not commonly available.
  c. People or organizational capabilities are featured when facilities/equipment are common among the competitive service suppliers.

Initially it might seem that facilities- and equipment-intensive service organizations would build their marketing programs around their facility or equipment capabilities. This should be the case, however, only when they can secure and maintain unique, superior facilities or equipment not possessed by their competitors. A few airlines took this action, for example, when they secured the extra-long-range 747 aircrafts. Hilton and Hyatt can do this when they first build new advance-designed and equipped hotels.

A pattern appears to be present among facility- and equipment-intensive services. Sequential stages are frequently followed. First, marketing strategies are built around superior facilities or equipment capabilities as these advantages are available. Second, as comparable facilities or equipment become more common among competitors, the marketing effort evolves to focus more on the ability of people to interact with the facilities and equipment to provide, in combination, a set of unique and desired capabilities and benefits. Finally, when no unique superior facilities and equipment capabilities remain, the focus is on the organizations' people and their capabilities to provide benefits.

While there are many possible illustrations (e.g., motel/hotel accommodations, new bank branches and equipment such as 24-hour automated teller machines), commercial air travel provides one of the most vivid ones. As major new airplanes become available, the first airlines to take delivery feature the airplanes and the unique service benefits they can provide. The equipment focus subsides as additional airlines take delivery, with the focus moving more to the benefits available to the customer based on the mixture of pilots, stewardesses, and other personnel that interface with the equipment. One international airline has, for example, shifted its advertising focus from its now less unique aircraft to the flight simulator training and 6-month checkups it requires of each of its pilots. In the final stage, when the airplanes no longer offer a differential advantage, they are virtually ignored.

> **Proposition 4:** *In the marketing of people-intensive services, major attention is focused on the organization's overall capabilities, key people and their capabilities (experience and training), the nature of methods/procedures used by the firm, and the immediate environment that can convey cues as to the successful provision of these services.*

People-intensive services—professional, personal, and business—frequently involve extensive and expensive equipment. However, the major marketing strategies appear to be built around the key people in the organizations. This seems to be common both in the acquisition of new clients and the expansion of additional services to present clients. It seems true when professional traditions and ethics involve the use of centers of influence. It also appears common of personal and business services which make extensive use of more visible promotional media.

People capabilities can be emphasized by focusing on training and/or degrees received, certifications, years of experience, prestigious affiliations with professional societies, awards won, and other similar indicators of the ability of, and likely quality of services rendered by, such individuals.

Overall organizational capabilities often are stressed by people-intensive service organizations. For instance, financial institutions typically *appear to* emphasize their financial stability-ability capabilities by focusing attention on balance sheets, financial size, worldwide operations, years of existence, and continued growth. Public accounting firms stress the number of partners, office locations, and international experience.

Impressive facilities, office environments, equipment, and prestigious locations also appear to be used to help market people-intensive services. Large, striking home office buildings often are featured in advertisements or promotional brochures by insurance companies and banks. Well-appointed reception areas, open chart rooms and libraries, sumptuous offices, certificates of degrees and awards, and other accouterments also are quite prominent. They, like other tangible cues, are used by consumers to draw inferences as to the capabilities of people and the organization as a whole. For instance, as part of the Bank of America's early and successful efforts to attract more hesitant small depositors and borrowers, loan officers' offices were placed in an open area rather than behind closed doors. This more open and friendly atmosphere set the tone for the interior design of many banks.

Research regarding the strategic management of tangible evidence in the promotion of people-intensive services has been limited. Wittreich (1966) suggests that providers of professional services have two major approaches available to them in utilizing tangible capabilities in advertising or otherwise promoting their services. The first is the *extrinsic* approach—such as, focusing on key personnel, particular methods used to satisfy clients' needs, and any actual successes achieved by these personnel or methods. Examples of such promotion can be seen in recent ads by public accountants and by business consultants (in particular, marketing research organizations). Some advertisements highlight personnel. Other advertisements focus on accounting, planning, or survey procedures and control checks and successes achieved in the use of these procedures.

The second and, according to Wittreich, superior approach combines extrinsic copy themes with intrinsic or benefits appeals. The combination approach conveys the specific client benefits likely to result from the possession of extrinsic or overall firm attributes. Uhl and Upah (1980a) outline a hierarchical approach for the advertising of public accounting services. Promotion-advertising begins with more general firm attributes and then progresses to more specific attributes as the overall capabilities begin to be established in the minds of prospective clients.

VIII. Research Regarding Consumer Choice Criteria for Services

There has been and continues to be a considerable amount of research and dialogue regarding (1) the usefulness of various attributes of service organizations in consumer decision making; and (2) the propriety of statements of possession of certain kinds of attributes by service providers. Before discussing our next set of propositions, we will review some of the research results and current thinking regarding consumers' decision criteria for services.

There have been some studies of consumer decision making for services. The majority of the marketing studies have pertained to the choice criteria or attributes used by individuals to select banks, physicians, attorneys, accountants, and consultants (e.g., Anderson et al., 1976; Sarkar and Saleh, 1974; Smith and Meyer, 1980; Wood and Ball, 1978). Often, however, the criteria, while intuitively relevant, are very global or subjective in nature. For instance, results from studies by Wood and Ball (1978) and Smith and Meyer (1980) suggest that when seeking public accountants and/or attorneys consumers are looking for such qualities as trustworthiness and competence.

One of the critical questions involved in developing useful guidelines for the advertising of highly people-intensive services—particularly professional services—is which specific and more objective attributes of the service organization are indicative, to the consumer, of the levels of the more general benefits sought. Major professional associations such as the American Institute of Certified Public Accountants (AICPA) have stated in advertising guidelines for their members that only "objectively verifiable" attributes should be used (Wood and Ball, 1978). Copy themes such as "we've earned your trust," "absolute integrity," "unsurpassed knowledge and competence in the field," i.e., matter-of-fact statements of possession of very subjective qualities, are presumably considered unprofessional and potentially misleading and thus not allowed by the AICPA.

One recent study has shown that a listing of professional attribute information (e.g., years in practice, educational background, location) had no significant limited impact on consumer (i.e., individual as opposed to organizational consumers) attitudes and behavioral intentions with respect to selection of physicians and attorneys (Kuehl and Ford, 1977). As might have been expected, personal recommendations or referrals did have a significant impact on both dependent measures (Kuehl and Ford, 1977). The authors suggest that other kinds of attribute information may have had a more significant impact. Furthermore, since only individual consumers were studied, the results may not be applicable to organizational clients for professional services. Organizations may be more sophisticated in their ability to utilize, and more impressed by, the attributes mentioned in the Kuehl and Ford study. One major question regarding the use of attribute information by individual consumers is not whether or not the attributes are good indicators of service quality or value, but whether or not consumers understand how to utilize these attributes.

This issue is reminiscent of a similar problem involved in providing more and "better" information about products (on labels, in brochures, in advertisements, etc.). As is the case for nutrient labeling, the question is not necessarily the worth of nutrient information, but rather the consumer's ability to effectively utilize often very complex information. Thus, the issue of either using less and/or simpler forms of information versus increasing the consumer's ability to use more complex forms of information (e.g., through public education) is raised.

IX. Implications of the Inability to Store Services

A. Managing Without Storage

Proposition 5: *In the marketing of services, close coordination of production capacity with market stimulation and demand is used to offset problems caused by the inability to store services.*

A second major difference between products and services is ability to store. Products, being tangible, can be stored, with perishability being largely a function of use and age. Services cannot be stored for any length of time. Haircuts, appendectomies, motel lodgings, travel, live entertainment—none of these, nor any other service, can be produced and stored in one year and consumed the next. This total lack of storage capability creates the need for a more exacting match between supply and demand for services than for products (Sasser, 1976).

Wyckham et al. (1975) and other persons who argue that service and product marketing are the same point out that perishability differences between products and services are merely short-term differences. They say that products, like services, can become obsolete or decay with age. We agree that the perishability difference is a difference of degree, not kind. However, we feel that Wyckham et al. understate the magnitude of this key difference between products and services. *All* service capacity is perishable and furthermore perishes with every instant of nonuse. Most products do not perish with nonuse, but retain their ability to be sold at full value—at least in the short term. Durable products such as houses, furniture, and automobiles retain their value for long periods of time.

Wyckham et al. also argue that to compensate for perishability, service capacity can be adjusted just as the hours of a retail store are adjusted according to seasonal demand. The crucial issue is that it is *much more critical* that service capacity be adjusted according to demand and vice versa. Unsold products can be used to satisfy future demand, but unused service capacity, because of its inability to be stored, cannot be recalled for future use. The following example will, hopefully, further illustrate this point.

A typical automobile dealer markets both cars and maintenance and repair services. Because of storage, a 25% over- or underorder of cars usually can be met without serious consequences. Cars not sold one week can be sold the next. Furthermore, although a larger inventory causes some increase in costs, the larger selection aids sales. This oversupply situation also can be remedied by transporting cars to other dealers. When demand exceeds supply, dealers can purchase additional cars being stored by other dealers or by the manufacturer.

A 25% over- or undercapacity in maintenance and repair services, however, can greatly impair profitability. Service capacity not used one week cannot be stored and used in weeks where demand exceeds capacity. Service capacity, unlike automobiles, is not easily transported to other dealers experiencing higher levels of demand. This overcapacity is idle capacity and adds to costs and not revenues. It also is more difficult (at least in the short term) to obtain additional service capacity (e.g., equipment, facilities, and trained personnel) when demand exceeds supply than to acquire additional automobiles (that is, assuming that the entire industry is not experiencing product shortages).

Profitability calls for the coordination of supply and demand for both the product and service sides of the business. The services, not being subject to storage, require far more exacting management than the products. Unfortunately, most car dealers concentrate on the management of the more glamorous product side and neglect the management of the more difficult service side of the business. Not surprisingly, they have traditionally made money on car sales and lost money on maintenance-repair services.[3]

The essential fact to remember is that services, not being storable, can only be produced when they are demanded. They require far more exacting management of supply and demand than do products. Demand for service must be met or lost. Demand that is met increases revenues; demand that is missed contributes no revenues. Service capacity that is available at the wrong time or place and, in turn, is idle continues to incur costs, but not revenues. This is the essence of managing without storage.

Kotler (1980) uses the term *synchromarketing* to describe efforts designed to resolve irregular demand—i.e., to better match levels of demand with supply. Our point, again, then, is that synchromarketing with respect to capacity and demand is more crucial in assuring economical utilization of capacity for service firms than product firms. Clearly, neither manufacturing firms nor product retailers want over- or undercapacity situations when producing and selling goods. However, there are buffers available to both of these organizations which are not available to most service organizations—i.e., the ability to store unused products and sell them at future dates with, at least in the short term, minimal or no loss in the value of those products. Stated in another way, service supply is, in general, often less flexible than the supply of products because of the inability to maintain or store service supply during periods of nonuse.

B. Adjusting Supply to Match Demand

How, then, do or should service firms attempt to achieve the close coordination of supply (i.e., service capacity) and demand necessitated by the inability to store services? Coordination of supply and demand may involve adjustments to supply, demand, or both. Proposition 6 suggests which supply-adjusting mechanisms seem to be most popular for services.

Proposition 6: *The management of short-run production capabilities for services is (1) a crucial determinant of efficiency; and (2) often accomplished by increased flowthrough rates and by service postponements, facility extensions, and shared capacities.*

Some service organizations can quickly alter their supply up and down. Others face more fixed supply situations in the short run. In any case, the altering of supply to match demand has traditionally been accomplished through a number of methods. Reduction in the time spent servicing individual customers (i.e., increasing flowthrough rates) is one means of increasing the amount of customers a facility can handle. Restaurants may accomplish this by faster and more attentive service.

Service firms can, of course, add capacity such as temporary help or rental equipment in peak periods. Capacity also can be expanded by merely extending the hours of operation of the firm to times that seem to be more convenient for certain customer segments. One dental partnership doubled its patient volume by employing two shifts extending from early morning to 7:30 in the evening (Smith, 1976). Some service needs, not requiring immediate attention, can be postponed until later periods when demand has slackened. Accounting firms handle tax preparation at tax time and work on estate and tax planning between May and January.

Apart from traditional demand stimulation activities, another increasingly used method of extending service capacity is to ask the consumer to assume more responsibility in the purchase of the service. Self-service gasoline stations, automated cafeterias, and automated bank tellers are prime examples of attempts to substitute the consumer's effort for the effort of a salaried employee. This substitution enables the service firm to reduce their labor force or divert it to other activities. It also provides benefits to the consumer such as more flexible service times or lower prices. However, it is obvious that not all customer segments will be willing to increase their own input in the acquisition of a service.

Service firms also can overcome over- or underutilization of capacity by sharing capacity with other firms. Airlines share gates, ramps, baggage-handling equipment, personnel, and even airplanes with other airlines (Sasser, 1976). Firms may share computer time with other firms.

C. Matching Demand to Level of Supply

The other means of equating demand and supply is to alter demand to match supply. Both fluctuations in demand and the magnitude of demand need to be managed. Managers prefer a steady flow of demand without extreme peaks or valleys. They desire a magnitude of demand that allows production and marketing to be efficient and profitable. Too little demand, either continuously or periodically, underutilizes plant and personnel and results in excessive costs. Surges of too much demand lead to lost sales and extra expense if the service suppliers cannot adapt capacity. Ongoing overdemand is usually welcome, particularly by suppliers who can react faster than competitors and so gain sales and market share.

Many of the demand-adjusting mechanisms used by service firms (e.g., pricing up or down) are identical to those used by product firms. However, some methods are fairly unique and their use arguably more important given the more severe problems of under- or overcapacity in services. This leads us to Proposition 7:

> **Proposition 7:** *The management of short-run demand for services is largely done by pricing, promotion, in-house alternative services, and demand-deflecting activities.*

Peak-load pricing is one of the most familiar means of demand management. Low prices at slack periods and high prices at peak periods have been used extensively by resort hotels, telephone companies, movie theatres, and airlines. Promotions such as double-stamp days, free parking days, and bat days also have been used to bolster demand in slack time. Bridge and highway tolls are often lower during nonpeak periods than during peak periods. Ski resorts alter their prices and service mix and offer golf, tennis, horseback riding, and even grass skiing to attract customers in nonwinter months.

Such demand-adjusting mechanisms work well when buyers are price-sensitive, have consumption time flexibilities, and do not perceive time differences in provision of the service as quality differences. However, such mechanisms are not effective demand adjusters for medical services, roadside repair, and burial services. Also, they may not be effective if buyers perceive no additional benefits from purchasing services during slack times. A lack of perceived quality differences caused problems for a cargo airline attempting to fill empty cargo space by offering lower rates for second- and third-day deliveries. Because the airline had overcapacity even with the promotion, much of the increased load was delivered on the first day. Shippers were quick to discover this and shifted most of their shipments to the lower-priced alternatives. The company experienced increased sales volume but lower profits (Sasser, 1976).

The use of advertising without sales promotion has been used by the U.S. Postal Service to get people to mail early at Christmastime. The Internal Revenue Service urges people to file early to lessen their peak load in April. These efforts and others have had impressive results in increasing the productivity of the respective services involved (Lovelock and Young, 1977).

Many service firms have adjusted demand by offering in-house alternatives for the heavily demanded service. Many fast-food restaurants with limited seating capacity have added drive-up windows or home delivery services. One resort solved a problem of overcrowded tennis facilities in peak hours by diverting guests to surfing, sailing, and other activities while they were waiting for tennis courts (Sasser, 1976).

Many service firms manage demand through appointment scheduling or reservations. Certain times, are, of course, "left open" for emergency needs such as occur for medical services. Some service firms also offer standby or walk-in services to take more customers should existing appointments or reservations fail to fully utilize existing capacity or when "no-shows" may be a problem.

Altering the timing of demand for services not only helps the service provider (i.e., in terms of better utilization of capacity and fewer lost customers due to lack of capacity or crowded facilities), but also may have a favorable impact on the consumer. Consumers receive more and better attention when service providers are in more favorable circumstances to provide that attention.

X. IMPLICATIONS OF THE INABILITY TO TRANSPORT SERVICES

Proposition 8: *Convenience-type services require the presence of numerous market-oriented facilities that combine both marketing and production activities.*

Products can be produced in one or more places and then transported to middlemen or final consumers for sale. Most services cannot be produced in one place and then transported to another. For these services, either the consumer must go to the production facility or the production facility must be brought to the consumer. The latter situation is exemplified by the ability of educators, lawyers, accountants, and sports teams to be transported to where they are needed. Some New York City area universities dispatch professors to teach classes on commuter trains going to and from Manhattan. Product representations of services such as consultants' reports, tax filings, and insurance policies can also be transported. Again, though, the actual services that give the papers meaning cannot be transported.

There are some services which, due principally to breakthroughs in technology, can, in essence, be transported. Educational services can be conveyed from university campuses to in-plant classrooms by closed-circuit television. Students who view lectures live are able to ask the instructor questions by means of direct telephone hookups. Physicians can guide paramedics in emergency medical treatment by radio. Despite such exceptions, however, most services which need to be received locally must be produced locally.

The inability of most services to be transported has implications for the location of service outlets and the marketing and production functions performed at those outlets. However, the effects of lack of transportability are mediated by the "convenience" or "nonconvenience" nature of the service.

As with convenience products, consumers are less willing to travel long distances or spend a great degree of search time for such convenience services as hair care, some banking services, dry cleaning, minor repair services, car washes, and fast-food service. This suggests that the distribution of such services be intensive—i.e., that the service be provided in numerous localities. As with convenience products, there are a large number of retail service outlets for convenience services. However, unlike a retailer selling products, the service retailer—whether owned independently or by a parent service firm—must promote *and* produce the service being offered. Because of the inability to transport services, intermediaries in service channels cannot take title to an already-produced service, store it, and then offer it for resale. Thus, channels for services only contain service producers and final customers, along with some agent intermediaries. When agents or brokers are used, they typically help producers to (1) inform prospective customers about the services; and (2) negotiate or transact the sale of the services. On occasion, agents or brokers also represent customers.

Producers of convenience services usually sell directly to their customers because they are right in their midst. About the only reason they use an agent or a broker is to gain greater selling coverage, expertise, or emphasis. Some apartment owners, for example, use real estate agents to negotiate the rental of their units.

Producers of nonconvenience services face less stringent requirements for the number and location of, and tasks performed at, local outlets. Nonconvenience-type services—i.e., those that are not purchased frequently and for which consumers are willing to spend considerably more search and/or travel time (as compared to convenience-type services)—can utilize more centralized production facilities. Customers are willing to travel considerable distance to reach such "shopping services" as long-distance air travel, professional theatre, and some professional services (e.g., general practice attorneys, physicians). This leads us to our next proposition.

Proposition 9: *Nonconvenience-type services facilities can be located at considerable distances from intended customers because (1) the services can be sold through the use of market-located sales offices, salespersons, or telephone or mail activities; (2) customers will seek more prepurchase information; (3) customers will travel considerable distances for the service; and/or (4) the service capability can be transported to the customer.*

Customers would be expected to engage in even more extensive search, be willing to travel longer distances, make purchase commitments in advance of use, and endure longer waiting times for specialty services. Services such as those provided by orthodontists, ophthalmologists, probate, tax, or patent attorneys; and heart, eye, or neurosurgeons could well be considered specialty services.

Since the actual production facilities or offices for shopping and specialty services may be located long distances from most customers, the use of brokers and agents (e.g., travel agents and other physicians or attorneys who refer their patients or clients) to promote, schedule, and negotiate the sale of such services is more common. Obviously, customers are less willing to travel long distances, wait for longer periods of time, and pay higher fees for these services without some prior indication that they will be able to obtain the desired benefits.

Some shopping or specialty services such as life insurance and stock brokering and some accounting and legal services may be produced at locations far from the consumer and may not require local agents. Through the use of mail or telephone, customers for these services can convey the necessary information for the service provider to act upon. Furthermore, the capability to provide these nonconvenience services can be transported. Insurance adjusters, attorneys, accountants, and consultants regularly provide on-site assistance.

XI. LIMITATIONS ON THE ABILITY TO MASS MARKET SERVICES

Organizations can mass-market products because centralized production, which allows for production economies and product quality control, is possible due to storage and transportation. Because services are intangible and cannot be stored or transported, there are special efforts required, and limits on the ability to, effectively mass-market services—i.e., mass-produce the service and promote it on a mass basis.

Proposition 10: *Organizations can mass-market convenience-type services (without meaningful economies of mass production) when organizational and control methods can be used to knit numerous market-oriented production-marketing facilities together in such ways to (1) install and maintain a uniform quality of services; (2) identify individual service outlets as members of the larger group; and (3) engage in and gain the economic benefits of large-scale advertising and other mass-marketing activities.*

The necessity for numerous local production facilities for convenience-type service reduces opportunities for economies of mass production. Just as important, it increases the difficulty of producing services of uniform quality—which is necessary for successful branding, advertising, and other mass-marketing activities. There is little occasion to gain meaningful economies of mass production. However, uniform quality can be achieved through the use of tightly controlled franchise, partnership, or chain ownership arrangements.

There are several examples of recent efforts by service organizations to do just this. Some of the new franchise systems in service industries include Century 21 in the real estate business; the Barbers, a hair styling franchise; Hyatt Legal Services and the Law Store, both franchise systems for attorneys; and dental clinics operated as leased departments in Sears stores. All of these franchise organizations benefit from (1) careful hiring and training of personnel; (2) development of standard operating procedures; (3) augmentation of employee efforts with the use of better machines and equipment; and (4) careful control procedures to see that requirements have been met (Upah, 1980). These mechanisms allow each member organization to benefit from (1) national or regional marketing efforts and the identity and credibility created by those efforts; and (2) the favorable experiences that consumers now in their area have had with other franchise outlets. Furthermore, because uniformity in quality is enhanced via these organizational control mechanisms, large-scale promotion highlighting consistent quality can be used. This is especially beneficial given the evidence for greater consumer dissatisfaction (or at least greater difficulties in achieving consumer satisfaction) with services than with products (Czepiel, 1980; Upah, 1980).

Thus, local production and the resulting difficulties in achieving uniform quality increase the difficulty of being able to utilize and benefit from mass promotion. However, mass marketing on this basis can be used.

Proposition 11: *Organizations can mass-market nonconvenience-type services, with some meaningful economies of mass production, when (1) they can attract large numbers of customers to their production facilities; or (2) the services are not dependent on the physical coming together of the service customer and the production facility.*

Many of the economies of both mass production and mass promotion can be attained when services can be provided through centralized production facilities. However, this is typically limited to two types of services. First are services for which people will journey long distances — by definition, shopping or specialty services. Illustrative of such services are major league sports entertainment, amusement such as that offered by Disney World and resort hotels, and specialized medical services. The task for these organizations is to provide continual encouragement to consumers to travel longer distances (e.g., through the use of travel packages) to reach the principal service facility.

Second are services that are not dependent on the physical coming together of customers and the production facilities. These may be convenience, shopping, or specialty services. Illustrative of these services are some types of insurance, photofinishing services, some dry-cleaning services, and possibly legal and/or accounting services. For these services, the customer-contact facilities may be separated from the actual service production facility. For instance, dry-cleaning and photo-processing firms use pickup points but provide cleaning and photofinishing at central processing plants. The Law Store legal franchise offers legal advice by telephone hookups in department stores. Thus, only customer-contact facilities are in multiple outlets. The central production facility allows the firm to achieve economies in production and to maintain a means of centralized quality control.

Service organizations which possess either of the two qualities described above can and do realize meaningful *production* economies. However, what options are left for those service organizations which are not in the specialty service category and which require the customer's presence for provision of the services received — i.e., customer-contact and production facilities are essentially one in the same? Several options have been outlined elsewhere (for a review of these options see Upah, 1980) and form the basis for our final proposition.

Proposition 12: *Service firms of all types can achieve some meaningful benefits of mass promotion through efforts to (1) substitute more vigorous promotions for fewer production outlets; (2) to locate near complementary organizations; (3) join complementary organizations in common facilities; (4) share service capacity with other firms; and (5) improve production procedures within individual production outlets.*

First, even sellers of convenience services can utilize fewer outlets but encourage customers to travel longer distances. Retailers of all types use selective promotional mechanisms specifically designed to attract customers outside the retailer's immediate trading area. Second, sellers of convenience services can locate their outlets near complementary outlets and/or join these outlets in forming a service "shopping center." Optometrists frequently locate their offices near professional or medical centers. Theatre owners have realized substantial benefits (for example, in land and building, projection operators, concessions people, and so forth) by turning from multiple locations for their theaters to theater complexes. Health centers in many cities combine hair styling and beauty care with exercise programs and tennis and racquetball courts. One dental practice has been located inside an iceskating rink. The basic rationale for these combinations of service outlets is that of any consolidation of retailers—increased pulling power. However, given their unique productivity problems, service firms may find such combinations even more beneficial.

There are still other means of improving production efficiency for services. Service firms may achieve productivity gains by reducing the range of services provided at individual outlets. Routine cases may be handled in some outlets (in the case of the Law Store by phone). More complex cases which increase waiting time for other customers and reduce customer volume can be handled elsewhere. The Law Store does this by handling complex cases by mail, personal consultation, or referral to local attorneys—for a 25% referral fee.

Service firms of all types may achieve increased economies by sharing service capacity with other firms. This strategy was discussed above in the context of managing supply/demand imbalances in services. Finally, and also mentioned above, service organizations with multiple production outlets can strive to improve the efficiency of production procedures in those outlets. Levitt (1972, 1976) sees a great deal of room for what he calls "taking a production line approach to" or "industrializing" service. Again, while many of these mechanisms are important to firms selling principally products as well as to those selling principally services, they are critically important in achieving production economies in what has been viewed as the less productive sector of the economy—the service sector.

XII. Suggestions for Futher Study

This paper has attempted to show that there are major differences between products and services and that these differences do lead to differences in marketing. However, the propositions for service marketing just discussed are only propositions. Accordingly, they need to be subjected to empirical testing and rigorous thought by scholars and practitioners. Several of the propositions seem amenable to hypothesis formulation and empirical testing. Others may be best verified by extensive observations of actual service marketing strategies with case-by-case support or rejection, noting exceptions and reasons for those exceptions. Of course, the mere fact that many firms are observed to be using a strategy does not mean that they should be using that strategy.

The discussion of product-service differences reported here and presented in the work of others reviewed above has furthered the development of positive and normative theory in service marketing. However, there is room for additional dialog on these and other product-service differences and resulting marketing implications. Propositions specific to particular types of services such as public accounting and medical and transportation services also might be developed. Because of the lack of emphasis on overt promotion in the professions, the development of strategic marketing guidelines for professionals would seem to be an interesting and useful research pursuit. Undoubtedly, the practitioners in the various professions have welcomed the recent surge of interest in their marketing opportunities and problems and would continue to welcome further input.

Another means of developing strategic service marketing implications is to focus not on product-service differences, but rather on differences among services. There have been at least three attempts to classify and differentiate services (Judd, 1964; Lovelock, 1980; Rathmell, 1974). Unfortunately there has been little development of the strategic marketing implications of various categorizations. Lovelock (1980), who provides the most comprehensive set of classification characteristics, does, however, provide some direction for the development of these implications. One major and potentially fruitful opportunity for further research, then, would be to first evaluate and refine Lovelock's classification schema. The various classification characteristics could then be combined in order to develop the most useful combinations for the development of strategic implications. Finally, the implications themselves could be developed. One current example of such an effort is provided by Ryans and Wittink (1977).

As pointed out above, fundamental research which focuses on the cues consumers use when selecting and evaluating services is very limited—that is, at least based on what is published in the marketing literature. A review and integration of contributions from other disciplines (e.g., sociology, medical sociology) would serve to form an even better basis for such an understanding as well as suggest new opportunities for marketing-oriented research on these issues. In order to do such research, however, standard research techniques which involve asking consumers direct questions about the attributes they look to most in evaluating a service may not be adequate. More creative direct and indirect measures (e.g., projective techniques) may be required to uncover decision criteria that consumers are unable or unwilling to articulate.

A good deal of service marketing research has focused on the development of strategies designed to enhance the productivity of service organizations (e.g., better management of perishable production capacity). However, there have been questions regarding the counterproductive or undesirable outcomes of using some of these strategies. For instance, one major set of issues yet to be fully addressed in the service marketing literature is the management of the trade-offs involved in efforts to increase productivity. These trade-offs included (1) increasing the structure and efficiency of service tasks versus reducing the attractiveness of the service task to employees (Sasser and Arbeit, 1976); (2) increasing the structure in, and uniformity of, service tasks versus reducing the personalized appeal of the service offering (Berry, 1975; George, 1977); (3) increasing utilization of consumer input in service delivery (e.g., self-service) versus decreasing the desirability of the service—especially for those services sought because of the lack of need for the consumer to expend certain efforts—to the consumer (Lovelock and Young, 1977, 1979); and (4) the substitution of machines for tasks formerly done by employees versus the loss of benefits from providing personal contact to customers (Berry, 1975). Additional research might proceed by categorizing those service industries for which the mechanization strategies would be most beneficial/detrimental to the appeal of the service to customers, which services lend themselves to more self-service activities, and so forth.

XIII. Conclusions

It is hoped that this paper has furthered the argument that service marketing is significantly different from product marketing. While many of the differences between products and services and the implications of these differences involve differences of degree rather than kind, they are nevertheless important. It is also hoped that this attempt to integrate existing knowledge as to the implications of these differences and to develop both descriptive and normative propositions for the marketing of services will help persons interested in service marketing to organize their thinking and experiences. Such results should lead to the development of better theory and practice for service marketing and marketing in general.

ENDNOTES

1. The authors choose to use the term *product* to indicate a tangible, physical object which is exchanged in a market transaction. The term will *not*, unless otherwise noted, refer to the total market offering (for example, the full range of product, service, and other related benefits which are exchanged in a market transaction).
2. This term, and the importance of recognizing the category of market offerings to which it refers, was suggested to us by Professor Tom Bonoma.
3. This point is based on National Automobile Dealer Association data. For a review of these data see Uhl and Upah (1980b).

REFERENCES

Anderson, W. Thomas, Jr., Cox, Eli P., III, and Fulcher, David G. Bank Selection Decisions and Market Segmentation. *Journal of Marketing*, January 1976, *40*, 40–45.

Barker, Roger G., *Ecological Psychology*. Stanford, CA. Stanford University Press, 1968.

Belk, Russell W., Situational Variables and Consumer Behavior. *Journal of Consumer Research*, December 1975, *2*, 157–64.

Berry, Leonard L., Personalizing The Bank: Key Opportunity in Bank Marketing. *Bank Marketing*. April 1975, 22–25.

Bloom, Paul N., Advertising in The Professions: The Critical Issues. *Journal of Marketing*. July 1977, *41*, 103–10.

Bonoma, Thomas V., and Mills, Michael K., Developmental Service Marketing. Unpublished Working Paper. Pittsburgh: Graduate School of Business, University of Pittsburgh, 1979.

Chase, Richard B., Where Does The Consumer Fit in a Service Operation? *Harvard Business Review*, November–December 1978, 137–42.

Currim, Imran, Weinberg, Charles B., and Wittink, Dick R., On the Design of Subscription Programs For A Performing Arts Series. *Journal of Consumer Research*, 1981.

Czepiel, John A., *Managing Customer Satisfaction in Consumer Service Businesses*. Report 80-107. Cambridge, MA: Marketing Sciences Institute, 1980.

Donnelly, James H., Jr., Marketing Intermediaries in Channels of Distribution for Services. *Journal of Marketing*, January 1976, *40*, 55–57.

Eiglier, Pierre, and Langeard, Eric. A New Approach To Service Marketing. In Pierre Eiglier, Eric Langeard, Christopher H. Lovelock, John E. G. Bateson and Robert F.

Young, *Marketing Consumer Services: New Insights*. Report 77-115, Cambridge, MA: Marketing Science Institute. 1977, 31–58.

Eiglier, Pierre, Langeard, Eric, Lovelock, Christopher H., Bateson, John E. G., and Young, Robert F., *Marketing Consumer Services: New Insights*. Report 77-115, Cambridge, MA: Marketing Science Institute, 1977.

George, William R., The Retailing of Services: A Challenging Future. *Journal of Retailing*, Fall 1977, *53*, 85–98.

Hall, Edward T., *The Silent Language*. Garden City, N.Y.: Doubleday, 1959.

Judd, Robert C., The Case for Redefining Services. *Journal of Marketing*, January 1964, *28*, 58–59.

Judd, Robert C., Similarities or Differences in Product and Service Retailing. *Journal of Marketing*, Winter, 1968, 32.

Kotler, Philip, *Marketing Management: Analysis, Planning and Control*. (4th ed.). Englewood Cliffs, NJ: Prentice-Hall, 1980.

Kotler, Philip, and Connor, Richard A., Jr., Marketing Professional Services. *Journal of Marketing*, January 1977, *41*, 71–76.

Kuehl, Philip G., and Ford, Gary T., The Promotion of Medical and Legal Services: An Experimental Study. In Barnett A. Greenberg, and Danny N. Bellanger (eds.), *Contemporary Marketing Thought*. Chicago: American Marketing Association, 1977, 39–44.

Levitt, Theodore, Production-Line Approach To Services. *Harvard Business Review*, September 1972, *50*, 41–52.

Levitt, Theodore, The Industrialization of Service. *Harvard Business Review*, September 1976, *54*, 63–74.

Lovelock, Christopher H., Toward a Classification of Services. In C. W. Lamb, and P. M. Dunne (eds.), *Theoretical Developments in Marketing*. Chicago: American Marketing Association, 1980, 72–78.

Lovelock, Christopher H., Look To Consumers To Increase Productivity. *Harvard Business Review*, November–December 1979, 168–78.

Lovelock, Christopher H., and Young, Robert F., Marketing's Potential For Improving Productivity in Service Industries. In Pierre Eiglier, Eric Langeard, Christopher H. Lovelock, John E. G. Bateson and Robert F. Young, *Marketing Consumer Services: New Insights*. Cambridge, MA: Marketing Science Institute, 1977, 105–20.

Nord, Walter R., and Peter, J. Paul, A Behavior Modification Perspective on Marketing. *Journal of Marketing*, Spring 1980, *44*, 36–47.

Rathmell, John M., *Marketing in The Service Sector*. Cambridge, MA: Winthrop, 1974.

Ryans, Adrian B., and Wittink, Dick R., The Marketing of Services: Categorization With Implications For Strategy. In Barnett A. Greenberg, and Danny N. Bellanger (eds.), *Contemporary Marketing Thought*, Chicago: American Marketing Association, 1977, 312–14.

Sarkar, A. K., and Saleh, F. A., The Buyer of Professional Services: An Examination of Some Key Variables in The Selection Process. *Journal of Purchasing and Materials Management*, February 1974, *10*, 22–32.

Sasser, W. Earl, Match Supply and Demand in Service Industries. *Harvard Business Review*, November–December 1976, *54*, 133–40.

Sasser, W. Earl, and Arbeit, Stephen P., Selling Jobs in The Service Sector. *Business Horizons*, June 1976, 61–65.

Shimp, Terence, and Dyer, Robert, How The Legal Profession Views Legal Service Advertising. *Journal of Marketing*, July 1978, *42*, 74–81.

Shostack, G. Lynn, Breaking Free From Product Marketing. *Journal of Marketing*, April 1977, *41*, 73–80.

Smith, Geoffrey, I Can Cut Gold Crowns Like You Wouldn't Believe. *Forbes*, November 1976, 88.

Smith, Robert E., and Meyer, Tiffany S., Attorney Advertising: A Consumer Perspective. *Journal of Marketing*, Spring 1980, *44*, 56–64.

Stern, Louis W., and El-Ansary, Adel H., *Marketing Channels*. Englewood Cliffs, NJ: Prentice-Hall, 1977.

Uhl, Kenneth P., and Upah, Gregory D., The Marketing of Services: A Set of Propositions. In Charles C. Slater and Philip D. White (eds.), *Macro-Marketing: Distributive Processes From A Societal Perspective, An Elaboration of Issues*. Boulder, CO: Graduate School of Business Administration, University of Colorado, August 1978, 411–33.

Uhl, Kenneth P., and Upah, Gregory D., A Sequential Approach to the Advertising of Accounting Services. Working Paper, Virginia Polytechnic Institute and State University, 1980. (a)

Uhl, Kenneth P., and Upah, Gregory D., Service Marketing: A Road Map For Research. Paper Presented at American Institute For Decision Sciences National Conference, November 1980. (b)

Upah, Gregory D., Mass Marketing in Service Retailing: A Review and Synthesis of Major Methods. *Journal of Retailing*, Fall 1980, *56*, 59–76.

Vaughn, Ronald L., Arora, Raj, and Hansotia, Behram, Marketing Urban Transit Systems: A Look at the Cognitive Structure of Users and Nonusers By Trip Purpose. Working Paper, College of Business Administration, November 1979.

Wilson, Aubrey, *The Marketing of Professional Services*. New York: McGraw-Hill, 1972.

Wittreich, Warren J., How To Buy/Sell Professional Services. *Harvard Business Review*. March–April 1966. 71–76.

Wood, Thomas David, and Ball, Donald A., New Rule 502 and Effective Advertising By CPA's. *Journal of Accountancy*, June 1978, 65–70.

Wyckham, R. G., Fitzroy, T. P., and Mandry, G. D., Marketing Services: An Evaluation of the Theory. *European Journal of Marketing*. 1975, *9*, 59–67.